# SECTION ONE

The Short Story
from its beginnings
to modern times

## Early

*Washington Irving* (1783–1859) was the first American writer to receive praise from Europeans for his literary achievements. Born in New York City, he was educated in Europe and traveled extensively there. He was admitted to the bar in 1806 but did not practice law, preferring to write instead. He first won literary recognition with *Diedrich Knickerbocker's History of New York* (1809). *The Sketch Book of Geoffrey Crayon,* published serially in Europe and in book form in the United States in 1820, is considered by some to be an initial landmark in the history of the short story. This was a collection of tales and sketches including Irving's masterpieces, "Rip Van Winkle" and "The Legend of Sleepy Hollow." There followed other collections of tales and sketches: *Bracebridge Hall* (1822), *Tales of a Traveller* (1824), and *The Alhambra* (1832). Though Irving believed that short stories require a unity of effect and a nicety of execution not required in longer works, his own stories are looser in structure than those written a few years later by Nathaniel Hawthorne. "The Legend of Sleepy Hollow" is, nevertheless, a delightful story, its cartoonlike characters having captured the imagination of generation after generation of readers.

# THE LEGEND OF SLEEPY HOLLOW

FOUND AMONG THE PAPERS OF THE LATE
DIEDRICH KNICKERBOCKER

*A pleasing land of drowsy head it was,*
*Of dreams that wave before the half-shut eye,*
*And of gay castles in the clouds that pass,*
*For ever flushing round a summer sky.*

CASTLE OF INDOLENCE

In the bosom of one of those spacious coves which indent the eastern shore of the Hudson, at that broad expansion of the river denominated by the ancient Dutch navigators the Tappan Zee, and where they always prudently shortened sail, and implored the protection of St. Nicholas when they crossed, there lies a small market-town or rural port, which by some is called Greensburgh, but which is more generally and properly known by the name of Tarry Town. This name was given, we are told, in former days, by the good housewives of the adjacent country, from the inveterate propensity of their husbands to linger about the village tavern on market days. Be that as it may, I do not vouch for the fact, but merely advert to it, for the sake of being precise and authentic. Not far from this village, perhaps about two miles, there is a little valley, or rather lap of land, among high hills, which is one of the quietest places in the whole world. A small brook glides through it, with just murmur enough to lull one to repose; and the occasional whistle of a quail, or tapping of a woodpecker, is almost the only sound that ever breaks in upon the uniform tranquillity.

I recollect that, when a stripling, my first exploit in squirrel-shooting was in a grove of tall walnut-trees that shades one side of the valley. I had wandered into it at noon time, when all nature is peculiarly quiet, and was startled by the roar of my own gun, as it broke the Sabbath stillness around, and was prolonged and reverberated by the angry echoes. If ever I should wish for a retreat, whither I might steal from the world and its distractions, and dream quietly away the remnant of a troubled life, I know of none more promising than this little valley.

From the listless repose of the place, and the peculiar character of its inhabitants, who are descendents from the original Dutch settlers, this sequestered glen has long been known by the name of SLEEPY HOLLOW, and its rustic lads are called the Sleepy Hollow Boys throughout all the neighboring country. A drowsy, dreamy influence seems to hang over the land, and to pervade the very atmosphere. Some say that the place was bewitched by a high German doctor, during the early days of the settlement; others, that an old Indian chief, the prophet or wizard of his tribe, held his powwows there before the country was discovered by Master Hendrick Hudson. Certain it is, the place still continues under the sway of some witching power, that holds a spell over the minds of the good people, causing them to walk in a continual reverie. They are given to all kinds of marvellous beliefs; are subject to trances and visions; and frequently see strange sights, and hear music and voices in the air. The whole neighborhood abounds with local tales, haunted spots, and twilight superstitions; stars shoot and meteors glare oftener across the valley than in any part of the country, and the nightmare, with her whole nine fold, seems to make it the favorite scene of her gambols.

The dominant spirit, however, that haunts this enchanted region, and seems to be commander-in-chief of all the powers of the air, is the apparition of a figure on horseback without a head. It is said by some to be the ghost of a Hessian trooper, whose head had been carried away by a cannon-ball, in some nameless battle during the revolutionary war; and who is ever and anon seen by the country folk, hurrying along in the gloom of night, as if on the wings of the wind. His haunts are not confined to the valley, but extend at times to the adjacent roads, and especially to the vicinity of a church at no great distance. Indeed, certain of the most authentic historians of those parts, who have been careful in collecting and collating the floating facts concerning this spectre, allege that the body of the trooper, having been buried in the church-yard, the ghost rides forth to the scene of battle in nightly quest of his head; and that the rushing speed with which he sometimes passes along the Hollow, like a midnight blast, is owing to his being belated, and in a hurry to get back to the church-yard before daybreak.

Such is the general purport of this legendary superstition, which has furnished materials for many a wild story in that region of shadows; and the spectre is known, at all the country firesides, by the name of the Headless Horseman of Sleepy Hollow.

It is remarkable that the visionary propensity I have mentioned is not confined to the native inhabitants of the valley, but is unconsciously imbibed by every one who resides there for a time. However wide awake they may have been before they entered that sleepy region, they are sure, in a little time, to inhale the witching influence of the air, and begin to grow imaginative—to dream dreams, and see apparitions.

I mention this peaceful spot with all possible laud; for it is in such little retired Dutch valleys, found here and there embosomed in the great State of New York, that population, manners, and customs, remain fixed; while the great torrent of migration and improvement, which is making such incessant changes in other parts of this restless country, sweeps by them unobserved. They are like those little nooks of still water which border a rapid stream; where we may see the straw and bubble riding quietly at anchor, or slowly revolving in their mimic harbor, undisturbed by the rush of the passing current. Though many years have elapsed since I trod the drowsy shades of Sleepy Hollow, yet I question whether I should not still find the same trees and the same families vegetating in its sheltered bosom.

In this by-place of nature, there abode, in a remote period of American history, that is to say, some thirty years since, a worthy wight of the name of Ichabod Crane; who sojourned, or, as he expressed it, "tarried," in Sleepy Hollow, for the purpose of instructing the children of the vicinity. He was a native of Connecticut; a State which supplies the Union with pioneers for the mind as well as for the forest, and sends forth yearly its legions of frontier woodsmen and country schoolmasters. The cognomen of Crane was not inapplicable to his person. He was tall, but exceedingly lank, with narrow shoulder, long arms and legs, hands that dangled a mile out of his sleeves, feet that might have served for shovels, and his whole frame most loosely hung together. His head was small, and flat at top, with huge ears, large green glassy eyes, and a long snipe nose, so that it looked like a weather-cock, perched upon his spindle neck, to tell which way the wind blew. To see him striding along the profile of a hill on a windy day, with his clothes bagging and fluttering about him, one might have mistaken him for the genius of famine descending upon the earth, or some scarecrow eloped from a cornfield.

His school-house was a low building of one large room, rudely constructed of logs; the windows partly glazed, and partly patched with leaves of old copybooks. It was most ingeniously secured at vacant hours, by a withe twisted in the handle of the door, and stakes set against the window shutters; so that, though a thief might get in with perfect ease, he would find some embarrassment in getting out; an idea most probably borrowed by the architect, Yost Van Houten, from the mystery of an eel-pot. The school-house stood in a rather lonely but pleasant situation, just at the foot of a woody hill, with a brook running close by, and a formidable birch tree growing at one end of it. From hence the low murmur of his pupils' voices, conning over their lessons, might be heard in a drowsy summer's day, like the hum of a bee-hive; interrupted now and then by the authoritative voice of the master, in the tone of menace or command; or, peradventure, by the appalling sound of the birch, as he urged some tardy loiterer along the flowery path of knowledge. Truth to say, he was a conscientious man, and ever bore in mind the golden maxim, "Spare the rod and spoil the child."—Ichabod Crane's scholars certainly were not spoiled.

I would not have it imagined, however, that he was one of those cruel potentates of the school, who joy in the smart of their subjects; on the contrary, he administered justice with discrimination rather than severity; taking the burthen off the backs of the weak, and laying it on those of the strong. Your mere puny stripling, that winced at the least flourish of the rod, was passed by with indulgence; but the claims of justice were satisfied by inflicting a double portion on some little, tough, wrong-headed, broad-skirted Dutch urchin, who sulked and swelled and grew dogged and sullen beneath the birch. All this he called "doing his duty by their parents"; and he never inflicted a chastisement without following it by the assurance, so consolatory to the smarting urchin, that "he would remember it, and thank him for it the longest day he had to live."

When school hours were over, he was even the companion and playmate of the larger boys; and on holiday afternoons would convoy some of the smaller ones home, who happened to have pretty sisters, or good housewives for mothers, noted for the comforts of the cupboard. Indeed it behooved him to keep on good terms with his pupils. The revenue arising from his school was small, and would have been scarcely sufficient to furnish him with daily bread, for he was a huge feeder, and though lank, had the dilating powers of an anaconda; but to help out his maintenance, he was, according to country custom in those parts, boarded and lodged at the houses of the farmers, whose children he instructed. With these he lived successively a week at a time; thus going the rounds of the neighborhood, with all his worldly effects tied up in a cotton handkerchief.

That all this might not be too onerous on the purses of his rustic patrons, who are apt to consider the costs of schooling a grievous burden, and schoolmasters as mere drones, he had various ways of rendering himself both useful and agreeable. He assisted the farmers occasionally in the lighter labors of their farms; helped to make hay; mended the fences; took the horses to water; drove the cows from pasture; and cut wood for the winter fire. He laid aside, too, all the dominant dignity and absolute sway with which he lorded it in his little empire, the school, and became wonderfully gentle and ingratiating. He found favor in the eyes of the mothers, by petting the children, particularly the youngest; and like the lion bold, which whilom so magnanimously the lamb did hold, he would sit with a child on one knee, and rock a cradle with his foot for whole hours together.

In addition to his other vocations, he was the singing-master of the neighborhood, and picked up many bright shillings by instructing the young folks in psalmody. It was a matter of no little vanity to him, on Sundays, to take his station in front of the church gallery, with a band of chosen singers; where, in his own mind, he completely carried away the psalm from the parson. Certain it is, his voice resounded far above all the rest of the congregation; and there are peculiar quavers still to be heard in that church, and which may even be heard half a mile off, quite to the opposite side of the mill-pond, on a still Sunday morning, which are said to be legitimately descended from the nose of Ichabod Crane. Thus, by divers little make-shifts in that ingenious way which is commonly denominated "by hook and by crook," the worthy pedagogue got on tolerably enough, and was thought, by all who understood nothing of the labor of headwork, to have a wonderfully easy life of it.

The schoolmaster is generally a man of some importance in the female circle of a rural neighborhood; being considered a kind of idle gentlemanlike personage, of vastly superior taste and accomplishments to the rough country swains, and, indeed, inferior in learning only to the parson. His appearance, therefore, is apt to occasion some little stir at the tea-table of a farmhouse, and the addition of a supernumerary dish of cakes or sweetmeats, or peradvanture, the parade of a silver tea-pot. Our man of letters, therefore, was peculiarly happy in the smiles of all the country damsels. How he would figure among them in the churchyard, between services on Sundays! gathering grapes for them from the wild vines that overrun the surrounding trees; reciting for their amusement all the epitaphs on the tombstones; or sauntering, with a whole bevy of them, along the banks of the adjacent mill-pond; while the more bashful country bumpkins hung sheepishly back, envying his superior elegance and address.

From his half itinerant life, also, he was a kind of travelling gazette, carrying the whole budget of local gossip from house to house; so that his appearance was always greeted with satisfaction. He was, moreover, esteemed by the women as a man of great erudition, for he had read several books quite through, and was a perfect master of Cotton Mather's history of New England Witchcraft, in which, by the way, he most firmly and potently believed.

He was, in fact, an odd mixture of small shrewdness and simple credulity. His appetite for the marvellous, and his powers of digesting it, were equally extraordinary; and both had been increased by his residence in this spellbound region. No tale was too gross or monstrous for his capacious swallow. It was often his delight, after his school was dismissed in the afternoon, to stretch himself on the rich bed of clover, bordering the little brook that whimpered by his school-house, and there con over old Mather's direful tales, until the gathering dusk of the evening made the printed page a mere mist before his eyes. Then, as he wended his way, by swamp and stream and awful woodland, to the farmhouse where he happened to be quartered, every sound of nature, at that witching hour, fluttered his excited imagination: the moan of the whip-poor-will from the hill-side; the boding cry of the tree-toad, that harbinger of storm; the dreary hooting of the screech-owl, or the sudden rustling in the thicket of birds frightened from their roost. The fire-flies, too, which sparkled most vividly in the darkest places, now and then startled him, as one of uncommon brightness would stream across his path; and if, by chance, a huge blockhead of a beetle came winging his blundering flight against him, the poor varlet was ready to give up the ghost, with the idea that he was struck with a witch's token. His only resource on such occasions, either to drown thought, or drive away evil spirits, was to sing psalm tunes;—and the good people of Sleepy Hollow, as they sat by their doors of an evening, were often filled with awe, at hearing his nasal melody, "in linked sweetness long drawn out," floating from the distant hill, or along the dusky road.

Another of his sources of fearful pleasure was, to pass long winter evenings with the old Dutch wives, as they sat spinning by the fire, with a row of apples roasting and spluttering along the hearth, and listen to their marvellous tales of ghosts and goblins, and haunted fields, and haunted brooks, and haunted bridges, and haunted houses, and particularly of the headless horseman, or galloping Hessian of the Hollow, as they sometimes called him. He would delight them equally by his anecdotes of witchcraft, and of the direful omens and portentous sights and sounds in the air, which prevailed in the earlier times of Connecticut; and would frighten them wofully with speculations upon comets and shooting stars; and with the alarming fact that the world did absolutely turn round, and that they were half the time topsy-turvy!

But if there was a pleasure in all this, while snugly cuddling in the chimney corner of a chamber that was all of a ruddy glow from the crackling wood fire, and where, of course, no spectre dared to show his face, it was dearly purchased by the terrors of his subsequent walk homewards. What fearful shapes and shadows beset his path amidst the dim and ghastly glare of a snowy night!—With what wistful look did he eye every trembling ray of light streaming across the waste fields from some distant window!—How often was he appalled by some shrub covered with snow, which, like a sheeted spectre, beset his very path!—How often did he shrink with curdling awe at the sound of his own steps on the frosty crust beneath his feet; and dread to look over his shoulder, lest he should behold some uncouth being tramping close behind him!—and how often was he thrown into complete dismay by some rushing blast, howling among the trees, in the idea that it was the Galloping Hessian on one of his nightly scourings!

All these, however, were mere terrors of the night, phantoms of the mind that walk in darkness; and though he had seen many spectres in his time, and been more than once beset by Satan in divers shapes, in his lonely perambulations, yet daylight put an end to all these evils; and he would have passed a pleasant life of it, in despite of the devil and all his works, if his path had not been crossed by a being that causes more perplexity to mortal man than ghosts, goblins, and the whole race of witches put together, and that was—a woman.

Among the musical disciples who assembled, one evening in each week, to receive his instructions in psalmody, was Katrina Van Tassel, the daughter and only child of a substantial Dutch farmer. She was a blooming lass of fresh eighteen; plump as a partridge; ripe and melting and rosy cheeked as one of her father's peaches, and universally famed, not merely for her beauty, but her vast expectations. She was withal a little of a coquette, as might be perceived even in her dress, which was a mixture of ancient and modern fashions, as most suited to set off her charms. She wore the ornaments of pure yellow gold, which her great-great-grandmother had brought over from Saardam; the tempting stomacher of the older time; and withal a provokingly short petticoat, to display the prettiest foot and ankle in the country round.

Ichabod Crane had a soft and foolish heart towards the sex; and it is not to be wondered at, that so tempting a morsel soon found favor in his eyes; more especially after he had visited her in her paternal mansion. Old Baltus Van Tassel was a perfect picture of a thriving, contented, liberal-hearted farmer. He seldom, it is true, sent either his eyes or his thoughts beyond the boundaries of his own farm; but within those every thing was snug, happy, and well-conditioned. He was satisfied with his wealth, but not proud of it; and piqued himself upon the hearty abundance, rather than the style in which he lived. His stronghold was situated on the banks of the Hudson, in one of those green sheltered, fertile nooks, in which the Dutch farmers are so fond of nestling. A great elm-tree spread its broad branches over it; at the foot of which bubbled up a spring of the softest and sweetest water, in a little well, formed of a barrel; and then stole sparkling away through the grass, to a neighboring brook, that bubbled along among alders and dwarf willows. Hard by the farmhouse was a vast barn, that might have served for a church; every window and crevice of which seemed bursting forth with the treasures of the farm; the flail was busily resounding within it from morning to night; swallows and martins skimmed twittering about the eaves; and rows of pigeons, some with one eye turned up, as if watching the weather, some with their heads under their wings, or buried in their bosoms, and others swelling, and cooing, and bowing about their dames, were enjoying the sunshine on the roof. Sleek unwieldy porkers were grunting in the repose and abundance of their pens; whence sallied forth, now and then, troops of sucking pigs, as if to snuff the air. A stately squadron of snowy geese were riding in an adjoining pond, convoying whole fleets of ducks; regiments of turkeys were gobbling through the farmyard, and guinea fowls fretting about it, like ill-tempered housewives, with their peevish discontented cry. Before the barn door strutted the gallant cock, that pattern of a husband, a warrior, and a fine gentleman, clapping his burnished wings, and crowing in the pride and gladness of his heart—sometimes tearing up the earth with his feet, and then generously calling his ever-hungry family of wives and children to enjoy the rich morsel which he had discovered.

The pedagogue's mouth watered, as he looked upon this sumptuous promise of luxurious winter fare. In his devouring mind's eye, he pictured to himself every roasting-pig running about with a pudding in his belly, and an apple in his mouth; the pigeons were snugly put to bed in a comfortable pie, and tucked in with a coverlet of crust; the geese were swimming in their own gravy; and the ducks pairing cosily in dishes, like snug married couples, with a decent competency of onion sauce. In the porkers he saw carved out the future sleek side of bacon, and juicy relishing ham; not a turkey but he beheld daintly trussed up, with its gizzard under its wing, and, peradventure, a necklace of savory sausages; and even bright chanticleer himself lay sprawling on his back, in a side-dish, with uplifted claws, as if craving that quarter which his chivalrous spirit disdained to ask while living.

As the enraptured Ichabod fancied all this, and as he rolled his great green eyes over the fat meadowlands, the rich fields of wheat, of rye, of buckwheat, and Indian corn, and the orchards burthened with ruddy fruit, which surrounded the warm tenement of Van Tassel, his heart yearned after the damsel who was to inherit these domains, and his imagination expanded with the idea, how they might be readily turned into cash, and the money invested in immense tracts of wild land, and shingle palaces in the wilderness. Nay, his busy fancy already realized his hopes, and presented to him the blooming Katrina, with a whole family of children, mounted on the top of a wagon loaded with household trumpery, with pots and kettles dangling beneath; and he beheld himself bestriding a pacing mare, with a colt at her heels, setting out for Kentucky, Tennessee, or the Lord knows where.

When he entered the house the conquest of his heart was complete. It was one of those spacious farmhouses, with high-ridged, but lowly-sloping roofs, built in the style handed down from the first Dutch settlers; the low projecting eaves forming a piazza along the front, capable of being closed up in bad weather. Under this were hung flails, harness, various utensils of husbandry, and nets for fishing in the neighboring river. Benches were built along the sides for summer use; and a great spinning-wheel at one end, and a churn at the other, showed the various uses to which this important porch might be devoted. From this piazza the wondering Ichabod entered the hall, which formed the centre of the mansion and the place of usual residence. Here, rows of resplendent pewter, ranged on a long dresser, dazzled his eyes. In one corner stood a huge bag of wool ready to be spun; in another a quantity of linsey-woolsey just from the loom; ears of Indian corn, and strings of dried apples and peaches, hung in gay festoons along the walls, mingled with the gaud of red peppers; and a door left ajar gave him a peep into the best parlor, where the claw-footed chairs, and dark mahogany tables, shone like mirrors; andirons, with their accompanying shovel and tongs, glistened from their covert of asparagus tops; mock-oranges and conch-shells decorated the mantel-piece; strings of various colored birds' eggs were suspended above it: a great ostrich egg was hung from the centre of the room, and a corner cupboard, knowingly left open, displayed immense treasures of old silver and well-mended china.

From the moment Ichabod laid his eyes upon these regions of delight, the peace of his mind was at an end, and his only study was how to gain the affections of the peerless daughter of Van Tassel. In this enterprise, however, he had more real difficulties than generally fell to the lot of a knight-errant of yore, who seldom had any thing but giants, enchanters, fiery dragons, and such like easily-conquered adversaries, to contend with; and had to make his way merely through gates of iron and brass, and walls of adamant, to the castle keep, where the lady of his heart was confined; all which he achieved as easily as a man would carve his way to the centre of a Christmas pie; and then the lady gave him her hand as a matter of course. Ichabod, on the contrary, had to win his way to the heart of a country coquette, beset with a labyrinth of whims and caprices, which were for ever presenting new difficulties and impediments; and he had to encounter a host of fearful adversaries of real flesh and blood, and numerous rustic admirers, who beset every portal to her heart; keeping a watchful and angry eye upon each other, but ready to fly out in the common cause against any new competitor.

Among these the most formidable was a burly, roaring, roystering blade, of the name of Abraham, or, according to the Dutch abbreviation, Brom Van

Brunt, the hero of the country round, which rang with his feats of strength and hardihood. He was broad-shouldered and double-jointed, with short curly black hair, and a bluff, but not unpleasant countenance, having a mingled air of fun and arrogance. From his Herculean frame and great powers of limb, he had received the nickname of BROM BONES, by which he was universally known. He was famed for great knowledge and skill in horsemanship, being as dexterous on horseback as a Tartar. He was foremost at all races and cock-fights; and, with the ascendency which bodily strength acquires in rustic life, was the umpire in all disputes, setting his hat on one side, and giving his decisions with an air and tone admitting of no gainsay or appeal. He was always ready for either a fight or a frolic; but had more mischief than ill-will in his composition; and, with all his over-bearing roughness, there was a strong dash of waggish good humor at bottom. He had three or four boon companions, who regarded him as their model, and at the head of whom he scoured the country, attending every scene of feud or merriment for miles round. In cold weather he was distinguished by a fur cap, surmounted with a flaunting fox's tail; and when folks at a country gathering described this well-known crest at a distance, whisking about among a squad of hard riders, they always stood by for a squall. Sometimes his crew would be heard dashing along past the farmhouses at midnight, with whoop and halloo, like a troop of Don Cossacks; and the old dames, startled out of their sleep, would listen for a moment till the hurry-scurry had clattered by, and then exclaim, "Ay, there goes Brom Bones and his gang!" The neighbors looked upon him with a mixture of awe, admiration, and good will; and when any madcap prank, or rustic brawl, occurred in the vicinity, always shook their heads, and warranted Brom Bones was at the bottom of it.

This rantipole hero had for some time singled out the blooming Katrina for the object of his uncouth gallantries, and though his amorous toyings were something like the gentle caresses and endearments of a bear, yet it was whispered that she did not altogether discourage his hopes. Certain it is, his advances were signals for rival candidates to retire, who felt no inclination to cross a lion in his amours; insomuch, that when his horse was seen tied to Van Tassel's paling, on a Sunday night, a sure sign that his master was courting, or, as it is termed, "sparking," within, all other suitors passed by in despair, and carried the war into other quarters.

Such was the formidable rival with whom Ichabod Crane had to contend, and, considering all things, a stouter man than he would have shrunk from the competition, and a wiser man would have despaired. He had, however, a happy mixture of pliability and perserverance in his nature; he was in form and spirit like a supple-jack—yielding, but tough; though he bent, he never broke; and though he bowed beneath the slightest pressure, yet, the moment it was away—jerk! he was as erect, and carried his head as high as ever.

To have taken the field openly against his rival would have been madness; for he was not a man to be thwarted in his amours, any more than the stormy lover, Achilles. Ichabod, therefore, made his advances in a quiet and gently-insinuating manner. Under cover of his character of singing-master, he made frequent visits at the farmhouse; not that he had any thing to apprehend from the meddlesome interference of parents, which is so often a stumbling-block in the path of lovers. Balt Van Tassel was an easy indulgent soul; he loved his daughter better even than his pipe, and like a reasonable man and an excellent father, let her have her way in every thing. His notable little wife, too, had enough to do to attend to her housekeeping and manage her poultry; for, as she sagely observed, ducks and geese are foolish things, and must be looked after, but girls can take care of themselves. Thus while the busy dame bustled about the house, or plied her spinning-wheel at one end of the piazza, honest Balt would sit smoking his evening pipe at the other, watching the achievements of a little wooden warrior, who, armed with a sword in each hand, was most valiantly fighting the wind on the pinnacle of the barn. In the mean time, Ichabod would carry on his suit with the daughter by the side of the spring under the great elm, or sauntering along in the twilight, that hour so favorable to the lover's eloquence.

I profess not to know how women's hearts are wooed and won. To me they have always been matters of riddle and admiration. Some seem to have but one vulnerable point, or door of access; while others have a thousand avenues, and may be captured in a thousand different ways. It is a great triumph of skill to gain the former, but a still greater proof of generalship to maintain possession of the latter, for the man must battle for his fortress at every door and window. He who wins a thousand common hearts is therefore entitled to some renown; but he who keeps undisputed sway over the heart of a coquette, is indeed a hero. Certain it is, that this was not the case with the redoubtable Brom Bones; and from the moment Ichabod Crane made his advances, the interests of the former evidently declined; his horse was no longer seen tied at the palings on Sunday nights, and a deadly feud gradually arose between him and the preceptor of Sleepy Hollow.

Brom, who had a degree of rough chivalry in his nature, would fain have carried matters to open warfare, and have settled their pretensions to the lady, according to the mode of those most concise and simple reasoners, the knights-errant of yore—by single combat; but Ichabod was too conscious of the superior might of his adversary to enter the lists against him: he had overheard a boast of Bones, that he would "double the schoolmaster up, and lay him on a shelf of his own school-house"; and he was too wary to give him an opportunity. There was something extremely provoking in this obstinately pacific system; it left Brom no alternative but to draw upon the funds of rustic waggery in his disposition, and to play off boorish practical jokes upon his rival: Ichabod became the object of whimsical persecution to Bones, and his gang of rough riders. They harried his hitherto peaceful domains; smoked out his singing school, by stopping up the chimney; broke into the school-house at night, in spite of its formidable fastenings of withe and window stakes, and turned every thing topsy-turvy: so that the poor schoolmaster began to think all the witches in the country held their meetings there. But what was still more annoying, Brom took all opportunities of turning him into ridicule in presence of his mistress, and had a scoundrel dog whom he taught to whine in the most ludicrous manner, and introduced as a rival of Ichabod's to instruct her in psalmody.

In this way matters went on for some time, without producing any material effect on the relative situation of the contending powers. On a fine autumnal afternoon, Ichabod, in pensive mood, sat enthroned on the lofty stool whence he usually watched all the concerns of his little literary realm. In his hand he swayed a ferule, that sceptre of despotic power; the birch of justice reposed on three nails, behind the throne, a constant terror to evil doers; while on the desk before him might be seen sundry contraband articles, and prohibited weapons, detected upon the persons of idle urchins; such as half-munched apples, popguns, whirligigs, fly-cages, and whole legions of rampant little paper game-cocks. Apparently there had been some appalling act of justice recently inflicted, for his scholars were all busily intent upon their books, or slyly whispering behind them with one eye kept upon the master; and a kind of buzzing stillness reigned throughout the schoolroom. It was suddenly interrupted by the appearance of a negro, in tow-cloth jacket and trowsers, a round-crowned fragment of a hat, like the cap of Mercury, and mounted on the back of a ragged, wild, half-broken colt, which he managed with a rope by way of halter. He came clattering up to the school door with an invitation to Ichabod to attend a merry-making or "quilting frolic," to be held that evening at Mynheer Van Tassel's; and having delivered his message with that air of importance, and effort at fine language, which a negro is apt to display on petty embassies of the kind, he dashed over the brook, and was seen scampering away up the hollow, full of the importance and hurry of his mission.

All was now bustle and hubbub in the late quiet schoolroom. The scholars were hurried through their lessons, without stopping at trifles; those who were nimble skipped over half with impunity, and those who were tardy, had a smart application now and then in the rear, to quicken their speed, or help them over a tall word. Books were flung aside without being put away on the shelves, ink-stands were overturned, benches thrown down, and the whole school was turned loose an hour before the usual time, bursting forth like a legion of young imps, yelping and racketing about the green, in joy at their early emancipation.

The gallant Ichabod now spent at least an extra hour at his toilet, brushing and furbishing up his best, and indeed only suit of rusty black, and arranging his looks* by a bit of broken looking-glass, that hung up in the school-house. That he might make his appearance before his mistress in the true style of a cavalier, he borrowed a horse from the farmer with whom he was domiciliated, a choleric old Dutchman, of the name of Hans Van Ripper, and, thus gallantly mounted, issued forth, like a knight-errant in quest of adventures. But it is meet I should, in the true spirit of romantic story, give some account of the looks and equipments of my hero and his steed. The animal he bestrode was a broken-down plough-horse, that had outlived almost every thing but his viciousness. He was gaunt and shagged, with a ewe neck and a head like a hammer; his rusty mane and tail was tangled and knotted with burrs; one eye had lost its pupil, and was glaring and spectral; but the other had the gleam of a genuine devil in it. Still

* Some versions of the story read *locks*.

he must have had fire and mettle in his day, if we may judge from the name he bore of Gunpowder. He had, in fact, been a favorite steed of his master's, the choleric Van Ripper, who was a furious rider, and had infused, very probably, some of his own spirit into the animal; for, old and broken-down as he looked, there was more of the lurking devil in him than in any young filly in the country.

Ichabod was a suitable figure for such a steed. He rode with short stirrups, which brought his knees nearly up to the pommel of the saddle; his sharp elbows stuck out like grasshoppers'; he carried his whip perpendicularly in his hand, like a sceptre, and, as his horse jogged on, the motion of his arms was not unlike the flapping of a pair of wings. A small wool hat rested on the top of his nose, for so his scanty strip of forehead might be called; and the skirts of his black coat fluttered out almost to the horse's tail. Such was the appearance of Ichabod and his steed, as they shambled out of the gate of Hans Van Ripper, and it was altogether such an apparition as is seldom to be met with in broad daylight.

It was, as I have said, a fine autumnal day, the sky was clear and serene, and nature wore that rich and golden livery which we always associate with the idea of abundance. The forests had put on their sober brown and yellow, while some trees of the tenderer kind had been nipped by the frosts into brilliant dyes of orange, purple, and scarlet. Streaming files of wild ducks began to make their appearance high in the air; the bark of the squirrel might be heard from the groves of beech and hickory nuts, and the pensive whistle of the quail at intervals from the neighboring stubble-field.

The small birds were taking their farewell banquets. In the fulness of their revelry, they fluttered, chirping and frolicking, from bush to bush, and tree to tree, capricious from the very profusion and variety around them. There was the honest cock-robin, the favorite game of stripling sportsmen, with its loud querulous note; and the twittering blackbirds flying in sable clouds; and the golden-winged woodpecker, with his crimson crest, his broad black gorget, and splendid plumage; and the cedar bird, with its red-tipt wings and yellow-tipt tail, and its little monteiro cap of feathers; and the blue jay, that noisy coxcomb, in his gay light-blue coat and white underclothes; screaming and chattering, nodding and bobbing and bowing, and pretending to be on good terms with every songster of the grove.

As Ichabod jogged slowly on his way, his eye, ever open to every symptom of culinary abundance, ranged with delight over the treasures of jolly autumn. On all sides he beheld vast store of apples; some hanging in oppressive opulence on the trees; some gathered into baskets and barrels for the market; others heaped up in rich piles for the cider-press. Farther on he beheld great fields of Indian corn, with its golden ears peeping from their leafy coverts, and holding out the promise of cakes and hasty pudding; and the yellow pumpkins lying beneath them, turning up their fair round bellies to the sun, and giving ample prospects of the most luxurious of pies; and anon he passed the fragant buckwheat fields, breathing the odor of the bee-hive, and as he beheld them, soft anticipations stole over his mind of dainty slapjacks, well buttered, and garnished with honey or treacle, by the delicate little dimpled hand of Katrina Van Tassel.

Thus feeding his mind with many sweet thoughts and "sugared suppositions," he journeyed along the sides of a range of hills which look out upon some of the goodliest scenes of the mighty Hudson. The sun gradually wheeled his broad disk down into the west. The wide bosom of the Tappan Zee lay motionless and glassy, excepting that here and there a gentle undulation waved and prolonged the blue shadow of the distant mountain. A few amber clouds floated in the sky, without a breath of air to move them. The horizon was of a fine golden tint, changing gradually into a pure apple green, and from that into the deep blue of the mid-heaven. A slanting ray lingered on the woody crests of the precipices that overhung some parts of the river, giving greater depth to the dark-gray and purple of their rocky sides. A sloop was loitering in the distance, dropping slowly down with the tide, her sail hanging uselessly against the mast; and as the reflection of the sky gleamed along the still water, it seemed as if the vessel was suspended in the air.

It was toward evening that Ichabod arrived at the castle of the Heer Van Tassel, which he found thronged with the pride and flower of the adjacent country. Old farmers, a spare leathern-faced race, in homespun coats and breeches, blue stockings, huge shoes, and magnificent pewter buckles. Their brisk withered little dames, in close crimped caps, longwaisted shortgowns, homespun petticoats, with scissors and pin-cushions, and gay calico pockets hanging on the outside. Buxom lasses, almost as antiquated as their mothers, excepting where a straw hat, a fine ribbon, or perhaps a white frock, gave symptoms of city innovation. The sons, in short square-skirted coats with rows of stupendous brass buttons, and their hair generally queued in the fashion of the times, especially if they could procure an eel-skin for the purpose, it being esteemed throughout the country, as a potent nourisher and strengthener of the hair.

Brom Bones, however, was the hero of the scene, having come to the gathering on his favorite steed Daredevil, a creature, like himself, full of mettle and mischief, and which no one but himself could manage. He was, in fact, noted for preferring vicious animals, given to all kinds of tricks, which kept the rider in constant risk of his neck, for he held a tractable well-broken horse as unworthy of a lad of spirit.

Fain would I pause to dwell upon the world of charms that burst upon the enraptured gaze of my hero, as he entered the state parlor of Van Tassel's mansion. Not those of the bevy of buxom lasses, with their luxurious display of red and white; but the ample charms of a genuine Dutch country tea-table, in the sumptuous time of autumn. Such heaped-up platters of cakes of various and almost indescribable kinds, known only to experienced Dutch housewives! There was the doughty dough-nut, the tenderer oly koek, and the crisp and crumbling cruller; sweet cakes and short cakes, ginger cakes and honey cakes, and the whole family of cakes. And then there were apple pies and peach pies and pumpkin pies; besides slices of ham and smoked beef; and moreover delectable dishes of preserved plums, and peaches, and pears, and quinces; not to mention broiled shad and roasted chicken; together with bowls of milk and cream, all mingled higgledy-piggledy, pretty much as I have enumerated them, with the motherly tea-pot sending up its clouds of vapor from the midst—Heaven bless the mark! I want breath and time to discuss this banquet as it deserves, and am too eager to get on with my story. Happily, Ichabod Crane was not in so great a hurry as his historian, but did ample justice to every dainty.

He was a kind and thankful creature, whose heart dilated in proportion as his skin was filled with good cheer; and whose spirits rose with eating as some men's do with drink. He could not help, too, rolling his large eyes round him as he ate, and chuckling with the possibility that he might one day be lord of all this scene of almost unimaginable luxury and splendor. Then, he thought, how soon he'd turn his back upon the old school-house; snap his fingers in the face of Hans Van Ripper, and every other niggardly patron, and kick any itinerant pedagogue out of doors that should dare to call him comrade!

Old Baltus Van Tassel moved about among his guests with a face dilated with content and good humor, round and jolly as the harvest moon. His hospitable attentions were brief, but expressive, being confined to a shake of a hand, a slap on the shoulder, a loud laugh, and a pressing invitation to "fall to, and help themselves."

And now the sound of the music from the common room, or hall, summoned to the dance. The musician was an old grayheaded negro, who had been the itinerant orchestra of the neighborhood for more than half a century. His instrument was as old and battered as himself. The greater part of the time he scraped on two or three strings, accompanying every movement of the bow with a motion of the head; bowing almost to the ground, and stamping with his foot whenever a fresh couple were to start.

Ichabod prided himself upon his dancing as much as upon his vocal powers. Not a limb, not a fibre about him was idle; and to have seen his loosely hung frame in full motion, and clattering about the room, you would have thought Saint Vitus himself, that blessed patron of the dance, was figuring before you in person. He was the admiration of all the negroes; who, having gathered, of all ages and sizes, from the farm and the neighborhood, stood forming a pyramid of shining black faces at every door and window, gazing with delight at the scene, rolling their white eye-balls, and showing grinning rows of ivory from ear to ear. How could the flogger of urchins be otherwise than animated and joyous? the lady of his heart was his partner in the dance, and smiling graciously in reply to all his amorous oglings; while Brom Bones, sorely smitten with love and jealousy, sat brooding by himself in one corner.

When the dance was at an end, Ichabod was attracted to a knot of the sager folks, who, with old Van Tassel, sat smoking at one end of the piazza, gossiping over former times, and drawing out long stories about the war.

This neighborhood, at the time of which I am speaking, was one of those highly-favored places which abound with chronicle and great men. The British and American line had run near it during the war; it had, therefore, been the scene of marauding, and infested with refugees, cow-boys, and all kinds of border chivalry. Just sufficient time had elapsed to enable each story-teller to dress up his tale with a little becoming fiction, and, in the indistinctness of his recollection, to make himself the hero of every exploit.

There was the story of Doffue Martling, a large blue-bearded Dutchman, who had nearly taken a British frigate with an old iron nine-pounder from a mud breastwork, only that his gun burst at the sixth discharge. And there was an old gentleman who shall be nameless, being too rich a mynheer to be lightly mentioned, who, in the battle of Whiteplains, being an excellent master of defence, parried a musket ball with a small sword, insomuch that he absolutely felt it whiz round the blade, and glance off at the hilt: in proof of which he was ready at any time to show the sword, with the hilt a little bent. There were several more that had been equally great in the field, not one of whom but was persuaded that he had a considerable hand in bringing the war to a happy termination.

But all these were nothing to the tales of ghosts and apparitions that succeeded. The neighborhood is rich in legendary treasures of the kind. Local tales and superstitions thrive best in these sheltered long-settled retreats; but are trampled under foot by the shifting throng that forms the population of most of our country places. Besides, there is no encouragement for ghosts in most of our villages, for they have scarcely had time to finish their first nap, and turn themselves in their graves, before their surviving friends have travelled away from the neighborhood; so that when they turn out at night to walk their rounds, they have no acquaintance left to call upon. This is perhaps the reason why we so seldom hear of ghosts except in our long-established Dutch communities.

The immediate cause, however, the prevalence of supernatural stories in these parts, was doubtless owing to the vicinity of Sleepy Hollow. There was a contagion in the very air that blew from that haunted region; it breathed forth an atmosphere of dreams and fancies infecting all the land. Several of the Sleepy Hollow people were present at Van Tassel's, and, as usual, were doling out their wild and wonderful legends. Many dismal tales were told about funeral trains, and mourning cries and wailings heard and seen about the great tree where the unfortunate Major André was taken, and which stood in the neighborhood. Some mention was made also of the woman in white, that haunted the dark glen at Raven Rock, and was often heard to shriek on winter nights before a storm, having perished there in the snow. The chief part of the stories, however, turned upon the favorite spectre of Sleepy Hollow, the headless horseman, who had been heard several times of late, patrolling the country; and, it was said, tethered his horse nightly among the graves in the churchyard.

The sequestered situation of this church seems always to have made it a favorite haunt of troubled spirits. It stands on a knoll, surrounded by locust-trees and lofty elms, from among which its decent whitewashed walls shine modestly forth, like Christian purity beaming through the shades of retirement. A gentle slope descends from it to a silver sheet of water, bordered by high trees, between which, peeps may be caught at the blue hills of the Hudson. To look upon its grass-grown yard, where the sunbeams seem to sleep so quietly, one would think that there at least the dead might rest in peace. On one side of the church extends a wide woody dell, along which raves a large brook among broken rocks and trunks of fallen trees. Over a deep black part of the stream, not far from the church, was formerly thrown a wooden bridge; the road that led to it, and the bridge itself, were thickly shaded by overhanging trees, which cast a gloom about it, even in the daytime; but occasioned a fearful darkness at night. This was one of the favorite haunts of the headless horseman; and the place where he was most frequently encountered. The tale was told of old Brouwer, a most heretical disbeliever in ghosts, how he met the horseman returning from his foray into Sleepy Hollow, and was obliged to get up behind him; how they galloped over bush and brake, over hill and swamp, until they reached the bridge; when the horseman suddenly turned into a skeleton, threw old Brouwer into the brook, and sprang away over the tree-tops with a clap of thunder.

This story was immediately matched by a thrice marvellous adventure of Brom Bones, who made light of the galloping Hessian as an arrant jockey. He affirmed that, on returning one night from the neighboring village of Sing Sing, he had been overtaken by this midnight trooper; that he had offered to race with him for a bowl of punch, and should have won it too, for Daredevil beat the goblin-horse all hollow, but, just as they came to the church-bridge, the Hessian bolted, and vanished in a flash of fire.

All these tales, told in that drowsy undertone with which men talk in the dark, the countenances of the listeners only now and then receiving a casual gleam from the glare of a pipe, sank deep in the mind of Ichabod. He repaid them in kind with large extracts from his invaluable author, Cotton Mather, and added many marvellous events that had taken place in his native State of Connecticut, and fearful sights which he had seen in his nightly walks about Sleepy Hollow.

The revel now gradually broke up. The old farmers gathered together their families in their wagons, and were heard for some time rattling along the hollow roads, and over the distant hills. Some of the damsels mounted on pillions behind their favorite swains, and their light-hearted laughter, mingling with the clatter of hoofs, echoed along the silent woodlands, sounding fainter and fainter until they gradually died away—and the late scene of noise and frolic was all silent and deserted. Ichabod only lingered behind, according to the custom of country lovers to have tête-à-tête with the heiress, fully convinced that he was now on the high road to success. What passed at this interview I will not pretend to say, for in fact I do not know. Something, however, I fear me, must have gone wrong, for he certainly sallied forth, after no very great interval, with an air quite desolate and chop-fallen.—Oh these women! these women! Could that girl have been playing off any of her coquettish tricks?—Was her encouragement of the poor pedagogue all a mere sham to secure her conquest of his rival?—Heaven only knows, not I!—Let it suffice to say, Ichabod stole forth with the air of one who had been sacking a hen-roost, rather than a fair lady's heart. Without looking to the right or left to notice the scene of rural wealth, on which he had so often gloated, he went straight to the stable, and with several hearty cuffs and kicks, roused his steed most uncourteously from the comfortable quarters in which he was soundly sleeping, dreaming of mountains of corn and oats, and whole valleys of timothy and clover.

It was the very witching time of night that Ichabod, heavy-hearted and crest-fallen, pursued his travel homewards, along the sides of the lofty hills which rise about Tarry Town, and which he had traversed so cheerily in the afternoon. The hour was as dismal as himself. Far below him, the Tappan Zee spread its dusky and indistinct waste of waters, with here and there the tall mast of a sloop, riding quietly at anchor under the land. In the dead hush of midnight, he could even hear the barking of the watchdog from the opposite shore of the Hudson; but it was so vague and faint as only to give an idea of his distance from this faithful companion of man. Now and then, too, the long-drawn crowing of a cock, accidentally awakened, would sound far, far off, from some farmhouse away among the hills—but it was like a dreaming sound in his ear. No signs of life occurred near him, but occasionally the melancholy chirp of a cricket, or perhaps the guttural twang of a bullfrog, from a neighboring marsh, as if sleeping uncomfortably, and turning suddenly in his bed.

All the stories of ghosts and goblins that he had heard in the afternoon, now came crowding upon his recollection. The night grew darker and darker; the stars seemed to sink deeper in the sky, and driving clouds occasionally hid them from his sight. He had never felt so lonely and dismal. He was, moreover, approaching the very place where many of the scenes of the ghost stories had been laid. In the centre of the road stood an enormous tulip-tree, which towered like a giant above all the other trees of the neighborhood, and formed a kind of landmark. Its limbs were gnarled, and fantastic, large enough to form trunks for ordinary trees, twisting down almost to the earth, and rising again into the air. It was connected with the tragical story of the unfortunate André, who had been taken prisoner hard by; and was universally known by the name of Major André's tree. The common people regarded it with a mixture of respect and superstition, partly out of sympathy for the fate of its ill-starred namesake, and partly from the tales of strange sights and doleful lamentations told concerning it.

As Ichabod approached this fearful tree, he began to whistle: he thought his whistle was answered—it was but a blast sweeping sharply through the dry branches. As he approached a little nearer, he thought he saw something white, hanging in the midst of the tree—he paused and ceased whistling; but on looking more narrowly, perceived that it was a place where the tree had been scathed by lightning, and the white wood laid bare. Suddenly he heard a groan—his teeth chattered and his knees smote against the saddle: it was but the rippling of one huge bough upon another, as they were swayed about by the breeze. He passed the tree in safety, but new perils lay befor him.

About two hundred yards from the tree a small brook crossed the road, and ran into a marshy and thickly-wooded glen, known by the name of Wiley's swamp. A few rough logs, laid side by side, served for a bridge over this stream. On that side of the road where the brook entered the wood, a group of oaks and chestnuts, matted thick with wild grapevines, threw a cavernous gloom over it. To pass this bridge was the severest trial. It was at this identical spot that the unfortunate André was captured, and under the covert of those chestnuts and vines were the sturdy yeomen concealed who surprised him. This has ever since been considered a haunted stream, and fearful are the feelings of the schoolboy who has to pass it alone after dark.

As he approached the stream his heart began to thump; he summoned up, however, all his resolution, gave his horse half a score of kicks in the ribs, and attempted to dash briskly across the bridge; but instead of starting forward, the perverse old animal made a lateral movement, and ran broadside against the fence. Ichabod, whose fears increased with the delay, jerked the reins on the other side, and kicked lustily with the contrary foot: it was all in vain; his steed started, it is true, but it was only to plunge to the opposite side of the road into a thicket of brambles and alder bushes. The schoolmaster now bestowed both whip and heel upon the starveling ribs of old Gunpowder, who dashed forward, snuffling and snorting, but came to a stand just by the bridge, with a suddenness that had nearly sent his rider sprawling over his head. Just at this moment a plashy tramp by the side of the bridge caught the sensitive ear of Ichabod. In the dark shadow of the grove, on the margin of the brook, he beheld something huge, misshapen, black and towering. It stirred not, but seemed gathered up in the gloom, like some gigantic monster ready to spring upon the traveller.

The hair of the affrighted pedagogue rose upon his head with terror. What was to be done? To turn and fly was now too late; and besides, what chance was there of escaping ghost or goblin, if such it was, which could ride upon the wings of the wind? Summoning up, therefore, a show of courage, he demanded in stammering accents—"Who are you?" He received no reply. He repeated his demand in a still more agitated voice. Still there was no answer. Once more he cudgelled the sides of the inflexible Gunpowder, and, shutting his eyes, broke forth with involuntary fervor into a psalm tune. Just then the shadowy object of alarm put itself in motion, and, with a scramble and a bound, stood at once in the middle of the road. Though the night was dark and dismal, yet the form of the unknown might now in some degree be ascertained. He appeared to be a horseman of large dimensions, and mounted on a black horse of powerful frame. He made no offer of molestation or sociability, but kept aloof on one side of the road, jogging along on the blind side of old Gunpowder, who had now got over his fright and waywardness.

Ichabod, who had no relish for this strange midnight companion, and bethought himself of the adventure of Brom Bones with the Galloping Hession, now quickened his steed, in hopes of leaving him behind. The stranger, however, quickened his horse to an equal pace. Ichabod pulled up, and fell into a walk, thinking to lag behind—the other did the same. His heart began to sink within him; he endeavored to resume his psalm tune, but his parched tongue clove to the roof of his mouth, and he could not utter a stave. There was something in the moody and dogged silence of this pertinacious companion, that was mysterious and appalling. It was soon fearfully accounted for. On mounting a rising ground, which brought the figure of his fellow-traveller in relief against the sky, gigantic in height, and muffled in a cloak, Ichabod was horror-struck, on perceiving that he was headless!—but his horror was still more increased, on observing that the head, which should have rested on his shoulders, was carried before him on the pommel of the saddle: his terror rose to desperation; he rained a shower of kicks and blows upon Gunpowder, hoping, by a sudden movement, to give his companion the slip—but the spectre started full jump with him. Away then they dashed, through thick and thin; stones flying, and sparks flashing at every bound. Ichabod's flimsy garments fluttered in the air, as he stretched his long lank body away over his horse's head, in the eagerness of his flight.

They had now reached the road which turns off to Sleepy Hollow; but Gunpowder, who seemed possessed with a demon, instead of keeping up it, made an opposite turn, and plunged headlong down hill to the left. This road leads through a sandy hollow, shaded by trees for about a quarter of a mile, where it crosses the bridge famous in goblin story, and just beyond swells the green knoll on which stands the whitewashed church.

As yet the panic of the steed had given his unskilful rider an apparent advantage in the chase; but just as he had got half way through the hollow, the girths of the saddle gave way, and he felt it slipping from under him. He seized it by the pommel, and endeavored to hold it firm, but in vain; and had just time to save himself by clasping old Gunpowder round the neck, when the saddle fell to the earth, and he heard it trampled under foot by his pursuer. For a moment the terror of Hans Van Ripper's wrath passed across his mind—for it was his Sunday saddle; but this was no time for petty fears; the goblin was hard on his haunches; and (unskilful rider that he was!) he had much ado to maintain his seat; sometimes slipping on one side, sometimes on another, and sometimes jolted on the high ridge of his horse's back-bone, with a violence that he verily feared would cleave him asunder.

An opening in the trees now cheered him with the hopes that the church bridge was at hand. The wavering reflection of a silver star in the bosom of the brook told him that he was not mistaken. He saw the walls of the church dimly glaring under the trees beyond. He recollected the place where Brom Bone's ghostly competitor had disappeared. "If I can but reach the bridge," thought Ichabod, "I am safe." Just then he heard the black steed panting and blowing close behind him; he even fancied that he felt his hot breath. Another convulsive kick in the ribs and old Gunpowder sprang upon the bridge; he thundered over the resounding planks; he gained the opposite side; and now Ichabod cast a look behind to see if his pursuer should vanish, according to rule, in a flash of fire and brimstone. Just then he saw the goblin rising in his stirrups, and in the very act of hurling his head at him. Ichabod endeavored to dodge the horrible missile, but too late. It encountered his cranium with a tremendous crash—he was tumbled headlong into the dust, and Gunpowder, the black steed, and the goblin rider, passed by like a whirlwind.

The next morning the old horse was found without his saddle, and with the bridle under his feet, soberly cropping the grass at his master's gate. Ichabod did not make his appearance at breakfast—dinner-hour came, but no Ichabod. The boys assembled at the school-house, and strolled idly about the banks of the brook; but no schoolmaster. Hans Van Ripper now began to feel some uneasiness about the fate of poor Ichabod, and his saddle. An inquiry was set on foot, and after diligent investigation they came upon his traces. In one part of the road leading to the church was found the saddle trampled in the dirt; the tracks of horses' hoofs deeply dented in the road, and evidently at furious speed, were traced to the bridge, beyond which, on the bank of a broad part of the brook, where the water ran deep and black, was found the hat of the unfortunate Ichabod, and close beside it a shattered pumpkin.

The brook was searched, but the body of the schoolmaster was not to be discovered. Hans Van Ripper, as executor of his estate, examined the bundle which contained all his worldly effects. They consisted of two shirts and a half;

two stocks for the neck; a pair or two of worsted stockings; an old pair of corduroy small-clothes; a rusty razor; a book of psalm tunes, full of dogs' ears; and a broken pitch-pipe. As to the books and furniture of the schoolhouse, they belonged to the community, excepting Cotton Mather's History of Witchcraft, a New England Almanac, and a book of dreams and fortune-telling; in which last was a sheet of foolscap much scribbled and blotted in several fruitless attempts to make a copy of verses in honor of the heiress of Van Tassel. These magic books and the poetic scrawl were forthwith consigned to the flames by Hans Van Ripper; who from that time forward determined to send his children no more to school; observing, that he never knew any good come of this same reading and writing. Whatever money the schoolmaster possessed, and he had received his quarter's pay but a day or two before, he must have had about his person at the time of his disappearance.

The mysterious event caused much speculation at the church on the following Sunday. Knots of gazers and gossips were collected in the churchyard, at the bridge, and at the spot where the hat and pumpkin had been found. The stories of Brouwer, of Bones, and a whole budget of others, were called to mind; and when they had diligently considered them all, and compared them with the symptoms of the present case, they shook their heads, and came to the conclusion that Ichabod had been carried off by the Galloping Hession. As he was a bachelor, and in nobody's debt, nobody troubled his head any more about him. The school was removed to a different quarter of the hollow, and another pedagogue reigned in his stead.

It is true, an old farmer, who had been down to New York on a visit several years after, and from whom this account of the ghostly adventure was received, brought home the intelligence that Ichabod Crane was still alive; that he had left the neighborhood, partly through fear of the goblin and Hans Van Ripper, and partly in mortification at having been suddenly dismissed by the heiress; that he had changed his quarters to a distant part of the country; had kept school and studied law at the same time, had been admitted to the bar, turned politician, electioneered, written for the newspapers, and finally had been made a justice of the Ten Pound Court. Brom Bones too, who, shortly after his rival's disappearance, conducted the blooming Katrina in triumph to the altar, was observed to look exceedingly knowing whenever the story of Ichabod was related, and always burst into a hearty laugh at the mention of the pumpkin; which led some to suspect that he knew more about the matter than he chose to tell.

The old country wives, however, who are the best judges of these matters, maintain to this day that Ichabod was spirited away by supernatural means; and it is a favorite story often told about the neighborhood round the winter evening fire. The bridge became more than ever an object of superstitious awe, and that may be the reason why the road has been altered of late years, so as to approach the church by the border of the mill-pond. The schoolhouse being deserted, soon fell to decay, and was reported to be haunted by the ghost of the unfortunate pedagogue; and the plough boy, loitering homeward of a still summer evening, has often fancied his voice at a distance, chanting a melancholy psalm tune among the tranquil solitudes of Sleepy Hollow.

POSTSCRIPT, FOUND IN THE HANDWRITING
OF MR. KNICKERBOCKER

The preceding Tale is given, almost in the precise words in which I heard it related at a Corporation meeting of the ancient city of Manhattoes, at which were present many of its sagest and most illustrious burghers. The narrator was a pleasant, shabby, gentlemanly old fellow, in pepper-and-salt clothes, with a sadly humorous face; and one whom I strongly suspected of being poor,—he made such efforts to be entertaining. When his story was concluded, there was much laughter and approbation, particularly from two or three deputy aldermen, who had been asleep the greater part of the time. There was, however, one tall, dry-looking old gentleman, with beetling eyebrows, who maintained a grave and rather severe face throughout: now and then folding his arms, inclining his head, and looking down upon the floor, as if turning a doubt over in his mind. He was one of your wary men, who never laugh, but upon good grounds—when they have reason and the law on their side. When the mirth of the rest of the company had subsided, and silence was restored, he leaned one arm on the elbow of his chair, and sticking the other akimbo, demanded, with a slight, but exceedingly sage motion of the head, and contraction of the brow, what was the moral of the story, and what it went to prove?

The story-teller, who was just putting a glass of wine to his lips, as a refreshment after his toils, paused for a moment, looked at his inquirer with an air of infinite deference, and, lowering the glass slowly to the table, observed, that the story was intended most logically to prove:—

"That there is no situation in life but has its advantages and pleasures—providing we will but take a joke as we find it:

"That, therefore, he that runs races wih goblin troopers is likely to have rough riding of it.

"Ergo, for a country schoolmaster to be refused the hand of a Dutch heires, is a certain step to high preferment, in the state."

The cautious old gentleman knit his brows tenfold closer after this explanation, being sorely puzzled by the ratiocination of the syllogism; while, methought, the one in pepper-and-salt eyed him with something of a triumphant leer. At length he observed, that all this was very well, but still he thought the story a little on the extravagant—there were one or two points on which he had his doubts.

"Faith, sir," replied the story-teller, "as to that matter, I don't believe one-half of it myself."

D. K.

1860–1861

## *Study questions*

1. *What do you think really happened to Ichabod? Is this a fair question?* 2. *List all the references to myths, dreams, and legends as they occur in the story. How*

*are these allusions important to the story?* 3. *At one point in the story Ichabod is presented as a parody of a knight errant on a romantic quest. Why does Irving make this identification? What is Ichabod's quest really for? What is Ichabod like?* 4. *What does the headless horseman represent? Reality? A fantastic projection of a nightmare Ichabod might have had? Both? Something else?* 5. *Why is Ichabod attracted to Katrina? What is she like?* 6. *What role does Brom Van Brunt play in the story? Are other names as suggestive of meaning as his is?* 7. *What is the function of the setting?* 8. *What is the role of the narrator in this story? Is he related to the events and the characters in some integral way, or does he merely report events and tell about characters?* 9. *What is the point of the postscript found in the handwriting of Diedrich Knickerbocker?*

*Nathaniel Hawthorne* (1804–1864), although one of the most important American authors in literary history, was never able to make a satisfactory living from his writings. Born in Salem, Massachusetts, where his ancestors had lived for several generations, he attended Bowdoin College, graduating in 1825. Determined to be a writer, for the next ten years while living in his family home, he practiced his craft. During this period he wrote a lot and destroyed much of what he wrote, but what remains suggests that it was during this time that he created both subject matter and techniques that would serve him throughout his literary career. Some of the stories he wrote during this period were collected in later volumes: *Twice-Told Tales* (1837), *Mosses from an Old Manse* (1846), *The Snow-Image and Other Twice-Told Tales* (1851). Other important publications include his novels: *Fanshawe* (1828), *The Scarlet Letter* (1850), *The House of the Seven Gables* (1851), *The Blithedale Romance* (1852), and *The Marble Faun* (1860).

"The Hollow of the Three Hills" (1830), "Roger Malvin's Burial" (1832), and "The Maypole of Merry Mount" (1836) are all early stories, but they are representative of the kind of short story which became the prototype for the form as it developed throughout its history. Hawthorne's themes, too, remain modern. Although most of his stories are set in Puritan times, he was no Calvinist. Indeed, though his stories often deal with guilt and repentance, he believed in no theology. His probing into what he called the human heart is similar to modern psychological probing into the subconscious, and his reliance in many of his stories on dreams and dream structures points the way to the contemporary.

## THE HOLLOW OF THE THREE HILLS

In those strange old times, when fantastic dreams and madmen's reveries were realized among the actual circumstances of life, two persons met together at an appointed hour and place. One was a lady, graceful in form and fair of feature, though pale and troubled, and smitten with an untimely blight in what should have been the fullest bloom of her years; the other was an ancient and meanly-dressed woman, of ill-favored aspects, and so withered, shrunken, and decrepit, that even the space since she began to decay must have exceeded the ordinary term of human existence. In the spot where they encountered, no mortal could observe them. Three little hills stood near each other, and down in the midst of them sunk a hollow basin, almost mathematically circular, two or three hundred feet in breadth, and of such depth that a stately cedar might but just be visible above the sides. Dwarf pines were numerous upon the hills, and partly fringed the outer verge of the intermediate hollow, within which there was nothing but the brown grass of October, and here and there a tree trunk that had fallen long ago, and lay mouldering with no green successor from its roots. One of these masses of decaying wood, formerly a majestic oak, rested close beside a pool of green and sluggish water at the bottom of the basin. Such scenes as this (so gray tradition tells) were once the resort of the Power of Evil and his plighted subjects; and here, at midnight or on the dim verge of evening, they were said to stand round the mantling pool, disturbing its putrid waters in the performance of an impious baptismal rite. The chill beauty of an autumnal sunset was now gilding the three hill-tops, whence a paler tint stole down their sides into the hollow.

"Here is our pleasant meeting come to pass," said the aged crone, "according as thou hast desired. Say quickly what thou wouldst have of me, for there is but a short hour that we may tarry here."

As the old withered woman spoke, a smile glimmered on her countenance, like lamplight on the wall of a sepulchre. The lady trembled, and cast her eyes upward to the verge of the basin, as if meditating to return with her purpose unaccomplished. But it was not so ordained.

"I am a stranger in this land, as you know," said she at length. "Whence I come it matters not; but I have left those behind me with whom my fate was intimately bound, and from whom I am cut off forever. There is a weight in my bosom that I cannot away with, and I have come hither to inquire of their welfare."

"And who is there by this green pool that can bring thee news from the ends of the earth?" cried the old woman, peering into the lady's face. "Not from my lips mayst thou hear these tidings; yet, be thou bold, and the daylight shall not pass away from yonder hill-top before thy wish be granted."

"I will do your bidding though I die," replied the lady desperately.

The old woman seated herself on the trunk of the fallen tree, threw aside the hood that shrouded her gray locks, and beckoned her companion to draw near.

"Kneel down," she said, "and lay your forehead on my knees."

She hesitated a moment, but the anxiety that had long been kindling burned fiercely up within her. As she knelt down, the border of her garment was dipped into the pool; she laid her forehead on the old woman's knees, and the latter drew a cloak about the lady's face, so that she was in darkness. Then she heard the muttered words of prayer, in the midst of which she started, and would have arisen.

"Let me flee,—let me flee and hide myself, that they may not look upon me!" she cried. But, with returning recollection, she hushed herself, and was still as death.

For it seemed as if other voices—familiar in infancy, and unforgotten through many wanderings, and in all the vicissitudes of her heart and fortune—were mingling with the accents of the prayer. At first the words were faint and indistinct, not rendered so by distance, but rather resembling the dim pages of a book which we strive to read by an imperfect and gradually brightening light. In such a manner, as the prayer proceeded, did those voices strengthen upon the ear; till at length the petition ended, and the conversation of an aged man, and of a woman broken and decayed like himself, became distinctly audible to the lady as she knelt. But those strangers appeared not to stand in the hollow depth between the three hills. Their voices were encompassed and reëchoed by the walls of a chamber, the windows of which were rattling in the breeze; the regular vibration of a clock, the crackling of a fire, and the tinkling of the embers as they fell among the ashes, rendered the scene almost as vivid as if painted to the eye. By a melancholy hearth sat these two old people, the man calmly despondent, the woman querulous and tearful, and their words were all of sorrow. They spoke of a daughter, a wanderer they knew not where, bearing dishonor along with her, and leaving shame and affliction to bring their gray heads to the grave. They alluded also to other and more recent woe, but in the midst of their talk their voices seemed to melt into the sound of the wind sweeping mournfully among the autumn leaves; and when the lady lifted her eyes, there was she kneeling in the hollow between three hills.

"A weary and lonesome time yonder old couple have of it," remarked the old woman, smiling in the lady's face.

"And did you also hear them?" exclaimed she, a sense of intolerable humiliation triumphing over her agony and fear.

"Yea; and we have yet more to hear," replied the old woman. "Wherefore, cover thy face quickly."

Again the withered hag poured forth the monotonous words of a prayer that was not meant to be acceptable in heaven; and soon, in the pauses of her breath, strange murmurings began to thicken, gradually increasing so as to drown and overpower the charm by which they grew. Shrieks pierced through the obscurity of sound, and were succeeded by the singing of sweet female voices, which, in their turn, gave way to a wild roar of laughter, broken suddenly by groanings and sobs, forming altogether a ghastly confusion of terror and mourning and mirth. Chains were rattling, fierce and stern voices uttered threats, and the scourge resounded at their command. All these noises deepened and became substantial to the listener's ear, till she could distinguish every soft and dreamy accent of the love songs that died causelessly into funeral hymns. She shuddered at the unprovoked wrath which blazed up like the spontaneous kindling of flame, and she grew faint at the fearful merriment raging miserably around her. In the midst of this wild scene, where unbound passions jostled each other in a drunken career, there was one solemn voice of a man, and a manly and melodious voice it might once have been. He went to and fro continually, and his feet sounded upon the floor. In each member of that frenzied company, whose own burning thoughts had become their exclusive world, he sought an auditor for the story of his individual wrong, and interpreted their laughter and tears as his reward of scorn or pity. He spoke of woman's perfidy, of a wife who had broken her holiest vows, of a home and heart made desolate. Even as he went on, the shout, the laugh, the shriek, the sob, rose up in unison, till they changed into the hollow, fitful, and uneven sound of the wind, as it fought among the pine-trees on those three lonely hills. The lady looked up, and there was the withered woman smiling in her face.

"Couldst thou have thought there were such merry times in a madhouse?" inquired the latter.

"True, true," said the lady to herself; "there is mirth within its walls, but misery, misery without."

"Wouldst thou hear more?" demanded the old woman.

"There is one other voice I would fain listen to again," replied the lady, faintly.

"Then, lay down thy head speedily upon my knees, that thou mayst get thee hence before the hour be past."

The golden skirts of day were yet lingering upon the hills, but deep shades obscured the hollow and the pool, as if sombre night were rising thence to overspread the world. Again that evil woman began to weave her spell. Long did it proceed unanswered, till the knolling of a bell stole in among the intervals of her words, like a clang that had travelled far over valley and rising ground, and was just ready to die in the air. The lady shook upon her companion's knees as she heard that boding sound. Stronger it grew and sadder, and deepened into the tone of a death bell, knolling dolefully from some ivy-mantled tower, and bearing tidings of mortality and woe to the cottage, to the hall, and to the solitary wayfarer, that all might weep for the doom appointed in turn to them. Then came a measured tread, passing slowly, slowly on, as of mourners with a coffin, their garments trailing on the ground, so that the ear could measure the length of their melancholy array. Before them went the priest, reading the burial service, while the leaves of his book were rustling in the breeze. And though no voice but in his was heard to speak aloud, still there were revilings and anathemas, whispered but distinct, from women and from men, breathed against the daughter who had wrung the aged hearts of her parents,—the wife who had betrayed the trusting fondnes of her husband,—the mother who had sinned against natural affection, and left her child to die. The sweeping sound of the funeral train faded away like a thin vapor, and the wind, that just before had seemed to shake the coffin pall, moaned sadly round the verge of the Hollow between three Hills. But when the old woman stirred the kneeling lady, she lifted not her head.

"Here has been a sweet hour's sport!" said the withered crone, chuckling to herself.

## *Study questions*

1. *Why does Hawthorne mention in his first paragraph "fantastic dreams and madmen's reveries"? How are these dreams tied to the rest of the story?* 2. *What is the point of the reference to "an impious baptismal rite"? Could the action in the story be a kind of baptism?* 3. *What is the relationship of the lady to the withered crone? Note the relative positions of the two people—the lady on her knees with her forehead resting on the old woman's lap, the border of the lady's skirt dipped into the pool and her face covered by a cloak.* 4. *Does the old woman create the dreams that appear or cause them to be delivered forth from the young woman's subconscious? Could the withered crone be a projection of what the young woman could become?* 5. *How does Hawthorne alternate dramatic scene and summary action? For what purpose?* 6. *Chart the development of the plot. Where do complications begin? Where is the climax? Is there a resolution?* 7. *What is the young woman's conflict? Why does she say: "I will do your bidding though I die"?*

# ROGER MALVIN'S BURIAL

One of the few incidents of Indian warfare naturally susceptible of the moonlight of romance was that exhibition undertaken for the defence of the frontiers in the year 1725, which resulted in the well-remembered "Lovell's Fight." Imagination, by casting certain circumstances judicially into the shade, may see much to admire in the heroism of a little band who gave battle to twice their number in the heart of the enemy's country. The open bravery displayed by both parties was in accordance with civilized ideas of valor; and chivalry itself might not blush to record the deeds of one or two individuals. The battle, though so fatal to those who fought, was not unfortunate in its consequences to the country; for it broke the strength of a tribe and conduced to the peace which subsisted during several ensuing years. History and tradition are unusually minute in their memorials of their affair; and the captain of a scouting party of frontier men has acquired as actual a military renown as many a victorious leader of thousands. Some of the incidents contained in the following pages will be recognized, notwithstanding the substitution of fictitious names, by such as have heard, from old men's lips, the fate of the few combatants who were in a condition to retreat after "Lovell's Fight."

The early sunbeams hovered cheerfully upon the tree-tops, beneath which two weary and wounded men had stretched their limbs the night before. Their bed of withered oak leaves was strewn upon the small level space, at the foot of a rock, situated near the summit of one of the gentle swells by which the face of the country is there diversified. The mass of granite, rearing its smooth, flat surface fifteen or twenty feet above their heads, was not unlike a gigantic gravestone, upon which the veins seemed to form an inscription in forgotten characters. On a tract of several acres around this rock, oaks and other hard-wood trees had supplied the place of the pines, which were the usual growth of the land; and a young and vigorous sapling stood close beside the travellers.

The severe wound of the elder man had probably deprived him of sleep; for, so soon as the first ray of sunshine rested on the top of the highest tree, he reared himself painfully from his recumbent posture and sat erect. The deep lines of his countenance and the scattered gray of his hair marked him as past the middle age; but his muscular frame would, but for the effect of his wound, have been as capable of sustaining fatigue as in the early vigor of life. Languor and exhaustion now sat upon his haggard features; and the despairing glance which he sent forward through the depths of the forest proved his own conviction that his pilgrimage was at an end. He next turned his eyes to the companion who reclined by his side. The youth—for he had scarcely attained the years of manhood—lay, with his head upon his arm, in the embrace of an unquiet sleep, which a thrill of pain from his wounds seemed each moment on the point of breaking. His right hand grasped a musket; and, to judge from the violent action of his features, his slumbers were bringing back a vision of the conflict of which he was one of the few survivors. A shout—deep and loud in his dreaming fancy

—found its way in an imperfect murmur to his lips: and, starting even at the slight sound of his own voice, he suddenly awoke. The first act of reviving recollection was to make anxious inquiries respecting the condition of his wounded fellow-traveller. The latter shook his head.

"Reuben, my boy," said he, "this rock beneath which we sit will serve for an old hunter's gravestone. There is many and many a long mile of howling wilderness before us yet; nor would it avail me anything if the smoke of my own chimney were but on the other side of that swell of land. The Indian bullet was deadlier than I thought."

"You are weary with our three days' travel," replied the youth, "and a little longer rest will recruit you. Sit you here while I search the woods for the herbs and roots that must be our sustenance; and, having eaten, you shall lean on me, and we will turn our faces homeward. I doubt not that, with my help, you can attain to some one of the frontier garrisons."

"There is not two days' life in me, Reuben," said the other, calmly, "and I will no longer burden you with my useless body, when you can scarcely support your own. Your wounds are deep and your strength is failing fast; yet, if you hasten onward alone, you may be preserved. For me there is no hope, and I will await death here."

"If it must be so, I will remain and watch by you," said Reuben, resolutely.

"No, my son, no," rejoined his companion. "Let the wish of a dying man have weight with you; give me one grasp of your hand and get you hence. Think you that my last moments will be eased by the thought that I leave you to die a more lingering death? I have loved you like a father, Reuben; and at a time like this I should have something of a father's authority. I charge you to be gone that I may die in peace."

"And because you have been a father to me, should I therefore leave you to perish and to lie unburied in the wilderness?" exclaimed the youth. "No; if your end be in truth approaching, I will watch by you and receive your parting words. I will dig a grave here by the rock, in which, if my weakness overcome me, we will rest together; or, if Heaven gives me strength, I will seek my way home."

"In the cities and wherever men dwell," replied the other, "they bury their dead in the earth; they hide them from the sight of the living; but here, where no step may pass perhaps for a hundred years, wherefore should I not rest beneath the open sky, covered only by the oak leaves when the autumn winds shall strew them? And for a monument, here is this gray rock, on which my dying hand shall carve the name of Roger Malvin; and the traveller in days to come will know that here sleeps a hunter and a warrior. Tarry not, then, for a folly like this, but hasten away, if not for your own sake, for hers who will else be desolate."

Malvin spoke the last few words in a faltering voice, and their effect upon his companion was strongly visible. They reminded him that there were other and less questionable duties than that of sharing the fate of a man whom his death could not benefit. Nor can it be affirmed that no selfish feeling strove to enter Reuben's heart, though the consciousness made him more earnestly resist his companion's entreaties.

"How terrible to wait the slow approach of death in this solitude!" exclaimed he. "A brave man does not shrink in the battle; and, when friends stand round the bed, even women may die composedly; but here"—

"I shall not shrink even here, Reuben Bourne," interrupted Malvin. "I am a man of no weak heart, and, if I were, there is a surer support than that of earthly friends. You are young, and life is dear to you. Your last moments will need comfort far more than mine; and when you have laid me in the earth, and are alone, and night is settling on the forest, you will feel all the bitterness of the death that may now be escaped. But I will urge no selfish motive to your generous nature. Leave me for my sake, that, having said a prayer for your safety, I may have space to settle my account undisturbed by worldly sorrows."

"And your daughter,—how shall I dare to meet her eye?" exclaimed Reuben. "She will ask the fate of her father, whose life I vowed to defend with my own. Must I tell her that he travelled three days' march with me from the field of battle and that then I left him to perish in the wilderness? Were it not better to lie down and die by your side than to return safe and say this to Dorcas?"

"Tell my daughter," said Roger Malvin, "that, though yourself sore wounded, and weak, and weary, you led my tottering footsteps many a mile, and left me only at my earnest entreaty, because I would not have your blood upon my soul. Tell her that through pain and danger you were faithful, and that, if your lifeblood could have saved me, it would have flowed to its last drop; and tell her that you will be something dearer than a father, and that my blessing is with you both, and that my dying eyes can see a long and pleasant path in which you will journey together."

As Malvin spoke he almost raised himself from the ground, and the energy of his concluding words seemed to fill the wild and lonely forest with a vision of happiness; but, when he sank exhausted upon his bed of oak leaves, the light which had kindled in Reuben's eye was quenched. He felt as if it were both sin and folly to think of happiness at such a moment. His companion watched his changing countenance, and sought with generous art to wile him to his own good.

"Perhaps I deceive myself in regard to the time I have to live," he resumed. "It may be that, with speedy assistance, I might recover of my wound. The foremost fugitives must, ere this, have carried tidings of our fatal battle to the frontiers, and parties will be out to succor those in like condition with ourselves. Should you meet one of these and guide them hither, who can tell but that I may sit by my own fireside again?"

A mournful smile strayed across the features of the dying man as he insinuated that unfounded hope,—which, however, was not without its effect on Reuben. No merely selfish motive, nor even the desolate condition of Dorcas, could have induced him to desert his companion at such a moment—but his wishes seized on the thought that Malvin's life might be preserved, and his sanguine nature heightened almost to certainty the remote possibility of procuring human aid.

"Surely there is reason, weighty reason, to hope that friends are not far distant," he said, half aloud. "There fled one coward, unwounded, in the beginning of the fight, and most probably he made good speed. Every true man on the frontier would shoulder his musket at the news; and, though no party may range so far into the woods as this, I shall perhaps encounter them in one day's march. Counsel me faithfully," he added, turning to Malvin, in distrust of his own motives. "Were your situation mine, would you desert me while life remained?"

"It is now twenty years," replied Roger Malvin,—sighing, however, as he secretly acknowledged the wide dissimilarity between the two cases,—"it is now twenty years since I escaped with one dear friend from Indian captivity near Montreal. We journeyed many days through the woods, till at length overcome with hunger and weariness, my friend lay down and besought me to leave him; for he knew that, if I remained, we both must perish; and, with but little hope of obtaining succor, I heaped a pillow of dry leaves beneath his head and hastened on."

"And did you return in time to save him?" asked Reuben, hanging on Malvin's words as if they were to be prophetic of his own success.

"I did," answered the other. "I came upon the camp of a hunting party before sunset of the same day. I guided them to the spot where my comrade was expecting death; and he is now a hale and hearty man upon his own farm, far within the frontiers, while I lie wounded here in the depths of the wilderness."

This example, powerful in affecting Reuben's decision, was aided, unconsciously to himself, by the hidden strength of many another motive. Roger Malvin perceived that the victory was nearly won.

"Now, go, my son, and Heaven prosper you!" he said. "Turn not back with your friends when you meet them, lest your wounds and weariness overcome you; but send hitherward two or three, that may be spared, to search for me; and believe me, Reuben, my heart will be lighter with every step you take towards home." Yet there was, perhaps, a change both in his countenance and voice as he spoke thus; for, after all, it was a ghastly fate to be left expiring in the wilderness.

Reuben Bourne, but half convinced that he was acting rightly, at length raised himself from the ground and prepared himself for his departure. And first, though contrary to Malvin's wishes, he collected a stock of roots and herbs, which had been their only food during the last two days. This useless supply he placed within reach of the dying man, for whom, also, he swept together a bed of dry oak leaves. Then climbing to the summit of the rock, which on one side was rough and broken, he bent the oak sapling downward, and bound his handkerchief to the topmost branch. This precaution was not unnecessary to direct any who might come in search of Malvin; for every part of the rock, except its broad, smooth front, was concealed at a little distance by the dense undergrowth of the forest. The handkerchief had been the bandage of a wound upon Reuben's arm; and, as he bound it to the tree, he vowed by the blood that stained it that he would return, either to save his companion's life or to lay his body in the grave. He then descended, and stood, with downcast eyes, to receive Roger Malvin's parting words.

The experience of the latter suggested much and minute advice respecting the youth's journey through the trackless forest. Upon this subject he spoke with calm earnestness, as if he were sending Reuben to the battle or the chase while he himself remained secure at home, and not as if the human countenance that was about to leave him were the last he would ever behold. But his firmness was shaken before he concluded.

"Carry my blessing to Dorcas, and say that my last prayer shall be for her and you. Bid her to have no hard thoughts because you left me here,"— Reuben's heart smote him,—"for that your life would not have weighed with you if its sacrifice could have done me good. She will marry you after she has mourned a little while for her father; and Heaven grant you long and happy days, and may your children's children stand round your death bed! And, Reuben," added he, as the weakness of mortality made its way at last, "return, when your wounds are healed and your weariness refreshed,— return to this wild rock, and lay my bones in the grave, and say a prayer over them."

An almost superstitious regard, arising perhaps from the customs of the Indians, whose war was with the dead as well as the living, was paid by the frontier inhabitants to the rites of sepulture; and there are many instances of the sacrifice of life in the attempt to bury those who had fallen by the "sword of the wilderness." Reuben, therefore, felt the full importance of the promise which he most solemnly made to return and perform Roger Malvin's obsequies. It was remarkable that the latter, speaking his whole heart in his parting words, no longer endeavored to persuade the youth that even the speediest succor might avail to the preservation of his life. Reuben was internally convinced that he should see Malvin's living face no more. His generous nature would fain have delayed him, at whatever risk, till the dying scene were past; but the desire of existence and the hope of happiness had strengthend in his heart, and he was unable to resist them.

"It is enough," said Roger Malvin, having listened to Reuben's promise. "Go, and God speed you!"

The youth pressed his hand in silence, turned, and was departing. His slow and faltering steps, however, had borne him but a little way before Malvin's voice recalled him.

"Reuben, Reuben," said he, faintly; and Reuben returned and knelt down by the dying man.

"Raise me, and let me lean against the rock," was his last request. "My face will be turned towards home, and I shall see you a moment longer as you pass among the trees."

Reuben, having made the desired alteration in his companion's posture, again began his solitary pilgrimage. He walked more hastily at first than was consistent with his strength; for a sort of guilty feeling, which sometimes torments men in their most justifiable acts, caused him to seek concealment from Malvin's eyes; but after he had trodden far upon the rustling forest leaves he crept back, impelled by a wild and painful curiosity, and, sheltered by the earthy roots of an uptorn tree, gazed earnestly at the desolate man. The morning sun was unclouded, and the trees and shrubs imbibed the sweet air of the month of May; yet there seemed a gloom on Nature's face, as if she sympathized with mortal pain and sorrow. Roger Malvin's hands were uplifted in a fervent prayer, some of the words of which stole through the stillness of the woods and entered Reuben's heart, torturing it with an unutterable pang. They were the broken accents of a petition for his own happiness and that of Dorcas; and, as the youth listened, conscience, or something in its similitude, pleaded strongly with him to return and lie down again by the rock. He felt how hard was the doom of the kind and generous being whom he had deserted in his extremity. Death would come like the slow approach of a corpse, stealing gradually towards him through the forest, and showing its ghastly and motionless features from behind a nearer and yet a nearer tree. But such must have been Reuben's own fate had he tarried another sunset; and who shall impute blame to him if he shrink from so useless a sacrifice? As he gave a parting look, a breeze waved the little banner upon the sapling oak and reminded Reuben of his vow.

Many circumstances combined to retard the wounded traveller in his way to the frontiers. On the second day the clouds, gathering densely over the sky, precluded the possibility of regulating his course by the position of the sun; and he knew not but that every effort of his almost exhausted strength was removing him farther from the home he sought. His scanty sustenance was supplied by the berries and other spontaneous products of the forest. Herds of deer, it is true, sometimes bounded past him, and partridges frequently whirred up before his footsteps; but his ammunition had been expended in the fight, and he had no means of slaying them. His wounds, irritated by the constant exertion in which lay the only hope of life, wore away his strength and at intervals confused his reason. But, even in the wanderings of intellect, Reuben's young heart clung strongly to existence; and it was only through absolute incapacity of motion that he at last sank down beneath a tree, compelled there to await death.

In this situation he was discovered by a party who, upon the first intelligence of the fight, had been despatched to the relief of the survivors. They conveyed him to the nearest settlement, which chanced to be that of his own residence.

Dorcas, in the simplicity of the olden time, watched by the bedside of her wounded lover, and administered all those comforts that are in the sole gift of woman's heart and hands. During several days Reuben's recollection strayed drowsily among the perils and hardships through which he had passed, and he was incapable of returning definite answers to the inquiries with which many were eager to harass him. No authentic particulars of the battle had yet been circulated; nor could mothers, wives, and children tell whether their loved ones were detained by captivity or by the stronger chain of death. Dorcas nourished her apprehensions in silence till one afternoon when Reuben awoke from an unquiet sleep, and seemed to recognize her more perfectly than at any previous time. She saw that his intellect had become composed, and she could no longer restrain her filial anxiety.

"My father, Reuben?" she began; but the change in her lover's countenance made her pause.

The youth shrank as if with a bitter pain, and the blood gushed vividly into his wan and hollow cheeks. His first impulse was to cover his face; but, apparently with a desperate effort, he half raised himself and spoke vehemently, defending himself against an imaginary accusation.

"Your father was sore wounded in the battle, Dorcas; and he bade me not burden myself with him, but only to lead him to the lakeside, that he might quench his thirst and die. But I would not desert the old man in his extremity, and, though bleeding myself, I supported him; I gave him half my strength, and led him away with me. For three days we journeyed on together, and your father was sustained beyond my hopes, but, awaking at sunrise on the fourth day, I found him faint and exhausted; he was unable to proceed; his life had ebbed away fast; and"—

"He died!" exclaimed Dorcas, faintly.

Reuben felt it impossible to acknowledge that his selfish love of life had hurried him away before her father's fate was decided. He spoke not; he only bowed his head; and between shame and exhaustion, sank back and hid his face in the pillow. Dorcas wept when her fears were thus confirmed; but the shock, as it had been long anticipated, was on that account the less violent.

"You dug a grave for my poor father in the wilderness, Reuben?" was the question by which her filial piety manifested itself.

"My hands were weak; but I did what I could," replied the youth in a smothered tone. "There stands a noble tombstone above his head; and I would to Heaven I slept as soundly as he!"

Dorcas, perceiving the wildness of his latter words, inquired no further at the time; but her heart found ease in the thought that Roger Malvin had not lacked such funeral rites as it was possible to bestow. The tale of Reuben's courage and fidelity lost nothing when she communicated it to her friends; and the poor youth, tottering from his sick chamber to breathe the sunny air, experienced from every tongue the miserable and humiliating torture of unmerited praise. All acknowledged that he might worthily demand the hand of the maiden to whose father he had been "faithful unto death;" and, as my tale is not of love, it shall suffice to say that in the space of a few months Reuben became the husband of Dorcas Malvin. During the marriage ceremony the bride was covered with blushes, but the bridegroom's face was pale.

There was now in the breast of Reuben Bourne an incommunicable thought—something which he was to conceal most heedfully from her whom he most loved and trusted. He regretted, deeply and bitterly, the moral cowardice that had restrained his words when he was about to disclose the truth to Dorcas; but pride, the fear of losing her affection, the dread of universal scorn, forbade him to rectify this falsehood. He felt that for leaving Roger Malvin he deserved no censure. His presence, the gratuitous sacrifice of his own life, would have added only another and a needless agony to the last moments of the dying man; but concealment had imparted to a justifiable act much of the secret effect of guilt; and Reuben, while reason told him that he had done right, experienced in no small degree the mental horrors which punish the perpetrator of undiscovered crime. By a certain association of ideas, he at times almost imagined himself a murderer. For years, also, a thought would occasionally recur, which, though he perceived all its folly and extravagance, he had not power to banish from his mind. It was a haunting and torturing fancy that his father-in-law was yet sitting at the foot of the rock, on the withered forest leaves, alive, and awaiting his pledged assistance. These mental deceptions, however, came and went, nor did he ever mistake them for realities, but in the calmest and clearest moods of his mind he was conscious that he had a deep vow unredeemed, and that an unburied corpse was calling to him out of the wilderness. Yet such was the consequence of his prevarication that he could not obey the call. It was now too late to require the assistance of Roger Malvin's friends in performing his long-deferred sepulture; and superstitious fears, of which none were more susceptible than the people of the outward settlements, forbade Reuben to go alone. Neither did he know where in the pathless and illimitable forest to seek that smooth and lettered rock at the base of which the body lay; his remembrance of every portion of his travel thence was indistinct, and the latter part had left no impression upon his mind. There was, however, a continual impulse, a voice audible only to himself, commanding him to go forth and redeem his vow; and he had a strange impression that, were he to make the trial, he would be led straight to Malvin's bones. But year after year that summons, unheard but felt, was disobeyed. His one secret thought became like a chain binding down his spirit and like a serpent gnawing into his heart; and he was transformed into a sad and downcast yet irritable man.

In the course of a few years after their marriage changes began to be visible in the external prosperity of Reuben and Dorcas. The only riches of the former had been his stout heart and strong arm; but the latter, her father's sole heiress, had made her husband master of a farm, under older cultivation, larger, and better stocked than most of the frontier establishments. Reuben Bourne, however, was a neglectful husbandman; and, while the lands of the other settlers became annually more fruitful, his deteriorated in the same proportion. The discouragements to agriculture were greatly lessened by the cessation of Indian war, during which men held the plough in one hand and the musket in the other, and were fortunate if the products of their dangerous labor were not destroyed, either in the field or in the barn, by the savage enemy. But Reuben did not profit by the altered condition of the country; nor can it be denied that his intervals of industrious attention to his affairs were but scantily rewarded with success. The irritability by which he had recently become distinguished was another cause of his declining prosperity, as it occasioned frequent quarrels in his unavoidable intercourse with the neighboring settlers. The results of these were innumerable lawsuits; for the people of New England, in the earliest stages and wildest circumstances of the country, adopted, whenever attainable, the legal mode of deciding their differences. To be brief, the world did not go well with Reuben Bourne; and, though not till many years after his marriage, he was finally a ruined man, with but one remaining expedient against the evil fate that had pursued him. He was to throw sunlight into some deep recess of the forest, and seek subsistence from the virgin bosom of the wilderness.

The only child of Reuben and Dorcas was a son, now arrived at the age of fifteen years, beautiful in youth, and giving promise of a glorious manhood. He was peculiarly qualified for, and already began to excel in, the wild accomplishments of frontier life. His foot was fleet, his aim true, his apprehension quick, his heart glad and high; and all who anticipated the return of Indian war spoke of Cyrus Bourne as a future leader in the land. The boy was loved by his father with a deep and silent strength, as if whatever was good and happy in his own nature had been transferred to his child, carrying his affections with it. Even Dorcas, though loving and beloved, was far less dear to him; for Reuben's secret thoughts and insulated emotions had gradually made him a selfish man, and he could no longer love deeply except where he saw or imagined some reflection or likeness of his own mind. In Cyrus he recognized what he had himself been in other days, and at intervals he seemed to partake of the boy's spirit, and to be revived with a fresh and happy life. Reuben was accompanied by his son in the expedition, for the purpose of selecting a tract of land and felling and burning the timber, which necessarily preceded the removal of the household goods. Two months of autumn were thus occupied, after which Reuben Bourne and his young hunter returned to spend their last winter in the settlements.

It was early in the month of May that the little family snapped asunder whatever tendrils of affections had clung to inanimate objects, and bade farewell to the few who, in the blight of fortune, called themselves their friends. The sadness of the parting moment had, to each of the pilgrims, its peculiar alleviations. Reuben, a moody man, and misanthropic because unhappy, strode onward with his usual stern brow and downcast eye, feeling few regrets and disdaining to acknowledge any. Dorcas, while she wept abundantly over the broken ties by which her simple and affectionate nature had bound itself to everything, felt that the inhabitants of her inmost heart moved on with her, and that all else would be supplied wherever she might go. And the boy dashed one teardrop from his eye, and thought of the adventurous pleasures of the untrodden forest.

Oh, who, in the enthusiasm of a daydream, has not wished that he were a wanderer in a world of summer wilderness, with one fair and gentle being hanging lightly on his arm? In youth his free and exulting step would know no barrier but the rolling ocean or the snow-topped mountains; calmer manhood would choose a home where Nature had strewn a double wealth in the vale of some transparent stream; and when hoary age, after long, long years of that pure life, stole on and found him there, it would find him the father of a race, the patriarch of a people, the founder of a mighty nation yet to be. When death, like the sweet sleep which we welcome after a day of happiness, came over him, his far descendants would mourn over the venerated dust. Enveloped by tradition in mysterious attributes, the men of future generations would call him godlike; and remote posterity would see him standing, dimly glorious, far up the valley of a hundred centuries.

The tangled and gloomy forest through which the personages of my tale were wandering differed widely from the dreamer's land of fantasy; yet there was something in their way of life that Nature asserted as her own, and the gnawing cares which went with them from the world were all that now obstructed their happiness. One stout and shaggy steed, the bearer of all their wealth, did not shrink from the added weight of Dorcas, although her hardy breeding sustained her, during the latter part of each day's journey, by her husband's side. Reuben and his son, their muskets on their shoulders and their axes slung behind them, kept an unwearied pace, each watching with a hunter's eye for the game that supplied their food. When hunger bade, they halted and prepared their meal on the bank of some unpolluted forest brook, which, as they knelt down with thirsty lips to drink, murmured a sweet unwillingness, like a maiden at love's first kiss. They slept beneath a hut of branches, and awoke at peep of light refreshed for the toils of another day. Dorcas and the boy went on joyously, and even Reuben's spirit shone at intervals with an outward gladness; but inwardly there was a cold, cold sorrow, which he compared to the snowdrifts lying deep in the glens and hollows of the rivulets while the leaves were brightly green above.

Cyrus Bourne was sufficiently skilled in the travel of the woods to observe that his father did not adhere to the course they had pursued in their expedition of the preceding autumn. They were now keeping father to the north, striking out more directly from the settlements, and into a region of which savage beasts and savage men were as yet the sole possessors. The boy sometimes hinted his opinions upon the subject, and Reuben listened attentively, and once or twice altered the direction of their march in accordance with his son's counsel; but, having so done, he seemed ill at ease. His quick and wandering glances were sent forward, apparently in search of enemies lurking behind the tree trunks; and, seing nothing there, he would cast his eyes backwards as if in fear of some pursuer. Cyrus, perceiving that his father gradually resumed the old direction, forebore to interfere; nor, though something began to weigh upon his heart, did his adventurous nature permit him to regret the increased length and the mystery of their way.

On the afternoon of the fifth day they halted, and made their simple encampment nearly an hour before sunset. The face of the country, for the last few miles, had been diversified by swells of land resembling huge waves of a petrified sea; and in one of the corresponding hollows, a wild and romantic spot, had the family reared their hut and kindled their fire. There is something chilling, and yet heart-warming, in the thought of these three, united by strong bonds of love and insulated from all that breathe beside. The dark and gloomy pines looked down upon them, and, as the wind swept through their tops, a pitying sound was heard in the forest; or did those old trees groan in fear that men were come to lay the axe to their roots at last? Reuben and his son, while Dorcas made ready their meal, proposed to wander out in search of game, of which that day's march had afforded no supply. The boy, promising not to quit the vicinity of the encampment, bounded off with a step as light and elastic as that of the deer he hoped to slay; while his father feeling a transient happiness as he gazed after him, was about to pursue an opposite direction. Dorcas, in the meanwhile, had seated herself near their fire of fallen branches, upon the mossgrown and mouldering trunk of a tree uprooted years before. Her employment, diversified by an occasional glance at the pot, now beginning to simmer over the blaze, was the perusal of the current year's Massachusetts Almanac, which, with the exception of an old black-letter Bible, comprised all the literary wealth of the family. None pay a greater regard to arbitrary divisions of time than those who are excluded from society; and Dorcas mentioned, as if the information were of importance, that it was now the twelfth of May. Her husband started.

"The twelfth of May! I should remember it well," muttered he, while many thoughts occasioned a momentary confusion in his mind. "Where am I? Whither am I wandering? Where did I leave him?"

Dorcas, too well accustomed to her husband's wayward moods to note any peculiarity of demeanor, now laid aside the almanac and addressed him in that mournful tone which the tender hearted appropriate to griefs long cold and dead.

"It was near this time of the month, eighteen years ago, that my poor father left this world for a better. He had a kind arm to hold his head and a kind voice to cheer him, Reuben, in his last moments; and the thought of the faithful care you took of him has comforted me many times since. Oh, death would have been awful to a solitary man in a wild place like this!"

"Pray Heaven, Dorcas," said Reuben, in a broken voice,—"pray Heaven that neither of us three dies solitary and lies unburied in this howling wilderness!" And he hastened away, leaving her to watch the fire beneath the gloomy pines.

Reuben Bourne's rapid pace gradually slackened as the pang, unintentionally inflicted by the words of Dorcas, became less acute. Many strange reflections, however, thronged upon him; and, straying onward rather like a sleep walker than a hunter, it was attributable to no care of his own that his devious course kept him in the vicinity of the encampment. His steps were imperceptibly led almost in a circle; nor did he observe that he was on the verge of a tract of land heavily timbered, but not with pine trees. The place of the latter was here supplied by oaks and other of the harder woods; and around their roots clustered a dense and bushy under-growth, leaving, however, barren spaces between the trees, thick strewn with withered leaves. Whenever the rustling of the branches or the creaking of the trunks made a sound, as if the forest were waking from slumber, Reuben instinctively raised the musket that rested on his arm, and cast a quick, sharp glance on every side; but, convinced by a partial observation that no animal was near, he would again give himself up to his thoughts. He was musing on the strange influence that had led him away from his premeditated course, and so far into the depths of the wilderness. Unable to penetrate to the secret place of his soul where his motives lay hidden, he believed that a supernatural voice had called him onward, and that a supernatural power had obstructed his retreat. He trusted that it was Heaven's intent to afford him an opportunity of expiating his sin; he hoped that he might find the bones so long unburied; and that, having laid the earth over them, peace would throw its sunlight into the sepulchre of his heart. From these thoughts he was aroused by a rustling in the forest at some distance from the spot to which he had wandered. Perceiving the motion of some object behind a thick veil of undergrowth, he fired, with the instinct of a hunter and the aim of a practised marksman. A low moan, which told his success, and by which even animals can express their dying agony, was unheeded by Reuben Bourne. What were the recollections now breaking upon him?

The thicket into which Reuben had fired was near the summit of a swell of land, and was clustered around the base of a rock, which, in the shape and smoothness of one of its surfaces, was not unlike a gigantic gravestone. As if reflected in a mirror, its likeness was in Reuben's memory. He even recognized the veins which seemed to form an inscription in forgotten characters: everything remained the same, except that a thick covert of bushes shrouded the lower part of the rock, and would have hidden Roger Malvin had he still been sitting there. Yet in the next moment Reuben's eye was caught by another change that time had effected since he last stood where he was now standing again behind the earthy roots of the uptorn tree. The sapling to which he had bound the blood-stained symbol of his vow had increased and strengthened into an oak, far indeed from its maturity, but with no mean spread of shadowy branches. There was one singularity observable in this tree which made Reuben tremble. The middle and lower branches were in luxuriant life, and an excess of vegetation had fringed the trunk almost to the ground; but a blight had apparently stricken the upper part of the oak, and the very topmost bough was withered, sapless, and utterly dead. Reuben remembered how the little banner had fluttered on that topmost bough, when it was green and lovely, eighteen years before. Whose guilt had blasted it?

Dorcas, after the departure of the two hunters, continued her preparations for their evening repast. Her sylvan table was the moss-covered trunk of a large fallen tree, on the broadest part of which she had spread a snow-white cloth and arranged what were left of the bright pewter vessels that had been her pride in the settlements. It had a strange aspect, that one little spot of homely comfort in the desolate heart of Nature. The sunshine yet lingered upon the higher branches of the trees that grew on rising ground; but the shadows of evening had deepened into the hollow where the encampment was made, and the firelight began to redden as it gleamed up the tall trunks of the pines or hovered on the dense and obscure mass of foliage that circled round the spot. The heart of Dorcas was not sad; for she felt that it was better to journey in the wilderness with two whom she loved than to be a lonely woman in a crowd that cared not for her. As she busied herself in arranging seats of mouldering wood, covered with leaves, for Reuben and her son, her voice danced through the gloomy forest in the measure of a song that she had learned in youth. The rude melody, the production of a bard who won no name, was descriptive of a winter evening in a frontier cottage, when, secured from savage inroad by the high-piled snow-drifts, the family rejoiced by their own fireside. The whole song possessed the nameless charm peculiar to unborrowed thought, but four continually-recurring lines shone out from the rest like the blaze of the hearth whose joys they celebrated. Into them, working magic with a few simple words, the poet had instilled the very essence of domestic love and household happiness, and they were poetry and picture joined in one. As Dorcas sang, the walls of her forsaken home seemed to encircle her; she no longer saw the gloomy pines, nor heard the wind which still, as she began each verse, sent a heavy breath through the branches, and died away in a hollow moan from the burden of the song. She was aroused by the report of a gun in the vicinity of the encampment; and either the sudden sound, or her loneliness by the glowing fire, caused her to tremble violently. The next moment she laughed in the pride of a mother's heart.

"My beautiful young hunter! My boy has slain a deer!" she exclaimed, recollecting that in the direction whence the shot proceeded Cyrus had gone to the chase.

She waited a reasonable time to hear her son's light step bounding over the rustling leaves to tell of his success. But he did not immediately appear; and she sent her cheerful voice among the trees in search of him.

"Cyrus! Cyrus!"

His coming was still delayed; and she determined, as the report had apparently been very near, to seek for him in person. Her assistance, also, might be necessary in bringing home the venison which she flattered herself he had obtained. She therefore set forward, directing her steps by the long-past sound, and singing as she went, in order that the boy might be aware of her approach and run to meet her. From behind the trunk of every tree, and from every hiding-place in the thick foliage of the undergrowth, she hoped to discover the countenance of her son, laughing with the sportive mischief that is born of affection. The sun was now beneath the horizon, and the light that came down among the leaves was sufficiently dim to create many illusions in her expecting fancy. Several times she seemed indistinctly to see his face gazing out from among the leaves; and once she imagined that he stood beckoning to her at the base of craggy rock. Keeping her eyes on this object, however, it proved to be no more than the trunk of an oak fringed to the very ground with little branches, one of which, thrust out farther than the rest, was shaken by the breeze. Making her way round the foot of the rock, she suddenly found herself close to her husband, who had approached in another direction. Leaning upon the butt of his gun, the muzzle of which rested upon the withered leaves, he was apparently absorbed in the contemplation of some object at his feet.

"How is this, Reuben? Have you slain the deer and fallen asleep over him?" exclaimed Dorcas, laughing cheerfully, on her first slight observation of his posture and appearance.

He stirred not, neither did he turn his eyes towards her; and a cold, shuddering fear, indefinite in its source and object, began to creep into her blood. She now perceived that her husband's face was ghastly pale, and his features were rigid, as if incapable of assuming any other expression than the strong despair which had hardened upon them. He gave not the slightest evidence that he was aware of her approach.

"For the love of Heaven, Reuben, speak to me!" cried Dorcas; and the strange sound of her own voice affrighted her even more than the dead silence.

Her husband started, stared into her face, drew her to the front of the rock, and pointed with his finger.

Oh, there lay the boy, asleep, but dreamless, upon the fallen forest leaves! His cheek rested upon his arm—his curled locks were thrown back from his brow—his limbs were slightly relaxed. Had a sudden weariness overcome the youthful hunter? Would his mother's voice arouse him? She knew that it was death.

"This broad rock is the gravestone of your near kindred, Dorcas," said her husband. "Your tears will fall at once over your father and your son."

She heard him not. With one wild shriek, that seemed to force its way from the sufferer's inmost soul, she sank insensible by the side of her dead boy. At that moment the withered topmost bough of the oak loosened itself in the still air, and fell in soft, light fragments upon the rock, upon the leaves, upon Reuben, upon his wife and child, and upon Roger Malvin's bones. Then Reuben's heart was stricken, and the tears gushed out like water from a rock. The vow that the wounded youth had made the blighted man had come to redeem. His sin was expiated,—the curse was gone from him; and in the hour when he had shed blood dearer to him than his own, a prayer, the first for years, went up to Heaven from the lips of Reuben Bourne.

## *Study questions*

1. *What are the details of the setting in which Reuben leaves Roger to die that became significant later in the story?* 2. *Why does Hawthorne make Reuben a youth who "had scarcely attained the years of manhood" and Roger an older man who speaks with "something of a father's authority"?* 3. *Why does Reuben leave Roger to die? Is Reuben fully conscious of all the reasons? What does Hawthorne mean when he says that Reuben's decision to leave "was aided, unconsciously to himself, by the hidden strength of many another motive"? What could be some hidden motives?* 4. *Is it significant that Reuben is engaged to marry Roger's daughter and will, thus, inherit Roger's possessions? Why does Reuben lie to Dorcas?* 5. *Why does Reuben imagine himself a murderer? Is the guilt that he feels tied to his losing all his possessions?* 6. *What role does Cyrus play?* 7. *What is the significance of Reuben's wandering in the forest?* 8. *What does Hawthorne mean when he says that Reuben is "unable to penetrate to the secret place of his soul where his motives lay hidden"?* 9. *How could a trained hunter and practiced marksman, as Reuben is, fire into the forest and accidentally kill his son? Is the killing something other than accidental?* 10. *How can expiation be complete after a man kills his only son?* 11. *How does the forest function, the oak tree, the granite rock?* 12. *Can this story have anything to do with the idea of the necessary sacrifice of a son to propitiate a father? If so, what religious implications are present?* 13. *What is the function of the first paragraph of the story?*

## THE MAYPOLE OF MERRY MOUNT

*There is an admirable foundation for a philosophic romance in the curious history of the early settlement of Mount Wollaston, or Merry Mount. In the slight sketch here attempted, the facts, recorded on the grave pages of our New England annalists, have wrought themselves, almost spontaneously, into a sort of allegory. The masques, mummeries, and festive customs, described in the text, are in accordance with the manners of the age. Authority on these points may be found in Strutt's Book of English Sports and Pastimes.*

Bright were the days at Merry Mount, when the Maypole was the banner staff of that gay colony! They who reared it, should their banner be triumphant, were to pour sunshine over New England's rugged hills, and scatter flower seeds throughout the soil. Jollity and gloom were contending for an empire. Midsummer eve had come, bringing deep verdure to the forest, and roses in her lap, of a more vivid hue than the tender buds of Spring. But May, or her mirthful spirit, dwelt all the year round at Merry Mount, sporting with the Summer months, and revelling with Autumn, and basking in the glow of Winter's fireside. Through a world of toil and care she flitted with a dreamlike smile, and came hither to find a home among the lightsome hearts of Merry Mount.

Never had the Maypole been so gayly decked as at sunset on midsummer eve. This venerated emblem was a pine-tree, which had preserved the slender grace of youth, while it equalled the loftiest height of the old wood monarchs. From its top streamed a silken banner, colored like the rainbow. Down nearly to the ground the pole was dressed with birchen boughs, and others of the liveliest green, and some with silvery leaves, fastened by ribbons that fluttered in fantastic knots of twenty different colors, but no sad ones. Garden flowers, and blossoms of the wilderness, laughed gladly forth amid the verdure, so fresh and dewy that they must have grown by magic on that happy pine-tree. Where this green and flowery splendor terminated, the shaft of the Maypole was stained with the seven brilliant hues of the banner at its top. On the lowest green bough hung an abundant wreath of roses, some that had been gathered in the sunniest spots of the forest, and others, of still richer blush, which the colonists had reared from English seed. O, people of the Golden Age, the chief of your husbandry was to raise flowers!

But what was the wild throng that stood hand in hand about the Maypole? It could not be that the fauns and nymphs, when driven from their classic groves and homes of ancient fable, had sought refuge, as all the persecuted did, in the fresh woods of the West. These were Gothic monsters, though perhaps of Grecian ancestry. On the shoulders of a comely youth uprose the head and branching antlers of a stag; a second, human in all other points, had the grim visage of a wolf; a third, still with the trunk and limbs of a mortal man, showed the beard and horns of a venerable he-goat. There was the likeness of a bear erect, brute in all but his hind legs, which were adorned with pink silk stockings.

And here again, almost as wondrous, stood a real bear of the dark forest, lending each of his forepaws to the grasp of a human hand, and as ready for the dance as any in that circle. His inferior nature rose half way, to meet his companions as they stooped. Other faces wore the similitude of man or woman, but distorted or extravagant, with red noses pendulous before their mouths, which seemed of awful depth, and stretched from ear to ear in an eternal fit of laughter. Here might be seen the Savage Man, well known in heraldry, hairy as a baboon, and girdled with green leaves. By his side, a noble figure, but still a counterfeit, appeared an Indian hunter, with feathery crest and wampum belt. Many of this strange company wore foolscaps, and had little bells appended to their garments, tinkling with a silvery sound, responsive to the inaudible music of their gleesome spirits. Some youths and maidens were of soberer garb, yet well maintained their places in the irregular throng by the expression of wild revelry upon their features. Such were the colonists of Merry Mount, as they stood in the broad smile of sunset round their venerated Maypole.

Had a wanderer, bewildered in the melancholy forest, heard their mirth, and stolen a half-affrighted glance, he might have fancied them the crew of Comus, some already transformed to brutes, some midway between man and beast, and the others rioting in the flow of tipsy jollity that foreran the change. But a band of Puritans, who watched the scene, invisible themselves, compared the masques to those devils and ruined souls with whom their superstition peopled the black wilderness.

Within the ring of monsters appeared the two airiest forms that had ever trodden on any more solid footing than a purple and golden cloud. One was a youth in glistening apparel, with a scarf of the rainbow pattern crosswise on his breast. His right hand held a gilded staff, the ensign of high dignity among the revellers, and his left grasped the slender fingers of a fair maiden, not less gayly decorated than himself. Bright roses glowed in contrast with the dark and glossy curls of each, and were scattered round their feet, or had sprung up spontaneously there. Behind this lightsome couple, so close to the Maypole that its boughs shaded his jovial face, stood the figure of an English priest, canonically dressed, yet decked with flowers, in heathen fashion, and wearing a chaplet of the native vine leaves. By the riot of his rolling eye, and the pagan decorations of his holy garb, he seemed the wildest monster there, and the very Comus of the crew.

"Votaries of the Maypole," cried the flower-decked priest, "merrily, all day long, have the woods echoed to your mirth. But be this your merriest hour, my hearts! Lo, here stand the Lord and Lady of the May, whom I, a clerk of Oxford, and high priest of Merry Mount, am presently to join in holy matrimony. Up with your nimble spirits, ye morris-dancers, green men, and glee maidens, bears and wolves, and horned gentlemen! Come; a chorus now, rich with the old mirth of Merry England, and the wilder glee of this fresh forest; and then a dance, to show the youthful pair what life is made of, and how airily they should go through it! All ye that love the Maypole, lend your voices to the nuptial song of the Lord and Lady of the May!"

This wedlock was more serious than most affairs of Merry Mount, where jest and delusion, trick and fantasy, kept up a continual carnival. The Lord and

Lady of the May, though their titles must be laid down at sunset, were really and truly to be partners for the dance of life, beginning the measure that same bright eve. The wreath of roses, that hung from the lowest green bough of the Maypole, had been twined for them, and would be thrown over both their heads, in symbol of their flowery union. When the priest had spoken, therefore, a riotous uproar burst from the rout of monstrous figures.

"Begin you the stave, reverend Sir," cried they all; "and never did the woods ring to such a merry peal as we of the Maypole shall send up!"

Immediately a prelude of pipe, cithern, and viol, touched with practised minstrelsy, began to play from a neighboring thicket, in such a mirthful cadence that the boughs of the Maypole quivered to the sound. But the May Lord, he of the gilded staff, chancing to look into his Lady's eyes, was wonder struck at the almost pensive glance that met his own.

"Edith, sweet Lady of the May," whispered he reproachfully, "is yon wreath of roses a garland to hang above our graves, that you look so sad? O, Edith, this is our golden time! Tarnish it not by any pensive shadow of the mind; for it may be that nothing of futurity will be brighter than the mere remembrance of what is now passing."

"That was the very thought that saddened me! How come it in your mind too?" said Edith, in a still lower tone than he, for it was high treason to be sad at Merry Mount. "Therefore do I sigh amid the festive music. And besides, dear Edgar, I struggle as with a dream, and fancy that these shapes of our jovial friends are visionary, and their mirth unreal, and that we are no true Lord and Lady of the May. What is the mystery in my heart?"

Just then, as if a spell had loosened them, down came a little shower of withering rose leaves from the Maypole. Alas, for the young lovers! No sooner had their hearts glowed with real passion than they were sensible of something vague and unsubstantial in their former pleasures, and felt a dreary presentiment of inevitable change. From the moment that they truly loved, they had subjected themselves to earth's doom of care and sorrow, and troubled joy, and had no more a home at Merry Mount. That was Edith's mystery. Now leave we the priest to marry them, and the masquers to sport round the Maypole, till the last sunbeam be withdrawn from its summit, and the shadows of the forest mingle gloomily in the dance. Meanwhile, we may discover who these gay people were.

Two hundred years ago, and more, the old world and its inhabitants became mutually weary of each other. Men voyaged by thousands to the West: some to barter glass beads, and such like jewels, for the furs of the Indian hunter; some to conquer virgin empires; and one stern band to pray. But none of these motives had much weight with the colonists of Merry Mount. Their leaders were men who had sported so long with life, that when Thought and Wisdom came, even these unwelcome guests were led astray by the crowd of vanities which they should have put to flight. Erring Thought and perverted Wisdom were made to put on masques, and play the fool. The men of whom we speak, after losing the heart's fresh gayety, imagined a wild philosophy of pleasure, and came hither to act out their latest day-dream. They gathered followers from all that giddy tribe whose whole life is like the festal days of soberer men. In their train were minstrels, not unknown in London streets; wandering players, whose theatres had been the halls of noblemen; mummers, rope-dancers, and mountebanks, who would long be missed at wakes, church ales, and fairs; in a word, mirth makers of every sort, such as abounded in that age, but now began to be discountenanced by the rapid growth of Puritanism. Light had their footsteps been on land, and as lightly they came across the sea. Many had been maddened by their previous troubles into a gay despair; others were as madly gay in the flush of youth, like the May Lord and his Lady; but whatever might be the quality of their mirth, old and young were gay at Merry Mount. The young deemed themselves happy. The elder spirits, if they knew that mirth was but the counterfeit of happiness, yet followed the false shadow wilfully, because at least her garments glittered brightest. Sworn triflers of a lifetime, they would not venture among the sober truths of life not even to be truly blest.

All the hereditary pastimes of Old England were transplanted hither. The King of Christmas was duly crowned, and the Lord of Misrule bore potent sway. On the Eve of St. John, they felled whole acres of the forest to make bonfires, and danced by the blaze all night, crowned with garlands, and throwing flowers into the flame. At harvest time, though their crop was of the smallest, they made an image with the sheaves of Indian corn, and wreathed it with autumnal garlands, and bore it home triumphantly. But what chiefly characterized the colonists of Merry Mount was their veneration for the Maypole. It has made their true history a poet's tale. Spring decked the hallowed emblem with young blossoms and fresh green boughs; Summer brought roses of the deepest blush, and the perfected foliage of the forest; Autumn enriched it with that red and yellow gorgeousness which converts each wildwood leaf into a painted flower; and Winter silvered it with sleet, and hung it round with icicles, till it flashed in the cold sunshine, itself a frozen sunbeam. Thus each alternate season did homage to the Maypole, and paid it a tribute of its own richest splendor. Its votaries danced round it, once, at least, in every month; sometimes they called it their religion, or their altar; but always, it was the banner staff of Merry Mount.

Unfortunately, there were men in the new world of a sterner faith than those Maypole worshippers. Not far from Merry Mount was a settlement of Puritans, most dismal wretches, who said their prayers before daylight, and then wrought in the forest or the cornfield till evening made it prayer time again. Their weapons were always at hand to shoot down the straggling savage. When they met in conclave, it was never to keep up the old English mirth, but to hear sermons three hours long, or to proclaim bounties on the heads of wolves and the scalps of Indians. Their festivals were fast days, and their chief pastime the singing of psalms. Woe to the youth or maiden who did but dream of a dance! The selectman nodded to the constable; and there sat the light-heeled reprobate in the stocks; or if he danced, it was round the whipping-post, which might be termed the Puritan Maypole.

A party of these grim Puritans, toiling through the difficult woods, each with a horseload of iron armor to burden his footsteps, would sometimes draw near the sunny precincts of Merry Mount. There were the silken colonists, sporting round their Maypole; perhaps teaching a bear to dance, or striving to communicate their mirth to the grave Indian; or masquerading in the skins of deer and wolves, which they had hunted for that especial purpose. Often, the whole colony were playing at blindman's buff, magistrates and all, with their eyes bandaged, except a single scapegoat, whom the blinded sinners pursued by the tinkling of the bells at his garments. Once, it is said, they were seen following a flower-decked corpse, with merriment and festive music, to his grave. But did the dead man laugh? In their quietest times, they sang ballads and told tales, for the edification of their pious visitors; or perplexed them with juggling tricks; or grinned at them through horse collars; and when sport itself grew wearisome, they made game of their own stupidity, and began a yawning match. At the very least of these enormities, the men of iron shook their heads and frowned so darkly that the revellers looked up imagining that a momentary cloud had overcast the sunshine, which was to be perpetual there. On the other hand, the Puritans affirmed that, when a psalm was pealing from their place of worship, the echo which the forest sent them back seemed often like the chorus of a jolly catch, closing with a roar of laughter. Who but the fiend, and his bond slaves, the crew of Merry Mount, had thus disturbed them? In due time, a feud arose, stern and bitter on one side, and as serious on the other as anything could be among such light spirits as had sworn allegiance to the Maypole. The future complexion of New England was involved in this important quarrel. Should the grizzly saints establish their jurisdiction over the gay sinners, then would their spirits darken all the clime, and make it a land of clouded visages, of hard toil, of sermon and psalm forever. But should the banner staff of Merry Mount be fortunate, sunshine would break upon the hills, and flowers would beautify the forest, and late posterity do homage to the Maypole.

After these authentic passages from history, we return to the nuptials of the Lord and Lady of the May. Alas! we have delayed too long, and must darken our tale too suddenly. As we glance again at the Maypole, a solitary sunbeam is fading from the summit, and leaves only a faint, golden tinge blended with the hues of the rainbow banner. Even that dim light is now withdrawn, relinquishing the whole domain of Merry Mount to the evening gloom, which has rushed so instantaneously from the black surrounding woods. But some of these black shadows have rushed forth in human shape.

Yes, with the setting sun, the last day of mirth had passed from Merry Mount. The ring of gay masquers was disordered and broken; the stag lowered his antlers in dismay; the wolf grew weaker than a lamb; the bells of the morris-dancers tinkled with tremulous affright. The Puritans had played a characteristic part in the Maypole mummeries. Their darksome figures were intermixed with the wild shapes of their foes, and made the scene a picture of the moment, when waking thoughts start up amid the scattered fantasies of a dream. The leader of the hostile party stood in the centre of the circle, while the route of monsters cowered around him, like evil spirts in the presence of a dread magician. No fantastic foolery could look him in the face. So stern was the energy of his aspect, that the whole man, visage, frame, and soul, seemed wrought of iron, gifted with life and thought, yet all of one substance with his headpiece and breastplate. It was the Puritan of Puritans; it was Endicott himself!

"Stand off, priest of Baal!" said he, with a grim frown, and laying no reverent hand upon the surplice. "I know thee, Blackstone!* Thou art the man who couldst not abide the rule even of thine own corrupted church, and hast come hither to preach iniquity, and to give example of it in thy life. But now shall it be seen that the Lord hath sanctified this wilderness for his peculiar people. Woe unto them that would defile it! And first, for this flower-decked abomination, the altar of thy worship!"

And with his keen sword Endicott assaulted the hallowed Maypole. Nor long did it resist his arm. It groaned with a dismal sound; it showered leaves and rosebuds upon the remorseless enthusiast; and finally, with all its green boughs and ribbons and flowers, symbolic of departed pleasures, down fell the banner staff of Merry Mount. As it sank, tradition says, the evening sky grew darker, and the woods threw forth a more sombre shadow.

"There," cried Endicott, looking triumphantly on his work, "there lies the only Maypole in New England! The thought is strong within me that, by its fall, is shadowed forth the fate of light and idle mirth makers, amongst us and our posterity. Amen, saith John Endicott."

"Amen!" echoed his followers.

But the votaries of the Maypole gave one groan for their idol. At the sound, the Puritan leader glanced at the crew of Comus, each a figure of broad mirth, yet, at this moment, strangely expressive of sorrow and dismay.

"Valiant captain," quoth Peter Palfrey, the Ancient of the band, "what order shall be taken with the prisoners?"

"I thought not to repent me of cutting down a Maypole," replied Endicott, "yet now I could find in my heart to plant it again, and give each of these bestial pagans one other dance round their idol. It would have served rarely for a whipping-post!"

"But there are pine-trees enow," suggested the lieutenant.

"True, good Ancient," said the leader. "Wherefore, bind the heathen crew, and bestow on them a small matter of stripes apiece, as earnest of our future justice. Set some of the rogues in the stocks to rest themselves, so soon as Providence shall bring us to one of our own well-ordered settlements where such accommodations may be found. Further penalties, such as branding and cropping of ears, shall be thought of hereafter."

"How many stripes for the priest?" inquired Ancient Palfrey.

"None as yet," answered Endicott, bending his iron frown upon the culprit. "It must be for the Great and General Court to determine, whether stripes and long imprisonment, and other grievous penalty, may atone for his transgressions. Let him look to himself! For such as violate our civil order, it may be permitted us to show mercy. But woe to the wretch that troubleth our religion."

* Did Governor Endicott speak less positively, we should suspect a mistake here. The Rev. Mr. Blackstone, though an eccentric, is not known to have been an immoral man. We rather doubt his identity with the priest of Merry Mount. [Hawthorne's note.]

"And this dancing bear," resumed the officer. "Must he share the stripes of his fellows?"

"Shoot him through the head!" said the energetic Puritan. "I suspect witchcraft in the beast."

"Here be a couple of shining ones," continued Peter Palfrey, pointing his weapon at the Lord and Lady of the May. "They seem to be of high station among these misdoers. Methinks their dignity will not be fitted with less than a double share of stripes."

Endicott rested on his sword, and closely surveyed the dress and aspect of the hapless pair. There they stood, pale, downcast, and apprehensive. Yet there was an air of mutual support and of pure affection, seeking aid and giving it, that showed them to be man and wife, with the sanction of a priest upon their love. The youth, in the peril of the moment, had dropped his gilded staff, and thrown his arm about the Lady of the May, who leaned against his breast, too lightly to burden him, but with weight enough to express that their destinies were linked together, for good or evil. They looked first at each other, and then into the grim captain's face. There they stood, in the first hour of wedlock, while the idle pleasures, of which their companions were the emblems, had given place to the sternest cares of life, personified by the dark Puritans. But never had their youthful beauty seemed so pure and high as when its glow was chastened by adversity.

"Youth," said Endicott, "ye stand in an evil case, thou and thy maiden wife. Make ready presently, for I am minded that ye shall both have a token to remember your wedding day!"

"Stern man," cried the May Lord, "how can I move thee? Were the means at hand, I would resist to the death. Being powerless, I entreat! Do with me as thou wilt, but let Edith go untouched!"

"Not so," replied the immitigable zealot. "We are not wont to show an idle courtesy to that sex, which requireth the stricter discipline. What sayest thou, maid? Shall thy silken bridegroom suffer thy share of the penalty, besides his own?"

"Be it death," said Edith, "and lay it all on me!"

Truly, as Endicott had said, the poor lovers stood in a woful case. Their foes were triumphant, their friends captive and abased, their home desolate, the benighted wilderness around them, and a rigorous destiny, in the shape of the Puritan leader, their only guide. Yet the deepening twilight could not altogether conceal that the iron man was softened; he smiled at the fair spectacle of early love; he almost sighed for the inevitable blight of early hopes.

"The troubles of life have come hastily on this young couple," observed Endicott. "We will see how they comport themselves under their present trials ere we burden them with greater. If, among the spoil, there be any garments of a more decent fashion, let them be put upon this May Lord and his Lady, instead of their glistening vanities. Look to it, some of you."

"And shall not the youth's hair be cut?" asked Peter Palfrey, looking with abhorrence at the lovelock and long glossy curls of the young man.

"Crop it forthwith, and that in the true pumpkin-shell fashion," answered the captain. "Then bring them along with us, but more gently than their fellows. There be qualities in the youth, which may make him valiant to fight, and sober to toil, and pious to pray; and in the maiden, that may fit her to become a mother in our Israel, bringing up babes in better nurture than her own hath been. Nor think ye, young ones, that they are the happiest, even in our lifetime of a moment, who misspend it in dancing round a Maypole!"

And Endicott, the severest Puritan of all who laid the rock foundation of New England, lifted the wreath of roses from the ruin of the Maypole, and threw it, with his own gauntleted hand, over the heads of the Lord and Lady of the May. It was a deed of prophecy. As the moral gloom of the world overpowers all systematic gayety, even so was their home of wild mirth made desolate amid the sad forest. They returned to it no more. But as their flowery garland was wreathed of the brightest roses that had grown there, so, in the tie that united them, were intertwined all the purest and best of their early joys. They went heavenward, supporting each other along the difficult path which it was their lot to tread, and never wasted one regretful thought on the vanities of Merry Mount.

## *Study questions*

1. *What are the people of Merry Mount like? Why does Hawthorne link them to primitive religious ceremonies and practices?* 2. *What does the maypole signify? Look it up in a dictionary of mythology.* 3. *What are Edith and Edgar like? Why does he wear "a scarf of the rainbow pattern crosswise on his breast"?* 4. *What is the significance of the marriage?* 5. *What are the Puritans like? Why does Hawthorne call them "most dismal wretches"?* 6. *How is the maypole likened to the whipping post? (Which, by the way, would you prefer?)* 7. *Could the Merry Mounters be seen as projections of a wish-fulfillment fantasy and the Puritans as projections of a nightmare?* 8. *What role does Endicott play?* 9. *How much dramtic action is the story actually composed of?* 10. *Who is the protagonist of this story? What is the conflict? How is it resolved?*

*Edgar Allan Poe* (1809–1849), born in Boston, Massachusetts, of theatrical parents, was adopted after the death of his mother by John Allan of Richmond, Virginia. As a boy Poe went to school in England and in Virginia, where he enrolled at the University of Virginia, leaving there, at John Allan's insistence, at the end of his first term because of the accumulation of gambling debts. A time in the army and at West Point followed. Allan then disowned him and Poe had to make his own way. Poe did make a living from his writings, and he worked hard at it, turning out stories, poems, essays, and critical reviews, and editing magazines. His activities belie the myth that surrounds him—that he was a haunted figure, nocturnal and spectral. Anyone who worked as hard as Poe did had to use most of the daytime hours. He was a remarkable man: His stories of ratiocination are prototypes for the Sherlock Holmes series and for the myriad successors in that genre; his tales of the future are prototypes for the H. G. Wells type of science-fiction story and for most that followed thereafter; his stories concerning abnormal or self-destructive states predate Dostoevsky's. He knew the death wish before Freud; he used the theme of the split personality before the term was invented; he investigated the surreal before André Breton defined it.

Poe's contributions to the short-story genre are immense. He was the first literary critic to theorize upon the form, and after better than a hundred years what he said is still quoted. His own stories are among the most popular in our literature. "The Fall of the House of Usher" is, perhaps, his best story. In it the reader is led by an ostensibly sane narrator into a nightmare that explores his own psyche. "Ligeia" is also a fantasy projection where distinctions between dream and reality blur. The famous "The Masque of the Red Death" is choreography for a *dance macabre.*

## THE FALL OF THE HOUSE OF USHER

*Son coeur est un luth suspendu;*
*Sitôt qu'on le touche il résonne.*
DE BÉRANGER

During the whole of a dull, dark, and soundless day in the autumn of the year, when the clouds hung oppressively low in the heavens, I had been passing alone, on horseback, through a singularly dreary tract of country; and at length found myself, as the shades of the evening drew on, within view of the melancholy House of Usher. I know not how it was—but, with the first glimpse of the building, a sense of insufferable gloom pervaded my spirit. I say insufferable; for the feeling was unrelieved by any of that half-pleasurable, because poetic, sentiment with which the mind usually receives even the sternest natural images of the desolate or terrible. I looked upon the scene before me—upon the mere house, and the simple landscape features of the domain—upon the bleak walls—upon the vacant eye-like windows—upon a few rank sedges—and upon a few white trunks of decayed trees—with an utter depression of soul which I can compare to no earthly sensation more properly than to the after-dream of the reveller upon opium—the bitter lapse into everyday life—the hideous dropping off of the veil. There was an iciness, a sinking, a sickening of the heart—an unredeemed dreariness of thought, which no goading of the imagination could torture into aught of the sublime. What was it—I paused to think—what was it that so unnerved me in the contemplation of the House of Usher? It was a mystery all insoluble; nor could I grapple with the shadowy fancies that crowded upon me as I pondered. I was forced to fall back upon the unsatisfactory conclusion, that while, beyond doubt, there *are* combinations of very simple natural objects which have the power of thus affecting us, still the analysis of this power lies among considerations beyond our depth. It was possible, I reflected, that a mere different arrangement of the particulars of the scene, of the details of the picture, would be sufficient to modify, or perhaps to annihilate, its capacity for sorrowful impression; and, acting upon this idea, I reined my horse to the precipitous brink of a black and lurid tarn that lay in unruffled lustre by the dwelling, and gazed down—but with a shudder even more thrilling than before—upon the remodeled and inverted images of the gray sedge, and the ghastly tree-stems, and the vacant and eye-like windows.

Nevertheless, in this mansion of gloom I now proposed to myself a sojourn of some weeks. Its proprietor, Roderick Usher, had been one of my boon companions in boyhood; but many years had elapsed since our last meeting. A letter, however, had lately reached me in a distant part of the country—a letter from him—which, in its wildly importunate nature, had admitted of no other than a personal reply. The MS. gave evidence of nervous agitation. The writer spoke of acute bodily illness—of a mental disorder which oppressed him—and of an earnest desire to see me, as his best, and indeed his only personal friend, with a view of attempting, by the cheerfulness of my society, some alleviation of his malady. It was the manner in which all this, and much more, was said—it was the apparent *heart* that went with his request—which allowed me no room for hesitation; and I accordingly obeyed forthwith what I still considered a very singular summons.

Although, as boys, we had been even intimate associates, yet I really knew little of my friend. His reserve had been always excessive and habitual. I was aware, however, that his very ancient family had been noted, time out of mind, for a peculiar sensibility of temperament, displaying itself, through long ages, in many works of exalted art, and manifested, of late, in repeated deeds of munificent yet unobtrusive charity, as well as in a passionate devotion to the intricacies, perhaps even more than to the orthodox and easily recognisable beauties, of musical science. I had learned, too, the very remarkable fact, that the stem of the Usher race, all time-honored as it was, had put forth, at no period, any enduring branch; in other words, that the entire family lay in the direct line of descent, and had always, with a very trifling and very temporary variation, so lain. It was this deficiency, I considered, while running over in thought the perfect keeping of the character of the premises with the accredited character of the people, and while speculating upon the possible influence which the one, in the long lapse of centuries, might have exercised upon the other—it was this deficiency, perhaps, of collateral issue, and the consequent undeviating transmission, from sire to son, of the patrimony with the name, which had, at length, so identified the two as to merge the original title of the estate in the quaint and equivocal appellation of the "House of Usher"—an appellation which seemed to include, in the minds of the peasantry who used it, both the family and the family mansion.

I have said that the sole effect of my somewhat childish experiment—that of looking down within the tarn—had been to deepen the first singular impression. There can be no doubt that the consciousness of the rapid increase of my superstition—for why should I not so term it?—served mainly to accelerate the increase itself. Such, I have long known, is the paradoxical law of all sentiments having terror as a basis. And it might have been for this reason only, that, when I again uplifted my eyes to the house itself, from its image in the pool, there grew in my mind a strange fancy—a fancy so ridiculous, indeed, that I but mention it to show the vivid force of the sensations which oppressed me. I had so worked upon my imagination as really to believe that about the whole mansion and domain there hung an atmosphere peculiar to themselves and their immediate vicinity—an atmosphere which had no affinity with the air of heaven, but which had reeked up from the decayed trees, and the gray wall, and the silent tarn—a pestilent and mystic vapour, dull, sluggish, faintly discernable, and leaden-hued.

Shaking off from my spirit what *must* have been a dream, I scanned more narrowly the real aspect of the building. Its principal feature seemed to be that of an excessive antiquity. The discoloration of ages had been great. Minute *fungi* overspread the whole exterior, hanging in a fine tangled web-work from the eaves. Yet all this was apart from any extraordinary dilapidation. No portion of the masonry had fallen; and there appeared to be a wild inconsistency between its still perfect adaptation of parts, and the crumbling condition of the individual stones. In this there was much that reminded me of the specious totality of old woodwork which has rotted for long years in some neglected vault, with no disturbance from the breath of the external air. Beyond this indication of extensive decay, however, the fabric gave little token of instability. Perhaps the eye of a scrutinising observer might have discovered a barely perceptible fissure, which, extending from the roof of the building in front, made its way down the wall in a zigzag direction, until it became lost in the sullen waters of the tarn.

Noticing these things, I rode over a short causeway to the house. A servant in waiting took my horse, and I entered the Gothic archway of the hall. A valet, of stealthy step, thence conducted me, in silence, through many dark and intricate passages in my progress to the *studio* of his master. Much that I encountered on the way contributed, I know not how, to heighten the vague sentiments of which I have already spoken. While the objects around me—while the carvings of the ceiling, the sombre tapestries of the walls, the ebon blackness of the floors, and the phantasmagoric armorial trophies which rattled as I strode, were but matters to which, or to such as which, I had been accustomed from my infancy—while I hesitated not to acknowledge how familiar was all this—I still wondered to find how unfamiliar was all this—I still wondered to find how unfamiliar were the fancies which ordinary images were stirring up. On one of the staircases, I met the physician of the family. His countenance, I thought, wore a mingled expression of low cunning and perplexity. He accosted me with trepidation and passed on. The valet now threw open a door and ushered me into the presence of his master.

The room in which I found myself was very large and lofty. The windows were long, narrow, and pointed, and at so vast a distance from the black oaken floor as to be altogether inaccessible from within. Feeble gleams of encrimsoned light made their way through the trellised panes, and served to render sufficiently distinct the more prominent objects around; the eye, however, struggled in vain to reach the remoter angles of the chamber, or the recesses of the vaulted and fretted ceiling. Dark draperies hung upon the walls. The general furniture was profuse, comfortless, antique, and tattered. Many books and musical instruments lay scattered about, but failed to give any vitality to the scene. I felt that I breathed an atmosphere of sorrow. An air of stern, deep, and irredeemable gloom hung over and pervaded all.

Upon my entrance, Usher arose from a sofa on which he had been lying at full length, and greeted me with a vivacious warmth which had much in it, I at first thought, of an overdone cordiality—of the constrained effort of the *ennuyé* man of the world. A glance, however, at his countenance, convinced me of his perfect sincerity. We sat down; and for some moments, while he spoke not, I gazed upon him with a feeling half of pity, half of awe. Surely, man had never before so terribly altered, in so brief a period, as had Roderick Usher! It was with difficulty that I could bring myself to admit the identity of the wan being before me with the companion of my early boyhood. Yet the character of his face had been at all times remarkable. A cadaverousness of complexion; an eye large, liquid, and luminous beyond comparison; lips somewhat thin and very pallid, but of a surpassingly beautiful curve; a nose of a delicate Hebrew model, but with a breadth of nostril unusual in similar formations; a finely moulded chin, speaking, in its want of prominence, of a want of moral energy; hair of a more than web-like softness and tenuity; these features, with an inordinate expansion above the regions of the temple, made up altogether a countenance not easily to be forgotten. And now in the mere exaggeration of the prevailing character of these features, and of the expression they were wont to convey, lay so much of change that I doubted to whom I spoke. The now ghastly pallor of the skin, and the now miraculous lustre of the eye, above all things startled and even awed me. The silken hair, too, had been suffered to grow all unheeded, and as, in its wild gossamer texture, it floated rather than fell above the face, I could not, even with effort, connect its Arabesque expression with any idea of simple humanity.

In the manner of my friend I was at once struck with an incoherence—an inconsistency; and I soon found this to arise from a series of feeble and futile struggles to overcome an habitual trepidancy—an excessive nervous agitation. For something of this nature I had indeed been prepared, no less by his letter, than by reminiscences of certain boyish traits, and by conclusions deduced from his peculiar physical conformation and temperament. His action was alternately vivacious and sullen. His voice varied rapidly from a tremulous indecision (when the animal spirits seemed utterly in abeyance) to that species of energetic concision—that abrupt, weighty, unhurried, and hollow-sounding enunciation, that leaden, self-balanced, and perfectly modulated guttural utterance, which may be observed in the lost drunkard, or the irreclaimable eater of opium, during the periods of his most intense excitement.

It was thus that he spoke of the object of my visit, of his earnest desire to see me, and of the solace he expected me to afford him. He entered, at some length, into what he conceived to be the nature of his malady. It was, he said, a constitutional and a family evil, and one for which he despaired to find a remedy—a mere nervous affection, he immediately added, which would undoubtedly soon pass off. It displayed itself in a host of unnatural sensations. Some of these, as he detailed them, interested and bewildered me; although, perhaps, the terms, and the general manner of the narration had their weight. He suffered much from a morbid acuteness of the senses; the most insipid food was alone endurable; he could wear only garments of certain texture; the odors of all flowers were oppressive; his eyes were tortured by even faint light; and there were but peculiar sounds, and these from stringed instruments, which did not inspire him with horror.

To an anomalous species of terror I found him a bounden slave. "I shall perish," said he, "I *must* perish in this deplorable folly. Thus, thus, and not otherwise, shall I be lost. I dread the events of the future, not in themselves, but in their results. I shudder at the thought of any, even the most trivial, incident, which may operate upon this intolerable agitation of soul. I have, indeed, no abhorrence of danger, except in its obsolute effect—in terror. In this unnerved—in this pitiable condition—I feel that the period will sooner or later arrive when I must abandon life and reason together in some struggle with the grim phantasm, FEAR."

I learned, moreover, at intervals, and through broken and equivocal hints, another singular feature of his mental condition. He was enchained by certain superstitious impressions in regard to the dwelling which he tenanted, and whence, for many years, he had never ventured forth—in regard to an influence whose supposititious force was conveyed in terms too shadowy here to be re-stated—an influence which some peculiarities in the mere form and substance of his family mansions, had, by dint of long sufferance, he said, obtained over his spirit—an effect which the *physique* of the gray walls and turrets, and of the dim tarn into which they all looked down, had, at length, brought about upon the *morale* of his existence.

He admitted, however, although with hesitation, that much of the peculiar gloom which thus afflicted him could be traced to a more natural and far more palpable origin—to the severe and long-continued illness—indeed to the evidently approaching dissolution—of a tenderly beloved sister—his sole companion for long years—his last and only relative on earth. "Her decease," he said, with a bitterness which I can never forget, "would leave him (him the hopless and the frail) the last of the ancient race of the Ushers." While he spoke, the lady Madeline (for so was she called) passed slowly through a remote portion of the apartment, and, without having noticed my presence, disappeared. I regarded her with an utter astonishment not unmingled with dread—and yet I found it impossible to account for such feelings. A sensation of stupor oppressed me, as my eyes followed her retreating steps. When a door, at length, closed upon her, my glance sought instinctively and eagerly the countenance of the brother—but he had buried his face in his hands, and I could only perceive that a far more than ordinary wanness had overspread the emaciated fingers through which trickled many passionate tears.

The disease of the lady Madeline had long baffled the skill of her physicians. A settled apathy, a gradual wasting away of the person, and frequent although transient affections of a partially cataleptical character, were the unusual diagnosis. Hitherto she had steadily borne up against the pressure of her malady, and had not betaken herself finally to bed; but, on the closing in of the evening of my arrival at the house, she succumbed (as her brother told me at night with inexpressible agitation) to the prostrating power of the destroyer; and I learned that the glimpse I had obtained of her person would thus probably be the last I should obtain—that the lady, at least while living, would be seen by me no more.

For several days ensuing, her name was unmentioned by either Usher or myself: and during this period I was busied in earnest endeavors to alleviate the melancholy of my friend. We painted and read together; or I listened, as if in a dream, to the wild improvisations of his speaking guitar. And thus, as a closer and still closer intimacy admitted me more unreservedly into the recesses of his spirit, the more bitterly did I perceive the futility of all attempts at cheering a mind from which darkness, as if an inherent positive quality, poured forth upon all objects of the moral and physical universe, in one unceasing radiation of gloom.

I shall ever bear about me a memory of the many solemn hours I thus spent alone with the master of the House of Usher. Yet I should fail in my attempt to convey an idea of the exact character of the studies, or of the occupations, in which he involved me, or led me the way. An excited and highly distempered ideality threw a sulphureous lustre over all. His long improvised dirges will ring forever in my ears. Among other things, I hold painfully in mind a certain singular perversion and amplification of the wild air of the last waltz of Von Weber. From the paintings over which his elaborate fancy brooded, and which grew, touch by touch, into vaguenesses at which I shuddered the more thrillingly, because I shuddered knowing not why;—from these paintings (vivid as their images are now are before me) I would in vain endeavour to educe more than a small portion which should lie within the compass of merely written words. By the utter simplicity, by the nakedness of his designs, he arrested and overawed attention. If ever mortal painted an idea, that mortal was Roderick Usher. For me at least—in the circumstances then surrounding me—there arose out of the pure abstractions which the hypochondriac contrived to throw upon his canvas, an intensity of intolerable awe, no shadow of which felt I ever yet in the contemplation of the certainly glowing yet too concrete reveries of Fuseli.

One of the phantasmagoric concepts of my friend, partaking not so rigidly of the spirit of abstraction, may be shadowed forth, although feebly, in words. A small picture presented the interior of an immensely long and rectangular vault or tunnel, with low walls, smooth, white, and without interruption or device. Certain accessory points of the design served well to convey the idea that this excavation lay at an exceeding depth below the surface of the earth. No outlet was observed in any portion of its vast extent, and no torch, or other artificial source of light was discernible; yet a flood of intense rays rolled throughout, and bathed the whole in a ghastly and inappropriate splendour.

I have just spoken of that morbid condition of the auditory nerve which rendered all music intolerable to the sufferer, with the exception of certain effects of stringed instruments. It was, perhaps, the narrow limits to which he thus confined himself upon the guitar, which gave birth, in great measure, to the fantastic character of his performances. But the fervid *facility* of his *impromptus* could not be so accounted for. They must have been, and were, in the notes, as well as in the words of his wild fantasies (for he not unfrequently accompanied himself with rhymed verbal improvisations), the result of that intense mental collectedness and concentration to which I have previously alluded as observable only in particular moments of the highest artificial excitement. The words of one of these rhapsodies I have easily remembered. I was, perhaps, the more forcibly impressed with it, as he gave it, because, in the under or mystic current of its meaning, I fancied that I perceived, and for the first time, a full consciousness on the part of Usher, of the tottering of his lofty reason upon her throne. The verses, which were entitled "The Haunted Palace," ran very nearly, if not accurately, thus:

I.

*In the greenest of our valleys,*
*By good angels tenanted,*
*Once a fair and stately palace—*
*Radiant palace—reared its head.*
*In the monarch Thought's dominion—*
*It stood there!*
*Never seraph spread a pinion*
*Over fabric half so fair.*

II.

*Banners yellow, glorious, golden,*
*On its roof did float and flow;*
*(This—all this—was in the olden*
*Time long ago)*
*And every gentle air that dallied,*
*In that sweet day,*
*Along the ramparts plumed and pallid,*
*A winged odour went away.*

III.

*Wanderers in that happy valley*
*Through two luminous windows saw*
*Spirits moving musically*
*To a lute's well-tuned law,*
*Round about a throne, where sitting,*
*(Porphyrogene!)*
*In state his glory well befitting,*
*The ruler of the realm was seen.*

IV.

*And all with pearl and ruby glowing*
*Was the fair palace door,*
*Through which came flowing, flowing, flowing,*
*And sparkling evermore,*
*A troop of Echoes whose sweet duty*
*Was but to sing,*
*In voices of surpassing beauty,*
*The wit and wisdom of their king.*

V.

*But evil things, in robes of sorrow,*
*Assailed the monarch's high estate;*
*(Ah, let us mourn, for never morrow*
*Shall dawn upon him, desolate!)*
*And, round about his home, the glory*
*That blushed and bloomed*
*Is but a dim-remembered story*
*Of the old time entombed.*

VI.

*And travellers now within that valley,*
*Through the red-litten window, see*
*Vast forms that move fantastically*
*To a discordant melody;*
*While, like a ghastly rapid river,*
*Through the pale door,*
*A hideous throng rush out forever,*
*And laugh—but smile no more.*

I well remember that suggestions arising from this ballad, led us into a train of thought wherein there became manifest an opinion of Usher's which I mention, not so much on account of its novelty, (for other men have thought thus,) as on account of the pertinacity with which he maintained it. This opinion, in its general form, was that of the sentience of all vegetable things. But, in his disordered fancy, the idea had assumed a more daring character, and trespassed, under certain conditions, upon the kingdom of inorganization. I lack words to express the full extent, or the earnest *abandon* of his persuasion. The belief, however, was connected (as I have previously hinted) with the gray stones of the home of his forefathers. The conditions of the sentience had been here, he imagined, fulfilled in the method of collocation of these stones—in the order of their arrangement, as well as in that of the many *fungi* which overspread them, and of the decayed trees which stood around—above all, in the long undisturbed endurance of this arrangement, and in its reduplication in the still waters of the tarn. Its evidence—the evidence of the sentience—was to be seen, he said (and I here started as he spoke,) in the gradual yet certain condensation of an atmosphere of their own about the water and the walls. The result was discoverable, he added, in the silent yet importunate and terrible influence which for centuries had moulded the destinies of his family, and which made *him* what I now saw him—what he was. Such opinions need no comment, and I will make none.

Our books—the books which for years had formed no small portion of the mental existence of the invalid—were, as might be supposed, in strict keeping with this character of phantasm. We pored together over such works as the Ververt and Chartreuse of Gresset; the Belphegor of Machiavelli; the Heaven and Hell of Swedenborg; the Subterranean Voyage of Nicholas Klimm by Holberg; the Chiromancy of Robert Flud, of Jean D'Indaginé, and of De la Chambre; the Journey into the Blue Distance of Tieck; and the City of the Sun of Campanella. One favourite volume was a small octavo edition of the *Directorium Inquisitorum,* by the Dominican Eymeric de Gironne; and there were passages in Pomponius Mela, about the old African Satyrs and Ægipans, over which Usher would sit dreaming for hours. His chief delight, however, was found in the perusal of an exceedingly rare and curious book in quarto Gothic—the manual of a forgotten church—the *Vigiliæ Mortuorum secundum Chorum Ecclesiæ Maguntinæ.*

I could not help thinking of the wild ritual of this work, and of its probable influence upon the hypochondriac, when, one evening, having informed me abruptly that the lady Madeline was no more, he stated his intention of preserving her corpse for a fortnight, (previously to its final interment,) in one of the numerous vaults within the main walls of the building. The wordly reason, however, assigned for this singular proceeding, was one which I did not feel at liberty to dispute. The brother had been led to his resolution (so he told me) by consideration of the unusual character of the malady of the deceased, of certain obtrusive and eager inquiries on the part of her medical men, and of the remote and exposed situation of the burial-ground of the family. I will not deny that when I called to mind the sinister countenance of the person whom I met upon the staircase, on the day of my arrival at the house, I had no desire to oppose what I regarded as at best but a harmless, and by no means an unnatural, precaution.

At the request of Usher, I personally aided him in the arrangement for the temporary entombment. The body having been encoffined, we two alone bore it to its rest. The vault in which we placed it (and which had been so long unopened that our torches, half smothered in its oppressive atmosphere, gave us little opportunity for investigation) was small, damp, and entirely without means of admission for light; lying, at great depth, immediately beneath that portion of the building in which was my own sleeping apartment. It had been used, apparently, in remote feudal times, for the worst purposes of a donjon-keep, and, in later days, as a place of deposit for powder, or some other highly combustible substance, as a portion of its floor, and the whole interior of a long archway through which we reached it, were carefully sheathed with copper. The door, of massive iron, had been, also, similarly protected. Its immense weight caused an unusually sharp grating sound, as it moved upon its hinges.

Having deposited our mournful burden upon tressels within this region of horror, we partially turned aside the yet unscrewed lid of the coffin, and looked upon the face of the tenant. A striking similitude between the brother and sister now first arrested my attention; and Usher, divining, perhaps, my thoughts, murmured out some few words from which I learned that the deceased and himself had been twins, and that sympathies of a scarcely intelligible nature had always existed between them. Our glances, however, rested not long upon the dead—for we could not regard her unawed. The disease which had thus entombed the lady in the maturity of youth, had left, as usual in all maladies of a strictly cataleptical character, the mockery of a faint blush upon the bosom and the face, and that suspiciously lingering smile upon the lip which is so terrible in death. We replaced and screwed down the lid, and having secured the door of iron, made our way, with toil, into the scarcely less gloomy apartments of the upper portion of the house.

And now, some days of bitter grief having elapsed, an observable change came over the features of the mental disorder of my friend. His ordinary manner had vanished. His ordinary occupations were neglected or forgotten. He roamed from chamber to chamber with hurried, unequal, and objectless step. The pallor of his countenance had assumed, if possible, a more ghastly hue—but the luminousness of his eye had utterly gone out. The once occasional huskiness of his tone was heard no more; and a tremulous quaver, as if of extreme terror, habitually characterized his utterance. There were times, indeed, when I thought his unceasingly agitated mind was labouring with some oppressive secret, to divulge which he struggled for the necessary courage. At times, again, I was obliged to resolve all into the mere inexplicable vagaries of madness, for I beheld him gazing upon vacancy for long hours, in an attitude of the profoundest attention, as if listening to some imaginary sound. It was no wonder that his condition terrified—that it infected me. I felt creeping upon me, by slow yet certain degrees, the wild influences of his own fantastic yet impressive superstitions.

It was, especially, upon retiring to bed late in the night of the seventh or eighth day after the placing of the lady Madeline within the donjon, that I experienced the full power of such feelings. Sleep came not near my couch—while the hours waned and waned away. I struggled to reason off the nervousness which had dominion over me. I endeavoured to believe that much, if not all of what I felt, was due to the bewildering influence of the gloomy furniture of the room—

of the dark and tattered draperies, which, tortured into motion by the breath of a rising tempest, swayed fitfully to and fro upon the walls, and rustled uneasily about the decorations of the bed. But my efforts were fruitless. An irrepressible tremour gradually pervaded my frame; and, at length, there sat upon my very heart an incubus of utterly causeless alarm. Shaking this off with a gasp and a struggle, I uplifted myself upon the pillows, and, peering earnestly within the intense darkness of the chamber, hearkened—I know not why, except that an instinctive spirit prompted me—to certain low and indefinite sounds which came, through the pauses of the storm, at long intervals, I knew not whence. Overpowered by an intense sentiment of horror, unaccountable yet unendurable, I threw on my clothes with haste (for I felt that I should sleep no more during the night), and endeavoured to arouse myself from the pitiable condition into which I had fallen, by pacing rapidly to and fro through the apartment.

I had taken but few turns in this manner, when a light step on an adjoining staircase arrested my attention. I presently recognized it as that of Usher. In an instant afterward he rapped, with a gentle touch, at my door, and entered, bearing a lamp. His countenance was, as usual, cadaverously wan—but, moreover, there was a species of mad hilarity in his eyes—an evidently restrained *hysteria* in his whole demeanour. His air appalled me—but anything was preferable to the solitude which I had so long endured, and I even welcome his presence as a relief.

"And you have not seen it?" he said abruptly, after having stared about him for some moments in silence—"you have not then seen it?—but, stay! you shall." Thus speaking, and having carefully shaded his lamp, he hurried to one of the casements, and threw it freely open to the storm.

The impetuous fury of the entering gust nearly lifted us from our feet. It was, indeed, a tempestuous yet sternly beautiful night, and one wildly singular in its terror and its beauty. A whirlwind had apparently collected its force in our vicinity; for there were frequent and violent alterations in the direction of the wind; and the exceeding density of the clouds (which hung so low as to press upon the turrets of the house) did not prevent our perceiving the life-like velocity with which they flew careering from all points against each other, without passing away into the distance. I say that even their exceeding density did not prevent our perceiving this—yet we had no glimpse of the moon or stars—nor was there any flashing forth of the lightning. But the under surfaces of the huge masses of agitated vapour, as well as all terrestrial objects immediately around us, were glowing in the unnatural light of a faintly luminous and distinctly visible gaseous exhalation which hung about and enshrouded the mansion.

"You must not—you shall not behold this!" said I, shudderingly, to Usher, as I led him with a gentle violence, from the window to a seat. "These appearances, which bewilder you, are merely electrical phenomena not uncommon—or it may be that they have their ghastly origin in the rank miasma of the tarn. Let us close this casement;—the air is chilling and dangerous to your frame. Here is one of your favorite romances. I will read, and you shall listen;—and so we will pass away this terrible night together."

The antique volume which I had taken up was the "Mad Trist" of Sir

Launcelot Canning; but I had called it a favourite of Usher's more in sad jest than in earnest; for, in truth, there is little in its uncouth and unimaginative prolixity which could have had interest for the lofty and spiritual ideality of my friend. It was, however, the only book immediately at hand; and I indulged a vague hope that the excitement which now agitated the hypochrondriac, might find relief (for the history of mental disorder is full of similar anomalies) even in the extremeness of the folly which I should read. Could I have judged, indeed, by the wild, overstrained air of vivacity with which he hearkened, or apparently hearkened, to the words of the tale, I might well have congratulated myself upon the success of my design.

I had arrived at that well-known portion of the story where Ethelred, the hero of the Trist, having sought in vain for peaceable admission into the dwelling of the hermit, proceeds to make good an entrance by force. Here, it will be remembered, the words of the narrative run thus:

"And Ethelred, who was by nature of a doughty heart, and who was now mighty withal, on account of the powerfulness of the wine which he had drunken, waited no longer to hold parley with the hermit, who, in sooth, was of an obstinate and maliceful turn, but, feeling the rain upon his shoulders, and fearing the rising of the tempest, unlifted his mace outright, and, with blows, made quickly room in the plankings of the door for his gauntleted hand; and now, pulling therewith sturdily, he so cracked, and ripped, and tore all asunder, that the noise of the dry and hollow-sounding wood alarumed and reverberated throughout the forest."

At the termination of this sentence I started, and for a moment, paused; for it appeared to me (although I at once concluded that my excited fancy had deceived me)—it appeared to me that, from some very remote portion of the mansion, there came, indistinctly, to my ears, what might have been, in its exact similarity of character, the echo (but a stifled and dull one certainly) of the very cracking and ripping sound which Sir Launcelot had so particularly described. It was, beyond doubt, the coincidence alone which had arrested my attention; for, amid the rattling of the sashes of the casements, and the ordinary commingled noises of the still increasing storm, the sound, in itself, had nothing, surely, which should have interested or disturbed me. I continued the story:

"But the good champion Ethelred, now entering within the door, was sore enraged and amazed to perceive no signal of the maliceful hermit; but, in the stead thereof, a dragon of a scaly and prodigious demeanour, and of a fiery tongue, which sate in guard before a palace of gold, with a floor of silver; and upon the wall there hung a shield of shining brass with this legend enwritten—

*Who entereth herein, a conqueror hath bin;*
*Who slayeth the dragon, the shield he shall win;*

And Ethelred uplifted his mace, and struck upon the head of the dragon, which fell before him, and gave up his pesty breath, with a shriek so horrid and harsh, and withal so piercing, that Ethelred had fain to close his ears with his hands against the dreadful noise of it, the like whereof was never before heard."

Here again I paused abruptly, and now with a feeling of wild amazement—for there could be no doubt whatever that, in this instance, I did actually hear (although from what direction it proceeded I found it impossible to say) a low and apparently distant, but harsh, protracted and most unusual screaming or grating sound—the exact counterpart of what my fancy had already conjured up for the dragon's unnatural shriek as described by the romancer.

Oppressed, as I certainly was, upon the occurrence of this second and most extraordinary coincidence, by a thousand conflicting sensations, in which wonder and extreme terror were predominant, I still retained sufficient presence of mind to avoid exciting, by any observation, the sensitive nervousness of my companion. I was by no means certain that he had noticed the sounds in question; although, assuredly, a strange alteration had, during the last few minutes, taken place in his demeanour. From a position fronting my own, he had gradually brought round his chair, so as to sit with his face to the door of the chamber; and thus I could but partially perceive his features, although I saw that his lips trembled as if he were murmuring inaudibly. His head had dropped upon his breast—yet I knew that he was not asleep, from the wide rigid opening of the eye as I caught a glance of it in profile.The motion of his body, too, was at variance with this idea—for he rocked from side to side with a gentle yet constant and uniform sway. Having rapidly taken notice of all this, I resumed the narrative of Sir Launcelot, which thus proceeded:

"And now, the champion, having escaped from the terrible fury of the dragon, bethinking himself of the brazen shield, and of the breaking up of the enchantment which was upon it, removed the carcass from out of the way before him, and approached valorously over the silver pavement of the castle to where the shield was upon the wall; which in sooth tarried not for his full coming, but fell down at his feet upon the silver floor, with a mighty great and terrible ringing sound."

No sooner had these syllables passed my lips, than—as if a shield of brass had indeed, at the moment, fallen heavily upon a floor of silver—I became aware of a distinct, hollow, metallic, and clangorous yet apparently muffled reverberation. Completely unnerved, I leaped to my feet; but the measured rocking movement of Usher was undisturbed. I rushed to the chair in which he sat. His eyes were bent fixedly before him, and throughout his whole countenance there reigned a stony rigidity. But, as I placed my hand upon his shoulder, there came a strong shudder over his whole person; a sickly smile quivered about his lips; and I saw that he spoke in a low, hurried, and gibbering murmur, as if unconscious of my presence. Bending closely over him, I at length drank in the hideous import of his words.

"Not hear it?—yes, I hear it, and *have* heard it. Long—long—long—many minutes, many hours, many days, have I heard it—yet I dared not—oh, pity me, miserable wretch that I am!—I dared not—I *dared* not speak! *We have put her living in the tomb!* Said I not that my senses were acute? I *now* tell you that I heard her first feeble movements in the hollow coffin. I heard them—many, many days ago—yet I dared not—*I dared not speak!* And now—to-night—Ethelred—ha! ha!—the breaking of the hermit's door, and the death-cry of the dragon, and the clangour of the shield!—say, rather, the rending of her coffin, and the grating of the iron hinges of her prison, and her struggles within the coppered archway of the vault! Oh whither shall I fly? Will she not be here anon? Is she not hurrying to upbraid me for my haste? Have I not heard her footstep on the stair? Do I not distinguish that heavy and horrible beating of her heart? MADMAN!" here he sprang furiously to his feet, and shrieked out his syllables, as if in the effort he were giving up his soul—"MADMAN! I TELL YOU THAT SHE NOW STANDS WITHOUT THE DOOR!"

As if in the superhuman energy of his utterance there had been found the potency of a spell—the huge antique panels to which the speaker pointed, threw slowly back, upon the instant, their ponderous and ebony jaws. It was the work of the rushing gust—but then without those doors there DID stand the lofty and enshrouded figure of the lady Madeline of Usher. There was blood upon her white robes, and the evidence of some bitter struggle upon every portion of her emaciated frame. For a moment she remained trembling and reeling to and fro upon the threshold, then, with a low moaning cry, fell heavily inward upon the person of her brother, and in her violent and now final death-agonies, bore him to the floor a corpse, and a victim to the terrors he had anticipated.

From that chamber, and from that mansion, I fled aghast. The storm was still abroad in all its wrath as I found myself crossing the old causeway. Suddenly there shot along the path a wild light, and I turned to see whence a gleam so unusual could have issued; for the vast house and its shadows were alone behind me. The radiance was that of the full, setting. and blood-red moon, which now shone vividly through that once barely-discernible fissure of which I have before spoken as extending from the roof of the building, in a zigzag direction, to the base. While I gazed, this fissure rapidly widened—there came a fierce breath of the whirlwind—the entire orb of the satellite burst at once upon my sight—my brain reeled as I saw the mighty walls rushing asunder—there was a long tumultuous shouting sound like the voice of a thousand waters—and the deep and dank tarn at my feet closed sullenly and silently over the fragments of the "HOUSE OF USHER."

## *Study questions*

1. *What do we learn about the narrator in the opening paragraphs of the story? What do we learn about the situation? How is the narrator related to the situation?* 2. *What details of the setting presented in the opening paragraphs become important as the story goes on?* 3. *What is Usher's house like? What is Usher like? Are the house and Usher related in some symbolic way?* 4. *What role does the lady Madeline play? Why does she disappear at the time the narrator comes to stay?* 5. *The house that is reduplicated in the tarn begins a line of images and motifs that suggests a kind of microcosmic duplication. How many scenes, objects, characters seem "doubles" of each other or mirror images?* 6. *At what point do the narrator and Usher begin to mirror each other? Why does the*

*narrator get so involved in Usher's troubles?* 7. *What is the function of the picture Usher painted? How it it related to the vault in which they bury the lady Madeline?* 8. *How do the details in the "Mad Trist" contribute to the story?* 9. *Why do they bury the lady Madeline alive?* 10. *What elements in the story suggest a dream pattern? Consider the mazes, for example, and the idea of suffocation.* 11. *What is Usher's conflict? How is it resolved?* 12. *How does Usher's conflict relate to the narrator?*

# LIGEIA

*And the will therein lieth, which dieth not. Who knoweth the mysteries of the will, with its vigor? For God is but a great will pervading all things by nature of its intentness. Man doth not yield himself to the angels, nor unto death utterly, save only through the weakness of his feeble will.*

JOSEPH GLANVILL

I cannot, for my soul, remember how, when, or even precisely where, I first became acquainted with the lady Ligeia. Long years have since elapsed, and my memory is feeble through much suffering. Or, perhaps, I cannot *now* bring these points to mind, because, in truth, the character of my beloved, her rare learning, her singular yet placid cast of beauty, and the thrilling and enthralling eloquence of her low musical language, made their way into my heart by paces so steadily and stealthily progressive that they have been unnoticed and unknown. Yet I believe that I met her first and most frequently in some large, old, decaying city near the Rhine. Of her family—I have surely heard her speak. That it is of a remotely ancient date cannot be doubted. Ligeia! Ligeia! Buried in studies of a nature more than all else adapted to deaden impressions of the outward world, it is by that sweet word alone—by Ligeia—that I bring before mine eyes in fancy the image of her who is no more. And now, while I write, a recollection flashes upon me that I have *never known* the paternal name of her who was my friend and my betrothed, and who became the partner of my studies, and finally the wife of my bosom. Was it a playful charge on the part of my Ligeia? or was it a test of my strength of affection, that I should institute no inquiries upon this point? or was it rather a caprice of my own—a wildly romantic offering on the shrine of the most passionate devotion? I but indistinctly recall the fact itself—what wonder that I have utterly forgotten the circumstances which originated or attended it? And, indeed, if ever that spirit which is entitled *Romance*—if ever she, the wan and the misty-winged *Ashtophet* of idolatrous Egypt, presided, as they tell, over marriages ill-omened, then most surely she presided over mine.

There is one dear topic, however, on which my memory fails me not. It is the *person* of Ligeia. In stature she was tall, somewhat slender, and, in her latter days, even emaciated. I would in vain attempt to portray the majesty, the quiet ease of her demeanor, or the incomprehensible lightness and elasticity of her footfall. She came and departed as a shadow. I was never made aware of her entrance into my closed study save by the dear music of her low sweet voice, as she placed her marble hand upon my shoulder. In beauty of face no maiden ever equalled her. It was the radiance of an opium-dream—an airy and spirit-lifting vision more wildly divine than the phantasies which hovered about the slumbering souls of the daughters of Delos. Yet her features were not of that regular mould which we have been falsely taught to worship in the classical labors of the heathen. "There is no exquisite beauty," says Bacon, Lord Verulam, speaking truly of all the forms and *genera* of beauty, "without some *strangeness* in the proportion." Yet, although I saw that the features of Ligeia were not of a classic regularity—although I perceived that her loveliness was indeed "exquisite," and felt that there was much of "strangeness' pervading it, yet I have tried in vain to detect the irregularity and to trace home my own perception of "the strange." I examined the contour of the lofty and pale forehead—it was faultless—how cold indeed that word when applied to a majesty so divine!—the skin rivalling the purest ivory, the commanding extent and respose, the gentle prominence of the regions above the temples; and then the raven-black, the glossy, the luxuriant and naturally-curling tresses, setting forth the full force of the Homeric epithet, "hyacinthine!" I looked at the delicate outlines of the nose—and nowhere but in the graceful medallions of the Hebrews had I beheld a similar perfection. There were the same luxurious smoothness of surface, the same scarcely perceptible tendency to the aquiline, the same harmoniously curved nostrils speaking the free spirit. I regarded the sweet mouth. Here was indeed the triumph of all things heavenly—the magnificent turn of the short upper lip—the soft, voluptuous slumber of the under—the dimples which sported, and the color which spoke—the teeth glancing back, with a brilliancy almost startling, every ray of the holy light which fell upon them in her serene and placid yet most exultingly radiant of all smiles. I scrutinized the formation of the chin—and, here too, I found the gentleness of breadth, the softness and the majesty, the fullness and the spirituality, of the Greek—the contour which the god Apollo revealed but in a dream to Cleomenes, the son of the Athenian. And then I peered into the large eyes of Ligeia.

For eyes we have no models in the remotely antique. It might have been, too, that in these eyes of my beloved lay the secret to which Lord Verulam alludes. They were, I must believe, far larger than the ordinary eyes of our own race. They were even fuller than the fullest of the gazelle eyes of the tribe of the valley of Nourjahad. Yet it was only at intervals—in moments of intense excitement—that this peculiarity became more than slightly noticeable in Ligeia. And at such moments was her beauty—in my heated fancy thus it appeared perhaps—the beauty of beings either above or apart from the earth—the beauty of the fabulous Houri of the Turk. The hue of the orbs was the most brilliant of black, and, far over them, hung jetty lashes of great length. The brows, slightly irregular in outline, had the same tint. The "strangeness," however, which I found in the eyes, was of a nature distinct from the formation, or the color, or the brilliancy of the features, and must, after all, be referred to the *expression.* Ah, word of no meaning! behind whose vast latitude of mere sound we intrench our ignorance of so much of the spiritual. The expression of the eyes of Ligeia! How for long hours have I pondered upon it! How have I, through the whole of a midsummer night, struggled to fathom it! What was it—that something more profound than the well of Democritus—which lay far within the pupils of my beloved? What *was* it? I was possessed with a passion to discover. Those eyes! those large, those shining, those divine orbs! they became to me twin stars of Leda, and I to them devoutest of astrologers.

There is no point, among the many incomprehensible anomalies of the science of mind, more thrillingly exciting than the fact—never, I believe, noticed in the schools—that in our endeavors to recall to memory something long forgotten, we often find ourselves *upon the very verge* of remembrance, without being able, in the end, to remember. And thus how frequently, in my intense scrutiny of Ligeia's eyes, have I felt approaching the full knowledge of their expression—felt it approaching—yet not quite be mine—and so at length entirely depart! And (strange, oh strangest mystery of all!) I found, in the commonest objects of the universe, a circle of analogies to that expression. I mean to say that, subsequently to the period when Ligeia's beauty passed into my spirit, there dwelling as in a shrine, I derived, from many existences in the material world, a sentiment such as I felt always aroused, within me, by her large and luminous orbs. Yet not the more could I define that sentiment, or analyze, or even steadily view it. I recognized it, let me repeat, sometimes in the survey of a rapidly growing vine—in the contemplation of a moth, a butterfly, a chrysalis, a stream of running water. I have felt it in the ocean; in the falling of a meteor. I have felt it in the glances of unusually aged people. And there are one or two stars in heaven—(one especially, a star of the sixth magnitude, double and changeable, to be found near the large star in Lyra) in a telescopic scrutiny of which I have been made aware of the feeling. I have been filled with it by certain sounds from stringed instruments, and not unfrequently by passages from books. Among innumerable other instances, I well remember something in a volume of Joseph Glanvill, which (perhaps from its quaintness—who shall say?) never failed to inspire me with the sentiment;—"And the will therein lieth, which dieth not. Who knoweth the mysteries of the will, with its vigor? For God is but a great will pervading all things by nature of its intentness. Man doth not yield him to the angels, nor unto death utterly, save only through the weakness of his feeble will."

Length of years and subsequent reflection, have enabled me to trace, indeed, some remote connection between the passage in the English moralist and a portion of the character of Ligeia. An *intensity* in thought, action, or speech, was possibly, in her, a result, or at least an index, of that gigantic volition which, during our long intercourse, failed to give other and more immediate evidence of its existence. Of all the women whom I have ever known, she, the outwardly calm, the ever-placid Ligeia, was the most violently a prey to the tumultuous vultures of stern passion. And of such passion I could form no estimate, save by the miraculous expansion of those eyes which at once so delighted and appalled me—by the almost magical melody, modulation, distinctness, and placidity of her very low voice—and by the fierce energy (rendered doubly effective by contrast with her manner of utterance) of the wild words which she habitually uttered.

I have spoken of the learning of Ligeia; it was immense—such as I have never known, in woman. In the classical tongues was she deeply proficient, and as far as my own acquaintance extended in regard to the modern dialects of Europe, I have never known her at fault. Indeed upon any theme of the most admired, because simply the most abstruse of the boasted erudition of the academy, have I *ever* found Ligeia at fault? How singularly—how thrilling, this one point in the nature of my wife has forced itself, at this late period only, upon my attention! I said her knowledge was such as I have never known in woman—but where breathes the man who has traversed, and successfully, *all* the wide areas of moral, physical, and mathematical science? I saw not then what I now clearly perceive, that the acquisitions of Ligeia were gigantic, were astounding; yet I was sufficiently aware of her infinite supremacy to resign myself, with a child-like confidence, to her guidance through the chaotic world of metaphysical investigation at which I was most busily occupied during the earlier years of our marriage. With how vast a triumph—with how vivid a delight—with how much of all that is etheral in hope—did I *feel,* as she bent over me in studies but little sought—but less known—that delicious vista by slow degrees expanding before me, down whose long, gorgeous, and all untrodden path, I might at length pass onward to the goal of a wisdom too divinely precious not to be forbidden!

How poignant, then, must have been the grief with which, after some years, I beheld my well-grounded expectations take wings to themselves and fly away! Without Ligeia I was but as a child groping benighted. Her presence, her readings alone, rendered vividly luminous the many mysteries of the transcendentalism in which we were immersed. Wanting the radiant lustre of her eyes, letters, lambent and golden, grew duller than Saturnian lead. And now those eyes shone less and less frequently upon the pages over which I pored. Ligeia grew ill. The wild eyes blazed with a too—too glorious effulgence; the pale fingers became of the transparent waxen hue of the grave; and the blue veins upon the lofty forehead swelled and sank impetuously with the tides of the most gentle emotion. I saw that she must die—and I struggled desperately in spirit with the grim Azrael. And the struggles of the passionate wife were, to my astonishment, even more energetic than my own. There had been much in her stern nature to impress me with the belief that, to her, death would have come without its terrors; but not so. Words are impotent to convey any just idea of the fierceness of resistance with which she wrestled with the Shadow. I groaned in anguish at the pitiable spectacle. I would have soothed—I would have reasoned; but, in the intensity of her wild desire for life,—for life—*but* for life—solace and reason were alike the uttermost folly. Yet not until the last instance, amid the most convulsive writhings of her fierce spirit, was shaken the external placidity of her demeanor. Her voice grew more gentle—grew more low—yet I would not wish to dwell upon the wild meaning of the quietly uttered words. My brain reeled as I hearkened entranced, to a melody more than mortal—to assumptions and aspirations which mortality had never before known.

That she loved me I should not have doubted; and I might have been easily aware that, in a bosom such as hers, love would have reigned no ordinary passion. But in death only was I fully impressed with the strength of her affection. For long hours, detaining my hand, would she pour out before me the overflowing of a heart whose more than passionate devotion amounted to idolatry. How had I deserved to be so blessed by such confessions?—how had I deserved to be so cursed with the removal of my beloved in the hour of her making them? But upon this subject I cannot bear to dilate. Let me say only, that in Ligeia's more than womanly abandonment to a love, alas! all unmerited, all unworthily bestowed, I at length recognized the principle of her longing with so wildly earnest a desire for the life which was now fleeting so rapidly away. It is this wild longing—it is this eager vehemence of desire for life—*but* for life—that I have no power to portray—no utterance capable of expressing.

At high noon of the night in which she departed, beckoning me, peremptorily, to her side, she bade me repeat certain verses composed by herself not many days before. I obeyed her.—They were these:

*Lo! 'tis a gala night*
*Within the lonesome latter years!*
*An angel throng, bewinged, bedight*
*In veils, and drowned in tears,*
*Sit in a theatre, to see*
*A play of hopes and fears,*
*While the orchestra breathes fitfully*
*The music of the spheres.*

*Mimes, in the form of God on high,*
*Mutter and mumble low,*
*And hither and thither fly—*
*Mere puppets they, who come and go*

*At bidding of vast formless things*
*That shift the scenery to and fro,*
*Flapping from out their Condor wings*
*Invisible Woe!*

*That motley drama!—oh, be sure*
*It shall not be forgot!*
*With its Phantom chased forever more,*
*By a crowd that seize it not,*
*Through a circle that ever returneth in*
*To the self-same spot,*
*And much of Madness and more of Sin*
*And Horror the soul of the plot.*

*But see, amid the mimic rout,*
*A crawling shape intrude!*
*A blood-red thing that writhes from out*
*The scenic solitude!*
*It writhes!—it writhes!—with mortal pangs*
*The mimes become its food,*
*And the seraphs sob at vermin fangs*
*In human gore imbued.*

*Out—out are the lights—out all!*
*And over each quivering form,*
*The curtain, a funeral pall,*
*Comes down with the rush of a storm.*
*And the angels, all pallid and wan,*
*Uprising, unveiling, affirm*
*That the play is the tragedy, "Man,"*
*And its hero the Conqueror Worm.*

"O God!" half shrieked Ligeia, leaping to her feet and extending her arms aloft with a spasmodic movement, as I made an end of these lines—"O God! O Divine Father!—shall these things be undeviatingly so?—shall this Conqueror be not once conquered? Are we not part and parcel in Thee? Who—who knoweth the mysteries of the will with its vigor? Man doth not yield him to the angels, *nor unto death utterly,* save only through the weakness of his feeble will."

And now, as if exhausted with emotion, she suffered her white arms to fall, and returned solemnly to her bed of death. And as she breathed her last sighs, there came mingled with them a low murmur from her lips. I bent to them my ear, and distinguished, again, the concluding words of the passage in Glanvill—*"Man doth not yield him to the angels, nor unto death utterly, save only through the weakness of his feeble will."*

She died;—and I, crushed into the very dust with sorrow, could no longer endure the lonely desolation of my dwelling in the dim and decaying city by the Rhine. I had no lack of what the world calls wealth. Ligeia had brought me far more, very far more than ordinarily falls to the lot of mortals. After a few months, therefore, of weary and aimless wandering, I purchased, and put in some repair, an abbey, which I shall not name, in one of the wildest and least frequented portions of fair England. The gloomy and dreary grandeur of the building, the almost savage aspect of the domain, the many melancholy and time-honored memories connected with both, had much in unison with the feelings of utter abandonment which had driven me into that remote and unsocial region of the country. Yet although the external abbey, with its verdant decay hanging about it, suffered but little alteration, I gave way, with a child-like perversity, and perchance with a faint hope of alleviating my sorrows, to a display of more than regal magnificence within.—For such follies, even in childhood, I had imbibed a taste, and now they came back to me as if in the dotage of grief. Alas, I feel how much even of incipient madness might have been discovered in the gorgeous and fantastic draperies, in the solemn carvings of Egypt, in the wild cornices and furniture, in the Bedlam patterns of the carpets of tufted gold! I had become a bounden slave in the trammels of opium, and my labors and orders had taken a coloring from my dreams. But these absurdities I must not pause to detail. Let me speak only of that one chamber, ever accursed, whither, in a moment of mental alienation, I led from the altar as my bride—as the successor of the unforgotten Ligeia—the fair-haired and blue-eyed Lady Rowena Trevanion, of Tremaine.

There is no individual portion of the architecture and decoration of that bridal chamber which is not now visibly before me. Where were the souls of the haughty family of the bride, when, through thirst of gold, they permitted to pass the threshold of an apartment *so* bedecked, a maiden and a daughter so beloved? I have said that I minutely remember the details of the chamber—yet I am sadly forgetful on topics of deep moment—and here there was no system, no keeping, in the fantastic display, to take hold upon the memory. The room lay in a high turret of the castellated abbey, was pentagonal in shape, and of capacious size. Occupying the whole southern face of the pentagon was the sole window—an immense sheet of unbroken glass from Venice—a single pane, and tinted of a leaden hue, so that the rays of either the sun or moon, passing through it, fell with a ghastly lustre on the objects within. Over the upper portion of this huge window, extended the trellis-work of an aged vine, which clambered up the massy walls of the turret. The ceiling, of gloomy-looking oak, was excessively lofty, vaulted, and elaborately fretted with the wildest and most grotesque specimens of a semi-Gothic, semi-Druidical device. From out the most central recess of this melancholy vaulting, depended, by a single chain of gold with long links, a huge censer of the same metal, Saracenic in pattern, and with many perforations so contrived that there writhed in and out of them, as if endued with a serpent vitality, a continual succession of parti-colored fires.

Some few ottomans and golden candelabra, of Eastern figure, were in various stations about—and there was the couch, too—the bridal couch—of an Indian model, and low, and sculptured of solid ebony, with a pall-like canopy above. In each of the angles of the chamber stood on end a gigantic sarcophagus of black granite, from the tombs of the kings over against Luxor, with their aged lids full of immemorial sculpture. But in the draping of the apartment lay, alas! the chief phantasy of all. The lofty walls, gigantic in height—even unproportionably so—were hung from summit to foot, in vast folds, with a heavy and massive-looking tapestry—tapestry of a material which was found alike as a carpet on the floor, as a covering for the ottomans and the ebony bed, as a canopy for the bed and as the gorgeous volutes of the curtains which partially shaded the window. The material was the richest cloth of gold. It was spotted all over, at irregular intervals, with arabesque figures, about a foot in diameter, and wrought upon the cloth in patterns of the most jetty black. But these figures partook of the true character of the arabesque only when regarded from a single point of view. By a contrivance now common, and indeed traceable to a very remote period of antiquity, they were made changeable in aspect. To one entering the room, they bore the appearance of simple monstrosities; but upon a farther advance, this appearance gradually departed; and step by step, as the visitor moved his station in the chamber, he saw himself surrounded by an endless succession of the ghastly forms which belong to the superstition of the Norman, or arise in the guilty slumbers of the monk. The phantasmagoric effect was vastly heightened by the artificial introduction of a strong continual current of wind behind the draperies—giving a hideous and uneasy animation to the whole.

In halls such as these—in a bridal chamber such as this—I passed, with the Lady of Tremaine, the unhallowed hours of the first month of our marriage—passed them with but little disquietude. That my wife dreaded the fierce moodiness of my temper—that she shunned me and loved me but little—I could not help perceiving; but it gave me rather pleasure than otherwise. I loathed her with a hatred belonging more to demon than to man. My memory flew back, (oh, with what intensity of regret!) to Ligeia, the beloved, the august, the beautiful, the entombed. I revelled in recollections of her purity, of her wisdom, of her lofty, her ethereal nature, of her passionate, her idolatrous love. Now, then, did my spirit fully and freely burn with more than all the fires of her own. In the excitement of my opium dreams (for I was habitually fettered in the shackles of the drug) I would call aloud upon her name, during the silence of the night, or among the sheltered recesses of the glens by day, as if, through the wild eagerness, the solemn passion, the consuming ardor of my longing for the departed, I could restore her to the pathways she had abandoned—ah, *could* it be forever?—upon the earth.

About the commencement of the second month of the marriage, the Lady Rowena was attacked with sudden illness, from which her recovery was slow. The fever which consumed her rendered her nights uneasy; and in her perturbed state of half-slumber, she spoke of sounds, and of motions, in and about the chamber of the turret, which I concluded had no origin save in the distemper of her fancy, or perhaps in the phantasmagoric influences of the chamber itself. She became at length convalescent—finally well. Yet but a brief period elapsed, ere a second more violent disorder again threw her upon a bed of suffering; and from this attack her frame, at all times feeble, never altogether recovered. Her illnesses were, after this epoch, of alarming character, and of more alarming recurrence, defying alike the knowledge and the great exertions of her physicians. With the increase of the chronic disease which had thus, apparently, taken too sure hold upon her constitution to be eradicated by human means, I could not fail to observe a similar increase in the nervous irritation of her temperament, and in her excitability by trival causes of fear. She spoke again, and now more frequently and pertinaciously, of the sounds—of the slight sounds—and of the unusual motions among the tapestries, to which she had formerly alluded.

One night, near the closing in of September, she pressed this distressing subject with more than usual emphasis upon my attention. She had just awakened from an unquiet slumber, and I had been watching, with feelings half of anxiety, half of vague terror, the workings of her emaciated countenance. I sat by the side of her ebony bed, upon one of the ottomans of India. She partly arose, and spoke, in an earnest low whisper, of sounds which she *then* heard, but which I could not hear—of motions which she *then* saw, but which I could not perceive.

The wind was rushing hurriedly behind the tapestries, and I wished to show her (what, let me confess it, I could not *all* believe) that those almost inarticulate breathings, and those very gentle variations of the figures upon the wall, were but the natural effects of that customary rushing of the wind. But a deadly pallor, overspreading her face, had proved to me that my exertions to reassure her would be fruitless. She appeared to be fainting, and no attendants were within call. I remembered where was deposited a decanter of light wine which had been ordered by her physicians, and hastened across the chamber to procure it. But, as I stepped beneath the light of the censer, two circumstances of a startling nature attracted my attention. I had felt that some palpable although invisible object had passed lightly by my person; and I saw that there lay upon the golden carpet, in the very middle of the rich lustre thrown from the censer, a shadow—a faint, indefinite shadow of angelic aspect—such as might be fancied for the shadow of a shade. But I was wild with the excitement of an immoderate dose of opium, and heeded these things but little, nor spoke of them to Rowena. Having found the wine, I recrossed the chamber, and poured out a goblet-ful, which I held to the lips of the fainting lady. She had now partially recovered, however, and took the vessel herself, while I sank upon an ottoman near me, with my eyes fastened upon her person. It was then that I became distinctly aware of a gentle foot-fall upon the carpet, and near the couch; and in a second thereafter, as Rowena was in the act of raising the wine to her lips, I saw, or may have dreamed that I saw, fall within the goblet, as if from some invisible spring in the atmosphere of the room, three or four large drops of a brilliant and ruby colored fluid. If this I saw—not so Rowena. She swallowed the wine unhesitatingly, and I forbore to speak to her of a circumstance which must, after all, I considered, have been but the suggestion of a vivid imagination, rendered morbidly active by the terror of the lady, by the opium, and by the hour.

Yet I cannot conceal it from my own perception that, immediately subsequent to the fall of the ruby-drops, a rapid change for the worse took place in the disorder of my wife; so that, on the third subsequent night, the hands of her menials prepared her for the tomb, and on the fourth, I sat alone, with her shrouded body, in that fantastic chamber which had received her as my bride.—Wild visions, opium-engendered, flitted, shadowlike, before me. I gazed with unquiet eye upon the sarcophagi in the angles of the room, upon the varying figures of the drapery, and upon the writhing of the parti-colored fires in the censer overhead. My eyes then fell, as I called to mind the circumstances of a former night, to the spot beneath the glare of the censer where I had seen the faint traces of the shadow. It was there, however, no longer; and breathing with greater freedom, I turned my glances to the pallid and rigid figure upon the bed. Then rushed upon me a thousand memories of Ligeia—and then came back upon my heart, with the turbulent violence of a flood, the whole of that unutterable woe with which I had regarded *her* thus enshrouded. The night waned; and still, with a bosom full of bitter thoughts of the one only and supremely beloved, I remained gazing upon the body of Rowena.

It might have been midnight, or perhaps earlier, or later, for I had taken no note of time, when a sob, low, gentle, but very distinct, startled me from my revery.—I *felt* that it came from the bed of ebony—the bed of death. I listened in an agony of superstitious terror—but there was no repetition of the sound. I strained my vision to detect any motion in the corpse—but there was not the slightest perceptible. Yet I could not have been deceived. I *had* heard the noise, however faint, and my soul was awakened within me. I resolutely and perseveringly kept my attention riveted upon the body. Many minutes elapsed before any circumstance occurred tending to throw light upon the mystery. At length it became evident that a slight, a very feeble, and barely noticeable tinge of color had flushed up within the cheeks, and along the sunken small veins of the eyelids. Through a species of unutterable horror and awe, for which the language of mortality has no sufficiently energetic expression, I felt my heart cease to beat, my limbs grow rigid where I sat. Yet a sense of duty finally operated to restore my self-possession. I could no longer doubt that we had been precipitate in our preparations—that Rowena still lived. It was necessary that some immediate exertion be made; yet the turret was altogether apart from the portion of the abbey tenanted by the servants—there were none within call—I had no means of summoning them to my aid without leaving the room for many minutes—and this I could not venture to do. I therefore struggled alone in my endeavors to call back the spirit still hovering. In a short period it was certain, however, that a relapse had taken place; the color disappeared from both eyelid and cheek, leaving a wanness even more than that of marble; the lips became doubly shrivelled and pinched up in the ghastly expression of death; a repulsive clamminess and coldness overspread rapidly the surface of the body; and all the usual rigorous stiffness immediately supervened. I fell back with a shudder upon the couch from which I had been so startlingly aroused, and again gave myself up to passionate waking visions of Ligeia.

An hour thus elapsed when (could it be possible?) I was a second time aware of some vague sound issuing from the region of the bed. I listened—in extremity of horror. The sound came again—it was a sigh. Rushing to the corpse, I saw—distinctly saw—a tremor upon the lips. In a minute afterward they relaxed, disclosing a bright line of the pearly teeth. Amazement now struggled in my bosom with the profound awe which had hitherto reigned there alone. I felt that my vision grew dim, that my reason wandered; and it was only by a violent effort that I at length succeeded in nerving myself to the task which duty thus once more had pointed out. There was now a partial glow upon the forehead and upon the cheek and throat; a perceptible warmth pervaded the whole frame; there was even a slight pulsation at the heart. The lady *lived;* and with redoubled ardor I betook myself to the task of restoration. I chafed and bathed the temples and the hands, and used every exertion which experience, and no little medical reading, could suggest. But in vain. Suddenly, the color fled, the pulsation ceased, the lips resumed the expression of the dead, and, in an instant afterward, the whole body took upon itself the icy chilliness, the livid hue, the intense rigidity, the sunken outline, and all the loathsome peculiarities of that which has been, for many days, a tenant of the tomb.

And again I sunk into visions of Ligeia and again, (what marvel that I shudder while I write?) *again* there reached my ears a low sob from the region of the ebony bed. But why shall I minutely detail the unspeakable horrors of that night? Why shall I pause to relate how, time after time, until near the period of the gray dawn, this hideous drama of revivification was repeated; how each terrific relapse was only into a sterner and apparently more irredeemable death; how each agony wore the aspect of a struggle with some invisible foe; and how each struggle was succeeded by I know not what of wild change in the personal appearance of the corpse? Let me hurry to a conclusion.

The greater part of the fearful night had worn away, and she who had been dead once again stirred—and now more vigorously than hitherto, although arousing from a dissolution more appalling in its utter hopelessness than any. I had long ceased to struggle or to move, and remained sitting rigidly upon the ottoman, a helpless prey to a whirl of violent emotions, of which extreme awe was perhaps the least terrible, the least consuming. The corpse, I repeat, stirred and now more vigorously than before. The hues of life flushed up with unwonted energy into the countenance—the limbs relaxed—and, save that the eyelids were yet pressed heavily together, and that the bandages and draperies of the grave still imparted their charnel character to the figure, I might have dreamed that Rowena had indeed shaken off, utterly, the fetters of Death. But if this idea was not, even then, altogether adopted, I could at least doubt no longer, when, arising from the bed, tottering, with feeble steps, with closed eyes, and with the manner of one bewildered in a dream, the thing that was enshrouded advanced boldly and palpably into the middle of the apartment.

I trembled not—I stirred not—for a crowd of unutterable fancies connected with the air, the stature, the demeanor of the figure, rushing hurriedly through my brain, had paralyzed—had chilled me into stone. I stirred not—but gazed upon the apparition. There was a mad disorder in my thoughts—a tumult unappeasable. Could it, indeed, be the *living* Rowena who confronted me? Could it, indeed be Rowena *at all*—the fair-haired, the blue-eyed Lady Rowena Trevanion of Tremaine? Why *why* should I doubt it? The bandage lay heavily about the mouth—but then might it not be the mouth of the breathing Lady of Tremaine? And the cheeks—there were the roses as in her noon of life—yes, these might indeed be the fair cheeks of the living Lady of Tremaine. And the chin, with its dimples, as in health, might it not be hers?—but *had she then grown taller since her malady?* What inexpressible madness seized me with that thought? One bound, and I had reached her feet! Shrinking from my touch, she let fall from her head, unloosened, the ghastly cerements which had confined it, and there streamed forth into the rushing atmosphere of the chamber huge masses of long and dishevelled hair, *it was blacker than the raven wings of midnight!* And now slowly opened *the eyes* of the figure which stood before me. "Here then, at least," I shrieked aloud, "can I never—can I never be mistaken—these are the full, and the black, and the wild eyes—of my lost love—of the Lady—of the LADY LIGEIA."

## *Study questions*

1. *Why can't the narrator remember where he first met Ligeia or remember her surname?* 2. *What does he remember about her? What attributes does he ascribe to her? What does she come to mean to him? What is the nature of their study?* 3. *What is the relevance of the poem Ligeia recites to him? Under what conditions does she die?* 4. *Under what conditions does the narrator marry the Lady Rowena? What is their bridal chamber like?* 5. *What causes the Lady Rowena's death? How does the narrator behave while she is dying?* 6. *Does Ligeia will herself to life again? What role does the narrator play?* 7. *Is the narrator sane? Is Ligeia real? the Lady Rowena? Are these questions relevant?*

# THE MASQUE OF THE RED DEATH

The "Red Death" had long devastated the country. No pestilence had ever been so fatal, or so hideous. Blood was its Avatar and its seal—the redness and the horror of blood. There were sharp pains, and sudden dizziness, and then profuse bleeding at the pores, with dissolution. The scarlet stains upon the body and especially upon the face of the victim, were the pest ban which shut him out from the aid and from the sympathy of his fellowmen. And the whole seizure, progress and termination of the disease, were the incidents of half an hour.

But the Prince Prospero was happy and dauntless and sagacious. When his dominions were half depopulated, he summoned to his presence a thousand hale and light-hearted friends from among the knights and dames of his court, and with these retired to the deep seculsion of one of his castellated abbeys. This was an extensive and magnificent structure, the creation of the prince's own eccentric yet august taste. A strong and lofty wall girdled it in. This wall had gates of iron. The courtiers, having entered, brought furnaces and massy hammers and welded the bolts. They resolved to leave means neither of ingress or egress to the sudden impulses of despair or frenzy from within. The abbey was amply provisioned. With such precautions the courtiers might bid defiance to contagion. The external world could take care of itself. In the meantime it was folly to grieve, or to think. The prince had provided all the appliances of pleasure. There were buffoons, there were improvisatori, there were ballet-dancers, there were musicians, there was Beauty, there was wine. All these and security were within. Without was the "Red Death."

It was toward the close of the fifth or sixth month of his seclusion, and while the pestilence raged most furiously abroad, that the Prince Prospero entertained his thousand friends at a masked ball of the most unusual magnificence.

It was a voluptuous scene, that masquerade. But first let me tell of the rooms in which it was held. There were seven—an imperial suite. In many palaces, however, such suites form a long and straight vista, while the folding doors slide back nearly to the walls on either hand, so that the view of the whole extent is scarcely impeded. Here the case was very different; as might have been expected from the duke's love of the *bizarre*. The apartments were so irregularly disposed that the vision embraced but little more than one at a time. There was a sharp turn at every twenty or thirty yards, and at each turn a novel effect. To the right and left, in the middle of each wall, a tall and narrow Gothic window looked out upon a closed corridor which pursued the windings of the suite. These windows were of stained glass whose color varied in accordance with the prevailing hue of the decorations of the chamber into which it opened. That at the eastern extremity was hung, for example, in blue—and vividly blue were its windows. The second chamber was purple in its ornaments and tapestries, and here the panes were purple. The third was green throughout, and so were the casements. The fourth was furnished and lighted with orange—the fifth with white—the sixth with violet. The seventh apartment was closely shrouded in black velvet tapestries that hung all over the ceiling and down the walls, falling in heavy folds upon a carpet of the same material and hue. But in this chamber only, the color of the windows failed to correspond with the decorations. The panes here were scarlet—a deep blood color. Now in no one of the seven apartments was there any lamp or candelabrum, amid the profusion of golden ornaments that lay scattered to and fro or depended from the roof. There was no light of any kind emanating from lamp or candle within the suite of chambers. But in the corridors that followed the suite, there stood, opposite to each window a heavy tripod, bearing a brazier of fire, that projected its rays through the tinted glass and so glaringly illumined the room. And thus were produced a multitude of gaudy and fantastic appearances. But in the western or black chamber the effect of the fire-light that streamed upon the dark hangings through the blood-tinted panes, was ghastly in the extreme, and produced so wild a look upon the countenances of those who entered, that there were few of the company bold enough to set foot within its precincts at all.

It was in this apartment, also, that there stood against the western wall, a gigantic clock of ebony. Its pendulum swung to and fro with a dull, heavy, monotonous clang; and when the minute-hand made the circuit of the face, and the hour was to be stricken, there came from the brazen lungs of the clock a sound which was clear and loud and deep and exceedingly musical, but of so peculiar a note and emphasis that, at each lapse of an hour, the musicians of the orchestra were constrained to pause, momentarily, in their performance, to hearken to the sound; and thus the waltzers perforce ceased their evolutions; and there was a brief disconcert of the whole gay company; and, while the chimes of the clock yet rang, it was observed that the giddiest grew pale, and the more aged and sedate passed their hands over their brows as if in confused revery or meditation. But when the echoes had fully ceased, a light laughter at once pervaded the assembly; the musicians looked at each other and smiled as if at their own nervousness and folly, and made whispering vows, each to the other, that the next chiming of the clock should produce in them no similar emotion; and then, after the lapse of sixty minutes, (which embrace three thousand and six hundred seconds of the Time that flies,) there came yet another chiming of the clock, and then were the same disconcert and tremulousness and meditation as before.

But, in spite of these things, it was a gay and magnificent revel. The tastes of the duke were peculiar. He had a fine eye for colors and effects. He disregarded the *decora* of mere fashion. His plans were bold and fiery, and his conceptions glowed with barbaric lustre. There are some who would have thought him mad. His followers felt that he was not. It was necessary to hear and see and touch him to be *sure* that he was not.

He had directed, in great part, the moveable embellishments of the seven chambers, upon occasion of this great *fête;* and it was his own guiding taste which had given character to the masqueraders. Be sure they were grotesque. There were much glare and glitter and piquancy and phantasm—much of what has been since seen in "Hernani." There were arabesque figures with unsuited limbs and appointments. There were delirious fancies such as the madman fashions. There were much of the beautiful, much of the wanton, much of the *bizarre,* something of the terrible, and not a little of that which might have excited disgust. To and fro in the seven chambers there stalked, in fact, a multitude of dreams. And these—the dreams—writhed in and about, taking hue from the rooms, and causing the wild music of the orchestra to seem as the echo of their steps. And, anon, there strikes the ebony clock which stands in the hall of the velvet. And then, for a moment, all is still, and all is silent save the voice of the clock. The dreams are stiff-frozen as they stand. But the echoes of the chime die away—they have endured but an instant—and a light, half-subdued laughter floats after them as they depart. And now again the music swells, and the dreams live, and writhe to and fro more merrily than ever, taking hue from the many-tinted windows through which stream the rays from the tripods. But to the chamber which lies most westwardly of the seven, there are now none of the maskers who venture; for the night is waning away; and there flows a ruddier light through the blood-colored panes; and the blackness of the sable drapery appals; and to him whose foot falls upon the sable carpet, there comes from the near clock of ebony a muffled peal more solemnly emphatic than any which reaches *their* ears who indulge in the more remote gaieties of the other apartments.

But these other apartments were densely crowded, and in them beat feverishly the heart of life. And the revel went whirlingly on, until at length there commenced the sounding of midnight upon the clock. And then the music ceased, as I have told; and the evolutions of the waltzers were quieted; and there was an uneasy cessation of all things as before. But now there were twelve strokes to be sounded by the bell of the clock; and thus it happened, perhaps, that more of thought crept, with more of time, into the meditations of the thoughtful among those who revelled. And thus, too, it happened, perhaps, that before the last echoes of the last chime had utterly sunk into silence, there were many individuals in the crowd who had found leisure to become aware of the presence of a masked figure which had arrested the attention of no single individual before. And the rumor of this new presence having spread itself whisperingly around, there arose at length from the whole company a buzz, or murmur, expressive of disapprobation and surprise—then, finally, of terror, of horror, and of disgust.

In an assembly of phantasms such as I have painted, it may well be supposed that no ordinary appearance could have excited such sensation. In truth the masquerade license of the night was nearly unlimited; but the figure in question had out-Heroded Herod, and gone beyond the bounds of even the prince's indefinite decorum. There are chords in the hearts of the most reckless which cannot be touched without emotion. Even with the utterly lost, to whom life and death are equally jests, there are matters of which no jest can be made. The whole company, indeed, seemed now deeply to feel that in the costume and bearing of the stranger neither wit nor propriety existed. The figure was tall and gaunt, and shrouded from head to foot in the habiliments of the grave. The mask which concealed the visage was made so nearly to resemble the countenance of a stiffened corpse that the closest scrutiny must have had difficulty in detecting the cheat. And yet all this might have been endured, if not approved, by the mad revellers around. But the mummer had gone so far as assume the type of the Red Death. His vesture was dabbled in *blood*—and his broad brow, with all the features of the face, was besprinkled with the scarlet horror.

When the eyes of Prince Prospero fell upon this spectral image (which with a slow and solemn movement, as if more fully to sustain its *rôle,* stalked to and fro among the waltzers) he was seen to be convulsed, in the first moment with a strong shudder either of terror or distaste; but, in the next, his brow reddened with rage.

"Who dares?" he demanded hoarsely of the courtiers who stood near him—"who dares insult us with this blasphemous mockery? Seize him and unmask him—that we may know whom we have to hang at sunrise, from the battlements!"

It was in the eastern or blue chamber in which stood the Prince Prospero as he uttered these words. They rang throughout the seven rooms loudly and clearly—for the prince was a bold and robust man, and the music had become hushed at the waving of his hand.

It was in the blue room where stood the prince, with a group of pale courtiers by his side. At first, as he spoke, there was a slight rushing movement of this group in the direction of the intruder, who at the moment was also near at hand, and now, with deliberate and stately step, made closer approach to the speaker. But from a certain nameless awe with which the mad assumptions of the mummer had inspired the whole party, there were found none who put forth hand to seize him; so that, unimpeded, he passed within a yard of the prince's person; and, while the vast assembly, as if with one impulse, shrank from the centres of the rooms to the walls, he made his way uninterruptedly, but with the same solemn and measured step which had distinguished him from the first, through the blue chamber to the purple—through the purple to the green—through the green to the orange—through this again to the white—and even thence to the violet, ere a decided movement had been made to arrest him. It was then, however, that the Prince Prospero, maddening with rage and the shame of his own momentary cowardice, rushed hurriedly through the six chambers, while none followed him on account of a deadly terror that had seized upon all. He bore aloft a drawn dagger, and had approached, in rapid impetuosity, to within three or four feet of the retreating figure, when the latter, having attained the extremity of the velvet apartment, turned suddenly and confronted his pursuer. There was a sharp cry—and the dagger dropped gleaming upon the sable carpet, upon which, instantly afterwards, fell prostrate in death the Prince Prospero. Then, summoning the wild courage of despair, a throng of the revellers at once threw themselves into the black apartment, and, seizing the mummer, whose tall figure stood erect and motionless within the shadow of the ebony clock, gasped in unutterable horror at finding the grave-cerements and corpse-like mask which they handled with so violent a rudeness, untenanted by any tangible form.

And now was acknowledged the presence of the Red Death. He had come like a thief in the night. And one by one dropped the revellers in the blood-bedewed halls of their revel, and died each in the despairing posture of his fall. And the life of the ebony clock went out with that of the last of the gay. And the flames of the tripods expired. And Darkness and Decay and the Red Death held illimitable dominion over all.

## *Study questions*

1. *How does Poe establish the mood of this story? Account for the fact that there are only two sentences of spoken dialogue.* 2. *What are the Prince Prospero and his followers trying to do? Can they succeed?* 3. *What is the significance of the title of the story? the setting? the colors and the arrangement of the rooms of the castle?* 4. *What is the function of time in the story?* 5. *Why does Poe choose to tell this story in the third person?*

*Nikolai Gogol* (1809–1852) was born in Sorochintzy in the Ukraine and attended a grammar school there. In 1828 he went to St. Petersburg as a civil servant. There he became a friend of the great Russian poet Alexander Pushkin and began to get involved in the literary life of the city. In 1831–1832 he published a two-volume collection of stories, *Evenings in a Village Near Dikenka.* In the stories collected in these volumes, Gogol draws on the legends and the traditions of the Ukrainian people in much the same way that Washington Irving drew on the legends and tales popular in his region. In 1835, Gogol published *Taras Bulba,* a historical novel. This was followed in 1836 by a play, *The Inspector General.* His masterpiece, a novel, *Dead Souls,* appeared in 1842. The most famous of his short stories, "The Nose" and "The Overcoat," appeared in a collection of his works published in 1842. "The Diary of a Madman" records the progression to madness of a minor clerk in a bureaucracy. As the clerk more and more loses contact with reality, it becomes clear that the world around him is as insane as he is.

## THE DIARY OF A MADMAN

*October 3*

An extraordinary thing happened today. I got up rather late, and when Marva brought my boots, I asked her the time. Hearing that ten had struck quite a while before, I dressed in a hurry. I must say I'd as soon have skipped the office altogether, knowing the sour look the Chief of my Division would give me. For a long time now he has been telling me: "How come, my man, you're always in such a muddle? Sometimes you dart around like a house on fire, and get your work in such a tangle the Devil himself couldn't put it straight; you're likely to start a new heading with a small letter and give no date or reference number." The vicious old crane! He must envy me for sitting in the Director's room and sharpening his quills. So I wouldn't have gone to the office if not in hopes of seeing the cashier and trying to get even a small advance on my salary out of the Jew. What a creature he is! The Last Judgment will come before you'll get a month's pay out of him in advance. Even if there's a dire emergency, you can beg till something bursts inside you; he won't give in, the hoary monster. Yet at home his own cook slaps him around. Everyone knows that. I see no advantage in working in our department. No side benefits whatever. It's not like working, say, for the City Administration or in the Justice Department. There you may see someone nesting in a corner and scribbling away. He may be wearing a shabby coat and have a snout that you'd want to spit at. But then, just take a look at the summer house he rents! And don't even think of offering him a gilt china cup: this, he'd say, may be all right for a doctor. But he—he must have a pair of horses maybe, or a carriage, or a beaver fur—300 rubles' worth or so. And he looks so quiet and sounds so deferential and polite: "Would you," he'll say, "be so kind as to lend me your penknife to sharpen my quill, if you please." But he'll strip a petitioner naked, except perhaps for his shirt. On the other hand, though, to work in our department carries more prestige. The people of the City Administration have never dreamt of such cleanliness. Then we have red mahogany tables and our superiors always address us politely. Yes, if it weren't for the prestige, I confess I'd have left the department long ago.

I put on my old overcoat and, as it was pouring rain, took my umbrella. The streets were quite deserted except for some peasant women, their skirts thrown over their heads, a few merchants under umbrellas, and a coachman here and there. As for decent people there was only our kind, the civil-service clerk, squelching along. I saw him at a street crossing. And as soon as I saw him I said to myself: "You're not on your way to the office, my man. You're after that one trotting ahead over there and it's her legs you're staring at." What a rogue your civil servant is! When it comes to such matters, he can take on an army officer any day. He'll try to pick up anything under a bonnet. I was passing by a store, thinking about all this, when a carriage stopped in front of it. I recognized it at once: it belonged to the Director of our Department, himself. But, I thought, he cannot possibly need anything here—it must be his daughter. I pressed myself against the wall. The footman opened the carriage door and she fluttered out like a little bird. Ah, how she looked around, first right, then left, how her eyes and eyebrows flashed past me! . . . Oh God, I'm lost, lost forever. And why did she have to drive out in the pouring rain? Try and deny after that, that women have a passion for clothing. She did not recognize me. Besides, I was trying to hide myself; my coat was quite stained and out of fashion too. Nowadays, they are wearing long collars on their coats while I had two very short ones, one on top of the other. Her lap dog was too slow to get into the store while the door was open and had to stay in the street. I know this little dog. She's called Madgie. Then, a minute or so later, I heard a thin little voice: "Hello, Madgie." I'll be damned! Who's that talking? I turned around and saw two ladies walking under their umbrellas: one old, the other young and pretty. But they had already passed when I heard again, just next to me: "You ought to be ashamed, Madgie!" What on earth was going on? I saw Madgie and a dog that had been following the two ladies sniffing at one another. "Maybe I'm drunk," I said to myself, "but it's not likely. It doesn't happen to me very often." "No, Fidele, you're wrong." With my own eyes I saw Madgie forming the words, "I was, bow-wow, I was, bow-ow-ow, very sick." Talk about a lap dog! I must say I was quite surprised to hear her talking. Later, however, when I had properly sized up the situation, I was no longer surprised. As a matter of fact, the world has seen many similar occurrences before. I've heard that, in England, a fish broke surface and uttered a couple of words in such an outlandish language that scholars have been trying to work out their meaning for three years—so far in vain. Then, too, I read in the newspapers about two cows who went into a store and asked for a pound of tea. But I'll confess that I was much more bewildered when Madgie said: "I *did* write you, Fidele. Perhaps Fido didn't give you my letter." Now, I'd be willing to forfeit a month's pay if I've ever heard of a dog that could write. Only a gentleman can write correctly anyway. Of course, one finds some scribbling shopkeepers—even serfs—but that sort of writing is mostly mechanical; no commas, periods, or spelling. So I was surprised. I'll confess that recently I have been seeing and hearing things that no one else has ever seen or heard. "Let's," I said to myself, "follow this little dog and find out who she is and what her thoughts are." I opened my umbrella and followed the ladies. We crossed Pea Street, from there on to Tradesman's Avenue, turned into Carpenter's Lane, and finally stopped before a large building near Cuckoo Bridge. "I know this house," I said to myself, "it's the Zverkov house." What a house! Who isn't to be found there! There are so many crooks, so many Poles! And it teems with my fellow civil servants; they sit there on top of one another, like dogs. I have a friend there who can play the trumpet quite well. The ladies went up to the fifth floor. "Fine," I thought, "I won't go in now. I'll make a note of the place and wait for the first opportunity."

*October 4*

Today is Wednesday and that's why I was in our Director's study at his home. I purposely came in early, settled down and sharpened all the quills. Our Director must be a very brilliant man. His study is crammed with bookcases. I looked at some of the titles: such erudition all over the place—cuts an ordinary person off completely; they're all in French or German. And just look into his face, good gracious! What a lot of importance shines in his eyes! I've never heard him utter an unnecessary word. Except, perhaps, when one hands him some documents, he may ask: "How's the weather outside?" "It's quite damp, sir." Yes, he's different from our kind. A public figure! Nevertheless, I feel that he has taken a special liking to me. If only his daughter . . . Ah, what a rogue I am! Never mind, never mind . . . Quiet! . . . I was reading the *Bee.* Aren't the French a stupider race? Whatever can they be driving at? I'd like to take them all and give each one of them a good thrashing. In the same journal I also read a very nice description ot a ball by a landowner from Kursk. Kursk landowners certainly write well. . . . Whereupon I noticed that it was striking twelve-thirty and our Director still hadn't left his bedroom. But then, around one-thirty, a thing happened that no pen can adequately describe. The door opened; I thought it was the Director and jumped up from my desk holding the documents in my hand; but it was her, in person! Holy Fathers, the way she was dressed! Her dress was white, all fluffy, like a swan, and when she looked at me, I swear it was like the sun! She nodded to me and said: "Hasn't Papa been in here?" What a voice! A canary, an absolute canary. "Ma'am," I was on the point of saying, "don't have me put to death. But if you do decide that I must die, let it be by your own aristocratic little hand."

But my tongue would not obey me and I only muttered, "No, ma'am." Her glance slid from me to the books and she dropped her handkerchief. I rushed like mad, slipped on the blasted parquet and almost smashed my nose. But somehow I recovered my balance and picked it up. Holy Saints, what a hanky! Such fine, delicate linen, and amber, sheer amber. It exuded aristocracy. She said, "Thank you" and smiled, but so faintly that her divine lips hardly moved, and then she left. I remained seated there and, after another hour, a footman came in and told me: "You may go home, the master has gone out." The flunky is the one thing I cannot stand. They're always sprawled out in the entrance hall, not even bothering to acknowledge my existence with a little nod. Once, one of those lumps actually offered me snuff, and without even getting up. Don't you know, you stupid flunky, that I am a civil servant and that I come from a respectable family? Still, I picked up my hat and pulled on my overcoat unaided since those gents wouldn't think of helping you, and left. At home, I lay on my bed most of the time. Then I copied an excellent poem:

*Without you one hour crept*
*Slowly like a year.*
*"Is my life worth while," I wept,*
*"When you are not near?"*

Sounds like Pushkin. In the evening, I put on my overcoat and walked over to the Director's house and waited by the gate for quite a while to see whether she wouldn't come out and get into her carriage. But she didn't.

### *November 6*

Something has got into the Chief of my Division. When I arrived at the office he called me and began as follows: "Now then, tell me. What's the matter with you?" "What do you mean? Nothing," I said. "Come, try to understand; aren't you over forty? Time to be a bit wiser. What do you fancy you are? Don't imagine I can't see what you're up to. I know you're trailing after the Director's daughter. Just look at yourself—what are you? Just nothing. You haven't a penny to your name. Look in the mirror. How can you even think of such things?" The hell with him! Just because he's got a face like a druggist's bottle and that quiff of hair on his head all curled and pomaded, and because he holds his head up in the air like that, he thinks he can get away with anything. I see through his indignation. He's envious; perhaps he's noticed the marks of favor bestowed upon me. A lot I care what he says. So he's a Divisional Chief, so what! So he hangs out his gold watch chain and has custom-made boots at thirty rubles. Let him be damned. Perhaps he imagines I had a shopkeeper or a tailor for a father. I'm a gentleman! And I can be promoted too. I'm only forty-two, an age when one's career is really just beginning. Wait, my friend, I'll go higher than you yet, and, God willing, very, very much higher. Then I'll have a social position beyond your dreams. Do you imagine you're the only one to have dignity? Give me a fashionable new coat, let me wear a tie like yours, and you won't be worthy to shine my shoes. My lack of means—that's the only trouble.

*November 8*

Went to the theater. The play was about the Russian fool Filatka. Laughed a lot. They had a vaudeville show as well, full of amusing verses lampooning lawyers, so outspoken that I wondered how it got past the censor; as to the merchants, it says plainly that they swindle the people, that their sons wallow in debauchery and elbow their way into society. There was also an amusing couplet which complained about the way newspapermen criticize everything and asked the audience for protection from them. Playwrights write very amusing plays nowadays. I love going to the theater. As soon as I get hold of a few pennies, I can't help myself, I go. But civil servants are such swine . . . you won't catch clods like them going to the theater, not even if they're given free tickets. One actress sang really well. . . . It made me think of . . . What a rogue I am! Never mind, never mind . . . silence!

*November 9*

Left for the office at eight. The Divisional Chief pretended he hadn't noticed me come in. And I also acted as though nothing had happened between us. I went through the papers and sorted them out. Left at four. On the way home, passed by the Director's house but didn't see anyone. After dinner, mostly lay on my bed.

Today, I sat in the Director's study and sharpened twenty-three quills for him, and four quills for . . . oh-oh . . . her. He likes to have as many quills to hand as possible. My, how brainy he must be! Usually he doesn't say much but I guess he must be weighing everything in that head of his. I'd like to know what he has on his mind most of the time, what's cooking up there. I'd like to have a closer look at these people, how they live, with all their subtle innuendoes and courtly jokes; I wish I knew how they behave and what they do among themselves. I've often tried to engage the Director in conversation but I'm damned if it's ever come off. I've managed to say it's warm or cold outside and that is absolutely as far as I've got. One day I'd like just to step into their drawing room. The door is ajar sometimes and from there I can see another door, leading to another room. That drawing room! You should see how it's decorated. All those mirrors and fine pieces of porcelain. I'd also like to see the part where her rooms are. That's where I'd really like to go! I'd like to peep into her boudoir, and see all those little jars and bottles of hers standing there amidst the sort of flowers one doesn't even dare breathe on; to have a glimpse at the dress she has thrown off, lying there looking more like air than a dress. It would be wonderful to glance into her bedroom. . . . Miracles must happen there. It's a paradise surpassing the heavenly one. What wouldn't I give to see the little stool upon which her delicate foot descends when she gets out of bed and watch how an incredibly fine, immaculate stocking is pulled up her leg. . . . Oh, the roguish thoughts! . . . Never mind . . . never mind . . . silence!

But today something suddenly became clear to me when I recalled the conversation between the two dogs I'd overheard on Nevsky Avenue. Fine, I said to myself, now I'll find out everything. I must get hold of the letters exchanged between those nasty mutts. I'm sure to find out something. Now I'll confess that, at one point, I almost called Madgie and said to her: "Listen, Madgie, we are alone now. If you wish, I'll even lock the door so that no one'll see us. Tell me everything you know about your mistress: what she's like and all that. And don't worry, I swear I'll not repeat a thing to anyone." But the sly little mutt just sort of shrank into herself, put her tail between her legs, and left the room in silence, as though she hadn't heard a thing. For a long time I've suspected that dogs are much more intelligent than men; I was even certain that they could speak and simply chose not to out of a peculiar stubbornness. A dog is an extraordinary politician and notices everything, every step a human takes. Still, whatever happens, tomorrow I'll go to the Zverkov house and question Fidele and, if possible, I'll lay my hand on Madgie's letters to her.

*November 12*

At 2:00 P.M. I went out determined to find Fidele and question her. I can't stand the smell of cabbage which comes pouring out of all the greengrocers along Tradesman's Avenue. This, and the infernal stench from under the gates of every house, sent me scurrying, holding my nose. And all the soot and smoke that they let pour out of the vile workshops make it a quite unsuitable place for a person of breeding to take a stroll. When I reached the sixth floor and rang the bell, out came a girl with little freckles and not too bad-looking at that. I recognized her at once. She was the one I had seen walking with the old woman. She blushed a little and I immediately saw through her: what you need, my dear, is a husband. "What do you want?" she asked. "I want to have a talk with your doggie."

The girl was stupid. I could see from the start how stupid she was! At that moment the mutt ran in yapping furiously and as I was trying to grab her, the repulsive creature almost caught my nose between her teeth. But then I saw her basket in the corner—which was just what I was looking for! I went over to it and felt under the straw and, to my great joy, I found a small bundle of papers. Seeing what I was doing, the nasty little cur first took a bite out of my calf; then, when upon further sniffing she found that I had taken her letters, she began whining and making up to me, but I told her, "Oh, no, my dear. See you later!" And off I went. I believe the girl mistook me for a madman—she seemed very frightened indeed.

Once home, I wanted to get down to work immediately, to have those letters sorted before dark, since I can't see too well by candlelight. But for some reason Marva decided to scrub the floor just then. Those stupid Finns succumb to their obsession for cleanliness at the worst moments. So I went out for a walk to think it all over. Now, finally, I'll find out everything about these intrigues and plots; I'll understand all the little wheels and springs and get to the bottom of the matter. These letters will explain. Dogs are a clever race. They know all about intrigue and so it's all bound to be in their letters: all there is to know about the Director's character and actions. And she, she too is sure to be mentioned . . . but never mind that . . . silence! I came home toward evening. Most of the time, I lay on my bed.

*November 13*

Let's see now. This letter looks quite legible, though there *is* something canine about the handwriting:

Dear Fidele, I still find it difficult to get accustomed to the commonness of your name. Couldn't they find a better one for you? Fidele, like Rose, is very ordinary, but all that's beside the point. I'm very glad we have decided to write to each other.

The spelling is very good. It's even punctuated correctly. This is considerably better than our Divisional Chief can do, although he claims to have gone to some university or other. Let's see further on:

I believe that sharing feelings and impressions with another is one of the main blessings in life. . . .

Hm! The thought is stolen from a work translated from the German. The author's name escapes me now.

I speak from experience although I've never been much further than the gates of our house. But then, isn't my life full of blessings? My young mistress, whom her papa calls Sophie, is crazy about me.

Ouch! Never mind, never mind. Silence!

Papa often pets me too. I drink tea and coffee with cream. I must tell you, my dear, that I am not in the least tempted by the half-gnawed bones which our Fido chews on in the kitchen. I only like the bones of game and, even then, only if the marrow hasn't seen sucked out by someone else. A mixture of sauces is nice as long as they contain no capers or vegetables. What I hate is people who give dogs the little pellets they knead out of bread. Some person sitting at the table, who has previously touched all sorts of filthy things, begins to knead a piece of bread with those same hands, then calls you and thrusts the pellet into your mouth. It is awkward somehow to refuse and, disgusted, you eat it up. . . .

What's that all about? What rubbish! As though there weren't more interesting things to write about. Let's see the next page. There may be something less stupid.

Now, I'll tell you with pleasure what goes on in this household. I have mentioned the main character, whom Sophie calls Papa. He's a very strange man. . . .

At last! I knew they had very shrewd judgment, whatever the subject. Let's see what Papa's like.

. . . a very strange man. He's usually silent. He speaks very little, but a week ago he never stopped saying to himself: Will I get it or not? Once he even asked me: What do you say, Madgie, will I get it or won't I? I could make no sense out of it so I smelled his shoe and left the room. Then, a week later, Papa came home overjoyed. All that morning formally dressed people came and congratulated him. At dinner Papa was gayer than I'd ever seen him before, and after dinner, he picked me up and held me level with his chest, saying: Look, Madgie, what's this? I saw some sort of a ribbon. I sniffed at it but it had no fragrance whatever. Finally, discreetly, I gave it a lick: slightly salty.

Hm. The mutt really goes too far . . . she needs a good whipping . . . So he is that vain is he? I must take it into account.

Good-bye, my dear, I must run along . . . blah-blah-blah-blah . . . will finish this letter tomorrow. Hello, I am back with you. Today my mistress, Sophie . . .

Aha! Let's see what she says about Sophie. I really *am* a rogue! But never mind, never mind. Let's go on.

. . . my mistress, Sophie, was in a terrific to-do. She was getting ready for a ball and I intended to take advantage of her absence and write to you. Sophie is always very happy when she's about to leave for a ball but is always very irritable while she's getting dressed for it. You know, my dear, I personally can see no pleasure in going to a ball. Sophie usually returns home from balls at 6 A.M., and I can tell by her pale and emaciated features that the poor thing hasn't been given a bite to eat. I confess I could never lead such a life. If I had to go without game in sauce or chicken-wing stews, I don't know what would become of me. A sauce is not at all bad with porridge. But nothing can make carrots, turnips, and artichokes palatable. . . .

The style is very jerky. You can see that it's not written by a man. She starts off all right and then lapses into dogginess. Let's see another letter. Looks rather long . . . hm . . . no date . . .

Oh, my dear, how strongly I feel the approach of spring. My heart beats as though it were waiting for something. In my ears, there's a constant buzz. Very often I listen so intently behind doors that I raise my front paw. And, confidentially, I have plenty of suitors. I often sit by the window and watch them. If only you could see some of them, they're so ugly. There is a horrible mongrel with stupidity written all over him, who swaggers along the street and imagines he is a person of breeding and that everyone is bound to admire him. I paid no attention to him, as though I hadn't even noticed him. Then you should have seen the terrifying Great Dane that stopped in front of my window! If that one stood up on his hind legs, which, incidentally, the clod is incapable of doing, he would be a head taller than Sophie's Papa, who's quite tall himself and fat besides. Moreover, the lump seems to be very arrogant. I growled at him but it didn't put him off in the least. He just hung his tongue out, drooped his huge ears, and kept staring at my window, the oaf! But, my dear, you don't really imagine, do you, that my heart is indifferent to all the hopefuls? . . . You should have seen the dashing young lover that came jumping over the fence into our courtyard. His name is Treasure and he has such a nice face. . . .

Ah, damn it all! What rubbish! How much of her letter is she going to fill with such stupid stuff? I'm after *people,* not dogs! I need spiritual food and I am served these inanities. . . . Let's skip a page, perhaps we'll find something more interesting. . . .

. . . Sophie was sitting at the table sewing something. I was looking out of the window; I like to watch people in the street. Suddenly the manservant came in and announced someone. "Show him in!" Sophie said. She hugged me hard and murmured, "Oh Madgie, darling, if you only knew who that is. He's a Guards officer, his hair is black and his eyes are so dark and so light at the same time . . . like fire." And Sophie rushed out. A minute later a young officer with black side whiskers appeared. He went to the mirror and smoothed his hair; then he looked around the room. I growled a little and settled down by my window. Soon Sophie came back, greeted him gaily, while I pretended to be busy looking out of the window. In fact, however, I turned my head sideways a little, so that I could catch what they said. You cannot imagine, Fidele dear, the silliness of that conversation. They spoke about some lady who, during a dance, kept doing a certain step instead of the one she was expected to do, then about somebody called Bobov, who looked like a stork and almost fell over, then about one Lidina, who thought she had blue eyes when they were really green, and so on and on. Oh no, I said to myself, this officer doesn't compare to Treasure. Heavens, what a difference! To start with, the officer has a wide face, quite bald except for his side whiskers which, in fact, look like a black kerchief tied around it, whereas Treasure's face is narrow and fine and he has a sweet white patch on his brow. Treasure's waist is incomparably slenderer than the officer's, and his eyes, his gestures, and his ways are vastly superior. Really, a tremendous difference! I wonder what she finds in her officer. What on earth can she admire in him? . . .

Yes, here I tend to agree. Something seems wrong. It is quite unbelieveable that this officer should have swept her off her feet. Let's see:

If she likes the officer, I think she'll soon be liking the civil-service clerk who sits in Papa's study. That one, my dear, is a real scarecrow. He looks a bit like a turtle caught in a bag. . . .

Which clerk can that be? . . .

He has a funny name and he's always sitting sharpening quills. The hair on his head is like straw. Papa sends him on errands like a servant. . . .

The filthy cur seems to be trying to get its own back! Why is my hair like straw?

Sophie can hardly control her laughter when she sees him.

You wretched, lying dog! What a filthy, poisonous tongue! As if I didn't know it's all your jealousy. I know whose tricks these are. I recognize the hand of the Divisional Chief here. For some reason, that man has sworn undying hatred for me and he is trying to harm me, to harm me every minute of the day and night. Still, let's see one more letter. It may make it clear.

My dear Fidele, forgive me for not writing to you all this time. I've been going around in absolute ecstasy. I agree, without reservation, with the philosopher who said that love is a second life. Moreover, a lot of things are changing in our household. The officer comes every day now. Sophie is madly in love with him. Papa is very gay. I even heard our Gregory, who always talks to himself while sweeping the floors, say that the wedding is close at hand, because Papa always wanted to see Sophie married to a high official or to an army officer with a brilliant career ahead of him. . . .

Hell! . . . I can't go on. . . . High officials, senior officers, they get all the best things in this world. You discover a crumb of happiness, you reach out for it and then along comes a high official or an officer and snatches it away. Goddammit! I would like so much to become a high official myself and not just to obtain her hand in marriage either. No, I'd like to be a high official just so that I could watch them jump around for my benefit; I'd listen for a while to their courtly jokes and innuendoes and then tell them what they could do with themselves. It hurts, though. Oh hell! . . . I tore the stupid little dog's letter to shreds.

*December 3*

Impossible! Lies! There can't be a wedding. So what if he had a commission in the Guards? That's nothing but position, you can't touch it with your hand. A Guards officer does not have a third eye in the middle of his forehead, his nose is not made of gold but the same stuff as mine or anyone else's and he uses it to sniff not to eat, for sneezing not for coughing. I've often tried to discover where all these differences lie. Why am I a clerk? Why should I be a clerk? Perhaps I'm really a general or a count and only seem to be a clerk? Maybe I don't really know who I am? There are plenty of instances in history when somebody quite ordinary, not necessarily an aristocrat, some middle-class person or even a peasant, suddenly turns out to be a public figure and perhaps even the ruler of a country. If a peasant can turn into someone so important, where are the limits to the possibilities for a man of breeding? Imagine, for instance, me, entering a room in a general's uniform. There's an epaulet on my right shoulder, an epaulet on my left, a blue ribbon across my chest. How would that be? What tune would my beauty sing then? And Papa himself, our Director, what would he say? Ow, he's so vain! He's a Mason, no mistake about it, although he may pretend to be this or that; I noticed from the start that when he shakes hands, he sticks out two fingers only. But I can't be promoted to general or governor or anything like that overnight. What I'd like to know is, why am I a clerk? Why precisely a clerk?

*December 5*

I read the newspapers all morning. Strange things are happening in Spain. I can't even make them out properly. They write that the throne has been vacated and that the ranking grandees are having difficulty in selecting an heir. It seems there's discontent. Sounds very strange to me. How can a throne be vacant? They say that some donna may accede. A donna cannot accede to a throne. It's absolutely impossible. A king should sit on a throne. But they say there is no king. It's impossible that there should be no king. There must be a king but he's hidden away somewhere in anonymity. It's even possible that he's around but is being forced to remain in hiding for family reasons or for fear of some neighboring country such as France. Or there may be other reasons.

*December 8*

I was on the point of going to the office but various considerations held me back. I couldn't get those Spanish affairs out of my head. How can a donna possibly become ruler? They won't allow it. In the first place, England won't stand for it. Then we must keep in mind the political setup of the rest of Europe: the Austrian Emperor, our Tsar. . . . I confess I was so perturbed and hurt by these events that I could do nothing all day. Marva remarked that I was very absent-minded during dinner. . . . In fact, I believe I absent-mindedly threw a couple of plates on the floor, where they broke at once. After dinner, I walked the streets, uphill and downhill. Came across nothing of interest. Then, mostly lay on my bed and thought about the Spanish question.

*Year 2000, April 43*

This is a day of great jubilation. Spain has a king. They've found him. *I* am the King. I discovered it today. It all came to me in a flash. It's incredible to me now that I could have imagined that I was a civil-service clerk. How could such a crazy idea ever have entered my head? Thank God no one thought of slapping me into a lunatic asylum. Now I see everything clearly, as clearly as if it lay in the palm of my hand. But what was happening to me before? Then things loomed at me out of a fog. Now, I believe that all troubles stem from the misconception that human brains are located in the head. They are not: human brains are blown in by the winds from somewhere around the Caspian Sea.

Marva was the first to whom I revealed my identity. When she heard that she was facing the King of Spain, she flung up her hands in awe. She almost died of terror. The silly woman had never seen a King of Spain before. However, I tried to calm her and, speaking graciously, did my best to assure her of my royal favor. I was not going to hold against her all the times she had failed to shine my boots properly. The masses are so ignorant. One can't talk to them on lofty subjects. Probably she was so frightened because she thought that all kings of Spain are like Philip II. But I carefully pointed out that I wasn't like Philip II at all. I didn't go to the office. The hell with it. No, my friends, you won't entice me there now; never again shall I copy your dreadful documents.

*Martober 86. Between Day And Night*

Today, our Divisional Chief sent someone to make me go to the office. I hadn't been there for over three weeks. I went, just for a lark. The Divisional Chief expected me to come apologizing to him but I just looked at him indifferently, with not too much ire, nor too much benevolence either; then I sat down in my usual place as though unaware of the people around me. I looked around at all that scribbling rabble and thought: If only you had an inkling of who's sitting here among you, oh Lord, what a fuss you'd make. There'd be a terrific to-do and the Divisional Chief himself would bow deeply to me, as he does to the Director. They put some papers in front of me which I was supposed to abstract or something. I didn't even stir. A few minutes later, there was a general commotion. They said the Director was on his way. Several clerks jumped up, hoping he'd notice them. But I didn't budge. When word came that the Director was about to pass through our Division, they all buttoned up their coats. I did nothing of the sort. What kind of a Director does he think he is? Who says I should get up for him? Never! He's an old cork, not a Director. Yes, just an ordinary cork, the kind used for stoppering a bottle. That's all he is. But the funniest thing of all was when they gave me a paper to sign. They expected I'd sign it in the corner: head clerk such and such. Well, let them think again. I wrote in the main space, the one reserved for the Director's signature: Ferdinand VIII. You should have witnessed the awed silence that followed; but I merely waved my hand graciously and said: "Dispense with the manifestation of allegiance!" and walked out of the room. From there, I went straight to the Director's house. He was not at home. The footman tried to stop me from going in but what I said made his arms drop limp at his sides. I went straight to her boudoir. She was sitting in front of her mirror. She jumped up and stepped back, away from me. Still I did not tell her that I was the King of Spain. I simply told her that she couldn't even imagine the happiness awaiting her and that despite all our enemies' intrigues, we would be together. I did not want to say more and left. Oh, women are such perfidious things! Only now did I understand what a woman is like. So far, no one has found out whom Woman is in love with. I was the first to discover it: Woman is in love with the Devil. And I'm not joking either. Physicists write a lot of drivel about her being this, that and the other. She loves only the Devil. Look, do you see over there, in the front tier of the boxes? She raises her lorgnette. You think she's looking at that fat man with the star over there? Nothing of the sort. She's staring at the Devil, the Devil hiding behind the fat man's back. See, now he has hidden himself in the star and he's beckoning to her with his finger! And she'll marry him too. She will for sure. As for all the rest of them, all those who lick boots and proclaim their patriotism, all they really want is annuities and more annuities. Some patriots! They'd sell their mother, their father, and their God for money, the strutting betrayers of Christ! And all this crazy ambition and vanity come from the little bubble under the tongue which has a tiny worm about the size of a pinhead in it, and it's all the work of a barber on Pea Street. I can't recall his name but the moving force behind it all is the Sultan of Turkey who pays the barber to spread Mohammedanism all over the world. They say that in France, already, the majority of the people have embraced the Mohammedan faith.

### *No Date. A Day Without Date*

Went along Nevsky Avenue incognito. Saw the Tsar riding past. Everybody was doffing his hat, and so did I. I gave no sign that I was the King of Spain. I thought it would be undignified to reveal my identity there, in front of all those people, that it would be more proper to be presented at Court first. What has prevented me so far is the fact that I haven't got Spanish royal attire. If only I could get hold of a royal mantle of some sort. I thought of having one made but tailors are so stupid. Besides, they don't seem to be interested in their trade nowadays and go in for speculation, so that most of them end up mending roads. I decided to make a mantle out of my best coat, which I had only worn twice. But I didn't want those good-for-nothings to mess it all up—I preferred to do it myself. I locked my door so as not to be seen. I had to cut my coat to ribbons with the scissors since a mantle has a completely different style.

### *Can't Remember The Day, Nor Was There A Month. Damned If I Know What's Been Going On*

The mantle is ready. Marva really let out a yell when I put it on. Even so, I still don't feel ready to be presented at Court. My retinue hasn't as yet arrived from Spain. The absence of a retinue would be incompatible with my dignity. I'm expecting them at any time.

### *1st Date*

I'm puzzled by the unaccountable delay in the arrival of my retinue. What can be holding them up? I went to the post office and inquired whether the Spanish delegates had arrived. But the postmaster is an utter fool and knows nothing: No, he says, there are no Spanish delegates around here but if you wish to mail a letter, we'll accept it. What the hell is he talking about? What letter? Letter my foot! Let druggists write letters. . . .

### *Madrid, Februarius The Thirtieth*

So I'm in Spain. It all happened so quickly that I hardly had time to realize it. This morning the Spanish delegation finally arrived for me and we all got into a carriage. I was somewhat bewildered by the extraordinary speed at which we traveled. We went so fast that in half an hour we reached the Spanish border. But then, nowadays there are railroads all over Europe and the ships go so fast too. Spain is a strange country. When we entered the first room, I saw a multitude of people with shaven heads. I soon realized, though, that these must be Dominican or Capuchin monks because they always shave their heads. I also thought that the manners of the King's Chancellor, who was leading me by the hand, were rather strange. He pushed me into a small room and said: "You sit quiet and don't you call yourself King Ferdinand again or I'll beat the nonsense out of your head." But I knew that I was just being tested and refused to submit. For this, the Chancellor hit me across the back with a stick, twice, so painfully that I almost let out a cry. But I contained myself, remembering that this is customary procedure among knights on initiation into an exalted order. To this day, they adhere to the chivalric code in Spain.

Left to myself, I decided to devote some time to affairs of state. I have discovered that China and Spain are the same thing and it's only ignorance that makes people take them for two separate countries. I advise anybody who doubts it to take a piece of paper and write the word "Spain" and they'll see for themselves that it comes out "China." I also gave much thought to a sad event that must occur tomorrow at seven o'clock. As foreseen by the famous English chemist Wellington, the Earth will mount the Moon. I confess I was deeply worried when I thought of the Moon's extraordinary sensitivity and fragility. The Moon, of course, is made in Hamburg, and I must say they do a very poor job. I wonder why England doesn't do something about it. It's a lame cooper that makes the Moon, and it's quite obvious that the fool has no conception of what the Moon should be. He uses tarred rope and olive oil and that's why the stench is so awful all over the Earth and we are forced to plug our noses. And that's why the Moon itself is such a delicate ball that men cannot live there—only noses. And that's why we can't see our own noses: they are all on the Moon. And when I thought what a heavy thing the Earth is and that, sitting down on the Moon, it would crush our noses into a powder, I became so worried that I put on my socks and shoes and rushed into the State Council Room to order my police force to stand by to prevent the Earth from mounting the Moon. The Capuchin monks I found in the State Council Room were very clever people and when I said, "Gentlemen, let's save the Moon, the Earth is preparing to mount it," they all rushed at once to execute my royal wish and many tried to climb the wall to reach the Moon. But at that moment, the Grand Chancellor came in. As soon as they saw him, they scattered. Being the King, I remained there alone. But to my surprise, the Chancellor hit me with his stick and chased me into my room. Such is the power of popular tradition in Spain!

*January Of The Same Year Which Happened After Februarius*

I still can't make out what sort of a place Spain is. The customs and the etiquette at the Court are quite incredible. I don't see, I don't grasp it, I don't understand at all! Today, they shaved my head, although I shouted with all my might that I did not want to become a monk. But then they began to drip cold water on my head and everything went blank. Never have I been through such hell. I just can't understand the point of this peculiar custom, so stupid, so senseless. And the irresponsibility of the kings who never got around to outlawing this custom is quite beyond me.

Some indications make me wonder whether I haven't fallen into the hands of the Inquisition. Maybe the man I took for the Chancellor is really the Grand Inquisitor himself? But then, I can't see how the King can be subjected to the Inquisition. True, this could be the work of France, especially Polignac. That Polignac is an absolute beast. He has sworn to drive me to my death. And so he maneuvers on and on. But I know, my fine fellow, that you in turn are being led by the English. The English are great politicians. They sow the seeds of dissension everywhere. The whole world knows that when England takes snuff, France sneezes.

*25th Date*

Today, the Grand Inquisitor entered my room. I heard his steps approaching while he was still far off and hid under a chair. He looked around and, not seeing me, he began to call out. First he shouted my name and civil-service rank. I remained silent. Then, Ferdinand VIII, King of Spain! I was about to stick my head out but thought to myself: No, they won't get me that way! They may want to pour cold water on my head again. But he saw me and chased me out from under the chair with his stick. His damn stick hurts dreadfully. But my very latest discovery made me feel better: I had found that every rooster has his own Spain and he has it under his feathers. The Grand Inquisitor left very angry, threatening me with some punishment or other. Of course, I completely ignored his helpless fury. I knew he was a puppet. A tool of England.

### *Da 34 Te Mnth Yr. Yraurbef 349*

No, I have no strength left. I can't stand any more. By God! What they're doing to me! They pour cold water on my head. They don't listen to me, they don't hear me, they don't see me. What have I done to them? Why do they torture me so? What do they want from me? What can I give them? I haven't anything to give. I have no strength, I cannot bear this suffering, my head is on fire, and everything goes around me in circles. Save me! Take me away from here! Give me a carriage with horses swift as wind! Drive on, coachman, let the harness bells ring! Soar upward, my horses, carry me away from this world! Further, further, where I will see nothing, nothing. There is the sky smoking before me. A star twinkles far away, the forest rushes past with its dark trees and the crescent moon. The violet fog is a carpet underfoot. I hear the twanging of a guitar string through the fog; on one side, the sea, and on the other, Italy. Then Russian huts come into sight. Perhaps that's my house over there, looking blue in the distance. And isn't that my mother sitting by the window? Mother, save your wretched son! Let your tears fall on his sick head! See how they torture him! Hold me, a poor waif, in your arms. There's no room for him in this world. They are chasing him. Mother, take pity on your sick child. . . .

And, by the way, have you heard that the Dey of Algiers has a wart right under his nose?

## *Study questions*

*1. What does the diary form contribute to the story? Are we, nevertheless, able to follow a plot line? 2. How does the narrator feel about himself? his job? his circumstances? Why does he keep referring to himself as a rogue? 3. What do we learn about the world in which the narrator lives? Can he be a reliable reporter? 4. Why does he decide that he is the King of Spain? Does it have anything to do with his belief that a woman cannot accede to a throne? How does the narrator feel about women? 5. Could there be any basis in fact for the narrator's assumption that he is in the hands of the Inquisition? 6. How does the setting function in this story? the tone? the mood?*

*Herman Melville* (1819–1891) was born in New York City of a fairly prosperous family, but after the death of his father, they had a difficult time making ends meet. With very little formal education and while still in his teens, Melville went to sea as a cabin boy. In 1841 he shipped out on a whaler and began to live a series of colorful adventures, many of which formed the basis for his early novels: *Typee* (1846), *Omoo* (1847), *Mardi* (1849), *Redburn* (1849), and *White-Jacket* (1850). These earlier works (with the exception of *Mardi*) were very successful, but his popularity dropped after the publication of his masterpiece, *Moby Dick* (1851), then considered a highly complex and difficult novel. Three other novels followed during his lifetime: *Pierre; or The Ambiguities* (1852), *Israel Potter* (1855), and *The Confidence Man* (1857). *Piazza Tales* (1856) contained the best of his short stories, including the finely crafted "Bartleby the Scrivener," "Benito Cereno," and "The Encantadas, or the Enchanted Isles." *Billy Budd* was published posthumously in 1924. Although Melville published several volumes of poetry between 1866 and 1891, his poems are seldom without flaw, and his reputation rests mainly on his fiction.

"Benito Cereno" is one of the best stories in the English language. An exerise in point of view, it shows how a kindly and practical American sea captain is unable to see the real conditions before him because he views the world from a limited and biased perspective. Ironically, it is his ignorance that saves him. The experienced Spanish sea captain, Don Benito Cereno, is doomed, because he has seen the world and knows it for what it is.

# BENITO CERENO

In the year 1799, Captain Amasa Delano, of Duxbury, in Massachusetts, commanding a large sealer and general trader, lay at anchor with a valuble cargo, in the harbour of Santa Maria—a small, desert, uninhabited island toward the southern extremity of the long coast of Chile. There he had touched for water.

On the second day, not long after dawn, while lying in his berth, his mate came below, informing him that a strange sail was coming into the bay. Ships were then not so plenty in those waters as now. He rose, dressed, and went on deck.

The morning was one peculiar to that coast. Everything was mute and calm; everything grey. The sea, though undulated into long roods of swells, seemed fixed, and was sleeked at the surface like waved lead that has cooled and set in the smelter's mould. The sky seemed a grey surtout. Flights of troubled grey fowl, kith and kin with flights of troubled grey vapours among which they were mixed, skimmed low and fitfully over the waters, as swallows over meadows before storms. Shadows present, foreshadowing deeper shadows to come.

To Captain Delano's surprise, the stranger, viewed through the glass, showed no colours; though to do so upon entering a haven, however uninhabited in its shores, where but a single other ship might be lying, was the custom among peaceful seamen of all nations. Considering the lawlessness and loneliness of the spot, and the sort of stories, at that day, associated with those seas, Captain Delano's surprise might have deepened into some uneasiness had he not been a person of a singularly undistrustful good nature, not liable, except on extraordinary and repeated incentives, and hardly then, to indulge in personal alarms, any way involving the imputation of malign evil in man. Whether, in view of what humanity is capable, such a trait implies, along with a benevolent heart, more than ordinary quickness and accuracy of intellectual perception, may be left to the wise to determine.

But whatever misgivings might have obtruded on first seeing the stranger, would almost, in any seaman's mind, have been dissipated by observing, that the ship, in navigating into the harbour, was drawing too near the land; a sunken reef making out off her bow. This seemed to prove her a stranger, indeed, not only to the sealer, but the island; consequently, she could be no wonted freebooter on that ocean. With no small interest, Captain Delano continued to watch her—a proceeding not much facilitated by the vapours partly mantling the hull, through which the far matin light from her cabin streamed equivocally enough; much like the sun—by this time hemisphered on the rim of the horizon, and apparently, in company with the strange ship entering the harbour—which, wimpled by the same low, creeping clouds, showed not unlike a Lima intriguante's one sinister eye peering across the Plaza from the Indian loop-hole of her dusk *saya-y-manto*.*

It might have been but a deception of the vapours, but, the longer the stranger was watched the more singular appeared her manœuvres. Ere long it seemed hard to decide whether she meant to come in or no—what she wanted, or what she was about. The wind, which had breezed up a little during the night, was not extremely light and baffling, which the more increased the apparent uncertainty of her movements.

Surmising, at last, that it might be a ship in distress, Captain Delano ordered his whale-boat to be dropped, and, much to the wary opposition of his mate, prepared to board her, and, at the least, pilot her in. On the night previous, a fishing party of the seamen had gone a long distance to some detached rocks out of sight from the sealer, and, an hour or two before daybreak, had returned, having met with no small success. Presuming that the stranger might have been long off soundings, the good captain put several baskets of the fish, for presents, into his boat, and so pulled away. From her continuing too near the sunken reef, deeming her in danger, calling to his men, he made all haste to apprise those on board of their situation. But, some time ere the boat came up, the wind, light though it was, having shifted, had headed the vessel off, as well as partly broken the vapours from about her.

* *Saya-y-manto:* Tunic-and-mantle.

Upon gaining a less remote view, the ship, when made signally visible on the verge of the leaden-hued swells, with the shreds of fog here and there raggedly furring her, appeared like a whitewashed monastery after a thunderstorm, seen perched upon some dun cliff among the Pyrenees. But it was no purely fanciful resemblance which now, for a moment, almost led Captain Delano to think that nothing less than a ship-load of monks was before him. Peering over the bulwarks were what really seemed, in the hazy distance, throngs of dark cows; while, fitfully revealed through the open portholes, other dark moving figures were dimly descried, as of Black Friars pacing the cloisters.

Upon a still nigher approach, this appearance was modified, and the true character of the vessel was plain—a Spanish merchantman of the first class, carrying negro slaves, amongst other valuable freight, from one colonial port to another. A very large, and, in its time, a very fine vessel, such as in those days were at intervals encountered along that main; sometimes superseded Acapulco treasure-ships, or retired frigates of the Spanish king's navy, which, like superannuated Italian palaces, still, under a decline of masters, preserved signs of former state.

As the whale-boat drew more and more nigh, the cause of the peculiar pipeclayed aspect of the stranger was seen in the slovenly neglect pervading her. The spars, ropes, and great part of the bulwarks, looked woolly, from long unacquaintance with the scraper, tar, and the bush. Her keel seemed laid, her ribs put together, and she launched, from Ezekiel's Valley of Dry Bones.

In the present business in which she was engaged, the ship's general model and rig appeared to have undergone no material change from their original warlike and Froissart pattern. However, no guns were seen.

The tops were large, and were railed about with what had once been octagonal net-work, all now in sad disrepair. These tops hung overhead like three ruinous aviaries, in one of which was seen perched, on a ratlin, a white noddy, a strange fowl, so called from its lethargic, somnambulistic character, being frequently caught by hand at sea. Battered and mouldy, the castellated forecastle seemed some ancient turret, long ago taken by assault, and then left to decay. Toward the stern, two high-raised quarter-galleries—the balustrades here and there covered with dry, tindery sea-moss—opening out from the unoccupied state-cabin, whose dead-lights, for all the mild weather, were hermetically closed and calked—these tenantless balconies hung over the sea as if it were the grand Venetian canal. But the principal relic of faded grandeur was the ample oval of the shield-like sternpiece, intricately carved with the arms of Castile and León, medallioned about by groups of mythological or symbolical devices; uppermost and central of which was a dark satyr in a mask, holding his foot on the prostrate neck of a writhing figure, likewise masked.

Whether the ship had a figure-head, or only a plain beak, was not quite certain, owing to canvas wrapped about that part, either to protect it while undergoing a refurbishing, or else decently to hide its decay. Rudely painted or chalked, as in a sailor freak, along the forward side of a sort of pedestal below the canvas was the sentence, *"Sequid vuestro jefe,"* (follow your leader); while upon the tarnished headboards, near by, appeared, in stately capitals, once gilt, the ship's name, "SAN DOMINICK," each letter streakingly corroded with tricklings of copper-spike rust; while, like mourning weeds, dark festoons of sea-grass slimily swept to and fro over the name, with every hearse-like roll of the hull.

As, at last, the boat was hooked from the bow along toward the gangway amidship, its keel, while yet some inches separated from the hull, harshly grated as on a sunken coral reef. It proved a huge bunch of conglobated barnacles adhering below the water to the side like a wen—a token of baffling airs and long calms passed somewhere in those seas.

Climbing the side, the visitor was at once surrounded by a clamorous throng of whites and blacks, but the latter outnumbering the former more than could have been expected, negro transportation-ship as the stranger in port was. But, in one language, and as with one voice, all poured out a common tale of suffering; in which the negresses, of whom there were not a few, exceeded the others in their dolorous vehemence. The survey, together with the fever, had swept off a great part of their number, more especially the Spaniards. Off Cape Horn they had narrowly escaped shipwreck; then, for days together, they had lain tranced without wind; their provisions were low; their water next to none; their lips that moment were baked.

While Captain Delano was thus made the mark of all eager tongues, his one eager glance took in all faces, with every other object about him.

Always upon first boarding a large and populous ship at sea, especially a foreign one, with a nondescript crew such as Lascars or Manila men, the impression varies in a peculiar way from that produced by first entering a strange house with strange inmates in a strange land. Both house and ship—the one by its walls and blinds, the other by its high bulwarks like ramparts—hoard from view their interiors till the last moment; but in the case of the ship there is this addition: that the living spectacle it contains, upon its sudden and complete disclosure, has, in contrast with the blank ocean which zones it, something of the effect of enchantment. The ship seems unreal; these strange costumes, gestures, and faces, but a shadowy tableau just emerged from the deep, which directly must receive back what it gave.

Perhaps it was some such influence, as above is attempted to be described, which, in Captain Delano's mind, heightened whatever, upon a staid scrutiny, might have seemed unusual; especially the conspicuous figures of four elderly grizzled negroes, their heads like black, doddered willow tops, who, in venerable contrast to the tumult below them, were couched, sphynx-like, one on the starboard cat-head, another on the larboard, and the remaining pair face to face on the opposite bulwarks above the main-chains. They each had bits of unstranded old junk in their hands, and, with a sort of stoical self-content, were picking the junk into oakum, a small heap of which lay by their sides. They accompanied the task with a continuous, low, monotonous chant; droning and drooling away like so many grey-headed bag-pipers playing a funeral march.

The quarter-deck rose into an ample elevated poop, upon the forward verge of which, lifted, like the oakum-pickers, some eight feet above the general throng, sat along in a row, separated by regular spaces, the cross-legged figures of six other blacks; each with a rusty hatchet in his hand, which, with a bit of brick and a rag, he was engaged like a scullion in scouring; while between each two was a small stack of hatchets, their rusted edges turned forward awaiting a like operation. Though occasionally the four oakum-pickers would briefly address some person or persons in the crowd below, yet the six hatchet-polishers neither spoke to others, nor breathed a whisper among themselves, but sat intent upon their task, except at intervals, when, with the peculiar love in negroes of uniting industry with pastime, two and two they sideways clashed their hatchets together, like cymbals, with a barbarous din. All six, unlike the generality, had the raw aspect of unsophisticated Africans.

But that first comprehensive glance which took in those ten figures, with scores less conspicuous, rested but an instant upon them, as, impatient of the hubbub of voices, the visitor turned in quest of whomsoever it might be that commanded the ship.

But as if not unwilling to let nature make known her own case among his suffering charge, or else in despair of restraining it for the time, the Spanish captain, a gentlemanly, reserved-looking, and rather young man to a stranger's eye, dressed with singular richness, but bearing plain traces of recent sleepless cares and disquietudes, stood passively by, leaning against the main-mast, at one moment casting a dreary, spiritless look upon his excited people, at the next an unhappy glance toward his visitor. By his side stood a black of small stature, in whose rude face, as occasionally, like a shepherd's dog, he mutely turned it up into the Spaniard's, sorrow and affection were equally blended.

Struggling through the throng, the American advanced to the Spaniard, assuring him of his sympathies, and offering to render whatever assistance might be in his power. To which the Spaniard returned for the present but grave and ceremonious acknowledgments, his national formality ducked by the saturnine mood of ill-health.

But losing no time in mere compliments, Captain Delano, returning to the gangway, had his baskets of fish brought up; and as the wind still continued light, so that some hours at least must elapse ere the ship could be brought to the anchorage, he bade his men return to the sealer, and fetch back as much water as the whale-boat could carry, with whatever soft bread the steward might have, all the remaining pumpkins on board, with a box of sugar, and a dozen of his private bottles of cider.

Not many minutes after the boat's pushing off, to the vexation of all, the wind entirely died away, and the tide turning, began drifting back the ship helplessly seaward. But trusting this would not long last, Captain Delano sought, with good hopes, to cheer up the strangers, feeling no small satisfaction that, with persons in their condition, he could—thanks to his frequent voyages along the Spanish Main—converse with some freedom in their native tongue.

While left alone with them, he was not long in observing some things tending to heighten his first impressions; but surprise was lost in pity, both for the Spaniards and blacks, alike evidently reduced from scarcity of water and provisions; while long-continued suffering seemed to have brought out the less good-natured qualities of the negroes, besides, at the same time, impairing the Spaniard's authority over them. But, under the circumstances, precisely this condition of things was to have been anticipated. In armies, navies, cities, or families, in nature herself, nothing more relaxes good order than misery. Still, Captain Delano was not without the idea, that had Benito Cereno been a man of greater energy, misrule would hardly have come to the present pass. But the debility, constitutional or induced by hardships, bodily and mental, of the Spanish captain, was too obvious to be overlooked. A prey to settled dejection, as if long mocked with hope he would not now indulge it, even when it had ceased to be a mock, the prospect of that day, or evening at furthest, lying at anchor, with plenty of water for his people, and a brother captain to counsel and befriend, seemed in no perceptible degree to encourage him. His mind appeared unstrung, if not still more seriously affected. Shut up in these oaken walls, chained to one dull round of command, whose unconditionality cloyed him, like some hypochondriac abbot he moved slowly about, at times suddenly pausing, starting, or staring, biting his lip, biting his finger-nail, flushing, paling, twitching his beard, with other symptoms of an absent or moody mind. This distempered spirit was lodged, as before hinted, in as distempered a frame. He was rather tall, but seemed never to have been robust, and now with nervous suffering was almost worn to a skeleton. A tendency to some pulmonary complaint appeared to have been lately confirmed. His voice was like that of one with lungs half gone—hoarsely suppressed, a husky whisper. No wonder that, as in this state he tottered about, his private servant apprehensively followed him. Sometimes the negro gave his master his arm, or took his handkerchief out of his pocket for him; performing these and similar offices with that affectionate zeal which transmutes into something filial or fraternal acts in themselves but menial; and which has gained for the negro the repute of making the most pleasing body-servant in the world; one, too, whom a master need be on no stiffly superior terms with, but may treat with familiar trust; less a servant than a devoted companion.

Marking the noisy indocility of the blacks in general, as well as what seemed the sullen inefficiency of the whites, it was not without humane satisfaction that Captain Delano witnessed the steady good conduct of Babo.

But the good conduct of Babo, hardly more than the ill-behaviour of others, seemed to withdraw the half-lunatic Don Benito from his cloudy languor. Not that such precisely was the impression made by the Spaniard on the mind of his visitor. The Spaniard's individual unrest was, for the present, but noted as a conspicuous feature in the ship's general affliction. Still, Captain Delano was not a little concerned at what he could not help taking for the time to be Don Benito's unfriendly indifference towards himself. The Spaniard's manner, too, conveyed a sort of sour and gloomy disdain, which he seemed at no pains to disguise. But this the American in charity ascribed to the harassing effects of sickness, since, in former instances, he had noted that there are peculiar natures on whom prolonged physical suffering seems to cancel every social instinct of kindness; as if, forced to black bread themselves, they deemed it but equity that each person coming nigh them should, indirectly, by some slight or affront, be made to partake of their fare.

But ere long Captain Delano bethought him that, indulgent as he was at the first, in judging the Spaniard, he might not, after all, have exercised charity enough. At bottom it was Don Benito's reserve which displeased him; but the same reserve was shown towards all but his faithful personal attendant. Even the formal reports which, according to sea-usage, were, at stated times, made to him by some petty underling, either a white, mulatto or black, he hardly had patience enough to listen to, without betraying contemptuous aversion. His manner upon such occasions was, in its degree, not unlike that which might be supposed to have been his imperial countryman's, Charles V, just previous to the anchoritish retirement of that monarch from the throne.

This splenetic disrelish of his place was evinced in almost every function pertaining to it. Proud as he was moody, he condescended to no personal mandate. Whatever special orders were necessary, their delivery was delegated to his body-servant, who in turn transferred them to their ultimate destination, through runners, alert Spanish boys or slave boys, like pages or pilot-fish within easy call continually hovering round Don Benito. So that to have beheld this undemonstrative invalid gliding about, apathetic and mute, no landsman could have dreamed that in him was lodged a dictatorship beyond which, while at sea, there was no earthly appeal.

Thus, the Spaniard, regarded in his reserve, seemed the involuntary victim of mental disorder. But, in fact, his reserve might, in some degree, have proceeded from design. If so, then here was evinced the unhealthy climax of that icy though conscientious policy, more or less adopted by all commanders of large ships, which, except in signal emergencies, obliterates alike the manifestation of sway with every trace of sociality; transforming the man into a block, or rather into a loaded cannon, which, until there is call for thunder, has nothing to say.

Viewing him in this light, it seemed but a natural token of the perverse habit induced by a long course of such hard self-restraint, that, notwithstanding the present condition of his ship, the Spaniard should still persist in a demeanour, which, however harmless, or, it may be, appropriate, in a well-appointed vessel, such as the *San Dominick* might have been at the outset of the voyage, was anything but judicious now. But the Spaniard, perhaps, thought that it was with captains as with gods: reserve, under all events, must still be their cue. But probably this appearance of slumbering dominion might have been but an attempted disguise to conscious imbecility—not deep policy, but shallow device. But be all this as it might, whether Don Benito's manner was designed or not, the more Captain Delano noted its pervading reserve, the less he felt uneasiness at any particular manifestation of that reserve towards himself.

Neither were his thoughts taken up by the captain alone. Wonted to the quiet orderliness of the sealer's comfortable family of a crew, the noisy confusion of the *San Dominick*'s suffering host repeatedly challenged his eye. Some prominent breaches, not only of discipline but of decency, were observed. These Captain Delano could not but ascribe, in the main, to the absence of those subordinate deck-officers to whom, along with higher duties, is intrusted what may be styled the police department of a populous ship. True, the old oakum-pickers appeared at times to act the part of monitorial constables to their countrymen, the blacks; but though occasionally succeeding in allaying trifling outbreaks now and then between man and man, they could do little or nothing toward establishing general quiet. The *San Dominick* was in the condition of a transatlantic emigrant ship, among whose multitude of living freight are some individuals, doubtless, as little troublesome as crates and bales; but the friendly remonstrances of such with their ruder companions are of not so much avail as the unfriendly arm of the mate. What the *San Dominick* wanted was, what the emigrant ship has, stern superior officers. But on these decks not so much as a fourth-mate was to be seen.

The visitor's curiosity was roused to learn the particulars of those mishaps which had brought about such absenteeism, with its consequences; because, though deriving some inkling of the voyage from the wails which at the first moment had greeted him, yet of the details no clear understanding had been had. The best account would, doubtless, be given by the captain. Yet at first the visitor was loth to ask it, unwilling to provoke some distant rebuff. But plucking up courage, he at last accosted Don Benito, renewing the expression of his benevolent interest, adding, that did he (Captain Delano) but know the particulars of the ship's misfortunes, he would, perhaps, be better able in the end to relieve them. Would Don Benito favour him with the whole story?

Don Benito faltered; then, like some somnambulist suddenly interfered with, vacantly stared at his visitor, and ended by looking down on the deck. He maintained this posture so long, that Captain Delano, almost equally disconcerted, and involuntarily almost as rude, turned suddenly from him, walking forward to accost one of the Spanish seamen for the desired information. But he had hardly gone five paces, when, with a sort of eagerness, Don Benito invited him back, regretting his momentary absence of mind, and professing readiness to gratify him.

While most part of the story was being given, the two captains stood on the after part of the main-deck, a privileged spot, no one being near but the servant.

"It is now a hundred and ninety days," began the Spaniard, in his husky whisper, "that this ship, well officered and well-manned, with several cabin passengers—some fifty Spaniards in all—sailed from Buenos Ayres bound to Lima, with a general cargo, hardware, Paraguay tea and the like—and," pointing forward, "that parcel of negroes, now not more than a hundred and fifty, as you see, but then numbering over three hundred souls. Off Cape Horn we had heavy gales. In one moment, by night, three of my best officers, with fifteen sailors, were lost, with the main-yard; the spar snapping under them in the slings, as they sought, with heavers, to beat down the icy sail. To lighten the hull, the heavier sacks of maté were thrown into the sea, with most of the water-pipes lashed on deck at the time. And this last necessity it was, combined with the prolonged detentions afterwards experienced, which eventually brought about our chief causes of suffering. When——."

Here there was a sudden fainting attack of his cough, brought on, no doubt, by his mental distress. His servant sustained him, and drawing a cordial from his pocket placed it to his lips. He a little revived. But unwilling to leave him unsupported while yet imperfectly restored, the black with one arm still encircled his master, at the same time keeping his eye fixed on his face, as if to watch for the first sign of complete restoration, or relapse, as the event might prove.

The Spaniard proceeded, but brokenly and obscurely, as one in a dream.

—"Oh, my God! rather than pass through what I have, with joy I would have hailed the most terrible gales; but——"

His cough returned and with increased violence; this subsiding, with reddened lips and closed eyes he fell heavily against his supporter.

"His mind wanders. He was thinking of the plague that followed the gales," plaintively sighed the servant; "my poor, poor master!" wringing one hand, and with the other wiping the mouth. "But be patient, Señor," again turning to Captain Delano, "these fits do not last long; master will soon be himself."

Don Benito reviving, went on; but as this portion of the story was very brokenly delivered, the substance only will here be set down.

It appeared that after the ship had been many days tossed in storms off the Cape, the scurvy broke out, carrying off numbers of the whites and blacks. When at last they had worked round into the Pacific, their spars and sails were so damaged, and so inadequately handled by the surviving mariners, most of whom were become invalids, that, unable to lay her northerly course by the wind which was powerful, the unmanageable ship, for successive days and nights, was blown northwestward, where the breeze suddenly deserted her, in unknown waters, to sultry calms. The absence of the water-pipes now proved as fatal to life as before their presence had menaced it. Induced, or at least aggravated, by the more than scanty allowance of water, a malignant fever followed the scurvy; with the excessive heat of the lengthened calm, making such short work of it as to sweep away, as by billows, whole families of the Africans, and a yet larger number, proportionably, of the Spaniards, including, by a luckless fatality, every remaining officer on board. Consequently, in the smart west winds eventually following the calm, the already rent sails, having to be simply dropped, not furled, at need, had been gradually reduced to the beggars' rags they were now. To procure substitutes for his lost sailors, as well as supplies of water and sails, the captain, at the earliest opportunity, had made for Valdivia, the southernmost civilized port of Chile and South America; but upon nearing the coast the thick weather had prevented him from so much as sighting that harbour. Since which period, almost without a crew, and almost without canvas and almost without water, and, at intervals, giving its added dead to the sea, the *San Dominick* had been battledored about by contrary winds, inveigled by currents, or grown weedy in calms. Like a man lost in woods, more than once she had doubled upon her own track.

"But throughout these calamities," huskily continued Don Benito, painfully turning in the half embrace of his servant, "I have to thank those negroes you see, who, though to your inexperienced eyes appearing unruly, have, indeed, conducted themselves with less of restlessness than even their owner could have thought possible under such circumstances."

Here he again fell faintly back. Again his mind wandered; but he rallied, and less obscurely proceeded.

"Yes, their owner was quite right in assuring me that no fetters would be needed with his blacks; so that while, as is wont in this transportation, those negroes have always remained upon deck—not thrust below, as in the Guineamen—they have, also, from the beginning, been freely permitted to range within given bounds at their pleasure."

Once more the faintness returned—his mind roved—but, recovering, he resumed:

"But it is Babo here to whom, under God, I owe not only my own preservation, but likewise to him, chiefly, the merit is due, of pacifying his more ignorant brethren, when at intervals tempted to murmurings."

"Ah, master," sighed the black, bowing his face, "don't speak of me; Babo is nothing; what Babo has done was but duty."

"Faithful fellow!" cried Captain Delano. "Don Benito, I envy you such a friend; slave I cannot call him."

As master and man stood before him, the black upholding the white, Captain Delano could not but bethink him of the beauty of that relationship which could present such a spectacle of fidelity on the one hand and confidence on the other. The scene was heightened by the contrast in dress, denoting their relative positions. The Spaniard wore a loose Chile jacket of dark velvet, white small-clothes and stockings, with silver buckles at the knee and instep; a high-crowned sombrero, of fine grass; a slender sword, silver mounted, hung from a knot in his sash—the last being an almost invariable adjunct, more for utility than ornament, of a South American gentleman's dress to this hour. Excepting when his occasional nervous contortions brought about disarray, there was a certain precision in his attire curiously at variance with the unsightly disorder around; especially in the belittered Ghetto, forward of the main-mast, wholly occupied by the blacks.

The servant wore nothing but wide trousers, apparently, from their coarseness and patches, made out of some old topsail; they were clean, and confined at the waist by a bit of unstranded rope, which, with his composed, deprecatory air at times, made him look something like a begging friar of St. Francis.

However unsuitable for the time and place, at least in the blunt-thinking American's eyes, and however strangely surviving in the midst of all his afflictions, the toilette of Don Benito might not, in fashion at least, have gone beyond the style of the day among South Americans of his class. Though on the present voyage sailing from Buenos Ayres, he had avowed himself a native and resident of Chile, whose inhabitants had not so generally adopted the plain coat and once plebeian pantaloons; but, with a becoming modification, adhered to their provincial costume, picturesque as any in the world. Still, relatively to the pale history of the voyage, and his pale face, there seemed something so incongruous in the Spaniard's apparel, as almost to suggest the image of an invalid courtier tottering about London streets in the time of the plague.

The portion of the narrative which, perhaps, most excited interest, as well as some surprise, considering the latitudes in question, was the long calms spoken of, and more particularly the ship's so long drifting about. Without communicating the opinion, of course, the American could not but impute at least part of the detentions both to clumsy seamanship and faulty navigation. Eyeing Don Benito's small, yellow hands, he easily inferred that the young captain had not got into command at the hawse-hole, but the cabin-window; and if so, why wonder at incompetence, in youth, sickness, and gentility united?

But drowning criticism in compassion, after a fresh repetition of his sympathies, Captain Delano, having heard out his story, not only engaged, as in the first place, to see Don Benito and his people supplied in their immediate bodily needs, but, also, now further promised to assist him in procuring a large permanent supply of water, as well as some sails and rigging, and, though it would involve no small embarrassment to himself, yet he would spare three of his best seamen for temporary deck-officers; so that without delay the ship might proceed to Concepcion, there fully to refit for Lima, her destined port.

Such generosity was not without its effect, even upon the invalid. His face lighted up; eager and hectic, he met the honest glance of his visitor. With gratitude he seemed overcome.

"This excitement is bad for master," whispered the servant, taking his arm, and with soothing words gently drawing him aside.

When Don Benito returned, the American was pained to observe that his hopefulness, like the sudden kindling in his cheek, was but febrile and transient.

Ere long, with a joyless mien, looking up towards the poop, the host invited his guest to accompany him there, for the benefit of what little breath of wind might be stirring.

As during the telling of the story, Captain Delano had once or twice started at the occasional cymballing of the hatchet-polishers, wondering why such an interruption should be allowed, especially in that part of the ship, and in the ears of an invalid; and moreover, as the hatchets had anything but an attractive look, and the handlers of them still less so, it was, therefore, to tell the truth, not without some lurking reluctance, or even shrinking, it may be, that Captain Delano, with apparent complaisance, acquiesced in his host's invitation. The more so, since, with an untimely caprice of punctilio, rendered distressing by his cadaverous aspect, Don Benito, with Castilian bows, solemnly insisted upon his guest's preceding him up the ladder leading to the elevation; where, one on each side of the last step, sat for armorial supporters and sentries two of the ominous file. Gingerly enough stepped good Captain Delano between them, and in the instant of leaving them behind, like one running the gauntlet, he felt an apprehensive twitch in the calves of his legs.

But when, facing about, he saw the whole file, like so many organ grinders, still stupidly intent on their work, unmindful of everything beside, he could not but smile at his late fidgety panic.

Presently, while standing with his host, looking forward upon the decks below, he was struck by one of the instances of insubordination previously alluded to. Three black boys, with two Spanish boys, were sitting together on the hatches, scraping a rude wooden platter, in which some scanty mess had recently been cooked. Suddenly, one of the black boys, enraged at a word dropped by one of his white companions, seized a knife, and, though called to forbear by one of the oakum-pickers, struck the lad over the head, inflicting a gash from which blood flowed.

In amazement, Captain Delano inquired what this meant. To which the pale Don Benito dully muttered, that it was merely the sport of the lad.

"Pretty serious sport, truly," rejoined Captain Delano. "Had such a thing happened on board the *Bachelor's Delight*, instant punishment would have followed."

At these words the Spaniard turned upon the American one of his sudden, staring, half-lunatic looks; then, relapsing into his torpor, answered, "Doubtless, doubtless, Señor."

Is it, thought Captain Delano, that this hapless man is one of those paper captains I've known, who by policy wink at what by power they cannot put down? I know no sadder sight than a commander who has little of command but the name.

"I should think, Don Benito," he now said, glancing towards the oakum-picker who had sought to interfere with the boys, "that you would find it advantageous to keep all your blacks employed, especially the younger ones, no matter at what useless task, and no matter what happens to the ship. Why, even with my little band, I find such a course indispensable. I once kept a crew on my quarter-deck thrumming mats for my cabin, when, for three days, I had given up my ship—mats, men, and all—for a speedy loss, owing to the violence of a gale, in which we could do nothing but helplessly drive before it."

"Doubtless, doubtless," muttered Don Benito.

"But," continued Captain Delano, again glancing upon the oakum-pickers and then at the hatchet-polishers, near by, "I see you keep some, at least, of your host employed."

"Yes," was again the vacant response.

"Those old men there, shaking their pows from their pulpits," continued Captain Delano, pointing to the oakum-pickers, "seem to act the part of old dominies to the rest, little heeded as their admonitions are at times. Is this voluntary on their part, Don Benito, or have you appointed them shepherds to your flock of black sheep?"

"What posts they fill, I appointed them," rejoined the Spaniard, in an acrid tone, as if resenting some supposed satiric reflection.

"And these others, these Ashantee conjurors here," continued Captain Delano, rather uneasily eyeing the brandished steel of the hatchet-polishers, where, in spots, it had been brought to a shine, "this seems a curious business they are at, Don Benito?"

"In the gales we met," answered the Spaniard, "what of our general cargo was not thrown overboard was much damaged by the brine. Since coming into calm weather, I have had several cases of knives and hatchets daily brought up for overhauling and cleaning."

"A prudent idea, Don Benito. You are part owner of ship and cargo, I presume; but none of the slaves, perhaps?"

"I am owner of all you see," impatiently returned Don Benito, "except the main company of blacks, who belonged to my late friend, Alexandro Aranda."

As he mentioned this name, his air was heart-broken; his knees shook; his servant supported him.

Thinking he divined the cause of such unusual emotion, to confirm his surmise, Captain Delano, after a pause, said: "And may I ask, Don Benito, whether—since a while ago you spoke of some cabin passengers—the friend whose loss so afflicts you, at the outset of the voyage accompanied his blacks?"

"Yes."

"But died of the fever?"

"Died of the fever. Oh, could I but—" Again quivering, the Spaniard paused.

"Pardon me," said Captain Delano, slowly, "but I think that, by a sympathetic experience, I conjecture, Don Benito, what it is that gives the keener edge to your grief. It was once my hard fortune to lose, at sea, a dear friend, my own brother then supercargo. Assured of the welfare of his spirit, its departure I could have borne like a man; but that honest eye, that honest hand—both of which had so often met mine—and that warm heart; all, all—like scraps to the dogs—to throw all to the sharks! It was then I vowed never to have for fellow-voyager a man I loved, unless, unbeknown to him, I had provided every requisite, in case of a fatality, for embalming his mortal part for interment on shore. Were your friend's remains now on board this ship, Don Benito, not thus strangely would the mention of his name affect you."

"On board this ship?" echoed the Spaniard. Then, with horrified gestures, as directed against some spectre, he unconsciously fell into the ready arms of his attendant, who, with a silent appeal toward Captain Delano, seemed beseeching him not again to broach a theme so unspeakably distressing to his master.

This poor fellow now, thought the pained American, is the victim of that sad superstition which associates goblins with the deserted body of man, as ghosts with an abandoned house. How unlike are we made! What to me, in like case, would have been a solemn satisfaction, the bare suggestion, even, terrifies the Spaniard into this trance. Poor Alexandro Aranda! what would you say could you here see your friend—who, on former voyages, when you, for months, were left behind, has, I dare say, often longed, and longed, for one peep at you —now transported with terror at the least thought of having you anyway nigh him.

At this moment, with a dreary grave-yard toll, betokening a flaw, the ship's forecastle bell, smote by one of the grizzled oakum-pickers, proclaimed ten o'clock, through the leaden calm; when Captain Delano's attention was caught by the moving figure of a gigantic black, emerging from the general crowd below, and slowly advancing towards the elevated poop. An iron collar was about his neck, from which depended a chain, thrice wound round his body; the terminating links padlocked together at a broad band of iron, his girdle.

"How like a mute Atufal moves," murmured the servant.

The black mounted the steps of the poop, and, like a brave prisoner, brought up to receive sentence, stood in unquailing muteness before Don Benito, now recovered from his attack.

At the first glimpse of his approach, Don Benito had started, a resentful shadow swept over his face; and, as with the sudden memory of bootless rage, his white lips glued together.

This is some mulish mutineer, thought Captain Delano, surveying, not without a mixture of admiration, the colossal form of the negro.

"See, he waits your question, master," said the servant.

Thus reminded, Don Benito, nervously averting his glance, as if shunning, by anticipation, some rebellious response, in a disconcerted voice, thus spoke:—

"Atufal, will you ask my pardon, now?"

The black was silent.

"Again, master," murmured the servant, with bitter upbraiding eyeing his countryman. "Again, master; he will bend to master yet."

"Answer," said Don Benito, still averting his glance, "say but the one word *pardon,* and your chains shall be off."

Upon this, the black, slowly raising both arms, let them lifelessly fall, his links clanking, his head bowed; as much as to say, "No, I am content."

"Go," said Don Benito, with inkept and unknown emotion.

Deliberately as he had come, the black obeyed.

"Excuse me, Don Benito," said Captain Delano, "but this scene surprises me; what means it, pray?"

"It means that the negro alone, of all the band, has given me peculiar cause of offence. I have put him in chains; I——"

Here he paused; his hand to his head, as if there were a swimming there, or a sudden bewilderment of memory had come over him; but meeting his servant's kindly glance seemed reassured, and proceeded:—

"I could not scourge such a form. But I told him he must ask my pardon. As yet he has not. At my command, every two hours he stands before me."

"And how long has this been?"

"Some sixty days."

"And obedient in all else? And respectful?"

"Yes."

"Upon my conscience, then," exclaimed Captain Delano, impulsively, "he has a royal spirit in him, this fellow."

"He may have some right to it," bitterly returned Don Benito, "he says he was king in his own land."

"Yes," said the servant, entering a word, "those slits in Atufal's ears once held wedges of gold; but poor Babo here, in his own land, was only a poor slave; a black man's slave was Babo, who now is the white's."

Somewhat annoyed by these conversational familiarities, Captain Delano turned curiously upon the attendant, then glanced inquiringly at his master; but, as if long wonted to these little informalities, neither master nor man seemed to understand him.

"What, pray, was Atufal's offence, Don Benito?" asked Captain Delano; "if it was not something very serious, take a fool's advice, and, in view of his general docility, as well as in some natural respect for his spirit, remit him his penalty."

"No, no, master never will do that," here murmured the servant to himself, "proud Atufal must first ask master's pardon. The slave there carries the padlock, but master here carries the key."

His attention thus directed, Captain Delano now noticed for the first time that, suspended by a slender silken cord, from Don Benito's neck, hung a key. At once, from the servant's muttered syllables, divining the key's purpose, he smiled and said:—"So, Don Benito—padlock and key—signficant symbols truly."

Biting his lip, Don Benito faltered.

Though the remark of Captain Delano, a man of such native simplicity as to be incapable of satire or irony, had been dropped in playful allusion to the Spaniard's singularly evidenced lordship over the black; yet the hypochondriac seemed some way to have taken it as a malicious reflection upon his confessed inability thus far to break down, at least, on a verbal summons, the entrenched will of the slave. Deploring this supposed misconception, yet despairing of correcting it, Captain Delano shifted the subject; but finding his companion more than ever withdrawn, as if still sourly digesting the lees of the presumed affront above-mentioned, by and by Captain Delano likewise became less talkative, oppressed, against his own will, by what seemed the secret vindictiveness of the morbidly sensitive Spaniard. But the good sailor, himself of a quite contrary disposition, refrained, on his part, alike from the appearance as from the feeling of resentment, and if silent, was only so from contagion.

Presently the Spaniard, assisted by his servant, somewhat discourteously crossed over from his guest; a procedure which, sensibly enough, might have been allowed to pass from idle caprice of ill-humour, had not master and man, lingering round the corner of the elevated skylight, begun whispering together in low voices. This was unpleasing. And more: the moody air of the Spaniard, which at times had not been without a sort of valetudinarian stateliness, now seemed anything but dignified; while the menial familiarity of the servant lost its original charm of simple-hearted attachment.

In his embarrassment, the visitor turned his face to the other side of the ship. By so doing, his glance accidentally fell on a young Spanish sailor, a coil of rope in his hand, just stepped from the deck to the first round of the mizzen-rigging. Perhaps the man would not have been particularly noticed, were it not that, during his ascent to one of the yards, he, with a sort of covert intentness, kept his eye fixed on Captain Delano, from whom, presently, it passed, as if by a natural sequence, to the two whisperers.

His own attention thus redirected to that quarter, Captain Delano gave a slight start. From something in Don Benito's manner just then, it seemed as if the visitor had, at least partly, been the subject of the withdrawn consultation going on—a conjecture as little agreeable to the guest as it was little flattering to the host.

The singular alternations of courtesy and ill-breeding in the Spanish captain were unaccountable, except on one of two suppositions—innocent lunacy, or wicked imposture.

But the first idea, though it might naturally have occurred to an indifferent observer, and, in some respect, had not hitherto been wholly a stranger to Captain Delano's mind, yet, now that, in an incipient way, he began to regard the stranger's conduct something in the light of an intentional affront, of course the idea of lunacy was virtually vacated. But if not a lunatic, what then? Under the circumstances, would a gentleman, nay, any honest boor, act the part now acted by his host? The man was an imposter. Some low-born adventurer, masquerading as an oceanic grandee; yet so ignorant of the first requisites of mere gentlemanhood as to be betrayed into the present remarkable indecorum. The strange ceremoniousness, too, at other times evinced, seemed not uncharacteristic of one playing a part above his real level. Benito Cereno—Don Benito Cereno—a sounding name. One, too, at that period, not unknown, in the surname, to supercargoes and sea captains trading along the Spanish Main, as belonging to one of the most enterprising and extensive mercantile families in all those provinces; several members of it having titles; a sort of Castilian Rothschild, with a noble brother, or cousin, in every great trading town of South America. The alleged Don Benito was in early manhood, about twenty-nine or thirty. To assume a sort of roving cadetship in the maritime affairs of such a house, what more likely scheme for a young knave of talent and spirit? But the Spaniard was a pale invalid. Never mind. For even to the degree of simulating mortal disease, the craft of some tricksters had been known to attain. To think that, under the aspect of infantile weakness, the most savage energies might be couched—those velvets of the Spaniard but the silky paw to his fangs.

From no train of thought did these fancies come; not from within, but from without; suddenly, too, and in one throng, like hoar frost; yet as soon to vanish as the mild sun of Captain Delano's good nature regained its meridian.

Glancing over once more towards his host—whose sideface, revealed above the skylight, was now turned towards him—he was struck by the profile, whose clearness of cut was refined by the thinness, incident to ill-health, as well as ennobled about the chin by the beard. Away with suspicion. He was a true off-shoot of a true hidalgo Cereno.

Relieved by these and other better thoughts, the visitor, lightly humming a tune, now began indifferently pacing the poop, so as not to betray to Don Benito that he had at all mistrusted incivility, much less duplicity; for such mistrust would yet be proved illusory, and by the event; though, for the present, the circumstance which had provoked that distrust remained unexplained. But when that little mystery should have been cleared up, Captain Delano thought he might extremely regret it, did he allow Don Benito to become aware that he had indulged in ungenerous surmises. In short, to the Spaniard's black-letter text, it was best, for a while, to leave open margin.

Presently, his pale face twitching and overcast, the Spaniard, still supported by his attendant, moved over towards his guest, when, with even more than his usual embarrassment, and a strange sort of intriguing intonation in his husky whisper, the following conversation began:—

"Señor, may I ask how long you have lain at this isle?"

"Oh, but a day or two, Don Benito."

"And from what port are you last?"

"Canton."

"And there, Señor, you exchanged your sealskins for teas and silks, I think you said?"

"Yes. Silks mostly."

"And the balance you took in specie, perhaps?"

Captain Delano, fidgeting a little, answered—

"Yes; some silver; not a very great deal, though."

"Ah—well. May I ask how many men have you, Señor?"

Captain Delano slightly started, but answered—

"About five-and-twenty, all told."

"And at present, Señor, all on board, I suppose?"

"All on board, Don Benito," replied the Captain, now with satisfaction.

"And will be to-night, Señor?"

At this last question, following so many pertinacious ones, for the soul of him Captain Delano could not but look very earnestly at the questioner, who, instead of meeting the glance, with every token of craven discomposure dropped his eyes to the deck; presenting an unworthy contrast to his servant, who, just then, was kneeling at his feet, adjusting a loose shoebuckle; his disengaged face meantime, with humble curiosity, turned openly up into his master's downcast one.

The Spaniard, still with a guilty shuffle, repeated his question:

"And—and will be to-night, Señor?"

"Yes, for aught I know," returned Captain Delano—"but nay," rallying himself into fearless truth, "some of them talked of going off on another fishing party about midnight."

"Your ships generally go—go more or less armed, I believe, Señor?"

"Oh, a six-pounder or two, in case of emergency," was the intrepidly indifferent reply, "with a small stock of muskets, sealing-spears, and cutlasses, you know."

As he thus responded, Captain Delano again glanced at Don Benito, but the latter's eyes were averted; while abruptly and awkwardly shifting the subject, he made some peevish allusion to the calm, and then, without apology, once more, with his attendant, withdrew to the opposite bulwarks, where the whispering was resumed.

At this moment, and ere Captain Delano could cast a cool thought upon what had just passed, the young Spanish sailor, before mentioned, was seen descending from the rigging. In act of stooping over to spring inboard to the deck, his voluminous, unconfined frock, or shirt, of coarse woolen, much spotted with tar, opened out far down the chest, revealing a soiled undergarment of what seemed the finest linen, edged, about the neck, with a narrow blue ribbon, sadly faded and worn. At this moment the young sailor's eye was again fixed on the whisperers, and Captain Delano thought he observed a lurking significance in it, as if silent signs, of some Freemason sort, had that instant been interchanged.

This once more impelled his own glance in the direction of Don Benito, and, as before, he could not but infer that himself formed the subject of the conference. He paused. The sound of the hatchet-polishing fell on his ears. He cast another swift side-look at the two. They had the air of conspirators. In connection with the late questionings, and the incident of the young sailor, these things now begat such return of involuntary suspicion, that the singular guilelessness of the American could not endure it. Plucking up a gay and humorous expression, he crossed over to the two rapidly saying:—"Ha, Don Benito, your black here seems high in your trust; a sort of privy-counsellor, in fact."

Upon this, the servant looked up with a good-natured grin, but the master started as from a venomous bite. It was a moment or two before the Spaniard sufficiently recovered himself to reply; which he did, at last, with cold constraint:—"Yes, Señor, I have trust in Babo."

Here Babo, changing his previous grin of mere animal humour into an intelligent smile, not ungratefully eyed his master.

Finding that the Spaniard now stood silent and reserved, as if involuntarily, or purposely giving hint that his guest's proximity was inconvenient just then, Captain Delano, unwilling to appear uncivil even to incivility itself, made some trivial remark and moved off; again and again turning over in his mind the mysterious demeanour of Don Benito Cereno.

He had descended from the poop, and, wrapped in thought, was passing near a dark hatchway, leading down into the steerage, when, perceiving motion there, he looked to see what moved. The same instant there was a sparkle in the shadowy hatchway, and he saw one of the Spanish sailors, prowling there, hurriedly placing his hand in the bosom of his frock, as if hiding something. Before the man could have been certain who it was that was passing, he slunk below out of sight. But enough was seen of him to make it sure that he was the same young sailor before noticed in the rigging.

What was that which so sparkled? though Captain Delano. It was no lamp—no match—no live coal. Could it have been a jewel? But how come sailors with jewels?—or with silk-trimmed under-shirts either? Has he been robbing the trunks of the dead cabin-passengers? But if so, he would hardly wear one of the stolen articles on board ship here. Ah, ah—if, now, that was, indeed, a secret sign I saw passing between this suspicious fellow and his captain awhile since; if I could only be certain that, in my uneasiness, my senses did not deceive me, then——

Here, passing from one suspicious thing to another, his mind revolved the strange questions put to him concerning his ship.

By a curious coincidence, as each point was recalled, the black wizards of Ashantee would strike up with their hatchets, as in ominous comment on the white stranger's thoughts. Pressed by such enigmas and portents, it would have been almost against nature, had not, even into the least distrustful heart, some ugly misgivings obtruded.

Observing the ship, now helplessly fallen into a current, with enchanted sails, drifting with increased rapidity seaward; and noting that, from a lately intercepted projection of the land, the sealer was hidden, the stout mariner began to quake at thoughts which he barely durst confess to himself. Above all, he began to feel a ghostly dread of Don Benito. And yet, when he roused himself, dilated his chest, felt himself strong on his legs, and coolly considered it—what did all these phantoms amount to?

Had the Spaniard any sinister scheme, it must have reference not so much to him (Captain Delano) as to his ship (the *Bachelor's Delight*). Hence the present drifting away of the one ship from the other, instead of favouring any such possible scheme, was, for the time, at least, opposed to it. Clearly any suspicion, combining such contradictions, must need be delusive. Besides, was it not absurd to think of a vessel in distress—a vessel by sickness almost dismanned of her crew—a vessel whose inmates were parched for water—was it not a thousand times absurd that such a craft should, at present, be of a piratical character; or her commander, either for himself or those under him, cherish any desire but for speedy relief and refreshment? But then, might not general distress, and thirst in particular, be affected? And might not that same undiminished Spanish crew, alleged to have perished off to a remnant, be at that very moment lurking in the hold? On heart-broken pretence of entreating a cup of cold water, fiends in human form had got into lonely dwellings, nor retired until a dark deed had been done. And among the Malay pirates, it was no unusual thing to lure ships after them into their treacherous harbours, or entice boarders from a declared enemy at sea, by the spectacle of thinly manned or vacant decks, beneath which prowled a hundred spears with yellow arms ready to upthrust them through the mats. Not that Captain Delano had entirely credited such things. He had heard of them—and now, as stories, they recurred. The present destination of the ship was the anchorage. There she would be near his own vessel. Upon gaining that vicinity, might not the *San Dominick*, like a slumbering volcano, suddenly let loose energies now hid?

He recalled the Spaniard's manner while telling his story. There was a gloomy hesitancy and subterfuge about it. It was just the manner of one making up his tale for evil purposes, as he goes. But if that story was not true, what was the truth? That the ship had unlawfully come into the Spaniard's possession? But in many of its details, especially in reference to the more calamitous parts, such as the fatalities among the seamen, the consequent prolonged beating about, the past sufferings from obstinate calms, and still continued suffering from thirst; in all these points, as well as others, Don Benito's story had corroborated not only the wailing ejaculations of the indiscriminate multitude, white and black, but likewise—what seemed impossible to be counterfeit—by the very expression and play of every human feature, which Captain Delano saw. If Don Benito's story was, throughout, an invention, then every soul on board, down to the youngest negress, was his carefully drilled recruit in the plot: an incredible inference. And yet, if there was ground for mistrusting his veracity, that inference was a legitimate one.

But those questions of the Spaniard. There, indeed, one might pause. Did they not seem put with much the same object with which the burglar or assassin, by day-time, reconnoitres the walls of a house? But, with ill purposes, to solicit such information openly of the chief person endangered, and so, in effect, setting him on his guard; how unlikely a procedure was that? Absurd, then, to suppose that those questions had been prompted by evil designs. Thus, the same conduct, which, in this instance, had raised the alarm, served to dispel it. In short, scarce any suspicion or uneasiness, however apparently reasonable at the time, which was not now, with equally apparent reason, dismissed.

At last he began to laugh at his former forebodings; and laugh at the strange ship for, in its aspect, someway siding with them, as it were; and laugh, too, at the odd-looking blacks, particularly those old scissors-grinders, the Ashantees; and those bed-ridden old knitting women, the oakum-pickers; and almost at the dark Spaniard himself, the central hobgoblin of all.

For the rest, whatever in a serious way seemed enigmatical, was now good-naturedly explained away by the thought that, for the most part, the poor invalid scarcely knew what he was about; either sulking in black vapours, or putting idle questions without sense of object. Evidently, for the present, the man was not fit to be intrusted with the ship. On some benevolent plea withdrawing the command from him, Captain Delano would yet have to send her to Concepcion, in charge of his second mate, a worthy person and good navigator—a plan not more convenient for the *San Dominick* than for Don Benito; for, relieved from all anxiety, keeping wholly to his cabin, the sick man, under the good nursing of his servant, would, probably, by the end of the passage, be in a measure restored to health, and with that he should also be restored to authority.

Such were the American's thoughts. They were tranquilizing. There was a difference between the idea of Don Benito's darkly pre-ordaining Captain Delano's fate, and Captain Delano's lightly arranging Don Benito's. Nevertheless, it was not without something of relief that the good seaman presently perceived his whale-boat in the distance. Its absence had been prolonged by unexpected detention at the sealer's side, as well as its returning trip lengthened by the continual recession of the goal.

The advancing speck was observed by the blacks. Their shouts attracted the attention of Don Benito, who, with a return of courtesy, approaching Captain Delano, expressed satisfaction at the coming of some supplies, slight and temporary as they must necessarily prove.

Captain Delano responded; but while doing so, his attention was drawn to something passing on the deck below: among the crowd climbing the landward bulwarks, anxiously watching the coming boat, two blacks, to all appearances accidentally incommoded by one of the sailors, violently pushed him aside, which the sailor someway resenting, they dashed him to the deck, despite the earnest cries of the oakum-pickers.

"Don Benito," said Captain Delano quickly, "do you see what is going on there? Look!"

But, seized by his cough, the Spaniard staggered, with both hands to his face, on the point of falling. Captain Delano would have supported him, but the servant was more alert, who, with one hand sustaining his master, with the other applied the cordial. Don Benito restored, the black withdrew his support, slipping aside a little, but dutifully remaining within call of a whisper. Such discretion was here evinced as quite wiped away, in the visitor's eyes, any blemish of impropriety which might have attached to the attendant, from the indecorous conferences before mentioned; showing, too, that if the servant were to blame, it might be more the master's fault than his own, since, when left to himself, he could conduct thus well.

His glance called away from the spectacle of disorder to the more pleasing one before him, Captain Delano could not avoid again congratulating his host upon possessing such a servant, who, though perhaps a little too forward now and then, must upon the whole be invaluable to one in the invalid's situation.

"Tell me, Don Benito," he added, with a smile—"I should like to have your man here, myself—what will you take for him? Would fifty doubloons be any object?"

"Master wouldn't part with Babo for a thousand doubloons," murmured the black, overhearing the offer, and taking it in earnest, and, with the strange vanity of a faithful slave, appreciated by his master, scorning to hear so paltry a valuation put upon him by a stranger. But Don Benito, apparently hardly yet completely restored, and again interrupted by his cough, made but some broken reply.

Soon his physical distress became so great, affecting his mind, too, apparently, that, as if to screen the sad spectacle, the servant gently conducted his master below.

Left to himself, the American, to while away the time till his boat should arrive, would have pleasantly accosted some one of the few Spanish seamen he saw; but recalling something that Don Benito had said touching their ill conduct, he refrained; as a shipmaster indisposed to countenance cowardice or unfaithfulness in seamen.

While, with these thoughts, standing with eye directed forward towards that handful of sailors, suddenly he thought that one or two of them returned the glance and with a sort of meaning. He rubbed his eyes, and looked again; but again seemed to see the same thing. Under a new form, but more obscure than any previous one, the old suspicions recurred, but, in the absence of Don Benito, with less of panic than before. Despite the bad account given of the sailors, Captain Delano resolved forthwith to accost one of them. Descending the poop, he made his way through the blacks, his movement drawing a queer a queer cry from the oakum-pickers, prompted by whom, the negroes, twitching each other aside, divided before him; but, as if curious to see what was the object of this deliberate visit to their Ghetto, closing in behind, in tolerable order, followed the white stranger up. His progress thus proclaimed as by mounted kings-at-arms, and escorted as by a Kaffir guard of honour, Captain Delano, assuming a good-humoured, off-handed air, continued to advance; now and then saying a blithe word to the negroes, and his eye curiously surveying the white faces, here and there sparsely mixed in with the blacks, like stray white pawns venturously involved in the ranks of the chessmen opposed.

While thinking which of them to select for his purpose, he chanced to observe a sailor seated on the deck engaged in tarring the strap of a large block, a circle of blacks squatted round him inquisitively eyeing the process.

The mean employment of the man was in contrast with something superior in his figure. His hand, black with continually thrusting it into the tar-pot held for him by a negro, seemed not naturally allied to his face, a face which would have been a very fine one but for its haggardness. Whether this haggardness had aught to do with criminality, could not be determined; since, as intense heat and cold, though unlike, produce like sensations, so innocence and guilt, when, through casual association with mental pain, stamping any visible impress, use one seal—a hacked one.

Not again that this reflection occurred to Captain Delano at the time, charitable man as he was. Rather another idea. Because observing so singular a haggardness combined with a dark eye, averted as in trouble and shame, and then again recalling Don Benito's confessed ill opinion of his crew, insensibly he was operated upon by certain general notions which, while disconnecting pain and abashment from virtue, invariably link them with vice.

If, indeed, there be any wickedness on board this ship, thought Captain Delano, be sure that man there has fouled his hand in it, even as now he fouls it in the pitch. I don't like to accost him. I will speak to this other, this old Jack here on the windlass.

He advanced to an old Barcelona tar, in ragged red breeches and dirty nightcap, cheeks trenched and bronzed, whiskers dense as thorn hedges. Seated between two sleepy-looking Africans, this mariner, like his younger shipmate, was employed upon some rigging—splicing a cable—the sleepy-looking blacks performing the inferior function of holding the outer parts of the ropes for him.

Upon Captain Delano's approach, the man at once hung his head below its previous level; the one necessary for business. It appeared as if he desired to be thought absorbed, with more than common fidelity, in his task. Being addressed, he glanced up, but with what seemed a furtive, diffident air, which sat strangely enough on his weather-beaten visage, much as if a grizzly bear, instead of growling and biting, should simper and cast sheep's eyes. He was asked several questions concerning the voyage—questions purposely referring to several particulars in Don Benito's narrative, not previously corroborated by those impulsive cries greeting the visitor on the first coming on board. The questions were briefly answered, confirming all that remained to be confirmed of the story. The negroes about the windlass joined in with the old sailor; but, as they became talkative, he by degrees became mute, and at length quite glum, seemed morosely unwilling to answer more questions, and yet, all the while, this ursine air was somehow mixed with his sheepish one.

Despairing of getting into unembarrassed talk with such a centaur, Captain Delano, after glancing round for a more promising countenance, but seeing none, spoke pleasantly to the blacks to make way for him; and so, amid various grins and grimaces, returned to the poop, feeling a little strange at first, he could hardly tell why, but upon the whole with regained confidence in Benito Cereno.

How plainly, thought he, did that old whiskerando yonder betray a consciousness of ill desert. No doubt, when he saw me coming, he dreaded lest I, appraised by his captain of the crew's general misbehaviour, came with sharp words for him, and so down with his head. And yet—and yet, now that I think of it, that very fellow, if I err not, was one of those who seemed so earnestly eyeing me here awhile since. Ah, these currents spin one's head round almost as much as they do the ship. Ha, there now's a pleasant sort of sunny sight; quite sociable, too.

His attention had been drawn back to a slumbering negress, partly disclosed through the lacework of some rigging, lying, with youthful limbs carelessly disposed, under the lee of the bulwarks, like a doe in the shade of a woodland rock. Sprawling at her lapped breasts was her wide-awake fawn, stark naked, its black little body half lifted from the deck, crosswise with its dam's; its hands, like two paws, clambering upon her; its mouth and nose ineffectually rooting to get at the mark; and meantime giving a vexatious half-grunt, blending with the composed snore of the negress.

The uncommon vigour of the child at length roused the mother. She started up, at a distance facing Captain Delano. But as if not at all concerned at the attitude in which she had been caught, delightedly she caught the child up, with maternal transports, covering it with kisses.

There's naked nature, now; pure tenderness and love, thought Captain Delano, well pleased.

This incident prompted him to remark the other negresses more particularly than before. He was gratified with their manners: like most uncivilized women, they seemed at once tender of heart and tough of constitution; equally ready to die for their infants or fight for them. Unsophisticated as leopardesses; loving as doves. Ah! thought Captain Delano, these, perhaps, are some of the very women whom Ledyard saw in Africa, and gave such a noble account of.

These natural sights somehow insensibly deepened his confidence and ease. At last he looked to see how his boat was getting on; but it was still pretty remote. He turned to see if Don Benito had returned; but he had not.

To change the scene, as well as to please himself with a leisurely observation of the coming boat, stepping over into the mizzen-chains, he clambered his way into the starboard quarter-gallery—one of those abandoned Venetian-looking water-balconies previously mentioned—retreats cut off from the deck. As his foot pressed the half-damp, half-dry sea-mosses matting the place, and a chance phantom cats-paw—an islet of breeze, unheralded, unfollowed—as this ghostly cats-paw came fanning his cheek; as his glance fell upon the row of small, round dead-lights—all closed like coppered eyes of the coffined—and the state-cabin door, once connecting with the gallery, even as the dead-lights had once looked out upon it, but now calked fast like a sarcophagus lid; and to a purple-black, tarred-over panel, threshold, and post; and he bethought him of the time, when that state-cabin and this state-balcony had heard the voices of the Spanish king's officers, and the forms of the Lima viceroy's daughters had perhaps leaned where he stood—as these and other images flitted through his mind, as the cats-paw through the calm, gradually he felt rising a dreamy inquietude, like that of one who alone on the prairie feels unrest from the repose of the noon.

He leaned against the carved balustrade, again looking off toward his boat; but found his eye falling upon the ribbon grass, trailing along the ship's waterline, straight as a border of green box; and parterres of seaweed, broad ovals and crescents, floating nigh and far, with what seemed long formal alleys between, crossing the terraces of swells, and sweeping round as if leading to the grottoes below. And overhanging all was the balustrade by his arm, which, partly stained with pitch and partly embossed with moss, seemed the charred ruin of some summer-house in a grand garden long running to waste.

Trying to break one charm, he was but becharmed anew. Though upon the wide sea, he seemed in some far inland country; prisoner in some deserted château, left to stare at empty grounds, and peer out at vague roads, where never wagon or wayfarer passed.

But these enchantments were a little disenchanted as his eye fell on the corroded main-chains. Of an ancient style, massy and rusty in link, shackle and bolt, they seemed even more fit for the ship's present business than the one for which she had been built.

Presently he thought something moved nigh the chains. He rubbed his eyes, and looked hard. Groves of rigging were about the chains; and there, peering from behind a great stay, like an Indian from behind a hemlock, a Spanish sailor, a marlingspike in his hand, was seen, who made what seemed an imperfect gesture towards the balcony, but immediately, as if alarmed by some advancing step along the deck within, vanished into the recesses of the hempen forest, like a poacher.

What meant this? Something the man had sought to communicate, unbeknown to any one, even to his captain. Did the secret involve aught unfavourable to his captain? Were those previous misgivings of Captain Delano's about to be verified? Or, in his haunted mood at the moment, had some random, unintentional motion of the man, while busy with the stay, as if repairing it, been mistaken for a significant beckoning?

Not unbewildered, again he gazed off for his boat. But it was temporarily hidden by a rocky spur of the isle. As with some eagerness he bent forward, watching for the first shooting view of its beak, the balustrade gave way before him like charcoal. Had he not clutched an outreaching rope he would have fallen into the sea. The crash, though feeble, and the fall, though hollow, of the rotten fragments, must have been overheard. He glanced up. With sober curiosity peering down upon him was one of the old oakum-pickers, slipped from his perch to an outside boom; while below the old negro, and, invisible to him, reconnoitring from a port-hole like a fox from the mouth of its den, crouched the Spanish sailor again. From something suddenly suggested by the man's air, the mad idea now darted into Captain Delano's mind, that Don Benito's plea of indisposition, in withdrawing below, was but a pretence: that he was engaged there maturing his plot, of which the sailor, by some means gaining an inkling, had a mind to warn the stranger against; incited, it may be, by gratitude for a kind word on first boarding the ship. Was it from foreseeing some possible interference like this, that Don Benito had, beforehand, given such a bad character of his sailors, while praising the negroes; though, indeed, the former seemed as docile as the latter the contrary? The whites, too, by nature, were the shrewder race. A man with some evil design, would he not be likely to speak well of that stupidity which was blind to his depravity, and malign that intelligence from which it might not be hidden? Not unlikely, perhaps. But if the whites had dark secrets concerning Don Benito, could then Don Benito be any way in complicity with the blacks? But they were too stupid. Besides, who ever heard of a white so far a renegade as to apostatize from his very species almost, by leaguing in against it with negroes? These difficulties recalled former ones. Lost in their mazes, Captain Delano, who had now regained the deck, was uneasily advancing along it, when he observed a new face; an aged sailor seated cross-legged near the main hatchway. His skin was shrunk up with wrinkles like a pelican's empty pouch; his hair frosted; his countenance grave and composed. His hands were full of ropes, which he was working into a large knot. Some blacks were about him obligingly dipping the strands for him, here and there, as the exigencies of the operation demanded.

Captain Delano crossed over to him, and stood in silence surveying the knot; his mind, by a not uncongenial transition, passing from its own entanglements to those of the hemp. For intricacy, such a knot he had never seen in an American ship, nor indeed any other. The old man looked like an Egyptian priest, making Gordian knots for the temple of Ammon. The knot seemed a combination of double-bowline-knot, treble-crown-knot, back-handed-well-knot, knot-in-and-out-knot, and jamming knot.

At last, puzzled to comprehend the meaning of such a knot, Captain Delano addressed the knotter:—

"What are you knotting there, my man?"

"The knot," was the brief reply, without looking up.

"So it seems; but what is it for?"

"For some one else to undo," muttered back the old man, plying his fingers harder than ever, the knot being now nearly completed.

While Captain Delano stood watching him, suddenly the old man threw the knot towards him, saying in broken English—the first heard in the ship—something to this effect: "Undo it, cut it, quick." It was said lowly, but with such condensation of rapidity, that the long, slow words in Spanish, which had preceded and followed, almost operated as covers to the brief English between.

For a moment, knot in hand, and knot in head, Captain Delano stood mute; while, without further heeding him, the old man was now intent upon other ropes. Presently there was a slight stir behind Captain Delano. Turning, he saw the chained negro, Atufal, standing quietly there. The next moment the old sailor rose, muttering, and, followed by his subordinate negroes, removed to the forward part of the ship, where in the crowd he disappeared.

An elderly negro, in a clout like an infant's, with a pepper-and-salt head, and a kind of attorney air, now approached Captain Delano. In tolerable Spanish, and with a good-natured, knowing wink, he informed him that the old knotter was simple-witted, but harmless; often playing his odd tricks. The negro concluded by begging the knot, for of course the stranger would not care to be troubled with it. Unconsciously, it was handed to him. With a sort of congé, the negro received it, and, turning his back, ferreted into it like a detective custom-house officer after smuggled laces. Soon, with some African word, equivalent to pshaw, he tossed the knot overboard.

All this is very queer now; thought Captain Delano, with a qualmish sort of emotion; but, as one feeling incipient sea-sickness, he strove, by ignoring the symptoms, to get rid of the malady. Once more he looked off for his boat. To his delight, it was now again in view, leaving the rocky spur astern.

The sensation here experienced, after at first relieving his uneasiness, with unforeseen efficacy soon began to remove it. The less distant sight of that well-known boat—showing it, not as before, half blended with the haze, but with outline defined, so that its individuality, like a man's, was manifest; that boat,

*Rover* by name, which, though now in strange seas, had often pressed the beach of Captain Delano's home, and, brought to its threshold for repairs, had familiarly lain there, as a Newfoundland dog; the sight of that household boat evoked a thousand trustful associations, which, contrasted with previous suspicions, filled him not only with lightsome confidence, but somehow with half-humorous self-reproaches at his former lack of it.

"What, I, Amasa Delano—Jack of the Beach, as they called me when a lad—I, Amasa; the same that, duck-satchel in hand, used to paddle along the water-side to the school-house made from the old hulk—I, little Jack of the Beach, that used to go berrying with cousin Nat and the rest; I to be murdered here at the ends of the earth, on board a haunted pirate-ship by a horrible Spaniard? Too nonsensical to think of! Who would murder Amasa Delano? His conscience is clean. There is someone above. Fie, fie, Jack of the Beach! you are a child indeed; a child of the second childhood, old boy; you are beginning to dote and drool, I'm afraid."

Light of heart and foot, he stepped aft, and there was met by Don Benito's servant, who, with a pleasing expression, responsive to his own present feelings, informed him that his master had recovered from the effects of his coughing fit, and had just ordered him to go present his compliments to his good guest. Don Amasa, and say that he (Don Benito) would soon have the happiness to rejoin him.

There now, do you mark that? again thought Captain Delano, walking the poop. What a donkey I was. This kind gentleman who here sends me his kind compliments, he, but ten minutes ago, dark-lantern in hand, was dodging round some old grindstone in the hold, sharpening a hatchet for me, I thought. Well, well; these long calms have a morbid effect on the mind, I've often heard, though I never believed it before. Ha! glancing towards the boat; there's *Rover;* good dog; a white bone in her mouth. A pretty big bone though, seems to me.—What? Yes, she has fallen afoul of the bubbling tide-rip there. It sets her the other way, too, for the time. Patience.

It was now about noon, though, from the greyness of everything, it seemed to be getting towards dusk.

The calm was confirmed. In the far distance away from the influence of land, the leaden ocean seemed laid out and leaded up, its course finished, soul gone, defunct. But the current from landward, where the ship was, increased; silently sweeping her further and further towards the tranced waters beyond.

Still, from his knowledge of those latitudes, cherishing hopes of a breeze, and a fair and fresh one, at any moment, Captain Delano, despite present prospects, buoyantly counted upon bringing the *San Dominick* safely to anchor ere night. The distance swept over was nothing; since, with a good wind, ten minutes' sailing would retrace more than sixty minutes' drifting. Meantime, one moment turning to mark *Rover* fighting the tide-rip, and the next to see Don Benito approaching, he continued walking the poop.

Gradually he felt a vexation arising from the delay of his boat; this soon merged into uneasiness; and at last—his eye falling continually, as from a stage-box into the pit, upon the strange crowd before and below him, and, by and by, recognizing there the face—now composed to indifference—of the Spanish sailor who had seemed to beckon from the main-chains—something of his old trepidations returned.

Ah, thought he—gravely enough—this is like the ague: because it went off, it follows not that it won't come back.

Though ashamed of the relapse, he could not altogether subdue it; and so, exerting his good nature to the utmost, insensibly he came to a compromise.

Yes, this is a strange craft; a strange history, too, and strange folks on board. But—nothing more.

By way of keeping his mind out of mischief till the boat should arrive, he tried to occupy it with turning over and over, in a purely speculative sort of way, some lesser peculiarities of the captain and crew. Among others, four curious points recurred:

First, the affair of the Spanish lad assailed with a knife by the slave boy; an act winked at by Don Benito. Second, the tyranny in Don Benito's treatment of Atufal, the black, as if a child should lead a bull of the Nile by the ring in his nose. Third, the trampling of the sailor by the two negroes; a piece of insolence passed over without so much as a reprimand. Fourth, the cringing submission to their master, of all the ship's underlings, mostly blacks; as if by the least inadvertence they feared to draw down his despotic displeasure.

Coupling these points, they seemed somewhat contradictory. But what then, thought Captain Delano, glancing towards his now nearing boat—what then? Why, Don Benito is a very capricious commander. But he is not the first of the sort I have seen; though it's true he rather exceeds any other. But as a nation—continued he in his reveries—these Spaniards are all an odd set; the very word Spaniard has a curious, conspirator, Guy-Fawkish twang to it. And yet, I dare say, Spaniards in the main are as good folks as any in Duxbury, Massachusetts. Ah, good! At last *Rover* has come.

As, with its welcome freight, the boat touched the side, the oakum-pickers, with venerable gestures, sought to restrain the blacks, who, at the sight of three gurried water casks in its bottom, and a pile of wilted pumpkins in its bow, hung over the bulwarks in disorderly raptures.

Don Benito, with his servant, now appeared; his coming, perhaps, hastened by hearing the noise. Of him Captain Delano sought permission to serve out the water, so that all might share alike, and none injure themselves by unfair excess. But sensible, and, on Don Benito's account, kind as this offer was, it was received with what seemed impatience; as if aware that he lacked energy as a commander, Don Benito, with the true jealousy of weakness, resented as an affront any intereference. So, at least, Captain Delano inferred.

In another moment the casks were being hoisted in, when some of the eager negroes accidently jostled Captain Delano, where he stood by the gangway; so that, unmindful of Don Benito, yielding to the impulse of the moment, with good-natured authority he bade the blacks stand back; to enforce his words making use of a half-mirthful, half-menacing gesture. Instantly the blacks paused, just where they were, each negro and negress suspended in his or her posture, exactly as the word had found them—for a few seconds continuing so—while, as between the responsive posts of a telegraph, an unknown syllable ran from man to man among the perched oakum-pickers. While the visitor's attention was fixed by this scene, suddenly the hatchet-polishers half rose, and a rapid cry came from Don Benito.

Thinking that at the signal of the Spaniard he was about to be massacred, Captain Delano would have sprung for his boat, but paused, as the oakum-pickers, dropping down into the crowd with earnest exclamations, forced every white and every negro back, at the same moment, with gestures friendly and familiar, almost jocose, bidding him, in substance, not be a fool. Simultaneously the hatchet-polishers resumed their seats, quietly as so many tailors, and at once, as if nothing had happened, the work of hoisting in the casks was resumed, whites and black singing at the tackle.

Captain Delano glanced towards Don Benito. As he saw his meagre form in the act of recovering itself from reclining in the servant's arms, into which the agitated invalid had fallen, he could not but marvel at the panic by which himself had been surprised, on the darting supposition that such a commander, who, upon a legitimate occasion, so trivial, too, as it now appeared, could lose all self-command, was, with energetic iniquity, going to bring about his murder.

The casks being on deck, Captain Delano was handed a number of jars and cups by one of the steward's aids, who, in the name of his captain, entreated him to do as he had proposed—dole out the water. He complied, with republican impartiality as to this republican element, which always seeks one level, serving the oldest white no better than the youngest black; excepting, indeed, poor Don Benito, whose condition, if not rank, demanded an extra allowance. To him, in the first place, Captain Delano presented a fair pitcher of the fluid; but, thirsting as he was for it, the Spaniard quaffed not a drop until after several grave bows and salutes. A reciprocation of courtesies which the sight-loving Africans hailed with clapping of hands.

Two of the less wilted pumpkins being reserved for the cabin table, the residue were minced up on the spot for the general regalement. But the soft bread, sugar, and bottled cider, Captain Delano would have given the whites alone, and in chief Don Benito; but the latter objected; which disinterestedness not a little pleased the American; and so mouthfuls all around were given alike to whites and blacks; excepting one bottle of cider, which Babo insisted upon setting aside for his master.

Here it may be observed that as, on the first visit of the boat, the American had not permitted his men to board the ship, neither did he now; being unwilling to add to the confusion of the decks.

Not uninfluenced by the peculiar good-humor at present prevailing, and for the time oblivious of any but benevolent thoughts, Captain Delano, who, from recent indications, counted upon a breeze within an hour or two at furthest, dispatched the boat back to the sealer, with orders for all the hands that could be spared immediately to set about rafting casks to the watering-place and filling them. Likewise he bade word be carried to his chief officer, that if, against present expectation, the ship was not brought to anchor by sunset, he need be under no concern; for as there was to be a full moon that night, he (Captain Delano) would remain on board ready to play the pilot, come the wind soon or late.

As the two captains stood together, observing the departing boat—the servant, as it happened, having just spied a spot on his master's velvet sleeve, and silently engaged rubbing it out—the American expressed his regrets that the *San Dominick* had no boats; none, at least, but the unseaworthy old hulk of the long-boat, which, warped as a camel's sketeton in the desert, and almost as bleached, lay pot-wise inverted amid-ships, one side a little tipped, furnishing a subterraneous sort of den for family groups of the blacks, mostly women and small children; who, squatting on old mats below, or perched above in the dark dome, on the elevated seats, were descried, some distance within, like a social circle of bats, sheltering in some friendly cave; at intervals, ebon flights of naked boys and girls, three or four years old, darting in and out of the den's mouth.

"Had you three or four boats now, Don Benito," said Captain Delano, "I think that, by tugging at the oars, your negroes here might help along matters some. Did you sail from port without boats, Don Benito?"

"They were stove in the gales, Señor."

"That was bad. Many men, too, you lost then. Boats and men. Those must have been hard gales, Don Benito."

"Past all speech," cringed the Spaniard.

"Tell me, Don Benito," continued his companion with increased interest, "tell me, were these gales immediately off the pitch of Cape Horn?"

"Cape Horn?—who spoke of Cape Horn?"

"Yourself did, when giving me an account of your voyage," answered Captain Delano, with almost equal astonishment at this eating of his own words, even as he ever seemed eating his own heart, on the part of the Spaniard. "You yourself, Don Benito, spoke of Cape Horn," he emphatically repeated.

The Spaniard turned, in a sort of stooping posture, pausing an instant, as one about to make a plunging exchange of elements, as from air to water.

At this moment a messenger-boy, a white, hurried by, in the regular performance of his function carrying the last expired half-hour forward to the forecastle, from the cabin time-piece, to have it struck at the ship's large bell.

"Master," said the servant, discontinuing his work on the coat sleeve, and addressing the rapt Spaniard with a sort of timid apprehensiveness, as one charged with a duty, the discharge of which, it was foreseen, would prove irksome to the very person who had imposed it, and for whose benefit it was intended, "master told me never mind where he was, or how engaged, always to remind him, to a minute, when shaving-time comes. Miguel has gone to strike the half-hour afternoon. It is *now*, master. Will master go into the cuddy?"

"Ah—yes," answered the Spaniard, starting, as from dreams into realities; then turning upon Captain Delano, he said that ere long he would resume the conversation.

"Then if master means to talk more to Don Amasa," said the servant, "why not let Don Amasa sit by master in the cuddy, and master can talk, and Don Amasa can listen, while Babo here lathers and strops."

"Yes," said Captain Delano, not unpleased with this sociable plan, "yes, Don Benito, unless you had rather not, I will go with you."

"Be it so, Señor."

As the three passed aft, the American could not but think it another strange instance of his host's capriciousness, this being shaved with such uncommon punctuality in the middle of the day. But he deemed it more than likely that the servant's anxious fidelity had something to do with the matter; inasmuch as the timely interruption served to rally his master from the mood which had evidently been coming upon him.

The place called the cuddy was a light deck-cabin formed by the poop, a sort of attic to the large cabin below. Part of it had formerly been the quarters of the officers; but since their death all the partitionings had been thrown down, and the whole interior converted into one spacious and airy marine hall; for absence of fine furniture and picturesque disarray of odd appurtenances, somewhat answering to the wide, cluttered hall of some eccentric bachelor-squire in the country, who hangs his shooting-jacket and tobacco-pouch on deer antlers, and keeps his fishing-rod, tongs, and walking-stick in the same corner.

The similitude was heightened, if not originally suggested, by glimpses of the surrounding sea; since, in one aspect, the country and the ocean seem cousins-german.

The floor of the cuddy was matted. Overhead, four or five old muskets were stuck into horizontal holes along the beams. On one side was a clawfooted old table lashed to the deck; a thumbed missal on it, and over it a small, meagre crucifix attached to the bulk-head. Under the table lay a dented cutlass or two, with a hacked harpoon, among some melancholy old rigging, like a heap of poor friars' girdles. There were also two long, sharp, ribbed settees of Malacca cane, black with age, and uncomfortable to look at as inquisitors' racks, with a large, misshapen arm-chair, which, furnished with a rude barber's crotch at the back, working with a screw, seemed some grotesque engine of torment. A flag-locker was in one corner, open, exposing various coloured bunting, some rolled up, others half unrolled, still others tumbled. Opposite was a cumbrous washstand, of black mahogany, all of one block, with a pedestal, like a font, and over it a railed shelf, containing combs, brushes, and other implements of the toilet. A torn hammock of stained grass swung near; the sheets tossed, and the pillow wrinkled up like a brow, as if whoever slept here slept but illy, with alternate visitations of sad thoughts and bad dreams.

The further extremity of the cuddy, overhanging the ship's stern, was pierced with three openings, windows or port-holes, according as men or cannon might peer, socially or unsocially, out of them. At present neither men nor cannon were seen, though huge ring-bolts and other rusty iron fixtures of the woodwork hinted of twenty-four-pounders.

Glancing towards the hammock as he entered, Captain Delano said, "You sleep here, Don Benito?"

"Yes, Señor, since we got into mild weather."

"This seems a sort of dormitory, sitting-room, sail-loft, chapel, armoury, and private closet altogether, Don Benito," added Captain Delano, looking round.

"Yes, Señor; events have not been favourable to much order in my arrangements."

Here the servant, napkin on arm, made a motion as if waiting his master's good pleasure. Don Benito signified his readiness, when, seating him in the

Malacca arm-chair, and for the guest's convenience drawing opposite one of the settees, the servant commenced operations by throwing back his master's collar and loosening his cravat.

There is something in the negro which, in a peculiar way, fits him for avocations about one's person. Most negroes are natural valets and hair-dressers; taking to the comb and brush congenially as to the castanets, and flourishing them apparently with almost equal satisfaction. There is, too, a smooth tact about them in this employment, with a marvellous, noiseless, gliding briskness, not ungraceful in its way, singularly pleasing to behold, and still more so to be the manipulated subject of. And above all is the great gift of good-humour. Not the mere grin or laugh is here meant. Those were unsuitable. But a certain easy cheerfulness, harmonious in every glance and gesture; as though God had set the whole negro to some pleasant tune.

When to this is added the docility arising from the unaspiring contentment of a limited mind, and that susceptibility of blind attachment sometimes inhering in indisputable inferiors, one readily perceives why those hypochondriacs, Johnson and Byron—it may be, something like the hypochondriac Benito Cereno—took to their hearts, almost to the exclusion of the entire white race, their serving men, the negroes, Barber and Fletcher. But if there be that in the negro which exempts him from the inflicted sourness of the morbid or cynical mind, how, in his most prepossessing aspects, must he appear to a benevolent one? When at ease with respect to exterior things, Captain Delano's nature was not only benign, but familiarly and humorously so. At home, he had often taken rare satisfaction in sitting in his door, watching some free man of colour at his work or play. If on a voyage he chanced to have a black sailor, invariably he was on chatty and half-gamesome terms with him. In fact, like most men of a good, blithe heart, Captain Delano took to negroes, not philanthropically, but genially, just as other men to Newfoundland dogs.

Hitherto, the circumstances in which he found the *San Dominick* had repressed the tendency. But in the cuddy, relieved from his former uneasiness, and, for various reasons, more sociably inclined than at any previous period of the day, and seeing the coloured servant, napkin on arm, so debonair about his master, in a business so familiar as that of shaving, too, all his old weakness for negroes returned.

Among other things, he was amused with an odd instance of the African love of bright colours and fine shows, in the black's informally taking from the flag-locker a great piece of bunting of all hues, and lavishly tucking it under his master's chin for an apron.

The mode of shaving among the Spaniards is a little different from what it is with other nations. They have a basin, specifically called a barber's basin, which on one side is scooped out, so as accurately to receive the chin, against which it is closely held in lathering; which is done, not with a brush, but with soap dipped in the water of the basin and rubbed on the face.

In the present instance salt-water was used for lack of better; and the parts lathered were only the upper lip, and low down under the throat, all the rest being cultivated beard.

The preliminaries being somewhat novel to Captain Delano, he sat curiously eyeing them, so that no conversation took place, nor, for the present, did Don Benito appear disposed to renew any.

Setting down his basin, the negro searched among the razors, as for the sharpest, and having found it, gave it an additional edge by expertly stropping it on the firm, smooth, oily skin of his open palm; he then made a gesture as if to begin, but midway stood suspended for an instant, one hand elevating the razor, the other professionally dabbling among the bubbling suds on the Spaniard's lank neck. Not unaffected by the close sight of the gleaming steel, Don Benito nervously shuddered; his usual ghastliness was heightened by the lather, which lather, again, was intensified in its hue by the contrasting sootiness of the negro's body. Altogether the scene was somewhat peculiar, at least to Captain Delano, nor, as he saw the two thus postured, could he resist the vagary, that in the black he saw a headsman, and in the white a man at the block. But this was one of those antic conceits, appearing and vanishing in a breath, from which, perhaps, the best regulated mind is not always free.

Meantime the agitation of the Spaniard had a little loosened the bunting from around him, so that one broad fold swept curtain-like over the chair-arm to the floor, revealing, amid a profusion of armorial bars and ground-colours—black, blue, and yellow—a closed castle in a blood-red field diagonal with a lion rampant in a white.

"The castle and the lion," exclaimed Captain Delano—"why, Don Benito, this is the flag of Spain you use here. It's well it's only I, and not the King, that see this," he added, with a smile, "but,"—turning towards the black—"it's all one, I suppose, so the colours be gay," which playful remark did not fail somewhat to tickle the negro.

"Now, master," he said, readjusting the flag, and pressing the head gently further back into the crotch of the chair; "now, master," and the steel glanced nigh that throat.

Again Don Benito faintly shuddered.

"You must not shake so, master. See, Don Amasa, master always shakes when I shave him. And yet master knows I never yet have drawn blood, though it's true, if master will shake so, I may some of these times. Now, master," he continued. "And now, Don Amasa, please go on with your talk about the gale, and all that; master can hear, and, between times, master can answer."

"Ah yes, these gales," said Captain Delano; "but the more I think of your voyage, Don Benito, the more I wonder, not at the gales, terrible as they must have been, but at the disastrous interval following them. For here, by your account, have you been these two months and more getting from Cape Horn to Santa Maria, a distance which I myself, with a good wind, have sailed in a few days. True, you had calms, and long ones, but to be becalmed for two months, that is, at least, unusual. Why, Don Benito, had almost any other gentleman told me such a story, I should have been half disposed to a little incredulity."

Here an involuntary expression came over the Spaniard, similiar to that just before on the deck, and whether it was the start he gave, or a sudden gawky roll of the hull in the calm, or a momentary unsteadiness of the servant's hand, however it was, just then the razor drew blood, spots of which stained the creamy lather under the throat: immediately the black barber drew back his steel, and, remaining in his professional attitude, back to Captain Delano, and face to Don Benito, held up the trickling razor, saying, with a sort of half-humorous sorrow, "See, master—you shook so—here's Babo's first blood."

No sword drawn before James the First of England, no assassination in that timid King's presence, could have produced a more terrified aspect than was now presented by Don Benito.

Poor fellow, thought Captain Delano, so nervous he can't even bear the sight of barber's blood; and this unstrung, sick man, is it credible that I should have imagined he meant to spill all my blood, who can't endure the sight of one little drop of his own? Surely, Amasa Delano, you have been beside yourself this day. Tell it not when you get home, sappy Amasa. Well, he looks like a murderer, doesn't he? More like as if himself were to be done for. Well, well, this day's experience shall be a good lesson.

Meantime, while these things were running through the honest seaman's mind, the servant had taken the napkin from under his arm, and to Don Benito had said—"But answer Don Amasa, please, master, while I wipe this ugly stuff off the razor, and strop it again."

As he said the words, his face was turned half round, so as to be alike visible to the Spaniard and the American, and seemed, by its expression, to hint, that he was desirous, by getting his master to go on with the conversation, considerately to withdraw his attention from the recent annoying accident. As if glad to snatch the offered relief, Don Benito resumed, rehearsing to Captain Delano, that not only were the calms of unusual duration, but the ship had fallen in with obstinate currents; and other things he added, some of which were but repetitions of former statements, to explain how it came to pass that the passage from Cape Horn to Santa Maria had been so exceedingly long; now and then mingling with his words, incidental praises, less qualified than before, to the blacks, for their general good conduct. These particulars were not given consecutively, the servant, at convenient times, using his razor, and so, between the intervals of shaving, the story and panegyric went on with more than usual huskiness.

To Captain Delano's imagination, now again not wholly at rest, there was something so hollow in the Spaniard's manner, with apparently some reciprocal hollowness in the servant's dusky comment of silence, that the idea flashed across him, that possibly master and man, for some unknown purpose, were acting out, both in word and deed, nay, to the very tremor of Don Benito's limbs, some juggling play before him. Neither did the suspicion of collusion lack apparent support, from the fact of those whispered conferences before mentioned. But then, what could be the object of enacting this play of the barber before him? At last, regarding the notion as a whimsy, insensibly suggested, perhaps, by the theatrical aspect of Don Benito in his harlequin ensign, Captain Delano speedily banished it.

The shaving over, the servant bestirred himself with a small bottle of scented waters, pouring a few drops on the head, and then diligently rubbing; the vehemence of the exercise causing the muscles of his face to twitch rather strangely.

His next operation was with comb, scissors, and brush; going round and round, smoothing a curl here, clipping an unruly whisker-hair there, giving a graceful sweep to the temple-lock, with other impromptu touches evincing the hand of a master; while, like any resigned gentleman in barber's hands, Don Benito bore all, much less uneasily, at least, than he had done the razoring; indeed, he sat so pale and rigid now, that the negro seemed a Nubian sculptor finishing off a white statue-head.

All being over at the last, the standard of Spain removed, tumbled up, and tossed back into the flag-locker, the negro's warm breath blowing away any stray hair which might have lodged down his master's neck; collar and cravat readjusted; a speck of lint whisked off the velvet lapel; all this being done, backing off a little space, and pausing with an expression of subdued self-complacency, the servant for a moment surveyed his master, as, in toilet at least, the creature of his own tasteful hands.

Captain Delano playfully complimented him upon his achievement; at the same time congratulating Don Benito.

But neither sweet waters, nor shampooing, nor fidelity, nor sociality, delighted the Spaniard. Seeing him relapsing into forbidding gloom, and still remaining seated, Captain Delano, thinking that his presence was undesired just then, withdrew, on pretence of seeing whether, as he had prophesied, any signs of a breeze were visible.

Walking forward to the main-mast, he stood awhile thinking over the scene, and not without some undefined misgivings, when he heard a noise near the cuddy, and turning, saw the negro, his hand to his cheek. Advancing, Captain Delano perceived that the cheek was bleeding. He was about to ask the cause, when the negro's wailing soliloquy enlightened him.

"Ah, when will master get better from his sickness; only the sour heart that sour sickness breeds made him serve Babo so; cutting Babo with the razor, because, only by accident, Babo had given master one little scratch; and for the first time in so many a day, too. Ah, ah, ah," holding his hand to his face.

It is possible, thought Captain Delano; was it to wreak in private his Spanish spite against this poor friend of his, that Don Benito, by his sullen manner, impelled me to withdraw? Ah, this slavery breeds ugly passions in man.—Poor fellow!

He was about to speak in sympathy to the negro, but with a timid reluctance he now re-entered the cuddy.

Presently master and man came forth; Don Benito leaning on his servant as if nothing had happened.

But a sort of love-quarrel, after all, thought Captain Delano.

He accosted Don Benito, and they slowly walked together. They had gone but a few paces, when the steward—a tall, rajah-looking mulatto, orientally set off with a pagoda turban formed by three or four Madras handkerchiefs wound about his head, tier on tier—approaching with a salaam, announced lunch in the cabin.

On their way thither, the two captains were preceded by the mulatto, who, turning round as he advanced, with continual smiles and bows, ushered them on, a display of elegance which quite completed the insignificance of the small bare-headed Babo, who, as if not unconscious of inferiority, eyed askance the graceful steward. But in part, Captain Delano imputed his jealous watchfulness to that peculiar feeling which the full-blooded African entertains from the adulterated one. As for the steward, his manner, if not bespeaking much dignity of self-respect, yet evidenced his extreme desire to please; which is doubly meritorious, as at once Christian and Chesterfieldian.

Captain Delano observed with interest that while the complexion of the mulatto was hybrid, his physiognomy was European—classically so.

"Don Benito," whispered he, "I am glad to see this usher-of-the-golden-rod of yours; the sight refutes an ugly remark once made to me by a Barbados planter; that when a mulatto has a regular European face, look out for him; he is a devil. But see, your steward here has features more regular than King George's of England; and yet there he nods, and bows, and smiles; a king, indeed—the king of kind hearts and polite fellows. What a pleasant voice he has, too."

"He has, Señor."

"But tell me, has he not, so far as you have known him, always proved a good, worthy fellow?" said Captain Delano, pausing, while with a final genuflection the steward disappeared into the cabin; "come, for the reason just mentioned, I am curious to know."

"Francesco is a good man," sort of sluggishly responded Don Benito, like a phlegmatic appreciator, who would neither find fault nor flatter.

"Ah, I thought so. For it were strange, indeed, and not very creditable to us white-skins, if a little of our blood mixed with the African's, should, far from improving the latter's quality, have the sad effect of pouring vitriolic acid into black broth; improving the hue, perhaps, but not the wholesomeness."

"Doubtless, doubtless, Señor, but,"—glancing at Babo—"not to speak of negroes, your planter's remark I have heard applied to the Spanish and Indian intermixtures in our provinces. But I know nothing about the matter," he listlessly added.

And here they entered the cabin.

The lunch was a frugal one. Some of Captain Delano's fresh fish and pumpkins, biscuit and salt beef, the reserved bottle of cider, and the *San Dominick*'s last bottle of Canary.

As they entered, Francesco, with two or three coloured aids, was hovering over the table giving the last adjustments. Upon perceiving their master they withdrew, Francesco making a smiling congé, and the Spaniard, without condescending to notice it, fastidiously remarking to his companion that he relished not superfluous attendance.

Without companions, host and guest sat down, like a childless married couple, at opposite ends of the table, Don Benito waving Captain Delano to his place, and, weak as he was, insisting upon that gentleman being seated before himself.

The negro placed a rug under Don Benito's feet, and a cushion behind his back, and then stood behind, not his master's chair, but Captain Delano's. At

first, this a little surprised the latter. But it was soon evident that, in taking his position, the black was still true to his master; since by facing him he could the more readily anticipate his slightest want.

"This is an uncommonly intelligent fellow of yours, Don Benito," whispered Captain Delano across the table.

"You say true, Señor."

During the repast, the guest again reverted to parts of Don Benito's story, begging further particulars here and there. He inquired how it was that the scurvy and fever should have committed such wholesale havoc upon the whites, while destroying less than half the blacks. As if this question reproduced the whole scenes of plague before the Spaniard's eyes, miserably reminding him of his solitude in a cabin where before he had had so many friends and officers round him, his hand shook, his face became hueless, broken words escaped; but directly the same memory of the past seemed replaced by insane terrors of the present. With starting eyes he stared before him at vacancy. For nothing was to be seen but the hand of his servant pushing the Canary over towards him. At length a few sips served partially to restore him. He made random reference to the different constitution of races, enabling one to offer more resistance to certain maladies than another. The thought was new to his companion.

Presently Captain Delano, intending to say something to his host concerning the pecuniary part of the business he had undertaken for him, especially—since he was strictly accountable to his owners—with reference to the new suite of sails, and other things of that sort; and naturally preferring to conduct such affairs in private, was desirous that the servant should withdraw; imagining that Don Benito for a few minutes could dispense with his attendance. He, however, waited awhile; thinking that, as the conversation proceeded, Don Benito, without being prompted, would perceive the propriety of the step.

But it was otherwise. At last catching his host's eye, Captain Delano, with a slight backward gesture of his thumb, whispered, "Don Benito, pardon me, but there is interference with the full expression of what I have to say to you."

Upon this the Spaniard changed countenance; which was imputed to his resenting the hint, as in some way a reflection upon his servant. After a moment's pause, he assured his guest that the black's remaining with them could be of no disservice; because since losing his officers he had made Babo (whose original office, it now appeared, had been captain of the slaves) not only his constant attendant and companion, but in all things his confidant.

After this, nothing more could be said; though, indeed, Captain Delano could hardly avoid some little tinge of irritation upon being left ungratified in so inconsiderable a wish, by one, too, for whom he intended such solid services. But it is only his querulousness, thought he; and so filling his glass he proceeded to business.

The price of the sails and other matters were fixed upon. But while this was being done, the American observed that, though his original offer of assistance had been hailed with hectic animation, yet now, when it was reduced to a

business transaction, indifference and apathy were betrayed. Don Benito, in fact, appeared to submit to hearing the details more out of regard to common propriety, than from any impression that weighty benefit to himself and his voyage was involved.

Soon, his manner became still more reserved. The effort was vain to seek to draw him into social talk. Gnawed by his splenetic mood, he sat twitching his beard, while to little purpose the hand of his servant, mute as that on the wall, slowly pushed over the Canary.

Lunch being over, they sat down on the cushioned transom; the servant placing a pillow behind his master. The long continuance of the calm had now affected the atmosphere. Don Benito sighed heavily, as if for breath.

"Why not adjourn to the cuddy?" said Captain Delano. "There is more air there." But the host sat silent and motionless.

Meantime his servant knelt before him, with a large fan of feathers. And Francesco coming in on tiptoes, handed the negro a little cup of aromatic waters, with which at intervals he chafed his master's brow; smoothing the hair along the temples as a nurse does a child's. He spoke no word. He only rested his eye on his master's, as if, amid all Don Benito's distress, a little to refresh his spirit by the silent sight of fidelity.

Presently the ship's bell sounded two o'clock; and through the cabin windows a slight rippling of the sea was discerned; and from the desired direction.

"There," exclaimed Captain Delano, "I told you so, Don Benito, look!"

He had risen to his feet, speaking in a very animated tone, with a view the more to rouse his companion. But though the crimson curtain of the stern-window near him that moment fluttered against his pale cheek, Don Benito seemed to have even less welcome for the breeze than the calm.

Poor fellow, thought Captain Delano, bitter experience has taught him that one ripple does not make a wind, any more than one swallow a summer. But he is mistaken for once. I will get his ship in for him, and prove it.

Briefly alluding to his weak condition, he urged his host to remain quietly where he was, since he (Captain Delano) would with pleasure take upon himself the responsibility of making the best use of the wind.

Upon gaining the deck, Captain Delano started at the unexpected figure of Atufal, monumentally fixed at the threshold, like one of those sculptured porters of black marble guarding the porches of Egyptian tombs.

But this time the start was, perhaps, purely physical. Atufal's presence, singularly attesting docility even in sullenness, was contrasted with that of the hatchet-polishers, who in patience evinced their industry; while both spectacles showed, that lax as Don Benito's general authority might be, still, whenever he chose to exert it, no man so savage or colossal but must, more or less, bow.

Snatching a trumpet which hung from the bulwarks, with a free step Captain Delano advanced to the forward edge of the poop, issuing his orders in his best Spanish. The few sailors and many negroes, all equally pleased, obediently set about heading the ship towards the harbour.

While giving some directions about setting a lower stu'n-sail, suddenly Captain Delano heard a voice faithfully repeating his orders. Turning, he saw

Babo, now for the time acting, under the pilot, his original part of the captain of the slaves. This assistance proved valuable. Tattered sails and warped yards were soon brought into some trim. And no brace or halyard was pulled but to the blithe songs of the inspirited negroes.

Good fellows, thought Captain Delano, a little training would make fine sailors of them. Why see, the very women pull and sing too. These must be some of those Ashantee negresses that make such capital soldiers, I've heard. But who's at the helm? I must have a good hand there.

He went to see.

The *San Dominick* steered with a cumbrous tiller, with large horizontal pulleys attached. At each pulley-end stood a subordinate black, and between them, at the tiller-head, the responsible post, a Spanish seaman, whose countenance evinced his due share in the general hopefulness and confidence at the oncoming of the breeze.

He proved the same man who had behaved with so shame-faced an air on the windlass.

"Ah,—it is you, my man," exclaimed Captain Delano—"well, no more sheep's eyes now;—look straight forward and keep the ship so. Good hand, I trust? And want to get into the harbour, don't you?

The man assented with an inward chuckle, grasping the tiller-head firmly. Upon this, unperceived by the American, the two blacks eyed the sailor intently.

Finding all right at the helm, the pilot went forward to the forecastle, to see how matters stood there.

The ship now had way enough to breast the current. With the approach of evening, the breeze would be sure to freshen.

Having done all that was needed for the present, Captain Delano, giving his last orders to the sailors, turned aft to report affairs to Don Benito in the cabin; perhaps additionally incited to rejoin him by the hope of snatching a moment's private chat while the servant was engaged upon deck.

From opposite sides, there were, beneath the poop, two approaches to the cabin; one further forward than the other, and consequently communicating with a longer passage. Marking the servant still above, Captain Delano, taking the nighest entrance—the one last named, and at whose porch Atufal still stood—hurried on his way, till, arrived at the cabin threshold, he paused an instant, a little to recover from his eagerness. Then, with the words of his intended business upon his lips, he entered. As he advanced toward the seated Spaniard, he heard another footstep, keeping time with his. From the opposite door, a salver in hand, the servant was likewise advancing.

"Confound the faithful fellow," thought Captain Delano; "what a vexatious coincidence."

Possibly, the vexation might have been something different, were it not for the brisk confidence inspired by the breeze. But even as it was, he felt a slight twinge, from a sudden indefinite association in his mind of Babo with Atufal.

"Don Benito," said he, "I give you joy; the breeze will hold, and will increase. By the way, your tall man and time-piece, Atufal, stands without. By your order, of course?"

Don Benito recoiled, as if at some bland satirical touch, delivered with such adroit garnish of apparent good breeding as to present no handle for retort.

He is like one flayed alive, thought Captain Delano; where may one touch him without causing a shrink?

The servant moved before his master, adjusting a cushion; recalled to civility, the Spaniard stiffly replied: "You are right. The slave appears where you saw him, according to my command; which is, that if at the given hour I am below, he must take his stand and abide my coming."

"Ah now, pardon me, but that is treating the poor fellow like an ex-king indeed. Ah, Don Benito," smiling, "for all the licence you permit in some things, I fear lest, at bottom, you are a bitter hard master."

Again Don Benito shrank; and this time, as the good sailor thought, from a genuine twinge of his conscience.

Again conversation became constrained. In vain Captain Delano called attention to the now perceptible motion of the keel gently cleaving the sea; with lack-lustre eye, Don Benito returned words few and reserved.

By and by, the wind having steadily risen, and still blowing right into the harbour, bore the *San Dominick* swiftly on. Rounding a point of land, the sealer at a distance came into open view.

Meantime Captain Delano had again repaired to the deck, remaining there some time. Having at last altered the ship's course, so as to give the reef a wide berth, he returned for a few moments below.

I will cheer up my poor friend, this time, thought he.

"Better and better, Don Benito," he cried as he blithely re-entered: "there will soon be an end to your cares, at least for a while. For when, after a long, sad voyage, you know, the anchor drops into the haven, all its vast weight seems lifted from the captain's heart. We are getting on famously, Don Benito. My ship is in sight. Look through this side-light here; there she is, all a-taunt-o! The *Bachelor's Delight*, my good friend. Ah, how this wind braces one up. Come, you must take a cup of coffee with me this evening. My old steward will give you as fine a cup as ever any sultan tasted. What say you, Don Benito, will you?"

At first, the Spaniard glanced feverishly up, casting a longing look towards the sealer, while with mute concern his servant gazed into his face. Suddenly the old ague of coldness returned, and dropping back to his cushions he was silent.

"You do not answer. Come, all day you have been my host; would you have hospitality all on one side?"

"I cannot go," was the response.

"What? It will not fatigue you. The ships will lie together as near as they can, without swinging foul. It will be little more than stepping from deck to deck; which is but as from room to room. Come, come, you must not refuse me."

"I cannot go," decisively and repulsively repeated Don Benito.

Renouncing all but the last appearance of courtesy, with a sort of cadaverous sullenness, and biting his thin nails to the quick he glanced, almost glared, at his guest, as if impatient that a stranger's presence should interfere with the full indulgence of his morbid hour. Meantime the sound of the parted waters came more and more gurglingly and merrily in at the windows; as reproaching

him for his dark spleen; as telling him that, sulk as he might, and go mad with it, nature cared not a jot; since, whose fault was it, pray?

But the foul mood was now at its depth, as the fair wind at its height.

There was something in the man so far beyond any mere unsociality or sourness previously evinced, that even the forebearing good-nature of his guest could no longer endure it. Wholly at a loss to account for such demeanour, and deeming sickness with eccentricity, however extreme, no adequate excuse, well satisfied, too, that nothing in his own conduct could justify it, Captain Delano's pride began to be roused. Himself became reserved. But all seemed one to the Spaniard. Quitting him, therefore, Captain Delano once more went to the deck.

The ship was now within less than two miles of the sealer. The whale-boat was seen darting over the interval.

To be brief, the two vessels, thanks to the pilot's skill, ere long in neighbourly style lay anchored together.

Before returning to his own vessel, Captain Delano had intended communicating to Don Benito the smaller details of the proposed services to be rendered. But, as it was, unwilling anew to subject himself to rebuffs, he resolved, now that he had seen the *San Dominick* safely moored, immediately to quit her, without further allusion to hospitality or business. Indefinitely postponing his ulterior plans, he would regulate his future actions according to future circumstances. His boat was ready to receive him; but his host still tarried below. Well, thought Captain Delano, if he has little breeding, the more need to show mine. He descended to the cabin to bid a ceremonious, and it may be, tacitly rebukeful adieu. But to his great satisfaction, Don Benito, as if he began to feel the weight of that treatment with which his slighted guest had, not indecorously, retaliated upon him, now supported by his servant, rose to his feet, and grasping Captain Delano's hand, stood tremulous; too much agitated to speak. But the good augury hence drawn was suddenly dashed, by his resuming all his previous reserve, with augmented gloom, as, with half-averted eyes, he silently reseated himself on his cushions. With a corresponding return of his own chilled feelings, Captain Delano bowed and withdrew.

He was hardly midway in the narrow corridor, dim as a tunnel, leading from the cabin to the stairs, when a sound, as of the tolling for execution in some jail-yard, fell on his ears. It was the echo of the ship's flawed bell, striking the hour, drearily reverberated in this subterranean vault. Instantly, by a fatality not to be withstood, his mind, responsive to the portent, swarmed with superstitious suspicions. He paused. In images far swifter than these sentences, the minutest details of all his former distrusts swept through him.

Hitherto, credulous good-nature had been too ready to furnish excuses for reasonable fears. Why was the Spaniard, so superfluously punctilious at times, now heedless of common propriety in not accompanying to the side his departing guest? Did indisposition forbid? Indisposition had not forbidden more irksome exertion that day. His last equivocal demeanour recurred. He had risen to his feet, grasped his guest's hand, motioned toward his hat; then, in an instant, all was eclipsed in sinister muteness and gloom. Did this imply one brief, repentant relenting at the final moment, from some iniquitous plot, followed by remorseless return to it? His last glance seemed to express a calamitous, yet acquiescent farewell to Captain Delano forever. Why decline the invitation to visit the sealer that evening? Or was the Spaniard less hardened than the Jew, who refrained not from supping at the board of him whom the same night he meant to betray? What imported all those day-long enigmas and contradictions, except they were intended to mystify, preliminary to some stealthy blow? Atufal, the pretended rebel, but punctual shadow, that moment lurked by the threshold without. He seemed a sentry, and more. Who, by his own confession, had stationed him there? Was the negro now lying in wait?

The Spaniard behind—his creature before: to rush from darkness to light was the involuntary choice.

The next moment, with clenched jaw and hand, he passed Atufal, and stood unharmed in the light. As he saw his trim ship lying peacefully at anchor, and almost within ordinary call; as he saw his household boat, with familiar faces in it, patiently rising and falling on the short waves by the *San Dominick*'s side; and then, glancing about the decks where he stood, saw the oakum-pickers still gravely plying their fingers; and heard the low, buzzing whistle and industrious hum of the hatchet-polishers, still bestirring themselves over their endless occupation; and more than all, as he saw the benign aspect of nature, taking her innocent repose in the evening; the screened sun in the quiet camp of the west shining out like the mild light from Abraham's tent; as charmed eye and ear took in all these, with the chained figure of the black, clenched jaw and hand relaxed. Once again he smiled at the phantoms which had mocked him, and felt something like a tinge of remorse, that, by harbouring them even for a moment, he should, by implication, have betrayed an atheist doubt of the ever-watchful Providence above.

There was a few minutes' delay, while, in obedience to his orders, the boat was being hooked along to the gangway. During this interval, a sort of saddened satisfaction stole over Captain Delano, at thinking of the kindly offices he had that day discharged for a stranger. Ah, thought he, after good actions one's conscience is never ungrateful, however much so the benefitted party may be.

Presently, his foot, in the first act of descent into the boat, pressed the first round of the side-ladder, his face presented inward upon the deck. In the same moment, he heard his name courteously sounded; and, to his pleased surprise, saw Don Benito advancing—an unwonted energy in his air, as if, at the last moment, intent upon making amends for his recent discourtesy. With instinctive good feeling, Captain Delano, withdrawing his foot, turned and reciprocally advanced. As he did so, the Spaniard's nervous eagerness increased, but his vital energy failed; so that, the better to support him, the servant, placing his master's hand on his naked shoulder, and gently holding it there, formed himself into a sort of crutch.

When the two captains met, the Spaniard again fervently took the hand of the American, at the same time casting an earnest glance into his eyes, but, as before, too much overcome to speak.

I have done him wrong, self-reproachfully thought Captain Delano; his apparent coldness has deceived me; in no instance has he meant to offend.

Meantime, as if fearful that the continuance of the scene might too much unstring his master, the servant seemed anxious to terminate it. And so still presenting himself as a crutch, and walking between the two captains, he advanced with them towards the gangway; while still, as if full of kindly contrition, Don Benito would not let go the hand of Captain Delano, but retained it in his, across the black's body.

Soon they were standing by the side, looking over into the boat, whose crew turned up their curious eyes. Waiting a moment for the Spaniard to relinquish his hold, the now embarrassed Captain Delano lifted his foot, to overstep the threshold of the open gangway; but still Don Benito would not let go his hand. And yet, with an agitated tone, he said, "I can go no further; here I must bid you adieu. Adieu, my dear, dear Don Amasa. Go—go!" suddenly tearing his hand loose, "go, and God guard you better than me, my best friend."

Not unaffected, Captain Delano would now have lingered; but catching the meekly admonitory eye of the servant, with a hasty farewell he descended into his boat, followed by the continual adieus of Don Benito, standing rooted in the gangway.

Seating himself in the stern, Captain Delano, making a last salute, ordered the boat shoved off. The crew had their oars on end. The bowsman pushed the boat a sufficient distance for the oars to be lengthwise dropped. The instant that was done, Don Benito sprang over the bulwarks, falling at the feet of Captain Delano; at the same time calling towards his ship, but in tones so frenzied, that none in the boat could understand him. But, as if not equally obtuse, three sailors, from three different and distant parts of the ship, splashed into the sea, swimming after their captain, as if intent upon his rescue.

The dismayed officer of the boat eagerly asked what this meant. To which, Captain Delano, turning a disdainful smile upon the unaccountable Spaniard, answered that, for his part, he neither knew nor cared; but it seemed as if Don Benito had taken it into his head to produce the impression among his people that the boat wanted to kidnap him. "Or else—give way for your lives," he wildly added, starting at a clattering hubbub in the ship, above which rang the tocsin of the hatchet-polishers; and seizing Don Benito by the throat he added, "this plotting pirate means murder!" Here, in apparent verification of the words the servant a dagger in his hand, was seen on the rail overhead, poised, in the act of leaping, as if with desperate fidelity to befriend his master to the last; while, seemingly to aid the black, the three white sailors were trying to clamber into the hampered bow. Meantime, the whole host of negroes, as if inflamed at the sight of their jeopardized captain, impended in one sooty avalanche over the bulwarks.

All this, with what preceded, and what followed, occurred with such involutions of rapidity, that past, present, and future seemed one.

Seeing the negro coming, Captain Delano had flung the Spaniard aside, almost in the very act of clutching him, and by the unconscious recoil, shifting his place, with arms thrown up, so promptly grappled the servant in his descent, that with dagger presented at Captain Delano's heart, the black seemed of purpose to have leaped there as to his mark. But the weapon was wrenched away, and the assailant dashed down into the bottom of the boat, which now, with disentangled oars, began to speed through the sea.

At this juncture, the left hand of Captain Delano, on one side, again clutched the half-reclining Don Benito, heedless that he was in a speechless faint, while his right foot, on the other side, ground the prostrate negro; and his right arm pressed for added speed on the after oar, his eye bent forward, encouraging his men to their utmost.

But here, the officer of the boat, who had at last succeeded in beating off the towing sailors, and was now, with face turned aft, assisting the bowsman at his oar, suddenly called to Captain Delano, to see what the black was about; while a Portuguese oarsman shouted to him to give heed to what the Spaniard was saying.

Glancing down at his feet, Captain Delano saw the freed hand of the servant aiming with a second dagger—a small one, before concealed in his wool—with this he was snakishly writhing up from the boat's bottom, at the heart of his master, his countenance lividly vindictive, expressing the centered purpose of his soul; while the Spaniard, half-choked, was vainly shrinking away, with husky words, incoherent to all but the Portuguese.

That moment, across the long-benighted mind of Captain Delano, a flash of revelation swept, illuminating, in unanticipated clearness, his host's whole mysterious demeanour, with every enigmatic event of the day, as well as the entire past voyage of the *San Dominick.* He smote Babo's hand down, but his own heart smote him harder. With infinite pity he withdraw his hold from Don Benito. Not Captain Delano, but Don Benito, the black, in leaping into the boat, had intended to stab.

Both the black's hands were held, as, glancing up towards the *San Dominick,* Captain Delano, now with scales dropped from his eyes, saw the negroes, not in misrule, not in tumult, not as if frantically concerned for Don Benito, but with mask torn away, flourishing hatchets, and knives, in ferocious piratical revolt. Like delirious black dervishes, the six Ashantees danced on the poop. Prevented by their foes from springing into the water, the Spanish boys were hurrying up to the top-most spars, while such of the few Spanish sailors, not already in the sea, less alert, were descried, helplessly mixed in, on deck, with the blacks.

Meantime Captain Delano hailed his own vessel, ordering the ports up, and the guns run out. But by this time the cable on the *San Dominick* had been cut; and the fag-end, in lashing out, whipped away the canvas shroud about the beak, suddenly revealing, as the bleached hull swung round towards the open ocean, death for the figure-head, in a human skeleton; chalky comment on the chalked words below, *"Follow your leader."*

At the sight, Don Benito, covering his face, wailed out:

" 'Tis he, Aranda! my murdered, unburied friend!"

Upon reaching the sealer, calling for ropes, Captain Delano bound the negro, who made no resistance, and had him hoisted to the deck. He would then have assisted the now almost helpless Don Benito up the side; but Don Benito, wan as he was, refused to move, or be moved, until the negro should have been first put below out of view. When, presently assured that it was done, he no more shrank from the ascent.

The boat was immediately dispatched back to pick up the three swimming sailors. Meantime, the guns were in readiness, though, owing to the *San Dominick* having glided somewhat astern of the sealer, only the aftermost one could be brought to bear. With this, they fired six times; thinking to cripple the fugitive ship by bringing down her spars. But only a few inconsiderable ropes were shot away. Soon the ship was beyond the gun's range, steering broad out of the bay; the blacks thickly clustering round the bowsprit, one moment with taunting cries towards the whites, the next with upthrown gestures hailing the now dusky moors of ocean—cawing crows escaped from the hand of the fowler.

The first impulse was to slip the cables and give chase. But, upon second thoughts, to pursue with whale-boat and yawl seemed more promising.

Upon inquiring of Don Benito what fire-arms they had on board the *San Dominick,* Captain Delano was answered that they had none that could be used; because, in the earlier stages of the mutiny, a cabin-passenger, since dead, had secretly put out of order the locks of what few muskets there were. But with all his remaining strength, Don Benito entreated the American not to give chase, either with ship or boat; for the negroes had already proved themselves such desperadoes, that, in case of a present assault, nothing but a total massacre of the whites could be looked for. But, regarding this warning as coming from one whose spirit had been crushed by misery, the American did not give up his design.

The boats were got ready and armed. Captain Delano ordered his men into them. He was going himself when Don Benito grasped his arm.

"What! have you saved my life, Señor, and are you now going to throw away your own?"

The officers also, for reasons connected with their interests and those of the voyage, and a duty owing to the owners, strongly objected against their commander's going. Weighing their remonstrances a moment, Captain Delano felt bound to remain; appointing his chief mate—an athletic and resolute man, who had been a privateer's-man—to head the party. The more to encourage the sailors, they were told, that the Spanish captain considered his ship good as lost; that she and her cargo, including some gold and silver, were worth more than a thousand doubloons. Take her, and no small part should be theirs. The sailors replied with a shout.

The fugitives had now almost gained an offing. It was nearly night; but the moon was rising. After hard, prolonged pulling, the boats came up on the ship's quarters, at a suitable distance laying upon their oars to discharge their muskets. Having no bullets to return, the negroes sent their yells. But, upon the second volley, Indian-like, they hurled their hatchets. One took off a sailor's fingers. Another struck the whale-boat's bow, cutting off the rope there, and remaining stuck in the gunwale like a woodman's axe. Snatching it, quivering from its lodgment, the mate hurled it back. The returned gauntlet now stuck in the ship's broken quarter-gallery, and so remained.

The negroes giving too hot a reception, the whites kept a more respectful distance. Hovering now just out of reach of the hurtling hatchets, they, with a view of the close encounter which must soon come, sought to decoy the blacks into entirely disarming themselves of their most murderous weapons in a hand-to-hand fight, by foolishly flinging them, as missiles, short of the mark, into the sea. But, ere long, perceiving the stratagem, the negroes desisted, though not before many of them had to replace their lost hatchets with handspikes; an exchange which, as counted upon, proved, in the end, favourable to the assailants.

Meantime, with a strong wind, the ship still clove the water; the boats alternately falling behind, and pulling up, to discharge fresh volleys.

The fire was mostly directed towards the stern, since there, chiefly, the negroes, at present, were clustering. But to kill or maim the negroes was not the object. To take them, with the ship, was the object. To do it, the ship must be boarded; which could not be done by boats while she was sailing so fast.

A thought now struck the mate. Observing the Spanish boys still aloft, high as they could get, he called to them to descend to the yards, and cut adrift the sails. It was done. About this time, owing to causes hereafter to be shown, two Spaniards, in the dress of sailors, and conspicuously showing themselves, were killed; not by volleys, but by deliberate marksman's shots; while, as it afterwards appeared, by one of the general discharges, Atufal, the black, and the Spaniard at the helm likewise were killed. What now, with the loss of sails, and loss of leaders, the ship became unmanageable to the negroes.

With creaking masts, she came heavily round to the wind; the prow slowly swinging into view of the boats, its skeleton gleaming in the horizontal moonlight, and casting a gigantic ribbed shadow upon the water. One extended arm of the ghost seemed beckoning the whites to avenge it.

"Follow your leader!" cried the mate; and, one on each bow, the boats boarded. Sealing-spears and cutlasses crossed hatchets and handspikes. Huddled upon the long-boat amidships, the negresses raised a wailing chant, whose chorus was the clash of the steel.

For a time, the attack wavered; the negroes wedging themselves to beat it back; the half-repelled sailors, as yet unable to gain a footing, fighting as troopers in the saddle, one leg sideways flung over the bulwarks, and one without, plying their cutlasses like carters' whips. But in vain. They were almost overborne, when, rallying themselves into a squad as one man, with a huzza, they sprang inboard, where, entangled, they involuntarily separated again. For a few breaths' space, there was a vague, muffled, inner sound, as of submerged sword-fish rushing hither and thither through shoals of black-fish. Soon, in a reunited band, and joined by the Spanish seamen, the whites came to the surface, irresitibly driving the negroes towards the stern. But a barricade of casks and sacks, from side to side, had been thrown up by the main-mast. Here the negroes faced about, and though scorning peace or truce, yet fain would have had respite. But, without pause, overleaping the barrier, the unflagging sailors again closed. Exhausted, the blacks now fought in despair. Their red tongues lolled, wolf-like, from their black mouths. But the pale sailors' teeth were set; not a word was spoken; and in five minutes more, the ship was won.

Nearly a score of the negroes were killed. Exclusive of those by the balls, many were mangled; their wounds—mostly inflicted by the long-edged sealing-spears, resembling those shaven ones of the English at Preston Pans, made by the poled scythes of the Highlanders. On the other side, none were killed, though several were wounded; some severely, including the mate. The surviving negroes were temporarily secured, and the ship, towed back into the harbour at midnight, once more lay anchored.

Omitting the incidents and arrangements ensuing, suffice it that, after two days spent in refitting, the ships sailed in company for Concepcion, in Chile, and thence for Lima, in Peru; where, before the vice-regal courts, the whole affair, from the beginning, underwent investigation.

Though, midway on the passage, the ill-fated Spaniard, relaxed from constraint, showed some signs of regaining health with free-will; yet, agreeably to his own foreboding, shortly before arriving at Lima, he relapsed finally becoming so reduced as to be carried ashore in arms. Hearing of his story and plight, one of the many religious institutions of the City of Kings opened an hospitable refuge to him, where both physician and priest were his nurses, and a member of the order volunteered to be his one special guardian and consoler, by night and by day.

The following extracts, translated from one of the official Spanish documents, will, it is hoped, shed light on the preceding narrative, as well as, in the first place, reveal the true port of departure and true history of the *San Dominick*'s voyage, down to the time of her touching at the island of Santa Maria.

But, ere the extracts come, it may be well to preface them with a remark.

The document selected, from among many others, for partial translation, contains the deposition of Benito Cereno; the first taken in the case. Some disclosures therein were, at the time, held dubious for both learned and natural reasons. The tribunal inclined to the opinion that the deponent, not undisturbed in his mind by recent events, raved of some things which could never have happened. But subsequent depositions of the surviving sailors, bearing out the revelations of their captain in several of the strangest particulars, gave credence to the rest. So that the tribunal, in its final decision, rested its capital sentences upon statements which, had they lacked confirmation, it would have deemed it but duty to reject.

*I, Don José de Abos and Padilla, His Majesty's Notary for the Royal Revenue, and Register of this Province, and Notary Public of the Holy Crusade of this Bishoprick, &c.*

*Do certify and declare, as much as is requisite in law, that, in the criminal cause commenced the twenty-fourth of the month of September, in the year seventeen hundred and ninety-nine, against the negroes of the ship* San Dominick, *the following declaration before me was made:*

*Declaration of the first Witness, Don Benito Cereno.*

*The same day and month and year, His Honour, Doctor Juan Martinez de Rozas, Councillor of the Royal Audience of this Kingdom, and learned in the law of this Intendency, ordered the captain of the ship* San Dominick, *Don Benito Cereno, to appear; which he did in his litter, attended by the monk Infelez; of whom he received the oath, which he took by God, our Lord, and a Sign of the Cross; under which he promised to tell the truth of whatever he should know and should be asked;—and being interrogated agreeably to the tenor of the act, commencing the process, he said, that on the twentieth of May last, he set sail with his ship from the port of Valparaiso, bound to that of Callao; loaded with the produce of the country beside thirty cases of hardware and one hundred and sixty blacks, of both sexes, mostly belonging to Don Alexandro Aranda, gentleman, of the City of Mendoza; that the crew of the ship consisted of thirty-six men, beside the persons who went as passengers; that the negroes were in part as follows:*

[Here, in the original, follows a list of some fifty names, descriptions, and ages, compiled from certain recovered documents of Aranda's and also from recollections of the deponent, from which portions only are extracted.]

*—One, from about eighteen to nineteen years, named José, and this was the man that waited upon his master, Don Alexandro, and who speaks well the Spanish, having served him four or five years . . . a mulatto, named Francesco, the cabin steward, of a good person and voice having sung in the Valparaiso churches, native of the province of Buenos Ayres, aged about thirty-five years. . . . A smart negro, named Dago, who had been for many years a grave-digger among the Spaniards, aged forty-six years. . . . Four old negroes, born in Africa, from sixty to seventy, but sound, calkers by trade, whose names are as follows:—the first was named Mure, and he was killed (as was also his son named Diamelo); the second, Nacta; the third, Yola, likewise killed; the fourth, Ghofan; and six full-grown negroes; aged from thirty to forty-five, all raw, and born among the Ashantees—Matinqui, Yau, Lecbe, Mapenda, Yambaio, Akim, four of whom were killed; . . . a powerful negro named Atufal, who being supposed to have been a chief in Africa, his owner set great store by him. . . . And a small negro of Senegal, but some years among the Spaniards, aged about thirty, which negro's name was Babo; . . . that he does not remember the names of the others, but that still expecting the residue of Don Alexandro's papers will be found, will then take due account of them all, and remit to the court; . . . and thirty-nine women and children of all ages.*

[The catalogue over, the deposition goes on:]

*. . . That all the negroes slept upon deck, as is customary in this navigation, and none wore fetters, because the owner, his friend Aranda, told him that they were all tractable; . . . that on the seventh day after leaving port, at three o'clock in the morning, all the Spaniards being asleep except two officers at the watch, who were the boat-swain, Juan Robles, and the carpenter, Juan Bautista Gayete, and the helmsman and his boy, the negroes revolted suddenly, wounded dangerously the boat-swain and the carpenter, and successively killed eighteen men of those who were sleeping upon deck, some with hand-spikes and hatchets, and others by throwing them alive overboard, after tying them; that of the Spaniards upon deck, they left about seven, as he thinks, alive and tied, to manœuvre the ship, and three or four more, who hid themselves, remained also alive. Although in the act of revolt the negroes made themselves masters of the hatchway, six or seven wounded went through it to the cockpit, without any hindrance on their part; that during the act of revolt, the mate and another person, whose name he does not recollect, attempted to come up through the hatchway, but being quickly wounded, were obliged to return to the cabin; that the deponent resolved at break of day to come up the companion-way, where the negro Babo was, being the ringleader, and Atufal, who assisted him, and having spoken to them, exhorted them to cease*

*committing such atrocities asking them, at the same time, what they wanted and intended to do, offering, himself, to obey their commands; that notwithstanding this, they threw, in his presence, three men, alive and tied, overboard; that they told the deponent to come up, and that they would not kill him; which having done, the negro Babo asked him whether there were in those seas any negro countries where they might be carried, and he answered them, No; that the negro Babo afterwards told him to carry them to Senegal, or to the neighboring islands of St. Nicholas; and he answered, that this was impossible, on account of the great distance, the necessity involved of rounding Cape Horn, the bad condition of the vessel, the want of provisions, sails, and water; but that the negro Babo replied to him he must carry them in any way; that they would do and conform themselves to anything the deponent should require as to eating and drinking; that after a long conference, being absolutely compelled to please them, for they threatened to kill all the whites if they were not, at all events, carried to Senegal, he told them that what was most wanting for the voyage was water; that they would go near the coast to take it, and thence they would proceed on their course; that the negro Babo agreed to it; and the deponent steered towards the intermediate ports, hoping to meet some Spanish or foreign vessel that would save them; that within ten or eleven days they saw the land, and continued their course by it in the vicinity of Nasca; that the deponent observed that the negroes were now restless and mutinous, because he did not effect the taking in of water, the negro Babo having required, with threats, that it should be done, without fail, the following day; he told him he saw plainly that the coast was steep, and the rivers designated in the maps were not to be found, with other reasons suitable to the circumstances; that the best way would be to go to the island of Santa Maria, where they might water easily, it being a solitary island, as the foreigners did; that the deponent did not go to Pisco, that was near, nor make any other port of the coast, because the negro Babo had intimated to him several times, that he would kill all the whites the very moment he should perceive any city, town, or settlement of any kind on the shores to which they should be carried: that having determined to go to the island of Santa Maria, as the deponent had planned, for the purpose of trying whether, on the passage or near the island itself, they could find any vessel that should favour them, or whether he could escape from it in a boat to the neighboring coast of Arauco, to adopt the necessary means he immediately changed his course, steering for the island; that the negroes Babo and Atufal held daily conferences, in which they discussed what was necessary for their design of returning to Senegal, whether they were to kill all the Spaniards, and particularly the deponent; that eight days after parting from the coast of Nasca, the deponent being on the watch a little after day-break, and soon after the negroes had their meeting, the negro Babo came to the place where the deponent was, and told him that he had determined to kill his master, Don Alexandro Aranda, both because he and his companions could not otherwise be sure of their liberty, and that to keep the seamen in subjection, he wanted to prepare a warning of what they should be made to take did they or any of them oppose him; and that, by means of the death of Don Alexandro, that warning would best be given; but, that what this last meant, the deponent did not at the time comprehend, nor could not, further than the death of Don Alexandro was intended; and moreover the negro Babo proposed to the deponent to call the mate Raneds, who was sleeping in the cabin, before the thing was done, for fear, as the deponent understood it, that the mate, who was a good navigator, should not be killed with Don Alexandro and the rest; that the deponent, who was the friend, from youth, of Don Alexandro, prayed and conjured, but all was useless; for the negro Babo answered him that the thing could not be prevented, and that all the Spaniards risked their death if they should attempt to frustrate his will in this matter, or any other; that, in this conflict, the deponent called the mate, Raneds, who was forced to go apart, and immediately the negro Babo commanded the Ashantee Matinqui and the Ashantee Lecbe to go and commit the murder; that those two went down with hatchets to the berth of Don Alexandro; that, yet half alive and mangled, they dragged him on deck; that they were going to throw him overboard in that state, but the negro Babo stopped them, bidding the murder be completed on the deck before him, which was done, when, by his orders, the body was carried below, forward; that nothing more was seen of it by the deponent for three days; . . . that Don Alonzo Sidonia, an old man, long resident at Valparaiso, and lately appointed to a civil office in Peru, whither he had taken passage, was at the time sleeping in the berth opposite Don Alexandro's; that awakening at his cries, surprised by them, and at the sight of the negroes with their bloody hatchets in their hands, he threw himself into the sea through a window which was near him, and was drowned, without it being in the power of the deponent to assist or take him up; . . . that a short time after killing Aranda, they brought upon deck his cousin-german, of middle-age, Don Francisco Masa, of Mendoza, and the young Don Joaquin, Marques de Aramboalaza, then lately from Spain, with his Spanish servant Ponce, and the three young clerks of Aranda, José Morairi, Lorenzo Bargas, and Hermenegildo Gandix, all of Cadiz; that Don Joaquin and Hermenegildo Gandix, the negro Babo, for purposes hereafter to appear, preserved alive; but Don Francisco Masa, José Morairi, and Lorenzo Bargas, with Ponce the servant, beside the boat-swain, Juan Robles, the boat-swain's mates, Manuel Viscaya and Roderigo Hurta, and four of the sailors, the negro Babo ordered to be thrown alive into the sea, although they made no resistance, nor begged for anything else but mercy; that the boat-swain Juan Robles, who knew how to swim, kept the longest above water, making acts of contrition, and, in the last words he uttered, charged this deponent to cause mass to be said for his soul to our Lady of Succour; . . . that, during the three days which followed, the deponent uncertain what fate had befallen the remains of Don Alexandro, frequently asked the negro Babo where they were, and, if still on board, whether they were to be preserved for interment ashore, entreating him so to order it; that the negro Babo answered nothing till the fourth day, when at sunrise, the deponent coming on deck, the negro Babo showed him a skeleton, which had been substituted for the ship's proper figurehead—the image of Cristobal Colon, the discoverer of the New World; that the negro Babo asked him whose skeleton that was, and whether from its whiteness, he should not think it a white's; that, upon his covering his face the negro Babo, coming close, said words to this effect: "Keep faith with the blacks from here to Senegal, or you shall in spirit, as now in body, follow your leader," pointing to the prow; . . . that the same morning the negro Babo took by succession each Spaniard forward, and asked him whose skeleton that was, and whether, from its whiteness, he should not think it a white's; that each Spaniard covered his face; that then to each the negro Babo repeated the words in the first place said to the deponent; . . . that they (the Spaniards), being then assembled aft, the negro Babo harangued them, saying that he had now done all; that the deponent (as navigator for the negroes) might pursue his course, warning him and all of them that they should, soul and body, go the way of Don Alexandro, if he saw them (the Spaniards) speak or plot anything against them (the negroes), a threat which was repeated every day; that, before the events last mentioned, they had tied the cook to throw him overboard, for it is not known what thing they heard him speak, but finally the negro Babo spared his life, at the request of the deponent; that a few days after, the deponent, endeavouring not to omit any means to preserve the lives of the remaining whites, spoke to the negroes peace and tranquillity, and agreed to draw up a paper, signed by the deponent and the sailors who could write, as also by the negro Babo, for himself and all the blacks, in which the deponent obliged himself to carry them to Senegal, and they not to kill any more, and he formally to make over to them the ship, with the cargo, with which they were for that time satisfied and quieted. . . . But the next day, the more surely to guard against the sailors' escape, the negro Babo commanded all the boats to be destroyed but the long-boat, which was unseaworthy, and another, a cutter in good condition, which knowing it would yet be wanted for towing the water casks, he had it lowered into the hold. . . .*

[Various particulars of the prolonged and perplexed navigation ensuing here follow, with incidents of a calamitous calm, from which portion one passage is extracted, to wit:]

*—That on the fifth day of the calm, all on board suffering much from the heat, and want of water, and five having died in fits, and mad, the negroes became irritable, and for a chance gesture, which they deemed suspicious—though it was harmless—made by the mate, Raneds, to the deponent in the act of handing a quadrant, they killed him; but that for this they afterwards were sorry, the mate being the only remaining navigator on board, except the deponent.*

❂ ❂ ❂

*—That omitting other events which daily happened, and which can only serve uselessly to recall past misfortunes and conflicts, after seventy-three days' navigation, reckoned from the time they sailed from Nasca, during which they navigated under a scanty allowance of water, and were afflicted with the calms before mentioned, they at last arrived at the island of Santa Maria, on the seventeenth of the month of August, at about six o'clock in the afternoon, at which hour they cast anchor very near the American ship,* Bachelor's Delight, *which lay in the same bay, commanded by the generous Captain Amasa Delano; but at six o'clock in the morning, they had already described the port, and the negroes became uneasy, as soon as at distance they saw the ship, not having expected to see one there; that the negro Babo pacified them, assuring them that no fear need be had; that straightway he ordered the figure on the bow to be covered with canvas, as for repairs, and had the decks a little set in order; that for a time the negro Babo and the negro Atufal conferred; that the negro Atufal was for sailing away, but the negro Babo would not, and, by himself, cast about what to do; that at last he came to the deponent, proposing to him to say and do all that the deponent declares to have said and done to the American captain; . . . that the negro Babo warned him that if he varied in the least, or uttered any word, or gave any look that should give the least intimation of the past events or present state, he would instantly kill him, with all his companions, showing a dagger, which he carried hid, saying something which, as he understood it, meant that that dagger would be alert as his eyes; that the negro Babo then announced the plan to all his companions, which pleased them; that he then, the better to disguise the truth, devised many expedients, in some of them uniting deceit and defense; that of this sort was the device of the six Ashantees before named, who were his bravoes; that*

*them he stationed on the break of the poop, as if to clean certain hatchets (in cases, which were part of the cargo), but in reality to use them, and distribute them at need, and at a given word he told them; that, among other devices, was the device of presenting Atufal, his right hand man, as chained, though in a moment the chains could be dropped; that in every particular he informed the deponent what part he was expected to enact in every device, and what story he was to tell on every occasion, always threatening him with instant death if he varied in the least: that, conscious that many of the negroes would be turbulent, the negro Babo appointed the four aged negroes who were calkers, to keep what domestic order they could on the decks; that again and again he harangued the Spaniards and his companions, informing them of his intent, and of his devices, and of the invented story that this deponent was to tell; charging them lest any of them varied from that story; that these arrangements were made and matured during the interval of two or three hours, between their first sighting the ship and the arrival on board of Captain Amasa Delano; that this happened about half-past seven o'clock in the morning, Captain Amasa Delano coming in his boat, and all gladly receiving him; that the deponent, as well as he could force himself, acting then the part of principal owner, and a free captain of the ship, told Captain Amasa Delano, when called upon, that he came from Buenos Ayres, bound to Lima, with three hundred negroes; that off Cape Horn, and in a subsequent fever, many negroes had died; that also, by similar casualties, all the sea-officers and the greatest part of the crew had died.*

✲ ✲ ✲

[And so the deposition goes on, circumstantially recounting the fictitious story dictated to the deponent by Babo, and through the deponent imposed upon Captain Delano; and also recounting the friendly offers of Captain Delano, with other things, but all of which is here omitted. After the fictitious story, etc., the deposition proceeds:]

*—that that generous Captain Delano remained on board all the day, till he left the ship anchored at six o'clock in the evening, deponent speaking to him always of his pretended misfortunes, under the forementioned principles, without having had it in his power to tell a single word, or give him the least hint, that he might know the truth and state of things; because the negro Babo, performing the office of an officious servant with all the appearance of submission of the humble slave, did not leave the deponent one moment; that this was in order to observe the deponent's actions and words, for the negro Babo understands well the Spanish; and besides, there were thereabouts some others who were constantly on the watch, and likewise understood the Spanish; . . . that upon one occasion, while deponent was standing on the deck conversing with Amasa Delano, by a secret sign the negro Babo drew him (the deponent) aside, the act appearing as if originating with the deponent; that then, he being drawn aside, the negro Babo proposed to him to gain from Amasa Delano full particulars about his ship, and crew, and arms; that the deponent asked "for what?" that the negro Babo answered he might conceive; that, grieved at the prospect of what might overtake the generous Captain Amasa Delano, the deponent at first refused to ask the desired questions, and used every argument to induce the negro Babo to give up this new design; that the negro Babo showed the point of his dagger; that, after the information had been*

*obtained, the negro Babo again drew him aside, telling him that that very night he (the deponent) would be captain of two ships, instead of one, for that, great part of the American's ship's crew being to be absent fishing, the six Ashantees without any one else, would easily take it; that at this time he said other things to the same purpose; that no entreaties availed; that, before Amasa Delano's coming on board, no hint had been given touching the capture of the American ship; that to prevent this project the deponent was powerless; . . . —that in some things his memory is confused, he cannot distinctly recall every event; . . . that as soon as they had cast anchor at six o'clock in the evening, as has before been stated, the American captain took leave, to return to his vessel; that upon a sudden impulse, which the deponent believes to have come from God and his angels, he, after the farewell had been said, followed the generous Captain Amasa Delano as far as the gunwale, where he stayed, under pretence of taking leave until Amasa Delano should have been seated in his boat; that on shoving off, the deponent sprang from the gunwale into the boat and fell into it, he knows not how, God guarding him; that—*

[Here, in the original, follows the account of what further happened at the escape, and how the *San Dominick* was retaken, and of the passage to the coast; including in the recital many expressions of "eternal gratitude" to the "generous Captain Amasa Delano." The deposition then proceeds with recapitulatory remarks, and a partial renumeration of the negroes, making record of their individual part in the past events, with a view to furnishing, according to command of the court, the data whereon to found the criminal sentences to be pronounced. From this portion is the following:]

*—That he believes that all the negroes, though not in the first place knowing to the design of revolt, when it was accomplished, approved it. . . . That the negro José, eighteen years old, and in the personal service of Don Alexandro, was the one who communicated the information to the negro Babo about the state of things in the cabin, before the revolt; that this is known, because, in the preceding nights, he used to come from his berth, which was under his master's, in the cabin, to the deck where the ringleader and his associates were, and had secret conversations with the negro Babo, in which he was several times seen by the mate; that one night, the mate drove him away twice; . . . that this same negro José was the one who, without being commanded to do so by the negro Babo, as Lecbe and Matinqui were, stabbed his master, Don Alexandro, after he had been dragged half lifeless to the deck; . . . that the mulatto steward, Francesco, was of the first band of revolters, that he was, in all things, the creature and tool of the negro Babo; that, to make his court, he, just before a repast in the cabin, proposed to the negro Babo, poisoning a dish for the generous Captain Amasa Delano; this is known and believed, because the negroes have said it; but that the negro Babo, having another design, forbade Francesco; . . . that the Ashantee Lecbe was one of the worst of them; for that, on the day the ship was retaken, he assisted in the defence of her, with a hatchet in each hand, with one of which he wounded in the breast, the chief mate of Amasa Delano, in the first act of boarding; this all knew; that, in sight of the deponent, Lecbe struck with a hatchet, Don Francisco Masa, when, by the negro Babo's orders, he was carrying him to throw him overboard alive, beside participating in the murder, before mentioned, of Don Alexandro Aranda, and others of the cabin-passengers; that, owing to the fury with which the*

*Ashantees fought in the engagement with the boats, but this Lecbe and Yau survived; that Yau was bad as Lecbe; that Yau was the man who, by Babo's command, willingly prepared the skeleton of Don Alexandro, in a way the negroes afterwards told the deponent, but which he, so long as reason is left him, can never divulge; that Yau and Lecbe were the two who, in a calm by night, riveted the skeleton to the bow; this also the negroes told him; that the negro Babo was he who traced the inscription below it; that the negro Babo was the plotter from first to last; he ordered every murder, and was the helm and keel of the revolt; that Atufal was his lieutenant in all; but Atufal, with his own hand, committed no murder; nor did the negro Babo; . . . that Atufal was shot, being killed in the fight with the boats, ere boarding; . . . that the negresses of age, were known to the revolt, and testified themselves satisfied at the death of their master, Don Alexandro; that, had the negroes not restrained them, they would have tortured to death, instead of simply killing, the Spaniards slain by command of the negro Babo; that the negresses used their utmost influence to have the deponent made away with; that, in the various acts of murder, they sang songs and danced—not gaily, but solemnly; and before the engagement with the boats, as well as during the action, they sang melancholy songs to the negroes, and that this melancholy tone was more inflaming than a different one would have been, and was so intended; that all this is believed, because the negroes have said it;—that of the thirty-six men of the crew, exclusive of the passengers (all of whom are now dead), which the deponent had knowledge of, six only remained alive, with four cabin-boys and ship-boys, not included with the crew; . . . —that the negroes broke an arm of one of the cabin-boys and gave him strokes with hatchets.*

[Then follow various random disclosures referring to various periods of time. The following are extracted:]

*—That during the presence of Captain Amasa Delano on board, some attempts were made by the sailors, and one by Hermenegildo Gandix, to convey hints to him of the true state of affairs; but that these attempts were ineffectual, owing to fear of incurring death, and furthermore, owing to the devices which offered contradictions to the true state of affairs, as well as the owing to the generosity and piety of Amasa Delano incapable of sounding such wickedness; . . . that Luys Galgo, a sailor about sixty years of age, and formerly of the King's navy, was one of those who sought to convey tokens to Captain Amasa Delano; but his intent, though undiscovered, being suspected, he was, on a pretence, made to retire out of sight, and at last into the hold and there was made away with. This the negroes have since said; . . . that one of the ship-boys, feeling from Captain Amasa Delano's presence, some hopes of release, and not having enough prudence, dropped some chance word respecting his expectations, which being overheard and understood by a slave-boy with whom he was eating at the time, the latter struck him on the head with a knife, inflicting a bad wound, but of which the boy is now healing; that likewise, not long before the ship was brought to anchor, one of the seamen, steering at the time, endangered himself by letting the blacks remark some expression in his countenance, arising from a similar cause to the above; but this sailor, by his heedful after conduct, escaped; . . . that these statements are made to show the court that from the beginning to the end of the revolt, it was impossible for the deponent and his men to act otherwise than they did; . . . —that the third clerk, Hermenegildo Gandix, who before had been forced to live*

*among the seamen, wearing a seaman's habit, and in all respects appearing to be one for the time, he, Gandix, was killed by a musket ball fired through mistake from the boats before boarding; having in his fright run up the mizzen-rigging, calling to the boats—"don't board," lest upon their boarding the negroes should kill him; that this inducing the Americans to believe he some way favoured the cause of the negroes, they fired two balls at him, so that he fell wounded from the rigging, and was drowned in the sea; . . . —that the young Don Joaquin, Marques de Aramboalaza, like Hermenegildo Gandix, the third clerk, was degraded to the office and appearance of a common seaman; that upon one occasion when Don Joaquin shrank, the negro Babo commanded the Ashantee Lecbe to take tar and heat it, and pour it upon Don Joaquin's hands; . . . —that Don Joaquin was killed owing to another mistake of the Americans, but one impossible to be avoided, as upon the approach of the boats, Don Joaquin, with a hatchet tied edge out and upright to his hand, was made by the negroes to appear on the bulwarks; whereupon, seen with arms in his hands, and in a questionable attitude, he was shot for a renegade seaman; . . . that on the person of Don Joaquin was found secreted a jewel, which, by papers that were discovered, proved to have been meant for the shrine of our Lady of Mercy in Lima; a votive offering, beforehand prepared and guarded, to attest his gratitude, when he should have landed in Peru, his last destination for the safe conclusion of his entire voyage from Spain; . . . —that the jewel, with the other effects of the late Don Joaquin, is in the custody of the Hospital de Sacerdotes, awaiting the disposition of the honourable court; . . . —that, owing to the condition of the deponent, as well as the haste in which the boats departed for the attack, the Americans were not forewarned that there were, among the apparent crew, a passenger and one of the clerks disguised by the negro Babo; . . . —that, beside the negroes killed in the action, some were killed after the capture and re-anchoring at night, when shackled to the ring-bolts on deck; that these deaths were committed by the sailors, ere they could be prevented. That so soon as informed of it, Captain Amasa Delano used all his authority, and in particular with his own hand, struck down Martinez Gola, who, having found a razor in the pocket of an old jacket of his, which one of the shackled negroes had on, was aiming it at the negro's throat; that the noble Captain Amasa Delano also wrenched from the hand of Bartholomew Barlo a dagger, secreted at the time of the massacre of the whites, with which he was in the act of stabbing a shackled negro, who, the same day, with another negro had thrown him down and jumped upon him; . . . —that, for all the events befalling through so long a time, during which the ship was in the hands of the negro Babo, he cannot here give account; but that, what he has said is the most substantial of what occurs to him at present, and is the truth under the oath which he has taken; which declaration he affirmed and ratified, after hearing it read to him.*

*He said that he is twenty-nine years of age, and broken in body and mind; that when finally dismissed by the court, he shall not return home to Chile, but betake himself to the monastery of Mount Agonia without; and signed with his honour, and crossed himself, and, for the time, departed as he came, in his litter, with the monk Infelez, to the Hospital de Sacerdotes.* Benito Cereno. Dr. Rozas.

If the Deposition have served as the key to fit into the lock of the complications which precede it, then, as a vault whose door has been flung back, the *San Dominick*'s hull lies open to-day.

Hitherto the nature of this narrative, besides rendering the intricacies in the beginning unavoidable, has more or less required that many things, instead of being set down in order of occurrence, should be retrospectively, or irregularly given; this last is the case with the following passages, which will conclude the account.

During the long, mild voyage to Lima, there was, as before hinted, a period during which the sufferer a little recovered his health, or, at least in some degree, his tranquillity. Ere the decided relapse which came, the two captains had many cordial conversations—their fraternal unreserve in similar contrast with former withdrawments.

Again and again it was repeated, how hard it had been to enact the part forced on the Spaniard by Babo.

"Ah, my dear friend," Don Benito once said, "at those very times you thought me so morose and ungrateful, nay, when, as you now admit, you have thought me plotting your murder, at those very times my heart was frozen; I could not look at you, thinking of what, both on board this ship and your own, hung, from other hands, over my kind benefactor. And as God lives, Don Amasa, I know not whether desire for my own safety alone could have nerved me to that leap into your boat, had it not been for the thought that, did you, unenlightened, return to your ship, you, my best friend, with all who might be with you, stolen upon, that night, in your hammocks, would never in this world have wakened again. Do but think how you walked this deck, how you sat in this cabin, every inch of ground mined into honey-combs under you. Had I dropped the least hint, made the least advance towards an understanding between us; death, explosive death—yours and mine—would have ended the scene."

"True, true," cried Captain Delano, starting, "you have saved my life, Don Benito, more than I yours; saved it, too, against my knowledge and will."

"Nay, my friend," rejoined the Spaniard, courteous even to the point of religion, "God charmed your life, but you saved mine. To think of some things you did—those smilings and chattings, rash pointings and gesturings. For less than these, they slew my mate, Raneds; but you had the Prince of Heaven's safe-conduct through all ambuscades."

"Yes, all is owing to Providence, I know: but the temper of my mind that morning was more than commonly pleasant, while the sight of so much suffering, more apparent than real, added to my good-nature, compassion, and charity, happily interweaving the three. Had it been otherwise, doubtless, as you hint, some of my interferences might have ended unhappily enough. Besides, those feelings I spoke of enabled me to get the better of momentary distrust, at times when acuteness might have cost me my life without saving another's. Only at the end did my suspicions get the better of me, and you know how wide of the mark they then proved."

"Wide, indeed," said Don Benito, sadly; "you were with me all day; stood with me, sat with me, talked with me, looked at me, ate with me, drank with me, and yet, your last act was to clutch for a monster, not only an innocent man, but the most pitiable of all men. To such degree may malign machinations and deceptions impose. So far may even the best man err, in judging the conduct of one with the recesses of whose condition he is not acquainted. But you were forced to it; and you were in time undeceived. Would that, in both respects, it was so ever, and with all men."

"You generalize, Don Benito; and mournfully enough. But the past is passed; why moralize upon it? Forget it. See, yon bright sun has forgotten it all, and the blue sea, and the blue sky; these have turned over new leaves."

"Because they have no memory," he dejectedly replied; "because they are not human."

"But these mild trades that now fan your cheek, do they not come with a human-like healing to you? Warm friends, steadfast friends are the trades."

"With their steadfastness they but waft me to my tomb, Señor," was the foreboding response.

"You are saved," cried Captain Delano, more and more astonished and pained; "You are saved: what has cast such a shadow upon you?"

"The negro."

There was silence, while the moody man sat, slowly and unconsciously gathering his mantle about him, as if it were a pall.

There was no more conversation that day.

But if the Spaniard's melancholy sometimes ended in muteness upon topics like the above, there were others upon which he never spoke at all; on which, indeed, all his old reserves were piled. Pass over the worst, and, only to elucidate, let an item or two of these be cited. The dress, so precise and costly, worn by him on the day whose events have been narrated, had not willingly been put on. And that silver-mounted sword, apparent symbol of despot command, was not, indeed, a sword, but the ghost of one. The scabbard, artificially stiffened, was empty.

As for the black—whose brain, not body, had schemed and led the revolt, with the plot—his slight frame, inadequate to that which it held, had at once yielded to the superior muscular strength of his captor, in the boat. Seeing all was over, he uttered no sound, and could not be forced to. His aspect seemed to say, since I cannot do deeds, I will not speak words. Put in irons in the hold, with the rest, he was carried to Lima. During the passage, Don Benito did not visit him. Nor then, nor at any time after would he look at him. Before the tribunal he refused. When pressed by the judges he fainted. On the testimony of the sailors alone rested the legal identity of Babo.

Some months after, dragged to the gibbet at the tail of a mule, the black met his voiceless end. The body was burned to ashes; but for many days, the head, that hive of subtlety, fixed on a pole in the Plaza, met, unabashed, the gaze of the whites; and across the Plaza looked towards St. Bartholomew's church, in whose vaults slept then, as now, the recovered bones of Aranda: and across the Rimac bridge looked towards the monastery, on Mount Agonia without; where, three months after being dismissed by the court, Benito Cereno, borne on the bier, did, indeed, follow his leader.

## *Study questions*

1. *How many facts are presented in the first two paragraphs?* 2. *Show how in the third paragraph facts begin to slide into metaphors. Notice the number of times the words* seem, appear, *and* like *occur in the story. What has this story to do with appearance and reality?* 3. *What does the fourth paragraph tell us about Captain Delano's character and intelligence? How is this information important as the story continues?* 4. *What is the importance of the sternpiece of the* San Dominick*? the figurehead? the motto?* 5. *What kind of man is Delano? Is his name significant? Does he typify an American sea captain? Why is his ship called the* Bachelor's Delight? 6. *What kind of man is Benito Cereno? Is his name significant? Does he typify a Spanish sea captain? Why is his ship called the* San Dominick? 7. *Is the behavior of the blacks a function of their culture and mores?* 8. *Is Babo's behavior any worse than the behavior of the slave owners, the behavior of the American seamen, or the behavior of the Spanish authorities?* 9. *How does Delano stereotype blacks and Spaniards? How does his stereotypic thinking prevent him from seeing the true conditions on the* San Dominick? 10. *At what point in the action does Melville leave Delano as point-of-view character? How is this change important? Does Melville set out deliberately to fool the reader? If so, how does he do it?* 11. *What is the function of the deposition?* 12. *What does Benito Cereno mean when he says at the climax of the story: "the negro"?* 13. *Who is master? slave? leader? What does it mean to "follow your leader"?* 14. *What does Delano learn?*

*Feodor Dostoevsky* (1821–1881) is chiefly known for his long works, among them such world-famous novels as *Crime and Punishment* (1866), *The Idiot* (1868), *The Possessed* (1871–1872), and *The Brothers Karamazov* (1879–1880). But his shorter works, such as *The Double* (1846) and *Notes from the Underground* (1864), are also impressive, as are such short stories as "The Eternal Husband," "A Gentle Creature," and "The Dream of a Ridiculous Man," all written in the 1870s.

Born in Moscow in the hospital for the poor, where his father was resident physician, Dostoevsky attended the St. Petersburg School for Military Engineering. In 1843, he joined the engineering department of the War Ministry, but by this time he had already begun writing. He established a literary reputation with the publication of *Poor Folk* in 1846. Dostoevsky's own life was not without turmoil. He was an epileptic and a compulsive gambler. In addition, in 1849, he was sentenced to death as a member of a revolutionary movement. At the last minute, at the moment when the guns were ready to fire, a reprieve was granted, and Dostoevsky was sent to Siberia at hard labor, where he stayed for four years.

In "The Dream of a Ridiculous Man," the protagonist confronts absurdity and passes beyond it to lucidity. The lucidity, however, is based not on logic but on a dream vision of a time before people were corrupted by their lusts and cupidities.

# THE DREAM OF A RIDICULOUS MAN

## 1

I am a ridiculous person. Now they call me a madman. That would be a promotion if it were not that I remain as ridiculous in their eyes as before. But now I do not resent it, they are all dear to me now, even when they laugh at me—and, indeed, it is just then that that they are particularly dear to me. I could join in their laughter—not exactly at myself, but through affection for them, if I did not feel so sad as I look at them. Sad because they do not know the truth and I do know it. Oh, how hard it is to be the only one who knows the truth! But they won't understand that. No, they won't understand it.

In old days I used to be miserable at seeming ridiculous. Not seeming, but being. I have always been ridiculous, and I have known it, perhaps, from the hour I was born. Perhaps from the time I was seven years old I knew I was ridiculous. Afterwards I went to school, studied at the university, and, do you know, the more I learned, the more thoroughly I understood that I was ridiculous. So that it seemed in the end as though all the sciences I studied at the university existed only to prove and make evident to me as I went more deeply into them that I was ridiculous. It was the same with life as it was with science. With every year the same consciousness of the ridiculous figure I cut in every relation grew and strengthened. Every one always laughed at me. But not one of them knew or guessed that if there were one man on earth who knew better than anybody else that I was absurd, it was myself, and what I resented most of all was that they did not know that. But that was my own fault; I was so proud that nothing would have ever induced me to tell it to any one. This pride grew in me with the years; and if it had happened that I allowed myself to confess to any one that I was ridiculous, I believe that I should have blown out my brains the same evening. Oh, how I suffered in my early youth from the fear that I might give way and confess it to my schoolfellows. But since I grew to manhood, I have for some unknown reason become calmer, though I realised my awful characteristic more fully every year. I say "unknown," for to this day I cannot tell why it was. Perhaps it was owing to the terrible misery that was growing in my soul through something which was of more consequence than anything else about me: that something was the conviction that had come upon me that *nothing in the world mattered.* I had long had an inkling of it, but the full realisation came last year almost suddenly. I suddenly felt that it was all the same to me whether the world existed or whether there had never been anything at all: I began to feel with all my being that there was *nothing existing.* At first I fancied that many things had existed in the past, but afterwards I guessed that there never had been anything in the past either, but that it had only seemed so for some reason. Little by little I guessed that there would be nothing in the future either. Then I left off being angry with people and almost ceased to notice them. Indeed this showed itself even in the pettiest trifles: I used, for instance, to knock against people in the street. And not so much from being lost in thought: what had I to think about? I had almost given up thinking by that time; nothing mattered to me. If at least I had solved my problems! Oh, I had not settled one of them, and how many they were! But I gave up caring about anything, and all the problems disappeared.

And it was after that that I found out the truth. I learnt the truth last November—on the third of November, to be precise—and I remember every instant since. It was a gloomy evening, one of the gloomiest possible evenings. I was going home at about eleven o'clock, and I remember that I thought that the evening could not be gloomier. Even physically. Rain had been falling all day, and it had been a cold, gloomy, almost menacing rain, with, I remember, an unmistakable spite against mankind. Suddenly between ten and eleven it had stopped, and was followed by a horrible dampness, colder and damper than the rain, and a sort of steam was rising from everything, from every stone in the street, and from every by-lane if one looked down it as far as one could. A thought suddenly occurred to me, that if all the street lamps had been put out it would have been less cheerless, that the gas made one's heart sadder because it lighted it all up. I had had scarcely any dinner that day, and had been spending the evening with an engineer, and two other friends had been there also. I sat silent—I fancy I bored them. They talked of something rousing and suddenly they got excited over it. But they did not really care, I could see that, and only made a show of being excited. I suddenly said as much to them. "My friends,"

I said, "you really do not care one way or the other." They were not offended, but they all laughed at me. That was because I spoke without any note of reproach, simply because it did not matter to me. They saw it did not, and it amused them.

As I was thinking about the gas lamps in the street I looked up at the sky. The sky was horribly dark, but one could distinctly see tattered clouds, and between them fathomless black patches. Suddenly I noticed in one of these patches a star, and began watching it intently. That was because that star gave me an idea: I decided to kill myself that night. I had firmly determined to do so two months before, and poor as I was, I bought a splendid revolver that very day, and loaded it. But two months had passed and it was still lying in my drawer; I was so utterly indifferent that I wanted to seize a moment when I would not be so indifferent—why, I don't know. And so for two months every night that I came home I thought I would shoot myself. I kept waiting for the right moment. And so now this star gave me a thought. I made up my mind that it should certainly be that night. And why the star gave me the thought I don't know.

And just as I was looking at the sky, this little girl took me by the elbow. The street was empty, and there was scarcely any one to be seen. A cabman was sleeping in the distance in his cab. It was a child of eight with a kerchief on her head, wearing nothing but a wretched little dress all soaked with rain, but I noticed particularly her wet broken shoes and I recall them now. They caught my eye particularly. She suddenly pulled me by the elbow and called me. She was not weeping, but was spasmodically crying out some words which she could not utter properly, because she was shivering and shuddering all over. She was in terror about something, and kept crying, "Mammy, mammy!" I turned facing her, I did not say a word and went on; but she ran, pulling at me, and there was that note in her voice which in frightened children means despair. I know that sound. Though she did not articulate the words, I understood that her mother was dying, or something of the sort was happening to them, and that she had run out to call some one, to find something to help her mother. I did not go with her; on the contrary, I had an impulse to drive her away. I told her first to go to a policeman. But clasping her hands, she ran beside me sobbing and gasping, and would not leave me. Then I stamped my foot, and shouted at her. She called out "Sir! sir! . . ." but suddenly abandoned me and rushed headlong across the road. Some other passer-by appeared there, and she evidently flew from me to him.

I mounted up to my fifth storey. I have a room in a flat where there are other lodgers. My room is small and poor, with a garret window in the shape of a semicircle. I have a sofa covered with American leather, a table with books on it, two chairs and a comfortable arm-chair, as old as old can be, but of the good old-fashioned shape. I sat down, lighted the candle, and began thinking. In the room next to mine, through the partition wall, a perfect Bedlam was going on. It had been going on for the last three days. A retired captain lived there, and he had half a dozen visitors, gentlemen of doubtful reputation, drinking vodka and playing *stoss* with old cards. The night before there had been a fight, and I know that two of them had been for a long time engaged in dragging each other about by the hair. The landlady wanted to complain, but she was in abject terror of the captain. There was only one other lodger in the flat, a thin little regimental lady, on a visit to Petersburg, with three little children who had been taken ill since they came into the lodgings. Both she and her children were in mortal fear of the captain, and lay trembling and crossing themselves all night, and the youngest child had a sort of fit from fright. That captain, I know for a fact, sometimes stops people in the Nevsky Prospect and begs. They won't take him into the service, but strange to say (that's why I am telling this), all this month that the captain has been here his behaviour has caused me no annoyance. I have, of course, tried to avoid his acquaintance from the very beginning, and he, too, was bored with me from the first; but I never care how much they shout the other side of the partition nor how many of them there are in there: I sit up all night and forget them so completely that I do not even hear them. I stay awake till daybreak, and have been going on like that for the last year. I sit up all night in my arm-chair at the table, doing nothing. I only read by day. I sit—don't even think; ideas of a sort wander through my mind and I let them come and go as they will. A whole candle is burnt every night. I sat down quietly at the table, took out the revolver and put it down before me. When I had put it down I asked myself, I remember, "Is that so?" and answered with complete conviction, "It is." That is, I shall shoot myself. I knew that I should shoot myself that night for certain, but how much longer I should go on sitting at the table I did not know. And no doubt I should have shot myself if it had not been for that little girl.

## 2

You see, though nothing mattered to me, I could feel pain, for instance. If any one had struck me it would have hurt me. It was the same morally: if anything very pathetic happened, I should have felt pity just as I used to do in old days when there were things in life that did matter to me. I had felt pity that evening. I should have certainly helped a child. Why, then, had I not helped the little girl? Because of an idea that occurred to me at the time: when she was calling and pulling at me, a question suddenly arose before me and I could not settle it. The question was an idle one, but I was vexed. I was vexed at the reflection that if I were going to make an end of myself that night, nothing in life ought to have mattered to me. Why was it that all at once I did not feel that nothing mattered and was sorry for the little girl? I remember that I was very sorry for her, so much so that I felt a strange pang, quite incongruous in my position. Really I do not know better how to convey my fleeting sensation at the moment, but the sensation persisted at home when I was sitting at the table, and I was very much irritated as I had not been for a long time past. One reflection followed another. I saw clearly that so long as I was still a human being and not nothingness, I was alive and so could suffer, be angry and feel shame at my actions. So be it. But if I am going to kill myself, in two hours, say, what is the little girl to me and what have I to do with shame or with anything else in the world? I shall turn into nothing, absolutely nothing. And can it really be true that the consciousness that I shall *completely* cease to exist immediately and so everything else will cease to exist, does not in the least affect my feeling of pity for the child nor the feeling of shame after a contemptible action? I stamped and shouted at the unhappy child as though to say—not only I feel no pity, but even if I behave inhumanly and contemptibly, I am free to, for in another two hours everything will be extinguished. Do you believe that that was why I shouted that? I am almost convinced of it now. It seemed clear to me that life and the world somehow depended upon me now. I may almost say that the world now seemed created for me alone: if I shot myself the world would cease to be at least for me. I say nothing of its being likely that nothing will exist for any one when I am gone, and that as soon as my consciousness is extinguished the whole world will vanish too and become void like a phantom, as a mere appurtenance of my consciousness, for possibly all this world and all these people are only me myself. I remember that as I sat and reflected, I turned all these new questions that swarmed one after another quite the other way, and thought of something quite new. For instance, a strange reflection suddenly occurred to me, that if I had lived before on the moon or on Mars and there had committed the most disgraceful and dishonourable action and had there been put to such shame and ignominy as one can only conceive and realise in dreams, in nightmares, and if, finding myself afterwards on earth, I were able to retain the memory of what I had done on the other planet and at the same time knew that I should never, under any circumstances, return there, then looking from the earth to the moon—*should I care or not?* Should I feel shame for that action or not? These were idle and superfluous questions for the revolver was already lying before me, and I knew in every fibre of my being that *it* would happen for certain, but they excited me and I raged. I could not die now without having first settled something. In short, the child had saved me, for I put off my pistol shot for the sake of these questions. Meanwhile the clamour had begun to subside in the captain's room: they had finished their game, were settling down to sleep, and meanwhile were grumbling and languidly winding up their quarrels. At that point I suddenly fell asleep in my chair at the table—a thing which had never happened to me before. I dropped asleep quite unawares.

Dreams, as we all know, are very queer things: some parts are presented with appalling vividness, with details worked up with the elaborate finish of jewellery, while others one gallops through, as it were, without noticing them at all, for instance, through space and time. Dreams seem to be spurred on not by reason but by desire, not by the head but by the heart, and yet what complicated tricks my reason has played sometimes in dreams, what utterly incomprehensible things happen to it! My brother died five years ago, for instance. I sometimes dream of him; he takes part in my affairs, we are very much interested, and yet all through my dream I quite know and remember that my brother is dead and buried. How is it that I am not surprised that, though he is dead, he is here beside me and working with me? Why is it that my reason fully accepts it? But enough. I will begin about my dream. Yes, I dreamed a dream, my dream of the third of November. They tease me now, telling me it was only a dream.

But does it matter whether it was a dream or reality, if the dream made known to me the truth? If once one has recognised the truth and seen it, you know that it is the truth and that there is no other and there cannot be, whether you are asleep or awake. Let it be a dream, so be it, but that real life of which you make so much I had meant to extinguish by suicide, and my dream, my dream—oh, it revealed to me a different life, renewed, grand and full of power!

Listen.

3

I have mentioned that I dropped asleep unawares and even seemed to be still reflecting on the same subjects. I suddenly dreamt that I picked up the revolver and aimed it straight at my heart—my heart, and not my head; and I had determined beforehand to fire at my head, at my right temple. After aiming at my chest I waited a second or two, and suddenly my candle, my table, and the wall in front of me began moving and heaving. I made haste to pull the trigger.

In dreams you sometimes fall from a height, or are stabbed, or beaten, but you never feel pain unless, perhaps, you really bruise yourself against the bedstead, then you feel pain and almost always wake up from it. It was the same in my dream. I did not feel any pain, but it seemed as though with my shot everything within me was shaken and everything was suddenly dimmed, and it grew horribly black around me. I seemed to be blinded and benumbed, and I was lying on something hard, stretched on my back; I saw nothing, and could not make the slightest movement. People were walking and shouting around me, the captain bawled, the landlady shrieked—and suddenly another break and I was being carried in a closed coffin. And I felt how the coffin was shaking and reflected upon it, and for the first time the idea struck me that I was dead, utterly dead, I knew it and had no doubt of it, I could neither see nor move and yet I was feeling and reflecting. But I was soon reconciled to the position, and as one usually does in a dream, accepted the facts without disputing them.

And now I was buried in the earth. They all went away, I was left alone, utterly alone. I did not move. Whenever before I had imagined being buried the one sensation I associated with the grave was that of damp and cold. So now I felt that I was very cold, especially the tips of my toes, but I felt nothing else.

I lay still, strange to say I expected nothing, accepting without dispute that a dead man had nothing to expect. But it was damp. I don't know how long a time passed—whether an hour, or several days, or many days. But all at once a drop of water fell on my closed left eye, making its way through a coffin lid; it was followed a minute later by a second, then a minute later by a third—and so on, regularly every minute. There was a sudden glow of profound indignation in my heart, and I suddenly felt in it a pang of physical pain. "That's my wound," I thought; "that's the bullet. . . ." And drop after drop every minute kept falling on my closed eyelid. And all at once, not with my voice, but with my whole being, I called upon the power that was responsible for all that was happening to me:

"Whoever you may be, if you exist, and if anything more rational than what is happening here is possible, suffer it to be here now. But if you are revenging yourself upon me for my senseless suicide by the hideousness and absurdity of this subsequent existence, then let me tell you that no torture could ever equal the contempt which I shall go on dumbly feeling, though my martyrdom may last a million years!"

I made this appeal and held my peace. There was a full minute of unbroken silence and again another drop fell, but I knew with infinite unshakable certainty that everything would change immediately. And behold my grave suddenly was rent asunder, that is, I don't know whether it was opened or dug up, but I was caught up by some dark and unknown being and we found ourselves in space. I suddenly regained my sight. It was the dead of night, and never, never had there been such darkness. We were flying through space far away from the earth. I did not question the being who was taking me; I was proud and waited. I assured myself that I was not afraid, and was thrilled with ecstasy at the thought that I was not afraid. I do not know how long we were flying, I cannot imagine; it happened as it always does in dreams when you skip over space and time, and the laws of thought and existence, and only pause upon the points for which the heart yearns. I remember that I suddenly saw in the darkness a star. "Is that Sirius?" I asked impulsively, though I had not meant to ask any questions.

"No, that is the star you saw between the clouds when you were coming home," the being who was carrying me replied.

I knew that it had something like a human face. Strange to say, I did not like that being, in fact I felt an intense aversion for it. I had expected complete non-existence, and that was why I had put a bullet through my heart. And here I was in the hands of a creature not human, of course, but yet living, existing. "And so there is life beyond the grave," I thought with the strange frivolity one has in dreams. But in its inmost depth my heart remained unchanged. "And if I have got to exist again," I thought, "and live once more under the control of some irresistible power, I won't be vanquished and humiliated."

"You know that I am afraid of you and despise me for that," I said suddenly to my companion, unable to refrain from the humiliating question which implied a confession, and feeling my humiliation stab my heart as with a pin. He did not answer my question, but all at once I felt that he was not even despising me, but was laughing at me and had no compassion for me, and that our journey had an unknown and mysterious object that concerned me only. Fear was growing in my heart. Something was mutely and painfully communicated to me from my silent companion, and permeated my whole being. We were flying through dark, unknown space. I had for some time lost sight of the constellations familiar to my eyes. I knew that there were stars in the heavenly spaces the light of which took thousands or millions of years to reach the earth. Perhaps we were already flying through those spaces. I expected something with a terrible anguish that tortured my heart. And suddenly I was thrilled by a familiar feeling that stirred me to the depths: I suddenly caught sight of our sun! I knew that it could not be *our sun,* that gave life to *our* earth, and that we were an infinite distance from our sun, but for some reason I knew in my whole being that it was a sun exactly like ours, a duplicate of it. A sweet, thrilling feeling resounded with ecstasy in my heart: the kindred power of the same light which had given me light stirred an echo in my heart and awakened it, and I had a sensation of life, the old life of the past for the first time since I had been in the grave.

"But if that is the sun, if that is exactly the same as our sun," I cried, "where is the earth?"

And my companion pointed to a star twinkling in the distance with an emerald light. We were flying straight towards it.

"And are such repetitions possible in the universe? Can that be the law of Nature? . . . And if that is an earth there, can it be just the same earth as ours . . . just the same, as poor, as unhappy, but precious and beloved for ever, arousing in the most ungrateful of her children the same poignant love for her that we feel for our earth?" I cried out, shaken by irresistible, ecstatic love for the old familiar earth which I had left. The image of the poor child whom I had repulsed flashed through my mind.

"You shall see it all," answered my companion, and there was a note of sorrow in his voice.

But we were rapidly approaching the planet. It was growing before my eyes; I could already distinguish the ocean, the outline of Europe; and suddenly a feeling of a great and holy jealousy glowed in my heart.

"How can it be repeated and what for? I love and can love only that earth which I have left, stained with my blood, when, in my ingratitude, I quenched my life with a bullet in my heart. But I have never, never ceased to love that earth, and perhaps on the very night I parted from it I loved it more than ever. Is there suffering upon this new earth? On our earth we can only love with suffering and through suffering. We cannot love otherwise, and we know of no other sort of love. I want suffering in order to love. I long, I thirst, this very instant, to kiss with tears the earth that I have left, and I don't want, I won't accept life on any other!"

But my companion had already left me. I suddenly, quite without noticing how, found myself on this other earth, in the bright light of a sunny day, fair as paradise. I believe I was standing on one of the islands that make up on our globe the Greek archipelago, or on the coast of the mainland facing that archipelago. Oh, everything was exactly as it is with us, only everything seemed to have a festive radiance, the splendour of some great, holy triumph attained at last. The caressing sea, green as emerald, splashed softly upon the shore and kissed it with manifest, almost conscious love. The tall, lovely trees stood in all the glory of their blossom, and their innumerable leaves greeted me, I am certain, with their soft, caressing rustle and seemed to articulate words of love. The grass glowed with bright and fragrant flowers. Birds were flying in flocks in the air, and perched fearlessly on my shoulders and arms and joyfully struck me with their darling, fluttering wings. And at last I saw and knew the people of this happy land. They came to me of themselves, surrounded me, kissed me. The children of the sun, the children of their sun—oh, how beautiful they were! Never had I seen on our own earth such beauty in mankind. Only perhaps in our children, in their earliest years, one might find some remote, faint reflection of this beauty. The eyes of these happy people shone with a clear brightness.

Their faces were radiant with the light of reason and fulness of a serenity that comes of perfect understanding, but those faces were gay; in their words and voices there was a note of childlike joy. Oh, from the first moment, from the first glance at them, I understood it all! It was the earth untarnished by the Fall; on it lived people who had not sinned. They lived just in such a paradise as that in which, according to all the legends of mankind, our first parents lived before they sinned; the only difference was that all this earth was the same paradise. These people, laughing joyfully, thronged round me and caressed me; they took me home with them, and each of them tried to reassure me. Oh, they asked me no questions, but they seemed, I fancied, to know everything without asking, and they wanted to make haste and smooth away the signs of suffering from my face.

## 4

And do you know what? Well, granted that it was only a dream, yet the sensation of the love of those innocent and beautiful people has remained with me for ever, and I feel as though their love is still flowing out to me from over there. I have seen them myself, have known them and been convinced; I loved them, I suffered for them afterwards. Oh, I understood at once even at the time that in many things I could not understand them at all; as an up-to-date Russian progressive and contemptible Petersburger, it struck me as inexplicable that, knowing so much, they had, for instance, no science like ours. But I soon realised that their knowledge was gained and fostered by intuitions different from those of us on earth, and that their aspirations, too, were quite different. They desired nothing and were at peace; they did not aspire to knowledge of life as we aspire to understand it, because their lives were full. But their knowledge was higher and deeper than ours; for our science seeks to explain what life is, aspires to understand it in order to teach others how to live, while they without science knew how to live; and that I understood, but I could not understand their knowledge. They showed me their trees, and I could not understand the intense love with which they looked at them; it was as though they were talking with creatures like themselves. And perhaps I shall not be mistaken if I say that they conversed with them. Yes, they had found their language, and I am convinced that the trees understood them. They looked at all Nature like that—at the animals who lived in peace with them and did not attack them, but loved them, conquered by their love. They pointed to the stars and told me something about them which I could not understand, but I am convinced that they were somehow in touch with the stars, not only in thought, but by some living channel. Oh, these people did not persist in trying to make me understand them, they loved me without that, but I knew that they would never understand me, and so I hardly spoke to them about our earth. I only kissed in their presence the earth on which they lived and mutely worshipped them themselves. And they saw that and let me worship them without being abashed at my adoration, for they themselves loved much. They were not unhappy on my account when at times I kissed their feet with tears, joyfully conscious of the love with which they would respond to mine. At times I asked myself with wonder how it was they were able never to offend a creature like me, and never once to arouse a feeling of jealousy or envy in me? Often I wondered how it could be that, boastful and untruthful as I was, I never talked to them of what I knew—of which, of course, they had no notion—that I was never tempted to do so by a desire to astonish or even to benefit them.

They were as gay and sportive as children. They wandered about their lovely woods and copses, they sang their lovely songs; their fare was light—the fruits of their trees, the honey from their woods, and the milk of the animals who loved them. The work they did for food and raiment was brief and not laborious. They loved and begot children, but I never noticed in them the impulse of that *cruel* sensuality which overcomes almost every man on this earth, all and each, and is the source of almost every sin of mankind on earth. They rejoiced at the arrival of children as new beings to share their happiness. There was no quarrelling, no jealousy among them, and they did not even know what the words meant. Their children were the children of all, for they all made up one family. There was scarcely any illness among them, though there was death; but their old people died peacefully, as though falling asleep, giving blessings and smiles to those who surrounded them to take their last farewell with bright and loving smiles. I never saw grief or tears on those occasions, but only love, which reached the point of ecstasy, but a calm ecstasy, made perfect and contemplative. One might think that they were still in contact with the departed after death, and that their earthly union was not cut short by death. They scarcely understood me when I questioned them about immortality, but evidently they were so convinced of it without reasoning that it was not for them a question at all. They had no temples, but they had a real living and uninterrupted sense of oneness with the whole of the universe; they had no creed, but they had a certain knowledge that when their earthly joy had reached the limits of earthly nature, then there would come for them, for the living and for the dead, a still greater fulness of contact with the whole of the universe. They looked forward to that moment with joy, but without haste, not pining for it, but seeming to have a foretaste of it in their hearts, of which they talked to one another.

In the evening before going to sleep they liked singing in musical and harmonious chorus. In those songs they expressed all the sensations that the parting day had given them, sang its glories and took leave of it. They sang the praises of nature, of the sea, of the woods. They liked making songs about one another, and praised each other like children; they were the simplest songs, but they sprang from their hearts and went to one's heart. And not only in their songs but in all their lives they seemed to do nothing but admire one another. It was like being in love with each other, but an all-embracing, universal feeling.

Some of their songs, solemn and rapturous, I scarcely understood at all. Though I understood the words I could never fathom their full significance. It remained, as it were, beyond the grasp of my mind, yet my heart unconsciously absorbed it more and more. I often told them that I had had a presentiment of it long before, that this joy and glory had come to me on our earth in the form of a yearning melancholy that at times approached insufferable sorrow; that I had a foreknowledge of them all and of their glory in the dreams of my heart and the visions of my mind; that often on our earth I could not look at the setting sun without tears . . . that in my hatred for the men of our earth there was always a yearning anguish: why could I not hate them without loving them? why could I not help forgiving them? and in my love for them there was a yearning grief: why could I not love them without hating them? They listened to me, and I saw they could not conceive what I was saying, but I did not regret that I had spoken to them of it: I knew that they understood the intensity of my yearning anguish over those whom I had left. But when they looked at me with their sweet eyes full of love, when I felt that in their presence my heart, too, became as innocent and just as theirs, the feeling of the fulness of life took my breath away, and I worshipped them in silence.

Oh, every one laughs in my face now, and assures me that one cannot dream of such details as I am telling now, that I only dreamed or felt one sensation that arose in my heart in delirium and made up the details myself when I woke up. And when I told them that perhaps it really was so, my God, how they shouted with laughter in my face, and what mirth I caused! Oh, yes, of course I was overcome by the mere sensation of my dream, and that was all that was preserved in my cruelly wounded heart; but the actual forms and images of my dreams, that is, the very ones I really saw at the very time of my dream, were filled with such harmony, were so lovely and enchanting and were so actual, that on awakening I was, of course, incapable of clothing them in our poor language, so that they were bound to become blurred in my mind; and so perhaps I really was forced afterwards to make up the details, and so of course to distort them in my passionate desire to convey some at least of them as quickly as I could. But on the other hand, how can I help believing that it was all true? It was perhaps a thousand times brighter, happier and more joyful than I describe it. Granted that I dreamed it, yet it must have been real. You know, I will tell you a secret: perhaps it was not a dream at all! For then something happened so awful, something so horribly true, that it could not have been imagined in a dream. My heart may have originated the dream, but would my heart alone have been capable of originating the awful event which happened to me afterwards? How could I alone have invented it or imagined it in my dream? Could my petty heart and my fickle, trivial mind have risen to such a revelation of truth? Oh, judge for yourselves: hitherto I have concealed it, but now I will tell the truth. The fact is that I . . . corrupted them all!

## *5*

Yes, yes it ended in my corrupting them all! How it could come to pass I do not know, but I remember it clearly. The dream embraced thousands of years and left in me only a sense of the whole. I only know that I was the cause of their sin and downfall. Like a vile trichina, like a germ of the plague infecting whole kingdoms, so I contaminated all this earth, so happy and sinless before my coming. They learnt to lie, grew fond of lying, and discovered the charm of falsehood. Oh, at first perhaps it began innocently, with a jest, coquetry, with amorous play, perhaps indeed with a germ, but that germ of falsity made its way into their hearts and pleased them. Then sensuality was soon begotten, sensuality begot jealousy, jealousy—cruelty. . . . Oh, I don't know, I don't remember; but soon, very soon the first blood was shed. They marvelled and were horrified, and began to be split up and divided. They formed into unions, but it was against one another. Reproaches, upbraidings followed. They came to know shame, and shame brought them to virtue. The conception of honour sprang up, and every union began waving its flags. They began torturing animals, and the animals withdrew from them into the forests and became hostile to them. They began to struggle for separation, for isolation, for individuality, for mine and thine. They began to talk in different languages. They became acquainted with sorrow and loved sorrow; they thirsted for suffering, and said that truth could only be attained through suffering. Then science appeared. As they became wicked they began talking of brotherhood and humanitarianism, and understood those ideas. As they became criminal, they invented justice and drew up whole legal codes in order to observe it, and to ensure their being kept, set up a guillotine. They hardly remembered what they had lost, in fact refused to believe that they had ever been happy and innocent. They even laughed at the possibility of this happiness in the past, and called it a dream. They could not even imagine it in definite form and shape, but, strange and wonderful to relate, though they lost all faith in their past happiness and called it a legend, they so longed to be happy and innocent once more that they succumbed to this desire like children, made an idol of it, set up temples and worshipped their own idea, their own desire; though at the same time they fully believed that it was unattainable and could not be realised, yet they bowed down to it and adored it with tears! Nevertheless, if it could have happened that they had returned to the innocent and happy condition which they had lost, and if some one had shown it to them again and had asked them whether they wanted to go back to it, they would certainly have refused. They answered me:

"We may be deceitful, wicked and unjust, we *know* it and weep over it, we grieve over it; we torment and punish ourselves more perhaps than that merciful Judge Who will judge us and whose Name we know not. But we have science, and by means of it we shall find the truth and we shall arrive at it consciously. Knowledge is higher than feeling, the consciousness of life is higher than life. Science will give us wisdom, wisdom will reveal the laws, and the knowledge of the laws of happiness is higher than happiness."

That is what they said, and after saying such things every one began to love himself better than any one else, and indeed they could not do otherwise. All became so jealous of the rights of their own personality that they did their very utmost to curtail and destroy them in others, and made that the chief thing in their lives. Slavery followed, even voluntary slavery; the weak eagerly submitted to the strong, on condition that the latter aided them to subdue the still weaker. Then there were saints who came to these people, weeping, and talked to them of their pride, of their loss of harmony and due proportion, of their loss of shame. They were laughed at or pelted with stones. Holy blood was shed on the threshold of the temples. Then there arose men who began to think how to bring all people together again, so that everybody, while still loving himself best of all, might not interfere with others, and all might live together in something like a harmonious society. Regular wars sprang up over this idea. All the combatants at the same time firmly believed that science, wisdom and the instinct of self-preservation would force men at last to unite into a harmonious and rational society; and so, meanwhile, to hasten matters, "the wise" endeavoured to exterminate as rapidly as possible all who were "not wise" and did not understand their idea, that the latter might not hinder its triumph. But the instinct of self-preservation grew rapidly weaker; there arose men, haughty and sensual, who demanded all or nothing. In order to obtain everything they resorted to crime, and if they did not succeed—to suicide. There arose religions with a cult of non-existence and self-destruction for the sake of the everlasting peace of annihilation. At last these people grew weary of their meaningless toil, and signs of suffering came into their faces, and then they proclaimed that suffering was a beauty, for in suffering alone was there meaning. They glorified suffering in their songs. I moved about among them, wringing my hands and weeping over them, but I loved them perhaps more than in old days when there was no suffering in their faces and when they were innocent and so lovely. I loved the earth they had polluted even more than when it had been a paradise, if only because sorrow had come to it. Alas! I always loved sorrow and tribulation, but only for myself, for myself; but I wept over them, pitying them. I stretched out my hands to them in despair, blaming, cursing and despising myself. I told them that all this was my doing, mine alone; that it was I had brought them corruption, contamination and falsity. I besought them to crucify me, I taught them how to make a cross. I could not kill myself, I had not the strength, but I wanted to suffer at their hands. I yearned for suffering, I longed that my blood should be drained to the last drop in these agonies. But they only laughed at me, and began at last to look upon me as crazy. They justified me, they declared that they had only got what they wanted themselves, and that all that now was could not have been otherwise. At last they declared to me that I was becoming dangerous and that they should lock me up in a madhouse if I did not hold my tongue. Then such grief took possession of my soul that my heart was wrung, and I felt as though I were dying; and then . . . then I awoke.

It was morning, that is, it was not yet daylight, but about six o'clock. I woke up in the same arm-chair; my candle had burnt out; every one was asleep in the captain's room, and there was a stillness all round, rare in our flat. First of all I leapt up in great amazement: nothing like this had ever happened to me before, not even in the most trivial detail; I had never, for instance, fallen asleep like this in my arm-chair. While I was standing and coming to myself I suddenly caught sight of my revolver lying loaded, ready—but instantly I thrust it away! Oh, now, life, life! I lifted up my hands and called upon eternal truth, not with words but with tears; ecstasy, immeasurable ecstasy flooded my soul. Yes, life and spreading the good tidings! Oh, I at that moment resolved to spread the tidings, and resolved it, of course, for my whole life. I go to spread the tidings, I want to spread the tidings—of what? Of the truth, for I have seen it, have seen it with my own eyes, have seen it in all its glory.

And since then I have been preaching! Moreover I love all those who laugh at me more than any of the rest. Why that is so I do not know and cannot explain, but so be it. I am told that I am vague and confused, and if I am vague and confused now, what shall I be later on? It is true indeed: I am vague and confused, and perhaps as times goes on I shall be more so. And of course I shall make many blunders before I find out how to preach, that is, find out what words to say, what things to do, for it is a very difficult task. I see all that as clear as daylight, but, listen, who does not make mistakes? And yet, you know, all are making for the same goal, all are striving in the same direction anyway, from the sage to the lowest robber, only by different roads. It is an old truth, but this is what is new: I cannot go far wrong. For I have seen the truth; I have seen and I know that people can be beautiful and happy without losing the power of living on earth. I will not and cannot believe that evil is the normal condition of mankind. And it is just this faith of mine that they laugh at. But how can I help believing it? I have seen the truth—it is not as though I had invented it with my mind, I have seen it, seen it, and *the living image* of it has filled my soul for ever. I have seen it in such full perfection that I cannot believe that it is impossible for people to have it. And so how can I go wrong? I shall make some slips no doubt, and shall perhaps talk in second-hand language, but not for long: the living image of what I saw will always be with me and will always correct and guide me. Oh, I am full of courage and freshness, and I will go on and on if it were for a thousand years! Do you know, at first I meant to conceal the fact that I corrupted them, but that was a mistake—that was my first mistake! But truth whispered to me that I was *lying,* and preserved me and corrected me. But how establish paradise—I don't know, because I do not know how to put it into words. After my dream I lost command of words. All the chief words, anyway, the most necessary ones. But never mind, I shall go and I shall keep talking, I won't leave off, for anyway I have seen it with my own eyes, though I cannot describe what I saw. But the scoffers do not understand that. It was a dream, they say, delirium, hallucination. Oh! As though that meant so much! And they are so proud! A dream! What is a dream? And is not our life a dream? I will say more. Suppose that this paradise will never come to pass (that I understand), yet I shall go on preaching it. And yet how simple it is: in one day, *in one hour* everything could be arranged at once! The chief thing is to love others like yourself, that's the great thing, and that's everything; nothing else is wanted—you will find out at once how to arrange it all. And yet it's an old truth which has been told and retold a billion times—but it has not formed part of our lives! The consciousness of life is higher than life, the knowledge of the laws of happiness is higher than happiness—that is what one must contend against. And I shall. If only every one wants it, it can all be arranged at once.

And I tracked out that little girl . . . and I shall go on and on!

## *Study questions*

1. *In a subtitle, Dostoevsky labels "The Dream of a Ridiculous Man" as "A Fantastic Story." What is fantastic about this story?* 2. *Why does the narrator consider himself a ridiculous man? Why at the end is he called a madman? Is there a relationship between the two conditions?* 3. *Why does the narrator consider that the world is absurd? What does he mean when he says: "I began to feel with all my being that there was* nothing existing*"?* 4. *Why does the narrator decide to kill himself? What stops him?* 5. *In his dream how does the narrator conceive the condition of death? What feelings do the death journey arouse in him?* 6. *The narrator's companion on the death journey leads him to a replication of earth. What is it like there? How does the narrator respond to it?* 7. *What happens in the paradise he discovers? How does he corrupt the people there?* 8. *After the corruption the "new" earth becomes a mirror image of the earth the narrator knew before his dream. Why does he take the full blame and implore the people to crucify him?* 9. *After his dream, why does the narrator assume the role of preacher in an attempt to deliver people to paradise?* 10. *What does the narrator mean when he says: "What is a dream? And is not our life a dream?"* 11. *How is it relevant to the theme of the story that the narrator cannot find appropriate words?* 12. *Is the narrator a madman?*

*Mark Twain* (SAMUEL LANGHORNE CLEMENS, 1835–1910), printer, riverboat pilot, prospector, reporter, and, of course, writer, is considered by some to be the representative American writer and his *Adventures of Huckleberry Finn* (1884) a central document of American culture. Born near Hannibal, Missouri, Twain immortalized the town in his fiction. His most popular early work is based on folk materials, such as the tall tale and the practical joke. As he grew older, however, he turned to pessimism and indicted the human race as wicked and perverse. A story like "The Mysterious Stranger," published posthumously in 1916, is a powerful statement about malevolent human force. Twain's short pieces are, however, usually no more than sketches, humorous, farcical, or gently satiric, not often getting beyond a surface level. Encouraged by Bret Harte, Twain published his first volume of short pieces, *The Celebrated Jumping Frog of Calaveras County and Other Sketches*, in 1867. His complete short stories were brought together in a volume edited by Charles Neider in 1957. In short fiction Twain's major accomplishment was his handling of the oral tale celebrating the vigorous language and rough features of frontier life. In this he may be grouped with the "local color" story writers like T. B. Thorpe and George Washington Harris. Another kind of local color writing comes down through the writings of people like William Gilmore Simms and Bret Harte, writers who used local scenes, customs, and dialects as background for their essentially romantic and often sentimental characters. "My Platonic Sweetheart" exhibits another side of Twain's character and aspect of his writing—his interest in so-called "sleep fancies." But in this story the narrator's recurrent dreams are of the order of wish-fulfillment fantasies and are not at all like the nightmares into which Hawthorne, Poe, and Gogol sometimes plunge us.

# MY PLATONIC SWEETHEART

I met her first when I was seventeen and she fifteen. It was in a dream. No, I did not meet her; I overtook her. It was in a Missourian village which I had never been in before, and was not in at that time, except dreamwise; in the flesh I was on the Atlantic seaboard ten or twelve hundred miles away. The thing was sudden, and without preparation—after the custom of dreams. There I was, crossing a wooden bridge that had a wooden rail and was untidy with scattered wisps of hay, and there she was, five steps in front of me; half a second previously neither of us was there. This was the exit of the village, which lay immediately behind us. Its last house was the blacksmith-shop; and the peaceful clinking of the hammers—a sound which nearly always seems remote, and is always touched with a spirit of loneliness and a feeling of soft regret for something, you don't know what—was wafted to my ears over my shoulder; in front of us was the winding country road, with woods on one side, and on the other a rail fence, with blackberry vines and hazel bushes crowding its angles; on an upper rail a bluebird, and scurrying toward him along the same rail a fox-squirrel with his tail bent high like a shepherd's crook; beyond the fence a rich field of grain, and far away a farmer in shirtsleeves and straw hat wading knee-deep through it; no other representatives of life, and no noise at all; everywhere a Sabbath stillness.

I remember it all—and the girl, too, and just how she walked, and how she was dressed. In the first moment I was five steps behind her; in the next one I was at her side—without either stepping or gliding; it merely happened; the transfer ignored space. I noticed that, but not with any surprise; it seemed a natural process.

I was at her side. I put my arm around her waist and drew her close to me, for I loved her; and although I did not know her, my behavior seemed to me quite natural and right, and I had no misgivings about it. She showed no surprise, no distress, no displeasure, but put an arm around my waist, and turned up her face to mine with a happy welcome in it, and when I bent down to kiss her she received the kiss as if she was expecting it, and as if it was quite natural for me to offer it and her to take it and have pleasure in it. The affection which I felt for her and which she manifestly felt for me was a quite simple fact; but the quality of it was another matter. It was not the affection of brother and sister—it was closer than that, more clinging, more endearing, more reverent; and it was not the love of sweethearts, for there was no fire in it. It was somewhere between the two, and was finer than either, and more exquisite, more profoundly contenting. We often experience this strange and gracious thing in our dream-loves; and we remember it as a feature of our childhood-loves, too.

We strolled along, across the bridge and down the road, chatting like the oldest friends. She called me George, and that seemed natural and right, though it was not my name; and I called her Alice, and she did not correct me, though without doubt it was not her name. Everything that happened seemed just natural and to be expected. Once I said, "What a dear little hand it is!" and without any words she laid it gracefully in mine for me to examine it. I did it, remarking upon its littleness, its delicate beauty, and its satin skin, then kissed it; she put it up to her lips without saying anything and kissed it in the same place.

Around a curve of the road, at the end of half a mile, we came to a log house, and entered it and found the table set and everything on it steaming hot—a roast turkey, corn in the ear, butterbeans, and the rest of the usual things—and a cat curled up asleep in a splint-bottomed chair by the fireplace; but no people; just emptiness and silence. She said she would look in the next room if I would wait for her. So I sat down, and she passed through a door, which closed behind her with a click of the latch. I waited and waited. Then I got up and followed, for I could not any longer bear to have her out of my sight. I passed through the door, and found myself in a strange sort of cemetery, a city of innumerable tombs and monuments stretching far and wide on every hand, and flushed with pink and gold lights flung from the sinking sun. I turned around, and the log house was gone. I ran here and there and yonder down the lanes between the rows of tombs, calling Alice; and presently the night closed down, and I could not find my way. Then I woke, in deep distress over my loss, and was in my bed in Philadelphia. And I was not seventeen, now, but nineteen.

Ten years afterward, in another dream, I found her. I was seventeen again, and she was still fifteen. I was in a grassy place in the twilight deeps of a magnolia forest some miles above Natchez, Mississippi; the trees were snowed over with great blossoms, and the air was loaded with their rich and strenuous fragrance; the ground was high, and through a rift in the wood a burnished patch of the river was visible in the distance. I was sitting on the grass, absorbed in thinking, when an arm was laid around my neck, and there was Alice sitting by my side and looking into my face. A deep and satisfied happiness and an unwordable gratitude rose in me, but with it there was no feeling of surprise; and there was no sense of a time-lapse; the ten years amounted to hardly even a yesterday; indeed, to hardly even a noticeable fraction of it. We dropped in the tranquilest way into affectionate caressings and pettings, and chatted along without a reference to the separation; which was natural, for I think we did not know there had been any that one might measure with either clock or almanac. She called me Jack and I called her Helen, and those seemed the right and proper names, and perhaps neither of us suspected that we had ever borne others; or, if we did suspect it, it was probably not a matter of consequence.

She had been beautiful ten years before; she was just as beautiful still; girlishly young and sweet and innocent, and she was still that now. She had blue eyes, a hair of flossy gold before; she had black hair now, and dark-brown eyes. I noted these differences, but they did not suggest change; to me she was the same girl she was before, absolutely. It never occurred to me to ask what became of the log house; I doubt if I even thought of it. We were living in a simple and natural and beautiful world where everything that happened was natural and right, and was not perplexed with the unexpected or with any forms of surprise, and so there was no occasion for explanations and no interest attaching to such things.

We had a dear and pleasant time together, and were like a couple of ignorant and contented children. Helen had a summer hat on. She took it off presently and said, "It was in the way; now you can kiss me better." It seemed to me merely a bit of courteous and considerate wisdom, nothing more; and a natural thing for her to think of and do. We went wandering through the woods, and came to a limpid and shallow stream a matter of three yards wide. She said:

"I must not get my feet wet, dear; carry me over."

I took her in my arms and gave her my hat to hold. This was to keep my own feet from getting wet. I did not know why this should have that effect; I merely knew it; and she knew it, too. I crossed the stream, and said I would go on carrying her, because it was so pleasant; and she said it was pleasant to her, too, and wished we had thought of it sooner. It seemed to me a pity that we should have walked so far, both of us on foot, when we could have been having this higher enjoyment; and I spoke of it regretfully, as a something lost which could never be got back. She was troubled about it, too, and said there must be some way to get it back; and she would think. After musing deeply a little while she looked up radiant and proud, and said she had found it.

"Carry me back and start over again."

I can see, now, that that was no solution, but at the time it seemed luminous with intelligence, and I believed that there was not another little head in the world that could have worked out that difficult problem with such swiftness and success.

I told her that, and it pleased her; and she said she was glad it all happened, so that I could see how capable she was. After thinking a moment she added that it was "quite atreous." The words seemed to mean something, I do not know why: in fact, it seemed to cover the whole ground and leave nothing more to say; I admired the nice aptness and the flashing felicity of the phrase, and was filled with respect for the marvelous mind that had been able to engender it. I think less of it now. It is a noticeable fact that the intellectual coinage of Dreamland often passes for more there than it would fetch here. Many a time in after years my dream-sweetheart threw off golden sayings which crumbled to ashes under my pencil when I was setting them down in my note-book after breakfast.

I carried her back and started over again; and all the long afternoon I bore her in my arms, miles upon miles, and it never occurred to either of us that there was anything remarkable in a youth like me being able to carry that sweet bundle around half a day without some sense of fatigue or need of rest. There are many dream-worlds, but none is so rightly and reasonably and pleasantly arranged as that one.

After dark we reached a great plantation-house, and it was her home. I carried her in, and the family knew me and I knew them, although we had not met before; and the mother asked me with ill disguised anxiety how much twelve times fourteen was, and I said a hundred and thirty-five, and she put it down on a piece of paper, saying it was her habit in the process of perfecting her education not to trust important particulars to her memory; and her husband was offering me a chair, but noticed that Helen was asleep, so he said it would be best not to disturb her; and he backed me softly against a wardrobe and said I could stand more easily now; then a negro came in, bowing humbly, with his slouch-hat in his hand, and asked me if I would have my measure taken. The question did not surprise me, but it confused me and worried me, and I said I should like to have advice about it. He started toward the door to call advisers; then he and the family and the lights began to grow dim, and in a few moments the place was pitch dark; but straightway there came a flood of moonlight and a gust of cold wind, and I found myself crossing a frozen lake, and my arms were empty. The wave of grief that swept through me woke me up, and I was sitting at my desk in the newspaper office in San Francisco, and I noticed by the clock that I had been asleep less than two minutes. And what was of more consequence, I was twenty-nine years old.

That was 1864. The next year and the year after I had momentary glimpses of my dream-sweetheart, but nothing more. These are set down in my note-books under their proper dates, but with no talks nor other particulars added; which is sufficient evidence to me that there were none to add. In both of these instances there was the sudden meeting and recognition, the eager approach, then the instant disappearance, leaving the world empty and of no worth. I remember the two images quite well; in fact I remember all the images of that spirit, and can bring them before me without help of my note-book. The habit of writing down my dreams of all sorts while they were fresh in my mind, and then studying them and rehearsing them and trying to find out what the source of dreams is, and which of the two or three separate persons inhabiting us is their architect, has given me a good dream-memory—a thing which is not usual with people, for few drill the dream-memory and, no memory can be kept strong without that.

I spent a few months in the Hawaiian Islands in 1866, and in October of that year I delivered my maiden lecture; it was in San Francisco. In the following January I arrived in New York, and had just completed my thirty-first year. In that year I saw my platonic dream-sweetheart again. In this dream I was again standing on the stage of the Opera House in San Francisco, ready to lecture, and with the audience vividly individualized before me in the strong light. I began, spoke a few words, and stopped, cold with fright; for I discovered that I had no subject, no text, nothing to talk about. I choked for a while, then got out a few words, a lame, poor attempt at humor. The house made no response. There was a miserable pause, then another attempt, and another failure. There were a few scornful laughs; otherwise the house was silent, unsmilingly austere, deeply offended. I was consuming with shame. In my distress I tried to work upon its pity. I began to make servile apologies, mixed with gross and ill-timed flatteries, and to beg and plead for forgiveness; this was too much, and the people broke into insulting cries, whistlings, hootings, and cat-calls, and in the midst of this they rose and began to struggle in a confused mass toward the door. I stood dazed and helpless, looking out over this spectacle, and thinking how everybody would be talking about it next day, and I could not show myself in the streets. When the house was become wholly empty and still, I sat down on the only chair that was on the stage and bent my head down on the reading-desk to shut out the look of that place. Soon that familiar dream-voice spoke my name, and swept all my troubles away:

"Robert!"

I answered:

"Agnes!"

The next moment we two were lounging up the blossomy gorge called the Iao Valley, in the Hawaiian Islands. I recognized, without any explanations, that Robert was not my name, but only a pet name, a common noun, and meant "dear"; and both of us knew that Agnes was not a name, but only a pet name, a common noun, whose spirit was affectionate, but not conveyable with the exactness in any but the dream-language. It was about the equivalent of "dear," but the dream-vocabulary shaves meanings finer and closer than do the world's daytime dictionaries. We did not know why those words should have those meanings; we had used words which had no existence in any known language, and had expected them to be understood, and they were understood. In my note-books there are several letters from this dream-sweetheart, in some unknown tongue—presumably dream-tongue—with translations added. I should like to be master of that tongue, then I could talk in shorthand. Here is one of those letters—the whole of it:

"Rax oha tal."

Translation.—"When you receive this it will remind you that I long to see your face and touch your hand, for the comfort of it and the peace."

It is swifter than waking thought; for thought is not thought at all, but only a vague and formless fog until it is articulated into words.

We wandered far up the fairy gorge, gathering the beautiful flowers of the ginger-plant and talking affectionate things, and tying and retying each other's ribbons and cravats, which didn't need it; and finally sat down in the shade of a tree and climbed the vine-hung precipices with our eyes, up and up and up toward the sky to where the drifting scarfs of white mist clove them across and left the green summits floating pale and remote, like spectral islands wandering in the deeps of space; and then we descended to earth and talked again.

"How still it is—and soft, and balmy, and reposeful! I could never tire of it. You like it, don't you, Robert?"

"Yes, and I like the whole region—all the islands. Maui. It is a darling island. I have been here before. Have you?"

"Once, but it wasn't an island then."

"What was it?"

"It was a sufa."

I understood. It was the dream-word for "part of a continent."

"What were the people like?"

"They hadn't come yet. There weren't any."

"Do you know, Agnes—that is Haleakala, the dead volcano, over there across the valley; was it here in your friend's time?"

"Yes, but it was burning."

"Do you travel much?"

"I think so. Not here much, but in the stars a good deal."

"Is it pretty there?"

She used a couple of dream-words for "You will go with me some time and you will see." Non-committal, as one perceives now, but I did not notice it then.

A man-of-war-bird lit on her shoulder; I put out my hand and caught it. Its feathers began to fall out, and it turned into a kitten; then the kitten's body began to contract itself to a ball and put out hairy, long legs, and soon it was a tarantula; I was going to keep it, but it turned into a star-fish, and I threw it away. Agnes said it was not worth while to try to keep things; there was no stability about them. I suggested rocks; but she said a rock was like the rest; it wouldn't stay. She picked up a stone, and it turned into a bat and flew away. These curious matters interested me, but that was all; they did not stir my wonder.

While we were sitting there in the Iao gorge talking, a Kanaka came along who was wrinkled and bent and white-headed, and he stopped and talked to us in the native tongue, and we understood him without trouble and answered him in his own speech. He said he was a hundred and thirty years old, and he remembered Captain Cook well, and was present when he was murdered; saw it with his own eyes, and also helped. Then he showed us his gun, which was of strange make, and he said it was his own invention and was to shoot arrows with, though one loaded it with powder and it had a percussion lock. He said it would carry a hundred miles. It seemed a reasonable statement; I had no fault to find with it, and it did not in any way surprise me. He loaded it and fired an arrow aloft, and it darted into the sky and vanished. Then he went his way, saying that the arrow would fall near us in half an hour, and would go many yards into the earth, not minding the rocks.

I took the time, and we waited, reclining upon the mossy slant at the base of a tree, and gazing into the sky. By and by there was a hissing sound, followed by a dull impact, and Agnes uttered a groan. She said, in a series of fainting gasps:

"Take me to your arms—it passed through me—hold me to your heart—

I am afraid to die—closer—closer. It is growing dark—I cannot see you. Don't leave me—where are you? You are not gone? You will not leave me? I would not leave you."

Then her spirit passed; she was clay in my arms.

The scene changed in an instant and I was awake and crossing Bond Street in New York with a friend, and it was snowing hard. We had been talking, and there had been no observable gaps in the conversation. I doubt if I had made any more than two steps while I was asleep. I am satisfied that even the most elaborate and incident-crowded dream is seldom more than a few seconds in length. It would not cost me very much of a strain to believe in Mohammed's seventy-year dream, which began when he knocked his glass over, and ended in time for him to catch it before the water was spilled.

Within a quarter of an hour I was in my quarters, undressed, ready for bed, and was jotting down my dream in my note-book. A striking thing happened now. I finished my notes, and was just going to turn out the gas when I was caught with a most strenuous gape, for it was very late and I was very drowsy. I fell asleep and dreamed again. What now follows occurred while I was asleep; and when I woke again the gape had completed itself, but not long before, I think, for I was still on my feet. I was in Athens—a city which I had not then seen, but I recognized the Parthenon from the pictures, although it had a fresh look and was in perfect repair. I passed by it and climbed a grassy hill toward a palatial sort of mansion which was built of red terra-cotta and had a spacious portico, whose roof was supported by a rank of fluted columns with Corinthian capitals. It was noonday, but I met no one. I passed into the house and entered the first room. It was very large and light, its walls were of polished and richly tinted and veined onyx, and its floor was a pictured pattern in soft colors laid in tiles. I noted the details of the furniture and the ornaments—a thing which I should not have been likely to do when awake—and they took sharp hold and remained in my memory; they are not really dim yet, and this was more than thirty years ago.

There was a person present—Agnes. I was not surprised to see her, but only glad. She was in the simple Greek costume, and her hair and eyes were different as to color from those she had had when she died in the Hawaiian Islands half an hour before, but to me she was exactly her own beautiful little self as I had always known her, and she was still fifteen, and I was seventeen once more. She was sitting on an ivory settee, crocheting something or other, and had her crewels in a shallow willow work-basket in her lap. I sat down by her and we began to chat in the usual way. I remembered her death, but the pain and the grief and the bitterness which had been so sharp and so desolating to me at the moment that it happened had wholly passed from me now, and had left not a scar. I was grateful to have her back, but there was no realizable sense that she had ever been gone, and so it did not occur to me to speak about it, and she made no reference to it herself. It may be that she had often died before, and knew that there was nothing lasting about it, and consequently nothing important enough in it to make conversation out of.

When I think of that house and its belongings, I recognize what a master in taste and drawing and color and arrangement is the dream-artist who resides in us. In my waking hours, when the inferior artist in me is in command, I cannot draw even the simplest picture with a pencil, nor do anything with a brush and colors; I cannot bring before my mind's eye the detail image of any building known to me except my own house at home; of St. Paul's, St. Peter's, the Eiffel Tower, the Taj, the Capitol at Washington, I can reproduce only portions, partial glimpses; the same with Niagara Falls, the Matterhorn, and other familiar things in nature; I cannot bring before my mind's eye the face or figure of any human being known to me; I have seen my family at breakfast within the past two hours; I cannot bring their images before me, I do not know how they look; before me, as I write, I see a little grove of young trees in the garden; high above them projects the slender lance of a young pine, beyond it is a glimpse of the upper half of a dull-white chimney covered by an A-shaped little roof shingled with brown-red tiles, and half a mile away is a hill-top densely wooded, and the red is cloven by a curved, wide vacancy, which is smooth and grass-clad; I cannot shut my eyes and reproduce that picture as a whole at all, nor any single detail of it except the grassy curve, and that but vaguely and fleetingly.

But my dream-artist can draw anything, and do it perfectly; he can paint with all the colors and all the shades, and do it with delicacy and truth; he can place before me vivid images of palaces, cities, hamlets, hovels, mountains, valleys, lakes, skies, glowing in sunlight or moonlight, or veiled in driving gusts of snow or rain, and he can set before me people who are intensely alive, and who feel, and express their feelings in their faces, and who also talk and laugh, sing and swear. And when I wake I can shut my eyes and bring back those people, and the scenery and the buildings; and not only in general view, but often in nice detail. While Agnes and I sat talking in that grand Athens house, several stately Greeks entered from another part of it, disputing warmly about something or other, and passed us by with courteous recognition; and among them was Socrates. I recognized him by his nose. A moment later the house and Agnes and Athens vanished away, and I was in my quarters in New York again and reaching for my note-book.

In our dreams—I know it!—we do make the journeys we seem to make; we do see the things we seem to see; the people, the horses, the cats, the dogs, the birds, the whales, are real, not chimeras; they are living spirits, not shadows; and they are immortal and indestructible. They go whither they will; they visit all resorts, all points of interest, even the twinkling suns that wander in the wastes of space. That is where those strange mountains are which slide from under our feet while we walk, and where those vast caverns are whose bewildering avenues close behind us and in front when we are lost, and shut us in. We know this because there are no such things here, and they must be there, because there is no other place.

This tale is long enough, and I will close it now. In the forty-four years that I have known my Dreamland sweetheart, I have seen her once in two years on an average. Mainly these were glimpses, but she was always immediately recognizable, notwithstanding she was so given to repair herself and getting up doubtful improvements in her hair and eyes. She was always fifteen, and looked it and acted it; and I was always seventeen, and never felt a day older. To me she is a real person, not a fiction, and her sweet and innocent society has been one of the prettiest and pleasantest experiences of my life. I know that to you her talk will not seem of the first intellectual order; but you should hear her in Dreamland—then you would see!

I saw her a week ago, just for a moment. Fifteen, as usual, and I seventeen, instead of going on sixty-three, as I was when I went to sleep. We were in India, and Bombay was in sight; also Windsor Castle, its towers and battlements veiled in a delicate haze, and from it the Thames flowed, curving and winding between its swarded banks, to our feet. I said:

"There is no question about it, England is the most beautiful of all the countries."

Her face lighted with approval, and she said, with that sweet and earnest irrelevance of hers:

"It is, because it is so marginal."

Then she disappeared. It was just as well; she could probably have added nothing to that rounded and perfect statement without damaging its symmetry.

This glimpse of her carries me back to Maui, and that time when I saw her gasp out her young life. That was a terrible thing to me at the time. It was preternaturally vivid; and the pain and the grief and the misery of it to me transcended many sufferings that I have known in waking life. For everything in a dream is more deep and strong and sharp and real than is ever its pale imitation in the unreal life which is ours when we go about awake and clothed with our artificial selves in this vague and dull-tinted artificial world. When we die we shall slough off this cheap intellect, perhaps, and go abroad into Dreamland clothed in our real selves, and aggrandized and enriched by the command over the mysterious mental magician who is here not our slave, but only our guest.

## *Study questions*

1. *What characteristics of dream structure does Twain use in this story?* 2. *Why does the narrator equate dream loves and childhood loves?* 3. *What similarities and differences occur in the dreams of the nineteen-year-old dreamer and the twenty-nine-year-old dreamer?* 4. *How does the increasing anxiety of the dreamer manifest itself in the dream of the thirty-one-year-old? What features remain the same? Continue to compare and contrast dreams.* 5. *What conflicts of the dreamer are manifest in his dreams?* 6. *What order of reality does he suggest dreams are?*

*Henry James* (1843–1916), born in New York City into a wealthy and distinguished family (his father was a philosopher and his brother, William, became a well-known psychologist), spent much of his life abroad, finally, in 1876, taking residence in England, and, just before his death, becoming a British subject. The body of his work is immense, including such novels as *The American* (1877), *The Portrait of a Lady* (1881), *The Awkward Age* (1899), and *The Ambassadors* (1903). His short stories were published in such collections as *The Lesson of the Master* (1892), *The Real Thing and Other Tales* (1893), *The Soft Side* (1900), and *The Better Sort* (1903). The complete stories were edited by Leon Edel in twelve volumes (1962–1964). James was also a brilliant theoretician on the art of fiction. One of his important contributions is the device he called the "central intelligence," a character through whom all of a story flows. Like his novels, James's short stories are rich in psychological realism, displaying subtle nuances attached to social situations and moral behavior. With few exceptions the surfaces of his stories are realistic, but details, forming patterns, move to the symbolic and the stories often become metaphors for a state of mind. James, like Twain and Crane, was influenced by William Dean Howells, whose "genteel realism" was succeeded by Hamlin Garland's "veritism," and by the naturalism of such writers as Frank Norris and Theodore Dreiser.

"The Tree of Knowledge" is a story about awareness. Restricted to the consciousness of the protagonist, Peter Brench, the sentence structure and subtle variations in tone and mood project an image of the psychological structure of his mind.

# THE TREE OF KNOWLEDGE

## 1

It was one of the secret opinions, such as we all have, of Peter Brench that his main success in life would have consisted in his never having committed himself about the work, as it was called, of his friend Morgan Mallow. This was a subject on which it was, to the best of his belief, impossible with veracity to quote him, and it was nowhere on record that he had, in the connexion, on any occasion and in any embarrassment, either lied or spoken the truth. Such a triumph had its honour even for a man of other triumphs—a man who had reached fifty, who had escaped marriage, who had lived within his means, who had been in love with Mrs. Mallow for years without breathing it, and who, last not least, had judged himself once for all. He had so judged himself in fact that he felt an extreme and general humility to be his proper portion; yet there was nothing that made him think so well of his parts as the course he had steered so often through the shallows just mentioned. It became thus a real wonder that the friends in whom he had most confidence were just those with whom he had most reserves. He couldn't tell Mrs. Mallow—or at least he supposed, excellent man, he couldn't—that she was the one beautiful reason he had never married; any more than he could tell her husband that the sight of the multiplied marbles in that gentleman's studio was an affliction of which even time had never blunted the edge. His victory, however, as I have intimated, in regard to these productions, was not simply in his not having let it out that he deplored them; it was, remarkably, in his not having kept it in by anything else.

The whole situation, among these good people, was verily a marvel, and there was probably not such another for a long way from the spot that engages us—the point at which the soft declivity of Hampstead began at that time to confess in broken accents to Saint John's Wood. He despised Mallow's statues and adored Mallow's wife, and yet was distinctly fond of Mallow, to whom, in turn, he was equally dear. Mrs. Mallow rejoiced in the statues—though she preferred, when pressed, the busts; and if she was visibly attached to Peter Brench it was because of his affection for Morgan. Each loved the other moreover for the love borne in each case to Lancelot, whom the Mallows respectively cherished as their only child and whom the friend of their fireside identified as the third—but decidedly the handsomest—of his godsons. Already in the old years it had come to that—that no one, for such a relation, could possibly have occurred to any of them, even to the baby itself, but Peter. There was luckily a certain independence, of the pecuniary sort, all round: the Master could never otherwise have spent his solemn *Wanderjahre* in Florence and Rome, and continued by the Thames as well as by the Arno and the Tiber to add unpurchased group to group and model, for what was too apt to prove in the event mere love, fancy-heads of celebrities either too busy or too buried—too much of the age or too little of it—to sit. Neither could Peter, lounging in almost daily, have found time to keep the whole complicated tradition so alive by his presence. He was massive but mild, the depositary of these mysteries—large and loose and ruddy and curly, with deep tones, deep eyes, deep pockets, to say nothing of the habit of long pipes, soft hats and brownish greyish weather-faded clothes, apparently always the same.

He had "written," it was known, but had never spoken, never spoken in particular of that; and he had the air (since, as was believed, he continued to write) of keeping it up in order to have something more—as if he hadn't at the worst enough—to be silent about. Whatever his air, at any rate, Peter's occasional unmentioned prose and verse were quite truly the result of an impulse to maintain the purity of his taste by establishing still more firmly the right relation of fame to feebleness. The little green door of his domain was in a garden-wall on which the discoloured stucco made patches, and in the small detached villa behind it everything was old, the furniture, the servants, the books, the prints, the immemorial habits and the new improvements. The Mallows, at Carrara Lodge, were within ten minutes, and the studio there was on their little land, to which they had added, in their happy faith, for building it. This was the good fortune, if it was not the ill, of her having brought him in marriage a portion that put them in a manner at their ease and enabled them thus, on their side, to keep it up. And they did keep it up—they always had—the infatuated sculptor and his wife, for whom nature had refined on the impossible by relieving them of the sense of the difficult. Morgan had at all events everything of the sculptor but the spirit of Phidias—the brown velvet, the becoming *beretto*, the "plastic" presence, the fine fingers, the beautiful accent in Italian and the old Italian factotum. He seemed to make up for everything when he addressed Egidio with the "tu" and waved him to turn one of the rotary pedestals of which the place was full. They were tremendous Italians at Carrara Lodge, and the secret of the part played by this fact in Peter's life was in a large degree that it gave him, sturdy Briton as he was, just the amount of "going abroad" he could bear. The Mallows were all his Italy, but it was in a measure for Italy he liked them. His one worry was that Lance—to which they had shortened his godson—was, in spite of a public school, perhaps a shade too Italian. Morgan meanwhile looked like somebody's flattering idea of somebody's own person as expressed in the great room provided at the Uffizi Museum for the general illustration of that idea by eminent hands. The Master's sole regret that he hadn't been born rather to the brush than to the chisel sprang from his wish that he might have contributed to that collection.

It appeared with time at any rate to be to the brush that Lance had been born; for Mrs. Mallow, one day when the boy was turning twenty, broke it to their friend, who shared, to the last delicate morsel, their problems and pains, that it seemed as if nothing would really do but that he should embrace the career. It had been impossible longer to remain blind to the fact that he was gaining no glory at Cambridge, where Brench's own college had for a year tempered its tone to him as for Brench's own sake. Therefore why renew the vain form of preparing him for the impossible? The impossible—it had become clear—was that he should be anything but an artist.

"Oh dear, dear!" said poor Peter.

"Don't you believe in it?" asked Mrs. Mallow, who still, at more than forty, had her violet velvet eyes, her creamy satin skin and her silken chestnut hair.

"Believe in what?"

"Why in Lance's passion."

"I don't know what you mean by 'believing in it.' I've never been unaware, certainly, of his disposition, from his earliest time, to daub and draw; but I confess I've hoped it would burn out."

"But why should it," she sweetly smiled, "with his wonderful heredity? Passion is passion—though of course indeed *you*, dear Peter, know nothing of that. Has the Master's ever burned out?"

Peter looked off a little and, in his familiar formless way, kept up for a moment a sound between a smothered whistle and a subdued hum. "Do you think he's going to be another Master?"

She seemed scarce prepared to go that length, yet she had on the whole a marvellous trust. "I know what you mean by that. Will it be a career to incur the jealousies and provoke the machinations that have been at times almost too much for his father? Well—say it may be, since nothing but clap-trap, in these dreadful days, *can*, it would seem, make its way, and since, with the curse of refinement and distinction, one may easily find one's self begging one's bread.

Put it at the worst—say he *has* the misfortune to wing his flight further than the vulgar taste of his stupid countrymen can follow. Think, all the same, of the happiness—the same the Master has had. He'll *know.*"

Peter looked rueful. "Ah but *what* will he know?"

"Quiet joy!" cried Mrs. Mallow, quite impatient and turning away.

## 2

He had of course before long to meet the boy himself on it and to hear that practically everything was settled. Lance was not to go up again, but to go instead to Paris where, since the die was cast, he would find the best advantages. Peter had always felt he must be taken as he was, but had never perhaps found him so much of that pattern as on this occasion. "You chuck Cambridge then altogether? Doesn't that seem rather a pity?"

Lance would have been like his father, to his friend's sense, had he had less humour, and like his mother had he had more beauty. Yet it was a good middle way for Peter that, in the modern manner, he was, to the eye, rather the young stockbroker than the young artist. The youth reasoned that it was a question of time—there was such a mill to go through, such an awful lot to learn. He had talked with fellows and had judged. "One has got, to-day," he said, "don't you see? to know."

His interlocutor, at this, gave a groan. "Oh hang it, *don't* know!"

Lance wondered. " 'Don't'? Then what's the use—?"

"The use of what?"

"Why of anything. Don't you think I've talent?"

Peter smoked away for a little in silence; then went on: "It isn't knowledge, it's ignorance that—as we've been beautifully told—is bliss."

"Don't you think I've talent?" Lance repeated.

Peter, with his trick of queer kind demonstrations, passed his arm round his godson and held him a moment. "How do I know?"

"Oh," said the boy, "if it's your own ignorance you're defending—!"

Again, for a pause, on the sofa, his godfather smoked. "It isn't. I've the misfortune to be omniscient."

"Oh well," Lance laughed again, "if you know *too* much—!"

"That's what I do, and it's why I'm so wretched."

Lance's gaiety grew. "Wretched? Come, I say!"

"But I forgot," his companion went on—"you're not to know about that. It would indeed for you too make the too much. Only I'll tell you what I'll do." And Peter got up from the sofa. "If you'll go up again I'll pay your way at Cambridge."

Lance stared, a little rueful in spite of being still more amused. "Oh Peter! You disapprove so of Paris?"

"Well, I'm afraid of it."

"Ah I see!"

"No, you don't see—yet. But you will—that is you would. And you mustn't."

The young man thought more gravely. "But one's innocence, already—!"

"Is considerably damaged? Ah that won't matter," Peter persisted—"we'll patch it up here."

"Here? Then you want me to stay at home?"

Peter almost confessed to it. "Well, we're so right—we four together—just as we are. We're so safe. Come, don't spoil it."

The boy, who had turned to gravity, turned from this, on the real pressure in his friend's tone, to consternation. "Then what's a fellow to be?"

"My particular care. Come, old man"—and Peter now fairly pleaded—"*I'll* look out for you."

Lance, who had remained on the sofa with his legs out and his hands in his pockets, watched him with eyes that showed suspicion. Then he got up. "You think there's something the matter with me—that I can't make a success."

"Well, what do you call a success?"

Lance thought again. "Why the best sort, I suppose, is to please one's self. Isn't that the sort that, in spite of cabals and things, is—in his own peculiar line—the Master's?"

There were so much too many things in this question to be answered at once that they practically checked the discussion, which became particularly difficult in the light of such renewed proof that, though the young man's innocence might, in the course of his studies, as he contended, somewhat have shrunken, the finer essence of it still remained. That was indeed exactly what Peter had assumed and what above all he desired; yet perversely enough it gave him a chill. The boy believed in the cabals and things, believed in the peculiar line, believed, to be brief, in the Master. What happened a month or two later wasn't that he went up again at the expense of his godfather, but that a fortnight after he had got settled in Paris this personage sent him fifty pounds.

He had meanwhile at home, this personage, made up his mind to the worst; and what that might be had never yet grown quite so vivid to him as when, on his presenting himself one Sunday night, as he never failed to do, for supper, the mistress of Carrara Lodge met him with an appeal as to—of all things in the world—the wealth of the Canadians. She was earnest, she was even excited. "Are many of them *really* rich?"

He had to confess he knew nothing about them, but he often thought afterwards of that evening. The room in which they sat was adorned with sundry specimens of the Master's genius, which had the merit of being, as Mrs. Mallow herself frequently suggested, of an unusually convenient size. They were indeed of dimensions not customary in the products of the chisel, and they had the singularity that, if the objects and features intended to be small looked too large, the objects and features intended to be large looked too small. The Master's idea, either in respect to this matter or to any other, had in almost any case, even after years, remained undiscoverable to Peter Brench. The creations that so failed to reveal it stood about on pedestals and brackets, on tables and shelves, a little staring white population, heroic, idyllic, allegoric, mythic, symbolic, in which "scale" had so strayed and lost itself that the public square and the chimney-piece seemed to have changed places, the monumental being all diminutive and the diminutive all monumental; branches at any rate, markedly, of a family in which stature was rather oddly irrespective of function, age and sex. They formed, like the Mallows themselves, poor Brench's own family—having at least to such a degree the note of familiarity. The occasion was one of those he had long ago learnt to know and to name—short flickers of the faint flame, soft gusts of a kinder air. Twice a year regularly the Master believed in his fortune, in addition to believing all the year round in his genius. This time it was to be made by a bereaved couple from Toronto, who had given him the handsomest order for a tomb to three lost children, each of whom they desired to see, in the composition, emblematically and characteristically represented.

Such was naturally the moral of Mrs. Mallow's question: if their wealth was to be assumed, it was clear, from the nature of their admiration, as well as from mysterious hints thrown out (they were a little odd!) as to other possibilities of the same mortuary sort, that their further patronage might be; and not less evident that should the Master become at all known in those climes nothing would be more inevitable than a run of Canadian custom. Peter had been present before at runs of custom, colonial and domestic—present at each of those of which the aggregation had left so few gaps in the marble company round him; but it was his habit never at these junctures to prick the bubble in advance. The fond illusion, while it lasted, eased the wound of elections never won, the long ache of medals and diplomas carried off, on every chance, by every one but the Master; it moreover lighted the lamp that would glimmer through the next eclipse. They lived, however, after all—as it was always beautiful to see—at a height scarce susceptible of ups and downs. They strained a point at times charmingly, strained it to admit that the public was here and there not too bad to buy; but they would have been nowhere without their attitude that the Master was always too good to sell. They were at all events deliciously formed, Peter often said to himself, for their fate; the Master had a vanity, his wife had a loyalty, of which success, depriving these things of innocence, would have diminished the merit and the grace. Any one could be charming under a charm, and as he looked about him at a world of prosperity more void of proportion even than the Master's museum he wondered if he knew another pair that so completely escaped vulgarity.

"What a pity Lance isn't with us to rejoice!" Mrs. Mallow on this occasion sighed at supper.

"We'll drink to the health of the absent," her husband replied, filling his friend's glass and his own and giving a drop to their companion; "but we must hope he's preparing himself for a happiness much less like this of ours this evening—excusable as I grant it to be!—than like the comfort we have always (whatever has happened or has not happened) been able to trust ourselves to enjoy. The comfort," the Master explained, leaning back in the pleasant lamplight and firelight, holding up his glass and looking round at his marble family, quartered more or less, a monstrous brood, in every room—"the comfort of art in itself!"

Peter looked a little shyly at his wine. "Well—I don't care what you may call it when a fellow doesn't—but Lance must learn to *sell,* you know. I drink to his acquisition of the secret of a base popularity!"

"Oh yes, *he* must sell," the boy's mother, who was still more, however, this seemed to give out, the Master's wife, rather artlessly allowed.

"Ah," the sculptor after a moment confidently pronounced, "Lance *will.* Don't be afraid. He'll have learnt."

"Which is exactly what Peter," Mrs. Mallow gaily returned—"why in the world were you so perverse, Peter?—wouldn't when he told him hear of."

Peter, when this lady looked at him with accusatory affection—a grace on her part not infrequent—could never find a word; but the Master, who was always all amenity and tact, helped him out now as he had often helped him before. "That's his old idea, you know—on which we've so often differed: his theory that the artist should be all impulse and instinct. *I* go in of course for a certain amount of school. Not too much—but a due proportion. There's where his protest came in," he continued to explain to his wife, "as against what *might,* don't you see? be in question for Lance."

"Ah well"—and Mrs. Mallow turned the violet eyes across the table at the subject of this discourse—"he's sure to have meant of course nothing but good. Only that wouldn't have prevented him, if Lance *had* taken his advice, from being in effect horribly cruel."

They had a sociable way of talking to him to his face as if he had been in the clay or—at most—in the plaster, and the Master was unfailingly generous. He might have been waving Egidio to make him revolve. "Ah but poor Peter wasn't so wrong as to what it may after all come to that he *will* learn."

"Oh but nothing artistically bad," she urged—still, for poor Peter, arch and dewy.

"Why just the little French tricks," said the Master: on which their friend had to pretend to admit, when pressed by Mrs. Mallow, that these aesthetic vices had been the objects of his dread.

## 3

"I know now," Lance said to him the next year, "why you were so much against it." He had come back supposedly for a mere interval and was looking about him at Carrara Lodge, where indeed he had already on two or three occasions since his expatriation briefly reappeared. This had the air of a longer holiday. "Something rather awful has happened to me. It *isn't* so very good to know."

"I'm bound to say high spirits don't show in your face," Peter was rather ruefully forced to confess. "Still, are you very sure you do know?"

"Well, I at least know about as much as I can bear." These remarks were exchanged in Peter's den, and the young man, smoking cigarettes, stood before the fire with his back against the mantel. Something of his bloom seemed really to have left him.

Poor Peter wondered. "You're clear then as to what in particular I wanted you not to go for?"

"In particular?" Lance thought. "It seems to me that in particular there can have been only one thing."

They stood for a little sounding each other. "Are you quite sure?"

"Quite sure I'm a beastly duffer? Quite—by this time."

"Oh!"—and Peter turned away as if almost with relief.

"It's *that* that isn't pleasant to find out."

"Oh I don't care for 'that,'" said Peter, presently coming round again. "I mean I personally don't."

"Yet I hope you can understand a little that I myself should!"

"Well, what do you mean by it?" Peter sceptically asked.

And on this Lance had to explain—how the upshot of his studies in Paris had inexorably proved a mere deep doubt of his means. These studies had so waked him up that a new light was in his eyes; but what the new light did was really to show him too much. "Do you know what's the matter with me? I'm too horribly intelligent. Paris was really the last place for me. I've learnt what I can't do."

Poor Peter stared—it was a staggerer; but even after they had had, on the subject, a longish talk in which the boy brought out to the full the hard truth of his lesson, his friend betrayed less pleasure than usually breaks into a face to the happy tune of "I told you so!" Poor Peter himself made now indeed so little a point of having told him so that Lance broke ground in a different place a day or two after. "What was it then that—before I went—you were afraid I should find out?" This, however, Peter refused to tell him—on the ground that if he hadn't yet guessed perhaps he never would, and that in any case nothing at all for either of them was to be gained by giving the thing a name. Lance eyed him on this an instant with the bold curiosity of youth—with the air indeed of having in his mind two or three names, of which one or other would be right. Peter nevertheless, turning his back again, offered no encouragement, and when they parted afresh it was with some show of impatience on the side of the boy. Accordingly on their next encounter Peter saw at a glance that he had now, in the interval, divined and that, to sound his note, he was only waiting till they should find themselves alone. This he had soon arranged and he then broke straight out. "Do you know your conundrum has been keeping me awake? But in the watches of the night the answer came over me—so that, upon my honour, I quite laughed out. Had you been supposing I had to go to Paris to learn *that?*" Even now, to see him still so sublimely on his guard, Peter's young friend had to laugh afresh. "You won't give a sign till you're sure? Beautiful old Peter!" But Lance at last produced it. "Why, hang it, the truth about the Master."

It made between them for some minutes a lively passage, full of wonder for each at the wonder of the other. "Then how long have you understood—"

"The true value of his work? I understood it," Lance recalled, "as soon as I began to understand anything. But I didn't begin fully to do that, I admit, till I got *là-bas.*"

"Dear, dear!"—Peter gasped with retrospective dread.

"But for what have you taken me? I'm a hopeless muff—that I *had* to have rubbed in. But I'm not such a muff as the Master!" Lance declared.

"Then why did you never tell me—?"

"That I hadn't after all"—the boy took him up—"remained such an idiot? Just because I never dreamed *you* knew. But I beg your pardon. I only wanted to spare you. And what I don't now understand is how the deuce then for so long you've managed to keep bottled."

Peter produced his explanation, but only after some delay and with a gravity not void of embarrassment. "It was for your mother."

"Oh!" said Lance.

"And that's the great thing now—since the murder *is* out. I want a promise from you. I mean"—and Peter almost feverishly followed it up—"a vow from you, solemn and such as you owe me here on the spot, that you'll sacrifice anything rather than let her ever guess—"

"That *I've* guessed?"—Lance took it in. "I see." He evidently after a moment had taken in much. "But what is it you've in mind that I may have a chance to sacrifice?"

"Oh one has always something."

Lance looked at him hard. "Do you mean that *you've* had—?" The look he received back, however, so put the question by that he found soon enough another. "Are you really sure my mother doesn't know?"

Peter, after renewed reflexion, was really sure. "If she does she's too wonderful."

"But aren't we all too wonderful?"

"Yes," Peter granted—"but in different ways. The thing's so desperately important because your father's little public consists only, as you know then," Peter developed—"well, of how many?"

"First of all," the Master's son risked, "of himself. And last of all too. I don't quite see of whom else."

Peter had an approach to impatience. "Of your mother, I say—*always*."

Lance cast it all up. "You absolutely feel that?"

"Absolutely."

"Well then with yourself that makes three."

"Oh *me!*"—and Peter, with a wag of his kind old head, modestly excused himself. "The number's at any rate small enough for any individual dropping out to be too dreadfully missed. Therefore, to put it in a nutshell, take care, my boy —that's all—that *you're* not!"

"I've got to keep on humbugging?" Lance wailed.

"It's just to warn you of the danger of your failing of that that I've seized this opportunity."

"And what do you regard in particular," the young man asked, "as the danger?"

"Why this certainty: that the moment your mother, who feels so strongly, should suspect your secret—well," said Peter desperately, "the fat would be on the fire."

Lance for a moment seemed to stare at the blaze. "She'd throw me over?"

"She'd throw *him* over."

"And come round to us?"

Peter, before he answered, turned away. "Come round to *you*." But he had said enough to indicate—and, as he evidently trusted, to avert—the horrid contingency.

## 4

Within six months again, none the less, his fear was on more occasions than one all before him. Lance had returned to Paris for another trial; then had reappeared at home and had had, with his father, for the first time in his life, one of the scenes that strike sparks. He described it with much expression to Peter, touching whom (since they had never done so before) it was the sign of a new reserve on the part of the pair at Carrara Lodge that they at present failed, on a matter of intimate interest, to open themselves—if not in joy then in sorrow—to their good friend. This produced perhaps practically between the parties a shade of alienation and a slight intermission of commerce—marked mainly indeed by the fact that to talk at his ease with his old playmate Lance had in general to come to see him. The closest if not quite the gayest relation they had yet known together was thus ushered in. The difficulty for poor Lance was a tension at home—begotten by the fact that his father wished him to be at least the sort of success he himself had been. He hadn't "chucked" Paris—though nothing appeared more vivid to him than that Paris had chucked him: he would go back again because of the fascination in trying, in seeing, in sounding the depths—in learning one's lesson, briefly, even if the lesson were simply that of one's impotence in the presence of one's larger vision. But what did the Master, all aloft in his senseless fluency, know of impotence, and what vision—to be called such—had he in all his blind life ever had? Lance, heated and indignant, frankly appealed to his godparent on this score.

His father, it appeared, had come down on him for having, after so long, nothing to show, and hoped that on his next return this deficiency would be repaired. *The* thing, the Master complacently set forth was—for any artist, however inferior to himself—at least to "do" something. "What can you do? That's all I ask!" *He* had certainly done enough, and there was no mistake about what he had to show. Lance had tears in his eyes when it came thus to letting his old friend know how great the strain might be on the "sacrifice" asked of him. It wasn't so easy to continue humbugging—as from son to parent—after feeling one's self despised for not grovelling in mediocrity. Yet a noble duplicity was what, as they intimately faced the situation, Peter went on requiring; and it was still for a time what his young friend, bitter and sore, managed loyally to comfort him with. Fifty pounds more than once again, it was true, rewarded both in London and in Paris the young friend's loyalty; none the less sensibly, doubtless, at the moment, that the money was a direct advance on a decent sum for which Peter had long since privately prearranged an ultimate function. Whether by these arts or others, at all events, Lance's just resentment was kept for a season—at bay. The day arrived when he warned his companion that he could hold out—or hold in—no longer. Carrara Lodge had had to listen to another lecture delivered from a great height—an infliction really heavier at last than, without striking back or in some way letting the Master have the truth, flesh and blood could bear.

"And what I don't see is," Lance observed with a certain irritated eye for what was after all, if it came to that, owing to himself too; "what I don't see is, upon my honour, how *you*, as things are going, can keep the game up."

"Oh the game for me is only to hold my tongue," said placid Peter. "And I have my reason."

"Still my mother?"

Peter showed a queer face as he had often shown it before—that is by turning it straight away. "What will you have? I haven't ceased to like her."

"She's beautiful—she's a dear of course," Lance allowed; "but what is she to you, after all, and what is it to you that, as to anything whatever, she should or she shouldn't?"

Peter, who had turned red, hung fire a little. "Well—it's all simply what I make of it."

There was now, however, in his young friend a strange, an adopted insistence. "What are you after all to *her?*"

"Oh nothing. But that's another matter."

"She cares only for my father," said Lance the Parisian.

"Naturally—and that's just why."

"Why you've wished to spare her?"

"Because she cares so tremendously much."

Lance took a turn about the room, but with his eyes still on his host. "How awfully—always—you must have liked her!"

"Awfully. Always," said Peter Brench.

The young man continued for a moment to muse—then stopped again in front of him. "Do you know how much she cares?" Their eyes met on it, but Peter, as if his own found something new in Lance's, appeared to hesitate, for the first time in an age, to say he did know. "*I've* only just found out," said Lance. "She came to my room last night, after being present, in silence and only with her eyes on me, at what I had had to take from him: she came—and she was with me an extraordinary hour."

He had paused again and they had again for a while sounded each other. Then something—and it made him suddenly turn pale—came to Peter. "She *does* know?"

"She does know. She let it all out to me—so as to demand of me no more than 'that,' as she said, of which she herself had been capable. She has always known," said Lance without pity.

Peter was silent a long time; during which his companion might have heard him gently breathe, and on touching him might have felt within him the vibration of a long low sound suppressed. By the time he spoke at last he had taken everything in. "Then I do see how tremendously much."

"Isn't it wonderful?" Lance asked.

"Wonderful," Peter mused.

"So that if your original effort to keep me from Paris was to keep me from knowledge—!" Lance exclaimed as if with a sufficient indication of this futility.

It might have been at the futility Peter appeared for a little to gaze. "I think it must have been—without my quite at the time knowing it—to keep *me!*" he replied at last as he turned away.

## *Study questions*

1. *How do we know that Peter Brench is prideful, though he thinks himself full of extreme and general humility?* 2. *What is gained by filtering this story through the consciousness of Peter Brench? What does the style of the story, the convoluted sentences, for example, reveal about the character of Peter Brench, his thinking patterns, and the structure of his mind and mode of perception?* 3. *What is Peter's relationship to the Mallow family? Is he protecting them or they him?* 4. *What is the significance of the Master's illusions? What other kinds of illusions are operative in the story?* 5. *Chart the plot line of this story. How and where do complications begin? Where is the exposition placed? What is the climax? What is the conflict? How and where is it resolved? Does the structure of the plot contribute to the meaning of the story?*

*Guy de Maupassant* (1850–1893) was born in Normandy of well-to-do parents. He attended school at Rouen and began to move into literary circles through his mother's friendship with Gustave Flaubert, whom Maupassant took as his mentor. Taking Flaubert's exacting craftsmanship as a model, Maupassant published nothing in his own name for seven years. With the publication of "Ball of Fat" in 1880, however, he won immediate literary recognition. Thereafter he wrote almost three hundred stories in a span of ten years. His most well known stories were collected in such volumes as *La Maison Tellier* (1881), *Mademoiselle Fifi* (1882), and *Contes et Nouvelles* (1885). By the time that Maupassant was writing, the realistic movement in France was well established, and Maupassant's narrative surfaces exhibit this influence. Although his best stories are precise and well controlled, they do not exhibit the complexity that derives from a tightly woven symbolic structure. In "La Mère Sauvage," for example, the theme of the story can be understood without reference to the central symbolic scene, though that scene does provide motivation for the savage mother's behavior.

# LA MÈRE SAUVAGE

I had not been at Virelogne for fifteen years. I went back there in the autumn, to shoot with my friend Serval, who had at last rebuilt his château, which had been destroyed by the Prussians.

I loved that district very much. It is one of those corners of the world which have a sensuous charm for the eyes. You love it with a bodily love. We, whom the country seduces, we keep tender memories for certain springs, for certain woods, for certain pools, for certain hills, seen very often, and which have stirred us like joyful events. Sometimes our thoughts turn back towards a corner in a forest, or the end of a bank, or an orchard powdered with flowers, seen but a single time, on some gay day; yet remaining in our hearts like the images of certain women met in the street on a spring morning, with bright transparent dresses; and leaving in soul and body an unappeased desire which is not to be forgotten, a feeling that you have just rubbed elbows with happiness.

At Virelogne I loved the whole countryside, dotted with little woods, and crossed by brooks which flashed in the sun and looked like veins, carrying blood to the earth. You fished in them for crawfish, trout, and eels! Divine happiness! You could bathe in places, and you often found snipe among the high grass which grew along the borders of these slender watercourses.

I was walking, lightly as a goat, watching my two dogs ranging before me. Serval, a hundred metres to my right, was beating a field of lucern. I turned the thicket which forms the boundary of the wood of Sandres, and I saw a cottage in ruins.

All of a sudden, I remembered it as I had seen it the last time, in 1869, neat, covered with vines, with chickens before the door. What is sadder than a dead house, with its skeleton standing upright, bare and sinister?

I also remembered that in it, one very tiring day, the good woman had given me a glass of wine to drink, and that Serval had then told me the history of its inhabitants. The father, an old poacher, had been killed by the gendarmes. The son, whom I had once seen, was a tall, dry fellow who also passed for a ferocious destroyer of game. People called them *"les Sauvage."*

Was that a name or a nickname?

I hailed Serval. He came up with his long strides like a crane.

I asked him:

"What's become of those people?"

And he told me this story:

When war was declared, the son Sauvage, who was then thirty-three years old, enlisted, leaving his mother alone in the house. People did not pity the old woman very much because she had money; they knew it.

But she remained quite alone in that isolated dwelling so far from the village, on the edge of the wood. She was not afraid, however, being of the same strain as her menfolk; a hardy old woman, tall and thin, who laughed seldom, and with whom one never jested. The women of the fields laugh but little in any case; that is men's business, that! But they themselves have sad and narrowed hearts, leading a melancholy, gloomy life. The peasants learn a little boisterous merriment at the tavern, but their helpmates remain grave, with countenances which are always severe. The muscles of their faces have never learned the movements of the laugh.

La Mère Sauvage continued her ordinary existence in her cottage, which was soon covered by the snows. She came to the village once a week, to get bread and a little meat; then she returned into her house. As there was talk of wolves, she went out with a gun upon her back—her son's gun, rusty, and with the butt worn by the rubbing of the hand; and she was strange to see, the tall "Sauvage," a little bent, going with slow strides over the snow, the muzzle of the piece extending beyond the black headdress, which pressed close to her head and imprisoned her white hair, which no one had ever seen.

One day a Prussian force arrived. It was billeted upon the inhabitants, according to the property and resources of each. Four were allotted to the old woman, who was known to be rich.

They were four great boys with blond skin, with blond beards, with blue eyes, who had remained stout notwithstanding the fatigues which they had endured already, and who also, though in a conquered country, had remained kind and gentle. Alone with this aged woman, they showed themselves full of consideration, sparing her, as much as they could, all expenses and fatigue. They would be seen, all four of them, making their toilet around the well, of a morning, in their shirt-sleeves, splashing with great swishes of water, under the crude daylight of the snowy weather, their pink-white Northman's flesh, while La Mère Sauvage went and came, making ready the soup. Then they would be seen cleaning the kitchen, rubbing the tiles, splitting wood, peeling potatoes, doing up all the housework, like four good sons about their mother.

But the old woman thought always of her own, so tall and thin, with his hooked nose and his brown eyes and his heavy mustache which made a roll of black hairs upon his lip. She asked each day of each of the soldiers who were installed beside her hearth:

"Do you know where the French Marching Regiment No. 23 was sent? My boy is in it."

They answered, "No, not know, not know at all." And, understanding her pain and her uneasiness (they, who had mothers too, there at home), they rendered her a thousand little services. She loved them well, moreover, her four enemies, since the peasantry feels no patriotic hatred; that belongs to the upper class alone. The humble, those who pay the most, because they are poor, and because every new burden crushes them down; those who are killed in masses, who make the true cannon's-meat, because they are so many; those, in fine, who suffer most cruelly the atrocious miseries of war, because they are the feeblest, and offer least resistance—they hardly understand at all those bellicose ardors, that excitable sense of honor, or those pretended political combinations which in six months exhaust two nations, the conqueror with the conquered.

They said on the countryside in speaking of the Germans of La Mère Sauvage:

"There are four who have found a soft place."

Now, one morning, when the old woman was alone in the house, she perceived far off on the plain a man coming towards her dwelling. Soon she recognized him; it was the postman charged to distribute the letters. He gave her a folded paper, and she drew out of her case the spectacles which she used for sewing; then she read:

Madame Sauvage,—The present letter is to tell you sad news. Your boy Victor was killed yesterday by a shell which near cut him in two. I was just by, seeing that we stood next each other in the company, and he would talk to me about you to let you know on the same day if anything happened to him.

I took his watch, which was in his pocket, to bring it back to you when the war is done.

I salute you very friendly.

CESAIRE RIVOT
Soldier of the 2nd class, March. Reg. No. 23

The letter was dated three weeks back.

She did not cry at all. She remained motionless, so seized and stupefied that she did not even suffer as yet. She thought: "V'la Victor who is killed now." Then little by little the tears mounted to her eyes, and the sorrow caught her heart. The ideas came to her, one by one, dreadful, torturing. She would never kiss him again, her child, her big boy, never again! The gendarmes had killed the father, the Prussians had killed the son. He had been cut in two by a cannon-ball. She seemed to see the thing, the horrible thing: the head falling, the eyes open, while he chewed the corner of his big mustache as he always did in moments of anger.

What had they done with his body afterwards? If they had only let her have her boy back as they had given her back her husband—with the bullet in the middle of his forehead!

But she heard a noise of voices. It was the Prussians returning from the village. She hid her letter very quickly in her pocket, and she received them quietly, with her ordinary face, having had time to wipe her eyes.

They were laughing, all four, delighted, since they brought with them a fine rabbit—stolen, doubtless—and they made signs to the old woman that there was to be something good to eat.

She set herself to work at once to prepare breakfast; but when it came to killing the rabbit, her heart failed her. And yet it was not the first. One of the soldiers struck it down with a blow of his fist behind the ears.

The beast once dead, she separated the red body from the skin; but the sight of the blood which she was touching, and which covered her hands, of the warm blood which she felt cooling and coagulating, made her tremble from head to foot; and she kept seeing her big boy cut in two, and quite red also, like this still-palpitating animal.

She set herself at table with the Prussians, but she could not eat, not even a mouthful. They devoured the rabbit without troubling themselves about her. She looked at them askance, without speaking, ripening a thought, and with a face so impassible that they perceived nothing.

All of a sudden she said: "I don't even know your names, and here's a whole month that we've been together." They understood, not without difficulty, what she wanted, and told their names. That was not sufficient; she had them written for her on a paper, with the addresses of their families, and, resting her spectacles on her great nose, she considered that strange handwriting, then folded the sheet and put it in her pocket, on top of the letter which told her of the death of her son.

When the meal was ended, she said to the men:

"I am going to work for you."

And she began to carry up hay into the loft where they slept.

They were astonished at her taking all this trouble; she explained to them that thus they would not be so cold; and they helped her. They heaped the trusses of hay as high as the straw roof; and in that manner they made a sort of great chamber with four walls of fodder, warm and perfumed, where they should sleep splendidly.

At dinner, one of them was worried to see that La Mère Sauvage still ate nothing. She told him that she had the cramps. Then she kindled a good fire to warm herself up, and the four Germans mounted to their lodging-place by the ladder which served them every night for this purpose.

As soon as they closed the trap, the old woman removed the ladder, then opened the outside door noiselessly, and went back to look for more bundles of straw, with which she filled her kitchen. She went barefoot in the snow, so softly that no sound was heard. From time to time she listened to the sonorous and unequal snoring of the four soldiers who were fast asleep.

When she judged her preparations to be sufficient, she threw one of the bundles into the fireplace, and when it was alight she scattered it all over the others. Then she went outside again and looked.

In a few seconds the whole interior of the cottage was illumined with a violent brightness and became a dreadful brasier, a gigantic fiery furnace, whose brilliance spouted out of the narrow window and threw a glittering beam upon the snow.

Then a great cry issued from the summit of the house; it was a clamor of human shriekings, heart-rending calls of anguish and of fear. At last, the trap having fallen in, a whirlwind of fire shot up into the loft, pierced the straw roof, rose to the sky like the immense flame of a torch; and all the cottage flared.

Nothing more was heard therein but the crackling of the fire, the crackling sound of the walls, the falling of the rafters. All of a sudden the roof fell in, and the burning carcass of the dwelling hurled a great plume of sparks into the air, amid a cloud of smoke.

The country, all white, lit up by the fire, shone like a cloth of silver tinted with red.

A bell, far off, began to toll.

The old "Sauvage" remained standing before her ruined dwelling, armed with her gun, her son's gun, for fear lest one of those men might escape.

When she saw that it was ended, she threw her weapon into the brasier. A loud report rang back.

People were coming, the peasants, the Prussians.

They found the woman seated on the trunk of a tree, calm and satisfied.

A German officer, who spoke French like a son of France, demanded of her:

"Where are your soldiers?"

She extended her thin arm towards the red heap of fire which was gradually going out, and she answered with a strong voice:

"There!"

They crowded round her. The Prussian asked:

"How did it take fire?"

She said:

"It was I who set it on fire."

They did not believe her, they thought that the sudden disaster had made her crazy. So, while all pressed round and listened, she told the thing from one end to the other, from the arrival of the letter to the last cry of the men who were burned with her house. She did not forget a detail of all which she had felt, nor of all which she had done.

When she had finished, she drew two pieces of paper from her pocket, and, to distinguish them by the last glimmers of the fire, she again adjusted her spectacles; then she said, showing one: "That, that is the death of Victor." Showing the other, she added, indicating the red ruins with a bend of the head:

"That, that is their names, so that you can write home." She calmly held the white sheet out to the officer, who held her by the shoulders, and she continued:

"You must write how it happened, and you must say to their mothers that it was I who did that, Victoire Simon, la Sauvage! Do not forget."

The officer shouted some orders in German. They seized her, they threw her against the walls of her house, still hot. Then twelve men drew quickly up before her, at twenty paces. She did not move. She had understood; she waited.

An order rang out, followed instantly by a long report. A belated shot went off by itself, after the others.

The old woman did not fall. She sank as though they had mowed off her legs.

The Prussian officer approached her. She was almost cut in two, and in her withered hand she held her letter bathed with blood.

My friend Serval added:

"It was by way of reprisal that the Germans destroyed the château of the district, which belonged to me."

As for me, I thought of the mothers of those four gentle fellows burned in the house; and of the atrocious heroism of that other mother shot against the wall.

And I picked up a little stone, still blackened by the flames.

## *Study questions*

1. *"La Mère Sauvage" has an unusual structure. An inner story in which the narrator takes omniscience is framed by an outer story told in the first person. How does the outer story relate to the inner story?* 2. *What kind of woman is* La mère sauvage? *Does she represent some evil force?* 3. *What are the Prussian soldiers like? Do they represent some evil force?* 4. *The central symbolic scene involves the killing and eating of the rabbit. How does this scene provide motivation for the mother's behavior? Does it operate in any other way?* 5. *What does the narrator say about who is responsible for war?* 6. *What is Serval's function in the story?* 7. *What is meant by the term "atrocious heroism" as it is attached to the behavior of the mother? How does the notion of "atrocious heroism" relate to the title of the story?* 8. *What is the function of the small rock that is blackened by the flames?*

*Joseph Conrad* (1857–1924) was born in the Ukraine region of Poland. Conrad knew few words in English until in 1878 he joined the British merchant marine, where he served until 1894. During this time he became more fluent in English than in Polish, and he later went on to become one of the great stylists in the English language. His first novel, *Almayer's Folly,* was published in 1895, after which he settled in England to live. Conrad published twenty-seven volumes of fiction, including such noted novels as *The Nigger of the Narcissus* (1897), *Lord Jim* (1900), *Nostromo* (1904), and *The Secret Agent* (1907). As a preface to *The Nigger of the Narcissus,* Conrad wrote his artistic credo in which he stated that his aim in writing was to make readers hear, feel, and, above all, make them see. A highly conscious literary artist, Conrad knew that great art has to be a perfect blending of form and substance. No exponent of the art for art's sake doctrine, Conrad believed that it is art which binds men to each other and all mankind to the visible world. Conrad's short-story masterpieces include "Heart of Darkness," "The Lagoon," "Youth," "An Outpost of Progress," and "The Secret Sharer." The stories, like the novels, are highly complex psychological studies, rich in symbolism and carefully crafted. "The Secret Sharer" is a "double" story, in the same mode as Poe's "William Wilson" and Dostoevsky's *The Double.*

# THE SECRET SHARER

## 1

On my right hand there were lines of fishing stakes resembling a mysterious system of half-submerged bamboo fences, incomprehensible in its division of the domain of tropical fishes, and crazy of aspect as if abandoned forever by some nomad tribe of fishermen now gone to the other end of the ocean; for there was no sign of human habitation as far as the eye could reach. To the left a group of barren islets, suggesting ruins of stone walls, towers, and block-houses, had its foundations set in a blue sea that itself looked solid, so still and stable did it lie below my feet; even the track of light from the westering sun shone smoothly, without that animated glitter which tells of an imperceptible ripple. And when I turned my head to take a parting glance at the tug which had just left us anchored outside the bar, I saw the straight line of the flat shore joined to the stable sea, edge to edge, and with a perfect and unmarked closeness, in one leveled floor half brown, half blue under the enormous dome of the sky. Corresponding in their insignificance to the islets of the sea, two small clumps of trees, one on each side of the only fault in the impeccable joint, marked the mouth of the river Meinam we had just left on the first preparatory stage of our homeward journey; and, far back on the inland level, a larger and loftier mass, the grove surrounding the great Paknam pagoda, was the only thing on which the eye could rest from the vain task of exploring the monotonous sweep of the horizon. Here and there gleams as of a few scattered pieces of silver marked the windings of the great river; and on the nearest of them, just within the bar, the tug steaming right into the land became lost to my sight, hull and funnel and masts, as though the impassive earth had swallowed her up without an effort, without a tremor. My eye followed the light cloud of her smoke, now here, now there, above the plain, according to the devious curves of the stream, but always fainter and farther away, till I lost it at last behind the miter-shaped hill of the great pagoda. And then I was left alone with my ship, anchored at the head of the Gulf of Siam.

She floated at the starting point of a long journey, very still in an immense stillness, the shadows of her spars flung far to the eastward by the setting sun. At that moment I was alone on her decks. There was not a sound in her—and around us nothing moved, nothing lived, not a canoe on the water, not a bird in the air, not a cloud in the sky. In this breathless pause at the threshold of a long passage we seemed to be measuring our fitness for a long and arduous enterprise, the appointed task of both our existences to be carried out, far from all human eyes, with only sky and sea for spectators and for judges.

There must have been some glare in the air to interfere with one's sight, because it was only just before the sun left us that my roaming eyes made out beyond the highest ridge of the principal islet of the group something which did away with the solemnity of perfect solitude. The tide of darkness flowed on swiftly; and with tropical suddenness a swarm of stars came out above the shadowy earth, while I lingered yet, my hand resting lightly on my ship's rail as if on the shoulder of a trusted friend. But, with all that multitude of celestial bodies staring down at one, the comfort of quiet communion with her was gone for good. And there were also disturbing sounds by this time—voices, footsteps forward; the steward flitted along the main deck, a busily ministering spirit; a hand bell tinkled urgently under the poop deck. . . .

I found my two officers waiting for me near the supper table, in the lighted cuddy. We sat down at once, and as I helped the chief mate, I said:

"Are you aware that there is a ship anchored inside the islands? I saw her mastheads above the ridge as the sun went down."

He raised sharply his simple face, overcharged by a terrible growth of whisker, and emitted his usual ejaculations: "Bless my soul, sir! You don't say so!"

My second mate was a round-cheeked, silent young man, grave beyond his years, I thought; but as our eyes happened to meet I detected a slight quiver on his lips. I looked down at once. It was not my part to encourage sneering on board my ship. It must be said, too, that I knew very little of my officers. In consequence of certain events of no particular significance, except to myself, I had been appointed to the command only a fortnight before. Neither did I know much of the hands forward. All these people had been together for eighteen months or so, and my position was that of the only stranger on board. I mention this because it has some bearing on what is to follow. But what I felt most was my being a stranger to the ship; and if all the truth must be told, I was somewhat of a stranger to myself. The youngest man on board (barring the second mate), and untried as yet by a position of the fullest responsibility, I was willing to take the adequacy of the others for granted. They had simply to be equal to their tasks; but I wondered how far I should turn out faithful to that ideal conception of one's own personality every man sets up for himself secretly.

Meantime the chief mate, with an almost visible effect of collaboration on the part of his round eyes and frightful whiskers, was trying to evolve a theory of the anchored ship. His dominant trait was to take all things into earnest consideration. He was of a painstaking turn of mind. As he used to say, he "liked to account to himself" for practically everything that came in his way, down to a miserable scorpion he had found in his cabin a week before. The why and the wherefore of that scorpion—how it got on board and came to select his room rather than the pantry (which was a dark place and more what a scorpion would be partial to), and how on earth it managed to drown itself in the inkwell of his writing desk—had exercised him infinitely. The ship within the islands was much more easily accounted for; and just as we were about to rise from the table he made his pronouncement. She was, he doubted not, a ship from home lately arrived. Probably she drew too much water to cross the bar except at the top of spring tides. Therefore she went into that natural harbor to wait for a few days in preference to remaining in an open roadstead.

"That's so," confirmed the second mate, suddenly, in his slightly hoarse voice. "She draws over twenty feet. She's the Liverpool ship *Sephora* with a cargo of coal. Hundred and twenty-three days from Cardiff."

We looked at him in surprise.

"The tugboat skipper told me when he came on board for your letters, sir," explained the young man. "He expects to take her up the river the day after tomorrow."

After thus overwhelming us with the extent of his information he slipped out of the cabin. The mate observed regretfully that he "could not account for that young fellow's whims." What prevented him telling us all about it at once, he wanted to know.

I detained him as he was making a move. For the last two days the crew had had plenty of hard work, and the night before they had very little sleep. I felt painfully that I—a stranger—was doing something unusual when I directed him to let all hands turn in without setting an anchor watch. I proposed to keep on deck myself till one o'clock or thereabouts. I would get the second mate to relieve me at that hour.

"He will turn out the cook and the steward at four," I concluded, "and then give you a call. Of course at the slightest sign of any sort of wind we'll have the hands up and make a start at once."

He concealed his astonishment. "Very well, sir." Outside the cuddy he put his head in the second mate's door to inform him of my unheard-of caprice to take a five hours' anchor watch on myself. I heard the other raise his voice incredulously. "What? The captain himself?" Then a few more murmurs, a door closed, then another. A few moments later I went on deck.

My strangeness, which had made me sleepless, had prompted that unconventional arrangement, as if I had expected in those solitary hours of the night to get on terms with the ship of which I knew nothing, manned by men of whom I knew very little more. Fast alongside a wharf, littered like any ship in port with a tangle of unrelated things, invaded by unrelated shore people, I had hardly seen her yet properly. Now, as she lay cleared for sea, the stretch of her main deck seemed to me very fine under the stars. Very fine, very roomy for her size, and very inviting. I descended the poop and paced the waist, my mind picturing to myself the coming passage through the Malay Archipelago, down the Indian Ocean, and up the Atlantic. All its phases were familiar enough to me, every characteristic, all the alternatives which were likely to face me on the high seas—everything! . . . except the novel responsibility of command. But I took heart from the reasonable thought that the ship was like other ships, the men like other men, and that the sea was not likely to keep any special surprises expressly for my discomfiture.

Arrived at that comforting conclusion, I bethought myself of a cigar and went below to get it. All was still down there. Everybody at the after end of the ship was sleeping profoundly. I came out again on the quarter-deck, agreeably at ease in my sleeping suit on that warm breathless night, barefooted, a glowing cigar in my teeth, and, going forward, I was met by the profound silence of the fore end of the ship. Only as I passed the door of the forecastle I heard a deep, quiet, trustful sigh of some sleeper inside. And suddenly I rejoiced in the great security of the sea as compared with the unrest of the land, in my choice of that untempted life presenting no disquieting problems, invested with an elementary moral beauty by the absolute straightforwardness of its appeal and by the singleness of its purpose.

The riding light in the fore-rigging burned with a clear, untroubled, as if symbolic, flame, confident and bright in the mysterious shades of the night. Passing on my way aft along the other side of the ship, I observed that the rope side ladder, put over, no doubt, for the master of the tug when he came to fetch away our letters, had not been hauled in as it should have been. I became annoyed at this, for exactitude in small matters is the very soul of discipline. Then I reflected that I had myself peremptorily dismissed my officers from duty, and by my own act had prevented the anchor watch being formally set and things properly attended to. I asked myself whether it was wise ever to interfere with the established routine of duties even from the kindest of motives. My action might have made me appear eccentric. Goodness only knew how that absurdly whiskered mate would "account" for my conduct, and what the whole ship thought of that informality of their new captain. I was vexed with myself.

Not from compunction certainly, but, as it were mechanically, I proceeded to get the ladder in myself. Now a side ladder of that sort is a light affair and comes in easily, yet my vigorous tug, which should have brought it flying on board, merely recoiled upon my body in a totally unexpected jerk. What the devil! . . . I was so astounded by the immovableness of that ladder that I remained stock-still, trying to account for it to myself like that imbecile mate of mine. In the end, of course, I put my head over the rail.

The side of the ship made an opaque belt of shadow on the darkling glassy shimmer of the sea. But I saw at once something elongated and pale floating very close to the ladder. Before I could form a guess a faint flash of phosphorescent light, which seemed to issue suddenly from the naked body of a man, flickered in the sleeping water with the elusive, silent play of summer lightning in a night sky. With a gasp I saw revealed to my stare a pair of feet, the long legs, a broad livid back immersed right up to the neck in a greenish cadaverous glow. One hand, awash, clutched the bottom rung of the ladder. He was complete but for the head. A headless corpse! The cigar dropped out of my gaping mouth with a tiny plop and a short hiss quite audible in the absolute stillness of all things under heaven. At that I suppose he raised up his face, a dimly pale oval in the shadow of the ship's side. But even then I could only barely make out down there the shape of his black-haired head. However, it was enough for the horrid, frost-bound sensation which had gripped me about the chest to pass off. The moment of vain exclamations was past, too. I only climbed on the spare spar and leaned over the rail as far as I could, to bring my eyes nearer to that mystery floating alongside.

As he hung by the ladder, like a resting swimmer, the sea lightning played about his limbs at every stir; and he appeared in it ghastly, silvery, fishlike. He remained as mute as a fish, too. He made no motion to get out of the water, either. It was inconceivable that he should not attempt to come on board, and strangely troubling to suspect that perhaps he did not want to. And my first words were prompted by just that troubled incertitude.

"What's the matter?" I asked in my ordinary tone, speaking down to the face upturned exactly under mine.

"Cramp," it answered, no louder. Then slightly anxious, "I say, no need to call anyone."

"I was not going to," I said.

"Are you alone on deck?"

"Yes."

I had somehow the impression that he was on the point of letting go the ladder to swim away beyond my ken—mysterious as he came. But, for the moment, this being appearing as if he had risen from the bottom of the sea (it was certainly the nearest land to the ship) wanted only to know the time. I told him. And he, down there, tentatively:

"I suppose your captain's turned in?"

"I'm sure he isn't," I said.

He seemed to struggle with himself, for I heard something like the low, bitter murmur of doubt. "What's the good?" His next words came out with a hesitating effort.

"Look here, my man. Could you call him out quietly?"

I thought the time had come to declare myself.

"*I* am the captain."

I heard a "By Jove!" whispered at the level of the water. The phosphorescence flashed in the swirl of the water all about his limbs, his other hand seized the ladder.

"My name's Leggatt."

The voice was calm and resolute. A good voice. The self-possession of that man had somehow induced a corresponding state in myself. It was very quietly that I remarked:

"You must be a good swimmer."

"Yes. I've been in the water practically since nine o'clock. The question for me now is whether I am to let go this ladder and go on swimming till I sink from exhaustion, or—to come on board here."

I felt this was no mere formula of desperate speech, but a real alternative in the view of a strong soul. I should have gathered from this that he was young; indeed, it is only the young who are ever confronted by such clear issues. But at the time it was pure intuition on my part. A mysterious communication was established already between us two—in the face of that silent, darkened tropical sea. I was young, too; young enough to make no comment. The man in the water began suddenly to climb up the ladder, and I hastened away from the rail to fetch some clothes.

Before entering the cabin I stood still, listening in the lobby at the foot of the stairs. A faint snore came through the closed door of the chief mate's room. The second mate's door was on the hook, but the darkness in there was absolutely soundless. He, too, was young and could sleep like a stone. Remained the steward, but he was not likely to wake up before he was called. I got a sleeping suit out of my room and, coming back on deck, saw the naked man from the sea sitting on the main hatch, glimmering white in the darkness, his elbows on his knees and his head in his hands. In a moment he had concealed his damp body in a sleeping suit of the same gray-stripe pattern as the one I was wearing and followed me like my double on the poop. Together we moved right aft, barefooted, silent.

"What is it?" I asked in a deadened voice, taking the lighted lamp out of the binnacle, and raising it to his face.

"An ugly business."

He had rather regular features; a good mouth; light eyes under somewhat heavy, dark eyebrows; a smooth, square forehead; no growth on his cheeks; a small, brown mustache, and a well-shaped, round chin. His expression was concentrated, meditative, under the inspecting light of the lamp I held up to his face; such as a man thinking hard in solitude might wear. My sleeping suit was just right for his size. A well-knit young fellow of twenty-five at most. He caught his lower lip with the edge of white, even teeth.

"Yes," I said, replacing the lamp in the binnacle. The warm, heavy tropical night closed upon his head again.

"There's a ship over there," he murmured.

"Yes, I know. The *Sephora*. Did you know of us?"

"Hadn't the slightest idea. I am the mate of her——" He paused and corrected himself. "I should say I *was*."

"Aha! Something wrong?"

"Yes. Very wrong indeed. I've killed a man."

"What do you mean? Just now?"

"No, on the passage. Weeks ago. Thirty-nine south. When I say a man——"

"Fit of temper," I suggested, confidently.

The shadowy, dark head, like mine, seemed to nod imperceptibly above the ghostly gray of my sleeping suit. It was, in the night, as though I had been faced by my own reflection in the depths of a somber and immense mirror.

"A pretty thing to have to own up to for a Conway boy," murmured my double, distinctly.

"You're a Conway boy?"

"I am," he said, as if startled. Then, slowly . . . "Perhaps you too——"

It was so; but being a couple of years older I had left before he joined. After a quick interchange of dates a silence fell; and I thought suddenly of my absurd mate with his terrific whiskers and the "Bless my soul—you don't say so" type of intellect. My double gave me an inkling of his thoughts by saying:

"My father's a parson in Norfolk. Do you see me before a judge and jury on that charge? For myself I can't see the necessity. There are fellows that an angel from heaven—— And I am not that. He was one of those creatures that are just simmering all the time with a silly sort of wickedness. Miserable devils that have no business to live at all. He wouldn't do his duty and wouldn't let anybody else do theirs. But what's the good of talking! You know well enough the sort of ill-conditioned snarling cur——"

He appealed to me as if our experiences had been as identical as our clothes. And I knew well enough the pestiferous danger of such a character where there are no means of legal repression. And I knew well enough also that my double there was no homicidal ruffian. I did not think of asking him for details, and he told me the story roughly in brusque, disconnected sentences. I needed no more. I saw it all going on as though I were myself inside that other sleeping suit.

"It happened while we were setting a reefed foresail, at dusk. Reefed foresail! You understand the sort of weather. The only sail we had left to keep the ship running; so you may guess what it had been like for days. Anxious sort of job, that. He gave me some of his cursed insolence at the sheet. I tell you I was overdone with this terrific weather that seemed to have no end to it. Terrific, I tell you—and a deep ship. I believe the fellow himself was half crazed with funk. It was no time for gentlemanly reproof, so I turned round and felled him like an ox. He up and at me. We closed just as an awful sea made for the ship. All hands saw it coming and took to the rigging, but I had him by the throat, and went on shaking him like a rat, the men above us yelling, 'Look out! look out!' Then a crash as if the sky had fallen on my head. They say that for over ten minutes hardly anything was to be seen of the ship—just the three masts and a bit of the forecastle head and of the poop all awash driving along in a smother of foam. It was a miracle that they found us, jammed together behind the forebits. It's clear that I meant business, because I was holding him by the throat still when they picked us up. He was black in the face. It was too much for them. It seems they rushed us aft together, gripped as we were, screaming 'Murder!' like a lot of lunatics, and broke into the cuddy. And the ship running for her life, touch and go all the time, any minute her last in a sea fit to turn your hair gray only a-looking at it. I understand that the skipper, too, started raving like the rest of them. The man had been deprived of sleep for more than a week, and to have this sprung on him at the height of a furious gale nearly drove him out of his mind. I wonder they didn't fling me overboard after getting the carcass of their precious shipmate out of my fingers. They had rather a job to separate us, I've been told. A sufficiently fierce story to make an old judge and a respectable jury sit up a bit. The first thing I heard when I came to myself was the maddening howling of that endless gale, and on that the voice of the old man. He was hanging on to my bunk, staring into my face out of his sou'wester.

" 'Mr. Leggatt, you have killed a man. You can act no longer as chief mate of this ship.' "

His care to subdue his voice made it sound monotonous. He rested a hand on the end of the skylight to steady himself with, and all that time did not stir a limb, so far as I could see. "Nice little tale for a quiet tea party," he concluded in the same tone.

One of my hands, too, rested on the end of the skylight; neither did I stir a limb, so far as I knew. We stood less than a foot from each other. It occurred to me that if old "Bless my soul—you don't say so" were to put his head up the companion and catch sight of us, he would think he was seeing double, or imagine himself come upon a scene of weird witchcraft; the strange captain having a quiet confabulation by the wheel with his own gray ghost. I became very much concerned to prevent anything of the sort. I heard the other's soothing undertone.

"My father's a parson in Norfolk," it said. Evidently he had forgotten he had told me this important fact before. Truly a nice little tale.

"You had better slip down into my stateroom now," I said, moving off stealthily. My double followed my movements; our bare feet made no sound; I let him in, closed the door with care, and, after giving a call to the second mate, returned on deck for my relief.

"Not much sign of any wind yet," I remarked when he approached.

"No, sir. Not much," he assented, sleepily, in his hoarse voice, with just enough deference, no more, and barely suppressing a yawn.

"Well, that's all you have to look out for. You have got your orders."

"Yes, sir."

I paced a turn or two on the poop and saw him take up his position face forward with his elbow in the ratlines of the mizzen-rigging before I went below. The mate's faint snoring was still going on peacefully. The cuddy lamp was burning over the table on which stood a vase with flowers, a polite attention from the ship's provision merchant—the last flowers we should see for the next three months at the very least. Two bunches of bananas hung from the beam symmetrically, one on each side of the rudder casing. Everything was as before in the ship—except that two of her captain's sleeping suits were simultaneously in use, one motionless in the cuddy, the other keeping very still in the captain's stateroom.

It must be explained here that my cabin had the form of the capital letter L, the door being within the angle and opening into the short part of the letter. A couch was to the left, the bed-place to the right, my writing desk and the chronometers' table faced the door. But anyone opening it, unless he stepped right inside, had no view of what I call the long (or vertical) part of the letter. It contained some lockers surmounted by a bookcase; and a few clothes, a thick jacket or two, caps, oilskin coat, and such like, hung on hooks. There was at the bottom of that part a door opening into my bathroom, which could be entered also directly from the saloon. But that way was never used.

The mysterious arrival had discovered the advantage of this particular shape. Entering my room, lighted strongly by a big bulkhead lamp swung on gimbals above my writing desk, I did not see him anywhere till he stepped out quietly from behind the coats hung in the recessed part.

"I heard somebody moving about, and went in there at once," he whispered.

I, too, spoke under my breath.

"Nobody is likely to come in here without knocking and getting permission."

He nodded. His face was thin and the sunburn faded, as though he had been ill. And no wonder. He had been, I heard presently, kept under arrest in his cabin for nearly seven weeks. But there was nothing sickly in his eyes or in his expression. He was not a bit like me, really; yet, as we stood leaning over my bed-place, whispering side by side, with our dark heads together and our backs to the door, anybody bold enough to open it stealthily would have been treated to the uncanny sight of a double captain busy talking in whispers with his other self.

"But all this doesn't tell me how you came to hang on to our side ladder," I inquired, in the hardly audible murmurs we used, after he had told me something more of the proceedings on board the *Sephora* once the bad weather was over.

"When we sighted Java Head I had had time to think all those matters out several times over. I had six weeks of doing nothing else, and with only an hour or so every evening for a tramp on the quarter-deck."

He whispered, his arms folded on the side of my bed-place, staring through the open port. And I could imagine perfectly the manner of this thinking out—a stubborn if not a steadfast operation; something of which I should have been perfectly incapable.

"I reckoned it would be dark before we closed with the land," he continued, so low that I had to strain my hearing, near as we were to each other, shoulder touching shoulder almost. "So I asked to speak to the old man. He always seemed very sick when he came to see me—as if he could not look me in the face. You know, that foresail saved the ship. She was too deep to have run long under bare poles. And it was I that managed to set it for him. Anyway, he came. When I had him in my cabin—he stood by the door looking at me as if I had the halter around my neck already—I asked him right away to leave my cabin door unlocked at night while the ship was going through Sunda Straits. There would be the Java coast within two or three miles, off Angier Point. I wanted nothing more. I've had a prize for swimming my second year in the Conway."

"I can believe it," I breathed out.

"God only knows why they locked me in every night. To see some of their faces you'd have thought they were afraid I'd go about at night strangling people. Am I a murdering brute? Do I look it? By Jove! if I had been he wouldn't have trusted himself like that into my room. You'll say I might have chucked him aside and bolted out, there and then—it was dark already. Well, no. And for the same reason I wouldn't think of trying to smash the door. There would have been a rush to stop me at the noise, and I did not mean to get into a confounded scrimmage. Somebody else might have got killed—for I would not have broken out only to get chucked back, and I did not want any more of that work. He refused, looking more sick than ever. He was afraid of the men, and also of that old second mate of his who had been sailing with him for years—a gray-headed old humbug; and his steward, too, had been with him devil knows how long—seventeen years or more—a dogmatic sort of loafer who hated me like poison, just because I was the chief mate. No chief mate ever made more than one voyage in the *Sephora,* you know. Those two old chaps ran the ship. Devil only knows what the skipper wasn't afraid of (all his nerve went to pieces altogether in that hellish spell of bad weather we had)—of what the law would do to him—of his wife, perhaps. Oh, yes! she's on board. Though I don't think she would have meddled. She would have been only too glad to have me out of the ship in any way. The 'brand of Cain' business, don't you see. That's all right. I was ready enough to go off wandering on the face of the earth—and that was price enough to pay for an Abel of that sort. Anyhow, he wouldn't listen to me. 'This thing must take its course. I represent the law here.' He was shaking like a leaf. 'So you won't?' 'No!' 'Then I hope you will be able to sleep on that,' I said, and turned my back on him. 'I wondered that *you* can,' cries he, and locks the door.

"Well, after that, I couldn't. Not very well. That was three weeks ago. We have had a slow passage through the Java Sea; drifted about Carimata for ten days. When we anchored here they thought, I suppose, it was all right. The nearest land (and that's five miles) is the ship's destination; the consul would soon set about catching me; and there would have been no object in bolting to these islets there. I don't suppose there's a drop of water on them. I don't know how it was, but tonight that steward, after bringing me my supper, went out to let me eat it, and left the door unlocked. And I ate it—all there was, too. After I had finished I strolled out on the quarter-deck. I don't know that I meant to do anything. A breath of fresh air was all I wanted, I believe. Then a sudden temptation came over me. I kicked off my slippers and was in the water before I had made up my mind fairly. Somebody heard the splash and they raised an awful hullabaloo. 'He's gone! Lower the boats! He's committed suicide! No, he's swimming.' Certainly I was swimming. It's not so easy for a swimmer like me to commit suicide by drowning. I landed on the nearest islet before the boat left the ship's side. I heard them pulling about in the dark, hailing, and so on, but after a bit they gave up. Everything quieted down and the anchorage became as still as death. I sat down on a stone and began to think. I felt certain they would start searching for me at daylight. There was no place to hide on those stony things—and if there had been, what would have been the good? But now I was clear of that ship, I was not going back. So after a while I took off all my clothes, tied them up in a bundle with a stone inside, and dropped them in the deep water on the outer side of that islet. That was suicide enough for me. Let them think what they liked, but I didn't mean to drown myself. I meant to swim till I sank—but that's not the same thing. I struck out for another of these little islands, and it was from that one that I first saw your riding light. Something to swim for. I went on easily, and on the way I came upon a flat rock a foot or two above water. In the daytime, I dare say, you might make it out with a glass from your poop. I scrambled up on it and rested myself for a bit. Then I made another start. That last spell must have been over a mile."

His whisper was getting fainter and fainter, and all the time he stared straight out through the porthole, in which there was not even a star to be seen. I had not interrupted him. There was something that made comment impossible in his narrative, or perhaps in himself; a sort of feeling, a quality, which I can't find a name for. And when he ceased, all I found was a futile whisper: "So you swam for our light?"

"Yes—straight for it. It was something to swim for. I couldn't see any stars low down because the coast was in the way, and I couldn't see the land, either. The water was like glass. One might have been swimming in a confounded thousand-feet deep cistern with no place for scrambling out anywhere; but what I didn't like was the notion of swimming round and round like a crazed bullock before I gave out; and as I didn't mean to go back . . . No. Do you see me being hauled back, stark naked, off one of these little islands by the scruff of the neck and fighting like a wild beast? Somebody would have got killed for certain, and I did not want any of that. So I went on. Then your ladder——"

"Why didn't you hail the ship?" I asked, a little louder.

He touched my shoulder lightly. Lazy footsteps came right over our heads and stopped. The second mate had crossed from the other side of the poop and might have been hanging over the rail, for all we knew.

"He couldn't hear us talking—could he?" My double breathed into my very ear, anxiously.

His anxiety was an answer, a sufficient answer, to the question I had put to him. An answer containing all the difficulty of that situation. I closed the porthole quietly, to make sure. A louder word might have been overheard.

"Who's that?" he whispered then.

"My second mate. But I don't know much more of the fellow than you do."

And I told him a little about myself. I had been appointed to take charge while I least expected anything of the sort, not quite a fortnight ago. I didn't know either the ship or the people. Hadn't had the time in port to look about me or size anybody up. And as to the crew, all they knew was that I was appointed to take the ship home. For the rest, I was almost as much of a stranger on board as himself, I said. And at the moment I felt it most acutely. I felt that it would take very little to make me a suspect person in the eyes of the ship's company.

He had turned about meantime; and we, the two strangers in the ship, faced each other in identical attitudes.

"Your ladder—" he murmured, after a silence. "Who'd have thought of finding a ladder hanging over at night in a ship anchored out here! I felt just then a very unpleasant faintness. After the life I've been leading for nine weeks, anybody would have got out of condition. I wasn't capable of swimming round as far as your rudder chains. And, lo and behold! there was a ladder to get hold of. After I gripped it I said to myself, 'What's the good?' When I saw a man's head looking over I thought I would swim away presently and leave him shouting—in whatever language it was. I didn't mind being looked at. I—I liked it. And then you speaking to me so quietly—as if you had expected me—made me hold on a little longer. It had been a confounded lonely time—I don't mean while swimming. I was glad to talk a little to somebody that didn't belong to the *Sephora.* As to asking for the captain, that was a mere impulse. It could have been no use, with all the ship knowing about me and the other people pretty certain to be round here in the morning. I don't know—I wanted to be seen, to talk with somebody, before I went on. I don't know what I would have said. . . . 'Fine night, isn't it?' or something of the sort."

"Do you think they will be round here presently?" I asked with some incredulity.

"Quite likely," he said, faintly.

He looked extremely haggard all of a sudden. His head rolled on his shoulders.

"H'm. We shall see then. Meantime get into that bed," I whispered. "Want help? There."

It was a rather high bed-place with a set of drawers underneath. This amazing swimmer really needed the lift I gave him by seizing his leg. He tumbled in, rolled over on his back, and flung one arm across his eyes. And then, with his face nearly hidden, he must have looked exactly as I used to look in that bed. I gazed upon my other self for a while before drawing across carefully the two green serge curtains which ran on a brass rod. I thought for a moment of pinning them together for greater safety, but I sat down on the couch, and once there I felt unwilling to rise and hunt for a pin. I would do it in a moment. I was extremely tired, in a peculiarly intimate way, by the strain of stealthiness, by the effort of whispering and the general secrecy of this excitement. It was three o'clock by now and I had been on my feet since nine, but I was not sleepy; I could not have gone to sleep. I sat there, fagged out, looking at the curtains, trying to clear my mind of the confused sensation of being in two places at once, and greatly bothered by an exasperating knocking in my head. It was a relief to discover suddenly that it was not in my head at all, but on the outside of the door. Before I could collect myself the words "Come in" were out of my mouth, and the steward entered with a tray, bringing in my morning coffee. I had slept, after all, and I was so frightened that I shouted, "This way! I am here, steward," as though he had been miles away. He put down the tray on the table next the couch and only then said very quietly, "I can see you are here, sir." I felt him give me a keen look, but I dared not meet his eyes just then. He must have wondered why I had drawn the curtains of my bed before going to sleep on the couch. He went out, hooking the door open as usual.

I heard the crew washing decks above me. I knew I would have been told at once if there had been any wind. Calm, I thought, and I was doubly vexed. Indeed, I felt dual more than ever. The steward reappeared suddenly in the doorway. I jumped up from the couch so quickly that he gave a start.

"What do you want here?"

"Close your port, sir—they are washing decks."

"It is closed," I said, reddening.

"Very well, sir." But he did not move from the doorway and returned my stare in an extraordinary, equivocal manner for a time. Then his eyes wavered, all his expression changed, and in a voice unusually gentle, almost coaxingly:

"May I come in to take the empty cup away, sir?"

"Of course!" I turned my back on him while he popped in and out. Then I unhooked and closed the door and even pushed the bolt. This sort of thing could not go on very long. The cabin was as hot as an oven, too. I took a peep at my double, and discovered that he had not moved, his arm was still over his eyes; but his chest heaved; his hair was wet; his chin glistened with perspiration. I reached over him and opened the port.

"I must show myself on deck," I reflected.

Of course, theoretically, I could do what I liked, with no one to say nay to me within the whole circle of the horizon; but to lock my cabin door and take the key away I did not dare. Directly I put my head out of the companion I saw the group of my two officers, the second mate barefooted, the chief mate in long india-rubber boots, near the break of the poop, and the steward halfway down the poop ladder talking to them eagerly. He happened to catch sight of me and dived, the second ran down on the main deck shouting some order or other, and the chief mate came to meet me, touching his cap.

There was a sort of curiosity in his eye that I did not like. I don't know whether the steward had told them that I was "queer" only, or downright drunk, but I know the man meant to have a good look at me. I watched him coming with a smile which, as he got into point-blank range, took effect and froze his very whiskers. I did not give him time to open his lips.

"Square the yards by lifts and braces before the hands go to breakfast."

It was the first particular order I had given on board that ship; and I stayed on deck to see it executed, too. I had felt the need of asserting myself without loss of time. That sneering young cub got taken down a peg or two on that occasion, and I also seized the opportunity of having a good look at the face of every foremast man as they filed past me to go to the after braces. At breakfast time, eating nothing myself, I presided with such frigid dignity that the two mates were only too glad to escape from the cabin as soon as decency permitted; and all the time the dual working of my mind distracted me almost to the point of insanity. I was constantly watching myself, my secret self, as dependent on my actions as my own personality, sleeping in that bed, behind that door which faced me as I sat at the head of the table. It was very much like being mad, only it was worse because one was aware of it.

I had to shake him for a solid minute, but when at last he opened his eyes it was in the full possession of his senses, with an inquiring look.

"All's well so far," I whispered. "Now you must vanish into the bathroom."

He did so, as noiseless as a ghost, and I then rang for the steward, and facing him boldly, directed him to tidy up my stateroom while I was having my bath—"and be quick about it." As my tone admitted of no excuses, he said, "Yes, sir," and ran off to fetch his dustpan and brushes. I took a bath and did most of my dressing, splashing, and whistling softly for the steward's edification, while the secret sharer of my life stood drawn up bolt upright in that little space, his face looking very sunken in daylight, his eyelids lowered under the stern, dark line of his eyebrows drawn together by a slight frown.

When I left him there to go back to my room the steward was finishing dusting. I sent for the mate and engaged him in some insignificant conversation. It was, as it were, trifling with the terrific character of his whiskers; but my object was to give him an opportunity for a good look at my cabin. And then I could at last shut, with a clear conscience, the door of my stateroom and get my double back into the recessed part. There was nothing else for it. He had to sit still on a small folding stool, half smothered by the heavy coats hanging there. We listened to the steward going into the bathroom out of the saloon, filling the water bottles there, scrubbing the bath, setting things to rights, whisk, bang, clatter—out again into the saloon—turn the key—click. Such was my scheme for keeping my second self invisible. Nothing better could be contrived under the circumstances. And there we sat; I at my writing desk ready to appear busy with some papers, he behind me, out of sight of the door. It would not have been prudent to talk in daytime; and I could not have stood the excitement of that queer sense of whispering to myself. Now and then, glancing over my shoulder, I saw him far back there, sitting rigidly on the low stool, his bare feet close together, his arms folded, his head hanging on his breast—and perfectly still. Anybody would have taken him for me.

I was fascinated by it myself. Every moment I had to glance over my shoulder. I was looking at him when a voice outside the door said:

"Beg pardon, sir."

"Well!" . . . I kept my eyes on him, and so, when the voice outside the door announced, "There's a ship's boat coming our way, sir," I saw him give a start—the first movement he had made for hours. But he did not raise his bowed head.

"All right. Get the ladder over."

I hesitated. Should I whisper something to him? But what? His immobility seemed to have been never disturbed. What could I tell him he did not know already? . . . Finally I went on deck.

## 2

The skipper of the *Sephora* had a thin red whisker all round his face, and the sort of complexion that goes with hair of that color; also the particular, rather smeary shade of blue in the eyes. He was not exactly a showy figure; his shoulders were high, his stature but middling—one leg slightly more bandy than the other. He shook hands, looking vaguely around. A spiritless tenacity was his main characteristic, I judged. I behaved with a politeness which seemed to disconcert him. Perhaps he was shy. He mumbled to me as if he were ashamed of what he was saying; gave his name (it was something like Archbold—but at this distance of years I hardly am sure), his ship's name, and a few other particulars of that sort, in the manner of a criminal making a reluctant and doleful confession. He had had terrible weather on the passage out—terrible—terrible—wife aboard, too.

By this time we were seated in the cabin and the steward brought in a tray with a bottle and glasses. "Thanks! No." Never took liquor. Would have some water, though. He drank two tumblerfuls. Terrible thirsty work. Ever since daylight had been exploring the islands round his ship.

"What was that for—fun?" I asked, with an appearance of polite interest.

"No!" He sighed. "Painful duty."

As he persisted in his mumbling and I wanted my double to hear every word, I hit upon the notion of informing him that I regretted to say I was hard of hearing.

"Such a young man, too!" he nodded, keeping his smeary blue, unintelligent eyes fastened upon me. What was the cause of it—some disease? he inquired, without the least sympathy and as if he thought that, if so, I'd got no more than I deserved.

"Yes; disease," I admitted in a cheerful tone which seemed to shock him. But my point was gained, because he had to raise his voice to give me his tale. It is not worth while to record that version. It was just over two months since all this had happened, and he had thought so much about it that he seemed completely muddled as to its bearings, but still immensely impressed.

"What would you think of such a thing happening on board your own ship? I've had the *Sephora* for these fifteen years. I am a well-known shipmaster."

He was densely distressed—and perhaps I should have sympathized with him if I had been able to detach my mental vision from the unsuspected sharer of my cabin as though he were my second self. There he was on the other side of the bulkhead, four or five feet from us, no more, as we sat in the saloon. I looked politely at Captain Archbold (if that was his name), but it was the other I saw, in a gray sleeping suit, seated on a low stool, his bare feet close together, his arms folded, and every word said between us falling into the ears of his dark head bowed on his chest.

"I have been at sea now, man and boy, for seven-and-thirty years, and I've never heard of such a thing happening in an English ship. And that it should be my ship. Wife on board, too."

I was hardly listening to him.

"Don't you think," I said, "that the heavy sea which, you told me, came aboard just then might have killed the man? I have seen the sheer weight of a sea kill a man very neatly, by simply breaking his neck."

"Good God!" he uttered, impressively, fixing his smeary blue eyes on me. "The sea! No man killed by the sea ever looked like that." He seemed positively scandalized at my suggestion. And as I gazed at him, certainly not prepared for anything original on his part, he advanced his head close to mine and thrust his tongue out at me so suddenly that I couldn't help starting back.

After scoring over my calmness in this graphic way he nodded wisely. If

I had seen the sight, he assured me, I would never forget it as long as I lived. The weather was too bad to give the corpse a proper sea burial. So next day at dawn they took it up on the poop, covering its face with a bit of bunting; he read a short prayer, and then, just as it was, in its oilskins and long boots, they launched it amongst those mountainous seas that seemed ready every moment to swallow up the ship herself and the terrified lives on board of her.

"That reefed foresail saved you," I threw in.

"Under God—it did," he exclaimed fervently. "It was by a special mercy, I firmly believe, that it stood some of those hurricane squalls."

"It was the setting of that sail which—" I began.

"God's own hand in it," he interrupted me. "Nothing less could have done it. I don't mind telling you that I hardly dared give the order. It seemed impossible that we could touch anything without losing it, and then our last hope would have been gone."

The terror of that gale was on him yet. I let him go on for a bit, then said, casually—as if returning to a minor subject:

"You were very anxious to give up your mate to the shore people, I believe?"

He was. To the law. His obscure tenacity on that point had in it something incomprehensible and a little awful; something, as it were, mystical, quite apart from his anxiety that he should not be suspected of "countenancing any doings of that sort." Seven-and-thirty virtuous years at sea, of which over twenty of immaculate command, and the last fifteen in the *Sephora,* seemed to have laid him under some pitiless obligation.

"And you know," he went on, groping shamefacedly amongst his feelings, "I did not engage that young fellow. His people had some interest with my owners. I was in a way forced to take him on. He looked very smart, very gentlemanly, and all that. But do you know—I never liked him, somehow. I am a plain man. You see, he wasn't exactly the sort for the chief mate of a ship like the *Sephora.*"

I had become so connected in thoughts and impressions with the secret sharer of my cabin that I felt as if I, personally, were being given to understand that I, too, was not the sort that would have done for the chief mate of a ship like the *Sephora.* I had no doubt of it in my mind.

"Not at all the style of man. You understand," he insisted, superfluously, looking hard at me.

I smiled urbanely. He seemed at a loss for a while.

"I suppose I must report a suicide."

"Beg pardon?"

"Sui-cide! That's what I'll have to write to my owners directly I get in."

"Unless you manage to recover him before tomorrow," I assented, dispassionately. . . . "I mean, alive."

He mumbled something which I really did not catch, and I turned my ear to him in a puzzled manner. He fairly bawled:

"The land—I say, the mainland is at least seven miles off my anchorage."

"About that."

My lack of excitement, of curiosity, of surprise, of any sort of pronounced interest, began to arouse his distrust. But except for the felicitous pretense of deafness I had not tried to pretend anything. I had felt utterly incapable of playing the part of ignorance properly, and therefore was afraid to try. It is also certain that he had brought some ready-made suspicions with him, and that he viewed my politeness as a strange and unnatural phenomenon. And yet how else could I have received him? Not heartily! That was impossible for psychological reasons, which I need not state here. My only object was to keep off his inquiries. Surlily? Yes, but surliness might have provoked a point-blank question. From its novelty to him and from its nature, punctilious courtesy was the manner best calculated to restrain the man. But there was the danger of his breaking through my defense bluntly. I could not, I think, have met him by a direct lie, also for psychological (not moral) reasons. If he had only known how afraid I was of his putting my feeling of identity with the other to the test! But, strangely enough—(I thought of it only afterward)—I believe that he was not a little disconcerted by the reverse side of that weird situation, by something in me that reminded him of the man he was seeking—suggested a mysterious similitude to the young fellow he had distrusted and disliked from the first.

However that might have been, the silence was not very prolonged. He took another oblique step.

"I reckon I had no more than a two-mile pull to your ship. Not a bit more."

"And quite enough, too, in this awful heat," I said.

Another pause full of mistrust followed. Necessity, they say, is mother of invention, but fear, too, is not barren of ingenious suggestions. And I was afraid he would ask me point-blank for news of my other self.

"Nice little saloon, isn't it?" I remarked, as if noticing for the first time the way his eyes roamed from one closed door to the other. "And very well fitted out, too. Here, for instance," I continued, reaching over the back of my seat negligently and flinging the door open, "is my bathroom."

He made an eager movement, but hardly gave it a glance. I got up, shut the door of the bathroom, and invited him to have a look around, as if I were very proud of my accommodation. He had to rise and be shown round, but he went through the business without any raptures whatever.

"And now we'll have a look at my stateroom," I declared, in a voice as loud as I dared to make it, crossing the cabin to the starboard side with purposely heavy steps.

He followed me in and gazed around. My intelligent double had vanished. I played my part.

"Very convenient—isn't it?"

"Very nice. Very comf . . ." He didn't finish, and went out brusquely as if to escape from some unrighteous wiles of mine. But it was not to be. I had been too frightened not to feel vengeful; I felt I had him on the run, and I meant to keep him on the run. My polite insistence must have had something menacing in it, because he gave in suddenly. And I did not let him off a single item; mate's room, pantry, storerooms, the very sail locker which was also under the poop—he had to look into them all. When at last I showed him out on the quarter-deck he drew a long, spiritless sigh, and mumbled dismally that he must really be going back to his ship now. I desired my mate, who had joined us, to see to the captain's boat.

The man of whiskers gave a blast on the whistle which he used to wear hanging round his neck, and yelled, "*Sephoras* away!" My double down there in my cabin must have heard, and certainly could not feel more relieved than I. Four fellows came running out from somewhere forward and went over the side, while my own men, appearing on deck too, lined the rail. I escorted my visitor to the gangway ceremoniously, and nearly overdid it. He was a tenacious beast. On the very ladder he lingered, and in that unique, guiltily conscientious manner of sticking to the point:

"I say . . . you . . . you don't think that——"

I covered his voice loudly:

"Certainly not. . . . I am delighted. Good-by."

I had an idea of what he meant to say, and just saved myself by the privilege of defective hearing. He was too shaken generally to insist, but my mate, close witness of that parting, looked mystified and his face took on a thoughtful cast. As I did not want to appear as if I wished to avoid all communication with my officers, he had the opportunity to address me.

"Seems a very nice man. His boat's crew told our chaps a very extraordinary story, if what I am told by the steward is true. I suppose you had it from the captain, sir?"

"Yes. I had a story from the captain."

"A very horrible affair—isn't it, sir?"

"It is."

"Beats all these tales we hear about murders in Yankee ships."

"I don't think it beats them. I don't think it resembles them in the least."

"Bless my soul—you don't say so! But of course I've no acquaintance whatever with American ships, not I, so I couldn't go against your knowledge. It's horrible enough for me. . . . But the queerest part is that those fellows seemed to have some idea the man was hidden aboard here. They had really. Did you ever hear of such a thing?"

"Preposterous—isn't it?"

We were walking to and fro athwart the quarter-deck. No one of the crew forward could be seen (the day was Sunday), and the mate pursued:

"There was some little dispute about it. Our chaps took offense. 'As if we would harbor a thing like that,' they said. 'Wouldn't you like to look for him in our coal hole?' Quite a tiff. But they made it up in the end. I suppose he did drown himself. Don't you, sir?"

"I don't suppose anything."

"You have no doubt in the matter, sir?"

"None whatever."

I left him suddenly. I felt I was producing a bad impression, but with my double down there it was most trying to be on deck. And it was almost as trying to be below. Altogether a nerve-trying situation. But on the whole I felt less torn in two when I was with him. There was no one in the whole ship whom I dared take into my confidence. Since the hands had got to know his story, it would have been impossible to pass him off for anyone else, and an accidental discovery was to be dreaded now more than ever. . . .

The steward being engaged in laying the table for dinner, we could talk only with our eyes when I first went down. Later in the afternoon we had a cautious try at whispering. The Sunday quietness of the ship was against us; the stillness of air and water around her was against us; the elements, the men were against us—everything was against us in our secret partnership; time itself—for this could not go on forever. The very trust in Providence was, I suppose, denied to his guilt. Shall I confess that this thought cast me down very much? And as to the chapter of accidents which counts for so much in the book of success, I could only hope that it was closed. For what favorable accident could be expected?

"Did you hear everything?" were my first words as soon as we took up our position side by side, leaning over my bed-place.

He had. And the proof of it was his earnest whisper, "The man told you he hardly dared to give the order."

I understood the reference to be to that saving foresail.

"Yes. He was afraid of it being lost in the setting."

"I assure you he never gave the order. He may think he did, but he never gave it. He stood there with me on the break of the poop after the maintopsail blew away, and whimpered about our last hope—positively whimpered about it and nothing else—and the night coming on! To hear one's skipper go on like that in such weather was enough to drive any fellow out of his mind. It worked me up into a sort of desperation. I just took it into my own hands and went away from him, boiling, and—. But what's the use telling you? *You* know! . . . Do you think that if I had not been pretty fierce with them I should have got the men to do anything? Not it! The bosun perhaps? Perhaps! It wasn't a heavy sea—it was a sea gone mad! I suppose the end of the world will be something like that; and a man may have the heart to see it coming once and be done with it—but to have to face it day after day—I don't blame anybody. I was precious little better than the rest. Only—I was an officer of that old coal-wagon, anyhow—"

"I quite understand," I conveyed that sincere assurance into his ear. He was out of breath with whispering; I could hear him pant slightly. It was all very simple. The same strung-up force which had given twenty-four men a chance, at least, for their lives, had, in a sort of recoil, crushed an unworthy mutinous existence.

But I had no leisure to weigh the merits of the matter—footsteps in the saloon, a heavy knock. "There's enough wind to get under way with, sir." Here was the call of a new claim upon my thoughts and even upon my feelings.

"Turn the hands up," I cried through the door. "I'll be on deck directly."

I was going out to make the acquaintance of my ship. Before I left the cabin our eyes met—the eyes of the only two strangers on board. I pointed to the recessed part where the little campstool awaited him and laid my finger on my lips. He made a gesture—somewhat vague—a little mysterious, accompanied by a faint smile, as if of regret.

This is not the place to enlarge upon the sensations of a man who feels for the first time a ship move under his feet to his own independent word. In my case they were not unalloyed. I was not wholly alone with my command; for there was that stranger in my cabin. Or rather, I was not completely and wholly with her. Part of me was absent. That mental feeling of being in two places at once affected me physically as if the mood of secrecy had penetrated my very soul. Before an hour had elapsed since the ship had begun to move, having occasion to ask the mate (he stood by my side) to take a compass bearing of the Pagoda, I caught myself reaching up to his ear in whispers. I say I caught myself, but enough had escaped to startle the man. I can't describe it otherwise than by saying that he shied. A grave, preoccupied manner, as though he were in possession of some perplexing intelligence, did not leave him henceforth. A little later I moved away from the rail to look at the compass with such a stealthy gait that the helmsman noticed it—and I could not help noticing the unusual roundness of his eyes. These are trifling instances, though it's to no commander's advantage to be suspected of ludicrous eccentricities. But I was also more seriously affected. There are to a seaman certain words, gestures, that should in given conditions come as naturally, as instinctively as the winking of a menaced eye. A certain order should spring on to his lips without thinking; a certain sign should get itself made, so to speak, without reflection. But all unconscious alertness had abandoned me. I had to make an effort of will to recall myself back (from the cabin) to the conditions of the moment. I felt that I was appearing an irresolute commander to those people who were watching me more or less critically.

And, besides, there were the scares. On the second day out, for instance, coming off the deck in the afternoon (I had straw slippers on my bare feet) I stopped at the open pantry door and spoke to the steward. He was doing something there with his back to me. At the sound of my voice he nearly jumped out of his skin, as the saying is, and incidentally broke a cup.

"What on earth's the matter with you?" I asked, astonished.

He was extremely confused. "Beg your pardon, sir. I made sure you were in your cabin."

"You see I wasn't."

"No, sir. I could have sworn I had heard you moving in there not a moment ago. It's most extraordinary . . . very sorry, sir."

I passed on with an inward shudder. I was so identified with my secret double that I did not even mention the fact in those scanty, fearful whispers we exchanged. I suppose he had made some slight noise of some kind or other. It would have been miraculous if he hadn't at one time or another. And yet, haggard as he appeared, he looked always perfectly self-controlled, more than calm—almost invulnerable. On my suggestion he remained almost entirely in the bathroom, which, upon the whole, was the safest place. There could be really no shadow of an excuse for anyone ever wanting to go in there, once the steward had done with it. It was a very tiny place. Sometimes he reclined on the floor, his legs bent, his head sustained on one elbow. At others I would find him on the campstool, sitting in his gray sleeping suit and with his cropped dark hair like a patient, unmoved convict. At night I would smuggle him into my bed-place, and we would whisper together, with the regular footfalls of the officer of the watch passing and repassing over our heads. It was an infinitely miserable time. It was lucky that some tins of fine preserves were stowed in a locker in my stateroom; hard bread I could always get hold of; and so he lived on stewed chicken, paté de foie gras, asparagus, cooked oysters, sardines—on all sorts of abominable sham delicacies out of tins. My early morning coffee he always drank; and it was all I dared do for him in that respect.

Every day there was the horrible maneuvering to go through so that my room and then the bathroom should be done in the usual way. I came to hate the sight of the steward, to abhor the voice of that harmless man. I felt that it was he who would bring on the disaster of discovery. It hung like a sword over our heads.

The fourth day out, I think (we were then working down the east side of the Gulf of Siam, tack for tack, in light winds and smooth water)—the fourth day, I say, of this miserable juggling with the unavoidable, as we sat at our evening meal, that man, whose slightest movement I dreaded, after putting down the dishes ran up on deck busily. This could not be dangerous. Presently he came down again; and then it appeared that he had remembered a coat of mine which I had thrown over a rail to dry after having been wetted in a shower which had passed over the ship in the afternoon. Sitting stolidly at the head of the table I became terrified at the sight of the garment on his arm. Of course he made for my door. There was no time to lose.

"Steward," I thundered. My nerves were so shaken that I could not govern my voice and conceal my agitation. This was the sort of thing that made my terrifically whiskered mate tap his forehead with his forefinger. I had detected him using that gesture while talking on deck with a confidential air to the carpenter. It was too far to hear a word, but I had no doubt that this pantomime could only refer to the strange new captain.

"Yes, sir," the pale-faced steward turned resignedly to me. It was this maddening course of being shouted at, checked without rhyme or reason, arbitrarily chased out of my cabin, suddenly called into it, sent flying out of his pantry on incomprehensible errands, that accounted for the growing wretchedness of his expression.

"Where are you going with that coat?"

"To your room, sir."

"Is there another shower coming?"

"I'm sure I don't know, sir. Shall I go up again and see, sir?"

"No! never mind."

My object was attained, as of course my other self in there would have heard everything that passed. During this interlude my two officers never raised their eyes off their respective plates; but the lip of that confounded cub, the second mate, quivered visibly.

I expected the steward to hook my coat on and come out at once. He was very slow about it; but I dominated my nervousness sufficiently not to shout after him. Suddenly I became aware (it could be heard plainly enough) that the fellow for some reason or other was opening the door of the bathroom. It was the end. The place was literally not big enough to swing a cat in. My voice died in my throat and I went stony all over. I expected to hear a yell of surprise and terror, and made a movement, but had not the strength to get on my legs. Everything remained still. Had my second self taken the poor wretch by the throat? I don't know what I would have done next moment if I had not seen the steward come out of my room, close the door, and then stand quietly by the sideboard.

Saved, I thought. But, no! Lost! Gone! He was gone!

I laid my knife and fork down and leaned back in my chair. My head swam. After a while, when sufficiently recovered to speak in a steady voice, I instructed my mate to put the ship round at eight o'clock himself.

"I won't come on deck," I went on. "I think I'll turn in, and unless the wind shifts I don't want to be disturbed before midnight. I feel a bit seedy."

"You did look middling bad a little while ago," the chief mate remarked without showing any great concern.

They both went out, and I stared at the steward clearing the table. There was nothing to be read on that wretched man's face. But why did he avoid my eyes I asked myself. Then I thought I should like to hear the sound of his voice.

"Steward!"

"Sir!" Startled as usual.

"Where did you hang up that coat?"

"In the bathroom, sir." The usual anxious tone. "It's not quite dry yet, sir."

For some time longer I sat in the cuddy. Had my double vanished as he had come? But of his coming there was an explanation, whereas his disappearance would be inexplicable. . . . I went slowly into my dark room, shut the door, lighted the lamp, and for a time dared not turn round. When at last I did I saw him standing bolt upright in the narrow recessed part. It would not be true to say I had a shock, but an irresistible doubt of his bodily existence flitted through my mind. Can it be, I asked myself, that he is not visible to other eyes than mine? It was like being haunted. Motionless, with a grave face, he raised his hands slightly at me in a gesture which meant clearly, "Heavens! what a narrow escape!" Narrow indeed. I think I had come creeping quietly as near insanity as any man who has not actually gone over the border. That gesture restrained me, so to speak.

The mate with the terrific whiskers was now putting the ship on the other tack. In the moment of profound silence which follows upon the hands going to their stations I heard on the poop his raised voice: "Hard alee!" and the distant shout of the order repeated on the maindeck. The sails, in that light breeze, made but a faint fluttering noise. It ceased. The ship was coming around slowly; I held my breath in the renewed stillness of expectation; one wouldn't have thought that there was a single living soul on her decks. A sudden brisk shout, "Mainsail haul!" broke the spell, and in the noisy cries and rush overhead of the men running away with the main brace we two, down in my cabin, came together in our usual position by the bed-place.

He did not wait for my question. "I heard him fumbling here and just managed to squat myself down in the bath," he whispered to me. "The fellow only opened the door and put his arm in to hang the coat up. All the same——"

"I never thought of that," I whispered back, even more appalled than before at the closeness of the shave, and marveling at that something unyielding in his character which was carrying him through so finely. There was no agitation in his whisper. Whoever was being driven distracted, it was not he. He was sane. And the proof of his sanity was continued when he took up the whispering again.

"It would never do for me to come to life again."

It was something that a ghost might have said. But what he was alluding to was his old captain's reluctant admission of the theory of suicide. It would obviously serve his turn—if I had understood at all the view which seemed to govern the unalterable purpose of his action.

"You must maroon me as soon as ever you can get amongst these islands off the Cambodje shore," he went on.

"Maroon you! We are not living in a boy's adventure tale," I protested. His scornful whispering took me up.

"We aren't indeed! There's nothing of a boy's tale in this. But there's nothing else for it. I want no more. You don't suppose I am afraid of what can be done to me? Prison or gallows or whatever they may please. But you don't see me coming back to explain such things to an old fellow in a wig and twelve respectable tradesmen, do you? What can they know whether I am guilty or not —or of *what* I am guilty, either? That's my affair. What does the Bible say? 'Driven off the face of the earth.' Very well. I am off the face of the earth now. As I came at night so I shall go."

"Impossible!" I murmured. "You can't."

"Can't? . . . Not naked like a soul on the Day of Judgment. I shall freeze on to this sleeping suit. The Last Day is not yet—and . . . you have understood thoroughly. Didn't you?"

I felt suddenly ashamed of myself. I may say truly that I understood—and my hesitation in letting that man swim away from my ship's side had been a mere sham sentiment, a sort of cowardice.

"It can't be done now till next night," I breathed out. "The ship is on the offshore tack and the wind may fail us."

"As long as I know that you understand," he whispered. "But of course you do. It's a great satisfaction to have got somebody to understand. You seem to have been there on purpose." And in the same whisper, as if we two whenever we talked had to say things to each other which were not fit for the world to hear, he added, "It's very wonderful."

We remained side by side talking in our secret way—but sometimes silent or just exchanging a whispered word or two at long intervals. And as usual he stared through the port. A breath of wind came now and again onto our faces. The ship might have been moored in dock, so gently and on an even keel she slipped through the water, that did not murmur even at our passage, shadowy and silent like a phantom sea.

At midnight I went on deck, and to my mate's great surprise put the ship round on the other tack. His terrible whiskers flitted round me in silent criticism. I certainly should not have done it if it had been only a question of getting out of that sleepy gulf as quickly as possible. I believe he told the second mate, who relieved him, that it was a great want of judgment. The other only yawned. That intolerable cub shuffled about so sleepily and lolled against the rails in such a slack, improper fashion that I came down on him sharply.

"Aren't you properly awake yet?"

"Yes, sir! I am awake."

"Well, then, be good enough to hold yourself as if you were. And keep a lookout. If there's any current we'll be closing with some islands before daylight."

The east side of the gulf is fringed with islands, some solitary, others in groups. On the blue background of the high coast they seem to float on silvery patches of calm water, arid and gray, or dark green and rounded like clumps of evergreen bushes, with the larger ones, a mile or two long, showing the outlines of ridges, ribs of gray rock under the dark mantle of matted leafage. Unknown to trade, to travel, almost to geography, the manner of life they harbor is an unsolved secret. There must be villages—settlements of fishermen at least—on the largest of them, and some communication with the world is probably kept up by native craft. But all the forenoon, as we headed for them, fanned along by the faintest of breezes, I saw no sign of man or canoe in the field of the telescope I kept on pointing at the scattered group.

At noon I gave no orders for a change of course, and the mate's whiskers became much concerned and seemed to be offering themselves unduly to my notice. At last I said:

"I am going to stand right in. Quite in—as far as I can take her."

The stare of extreme surprise imparted an air of ferocity also to his eyes, and he looked truly terrific for a moment.

"We're not doing well in the middle of the gulf," I continued, casually. "I am going to look for the land breezes tonight."

"Bless my soul! Do you mean, sir, in the dark amongst the lot of all them islands and reefs and shoals?"

"Well—if there are any regular land breezes at all on this coast one must get close inshore to find them, mustn't one?"

"Bless my soul!" he exclaimed again under his breath. All that afternoon he wore a dreamy, contemplative appearance which in him was a mark of perplexity. After dinner I went into my stateroom as if I meant to take some rest. There we two bent our dark heads over a half-unrolled chart lying on my bed.

"There," I said. "It's got to be Koh-ring. I've been looking at it ever since sunrise. It has got two hills and a low point. It must be inhabited. And on the coast opposite there is what looks like the mouth of a biggish river—with some town, no doubt, not far up. It's the best chance for you that I can see."

"Anything. Koh-ring let it be."

He looked thoughtfully at the chart as if surveying chances and distances from a lofty height—and following with his eyes his own figure wandering on the blank land of Cochin-China, and then passing off that piece of paper clean out of sight into uncharted regions. And it was as if the ship had two captains to plan her course for her. I had been so worried and restless running up and down that I had not had the patience to dress that day. I had remained in my sleeping suit, with straw slippers and a soft floppy hat. The closeness of the heat in the gulf had been most oppressive, and the crew were used to see me wandering in that airy attire.

"She will clear the south point as she heads now," I whispered into his ear. "Goodness only knows when, though, but certainly after dark. I'll edge her in to half a mile, as far as I may be able to judge in the dark——"

"Be careful," he murmured, warningly—and I realized suddenly that all my future, the only future of which I was fit, would perhaps go irretrievably to pieces in any mishap to my first command.

I could not stop a moment longer in the room. I motioned him to get out of sight and made my way on the poop. That unplayful cub had the watch. I walked up and down for a while thinking things out, then beckoned him over.

"Send a couple of hands to open the two quarter-deck ports," I said, mildly.

He actually had the impudence, or else so forgot himself in his wonder at such an incomprehensible order, as to repeat:

"Open the quarter-deck ports! What for, sir?"

"The only reason you need concern yourself about is because I tell you to do so. Have them open wide and fastened properly."

He reddened and went off, but I believe made some jeering remark to the carpenter as to the sensible practice of ventilating a ship's quarter-deck. I know he popped into the mate's cabin to impart the fact to him because the whiskers came on deck, as it were by chance, and stole glances at me from below—for signs of lunacy or drunkenness, I suppose.

A little before supper, feeling more restless than ever, I rejoined, for a moment, my second self. And to find him sitting so quietly was surprising, like something against nature, inhuman.

I developed my plan in a hurried whisper.

"I shall stand in as close as I dare and then put her round. I shall presently find means to smuggle you out of here into the sail locker, which communicates with the lobby. But there is an opening, a sort of square for hauling the sails out, which gives straight on the quarter-deck and which is never closed in fine weather, so as to give air to the sails. When the ship's way is deadened in stays and all the hands are aft at the main braces you shall have a clear road to slip out and get overboard through the open quarter-deck port. I've had them both fastened up. Use a rope's end to lower yourself into the water so as to avoid a splash—you know. It could be heard and cause some beastly complication."

He kept silent for a while, then whispered, "I understand."

"I won't be there to see you go," I began with an effort. "The rest . . . I only hope I have understood, too."

"You have. From first to last," and for the first time there seemed to be a faltering, something strained in his whisper. He caught hold of my arm, but the ringing of the supper bell made me start. He didn't, though; he only released his grip.

After supper I didn't come below again till well past eight o'clock. The faint, steady breeze was loaded with dew; and the wet, darkened sails held all there was of propelling power in it. The night, clear and starry, sparkled darkly, and the opaque, lightless patches shifting slowly against the low stars were the drifting islets. On the port bow there was a big one more distant and shadowily imposing by the great space of sky it eclipsed.

On opening the door I had a back view of my very own self looking at a chart. He had come out of the recess and was standing near the table.

"Quite dark enough," I whispered.

He stepped back and leaned against my bed with a level, quiet glance. I sat on the couch. We had nothing to say to each other. Over our heads the officer of the watch moved here and there. Then I heard him move quickly. I knew what that meant. He was making for the companion; and presently his voice was outside my door.

"We are drawing in pretty fast, sir. Land looks rather close."

"Very well," I answered. "I am coming on deck directly."

I waited till he was gone out of the cuddy, then rose. My double moved too. The time had come to exchange our last whispers, for neither of us was ever to hear each other's natural voice.

"Look here!" I opened a drawer and took out three sovereigns. "Take this, anyhow. I've got six and I'd give you the lot, only I must keep a little money to buy some fruit and vegetables for the crew from native boats as we go through Sunda Straits."

He shook his head.

"Take it," I urged him, whispering desperately. "No one can tell what——"

He smiled and slapped meaningly the only pocket of the sleeping jacket. It was not safe, certainly. But I produced a large old silk handkerchief of mine, and tying the three pieces of gold in a corner, pressed it on him. He was touched, I suppose, because he took it at last and tied it quickly round his waist under the jacket, on his bare skin.

Our eyes met; several seconds elapsed, till, our glances still mingled, I extended my hand and turned the lamp out. Then I passed through the cuddy, leaving the door of my room wide open. . . . "Steward!"

He was still lingering in the pantry in the greatness of his zeal, giving a rub-up to a plated cruet stand the last thing before going to bed. Being careful not to wake up the mate, whose room was opposite, I spoke in an undertone.

He looked round anxiously. "Sir!"

"Can you get me a little hot water from the galley?"

"I am afraid, sir, the galley fire's been out for some time now."

"Go and see."

He fled up the stairs.

"Now," I whispered, loudly, into the saloon—too loudly, perhaps, but I was afraid I couldn't make a sound. He was by my side in an instant—the double captain slipped past the stairs—through the tiny dark passage . . . a sliding door. We were in the sail locker, scrambling on our knees over the sails. A sudden thought struck me. I saw myself wandering barefooted, bareheaded, the sun beating on my dark poll. I snatched off my floppy hat and tried hurriedly in the dark to ram it on my other self. He dodged and fended off silently. I wonder what he thought had come to me before he understood and suddenly desisted. Our hands met gropingly, lingered united in a steady, motionless clasp for a second. . . . No word was breathed by either of us when they separated.

I was standing quietly by the pantry door when the steward returned.

"Sorry, sir. Kettle barely warm. Shall I light the spirit lamp?"

"Never mind."

I came out on deck slowly. It was now a matter of conscience to shave the land as close as possible—for now he must go overboard whenever the ship was put in stays. Must! There could be no going back for him. After a moment I walked over to leeward and my heart flew into my mouth at the nearness of the land on the bow. Under any other circumstances I would not have held on a minute longer. The second mate had followed me anxiously.

I looked on till I felt I could command my voice.

"She will weather," I said then in a quiet tone.

"Are you going to try that, sir?" he stammered out incredulously.

I took no notice of him and raised my tone just enough to be heard by the helmsman.

"Keep her good full."

"Good full, sir."

The wind fanned my cheek, the sails slept, the world was silent. The strain of watching the dark loom of the land grow bigger and denser was too much for me. I had shut my eyes—because the ship must go closer. She must! The stillness was intolerable. Were we standing still?

When I opened my eyes the second view started my heart with a thump. The black southern hill of Koh-ring seemed to hang right over the ship like a towering fragment of the everlasting night. On that enormous mass of blackness there was not a gleam to be seen, not a sound to be heard. It was gliding irresistibly toward us and yet seemed already within reach of the hand. I saw the vague figures of the watch grouped in the waist, gazing in awed silence.

"Are you going on, sir?" inquired an unsteady voice at my elbow.

I ignored it. I had to go on.

"Keep her full. Don't check her way. That won't do now," I said warningly.

"I can't see the sails very well," the helmsman answered me, in strange, quavering tones.

Was she close enough? Already she was, I won't say in the shadow of the land, but in the very blackness of it, already swallowed up as it were, gone too close to be recalled, gone from me altogether.

"Give the mate a call," I said to the young man who stood at my elbow as still as death. "And turn all hands up."

My tone had a borrowed loudness reverberated from the height of the land. Several voices cried out together: "We are all on deck, sir."

Then stillness again, with the great shadow gliding closer, towering higher, without a light, without a sound. Such a hush had fallen on the ship that she might have been a bark of the dead floating in slowly under the very gate of Erebus.

"My God! Where are we?"

It was the mate moaning at my elbow. He was thunderstruck, and as it were deprived of the moral support of his whiskers. He clapped his hands and absolutely cried out, "Lost!"

"Be quiet," I said sternly.

He lowered his tone, but I saw the shadowy gesture of his despair. "What are we doing here?"

"Looking for the land wind."

He made as if to tear his hair, and addressed me recklessly.

"She will never get out. You have done it, sir. I knew it'd end in something like this. She will never weather, and you are too close now to stay. She'll drift ashore before she's round. O my God!"

I caught his arm as he was raising it to batter his poor devoted head, and shook it violently.

"She's ashore already," he wailed, trying to tear himself away.

"Is she? . . . Keep good full there!"

"Good full, sir," cried the helmsman in a frightened, thin childlike voice.

I hadn't let go the mate's arm and went on shaking it. "Ready about, do you hear? You go forward"—shake—"and stop there"—shake—"and hold your noise"—shake—"and see these head sheets properly overhauled"—shake, shake —shake.

And all the time I dared not look toward the land lest my heart should fail me. I released my grip at last and he ran forward as if fleeing for dear life.

I wondered what my double there in the sail locker thought of this commotion. He was able to hear everything and perhaps he was able to understand why, on my conscience, it had to be thus close—no less. My first order "Hard alee!" re-echoed ominously under the towering shadow of Koh-ring as if I had shouted in a mountain gorge. And then I watched the land intently. In that smooth water and light wind it was impossible to feel the ship coming-to. No! I could not feel her. And my second self was making now ready to slip out and lower himself overboard. Perhaps he was gone already . . . ?

The great black mass brooding over our very mastheads began to pivot away from the ship's side silently. And now I forgot the secret stranger ready to depart, and remembered only that I was a total stranger to the ship. I did not know her. Would she do it? How was she to be handled?

I swung the mainyard and waited helplessly. She was perhaps stopped, and her very fate hung in the balance, with the black mass of Koh-ring like the gate of the everlasting night towering over her taffrail. What would she do now? Had she way on her yet? I stepped to the side swiftly, and on the shadowy water I could see nothing except a faint phosphorescent flash revealing the glassy smoothness of the sleeping surface. It was impossible to tell—and I had not learned yet the feel of my ship. Was she moving? What I needed was something easily seen, a piece of paper, which I could throw overboard and watch. I had nothing on me. To run down for it I didn't dare. There was no time. All at once my strained, yearning stare distinguished a white object floating within a yard of the ship's side. White on the black water. A phosphorescent flash passed under it. What was that thing? . . . I recognized my own floppy hat. It must have fallen off his head . . . and he didn't bother. Now I had what I wanted—the saving mark for my eyes. But I hardly thought of my other self, now gone from the ship, to be hidden forever from all friendly faces, to be a fugitive and a vagabond on the earth, with no brand of the curse on his sane forehead to stay a slaying hand . . . too proud to explain.

And I watched the hat—the expression of my sudden pity for his mere flesh. It had been meant to save his homeless head from the dangers of the sun. And now—behold—it was saving the ship, by serving me for a mark to help out the ignorance of my strangeness. Ha! It was drifting forward, warning me just in time that the ship had gathered sternway.

"Shift the helm," I said in a low voice to the seaman standing still like a statue.

The man's eyes glistened wildly in the binnacle light as he jumped round to the other side and spun round the wheel.

I walked to the break of the poop. On the overshadowed deck all hands stood by the forebraces waiting for my order. The stars ahead seemed to be gliding from right to left. And all was so still in the world that I heard the quiet remark "She's round," passed in a tone of intense relief between two seamen.

"Let go and haul."

The foreyards ran round with a great noise, amidst cheery cries. And now the frightful whiskers made themselves heard giving various orders. Already the ship was drawing ahead. And I was alone with her. Nothing! no one in the world should stand now between us, throwing a shadow on the way of silent knowledge and mute affection, the perfect communion of a seaman with his first command.

Walking to the taffrail, I was in time to make out, on the very edge of a darkness thrown by a towering black mass like the very gateway of Erebus—yes, I was in time to catch an evanescent glimpse of my white hat left behind to mark the spot where the secret sharer of my cabin and of my thoughts, as though he were my second self, had lowered himself into the water to take his punishment: a free man, a proud swimmer striking out for a new destiny.

## *Study questions*

1. *How does the captain feel about his first command? Does the statement "And I was alone with her [the ship] . . ." have symbolic dimensions? What is the captain's conflict? Is this an initiation story?* 2. *Conrad uses the word* double *at least twenty times in the story. In how many ways are the captain and Leggatt alike? different?* 3. *What is the significance of the fact that Leggatt has killed*

*a man? Is it possible to call Leggatt a murderer? If so, how can we justify on moral grounds the captain's refusal to turn him over to the authorities?* 4. *At what point in the story does the captain come close to violence? How is this action significant?* 5. *What is the relevance of the L-shaped room? of the white hat?* 6. *Why is Leggatt compared to a "headless corpse" while he is in the water?* 7. *How do the captain and crew of the* Sephora *function?* 8. *What change takes place in the captain?* 9. *Trace the images of light and dark throughout the story. How does this motif function?*

*Stephen Crane* (1871–1900), whose career was cut short by tuberculosis, spent most of his adult life as a correspondent, though he managed, also, to write an impressive number of stories. His most famous novel, *The Red Badge of Courage,* was published in 1895 and won for him immediate literary recognition. Born in Newark, New Jersey, he attended Lafayette College for a year and then went to Syracuse University, but he was unable to continue because of financial difficulties. He then went to New York City, where he tried to support himself with various reporting jobs. His experience in New York formed the basis for his first novel, *Maggie: A Girl of the Streets* (1893), which he published at his own expense. Other volumes of prose fiction, published after his success with *The Red Badge of Courage,* include *George's Mother* (1896), *The Open Boat and Other Tales of Adventure* (1898), *The Monster and Other Stories* (1899), *Whilomville Stories* (1900), and *Wounds in the Rain: War Stories* (1900). Probably his most famous short stories are "The Bride Comes to Yellow Sky," "The Blue Hotel," and "The Open Boat." Characteristically, his stories operate by means of a realistic rendering of the extensional world and a traditional plot line, but the details are charged with symbolic values. "The Open Boat" is the story of the aftermath of a wreck at sea when a group of men learn that the ethical content of their relationship with each other provides the base for any meaning in life. By the end of the story the correspondent is able to be an interpreter of the events and the reader of the microcosm Crane presents.

# THE OPEN BOAT

*A Tale Intended to be after the Fact:*
*Being the Experience of Four Men*
*from the Sunk Steamer 'Commodore'*

## 1

None of them knew the colour of the sky. Their eyes glanced level, and were fastened upon the waves that swept toward them. These waves were of the hue of slate, save for the tops, which were of foaming white, and all of the men knew the colours of the sea. The horizon narrowed and widened, and dipped and rose, and at all times its edge was jagged with waves that seemed thrust up in points like rocks.

Many a man ought to have a bathtub larger than the boat which here rode upon the sea. These waves were most wrongfully and barbarously abrupt and tall, and each froth-top was a problem in small-boat navigation.

The cook squatted in the bottom, and looked with both eyes at the six inches of gunwale which separated him from the ocean. His sleeves were rolled over his fat forearms, and the two flaps of his unbuttoned vest dangled as he bent to bail out the boat. Often he said, "Gawd! that was a narrow clip." As he remarked it he invariably gazed eastward over the broken sea.

The oiler, steering with one of the two oars in the boat, sometimes raised himself suddenly to keep clear of water that swirled in over the stern. It was a thin little oar, and it seemed often ready to snap.

The correspondent, pulling at the other oar, watched the waves and wondered why he was there.

The injured captain, lying in the bow, was at this time buried in that profound dejection and indifference which comes, temporarily at least, to even the bravest and most enduring when, willy-nilly, the firm fails, the army loses, the ship goes down. The mind of the master of a vessel is rooted deep in the timbers of her, though he command for a day or a decade; and this captain had on him the stern impression of a scene in the greys of dawn of seven turned faces, and later a stump of a topmast with a white ball on it, that slashed to and fro at the waves, went low and lower, and down. Thereafter there was something strange in his voice. Although steady, it was deep with mourning, and of a quality beyond oration or tears.

"Keep 'er a little more south, Billie," said he.

"A little more south, sir," said the oiler in the stern.

A seat in his boat was not unlike a seat upon a bucking broncho, and by the same token a broncho is not much smaller. The craft pranced and reared and plunged like an animal. As each wave came, and she rose for it, she seemed like a horse making at a fence outrageously high. The manner of her scramble over these walls of water is a mystic thing, and, moreover, at the top of them were ordinarily these problems in white water, the foam racing down from the summit of each wave requiring a new leap, and a leap from the air. Then, after scornfully bumping a crest, she would slide and race and splash down a long incline, and arrive bobbing and nodding in front of the next menace.

A singular disadvantage of the sea lies in the fact that after successfully surmounting one wave you discover that there is another behind it just as important and just as nervously anxious to do something effective in the way of swamping boats. In a ten-foot dinghy one can get an idea of the resources of the sea in the line of waves that is not probable to the average experience which is never at sea in a dinghy. As each slaty wall of water approached, it shut all else from the view of the men in the boat, and it was not difficult to imagine that this particular wave was the final outburst of the ocean, the last effort of the grim water. There was a terrible grace in the move of the waves, and they came in silence, save for the snarling of the crests.

In the wan light the faces of the men must have been grey. Their eyes must have glinted in strange ways as they gazed steadily astern. Viewed from a balcony, the whole thing would doubtless have been weirdly picturesque. But the men in the boat had no time to see it, and if they had had leisure, there were other things to occupy their minds. The sun swung steadily up the sky, and they knew it was broad day because the colour of the sea changed from slate to emerald green streaked with amber lights, and the foam was like tumbling snow. The process of the breaking day was unknown to them. They were aware only of this effect upon the colour of the waves that rolled toward them.

In disjointed sentences the cook and the correspondent argued as to the difference between a life-saving station and a house of refuge. The cook had said: "There's a house of refuge just north of the Mosquito Inlet Light, and as soon as they see us they'll come off in their boat and pick us up."

"As soon as who see us?" said the correspondent.

"The crew," said the cook.

"Houses of refuge don't have crews," said the correspondent. "As I understand them, they are only places where clothes and grub are stored for the benefit of shipwrecked people. They don't carry crews."

"Oh, yes, they do," said the cook.

"No, they don't," said the correspondent.

"Well, we're not there yet, anyhow," said the oiler, in the stern.

"Well," said the cook, "perhaps it's not a house of refuge that I'm thinking of as being near Mosquito Inlet Light; perhaps it's a life-saving station."

"We're not there yet," said the oiler in the stern.

## 2

As the boat bounced from the top of each wave the wind tore through the hair of the hatless men, and as the craft plopped her stern down again the spray slashed past them. The crest of each of these waves was a hill, from the top of which the men surveyed for a moment a broad tumultuous expanse, shining and wind-riven. It was probably splendid, it was probably glorious, this play of the free sea, wild with lights of emerald and white and amber.

"Bully good thing it's an on-shore wind," said the cook. "If not, where would we be? Wouldn't have a show."

"That's right," said the correspondent.

The busy oiler nodded his assent.

Then the captain, in the bow, chuckled in a way that expressed humour, contempt, tragedy, all in one. "Do you think we've got much of a show now, boys?" said he.

Whereupon the three were silent, save for a trifle of hemming and hawing. To express any particular optimism at this time they felt to be childish and stupid, but they all doubtless possessed this sense of the situation in their minds. A young man thinks doggedly at such times. On the other hand, the ethics of their condition was decidedly against any open suggestion of hopelessness. So they were silent.

"Oh, well," said the captain, soothing his children, "we'll get ashore all right."

But there was that in his tone which made them think; so the oiler quoth, "Yes! if this wind holds."

The cook was bailing. "Yes! if we don't catch hell in the surf."

Canton-flannel gulls flew near and far. Sometimes they sat down on the sea, near patches of brown seaweed that rolled over the waves with a movement like carpets on a line in a gale. The birds sat comfortably in groups, and they were envied by some in the dinghy, for the wrath of the sea was no more to them than it was to a covey of prairie chickens a thousand miles inland. Often they came very close and stared at the men with black bead-like eyes. At these times they were uncanny and sinister in their unblinking scrutiny, and the men hooted angrily at them, telling them to be gone. One came, and evidently decided to alight on the top of the captain's head. The bird flew parallel to the boat and did not circle, but made short sidelong jumps in the air in chicken-fashion. His black eyes were wistfully fixed upon the captain's head. "Ugly brute," said the oiler to the bird. "You look as if you were made with a jackknife." The cook and the correspondent swore darkly at the creature. The captain naturally wished to knock it away with the end of the heavy painter, but he did not dare do it, because anything resembling an emphatic gesture would have capsized this freighted boat; and so, with his open hand, the captain gently and carefully waved the gull away. After it had been discouraged from the pursuit the captain breathed easier on account of his hair, and others breathed easier because the bird struck their minds at this time as being somehow gruesome and ominous.

In the meantime the oiler and the correspondent rowed. And also they rowed. They sat together in the same seat, and each rowed an oar. Then the oiler took both oars; then the correspondent took both oars; then the oiler; then the correspondent. They rowed and they rowed. The very ticklish part of the business was when the time came for the reclining one in the stern to take his turn at the oars. By the very last star of truth, it is easier to steal eggs from under a hen than it was to change seats in the dinghy. First the man in the stern slid his hand along the thwart and moved with care, as if he were of Sèvres. Then the man in the rowing-seat slid his hand along the other thwart. It was all done with the most extraordinary care. As the two sidled past each other, the whole party kept watchful eyes on the coming wave, and the captain cried: "Look out, now! Steady, there!"

The brown mats of seaweed that appeared from time to time were like islands, bits of earth. They were travelling, apparently, neither one way nor the other. They were, to all intents, stationary. They informed the men in the boat that it was making progress slowly toward the land.

The captain, rearing cautiously in the bow after the dinghy soared on a great swell, said that he had seen the lighthouse at Mosquito Inlet. Presently the cook remarked that he had seen it. The correspondent was at the oars then, and for some reason he too wished to look at the lighthouse; but his back was toward the far shore, and the waves were important, and for some time he could not seize an opportunity to turn his head. But at last there came a wave more gentle than the others, and when at the crest of it he swiftly scoured the western horizon.

"See it?" said the captain.

"No," said the correspondent, slowly; "I didn't see anything."

"Look again," said the captain. He pointed. "It's exactly in that direction."

At the top of another wave the correspondent did as he was bid, and this time his eyes chanced on a small, still thing on the edge of the swaying horizon.

It was precisely like the point of a pin. It took an anxious eye to find a lighthouse so tiny.

"Think we'll make it, Captain?"

"If this wind holds and the boat don't swamp, we can't do much else," said the captain.

The little boat, lifted by each towering sea and splashed viciously by the crests, made progress that in the absence of seaweed was not apparent to those in her. She seemed just a wee thing wallowing, miraculously top up, at the mercy of five oceans. Occasionally a great spread of water, like white flames, swarmed into her.

"Bail her, cook," said the captain, serenely.

"All right, Captain," said the cheerful cook.

## 3

It would be difficult to describe the subtle brotherhood of men that was here established on the seas. No one said that it was so. No one mentioned it. But it dwelt in the boat, and each man felt it warm him. They were a captain, an oiler, a cook, and a correspondent, and they were friends—friends in a more curiously iron-bound degree than may be common. The hurt captain, lying against the water-jar in the bow, spoke always in a low voice and calmly; but he could never command a more ready and swiftly obedient crew than the motley three of the dinghy. It was more than a mere recognition of what was best for the common safety. There was surely in it a quality that was personal and heart-felt. And after this devotion to the commander of the boat, there was this comradeship, that the correspondent, for instance, who had been taught to be cynical of men, knew even at the time was the best experience of his life. But no one said that it was so. No one mentioned it.

"I wish we had a sail," remarked the captain. "We might try my overcoat on the end of an oar, and give you two boys a chance to rest." So the cook and the correspondent held the mast and spread wide the overcoat; the oiler steered; and the little boat made good way with her new rig. Sometimes the oiler had to scull sharply to keep a sea from breaking into the boat, but otherwise sailing was a success.

Meanwhile the lighthouse had been growing slowly larger. It had now almost assumed colour, and appeared like a little grey shadow on the sky. The man at the oars could not be prevented from turning his head rather often to try for a glimpse of this little grey shadow.

At last, from the top of each wave, the men in the tossing boat could see land. Even as the lighthouse was an upright shadow on the sky, this land seemed but a long black shadow on the sea. It certainly was thinner than paper. "We must be about opposite New Smyrna," said the cook, who had coasted this shore often in schooners. "Captain, by the way, I believe they abandoned that life-saving station there about a year ago."

"Did they?" said the captain.

The wind slowly died away. The cook and the correspondent were not now obliged to slave in order to hold high the oar. But the waves continued their old impetuous swooping at the dinghy, and the little craft, no longer under way, struggled woundily over them. The oiler or the correspondent took the oars again.

Shipwrecks are apropos of nothing. If men could only train for them and have them occur when the men had reached pink condition, there would be less drowning at sea. Of the four in the dinghy none had slept any time worth mentioning for two days and two nights previous to embarking in the dinghy, and in the excitement of clambering about the deck of a foundering ship they had also forgotten to eat heartily.

For these reasons, and for others, neither the oiler nor the correspondent was fond of rowing at this time. The correspondent wondered ingenuously how in the name of all that was sane could there be people who thought it amusing to row a boat. It was not an amusement; it was a diabolical punishment, and even a genius of mental aberrations could never conclude that it was anything but a horror to the muscles and a crime against the back. He mentioned to the boat in general how the amusement of rowing struck him, and the weary-faced oiler smiled in full sympathy. Previously to the foundering, by the way, the oiler had worked a double watch in the engine-room of the ship.

"Take her easy now, boys," said the captain. "Don't spend yourselves. If we have to run a surf you'll need all your strength, because we'll sure have to swim for it. Take your time."

Slowly the land arose from the sea. From a black line it became a line of black and a line of white—trees and sand. Finally the captain said that he could make out a house on the shore. "That's the house of refuge, sure," said the cook. "They'll see us before long, and come out after us."

The distant lighthouse reared high. "The keeper ought to be able to make us out now, if he's looking through a glass," said the captain. "He'll notify the life-saving people."

"None of those other boats could have got ashore to give word of this wreck," said the oiler, in a low voice, "else the life-boat would be out hunting us."

Slowly and beautifully the land loomed out of the sea. The wind came again. It had veered from the north-east to the south-east. Finally a new sound struck the ears of the men in the boat. It was the low thunder of the surf on the shore. "We'll never be able to make the lighthouse now," said the captain. "Swing her head a little more north, Billie."

"A little more north, sir," said the oiler.

Whereupon the little boat turned her nose once more down the wind, and all but the oarsman watched the shore grow. Under the influence of this expansion doubt and direful apprehension were leaving the minds of the men. The management of the boat was still most absorbing, but it could not prevent a quiet cheerfulness. In an hour, perhaps, they would be ashore.

Their backbones had become thoroughly used to balancing in the boat, and they now rode this wild colt of a dinghy like circus men. The correspondent thought that he had been drenched to the skin, but happening to feel in the top pocket of his coat, he found therein eight cigars. Four of them were soaked with sea-water; four were perfectly scatheless. After a search, somebody produced three dry matches; and thereupon the four waifs rode impudently in their little boat and, with an assurance of an impending rescue shining in their eyes, puffed at the big cigars, and judged well and ill of all men. Everybody took a drink of water.

## 4

"Cook," remarked the captain, "there don't seem to be any signs of life about your house of refuge."

"No," replied the cook. "Funny they don't see us!"

A broad stretch of lowly coast lay before the eyes of the men. It was of low dunes topped with dark vegetation. The roar of the surf was plain, and sometimes they could see the white lip of a wave as it spun up the beach. A tiny house was blocked out black upon the sky. Southward, the slim lighthouse lifted its little grey length.

Tide, wind, and waves were swinging the dinghy northward. "Funny they don't see us," said the men.

The surf's roar was here dulled, but its tone was nevertheless thunderous and mighty. As the boat swam over the great rollers the men sat listening to this roar. "We'll swamp sure," said everybody.

It is fair to say here that there was not a life-saving station within twenty miles in either direction; but the men did not know this fact, and in consequence they made dark and opprobrious remarks concerning the eyesight of the nation's life-savers. Four scowling men sat in the dinghy and surpassed records in the invention of epithets.

"Funny they don't see us."

The light-heartedness of a former time had completely faded. To their sharpened minds it was easy to conjure pictures of all kinds of incompetency and blindness and, indeed, cowardice. There was the shore of the populous land, and it was bitter and bitter to them that from it came no sign.

"Well," said the captain, ultimately, "I suppose we'll have to make a try for ourselves. If we stay out here too long, we'll none of us have strength left to swim after the boat swamps."

And so the oiler, who was at the oars, turned the boat straight for the shore. There was a sudden tightening of muscles. There was some thinking.

"If we don't all get ashore," said the captain—"if we don't all get ashore, I suppose you fellows know where to send news of my finish?"

They then briefly exchanged some addresses and admonitions. As for the reflections of the men, there was a great deal of rage in them. Perchance they might be formulated thus: "If I am going to be drowned—if I am going to be drowned—if I am going to be drowned, why, in the name of the seven mad gods who rule the sea, was I allowed to come thus far and contemplate sand and trees? Was I brought here merely to have my nose dragged away as I was about to nibble the sacred cheese of life? It is preposterous. If this old ninny-woman, Fate, cannot do better than this, she should be deprived of the management of men's fortunes. She is an old hen who knows not her intention. If she has decided to drown me, why did she not do it in the beginning and save me all this trouble? The whole affair is absurd.—But no; she cannot mean to drown me. She dare not drown me. She cannot drown me. Not after all this work." Afterward the man might have had an impulse to shake his fist at the clouds. "Just you drown me, now, and then hear what I call you!"

The billows that came at this time were more formidable. They seemed always just about to break and roll over the little boat in a turmoil of foam. There was a preparatory and long growl in the speech of them. No mind unused to the sea would have concluded that the dinghy could ascend these sheer heights in time. The shore was still afar. The oiler was a wily surfman. "Boys," he said swiftly, "she won't live three minutes more, and we're too far out to swim. Shall I take her to sea again, Captain?"

"Yes; go ahead!" said the captain.

This oiler, by a series of quick miracles and fast and steady oarsmanship, turned the boat in the middle of the surf and took her safely to sea again.

There was a considerable silence as the boat bumped over the furrowed sea to deeper water. Then somebody in gloom spoke: "Well, anyhow, they must have seen us from the shore by now."

The gulls went in slanting flight up the wind toward the grey, desolate east. A squall, marked by dingy clouds and clouds brick-red like smoke from a burning building, appeared from the south-east.

"What do you think of those life-saving people? Ain't they peaches?"

"Funny they haven't seen us."

"Maybe they think we're out here for sport! Maybe they think we're fishin'. Maybe they think we're damned fools."

It was a long afternoon. A changed tide tried to force them southward, but wind and wave said northward. Far ahead, where coast-line, sea, and sky formed their mighty angle, there were little dots which seemed to indicate a city on the shore.

"St. Augustine?"

The captain shook his head. "Too near Mosquito Inlet."

And the oiler rowed, and then the correspondent rowed; then the oiler rowed. It was a weary business. The human back can become the seat of more aches and pains than are registered in books for the composite anatomy of a regiment. It is a limited area, but it can become the theatre of innumerable muscular conflicts, tangles, wrenches, knots, and other comforts.

"Did you ever like to row, Billie?" asked the correspondent.

"No," said the oiler; "hang it!"

When one exchanged the rowing-seat for a place in the bottom of the boat, he suffered a bodily depression that caused him to be careless of everything save an obligation to wiggle one finger. There was cold sea-water swashing to and fro in the boat, and he lay in it. His head, pillowed on a thwart, was within an inch of the swirl of a wave-crest, and sometimes a particularly obstreperous sea came inboard and drenched him once more. But these matters did not annoy him. It is almost certain that if the boat had capsized he would have tumbled comfortably out upon the ocean as if he felt sure that it was a great soft mattress.

"Look! There's a man on the shore!"

"Where?"

"There! See 'im? See 'im?"

"Yes, sure! He's walking along."

"Now he's stopped. Look! He's facing us!"

"He's waving at us!"

"So he is! By thunder!"

"Ah, now we're all right! Now we're all right! There'll be a boat out here for us in half an hour."

"He's going on. He's running. He's going up to that house there."

The remote beach seemed lower than the sea, and it required a searching glance to discern the little black figure. The captain saw a floating stick, and they rowed to it. A bath towel was by some weird chance in the boat, and, tying this on the stick, the captain waved it. The oarsman did not dare turn his head, so he was obliged to ask questions.

"What's he doing now?"

"He's standing still again. He's looking, I think.—There he goes again—toward the house.—Now he's stopped again."

"Is he waving at us?"

"No, not now; he was, though."

"Look! There comes another man!"

"He's running."

"Look at him go, would you!"

"Why, he's on a bicycle. Now he's met the other man. They're both waving at us. Look!"

"There comes something up the beach."

"What the devil is that thing?"

"Why, it looks like a boat."

"Why, certainly, it's a boat."

"No; it's on wheels."

"Yes, so it is. Well, that must be the life-boat. They drag them along shore on a wagon."

"That's the life-boat, sure."

"No, by God, it's—it's an omnibus."

"I tell you it's a life-boat."

"It is not! It's an omnibus. I can see it plain. See? One of these big hotel omnibuses."

"By thunder, you're right. It's an omnibus, sure as fate. What do you suppose they are doing with an omnibus? Maybe they are going around collecting the life-crew, hey?"

"That's it, likely. Look! There's a fellow waving a little black flag. He's standing on the steps of the omnibus. There come those other two fellows. Now they're all talking together. Look at the fellow with the flag. Maybe he ain't waving it!"

"That ain't a flag, is it? That's his coat. Why, certainly, that's his coat."

"So it is; it's his coat. He's taken it off and is waving it around his head. But would you look at him swing it!"

"Oh, say, there isn't any life-saving station there. That's just a winter-resort hotel omnibus that has brought over some of the boarders to see us drown."

"What's that idiot with the coat mean? What's he signalling, anyhow?"

"It looks as if he were trying to tell us to go north. There must be a life-saving station up there."

"No; he thinks we're fishing. Just giving us a merry hand. See? Ah, there, Willie!"

"Well, I wish I could make something out of those signals. What do you suppose he means?"

"He don't mean anything; he's just playing."

"Well, if he'd just signal us to try the surf again, or to go to sea and wait, or go north, or go south, or go to hell, there would be some reason in it. But look at him! He just stands there and keeps his coat revolving like a wheel. The ass!"

"There come more people."

"Now there's quite a mob. Look! Isn't that a boat?"

"Where? Oh, I see where you mean. No, that's no boat."

"That fellow is still waving his coat."

"He must think we like to see him do that. Why don't he quit it? It don't mean anything."

"I don't know. I think he is trying to make us go north. It must be that there's a life-saving station there somewhere."

"Say, he ain't tired yet. Look at 'im wave!"

"Wonder how long he can keep that up. He's been revolving his coat ever since he caught sight of us. He's an idiot. Why aren't they getting men to bring a boat out? A fishing-boat—one of those big yawls—could come out here all right. Why don't he do something?"

"Oh, it's all right now."

"They'll have a boat out here for us in less than no time, now that they've seen us."

A faint yellow tone came into the sky over the low land. The shadows on the sea slowly deepened. The wind bore coldness with it, and the men began to shiver.

"Holy smoke!" said one, allowing his voice to express his impious mood, "if we keep on monkeying out here! If we've got to flounder out here all night!"

"Oh, we'll never have to stay here all night! Don't you worry. They've seen us now, and it won't be long before they'll come chasing out after us."

The shore grew dusky. The man waving a coat blended gradually into this gloom, and it swallowed in the same manner the omnibus and the group of people. The spray, when it dashed uproariously over the side, made the voyagers shrink and swear like men who were being branded.

"I'd like to catch the chump who waved the coat. I feel like socking him one, just for luck."

"Why? What did he do?"

"Oh, nothing, but then he seemed so damned cheerful."

In the meantime the oiler rowed, and then the correspondent rowed, and then the oiler rowed. Grey-faced and bowed forward, they mechanically, turn by turn, plied the leaden oars. The form of the lighthouse had vanished from the southern horizon, but finally a pale star appeared, just lifting from the sea. The streaked saffron in the west passed before the all-merging darkness, and the sea to the east was black. The land had vanished, and was expressed only by the low and drear thunder of the surf.

"If I am going to be drowned—if I am going to be drowned—if I am going to be drowned, why, in the name of the seven mad gods who rule the sea, was I allowed to come thus far and contemplate sand and trees? Was I brought here merely to have my nose dragged away as I was about to nibble the sacred cheese of life?"

The patient captain, drooped over the water-jar, was sometimes obliged to speak to the oarsman.

"Keep her head up! Keep her head up!"

"Keep her head up, sir." The voices were weary and low.

This was surely a quiet evening. All save the oarsman lay heavily and listlessly in the boat's bottom. As for him, his eyes were just capable of noting the tall black waves that swept forward in a most sinister silence, save for an occasional subdued growl of a crest.

The cook's head was on a thwart, and he looked without interest at the water under his nose. He was deep in other scenes. Finally he spoke. "Billie," he murmured, dreamfully, "what kind of pie do you like best?"

## 5

"Pie!" said the oiler and the correspondent, agitatedly. "Don't talk about those things, blast you!"

"Well," said the cook, "I was just thinking about ham sandwiches and—"

A night on the sea in an open boat is a long night. As darkness settled finally, the shine of the light, lifting from the sea in the south, changed to full gold. On the northern horizon a new light appeared, a small bluish gleam on the edge of the waters. These two lights were the furniture of the world. Otherwise there was nothing but waves.

Two men huddled in the stern, and distances were so magnificent in the dinghy that the rower was enabled to keep his feet partly warm by thrusting them under his companions. Their legs indeed extended far under the rowing-seat until they touched the feet of the captain forward. Sometimes, despite the efforts of the tired oarsman, a wave came piling into the boat, an icy wave of the night, and the chilling water soaked them anew. They would twist their bodies for a moment and groan, and sleep the dead sleep once more, while the water in the boat gurgled about them as the craft rocked.

The plan of the oiler and the correspondent was for one to row until he lost the ability, and then arouse the other from his sea-water couch in the bottom of the boat.

The oiler plied the oars until his head drooped forward and the overpowering sleep blinded him; and he rowed yet afterward. Then he touched a man in the bottom of the boat, and called his name. "Will you spell me for a little while?" he said, meekly.

"Sure, Billie," said the correspondent, awaking and dragging himself to a sitting position. They exchanged places carefully, and the oiler, cuddling down in the sea-water at the cook's side, seemed to go to sleep instantly.

The particular violence of the sea had ceased. The waves came without snarling. The obligation of the man at the oars was to keep the boat headed so that the tilt of the rollers would not capsize her, and to preserve her from filling when the crests rushed past. The black waves were silent and hard to be seen in the darkness. Often one was almost upon the boat before the oarsman was aware.

In a low voice the correspondent addressed the captain. He was not sure that the captain was awake, although this iron man seemed to be always awake. "Captain, shall I keep her making for that light north, sir?"

The same steady voice answered him. "Yes. Keep it about two points off the port bow."

The cook had tied a life-belt around himself in order to get even the warmth which this clumsy cork contrivance could donate, and he seemed almost stove-like when a rower, whose teeth invariably chattered wildly as soon as he ceased his labour, dropped down to sleep.

The correspondent, as he rowed, looked down at the two men sleeping underfoot. The cook's arm was around the oiler's shoulders, and, with their fragmentary clothing and haggard faces, they were the babes of the sea—a grotesque rendering of the old babes in the wood.

Later he must have grown stupid at his work, for suddenly there was a growling of water, and a crest came with a roar and a swash into the boat, and it was a wonder that it did not set the cook afloat in his life-belt. The cook continued to sleep, but the oiler sat up, blinking his eyes and shaking with the new cold.

"Oh, I'm awful sorry, Billie," said the correspondent, contritely.

"That's all right, old boy," said the oiler, and lay down again and was asleep.

Presently it seemed that even the captain dozed, and the correspondent thought that he was the one man afloat on all the oceans. The wind had a voice as it came over the waves, and it was sadder than the end.

There was a long, loud swishing astern of the boat, and a gleaming trail of phosphorescence, like blue flame, was furrowed on the black waters. It might have been made by a monstrous knife.

Then there came a stillness, while the correspondent breathed with open mouth and looked at the sea.

Suddenly there was another swish and another long flash of bluish light, and this time it was alongside the boat, and might almost been reached with an oar. The correspondent saw an enormous fin speed like a shadow through the water, hurling the crystalline spray and leaving the long glowing trail.

The correspondent looked over his shoulder at the captain. His face was hidden, and he seemed to be asleep. He looked at the babes of the sea. They certainly were asleep. So, being bereft of sympathy, he leaned a little way to one side and swore softly into the sea.

But the thing did not then leave the vicinity of the boat. Ahead or astern, on one side or the other, at intervals long or short, fled the long sparkling streak, and there was to be heard the *whirroo* of the dark fin. The speed and power of the thing was greatly to be admired. It cut the water like a gigantic and keen projectile.

The presence of this biding thing did not affect the man with the same horror that it would if he had been a picnicker. He simply looked at the sea dully and swore in an undertone.

Nevertheless, it is true that he did not wish to be alone with the thing. He wished one of his companions to awake by chance and keep him company with it. But the captain hung motionless over the water-jar, and the oiler and the cook in the bottom of the boat were plunged in slumber.

## 6

"If I am going to be drowned—if I am going to be drowned—if I am going to be drowned, why, in the name of the seven mad gods who rule the sea, was I allowed to come thus far and contemplate sand and trees?"

During this dismal night, it may be remarked that a man would conclude that it was really the intention of the seven mad gods to drown him, despite the abominable injustice of it. For it was certainly an abominable injustice to drown a man who had worked so hard, so hard. The man felt it would be a crime most unnatural. Other people had drowned at sea since galleys swarmed with painted sails, but still—

When it occurs to a man that nature does not regard him as important, and that she feels she would not maim the universe by disposing of him, he at first wishes to throw bricks at the temple, and he hates deeply the fact that there are no bricks and no temples. Any visible expression of nature would surely be pelleted with his jeers.

Then, if there be no tangible thing to hoot, he feels, perhaps, the desire to confront a personification and indulge in pleas, bowed to one knee, and with hands supplicant, saying, "Yes, but I love myself."

A high cold star on a winter's night is the word he feels that she says to him. Thereafter he knows the pathos of his situation.

The men in the dinghy had not discussed these matters, but each had, no doubt, reflected upon them in silence and according to his mind. There was seldom any expression upon their faces save the general one of complete weariness. Speech was devoted to the business of the boat.

To chime the notes of his emotion, a verse mysteriously entered the correspondent's head. He had even forgotten that he had forgotten this verse, but it suddenly was in mind.

*A soldier of the Legion lay dying in Algiers;*
*There was lack of woman's nursing, there was dearth of woman's tears;*

*But a comrade stood beside him, and he took that comrade's hand,*
*And he said, "I never more shall see my own, my native land."*

In his childhood the correspondent had been made acquainted with the fact that a soldier of the Legion lay dying in Algiers, but he had never regarded the fact as important. Myriads of his school-fellows had informed him of the soldier's plight, but the dinning had naturally ended by making him perfectly indifferent. He had never considered it his affair that a soldier of the Legion lay dying in Algiers, nor had it appeared to him as a matter for sorrow. It was less to him than the breaking of a pencil's point.

Now, however, it quaintly came to him as a human, living thing. It was no longer merely a picture of a few throes in the breast of a poet, meanwhile drinking tea and warming his feet at the grate; it was an actuality—stern, mournful, and fine.

The correspondent plainly saw the soldier. He lay on the sand with his feet out straight and still. While his pale left hand was upon his chest in an attempt to thwart the going of his life, the blood came between his fingers. In the far Algerian distance, a city of low square forms was set against a sky that was faint with the last sunset hues. The correspondent, plying the oars and dreaming of the slow and slower movements of the lips of the soldier, was moved by a profound and perfectly impersonal comprehension. He was sorry for the soldier of the Legion who lay dying in Algiers.

The thing which had followed the boat and waited had evidently grown bored at the delay. There was no longer to be heard the slash of the cutwater, and there was no longer the flame of the long trail. The light in the north still glimmered, but it was apparently no nearer to the boat. Sometimes the boom of the surf rang in the correspondent's ears, and he turned the craft seaward then and rowed harder. Southward, some one had evidently built a watch-fire on the beach. It was too low and too far to be seen, but it made a shimmering, roseate reflection upon the bluff in back of it, and this could be discerned from the boat. The wind came stronger, and sometimes a wave suddenly raged out like a mountain cat, and there was to be seen the sheen and sparkle of a broken crest.

The captain, in the bow, moved on his water-jar and sat erect. "Pretty long night," he observed to the correspondent. He looked at the shore. "Those life-saving people take their time."

"Did you see that shark playing around?"

"Yes, I saw him. He was a big fellow, all right."

"Wish I had known you were awake."

Later the correspondent spoke into the bottom of the boat. "Billie!" There was a slow and gradual disentanglement. "Billie, will you spell me?"

"Sure," said the oiler.

As soon as the correspondent touched the cold, comfortable sea-water in the bottom of the boat and had huddled close to the cook's life-belt he was deep in sleep, despite the fact that his teeth played all the popular airs. This sleep was so good to him that it was but a moment before he heard a voice call his name in a tone that demonstrated the last stages of exhaustion. "Will you spell me?"

"Sure, Billie."

The light in the north had mysteriously vanished, but the correspondent took his course from the wide-awake captain.

Later in the night they took the boat farther out to sea, and the captain directed the cook to take one oar at the stern and keep the boat facing the seas. He was to call out if he should hear the thunder of the surf. This plan enabled the oiler and the correspondent to get respite together. "We'll give those boys a chance to get into shape again," said the captain. They curled down and, after a few preliminary chatterings and trembles, slept once more the dead sleep. Neither knew they had bequeathed to the cook the company of another shark, or perhaps the same shark.

As the boat caroused on the waves, spray occasionally bumped over the side and gave them a fresh soaking, but this had no power to break their repose. The ominous slash of the wind and the water affected them as it would have affected mummies.

"Boys," said the cook, with the notes of every reluctance in his voice, "she's drifted in pretty close. I guess one of you had better take her to sea again." The correspondent, aroused, heard the crash of the toppled crests.

As he was rowing, the captain gave him some whisky-and-water, and this steadied the chills out of him. "If I ever get ashore and anybody shows me even a photograph of an oar—"

At last there was a short conversation.

"Billie!—Billie, will you spell me?"

"Sure," said the oiler.

## 7

When the correspondent again opened his eyes, the sea and the sky were each of the grey hue of the dawning. Later, carmine and gold was painted upon the waters. The morning appeared finally, in its splendour, with a sky of pure blue, and the sunlight flamed on the tips of the waves.

On the distant dunes were set many little black cottages, and a tall white windmill reared above them. No man, nor dog, nor bicycle appeared on the beach. The cottages might have formed a deserted village.

The voyagers scanned the shore. A conference was held in the boat. "Well," said the captain, "if no help is coming, we might better try a run through the surf right away. If we stay out here much longer we will be too weak to do anything for ourselves at all." The others silently acquiesced in this reasoning. The boat was headed for the beach. The correspondent wondered if none ever ascended the tall wind-tower, and if then they never looked seaward. This tower was a giant, standing with its back to the plight of the ants. It represented in a degree, to the correspondent, the serenity of nature amid the struggles of the individual—nature in the wind, and nature in the vision of men. She did not seem cruel to him then, nor beneficent, nor treacherous, nor wise. But she was indifferent, flatly indifferent. It is, perhaps, plausible that a man in this situation, impressed with the unconcern of the universe, should see the innumerable flaws of his life, and have them taste wickedly in his mind, and wish for another chance. A distinction between right and wrong seems absurdly clear to him, then, in this new ignorance of the grave-edge, and he understands that if he were given another opportunity he would mend his conduct and his words, and be better and brighter during an introduction or at a tea.

"Now, boys," said the captain, "she is going to swamp sure. All we can do is to work her in as far as possible, and then when she swamps, pile out and scramble for the beach. Keep cool now, and don't jump until she swamps sure."

The oiler took the oars. Over his shoulders he scanned the surf. "Captain," he said, "I think I'd better bring her about and keep her head-on to the seas and back her in."

"All right, Billie," said the captain. "Back her in." The oiler swung the boat then, and, seated in the stern, the cook and the correspondent were obliged to look over their shoulders to contemplate the lonely and indifferent shore.

The monstrous inshore rollers heaved the boat high until the men were again enabled to see the white sheets of water scudding up the slanted beach. "We won't get in very close," said the captain. Each time a man could wrest his attention from the rollers, he turned his glance toward the shore, and in the expression of the eyes during this contemplation there was a singular quality. The correspondent, observing the others, knew that they were not afraid, but the full meaning of their glances was shrouded.

As for himself, he was too tired to grapple fundamentally with the fact. He tried to coerce his mind into thinking of it, but the mind was dominated at this time by the muscles, and the muscles said they did not care. It merely occurred to him that if he should drown it would be a shame.

There were no hurried words, no pallor, no plain agitation. The men simply looked at the shore. "Now, remember to get well clear of the boat when you jump," said the captain.

Seaward the crest of a roller suddenly fell with a thunderous crash, and the long white comber came roaring down upon the boat.

"Steady now," said the captain. The men were silent. They turned their eyes from the shore to the comber and waited. The boat slid up the incline, leaped at the furious top, bounced over it, and swung down the long back of the wave. Some water had been shipped, and the cook bailed it out.

But the next crest crashed also. The tumbling, boiling flood of white water caught the boat and whirled it almost perpendicular. Water swarmed in from all sides. The correspondent had his hands on the gunwale at this time, and when the water entered at that place he swiftly withdrew his fingers, as if he objected to wetting them.

The little boat, drunken with this weight of water, reeled and snuggled deeper into the sea.

"Bail her out, cook! Bail her out!" said the captain.

"All right, Captain," said the cook.

"Now, boys, the next one will do for us sure," said the oiler. "Mind to jump clear of the boat."

The third wave moved forward, huge, furious, implacable. It fairly swallowed the dinghy, and almost simultaneously the men tumbled into the sea. A piece of life-belt had lain in the bottom of the boat, and as the correspondent went overboard he held this to his chest with his left hand.

The January water was icy, and he reflected immediately that it was colder than he had expected to find it off the coast of Florida. This appeared to his dazed mind as a fact important enough to be noted at the time. The coldness of the water was sad; it was tragic. This fact was somehow mixed and confused with his opinion of his own situation, so that it seemed almost a proper reason for tears. The water was cold.

When he came to the surface he was conscious of little but the noisy water. Afterward he saw his companions in the sea. The oiler was ahead in the race. He was swimming strongly and rapidly. Off to the correspondent's left, the cook's great white and corked back bulged out of the water; and in the rear the captain was hanging with his one good hand to the keel of the overturned dinghy.

There is a certain immovable quality to a shore, and the correspondent wondered at it amid the confusion of the sea.

It seemed also very attractive; but the correspondent knew that it was a long journey, and he paddled leisurely. The piece of life-preserver lay under him, and sometimes he whirled down the incline of a wave as if he were on a hand-sled.

But finally he arrived at a place in the sea where travel was beset with difficulty. He did not pause swimming to inquire what manner of current had caught him, but there his progress ceased. The shore was set before him like a bit of scenery on a stage, and he looked at it and understood with his eyes each detail of it.

As the cook passed, much farther to the left, the captain was calling to him, "Turn over on your back, cook! Turn over on your back and use the oar."

"All right, sir." The cook turned on his back, and, paddling with an oar, went ahead as if he were a canoe.

Presently the boat also passed to the left of the correspondent, with the captain clinging with one hand to the keel. He would have appeared like a man raising himself to look over a board fence if it were not for the extraordinary gymnastics of the boat. The correspondent marvelled that the captain could still hold to it.

They passed on nearer to shore—the oiler, the cook, the captain—and following them went the water-jar, bouncing gaily over the seas.

The correspondent remained in the grip of this strange new enemy—a current. The shore, with its white slope of sand and its green bluff topped with little silent cottages, was spread like a picture before him. It was very near to him then, but he was impressed as one who, in a gallery, looks at a scene from Brittany or Holland.

He thought: "I am going to drown? Can it be possible? Can it be possible? Can it be possible?" Perhaps an individual must consider his own death to be the final phenomenon of nature.

But later a wave perhaps whirled him out of this small deadly current, for he found suddenly that he could again make progress toward the shore. Later still he was aware that the captain, clinging with one hand to the keel of the dinghy, had his face turned away from the shore and toward him, and was calling his name. "Come to the boat! Come to the boat!"

In his struggle to reach the captain and the boat, he reflected that when one gets properly wearied drowning must really be a comfortable arrangement—a cessation of hostilities accompanied by a large degree of relief; and he was glad of it, for the main thing in his mind for some moments had been horror of the temporary agony. He did not wish to be hurt.

Presently he saw a man running along the shore. He was undressing with most remarkable speed. Coat, trousers, shirt, everything flew magically off him.

"Come to the boat!" called the captain.

"All right, Captain." As the correspondent paddled, he saw the captain let himself down to bottom and leave the boat. Then the correspondent performed his one little marvel of the voyage. A large wave caught him and flung him with ease and supreme speed completely over the boat and far beyond it. It struck him even then as an event in gymnastics and a true miracle of the sea. An overturned boat in the surf is not a plaything to a swimming man.

The correspondent arrived in water that reached only to his waist, but his condition did not enable him to stand for more than a moment. Each wave knocked him into a heap, and the undertow pulled at him.

Then he saw the man who had been running and undressing, and undressing and running, come bounding into the water. He dragged ashore the cook, and then waded toward the captain; but the captain waved him away and sent him to the correspondent. He was naked—naked as a tree in winter; but a halo was about his head, and he shone like a saint. He gave a strong pull, and a long drag, and a bully heave at the correspondent's hand. The correspondent, schooled in the minor formulae, said, "Thanks, old man." But suddenly the man cried, "What's that?" He pointed a swift finger. The correspondent said, "Go."

In the shallows, face downward, lay the oiler. His forehead touched sand that was periodically, between each wave, clear of the sea.

The correspondent did not know all that transpired afterward. When he achieved safe ground he fell, striking the sand with each particular part of his body. It was as if he had dropped from a roof, but the thud was grateful to him.

It seemed that instantly the beach was populated with men with blankets, clothes, and flasks, and women with coffee-pots and all the remedies sacred to their minds. The welcome of the land to the men from the sea was warm and generous; but a still and dripping shape was carried slowly up the beach, and the land's welcome for it could only be the different and sinister hospitality of the grave.

When it came night, the white waves paced to and fro in the moonlight, and the wind brought the sound of the great sea's voice to the men on the shore, and they felt that they could then be interpreters.

## *Study questions*

1. *The initial sentence of this story is one of the most famous in all literature. Speculate as to why.* 2. *There is an up-and-down, backward-and-forward, and in-and-out movement in the story. How does it function and how is it accomplished?* 3. *The open boat is a microcosm. What are the conditions and dimen-*

*sions of the world it describes?* 4. *Who is the protagonist of this story? Are the characters symbolic?* 5. *What kinds of repetitive motifs are found in the story? Is there a rhythmic arrangement of these motifs? How do they function? Consider them one at a time.* 6. *What is the relevance of the "soldier of the Legion who lay dying in Algiers"?* 7. *How do the men get along with one another? What is their relationship to the sharks? the gulls?* 8. *What is the function of the man on the shore? Explain his behavior.* 9. *Why does the oiler have to die?* 10. *If there is no beneficent God and if nature is indifferent to the needs of man, how is moral behavior possible? What constitutes moral behavior?* 11. *What is the conflict in the story? How is it resolved?*

SECTION TWO

# *Modern*

*Anton Chekhov* (1860–1904), born in Taganrog in southern Russia, the grandson of a serf and the son of an unsuccessful grocer, began to write in order to pay expenses for himself and his family. He received a degree from the medical school at the University of Moscow in 1884, the same year he published his first collection of short stories. Although he began to practice medicine, he did not continue for too long, but, because of pressing money problems, turned back to writing. Considered Russia's greatest writer of short fiction, he published successive volumes of short stories until 1900. But he was also a very fine dramatist, producing *The Sea Gull* (1896), *Uncle Vanya* (1899), *The Three Sisters* (1901), and his masterpiece, *The Cherry Orchard* (1904). He died of tuberculosis at the age of forty-four. Considered by some to be the father of the modern short story, Chekhov, like Katherine Mansfield and James Joyce who followed him, turned the short story away from a heavy reliance on plot line and concentrated on ordinary people in everyday experiences. "A Trifle from Real Life" is one of the first stories to use a child as protagonist in a situation common to most children. The trifle, of course, means much to the child but nothing to the adult who betrays him. "La Cigale" uses the cicada as the major metaphor in a story about how ordinary people feed upon each other. Olga consumes her husband until there is nothing left of him except a shell. In "Dreams" three men respond to a fantasy of human freedom and happiness but realize that the dream is impossible to attain.

## A TRIFLE FROM REAL LIFE

Nikolai Ilitch Belayeff was a young gentleman of St. Petersburg, aged thirty-two, rosy, well fed, and a patron of the race-tracks. Once, toward evening, he went to pay a call on Olga Ivanovna with whom, to use his own expression, he was dragging through a long and tedious love-affair. And the truth was that the first thrilling, inspiring pages of this romance had long since been read, and that the story was now dragging wearily on, presenting nothing that was either interesting or novel.

Not finding Olga at home, my hero threw himself upon a couch and prepared to await her return.

"Good evening, Nikolai Ilitch!" he heard a child's voice say. "Mamma will soon be home. She has gone to the dressmaker's with Sonia."

On the divan in the same room lay Aliosha, Olga's son, a small boy of eight, immaculately and picturesquely dressed in a little velvet suit and long black stockings. He had been lying on a satin pillow, mimicking the antics of an acrobat he had seen at the circus. First he stretched up one pretty leg, then another; then, when they were tired, he brought his arms into play, and at last jumped up galvanically, throwing himself on all fours in an effort to stand on his head. He went through all these motions with the most serious face in the world, puffing like a martyr, as if he himself regretted that God had given him such a restless little body.

"Ah, good evening, my boy!" said Belayeff. "Is that you? I did not know you were here. Is mamma well?"

Aliosha seized the toe of his left shoe in his right hand, assumed the most unnatural position in the world, rolled over, jumped up, and peeped out at Belayeff from under the heavy fringes of the lampshade.

"Not very," he said shrugging his shoulders. "Mamma is never really well. She is a woman, you see, and women always have something the matter with them."

From lack of anything better to do, Belayeff began scrutinizing Aliosha's face. During all his acquaintance with Olga he had never bestowed any consideration upon the boy or noticed his existence at all. He had seen the child about, but what he was doing there Belayeff, somehow, had never cared to think.

Now, in the dusk of evening, Aliosha's pale face and fixed, dark eyes unexpectedly reminded Belayeff of Olga as she had appeared in the first pages of their romance. He wanted to pet the boy.

"Come here, little monkey," he said, "and let me look at you!"

The boy jumped down from the sofa and ran to Belayeff.

"Well," the latter began, laying his hand on the boy's thin shoulder. "And how are you? Is everything all right with you?"

"No, not very. It used to be much better."

"In what way?"

"That's easy to answer. Sonia and I used to learn only music and reading before, but now we have French verses, too. You have cut your beard!"

"Yes."

"So I noticed. It is shorter than it was. Please let me touch it—does that hurt?"

"No, not a bit."

"Why does it hurt if you pull one hair at a time, and not a bit if you pull lots? Ha! Ha! I'll tell you something. You ought to wear whiskers! You could shave here on the sides, here, and here you could let the hair grow——"

The boy nestled close to Belayeff and began to play with his watch-chain.

"Mamma is going to give me a watch when I go to school, and I am going to ask her to give me a chain just like yours—— Oh, what a lovely locket! Papa has a locket just like that; only yours has little stripes on it, and papa's has letters. He has a portrait of mamma in his locket. Papa wears another watch-chain now made of ribbon."

"How do you know? Do you ever see your papa?"

"I—n-no—I——"

Aliosha blushed deeply at being caught telling a fib and began to scratch the locket furiously with his nail. Belayeff looked searchingly into his face and repeated:

"Do you ever see your papa?"

"N-no!"

"Come, tell me honestly! I can see by your face that you are not telling the truth. It's no use quibbling now that the cat is out of the bag. Tell me, do you see him? Now then, as between friends!"

Aliosha reflected.

"You won't tell mamma?" he asked.

"What an idea!"

"Honour bright?"

"Honour bright!"

"Promise!"

"Oh, you insufferable child! What do you take me for?"

Aliosha glanced around, opened his eyes wide, and said:

"For heaven's sake don't tell mamma! Don't tell a soul, because it's a secret. I don't know what would happen to Sonia and Pelagia and me if mamma should find out. Now, listen. Sonia and I see papa every Thursday and every Friday. When Pelagia takes us out walking before dinner we go to Anfel's confectionery and there we find papa already waiting for us. He is always sitting in the little private room with the marble table and the ash-tray that's made like a goose without a back."

"What do you do in there?"

"We don't do anything. First we say how do you do, and then papa orders coffee and pasties for us. Sonia likes pasties with meat, you know, but I can't abide them with meat. I like mine with cabbage or eggs. We eat so much that we have a hard time eating our dinner afterward so that mamma won't guess anything."

"What do you talk about?"

"With papa? Oh, about everything. He kisses us and hugs us and tells us the funniest jokes. Do you know what? He says that when we grow bigger he is going to take us to live with him. Sonia doesn't want to go, but I wouldn't mind. Of course it would be lonely without mamma, but I could write letters to her. Isn't it funny, we might go and see her then on Sundays, mightn't we? Papa says, too, he is going to buy me a pony. He is such a nice man! I don't know why mamma doesn't ask him to live with her and why she won't let us see him. He loves mamma very much. He always asks how she is and what she has been doing. When she was ill he took hold of his head just like this—and ran about the room. He always asks us whether we are obedient and respectful to her. Tell me, is it true that we are unfortunate?"

"H'm—why do you ask?"

"Because papa says we are. He says we are unfortunate children, and that he is unfortunate, and that mamma is unfortunate. He tells us to pray to God for her and for ourselves."

Aliosha fixed his eyes on the figure of a stuffed bird, and became lost in thought.

"Well, I declare——" muttered Belayeff. "So, that's what you do, you hold meetings at a confectioner's? And your mamma doesn't know it?"

"N-no. How could she? Pelagia wouldn't tell her for the world. Day before yesterday papa gave us pears. They were as sweet as sugar. I ate two!"

"H'm. But—listen to me, does papa ever say anything about me?"

"About you? What shall I say?" Aliosha looked searchingly into Belayeff's face and shrugged his shoulders. "Nothing special," he answered.

"Well, what does he say, for instance?"

"You won't be angry if I tell you?"

"What an idea! Does he abuse me?"

"No, he doesn't abuse you, but, you know, he is angry with you. He says that it is your fault that mamma is unhappy, and that you have ruined mamma. He is such a funny man! I tell him that you are kind and that you never scold mamma, but he only shakes his head."

"So he says I have ruined her?"

"Yes—don't be angry, Nikolai Ilitch!"

Belayeff rose and began pacing up and down the room.

"How strange this is—and how ridiculous!" he muttered shrugging his shoulders and smiling sarcastically. "It is all *his* fault and yet he says *I* have ruined her! What an innocent baby this is! And so he told you I had ruined your mother?"

"Yes, but—you promised not to be angry!"

"I'm not angry and—and it is none of your business anyway. Yes, this is—this is really ridiculous! Here I have been caught like a mouse in a trap, and now it seems it is all my fault!"

The door-bell rang. The boy tore himself from Belayeff's arms and ran out of the room. A moment later a lady entered with a little girl. It was Aliosha's mother, Olga Ivanovna. Aliosha skipped into the room behind her, singing loudly and clapping his hands. Belayeff nodded and continued to walk up and down.

"Of course!" he muttered. "Whom should he blame but me? He has right on his side! He is the injured husband."

"What is that you are saying?" asked Olga Ivanovna.

"What am I saying? Just listen to what your young hopeful here has been preaching. It appears that I am a wicked scoundrel and that I have ruined you and your children. You are all unhappy, and I alone am frightfully happy. Frightfully, frightfully happy!"

"I don't understand you, Nikolai. What is the matter?"

"Just listen to what this young gentleman here has to say!" cried Belayeff pointing to Aliosha.

Aliosha flushed and then grew suddenly pale and his face became distorted with fear.

"Nikolai Ilitch!" he whispered loudly. "Hush!"

Olga Ivanovna looked at Aliosha in surprise, and then at Belayeff, and then back again at Aliosha.

"Ask him!" Belayeff continued. "That idiot of yours, Pelagia, takes them to a confectioner's and arranges meetings there between them and their papa. But that isn't the point. The point is that papa is the victim, and that I am an abandoned scoundrel who has wrecked the lives of both of you!"

"Nikolai Ilitch!" groaned Aliosha. "You gave me your word of honour!"

"Leave me alone!" Belayeff motioned to him impatiently. "This is more important than words of honour. This hypocrisy, these lies are intolerable!"

"I don't understand!" cried Olga Ivanovna, the tears glistening in her eyes. "Listen, Aliosha," she asked, turning to her son. "Do you really see your father?"

But Aliosha did not hear her, his eyes were fixed with horror on Belayeff.

"It cannot be possible!" his mother exclaimed, "I must go and ask Pelagia."

Olga Ivanovna left the room.

"But Nikolai Ilitch, you gave me your word of honour!" cried Aliosha trembling all over.

Belayeff made an impatient gesture and went on pacing the floor. He was absorbed in thoughts of the wrong that had been done him, and, as before, was unconscious of the boy's presence: a serious, grown-up person like him could not be bothered with little boys. But Aliosha crept into a corner and told Sonia with horror how he had been deceived. He trembled and hiccoughed and cried. This was the first time in his life that he had come roughly face to face with deceit; he had never imagined till now that there were things in this world besides pasties and watches and sweet pears, things for which no name could be found in the vocabulary of childhood.

### *Study questions*

1. *What details does Chekhov use to characterize Belayeff? Why does he begin to pay attention to Aliosha?* 2. *What details does Chekhov use to characterize Aliosha? Why does he respond to Nikolai?* 3. *Why does Aliosha confide in Nikolai?* 4. *What is the climax of this story? What will happen to Aliosha?* 5. *How does Aliosha's mother function in the story? his father?*

## LA CIGALE

### *1*

To Olga Ivanovna's wedding came all her friends and acquaintances.

"Look at him! Isn't it true there is something in him?" she said to them, nodding towards her husband, as if to justify her marriage to this simple, commonplace, in no way remarkable man.

The bridegroom, Osip Stepanuitch Duimoff, was a doctor, with the rank of Titular Councillor. He worked at two hospitals; in one as supernumerary ordinator; as dissector in the other. At one, from nine in the morning till midday, he received out-patients and worked in the wards; and, finished with this, he took a tram to the second hospital, and dissected bodies. His private practice was small, worth some five hundred roubles a year. That was all. What more could be said of him? On the other hand, Olga Ivanovna, her friends and acquaintances, were by no means ordinary. All were noted for something, and fairly well known; they had names; they were celebrated, or if not celebrated yet, they inspired great hope for the future. A talented actor, clever, modest, a fine gentleman, a master of declamation, who taught Olga Ivanovna to recite; a good-humoured opera-singer who told Olga Ivanovna with a sigh that she was throwing herself away—if she gave up idling and took herself in hand, she would make a famous singer; a few artists, chief of them the genre-ist, animal-, and landscape-painter Riabovsky, handsome, fair-haired, twenty-five, successful at exhibitions, who sold his last picture for five hundred roubles—he touched up Olga Ivanovna's *études,* and predicted a future for her; a violoncellist, whose instrument wept, who frankly said that of all the women he knew Olga Ivanovna alone could accompany; a man of letters, young, but already known for his short stories, sketches, and plays. Who else? Yes, Vassili Vassiluitch, country gentleman, dilettante illustrator and vignettist, with his love of the national epos and his passion for old Russian art—on paper, china, and smoked plates he turned out veritable masterpieces. In such society—artistic, free, and spoiled by fate; and (though delicate and modest) oblivious of doctors save when ill; to whom "Duimoff" sounded as impersonal as "Tarasoff" or "Sidoroff"—in such society, the bridegroom seemed out-of-place, needless, and even insignificant, although he was really a very tall and very broad-shouldered man. His evening dress seemed made for some one else. His beard was like a shopman's. Though it is true that had he been a writer or artist, this beard would have reminded them of Zola.

The artist told Olga Ivanovna that with her flaxen hair and wedding dress she was a graceful cherry-tree covered with tender, white blossoms in spring.

"No, but listen!" replied Olga Ivanovna, seizing his hand. "How suddenly all this happened! Listen, listen! . . . I should tell you that Duimoff and my father were at the same hospital. While my poor father was ill, Duimoff watched day and night at his bedside. Such self-sacrifice! Listen, Riabovsky! . . . And you, writer, listen—this is very interesting! Come nearer! Such sacrifice of self, such sincere concern! I myself could not sleep at night, and sat at my father's bedside, and suddenly! . . . I captivated the poor young man! My Duimoff was up to his neck in love! In truth, things happen strangely. Well, after my father's death we sometimes met in the street; he paid me occasional visits, and one fine evening suddenly—he proposed to me! . . . I cried all night, and myself fell in love with him. And now, you see, I am married. Don't you think there is something in him? Something strong, mighty, leonine! Just now his face is turned three-quarters from us and the light is bad, but when he turns round just look at his forehead! Riabovsky, what do you think of his forehead? Duimoff, we are speaking of you." She turned to her husband. "Come here! Give your honest hand to Riabovsky. . . . That's right. Be friends!"

With a simple, kindly smile, Duimoff gave his hand to the artist, and said—

"I'm delighted! There was a Riabovsky at college with me. Was he a relation of yours?"

## 2

Olga Ivanovna was twenty-two years old, Duimoff thirty-one. After the marriage they lived well. Olga Ivanovna hung the drawing-room with drawings, her own and her friends', framed and unframed; and about the piano and furniture, arranged in pretty confusion Chinese parasols, easels, many-coloured draperies, poniards, busts, photographs. The dining-room she decked with the bright-coloured oleographs beloved by peasants, bast-shoes and sickles, and these, with the scythe and hay-rake in the corner, made a room in national style. To make her bedroom like a cave, she draped the ceiling and walls with dark cloth, hung a Venetian lantern over the bed, and set near the door a figure with a halberd. And every one agreed that the young couple had a charming flat.

Rising every day at eleven, Olga Ivanovna sat at the piano, or, if the sun shone, painted in oils. At one o'clock she drove to her dressmaker's. As neither she nor Duimoff was rich, many ingenious shifts were resorted to to keep her in the new-looking dresses which made such an impression on all. Pieces of old dyed cloth; worthless patches of tulle, lace, plush, and silk, came back from the dressmaker miracles, not dresses but ravishing dreams. Done with the dressmaker, Olga Ivanovna drove to some actress friend to learn theatrical news and get tickets for first-nights or benefits; thence to an artist's studio or picture gallery, ending up with some other celebrity whom she invited to visit her, or simply gossiped to. And those whom she counted celebrities and great men received her as an equal, and told her in one voice that if she did not throw away her opportunities, her talents, taste, and intellect would yield something really great. She sang, played, painted, modelled, acted in amateur theatricals; and did everything well: if she merely made lanterns for illuminations, or dressed herself up, or tied some one's necktie, the result was invariably graceful, artistic, charming. But none of her talents outshone her skill in meeting and getting on terms of intimacy with men of note. Let a man get the least reputation, or even be talked about, and in a single day she had met him, established friendly relations, and invited him to her home. And each new acquaintance was a festival in himself. She worshipped the well-known, was proud of them, and dreamed of them all night. Her thirst was insatiable. The old celebrities departed and were forgotten, and new celebrities replaced them; and to these last she grew accustomed in time; they lost their charm, so that she sought for more.

She dined at home with her husband at five o'clock. She was in ecstasies over his simplicity, common sense, and good humour. She jumped up from her chair, embraced his head, and covered it with kisses.

"You are a clever, a noble man, Duimoff!" she exclaimed. "You have only one drawback. You take no interest in art. You deny music and painting."

"I don't understand them," he answered kindly. "All my life I have studied only science and medicine. I have no time for art."

"But that is awful, Duimoff!"

"Why awful? Your friends know nothing of science or medicine, yet you don't blame them for that. To each man his own! I don't understand landscapes or operas, but I look at the matter thus: if talented men devote their lives to such things, and clever men pay vast sums for them, that means they are useful. I don't understand them, but not to understand does not mean to deny."

"Give me your hand! Let me press your honest hand!"

After dinner Olga Ivanovna drove away to her friends; after that followed theatres or concerts. She returned after midnight. And so every day.

On Wednesdays she gave evening parties. There were no cards and no dancing. Hostess and guests devoted themselves to art. The actor recited, the singer sang, artists sketched in Olga Ivanovna's numberless albums; the hostess painted, modelled, accompanied, and sang. In the pauses between these recreations, they talked of books, the theatre, and art. No women were present, because Olga Ivanovna considered all women, except actresses and dressmakers, tiresome and contemptible. When the hall bell rang the hostess started, and exclaimed triumphantly, "It's he!" meaning thereby some newly met celebrity. Duimoff kept out of sight, and few remembered his existence. But at half-past eleven the dining-room door flew open, and Duimoff appeared with a kindly smile, rubbed his hands, and said—

"Come, gentlemen, to supper!"

Whereupon all thronged to the dining-room, and each time found awaiting them the same things: a dish of oysters, a joint of ham or veal, sardines, cheese, caviare, mushrooms, vodka, and two decanters of wine.

"My dear *maître d'hôtel!*" cried Olga Ivanovna, waving her hands ecstatically. "You are simply adorable! Gentlemen, look at his forehead! Duimoff, show us your profile. Look at him, gentlemen: it is the face of a Bengal tiger with an expression as kind and good as a deer's. My sweetheart!"

And the guests ate steadily and looked at Duimoff. But soon they forgot his presence, and returned to theatre, music, and art.

The young couple were happy. Their life, it seemed, flowed as smoothly as oil. But the third week of the honeymoon was crossed by a cloud. Duimoff got erysipelas at the hospital, and his fine black hair was cut off. Olga Ivanovna sat with him and cried bitterly, but when he got better she bound a white handkerchief around his head and sketched him as a Bedouin. And both were happy. Three days after he had returned to hospital a second misfortune occurred.

"I am in bad luck, mama!" he said at dinner. "To-day I had four dissections, and I cut two fingers. I noticed it only just now."

Olga Ivanovna was frightened. But Duimoff smiled, dismissed the accident as a trifle, and said that he cut himself often.

"I am carried away by my work, mama, and forget what I'm about."

Olga Ivanovna dreaded blood-poisoning, and at night prayed to God. But no consequences followed, and life, serene and happy, flowed without trouble or alarm. The present was all delight, and behind it came spring—spring already near, beaming and beckoning, with a thousand joys. Pleasures it promised without end. In April, May, and June a villa far from town, with walks, fishing, studies, nightingales. From June till autumn the artists' tour on the Volga, and in this tour, as member of the Artists' Association, Olga Ivanovna would take part. She had already ordered two expensive dresses of gingham, and laid in a stock of colours, brushes, canvas, and a new palette. Almost every day came

Riabovsky to watch her progress in painting. When she showed him her work he thrust his hands deep in his pockets, compressed tightly his lips, grunted, and said—

"So! . . . This cloud of yours glares; the light is not right for evening. The foreground is somehow chewed up, and there is something, you understand. . . . And the cabin is somehow crushed . . . you should make that corner a little darker. But on the whole it's not bad. . . . I can praise it."

And the less intelligibly he spoke the better Olga Ivanovna understood.

## 3

After dinner, on the second day of Trinity week, Duimoff bought some *hors d'oeuvres* and sweets and took the train for his villa in the country. Two whole weeks he had not seen his wife, and he longed to be with her again. During the journey and afterwards, as he searched for the villa in a big wood, he felt hungry and fatigued, and rejoiced at the thought of supping in freedom with his wife and having a sound sleep. So, looking at his parcel of caviare, cheese, and white-fish, he felt happy.

Before he found the villa the sun had begun to set. The old servant said that her mistress was not at home, but that she would soon return. The villa, a very ugly villa, with low ceilings, papered with writing-paper, and uneven, chinky floors, contained only three rooms. In one was a bed, in another canvas, brushes, dirty paper, and men's clothes and hats scattered on chairs and window-sills; and in the third Duimoff found three strangers, two dark and bearded, the third —evidently an actor—clean-shaven and stout.

"What do you want?" asked the actor in a bass voice, looking at Duimoff shyly. "You want Olga Ivanovna? Wait; she'll be back shortly."

Duimoff sat down and waited. One of the dark men, looking at him drowsily and lazily, poured tea into his glass and asked—

"Would you like some tea?"

Duimoff wanted both to eat and drink, but, fearing to spoil his appetite, he refused the tea. Soon afterwards came footsteps and a familiar laugh; the door flew open, and in came Olga Ivanovna wearing a big hat. On her arm hung a basket, and behind her, with a big parasol and a deck-chair, came merry, rosy-cheeked Riabovsky.

"Duimoff!" cried Olga Ivanovna, radiant with joy. "Duimoff!" she repeated, laying her head and both hands on his shoulder. "It is you? Why did you not come sooner? Why? Why?"

"I couldn't, mama! I am always busy, and when I end my work there's generally no train."

"How glad I am you've come! I dreamed of you all, all last night. *Akh,* if you knew how I love you—and how opportunely you've come! You are my saviour! To-morrow we have a most original wedding." She laughed and re-tied her husband's tie. "A young telegraphist at the station, a certain Tchikeldeyeff, is going to be married. A handsome boy, not at all stupid; in his face, you know, there's something strong, bearish. . . . He'd sit admirably as model for a

Varangian. We are all interested in him, and promised to come to the wedding. . . . He is a poor man, solitary and shy, and it would be a sin to refuse. Imagine! . . . after church there'll be the wedding, then all go to the bride's house . . . you understand . . . the woods, the birds' songs, sun-spots on the grass, and we ourselves—variegated spots on a bright green background. . . . Most original, quite in the style of the French impressionists! But what am I to wear, Duimoff? I have nothing here, literally nothing. . . . No dress, no flowers, no gloves! . . . You must save me. Your arrival means that fate is on my side. Here are the keys, sweetheart! take the train home and bring my rose-coloured dress from the wardrobe. You know it; it's the first you'll see. Then in the chest of drawers —the bottom right-hand drawer—you'll find two boxes. At the top there's only tulle and other rags, but underneath you'll find flowers. Bring all the flowers—carefully! I don't know . . . then I'll choose. . . . And buy me some gloves."

"All right," said Duimoff. "I'll get them to-morrow!"

"How to-morrow?" asked Olga Ivanovna, looking at him with surprise. "You can't do it to-morrow. The first train leaves at nine, and the wedding is at eleven. No, dear; go to-night! If you can't get back yourself to-morrow send a messenger. The train is nearly due. Don't miss it, my soul!"

"All right!"

"*Akh,* how sorry I am to have to send you!" she said, and tears came into her eyes. "Why did I promise the telegraph clerk, like a fool!"

Duimoff hastily gulped down a glass of tea, and, still smiling kindly, returned to the station. And the caviare, the cheese, and the white-fish were eaten by the actor and the two dark men.

## 4

It was a still moonlight night of July. Olga Ivanovna stood on the deck of a Volga steamer and looked now at the river, now at its beautiful banks. Beside her stood Riabovsky, and affirmed that the black shadows on the water were not shadows but a dream; that this magic stream with its fantastic shimmer, this unfathomable sky, these mournful banks—which expressed but the vanity of life, and the existence of something higher, something eternal, something blessed—called to us to forget ourselves, to die, to fade into memories. The past was trivial and tedious, the future insignificant; and this magic night, this one night of life, would soon be past, would have hurried into eternity. Why, then, live?

And Olga Ivanovna listened, first to Riabovsky's voice, then to the midnight silence, and thought that she was immortal, and would never die. The river's turquoise hue, a hue she had never seen before, the sky, the banks, the black shadows, and the irresponsible joy which filled her heart, all whispered to her that she would become a great artist, that somewhere far away, beyond these distances, beyond the moonlight night, somewhere in infinite space there awaited success and glory, and the love of the world. When she looked earnestly into the distance, she saw crowds, lights; she heard solemn music and cries of rapture; she saw herself in a white dress surrounded by flowers cast at her from all sides. And she believed that here beside her, leaning on the bulwark, stood a really great man, a genius, the elected of God. He had already accomplished things beautiful, new, uncommon; what he would do when time had ripened his great talents would be greater immeasurably—that was written legibly in his face, his expressions, his relations to the world around. Of the shadows, the hues of nights, the moonlight, he spoke in language all his own, and unconsciously betrayed the power of his magic mastery over Nature. He was handsome and original; and his life, unhampered, free, alien to the trifles of the world, seemed the life of a bird.

"It is getting cold!" said Olga Ivanovna, shuddering.

Riabovsky wrapped her in his cloak and said mournfully—

"I feel myself in your power. I am a slave. Why are you so ravishing to-night?"

He looked at her steadily, and his eyes were so terrible that she feared to look at him.

"I love you madly . . ." he whispered, breathing against her cheek. "Say to me but one word, and I will not live . . . I will abandon my art. . . ." He stammered in his extreme agitation. "Love me, love. . . ."

"Don't speak in that way!" said Olga Ivanovna, closing her eyes. "It is terrible. And Duimoff?"

"What is Duimoff? Why Duimoff? What have I to do with Duimoff? The Volga, the moon, beauty, my love, my raptures . . . and no Duimoff at all! . . . *Akh,* I know nothing. . . . I do not want the past; give me but one moment . . . one second!"

Olga Ivanovna's heart beat quickly. She tried to think of her husband; but her whole past, her marriage, Duimoff, even the evening parties seemed to her trivial, contemptible, dull, needless, and remote. . . . And, indeed, who was Duimoff? Why Duimoff? What had she to do with Duimoff? Did he exist really in Nature; was he only a dream?

"He has had more happiness than he could expect, a simple and ordinary man," she thought, closing her eyes. "Let them condemn me, let them curse me; but I will take all and perish, take all and perish. . . . We must experience everything in life. . . . Lord, how painful and how good!"

"Well, what? What?" stammered the artist, embracing her. He kissed her hands greedily, while she strove to withdraw them. "You love me? Yes? Yes? O, what a night! O night divine!"

"Yes, what a night!" she whispered, looking into his eyes which glittered with tears. Then she looked around her, clasped her arms about him, and kissed him firmly on the lips.

"We are near Kineshma," said a voice somewhere across the deck.

Heavy footfalls echoed behind them. A waiter passed from the buffet.

"Waiter!" cried Olga Ivanovna, laughing and crying in her joy. "Bring us some wine."

Pale with excitement, the artist sat on a bench, and stared at Olga Ivanovna with grateful, adoring eyes. But in a moment he shut these eyes, and said with a weary smile—

"I am tired."

And he leaned his head against the bulwark.

## 5

The second of September was warm and windless but dull. Since early morning a light mist had wandered across the Volga, and at nine o'clock it began to rain. There was no hope of a clear sky. At breakfast Riabovsky told Olga Ivanovna that painting was the most thankless and tedious of arts, that he was no artist, and that only fools thought him talented. Then, for no cause whatever, he seized a knife and cut to pieces his best study. After breakfast, in bad humour, he sat at a window and looked at the river, and found it without life—dull, dead, and cold. All around spoke of frowning autumn's approach. It seemed already that the green carpet on the banks, the diamond flashes from the water, the clear blue distances—all the vanity and parade of Nature had been taken from the Volga and packed in a box until the coming spring; and that the ravens flying over the river mocked it and cried, "Naked! Naked!" Riabovsky listened to their cry, and brooded on the exhaustion and loss of his talent: and he thought that all the world was conditional, relative, and stupid, and that he should not have tied himself up with this woman. In one word he was out of spirits, and sulked.

On her bed behind the partition, pulling at her pretty hair, sat Olga Ivanovna; and pictured herself at home, first in the drawing-room, then in her bedroom, then in her husband's study; imagination bore her to theatres, to her dressmaker, to her friends. What was Duimoff doing now? Did he think of her? The season had already begun; it was time to think of the evening parties. And Duimoff? Dear Duimoff! How kindly, with what infantile complaints, he begged her in his letters to come home! Every month he sent her seventy-five roubles, and when she wrote that she had borrowed a hundred from the artists he sent her also that hundred. The good, the generous man! Olga Ivanovna was tired of the tour; she suffered from tedium, and wished to escape as soon as possible from the muzhiks, from the river damp, from the feeling of physical uncleanliness caused by living in huts and wandering from village to village. Had Riabovsky not promised his brother artists to stay till the twentieth of September, they might have left at once. And how good it would be to leave!

"My God!" groaned Riabovsky. "Will the sun ever come out? I cannot paint a landscape without the sun!"

"But your study of a cloudy sky?" said Olga Ivanovna, coming from behind the partition. "You remember, the one with the trees in the foreground to the right, and the cows and geese at the left. You could finish that."

"What?" The artist frowned. "Finish it? Do you really think I'm so stupid that I don't know what to do?"

"What I do think is that you've changed to me!" sighed Olga Ivanovna.

"Yes; and that's all right."

Olga Ivanovna's face quivered; she went to the stove and began to cry.

"We only wanted tears to complete the picture! Do stop! I have a thousand reasons for crying, but I don't cry."

"A thousand reasons!" burst out Olga Ivanovna. "The chief reason is that you are tired of me. Yes!" She began to sob. "I will tell you the truth: you are ashamed of your love. You try to hide it, to prevent the others noticing, but that is useless, because they knew about it long ago."

"Olga, I ask only one thing," said the artist imploringly. He put his hand to his ear. "One thing only; do not torture me! I want nothing more from you!"

"Then swear to me that you love me still!"

"This is torture!" hissed Riabovsky through his teeth. He jumped up. "It will end in my throwing myself into the Volga, or going out of my mind. Leave me alone!"

"Then kill me! Kill me!" cried Olga Ivanovna. "Kill me!"

She again sobbed, and retired behind the partition. Raindrops pattered on the cabin roof. Riabovsky with his hands to his head walked from corner to corner; then with a determined face, as if he wanted to prove something, put on his cap, took his gun, and went out of the hut.

When he left, Olga Ivanovna lay on her bed and cried. At first she thought that it would be good to take poison, so that Riabovsky on his return would find her dead. But soon her thoughts bore her back to the drawing-room and to her husband's study; and she fancied herself sitting quietly beside Duimoff, enjoying physical rest and cleanliness; and spending the evening listening to *Cavalleria Rusticana.* And a yearning for civilisation, for the sound of cities, for celebrities filled her heart. A peasant woman entered the hut, and lazily prepared the stove for dinner. There was a smell of soot, and the air turned blue from smoke. Then in came several artists in muddy top boots, their faces wet with rain; and they looked at the drawings, and consoled themselves by saying that even in bad weather the Volga had its especial charm. The cheap clock on the wall ticked away; half-frozen flies swarmed in the ikon-corner and buzzed; and cockroaches could be heard under the benches.

Riabovsky returned at sunset. He flung his cap on the table, and, pale, tired, and muddy, dropped on a bench and shut his eyes.

"I am tired," he said, and wrinkled his brows, trying to open his eyes.

To show him kindness, and prove that her anger had passed, Olga Ivanovna came up to him, kissed him silently, and drew a comb through his long, fair hair.

"What are you doing?" he asked, starting as if something cold had touched him. He opened his eyes. "What are you doing? Leave me alone, I beg of you!"

He repulsed her with both hands; and his face seemed to express repugnance and vexation. The peasant woman cautiously brought him a plate, and Olga Ivanovna noticed how she stuck her big fingers in the soup. And the dirty peasant woman with her pendent stomach, the soup which Riabovsky ate greedily, the hut, which she had loved at first for its plainness and artistic disorder, seemed to her unbearable. She felt a deep sense of offence, and said coldly—

"We must part for a time, otherwise we'll only quarrel seriously out of sheer tedium. I am tired of this. I am going to-day."

"Going, how? On the steamer?"

"To-day is Thursday—there is a steamer at half-past nine."

"Eh? Yes! . . . All right, go," said Riabovsky softly, using a towel for a table-napkin. "It's tiresome here for you, and there's nothing to do. Only a great egoist would try to keep you. Go . . . we will meet after the twentieth."

Olga Ivanovna, in good spirits, packed her clothes. Her cheeks burnt with pleasure. "Is it possible?" she asked herself. "Is it possible I shall soon paint in the drawing-room and sleep in a bedroom and dine off a tablecloth?" Her heart grew lighter, and her anger with the artist disappeared.

"I'll leave you the colours and brushes, Riabusha," she said. "You'll bring everything. . . . And, mind, don't idle when I am gone; don't sulk, but work. You are my boy, Riabusha!"

At ten o'clock Riabovsky kissed her good-bye in the hut, to avoid—as she saw—kissing her on the landing-stage in the presence of others. Soon afterwards the steamer arrived and took her away.

Two and a half days later she reached home. Still in her hat and waterproof cloak, panting with excitement, she went through the drawing-room into the dining-room. In his shirt-sleeves, with unbuttoned waistcoat, Duimoff sat at the table and sharpened a knife; on a plate before him was a grouse. As Olga Ivanovna entered the house she resolved to hide the truth from her husband, and felt that she was clever and strong enough to succeed. But when she saw his broad, kindly, happy smile and his bright, joyful eyes, she felt that to deceive such a man would be base and impossible, as impossible as to slander, steal, or kill; and she made up her mind in a second to tell him the whole story. When he had kissed and embraced her she fell upon her knees and hid her face.

"What? What is it, mama?" he asked tenderly. "You got tired of it?"

She raised her face, red with shame, and looked at him guiltily and imploringly. But fear and shame forbade her to tell the truth.

"It is nothing," she said. "I only . . ."

"Sit down here!" he said, lifting her and seating her at the table. "There we are! Eat the grouse! You are starving, of course, poor child!"

She breathed in greedily her native air and ate the grouse. And Duimoff looked at her with rapture and smiled merrily.

## 6

Apparently about the middle of winter Duimoff first suspected his wife's unfaithfulness. He behaved as if his own conscience reproached him. He no longer looked her straight in the face; no longer smiled radiantly when she came in sight; and, to avoid being alone with her, often brought home to dinner his colleague, Korosteleff, a little short-haired man, with a crushed face, who showed his confusion in Olga Ivanovna's society by buttoning and unbuttoning his coat and pinching his right moustache. During dinner the doctors said that when the diaphragm rises abnormally high the heart sometimes beats irregularly, that neuritis had greatly increased, and they discussed Duimoff's discovery made during dissection that a case of cancer of the pancreas had been wrongly diagnosed as "malignant anaemia." And it was plain that both men spoke only of medicine in order that Olga Ivanovna might be silent and tell no lies. After dinner, Korosteleff sat at the piano, and Duimoff sighed and said to him—

"*Akh,* brother! Well! Play me something mournful."

Whereupon, raising his shoulders and spreading his hands, Korosteleff strummed a few chords and sang in tenor, "Show me but one spot where Russia's peasants do not groan!" and Duimoff sighed again, rested his head on his hands, and seemed lost in thought.

Of late Olga Ivanovna had behaved recklessly. She awoke each morning in bad spirits, tortured by the thought that Riabovsky no longer loved her, that —thanks to the Lord, all the same!—all was over. But as she drank her coffee she reasoned that Riabovsky had stolen her from her husband, and that now she belonged to neither. Then she remembered a friend's remark that Riabovsky was getting ready for the exhibition a striking picture, a mixture of landscape and *genre,* in the style of Polienoff, and that this picture sent every one into raptures; this, she consoled herself, he had done under her influence. Thanks to her influence, indeed, he had on the whole changed for the better, and deprived of it, he would probably perish. She remembered that when last he visited her he came in a splashed cloth coat and a new tie and asked her languidly, "Am I good-looking?" And, in truth, elegant Riabovsky with his blue eyes and long curls was very good-looking—or, it may be, he merely seemed so—and he had treated her with affection.

Having remembered and reasoned much, Olga Ivanovna dressed, and in deep agitation drove to Riabovsky's studio. He was in good humour, delighted with what was indeed a fine picture; he hopped, played the fool, and answered every serious question with a joke. Olga Ivanovna was jealous of the picture, and hated it, but for the sake of good manners, she stood before it five minutes, and, sighing as people sigh before holy things, said softly—

"Yes, you never painted like that before. Do you know, it almost frightens me."

And she began to implore him to love her, not to forsake her, to pity her —poor and unfortunate! She kissed his hand, cried, made him swear his love, and boasted that without her influence he would go off the track and perish utterly. Thus having spoilt his good humour, and humiliated herself, she would drive away to a dressmaker, or to some actress friend to ask for free tickets.

Once when she found Riabovsky out she left a note swearing that if he did not visit her at once she would take poison. And he, frightened, came and stayed to dinner. Ignoring her husband's presence, he spoke to her impudently; and she answered in the same tone. They felt chained to one another; they were despots and foes; and their anger hid from them their own rudeness, which even close-clipped Korosteleff remarked. After dinner Riabovsky said good-bye hastily and went.

"Where are you going?" asked Olga Ivanovna. She stood in the hall, and looked at him with hatred.

Riabovsky frowned and blinked, and named a woman she knew, and it was plain that he enjoyed her jealousy, and wished to annoy her. Olga Ivanovna went to her bedroom and lay on her bed; from jealousy, anger, and a sense of humiliation and shame, she bit her pillow, and sobbed aloud. Duimoff left

Korosteleff alone, came into the bedroom, and, confused and abstracted, said softly—

"Don't cry so loudly, mama! . . . What good is it? We must keep silence about this. . . . People mustn't see. . . . You know yourself that what has happened is beyond recall."

Unable to appease the painful jealousy which made her temples throb, thinking, nevertheless, that what had happened was not beyond recall, she washed and powdered her face, and flew off to the woman friend. Finding no Riabovsky there she drove to another, then to a third. . . . At first she felt ashamed of these visits, but she soon reconciled herself; and one evening even called on every woman she knew and sought Riabovsky; and all of them understood her.

Of her husband she said to Riabovsky—

"This man tortures me with his magnanimity."

And this sentence so pleased her that, meeting artists who knew of her affair with Riabovsky, she repeated with an emphatic gesture—

"This man tortures me with his magnanimity."

In general, her life remained unchanged. She resumed her Wednesday-evening parties. The actor declaimed, the painters sketched, the violoncellist played, the singers sang; and invariably half an hour before midnight the dining-room door opened, and Duimoff said with a smile—

"Come gentlemen, supper is ready."

As before, Olga Ivanovna sought celebrities, found them, and, insatiable, sought for more. As before, she returned home late. But Duimoff, no longer sleeping as of old, sat in his study and worked. He went to bed at three, and rose at eight.

Once as she stood before the pier-glass dressing for the theatre, Duimoff, in evening dress and a white tie, came into the room. He smiled kindly, with his old smile, and looked his wife joyfully in the face. His face shone.

"I have just defended my dissertation," he said. He sat down and stroked his leg.

"Your dissertation?" said Olga Ivanovna.

"Yes," he laughed. He stretched forward so as to see in the mirror the face of his wife, who continued to stand with her back to him and dress her hair. "Yes," he repeated. "Do you know what? I expect to be offered a privat-docentship in general pathology. That is something."

It was plain from his radiant face that had Olga Ivanovna shared his joy and triumph he would have forgiven and forgotten everything. But "privat-docentship" and "general pathology" had no meaning for her, and, what's more, she feared to be late for the theatre. She said nothing.

Duimoff sat still for a few minutes, smiled guiltily, and left the room.

## 7

This was an evil day.

Duimoff's head ached badly; he ate no breakfast, and did not go to the hospital, but lay on the sofa in his study. At one o'clock Olga Ivanovna went to Riabovsky's, to show him her *Nature morte,* and ask why he had not come the day before. The *Nature morte* she herself did not take seriously; she had painted it only as an excuse to visit the artist.

She went to his apartment unannounced. As she took off her goloshes in the hall she heard hasty footsteps, and the rustle of a woman's dress; and as she hurried into the studio a brown skirt flashed for a moment before her and vanished behind a big picture, which together with its easel was hung with black calico. There was no doubt that a woman hid there. How often had Olga Ivanovna herself hidden behind that picture! Riabovsky, in confusion, stretched out both hands as if surprised at her visit, and said with a constrained smile—

"Ah, I am glad to see you. What is the news?" Olga Ivanovna's eyes filled with tears. She was ashamed and angered, and would have given millions to be spared speaking before the strange woman, the rival, the liar, who hid behind the picture and tittered, no doubt, maliciously.

"I have brought a study . . ." she said in a thin, frightened voice. Her lips trembled. *"Nature morte."*

"What? What? A study?"

The artist took the sketch, looked at it, and walked mechanically into another room. Olga Ivanovna followed submissively.

*"Nature morte . . ."* he stammered, seeking rhymes. *"Kurort . . . sort . . . porte . . ."*

From the studio came hasty footfalls and the rustle of a skirt. She had gone. Olga Ivanovna felt impelled to scream and strike the artist on the head; but tears blinded her, she was crushed by her shame, and felt as if she were not Olga Ivanovna the artist, but a little beetle.

"I am tired . . ." said Riabovsky languidly. He looked at the study, and shook his head as if to drive away sleep. "This is charming, of course, but . . . it is study to-day, and study to-morrow, and study last year, and study it will be again in a month. . . . How is it you don't get tired? If I were you, I should give up painting, and take up seriously music, or something else. . . . You are not an artist but a musician. You cannot imagine how tired I am. Let me order some tea. Eh?"

He left the room, and Olga Ivanovna heard him giving an order. To avoid good-byes and explanations, still more to prevent herself sobbing, she went quickly into the hall, put on her goloshes, and went out. Once in the street she sighed faintly. She felt that she was for ever rid of Riabovsky and painting, and the heavy shame which had crushed her in the studio. All was over! She drove to her dressmaker, then to Barnay, who had arrived the day before, and from Barnay to a music shop, thinking all the time how she would write Riabovsky a cold, hard letter, full of her own worth; and that the spring and summer she would spend with Duimoff in the Crimea, free herself for ever from the past, and begin life anew.

On her return, late as usual, she sat in her street clothes in the drawing-room, and prepared to write. Riabovsky had told her she was no artist; in revenge she would write that he painted every year one and the same tiresome thing, that he had exhausted himself, and would never again produce original work. She would write also that he owed much to her beneficent influence; and that if he made mistakes it was only because her influence was paralysed by various ambiguous personages who hid behind his pictures.

"Mama!" cried Duimoff from his study, without opening the door.

"What is it?"

"Mama, don't come in, but just come to the door. It is this. The day before yesterday I took diphtheria at the hospital, and now . . . I feel bad. Send at once for Korosteleff."

Olga Ivanovna called her husband and men-friends by their surnames; she disliked his name Osip, which reminded her of Gogol's Osip, and the pun "*Osip okrip, a Arkhip osip.*" But this time she cried—

"Osip, that is impossible!"

"Send! I am ill," said Duimoff from behind the door; and she heard him walking to the sofa and lying down. "Send!" came his hoarse voice.

"What can it be," thought Olga Ivanovna, chilled with fear. "Why this is dangerous!"

Without any aim she took a candle, and went into her room, and there, wondering what she should do, she saw herself unexpectedly in the glass. With her pale, terrified face, her high-sleeved jacket with the yellow gathers on the breast, her skirt with its strange stripes, she seemed to herself frightful and repulsive. And suddenly she felt sorry for Duimoff, sorry for his infinite love, his young life, the forsaken bed on which he had not slept so long. And remembering his kindly, suppliant smile, she cried bitterly, and wrote Korosteleff an imploring letter. It was two o'clock in the morning.

## *8*

When at eight next morning Olga Ivanovna, heavy from sleeplessness, untidy, unattractive, and guilty-faced, came out of her bedroom, an unknown, black-bearded man, obviously a doctor, passed her in the hall. There was a smell of drugs. Outside Duimoff's study stood Korosteleff, twisting his left moustache with his right hand.

"Excuse me, I cannot let you in," he said, looking at her savagely. "You might catch the disease. And in any case, what's the use? He's raving."

"Is it really diphtheria?" whispered Olga Ivanovna.

"People who do foolish things ought to pay for them," muttered Korosteleff, ignoring Olga Ivanovna's question. "Do you know how he got this diphtheria? On Tuesday he sucked through a tube the diphtheria laminae from a boy's throat. And why? Stupid. . . . Like a fool!"

"Is it dangerous? Very?" asked she.

"Yes, it's a very bad form, they say. We must send for Schreck, we must. . . ."

First came a little, red-haired, long-nosed man with a Jewish accent; then a tall, stooping, untidy man like a proto-deacon; lastly a young, very stout, red-faced man with spectacles. All these doctors came to attend their sick colleague.

Korosteleff, having served his turn, remained in the house, wandering about like a shadow. The maid-servant was kept busy serving the doctors with tea, and running to the apothecary's, and no one tidied the rooms. All was still and sad.

Olga Ivanovna sat in her room, and reflected that God was punishing her for deceiving her husband. That silent, uncomplaining, inexplicable man—impersonified, it seemed, by kindness and mildness, weak from excessive goodness—lay on his sofa and suffered alone, uttering no groan. And if he did complain in his delirium, the doctors would guess that the diphtheria was not the only culprit. They would question Korosteleff, who knew all, and not without cause looked viciously at his friend's wife as if she were chief and real offender, and disease only her accomplice. She no longer thought of the moonlight Volga night, the love avowal, the romance of life in the peasant's hut; she remembered only that from caprice and selfishness she had smeared herself from head to feet with something vile and sticky which no washing would wash away.

"*Akh,* how I lied to him!" she said, remembering her restless love of Riabovsky. "May it be accursed!"

At four o'clock she dined with Korosteleff, who ate nothing, but drank red wine, and frowned. She too ate nothing. But she prayed silently, and vowed to God that if Duimoff only recovered, she would love him again and be his faithful wife. Then, forgetting herself for a moment, she looked at Korosteleff and thought: "How tiresome it is to be such a simple, undistinguished, obscure man, and to have such bad manners." It seemed to her that God would strike her dead for her cowardice in keeping away from her husband. And altogether she was oppressed by a dead melancholy, and a feeling that her life was ruined, and that nothing now would mend it.

After dinner, darkness. Olga Ivanovna went into the drawing-room, and found Korosteleff asleep on a couch, his head resting on a silk cushion embroidered with gold. He snored loudly.

Alone the doctors, coming on and off duty, ignored the disorder. The strange man sleeping and snoring in the drawing-room, the studies on the walls, the wonderful decorations, the mistress's dishevelled hair and untidy dress—none of these awakened the least interest. One of the doctors laughed; and this laugh had such a timid sound that it was painful to hear.

When next Olga Ivanovna entered the drawing-room Korosteleff was awake. He sat up and smoked.

"He has got diphtheria . . . in the nasal cavity," he said quietly. "Yes . . . and his heart is weak. . . . It is a bad business."

"Better send for Schreck," said Olga Ivanovna.

"He's been. It was he noticed that the diphtheria had got into the nose. Yes . . . but what is Schreck? In reality, Schreck is nothing. He is Schreck, I am Korosteleff, and nothing more!"

Time stretched into eternity. Olga Ivanovna lay dressed on her unmade bed, and slumbered. She felt that the whole flat from floor to ceiling was filled with a giant block of iron, and that if the iron were only removed, all would be well again. But then she remembered that there was no iron, but only Duimoff's illness.

"*Nature morte* . . ." she thought, again losing consciousness. "Sport, *kurort.*

. . . And what about Schreck? Schreck, greck, vreck, kreck. Where are my friends now? Do they know of the sorrow that has overtaken us? O Lord, save . . . deliver us! Schreck, greck. . . ."

And again the iron. Time stretched into eternity, and the clock downstairs struck innumerable times. Now and then the bell was rung. Doctors came. . . . In came the servant with an empty glass on a salver, and said—

"Shall I make the bed, ma'am?"

And, receiving no answer, she went out. Again the clock struck—dreams of rain on the Volga—and again some one arrived, this time, it seemed, a stranger. Olga Ivanovna started, and saw Korosteleff.

"What time is it?" she asked.

"About three."

"Well, what?"

"Just that. I came to say that he's dying."

He sobbed, sat down on her bed, and wiped away his tears with his sleeve. At first Olga Ivanovna understood nothing; then she turned cold, and began to cross herself.

"He is dying," he repeated in a thin voice; and again he sobbed. "He is dying—because he sacrificed himself. What a loss to science!" He spoke bitterly. "This man, compared with the best of us, was a great man, an exceptional man! What gifts! What hopes he awakened in us all!" Korosteleff wrung his hands. "Lord, my God, you will not find such a scholar if you search till judgment day! Oska Duimoff, Oska Duimoff, what have you done? My God!"

In despair he covered his face with his hands and shook his head.

"And what moral fortitude!" he continued, each second increasing in anger. "Good, pure, loving soul—not a man, but a crystal! How he served his science, how he's died for it. Worked—day and night—like an ox, sparing himself never; and he, the young scholar, the coming professor, was forced to seek a practice and spend his nights translating to pay for these . . . these dirty rags!"

Korosteleff looked fiendishly at Olga Ivanovna, seized the sheet with both hands, and tore it as angrily as if it, and not she, were guilty.

"And he never spared himself . . . nor did others spare him. And for what purpose . . . why?"

"Yes, a man in a hundred!" came a deep voice from the dining-room.

Olga Ivanovna recalled her life with Duimoff, from beginning to end, in all its details; and suddenly she realised that her husband was indeed an exceptional man, a rare—compared with all her other friends—a great man. And remembering how he was looked up to by her late father and by all his colleagues, she understood that there was indeed good reason to predict for him future fame. The walls, the ceiling, the lamp, the carpet winked at her derisively, as if saying, "You have let it slip by, slip by!" With a cry, she rushed out of the room, slipped past some unknown man in the dining-room, and rushed into her husband's study. Covered with a counterpane to the waist, Duimoff lay, motionless, on the couch. His face had grown thin, and was a greyish-yellow never seen on the living; his black eyebrows and his kindly smile were all that remained of Duimoff. She felt his chest, his forehead, his hands. His chest was still warm, his forehead and hands were icy. And his half-closed eyes looked not at Olga Ivanovna, but down at the counterpane.

"Duimoff!" she cried loudly. "Duimoff!"

She wished to explain to him that the past was but a mistake; that all was not yet lost; that life might yet be happy and beautiful; that he was a rare, an uncommon, a great man; that she would worship him from this day forth, and pray, and torture herself with holy dread. . . .

"Duimoff!" she cried, tapping his shoulder, refusing to believe that he would never awaken. "Duimoff! Duimoff!"

But in the drawing-room Korosteleff spoke to the maid-servant.

"Don't ask silly questions! Go at once to the church watchman, and get the women's address. They will wash the body, and lay it out, and do all that's wanted."

## *Study questions*

1. *Why does Olga marry Duimoff? Why does Duimoff marry her?* 2. *Account for the fact that Olga has no women friends. What does Olga find attractive in artists? What do they find attractive in her? Are these people true artists?* 3. *Point out details of the setting that act also to characterize Olga and Duimoff.* 4. *Locate all the times in the story that eating is mentioned. How does this motif function? How does it relate to the theme?* 5. *Why does Duimoff hurt himself so much? Does he willingly sacrifice himself?* 6. *What is the significance of Olga's relationship with Riabovsky? Why is he tired?* 7. *How many characters are identified with the cicada? What are the characteristics of the cicada that make it particularly relevant for use as a symbol in this story?*

# DREAMS

Two soldiers are escorting to the country town a vagrant who does not remember who he is. One of them is black-bearded and thick-set, with legs so uncommonly short that, seen from hehind, they seem to begin much lower down than those of other men; the other is long, lank, spare, and straight as a stick, with a thin beard of a dark-reddish hue. The first waddles along, looking from side to side and sucking now a straw and now the sleeve of his coat. He slaps his thigh and hums to himself, and looks, on the whole, light-hearted and care-free. The other, with his lean face and narrow shoulders, is staid and important-looking; in build and in the expression of his whole person he resembles a priest of the Starover Faith or one of those warriors depicted on antique icons. "For his wisdom God has enlarged his brow," that is to say, he is bald, which still more enhances the resemblance. The first soldier is called Andrew Ptaka, the second Nikander Sapojnikoff.

The man they are escorting is not in the least like what every one imagines a tramp should be. He is small and sickly and feeble, with little, colourless, absolutely undefined features. His eyebrows are thin, his glance is humble and mild, and his whiskers have barely made their appearance though he is already past thirty. He steps timidly along, stooping, with his hands thrust into his sleeves. The collar of his threadbare, unpeasant-like little coat is turned right up to the brim of his cap, so that all that can venture to peep out at the world is his little red nose. When he speaks, it is in a high, obsequious little voice, and then he immediately coughs. It is hard, very hard to recognise in him a vagabond who is hiding his name. He looks more like some impoverished, God-forsaken son of a priest, or a clerk discharged for intemperance, or a merchant's son who has essayed his puny strength on the stage and is now returning to his home to play out the last act of the parable of the prodigal son. Perhaps, judging from the dull patience with which he battles with the clinging autumn mud, he is a fanatic; some youth trained for a monk who is wandering from one monastery to another all over Russia, doggedly seeking "a life of peace and freedom from sin," which he cannot find.

The wayfarers have been walking a long time, but for all their efforts they cannot get away from the same spot of ground. Before them lie ten yards of dark-brown, muddy road, behind them lies as much; beyond that, wherever they turn, rises a dense wall of white fog. They walk and walk, but the ground they walk on is always the same; the wall comes no nearer; the spot remains a spot. Now and then they catch glimpses of white, irregular cobblestones, a dip in the road, or an armful of hay dropped by some passing wagon; a large pool of muddy water gleams for a moment, or a shadow, vaguely outlined, suddenly and unexpectedly appears before them. The nearer they come to this, the smaller and darker it grows; they come nearer still, and before them rises a crooked mile-post with its numbers effaced, or a woebegone birch-tree, naked and wet, like a wayside beggar. The birch-tree is whispering something with the remains of its yellow foliage; one leaf breaks off and flutters sluggishly to the ground, and then again there come fog and mud and the brown grass by the roadside. Dim, evil tears hang on these blades—not the tears of quiet joy that the earth weeps when she meets and accompanies the summer sun, and with which at dawn she quenches the thirst of quail and rails and graceful, long-billed snipe! The feet of the travellers are caught by the thick, sticky mud; every step costs them an effort.

Andrew Ptaka is a trifle provoked. He is scrutinising the vagrant and trying to understand how a live, sober man could forget his name.

"You belong to the Orthodox Church, don't you?" he asks.

"I do," answers the tramp briefly.

"H'm—have you been christened?"

"Of course I have; I'm not a Turk! I go to church and observe the fasts and don't eat flesh when it's forbidden to do so——"

"Well, then, what name shall I call you by?"

"Call me what you please, lad."

Ptaka shrugs his shoulders and slaps his thigh in extreme perplexity. The other soldier, Nikander, preserves a sedate silence. He is not so simple as Ptaka, and evidently knows very well reasons which might induce a member of the Orthodox Church to conceal his identity. His expressive face is stern and cold. He walks apart and disdains idle gossip with his companions. He seems to be endeavouring to show to every one and everything, even to the mist, how grave and sensible he is.

"The Lord only knows what to think about you!" pursues Ptaka. "Are you a peasant or not? Are you a gentleman or not? Or are you something between the two? I was rinsing out a sieve in a pond one day and caught a little monster as long as my finger here, with gills and a tail. Thinks I—it's a fish! Then I take another look at it—and I'll be blessed if it didn't have feet! It wasn't a fish and it wasn't a reptile—the devil only knows what it was! That's just what you are. What class do you belong to?"

"I am a peasant by birth," sighs the tramp. "My mother was a house serf. In looks I'm not a peasant, and that is because fate has willed it so, good man. My mother was a nurse in a gentleman's house and had every pleasure the heart could desire, and I, as her flesh and blood, belonged, in her lifetime, to the household. They petted me and spoiled me and beat me till they beat me from common to well-bred. I slept in a bed, had a real dinner every day, and wore trousers and low shoes like any little noble. Whatever my mother had to eat, I had. They gave her dresses and dressed me, too. Oh, we lived well! The candy and cake I ate in my childhood would buy a good horse now if I could sell them! My mother taught me to read and write, and from the time I was a baby instilled the fear of God into me and trained me so well that to this day I couldn't use an impolite, peasant word. I don't drink vodka, boy, and I dress cleanly and can make a respectable appearance in good society. God give her health if she is still alive; if she is dead, take her soul, O Lord, to rest in thy heavenly kingdom where the blessed find peace!"

The tramp uncovers his head, with its sparse bristles, casts his eyes upward, and makes the sign of the cross twice.

"Give her peace, O Lord, in green places!" he says in a drawling voice, more like an old woman's than a man's. "Keep thy slave Keenia in all thy ways, O Lord! If it had not been for my good mother I should have been a simple peasant now, not knowing a thing. As it is, lad, ask me what you please; I know everything: the Holy Scriptures, all godly things, all the prayers, and the Catechisms. I live according to the Scriptures; I do wrong to no one; I keep my body pure; I observe the fasts and eat as it is ordered. Some men find pleasure only in vodka and brawling, but when I have time I sit in a corner and read a book, and as I read I cry and cry——"

"Why do you cry?"

"Because the things they tell of are so pitiful. Sometimes you pay only five copecks for a book and weep and wail over it to despair——"

"Is your father dead?" asks Ptaka.

"I don't know, lad. It's no use hiding a sin; I don't know who my father was. What I think is that I was an illegitimate son of my mother's. My mother lived all her life with the gentry and never would marry a common peasant."

"So she flew higher, up to his master!" laughs Ptaka.

"That is so. My mother was pious and godly, and of course it is a sin, a great sin, to say so, but, nevertheless, maybe I have noble blood in my veins. Maybe I am a peasant in station only and am really a high-born gentleman."

The "high-born gentleman" utters all this in a soft, sickly sweet voice, wrinkling his narrow brows and emitting squeaky noises from his cold, red, little nose.

Ptaka listens to him, eyes him with astonishment, and still shrugs his shoulders.

After going four miles the soldiers and the tramp sit down on a little knoll to rest.

"Even a dog can remember his name," mutters Ptaka. "I am called Andrew and he is called Nikander; every man has his God-given name and no one could possibly forget it—not possibly!"

"Whose business is it of any one's to know who I am?" sighs the tramp, leaning his cheek on his hand. "And what good would it do me if they knew? If I were allowed to go wherever I liked I should be worse off than I am now. I know the law, my Christian friends—now I am a vagrant who does not remember his name, and the worst they could do to me would be to send me to eastern Siberia with thirty or forty lashes, but if I should tell them my real name and station I should be sent to hard labour again—I know!"

"You mean to say you have been a convict?"

"I have, my good friend. My head was shaved and I wore chains for four years."

"What for?"

"For murder, good man. When I was still a boy, about eighteen years old, my mother put arsenic into our master's glass by mistake instead of soda. There were a great many different little boxes in the storeroom and it was not hard to mistake them."

The tramp sighs, shakes his head, and continues:

"She was a godly woman, but who can say? The soul of another is a dark forest. Maybe she did it by mistake. Maybe it was because her master had attached another servant to himself and her heart could not forgive the insult. Perhaps she did put it in on purpose—God only knows! I was young then and couldn't understand everything. I remember now that our master did, in fact, take another mistress at that time and that my mother was deeply hurt. Our trial went on for two years after that. My mother was condemned to twenty years' penal servitude and I to seven on account of my youth."

"And what charge were you convicted on?"

"For being an accomplice. I handed our master the glass. It was always that way: my mother would prepare the soda and I would hand him the glass. But

I am confessing all this before you, brothers, as before God. You won't tell any one——"

"No one will ever ask us," says Ptaka. "So that means you ran away from prison, does it?"

"Yes, I ran away, good friend. Fourteen of us escaped. God be with them! They ran away and took me along, too. Now judge for yourself, lad, and tell me honestly whether I have any reason for telling my name? I should be condemned to penal servitude again; and what sort of a convict am I? I am delicate and sickly; I like cleanliness in my food and in the places where I sleep. When I pray to God I like to have a little shrine lamp or a candle burning, and I don't like to have noises going on round me when I'm praying. When I prostrate myself I don't like to have the floor all filthy and spat over, and I prostrate myself forty times morning and night for my mother's salvation."

The tramp takes off his cap and crosses himself.

"But let them send me to eastern Siberia if they want to!" he cries. "I'm not afraid of that."

"What? Is that better?"

"It is an entirely different affair. At hard labour you are no better off than a crab in a basket. You are crowded and pushed and hustled; there's not a quiet corner to take breath; it's a hell on earth—the Mother of God forbid it! A ruffian you are, and a ruffian's treatment you receive—worse than any dog's. You get nothing to eat; there is nowhere to sleep and nowhere to say your prayers. In exile it's different. You first enroll yourself in the company, as every one else does. The government is compelled by law to give you your share of land. Yes, indeed! Land, they say, is cheap there, as cheap as snow. You can take all you want! They would give me land for farming, lad, and land for a garden, and land for a house. Then I would plough and sow, as other men do, raise cattle and bees and sheep and dogs—I'd get myself a Siberian cat to keep the rats and mice from eating my property, I'd build me a house, brothers, and buy icons; and, God willing, I'd marry and have children——"

The tramp is murmuring to himself now and has ceased looking at his listeners; he is gazing off somewhere to one side. Artless as his reveries are, he speaks with such sincerity and such heartfelt earnestness that it is hard not to believe what he says. The little mouth of the vagrant is twisted by a smile, and his whole face, his eyes, and his nose are numbed and paralysed by the foretaste of far-off happiness. The soldiers listen and regard him earnestly, not without compassion. They also believe what he says.

"I am not afraid of Siberia," the tramp murmurs on. "Siberia and Russia are the same thing. They have the same God there as here, and the same Czar, and they speak the language of Orthodox Christians, as I am speaking with you; only there is greater plenty, and the people are richer. Everything is better there. Take, for example, the rivers. They are a thousand times finer than ours. And fish! The fishing in them is simply beyond words! Fishing, brothers, is the greatest joy of my life. I don't ask for bread; only let me sit and hold a fishing-line! Indeed, that is true! I catch fish on a hook and line and in pots and with bow nets, and when the ice comes I use cast nets. I am not strong enough to fish with a cast net myself; so I have to hire a peasant for five copecks to do that for me. Heavens, what fun it is! It's like seeing your own brother again to catch an eel or a mudfish! And you have to treat every fish differently, I can tell you. You use a minnow for one, and a worm for another, and a frog or a grasshopper for a third; you've got to know all that. Take, for example, the eel. The eel isn't a dainty fish; it will take even a newt. Pikes like earthworms—garfish, butterflies. There is no greater joy on earth than fishing for chubs in swift water. You bait your hook with a butterfly or a beetle, so that it will float on the surface; and you let your line run out some twenty or thirty yards without a sinker; then you stand in the water without your trousers and let the bait float down with the current till—tug! and there's a chub on the hook! Then you have to watch ever so closely for just the right moment to hook it or the confounded thing will go off with your bait. The moment it twitches the line you've got to pull; there isn't a second to lose! The number of fish I have caught in my life is a caution! When we were escaping and the other convicts were asleep in the forest, I couldn't sleep and would go off in search of a river. The rivers there are so wide and swift and steep-banked—it's a caution. And all along their shores lie dense forests. The trees are so high that it makes your head swim to look up to the top of them. According to prices here every one of those pine-trees is worth ten roubles——"

Under the confused stress of his imagination, the dream pictures of the past, and the sweet foretaste of happiness, the piteous little man stops speaking and only moves his lips as if whispering to himself. The feeble, beatific smile does not leave his face. The soldiers say nothing. Their heads have sunk forward onto their breasts, and they are lost in meditation. In the autumn silence, when a chill, harsh fog from the earth settles on the soul and rises like a prison wall before one to testify to the narrow limits of man's freedom, ah! then it is sweet to dream of wide, swift rivers with bold, fertile banks, of dense forests, of boundless plains! Idly, peacefully, the fancy pictures to itself a man, a tiny speck, appearing on the steep, uninhabited bank of a river in the early morning, before the flush of dawn has faded from the sky. The summits of the everlasting pines rise piled high in terraces on either side of the stream and, muttering darkly, look sternly at that free man. Roots, great rocks, and thorny bushes obstruct his path, but he is strong of body and valiant of heart and fears neither the pines nor the rocks nor the solitude nor the rolling echoes that reiterate every footfall.

The imagination of the soldiers is painting for them pictures of a free life which they have never lived. Is it that they darkly recall images of things heard long ago? Or have these visions of a life of liberty come down to them with their flesh and blood as an inheritance from their remote, wild ancestors? God only knows!

The first to break the silence is Nikander, who until now has not let fall a word. Perhaps he is jealous of the vagrant's visionary happiness; perhaps he feels in his heart that dreams of bliss are incongruous amidst surroundings of grey mist and brown-black mud—at any rate, he looks sternly at the tramp and says:

"That is all very well, brother; that is all very fine, but you'll never reach that land of plenty! How could you? You would go thirty miles and then give up the ghost—a little half-dead creature like you! You've only walked four miles to-day and yet, look at you! You can't seem to get rested at all!"

The tramp turns slowly to Nikander and the blissful smile fades from his face. He looks with dismay at the grave countenance of the soldier as if he had been caught doing wrong and seems to have recollected something, for he nods his head. Silence falls once more. All three are busy with their own thoughts. The soldiers are trying to force their minds to grasp what perhaps God alone can conceive of: the terrible expanse that lies between them and that land of freedom. Images more clear, precise, and terrifying are crowding into the vagrant's head—courts of justice, dungeons for exiles and for convicts, prison barracks, weary halts along the road, the cold of winter, illness, the death of his companions—all rise vividly before him.

The tramp blinks, and little drops stand out upon his brow. He wipes his forehead with his sleeve, draws a deep breath as if he had just jumped out of a hot oven, wipes his forehead with the other sleeve, and glances fearfully behind him.

"It is quite true that you could never get there," Ptaka assents. "You're not a walker! Look at yourself—all skin and bone! It would kill you, brother."

"Of course it would kill him; he couldn't possibly do it," declares Nikander. "He'll be sent straight to the hospital, anyway, as it is. That's a fact!"

The nameless wanderer looks with terror at the stern, impassive faces of his evil-boding fellow travellers; then, lowering his eyes, he rapidly crosses himself without taking off his cap. He is trembling all over, his head is shaking, and he is beginning to writhe like a caterpillar that some one has stepped on.

"Come on! Time to go!" cries Nikander, rising. "We have rested long enough!"

Another minute and the travellers are plodding along the muddy road. The tramp is stooping more than before and has thrust his hands still deeper into the sleeves of his coat. Ptaka is silent.

## *Study questions*

1. *Why does Chekhov spend so much time describing the three men?* 2. *How does the road on which they are walking function as symbol?* 3. *Why does the protagonist prefer to go to Siberia?* 4. *Explain why the soldiers respond as they do to the protagonist's "dream pictures."* 5. *Chart the plot of this story. Is there exposition? rising action? complication? Where is the climax of the story?*

*Miguel de Unamuno* (1864–1936), considered by many scholars to be the most controversial figure in Spanish literature, was born in Bilbao. After receiving a doctorate at the University of Madrid, he went to the University of Salamanca to become professor of Greek. Ten years later he assumed the post of rector of the university. A philosopher, poet, fiction writer, dramatist, and essayist, he was also a polemicist, continually involved in controversial arguments. He was twice relieved of his position as rector because of political statements, the second time because of his opposition to Franco at the onset of the Spanish Civil War. Unamuno called his short stories "*novelas ejemplars*"—exempla. For him, fiction was a means of concretizing thought and then of bringing it to life. He believed that reason annihilates and kills, but imagination integrates and gives life. "Juan Manso: A Dead Man's Tale" is a humorous but telling allegory about the best way to get along on this earth.

## JUAN MANSO: A DEAD MAN'S TALE

And now for a story.

While he was on this wicked earth Juan Manso was a simple soul, a harmless fellow who during his whole life had never hurt a fly. As a child, when he played donkey with his friends, he was always the donkey. Later, his comrades confided in him about their love affairs, and when he grew to full manhood his acquaintances still used to greet him with an affectionate "Hello, little Johnny!"

His favorite maxim was from the Chinese: "Never commit yourself, and stick to the person who can help you the most."

He loathed politics, hated business, and avoided everything that might upset the even tenor of his ways.

He lived on a small income which he spent in its entirety without ever touching the capital. He was quite devout, would never contradict anyone, and as he had a bad opinion of everybody he spoke well of them.

If you mentioned politics to him he would say: "I'm nothing—neither one side nor the other: I don't care which party runs the government. I'm just a poor sinner who wants to live at peace with everyone."

His meekness, however, was of no avail against the finality of death. It was the only definite thing he ever did in his life.

An angel armed with a great flaming sword was sorting out souls according to the sign made upon them as they went by an enrollment desk which they had to pass as they departed from this world and went through a kind of immigration control where angels and devils were sitting side by side in friendly fashion examining documents to see if they were all in order.

The entrance to the registration room looked like the scene outside the box office on the day of a big bullfight. There were so many people milling around, pushing and shoving, with everyone in such a hurry to learn his fate, and such was the hubbub raised by the curses, entreaties, insults and excuses in the thousands of languages, dialects and jargons of this world, that Juan Manso said to himself:

"Who says I have to get mixed up in all this? There must be some very rough characters around here."

He said this *sotto voce,* so no one could hear him. The fact is that the angel with the great flaming sword paid not the slightest attention to him, so he was able to slip past and start on his way to Heaven.

He walked along very quietly all by himself. From time to time happy groups would pass by, chanting litanies; some were dancing wildly, which seemed to him not quite a proper thing for the blessed to be doing on their way up to Heaven. When he reached the heights he found a long line of people standing beside the walls of Paradise, and a few angels keeping order like policemen on earth. Juan Manso got on the very end of the line.

Shortly a humble Franciscan friar came along, and he was so clever in advancing pathetic arguments as to why he was in such a hurry to get inside right away that Juan Manso gave him his place in line, saying to himself:

"It's a good idea to make friends for yourself even in Heaven."

The next man to come along, though not a Franciscan, wanted the same privilege, and the same thing happened. In short, there wasn't a pious soul who did not trick Juan Manso out of his place; his reputation for meekness ran along the whole line, and was handed down as a continuing tradition among the constantly-changing crowd there. And Juan Manso stayed where he was, the prisoner of his own good reputation.

Centuries went by—or so it seemed to Juan Manso, for it took that much time for the meek little lamb to begin to lose his patience. Finally one day he happened to meet a wise and saintly bishop who turned out to be the great-great-grandson of one of Manso's brothers. Juan voiced his complaints to his great-great-grandnephew, and the wise and saintly bishop offered to intercede for him when he came before the Eternal Father. On the strength of this, Juan yielded his place to the wise and saintly bishop who, when he entered Heaven, quite properly went straight to the Eternal Father to pay Him his respects. He concluded his little talk with The Almighty, who listened absent-mindedly and said:

"Wasn't there something else you wanted to say?"

And with His glance He searched the depths of the bishop's heart.

"Lord, permit me to intercede for one of Thy servants who is out there at the very tip end of the line. . . ."

"Don't beat about the bush," thundered The Lord. "You mean Juan Manso."

"Yes, Lord, he is the one; Juan Manso, who . . . ."

"All right! All right! Let him look out for himself, and don't you get mixed up again in other people's affairs!" And turning to the angel who was introducing souls, He added: "Let the next one in!"

If anything is capable of marring the eternal happiness of a soul in everlasting bliss, we could say that the soul of the wise and saintly bishop was troubled. But at least, moved by pity, he went to Heaven's walls, next to which the long line was standing. He climbed up, and calling to Juan Manso he said:

"Great-great-uncle, how sad I am about this—how very sad, my dear man! The Lord told me that you should look out for yourself, and that I shouldn't get mixed up in other people's affairs again. But . . . are you still at the end of the line? Come now, my dear man! Summon up some courage and don't yield your place again."

"Now he tells me!" exclaimed Juan Manso, shedding tears as big as chick-peas. But it was too late, for the tragic tradition was now attached to him: people no longer even asked him for his place, they just took it.

Crestfallen, he abandoned the line and began to wander about the lonely wastelands beyond the grave until he came upon many people, all downcast, walking along a road. He followed their footsteps and found himself at the gates of Purgatory.

"It will be easier to get in here," he said to himself, "and once inside they will send me directly to Heaven after I have been purified."

"Hey! Where are you going, my friend?"

Juan Manso turned around and found himself face to face with an angel who was wearing an academic mortarboard and had a pen behind his ear. He looked at Juan over the top of his glasses, had him turn around, and after examining him from head to foot frowned and said:

"H-m-m! *Malorum causa*—the root of all ills! You are completely grey, and I'm afraid to put you through our procedures for fear you'll melt. You would do better to go to Limbo."

"To Limbo!"

Upon hearing this, Juan Manso became indignant for the first time, for no man is so patient and long-suffering that he will stand for having an angel treat him like a complete idiot.

In desperation, he set out for Hell. Here there was no waiting line, nor anything like one. It had a broad entrance, from which came puffs of thick smoke and an infernal din. At the door a poor devil was playing a hand-organ and shrieking at the top of his voice:

"Come inside, gentlemen, step inside . . . Here you will see the human comedy . . . Anyone may enter. . . ."

Juan Manso closed his eyes.

"Hey, young man! Stop!" the poor devil said to him.

"Didn't you say that anyone might enter?"

"Yes, but . . . Look," said the poor devil earnestly, as he stroked his tail, "we still have some slight spark of conscience . . . and, after all . . . you?"

"All right, all right!" said Juan Manso, turning away because he could not stand the smoke.

And he heard the devil mutter to himself, "Poor fellow!"

"Poor fellow? Even the devil pities me!"

Desperate now to the point of madness, he began to bob around like a cork in mid-ocean as he crossed the vast spaces beyond the grave. From time to time he would meet other legendary lost souls.

One day, attracted by the appetizing odor that was coming from Heaven, he approached its walls to see what they were cooking inside. It was about time for sunset, and he saw that The Lord was coming out to enjoy the cool air in the gardens of Paradise. Juan Manso waited for Him near the wall, and when he saw His noble head he opened his arms wide in supplication and said in a rather indignant tone:

"Lord, Lord, didst Thou not promise the Kingdom of Heaven to the meek?"

"Yes, but to the enterprising, not to the weak-kneed."

And He turned His back on Juan.

An old legend recounts that The Lord, taking pity on Juan Manso, let him return to this wicked world, and that when he got here again he began to push people around right and left. When he died a second time, he shoved his way right past the famous line and slipped boldly into Paradise.

Now inside, he keeps repeating:

"Man has to fight his way through life on earth!"

## *Study questions*

1. *What is the purpose of the first sentence?* 2. *What was Juan Manso like before he died? after?* 3. *Why does the "wise and saintly" bishop intercede for Juan?* 4. *Why won't they accept Juan in Purgatory?* 5. *Why does the devil turn Juan away?* 6. *How does the story suggest we should live our lives on earth?*

*Luigi Pirandello* (1867–1936), winner of the Nobel Prize in 1934, was the author of more than thirty plays, won international fame in 1921 for *Six Characters in Search of an Author*, and continued his success in 1922 with *Henry IV*. He wrote seven novels, of which the best known is *The Late Mattia Pascal* (1904). He is also the author of fifteen volumes of short stories, which in English translation were published as *Short Stories* (1959), *The Merry-Go-Round of Love and Selected Stories* (1964), and *Short Stories* (1965). He was born in Agrigento, Sicily, educated in Rome, and received a doctorate at the University of Bonn in 1891. Thereafter, financial problems forced him to teach at the Rome Normal College for Women. He began writing in 1900 and by 1921 was able to live on royalties produced from his writings. His works characteristically explore the subjective with a subtle and grim humor. Some of his best-known short stories are "The Jar," "The Soft Touch of Grass," "The Reserved Coffin," and "War." "Horse in the Moon" equates desire and death by means of a set of powerful images.

## HORSE IN THE MOON

In September, upon that high and arid clayey plain, jutting perilously over the African sea, the melancholy countryside still lay parched from the merciless summer sun; it was still shaggy with blackened stubble, while a sprinkling of almond trees and a few aged olive trunks were to be seen here and there. Nevertheless, it had been decided that the bridal pair should spend at least the first few days of their honeymoon in this place, to oblige the bridegroom.

The wedding feast, which was held in a room of the old deserted villa, was far from being a festive occasion for the invited guests. None of those present was able to overcome the embarrassment, or rather the feeling of dismay inspired in him by the aspect and bearing of that fleshy youth, barely twenty years of age, with the purplish face and with the little darting black eyes, which were preternaturally bright, like a madman's. The latter no longer heard what was being said around him; he did not eat, and he did not drink, but became, from moment to moment, redder and more purple of countenance.

Everyone knew that he had been madly in love with the one who now sat beside him as his bride, and that he had done perfectly mad things on her account, even to the point of attempting to kill himself. He was very rich, the sole heir to the Bernardi fortune, while she, after all, was only the daughter of an infantry colonel who had come there the year before, with his regiment, from Sicily. But in spite of this, the colonel, who had been warned against the inhabitants of the island, had been reluctant about giving his consent to this match, for the reason that he had not wanted to leave his daughter there among people that were little better than savages.

The dismay which the bridegroom's aspect and actions inspired in the guests increased when the latter came to contrast him with his extremely young bride. She was really but a child, fresh, vivacious and aloof; it seemed that she always shook off every unpleasant thought with a liveliness that was, at once, charming, ingenuous and roguish. Roguish as that of a little tomboy who as yet knows nothing of the world. A half-orphan, she had grown up without a mother's care; and indeed, it was all too evident that she was going into matrimony without any preparation whatsoever. Everyone smiled, but everyone felt a chill, when, at the end of the meal, she turned to the bridegroom and exclaimed:

"For goodness' sake, Nino, why do you make those little tiny eyes? Let me—no, they burn! Why do your hands burn like that? Feel, Papa, feel how hot his hands are—Do you suppose he has fever?"

The colonel, on pins and needles, did what he could to speed up the departure of the countryside guests. He wanted to put an end to a spectacle that impressed him as being indecent. They all piled into a half-dozen carriages. The one in which the colonel and the bridegroom's widowed mother rode proceeded slowly down the lane and lagged a little behind, for the reason that the bridal couple, one on one side and one on the other, holding hands with the mother and father, had wanted to follow a short distance on foot, down to where the highway which led to the distant city began. At that point, the colonel leaned down and kissed his daughter on the head; he coughed and muttered: "Good-bye, Nino."

"Good-bye, Ida," said the bridegroom's mother with a laugh; and the carriage rattled away at a good pace, in order to overtake the others.

The two stood there for a moment gazing after it. But it was really only Ida who gazed; for Nino saw nothing, was conscious of nothing; his eyes were fastened upon his bride as she stood there, alone with him at last—his, all his—But what was this? Was she weeping?

"Daddy—" said Ida, as she waved her handkerchief in farewell. "There, do you see? He, too——"

"No, Ida—Ida dear—" and stammering, almost sobbing, trembling violently, Nino made an effort to embrace her.

Ida pushed him away.

"No, let me alone, please."

"I just wanted to dry your eyes——"

"Thanks, my dear; I'll dry them myself."

Nino stood there awkwardly. His face, as he looked at her, was pitiful to behold, and his mouth was half-open. Ida finished drying her eyes.

"But what's the matter?" she asked him. "You're trembling all over—No, no, Nino, for heaven's sake, no; don't stand there like that! You make me laugh. And if I once start laughing—you'll see—I'll never stop! Wait a minute; I'll wake you up."

She put her hands on his temples and blew in his eyes. At the touch of those fingers, at the breath from those lips, he felt his legs giving way beneath him; he was about to sink down on one knee, but she held him up and burst into a loud laugh:

"Upon the highway? Are you crazy? Come on, let's go! Look at that little hill over there! We shall be able to see the carriages still. Let's go look!"

And she impetuously dragged him away by one arm.

From all the countryside round about, where so many weeds and grasses, so many things dispersed by the hand of time lay withered, there mounted into the heat-ridden air something like a dense and ancient drouth, mingling with the warm, heavy odor of the manure that lay fermenting in little piles upon the fallow fields, and with the sharper fragrance of sage and wild-mint. Of that dense drouth, those warm and heavy odors, that piercing fragrance, he alone was aware. She, as she ran, could hear how gaily the wood-larks sang up to the sun, from behind the thick hedges and from between the rugged yellowish tufts of burnt-over stubble; she could hear, too, in that impressive silence, the prophetic crow of cocks from distant barnyards; and she felt herself wrapped, every now and again, in the cool, keen breath that came up from the neighboring sea, to stir the few tired and yellowed leaves that were left on the almond trees, and the close-clustering, sharp-pointed, ashen-hued olive leaves.

It did not take them long to reach the hilltop; but he was so exhausted from running that he could no longer stand; he wanted to sit down, and tried to make her sit down also, there on the ground beside him, with his arm about her waist. But Ida put him off with "Let me have a look first."

She was beginning to feel restless inside, but she did not care to show it. Irritated by a certain strange and curious stubbornness on his part, she could not, she would not stand still, but longed to keep on fleeing, still farther away; she wanted to shake him up, to distract him, and to distract herself as well, so long as the day lasted.

Down there, on the other side of the hill, there stretched away a devastated plain, a sea of stubble, amid which one could make out occasionally the black and meandering traces of wood-ashes that had been sprinkled there; now and again, too, the crude yellow gleam was broken by a few clumps of caper or of liquorice. Away over there, as if on the other shore of that vast yellow sea, the roofs of a hamlet rose from the tall dark poplars.

And now Ida suggested to her husband that they go over there, all the way over to that hamlet. How long would it take? An hour or less. It was not more than five o'clock. Back home, in the villa, the servants must still be busy clearing away the things. They would be home before evening.

Nino made a feeble attempt at opposition, but she took him by the hands and dragged him to his feet; in a moment, she was running down the side of the hill and was off through that sea of stubble, as light and quick as a young doe. He was not fast enough to keep up with her, but, redder-faced than ever and seemingly stunned by it all, ran after her, pantingly and perspiringly, and kept calling to her to wait and give him her hand.

"Give me your hand, at least! At least, give me your hand!" he shouted.

All of a sudden, she uttered a cry and stopped short. A flock of cawing ravens had just flown up from in front of her. And there in front of her, stretched out upon the earth, was a dead horse. Dead? No, no, it wasn't dead; it had its eyes open. Heavens, what eyes! What eyes! A skeleton, that was what it was. And those ribs! And those flanks!

Nino came up, fuming and fretting:

"Come on, let's go—let's go back—at once!"

"It's alive, look!" cried Ida, shivering from compassion. "Lift its head—heavens, what eyes! Look, Nino!"

"Yes, yes," said he, panting still. "They've just put it out here—Leave it alone; let's go! What a sight! Don't you smell——?"

"And those ravens!" she exclaimed with a shudder. "Are those ravens going to eat it alive?"

"But, Ida, for heaven's sake!" he implored her, clasping his hands.

"Nino, that will do!" she cried. It was more than she could endure to see him so stupid and so contrite. "Answer me: what if they eat it alive?"

"What do I know about whether or not they'll eat it? They'll wait——"

"Until it dies here, of hunger, of thirst?" Her face was all drawn with horror and pity. "Just because it's old? Because it can't work any more? Ah, poor beast! What a shame! What a shame! Haven't they any heart, those peasants? Haven't you any heart, standing there like that?"

"Excuse me," he said, losing his temper, "but you feel so much sympathy for an animal——"

"And oughtn't I to?"

"But you don't feel any for me!"

"And are you an animal? Are you dying of hunger and thirst as you sit there in the stubble? You feel—Oh, look at the ravens. Nino, look, up there, circling around—Oh, what a horrible, shameful, monstrous thing!—Look—Oh, the poor beast—try to lift him up! Come, Nino, get up; maybe he can still walk—Nino, get up, help me—shake yourself out of it!"

"But what do you expect me to do?" he burst out, exasperatedly. "Do you expect me to drag him back? Put him on my shoulders? What's a horse more or less? How do you think he is going to walk? Can't you see he's half-dead?"

"But if we brought him something to eat?"

"And to drink, too!"

"Oh, Nino, you're wicked!" And the tears stood in Ida's eyes.

Overcoming her shudders, she bent over very gently to caress the horse's head. The animal, with a great effort, had managed to get to its knees; and even in its last degrading agony, it showed the traces of a noble beauty in head and neck.

Nino, owing possibly to the blood that was pounding in his veins, possibly owing to the bitterness and contempt she had manifested, or to the perspiration that was trickling from him, now suddenly felt his breath failing him; he grew giddy, his teeth began chattering, and he was conscious of a weird trembling all over his body. He instinctively turned up his coat collar, and with his hands in his pockets, went over and huddled down in gloomy despair upon a rock some distance away.

The sun had already set, and from the distant highway could be heard the occasional sound of horses' bells.

Why were his teeth chattering like that? For his forehead was burning up, the blood in his veins stung him, and there was a roaring in his ears. It seemed to him that he could hear so many far-away bells. All that anxiety, that spasm of expectation, her coldness and caprice, that last foot-race, and that horse there, that cursed horse—Oh, God! was it a dream? A nightmare within a dream? Did he have a fever? Or perhaps, a worse illness? Ah! How dark it was, God—how dark! And now, his sight was clouding over. And he could not speak, he could not cry out. He tried to call "Ida! Ida!" but he could not get the words out of his parched throat.

Where was Ida? What was she doing?

She had gone off to the distant hamlet, to seek aid for that horse; she did not stop to think that the peasants had brought the animal there to die.

He remained there, alone upon the rock, a prey to those growing tremors; and as he sat there, huddled to himself like a great owl upon a perch, he suddenly beheld a sight that seemed—Ah, yes—he could see it plainly enough now—an atrocious sight, like a vision from another world. The moon. A huge moon, coming slowly up from behind that sea of stubble. And black against that enormous, vapory copper disk, the headstrong head of that horse, waiting still with its neck stretched out—it had, perhaps, been waiting like that always, darkly etched upon that copper disk, while from far up in the sky could be heard the caw of circling ravens.

When Ida, angry and disillusioned, came groping her way back over the plain, calling "Nino! Nino!" the moon had already risen; the horse had dropped down as if dead; and Nino—where was Nino? Oh, there he was over there; he was on the ground, too.

Had he fallen asleep there?

She ran up to him, and found him with a death-rattle in his throat. His face, also, was on the ground; it was almost black, and his eyes, nearly closed, were puffed and bloodshot.

"Oh, God!"

She looked about her, as if in a swoon. She opened her hands which held a few dried beans that she had brought from the hamlet over there to feed to the horse. She looked at the moon, then at the horse, and then at the man lying on the ground as if dead. She felt faint, assailed as she was by the sudden suspicion that everything she saw was unreal. Terrified, she fled back to the villa, calling in a loud voice for her father, her father—to come and take her away, Oh, God! away from that man with the rattle in his throat—that rattle, the meaning of which she did not understand! away from that horse, away from under that mad moon, away from under those cawing ravens in the sky—away, away, away——

## *Study questions*

1. *What is the significance of the stark and barren setting? How is it related to Nino? to Ida?* 2. *Why are Ida's father and the wedding guests embarrassed at the wedding?* 3. *Is Ida's innocence credible? Why does she try to postpone physical contact with Nino?* 4. *What is the significance of the dying horse and the rising moon? of Nino's being compared to an owl? of the horse's head against the moon being projected as a vision from another world?* 5. *Why does Ida run away from the "man with the rattle in his throat" and from the "mad moon"?* 6. *What is the significance of the few dried beans she carries to feed the horse?* 7. *What happens to Nino? Is it adequately foreshadowed?* 8. *Why does Nino think of what is happening as a "nightmare within a dream"?*

*Thomas Mann* (1875–1955), the son of a prosperous merchant and senator, was born in Lubeck, Germany. His first novel, *Buddenbrooks*, was published in 1901, when he was twenty-five. Other important novels include *The Magic Mountain* (1924), *Joseph and His Brothers*, a tetralogy (1933–1943), and *Doktor Faustus* (1947). His stories were collected in 1936 in a volume titled *Stories of Three Decades*. A world-famous writer, Mann was awarded the Nobel Prize in 1929. Repelled by Nazi Germany, he left his home and traveled to the United States. In retaliation, the Nazis revoked his citizenship and burned his books. He lived in California from 1942 to 1952, becoming a citizen in 1944. Then, troubled by increasing political tensions during the McCarthy era, Mann left this country to settle in Zurich, Switzerland. Mann's characteristic themes involve cultural and psychological problems, particularly in the area of creativity and neurosis, genius and disease. Some of his major stories are "Death in Venice," "Mario and the Magician," "Disorder and Early Sorrow," and "Gladius Dei." "The Infant Prodigy" is characteristic of Mann's concern with artists, art, and performance.

# THE INFANT PRODIGY

The infant prodigy entered. The hall became quiet.

It became quiet and then the audience began to clap, because somewhere at the side a leader of mobs, a born organizer, clapped first. The audience had heard nothing yet, but they applauded; for a mighty publicity organization had heralded the prodigy and people were already hypnotized, whether they knew it or not.

The prodigy came from behind a splendid screen embroidered with Empire garlands and great conventionalized flowers, and climbed nimbly up the steps to the platform, diving into the applause as into a bath; a little chilly and shivering, but yet as though into a friendly element. He advanced to the edge of the platform and smiled as though he were about to be photographed; he made a shy, charming gesture of greeting, like a little girl.

He was dressed entirely in white silk, which the audience found enchanting. The little white jacket was fancifully cut, with a sash underneath it, and even his shoes were made of white silk. But against the white socks his bare little legs stood out quite brown; for he was a Greek boy.

He was called Bibi Saccellaphylaccas. And such indeed was his name. No one knew what Bibi was the pet name for, nobody but the impresario, and he regarded it as a trade secret. Bibi had smooth black hair reaching to his shoulders; it was parted on the side and fastened back from the narrow domed forehead by a little silk bow. His was the most harmless childish countenance in the world, with an unfinished nose and guileless mouth. The area beneath his pitch-black mouselike eyes was already a little tired and visibly lined. He looked as though he were nine years old but was really eight and given out for seven. It was hard to tell whether to believe this or not. Probably everybody knew better and still believed it, as happens about so many things. The average man thinks that a little falseness goes with beauty. Where should we get any excitement out of our daily life if we were not willing to pretend a bit? And the average man is quite right, in his average brains!

The prodigy kept on bowing until the applause died down, then he went up to the grand piano, and the audience cast a last look at its programmes. First came a *Marche solonnelle,* then a *Rêverie,* and then *Le Hibou et les moineaux*—all by Bibi Saccellaphylaccas. The whole programme was by him, they were all his compositions. He could not score them, of course, but he had them all in his extraordinary little head and they possessed real artistic significance, or so it said, seriously and objectively, in the programme. The programme sounded as though the impresario had wrested these concessions from his critical nature after a hard struggle.

The prodigy sat down upon the revolving stool and felt with his feet for the pedals, which were raised by means of a clever device so that Bibi could reach them. It was Bibi's own piano, he took it everywhere with him. It rested upon wooden trestles and its polish was somewhat marred by the constant transportation—but all that only made things more interesting.

Bibi put his silk-shod feet on the pedals; then he made an artful little face, looked straight ahead of him, and lifted his right hand. It was a brown, childish little hand; but the wrist was strong and unlike a child's, with well-developed bones.

Bibi made his face for the audience because he was aware that he had to entertain them a little. But he had his own private enjoyment in the thing too, an enjoyment which he could never convey to anybody. It was that prickling delight, that secret shudder of bliss which ran through him every time he sat at an open piano—it would always be with him. And here was the keyboard again, these seven black and white octaves, among which he had so often lost himself in abysmal and thrilling adventures—and yet it always looked as clean and untouched as a newly washed blackboard. This was the realm of music that lay before him. It lay spread out like an inviting ocean, where he might plunge in and blissfully swim, where he might let himself be borne and carried away, where he might go under in night and storm, yet keep the mastery: control, ordain—he held his right hand poised in the air.

A breathless stillness reigned in the room—the tense moment before the first note came. . . . How would it begin? It began so. And Bibi, with his index finger, fetched the first note out of the piano, a quite unexpectedly powerful first note in the middle register, like a trumpet blast. Others followed, an introduction developed—the audience relaxed.

The concert was held in the palatial hall of a fashionable first-class hotel. The walls were covered with mirrors framed in gilded arabesques, between frescoes of the rosy and fleshly school. Ornamental columns supported a ceiling that displayed a whole universe of electric bulbs, in clusters darting a brilliance far brighter than day and filling the whole space with thin, vibrating golden light. Not a seat was unoccupied, people were standing in the side aisles and at the back. The front seats cost twelve marks; for the impresario believed that anything worth having was worth paying for. And they were occupied by the best society, for it was in the upper classes, of course, that the greatest enthusiasm was felt. There were even some children, with their legs hanging down demurely from their chairs and their shining eyes staring at their gifted little white-clad contemporary.

Down in front on the left side sat the prodigy's mother, an extremely obese woman with a powdered double chin and a feather on her head. Beside her was the impresario, a man of oriental appearance with large gold buttons on his conspicuous cuffs. The princess was in the middle of the front row—a wrinkled, shrivelled little old princess but still a patron of the arts, especially everything full of sensibility. She sat in a deep, velvet-upholstered arm chair, and a Persian carpet was spread before her feet. She held her hands folded over her grey striped-silk breast, put her head on one side, and presented a picture of elegant composure as she sat looking up at the performing prodigy. Next to her sat her lady-in-waiting, in a green striped-silk gown. Being only a lady-in-waiting she had to sit up very straight in her chair.

Bibi ended in a grand climax. With what power this wee manikin belaboured the keyboard! The audience could scarcely trust its ears. The march theme, an infectious, swinging tune, broke out once more, fully harmonized, bold and showy; with every note Bibi flung himself back from the waist as though he were marching in a triumphal procession. He ended *fortissimo,* bent over, slipped sideways off the stool, and stood with a smile awaiting the applause.

And the applause burst forth, unanimously, enthusiastically; the child made his demure little maidenly curtsy and people in the front seat thought: "Look what slim little hips he has! Clap, clap! Hurrah, bravo, little chap, Saccophylax or whatever your name is! Wait, let me take off my gloves—what a little devil of a chap he is!"

Bibi had to come out three times from behind the screen before they would stop. Some latecomers entered the hall and moved about looking for seats. Then the concert continued. Bibi's *Rêverie* murmured its numbers, consisting almost entirely of arpeggios, above which a bar of melody rose now and then, weak-winged. Then came *Le Hibou et les moineaux.* This piece was brilliantly successful, it made a strong impression; it was an effective childhood fantasy, remarkably well envisaged. The bass represented the owl, sitting morosely rolling his filmy eyes; while in the treble the impudent, half-frightened sparrows chirped. Bibi received an ovation when he finished, he was called out four times. A hotel page with shiny buttons carried up three great laurel wreaths onto the stage and proffered them from one side while Bibi nodded and expressed his thanks. Even the princess shared in the applause, daintily and noiselessly pressing her palms together.

Ah, the knowing little creature understood how to make people clap! He stopped behind the screen, they had to wait for him; lingered a little on the steps of the platform, admired the long streamers on the wreaths—although actually such things bored him stiff by now. He bowed with the utmost charm, he gave the audience plenty of time to rave itself out, because applause is valuable and must not be cut short. "*Le Hibou* is my drawing card," he thought—this expression he had learned from the impresario. "Now I will play the fantasy, it is a lot better than *Le Hibou,* of course, especially the C-sharp passage. But you idiots dote on the *Hibou,* though it is the first and the silliest thing I wrote." He continued to bow and smile.

Next came a *Méditation* and then an *Étude*—the programme was quite comprehensive. The *Méditation* was very like the *Rêverie*—which was nothing against it—and the *Étude* displayed all of Bibi's virtuosity, which naturally fell a little short of his inventiveness. And then the *Fantaisie.* This was his favourite; he varied it a little each time, giving himself free rein and sometimes surprising even himself, on good evenings, by his own inventiveness.

He sat and played, so little, so white and shining, against the great black grand piano, elect and alone, above that confused sea of faces, above the heavy, insensitive mass soul, upon which he was labouring to work with his individual, differentiated soul. His lock of soft black hair with the white silk bow had fallen over his forehead, his trained and bony little wrists pounded away, the muscles stood out visibly on his brown childish cheeks.

Sitting there he sometimes had moments of oblivion and solitude, when the gaze of his strange little mouselike eyes with the big rings beneath them would lose itself and stare through the painted stage into space that was peopled with strange vague life. Then out of the corner of his eye he would give a quick look back into the hall and be once more with his audience.

"Joy and pain, the heights and the depths—that is my *Fantaisie,*" he thought lovingly. "Listen, here is the C-sharp passage." He lingered over the approach, wondering if they would notice anything. But no, of course not, how should they? And he cast his eyes up prettily at the ceiling so that at least they might have something to look at.

All these people sat there in their regular rows, looking at the prodigy and thinking all sorts of things in their regular brains. An old gentleman with a white beard, a seal ring on his finger and a bulbous swelling on his bald spot, a growth if you like, was thinking to himself: "Really, one ought to be ashamed." He had never got any further than "Ah, thou dearest Augustin" on the piano, and here he sat now, a grey old man, looking on while this little hop-o'-my-thumb performed miracles. Yes, yes, it is a gift of God, we must remember that. God grants His gifts, or He withholds them, and there is no shame in being an ordinary man. Like with the Christ Child.—Before a child one may kneel without feeling ashamed. Strange that thoughts like these should be so satisfying—he would even say so sweet, if it was not too silly for a tough old man like him to use the word. That was how he felt, anyhow.

Art . . . the business man with the parrot-nose was thinking. "Yes, it adds something cheerful to life, a little good white silk and a little tumty-ti-ti-tum. Really he does not play so badly. Fully fifty seats, twelve marks apiece, that makes six hundred marks—and everything else besides. Take off the rent of the hall, the lighting and the programmes, you must have fully a thousand marks profit. That is worth while."

That was Chopin he was just playing, thought the piano teacher, a lady with a pointed nose; she was of an age when the understanding sharpens as the hopes decay. "But not very original—I will say that afterwards, it sounds well. And his hand position is entirely amateur. One must be able to lay a coin on the back of the hand—I would use a ruler on him."

Then there was a young girl, at that self-conscious and chlorotic time of life when the most ineffable ideas come into the mind. She was thinking to herself: "What is it he is playing? It is expressive of passion, yet he is a child. If he kissed me it would be as though my little brother kissed me—no kiss at all. Is there such a thing as passion all by itself, without any earthly object, a sort of child's-play of passion? What nonsense! If I were to say such things aloud they would just be at me with some more cod-liver oil. Such is life."

An officer was leaning against a column. He looked on at Bibi's success and thought: "Yes, you are something and I am something, each in his own way." So he clapped his heels together and paid to the prodigy the respect which he felt to be due to all the powers that be.

Then there was a critic, an elderly man in a shiny black coat and turned-up trousers splashed with mud. He sat in his free seat and thought: "Look at him, this young beggar of a Bibi. As an individual he has still to develop, but as a type he is already quite complete, the artist *par excellence*. He has in himself all the artist's exaltation and his utter worthlessness, his charlatanry and his sacred fire, his burning contempt and his secret raptures. Of course I can't write all that, it is too good. Of course, I should have been an artist myself if I had not seen through the whole business so clearly."

Then the prodigy stopped playing and a perfect storm arose in the hall. He had to come out again and again from behind his screen. The man with the shiny buttons carried up more wreaths: four laurel wreaths, a lyre made of violets, a bouquet of roses. He had not arms enough to convey all these tributes, the impresario himself mounted the stage to help him. He hung a laurel wreath round Bibi's neck, he tenderly stroked the black hair—and suddenly as though overcome he bent down and gave the prodigy a kiss, a resounding kiss, square on the mouth. And then the storm became a hurricane. That kiss ran through the room like an electric shock, it went direct to people's marrow and made them shiver down their backs. They were carried away by a helpless compulsion of sheer noise. Loud shouts mingled with the hysterical clapping of hands. Some of Bibi's commonplace little friends down there waved their handkerchiefs. But the critic thought: "Of course that kiss had to come—it's a good old gag. Yes, good Lord, if only one did not see through everything quite so clearly—"

And so the concert drew to a close. It began at half past seven and finished at half past eight. The platform was laden with wreaths and two little pots of flowers stood on the lamp stands of the piano. Bibi played as his last number his *Rhapsodie grecque,* which turned into the Greek national hymn at the end. His fellow-countrymen in the audience would gladly have sung it with him if the company had not been so august. They made up for it with a powerful noise and hullabaloo, a hot-blooded national demonstration. And the aging critic was thinking: "Yes, the hymn had to come too. They have to exploit every vein—publicity cannot afford to neglect any means to its end. I think I'll criticize that as inartistic. But perhaps I am wrong, perhaps that is the most artistic thing of all. What is the artist? A jack-in-the-box. Criticism is on a higher plane. But I can't say that." And away he went in his muddy trousers.

After being called out nine or ten times the prodigy did not come any more from behind the screen but went to his mother and the impresario down in the hall. The audience stood about among the chairs and applauded and pressed forward to see Bibi close at hand. Some of them wanted to see the princess too. Two dense circles formed, one round the prodigy, the other round the princess, and you could actually not tell which of them was receiving more homage. But the court lady was commanded to go over to Bibi; she smoothed down his silk jacket a bit to make it look suitable for a court function, led him by the arm to the princess, and solemnly indicated to him that he was to kiss the royal hand. "How do you do it, child?" asked the princess. "Does it come into your head of itself when you sit down?" *"Oui, madame,"* answered Bibi. To himself he thought: "Oh, what a stupid old princess!" Then he turned round shyly and uncourtierlike and went back to his family.

Outside in the cloak room there was a crowd. People held up their numbers and received with open arms furs, shawls, and galoshes. Somewhere among her acquaintances the piano teacher stood making her critique. "He is not very original," she said audibly and looked about her.

In front of one of the great mirrors an elegant young lady was being arrayed in her evening cloak and fur shoes by her brothers, two lieutenants. She was exquisitely beautiful, with her steel-blue eyes and her clean-cut, well-bred face. A really noble dame. When she was ready she stood waiting for her brothers. "Don't stand so long in front of the glass, Adolf," she said softly to one of them, who could not tear himself away from the sight of his simple, good-looking young features. But Lieutenant Adolf thinks: What cheek! He would button his overcoat in front of the glass, just the same. Then they went out on the street where the arc lights gleamed cloudily through the white mist. Lieutenant Adolf struck up a little nigger dance on the frozen snow to keep warm, with his hands in his slanting overcoat pockets and his collar turned up.

A girl with untidy hair and swinging arms, accompanied by a gloomy-faced youth, came out just behind them. A child! she thought. A charming child. But in there he was an awe-inspiring . . . and aloud in a toneless voice she said: "We are all infant prodigies, we artists."

"Well, bless my soul!" thought the old gentleman who had never got further than Augustin on the piano, and whose boil was now concealed by a top hat. "What does all that mean? She sounds very oracular." But the gloomy youth understood. He nodded his head slowly.

Then they were silent and the untidy-haired girl gazed after the brothers and sister. She rather despised them, but she looked after them until they had turned the corner.

## *Study questions*

1. *What elements of the perverse are attached to Bibi and his performance?* 2. *Is Bibi's performance the only thing the audience responds to?* 3. *How good is Bibi as pianist? composer? performer? Are the three related?* 4. *What role does the impresario play?* 5. *Do the various members of the audience respond to the art? If not to the art, then to what?* 6. *At the end of the story the girl with the untidy hair says: "We are all infant prodigies." What does she mean? What does Mann mean when he has her say it?* 7. *In terms of this story, what is art?*

*Sherwood Anderson* (1876–1941) was born in Camden, Ohio, the son of a sign painter. He left school at the age of twelve to try to make his own way, worked at odd jobs, mostly as a laborer, then volunteered for the Spanish-American War. Afterward he worked for an advertising agency and managed a paint factory, which he partially owned. During this time he was also trying to write. When frustration became intense, he responded with a nervous breakdown, after which, in 1912, he abandoned his factory and his family, and went to Chicago to devote himself to writing. Two novels and a volume of poems went largely unnoticed before *Winesburg, Ohio* was published in 1919. This collection of short stories, interrelated around the young reporter George Willard and presenting people trapped by repressions and inhibitions and stifled in a small Midwestern town, at once made Anderson famous. There followed other novels, including *Poor White* (1920) and *Dark Laughter* (1925), and such collections of stories as *The Triumph of the Egg* (1921), *Horses and Men* (1923), and *Death in the Woods* (1933). Anderson's most important contribution, however, is to the short story in America: appearing after a period of moribundity, his stories revitalized the form. "Death in the Woods" takes its place among other stories whose myth-making propensities bring them close to legend.

# DEATH IN THE WOODS

## *1*

She was an old woman and lived on a farm near the town in which I lived. All country and small-town people have seen such old women, but no one knows much about them. Such an old woman comes into town driving an old worn-out horse or she comes afoot carrying a basket. She may own a few hens and have eggs to sell. She brings them in a basket and takes them to a grocer. There she trades them in. She gets some salt pork and some beans. Then she gets a pound or two of sugar and some flour.

Afterwards she goes to the butcher's and asks for some dog meat. She may spend ten or fifteen cents, but when she does she asks for something. Formerly the butchers gave liver to anyone who wanted to carry it away. In our family we were always having it. Once one of my brothers got a whole cow's liver at the slaughterhouse near the fairgrounds in our town. We had it until we were sick of it. It never cost a cent. I have hated the thought of it ever since.

The old farm woman got some liver and a soupbone. She never visited with anyone, and as soon as she got what she wanted she lit out for home. It made quite a load for such an old body. No one gave her a lift. People drive right down a road and never notice an old woman like that.

There was such an old woman who used to come into town past our house one summer and fall when I was a young boy and was sick with what was called inflammatory rheumatism. She went home later carrying a heavy pack on her back. Two or three large gaunt-looking dogs followed at her heels.

The old woman was nothing special. She was one of the nameless ones that hardly anyone knows, but she got into my thoughts. I have just suddenly now, after all these years, remembered her and what happened. It is a story. Her name was Grimes, and she lived with her husband and son in a small unpainted house on the bank of a small creek four miles from town.

The husband and son were a tough lot. Although the son was but twenty-one, he had already served a term in jail. It was whispered about that the woman's husband stole horses and ran them off to some other county. Now and then, when a horse turned up missing, the man had also disappeared. No one ever caught him. Once, when I was loafing at Tom Whitehead's livery barn, the man came there and sat on the bench in front. Two or three other men were there, but no one spoke to him. He sat for a few minutes and then got up and went away. When he was leaving he turned around and stared at the men. There was a look of defiance in his eyes. "Well, I have tried to be friendly. You don't want to talk to me. It has been so wherever I have gone in this town. If, some day, one of your fine horses turns up missing, well, then what?" He did not say anything actually. "I'd like to bust one of you on the jaw," was about what his eyes said. I remember how the look in his eyes made me shiver.

The old man belonged to a family that had had money once. His name was Jake Grimes. It all comes back clearly now. His father, John Grimes, had owned a sawmill when the country was new, and had made money. Then he got to drinking and running after women. When he died there wasn't much left.

Jake blew in the rest. Pretty soon there wasn't any more lumber to cut and his land was nearly all gone.

He got his wife off a German farmer, for whom he went to work one June day in the wheat harvest. She was a young thing then and scared to death. You see, the farmer was up to something with the girl—she was, I think, a bound girl and his wife had her suspicions. She took it out on the girl when the man wasn't around. Then, when the wife had to go off to town for supplies, the farmer got after her. She told young Jake that nothing really ever happened, but he didn't know whether to believe it or not.

He got her pretty easy himself, the first time he was out with her. He wouldn't have married her if the German farmer hadn't tried to tell him where to get off. He got her to go riding with him in his buggy one night when he was threshing on the place, and then he came for her the next Sunday night.

She managed to get out of the house without her employer's seeing, but when she was getting into the buggy he showed up. It was almost dark, and he just popped up suddenly at the horse's head. He grabbed the horse by the bridle and Jake got out his buggy whip.

They had it out all right! The German was a tough one. Maybe he didn't care whether his wife knew or not. Jake hit him over the face and shoulders with the buggy whip, but the horse got to acting up and he had to get out.

Then the two men went for it. The girl didn't see it. The horse started to run away and went nearly a mile down the road before the girl got him stopped. Then she managed to tie him to a tree beside the road. (I wonder how I know all this. It must have stuck in my mind from small-town tales when I was a boy.) Jake found her there after he got through with the German. She was huddled up in the buggy seat, crying, scared to death. She told Jake a lot of stuff, how the German had tried to get her, how he chased her once into the barn, how another time, when they happened to be alone in the house together, he tore her dress open clear down the front. The German, she said, might have got her that time if he hadn't heard his old woman drive in at the gate. She had been off to town for supplies. Well, she would be putting the horse in the barn. The German managed to sneak off to the fields without his wife seeing. He told the girl he would kill her if she told. What could she do? She told a lie about ripping her dress in the barn when she was feeding the stock. I remember now that she was a bound girl and did not know where her father and mother were. Maybe she did not have any father. You know what I mean.

Such bound children were often enough cruelly treated. They were children who had no parents, slaves really. There were very few orphan homes then. They were legally bound into some home. It was a matter of pure luck how it came out.

## 2

She married Jake and had a son and a daughter, but the daughter died.

Then she settled down to feed stock. That was her job. At the German's place she had cooked the food for the German and his wife. The wife was a strong woman with big hips and worked most of the time in the fields with her husband. She fed them and fed the cows in the barn, fed the pigs, the horses and the chickens. Every moment of every day, as a young girl, was spent feeding something.

Then she married Jake Grimes and he had to be fed. She was a slight thing, and when she had been married for three or four years, and after the two children were born, her slender shoulders became stooped.

Jake always had a lot of big dogs around the house, that stood near the unused sawmill near the creek. He was always trading horses when he wasn't stealing something and had a lot of poor bony ones about. Also he kept three or four pigs and a cow. They were all pastured in the few acres left of the Grimes place and Jake did little enough work.

He went into debt for a threshing outfit and ran it for several years, but it did not pay. People did not trust him. They were afraid he would steal the grain at night. He had to go a long way off to get work and it cost too much to get there. In the winter he hunted and cut a little firewood, to be sold in some nearby town. When the son grew up he was just like the father. They got drunk together. If there wasn't anything to eat in the house when they came home the old man gave his old woman a cut over the head. She had a few chickens of her own and had to kill one of them in a hurry. When they were all killed she wouldn't have any eggs to sell when she went to town, and then what would she do?

She had to scheme all her life about getting things fed, getting the pigs fed so they would grow fat and could be butchered in the fall. When they were butchered her husband took most of the meat off to town and sold it. If he did not do it first, the boy did. They fought sometimes and when they fought the old woman stood aside trembling.

She had got the habit of silence anyway—that was fixed. Sometimes, when she began to look old—she wasn't forty yet—and when the husband and son were both off, trading horses or drinking or hunting or stealing, she went around the house and the barnyard muttering to herself.

How was she going to get everything fed?—that was her problem. The dogs had to be fed. There wasn't enough hay in the barn for the horses and the cow. If she didn't feed the chickens how could they lay eggs? Without eggs to sell how could she get things in town, things she had to have to keep the life of the farm going? Thank heaven, she did not have to feed her husband—in a certain way. That hadn't lasted long after their marriage and after the babies came. Where he went on his long trips she did not know. Sometimes he was gone from home for weeks, and after the boy grew up they went off together.

They left everything at home for her to manage and she had no money. She knew no one. No one ever talked to her in town. When it was winter she had to gather sticks of wood for her fire, had to try to keep the stock fed with very little grain.

The stock in the barn cried to her hungrily, the dogs followed her about. In the winter the hens laid few enough eggs. They huddled in the corners of the barn and she kept watching them. If a hen lays an egg in the barn in the winter and you do not find it, it freezes and breaks.

One day in winter the old woman went off to town with a few eggs and the dogs followed her. She did not get started until nearly three o'clock and the snow was heavy. She hadn't been feeling very well for several days and so she went muttering along, scantily clad, her shoulders stooped. She had an old grain bag in which she carried her eggs, tucked away down in the bottom. There weren't many of them, but in winter the price of eggs is up. She would get a little meat in exchange for the eggs, some salt pork, a little sugar, and some coffee perhaps. It might be the butcher would give her a piece of liver.

When she had got to town and was trading in her eggs the dogs lay by the door outside. She did pretty well, got the things she needed, more than she had hoped. Then she went to the butcher and he gave her some liver and some dog meat.

It was the first time anyone had spoken to her in a friendly way for a long time. The butcher was alone in his shop when she came in and was annoyed by the thought of such a sick-looking old woman out on such a day. It was bitter cold and the snow, that had let up during the afternoon, was falling again. The butcher said something about her husband and her son, swore at them, and the old woman stared at him, a look of mild surprise in her eyes as he talked. He said that if either the husband or the son were going to get any of the liver or the heavy bones with scraps of meat hanging to them that he had put into the grain bag, he'd see him starve first.

Starve, eh? Well, things had to be fed. Men had to be fed, and the horses that weren't any good but maybe could be traded off, and the poor thin cow that hadn't given any milk for three months.

Horses, cows, pigs, dogs, men.

*3*

The old woman had to get back before darkness came if she could. The dogs followed at her heels, sniffing at the heavy grain bag she had fastened on her back. When she got to the edge of town she stopped by a fence and tied the bag on her back with a piece of rope she had carried in her dress pocket for just that purpose. That was an easier way to carry it. Her arms ached. It was hard when she had to crawl over fences and once she fell over and landed in the snow. The dogs went frisking about. She had to struggle to get to her feet again, but she made it. The point of climbing over the fences was that there was a short cut over a hill and through a woods. She might have gone around by the road, but it was a mile farther that way. She was afraid she couldn't make it. And then, besides, the stock had to be fed. There was a little hay left and a little corn. Perhaps her husband and son would bring some home when they came. They had driven off in the only buggy the Grimes family had, a rickety thing, a rickety horse hitched to the buggy, two other rickety horses led by halters. They were going to trade horses, get a little money if they could. They might come home drunk. It would be well to have something in the house when they came back.

The son had an affair on with a woman at the county seat, fifteen miles away. She was a rough enough woman, a tough one. Once, in the summer, the son had brought her to the house. Both she and the son had been drinking. Jake Grimes was away and the son and his woman ordered the old woman about like a servant. She didn't mind much; she was used to it. Whatever happened she never said anything. That was her way of getting along. She had managed that way when she was a young girl at the German's and ever since she had married Jake. That time her son brought his woman to the house they stayed all night, sleeping together just as though they were married. It hadn't shocked the old woman, not much. She had got past being shocked early in life.

With the pack on her back she went painfully along across an open field, wading in the deep snow, and got into the woods.

There was a path, but it was hard to follow. Just beyond the top of the hill, where the woods was thickest, there was a small clearing. Had someone once thought of building a house there? The clearing was as large as a building lot in town, large enough for a house and a garden. The path ran along the side of the clearing, and when she got there the old woman sat down to rest at the foot of a tree.

It was a foolish thing to do. When she got herself placed, the pack against the tree's trunk, it was nice, but what about getting up again? She worried about that for a moment and then quietly closed her eyes.

She must have slept for a time. When you are about so cold you can't get any colder. The afternoon grew a little warmer and the snow came thicker than ever. Then after a time the weather cleared. The moon even came out.

There were four Grimes dogs that had followed Mrs. Grimes into town, all tall gaunt fellows. Such men as Jake Grimes and his son always kept just such dogs. They kick and abuse them, but they stay. The Grimes dogs, in order to keep from starving, had to do a lot of foraging for themselves, and they had been at it while the old woman slept with her back to the tree at the side of the clearing. They had been chasing rabbits in the woods and in adjoining fields and in their ranging had picked up three other farm dogs.

After a time all the dogs came back to the clearing. They were excited about something. Such nights, cold and clear and with a moon, do things to dogs. It may be that some old instinct, come down from the time when they were wolves and ranged the woods in packs on winter nights, comes back into them.

The dogs in the clearing, before the old woman, had caught two or three rabbits and their immediate hunger had been satisfied. They began to play, running in circles in the clearing. Round and round they ran, each dog's nose at the tail of the next dog. In the clearing, under the snow-laden trees and under the wintry moon they made a strange picture, running thus silently, in a circle their running had beaten in the soft snow. The dogs made no sound. They ran around and around in the circle.

It may have been that the old woman saw them doing that before she died. She may have awakened once or twice and looked at the strange sight with dim old eyes.

She wouldn't be very cold now, just drowsy. Life hangs on a long time. Perhaps the old woman was out of her head. She may have dreamed of her girlhood, at the German's, and before that, when she was a child and before her mother lit out and left her.

Her dreams couldn't have been very pleasant. Not many pleasant things have happened to her. Now and then one of the Grimes dogs left the running circle and came to stand before her. The dog thrust his face close to her face. His red tongue was hanging out.

The running of the dogs may have been a kind of death ceremony. It may have been that the primitive instinct of the wolf, having been aroused in the dogs by the night and the running, made them somehow afraid.

"Now we are no longer wolves. We are dogs, the servants of men. Keep alive, man! When man dies we become wolves again."

When one of the dogs came to where the old woman sat with her back against the tree and thrust his nose close to her face he seemed satisfied and went back to run with the pack. All the Grimes dogs did it at some time during the evening, before she died. I knew all about it afterward, when I grew to be a man, because once in a woods in Illinois, on another winter night, I saw a pack of dogs act just like that. The dogs were waiting for me to die as they had waited for the old woman that night when I was a child, but when it happened to me I was a young man and had no intention whatever of dying.

The old woman died softly and quietly. When she was dead and when one of the Grimes dogs had come to her and had found her dead all the dogs stopped running.

They gathered about her.

Well, she was dead now. She had fed the Grimes dogs when she was alive, what about now?

There was the pack on her back, the grain bag containing the piece of salt pork, the liver the butcher had given her, the dog meat, the soupbones. The butcher in town, having been suddenly overcome with a feeling of pity, had loaded her grain bag heavily. It had been a big haul for the old woman.

It was a big haul for the dogs now.

4

One of the Grimes dogs sprang suddenly out from among the others and began worrying the pack on the old woman's back. Had the dogs really been wolves, that one would have been the leader of the pack. What he did, all the others did.

All of them sank their teeth into the grain bag the old woman had fastened with ropes to her back.

They dragged the old woman's body out into the open clearing. The worn-out dress was quickly torn from her shoulders. When she was found, a day or two later, the dress had been torn from her body clear to the hips, but the dogs had not touched her body. They had got the meat out of the grain bag, that was all. Her body was frozen stiff when it was found, and the shoulders were so narrow and the body so slight that in death it looked like the body of some charming young girl.

Such things happened in towns of the Middle West, on farms near town, when I was a boy. A hunter out after rabbits found the old woman's body and did not touch it. Something, the beaten round path in the little snow-covered clearing, the silence of the place, the place where the dogs had worried the body trying to pull the grain bag away or tear it open—something startled the man and he hurried off to town.

I was in Main Street with one of my brothers who was town newsboy and who was taking the afternoon papers to the stores. It was almost night.

The hunter came into a grocery and told his story. Then he went to a hardware shop and into a drugstore. Men began to gather on the sidewalks. Then they started out along the road to the place in the woods.

My brother should have gone on about his business of distributing papers but he didn't. Everyone was going to the woods. The undertaker went and the town marshal. Several men got on a dray and rode out to where the path left the road and went into the woods, but the horses weren't very sharply shod and slid about on the slippery roads. They made no better time than those of us who walked.

The town marshal was a large man whose leg had been injured in the Civil War. He carried a heavy cane and limped rapidly along the road. My brother and I followed at his heels, and as we went other men and boys joined the crowd.

It had grown dark by the time we got to where the old woman had left the road, but the moon had come out. The marshal was thinking there might have been a murder. He kept asking the hunter questions. The hunter went along with his gun across his shoulders, a dog following at his heels. It isn't often a rabbit hunter has a chance to be so conspicuous. He was taking full advantage of it, leading the procession with the town marshal. "I didn't see any wounds. She was a beautiful young girl. Her face was buried in the snow. No, I didn't know her." As a matter of fact, the hunter had not looked closely at the body. He had been frightened. She might have been murdered and someone might spring out from behind a tree and murder him. In a woods, in the late afternoon, when the trees are all bare and there is white snow on the ground, when all is silent, something creepy steals over the mind and body. If something strange or uncanny has happened in the neighborhood all you think about is getting away from there as fast as you can.

The crowd of men and boys had got to where the old woman had crossed the field and went, following the marshal and the hunter, up the slight incline and into the woods.

My brother and I were silent. He had his bundle of papers in a bag slung across his shoulder. When he got back to town he would have to go on distributing his papers before he went home to supper. If I went along, as he had no doubt already determined I should, we would both be late. Either Mother or our older sister would have to warm our supper.

Well, we would have something to tell. A boy did not get such a chance very often. It was lucky we just happened to go into the grocery when the hunter came in. The hunter was a country fellow. Neither of us had ever seen him before.

Now the crowd of men and boys had got to the clearing. Darkness comes quickly on such winter nights, but the full moon made everything clear. My brother and I stood near the tree beneath which the old woman had died.

She did not look old, lying there in that light, frozen and still. One of the men turned her over in the snow and I saw everything. My body trembled with some strange mystical feeling and so did my brother's. It might have been the cold.

Neither of us had ever seen a woman's body before. It may have been the snow, clinging to the frozen flesh, that made it look so white and lovely, so like marble. No woman had come with the party from town; but one of the men, he was the town blacksmith, took off his overcoat and spread it over her. Then he gathered her into his arms and started off to town, all the others following silently. At that time no one knew who she was.

## *5*

I had seen everything, had seen the oval in the snow, like a miniature race track, where the dogs had run, had seen how the men were mystified, had seen the white bare young-looking shoulders, had heard the whispered comments of the men.

The men were simply mystified. They took the body to the undertaker's, and when the blacksmith, the hunter, the marshal and several others had got inside they closed the door. If Father had been there perhaps he could have got in, but we boys couldn't.

I went with my brother to distribute the rest of the papers and when we got home it was my brother who told the story.

I kept silent and went to bed early. It may have been I was not satisfied with the way he told it.

Later, in the town, I must have heard other fragments of the old woman's story. She was recognized the next day and there was an investigation.

The husband and son were found somewhere and brought to town and there was an attempt to connect them with the woman's death, but it did not work. They had perfect enough alibis.

However, the town was against them. They had to get out. Where they went I never heard.

I remember only the picture there in the forest, the men standing about, the naked girlish-looking figure, face down in the snow, the tracks made by the running dogs and the clear cold winter sky above. White fragments of clouds were drifting across the sky. They went racing across the little open space among the trees.

The scene in the forest had become for me, without my knowing it, the foundation for the real story I am now trying to tell. The fragments, you see, had to be picked up slowly, long afterward.

Things happened. When I was a young man I worked on the farm of a German. The hired girl was afraid of her employer. The farmer's wife hated her.

I saw things at that place. Once later, I had a half-uncanny, mystical adventure with dogs in an Illinois forest on a clear, moonlit winter night. When I was a schoolboy, and on a summer day, I went with a boy friend out along a creek some miles from town and came to the house where the old woman had lived. No one had lived in the house since her death. The doors were broken from the hinges; the window lights were all broken. As the boy and I stood in the road outside, two dogs, just roving farm dogs no doubt, came running around the corner of the house. The dogs were tall, gaunt fellows and came down to the fence and glared through at us, standing in the road.

The whole thing, the story of the old woman's death, was to me as I grew older like music heard from far off. The notes had to be picked up slowly one at a time. Something had to be understood.

The woman who died was one destined to feed animal life. Anyway, that is all she ever did. She was feeding animal life before she was born, as a child, as a young woman working on the farm of the German, after she married, when she grew old, and when she died. She fed animal life in cows, in chickens, in pigs, in horses, in dogs, in men. Her daughter had died in childhood and with her one son she had no articulate relations. On the night when she died she was hurrying homeward, bearing on her body food for animal life.

She died in the clearing in the woods and even after her death continued feeding animal life.

You see, it is likely that when my brother told the story that night when we got home and my mother and sister sat listening I did not think he got the point. He was too young and so was I. A thing so complete has its own beauty.

I shall not try to emphasize the point. I am only explaining why I was dissatisfied then and have been ever since. I speak of that only that you may understand why I have been impelled to try to tell the simple story over again.

## *Study questions*

1. *How much of the story about the old woman does the narrator know and how much does he construct from imagination or related experiences?* 2. *Why is he compelled to tell the story over again? What could be beautiful about the death of the woman? Is the narrator satisfied with his retelling of the story?* 3. *What symbolism is attached to the old woman? to the dogs? to the ritual-like death?* 4. *What is the tone of the story? the mood?* 5. *Justify the use of the point of view used in this story. Is the narrator reliable?*

*James Joyce* (1882–1941) is considered by many people to be the greatest writer of prose fiction in English of this century. His reputation rests on what is basically a small volume of work—a book of short stories and three novels, at least one of which most people find impossible to read. Born in Dublin and educated by the Jesuits, Joyce is a perfect example of the alienated artist. He turned against the church, his family, and his country, leaving Ireland in 1904. The last two thirds of his life was spent in self-imposed exile in Trieste, Zurich, Rome, and Paris. Impoverished and toward the end of his life partially blind, he supported himself as a teacher of languages for the Berlitz schools. Although he was recognized early for his creative genius by a few critics and fellow artists, his great reputation did not come about until after his death. To add to his troubles, he was plagued most of his life by censorship problems and pirated editions of his works. Joyce published a volume of poems, *Chamber Music*, in 1907 and a play, *Exiles*, in 1918, but his reputation rests on his fiction. *Dubliners*, a collection of stories, was completed in 1906 but not published until 1914; *A Portrait of the Artist as a Young Man* was published in 1916, and *Ulysses* in 1922, although the latter novel was banned in England and the United States until the early 1930s. The surreal *Finnegans Wake*, begun in 1922 and published in 1939, completes the corpus of his work. The fifteen stories in *Dubliners* can be read separately and also as a group, since they are interrelated. The surfaces of the stories are realistic; plots are truncated, usually ending on an epiphany—a coming together; and details are heavily symbolic, suggesting meaning on several levels. "An Encounter," "Two Gallants," and "Clay" exhibit the structure of a typical Joyce story.

## AN ENCOUNTER

It was Joe Dillon who introduced the Wild West to us. He had a little library made up of old numbers of *The Union Jack, Pluck* and *The Halfpenny Marvel.* Every evening after school we met in his back garden and arranged Indian battles. He and his fat young brother Leo the idler held the loft of the stable while we tried to carry it by storm; or we fought a pitched battle on the grass. But, however well we fought, we never won siege or battle and all our bouts ended with Joe Dillon's war dance of victory. His parents went to eight-o'clock mass every morning in Gardiner Street and the peaceful odour of Mrs Dillon was prevalent in the hall of the house. But he played too fiercely for us who were younger and more timid. He looked like some kind of an Indian when he capered round the garden, an old tea-cosy on his head, beating a tin with his fist and yelling:

—Ya! yaka, yaka, yaka!

Everyone was incredulous when it was reported that he had a vocation for the priesthood. Nevertheless it was true.

A spirit of unruliness diffused itself among us and, under its influence, differences of culture and constitution were waived. We banded ourselves together, some boldly, some in jest and some almost in fear: and of the number of these latter, the reluctant Indians who were afraid to seem studious or lacking in robustness, I was one. The adventures related in the literature of the Wild West were remote from my nature but, at least, they opened doors of escape. I liked better some American detective stories which were traversed from time to time by unkempt fierce and beautiful girls. Though there was nothing wrong in these stories and though their intention was sometimes literary they were circulated secretly at school. One day when Father Butler was hearing the four pages of Roman History clumsy Leo Dillon was discovered with a copy of *The Halfpenny Marvel.*

—This page or this page? This page? Now, Dillon, up! *Hardly had the day* . . . Go on! What day? *Hardly had the day dawned* . . . Have you studied it? What have you there in your pocket?

Everyone's heart palpitated as Leo Dillon handed up the paper and everyone assumed an innocent face. Father Butler turned over the pages, frowning.

—What is this rubbish? he said. *The Apache Chief!* Is this what you read instead of studying your Roman History? Let me not find any more of this wretched stuff in this college. The man who wrote it, I suppose, was some wretched scribbler that writes these things for a drink. I'm surprised at boys like you, educated, reading such stuff. I could understand it if you were . . . National School boys. Now, Dillon, I advise you strongly, get at your work or . . .

This rebuke during the sober hours of school paled much of the glory of the Wild West for me and the confused puffy face of Leo Dillon awakened one of my consciences. But when the restraining influence of the school was at a distance I began to hunger again for wild sensations, for the escape which those chronicles of disorder alone seemed to offer me. The mimic warfare of the evening became at last as wearisome to me as the routine of school in the morning because I wanted real adventures to happen to myself. But real adventures, I reflected, do not happen to people who remain at home: they must be sought abroad.

The summer holidays were near at hand when I made up my mind to break out of the weariness of school-life for one day at least. With Leo Dillon and a boy named Mahony I planned a day's miching. Each of us saved up sixpence. We were to meet at ten in the morning on the Canal Bridge. Mahony's big sister was to write an excuse for him and Leo Dillon was to tell his brother to say he was sick. We arranged to go along the Wharf Road until we came to the ships, then to cross in the ferryboat and walk out to see the Pigeon House. Leo Dillon was afraid we might meet Father Butler or someone out of the college; but Mahony asked, very sensibly, what would Father Butler be doing out at the Pigeon House. We were reassured: and I brought the first stage of the plot to an end by collecting sixpence from the other two, at the same time showing them my own sixpence. When we were making the last arrangements on the eve we were all vaguely excited. We shook hands, laughing, and Mahony said:

—Till to-morrow, mates.

That night I slept badly. In the morning I was firstcomer to the bridge as I lived nearest. I hid my books in the long grass near the ashpit at the end of the garden where nobody ever came and hurried along the canal bank. It was a mild sunny morning in the first week of June. I sat up on the coping of the bridge admiring my frail canvas shoes which I had diligently pipeclayed overnight and watching the docile horses pulling a tramload of business people up the hill. All the branches of the tall trees which lined the mall were gay with little light green leaves and the sunlight slanted through them on to the water. The granite stone of the bridge was beginning to be warm and I began to pat it with my hands in time to an air in my head. I was very happy.

When I had been sitting there for five or ten minutes I saw Mahony's grey suit approaching. He came up the hill, smiling, and clambered up beside me on the bridge. While we were waiting he brought out the catapult which bulged from his inner pocket and explained some improvements which he had made in it. I asked him why he had brought it and he told me he had brought it to have some gas with the birds. Mahony used slang freely, and spoke of Father Butler as Bunsen Burner. We waited on for a quarter of an hour more but still there was no sign of Leo Dillon. Mahony, at last, jumped down and said:

—Come along. I knew Fatty'd funk it.

—And his sixpence . . . ? I said.

—That's forfeit, said Mahony. And so much the better for us—a bob and a tanner instead of a bob.

We walked along the North Strand Road till we came to the Vitriol Works and then turned to the right along the Wharf Road. Mahony began to play the Indian as soon as we were out of public sight. He chased a crowd of ragged girls, brandishing his unloaded catapult and, when two ragged boys began, out of chivalry, to fling stones at us, he proposed that we should charge them. I objected that the boys were too small, and so we walked on, the ragged troop screaming after us: *Swaddlers! Swaddlers!* thinking that we were Protestants because Mahony, who was dark-complexioned, wore the silver badge of a cricket club in his cap. When we came to the Smoothing Iron we arranged a siege; but it was a failure because you must have at least three. We revenged ourselves on Leo Dillon by saying what a funk he was and guessing how many he would get at three o'clock from Mr Ryan.

We came then near the river. We spent a long time walking about the noisy streets flanked by high stone walls, watching the working of cranes and engines and often being shouted at for our immobility by the drivers of groaning carts. It was noon when we reached the quays and, as all the labourers seemed to be eating their lunches, we bought two big currant buns and sat down to eat them on some metal piping beside the river. We pleased ourselves with the spectacle of Dublin's commerce—the barges signalled from far away by their curls of woolly smoke, the brown fishing fleet beyond Ringsend, the big white sailing-vessel which was being discharged on the opposite quay. Mahony said it would be right skit to run away to sea on one of those big ships and even I, looking at the high masts, saw, or imagined, the geography which had been scantily dosed to me at school gradually taking substance under my eyes. School and home seemed to recede from us and their influences upon us seemed to wane.

We crossed the Liffey in the ferryboat, paying our toll to be transported in the company of two labourers and a little Jew with a bag. We were serious to the point of solemnity, but once during the short voyage our eyes met and we laughed. When we landed we watched the discharging of the graceful threemaster which we had observed from the other quay. Some bystander said that she was a Norwegian vessel. I went to the stern and tried to decipher the legend upon it but, failing to do so, I came back and examined the foreign sailors to see had any of them green eyes for I had some confused notion. . . . The sailors' eyes were blue and grey and even black. The only sailor whose eyes could have been called green was a tall man who amused the crowd on the quay by calling out cheerfully every time the planks fell:

—All right! All right!

When we were tired of this sight we wandered slowly into Ringsend. The day had grown sultry, and in the windows of the grocers' shops musty biscuits lay bleaching. We bought some biscuits and chocolate which we ate sedulously as we wandered through the squalid streets where the families of the fishermen live. We could find no dairy and so we went into a huckster's shop and bought a bottle of raspberry lemonade each. Refreshed by this, Mahony chased a cat down a lane, but the cat escaped into a wide field. We both felt rather tired and when we reached the field we made at once for a sloping bank over the ridge of which we could see the Dodder.

It was too late and we were too tired to carry out our project of visiting the Pigeon House. We had to be home before four o'clock lest our adventure should be discovered. Mahony looked regretfully at his catapult and I had to suggest going home by train before he regained any cheerfulness. The sun went in behind some clouds and left us to our jaded thoughts and the crumbs of our provisions.

There was nobody but ourselves in the field. When we had lain on the bank for some time without speaking I saw a man approaching from the far end of the field. I watched him lazily as I chewed one of those green stems on which girls tell fortunes. He came along by the bank slowly. He walked with one hand upon his hip and in the other hand he held a stick with which he tapped the turf lightly. He was shabbily dressed in a suit of greenish-black and wore what we used to call a jerry hat with a high crown. He seemed to be fairly old for his moustache was ashen-grey. When he passed at our feet he glanced up at us quickly and then continued his way. We followed him with our eyes and saw that when he had gone on for perhaps fifty paces he turned about and began to retrace his steps. He walked towards us very slowly, always tapping the ground with his stick, so slowly that I thought he was looking for something in the grass.

He stopped when he came level with us and bade us good-day. We answered him and he sat down beside us on the slope slowly and with great care. He began to talk of the weather, saying that it would be a very hot summer and adding that the seasons had changed greatly since he was a boy—a long time ago. He said that the happiest time of one's life was undoubtedly one's schoolboy days and that he would give anything to be young again. While he expressed these sentiments which bored us a little we kept silent. Then he began to talk of school and of books. He asked us whether we had read the poetry of Thomas Moore or the works of Sir Walter Scott and Lord Lytton. I pretended that I had read every book he mentioned so that in the end he said:

—Ah, I can see you are a bookworm like myself. Now, he added, pointing to Mahony who was regarding us with open eyes, he is different; he goes in for games.

He said he had all Sir Walter Scott's works and all Lord Lytton's works at home and never tired of reading them. Of course, he said, there were some of Lord Lytton's works which boys couldn't read. Mahony asked why couldn't boys read them—a question which agitated and pained me because I was afraid the man would think I was as stupid as Mahony. The man, however, only smiled. I saw that he had great gaps in his mouth between his yellow teeth. Then he asked us which of us had the most sweethearts. Mahony mentioned lightly that he had three totties. The man asked me how many had I. I answered that I had none. He did not believe me and said he was sure I must have one. I was silent.

—Tell us, said Mahony pertly to the man, how many have you yourself?

The man smiled as before and said that when he was our age he had lots of sweethearts.

—Every boy, he said, has a little sweetheart.

His attitude on this point struck me as strangely liberal in a man of his age. In my heart I thought that what he said about boys and sweethearts was reasonable. But I disliked the words in his mouth and I wondered why he shivered once or twice as if he feared something or felt a sudden chill. As he proceeded I noticed that his accent was good. He began to speak to us about girls, saying what nice soft hair they had and how soft their hands were and how all girls were not so good as they seemed to be if one only knew. There was nothing he liked, he said, so much as looking at a nice young girl, at her nice white hands and her beautiful soft hair. He gave me the impression that he was repeating something which he had learned by heart or that, magnetised by some words of his own speech, his mind was slowly circling round and round in the same orbit. At times he spoke as if he were simply alluding to some fact that everybody knew, and at times he lowered his voice and spoke mysteriously as if he were telling us something secret which he did not wish others to overhear. He repeated his phrases over and over again, varying them and surrounding them with his monotonous voice. I continued to gaze towards the foot of the slope, listening to him.

After a long while his monologue paused. He stood up slowly, saying that he had to leave us for a minute or so, a few minutes, and, without changing the direction of my gaze, I saw him walking slowly away from us towards the near end of the field. We remained silent when he had gone. After a silence of a few minutes I heard Mahony exclaim:

—I say! Look what he's doing!

As I neither answered nor raised my eyes Mahony exclaimed again:

—I say . . . He's a queer old josser!

—In case he asks us for our names, I said, let you be Murphy and I'll be Smith.

We said nothing further to each other. I was still considering whether I would go away or not when the man came back and sat down beside us again. Hardly had he sat down when Mahony, catching sight of the cat which had escaped him, sprang up and pursued her across the field. The man and I watched the chase. The cat escaped once more and Mahony began to throw stones at the wall she had escaladed. Desisting from this, he began to wander about the far end of the field, aimlessly.

After an interval the man spoke to me. He said that my friend was a very rough boy and asked did he get whipped often at school. I was going to reply indignantly that we were not National School boys to be *whipped,* as he called it; but I remained silent. He began to speak on the subject of chastising boys. His mind, as if magnetised again by his speech, seemed to circle slowly round and round its new centre. He said that when boys were that kind they ought to be whipped and well whipped. When a boy was rough and unruly there was nothing would do him any good but a good sound whipping. A slap on the hand or a box on the ear was no good: what he wanted was to get a nice warm whipping. I was surprised at this sentiment and involuntarily glanced up at his face. As I did so I met the gaze of a pair of bottle-green eyes peering at me from under a twitching forehead. I turned my eyes away again.

The man continued his monologue. He seemed to have forgotten his recent liberalism. He said that if ever he found a boy talking to girls or having a girl for a sweetheart he would whip him and whip him; and that would teach him not to be talking to girls. And if a boy had a girl for a sweetheart and told lies about it then he would give him such a whipping as no boy ever got in this world. He said that there was nothing in this world he would like so well as that. He described to me how he would whip such a boy as if he were unfolding some elaborate mystery. He would love that, he said, better than anything in this world; and his voice, as he led me monotonously through the mystery, grew almost affectionate and seemed to plead with me that I should understand him.

I waited till his monologue paused again. Then I stood up abruptly. Lest I should betray my agitation I delayed a few moments pretending to fix my shoe properly and then, saying that I was obliged to go, I bade him good-day. I went up the slope calmly but my heart was beating quickly with fear that he would seize me by the ankles. When I reached the top of the slope I turned round and, without looking at him, called loudly across the field:

—Murphy!

My voice had an accent of forced bravery in it and I was ashamed of my paltry stratagem. I had to call the name again before Mahony saw me and hallooed in answer. How my heart beat as he came running across the field to me! He ran as if to bring me aid. And I was penitent; for in my heart I had always despised him a little.

## *Study questions*

1. *How do the school the boys attend and the war games they play set the stage for the encounter with the mysterious stranger?* 2. *What is significant about the fact that Joe Dillon "had a vocation for the priesthood"?* 3. *Why does Father Butler respond as he does to the book Leo is reading?* 4. *Locate the variations in the color green. How does Joyce use this color in the story?* 5. *Who is the mysterious stranger? What does he represent?* 6. *Who is the protagonist? What is his conflict? How is it resolved?* 7. *Summarize the plot of this story. Does it hold any meaning in itself?*

# TWO GALLANTS

The grey warm evening of August had descended upon the city and a mild warm air, a memory of summer, circulated in the streets. The streets, shuttered for the repose of Sunday, swarmed with a gaily coloured crowd. Like illumined pearls the lamps shone from the summits of their tall poles upon the living texture below which, changing shape and hue unceasingly, sent up into the warm grey evening air an unchanging unceasing murmur.

Two young men came down the hill of Rutland Square. One of them was just bringing a long monologue to a close. The other, who walked on the verge of the path and was at times obliged to step on to the road, owing to his companion's rudeness, wore an amused listening face. He was squat and ruddy. A yachting cap was shoved far back from his forehead and the narrative to which he listened made constant waves of expression break forth over his face from the corners of his nose and eyes and mouth. Little jets of wheezing laughter followed one another out of his convulsed body. His eyes, twinkling with cunning enjoyment, glanced at every moment towards his companion's face. Once or twice he rearranged the light waterproof which he had slung over one shoulder in toreador fashion. His breeches, his white rubber shoes and his jauntily slung waterproof expressed youth. But his figure fell into rotundity at the waist, his hair was scant and grey and his face, when the waves of expression had passed over it, had a ravaged look.

When he was quite sure that the narrative had ended he laughed noiselessly for fully half a minute. Then he said:

—Well! . . . That takes the biscuit!

His voice seemed winnowed of vigour; and to enforce his words he added with humour:

—That takes the solitary, unique, and, if I may so call it, *recherché* biscuit!

He became serious and silent when he had said this. His tongue was tired for he had been talking all the afternoon in a public-house in Dorset Street. Most people considered Lenehan a leech but, in spite of this reputation, his adroitness and eloquence had always prevented his friends from forming any general policy against him. He had a brave manner of coming up to a party of them in a bar and of holding himself nimbly at the borders of the company until he was included in a round. He was a sporting vagrant armed with a vast stock of stories, limericks and riddles. He was insensitive to all kinds of discourtesy. No one knew how he achieved the stern task of living, but his name was vaguely associated with racing tissues.

—And where did you pick her up, Corley? he asked.

Corley ran his tongue swiftly along his upper lip.

—One night, man, he said, I was going along Dame Street and I spotted a fine tart under Waterhouse's clock and said good-night, you know. So we went for a walk round by the canal and she told me she was a slavey in a house in Baggot Street. I put my arm round her and squeezed her a bit that night. Then next Sunday, man, I met her by appointment. We went out to Donnybrook and I brought her into a field there. She told me she used to go with a dairyman.... It was fine, man. Cigarettes every night she'd bring me and paying the tram out and back. And one night she brought me two bloody fine cigars—O, the real cheese, you know, that the old fellow used to smoke.... I was afraid, man, she'd get in the family way. But she's up to the dodge.

—Maybe she thinks you'll marry her, said Lenehan.

—I told her I was out of a job, said Corley. I told her I was in Pim's. She doesn't know my name. I was too hairy to tell her that. But she thinks I'm a bit of class, you know.

Lenehan laughed again, noiselessly.

—Of all the good ones ever I heard, he said, that emphatically takes the biscuit.

Corley's stride acknowledged the compliment. The swing of his burly body made his friend execute a few light skips from the path to the roadway and back again. Corley was the son of an inspector of police and he had inherited his father's frame and gait. He walked with his hands by his sides, holding himself erect and swaying his head from side to side. His head was large, globular and oily; it sweated in all weathers; and his large round hat, set upon it sideways, looked like a bulb which had grown out of another. He always stared straight before him as if he were on parade and, when he wished to gaze after someone in the street, it was necessary for him to move his body from the hips. At present he was about town. Whenever any job was vacant a friend was always ready to give him the hard word. He was often to be seen walking with policemen in plain clothes, talking earnestly. He knew the inner side of all affairs and was fond of delivering final judgments. He spoke without listening to the speech of his companions. His conversation was mainly about himself: what he had said to such a person and what such a person had said to him and what he had said to settle the matter. When he reported these dialogues he aspirated the first letter of his name after the manner of Florentines.

Lenehan offered his friend a cigarette. As the two young men walked on through the crowd Corley occasionally turned to smile at some of the passing girls but Lenehan's gaze was fixed on the large faint moon circled with a double halo. He watched earnestly the passing of the grey web of twilight across its face. At length he said:

—Well . . . tell me, Corley, I suppose you'll be able to pull it off all right, eh?

Corley closed one eye expressively as an answer.

—Is she game for that? asked Lenehan dubiously. You can never know women.

—She's all right, said Corley. I know the way to get around her, man. She's a bit gone on me.

—You're what I call a gay Lothario, said Lenehan. And the proper kind of a Lothario, too!

A shade of mockery relieved the servility of his manner. To save himself he had the habit of leaving his flattery open to the interpretation of raillery. But Corley had not a subtle mind.

—There's nothing to touch a good slavey, he affirmed. Take my tip for it.

—By one who has tried them all, said Lenehan.

—First I used to go with girls, you know, said Corley, unbosoming; girls off the South Circular. I used to take them out, man, on the tram somewhere and pay the tram or take them to a band or a play at the theatre or buy them chocolate and sweets or something that way. I used to spend money on them right enough, he added, in a convincing tone, as if he were conscious of being disbelieved.

But Lenehan could well believe it; he nodded gravely.

—I know that game, he said, and it's a mug's game.

—And damn the thing I ever got out of it, said Corley.

—Ditto here, said Lenehan.

—Only off of one of them, said Corley.

He moistened his upper lip by running his tongue along it. The recollection brightened his eyes. He too gazed at the pale disc of the moon, now nearly veiled, and seemed to meditate.

—She was . . . a bit of all right, he said regretfully.

He was silent again. Then he added:

—She's on the turf now. I saw her driving down Earl Street one night with two fellows with her on a car.

—I suppose that's your doing, said Lenehan.

—There was others at her before me, said Corley philosophically.

This time Lenehan was inclined to disbelieve. He shook his head to and fro and smiled.

—You know you can't kid me, Corley, he said.

—Honest to God! said Corley. Didn't she tell me herself?

Lenehan made a tragic gesture.

—Base betrayer! he said.

As they passed along the railings of Trinity College, Lenehan skipped out into the road and peered up at the clock.

—Twenty after, he said.

—Time enough, said Corley. She'll be there all right. I always let her wait a bit.

Lenehan laughed quietly.

—Ecod! Corley, you know how to take them, he said.

—I'm up to all their little tricks, Corley confessed.

—But tell me, said Lenehan again, are you sure you can bring it off all right? You know it's a ticklish job. They're damn close on that point. Eh? . . . What?

His bright, small eyes searched his companion's face for reassurance. Corley swung his head to and fro as if to toss aside an insistent insect, and his brows gathered.

—I'll pull it off, he said. Leave it to me, can't you?

Lenehan said no more. He did not wish to ruffle his friend's temper, to be sent to the devil and told that his advice was not wanted. A little tact was necessary. But Corley's brow was soon smooth again. His thoughts were running another way.

—She's a fine decent tart, he said, with appreciation; that's what she is.

They walked along Nassau Street and then turned into Kildare Street. Not far from the porch of the club a harpist stood in the roadway, playing to a little ring of listeners. He plucked at the wires heedlessly, glancing quickly from time to time at the face of each new-comer and from time to time, wearily, also, at the sky. His harp too, heedless that her coverings had fallen about her knees, seemed weary alike of the eyes of strangers and of her master's hands. One hand played in the bass the melody of *Silent, O Moyle,* while the other hand careered in the treble after each group of notes. The notes of the air throbbed deep and full.

The two young men walked up the street without speaking, the mournful music following them. When they reached Stephen's Green they crossed the road. Here the noise of trams, the lights and the crowd released them from their silence.

—There she is! said Corley.

At the corner of Hume Street a young woman was standing. She wore a blue dress and a white sailor hat. She stood on the curbstone, swinging a sunshade in one hand. Lenehan grew lively.

—Let's have a squint at her, Corley, he said.

Corley glanced sideways at his friend and an unpleasant grin appeared on his face.

—Are you trying to get inside me? he asked.

—Damn it! said Lenehan boldly, I don't want an introduction. All I want is to have a look at her. I'm not going to eat her.

—O . . . A look at her? said Corley, more amiably. Well . . . I'll tell you what. I'll go over and talk to her and you can pass by.

—Right! said Lenehan.

Corley had already thrown one leg over the chains when Lenehan called out:

—And after? Where will we meet?

—Half ten, answered Corley, bringing over his other leg.

—Where?

—Corner of Merrion Street. We'll be coming back.

—Work it all right now, said Lenehan in farewell.

Corley did not answer. He sauntered across the road swaying his head from side to side. His bulk, his easy pace, and the solid sound of his boots had something of the conqueror in them. He approached the young woman and, without saluting, began at once to converse with her. She swung her sunshade more quickly and executed half turns on her heels. Once or twice when he spoke to her at close quarters she laughed and bent her head.

Lenehan observed them for a few minutes. Then he walked rapidly along beside the chains to some distance and crossed the road obliquely. As he approached Hume Street corner he found the air heavily scented and his eyes made a swift anxious scrutiny of the young woman's appearance. She had her Sunday finery on. Her blue serge skirt was held at the waist by a belt of black leather. The great silver buckle of her belt seemed to depress the centre of her body, catching the light stuff of her white blouse like a clip. She wore a short black jacket with mother-of-pearl buttons and a ragged black boa. The ends of her tulle collarette had been carefully disordered and a big bunch of red flowers was pinned in her bosom, stems upwards. Lenehan's eyes noted approvingly her stout short muscular body. Frank rude health glowed in her face, on her fat red cheeks and in her unabashed blue eyes. Her features were blunt. She had broad nostrils, a straggling mouth which lay open in a contented leer, and two projecting front teeth. As he passed Lenehan took off his cap and, after about ten seconds, Corley returned a salute to the air. This he did by raising his hand vaguely and pensively changing the angle of position of his hat.

Lenehan walked as far as the Shelbourne Hotel where he halted and waited. After waiting for a little time he saw them coming towards him and, when they turned to the right, he followed them, stepping lightly in his white shoes, down one side of Merrion Square. As he walked on slowly, timing his pace to theirs, he watched Corley's head which turned at every moment towards the young woman's face like a big ball revolving on a pivot. He kept the pair in view until he had seen them climbing the stairs of the Donnybrook tram; then he turned about and went back the way he had come.

Now that he was alone his face looked older. His gaiety seemed to forsake him, and, as he came by the railings of the Duke's Lawn, he allowed his hand to run along them. The air which the harpist had played began to control his movements. His softly padded feet played the melody while his fingers swept a scale of variations idly along the railings after each group of notes.

He walked listlessly round Stephen's Green and then down Grafton Street. Though his eyes took note of many elements of the crowd through which he passed they did so morosely. He found trivial all that was meant to charm him and did not answer the glances which invited him to be bold. He knew that he would have to speak a great deal, to invent and to amuse, and his brain and throat were too dry for such a task. The problem of how he could pass the hours till he met Corley again troubled him a little. He could think of no way of passing them but to keep on walking. He turned to the left when he came to the corner of Rutland Square and felt more at ease in the dark quiet street, the sombre look of which suited his mood. He paused at last before the window of a poor-looking shop over which the words *Refreshment Bar* were printed in white letters. On the glass of the window were two flying inscriptions: *Ginger Beer* and *Ginger Ale.* A cut ham was exposed on a great blue dish while near it on a plate lay a segment of very light plum-pudding. He eyed this food earnestly for some time and then, after glancing warily up and down the street, went into the shop quickly.

He was hungry for, except some biscuits which he had asked two grudging curates to bring him, he had eaten nothing since breakfast-time. He sat down at an uncovered wooden table opposite two work-girls and a mechanic. A slatternly girl waited on him.

—How much is a plate of peas? he asked.

—Three halfpence, sir, said the girl.

—Bring me a plate of peas, he said, and a bottle of ginger beer.

He spoke roughly in order to belie his air of gentility for his entry had been followed by a pause of talk. His face was heated. To appear natural he pushed his cap back on his head and planted his elbows on the table. The mechanic and the two work-girls examined him point by point before resuming their conversation in a subdued voice. The girl brought him a plate of hot grocer's peas, seasoned with pepper and vinegar, a fork and his ginger beer. He ate his food greedily and found it so good that he made a note of the shop mentally. When he had eaten all the peas he sipped his ginger beer and sat for some time thinking of Corley's adventure. In his imagination he beheld the pair of lovers walking along some dark road; he heard Corley's voice in deep energetic gallantries and saw again the leer of the young woman's mouth. This vision made him feel keenly his own poverty of purse and spirit. He was tired of knocking about, of pulling the devil by the tail, of shifts and intrigues. He would be thirty-one in November. Would he never get a good job? Would he never have a home of his own? He thought how pleasant it would be to have a warm fire to sit by and a good dinner to sit down to. He had walked the streets long enough with friends and with girls. He knew what those friends were worth: he knew the girls too. Experience had embittered his heart against the world. But all hope had not left him. He felt better after having eaten than he had felt before, less weary of his life, less vanquished in spirit. He might yet be able to settle down in some snug corner and live happily if he could only come across some good simple-minded girl with a little of the ready.

He paid twopence halfpenny to the slatternly girl and went out of the shop to begin his wandering again. He went into Capel Street and walked along towards the City Hall. Then he turned into Dame Street. At the corner of George's Street he met two friends of his and stopped to converse with them. He was glad that he could rest from all his walking. His friends asked him had he seen Corley and what was the latest. He replied that he had spent the day with Corley. His friends talked very little. They looked vacantly after some figures in the crowd and sometimes made a critical remark. One said that he had seen Mac an hour before in Westmoreland Street. At this Lenehan said that he had been with Mac the night before in Egan's. The young man who had seen Mac in Westmoreland Street asked was it true that Mac had won a bit over a billiard match. Lenehan did not know: he said that Holohan had stood them drinks in Egan's.

He left his friends at a quarter to ten and went up George's Street. He turned to the left at the City Markets and walked on into Grafton Street. The crowd of girls and young men had thinned and on his way up the street he heard many groups and couples bidding one another good-night. He went as far as the clock of the College of Surgeons: it was on the stroke of ten. He set off briskly along the northern side of the Green, hurrying for fear Corley should return too soon. When he reached the corner of Merrion Street he took his stand in the shadow of a lamp and brought out one of the cigarettes which he had reserved and lit it. He leaned against the lamp-post and kept his gaze fixed on the part from which he expected to see Corley and the young woman return.

His mind became active again. He wondered had Corley managed it successfully. He wondered if he had asked her yet or if he would leave it to the last. He suffered all the pangs and thrills of his friend's situation as well as those of his own. But the memory of Corley's slowly revolving head calmed him somewhat: he was sure Corley would pull it off all right. All at once the idea struck him that perhaps Corley had seen her home by another way and given him the slip. His eyes searched the street: there was no sign of them. Yet it was surely half-an-hour since he had seen the clock of the College of Surgeons. Would Corley do a thing like that? He lit his last cigarette and began to smoke it nervously. He strained his eyes as each tram stopped at the far corner of the square. They must have gone home by another way. The paper of his cigarette broke and he flung it into the road with a curse.

Suddenly he saw them coming towards him. He started with delight and, keeping close to his lamp-post, tried to read the result in their walk. They were walking quickly, the young woman taking quick short steps, while Corley kept beside her with his long stride. They did not seem to be speaking. An intimation of the result pricked him like the point of a sharp instrument. He knew Corley would fail; he knew it was no go.

They turned down Baggot Street and he followed them at once, taking the other footpath. When they stopped he stopped too. They talked for a few moments and then the young woman went down the steps into the area of a house. Corley remained standing at the edge of the path, a little distance from the front steps. Some minutes passed. Then the hall-door was opened slowly and cautiously. A woman came running down the front steps and coughed. Corley turned and went towards her. His broad figure hid hers from view for a few seconds and then she reappeared running up the steps. The door closed on her and Corley began to walk swiftly towards Stephen's Green.

Lenehan hurried on in the same direction. Some drops of light rain fell. He took them as a warning and, glancing back towards the house which the young woman had entered to see that he was not observed, he ran eagerly across the road. Anxiety and his swift run made him pant. He called out:

—Hallo, Corley!

Corley turned his head to see who had called him, and then continued walking as before. Lenehan ran after him, settling the waterproof on his shoulders with one hand.

—Hallo, Corley! he cried again.

He came level with his friend and looked keenly in his face. He could see nothing there.

—Well? he said. Did it come off?

They had reached the corner of Ely Place. Still without answering Corley swerved to the left and went up the side street. His features were composed in stern calm. Lenehan kept up with his friend, breathing uneasily. He was baffled and a note of menace pierced through his voice.

—Can't you tell us? he said. Did you try her?

Corley halted at the first lamp and stared grimly before him. Then with a grave gesture he extended a hand towards the light and, smiling, opened it slowly to the gaze of his disciple. A small gold coin shone in the palm.

## *Study questions*

1. *This story operates as a microcosm of Irish society. What is the Ireland that Joyce pictures like?* 2. *How is the behavior of the two gallants the antithesis of the conventional pattern of "gallant" behavior?* 3. *Why is Corley described in militaristic terms?* 4. *Lenehan circles around the city. What is the significance of this aimless wandering?* 5. *Locate some of the religious allusions. How do they function?* 6. *Why does Lenehan take such prurient interest in Corley's affair?* 7. *The story ends on an epiphany. How does the ending function to tie together various motifs in the story?*

# CLAY

The matron had given her leave to go out as soon as the women's tea was over and Maria looked forward to the evening out. The kitchen was spick and span: the cook said you could see yourself in the big copper boilers. The fire was nice and bright and on one of the side-tables were four very big barmbracks. These barmbracks seemed uncut; but if you went closer you would see that they had been cut into long thick even slices and were ready to be handed round at tea. Maria had cut them herself.

Maria was a very, very small person indeed but she had a very long nose and a very long chin. She talked a little through her nose, always soothingly: *Yes, my dear,* and *No, my dear.* She was always sent for when the women quarrelled over their tubs and always succeeded in making peace. One day the matron had said to her:

—Maria, you are a veritable peace-maker!

And the sub-matron and two of the Board ladies had heard the compliment. And Ginger Mooney was always saying what she wouldn't do to the dummy who had charge of the irons if it wasn't for Maria. Everyone was so fond of Maria.

The women would have their tea at six o'clock and she would be able to get away before seven. From Ballsbridge to the Pillar, twenty minutes; from the Pillar to Drumcondra, twenty minutes; and twenty minutes to buy the things. She would be there before eight. She took out her purse with the silver clasps and read again the words *A Present from Belfast*. She was very fond of that purse because Joe had brought it to her five years before when he and Alphy had gone to Belfast on a Whit-Monday trip. In the purse were two half-crowns and some coppers. She would have five shillings clear after paying tram fare. What a nice evening they would have, all the children singing! Only she hoped that Joe wouldn't come in drunk. He was so different when he took any drink.

Often he had wanted her to go and live with them; but she would have felt herself in the way (though Joe's wife was ever so nice with her) and she had become accustomed to the life of the laundry. Joe was a good fellow. She had nursed him and Alphy too; and Joe used often say:

—Mamma is mamma but Maria is my proper mother.

After the break-up at home the boys had got her that position in the *Dublin by Lamplight* laundry, and she liked it. She used to have such a bad opinion of Protestants but now she thought they were very nice people, a little quiet and serious, but still very nice people to live with. Then she had her plants in the conservatory and she liked looking after them. She had lovely ferns and wax-plants and, whenever anyone came to visit her, she always gave the visitor one or two slips from her conservatory. There was one thing she didn't like and that was the tracts on the walls; but the matron was such a nice person to deal with, so genteel.

When the cook told her everything was ready she went into the women's room and began to pull the big bell. In a few minutes the women began to come in by twos and threes, wiping their steaming hands in their petticoats and pulling down the sleeves of their blouses over their red steaming arms. They settled down before their huge mugs which the cook and the dummy filled up with hot tea, already mixed with milk and sugar in huge tin cans. Maria superintended the distribution of the barmbrack and saw that every woman got her four slices. There was a great deal of laughing and joking during the meal. Lizzie Fleming said Maria was sure to get the ring and, though Fleming had said that for so many Hallow Eves, Maria had to laugh and say she didn't want any ring or man either; and when she laughed her grey-green eyes sparkled with disappointed shyness and the tip of her nose nearly met the tip of her chin. Then Ginger Mooney lifted up her mug of tea and proposed Maria's health while all the other women clattered with their mugs on the table, and said she was sorry she hadn't a sup of porter to drink it in. And Maria laughed again till the tip of her nose nearly met the tip of her chin and till her minute body nearly shook itself asunder because she knew that Mooney meant well though, of course, she had the notions of a common woman.

But wasn't Maria glad when the women had finished their tea and the cook and the dummy had begun to clear away the tea-things! She went into her little bedroom and, remembering that the next morning was a mass morning, changed the hand of the alarm from seven to six. Then she took off her working skirt and her house-boots and laid her best skirt out on the bed and her tiny dress-boots beside the foot of the bed. She changed her blouse too and, as she stood before the mirror, she thought of how she used to dress for mass on Sunday morning when she was a young girl; and she looked with quaint affection at the diminutive body which she had so often adorned. In spite of its years she found it a nice tidy little body.

When she got outside the streets were shining with rain and she was glad of her old brown raincloak. The tram was full and she had to sit on the little stool at the end of the car, facing all the people, with her toes barely touching the floor. She arranged in her mind all she was going to do and thought how much better it was to be independent and to have your own money in your pocket. She hoped they would have a nice evening. She was sure they would but she could not help thinking what a pity it was Alphy and Joe were not speaking. They were always falling out now but when they were boys together they used to be the best of friends: but such was life.

She got out of her tram at the Pillar and ferreted her way quickly among the crowds. She went into Downes's cakeshop but the shop was so full of people that it was a long time before she could get herself attended to. She bought a dozen of mixed penny cakes, and at last came out of the shop laden with a big bag. Then she thought what else would she buy: she wanted to buy something really nice. They would be sure to have plenty of apples and nuts. It was hard to know what to buy and all she could think of was cake. She decided to buy some plumcake but Downes's plumcake had not enough almond icing on top of it so she went over to a shop in Henry Street. Here she was a long time in suiting herself and the stylish young lady behind the counter, who was evidently a little annoyed by her, asked her was it wedding-cake she wanted to buy. That made Maria blush and smile at the young lady; but the young lady took it all very seriously and finally cut a thick slice of plumcake, parcelled it up and said:

—Two-and-four, please.

She thought she would have to stand in the Drumcondra tram because none of the young men seemed to notice her but an elderly gentleman made room for her. He was a stout gentleman and he wore a brown hard hat; he had a square red face and a greyish moustache. Maria thought he was a colonel-looking gentleman and she reflected how much more polite he was than the young men who simply stared straight before them. The gentleman began to chat with her about Hallow Eve and the rainy weather. He supposed the bag was full of good things for the little ones and said it was only right that the youngsters should enjoy themselves while they were young. Maria agreed with him and favoured him with demure nods and hems. He was very nice with her, and when she was getting out at the Canal Bridge she thanked him and bowed, and he bowed to her and raised his hat and smiled agreeably; and while she was going up along the terrace, bending her tiny head under the rain, she thought how easy it was to know a gentleman even when he has a drop taken.

Everybody said: *O, here's Maria!* when she came to Joe's house. Joe was there, having come home from business, and all the children had their Sunday dresses on. There were two big girls in from next door and games were going on. Maria gave the bag of cakes to the eldest boy, Alphy, to divide and Mrs Donnelly said it was too good of her to bring such a big bag of cakes and made all the children say:

—Thanks, Maria.

But Maria said she had brought something special for papa and mamma, something they would be sure to like, and she began to look for her plumcake. She tried in Downes's bag and then in the pockets of her raincloak and then on the hallstand but nowhere could she find it. Then she asked all the children had any of them eaten it—by mistake, of course—but the children all said no and looked as if they did not like to eat cakes if they were to be accused of stealing. Everybody had a solution for the mystery and Mrs Donnelly said it was plain that Maria had left it behind her in the tram. Maria, remembering how confused the gentleman with the greyish moustache had made her, coloured with shame and vexation and disappointment. At the thought of the failure of her little surprise and of the two and fourpence she had thrown away for nothing she nearly cried outright.

But Joe said it didn't matter and made her sit down by the fire. He was very nice with her. He told her all that went on in his office, repeating for her a smart answer which he had made to the manager. Maria did not understand why Joe laughed so much over the answer he had made but she said that the manager must have been a very overbearing person to deal with. Joe said he wasn't so bad when you knew how to take him, that he was a decent sort so long as you didn't rub him the wrong way. Mrs Donnelly played the piano for the children and they danced and sang. Then the two next-door girls handed round the nuts. Nobody could find the nutcrackers and Joe was nearly getting cross over it and asked how did they expect Maria to crack nuts without a nutcracker. But Maria said she didn't like nuts and that they weren't to bother about her. Then Joe asked would she take a bottle of stout and Mrs Donnelly said there was port wine too in the house if she would prefer that. Maria said she would rather they didn't ask her to take anything: but Joe insisted.

So Maria let him have his way and they sat by the fire talking over old times and Maria thought she would put in a good word for Alphy. But Joe cried that God might strike him stone dead if ever he spoke a word to his brother again and Maria said she was sorry she had mentioned the matter. Mrs Donnelly told her husband it was a great shame for him to speak that way of his own flesh and blood but Joe said that Alphy was no brother of his and there was nearly being a row on the head of it. But Joe said he would not lose his temper on account of the night it was and asked his wife to open some more stout. The two next-door girls had arranged some Hallow Eve games and soon everything was merry again. Maria was delighted to see the children so merry and Joe and his wife in such good spirits. The next-door girls put some saucers on the table and then led the children up to the table, blindfold. One got the prayer-book and the other three got the water; and when one of the next-door girls got the ring Mrs Donnelly shook her finger at the blushing girl as much as to say: *O, I know all about it!* They insisted then on blindfolding Maria and leading her up to the table to see what she would get; and, while they were putting on the bandage, Maria laughed and laughed again till the tip of her nose nearly met the tip of her chin.

They led her up to the table amid laughing and joking and she put her hand out in the air as she was told to do. She moved her hand about here and there in the air and descended on one of the saucers. She felt a soft wet substance with her fingers and was surprised that nobody spoke or took off her bandage. There was a pause for a few seconds; and then a great deal of scuffling and whispering. Somebody said something about the garden, and at last Mrs Donnelly said something very cross to one of the next-door girls and told her to throw it out at once: that was no play. Maria understood that it was wrong that time and so she had to do it over again: and this time she got the prayer-book.

After that Mrs Donnelly played Miss McCloud's Reel for the children and Joe made Maria take a glass of wine. Soon they were all quite merry again and Mrs Donnelly said Maria would enter a convent before the year was out because she had got the prayer-book. Maria had never seen Joe so nice to her as he was that night, so full of pleasant talk and reminiscences. She said they were all very good to her.

At last the children grew tired and sleepy and Joe asked Maria would she not sing some little song before she went, one of the old songs. Mrs Donnelly said *Do, please, Maria!* and so Maria had to get up and stand beside the piano. Mrs Donnelly bade the children be quiet and listen to Maria's song. Then she played the prelude and said *Now, Maria!* and Maria, blushing very much, began to sing in a tiny quavering voice. She sang *I Dreamt that I Dwelt,* and when she came to the second verse she sang again:

*I dreamt that I dwelt in marble halls*
*With vassals and serfs at my side*
*And of all who assembled within those walls*
*That I was the hope and the pride.*
*I had riches too great to count, could boast*
*Of a high ancestral name,*
*But I also dreamt, which pleased me most,*
*That you loved me still the same.*

But no one tried to show her her mistake; and when she had ended her song Joe was very much moved. He said that there was no time like the long ago and no music for him like poor old Balfe, whatever other people might say;

and his eyes filled up so much with tears that he could not find what he was looking for and in the end he had to ask his wife to tell him where the corkscrew was.

## *Study questions*

1. *How does the style Joyce uses in the story help to characterize Maria?* 2. *How does Maria feel about the life she leads? How do our perceptions about Maria's life differ from her perceptions?* 3. *What is the function of the scene in the bakery when the saleslady is rude to Maria?* 4. *What is the function of the scene in the tram? Why does Maria forget the cake she bought?* 5. *How does Maria feel about Joe and his family? How do we know that Joe and his family are going through motions without real feelings for Maria?* 6. *Why does Joyce cause Maria to look like a witch? Is it significant that the action takes place on All Hallows' Eve?* 7. *Locate the number of times in the story that Maria "had" to do something or was "made" to do something. How does this motif relate to the title of the story? What other meanings are attached to clay?* 8. *The second verse of "I Dreamt that I Dwelt" follows. Why does Maria make her mistake? How does the song relate to the story?*

*I dreamt that suitors besought my hand,*
*That knights upon bended knee.*
*And with vows no maiden heart could withstand,*
*That they pledged their faith to me.*
*And I dreamt that one of this noble host*
*Came forth my hand to claim;*
*Yet I also dreamt, which charmed me most,*
*That you lov'd me still the same.*

9. *What is the point of the end of the story?*

*D. H. Lawrence* (1885–1930), a major force in modern British literature, was born in Eastwood, Nottingham, England, the son of a coal miner. As a young man he spent some time as a clerk and taught school briefly before leaving England in 1919 and traveling extensively to, among other places, Italy, Australia, Mexico, the southwest United States, and France, where he died at the age of forty-five of tuberculosis. His most important novels include *Sons and Lovers* (1913), *The Rainbow* (1915), *Women in Love* (1920), and *Lady Chatterley's Lover* (1928). A highly controversial figure because of his graphic presentation of sexual matters and his insistence that a reevaluation of the relationship between the sexes was needed, Lawrence was often bothered by censorship problems. Besides novels, Lawrence wrote poems, plays, travel essays, literary criticism, and, of course, short stories. Indeed, many critics believe that his short stories, as works of art, are superior to his novels, since they are more often characterized by a totality of effect and a tighter structure. Among his best short stories are "The Rocking-Horse Winner," "Wintry Peacock," "Two Blue Birds," "Tickets, Please," "The Shadow in the Rose Garden," and "The Prussian Officer." "The Prussian Officer" is a powerful story showing the effects of sexual repression on two men.

# THE PRUSSIAN OFFICER

## *1*

They had marched more than thirty kilometres since dawn, along the white, hot road where occasional thickets of trees threw a moment of shade, then out into the glare again. On either hand, the valley, wide and shallow, glittered with heat; dark green patches of rye, pale young corn, fallow and meadow and black pine woods spread in a dull, hot diagram under a glistening sky. But right in front the mountains ranged across, pale blue and very still, snow gleaming gently out of the deep atmosphere. And towards the mountains, on and on, the regiment marched between the rye fields and the meadows, between the scraggy fruit trees set regularly on either side the high road. The burnished, dark green rye threw off a suffocating heat, the mountains drew gradually nearer and more distinct. While the feet of the soldiers grew hotter, sweat ran through their hair under their helmets, and their knapsacks could burn no more in contact with their shoulders, but seemed instead to give off a cold, prickly sensation.

He walked on and on in silence, staring at the mountains ahead, that rose sheer out of the land and stood fold behind fold, half earth, half heaven, the heaven, the barrier with slits of soft snow, in the pale, bluish peaks.

He could now walk almost without pain. At the start, he had determined not to limp. It had made him sick to take the first steps, and during the first mile or so, he had compressed his breath, and the cold drops of sweat had stood on his forehead. But he had walked it off. What were they after all but bruises! He had looked at them, as he was getting up: deep bruises on the backs of his thighs. And since he had made his first step in the morning, he had been conscious of them, till now he had a tight, hot place in his chest, with suppressing the pain, and holding himself in. There seemed no air when he breathed. But he walked almost lightly.

The Captain's hand had trembled at taking his coffee at dawn: his orderly saw it again. And he saw the fine figure of the Captain wheeling on horseback at the farmhouse ahead, a handsome figure in pale blue uniform with facings of scarlet, and the metal gleaming on the black helmet and the sword-scabbard, and dark streaks of sweat coming on the silky bay horse. The orderly felt he was connected with that figure moving so suddenly on horseback: he followed it like a shadow, mute and inevitable and damned by it. And the officer was always aware of the tramp of the company behind, the march of his orderly among the men.

The Captain was a tall man of about forty, grey at the temples. He had a handsome, finely knit figure, and was one of the best horsemen in the West. His orderly, having to rub him down, admired the amazing riding-muscles of his loins.

For the rest, the orderly scarcely noticed the officer any more than he noticed himself. It was rarely he saw his master's face: he did not look at it. The Captain had reddish-brown, stiff hair that he wore short upon his skull. His moustache was also cut short and bristly over a full, brutal mouth. His face was rather rugged, the cheeks thin. Perhaps the man was the more handsome for the deep lines in his face, the irritable tension of his brow, which gave him the look of a man who fights with life. His fair eyebrows stood bushy over light blue eyes that were always flashing with cold fire.

He was a Prussian aristocrat, haughty and overbearing. But his mother had been a Polish Countess. Having made too many gambling debts when he was young, he had ruined his prospects in the Army, and remained an infantry captain. He had never married: his position did not allow of it, and no woman had ever moved him to it. His time he spent riding—occasionally he rode one of his own horses at the races—and at the officers' club. Now and then he took himself a mistress. But after such an event, he returned to duty with his brow still more tense, his eyes still more hostile and irritable. With the men, however, he was merely impersonal, though a devil when roused; so that, on the whole, they feared him, but had no great aversion from him. They accepted him as the inevitable.

To his orderly he was at first cold and just and indifferent: he did not fuss over trifles. So that his servant knew practically nothing about him, except just what orders he would give, and how he wanted them obeyed. That was quite simple. Then the change gradually came.

The orderly was a youth of about twenty-two, of medium height, and well built. He had strong, heavy limbs, was swarthy, with a soft, black, young moustache. There was something altogether warm and young about him. He had firmly marked eyebrows over dark, expressionless eyes that seemed never to have thought, only to have received life direct through his senses, and acted straight from instinct.

Gradually the officer had become aware of his servant's young, vigorous, unconscious presence about him. He could not get away from the sense of the youth's person, while he was in attendance. It was like a warm flame upon the older man's tense, rigid body, that had become almost unliving, fixed. There was something so free and self-contained about him, and something in the young fellow's movement, that made the officer aware of him. And this irritated the Prussian. He did not choose to be touched into life by his servant. He might easily have changed his man, but he did not. He now very rarely looked direct at his orderly, but kept his face averted, as if to avoid seeing him. And yet as the young soldier moved unthinking about the apartment, the elder watched him, and would notice the movement of his strong young shoulders under the blue cloth, the bend of his neck. And it irritated him. To see the soldier's young, brown, shapely peasant's hand grasp the loaf or the wine-bottle sent a flash of hate or of anger through the elder man's blood. It was not that the youth was clumsy: it was rather the blind, instinctive sureness of movement of an unhampered young animal that irritated the officer to such a degree.

Once, when a bottle of wine had gone over, and the red gushed out on to the tablecloth, the officer had started up with an oath, and his eyes, bluey like fire, had held those of the confused youth for a moment. It was a shock for the young soldier. He felt something sink deeper, deeper into his soul, where nothing had ever gone before. It left him rather blank and wondering. Some of his natural completeness in himself was gone, a little uneasiness took its place. And from that time an undiscovered feeling had held between the two men.

Henceforward the orderly was afraid of really meeting his master. His subconsciousness remembered those steely blue eyes and the harsh brows, and did not intend to meet them again. So he always stared past his master and avoided him. Also, in a little anxiety, he waited for the three months to have gone, when his time would be up. He began to feel a constraint in the Captain's presence, and the soldier even more than the officer wanted to be left alone, in his neutrality as servant.

He had served the Captain for more than a year, and knew his duty. This he performed easily, as if it were natural to him. The officer and his commands he took for granted, as he took the sun and the rain, and he served as a matter of course. It did not implicate him personally.

But now if he were going to be forced into a personal interchange with his master he would be like a wild thing caught, he felt he must get away.

But the influence of the young soldier's being had penetrated through the officer's stiffened discipline, and perturbed the man in him. He, however, was a gentleman, with long, fine hands and cultivated movements, and was not going to allow such a thing as the stirring of his innate self. He was a man of passionate temper, who had always kept himself suppressed. Occasionally there had been a duel, an outburst before the soldiers. He knew himself to be always on the point of breaking out. But he kept himself hard to the idea of the Service. Whereas the young soldier seemed to live out his warm, full nature, to give it off in his very movements, which had a certain zest, such as wild animals have in free movement. And this irritated the officer more and more.

In spite of himself, the Captain could not regain his neutrality of feeling towards his orderly. Nor could he leave the man alone. In spite of himself, he watched him, gave him sharp orders, tried to take up as much of his time as possible. Sometimes he flew into a rage with the young soldier, and bullied him. Then the orderly shut himself off, as it were out of earshot, and waited, with sullen, flushed face, for the end of the noise. The words never pierced to his intelligence, he made himself, protectively, impervious to the feelings of his master.

He had a scar on his left thumb, a deep seam going across the knuckle. The officer had long suffered from it, and wanted to do something to it. Still it was there, ugly and brutal on the young, brown hand. At last the Captain's reserve gave away. One day, as the orderly was smoothing out the tablecloth, the officer pinned down his thumb with a pencil, asking:

"How did you come by that?"

The young man winced and drew back at attention.

"A wood axe, Herr Hauptmann," he answered.

The officer waited for further explanation. None came. The orderly went about his duties. The elder man was sullenly angry. His servant avoided him. And the next day he had to use all his will-power to avoid seeing the scarred thumb. He wanted to get hold of it and—A hot flame ran in his blood.

He knew his servant would soon be free, and would be glad. As yet, the soldier had held himself off from the elder man. The Captain grew madly irritable. He could not rest when the soldier was away, and when he was present, he glared at him with tormented eyes. He hated those fine black brows over the unmeaning dark eyes, he was infuriated by the free movement of the handsome limbs, which no military discipline could make stiff. And he became harsh and cruelly bullying, using contempt and satire. The young soldier only grew more mute and expressionless.

"What cattle were you bred by, that you can't keep straight eyes? Look me in the eyes when I speak to you."

And the soldier turned his dark eyes to the other's face, but there was no sight in them: he stared with the slightest possible cast, holding back his sight, perceiving the blue of his master's eyes, but receiving no look from them. And the elder man went pale, and his reddish eyebrows twitched. He gave his order, barrenly.

Once he flung a heavy military glove into the young soldier's face. Then he had the satisfaction of seeing the black eyes flare up into his own, like a blaze when straw is thrown on a fire. And he had laughed with a little tremor and a sneer.

But there were only two months more. The youth instinctively tried to keep himself intact: he tried to serve the officer as if the latter were an abstract authority and not a man. All his instinct was to avoid personal contact, even definite hate. But in spite of himself the hate grew, responsive to the officer's passion. However, he put it in the background. When he had left the Army, he could dare acknowledge it. By nature he was active, and had many friends. He thought what amazing good fellows they were. But, without knowing it, he was alone. Now this solitariness was intensified. It would carry him through his term. But the officer seemed to be going irritably insane, and the youth was deeply frightened.

The soldier had a sweetheart, a girl from the mountains, independent and primitive. The two walked together, rather silently. He went with her, not to talk, but to have his arm around her, and for the physical contact. This eased him, made it easier for him to ignore the Captain; for he could rest with her held fast against his chest. And she, in some unspoken fashion, was there for him. They loved each other.

The Captain perceived it, and was mad with irritation. He kept the young man engaged all the evenings long, and took pleasure in the dark look that came on his face. Occasionally, the eyes of the two men met, those of the younger sullen and dark, doggedly unalterable, those of the elder sneering with restless contempt.

The officer tried hard not to admit the passion that had got hold of him. He would not know that his feeling for his orderly was anything but that of a man incensed by his stupid, perverse servant. So, keeping quite justified and conventional in his consciousness, he let the other thing run on. His nerves, however, were suffering. At last he slung the end of a belt in his servant's face. When he saw the youth start back, the pain-tears in his eyes and the blood on his mouth, he had felt at once a thrill of deep pleasure and of shame.

But this, he acknowledged to himself, was a thing he had never done before. The fellow was too exasperating. His own nerves must be going to pieces. He went away for some days with a woman.

It was a mockery of pleasure. He simply did not want the woman. But he stayed on for his time. At the end of it, he came back in an agony of irritation, torment, and misery. He rode all the evening, then came straight into supper. His orderly was out. The officer sat with his long, fine hands lying on the table, perfectly still, and all his blood seemed to be corroding.

At last his servant entered. He watched the strong, easy young figure, the fine eyebrows, the thick black hair. In a week's time the youth had got back his old well-being. The hands of the officer twitched and seemed to be full of mad flame. The young man stood at attention, unmoving, shut off.

The meal went in silence. But the orderly seemed eager. He made a clatter with the dishes.

"Are you in a hurry?" asked the officer, watching the intent, warm face of his servant. The other did not reply.

"Will you answer my question?" said the Captain.

"Yes, sir," replied the orderly, standing with his pile of deep Army plates. The Captain waited, looked at him, then asked again:

"Are you in a hurry?"

"Yes, sir," came the answer, that sent a flash through the listener.

"For what?"

"I was going out, sir."

"I want you this evening."

There was a moment's hesitation. The officer had a curious stiffness of countenance.

"Yes, sir," replied the servant, in his throat.

"I want you tomorrow evening also—in fact, you may consider your evenings occupied, unless I give you leave."

The mouth with the young moustache set close.

"Yes, sir," answered the orderly, loosening his lips for a moment.

He again turned to the door.

"And why have you a piece of pencil in your ear?"

The orderly hesitated, then continued on his way without answering. He set the plates in a pile outside the door, took the stump of pencil from his ear, and put it in his pocket. He had been copying a verse for his sweetheart's birthday card. He returned to finish clearing the table. The officer's eyes were dancing, he had a little, eager smile.

"Why have you a piece of pencil in your ear?" he asked.

The orderly took his hands full of dishes. His master was standing near the great green stove, a little smile on his face, his chin thrust forward. When the young soldier saw him his heart suddenly ran hot. He felt blind. Instead of answering, he turned dazedly to the door. As he was crouching to set down the dishes, he was pitched forward by a kick from behind. The pots went in a stream down the stairs, he clung to the pillar of the banisters. And as he was rising he was kicked heavily again, and again, so that he clung sickly to the post for some moments. His master had gone swiftly into the room and closed the door. The maid-servant downstairs looked up the staircase and made a mocking face at the crockery disaster.

The officer's heart was plunging. He poured himself a glass of wine, part of which he spilled on the floor, and gulped the remainder, leaning against the cool, green stove. He heard his man collecting the dishes from the stairs. Pale, as if intoxicated, he waited. The servant entered again. The Captain's heart gave a pang, as of pleasure, seeing the young fellow bewildered and uncertain on his feet, with pain.

"Schöner!" he said.

The soldier was a little slower in coming to attention.

"Yes, sir!"

The youth stood before him, with pathetic young moustache, and fine eyebrows very distinct on his forehead of dark marble.

"I asked you a question."

"Yes, sir."

The officer's tone bit like acid.

"Why had you a pencil in your ear?"

Again the servant's heart ran hot, and he could not breathe. With dark, strained eyes, he looked at the officer, as if fascinated. And he stood there sturdily planted, unconscious. The withering smile came into the Captain's eyes, and he lifted his foot.

"I—I forgot it—sir," panted the soldier, his dark eyes fixed on the other man's dancing blue ones.

"What was it doing there?"

He saw the young man's breast heaving as he made an effort for words.

"I had been writing."

"Writing what?"

Again the soldier looked him up and down. The officer could hear him panting. The smile came into the blue eyes. The soldier worked his dry throat, but could not speak. Suddenly the smile lit like a flame on the officer's face, and a kick came heavily against the orderly's thigh. The youth moved a pace sideways. His face went dead, with two black, staring eyes.

"Well?" said the officer.

The orderly's mouth had gone dry, and his tongue rubbed in it as on dry brown-paper. He worked his throat. The officer raised his foot. The servant went stiff.

"Some poetry, sir," came the crackling, unrecognizable sound of his voice.

"Poetry, what poetry?" asked the Captain, with a sickly smile.

Again there was the working in the throat. The Captain's heart had suddenly gone down heavily, and he stood sick and tired.

"For my girl, sir," he heard the dry, inhuman sound.

"Oh!" he said, turning away. "Clear the table."

"Click!" went the soldier's throat; then again, "Click!" and then the half-articulate:

"Yes, sir."

The young soldier was gone, looking old, and walking heavily.

The officer, left alone, held himself rigid, to prevent himself from thinking. His instinct warned him that he must not think. Deep inside him was the intense gratification of his passion, still working powerfully. Then there was a counteraction, a horrible breaking down of something inside him, a whole agony of reaction. He stood there for an hour motionless, a chaos of sensations, but rigid with a will to keep blank his consciousness, to prevent his mind grasping. And he held himself so until the worst of the stress had passed, when he began to drink, drank himself to an intoxication, till he slept obliterated. When he woke in the morning he was shaken to the base of his nature. But he had fought off the realization of what he had done. He had prevented his mind from taking it in, had suppressed it along with his instincts, and the conscious man had nothing to do with it. He felt only as after a bout of intoxication, weak, but the affair itself all dim and not to be recovered. Of the drunkenness of his passion he successfully refused remembrance. And when his orderly appeared with coffee, the officer assumed the same self he had had the morning before. He refused the event of the past night—denied it had ever been—and was successful in his denial. He had not done any such thing—not he himself. Whatever there might be, lay at the door of a stupid, insubordinate servant.

The orderly had gone about in a stupor all the evening. He drank some beer because he was parched, but not much, the alcohol made his feeling come back, and he could not bear it. He was dulled, as if nine-tenths of the ordinary man in him were inert. He crawled about disfigured. Still, when he thought of the kicks, he went sick, and when he thought of the threat of more kicking, in the room afterwards, his heart went hot and faint, and he panted, remembering the one that had come. He had been forced to say, "For my girl." He was much too done even to want to cry. His mouth hung slightly open, like an idiot's. He felt vacant, and wasted. So, he wandered at his work, painfully, and very slowly and clumsily, fumbling blindly with the brushes, and finding it difficult, when he sat down, to summon the energy to move again. His limbs, his jaw, were slack and nerveless. But he was very tired. He got to bed at last, and slept inert, relaxed, in a sleep that was rather stupor than slumber, a dead night of stupefaction shot through with gleams of anguish.

In the morning were the manoeuvres. But he woke even before the bugle sounded. The painful ache in his chest, the dryness of his throat, the awful steady feeling of misery made his eyes come awake and dreary at once. He knew, without thinking, what had happened. And he knew that the day had come again, when he must go on with his round. The last bit of darkness was being pushed out of the room. He would have to move his inert body and go on. He was so young, and had known so little trouble, that he was bewildered. He only wished it would stay night, so that he could lie still, covered up by the darkness. And yet nothing would prevent the day from coming, nothing would save him from having to get up and saddle the Captain's horse, and make the Captain's coffee. It was there, inevitable. And then, he thought, it was impossible. Yet they would not leave him free. He must go and take the coffee to the Captain. He was too stunned to understand it. He only knew it was inevitable—inevitable, however long he lay inert.

At last, after heaving at himself, for he seemed to be a mass of inertia, he got up. But he had to force every one of his movements from behind, with his will. He felt lost, and dazed, and helpless. Then he clutched hold of the bed, the pain was so keen. And looking at his thighs, he saw the darker bruises on his swarthy flesh and he knew that, if he pressed one of his fingers on one of the bruises, he should faint. But he did not want to faint—he did not want anybody to know. No one should ever know. It was between him and the Captain. There were only the two people in the world now—himself and the Captain.

Slowly, economically, he got dressed and forced himself to walk. Everything was obscure, except just what he had his hands on. But he managed to get through his work. The very pain revived his dull senses. The worst remained yet. He took the tray and went up to the Captain's room. The officer, pale and heavy, sat at the table. The orderly, as he saluted, felt himself put out of existence. He stood still for a moment submitting to his own nullification—then he gathered himself, seemed to regain himself, and then the Captain began to grow vague, unreal, and the younger soldier's heart beat up. He clung to this situation—that the Captain did not exist—so that he himself might live. But when he saw his officer's hand tremble as he took the coffee, he felt everything falling shattered. And he went away, feeling as if he himself were coming to pieces, disintegrated. And when the Captain was there on horseback, giving orders, while he himself stood, with rifle and knapsack, sick with pain, he felt as if he must shut his eyes—as if he must shut his eyes on everything. It was only the long agony of marching with a parched throat that filled him with one single, sleep-heavy intention: to save himself.

## 2

He was getting used even to his parched throat. That the snowy peaks were radiant among the sky, that the whity-green glacier-river twisted through its pale shoals in the valley below, seemed almost supernatural. But he was going mad with fever and thirst. He plodded on uncomplaining. He did not want to speak, not to anybody. There were two gulls, like flakes of water and snow, over the river. The scent of green rye soaked in sunshine came like a sickness. And the march continued, monotonously, almost like a bad sleep.

At the next farm-house, which stood low and broad near the high road, tubs of water had been put out. The soldiers clustered round to drink. They took off their helmets, and the steam mounted from their wet hair. The Captain sat on horseback, watching. He needed to see his orderly. His helmet threw a dark shadow over his light, fierce eyes, but his moustache and mouth and chin were distinct in the sunshine. The orderly must move under the presence of the figure of the horseman. It was not that he was afraid, or cowed. It was as if he was disembowelled, made empty, like an empty shell. He felt himself as nothing, a shadow creeping under the sunshine. And, thirsty as he was, he could scarcely drink, feeling the Captain near him. He would not take off his helmet to wipe his wet hair. He wanted to stay in shadow, not to be forced into consciousness. Starting, he saw the light heel of the officer prick the belly of the horse; the Captain cantered away, and he himself could relapse into vacancy.

Nothing, however, could give him back his living place in the hot, bright morning. He felt like a gap among it all. Whereas the Captain was prouder, overriding. A hot flash went through the young servant's body. The Captain was firmer and prouder with life, he himself was empty as a shadow. Again the flash went through him, dazing him out. But his heart ran a little firmer.

The company turned up the hill, to make a loop for the return. Below, from among the trees, the farm-bell clanged. He saw the labourers, mowing barefoot at the thick grass, leave off their work and go downhill, their scythes hanging over their shoulders, like long, bright claws curving down behind them. They seemed like dream-people, as if they had no relation to himself. He felt as in a blackish dream: as if all the other things were there and had form, but he himself was only a consciousness, a gap that could think and perceive.

The soldiers were tramping silently up the glaring hillside. Gradually his head began to revolve, slowly, rhythmically. Sometimes it was dark before his eyes, as if he saw this world through a smoked glass, frail shadows and unreal. It gave him a pain in his head to walk.

The air was too scented, it gave no breath. All the lush green-stuff seemed to be issuing its sap, till the air was deathly, sickly with the smell of greenness. There was the perfume of clover, like pure honey and bees. Then there grew a faint acrid tang—they were near the beeches; and then a queer clattering noise, and a suffocating, hideous smell; they were passing a flock of sheep, a shepherd in a black smock, holding his crook. Why should the sheep huddle together under this fierce sun? He felt that the shepherd would not see him, though he could see the shepherd.

At last there was the halt. They stacked rifles in a conical stack, put down their kit in a scattered circle around it, and dispersed a little, sitting on a small knoll high on the hillside. The chatter began. The soldiers were steaming with heat, but were lively. He sat still, seeing the blue mountains rising upon the land, twenty kilometres away. There was a blue fold in the ranges, then out of that, at the foot, the broad, pale bed of the river, stretches of whity-green water between pinkish-grey shoals among the dark pine woods. There it was, spread out a long way off. And it seemed to come downhill, the river. There was a raft being steered, a mile away. It was a strange country. Nearer, a red-roofed, broad farm with white base and square dots of windows crouched beside the wall of beech foliage on the wood's edge. There were long strips of rye and clover and pale green corn. And just at his feet, below the knoll, was a darkish bog, where globe flowers stood breathless still on their slim stalks. And some of the pale gold bubbles were burst, and a broken fragment hung in the air. He thought he was going to sleep.

Suddenly something moved into this coloured mirage before his eyes. The Captain, a small, light-blue and scarlet figure, was trotting evenly between the strips of corn, along the level brow of the hill. And the man making flag-signals was coming on. Proud and sure moved the horseman's figure, the quick, bright thing, in which was concentrated all the light of this morning, which for the rest lay a fragile, shining shadow. Submissive, apathetic, the young soldier sat and stared. But as the horse slowed to a walk, coming up the last steep path, the great flash flared over the body and soul of the orderly. He sat waiting. The back of his head felt as if it were weighted with a heavy piece of fire. He did not want to eat. His hands trembled slightly as he moved them. Meanwhile the officer on horseback was approaching slowly and proudly. The tension grew in the orderly's soul. Then again, seeing the Captain ease himself on the saddle, the flash blazed through him.

The Captain looked at the patch of light blue and scarlet, and dark heads, scattered closely on the hill-side. It pleased him. The command pleased him. And he was feeling proud. His orderly was among them in common subjection. The officer rose a little on his stirrups to look. The young soldier sat with averted, dumb face. The Captain relaxed on his seat. His slim-legged, beautiful horse, brown as a beechnut, walked proudly uphill. The Captain passed into the zone of the company's atmosphere: a hot smell of men, of sweat, of leather. He knew it very well. After a word with the lieutenant, he went a few paces higher, and sat there, a dominant figure, his sweat-marked horse swishing its tail, while he looked down on his men, on his orderly, a nonentity among the crowd.

The young soldier's heart was like fire in his chest, and he breathed with difficulty. The officer, looking downhill, saw three of the young soldiers, two pails of water between them, staggering across a sunny green field. A table had been set up under a tree, and there the slim lieutenant stood, importantly busy.

Then the Captain summoned himself to an act of courage. He called his orderly.

The flame leaped into the young soldier's throat as he heard the command, and he rose blindly, stifled. He saluted, standing below the officer. He did not look up. But there was the flicker in the Captain's voice.

"Go to the inn and fetch me . . ." the officer gave his commands. "Quick!" he added.

At the last word, the heart of the servant leapt with a flash, and he felt the strength come over his body. But he turned in mechanical obedience, and set off at a heavy run downhill, looking almost like a bear, his trousers bagging over his military boots. And the officer watched this blind, plunging run all the way.

But it was only the outside of the orderly's body that was obeying so humbly and mechanically. Inside had gradually accumulated a core into which all the energy of that young life was compact and concentrated. He executed his commission, and plodded quickly back uphill. There was a pain in his head, as he walked, that made him twist his features unknowingly. But hard there in the centre of his chest was himself, himself, firm, and not to be plucked to pieces.

The Captain had gone up into the wood. The orderly plodded through the hot, powerfully smelling zone of the company's atmosphere. He had a curious mass of energy inside him now. The Captain was less real than himself. He approached the green entrance to the wood. There, in the half-shade, he saw the horse standing, the sunshine and the flickering shadow of leaves dancing over his brown body. There was a clearing where timber had lately been felled. Here, in the gold-green shade beside the brilliant cup of sunshine, stood two figures, blue and pink, the bits of pink showing out plainly. The Captain was talking to his lieutenant.

The orderly stood on the edge of the bright clearing, where great trunks of trees, stripped and glistening, lay stretched like naked, brown-skinned bodies. Chips of wood littered the trampled floor, like splashed light, and the bases of the felled trees stood here and there, with their raw, level tops. Beyond was the brilliant, sunlit green of a beech.

"Then I will ride forward," the orderly heard his Captain say. The lieutenant saluted and strode away. He himself went forward. A hot flash passed through his belly, as he tramped towards his officer.

The Captain watched the rather heavy figure of the young soldier stumble forward, and his veins, too, ran hot. This was to be man to man between them. He yielded before the solid, stumbling figure with bent head. The orderly stopped and put the food on a level-sawn tree-base. The Captain watched the glistening, sun-inflamed, naked hands. He wanted to speak to the young soldier but could not. The servant propped a bottle against his thigh, pressed open the cork, and poured out the beer into the mug. He kept his head bent. The Captain accepted the mug.

"Hot!" he said, as if amiably.

The flame sprang out of the orderly's heart, nearly suffocating him.

"Yes, sir," he replied, between shut teeth.

And he heard the sound of the Captain's drinking, and he clenched his fists, such a strong comment came into his wrists. Then came the faint clang of the closing of the pot-lid. He looked up. The Captain was watching him. He glanced swiftly away. Then he saw the officer stoop and take a piece of bread from the tree-base. Again the flash of flame went through the young soldier, seeing the stiff body stoop beneath him, and his hands jerked. He looked away. He could feel the officer was nervous. The bread fell as it was being broken. The officer ate the other piece. The two men stood tense and still, the master laboriously chewing his bread, the servant staring with averted face, his fist clenched.

Then the young soldier started. The officer had pressed open the lid of the mug again. The orderly watched the lid of the mug, and the white hand that clenched the handle, as if he were fascinated. It was raised. The youth followed it with his eyes. And then he saw the thin, strong throat of the elder man moving up and down as he drank, the strong jaw working. And the instinct which had been jerking at the young man's wrists suddenly jerked free. He jumped, feeling as if it were rent in two by a strong flame.

The spur of the officer caught in a tree-root, he went down backwards with a crash, the middle of his back thudding sickeningly against a sharp-edged tree-base, the pot flying away. And in a second the orderly, with serious, earnest young face, and underlip between his teeth, had got his knee in the officer's chest and was pressing the chin backward over the farther edge of the tree-stump, pressing, with all his heart behind in a passion of relief, the tension of his wrists exquisite with relief. And with the base of his palms he shoved at the chin, with all his might. And it was pleasant, too, to have that chin, that hard jaw already slightly rough with beard, in his hands. He did not relax one hair's breadth, but, all the force of all his blood exulting in his thrust, he shoved back the head of the other man, till there was a little "cluck" and a crunching sensation. Then he felt as if his head went to vapour. Heavy convulsions shook the body of the officer, frightening and horrifying the young soldier. Yet it pleased him, too, to repress them. It pleased him to keep his hands pressing back the chin, to feel the chest of the other man yield in expiration to the weight of his strong, young knees, to feel the hard twitchings of the prostrate body jerking his own whole frame, which was pressed down on it.

But it went still. He could look into the nostrils of the other man, the eyes he could scarcely see. How curiously the mouth was pushed out, exaggerating the full lips, and the moustache bristling up from them. Then, with a start, he noticed the nostrils gradually filled with blood. The red brimmed, hesitated, ran over, and went in a thin trickle down the face to the eyes.

It shocked and distressed him. Slowly, he got up. The body twitched and sprawled there, inert. He stood and looked at it in silence. It was a pity *it* was broken. It represented more than the thing which had kicked and bullied him. He was afraid to look at the eyes. They were hideous now, only the whites showing, and the blood running to them. The face of the orderly was drawn with horror at the sight. Well, it was so. In his heart he was satisfied. He had hated the face of the Captain. It was extinguished now. There was a heavy relief in the orderly's soul. That was as it should be. But he could not bear to see the long, military body lying broken over the tree-base, the fine fingers crisped. He wanted to hide it away.

Quickly, busily, he gathered it up and pushed it under the felled tree-trunks, which rested their beautiful, smooth length either end on logs. The face was horrible with blood. He covered it with the helmet. Then he pushed the limbs straight and decent, and brushed the dead leaves off the fine cloth of the uniform. So, it lay quite still in the shadow under there. A little strip of sunshine ran along the breast, from a chink between the logs. The orderly sat by it for a few moments. Here his own life also ended.

Then, through his daze, he heard the lieutenant, in a loud voice, explaining to the men outside the wood, that they were to suppose the bridge on the river below was held by the enemy. Now they were to march to the attack in such and such a manner. The lieutenant had no gift of expression. The orderly, listening from habit, got muddled. And when the lieutenant began it all again he ceased to hear.

He knew he must go. He stood up. It surprised him that the leaves were glittering in the sun, and the chips of wood reflecting white from the ground. For him a change had come over the world. But for the rest it had not—all seemed the same. Only he had left it. And he could not go back. It was his duty to return with the beer-pot and the bottle. He could not. He had left all that. The lieutenant was still hoarsely explaining. He must go, or they would overtake him. And he could not bear contact with anyone now.

He drew his fingers over his eyes, trying to find out where he was. Then he turned away. He saw the horse standing in the path. He went up to it and mounted. It hurt him to sit in the saddle. The pain of keeping his seat occupied him as they cantered through the wood. He would not have minded anything, but he could not get away from the sense of being divided from the others. The path led out of the trees. On the edge of the wood he pulled up and stood watching. There in the spacious sunshine of the valley soldiers were moving in a little swarm. Every now and then, a man harrowing on a strip of fallow shouted to his oxen, at the turn. The village and the white-towered church was small in the sunshine. And he no longer belonged to it—he sat there, beyond, like a man outside in the dark. He had gone out from everyday life into the unknown, and he could not, he even did not want to go back.

Turning from the sun-blazing valley, he rode deep into the wood. Tree-trunks, like people standing grey and still, took no notice as he went. A doe, herself a moving bit of sunshine and shadow, went running through the flecked shade. There were bright green rents in the foliage. Then it was all pine wood, dark and cool. And he was sick with pain, he had an intolerable great pulse in his head, and he was sick. He had never been ill in his life. He felt lost, quite dazed with all this.

Trying to get down from the horse, he fell, astonished at the pain and his lack of balance. The horse shifted uneasily. He jerked its bridle and sent it cantering jerkily away. It was his last connection with the rest of things.

But he only wanted to lie down and not be disturbed. Stumbling through the trees, he came on a quiet place where beeches and pine trees grew on a slope. Immediately he had lain down and closed his eyes, his consciousness went racing on without him. A big pulse of sickness beat in him as if it throbbed through the whole earth. He was burning with dry heat. But he was too busy, too tearingly active in the incoherent race of delirium to observe.

## 3

He came to with a start. His mouth was dry and hard, his heart beat heavily, but he had not the energy to get up. His heart beat heavily. Where was he?—the barracks—at home? There was something knocking. And, making an effort, he looked round—trees, and litter of greenery, and reddish, bright, still pieces of sunshine on the floor. He did not believe he was himself, he did not believe what he saw. Something was knocking. He made a struggle towards consciousness, but relapsed. Then he struggled again. And gradually his surroundings fell into relationship with himself. He knew, and a great pang of fear went through his heart. Somebody was knocking. He could see the heavy, black rags of a fir tree overhead. Then everything went black. Yet he did not believe he had closed his eyes. He had not. Out of the blackness sight slowly emerged again. And someone was knocking. Quickly, he saw the blood-disfigured face of his Captain, which he hated. And he held himself still with horror. Yet, deep inside, he knew that it was so, the Captain should be dead. But the physical delirium got hold of him. Someone was knocking. He lay perfectly still, as if dead, with fear. And he went unconscious.

When he opened his eyes again, he started, seeing something creeping swiftly up a tree-trunk. It was a little bird. And the bird was whistling overhead. Tap-tap-tap—it was the small, quick bird rapping the tree-trunk with its beak, as if its head were a little round hammer. He watched it curiously. It shifted sharply, in its creeping fashion. Then, like a mouse, it slid down the bare trunk. Its swift creeping sent a flash of revulsion through him. He raised his head. It felt a great weight. Then, the little bird ran out of the shadow across a still patch of sunshine, its little head bobbing swiftly, its white legs twinkling brightly for a moment. How neat it was in its build, so compact, with pieces of white on its wings. There were several of them. They were so pretty—but they crept like swift, erratic mice, running here and there among the beech-mast.

He lay down again exhausted, and his consciousness lapsed. He had a horror of the little creeping birds. All his blood seemed to be darting and creeping in his head. And yet he could not move.

He came to with a further ache of exhaustion. There was the pain in his head, and the horrible sickness, and his inability to move. He had never been ill in his life. He did not know where he was or what he was. Probably he had got sunstroke. Or what else?—he had silenced the Captain for ever—some time ago—oh, a long time ago. There had been blood on his face, and his eyes had turned upwards. It was all right, somehow. It was peace. But now he had got beyond himself. He had never been here before. Was it life, or not life? He was by himself. They were in a big, bright place, those others, and he was outside. The town, all the country, a big bright place of light: and he was outside, here, in the darkened open beyond, where each thing existed alone. But they would all have to come out there sometime, those others. Little, and left behind him, they all were. There had been father and mother and sweetheart. What did they all matter? This was the open land.

He sat up. Something scuffled. It was a little brown squirrel running in lovely, undulating bounds over the floor, its red tail completing the undulation of its body—and then, as it sat up, furling and unfurling. He watched it, pleased. It ran on again, friskily, enjoying itself. It flew wildly at another squirrel, and they were chasing each other, and making little scolding, chattering noises. The soldier wanted to speak to them. But only a hoarse sound came out of his throat. The squirrels burst away—they flew up the trees. And then he saw the one peeping round at him, half-way up a tree-trunk. A start of fear went through him, though, in so far as he was conscious, he was amused. It still stayed, its little, keen face staring at him half-way up the tree-trunk, its little ears pricked up, its clawey little hands clinging to the bark, its white breast reared. He started from it in panic.

Struggling to his feet, he lurched away. He went on walking, walking, looking for something—for a drink. His brain felt hot and inflamed for want of water. He stumbled on. Then he did not know anything. He went unconscious as he walked. Yet he stumbled on, his mouth open.

When, to his dumb wonder, he opened his eyes on the world again, he no longer tried to remember what it was. There was thick, golden light behind golden-green glitterings, and tall, grey-purple shafts, and darknesses further off, surrounding him, growing deeper. He was conscious of a sense of arrival. He was amid the reality, on the real, dark bottom. But there was the thirst burning in his brain. He felt lighter, not so heavy. He supposed it was newness. The air was muttering with thunder. He thought he was walking wonderfully swiftly and was coming straight to relief—or was it to water.

Suddenly he stood still with fear. There was a tremendous flare of gold, immense—just a few dark trunks like bars between him and it. All the young level wheat was burnished gold glaring on its silky green. A woman, full-skirted, a black cloth on her head for headdress, was passing like a block of shadow through the glistening green corn, into the full glare. There was a farm, too, pale blue in shadow, and the timber black. And there was a church spire, nearly fused away in the gold. The woman moved on, away from him. He had no language with which to speak to her. She was the bright, solid unreality. She would make a noise of words that would confuse him, and her eyes would look at him without seeing him. She was crossing there to the other side. He stood against a tree.

When at last he turned, looking down the long, bare grove whose flat bed was already filling dark, he saw the mountains in a wonder-light, not far away, and radiant. Behind the soft, grey ridge of the nearest range the further mountains stood golden and pale grey, the snow all radiant like pure, soft gold. So still, gleaming in the sky, fashioned pure out of the ore of the sky, they shone in their silence. He stood and looked at them, his face illuminated. And like the golden, lustrous gleaming of the snow he felt his own thirst bright in him. He stood and gazed, leaning against a tree. And then everything slid away into space.

During the night the lightning fluttered perpetually, making the whole sky white. He must have walked again. The world hung livid round him for moments, fields a level sheen of grey-green light, trees in dark bulk, and the range of clouds black across a white sky. Then the darkness fell like a shutter, and the night was whole. A faint flutter of a half-revealed world, that could not quite leap out of the darkness!—Then there again stood a sweep of pallor for the land, dark shapes looming, a range of clouds hanging overhead. The world was a ghostly shadow, thrown for a moment upon the pure darkness, which returned ever whole and complete.

And the mere delirium of sickness and fever went on inside him—his brain opening and shutting like the night—then sometimes convulsions of terror from something with great eyes that stared round a tree—then the long agony of the march, and the sun decomposing his blood—then the pang of hate for the Captain, followed by a pang of tenderness and ease. But everything was distorted, born of an ache and resolving into an ache.

In the morning he came definitely awake. Then his brain flamed with the sole horror of thirstiness! The sun was on his face, the dew was steaming from his wet clothes. Like one possessed, he got up. There, straight in front of him, blue and cool and tender, the mountains ranged across the pale edge of the morning sky. He wanted them—he wanted them alone—he wanted to leave himself and be identified with them. They did not move, they were still and soft, with white, gentle markings of snow. He stood still, mad with suffering, his hands crisping and clutching. Then he was twisting in a paroxysm on the grass.

He lay still, in a kind of dream of anguish. His thirst seemed to have separated itself from him, and to stand apart, a single demand. Then the pain he felt was another single self. Then there was the clog of his body, another separate thing. He was divided among all kinds of separate beings. There was some strange, agonized connection between them, but they were drawing further apart. Then they would all split. The sun, drilling down on him, was drilling through the bond. Then they would all fall, fall through the everlasting lapse of space. Then again, his consciousness reasserted itself. He roused on to his elbow and stared at the gleaming mountains. There they ranked, all still and wonderful between earth and heaven. He stared till his eyes went black, and the mountains, as they stood in their beauty, so clean and cool, seemed to have it, that which was lost in him.

## 4

When the soldiers found him, three hours later, he was lying with his face over his arm, his black hair giving off heat under the sun. But he was still alive. Seeing the open, black mouth, the young soldiers dropped him in horror.

He died in the hospital at night, without having seen again.

The doctors saw the bruises on his legs, behind, and were silent.

The bodies of the two men lay together, side by side, in the mortuary, the one white and slender, but laid rigidly at rest, the other looking as if every moment it must rouse into life again, so young and unused, from a slumber.

## *Study questions*

1. *How many senses are evoked in the first paragraph? What effect is achieved? Does Lawrence continue with this line of images?* 2. *What is the captain like? the orderly? List their confrontations prior to the murder. Is there a climactic order?* 3. *What kind of conflict is going on between the two men? Why is the military setting significant?* 4. *Why does the orderly kill the captain? How does the immediate setting relate to the murder? What particular actions trigger the murder?* 5. *How does the orderly feel immediately after the murder? later?* 6. *How does the orderly begin to respond to living things?* 7. *What details of the setting let us know that the orderly is moving in and out of consciousness.* 8. *What do the mountains signify? the heat?* 9. *Why does the orderly have to die?* 10. *How does Lawrence handle the chronology of this story? Why?*

*Katherine Mansfield* (1888–1923) was born Kathleen Mansfield Beauchamp in Wellington, New Zealand, and went to England to study music at Queen's College in London, where she stayed for four years. After a brief trip home, where she convinced her father to grant her a small subsidy so that she could live and write in London, she returned to England and took up residence there. Ill most of her adult life, she made frequent trips abroad in search of warm climates. In 1918 she married the noted critic John Middleton Murry. She died of tuberculosis at the age of thirty-five at the Gurdjieff Institute, near Paris, where, ironically, she thought she was at the point of recovery. Mansfield published her first collection of stories, *In a German Pension,* in 1911 but did not receive critical attention until after the publication of *Bliss* in 1920. Other volumes of stories include *The Garden Party* (1922), *The Doves' Nest* (1923), and *Something Childish* (1924). Her complete stories were edited and published by Murry in 1937. A conscious literary artist, Mansfield acknowledged a debt to Chekhov in her *Journal,* which also contains a record of her thoughts on matters of short-story technique. Perhaps because she wrote no novels, her reputation is not nearly so great as Joyce's, but her contribution to the form of the short story is immense. Relatively plotless, her stories record brief experiences in the lives of ordinary people, but by means of repetitive patterns she expands the moments to include all time. "The Wind Blows" uses the wind to concretize an adolescent girl's emotional turmoil as she is swept from girlhood to a time projected in the future. "The Daughters of the Late Colonel" manages through montage patterns to show two women in past, present, and future time. "The Man Without a Temperament" captures the poignancy and frustration of a couple who have no time.

## THE WIND BLOWS

Suddenly—dreadfully—she wakes up. What has happened? Something dreadful has happened. No—nothing has happened. It is only the wind shaking the house, rattling the windows, banging a piece of iron on the roof and making her bed tremble. Leaves flutter past the window, up and away; down in the avenue a whole newspaper wags in the air like a lost kite and falls, spiked on a pine tree. It is cold. Summer is over—it is autumn—everything is ugly. The carts rattle by, swinging from side to side; two Chinamen lollop along under their wooden yokes with the straining vegetable baskets—their pigtails and blue blouses fly out in the wind. A white dog on three legs yelps past the gate. It is all over! What is? Oh, everything! And she begins to plait her hair with shaking fingers, not daring to look in the glass. Mother is talking to grandmother in the hall.

"A perfect idiot! Imagine leaving anything out on the line in weather like this. . . . Now my best little Teneriffe-work teacloth is simply in ribbons. *What* is that extraordinary smell? It's the porridge burning. Oh, heavens—this wind!"

She has a music lesson at ten o'clock. At the thought the minor movement of the Beethoven begins to play in her head, the trills long and terrible like little rolling drums. . . . Marie Swainson runs into the garden next door to pick the "chrysanths" before they are ruined. Her skirt flies up above her waist; she tries to beat it down, to tuck it between her legs while she stoops, but it is no use—up it flies. All the trees and bushes beat about her. She picks as quickly as she can, but she is quite distracted. She doesn't mind what she does—she pulls the plants up by the roots and bends and twists them, stamping her foot and swearing.

"For heaven's sake keep the front door shut! Go round to the back," shouts someone. And then she hears Bogey:

"Mother, you're wanted on the telephone. Telephone, Mother. It's the butcher."

How hideous life is—revolting, simply revolting. . . . And now her hat-elastic's snapped. Of course it would. She'll wear her old tam and slip out the back way. But Mother has seen.

"Matilda. Matilda. Come back im-me-diately! What on earth have you got on your head? It looks like a tea cosy. And why have you got that mane of hair on your forehead."

"I can't come back, Mother. I'll be late for my lesson."

"Come back immediately!"

She won't. She won't. She hates Mother. "Go to hell," she shouts, running down the road.

In waves, in clouds, in big round whirls the dust comes stinging, and with it little bits of straw and chaff and manure. There is a loud roaring sound from the trees in the gardens, and standing at the bottom of the road outside Mr. Bullen's gate she can hear the sea sob: "Ah! . . . Ah! . . . Ah-h!" But Mr. Bullen's drawing-room is as quiet as a cave. The windows are closed, the blinds half pulled, and she is not late. The-girl-before-her has just started playing MacDowell's "To an Iceberg." Mr. Bullen looks over at her and half smiles.

"Sit down," he says. "Sit over there in the sofa corner, little lady."

How funny he is. He doesn't exactly laugh at you . . . but there is just something. . . . Oh, how peaceful it is here. She likes this room. It smells of art serge and stale smoke and chrysanthemums . . . there is a big vase of them on the mantelpiece behind the pale photograph of Rubenstein . . . *à mon ami Robert Bullen*. . . . Over the black glittering piano hangs "Solitude"—a dark tragic woman draped in white, sitting on a rock, her knees crossed, her chin on her hands.

"No, no!" says Mr. Bullen, and he leans over the other girl, puts his arms over her shoulders and plays the passage for her. The stupid—she's blushing! How ridiculous!

Now the-girl-before-her has gone; the front door slams. Mr. Bullen comes back and walks up and down, very softly, waiting for her. What an extraordinary thing. Her fingers tremble so that she can't undo the knot in the music satchel. It's the wind. . . . And her heart beats so hard she feels it must lift her blouse up and down. Mr. Bullen does not say a word. The shabby red piano seat is long enough for two people to sit side by side. Mr. Bullen sits down by her.

"Shall I begin with scales," she asks, squeezing her hands together. "I had some arpeggios, too."

But he does not answer. She doesn't believe he even hears . . . and then suddenly his fresh hand with the ring on it reaches over and opens Beethoven.

"Let's have a little of the old master," he says.

But why does he speak so kindly—so awfully kindly—and as though they had known each other for years and years and knew everything about each other.

He turns the page slowly. She watches his hand—it is a very nice hand and always looks as though it had just been washed.

"Here we are," says Mr. Bullen.

Oh, that kind voice—Oh, that minor movement. Here come the little drums. . . .

"Shall I take the repeat?"

"Yes, dear child."

His voice is far, far too kind. The crotchets and quavers are dancing up and down the stave like little black boys on a fence. Why is he so . . . She will not cry—she has nothing to cry about. . . .

"What is it, dear child?"

Mr. Bullen takes her hands. His shoulder is there—just by her head. She leans on it ever so little, her cheek against the springy tweed.

"Life is so dreadful," she murmurs, but she does not feel it's dreadful at all. He says something about "waiting" and "marking time" and "that rare thing, a woman," but she does not hear. It is so comfortable . . . for ever . . .

Suddenly the door opens and in pops Marie Swainson, hours before her time.

"Take the allegretto a little faster," says Mr. Bullen, and gets up and begins to walk up and down again.

"Sit in the sofa corner, little lady," he says to Marie.

The wind, the wind. It's frightening to be here in her room by herself. The bed, the mirror, the white jug and basin gleam like the sky outside. It's the bed that is frightening. There it lies, sound asleep. . . . Does Mother imagine for one moment that she is going to darn all those stockings knotted up on the quilt like a coil of snakes? She's not. No, Mother. I do not see why I should. . . . The wind—the wind! There's a funny smell of soot blowing down the chimney. Hasn't anyone written poems to the wind? . . . "I bring fresh flowers to the leaves and showers." . . . What nonsense.

"Is that you, Bogey?"

"Come for a walk round the esplanade, Matilda. I can't stand this any longer."

"Right-o. I'll put on my ulster. Isn't it an awful day!" Bogey's ulster is just like hers. Hooking the collar she looks at herself in the glass. Her face is white, they have the same excited eyes and hot lips. Ah, they know those two in the glass. Good-bye, dears; we shall be back soon.

"This is better, isn't it?"

"Hook on," says Bogey.

They cannot walk fast enough. Their heads bent, their legs just touching, they stride like one eager person through the town, down the asphalt zigzag where the fennel grows wild and on to the esplanade. It is dusky—just getting dusky. The wind is so strong that they have to fight their way through it, rocking like two old drunkards. All the poor little pahutukawas on the esplanade are bent to the ground.

"Come on! Come on! Let's get near."

Over by the breakwater the sea is very high. They pull off their hats and her hair blows across her mouth, tasting of salt. The sea is so high that the waves do not break at all; they thump against the rough stone wall and suck up the weedy, dripping steps. A fine spray skims from the water right across the esplanade. They are covered with drops; the inside of her mouth tastes wet and cold.

Bogey's voice is breaking. When he speaks he rushes up and down the scale. It's funny—it makes you laugh—and yet it just suits the day. The wind carries their voices—away fly the sentences like little narrow ribbons.

"Quicker! Quicker!"

It is getting very dark. In the harbour the coal hulks show two lights—one high on a mast, and one from the stern.

"Look, Bogey. Look over there."

A big black steamer with a long loop of smoke streaming, with the portholes lighted, with lights everywhere, is putting out to sea. The wind does not stop her; she cuts through the waves, making for the open gate between the pointed rocks that leads to . . . It's the light that makes her look so awfully beautiful and mysterious. . . . *They* are on board leaning over the rail arm in arm.

". . . Who are they?"

". . . Brother and sister."

"Look, Bogey, there's the town. Doesn't it look small? There's the post office clock chiming for the last time. There's the esplanade where we walked that windy day. Do you remember? I cried at my music lesson that day—how many years ago! Good-bye, little island, good-bye. . . ."

Now the dark stretches a wing over the tumbling water. They can't see those two any more. Good-bye, good-bye. Don't forget. . . . But the ship is gone, now.

The wind—the wind.

## *Study questions*

1. *Analyze the style of the first paragraph. What does it tell us of Matilda's feelings?* 2. *What is Matilda's relationship with her mother? How is it significant?* 3. *How is Mr. Bullen's drawing room different? How does Matilda feel about Mr. Bullen? How does he feel about her? the other girls?* 4. *What is the significance of the painting called "Solitude"? the minor movement of the Beethoven piece? the sob of the sea? Why does Matilda cry at her music lesson?* 5. *Does the mirror function in the story?* 6. *At what point in time does the last episode occur? Explain.* 7. *What is the significance of the steamer putting out to sea, cutting through the waves, making for the open gate between the pointed rocks?* 8. *How old is Matilda? What is her conflict? How does the wind relate to her conflict?*

# THE DAUGHTERS OF THE LATE COLONEL

## 1

The week after was one of the busiest weeks of their lives. Even when they went to bed it was only their bodies that lay down and rested; their minds went on, thinking things out, talking things over, wondering, deciding, trying to remember where . . .

Constantia lay like a statue, her hands by her sides, her feet just overlapping each other, the sheet up to her chin. She stared at the ceiling.

"Do you think father would mind if we gave his top-hat to the porter?"

"The porter?" snapped Josephine. "Why ever the porter? What a very extraordinary idea!"

"Because," said Constantia slowly, "he must often have to go to funerals. And I noticed at—at the cemetery that he only had a bowler." She paused. "I thought then how very much he'd appreciate a top-hat. We ought to give him a present, too. He was always very nice to father."

"But," cried Josephine, flouncing on her pillow and staring across the dark at Constantia, "father's head!" And suddenly, for one awful moment, she nearly giggled. Not, of course, that she felt in the least like giggling. It must have been habit. Years ago, when they had stayed awake at night talking, their beds had simply heaved. And now the porter's head, disappearing, popped out, like a candle, under father's hat. . . . The giggle mounted, mounted; she clenched her hands; she fought it down; she frowned fiercely at the dark and said "Remember" terribly sternly.

"We can decide to-morrow," she sighed.

Constantia had noticed nothing; she sighed.

"Do you think we ought to have our dressing-gowns dyed as well?"

"Black?" almost shrieked Josephine.

"Well, what else?" said Constantia. "I was thinking—it doesn't seem quite sincere, in a way, to wear black out of doors and when we're fully dressed, and then when we're at home—"

"But nobody sees us," said Josephine. She gave the bedclothes such a twitch that both her feet became uncovered, and she had to creep up the pillows to get them well under again.

"Kate does," said Constantia. "And the postman very well might."

Josephine thought of her dark-red slippers, which matched her dressing-gown, and of Constantia's favourite indefinite green ones which went with hers. Black! Two black dressing-gowns and two pairs of black woolly slippers, creeping off to the bathroom like black cats.

"I don't think it's absolutely necessary," said she.

Silence. Then Constantia said, "We shall have to post the papers with the notice in them to-morrow to catch the Ceylon mail. . . . How many letters have we had up till now?"

"Twenty-three."

Josephine had replied to them all, and twenty-three times when she came to "We miss our dear father so much" she had broken down and had to use her handkerchief, and on some of them even to soak up a very light-blue tear with an edge of blotting-paper. Strange! She couldn't have put it on—but twenty-three times. Even now, though, when she said over to herself sadly "We miss our dear father so much" she could have cried if she'd wanted to.

"Have you got enough stamps?" came from Constantia.

"Oh, how can I tell?" said Josephine crossly. "What's the good of asking me that now?"

"I was just wondering," said Constantia mildly.

Silence again. There came a little rustle, a scurry, a hop.

"A mouse," said Constantia.

"It can't be a mouse because there aren't any crumbs," said Josephine.

"But it doesn't know there aren't," said Constantia.

A spasm of pity squeezed her heart. Poor little thing! She wished she'd left a tiny piece of biscuit on the dressing-table. It was awful to think of it not finding anything. What would it do?

"I can't think how they manage to live at all," she said slowly.

"Who?" demanded Josephine.

And Constantia said more loudly than she meant to, "Mice."

Josephine was furious. "Oh, what nonsense, Con!" she said. "What have mice got to do with it? You're asleep."

"I don't think I am," said Constantia. She shut her eyes to make sure. She was.

Josephine arched her spine, pulled up her knees, folded her arms so that her fists came under her ears, and pressed her cheek hard against the pillow.

## *2*

Another thing which complicated matters was they had Nurse Andrews staying on with them that week. It was their own fault; they had asked her. It was Josephine's idea. On the morning—well, on the last morning, when the doctor had gone, Josephine had said to Constantia, "Don't you think it would be rather nice if we asked Nurse Andrews to stay on for a week as our guest?"

"Very nice," said Constantia.

"I thought," went on Josephine quickly, "I should just say this afternoon, after I've paid her, 'My sister and I would be very pleased, after all you've done for us, Nurse Andrews, if you would stay on for a week as our guest.' I'd have to put that in about being our guest in case—"

"Oh, but she could hardly expect to be paid!" cried Constantia.

"One never knows," said Josephine sagely.

Nurse Andrews had, of course, jumped at the idea. But it was a bother. It meant they had to have regular sit-down meals at the proper times, whereas if they'd been alone they could just have asked Kate if she wouldn't have minded bringing them a tray wherever they were. And meal-times now that the strain was over were rather a trial.

Nurse Andrews was simply fearful about butter. Really they couldn't help feeling that about butter, at least, she took advantage of their kindness. And she had that maddening habit of asking for just an inch more bread to finish what she had on her plate, and then, at the last mouthful, absent-mindedly—of course it wasn't absent-mindedly—taking another helping. Josephine got very red when this happened, and she fastened her small, bead-like eyes on the table-cloth as if she saw a minute strange insect creeping through the web of it. But Constantia's long, pale face lengthened and set, and she gazed away—away—far over the desert, to where that line of camels unwound like a thread of wool. . . .

"When I was with Lady Tukes," said Nurse Andrews, "she had such a dainty little contrayvance for the buttah. It was a silvah Cupid balanced on the—on the bordah of a glass dish, holding a tayny fork. And when you wanted some buttah you simply pressed his foot and he bent down and speared you a piece. It was quite a gayme."

Josephine could hardly bear that. But "I think those things are very extravagant" was all she said.

"But whey?" asked Nurse Andrews, beaming through her eye-glasses. "No one, surely, would take more buttah than one wanted—would one?"

"Ring, Con," cried Josephine. She couldn't trust herself to reply.

And proud young Kate, the enchanted princess, came in to see what the old tabbies wanted now. She snatched away their plates of mock something or other and slapped down a white, terrified blancmange.

"Jam, please, Kate," said Josephine kindly.

Kate knelt and burst open the sideboard, lifted the lid of the jam-pot, saw it was empty, put it on the table, and stalked off.

"I'm afraid," said Nurse Andrews a moment later, "there isn't any."

"Oh, what a bother!" said Josephine. She bit her lip. "What had we better do?"

Constantia looked dubious. "We can't disturb Kate again," she said softly.

Nurse Andrews waited, smiling at them both. Her eyes wandered, spying at everything behind her eye-glasses. Constantia in despair went back to her camels. Josephine frowned heavily—concentrated. If it hadn't been for this idiotic woman she and Con would, of course, have eaten their blancmange without. Suddenly the idea came.

"I know," she said. "Marmalade. There's some marmalade in the sideboard. Get it, Con."

"I hope," laughed Nurse Andrews, and her laugh was like a spoon tinkling against a medicine-glass—"I hope it's not very bittah marmalayde."

### *3*

But, after all, it was not long now, and then she'd be gone for good. And there was no getting over the fact that she had been very kind to father. She had nursed him day and night at the end. Indeed, both Constantia and Josephine felt privately she had rather overdone the not leaving him at the very last. For when they had gone in to say good-bye Nurse Andrews had sat beside his bed the whole time, holding his wrist and pretending to look at her watch. It couldn't have been necessary. It was so tactless, too. Supposing father had wanted to say something—something private to them. Not that he had. Oh, far from it! He lay there, purple, a dark, angry purple in the face, and never even looked at them when they came in. Then, as they were standing there, wondering what to do, he had suddenly opened one eye. Oh, what a difference it would have made, what a difference to their memory of him, how much easier to tell people about it, if he had only opened both! But no—one eye only. It glared at them a moment and then . . . went out.

## 4

It had made it very awkward for them when Mr. Farolles, of St. John's, called the same afternoon.

"The end was quite peaceful, I trust?" were the first words he said as he glided towards them through the dark drawing-room.

"Quite," said Josephine faintly. They both hung their heads. Both of them felt certain that eye wasn't at all a peaceful eye.

"Won't you sit down?" said Josephine.

"Thank you, Miss Pinner," said Mr. Farolles gratefully. He folded his coat-tails and began to lower himself into father's armchair, but just as he touched it he almost sprang up and slid into the next chair instead.

He coughed. Josephine clasped her hands; Constantia looked vague.

"I want you to feel, Miss Pinner," said Mr. Farolles, "and you, Miss Constantia, that I'm trying to be helpful. I want to be helpful to you both, if you will let me. These are the times," said Mr. Farolles, very simply and earnestly, "when God means us to be helpful to one another."

"Thank you very much, Mr. Farolles," said Josephine and Constantia.

"Not at all," said Mr. Farolles gently. He drew his kid gloves through his fingers and leaned forward. "And if either of you would like a little Communion, either or both of you, here *and* now, you have only to tell me. A little Communion is often very help—a great comfort," he added tenderly.

But the idea of a little Communion terrified them. What! In the drawing-room by themselves—with no—no altar or anything! The piano would be much to high, thought Constantia, and Mr. Farolles could not possibly lean over it with the chalice. And Kate would be sure to come bursting in and interrupt them, thought Josephine. And supposing the bell rang in the middle? It might be somebody important—about their mourning. Would they get up reverently and go out, or would they have to wait . . . in torture?

"Perhaps you will send round a note by your good Kate if you would care for it later," said Mr. Farolles.

"Oh yes, thank you very much!" they both said.

Mr. Farolles got up and took his black straw hat from the round table.

"And about the funeral," he said softly. "I may arrange that—as your dear father's old friend and yours, Miss Pinner—and Miss Constantia?"

Josephine and Constantia got up too.

"I should like it to be quite simple," said Josephine firmly, "and not too expensive. At the same time, I should like—"

"A good one that will last," thought dreamy Constantia, as if Josephine were buying a nightgown. But of course Josephine didn't say that. "One suitable to our father's position." She was very nervous.

"I'll run round to our good friend Mr. Knight," said Mr. Farolles soothingly. "I will ask him to come and see you. I am sure you will find him very helpful indeed."

*5*

Well, at any rate, all that part of it was over, though neither of them could possibly believe that father was never coming back. Josephine had had a moment of absolute terror at the cemetery, while the coffin was lowered, to think that she and Constantia had done this thing without asking his permission. What would father say when he found out? For he was bound to find out sooner or later. He always did. "Buried. You two girls had me *buried!*" She heard his stick thumping. Oh, what would they say? What possible excuse could they make? It sounded such an appallingly heartless thing to do. Such a wicked advantage to take of a person because he happened to be helpless at the moment. The other people seemed to treat it all as a matter of course. They were strangers; they couldn't be expected to understand that father was the very last person for such a thing to happen to. No, the entire blame for it all would fall on her and Constantia. And the expense, she thought, stepping into the tight-buttoned cab. When she had to show him the bills. What would he say then?

She heard him absolutely roaring, "And do you expect me to pay for this gimcrack excursion of yours?"

"Oh," groaned poor Josephine aloud, "we shouldn't have done it, Con!"

And Constantia, pale as a lemon in all that blackness, said in a frightened whisper, "Done what, Jug?"

"Let them bu-bury father like that," said Josephine, breaking down and crying into her new, queer-smelling mourning handkerchief.

"But what else could we have done?" asked Constantia wonderingly. "We couldn't have kept him, Jug—we couldn't have kept him unburied. At any rate, not in a flat that size."

Josephine blew her nose; the cab was dreadfully stuffy.

"I don't know," she said forlornly. "It is all so dreadful. I feel we ought to have tried to, just for a time at least. To make perfectly sure. One thing's certain"—and her tears sprang out again—"father will never forgive us for this—never!"

*6*

Father would never forgive them. That was what they felt more than ever when, two mornings later, they went into his room to go through his things. They had discussed it quite calmly. It was even down on Josephine's list of things to be done. *Go through father's things and settle about them.* But that was a very different matter from saying after breakfast:

"Well, are you ready, Con?"

"Yes, Jug—when you are."

"Then I think we'd better get it over."

It was dark in the hall. It had been a rule for years never to disturb father in the morning, whatever happened. And now they were going to open the door without knocking even. . . . Constantia's eyes were enormous at the idea; Josephine felt weak in the knees.

"You—you go first," she gasped, pushing Constantia.

But Constantia said, as she always had said on those occasions, "No, Jug, that's not fair. You're eldest."

Josephine was just going to say—what at other times she wouldn't have owned to for the world—what she kept for her very last weapon, "But you're tallest," when they noticed that the kitchen door was open, and there stood Kate. . . .

"Very stiff," said Josephine, grasping the door-handle and doing her best to turn it. As if anything ever deceived Kate!

It couldn't be helped. That girl was . . . Then the door was shut behind them, but—but they weren't in father's room at all. They might have suddenly walked through the wall by mistake into a different flat altogether. Was the door just behind them? They were too frightened to look. Josephine knew that if it was it was holding itself tight shut; Constantia felt that, like the doors in dreams, it hadn't any handle at all. It was the coldness which made it so awful. Or the whiteness—which? Everything was covered. The blinds were down, a cloth hung over the mirror, a sheet hid the bed; a huge fan of white paper filled the fireplace. Constantia timidly put out her hand; she almost expected a snowflake to fall. Josephine felt a queer tingling in her nose, as if her nose was freezing. Then a cab klop-klopped over the cobbles below, and the quiet seemed to shake into little pieces.

"I had better pull up a blind," said Josephine bravely.

"Yes, it might be a good idea," whispered Constantia.

They only gave the blind a touch, but it flew up and the cord flew after, rolling round the blindstick, and the little tassel tapped as if trying to get free. That was too much for Constantia.

"Don't you think—don't you think we might put it off for another day?" she whispered.

"Why?" snapped Josephine, feeling, as usual, much better now that she knew for certain that Constantia was terrified. "It's got to be done. But I do wish you wouldn't whisper, Con."

"I didn't know I was whispering," whispered Constantia.

"And why do you keep on staring at the bed?" said Josephine, raising her voice almost defiantly. "There's nothing *on* the bed."

"Oh, Jug, don't say so!" said poor Connie. "At any rate, not so loudly."

Josephine felt herself that she had gone too far. She took a wide swerve over to the chest of drawers, put out her hand, but quickly drew it back again.

"Connie!" she gasped, and she wheeled round and leaned with her back against the chest of drawers.

"Oh, Jug—what?"

Josephine could only glare. She had the most extraordinary feeling that she had just escaped something simply awful. But how could she explain to Constantia that father was in the chest of drawers? He was in the top drawer with his handkerchiefs and neckties, or in the next with his shirts and pyjamas, or in the lowest of all with his suits. He was watching there, hidden away—just behind the door-handle—ready to spring.

She pulled a funny old-fashioned face at Constantia, just as she used to in the old days when she was going to cry.

"I can't open," she nearly wailed.

"No, don't, Jug," whispered Constantia earnestly. "It's much better not to. Don't let's open anything. At any rate, not for a long time."

"But—but it seems so weak," said Josephine, breaking down.

"But why not be weak for once, Jug?" argued Constantia, whispering quite fiercely. "If it is weak." And her pale stare flew from the locked writing-table—so safe—to the huge glittering wardrobe, and she began to breathe in a queer, panting way. "Why shouldn't we be weak for once in our lives, Jug? It's quite excusable. Let's be weak—be weak, Jug. It's much nicer to be weak than to be strong."

And then she did one of those amazingly bold things that she'd done about twice before in their lives; she marched over to the wardrobe, turned the key, and took it out of the lock. Took it out of the lock and held it up to Josephine, showing Josephine by her extraordinary smile that she knew what she'd done, she'd risked deliberately father being in there among his overcoats.

If the huge wardrobe had lurched forward, had crashed down on Constantia, Josephine wouldn't have been surprised. On the contrary, she would have thought it the only suitable thing to happen. But nothing happened. Only the room seemed quieter than ever, and bigger flakes of cold air fell on Josephine's shoulders and knees. She began to shiver.

"Come, Jug," said Constantia, still with that awful callous smile, and Josephine followed just as she had that last time, when Constantia had pushed Benny into the round pond.

## *7*

But the strain told on them when they were back in the dining-room. They sat down, very shaky, and looked at each other.

"I don't feel I can settle to anything," said Josephine, "until I've had something. Do you think we could ask Kate for two cups of hot water?"

"I really don't see why we shouldn't," said Constantia carefully. She was quite normal again. "I won't ring. I'll go to the kitchen door and ask her."

"Yes, do," said Josephine, sinking down into a chair. "Tell her, just two cups, Con, nothing else—on a tray."

"She needn't even put the jug on, need she?" said Constantia, as though Kate might very well complain if the jug had been there.

"Oh no, certainly not! The jug's not at all necessary. She can pour it direct out of the kettle," cried Josephine, feeling that would be a labour-saving indeed.

Their cold lips quivered at the greenish brims. Josephine curved her small red hands round the cup; Constantia sat up and blew on the wavy stream, making it flutter from one side to the other.

"Speaking of Benny," said Josephine.

And though Benny hadn't been mentioned Constantia immediately looked as though he had.

"He'll expect us to send him something of father's, of course. But it's so difficult to know what to send to Ceylon."

"You mean things get unstuck so on the voyage," murmured Constantia.

"No, lost," said Josephine sharply. "You know there's no post. Only runners."

Both paused to watch a black man in white linen drawers running through the pale fields for dear life, with a large brown-paper parcel in his hands. Josephine's black man was tiny; he scurried along glistening like an ant. But there was something blind and tireless about Constantia's tall, thin fellow, which made him, she decided, a very unpleasant person indeed. . . . On the veranda, dressed all in white and wearing a cork helmet, stood Benny. His right hand shook up and down, as father's did when he was impatient. And behind him, not in the least interested, sat Hilda, the unknown sister-in-law. She swung in a cane rocker and flicked over the leaves of the *Tatler*.

"I think his watch would be the most suitable present," said Josephine.

Constantia looked up; she seemed surprised.

"Oh, would you trust a gold watch to a native?"

"But of course I'd disguise it," said Josephine. "No one would know it was a watch." She liked the idea of having to make a parcel such a curious shape that no one could possibly guess what it was. She even thought for a moment of hiding the watch in a narrow cardboard corset-box that she'd kept by her for a long time, waiting for it to come in for something. It was such beautiful firm cardboard. But, no, it wouldn't be appropriate for this occasion. It had lettering on it: *Medium Women's 28. Extra Firm Busks.* It would be almost too much of a surprise for Benny to open that and find father's watch inside.

"And of course it isn't as though it would be going—ticking, I mean," said Constantia, who was still thinking of the native love of jewellery. "At least," she added, "it would be very strange if after all that time it was."

## *8*

Josephine made no reply. She had flown off on one of her tangents. She had suddenly thought of Cyril. Wasn't it more usual for the only grandson to have the watch? And then dear Cyril was so appreciative, and a gold watch meant so much to a young man. Benny, in all probability, had quite got out of the habit of watches; men so seldom wore waistcoats in those hot climates. Whereas Cyril in London wore them from year's end to year's end. And it would be so nice for her and Constantia, when he came to tea, to know it was there. "I see you've got on grandfather's watch, Cyril." It would be somehow so satisfactory.

Dear boy! What a blow his sweet, sympathetic little note had been! Of course they quite understood; but it was most unfortunate.

"It would have been such a point, having him," said Josephine.

"And he would have enjoyed it so," said Constantia, not thinking what she was saying.

However, as soon as he got back he was coming to tea with his aunties. Cyril to tea was one of their rare treats.

"Now, Cyril, you mustn't be frightened of our cakes. Your Auntie Con and I bought them at Buszard's this morning. We know what a man's appetite is. So don't be ashamed of making a good tea."

Josephine cut recklessly into the rich dark cake that stood for her winter gloves or the soling and heeling of Constantia's only respectable shoes. But Cyril was most unmanlike in appetite.

"I say, Aunt Josephine, I simply can't. I've only just had lunch, you know."

"Oh, Cyril, that can't be true! It's after four," cried Josephine. Constantia sat with her knife poised over the chocolate-roll.

"It is, all the same," said Cyril. "I had to meet a man at Victoria, and he kept me hanging about till . . . there was only time to get lunch and to come on here. And he gave me—phew"—Cyril put his hand to his forehead—"a terrific blow-out," he said.

It was disappointing—to-day of all days. But still he couldn't be expected to know.

"But you'll have a meringue, won't you, Cyril?" said Aunt Josephine. "These meringues were bought specially for you. Your dear father was so fond of them. We were sure you are, too."

"I *am,* Aunt Josephine," cried Cyril ardently. "Do you mind if I take half to begin with?"

"Not at all, dear boy; but we mustn't let you off with that."

"Is your dear father still so fond of meringues?" asked Auntie Con gently. She winced faintly as she broke through the shell of hers.

"Well, I don't quite know, Auntie Con," said Cyril breezily.

At that they both looked up.

"Don't know?" almost snapped Josephine. "Don't know a thing like that about your own father, Cyril?"

"Surely," said Auntie Con softly.

Cyril tried to laugh it off. "Oh, well," he said, "it's such a long time since—" He faltered. He stopped. Their faces were too much for him.

"Even *so,*" said Josephine.

And Auntie Con looked.

Cyril put down his teacup. "Wait a bit," he cried. "Wait a bit, Aunt Josephine. What am I thinking of?"

He looked up. They were beginning to brighten. Cyril slapped his knee.

"Of course," he said, "it was meringues. How could I have forgotten? Yes, Aunt Josephine, you're perfectly right. Father's most frightfully keen on meringues."

They didn't only beam. Aunt Josephine went scarlet with pleasure; Auntie Con gave a deep, deep sigh.

"And now, Cyril, you must come and see father," said Josephine. "He knows you were coming to-day."

"Right," said Cyril, very firmly and heartily. He got up from his chair; suddenly he glanced at the clock.

"I say, Auntie Con, isn't your clock a bit slow? I've got to meet a man at—at Paddington just after five. I'm afraid I shan't be able to stay very long with grandfather."

"Oh, he won't expect you to stay *very* long!" said Aunt Josephine.

Constantia was still gazing at the clock. She couldn't make up her mind if it was fast or slow. It was one or the other, she felt almost certain of that. At any rate, it had been.

Cyril still lingered. "Aren't you coming along, Auntie Con?"

"Of course," said Josephine, "we shall all go. Come on, Con."

### *9*

They knocked at the door, and Cyril followed his aunts into grandfather's hot, sweetish room.

"Come on," said Grandfather Pinner. "Don't hang about. What is it? What've you been up to?"

He was sitting in front of a roaring fire, clasping his stick. He had a thick rug over his knees. On his lap there lay a beautiful pale yellow silk handkerchief.

"It's Cyril, father," said Josephine shyly. And she took Cyril's hand and led him forward.

"Good afternoon, grandfather," said Cyril, trying to take his hand out of Aunt Josephine's. Grandfather Pinner shot his eyes at Cyril in the way he was famous for. Where was Auntie Con? She stood on the other side of Aunt Josephine; her long arms hung down in front of her; her hands were clasped. She never took her eyes off grandfather.

"Well," said Grandfather Pinner, beginning to thump, "what have you got to tell me?"

What had he, what had he got to tell him? Cyril felt himself smiling like a perfect imbecile. The room was stifling, too.

But Aunt Josephine came to his rescue. She cried brightly, "Cyril says his father is still very fond of meringues, father dear."

"Eh?" said Grandfather Pinner, curving his hand like a purple meringue-shell over one ear.

Josephine repeated, "Cyril says his father is still very fond of meringues."

"Can't hear," said old Colonel Pinner. And he waved Josephine away with his stick, then pointed with his stick to Cyril. "Tell me what she's trying to say," he said.

(My God!) "Must I?" said Cyril, blushing and staring at Aunt Josephine.

"Do, dear," she smiled. "It will please him so much."

"Come on, out with it!" cried Colonel Pinner testily, beginning to thump again.

And Cyril leaned forward and yelled, "Father's still very fond of meringues."

At that Grandfather Pinner jumped as though he had been shot.

"Don't shout!" he cried. "What's the matter with the boy? *Meringues!* What about 'em?"

"Oh, Aunt Josephine, must we go on?" groaned Cyril desperately.

"It's quite all right, dear boy," said Aunt Josephine, as though he and she were at the dentist's together. "He'll understand in a minute." And she whispered to Cyril, "He's getting a bit deaf, you know." Then she leaned forward and really bawled at Grandfather Pinner, "Cyril only wanted to tell you, father dear, that *his* father is still very fond of meringues."

Colonel Pinner heard that time, heard and brooded, looking Cyril up and down.

"What an esstrordinary thing!" said old Grandfather Pinner. "What an esstrordinary thing to come all this way here to tell me!"

And Cyril felt it *was.*

"Yes, I shall send Cyril the watch," said Josephine.

"That would be very nice," said Constantia. "I seem to remember last time he came there was some little trouble about the time."

## *10*

Josephine gazed at Constantia; she raised her pale eyebrows until they rippled away into her pale hair. She got up. She said in a very lofty, imposing way, "Do you mind following me into the drawing-room, Constantia? I've something of great importance to discuss with you."

For it was always to the drawing-room they retired when they wanted to talk over Kate.

Josephine closed the door meaningly. "Sit down, Constantia," she said, still

They were interrupted by Kate bursting through the door in her usual fashion, as though she had discovered some secret panel in the wall.

"Fried or boiled?" asked the bold voice.

Fried or boiled? Josephine and Constantia were quite bewildered for the moment. They could hardly take it in.

"Fried or boiled what, Kate?" asked Josephine, trying to begin to concentrate.

Kate gave a loud sniff. "Fish."

"Well, why didn't you say so immediately?" Josephine reproached her gently. "How could you expect us to understand, Kate? There are a great many things in this world, you know, which are fried or boiled." And after such a display of courage she said quite brightly to Constantia, "Which do you prefer, Con?"

"I think it might be nice to have it fried," said Constantia. "On the other hand, of course boiled fish is very nice. I think I prefer both equally well . . . Unless you . . . In that case—"

"I shall fry it," said Kate, and she bounced back, leaving their door open and slamming the door of her kitchen.

Josephine gazed at Constantia; she raised her pale eyebrows until they rippled away into her pale hair. She got up. She said in a very lofty, imposing way, "Do you mind following me into the drawing-room, Constantia? I've something of great importance to discuss with you."

For it was always to the drawing-room they retired when they wanted to talk over Kate.

Josephine closed the door meaningly. "Sit down, Constantia," she said, still very grand. She might have been receiving Constantia for the first time. And Con looked round vaguely for a chair, as though she felt indeed quite a stranger.

"Now the question is," said Josephine, bending forward, "whether we shall keep her or not."

"That is the question," agreed Constantia.

"And this time," said Josephine firmly, "we must come to a definite decision."

Constantia looked for a moment as though she might begin going over all the other times, but she pulled herself together and said, "Yes, Jug."

"You see, Con," explained Josephine, "everything is so changed now." Constantia looked up quickly. "I mean," went on Josephine, "we're not dependent on Kate as we were." And she blushed faintly. "There's not father to cook for."

"That is perfectly true," agreed Constantia. "Father certainly doesn't want any cooking now, whatever else—"

Josephine broke in sharply. "You're not sleepy, are you, Con?"

"Sleepy, Jug?" Constantia was wide-eyed.

"Well, concentrate more," said Josephine sharply, and she returned to the subject. "What it comes to is, if we did"—and this she barely breathed, glancing at the door—"give Kate notice"—she raised her voice again—"we could manage our own food."

"Why not?" cried Constantia. She couldn't help smiling. The idea was so exciting. She clasped her hands. What should we live on, Jug?"

"Oh, eggs in various forms!" said Jug, lofty again. "And, besides, there are all the cooked foods."

"But I've always heard," said Constantia, "they are considered so very expensive."

"Not if one buys them in moderation," said Josephine. But she tore herself away from this fascinating bypath and dragged Constantia after her.

"What we've got to decide now, however, is whether we really do trust Kate or not."

Constantia leaned back. Her flat little laugh flew from her lips.

"Isn't it curious, Jug," she said, "that just on this one subject I've never been able to quite make up my mind?"

## 11

She never had. The whole difficulty was to prove anything. How did one prove things, how could one? Suppose Kate had stood in front of her and deliberately made a face. Mightn't she very well have been in pain? Wasn't it impossible, at any rate, to ask Kate if she was making a face at her? If Kate answered "No"—and of course she would say "No"—what a position! How undignified! Then again Constantia suspected, she was almost certain that Kate went to her chest of drawers when she and Josephine were out, not to take things but to spy. Many times she had come back to find her amethyst cross in the most unlikely places, under her lace ties or on top of her evening Bertha. More than once she had laid a trap for Kate. She had arranged things in a special order and then called Josephine to witness.

"You see, Jug?"

"Quite, Con."

"Now we shall be able to tell."

But, oh dear, when she did go to look, she was as far off from a proof as ever! If anything was displaced, it might so very well have happened as she closed the drawer; a jolt might have done it so easily.

"You come, Jug, and decide. I really can't. It's too difficult."

But after a pause and a long glare Josephine would sigh, "Now you've put the doubt into my mind, Con, I'm sure I can't tell myself."

"Well, we can't postpone it again," said Josephine. "If we postpone it this time—"

*12*

But at that moment in the street below a barrel-organ struck up. Josephine and Constantia sprang to their feet together.

"Run, Con," said Josephine. "Run quickly. There's sixpence on the—"

Then they remembered. It didn't matter. They would never have to stop the organ-grinder again. Never again would she and Constantia be told to make that monkey take his noise somewhere else. Never would sound that loud, strange bellow when father thought they were not hurrying enough. The organ-grinder might play there all day and the stick would not thump.

*It never will thump again,*
*It never will thump again,*

played the barrel-organ.

What was Constantia thinking? She had such a strange smile; she looked different. She couldn't be going to cry.

"Jug, Jug," said Constantia softly, pressing her hands together. "Do you know what day it is? It's Saturday. It's a week to-day, a whole week."

*A week since father died,*
*A week since father died,*

cried the barrel-organ. And Josephine, too, forgot to be practical and sensible; she smiled faintly, strangely. On the Indian carpet there fell a square of sunlight, pale red; it came and went and came—and stayed, deepened—until it shone almost golden.

"The sun's out," said Josephine, as though it really mattered.

A perfect fountain of bubbling notes shook from the barrel-organ, round, bright notes, carelessly scattered.

Constantia lifted her big, cold hands as if to catch them, and then her hands fell again. She walked over to the mantelpiece to her favourite Buddha. And the stone and gilt image, whose smile always gave her such a queer feeling, almost a pain and yet a pleasant pain, seemed to-day to be more than smiling. He knew something; he had a secret. "I know something that you don't know," said her Buddha. Oh, what was it, what could it be? And yet she had always felt there was . . . something.

The sunlight pressed through the windows, thieved its way in, flashed its light over the furniture and the photographs. Josephine watched it. When it came to mother's photograph, the enlargement over the piano, it lingered as though puzzled to find so little remained of mother, except the earrings shaped like tiny pagodas and a black feather boa. Why did the photographs of dead people always fade so? wondered Josephine. As soon as a person was dead their photograph died too. But, of course, this one of mother was very old. It was thirty-five years old. Josephine remembered standing on a chair and pointing out that feather boa to Constantia and telling her that it was a snake that had killed their mother in Ceylon. . . . Would everything have been different if mother hadn't died? She didn't see why. Aunt Florence had lived with them until they had left school, and they had moved three times and had their yearly holiday and . . . and there'd been changes of servants, of course.

Some little sparrows, young sparrows they sounded, chirped on the window-ledge. *Yeep—eyeep—yeep.* But Josephine felt they were not sparrows, not on the window-ledge. It was inside her, that queer little crying noise. *Yeep—eyeep—yeep.* Ah, what was it crying, so weak and forlorn?

If mother had lived, might they have married? But there had been nobody for them to marry. There had been father's Anglo-Indian friends before he quarrelled with them. But after that she and Constantia never met a single man except clergymen. How did one meet men? Or even if they'd met them, how could they have got to know men well enough to be more than strangers? One read of people having adventures, being followed, and so on. But nobody had ever followed Constantia and her. Oh yes, there had been one year at Eastbourne a mysterious man at their boarding-house who had put a note on the jug of hot water outside their bedroom door! But by the time Connie had found it the steam had made the writing too faint to read; they couldn't even make out to which of them it was addressed. And he had left next day. And that was all. The rest had been looking after father, and at the same time keeping out of father's way. But now? But now? The thieving sun touched Josephine gently. She lifted her face. She was drawn over to the window by gentle beams. . . .

Until the barrel-organ stopped playing Constantia stayed before the Buddha, wondering, but not as usual, not vaguely. This time her wonder was like longing. She remembered the times she had come in here, crept out of bed in her night-gown when the moon was full, and lain on the floor with her arms outstretched, as though she was crucified. Why? The big, pale moon had made her do it. The horrible dancing figures on the carved screen had leered at her and she hadn't minded. She remembered too how, whenever they were at the seaside, she had gone off by herself and got as close to the sea as she could, and sung something,

something she had made up, while she gazed all over that restless water. There had been this other life, running out, bringing things home in bags, getting things on approval, discussing them with Jug, and taking them back to get more things on approval, and arranging father's trays and trying not to annoy father. But it all seemed to have happened in a kind of tunnel. It wasn't real. It was only when she came out of the tunnel into the moonlight or by the sea or into a thunderstorm that she really felt herself. What did it mean? What was it she was always wanting? What did it all lead to? Now? Now?

She turned away from the Buddha with one of her vague gestures. She went over to where Josephine was standing. She wanted to say something to Josephine, something frightfully important, about—about the future and what . . .

"Don't you think perhaps—" she began.

But Josephine interrupted her. "I was wondering if now—" she murmured. They stopped; they waited for each other.

"Go on, Con," said Josephine.

"No, no, Jug; after you," said Constantia.

"No, say what you were going to say. You began," said Josephine.

"I . . . I'd rather hear what you were going to say first," said Constantia.

"Don't be absurd, Con."

"Really, Jug."

"Connie!"

"Oh, *Jug!*"

A pause. Then Constantia said faintly, "I can't say what I was going to say, Jug, because I've forgotten what it was . . . that I was going to say."

Josephine was silent for a moment. She stared at a big cloud where the sun had been. Then she replied shortly, "I've forgotten too."

## *Study questions*

1. *How old are Josephine and Constantia? How do we know? Why does Mansfield make them sound like adolescents one minute and senile another?* 2. *What is significant about the fact that their father was a colonel? What was he like? How do we know? What was the relationship between father and daughters?* 3. *How are Josephine and Constantia alike? different?* 4. *What is the function of Nurse Andrews? proud young Kate? Mr. Farolles?* 5. *How do the episodes with Cyril function?* 6. *Why do the sisters have such difficulty in making up their minds?* 7. *The last episode of the story is the point where all the motifs fall together. Go over it carefully. What does the organ grinder's song represent? the sunlight? the sparrows? the moonlight? the Buddha?* 8. *Why is Josephine associated with the sun and Constantia with the moon? Are their names significant?* 9. *What will happen to them?* 10. *How does Mansfield manage to walk a fine line between humor and pathos?*

## THE MAN WITHOUT A TEMPERAMENT

He stood at the hall door turning the ring, turning the heavy signet ring upon his little finger while his glance travelled coolly, deliberately, over the round tables and basket chairs scattered about the glassed-in verandah. He pursed his lips—he might have been going to whistle—but he did not whistle—only turned the ring—turned the ring on his pink, freshly washed hands.

Over in the corner sat The Two Topknots, drinking a decoction they always drank at this hour—something whitish, greyish, in glasses, with little husks floating on the top—and rooting in a tin full of paper shavings for pieces of speckled biscuit, which they broke, dropped into the glasses and fished for with spoons. Their two coils of knitting, like two snakes, slumbered beside the tray.

The American Woman sat where she always sat against the glass wall, in the shadow of a great creeping thing with wide open purple eyes that pressed—that flattened itself against the glass, hungrily watching her. And she knoo it was there—she knoo it was looking at her just that way. She played up to it; she gave herself little airs. Sometimes she even pointed at it, crying: "Isn't that the most terrible thing you've ever seen! Isn't that ghoulish!" It was on the other side of the verandah, after all . . . and besides it couldn't touch her, could it, Klaymongso? She was an American Woman, wasn't she Klaymongso, and she'd just go right away to her Consul. Klaymongso, curled in her lap, with her torn antique brocade bag, a grubby handkerchief, and a pile of letters from home on top of him, sneezed for reply.

The other tables were empty. A glance passed between the American and the Topknots. She gave a foreign little shrug; they waved an understanding biscuit. But he saw nothing. Now he was still, now from his eyes you saw he listened. "Hoo-e-zip-zoo-oo!" sounded the lift. The iron cage clanged open. Light dragging steps sounded across the hall, coming towards him. A hand, like a leaf, fell on his shoulder. A soft voice said: "Let's go and sit over there—where we can see the drive. The trees are so lovely." And he moved forward with the hand still on his shoulder, and the light, dragging steps beside his. He pulled out a chair and she sank into it, slowly, leaning her head against the back, her arms falling along the sides.

"Won't you bring the other up closer? It's such miles away." But he did not move.

"Where's your shawl?" he asked.

"Oh!" She gave a little groan of dismay. "How silly I am, I've left it upstairs on the bed. Never mind. Please don't go for it. I shan't want it, I know I shan't."

"You'd better have it." And he turned and swiftly crossed the verandah into the dim hall with its scarlet plush and gilt furniture—conjuror's furniture—its Notice of Services at the English Church, its green baize board with the unclaimed letters climbing the black lattice, huge "Presentation" clock that struck the hours at the half-hours, bundles of sticks and umbrellas and sunshades in the clasp of a brown wooden bear, past the two crippled palms, two ancient beggars at the foot of the staircase, up the marble stairs three at a time, past the life-size group on the landing of two stout peasant children with their marble pinnies full of marble grapes, and along the corridor, with its piled-up wreckage of old tin boxes, leather trunks, canvas hold-alls, to their room.

The servant girl was in their room, singing loudly while she emptied soapy water into a pail. The windows were open wide, the shutters put back, and the light glared in. She had thrown the carpets and the big white pillows over the balcony rails; the nets were looped up from the beds; on the writing table there stood a pan of fluff and match-ends. When she saw him her small impudent eyes snapped and her singing changed to humming. But he gave no sign. His eyes searched the glaring room. Where the devil was the shawl!

"*Vous désirez, Monsieur?*" mocked the servant girl.

No answer. He had seen it. He strode across the room, grabbed the grey cobweb and went out, banging the door. The servant girl's voice at its loudest and shrillest followed him along the corridor.

"Oh, there you are. What happened? What kept you? The tea's here, you see. I've just sent Antonio off for the hot water. Isn't it extraordinary? I must have told him about it sixty times at least, and still he doesn't bring it. Thank you. That's very nice. One does just feel the air when one bends forward."

"Thanks." He took his tea and sat down in the other chair. "No, nothing to eat."

"Oh do! Just one, you had so little at lunch and it's hours before dinner."

Her shawl dropped off as she bent forward to hand him the biscuits. He took one and put it in his saucer.

"Oh, those trees along the drive," she cried, "I could look at them for ever. They are like the most exquisite huge ferns. And you see that one with the grey-silver bark and the clusters of cream coloured flowers, I pulled down a head of them yesterday to smell and the scent"—she shut her eyes at the memory and her voice thinned away, faint, airy—"was like freshly ground nutmegs." A little pause. She turned to him and smiled. "You do know what nutmegs smell like—do you, Robert?"

And he smiled back at her. "Now how am I going to prove to you that I do?"

Back came Antonio with not only the hot water—with letters on a salver and three rolls of paper.

"Oh, the post! Oh, how lovely! Oh, Robert, they mustn't be all for you! Have they just come, Antonio?" Her thin hands flew up and hovered over the letters that Antonio offered her, bending forward.

"Just this moment, Signora," grinned Antonio. "I took-a them from the postman myself. I made-a the postman give them for me."

"Noble Antonio!" laughed she. "There—those are mine, Robert; the rest are yours."

Antonio wheeled sharply, stiffened, the grin went out of his face. His striped linen jacket and his flat gleaming fringe made him look like a wooden doll.

Mr. Salesby put the letters into his pocket; the papers lay on the table. He turned the ring, turned the signet ring on his little finger and stared in front of him, blinking, vacant.

But she—with her teacup in one hand, the sheets of thin paper in the other, her head tilted back, her lips open, a brush of bright colour on her cheek-bones, sipped, sipped, drank . . . drank. . . .

"From Lottie," came her soft murmur. "Poor dear . . . such trouble . . . left foot. She thought . . . neuritis . . . Doctor Blyth . . . flat foot . . . massage. So many robins this year . . . maid most satisfactory . . . Indian Colonel . . . every grain of rice separate . . . very heavy fall of snow." And her wide lighted eyes looked up from the letter. "Snow, Robert! Think of it!" And she touched the little dark violets pinned on her thin bosom and went back to the letter.

. . . Snow. Snow in London. Millie with the early morning cup of tea. "There's been a terrible fall of snow in the night, Sir." "Oh, has there, Millie?" The curtains ring apart, letting in the pale, reluctant light. He raises himself in the bed; he catches a glimpse of the solid houses opposite framed in white, of their window boxes full of great sprays of white coral. . . . In the bathroom—overlooking the back garden. Snow—heavy snow over everything. The lawn is covered with a wavy pattern of cat's paws; there is a thick, thick icing on the garden table; the withered pods of the laburnum tree are white tassels; only here and there in the ivy is a dark leaf showing. . . . Warming his back at the dining-room fire, the paper drying over a chair. Millie with the bacon. "Oh, if you please, Sir, there's two little boys come as will do the steps and front for a shilling, shall I let them?" . . . And then flying lightly, lightly down the stairs—Jinnie. "Oh, Robert, isn't it wonderful! Oh, what a pity it has to melt. Where's the pussy-wee?" "I'll get him from Millie" . . . "Millie, you might just hand me up the kitten if you've got him down there." "Very good, Sir." He feels the little beating heart under his hand. "Come on old chap, your Missus wants you." "Oh, Robert, do show him the snow—his first snow. Shall I open the window and give him a little piece on his paw to hold? . . ."

"Well, that's very satisfactory on the whole—very. Poor Lottie! Darling Anne! How I only wish I could send them something of this," she cried, waving her letters at the brilliant, dazzling garden. "More tea, Robert? Robert dear, more tea."

"No, thanks, no. It was very good," he drawled.

"Well mine wasn't. Mine was just like chopped hay. Oh, here comes the Honeymoon Couple."

Half striding, half running, carrying a basket between them and rods and lines, they came up the drive, up the shallow steps.

"My! have you been out fishing?" cried the American Woman.

They were out of breath, they panted: "Yes, yes, we have been out in a little boat all day. We have caught seven. Four are good to eat. But three we shall give away. To the children."

Mrs. Salesby turned her chair to look; the Topknots laid the snakes down. They were a very dark young couple—black hair, olive skin, brilliant eyes and teeth. He was dressed "English fashion" in a flannel jacket, white trousers and shoes. Round his neck he wore a silk scarf; his head, with his hair brushed back, was bare. And he kept mopping his forehead, rubbing his hands with a brilliant handkerchief. Her white skirt had a patch of wet; her neck and throat were stained a deep pink. When she lifted her arms big half-hoops of perspiration showed under her armpits; her hair clung in wet curls to her cheeks. She looked as though her young husband had been dipping her in the sea, and fishing her out again to dry in the sun and then—in with her again—all day.

"Would Klaymongso like a fish?" they cried. Their laughing voices charged with excitement beat against the glassed-in verandah like birds, and a strange saltish smell came from the basket.

"You will sleep well to-night," said a Topknot, picking her ear with a knitting needle while the other Topknot smiled and nodded.

The Honeymoon Couple looked at each other. A great wave seemed to go over them. They gasped, gulped, staggered a little and then came up laughing —laughing.

"We cannot go upstairs, we are too tired. We must have tea just as we are. Here—coffee. No—tea. No—coffee. Tea—coffee, Antonio!" Mrs. Salesby turned.

"Robert! Robert!" Where was he? He wasn't there. Oh, there he was at the other end of the verandah, with his back turned, smoking a cigarette. "Robert, shall we go for our little turn?"

"Right." He stumped the cigarette into an ash-tray and sauntered over, his eyes on the ground. "Will you be warm enough?"

"Oh, quite."

"Sure?"

"Well, she put her hand on his arm, "perhaps"—and gave his arm the faintest pressure—"it's not upstairs, it's only in the hall—perhaps you'd get me my cape. Hanging up."

He came back with it and she bent her small head while he dropped it on her shoulders. Then, very stiff, he offered her his arm. She bowed sweetly to the people on the verandah while he just covered a yawn, and they went down the steps together.

*"Vous avez voo ça!"* said the American Woman.

"He is not a man," said the Two Topknots, "he is an ox. I say to my sister in the morning and at night when we are in bed, I tell her—*No* man is he, but an ox!"

Wheeling, tumbling, swooping, the laughter of the Honeymoon Couple dashed against the glass of the verandah.

The sun was still high. Every leaf, every flower in the garden lay open, motionless, as if exhausted, and a sweet, rich, rank smell filled the quivering air. Out of the thick, fleshy leaves of a cactus there rose an aloe stem loaded with pale flowers that looked as though they had been cut out of butter; light flashed upon the lifted spears of the palms; over a bed of scarlet waxen flowers some big black insects "zoom-zoomed"; a great, gaudy creeper, orange splashed with jet, sprawled against a wall.

"I don't need my cape after all," said she. "It's really too warm." So he took it off and carried it over his arm. "Let us go down this path here. I feel so well to-day—marvellously better. Good heavens—look at those children! And to think it's November!"

In a corner of the garden there were two brimming tubs of water. Three little girls, having thoughtfully taken off their drawers and hung them on a bush, their skirts clasped to their waists, were standing in the tubs and tramping up and down. They screamed, their hair fell over their faces, they splashed one another. But suddenly, the smallest, who had a tub to herself, glanced up and saw who was looking. For a moment she seemed overcome with terror, then clumsily she struggled and strained out of the tub, and still holding her clothes above her waist. "The Englishman! The Englishman!" she shrieked and fled away to hide. Shrieking and screaming, the other two followed her. In a moment they were gone; in a moment there was nothing but the two brimming tubs and their little drawers on the bush.

"How—very—extraordinary!" said she. "What made them so frightened? Surely they were much too young to . . ." She looked up at him. She thought he looked pale—but wonderfully handsome with that great tropical tree behind him with its long, spiked thorns.

For a moment he did not answer. Then he met her glance, and smiling his slow smile, "*Très* rum!" said he.

*Très* rum! Oh, she felt quite faint. Oh, why should she love him so much just because he said a thing like that. *Très* rum! That was Robert all over. Nobody else but Robert could ever say such a thing. To be so wonderful, so brilliant, so learned, and then to say in that queer, boyish voice. . . . She could have wept.

"You know you're very absurd, sometimes," said she.

"I am," he answered. And they walked on.

But she was tired. She had had enough. She did not want to walk any more.

"Leave me here and go for a little constitutional, won't you? I'll be in one of these long chairs. What a good thing you've got my cape; you won't have to go upstairs for a rug. Thank you, Robert, I shall look at that delicious heliotrope. . . . You won't be gone long?"

"No—no. You don't mind being left?"

"Silly! I want you to go. I can't expect you to drag after your invalid wife every minute. . . . How long will you be?"

He took out his watch. "It's just after half-past four. I'll be back at a quarter past five."

"Back at a quarter past five," she repeated, and she lay still in the long chair and folded her hands.

He turned away. Suddenly he was back again. "Look here, would you like my watch?" And he dangled it before her.

"Oh!" She caught her breath. "Very, very much." And she clasped the watch, the warm watch, the darling watch in her fingers. "Now go quickly."

The gates of the Pension Villa Excelsior were open wide, jammed open against some bold geraniums. Stooping a little, staring straight ahead, walking swiftly, he passed through them and began climbing the hill that wound behind the town like a great rope looping the villas together. The dust lay thick. A carriage came bowling along driving towards the Excelsior. In it sat the General and the Countess; they had been for his daily airing. Mr. Salesby stepped to one side but the dust beat up, thick, white, stifling like wool. The Countess just had time to nudge the General.

"There he goes," she said spitefully.

But the General gave a loud caw and refused to look.

"It is the Englishman," said the driver, turning round and smiling. And the Countess threw up her hands and nodded so amiably that he spat with satisfaction and gave the stumbling horse a cut.

On—on—past the finest villas in the town, magnificent palaces, palaces worth coming any distance to see, past the public gardens with the carved grottoes and statues and stone animals drinking at the fountain, into a poorer quarter. Here the road ran narrow and foul between high lean houses, the ground floors of which were scooped and hollowed into stables and carpenters' shops. At a fountain ahead of him two old hags were beating linen. As he passed them they squatted back on their haunches, stared, and then their "A-hak-kak-kak!" with the slap, slap, of the stone on the linen sounded after him.

He reached the top of the hill; he turned a corner and the town was hidden. Down he looked into a deep valley with a dried up river bed at the bottom. This side and that was covered with small dilapidated houses that had broken stone verandahs where the fruit lay drying, tomato lanes in the garden, and from the gates to the doors a trellis of vines. The late sunlight, deep, golden, lay in the cup of the valley; there was a smell of charcoal in the air. In the gardens the men were cutting grapes. He watched a man standing in the greenish shade, raising up, holding a black cluster in one hand, taking the knife from his belt, cutting, laying the bunch in a flat boat-shaped basket. The man worked leisurely, silently, taking hundreds of years over the job. On the hedges on the other side of the road there were grapes small as berries, growing wild, growing among the stones. He leaned against a wall, filled his pipe, put a match to it. . . .

Leaned across a gate, turned up the collar of his mackintosh. It was going to rain. It didn't matter, he was prepared for it. You didn't expect anything else in November. He looked over the bare field. From the corner by the gate there came the smell of swedes, a great stack of them, wet, rank coloured. Two men passed walking towards the straggling village. "Good day!" "Good day!" By Jove! he had to hurry if he was going to catch that train home. Over the gate, across a field, over the stile, into the lane, swinging along in the drifting rain and dusk. . . . Just home in time for a bath and a change before supper. . . . In the drawing-room; Jinnie is sitting pretty nearly in the fire. "Oh, Robert, I didn't hear you come in. Did you have a good time? How nice you smell! A present?" "Some bits of blackberry I picked for you. Pretty colour." "Oh, lovely, Robert! Dennis and Beaty are coming to supper." Supper—cold beef, potatoes in their jackets, claret, household bread. They are gay—everybody's laughing. "Oh, we all know Robert," says Dennis, breathing on his eye-glasses and polishing them. "By the way, Dennis, I picked up a very jolly little edition of . . ."

A clock struck. He wheeled sharply. What time was it. Five? A quarter past? Back, back the way he came. As he passed through the gates he saw her on the look-out. She got up, waved and slowly she came to meet him, dragging the heavy cape. In her hand she carried a spray of heliotrope.

"You're late," she cried gaily. "You're three minutes late. Here's your watch, it's been very good while you were away. Did you have a nice time? Was it lovely? Tell me. Where did you go?"

"I say—put this *on*," he said, taking the cape from her.

"Yes, I will. Yes, it's getting chilly. Shall we go up to our room?"

When they reached the lift she was coughing. He frowned.

"It's nothing. I haven't been out too late. Don't be cross." She sat down on one of the red plush chairs while he rang and rang, and then, getting no answer, kept his finger on the bell.

"Oh, Robert, do you think you ought to?"

"Ought to what?"

The door of the *salon* opened. "What is that? Who is making that noise?" sounded from within. Klaymongso began to yelp. "Caw! Caw! Caw!" came from the General. A Topknot darted out with one hand to her ear, opened the staff door, "Mr. Queet! Mr. Queet!" she bawled. That brought the manager up at a run.

"Is that you ringing the bell, Mr. Salesby? Do you want the lift? Very good, Sir. I'll take you up myself. Antonio wouldn't have been a minute, he was just taking off his apron—" And having ushered them in, the oily manager went to the door of the *salon*. "Very sorry you should have been troubled, ladies and gentlemen." Salesby stood in the cage, sucking in his cheeks, staring at the ceiling and turning the ring, turning the signet ring on his little finger. . . .

Arrived in their room he went swiftly over to the washstand, shook the bottle, poured her out a dose and brought it across.

"Sit down. Drink it. And don't talk." And he stood over her while she obeyed. Then he took the glass, rinsed it and put it back in its case. "Would you like a cushion?"

"No, I'm quite all right. Come over here. Sit down by me just a minute, will you, Robert? Ah, that's very nice." She turned and thrust the piece of heliotrope in the lapel of his coat. "That," she said, "is most becoming." And then she leaned her head against his shoulder, and he put his arm round her.

"Robert—" her voice like a sigh—like a breath.

"Yes—"

They sat there for a long while. The sky flamed, paled; the two white beds were like two ships. . . . At last he heard the servant girl running along the corridor with the hot water cans, and gently he released her and turned on the light.

"Oh, what time is it? Oh, what a heavenly evening. Oh, Robert, I was thinking while you were away this afternoon . . ."

They were the last couple to enter the dining-room. The Countess was there with her lorgnette and her fan, the General was there with his special chair and the air cushion and the small rug over his knees. The American Woman was there showing Klaymongso a copy of the *Saturday Evening Post*. . . . "We're having a feast of reason and a flow of soul." The Two Topknots were there feeling over the peaches and the pears in their dish of fruit, and putting aside all they considered unripe or overripe to show to the manager, and the Honeymoon Couple leaned across the table, whispering, trying not to burst out laughing.

Mr. Queet, in everyday clothes and white canvas shoes, served the soup, and Antonio, in full evening dress, handed it round.

"No," said the American Woman, "take it away, Antonio. We can't eat soup. We can't eat anything mushy, can we, Klaymongso?"

"Take them back and fill them to the rim!" said the Topknots, and they turned and watched while Antonio delivered the message.

"What is it? Rice? Is it cooked?" The Countess peered through her lorgnette. "Mr. Queet, the General can have some of this soup if it is cooked."

"Very good, Countess."

The Honeymoon Couple had their fish instead.

"Give me that one. That's the one I caught. No it's not. Yes, it is. No it's not. Well, it's looking at me with its eye so it must be. Tee! Hee! Hee!" Their feet were locked together under the table.

"Robert, you're not eating again. Is anything the matter?"

"No. Off food, that's all."

"Oh, what a bother. There are eggs and spinach coming. You don't like spinach, do you. I must tell them in future . . ."

An egg and mashed potatoes for the General.

"Mr. Queet! Mr. Queet!"

"Yes, Countess."

"The General's egg's too hard again."

"Caw! Caw! Caw!"

"Very sorry, Countess. Shall I have you another cooked, General?"

. . . They are the first to leave the dining-room. She rises, gathering her shawl and he stands aside waiting for her to pass, turning the ring, turning the signet ring on his little finger. In the hall Mr. Queet hovers. "I thought you might not want to wait for the lift. Antonio's just serving the finger bowls. And I'm sorry the bell won't ring, it's out of order. I can't think what's happened."

"Oh, I do hope . . ." from her.

"Get in," says he.

Mr. Queet steps after them and slams the door. . . .

. . . "Robert, do you mind if I go to bed very soon? Won't you go down to the *salon* or out into the garden? Or perhaps you might smoke a cigar on the balcony. It's lovely out there. And I like cigar smoke. I always did. But if you'd rather . . ."

"No, I'll sit here."

He takes a chair and sits on the balcony. He hears her moving about in the room, lightly, lightly, moving and rustling. Then she comes over to him. "Good night, Robert."

"Good night." He takes her hand and kisses the palm. "Don't catch cold."

The sky is the colour of jade. There are a great many stars; an enormous white moon hangs over the garden. Far away lightning flutters—flutters like a wing—flutters like a broken bird that tries to fly and sinks again and again struggles.

The lights from the *salon* shine across the garden path and there is the sound of a piano. And once the American Woman, opening the French window to let Klaymongso into the garden, cries: "Have you seen this moon?" But nobody answers.

He gets very cold sitting there, staring at the balcony rail. Finally he comes inside. The moon—the room is painted white with moonlight. The light trembles in the mirrors; the two beds seem to float. She is asleep. He sees her through the nets, half sitting, banked up with pillows, her white hands crossed on the sheet. Her white cheeks, her fair hair pressed against the pillow, are silvered over. He undresses quickly, stealthily and gets into bed. Lying there, his hands clasped behind his head. . . .

. . . In his study. Late summer. The virginia creeper just on the turn. . . .

"Well, my dear chap, that's the whole story. That's the long and the short of it. If she can't cut away for the next two years and give a decent climate a chance she don't stand a dog's—h'm—show. Better be frank about these things." "Oh, certainly. . . ." "And hang it all, old man, what's to prevent you going with her? It isn't as though you've got a regular job like us wage earners. You can do what you do wherever you are—" "Two years." "Yes, I should give it two years. You'll have no trouble about letting this house you know. As a matter of fact . . ."

. . . He is with her. "Robert, the awful thing is—I suppose it's my illness—I simply feel I could not go alone. You see—you're everything. You're bread and wine, Robert, bread and wine. Oh, my darling—what am I saying? Of course I could, of course I won't take you away. . . ."

He hears her stirring. Does she want something?

"Boogles?"

Good Lord! She is talking in her sleep. They haven't used that name for years.

"Boogles. Are you awake?"

"Yes, do you want anything?"

"Oh, I'm going to be a bother. I'm so sorry. Do you mind? There's a wretched mosquito inside my net—I can hear him singing. Would you catch him? I don't want to move because of my heart."

"No, don't move. Stay where you are." He switches on the light, lifts the net. "Where is the little beggar? Have you spotted him?"

"Yes, there, over by the corner. Oh, I do feel such a fiend to have dragged you out of bed. Do you mind dreadfully?"

"No, of course not." For a moment he hovers in his blue and white pyjamas. Then, "got him," he said.

"Oh, good. Was he a juicy one?"

"Beastly." He went over to the washstand and dipped his fingers in water. "Are you all right now? Shall I switch off the light?"

"Yes, please. No. Boogles! Come back here a moment. Sit down by me. Give me your hand." She turns his signet ring. "Why weren't you asleep? Boogles, listen. Come closer. I sometimes wonder—do you mind awfully being out here with me?"

He bends down. He kisses her. He tucks her in, he smoothes the pillow. "Rot!" he whispers.

## *Study questions*

1. *What kind of hotel is pictured here? How does the Honeymoon Couple stand out from the rest of the guests?* 2. *What is the matter with Robert? Is he without a temperament? Why does he turn his ring?* 3. *What role is played by the Two Topknots? the American Woman?* 4. *What is the matter with Millie? Is her relationship with Robert an extension of a former relationship? Look to the flashbacks for an answer.* 5. *Eating is a recurrent motif in the story. How does it function?* 6. *What is the symbolic significance of the garden? How does it relate to the scene with the maid and the scene with the little girls?* 7. *What is the importance of the watch?* 8. *The epiphany in this story occurs when Robert kills the mosquito. Explain the scene and the end of the story.*

*Jean Toomer* (1894–1967), raised in Washington, D.C., published *Cane* in 1923, when he was twenty-eight years old. Its publication brought him immediate recognition as a rising star of the Harlem Renaissance. But it was printed in a small edition and reprinted only once during his lifetime; and, since he dropped out of sight, publishing during the rest of his life only a few stories, poems, essays, and a privately printed book of aphorisms, Toomer's star dimmed almost as quickly as it had risen. In time, however, *Cane* was found again. It has gone through several printings in the last decade and is now ranked as the literary masterpiece of the Harlem Renaissance. The book must also take a significant place in the history of the short story. A collection of stories and poems, interrelated by recurring themes, images, and motifs, the book records what Toomer believed was the swan song of a particular way of life for black people. Some of the stories, like "Karintha" and "Carma," no longer than two pages, are close to poetry but still narratives, with characters in conflict and plots that can be deduced from the images and recurrent motifs. Other stories, like "Box-Seat," are shaped by means of a plot structure similar to that employed by Katherine Mansfield and James Joyce. "Blood-Burning Moon" is a powerful story, its lyrical style set in juxtaposition with violent action, the two combining to create a witch's brew.

## BLOOD-BURNING MOON

### 1

Up from the skeleton stone walls, up from the rotting floor boards and the solid hand-hewn beams of oak of the pre-war cotton factory, dusk came. Up from the dusk the full moon came. Glowing like a fired pine-knot, it illumined the great door and soft showered the Negro shanties aligned along the single street of factory town. The full moon in the great door was an omen. Negro women improvised songs against its spell.

Louisa sang as she came over the crest of the hill from the white folks' kitchen. Her skin was the color of oak leaves on young trees in fall. Her breasts, firm and up-pointed like ripe acorns. And her singing had the low murmur of winds in fig trees. Bob Stone, younger son of the people she worked for, loved her. By the way the world reckons things, he had won her. By measure of that warm glow which came into her mind at thought of him, he had won her. Tom Burwell, whom the whole town called Big Boy, also loved her. But working in the fields all day, and far away from her, gave him no chance to show it. Though often enough of evenings he had tried to. Somehow, he never got along. Strong as he was with hands upon the ax or plow, he found it difficult to hold her. Or so he thought. But the fact was that he held her to factory town more firmly than he thought for. His black balanced, and pulled against, the white of Stone, when she thought of them. And her mind was vaguely upon them as she came over the crest of the hill, coming from the white folks' kitchen. As she sang softly at the evil face of the full moon.

A strange stir was in her. Indolently, she tried to fix upon Bob or Tom as the cause of it. To meet Bob in the canebrake, as she was going to do an hour or so later, was nothing new. And Tom's proposal which she felt on its way to her could be indefinitely put off. Separately, there was no unusual significance to either one. But for some reason, they jumbled when her eyes gazed vacantly at the rising moon. And from the jumble came the stir that was strangely within her. Her lips trembled. The slow rhythm of her song grew agitant and restless. Rusty black and tan spotted hounds, lying in the dark corners of porches or prowling around back yards, put their noses in the air and caught its tremor. They began plaintively to yelp and howl. Chickens woke up and cackled. Intermittently, all over the countryside dogs barked and roosters crowed as if heralding a weird dawn or some ungodly awakening. The women sang lustily. Their songs were cotton-wads to stop their ears. Louisa came down into factory town and sank wearily upon the step before her home. The moon was rising towards a thick cloud-bank which soon would hide it.

*Red nigger moon. Sinner!*
*Blood-burning moon. Sinner!*
*Come out that fact'ry door.*

2

Up from the deep dusk of a cleared spot on the edge of the forest a mellow glow arose and spread fan-wise into the low-hanging heavens. And all around the air was heavy with the scent of boiling cane. A large pile of cane-stalks lay like ribboned shadows upon the ground. A mule, harnessed to a pole, trudged lazily round and round the pivot of the grinder. Beneath a swaying oil lamp, a Negro alternately whipped out at the mule, and fed cane-stalks to the grinder. A fat boy waddled pails of fresh ground juice between the grinder and the boiling stove. Steam came from the copper boiling pan. The scent of cane came from the copper pan and drenched the forest and the hill that sloped to factory town, beneath its fragrance. It drenched the men in the circle seated around the stove. Some of them chewed at the white pulp of stalks, but there was no need for them to, if all they wanted was to taste the cane. One tasted it in factory town. And from factory town one could see the soft haze thrown by the glowing stove upon the low-hanging heavens.

Old David Georgia stirred the thickening syrup with a long ladle, and ever so often drew it off. Old David Georgia tended his stove and told tales about the white folks, about moon-shining and cotton picking, and about sweet nigger gals, to the men who sat there about his stove to listen to him. Tom Burwell chewed cane-stalk and laughed with the others till someone mentioned Louisa. Till some one said something about Louisa and Bob Stone, about the silk stockings she must have gotten from him. Blood ran up Tom's neck hotter than the glow that flooded from the stove. He sprang up. Glared at the men and said, "She's my gal." Will Manning laughed. Tom strode over to him. Yanked him up and knocked him to the ground. Several of Manning's friends got up to fight for him. Tom whipped out a long knife and would have cut them to shreds if they hadnt ducked into the woods. Tom had had enough. He nodded to Old David Georgia and swung down the path to factory town. Just then, the dogs started barking and the roosters began to crow. Tom felt funny. Away from the fight, away from the stove, chill got to him. He shivered. He shuddered when he saw the full moon rising towards the cloud-bank. He who didnt give a godam for the fears of old women. He forced his mind to fasten on Louisa. Bob Stone. Better not be. He turned into the street and saw Louisa sitting before her home. He went towards her, ambling, touched the brim of a marvelously shaped, spotted, felt hat, said he wanted to say something to her, and then found that he didnt know what he had to say, or if he did, that he couldnt say it. He shoved his big fists in his overalls, grinned, and started to move off.

"Youall want me, Tom?"

"Thats what us wants, sho, Louisa."

"Well, here I am—"

"An here I is, but that aint ahelpin none, all th same."

"You wanted to say something? . ."

"I did that, sho. But words is like th spots on dice: no matter how y fumbles em, there's times when they jes wont come. I dunno why. Seems like th love I feels fo yo done stole m tongue. I got it now. Whee! Louisa, honey, I oughtnt tell y, I feel I oughtnt cause yo is young an goes t church an I has had other gals, but Louisa I sho do love y. Lil gal, Ise watched y from them first days when youall sat right here befo yo door befo th well an sang sometimes in a way that like t broke m heart. Ise carried y with me into th fields, day after day, an after that, an I sho can plow when yo is there, an I can pick cotton. Yassur! Come near beatin Barlo yesterday. I sho did. Yassur! An next year if ole Stone'll trust me, I'll have a farm. My own. My bales will buy yo what y gets from white folks now. Silk stockings an purple dresses—course I dont believe what some folks been whisperin as t how y gets them things now. White folks always did do for niggers what they likes. An they jes cant help alikin yo, Louisa. Bob Stone likes y. Course he does. But not th way folks is awhisperin. Does he, hon?"

"I dont know what you mean, Tom."

"Course y dont. Ise already cut two niggers. Had t hon, t tell em so. Niggers always tryin t make somethin out a nothin. An then besides, white folks aint up t them tricks so much nowadays. Godam better not be. Leastawise not with yo. Cause I wouldnt stand f it. Nassur."

"What would you do, Tom?"

"Cut him jes like I cut a nigger."

"No, Tom—"

"I said I would an there aint no mo to it. But that aint th talk f now. Sing, honey, Louisa, an while I'm listenin t y I'll be makin love."

Tom took her hand in his. Against the tough thickness of his own, hers felt soft and small. His huge body slipped down to the step beside her. The full moon sank upward into the deep purple of the cloud-bank. An old woman brought a lighted lamp and hung it on the common well whose bulky shadow squatted in the middle of the road, opposite Tom and Louisa. The old woman lifted the well-lid, took hold the chain, and began drawing up the heavy bucket. As she did so, she sang. Figures shifted, restless-like, between lamp and window in the front rooms of the shanties. Shadows of the figures fought each other on the gray dust of the road. Figures raised the windows and joined the old woman in song. Louisa and Tom, the whole street, singing:

*Red nigger moon. Sinner!*
*Blood-burning moon. Sinner!*
*Come out that fact'ry door.*

*3*

Bob Stone sauntered from his veranda out into the gloom of fir trees and magnolias. The clear white of his skin paled, and the flush of his cheeks turned purple. As if to balance this outer change, his mind became consciously a white man's. He passed the house with its huge open hearth which, in the days of slavery, was the plantation cookery. He saw Louisa bent over that hearth. He went in as a master should and took her. Direct, honest, bold. None of this sneaking that he had to go through now. The contrast was repulsive to him. His family had lost ground. Hell no, his family still owned the niggers, practically. Damned if they did, or he wouldnt have to duck around so. What would they think if they knew? His mother? His sister? He shouldnt mention them, shouldnt think of them in this connection. There in the dusk he blushed at doing so. Fellows about town were all right, but how about his friends up North? He could see them incredible, repulsed. They didnt know. The thought first made him laugh. Then, with their eyes still upon him, he began to feel embarrassed. He felt the need of explaining things to them. Explain hell. They wouldnt understand, and moreover, who ever heard of a Southerner getting on his knees to any Yankee, or anyone. No sir. He was going to see Louisa to-night, and love her. She was lovely—in her way. Nigger way. What way was that? Damned if he knew. Must know. He'd known her long enough to know. Was there something about niggers that you couldnt know? Listening to them at church didnt tell you anything. Looking at them didnt tell you anything. Talking to them didnt tell you anything—unless it was gossip, unless they wanted to talk. Of course, about farming, and licker, and craps—but those werent nigger. Nigger was something more. How much more? Something to be afraid of, more? Hell no. Who ever heard of being afraid of a nigger? Tom Burwell. Cartwell had told him that Tom went with Louisa after she reached home. No sir. No nigger had ever been with his girl. He'd like to see one try. Some position for him to be in. Him, Bob Stone, of the old Stone family, in a scrap with a nigger over a nigger girl. In the good old days. . . Ha! Those were the days. His family had lost ground.

Not so much, though. Enough for him to have to cut through old Lemon's canefield by way of the woods, that he might meet her. She was worth it. Beautiful nigger gal. Why nigger? Why not, just gal? No, it was because she was nigger that he went to her. Sweet. . . The scent of boiling cane came to him. Then he saw the rich glow of the stove. He heard the voices of the men circled around it. He was about to skirt the clearing when he heard his own name mentioned. He stopped. Quivering. Leaning against a tree, he listened.

"Bad nigger. Yassur, he sho is one bad nigger when he gets started."

"Tom Burwell's been on th gang three times fo cuttin men."

"What y think he's agwine t do t Bob Stone?"

"Dunno yet. He aint found out. When he does—Baby!"

"Aint no tellin."

"Young Stone aint no quitter an I ken tell y that. Blood of th old uns in his veins."

"Thats right. He'll scrap, sho."

"Be gettin too hot f niggers round this away."

"Shut up, nigger. Y dont know what y talkin bout."

Bob Stone's ears burned as though he had been holding them over the stove. Sizzling heat welled up within him. His feet felt as if they rested on red-hot coals. They stung him to quick movement. He circled the fringe of the glowing. Not a twig cracked beneath his feet. He reached the path that led to factory town. Plunged furiously down it. Halfway along, a blindness within him veered him aside. He crashed into the bordering canebrake. Cane leaves cut his face and lips. He tasted blood. He threw himself down and dug his fingers in the ground. The earth was cool. Cane-roots took the fever from his hands. After a long while, or so it seemed to him, the thought came to him that it must be time to see Louisa. He got to his feet and walked calmly to their meeting place. No Louisa. Tom Burwell had her. Veins in his forehead bulged and distended. Saliva moistened the dried blood on his lips. He bit down on his lips. He tasted blood. Not his own blood; Tom Burwell's blood. Bob drove through the cane and out again upon the road. A hound swung down the path before him towards factory town. Bob couldnt see it. The dog loped aside to let him pass. Bob's blind rushing made him stumble over it. He fell with a thud that dazed him. The hound yelped. Answering yelps came from all over the countryside. Chickens cackled. Roosters crowed, heralding the bloodshot eyes of southern awakening. Singers in the town were silenced. They shut their windows down. Palpitant between the rooster crows, a chill hush settled upon the huddled forms of Tom and Louisa. A figure rushed from the shadow and stood before them. Tom popped to his feet.

"Whats y want?"

"I'm Bob Stone."

"Yassur—an I'm Tom Burwell. Whats y want?"

Bob lunged at him. Tom side-stepped, caught him by the shoulder, and flung him to the ground. Straddled him.

"Let me up."

"Yassur—but watch yo doins, Bob Stone."

A few dark figures, drawn by the sound of scuffle, stood about them. Bob sprang to his feet.

"Fight like a man, Tom Burwell, an I'll lick y."

Again he lunged. Tom side-stepped and flung him to the ground. Straddled him.

"Get off me, you godam nigger you."

"Yo sho has started somethin now. Get up."

Tom yanked him up and began hammering at him. Each blow sounded as if it smashed into a precious, irreplaceable soft something. Beneath them, Bob staggered back. He reached in his pocket and whipped out a knife.

"Thats my game, sho."

Blue flash, a steel blade slashed across Bob Stone's throat. He had a sweetish sick feeling. Blood began to flow. Then he felt a sharp twitch of pain. He let his knife drop. He slapped one hand against his neck. He pressed the other on top of his head as if to hold it down. He groaned. He turned, and staggered towards the crest of the hill in the direction of white town. Negroes who had seen the fight slunk into their homes and blew the lamps out. Louisa, dazed, hysterical, refused to go indoors. She slipped, crumbled, her body loosely propped against the woodwork of the well. Tom Burwell leaned against it. He seemed rooted there.

Bob reached Broad Street. White men rushed up to him. He collapsed in their arms.

"Tom Burwell. . . ."

White men like ants upon a forage rushed about. Except for the taut hum of their moving, all was silent. Shotguns, revolvers, rope, kerosene, torches. Two high-powered cars with glaring search-lights. They came together. The taut hum rose to a low roar. Then nothing could be heard but the flop of their feet in the thick dust of the road. The moving body of their silence preceded them over the crest of the hill into factory town. It flattened the Negroes beneath it. It rolled to the wall of the factory, where it stopped. Tom knew that they were coming. He couldnt move. And then he saw the search-lights of the two cars glaring down on him. A quick shock went through him. He stiffened. He started to run. A yell went up from the mob. Tom wheeled about and faced them. They poured down on him. They swarmed. A large man with dead-white face and flabby cheeks came to him and almost jabbed a gun-barrel through his guts.

"Hands behind y, nigger."

Tom's wrists were bound. The big man shoved him to the well. Burn him over it, and when the woodwork caved in, his body would drop to the bottom. Two deaths for a godam nigger. Louisa was driven back. The mob pushed in. Its pressure, its momentum was too great. Drag him to the factory. Wood and stakes already there. Tom moved in the direction indicated. But they had to drag him. They reached the great door. Too many to get in there. The mob divided and flowed around the walls to either side. The big man shoved him through the door. The mob pressed in from the sides. Taut humming. No words. A stake was sunk into the ground. Rotting floor boards piled around it. Kerosene poured on the rotting floor boards. Tom bound to the stake. His breast was bare. Nails scratches let little lines of blood trickle down and mat into the hair. His face, his eyes were set and stony. Except for irregular breathing, one would have thought him already dead. Torches were flung onto the pile. A great flare muffled in black smoke shot upward. The mob yelled. The mob was silent. Now Tom could be seen within the flames. Only his head, erect, lean, like a blackened stone. Stench of burning flesh soaked the air. Tom's eyes popped. His head settled downward. The mob yelled. Its yell echoed against the skeleton stone walls and sounded like a hundred yells. Like a hundred mobs yelling. Its yell thudded against the thick front wall and fell back. Ghost of a yell slipped through the flames and out the great door of the factory. It fluttered like a dying thing down the single street of factory town. Louisa, upon the step before her home, did not hear it, but her eyes opened slowly. They saw the full moon glowing in the great door. The full moon, an evil thing, an omen, soft showering the homes of folks she knew. Where were they, these people? She'd sing, and perhaps they'd come out and join her. Perhaps Tom Burwell would come. At any rate, the full moon in the great door was an omen which she must sing to:

*Red nigger moon. Sinner!*
*Blood-burning moon. Sinner!*
*Come out that fact'ry door.*

## *Study questions*

1. *How does the moon in its various manifestations contribute to the story?* 2. *Does the barking of the dogs, the cackling of the chickens, etc., contribute to the action?* 3. *Is there a suggestion of some kind of fatal necessity in operation? Did what happened here have to happen?* 4. *What is the significance of the boiling cane? the men seated in a circle around the stove? Notice that both Tom and Bob hear about Louisa from these men.* 5. *Who is the protagonist of this story? What is the conflict?* 6. *Does Louisa know what she is doing? Is she aware of what happened to Tom?* 7. *How is Louisa related to the moon?*

*Katherine Anne Porter* (b. 1890) has published only one novel, *Ship of Fools* (1962), which was many years in preparation and upon its publication widely acclaimed. But it is for her achievement in the short story that she is most often recognized. A collected edition of her stories won for her in 1966 both the National Book Award and the Pulitzer Prize for Fiction. Born in Indian Creek, Texas, she was educated in private schools in Texas and in Ursuline Convent in Louisiana. After graduating she traveled extensively through North America and Europe. In 1922, she published her first story, *"María Concepción."* Thereafter followed volumes of collected stories: *Flowering Judas* (1930), *Hacienda* (1934), *Noon Wine* (1937), *Pale Horse, Pale Rider* (1939), and *The Leaning Tower* (1944). Beautifully crafted, dense, and evocative, her stories enrich our literature. "The Fig Tree" was meant to appear in *The Leaning Tower* in the sequence of related stories collectively called "The Old Order," but it was lost in a box of unfinished manuscripts and not found again until 1961. Meant to precede her famous "The Grave" in the sequence, "The Fig Tree" features more characters, though Miranda is still protagonist and point-of-view character. In "The Fig Tree," Miranda seeks reassurance from her Great-Aunt Eliza and finds it in the singing of tree frogs. Though short, the story develops Miranda's character and conflict in vivid detail.

# THE FIG TREE

Old Aunt Nannie had a habit of gripping with her knees to hold Miranda while she brushed her hair or buttoned her dress down the back. When Miranda wriggled, Aunt Nannie squeezed still harder, and Miranda wriggled more, but never enough to get away. Aunt Nannie gathered up Miranda's scalp lock firmly, snapped a rubber band around it, jammed a freshly starched white chambray bonnet over her ears and forehead, fastened the crown to the lock with a large safety pin, and said: "Got to hold you still someways. Here now, don't you take this off your head till the sun go down."

"I didn't want a bonnet, it's too hot, I wanted a hat," said Miranda.

"You not goin' to get a hat, you goin' to get just what you got," said Aunt Nannie in the bossy voice she used for washing and dressing time, "and mo'over some of these days I'm goin' to *sew* this bonnet to your topknot. Your daddy says if you get freckles he blame me. Now, you're all ready to set out."

"Where are we going, Aunty?" Miranda could never find out about anything until the last minute. She was always being surprised. Once she went to sleep in her bed with her kitten curled on the pillow purring, and woke up in a stuffy tight bed in a train, hugging a hot-water bottle; and there was Grandmother stretched out beside her in her McLeod tartan dressing-gown, her eyes wide open. Miranda thought something wonderful had happened. "My goodness, Grandmother, where are we going?" And it was only for another trip to El Paso to see Uncle Bill.

Now Tom and Dick were hitched to the carry-all standing outside the gate with boxes and baskets tied on everywhere. Grandmother was walking alone through the house very slowly, taking a last look at everything. Now and then she put something else in the big leather portmoney on her arm until it was pretty bulgy. She carried a long black mohair skirt on her other arm, the one she put on over her other skirt when she rode horseback. Her son Harry, Miranda's father, followed her saying: "I can't see the sense in rushing off to Halifax on five minutes' notice."

Grandmother said, walking on: "It's five hours exactly." Halifax wasn't the name of Grandmother's farm at all, it was Cedar Grove, but Father always called it Halifax. "Hot as Halifax," he would say when he wanted to describe something very hot. Cedar Grove was very hot, but they went there every summer because Grandmother loved it. "I went to Cedar Grove for fifty summers before you were born," she told Miranda, who remembered last summer very well, and the summer before a little. Miranda liked it for watermelons and grasshoppers and the long rows of blooming chinaberry trees where the hounds flattened themselves out and slept. They whined and winked their eyelids and worked their feet and barked faintly in their sleep, and Uncle Jimbilly said it was because dogs always dreamed they were chasing something. In the middle of the day when Miranda looked down over the thick green fields towards the spring she could simply see it being hot: everything blue and sleepy and the mourning doves calling.

"Are we going to Halifax, Aunty?"

"Now just ask your dad if you wanta know so much."

"Are we going to Halifax, Dad?"

Her father twitched her bonnet straight and pulled her hair forward so it would show. "You mustn't get sunburned. No, let it alone. Show the pretty curls. You'll be wading in Whirlypool before supper this evening."

Grandmother said, "Don't say Halifax, child, say Cedar Grove. Call things by their right names."

"Yes, ma'am," said Miranda. Grandmother said again, to her son, "It's five hours, exactly, and your Aunt Eliza has had plenty of time to pack up her telescope, and take my saddle horse. She's been there three hours by now. I imagine she's got the telescope already set up on the hen-house roof. I hope nothing happens."

"You worry too much, Mammy," said her son, trying to conceal his impatience.

"I am not worrying," said Grandmother, shifting her riding skirt to the arm carrying the portmoney. "It will scarcely be any good taking this," she said; "I might in fact as well throw it away for this summer."

"Never mind, Mammy, we'll send to the Black Farm for Pompey, he's a good easy saddler."

"You may ride him yourself," said Grandmother. "I'll never mount Pompey while Fiddler is alive. Fiddler is my horse, and I hate having his mouth spoiled by a careless rider. Eliza never could ride, and she never will. . . ."

Miranda gave a little skip and ran away. So they were going to Cedar Grove. Miranda never got over being surprised at the way grown-up people simply did not seem able to give anyone a straight answer to any question, unless the answer was "No." Then it popped out with no trouble at all. At a little distance, she heard her grandmother say, "Harry, have you seen my riding crop lately?" and her father answered, at least maybe he thought it was an answer, "Now, Mammy, for God's sake let's get this thing over with." That was it, exactly.

Another strange way her father had of talking was calling Grandmother "Mammy." Aunt Jane was Mammy. Sometimes he called Grandmother "Mama," but she wasn't Mama either, she was really Grandmother. Mama was dead. Dead meant gone away forever. Dying was something that happened all the time, to people and everything else. Somebody died, and there was a long string of carriages going at a slow walk over the rocky ridge of the hill towards the river while the bell tolled and tolled, and that person was never seen again by anybody. Kittens and chickens and specially little turkeys died much oftener, and sometimes calves, but hardly ever cows or horses. Lizards on rocks turned into shells, with no lizard inside at all. If caterpillars all curled up and furry didn't move when you poked them with a stick, that meant they were dead—it was a sure sign.

When Miranda found any creature that didn't move or make a noise, or looked somehow different from the live one, she always buried it in a little grave with flowers on top and a smooth stone at the head. Even grasshoppers. Everything dead had to be treated this way. "This way and no other!" Grandmother always said when she was laying down the law about all kinds of things. "It must be done *this* way, and no other!"

Miranda went down the crooked flat-stone walk hopping zigzag between the grass tufts. First there were pomegranate and cape jessamine bushes mixed together; then it got very dark and shady and that was the fig grove. She went to her favorite fig tree where the deep branches bowed down level with her chin, and she could gather figs without having to climb and skin her knees. Grandmother hadn't remembered to take any figs to the country the last time, she said there were plenty of them at Cedar Grove. But the ones at Cedar Grove were big soft greenish white ones, and these at home were black and sugary. It was strange that Grandmother did not seem to notice the difference. The air was sweet among the fig trees, and chickens were always getting out of the run and rushing there to eat the figs off the ground. One mother hen was scurrying around scratching and clucking. She would scratch around a fig lying there in plain sight and cluck to her children as if it was a worm and she had dug it up for them.

"Old smarty," said Miranda, "you're just pretending."

When the little chickens all ran to their mother under Miranda's fig tree, one little chicken did not move. He was spread out on his side with his eyes shut and his mouth open. He was yellow fur in spots and pinfeathers in spots, and the rest of him was naked and sunburned. "Lazy," said Miranda, poking him with her toe. Then she saw that he was dead.

Oh, and in no time at all they'd be setting out for Halifax. Grandmother never went away, she always set out for somewhere. She'd have to hurry like anything to get him buried properly. Back into the house she went on tiptoe hoping not to be seen, for Grandmother always asked: "Where are you going, child? What are you doing? What is that you're carrying? Where did you get it? Who gave you permission?" and after Miranda had explained all that, even if there turned out not to be anything wrong in it, nothing ever seemed so nice any more. Besides it took forever to get away.

Miranda slid open her bureau drawer, third down, left-hand side where her new shoes were still wrapped in tissue paper in a nice white box the right size for a chicken with pinfeathers. She pushed the rustling white folded things and the lavender bags out of the way and trembled a little. Down in front the carry-all wheels screeched and crunched on the gravel, with Old Uncle Jimbilly yelling like a foghorn, "Hiyi, thar, back up, you steeds! Back up thar, you!" and of course, that meant he was turning Tom and Dick around so they would be pointing towards Halifax. They'd be after her, calling and hurrying her, and she wouldn't have time for anything and they wouldn't listen to a word.

❂ ❂ ❂

It wasn't hard work digging a hole with her little spade in the loose dry soil. Miranda wrapped the slimpsy chicken in tissue paper, trying to make it look pretty, laid it in the box carefully, and covered it up with a nice mound, just like people's. She had hardly got it piled up grave shape, kneeling and leaning to smooth it over, when a strange sound came from somewhere, a very sad little crying sound. It said Weep, weep, weep, three times like that slowly, and it seemed to come from the mound of dirt. "My goodness," Miranda asked herself aloud, "what's that?" She pushed her bonnet off her ears and listened hard. "Weep, weep," said the tiny sad voice. And People began calling and urging her, their voices coming nearer. She began to clamor, too.

"Yes, Aunty, wait a minute, Aunty!"

"You come right on here this minute, we're goin'!"

"You *have* to wait, Aunty!"

Her father was coming along the edge of the fig trees. "Hurry up, Baby, you'll get left!"

Miranda felt she couldn't bear to be left. She ran all shaking with fright. Her father gave her the annoyed look he always gave her when he said something to upset her and then saw that she was upset. His words were kind but his voice scolded: "Stop getting so excited, Baby, you know we wouldn't leave you for anything." Miranda wanted to talk back: "Then why did you say so?" but she was still listening for that tiny sound: "Weep, weep." She lagged and pulled backward, looking over her shoulder, but her father hurried her towards the carry-all. But things didn't make sounds if they were dead. They couldn't. That was one of the signs. Oh, but she had heard it.

Her father sat in front and drove, and old Uncle Jimbilly didn't do anything but get down and open gates. Grandmother and Aunt Nannie sat in the back seat, with Miranda between them. She loved setting out somewhere, with everybody smiling and settling down and looking up at the weather, with the horses bouncing and pulling on the reins, the springs jolting and swaying with a creaky noise that made you feel sure you were traveling. That evening she would go wading with Maria and Paul and Uncle Jimbilly, and that very night she would lie out on the grass in her nightgown to cool off, and they would all drink lemonade before going to bed. Sister Maria and Brother Paul would already be burned like muffins because they were sent on ahead the minute school was out. Sister Maria had got freckled and Father was furious. "Keep your bonnet on," he said to Miranda, sternly. "Now remember. I'm not going to have that face ruined, too." But oh, what had made that funny sound? Miranda's ears buzzed and she had a dull round pain in her just under her front ribs. She had to go back and let him out. He'd never get out by himself, all tangled up in tissue paper and that shoebox. He'd never get out without her.

"Grandmother, I've got to go back. Oh, I've *got* to go back!"

Grandmother turned Miranda's face around by the chin and looked at her closely, the way grown folks did. Grandmother's eyes were always the same. They never looked kind or sad or angry or tired or anything. They just looked, blue and still. "What is the matter with you, Miranda, what happened?"

"Oh, I've got to go back—I forg-got something important."

"Stop that silly crying and tell me what you want."

Miranda couldn't stop. Her father looked very anxious. "Mammy, maybe the Baby's sick." He reached out his handkerchief to her face. "What's the matter with my honey? Did you eat something?"

Miranda had to stand up to cry as hard as she wanted to. The wheels went grinding round in the road, the carry-all wobbled so that Grandmother had to take her by one arm, and her father by the other. They stared at each other over Miranda's head with a moveless gaze that Miranda had seen often, and their eyes looked exactly alike. Miranda blinked up at them, waiting to see who would win. Then Grandmother's hand fell away, and Miranda was handed over to her father. He gave the reins to Uncle Jimbilly, and lifted her over the top of the seat. She sprawled against his chest and knees as if he were an armchair and stopped crying at once. "We can't go back just for notions," he told her in the reasoning tone he always talked in when Grandmother scolded, and held the muffly handkerchief for her. "Now, blow hard. What did you forget, honey? We'll find another. Was it your doll?"

Miranda hated dolls. She never played with them. She always pulled the wigs off and tied them on the kittens, like hats. The kittens pulled them off instantly. It was fun. She put the doll clothes on the kittens and it took any one of them just half a minute to get them all off again. Kittens had sense. Miranda wailed suddenly, "Oh, I want my doll!" and cried again, trying to drown out the strange little sound, "Weep, weep"—

"Well now, if that's all," said her father comfortably, "there's a raft of dolls at Cedar Grove, and about forty fresh kittens. How'd you like that?"

"Forty?" asked Miranda.

"About," said Father.

Old Aunt Nannie leaned and held out her hand. "Look, honey, I toted you some nice black figs."

Her face was wrinkled and black and it looked like a fig upside down with a white ruffled cap. Miranda clenched her eyes tight and shook her head.

"Is that a pretty way to behave when Aunt Nannie offers you something nice?" asked Grandmother in her gentle reminding tone of voice.

"No, ma'am," said Miranda meekly. "Thank you, Aunt Nannie." But she did not accept the figs.

Great-Aunt Eliza, half way up a stepladder pitched against the flat-roofed chicken house, was telling Hinry just how to set up her telescope. "For a fellow who never saw or heard of a telescope," Great-Aunt Eliza said to Grandmother, who was really her sister Sophia Jane, "he doesn't do so badly so long as I tell him."

"I do wish you'd stop clambering up stepladders, Eliza," said Grandmother, "at your time of life."

"You're nothing but a nervous wreck, Sophia, I declare. When did you ever know me to get hurt?"

"Even so," said Grandmother tartly, "there is such a thing as appropriate behavior at your time of . . ."

Great-Aunt Eliza seized a fold of her heavy brown pleated skirt with one hand, with the other she grasped the ladder one rung higher and ascended another step. "Now Hinry," she called, "just swing it around facing west and leave it level. I'll fix it the way I want when I'm ready. You can come on down now." She came down then herself, and said to her sister: "So long as you can go bouncing off on that horse of yours, Sophia Jane, I s'pose I can climb ladders. I'm three years younger than you, and *at your time of life* that makes all the difference!"

Grandmother turned pink as the inside of a seashell, the one on her sewing table that had the sound of the sea in it; Miranda knew that she had always been the pretty one, and she was pretty still, but Great-Aunt Eliza was not pretty now and never had been. Miranda, watching and listening—for everything in the world was strange to her and something she had to know about—saw two old women, who were proud of being grandmothers, who spoke to children always as if they knew best about everything and children knew nothing, and they told children all day long to come here, go there, do this, do not do that, and they were always right and children never were except when they did anything they were told right away without a word. And here they were bickering like two little girls at school, or even the way Miranda and her sister Maria bickered and nagged and picked on each other and said things on purpose to hurt each other's feelings. Miranda felt sad and strange and a little frightened. She began edging away.

"Where are you going, Miranda?" asked Grandmother in her everyday voice.

"Just to the house," said Miranda, her heart sinking.

"Wait and walk with us," said Grandmother. She was very thin and pale and had white hair. Beside her, Great-Aunt Eliza loomed like a mountain with her grizzled iron-colored hair like a curly wig, her steel-rimmed spectacles over her snuff-colored eyes, and snuff-colored woollen skirts billowing about her, and her smell of snuff. When she came through the door she quite filled it up. When she sat down the chair disappeared under her, and she seemed to be sitting solidly on herself from her waistband to the floor.

Now with Grandmother sitting across the room rummaging in her work basket and pretending not to see anything, Great-Aunt Eliza took a small brown bottle out of her pocket, opened it, took a pinch of snuff in each nostril, sneezed loudly, wiped her nose with a big white starchy-looking handkerchief, pushed her spectacles up on her forehead, took a little twig chewed into a brush at one end, dipped and twisted it around in the little bottle, and placed it firmly between her teeth. Miranda had heard of this shameful habit in women of the lower classes, but no lady had been known to "dip snuff," and surely not in the family. Yet here was Great-Aunt Eliza, a lady even if not a very pretty one, dipping snuff. Miranda knew how her grandmother felt about it; she stared fascinated at Great-Aunt Eliza until her eyes watered. Great-Aunt Eliza stared back in turn.

"Look here, young one, d'ye s'pose if I gave you a gumdrop you'd get out from underfoot?"

She reached in the other pocket and took out a roundish, rather crushed-looking pink gumdrop with the sugar coating pretty badly crackled. "Now take this, and don't let me lay eyes on you any more today."

Miranda hurried away, clenching the gumdrop in her palm. When she reached the kitchen it was oozing through her fingers. She went to the tap and held her hand under the water and tried to wash off the snuffy smell. After this crime she did not really dare go near Great-Aunt Eliza again soon. "What did you do with that gumdrop so quickly, child?" she could almost hear her asking.

Yet Miranda almost forgot her usual interests, such as kittens and other little animals on the place, pigs, chickens, rabbits, anything at all so it was a baby and would let her pet and feed it, for Great-Aunt Eliza's ways and habits kept Miranda following her about, gazing, or sitting across the dining-table, gazing, for when Great-Aunt Eliza was not on the roof before her telescope, always just before daylight or just after dark, she was walking about with a microscope and a burning glass, peering closely at something she saw on a tree trunk, something she found in the grass; now and then she collected fragments that looked like dried leaves or bits of bark, brought them in the house, spread them out on a sheet of white paper, and sat there, poring, as still as if she were saying her prayers. At table she would dissect a scrap of potato peeling or anything else she might be eating, and sit there, bowed over, saying, "Hum," from time to time. Grandmother, who did not allow the children to bring anything to the table to play with and who forbade them to do anything but eat while they were there, ignored her sister's manners as long as she could, then remarked one day, when Great-Aunt Eliza was humming like a bee to herself over what her microscope had found in a raisin, "Eliza, if it is interesting save it for me to look at after dinner. Or tell me what it is."

"You wouldn't know if I told you," said Great-Aunt Eliza, coolly, putting her microscope away and finishing off her pudding.

When at last, just before they were all going back to town again, Great-Aunt Eliza invited the children to climb the ladder with her and see the stars through her telescope, they were so awed they looked at each other like strangers, and did not exchange a word. Miranda saw only a great pale flaring disk of cold light, but she knew it was the moon and called out in pure rapture, "Oh, it's like another world!"

"Why, of course, child," said Great-Aunt Eliza, in her growling voice, but kindly, "other worlds, a million other worlds."

"Like this one?" asked Miranda, timidly.

"Nobody knows, child. . . ."

"Nobody knows, nobody knows," Miranda sang to a tune in her head, and when the others walked on, she was so dazzled with joy she fell back by herself, walking a little distance behind Great-Aunt Eliza's swinging lantern and her wide-swinging skirts. They took the dewy path through the fig grove, much like the one in town, with the early dew bringing out the sweet smell of the milky leaves. They passed a fig tree with low hanging branches, and Miranda reached up by habit and touched it with her fingers for luck. From the earth beneath her feet came a terrible, faint troubled sound. "Weep weep, weep weep . . ." murmured a little crying voice from the smothering earth, the grave.

Miranda bounded like a startled pony against the back of Great-Aunt Eliza's knees, crying out, "Oh, oh, oh, wait . . ."

"What on earth's the matter, child?"

Miranda seized the warm snuffy hand held out to her and hung on hard. "Oh, there's something saying 'weep weep' out of the ground!"

Great-Aunt Eliza stooped, put her arm around Miranda and listened carefully, for a moment. "Hear them?" she said. "They're not in the ground at all. They are the first tree frogs, means it's going to rain," she said, "weep weep—hear them?"

Miranda took a deep trembling breath and heard them. They were in the trees. They walked on again, Miranda holding Great-Aunt Eliza's hand.

"Just think," said Great-Aunt Eliza, in her most scientific voice, "when tree frogs shed their skins, they pull them off over their heads like little shirts, and they eat them. Can you imagine? They have the prettiest little shapes you ever saw—I'll show you one some time under the microscope."

"Thank you, ma'am," Miranda remembered finally to say through her fog of bliss at hearing the tree frogs sing, "Weep weep . . ."

## *Study questions*

1. *How old is Miranda? What is her position in the family? How many people tell Miranda what to do and how to behave?* 2. *Why is Miranda continually*

*surprised? What kinds of things surprise her?* 3. *Account for Miranda's interest in death. Why does she have to bury the dead little chicken? Why doesn't she tell anyone what she is doing?* 4. *How does the "sad little crying sound" affect Miranda? How is the fact that the sound is "Weep, weep" significant?* 5. *Does Miranda really believe that her family will go off and leave her behind? Why does she cry for a doll though she hates dolls?* 6. *How is Great-Aunt Eliza different from Grandmother? What surprises Miranda about the relationship between the two women? What surprises Miranda about the behavior of Great-Aunt Eliza?* 7. *What is the significance of Great-Aunt Eliza's telescope and microscope?* 8. *Why is Miranda dazzled with joy when Great-Aunt Eliza says, "Nobody knows, child"?* 9. *How do the tree frogs function? the fig trees?*

*F. Scott Fitzgerald* (1896–1940), chronicler of the Jazz Age and its interpreter, achieved fame and monetary success with the publication of his first novel, *This Side of Paradise,* in 1920, when he was twenty-four years old. Born in St. Paul, Minnesota, he attended private schools, preparatory to his matriculation at Princeton University. Before he graduated, however, he took a commission in the United States Army, where he served until 1919. After the success of his first novel, he followed with the publication of *The Beautiful and Damned* (1921), *The Great Gatsby* (1925), and *Tender Is the Night* (1934). His stories were collected in *Flappers and Philosophers* (1920), *Tales of the Jazz Age* (1922), *All the Sad Young Men* (1926), and *Taps at Reveille* (1935). Toward the end of his life he went into a decline, brought on by ill-health and intense personal problems, many of which he discussed in "The Crack-Up" (1936). He died at the age of forty-four. Though at the time of his death he was out of literary favor, his stories and novels have, nevertheless, often been reprinted, and he is continually read. *The Last Tycoon* (1941) was published posthumously. "The Baby Party" shows both the ridiculous behavior adults can indulge in when their children are "put down" and the love that motivates their behavior.

## THE BABY PARTY

When John Andros felt old he found solace in the thought of life continuing through his child. The dark trumpets of oblivion were less loud at the patter of his child's feet or at the sound of his child's voice babbling mad non sequiturs to him over the telephone. The latter incident occurred every afternoon at three when his wife called the office from the country, and he came to look forward to it as one of the vivid minutes of his day.

He was not physically old, but his life had been a series of struggles up a series of rugged hills, and here at thirty-eight having won his battles against ill-health and poverty he cherished less than the usual number of illusions. Even his feeling about his little girl was qualified. She had interrupted his rather intense love-affair with his wife, and she was the reason for their living in a suburban town, where they paid for country air with endless servant troubles and the weary merry-go-round of the commuting train.

It was little Ede as a definite piece of youth that chiefly interested him. He liked to take her on his lap and examine minutely her fragrant, downy scalp and her eyes with their irises of morning blue. Having paid this homage John was content that the nurse should take her away. After ten minutes the very vitality of the child irritated him; he was inclined to lose his temper when things were broken, and one Sunday afternoon when she had disrupted a bridge game by permanently hiding up the ace of spades, he had made a scene that had reduced his wife to tears.

This was absurd and John was ashamed of himself. It was inevitable that such things would happen, and it was impossible that little Ede should spend all her indoor hours in the nursery up-stairs when she was becoming, as her mother said, more nearly a "real person" every day.

She was two and a half, and this afternoon, for instance, she was going to a baby party. Grown-up Edith, her mother, had telephoned the information to the office, and little Ede had confirmed the business by shouting "I yam going to a *pantry!*" into John's unsuspecting left ear.

"Drop in at the Markeys' when you get home, won't you, dear?" resumed her mother. "It'll be funny. Ede's going to be all dressed up in her new pink dress——"

The conversation terminated abruptly with a squawk which indicated that the telephone had been pulled violently to the floor. John laughed and decided to get an early train out; the prospect of a baby party in some one else's house amused him.

"What a peach of a mess!" he thought humorously. "A dozen mothers, and each one looking at nothing but her own child. All the babies breaking things and grabbing at the cake, and each mama going home thinking about the subtle superiority of her own child to every other child there."

He was in a good humor to-day—all the things in his life were going better than they had ever gone before. When he got off the train at his station he shook his head at an importunate taxi man, and began to walk up the long hill toward his house through the crisp December twilight. It was only six o'clock but the moon was out, shining with proud brilliance on the thin sugary snow that lay over the lawns.

As he walked along drawing his lungs full of cold air his happiness increased, and the idea of a baby party appealed to him more and more. He began to wonder how Ede compared to other children of her own age, and if the pink dress she was to wear was something radical and mature. Increasing his gait he came in sight of his own house, where the lights of a defunct Christmas-tree still blossomed in the window, but he continued on past the walk. The party was at the Markeys' next door.

As he mounted the brick step and rang the bell he became aware of voices inside, and he was glad he was not too late. Then he raised his head and listened —the voices were not children's voices, but they were loud and pitched high with anger; there were at least three of them and one, which rose as he listened to a hysterical sob, he recognized immediately as his wife's.

"There's been some trouble," he thought quickly.

Trying the door, he found it unlocked and pushed it open.

The baby party began at half past four, but Edith Andros, calculating shrewdly that the new dress would stand out more sensationally against vestments already rumpled, planned the arrival of herself and little Ede for five. When they appeared it was already a flourishing affair. Four baby girls and nine baby boys, each one curled and washed and dressed with all the care of a proud and jealous heart, were dancing to the music of a phonograph. Never more than two or three were dancing at once, but as all were continually in motion running to and from their mothers for encouragement, the general effect was the same.

As Edith and her daughter entered, the music was temporarily drowned out by a sustained chorus, consisting largely of the word *cute* and directed toward little Ede, who stood looking timidly about and fingering the edges of her pink dress. She was not kissed—this is the sanitary age—but she was passed along a row of mamas each one of whom said "cu-u-ute" to her and held her pink little hand before passing her on to the next. After some encouragement and a few mild pushes she was absorbed into the dance, and became an active member of the party.

Edith stood near the door talking to Mrs. Markey, and keeping one eye on the tiny figure in the pink dress. She did not care for Mrs. Markey; she considered her both snippy and common, but John and Joe Markey were congenial and went in together on the commuting train every morning, so the two women kept up an elaborate pretense of warm amity. They were always reproaching each other for "not coming to see me," and they were always planning the kind of parties that began with "You'll have to come to dinner with us soon, and we'll go in to the theatre," but never matured further.

"Little Ede looks perfectly darling," said Mrs. Markey, smiling and moistening her lips in a way that Edith found particularly repulsive. "So *grown-up*—I can't *believe* it!"

Edith wondered if "little Ede" referred to the fact that Billy Markey, though several months younger, weighed almost five pounds more. Accepting a cup of tea she took a seat with two other ladies on a divan and launched into the real business of the afternoon, which of course lay in relating the recent accomplishments and insouciances of her child.

An hour passed. Dancing palled and the babies took to sterner sport. They ran into the dining-room, rounded the big table, and essayed the kitchen door, from which they were rescued by an expeditionary force of mothers. Having been rounded up they immediately broke loose, and rushing back to the dining-room tried the familiar swinging door again. The word "overheated" began to be used, and small white brows were dried with small white handkerchiefs. A general attempt to make the babies sit down began, but the babies squirmed off laps with peremptory cries of "Down! Down!" and the rush into the fascinating dining-room began anew.

This phase of the party came to an end with the arrival of refreshments, a large cake with two candles, and saucers of vanilla ice-cream. Billy Markey, a stout laughing baby with red hair and legs somewhat bowed, blew out the candles, and placed an experimental thumb on the white frosting. The refreshments were distributed, and the children ate, greedily but without confusion—they had behaved remarkedly well all afternoon. They were modern babies who ate and slept at regular hours, so their dispositions were good, and their faces healthy and pink—such a peaceful party would not have been possible thirty years ago.

After the refreshments a gradual exodus began. Edith glanced anxiously at her watch—it was almost six, and John had not arrived. She wanted him to see Ede with the other children—to see how dignified and polite and intelligent she was, and how the only ice-cream spot on her dress was some that had dropped from her chin when she was joggled from behind.

"You're a darling," she whispered to her child, drawing her suddenly against her knee. "Do you know you're a darling? Do you *know* you're a darling?"

Ede laughed. "Bow-wow," she said suddenly.

"Bow-wow?" Edith looked around. "There isn't any bow-wow."

"Bow-wow," repeated Ede. "I want a bow-wow."

Edith followed the small pointing finger.

"That isn't a bow-wow, dearest, that's a teddy-bear."

"Bear?"

"Yes, that's a teddy-bear, and it belongs to Billy Markey. You don't want Billy Markey's teddy-bear, do you?"

Ede did want it.

She broke away from her mother and approached Billy Markey, who held the toy closely in his arms. Ede stood regarding him with inscrutable eyes, and Billy laughed.

Grown-up Edith looked at her watch again, this time impatiently.

The party had dwindled until, besides Ede and Billy, there were only two babies remaining—and one of the two remained only by virtue of having hidden himself under the dining-room table. It was selfish of John not to come. It showed so little pride in the child. Other fathers had come, half a dozen of them, to call for their wives, and they had stayed for a while and looked on.

There was a sudden wail. Ede had obtained Billy's teddy-bear by pulling it forcibly from his arms, and on Billy's attempt to recover it, she had pushed him casually to the floor.

"Why, Ede!" cried her mother, repressing an inclination to laugh.

Joe Markey, a handsome, broad-shouldered man of thirty-five, picked up his son and set him on his feet. "You're a fine fellow," he said jovially. "Let a girl knock you over! You're a fine fellow."

"Did he bump his head?" Mrs. Markey returned anxiously from bowing the next to last remaining mother out the door.

"No-o-o-o," exclaimed Markey. "He bumped something else, didn't you, Billy? He bumped something else."

Billy had so far forgotten the bump that he was already making an attempt to recover his property. He seized a leg of the bear which projected from Ede's enveloping arms and tugged at it but without success.

"No," said Ede emphatically.

Suddenly, encouraged by the success of her former half-accidental manoeuvre, Ede dropped the teddy-bear, placed her hands on Billy's shoulders and pushed him backward off his feet.

This time he landed less harmlessly; his head hit the bare floor just off the rug with a dull hollow sound, whereupon he drew in his breath and delivered an agonized yell.

Immediately the room was in confusion. With an exclamation Markey hurried to his son, but his wife was first to reach the injured baby and catch him up into her arms.

"Oh, *Billy*," she cried, "what a terrible bump! She ought to be spanked."

Edith, who had rushed immediately to her daughter, heard this remark, and her lips came sharply together.

"Why, Ede," she whispered perfunctorily, "you bad girl!"

Ede put back her little head suddenly and laughed. It was a loud laugh, a triumphant laugh with victory in it and challenge and contempt. Unfortunately it was also an infectious laugh. Before her mother realized the delicacy of the situation, she too had laughed, an audible, distinct laugh not unlike the baby's, and partaking of the same overtones.

Then, as suddenly, she stopped.

Mrs. Markey's face had grown red with anger, and Markey, who had been feeling the back of the baby's head with one finger, looked at her, frowning.

"It's swollen already," he said with a note of reproof in his voice. "I'll get some witch-hazel."

But Mrs. Markey had lost her temper. "I don't see anything funny about a child being hurt!" she said in a trembling voice.

Little Ede meanwhile had been looking at her mother curiously. She noted that her own laugh had produced her mother's and she wondered if the same cause would always produce the same effect. So she chose this moment to throw back her head and laugh again.

To her mother the additional mirth added the final touch of hysteria to the situation. Pressing her handkerchief to her mouth she giggled irrepressibly. It was more than nervousness—she felt that in a peculiar way she was laughing with her child—they were laughing together.

It was in a way a defiance—those two against the world.

While Markey rushed up-stairs to the bathroom for ointment, his wife was walking up and down rocking the yelling boy in her arms.

"Please go home!" she broke out suddenly. "The child's badly hurt, and if you haven't the decency to be quiet, you'd better go home."

"Very well," said Edith, her own temper rising. "I've never seen any one make such a mountain out of——"

"Get out!" cried Mrs. Markey frantically. "There's the door, get out—I never want to see you in our house again. You or your brat either!"

Edith had taken her daughter's hand and was moving quickly toward the door, but at this remark she stopped and turned around, her face contracting with indignation.

"Don't you dare call her that!"

Mrs. Markey did not answer but continued walking up and down, muttering to herself and to Billy in an inaudible voice.

Edith began to cry.

"I will get out!" she sobbed, "I've never heard anybody so rude and c-common in my life. I'm glad your baby did get pushed down—he's nothing but a f-fat little fool anyhow."

Joe Markey reached the foot of the stairs just in time to hear this remark.

"Why, Mrs. Andros," he said sharply, "can't you see the child's hurt? You really ought to control yourself."

"Control m-myself!" exclaimed Edith brokenly. "You better ask her to c-control herself. I've never heard anybody so c-common in my life."

"She's insulting me!" Mrs. Markey was now livid with rage. "Did you hear what she said, Joe? I wish you'd put her out. If she won't go, just take her by the shoulders and put her out!"

"Don't you dare touch me!" cried Edith. "I'm going just as quick as I can find my c-coat!"

Blind with tears she took a step toward the hall. It was just at this moment that the door opened and John Andros walked anxiously in.

"John!" cried Edith, and fled to him wildly.

"What's the matter? Why, what's the matter?"

"They're—they're putting me out!" she wailed, collapsing against him. "He'd just started to take me by the shoulders and put me out. I want my coat!"

"That's not true," objected Markey hurriedly. "Nobody's going to put you out." He turned to John. "Nobody's going to put her out," he repeated. "She's——"

"What do you mean 'put her out'?" demanded John abruptly. "What's all this talk, anyhow?"

"Oh, let's go!" cried Edith. "I want to go. They're so *common*, John!"

"Look here!" Markey's face darkened. "You've said that about enough. You're acting sort of crazy."

"They called Ede a brat!"

For the second time that afternoon little Ede expressed emotion at an inopportune moment. Confused and frightened at the shouting voices, she began to cry, and her tears had the effect of conveying that she felt the insult in her heart.

"What's the idea of this?" broke out John. "Do you insult your guests in your own house?"

"It seems to me it's your wife that's done the insulting!" answered Markey crisply. "In fact, your baby there started all the trouble."

John gave a contemptuous snort. "Are you calling names at a little baby?" he inquired. "That's a fine manly business!"

"Don't talk to him, John," insisted Edith. "Find my coat!"

"You must be in a bad way," went on John angrily, "if you have to take out your temper on a helpless little baby."

"I never heard anything so damn twisted in my life," shouted Markey. "If that wife of yours would shut her mouth for a minute——"

"Wait a minute! You're not talking to a woman and child now——"

There was an incidental interruption. Edith had been fumbling on a chair for her coat, and Mrs. Markey had been watching her with hot, angry eyes. Suddenly she laid Billy down on the sofa, where he immediately stopped crying and pulled himself upright, and coming into the hall she quickly found Edith's coat and handed it to her without a word. Then she went back to the sofa, picked up Billy, and rocking him in her arms looked again at Edith with hot, angry eyes. The interruption had taken less than half a minute.

"Your wife comes in here and begins shouting around about how common we are!" burst out Markey violently. "Well, if we're so damn common, you'd better stay away! And, what's more, you'd better get out now!"

Again John gave a short, contemptuous laugh.

"You're not only common," he returned, "you're evidently an awful bully —when there's any helpless women and children around." He felt for the knob and swung the door open. "Come on, Edith."

Taking up her daughter in her arms, his wife stepped outside and John, still looking contemptuously at Markey, started to follow.

"Wait a minute!" Markey took a step forward; he was trembling slightly, and two large veins on his temple were suddenly full of blood. "You don't think you can get away with that, do you? With me?"

Without a word John walked out the door, leaving it open.

Edith, still weeping, had started for home. After following her with his eyes until she reached her own walk, John turned back toward the lighted doorway where Markey was slowly coming down the slippery steps. He took off his overcoat and hat, tossed them off the path onto the snow. Then, sliding a little on the iced walk, he took a step forward.

At the first blow, they both slipped and fell heavily to the sidewalk, half rising then, and again pulling each other to the ground. They found a better foothold in the thin snow to the side of the walk and rushed at each other, both swinging wildly and pressing out the snow into a pasty mud underfoot.

The street was deserted, and except for their short tired gasps and the padded sound as one or the other slipped down into the slushy mud, they fought in silence, clearly defined to each other by the full moonlight as well as by the amber glow that shone out of the open door. Several times they both slipped down together, and then for a while the conflict threshed about wildly on the lawn.

For ten, fifteen, twenty minutes they fought there senselessly in the moonlight. They had both taken off coats and vests at some silently agreed upon interval and now their shirts dripped from their backs in wet pulpy shreds. Both were torn and bleeding and so exhausted that they could stand only when by their position they mutually supported each other—the impact, the mere effort of a blow, would send them both to their hands and knees.

But it was not weariness that ended the business, and the very meaninglessness of the fight was a reason for not stopping. They stopped because once when they were straining at each other on the ground, they heard a man's footsteps coming along the sidewalk. They had rolled somehow into the shadow, and when they heard these footsteps they stopped fighting, stopped moving, stopped breathing, lay huddled together like two boys playing Indian until the footsteps had passed. Then, staggering to their feet, they looked at each other like two drunken men.

"I'll be damned if I'm going on with this thing any more," cried Markey thickly.

"I'm not going on any more either," said John Andros. "I've had enough of this thing."

Again they looked at each other, sulkily this time, as if each suspected the other of urging him to a renewal of the fight. Markey spat out a mouthful of blood from a cut lip; then he cursed softly, and picking up his coat and vest, shook off the snow from them in a surprised way, as if their comparative dampness was his only worry in the world.

"Want to come in and wash up?" he asked suddenly.

"No, thanks," said John. "I ought to be going home—my wife'll be worried."

He too picked up his coat and vest and then his overcoat and hat. Soaking wet and dripping with perspiration, it seemed absurd that less than half an hour ago he had been wearing all these clothes.

"Well—good night," he said hesitantly.

Suddenly they both walked toward each other and shook hands. It was no perfunctory hand-shake: John Andros's arm went around Markey's shoulder, and he patted him softly on the back for a little while.

"No harm done," he said brokenly.

"No—you?"

"No, no harm done."

"Well," said John Andros after a minute, "I guess I'll say good night."

Limping slightly and with his clothes over his arm, John Andros turned away. The moonlight was still bright as he left the dark patch of trampled ground and walked over the intervening lawn. Down at the station, half a mile away, he could hear the rumble of the seven o'clock train.

"But you must have been crazy," cried Edith brokenly. "I thought you were going to fix it all up there and shake hands. That's why I went away."

"Did you want us to fix it up?"

"Of course not, I never want to see them again. But I thought of course that was what you were going to do." She was touching the bruises on his neck and back with iodine as he sat placidly in a hot bath. "I'm going to get the doctor," she said insistently. "You may be hurt internally."

He shook his head. "Not a chance," he answered. "I don't want this to get all over town."

"I don't understand yet how it all happened."

"Neither do I." He smiled grimly. "I guess these baby parties are pretty rough affairs."

"Well, one thing—" suggested Edith hopefully, "I'm certainly glad we have beefsteak in the house for to-morrow's dinner."

"Why?"

"For your eye, of course. Do you know I came within an ace of ordering veal? Wasn't that the luckiest thing?"

Half an hour later, dressed except that his neck would accommodate no collar, John moved his limbs experimentally before the glass. "I believe I'll get myself in better shape," he said thoughtfully. "I must be getting old."

"You mean so that next time you can beat him?"

"I did beat him," he announced. "At least, I beat him as much as he beat me. And there isn't going to be any next time. Don't you go calling people common any more. If you get in any trouble, you just take your coat and go home. Understand?"

"Yes, dear," she said meekly. "I was very foolish and now I understand."

Out in the hall, he paused abruptly by the baby's door.

"Is she asleep?"

"Sound asleep. But you can go in and peek at her—just to say good night."

They tiptoed in and bent together over the bed. Little Ede, her cheeks flushed with health, her pink hands clasped tight together, was sleeping soundly in the cool, dark room. John reached over the railing of the bed and passed his hand lightly over the silken hair.

"She's asleep," he murmured in a puzzled way.

"Naturally, after such an afternoon."

"Miz Andros," the colored maid's stage whisper floated in from the hall, "Mr. and Miz Markey downstairs an' want to see you. Mr. Markey he's all cut up in pieces, ma'am. His face look like a roast beef. An' Miz Markey she 'pear mighty mad."

"Why, what incomparable nerve!" exclaimed Edith. "Just tell them we're not home. I wouldn't go down for anything in the world."

"You most certainly will." John's voice was hard and set.

"What?"

"You'll go down right now, and, what's more, whatever that other woman does, you'll apologize for what you said this afternoon. After that you don't ever have to see her again."

"Why—John, I can't."

"You've got to. And just remember that she probably hated to come over here just twice as much as you hate to go downstairs."

"Aren't you coming? Do I have to go alone?"

"I'll be down—in just a minute."

John Andros waited until she had closed the door behind her; then he reached over into the bed, and picking up his daughter, blankets and all, sat down in the rocking-chair holding her tightly in his arms. She moved a little, and he held his breath, but she was sleeping soundly, and in a moment she was resting quietly in the hollow of his elbow. Slowly he bent his head until his cheek was against her bright hair. "Dear little girl," he whispered. "Dear little girl, dear little girl."

John Andros knew at length what it was he had fought for so savagely that evening. He had it now, he possessed it forever, and for some time he sat there rocking very slowly to and fro in the darkness.

## *Study questions*

1. *In this story the voice of a narrator can be heard apart from the thoughts of the characters. What kind of tone does this voice provide? Is the tone relevant to the action?* 2. *At the beginning of the story, how does John Andros feel about Ede? Have his feelings changed at the end?* 3. *Account for the fight between the women. How is it resolved?* 4. *Account for the fight between the men. How is it resolved?* 5. *Are sex roles operative in this story? status roles?*

*William Faulkner* (1897–1962), certainly the greatest American novelist of the first half of this century, was born in New Albany, Mississippi, but soon moved to Oxford, Mississippi, where he spent most of his life. He attended the University of Mississippi for about a year and then joined the British Royal Air Force in Canada for a short stint. Though he traveled abroad and went to New York, New Orleans (where he met Sherwood Anderson), and Hollywood, he was never away from Oxford for long. His best novels—*The Sound and the Fury, As I Lay Dying,* and *Absalom, Absalom!*—were written in the 1920s and 1930s, but his great literary achievement was not recognized until the 1940s. He received the Nobel Prize in 1949 and the Pulitzer Prize for *A Fable* in 1954 and *The Reivers* in 1963. A volume of *Collected Stories,* for which he received the National Book Award, was published in 1950. Faulkner's home town of Oxford became a model for the fictional town of Jefferson in Yoknapatawpha County, which was the setting for most of his fiction, both novels and short stories. His most frequently anthologized short stories include "A Rose for Emily," "Spotted Horses," "The Old People," "Dry September," "That Evening Sun," "Delta Autumn," and "Wash," which, taken together, show the range of his writing style. "A Rose for Emily" scrambles chronology and makes use of montage patterns to present Emily as both individual and symbol, as the narrator says, "dear, inescapable, impervious, tranquil, and perverse."

# A ROSE FOR EMILY

## *1*

When Miss Emily Grierson died, our whole town went to her funeral: the men through a sort of respectful affection for a fallen monument, the women mostly out of curiosity to see the inside of her house, which no one save an old manservant—a combined gardener and cook—had seen in at least ten years.

It was a big, squarish frame house that had once been white, decorated with cupolas and spires and scrolled balconies in the heavily lightsome style of the seventies, set on what had once been our most select street. But garages and cotton gins had encroached and obliterated even the august names of that neighborhood; only Miss Emily's house was left, lifting its stubborn and coquettish decay above the cotton wagons and the gasoline pumps—an eyesore among eyesores. And now Miss Emily had gone to join the representatives of those august names where they lay in the cedar-bemused cemetery among the ranked and anonymous graves of Union and Confederate soldiers who fell at the battle of Jefferson.

Alive, Miss Emily had been a tradition, a duty, and a care; a sort of hereditary obligation upon the town, dating from that day in 1894 when Colonel

Sartoris, the mayor—he who fathered the edict that no Negro woman should appear on the streets without an apron—remitted her taxes, the dispensation dating from the death of her father on into perpetuity. Not that Miss Emily would have accepted charity. Colonel Sartoris invented an involved tale to the effect that Miss Emily's father had loaned money to the town, which the town, as a matter of business, preferred this way of repaying. Only a man of Colonel Sartoris' generation and thought could have invented it, and only a woman could have believed it.

When the next generation, with its more modern ideas, became mayors and aldermen, this arrangement created some little dissatisfaction. On the first day of the year they mailed her a tax notice. February came, and there was no reply. They wrote her a formal letter, asking her to call at the sheriff's office at her convenience. A week later the mayor wrote her himself, offering to call or to send his car for her, and received in reply a note on paper of an archaic shape, in a thin, flowing calligraphy in faded ink, to the effect that she no longer went out at all. The tax notice was also enclosed, without comment.

They called a special meeting of the Board of Aldermen. A deputation waited upon her, knocked at the door through which no visitor had passed since she ceased giving china-painting lessons eight or ten years earlier. They were admitted by the old Negro into a dim hall from which a stairway mounted into still more shadow. It smelled of dust and disuse—a close, dank smell. The Negro led them into the parlor. It was furnished in heavy, leather-covered furniture. When the Negro opened the blinds of one window, they could see that the leather was cracked; and when they sat down, a faint dust rose sluggishly about their thighs, spinning with slow motes in the single run-ray. On a tarnished gilt easel before the fireplace stood a crayon portrait of Miss Emily's father.

They rose when she entered—a small, fat woman in black, with a thin gold chain descending to her waist and vanishing into her belt, leaning on an ebony cane with a tarnished gold head. Her skeleton was small and spare; perhaps that was why what would have been merely plumpness in another was obesity in her. She looked bloated, like a body long submerged in motionless water, and of that pallid hue. Her eyes, lost in the fatty ridges of her face, looked like two small pieces of coal pressed into a lump of dough as they moved from one face to another while the visitors stated their errand.

She did not ask them to sit. She just stood in the door and listened quietly until the spokesman came to a stumbling halt. Then they could hear the invisible watch ticking at the end of the gold chain.

Her voice was dry and cold. "I have no taxes in Jefferson. Colonel Sartoris explained it to me. Perhaps one of you can gain access to the city records and satisfy yourselves."

"But we have. We are the city authorities, Miss Emily. Didn't you get a notice from the sheriff, signed by him?"

"I received a paper, yes," Miss Emily said. "Perhaps he considers himself the sheriff . . . I have no taxes in Jefferson."

"But there is nothing on the books to show that, you see. We must go by the—"

"See Colonel Sartoris. I have no taxes in Jefferson."

"But, Miss Emily—"

"See Colonel Sartoris." (Colonel Sartoris had been dead almost ten years.) "I have no taxes in Jefferson. Tobe!" The Negro appeared. "Show these gentlemen out."

## 2

So she vanquished them, horse and foot, just as she had vanquished their fathers thirty years before about the smell. That was two years after her father's death and a short time after her sweetheart—the one we believed would marry her—had deserted her. After her father's death she went out very little; after her sweetheart went away, people hardly saw her at all. A few of the ladies had the temerity to call, but were not received, and the only sign of life about the place was the Negro man—a young man then—going in and out with a market basket.

"Just as if a man—any man—could keep a kitchen properly," the ladies said; so they were not surprised when the smell developed. It was another link between the gross, teeming world and the high and mighty Griersons.

A neighbor, a woman, complained to the mayor, Judge Stevens, eighty years old.

"But what will you have me do about it, madam?" he said.

"Why, send her word to stop it," the woman said. "Isn't there a law?"

"I'm sure that won't be necessary," Judge Stevens said. "It's probably just a snake or a rat that nigger of hers killed in the yard. I'll speak to him about it."

The next day he received two more complaints, one from a man who came in diffident deprecation. "We really must do something about it, Judge. I'd be the last one in the world to bother Miss Emily, but we've got to do something." That night the Board of Aldermen met—three graybeards and one younger man, a member of the rising generation.

"It's simple enough," he said. "Send her word to have her place cleaned up. Give her a certain time to do it in, and if she don't . . ."

"Dammit, sir," Judge Stevens said, "will you accuse a lady to her face of smelling bad?"

So the next night, after midnight, four men crossed Miss Emily's lawn and slunk about the house like burglars, sniffing along the base of the brickwork and at the cellar openings while one of them performed a regular sowing motion with his hand out of a sack slung from his shoulder. They broke open the cellar door and sprinkled lime there, and in all the outbuildings. As they recrossed the lawn, a window that had been dark was lighted and Miss Emily sat in it, the light behind her, and her upright torso motionless as that of an idol. They crept quietly across the lawn and into the shadow of the locusts that lined the street. After a week or two the smell went away.

That was when people had begun to feel really sorry for her. People in our town, remembering how old lady Wyatt, her great-aunt, had gone completely crazy at last, believed that the Griersons held themselves a little too high for what they really were. None of the young men were quite good enough for Miss

Emily and such. We had long thought of them as a tableau; Miss Emily a slender figure in white in the background, her father a spraddled silhouette in the foreground, his back to her and clutching a horsewhip, the two of them framed by the back-flung front door. So when she got to be thirty and was still single, we were not pleased exactly, but vindicated; even with insanity in the family she wouldn't have turned down all of her chances if they had really materialized.

When her father died, it got about that the house was all that was left to her; and in a way, people were glad. At last they could pity Miss Emily. Being left alone, and a pauper, she had become humanized. Now she too would know the old thrill and the old despair of a penny more or less.

The day after his death all the ladies prepared to call at the house and offer condolence and aid, as is our custom. Miss Emily met them at the door, dressed as usual and with no trace of grief on her face. She told them that her father was not dead. She did that for three days, with the ministers calling on her, and the doctors, trying to persuade her to let them dispose of the body. Just as they were about to resort to law and force, she broke down, and they buried her father quickly.

We did not say she was crazy then. We believed she had to do that. We remembered all the young men her father had driven away, and we knew that with nothing left, she would have to cling to that which had robbed her, as people will.

## *3*

She was sick for a long time. When we saw her again, her hair was cut short, making her look like a girl, with a vague resemblance to those angels in colored church windows—sort of tragic and serene.

The town had just let the contracts for paving the sidewalks, and in the summer after her father's death they began the work. The construction company came with niggers and mules and machinery, and a foreman named Homer Barron, a Yankee—a big, dark, ready man, with a big voice and eyes lighter than his face. The little boys would follow in groups to hear him cuss the niggers, and the niggers singing in time to the rise and fall of picks. Pretty soon he knew everybody in town. Whenever you heard a lot of laughing anywhere about the square, Homer Barron would be in the center of the group. Presently we began to see him and Miss Emily on Sunday afternoons driving in the yellow-wheeled buggy and the matched team of bays from the livery stable.

At first we were glad that Miss Emily would have an interest, because the ladies all said, "Of course a Grierson would not think seriously of a Northerner, a day laborer." But there were still others, older people, who said that even grief could not cause a real lady to forget *noblesse oblige*—without calling it *noblesse oblige*. They just said, "Poor Emily. Her kinsfolk should come to her." She had some kin in Alabama; but years ago her father had fallen out with them over the estate of old lady Wyatt, the crazy woman, and there was no communication between the two families. They had not even been represented at the funeral.

And as soon as the old people said, "Poor Emily," the whispering began. "Do you suppose it's really so?" they said to one another. "Of course it is. What else could . . ." This behind their hands; rustling of craned silk and satin behind jalousies closed upon the sun of Sunday afternoon as the thin, swift clop-clop-clop of the matched team passed: "Poor Emily."

She carried her head high enough—even when we believed that she was fallen. It was as if she demanded more than ever the recognition of her dignity as the last Grierson; as if it had wanted that touch of earthiness to reaffirm her imperviousness. Like when she bought the rat poison, the arsenic. That was over a year after they had begun to say "Poor Emily," and while the two female cousins were visiting her.

"I want some poison," she said to the druggist. She was over thirty then, still a slight woman, though thinner than usual, with cold, haughty black eyes in a face the flesh of which was strained across the temples and about the eye-sockets as you imagine a lighthouse-keeper's face ought to look. "I want some poison," she said.

"Yes, Miss Emily. What kind? For rats and such? I'd recom—"

"I want the best you have. I don't care what kind."

The druggist named several. "They'll kill anything up to an elephant. But what you want is—"

"Arsenic," Miss Emily said. "Is that a good one?"

"Is . . . arsenic? Yes, ma'am. But what you want—"

"I want arsenic."

The druggist looked down at her. She looked back at him, erect, her face like a strained flag. "Why, of course," the druggist said. "If that's what you want. But the law requires you to tell what you are going to use it for."

Miss Emily just stared at him, her head tilted back in order to look him eye for eye, until he looked away and went and got the arsenic and wrapped it up. The Negro delivery boy brought her the package; the druggist didn't come back. When she opened the package at home there was written on the box, under the skull and bones: "For rats."

## 4

So the next day we all said "She will kill herself"; and we said it would be the best thing. When she had first begun to be seen with Homer Barron, we had said, "She will marry him." Then we said, "She will persuade him yet," because Homer himself had remarked—he liked men, and it was known that he drank with the younger men in the Elks' Club—that he was not a marrying man. Later we said, "Poor Emily" behind the jalousies as they passed on Sunday afternoon in the glittering buggy, Miss Emily with her head high and Homer Barron with his hat cocked and a cigar in his teeth, reins and whip in a yellow glove.

Then some of the ladies began to say that it was a disgrace to the town and a bad example to the young people. The men did not want to interfere, but at last the ladies forced the Baptist minister—Miss Emily's people were Episcopal—to call upon her. He would never divulge what happened during that interview, but he refused to go back again. The next Sunday they again drove about the streets, and the following day the minister's wife wrote to Miss Emily's relations in Alabama.

So she had blood-kin under her roof again and we sat back to watch developments. At first nothing happened. Then we were sure that they were to be married. We learned that Miss Emily had been to the jeweler's and ordered a man's toilet set in silver, with the letters H. B. on each piece. Two days later we learned that she had bought a complete outfit of men's clothing, including a nightshirt, and we said, "They are married." We were really glad. We were glad because the two female cousins were even more Grierson than Miss Emily had ever been.

So we were not surprised when Homer Barron—the streets had been finished some time since—was gone. We were a little disappointed that there was not a public blowing-off, but we believed that he had gone on to prepare for Miss Emily's coming, or to give her a chance to get rid of the cousins. (By that time it was a cabal, and we were all Miss Emily's allies to help circumvent the cousins.) Sure enough, after another week they departed. And, as we had expected all along, within three days Homer Barron was back in town. A neighbor saw the Negro man admit him at the kitchen door at dusk one evening.

And that was the last we saw of Homer Barron. And of Miss Emily for some time. The Negro man went in and out with the market basket, but the front door remained closed. Now and then we would see her at a window for a moment, as the men did that night when they sprinkled the lime, but for almost six months she did not appear on the streets. Then we knew that this was to be expected too; as if that quality of her father which had thwarted her woman's life so many times had been too virulent and too furious to die.

When we next saw Miss Emily, she had grown fat and her hair was turning gray. During the next few years it grew grayer and grayer until it attained an even pepper-and-salt iron-gray, when it ceased turning. Up to the day of her death at seventy-four it was still that vigorous iron-gray, like the hair of an active man.

From that time on her front door remained closed, save for a period of six or seven years, when she was about forty, during which she gave lessons in china-painting. She fitted up a studio in one of the downstairs rooms, where the daughters and granddaughters of Colonel Sartoris' contemporaries were sent to her with the same regularity and in the same spirit that they were sent to church on Sundays with a twenty-five cent piece for the collection plate. Meanwhile her taxes had been remitted.

Then the newer generation became the backbone and the spirit of the town, and the painting pupils grew up and fell away and did not send their children to her with boxes of color and tedious brushes and pictures cut from the ladies' magazines. The front door closed upon the last one and remained closed for good. When the town got free postal delivery, Miss Emily alone refused to let them fasten the metal numbers above her door and attach a mailbox to it. She would not listen to them.

Daily, monthly, yearly we watched the Negro grow grayer and more stooped, going in and out with the market basket. Each December we sent her a tax notice, which would be returned by the post office a week later, unclaimed. Now and then we would see her in one of the downstairs windows—she had evidently shut up the top floor of the house—like the carven torso of an idol in a niche, looking or not looking at us, we could never tell which. Thus she passed from generation to generation—dear, inescapable, impervious, tranquil, and perverse.

And so she died. Fell ill in the house filled with dust and shadows, with only a doddering Negro man to wait on her. We did not even know she was sick; we had long since given up trying to get any information from the Negro. He talked to no one, probably not even to her, for his voice had grown harsh and rusty, as if from disuse.

She died in one of the downstairs rooms, in a heavy walnut bed with a curtain, her gray head propped on a pillow yellow and moldy with age and lack of sunlight.

## *5*

The Negro met the first of the ladies at the front door and let them in, with their hushed, sibilant voices and their quick, curious glances, and then he disappeared. He walked right through the house and out the back and was not seen again.

The two female cousins came at once. They held the funeral on the second day, with the town coming to look at Miss Emily beneath a mass of bought flowers, with the crayon face of her father musing profoundly above the bier and the ladies sibilant and macabre; and the very old men—some in their brushed Confederate uniforms—on the porch and the lawn, talking of Miss Emily as if she had been a contemporary of theirs, believing that they had danced with her and courted her perhaps, confusing time with its mathematical progression, as the old do, to whom all the past is not a diminishing road but, instead, a huge meadow which no winter ever quite touches, divided from them now by the narrow bottle-neck of the most recent decade of years.

Already we knew that there was one room in that region above stairs which no one had seen in forty years, and which would have to be forced. They waited until Miss Emily was decently in the ground before they opened it.

The violence of breaking down the door seemed to fill this room with pervading dust. A thin, acrid pall as of the tomb seemed to lie everywhere upon this room decked and furnished as for a bridal: upon the valence curtains of faded rose color, upon the rose-shaded lights, upon the dressing table, upon the delicate array of crystal and the man's toilet things backed with tarnished silver, silver so tarnished that the monogram was obscured. Among them lay a collar and tie, as if they had just been removed, which, lifted, left upon the surface a pale crescent in the dust. Upon a chair hung the suit, carefully folded; beneath it the two mute shoes and the discarded socks.

The man himself lay in the bed.

For a long while we just stood there, looking down at the profound and fleshless grin. The body had apparently once lain in the attitude of an embrace, but now the long sleep that outlasts love, that conquers even the grimace of love, had cuckolded him. What was left of him, rotted beneath what was left of the nightshirt, had become inextricable from the bed in which he lay; and upon him and upon the pillow beside him lay that even coating of the patient and biding dust.

Then we noticed that in the second pillow was the indentation of a head. One of us lifted something from it, and leaning forward, that faint and invisible dust dry and acrid in the nostrils, we saw a long strand of iron-gray hair.

## *Study questions*

1. *What is the significance of the title of the story?* 2. *What is the point of view? How does it function?* 3. *Why does Faulkner scramble the chronology of the story?* 4. *If you were reading this story for the first time, were you surprised by the ending? Why or why not?* 5. *What role does Emily's father play in the story? Are there any relationships between Emily's father and Homer Barron?* 6. *In this story, Emily is both an individual and a symbol for the Old South. Account for her behavior on both levels.* 7. *What do the townspeople feel about Emily before they know about the necrophilia? after?* 8. *How does the dust operate as symbol? the heat?* 9. *Is it possible to admire Emily? Can she be seen as a tragic hero?* 10. *Why doesn't Faulkner dramatize the scene with the Baptist minister? Why does he dramatize the scene with the druggist?*

*Ernest Hemingway* (1899–1961) was a legend during his lifetime and one of the most popular American writers of all time; a world traveler, big game hunter, deep sea fisherman, a follower of the bullfight, winner of the Pulitzer Prize for Fiction in 1953 for *The Old Man and the Sea* and of the Nobel Prize in 1954. Hemingway committed suicide in Ketchum, Idaho, at the age of sixty-two. His life had been spectacular, his fiction timely and marvelously wrought. He was born in Oak Park, Illinois, a suburb of Chicago. His father was a doctor, but Hemingway left school to undertake a brief career as a reporter before volunteering in Italy as an ambulance driver during World War I. He was badly wounded in action. After the war he moved to Paris and joined with other Americans of the so-called lost generation. Encouraged by Ezra Pound and Gertrude Stein, he published his first volume of stories, *In Our Time,* in 1925, but it was not until the publication of *The Sun Also Rises* in 1926 that his reputation began to grow. Other novels and collections of short stories followed, including such notable works as *Men Without Women* (1927), *A Farewell to Arms* (1929), *Winner Take Nothing* (1933), *For Whom the Bell Tolls* (1940), and *A Moveable Feast* (1964). His style—terse but evocative—was much imitated. No anthology is complete without one of his stories. "In Another Country" is one of the most famous. In it image patterns build, situations recur, characters are juxtaposed one with another until finally a microcosm of a modern wasteland appears.

## IN ANOTHER COUNTRY

In the fall the war was always there, but we did not go to it any more. It was cold in the fall in Milan and the dark came very early. Then the electric lights came on, and it was pleasant along the streets looking in the windows. There was much game hanging outside the shops, and the snow powdered in the fur of the foxes and the wind blew their tails. The deer hung stiff and heavy and empty, and small birds blew in the wind and the wind turned their feathers. It was a cold fall and the wind came down from the mountains.

We were all at the hospital every afternoon, and there were different ways of walking across the town through the dusk to the hospital. Two of the ways were alongside canals, but they were long. Always, though, you crossed a bridge across a canal to enter the hospital. There was a choice of three bridges. On one of them a woman sold roasted chestnuts. It was warm, standing in front of her charcoal fire, and the chestnuts were warm afterward in your pocket. The hospital was very old and very beautiful, and you entered through a gate and walked across a courtyard and out a gate on the other side. There were usually funerals starting from the courtyard. Beyond the old hospital were the new brick pavilions, and there we met every afternoon and were all very polite and interested in what was the matter, and sat in the machines that were to make so much difference.

The doctor came up to the machine where I was sitting and said: "What did you like best to do before the war? Did you practise a sport?"

I said: "Yes, football."

"Good," he said. "You will be able to play football again better than ever."

My knee did not bend and the leg dropped straight from the knee to the ankle without a calf, and the machine was to bend the knee and make it move as in riding a tricycle. But it did not bend yet, and instead the machine lurched when it came to the bending part. The doctor said: "That will all pass. You are a fortunate young man. You will play football again like a champion."

In the next machine was a major who had a little hand like a baby's. He winked at me when the doctor examined his hand, which was between two leather straps that bounced up and down and flapped the stiff fingers, and said: "And will I too play football, captain-doctor?" He had been a very great fencer, and before the war the greatest fencer in Italy.

The doctor went to his office in a back room and brought a photograph which showed a hand that had been withered almost as small as the major's, before it had taken a machine course, and after was a little larger. The major held the photograph with his good hand and looked at it very carefully. "A wound?" he asked.

"An industrial accident," the doctor said.

"Very interesting, very interesting," the major said, and handed it back to the doctor.

"You have confidence?"

"No," said the major.

There were three boys who came each day who were about the same age I was. They were all three from Milan, and one of them was to be a lawyer, and one was to be a painter, and one had intended to be a soldier, and after we were finished with the machines, sometimes we walked back together to the Café Cova, which was next door to the Scala. We walked the short way through the communist quarter because we were four together. The people hated us because we were officers, and from a wine-shop some one would call out, "A basso gli ufficiali!" as we passed. Another boy who walked with us sometimes and made us five wore a black silk handkerchief across his face because he had no nose then and his face was to be rebuilt. He had gone out to the front from the military academy and been wounded within an hour after he had gone into the front line for the first time. They rebuilt his face, but he came from a very old family and they could never get the nose exactly right. He went to South America and worked in a bank. But this was a long time ago, and then we did not any of us know how it was going to be afterward. We only knew then that there was always the war, but that we were not going to it any more.

We all had the same medals, except the boy with the black silk bandage across his face, and he had not been at the front long enough to get any medals. The tall boy with a very pale face who was to be a lawyer had been a lieutenant of Arditi and had three medals of the sort we each had only one of. He had lived a very long time with death and was a little detached. We were all a little detached, and there was nothing that held us together except that we met every afternoon at the hospital. Although, as we walked to the Cova through the tough part of town, walking in the dark, with light and singing coming out of the wine-shops, and sometimes having to walk into the street when the men and women would crowd together on the sidewalk so that we would have had to jostle them to get by, we felt held together by there being something that had happened that they, the people who disliked us, did not understand.

We ourselves all understood the Cova, where it was rich and warm and not too brightly lighted, and noisy and smoky at certain hours, and there were always girls at the tables and the illustrated papers on a rack on the wall. The girls at the Cova were very patriotic, and I found that the most patriotic people in Italy were the café girls—and I believe they are still patriotic.

The boys at first were very polite about my medals and asked me what I had done to get them. I showed them the papers, which were written in very beautiful language and full of *fratellanza* and *abnegazione,* but which really said, with the adjectives removed, that I had been given the medals because I was an American. After that their manner changed a little toward me, although I was their friend against outsiders. I was a friend, but I was never really one of them after they had read the citations, because it had been different with them and they had done very different things to get their medals. I had been wounded, it was true; but we all knew that being wounded, after all, was really an accident. I was never ashamed of the ribbons, though, and sometimes, after the cocktail hour, I would imagine myself having done all the things they had done to get their medals; but walking home at night through the empty streets with the cold wind and all the shops closed, trying to keep near the street lights, I knew that I would never have done such things, and I was very much afraid to die, and often lay in bed at night by myself, afraid to die and wondering how I would be when I went back to the front again.

The three with the medals were like hunting-hawks; and I was not a hawk, although I might seem a hawk to those who had never hunted; they, the three, knew better and so we drifted apart. But I stayed good friends with the boy who had been wounded his first day at the front, because he would never know now how he would have turned out; so he could never be accepted either, and I liked him because I thought perhaps he would not have turned out to be a hawk either.

The major, who had been the great fencer, did not believe in bravery, and spent much time while we sat in the machines correcting my grammar. He had complimented me on how I spoke Italian, and we talked together very easily. One day I had said that Italian seemed such an easy language to me that I could not take a great interest in it; everything was so easy to say. "Ah, yes," the major said. "Why, then, do you not take up the use of grammar?" So we took up the use of grammar, and soon Italian was such a difficult language that I was afraid to talk to him until I had the grammar straight in my mind.

The major came very regularly to the hospital. I do not think he ever missed a day, although I am sure he did not believe in the machines. There was a time when none of us believed in the machines, and one day the major said it was all nonsense. The machines were new then and it was we who were to prove them. It was an idiotic idea, he said, "a theory, like another." I had not learned my grammar, and he said I was a stupid impossible disgrace, and he was a fool to have bothered with me. He was a small man and he sat straight up in his chair with his right hand thrust into the machine and looked straight ahead at the wall while the straps thumped up and down with his fingers in them.

"What will you do when the war is over if it is over?" he asked me. "Speak grammatically!"

"I will go to the States."

"Are you married?"

"No, but I hope to be."

"The more of a fool you are," he said. He seemed very angry. "A man must not marry."

"Why, Signor Maggiore?"

"Don't call me 'Signor Maggiore.' "

"Why must not a man marry?"

"He cannot marry. He cannot marry," he said angrily. "If he is to lose everything, he should not place himself in a position to lose that. He should not place himself in a position to lose. He should find things he cannot lose."

He spoke very angrily and bitterly, and looked straight ahead while he talked.

"But why should he necessarily lose it?"

"He'll lose it," the major said. He was looking at the wall. Then he looked down at the machine and jerked his little hand out from between the straps and slapped it hard against his thigh. "He'll lose it," he almost shouted. "Don't argue with me!" Then he called to the attendant who ran the machines. "Come and turn this damned thing off."

He went back into the other room for the light treatment and the massage. Then I heard him ask the doctor if he might use his telephone and he shut the door. When he came back into the room, I was sitting in another machine. He was wearing his cape and had his cap on, and he came directly toward my machine and put his arm on my shoulder.

"I am so sorry," he said, and patted me on the shoulder with his good hand. "I would not be rude. My wife has just died. You must forgive me."

"Oh—" I said, feeling sick for him. "I am *so* sorry."

He stood there biting his lower lip. "It is very difficult," he said. "I cannot resign myself."

He looked straight past me and out through the window. Then he began to cry. "I am utterly unable to resign myself," he said and choked. And then crying, his head up looking at nothing, carrying himself straight and soldierly, with tears on both his cheeks and biting his lips, he walked past the machines and out the door.

The doctor told me that the major's wife, who was very young and whom he had not married until he was definitely invalided out of the war, had died of pneumonia. She had been sick only a few days. No one expected her to die. The major did not come to the hospital for three days. Then he came at the usual hour, wearing a black band on the sleeve of his uniform. When he came back, there were large framed photographs around the wall, of all sorts of wounds before and after they had been cured by the machines. In front of the machine the major used were three photographs of hands like his that were completely restored. I do not know where the doctor got them. I always understood we were the first to use the machines. The photographs did not make much difference to the major because he only looked out of the window.

## *Study questions*

1. *What is the significance of the title? How many conditions of isolation are worked into the story?* 2. *The wasteland is one of the dominant images of modern literature. It is a microcosm of a world that is characterized by the cold and dark of a barren land (or a desert where nothing grows), where men are impotent and isolated, and where, though they cling to hope of recovery, they know at the same time there is no hope. Show how images, repetitive patterns, recurrent situations, tone, and mood contribute to the building of this microcosm.* 3. *How do the details and style of the first paragraph function with reference to the whole story?* 4. *What is the function of the machines? Is the war a kind of machine also? If so, is some kind of dreadful cycle in operation?* 5. *Why do the townspeople hate the soldiers? Why does the narrator feel detached from his companions?* 6. *What role does the major play? How does he tie into the major symbolism?* 7. *What is the nature of the wounds the men received in the war? Are they similar in some symbolic way?*

*John Steinbeck* (1902–1968), winner of the Nobel Prize in 1962 and the Pulitzer Prize for *The Grapes of Wrath* in 1940, was born in Salinas, California, near Monterey, and he wrote about the place of his birth and its surrounding areas in story after story. He was a popular writer, and many of his novels became movies—*Tortilla Flat* (published in 1935), *Of Mice and Men* (1937), *The Grapes of Wrath* (1939), *The Moon Is Down* (1942), *The Wayward Bus* (1947), and *East of Eden* (1952). A storyteller of great skill and compassion, he celebrated the simple human virtues of kindness, justice, courage, and love. Steinbeck's short stories, collected in such volumes as *The Long Valley* (1938) and *The Red Pony* (1945), comprise a small part of his total output, but several of the stories are masterworks: "The Chrysanthemums," "The Red Pony," "Flight." The latter explores the time when a boy becomes a man.

# FLIGHT

About fifteen miles below Monterey, on the wild coast, the Torres family had their farm, a few sloping acres above a cliff that dropped to the brown reefs and to the hissing white waters of the ocean. Behind the farm the stone mountains stood up against the sky. The farm buildings huddled like little clinging aphids on the mountain skirts, crouched low to the ground as though the wind might blow them into the sea. The little shack, the rattling, rotting barn were gray-bitten with sea salt, beaten by the damp wind until they had taken on the color of the granite hills. Two horses, a red cow and a red calf, half a dozen pigs and a flock of lean, multicolored chickens stocked the place. A little corn was raised on the sterile slope, and it grew short and thick under the wind, and all the cobs formed on the landward sides of the stalks.

Mama Torres, a lean, dry woman with ancient eyes, had ruled the farm for ten years, ever since her husband tripped over a stone in the field one day and fell full length on a rattlesnake. When one is bitten on the chest there is not much that can be done.

Mama Torres had three children, two undersized black ones of twelve and fourteen, Emilio and Rosy, whom Mama kept fishing on the rocks below the farm when the sea was kind and when the truant officer was in some distant part of Monterey County. And there was Pepé, the tall smiling son of nineteen, a gentle, affectionate boy, but very lazy. Pepé had a tall head, pointed at the top, and from its peak, coarse black hair grew down like a thatch all around. Over his smiling little eyes, Mama cut a straight bang so he could see. Pepé had sharp Indian cheek bones and an eagle nose, but his mouth was as sweet and shapely as a girl's mouth, and his chin was fragile and chiseled. He was loose and gangling, all legs and feet and wrists, and he was very lazy. Mama thought him fine and brave, but she never told him so. She said, "Some lazy cow must have got into thy father's family, else how could I have a son like thee." And she said, "When I carried thee, a sneaking lazy coyote came out of the brush and looked at me one day. That must have made thee so."

Pepé smiled sheepishly and stabbed at the ground with his knife to keep the blade sharp and free from rust. It was his inheritance, that knife, his father's knife. The long heavy blade folded back into the black handle. There was a button on the handle. When Pepé pressed the button, the blade leaped out ready for use. The knife was with Pepé always, for it had been his father's knife.

One sunny morning when the sea below the cliff was glinting and blue and the white surf creamed on the reef, when even the stone mountains looked kindly, Mama Torres called out the door of the shack, "Pepé, I have a labor for thee."

There was no answer. Mama listened. From behind the barn she heard a burst of laughter. She lifted her full long skirt and walked in the direction of the noise.

Pepé was sitting on the ground with his back against a box. His white teeth glistened. On either side of him stood the two black ones, tense and expectant. Fifteen feet away a redwood post was set in the ground. Pepé's right hand lay limply in his lap, and in the palm the big black knife rested. The blade was closed back into the handle. Pepé looked smiling at the sky.

Suddenly Emilio cried, "Ya!"

Pepé's wrist flicked like the head of a snake. The blade seemed to fly open in mid-air, and with a thump the point dug into the redwood post, and the black handle quivered. The three burst into excited laughter. Rosy ran to the post and pulled out the knife and brought it back to Pepé. He closed the blade and settled the knife carefully in his listless palm again. He grinned self-consciously at the sky.

"Ya!"

The heavy knife lanced out and sunk into the post again. Mama moved forward like a ship and scattered the play.

"All day you do foolish things with the knife, like a toy-baby," she stormed. "Get up on thy huge feet that eat up shoes. Get up!" She took him by one loose shoulder and hoisted at him. Pepé grinned sheepishly and came half-heartedly to his feet. "Look!" Mama cried. "Big lazy, you must catch the horse and put on him thy father's saddle. You must ride to Monterey. The medicine bottle is empty. There is no salt. Go thou now, Peanut! Catch the horse."

A revolution took place in the relaxed figure of Pepé. "To Monterey, me? Alone? *Sí,* Mama."

She scowled at him. "Do not think, big sheep, that you will buy candy. No, I will give you only enough for the medicine and the salt."

Pepé smiled. "Mama, you will put the hatband on the hat?"

She relented then. "Yes, Pepé. You may wear the hatband."

His voice grew insinuating, "And the green handkerchief, Mama?"

"Yes, if you go quickly and return with no trouble, the silk green handkerchief will go. If you make sure to take off the handkerchief when you eat so no spot may fall on it. . . ."

"*Sí,* Mama. I will be careful. I am a man."

"Thou? A man? Thou art a peanut."

He went into the rickety barn and brought out a rope, and he walked agilely enough up the hill to catch the horse.

When he was ready and mounted before the door, mounted on his father's saddle that was so old that the oaken frame showed through torn leather in many places, then Mama brought out the round black hat with the tooled leather band, and she reached up and knotted the green silk handkerchief about his neck. Pepé's blue denim coat was much darker than his jeans, for it had been washed much less often.

Mama handed up the big medicine bottle and the silver coins. "That for the medicine," she said, "and that for the salt. That for a candle to burn for the papa. That for *dulces* for the little ones. Our friend Mrs. Rodriguez will give you dinner and maybe a bed for the night. When you go to the church say only ten Paternosters and only twenty-five Ave Marias. Oh! I know, big coyote. You would sit there flapping your mouth over Aves all day while you looked at the candles and the holy pictures. That is not good devotion to stare at the pretty things."

The black hat, covering the high pointed head and black thatched hair of Pepé, gave him dignity and age. He sat the rangy horse well. Mama thought how handsome he was, dark and lean and tall. "I would not send thee now alone, thou little one, except for the medicine," she said softly. "It is not good to have no medicine, for who knows when the toothache will come, or the sadness of the stomach. These things are."

"Adios, Mama," Pepé cried. "I will come back soon. You may send me often alone. I am a man."

"Thou art a foolish chicken."

He straightened his shoulders, flipped the reins against the horse's shoulder and rode away. He turned once and saw that they still watched him, Emilio and Rosy and Mama. Pepé grinned with pride and gladness and lifted the tough buckskin horse to a trot.

When he had dropped out of sight over a little dip in the road, Mama turned to the black ones, but she spoke to herself. "He is nearly a man now," she said. "It will be a nice thing to have a man in the house again." Her eyes sharpened on the children. "Go to the rocks now. The tide is going out. There will be abalones to be found." She put the iron hooks into their hands and saw them down the steep trail to the reefs. She brought the smooth stone *metate* to the doorway and sat grinding her corn to flour and looking occasionally at the road over which Pepé had gone. The noonday came and then the afternoon, when the little ones beat the abalones on a rock to make them tender and Mama patted the tortillas to make them thin. They ate their dinner as the red sun was plunging down toward the ocean. They sat on the doorsteps and watched the big white moon come over the mountain tops.

Mama said, "He is now at the house of our friend Mrs. Rodriguez. She will give him nice things to eat and maybe a present."

Emilio said, "Some day I too will ride to Monterey for medicine. Did Pepé come to be a man today?"

Mama said wisely, "A boy gets to be a man when a man is needed. Remember this thing. I have known boys forty years old because there was no need for a man."

Soon afterwards they retired, Mama in her big oak bed on one side of the room, Emilio and Rosy in their boxes full of straw and sheepskins on the other side of the room.

The moon went over the sky and the surf roared on the rocks. The roosters crowed the first call. The surf subsided to a whispering surge against the reef. The moon dropped toward the sea. The roosters crowed again.

The moon was near down to the water when Pepé rode on a winded horse to his home flat. His dog bounced out and circled the horse yelping with pleasure. Pepé slid off the saddle to the ground. The weathered little shack was silver in the moonlight and the square shadow of it was black to the north and east. Against the east the piling mountains were misty with light; their tops melted into the sky.

Pepé walked wearily up the three steps and into the house. It was dark inside. There was a rustle in the corner.

Mama cried out from her bed. "Who comes? Pepé, is it thou?"

"*Sí*, Mama."

"Did you get the medicine?"

"*Sí*, Mama."

"Well, go to sleep, then. I thought you would be sleeping at the house of Mrs. Rodriguez." Pepé stood silently in the dark room. "Why do you stand there, Pepé? Did you drink wine?"

"*Sí*, Mama."

"Well, go to bed then and sleep out the wine."

His voice was tired and patient, but very firm. "Light the candle, Mama. I must go away into the mountains."

"What is this, Pepé? You are crazy." Mama struck a sulphur match and held the little blue burr until the flame spread up the stick. She set light to the candle on the floor beside her bed. "Now, Pepé, what is this you say?" She looked anxiously into his face.

He was changed. The fragile quality seemed to have gone from his chin. His mouth was less full than it had been, the lines of the lips were straighter, but in his eyes the greatest change had taken place. There was no laughter in them any more, nor any bashfulness. They were sharp and bright and purposeful.

He told her in a tired monotone, told her everything just as it had happened. A few people came into the kitchen of Mrs. Rodriguez. There was wine to drink. Pepé drank wine. The little quarrel—the man started toward Pepé and then the knife—it went almost by itself. It flew, it darted before Pepé knew it. As he talked, Mama's face grew stern, and it seemed to grow more lean. Pepé finished. "I am a man now, Mama. The man said names to me I could not allow."

Mama nodded. "Yes, thou art a man, my poor little Pepé. Thou art a man. I have seen it coming on thee. I have watched you throwing the knife into the post, and I have been afraid." For a moment her face had softened, but now it grew stern again. "Come! We must get you ready. Go. Awaken Emilio and Rosy. Go quickly."

Pepé stepped over to the corner where his brother and sister slept among the sheepskins. He leaned down and shook them gently. "Come, Rosy! Come, Emilio! The mama says you must arise."

The little black ones sat up and rubbed their eyes in the candlelight. Mama was out of bed now, her long black skirt over her nightgown. "Emilio," she cried. "Go up and catch the other horse for Pepé. Quickly, now! Quickly." Emilio put his legs in his overalls and stumbled sleepily out the door.

"You heard no one behind you on the road?" Mama demanded.

"No, Mama. I listened carefully. No one was on the road."

Mama darted like a bird about the room. From a nail on the wall she took a canvas water bag and threw it on the floor. She stripped a blanket from her bed and rolled it into a tight tube and tied the ends with string. From a box beside the stove she lifted a flour sack half full of black stringy jerky. "Your father's black coat, Pepé. Here, put it on."

Pepé stood in the middle of the floor watching her activity. She reached behind the door and brought out the rifle, a long 38–56, worn shiny the whole length of the barrel. Pepé took it from her and held it in the crook of his elbow. Mama brought a little leather bag and counted the cartridges into his hand. "Only ten left," she warned. "You must not waste them."

Emilio put his head in the door. " '*Qui 'st 'l caballo,* Mama."

"Put on the saddle from the other horse. Tie on the blanket. Here, tie the jerky to the saddle horn."

Still Pepé stood silently watching his mother's frantic activity. His chin looked hard, and his sweet mouth was drawn and thin. His little eyes followed Mama about the room almost suspiciously.

Rosy asked softly, "Where goes Pepé?"

Mama's eyes were fierce. "Pepé goes on a journey. Pepé is a man now. He has a man's thing to do."

Pepé straightened his shoulders. His mouth changed until he looked very much like Mama.

At last the preparation was finished. The loaded horse stood outside the door. The water bag dripped a line of moisture down the bay shoulder.

The moonlight was being thinned by the dawn and the big white moon was near down to the sea. The family stood by the shack. Mama confronted Pepé. "Look, my son! Do not stop until it is dark again. Do not sleep even though you are tired. Take care of the horse in order that he may not stop of weariness. Remember to be careful with the bullets—there are only ten. Do not fill thy stomach with jerky or it will make thee sick. Eat a little jerky and fill thy stomach with grass. When thou comest to the high mountains, if thou seest any of the dark watching men, go not near to them nor try to speak to them. And forget not thy prayers." She put her lean hands on Pepé's shoulders, stood on her toes and kissed him formally on both cheeks, and Pepé kissed her on both cheeks. Then he went to Emilio and Rosy and kissed both of their cheeks.

Pepé turned back to Mama. He seemed to look for a little softness, a little weakness in her. His eyes were searching, but Mama's face remained fierce. "Go now," she said. "Do not wait to be caught like a chicken."

Pepé pulled himself into the saddle. "I am a man," he said.

It was the first dawn when he rode up the hill toward the little canyon which let a trail into the mountains. Moonlight and daylight fought with each other, and the two warring qualities made it difficult to see. Before Pepé had gone a hundred yards, the outlines of his figure were misty; and long before he entered the canyon, he had become a gray, indefinite shadow.

Mama stood stiffly in front of her doorstep, and on either side of her stood Emilio and Rosy. They cast furtive glances at Mama now and then.

When the gray shape of Pepé melted into the hillside and disappeared, Mama relaxed. She began the high, whining keen of the death wail. "Our beautiful—our brave," she cried. "Our protector, our son is gone." Emilio and Rosy moaned beside her. "Our beautiful—our brave, he is gone." It was the formal wail. It rose to a high piercing whine and subsided to a moan. Mama raised it three times and then she turned and went into the house and shut the door.

Emilio and Rosy stood wondering in the dawn. They heard Mama whimpering in the house. They went out to sit on the cliff above the ocean. They touched shoulders. "When did Pepé come to be a man?" Emilio asked.

"Last night," said Rosy. "Last night in Monterey." The ocean clouds turned red with the sun that was behind the mountains.

"We will have no breakfast," said Emilio. "Mama will not want to cook." Rosy did not answer him. "Where is Pepé gone?" he asked.

Rosy looked around at him. She drew her knowledge from the quiet air. "He has gone on a journey. He will never come back."

"Is he dead? Do you think he is dead?"

Rosy looked back at the ocean again. A little steamer, drawing a line of smoke sat on the edge of the horizon. "He is not dead," Rosy explained. "Not yet."

Pepé rested the big rifle across the saddle in front of him. He let the horse walk up the hill and he didn't look back. The stony slope took on a coat of short brush so that Pepé found the entrance to a trail and entered it.

When he came to the canyon opening, he swung once in his saddle and looked back, but the houses were swallowed in the misty light. Pepé jerked forward again. The high shoulder of the canyon closed in on him. His horse stretched out its neck and sighed and settled to the trail.

It was a well-worn path, dark soft leaf-mould earth strewn with broken pieces of sandstone. The trail rounded the shoulder of the canyon and dropped steeply into the bed of the stream. In the shallows the water ran smoothly, glinting in the first morning sun. Small round stones on the bottom were as brown as rust with sun moss. In the sand along the edges of the stream the tall, rich wild mint grew, while in the water itself the cress, old and tough, had gone to heavy seed.

The path went into the stream and emerged on the other side. The horse sloshed into the water and stopped. Pepé dropped his bridle and let the beast drink of the running water.

Soon the canyon sides became steep and the first giant sentinel redwoods guarded the trail, great round red trunks bearing foliage as green and lacy as ferns. Once Pepé was among the trees, the sun was lost. A perfumed and purple light lay in the pale green of the underbrush. Gooseberry bushes and blackberries and tall ferns lined the stream, and overhead the branches of the redwoods met and cut off the sky.

Pepé drank from the water bag, and he reached into the flour sack and brought out a black string of jerky. His white teeth gnawed at the string until the tough meat parted. He chewed slowly and drank occasionally from the water bag. His little eyes were slumberous and tired, but the muscles of his face were hard set. The earth of the trail was black now. It gave up a hollow sound under the walking hoofbeats.

The stream fell more sharply. Little waterfalls splashed on the stones. Five-fingered ferns hung over the water and dripped spray from their fingertips. Pepé rode half over in his saddle, dangling one leg loosely. He picked a bay leaf from a tree beside the way and put it into his mouth for a moment to flavor the dry jerky. He held the gun loosely across the pommel.

Suddenly he squared in his saddle, swung the horse from the trail and kicked it hurriedly up behind a big redwood tree. He pulled up the reins tight against the bit to keep the horse from whinnying. His face was intent and his nostrils quivered a little.

A hollow pounding came down the trail, and a horseman rode by, a fat man with red cheeks and a white stubble beard. His horse put down its head and blubbered at the trail when it came to the place where Pepé had turned off. "Hold up!" said the man and he pulled up his horse's head.

When the last sound of the hoofs died away, Pepé came back into the trail again. He did not relax in the saddle any more. He lifted the big rifle and swung the lever to throw a shell into the chamber, and then he let down the hammer to half cock.

The trail grew very steep. Now the redwood trees were smaller and their tops were dead, bitten dead where the wind reached them. The horse plodded on; the sun went slowly overhead and started down toward the afternoon.

Where the stream came out of a side canyon, the trail left it. Pepé dismounted and watered his horse and filled up his water bag. As soon as the trail had parted from the stream, the trees were gone and only the thick brittle sage and manzanita and chaparral edged the trail. And the soft black earth was gone, too, leaving only the light tan broken rock for the trail bed. Lizards scampered away into the brush as the horse rattled over the little stones.

Pepé turned in his saddle and looked back. He was in the open now: he could be seen from a distance. As he ascended the trail the country grew more rough and terrible and dry. The way wound about the bases of great square rocks. Little gray rabbits skittered in the brush. A bird made a monotonous high creaking. Eastward the bare rock mountaintops were pale and powder-dry under the dropping sun. The horse plodded up and up the trail toward a little V in the ridge which was the pass.

Pepé looked suspiciously back every minute or so, and his eyes sought the tops of the ridges ahead. Once, on a white barren spur, he saw a black figure for a moment, but he looked quickly away, for it was one of the dark watchers. No one knew who the watchers were, nor where they lived, but it was better to ignore them and never to show interest in them. They did not bother one who stayed on the trail and minded his own business.

The air was parched and full of light dust blown by the breeze from the eroding mountains. Pepé drank sparingly from his bag and corked it tightly and hung it on the horn again. The trail moved up the dry shale hillside, avoiding rocks, dropping under clefts, climbing in and out of old water scars. When he arrived at the little pass he stopped and looked back for a long time. No dark watchers were to be seen now. The trail behind was empty. Only the high tops of the redwoods indicated where the stream flowed.

Pepé rode on through the pass. His little eyes were nearly closed with weariness, but his face was stern, relentless and manly. The high mountain wind coasted sighing through the pass and whistled on the edges of the big blocks of broken granite. In the air, a red-tailed hawk sailed over close to the ridge and screamed angrily. Pepé went slowly through the broken jagged pass and looked down on the other side.

The trail dropped quickly, staggering among broken rock. At the bottom of the slope there was a dark crease, thick with brush, and on the other side of the crease a little flat, in which a grove of oak trees grew. A scar of green grass cut across the flat. And behind the flat another mountain rose, desolate with dead rocks and starving little black bushes. Pepé drank from the bag again for the air was so dry that it encrusted his nostrils and burned his lips. He put the horse down the trail. The hooves slipped and struggled on the steep way, starting little stones that rolled off into the brush. The sun was gone behind the westward mountain now, but still it glowed brilliantly on the oaks and on the grassy flat. The rocks and the hillsides still sent up waves of the heat they had gathered from the day's sun.

Pepé looked up to the top of the next dry withered ridge. He saw a dark form against the sky, a man's figure standing on top of a rock, and he glanced away quickly not to appear curious. When a moment later he looked up again, the figure was gone.

Downward the trail was quickly covered. Sometimes the horse floundered for footing, sometimes set his feet and slid a little way. They came at last to the bottom where the dark chaparral was higher than Pepé's head. He held up his rifle on one side and his arm on the other to shield his face from the sharp brittle fingers of the brush.

Up and out of the crease he rode, and up a little cliff. The grassy flat was before him, and the round comfortable oaks. For a moment he studied the trail down which he had come, but there was no movement and no sound from it. Finally he rode out over the flat, to the green streak, and at the upper end of the damp he found a little spring welling out of the earth and dropping into a dug basin before it seeped out over the flat.

Pepé filled his bag first, and then he let the thirsty horse drink out of the pool. He led the horse to the clump of oaks, and in the middle of the grove, fairly protected from sight on all sides, he took off the saddle and the bridle and laid them on the ground. The horse stretched his jaws sideways and yawned. Pepé knotted the lead rope about the horse's neck and tied him to a sapling among the oaks, where he could graze in a fairly large circle.

When the horse was gnawing hungrily at the dry grass, Pepé went to the saddle and took a black string of jerky from the sack and strolled to an oak tree on the edge of the grove, from under which he could watch the trail. He sat down in the crisp dry oak leaves and automatically felt for his big black knife to cut the jerky, but he had no knife. He leaned back on his elbow and gnawed at the tough strong meat. His face was blank, but it was a man's face.

The bright evening light washed the eastern ridge, but the valley was darkening. Doves flew down from the hills to the spring, and the quail came running out of the brush and joined them, calling clearly to one another.

Out of the corner of his eye Pepé saw a shadow grow out of the bushy crease. He turned his head slowly. A big spotted wildcat was creeping toward the spring, belly to the ground, moving like thought.

Pepé cocked his rifle and edged the muzzle slowly around. Then he looked apprehensively up the trail and dropped the hammer again. From the ground beside him he picked an oak twig and threw it toward the spring. The quail flew up with a roar and the doves whistled away. The big cat stood up: for a long moment he looked at Pepé with cold yellow eyes, and then fearlessly walked back into the gulch.

The dusk gathered quickly in the deep valley. Pepé muttered his prayers, put his head down on his arm and went instantly to sleep.

The moon came up and filled the valley with cold blue light, and the wind swept rustling down from the peaks. The owls worked up and down the slopes looking for rabbits. Down in the brush of the gulch a coyote gabbled. The oak trees whispered softly in the night breeze.

Pepé started up, listening. His horse had whinnied. The moon was just slipping behind the western ridge, leaving the valley in darkness behind it. Pepé sat tensely gripping his rifle. From far up the trail he heard an answering whinny and the crash of shod hooves on the broken rock. He jumped to his feet, ran to his horse and led it under the trees. He threw on the saddle and cinched it tight for the steep trail, caught the unwilling head and forced the bit into the mouth. He felt the saddle to make sure the water bag and the sack of jerky were there. Then he mounted and turned up the hill.

It was velvet dark. The horse found the entrance to the trail where it left the flat, and started up, stumbling and slipping on the rocks. Pepé's hand rose up to his head. His hat was gone. He had left it under the oak tree.

The horse had struggled far up the trail when the first change of dawn came into the air, a steel grayness as light mixed thoroughly with dark. Gradually the sharp snaggled edge of the ridge stood out above them, rotten granite tortured and eaten by the winds of time. Pepé had dropped his reins on the horn, leaving direction to the horse. The brush grabbed at his legs in the dark until one knee of his jeans was ripped.

Gradually the light flowed down over the ridge. The starved brush and rocks stood out in the half light, strange and lonely in high perspective. Then there came warmth into the light. Pepé drew up and looked back, but he could see nothing in the darker valley below. The sky turned blue over the coming sun. In the waste of the mountainside, the poor dry brush grew only three feet high. Here and there, big outcroppings of unrotted granite stood up like mouldering houses. Pepé relaxed a little. He drank from his water bag and bit off a piece of jerky. A single eagle flew over, high in the light.

Without warning Pepé's horse screamed and fell on its side. He was almost down before the rifle crash echoed up from the valley. From a hole behind the struggling shoulder, a stream of bright crimson blood pumped and stopped and pumped and stopped. The hooves threshed on the ground. Pepé lay half stunned beside the horse. He looked slowly down the hill. A piece of sage clipped off beside his head and another crash echoed up from side to side of the canyon. Pepé flung himself frantically behind a bush.

He crawled up the hill on his knees and one hand. His right hand held the rifle up off the ground and pushed it ahead of him. He moved with the instinctive care of an animal. Rapidly he wormed his way toward one of the big outcroppings of granite on the hill above him. Where the brush was high he doubled up and ran, but where the cover was slight he wiggled forward on his stomach, pushing the rifle ahead of him. In the last little distance there was no cover at all. Pepé poised and then he darted across the space and flashed around the corner of the rock.

He leaned panting against the stone. When his breath came easier he moved along behind the big rock until he came to a narrow split that offered a thin section of vision down the hill. Pepé lay on his stomach and pushed the rifle barrel through the slit and waited.

The sun reddened the western ridges now. Already the buzzards were settling down toward the place where the horse lay. A small brown bird scratched in the dead sage leaves directly in front of the rifle muzzle. The coasting eagle flew back toward the rising sun.

Pepé saw a little movement in the brush far below. His grip tightened on the gun. A little brown doe stepped daintily out on the trail and crossed it and disappeared into the brush again. For a long time Pepé waited. Far below he could see the little flat and the oak trees and the slash of green. Suddenly his eyes flashed back at the trail again. A quarter of a mile down there had been a quick movement in the chaparral. The rifle swung over. The front sight nestled in the v of the rear sight. Pepé studied for a moment and then raised the rear sight a notch. The little movement in the brush came again. The sight settled on it. Pepé squeezed the trigger. The explosion crashed down the mountain and up the other side, and came rattling back. The whole side of the slope grew still. No more movement. And then a white streak cut into the granite of the slit and a bullet whined away and a crash sounded up from below. Pepé felt a sharp pain in his right hand. A sliver of granite was sticking out from between his first and second knuckles and the point protruded from his palm. Carefully he pulled out the sliver of stone. The wound bled evenly and gently. No vein nor artery was cut.

Pepé looked into a little dusty cave in the rock and gathered a handful of spider web, and he pressed the mass into the cut, plastering the soft web into the blood. The flow stopped almost at once.

The rifle was on the ground. Pepé picked it up, levered a new shell into the chamber. And then he slid into the brush on his stomach. Far to the right he crawled, and then up the hill, moving slowly and carefully, crawling to cover and resting and then crawling again.

In the mountains the sun is high in its arc before it penetrates the gorges. The hot face looked over the hill and brought instant heat with it. The white light beat on the rocks and reflected from them and rose up quivering from the earth again, and the rocks and bushes seemed to quiver behind the air.

Pepé crawled in the general direction of the ridge peak, zig-zagging for cover. The deep cut between his knuckles began to throb. He crawled close to a rattlesnake before he saw it, and when it raised its dry head and made a soft beginning whirr, he backed up and took another way. The quick gray lizards flashed in front of him, raising a tiny line of dust. He found another mass of spider web and pressed it against his throbbing hand.

Pepé was pushing the rifle with his left hand now. Little drops of sweat ran to the ends of his coarse black hair and rolled down his cheeks. His lips and tongue were growing thick and heavy. His lips writhed to draw saliva into his mouth. His little dark eyes were uneasy and suspicious. Once when a gray lizard paused in front of him on the parched ground and turned its head sideways he crushed it flat with a stone.

When the sun slid past noon he had not gone a mile. He crawled exhaustedly a last hundred yards to a patch of high sharp manzanita, crawled desperately, and when the patch was reached he wriggled in among the tough gnarly trunks and dropped his head on his left arm. There was little shade in the meager brush, but there was cover and safety. Pepé went to sleep as he lay and the sun beat on his back. A few little birds hopped close to him and peered and hopped away. Pepé squirmed in his sleep and he raised and dropped his wounded hand again and again.

The sun went down behind the peaks and the cool evening came, and then the dark. A coyote yelled from the hillside, Pepé started awake and looked about with misty eyes. His hand was swollen and heavy; a little thread of pain ran up the inside of his arm and settled in a pocket in his armpit. He peered about and then stood up, for the mountains were black and the moon had not yet risen. Pepé stood up in the dark. The coat of his father pressed on his arm. His tongue was swollen until it nearly filled his mouth. He wriggled out of the coat and dropped it in the brush, and then he struggled up the hill, falling over rocks and tearing his way through the brush. The rifle knocked against stones as he went. Little dry avalanches of gravel and shattered stone went whispering down the hill behind him.

After a while the old moon came up and showed the jagged ridge top ahead of him. By moonlight Pepé traveled more easily. He bent forward so that his throbbing arm hung away from his body. The journey uphill was made in dashes and rests, a frantic rush up a few yards and then a rest. The wind coasted down the slope rattling the dry stems of the bushes.

The moon was at meridian when Pepé came at last to the sharp backbone of the ridge top. On the last hundred yards of the rise no soil had clung under the wearing winds. The way was on solid rock. He clambered to the top and looked down on the other side. There was a draw like the last below him, misty with moonlight, brushed with dry struggling sage and chaparral. On the other side the hill rose up sharply and at the top the jagged rotten teeth of the mountain showed against the sky. At the bottom of the cut the brush was thick and dark.

Pepé stumbled down the hill. His throat was almost closed with thirst. At first he tried to run, but immediately he fell and rolled. After that he went more carefully. The moon was just disappearing behind the mountains when he came to the bottom. He crawled into the heavy brush feeling with his fingers for water. There was no water in the bed of the stream, only damp earth. Pepé laid his gun down and scooped up a handful of mud and put it in his mouth, and then he spluttered and scraped the earth from his tongue with his finger, for the mud drew at his mouth like a poultice. He dug a hole in the stream bed with his fingers, dug a little basin to catch water; but before it was very deep his head fell forward on the damp ground and he slept.

The dawn came and the heat of the day fell on the earth, and still Pepé slept. Late in the afternoon his head jerked up. He looked slowly around. His eyes were slits of wariness. Twenty feet away in the heavy brush a big tawny mountain lion stood looking at him. Its long thick tail waved gracefully, its ears were erect with interest, not laid back dangerously. The lion squatted down on its stomach and watched him.

Pepé looked at the hole he had dug in the earth. A half inch of muddy water had collected in the bottom. He tore the sleeve from his hurt arm, with his teeth ripped out a little square, soaked it in the water and put it in his mouth. Over and over he filled the cloth and sucked it.

Still the lion sat and watched him. The evening came down but there was no movement on the hills. No birds visited the dry bottom of the cut. Pepé looked occasionally at the lion. The eyes of the yellow beast drooped as though he were about to sleep. He yawned and his long thin red tongue curled out. Suddenly his head jerked around and his nostrils quivered. His big tail lashed. He stood up and slunk like a tawny shadow into the thick brush.

A moment later Pepé heard the sound, the faint far crash of horses' hooves on gravel. And he heard something else, a high whining yelp of a dog.

Pepé took his rifle in his left hand and he glided into the brush almost as quietly as the lion had. In the darkening evening he crouched up the hill toward the next ridge. Only when the dark came did he stand up. His energy was short. Once it was dark he fell over the rocks and slipped to his knees on the steep slope, but he moved on and on up the hill, climbing and scrabbling over the broken hillside.

When he was far up toward the top, he lay down and slept for a little while. The withered moon, shining on his face, awakened him. He stood up and moved up the hill. Fifty yards away he stopped and turned back, for he had forgotten his rifle. He walked heavily down and poked about in the brush, but he could not find his gun. At last he lay down to rest. The pocket of pain in his armpit had grown more sharp. His arm seemed to swell out and fall with every heartbeat. There was no position lying down where the heavy arm did not press against his armpit.

With the effort of a hurt beast, Pepé got up and moved again toward the top of the ridge. He held his swollen arm away from his body with his left hand. Up the steep hill he dragged himself, a few steps and a rest, and a few more steps. At last he was nearing the top. The moon showed the uneven sharp back of it against the sky.

Pepé's brain spun in a big spiral up and away from him. He slumped to the ground and lay still. The rock ridge top was only a hundred feet above him.

The moon moved over the sky. Pepé half turned on his back. His tongue tried to make words, but only a thick hissing came from between his lips.

When the dawn came, Pepé pulled himself up. His eyes were sane again. He drew his great puffed arm in front of him and looked at the angry wound. The black line ran up from his waist to his armpit. Automatically he reached in his pocket for the big black knife, but it was not there. His eyes searched the ground. He picked up a sharp blade of stone and scraped at the wound, sawed at the proud flesh and then squeezed the green juice out in big drops. Instantly he threw back his head and whined like a dog. His whole right side shuddered at the pain, but the pain cleared his head.

In the gray light he struggled up the last slope to the ridge and crawled over and lay down behind a line of rocks. Below him lay a deep canyon exactly like the last, waterless and desolate. There was no flat, no oak trees, not even heavy brush in the bottom of it. And on the other side a sharp ridge stood up, thinly brushed with starving sage, littered with broken granite. Strewn over the hill there were giant outcroppings, and on the top the granite teeth stood out against the sky.

The new day was light now. The flame of the sun came over the ridge and fell on Pepé where he lay on the ground. His coarse black hair was littered with twigs and bits of spider web. His eyes had retreated back into his head. Between his lips the tip of his black tongue showed.

He sat up and dragged his great arm into his lap and nursed it, rocking his body and moaning in his throat. He threw back his head and looked up into the pale sky. A big black bird circled nearly out of sight, and far to the left another was sailing near.

He lifted his head to listen, for a familiar sound had come to him from the valley he had climbed out of; it was the crying yelp of hounds, excited and feverish, on a trail.

Pepé bowed his head quickly. He tried to speak rapid words but only a thick hiss came from his lips. He drew a shaky cross on his breast with his left hand. It was a long struggle to get to his feet. He crawled slowly and mechanically to the top of a big rock on the ridge peak. Once there, he arose slowly, swaying to his feet, and stood erect. Far below he could see the dark brush where he had slept. He braced his feet and stood there, black against the morning sky.

There came a ripping sound at his feet. A piece of stone flew up and a bullet droned off into the next gorge. The hollow crash echoed up from below. Pepé looked down for a moment and then pulled himself straight again.

His body jarred back. His left hand fluttered helplessly toward his breast. The second crash sounded from below. Pepé swung forward and toppled from the rock. His body struck and rolled over and over, starting a little avalanche. And when at last he stopped against a bush, the avalanche slid slowly down and covered up his head.

## *Study questions*

1. *Show how every detail in the first paragraph is important to the rest of the story.* 2. *What is Mama Torres like? Pepé? What roles do Emilio and Rosy play?* 3. *Is it important that Pepé's father was killed by a snake? Chart the number of times a snake or something similar recurs in the story. How does the snake imagery function?* 4. *What is the symbolic significance of Pepé's inheritance from his father?* 5. *Why does Steinbeck choose not to dramatize the murder scene?* 6. *At what point does Mama Torres agree that her son is a man? What kind of qualifications are attached to her statement?* 7. *What do his father's possessions mean to Pepé? During the flight what happens to the father's possessions?* 8. *How is the changing terrain significant?* 9. *Why are the pursuers never identified? Who are the dark watchers? How are they related to Pepé?* 10. *At what point does Pepé become a man?* 11. *Why does Pepé have to die in just the way he does?*

*Frank O'Connor* (1903–1966), born Michael John O'Donovan in Cork, Ireland, and mostly self-educated, fought with the I.R.A. against the British during the civil war of the early 1920s. Later he worked as a librarian to support himself while he was writing. His first volume of short stories was published in 1931—*Guests of the Nation.* Thereafter he published more than twenty volumes of stories, many of them collected and published in the United States: *The Stories of Frank O'Connor* (1952), *More Stories* (1954), and *Domestic Relations* (1957). Besides writing short stories, O'Connor also wrote literary criticism, plays, novels, and an autobiography titled *An Only Child* (1961). He became director of the famous Abbey Theatre in Dublin, a member of the Irish Academy of Letters, and received the D.Litt. from the University of Dublin. During his later years he traveled to the United States, where he lectured and taught at Harvard, Northwestern, and Stanford universities. Some of his frequently anthologized stories are "Guests of the Nation," "First Confession," "My Oedipus Complex," "Christmas Morning," and "Judas." "Judas" is a lighthearted portrayal of a young man who falls in love for the first time and feels that he has betrayed his mother.

## JUDAS

I'll forget a lot of things before I forget that night. As I was going out the mother said: "Sure, you won't be late, Jerry?" and I only laughed at her and said: "Am I ever late?" As I went down the road I was thinking it was months since I had taken her to the pictures. You might think that funny, Michael John, but after the father's death we were thrown together a lot. And I knew she hated being alone in the house after dark.

At the same time I had troubles of my own. You see, Michael John, being an only child, I never knocked round with girls the way others did. All the chaps in the office went with girls, or at any rate they let on they did. They said: "Who was the old doll I saw you with last night, Jerry? Aha, Jerry, you'd better mind yourself, boy, or you'll be getting into trouble!" Paddy Kinnane, for instance, talked like that, and he never saw how it upset me. I think he thought it was a great compliment. It wasn't until years after that I began to suspect that Paddy's acquaintance with dolls was about of one kind with my own.

Then I met Kitty Doherty. Kitty was a hospital nurse, and all the chaps in the office said a fellow should never go with hospital nurses—they knew too much. I knew when I met Kitty that that was a lie. She was a well-educated, superior girl; she lived up the river in a posh locality, and her mother was on all sorts of councils and committees. She was small and wiry; a good-looking girl, always in good humor, and when she talked, she hopped from one thing to another like a robin on a frosty morning.

Anyway, she had me dazzled. I used to meet her in the evenings up the river road, as if I was walking there by accident and very surprised to see her. "Fancy meeting you!" I'd say, or "Well, well, isn't this a great surprise?" Then we'd stand talking for half an hour and I'd see her home. Several times she asked me in, but I was too nervous. I knew I'd lose my head, break the china, use some dirty word, and then go home and cut my throat. Of course, I never asked her to come to the pictures or anything like that. I knew she was above that. My only hope was that if I waited long enough I might be able to save her from drowning, the White Slave Traffic, or something of the sort. That would show in a modest, dignified way how I felt about her. Of course, I knew at the same time I ought to stay at home more with the mother, but the very thought that I might be missing an opportunity like that would be enough to spoil a whole evening on me.

This night in particular I was nearly distracted. It was three weeks since I'd seen Kitty. You know what three weeks are at that age. I was sure that at the very least the girl was dying and asking for me and that no one knew my address. A week before, I'd felt I simply couldn't bear it any longer, so I made an excuse and went down to the post-office. I rang up the hospital and asked for her. I fully expected them to say that she was dead, and I got a shock when the girl at the other end asked my name. "I'm afraid," I said, "I'm a stranger to Miss Doherty, but I have an important message for her." Then I got completely panic-stricken. What could a girl like Kitty make of a damned deliberate lie like that? What else was it but a trap laid by an old and cunning hand. I held the receiver out and looked at it. "Moynihan," I said to it, "you're mad. An asylum, Moynihan, is the only place for a fellow like you." Then I heard her voice, not in my ear at all, but in the telephone booth as if she were standing before me, and I nearly dropped the receiver with terror. I put it to my ear and asked in a disguised voice: "Who is that speaking, please?" "This is Kitty Doherty," she said rather impatiently. "Who are you?" "I am Monsieur Bertrand," said I, speaking in what I hoped was a French accent. "I am afraid I have de wrong number." Then I put down the receiver carefully and thought how nice it would be if only I had a penknife handy to cut my throat with. It's funny, but from the moment I met Kitty I was always coveting sharp things like razors and penknives.

After that an awful idea dawned on my mind. Of course, I should have thought of it before, but, as you've probably guessed, I wasn't exactly knowledgeable. I began to see that I wasn't meeting Kitty for the very good reason that Kitty didn't want to meet me. That filled me with terror. I examined my conscience to find out what I might have said to her. You know what conscience is at that age. I remembered every remark I'd made and they were all brutal, indecent or disgusting. I had talked of Paddy Kinnane as a fellow who "went with dolls." What could a pure-minded girl think of a chap who naturally used such a phrase except—what, unfortunately, was true—that he had a mind like a cesspit.

It was a lovely summer evening, with views of hillsides and fields between the gaps in the houses, and that raised my spirits a bit. Maybe I was wrong, maybe she hadn't found out the sort I was and wasn't avoiding me, maybe we might meet and walk home together. I walked the full length of the river road and back, and then started off to walk it again. The crowds were thinning out as fellows and girls slipped off up the lanes or down to the river. As the streets went out like lamps about me I grew desperate. I saw clearly that she was avoiding me; that she knew I wasn't the quiet, good-natured chap I let on to be but a volcano of brutality and lust. "Lust, lust, lust!" I hissed to myself, clenching my fists.

Then I glanced up and saw her on a tram. I forgot instantly about the lust and smiled and waved my cap at her, but she was looking ahead and didn't see me. I ran after the car, intending to jump on it, to sit on one of the back seats on top and then say as she was getting off: "Fancy meeting you here!" (Trams were always a bit of a problem. If you sat beside a girl and paid for her, it might be considered forward; if you didn't, it looked mean. I never quite knew.) But as if the driver knew what was in my mind, he put on speed and away went the tram, tossing and screeching down the straight, and I stood panting in the middle of the road, smiling as if missing a tram was the best joke in the world and wishing all the time I had the penknife and the courage to use it. My position was hopeless. Then I must have gone a bit mad, for I started to race the tram. There were still lots of people out walking, and they stared after me, so I lifted my fists to my chest in the attitude of a professional runner and dropped into a comfortable stride which I hoped vaguely would delude them into the belief that I was training for a big race.

Between the running and the halts I just managed to keep the tram in view all the way through town and out at the other side. When I saw Kitty get off and go up a hilly street I collapsed and was just able to drag myself after her. When she went into a house on a terrace I sat on the curb with my head between my knees till the panting stopped. At any rate I felt safe. I could now walk up and down before the house till she came out, and accost her with an innocent smile and say: "Fancy meeting you!"

But my luck was dead out that night. As I was walking up and down out of range of the house I saw a tall chap come strolling up at the opposite side and my heart sank. It was Paddy Kinnane.

"Hullo, Jerry," he chuckled with that knowing grin he put on whenever he wanted to compliment you on being discovered in a compromising situation, "what are you doing here?"

"Ah, just waiting for a chap I had a date with, Paddy," I said, trying to sound casual.

"Begor," said Paddy, "you look to me more like a man that was waiting for an old doll. Still waters run deep. . . . What time are you supposed to be meeting him?"

"Half eight," I said at random.

"Half eight?" said Paddy in surprise. " 'Tis nearly nine now."

"I know," said I, "but as I waited so long I may as well give him another few minutes."

"Ah, I'll wait along with you," said Paddy, leaning against the wall and taking out a packet of fags. "You might find yourself stuck by the end of the evening. There's people in this town and they have no consideration for anyone."

That was Paddy all out; no trouble too much for him if he could do you a good turn.

"As he kept me so long," I said hastily, "I don't think I'll bother with him. It only struck me this very minute that there's a chap up the Asragh road that I have to see on urgent business. You'll excuse me, Paddy. I'll tell you about it another time."

And away I went hell for leather to the tram. When I reached the tram-stop below Kitty's house I sat on the river wall in the dusk. The moon was rising, and every quarter of an hour the trams came grunting and squeaking over the old bridge and then went black out while the conductors switched the trolleys. I stood on the curb in the moonlight searching for Kitty. Then a bobby came along, and as he seemed to be watching me, I slunk slowly off up the hill and stood against a wall in the shadow. There was a high wall at the other side too, and behind it the roofs of a house shining in the moon. Every now and then a tram would come in and people would pass in the moonlight, and the snatches of conversation I caught were like the warmth from an open door to the heart of a homeless man. It was quite clear now that my position was hopeless. The last tram came and went, and still there was no Kitty and still I hung on.

Then I heard a woman's step. I couldn't even pretend to myself that it might be Kitty till she shuffled past me with that hasty little walk of hers. I started and called out her name; she glanced over her shoulder and, seeing a man emerging from the shadow, took fright and ran. I ran too, but she put on speed and began to outdistance me. At that I despaired. I stood on the pavement and shouted after her at the top of my voice.

"Kitty!" I cried. "Kitty, for God's sake, wait for me!"

She ran a few steps further and then halted, turned, and came back slowly down the path.

"Jerry Moynihan!" she whispered, lifting her two arms to her breasts as if I had found her with nothing on. "What in God's name are you doing here?"

I was summoning up strength to tell her that I just happened to be taking a stroll in that direction and was astonished to see her when I realized the improbability of it and began to cry instead. Then I laughed. I suppose it was nerves. But Kity had had a bad fright and now that she was geting over it she was as cross as two sticks.

"What's wrong with you, I say," she snapped. "Are you out of your senses or what?"

"Well, you see," I stammered awkwardly, half in dread I was going to cry again, "I didn't see you in town."

"No," she replied with a shrug, "I know you didn't. I wasn't out. What about it?"

"I thought it might be something I said to you," I said desperately.

"No," said Kitty candidly, "it wasn't anything to do with you. It's Mother."

"Why?" I asked almost joyously. "Is there something wrong with her?"

"I don't mean that," said Kitty impatiently. "It's just that she made such a fuss, I felt it wasn't worth it."

"But what did she make a fuss about?" I asked.

"About you, of course," said Kitty in exasperation. "What did you think?"

"But what did I do?" I asked, clutching my head. This was worse than anything I'd ever imagined. This was terrible.

"You didn't do anything," said Kitty, "but people were talking about us. And you wouldn't come in and be introduced to her like anyone else. I know she's a bit of a fool, and her head is stuffed with old nonsense about her family. I could never see that they were different to anyone else, and anyway, she married a commercial herself, so she has nothing much to boast about. Still, you needn't be so superior. There's no obligation to buy, you know."

I didn't. There were cold shivers running through me. I had thought of Kitty as a secret between God, herself, and me and that she only knew the half of it. Now it seemed I didn't even know the half. People were talking about us! I was superior! What next?

"But what has she against me?" I asked despairingly.

"She thinks we're doing a tangle, of course," snapped Kitty as if she was astonished at my stupidity, "and I suppose she imagines you're not grand enough for a great-great-grandniece of Daniel O'Connell. I told her you were a different sort of fellow entirely and above all that sort of thing, but she wouldn't believe me. She said I was a deep, callous, crafty little intriguer and that I hadn't a drop of Daniel O'Connell's blood in my veins." Kitty began to giggle at the thought of herself as an intriguer.

"That's all she knows," I said bitterly.

"I know," said Kitty with a shrug. "The woman has no sense. And anyway she has no reason to think I'm telling lies. Cissy and I always had fellows, and we spooned with them all over the shop under her very nose, so why should she think I'm lying to her now?"

At that I began to laugh like an idiot. This was worse than appalling. This was a nightmare. Kitty, whom I had thought so angelic, talking in cold blood about "spooning" with fellows all over the house. Even the bad women in the books I'd read didn't talk about love in that cold-blooded way. Madame Bovary herself had at least the decency to pretend that she didn't like it. It was like another door opening on the outside world, but Kitty thought I was laughing at her and started to apologize.

"Of course I had no sense," she said. "You're the first fellow I ever met that treated me properly. The others only wanted to fool around with me, and now because I don't like it, Mother thinks I'm getting stuck-up. I told her I liked you better than any fellow I knew, but that I'd grown out of all that sort of thing."

"And what did she say to that?" I asked fiercely. It was—how can I describe it?—like a man who'd lived all his life in a dungeon getting into the sunlight for the first time and afraid of every shadow.

"Ah, I told you the woman was silly," said Kitty, getting embarrassed.

"Go on!" I shouted. "I want to know everything. I insist on knowing everything."

"Well," said Kitty with a demure little grin, "she said you were a deep, designing guttersnipe who knew exactly how to get round feather-pated little idiots like me. . . . You see," she added with another shrug, "it's quite hopeless. The woman is common. She doesn't understand."

"But I tell you she does understand," I shouted frantically. "She understands better than you do. I only wish to God I was deep and designing so that I'd have some chance with you."

"Do you really?" asked Kitty, opening her eyes wide. "To tell you the truth," she added after a moment, "I thought you were a bit keen the first time, but then I didn't know. When you didn't kiss me or anything, I mean."

"God," I said bitterly, "when I think of what I've been through in the past couple of weeks!"

"I know," said Kitty, biting her lip. "I was the same." And then we said nothing for a few moments.

"You're sure you're serious?" she asked suspiciously.

"I tell you, girl," I shouted, "I was on the point of committing suicide."

"What good would that be?" she asked with another shrug, and then she looked at me and laughed outright—the little jade!

It is all as clear in my mind as if it had happened last night. I told Kitty about my prospects. She didn't care, but I insisted on telling her. It was as if a stone had been lifted off my heart, and I went home in the moonlight singing. Then I heard the clock strike, and the singing stopped. I remembered the mother at home, waiting, and began to run again. This was desperation too, but a different sort.

The door was ajar and the kitchen in darkness. I saw her sitting before the fire by herself, and just as I was going to throw my arms about her, I smelt Kitty's perfume round me and was afraid to go near her. God help us, as if it would have told her anything!

"Hallo, Mum," I said with a laugh, rubbing my hands, "you're all in darkness."

"You'll have a cup of tea?" she said.

"I might as well," said I.

"What time is it?" she said, lighting the gas. "You're very late."

"Ah, I met a fellow from the office," I said, but at the same time I was stung by the complaint in her tone.

"You frightened me," she said with a little whimper. "I didn't know what happened you. What kept you at all?"

"Oh, what do you think?" I said, goaded into retorting. "Drinking and blackguarding as usual."

I could have bitten my tongue off when I'd said it; it sounded so cruel, as if some stranger had said it instead of me. She turned to me for a moment with a frightened stare as if she was seeing the stranger too, and somehow I couldn't bear it.

"God Almighty," I said, "a fellow can have no life in his own house," and away with me upstairs.

I lit the candle, undressed and got into bed. I was wild. A chap could be a drunkard and blackguard and not be made to suffer more reproach than I was for being late one single night. That, I felt, was what you got for being a good son.

"Jerry," she called from the foot of the stairs, "will I bring you up your cup?"

"I don't want it now, thanks," I said.

I heard her give a heavy sigh and turn away. Then she locked the two doors front and back. She didn't wash up, and I knew my cup of tea was standing there on the table with a saucer on top in case I changed my mind. She came slowly up the stairs, and she walked like an old woman. I blew out the candle before she reached the landing in case she came in to ask me if I wanted anything else, and the moonlight came in the attic window and brought me memories of Kitty. But every time I tried to imagine her face while she grinned up at me, waiting for me to kiss her, it was the mother's face that came up with that look like a child's when you strike him the first time—as if he suddenly saw the stranger in you. I remembered all our life together from the night the father—God rest him!—died; our early Mass on Sunday; our visits to the pictures; our plans for the future, and Christ, Michael John, it was as if I was inside her mind and she sitting by the fire, waiting for the blow to fall! And now it had fallen, and I was a stranger to her, and nothing I ever did could make us the same to each other again. There was something like a cannon-ball stuck in my chest, and I lay awake till the cocks started crowing. Then I couldn't bear it any longer. I went out on to the landing and listened.

"Are you awake, Mother?" I asked in a whisper.

"What is it, Jerry?" she said in alarm, and I knew she hadn't slept any more than I had.

"I only came to say I was sorry," I said, opening the room door, and then as I saw her sitting up in bed under the Sacred Heart lamp, the cannon-ball burst inside me and I began to bawl like a kid.

"Oh, child, child," she cried out, "what are you crying for at all, my little boy?" and she spread out her arms to me. I went to her and she hugged me and rocked me just as she did when I was only a nipper. "Oh, oh, oh," she was saying to herself in a whisper, "my storeen bawn, my little man!"—all the names she hadn't called me since I was a kid. That was all we said. I couldn't bring myself to tell her what I'd done, and she wouldn't confess to me that she was jealous; all she could do was to try and comfort me for the way I'd hurt her, to make up to me for the nature she'd given me. "My storeen bawn," she said. "My little man!"

## *Study questions*

1. *Who is Michael John? How does he function in the story? How old is the narrator? What is the effect of the point of view O'Connor uses here?* 2. *What is the narrator like before he meets Kitty? after?* 3. *Why does he covet knives and razors?* 4. *How is Kitty different from what the narrator expected? How does he react to this new knowledge?* 5. *Why does he believe himself a Judas?*

*Isaac Bashevis Singer* (b. 1904) was born in Radzymin, Poland, and grew up in Warsaw. He studied at the Rabbinical Seminary and then turned to journalism, working for the Yiddish press. He came to the United States in 1935 and became a citizen in 1943. Considered to be the foremost American writer in Yiddish, he has authored novels, short stories, and essays. His novels include *The Family Moskat* (1950), *The Magician of Lublin* (1960), *The Slave* (1962), *The Manor* (1967), *The Estate* (1969), and *Enemies: A Love Story* (1972). A children's book, *A Day of Pleasure,* won the National Book Award in 1970. A two-volume autobiography, *A Young Man in Search of Love,* appeared in 1978. His short stories have been collected in *Gimpel the Fool* (1957), *The Spinoza of Market Street* (1961), *Short Friday* (1964), *The Séance* (1968), *A Friend of Kafka* (1970), and *A Crown of Feathers* (1973), for which he won the National Book Award. In 1978 he was declared winner of the Nobel Prize for Literature. "The Black Wedding" operates on what is apparently two mutually exclusive planes of reality. "Normal" perception might insist that Hindele is insane, but the story really does not say. Rather, Singer allows the alternate possibilities to remain.

# THE BLACK WEDDING

## 1

Aaron Naphtali, Rabbi of Tzivkev, had lost three-fourths of his followers. There was talk in the rabbinical courts that Rabbi Aaron Naphtali alone had been responsible for driving away his Chassidim. A rabbinical court must be vigilant, more adherents must be acquired. One has to find devices so that the following will not diminish. But Rabbi Aaron Naphtali was apathetic. The study house was old and toadstools grew unmolested on the walls. The ritual bath fell to ruin. The beadles were tottering old men, deaf and half-blind. The rabbi passed his time practicing miracle-working cabala. It was said that Rabbi Aaron Naphtali wanted to imitate the feats of the ancient ones, to tap wine from the wall and create pigeons through combinations of holy names. It was even said that he molded a golem secretly in his attic. Moreover, Rabbi Naphtali had no son to succeed him, only one daughter named Hindele. Who would be eager to follow a rabbi under these circumstances? His enemies contended that Rabbi Aaron Naphtali was sunk in melancholy, as were his wife and Hindele. The latter, at fifteen, was already reading esoteric books and periodically went into seclusion like the holy men. It was rumored that Hindele wore a fringed garment underneath her dress like that worn by her saintly grandmother after whom she had been named.

Rabbi Aaron Naphtali had strange habits. He shut himself in his chamber for days and would not come out to welcome visitors. When he prayed, he put on two pairs of phylacteries at once. On Friday afternoons, he read the prescribed section of the Pentateuch—not from a book but from the parchment scroll itself. The rabbi had learned to form letters with the penmanship of the ancient scribes, and he used this script for writing amulets. A little bag containing one of these amulets hung from the neck of each of his followers. It was known that the rabbi warred constantly with the evil ones. His grandfather, the old Rabbi of Tzivkev, had exorcised a dybbuk from a young girl and the evil spirits had revenged themselves upon the grandson. They had not been able to bring harm to the old man because he had been blessed by the Saint of Kozhenitz. His son, Rabbi Hirsch, Rabbi Aaron Naphtali's father, died young. The grandson, Rabbi Aaron Naphtali, had to contend with the vengeful devils all his life. He lit a candle, they extinguished it. He placed a volume on the bookshelf, they knocked it off. When he undressed in the ritual bath, they hid his silk coat and his fringed garment. Often, sounds of laughter and wailing seemed to come from the rabbi's chimney. There was a rustling behind the stove. Steps were heard on the roof. Doors opened by themselves. The stairs would screech although nobody had stepped on them. Once the rabbi laid his pen on the table and it sailed out through the open window as if carried by an unseen hand. The rabbi's hair turned white at forty. His back was bent, his hands and feet trembled like those of an ancient man. Hindele often suffered attacks of yawning; red flushes spread over her face, her throat ached, there was a buzzing in her ears. At such times incantations had to be made to drive away the evil eye.

The rabbi used to say, "They will not leave me in peace, not even for a moment." And he stamped his foot and asked the beadle to give him his grandfather's cane. He rapped it against each corner of the room and cried out, "You will not work your evil tricks on me!"

But the black hosts gained ascendency just the same. One autumn day the rabbi became ill with erysipelas and it was soon apparent that he would not recover from his sickness. A doctor was sent for from a nearby town, but on the way the axle of his coach broke and he could not complete the journey. A second physician was called for, but a wheel of his carriage came loose and rolled into a ditch, and the horse sprained his leg. The rabbi's wife went to the memorial chapel of her husband's deceased grandfather to pray, but the vindictive demons tore her bonnet from her head. The rabbi lay in bed with a swollen face and a shrunken beard, and for two days he did not speak a word. Quite suddenly he opened an eye and cried out, "They have won!"

Hindele, who would not leave her father's bed, wrung her hands and began to wail in despair, "Father, what's to become of me?"

The rabbi's beard trembled. "You must keep silent if you are to be spared."

There was a great funeral. Rabbis had come from half of Poland. The women predicted that the rabbi's widow would not last much longer. She was white as a corpse. She hadn't enough strength in her feet to follow the hearse and two women had to support her. At the burial she tried to throw herself into the grave and they could barely restrain her. All through the Seven Days of Mourning, she ate nothing. They tried to force a spoon of chicken broth into her mouth, but she was unable to swallow it. When the Thirty Days of Mourning had passed, the rabbi's wife still had not left her bed. Physicians were brought to her but to no avail. She herself foresaw the day of her death and she foretold it to the minute. After her funeral, the rabbi's disciples began to look around for a young man for Hindele. They had tried to find a match for her even before her father's death, but her father had been difficult to please. The son-in-law would eventually have to take the rabbi's place and who was worthy to sit in the Tzivkev rabbinical chair? Whenever the rabbi finally gave his approval, his wife found fault with the young man. Besides, Hindele was known to be sick, to keep too many fast days and to fall into a swoon when things did not go her way. Nor was she attractive. She was short, frail, had a large head, a skinny neck, and flat breasts. Her hair was bushy. There was an insane look in her black eyes. However, since Hindele's dowry was a following of thousands of Chassidim, a candidate was found, Reb Simon, son of the Yampol Rabbi. His older brother having died, Reb Simon would become Rabbi of Yampol after his father's death. Yampol and Tzivkev had much in common. If they were to unite, the glory of former times would return. True, Reb Simon was a divorced man with five children. But as Hindele was an orphan, who would protest? The Tzivkev Chassidim had one stipulation—that after his father's death, Reb Simon should reside in Tzivkev.

Both Tzivkev and Yampol were anxious to bring the union about. Immediately after the marriage contract was written, wedding preparations were begun, because the Tzivkev rabbinical chair had to be filled. Hindele had not yet seen her husband-to-be. She was told that he was a widower, and nothing was said about the five children. The wedding was a noisy one. Chassidim came from all parts of Poland. The followers of the Yampol court and those of the Tzivkev court began to address one another by the familiar "thou." The inns were full. The innkeeper brought straw mattresses down from the attic and put them out in corridors, granaries, and tool sheds, to accommodate the large crowd. Those who opposed the match foretold that Yampol would engulf Tzivkev. The Chassidim of Yampol were known for their crudeness. When they played, they became boisterous. They drank long draughts of brandy from tin mugs and became drunk. When they danced, the floors heaved under them. When an adversary of Yampol spoke harshly of their rabbi, he was beaten. There was a custom in Yampol that when the wife of a young man gave birth to a girl, the father was placed on a table and lashed thirty-nine times with a strap.

Old women came to Hindele to warn her that it would not be easy to be a daughter-in-law in the Yampol court. Her future mother-in-law, an old woman, was known for her wickedness. Reb Simon and his younger brothers had wild ways. The mother had chosen large women for her sons and the frail Hindele would not please her. Reb Simon's mother had consented to the match only because of Yampol's ambitions regarding Tzivkev.

From the time that the marriage negotiations started until the wedding,

Hindele did not stop crying. She cried at the celebration of the writing of the marriage contract, she cried when the tailors fitted her trousseau, she cried when she was led to the ritual bath. There she was ashamed to undress for the immersion before the attendants and the other women, and they had to tear off her stays and her underpants. She would not let them remove from her neck the little bag which contained an amber charm and the tooth of a wolf. She was afraid to immerse herself in the water. The two attendants who led her into the bath, held her tightly by her wrists and she trembled like the sacrificial chicken the day before Yom Kippur. When Reb Simon lifted the veil from Hindele's face after the wedding, she saw him for the first time. He was a tall man with a broad fur hat, a pitch-black disheveled beard, wild eyes, a broad nose, thick lips, and a long moustache. He gazed at her like an animal. He breathed noisily and smelled of perspiration. Clusters of hair grew out of his nostrils and ears. His hands, too, had a growth of hair as thick as fur. The moment Hindele saw him she knew what she had suspected long before—that her bridegroom was a demon and that the wedding was nothing but black magic, a satanic hoax. She wanted to call out "Hear, O Israel" but she remembered her father's death-bed admonition to keep silent. How strange that the moment Hindele understood that her husband was an evil spirit, she could immediately discern what was true and what was false. Although she saw herself sitting in her mother's living room, she knew she was really in a forest. It appeared to be light, but she knew it was dark. She was surrounded by Chassidim with fur hats and satin gabardines, as well as by women who wore silk bonnets and velvet capes, but she knew it was all imaginary and that the fancy garments hid heads grown with elf-locks, goose-feet, unhuman navels, long snouts. The sashes of the young men were snakes in reality, their sable hats were actually hedgehogs, their beards clusters of worms. The men spoke Yiddish and sang familiar songs, but the noise they made was really the bellowing of oxen, the hissing of vipers, the howling of wolves. The musicians had tails, and horns grew from their heads. The maids who attended Hindele had canine paws, hoofs of calves, snouts of pigs. The wedding jester was all beard and tongue. The so-called relatives on the groom's side were lions, bears, boars. It was raining in the forest and a wind was blowing. It thundered and flashed lightning. Alas, this was not a human wedding, but a Black Wedding. Hindele knew, from reading holy books, that demons sometimes married human virgins whom they later carried away behind the black mountains to cohabit with them and sire their children. There was only one thing to do in such a case—not to comply with them, never willingly submit to them, to let them get everything by force as one kind word spoken to Satan is equivalent to sacrificing to the idols. Hindele remembered the story of Joseph De La Rinah and the misfortune that befell him when he felt sorry for the evil one and gave him a pinch of tobacco.

## 2

Hindele did not want to march to the wedding canopy, and she planted her feet stubbornly on the floor, but the bridesmaids dragged her. They half-pulled her, half-carried her. Imps in the images of girls held the candles and formed an aisle for her. The canopy was a braid of reptiles. The rabbi who performed the ceremony was under contract to Samael. Hindele submitted to nothing. She refused to hold out her finger for the ring and had to be forced to do so. She would not drink from the goblet and they poured some wine into her mouth. Hobgoblins performed all the wedding rites. The evil spirit who appeared in the likeness of Reb Simon was wearing a white robe. He stepped on the bride's foot with his hoof so that he might rule over her. Then he smashed the wine glass. After the ceremony, a witch danced toward the bride carrying a braided bread. Presently the bride and groom were served the so-called soup, but Hindele spat everything into her handkerchief. The musicians played a Kossack, an Angry Dance, a Scissors Dance and a Water Dance. But their webbed roosters' feet peeped out from under their robes. The wedding hall was nothing but a forest swamp, full of frogs, moon-calves, monsters, each with his ticks and grimaces. The Chassidim presented the couple with assorted gifts, but these were devices to ensnare Hindele in the net of evil. The wedding jester recited sad poems and funny poems, but his voice was that of a parrot.

They called Hindele to dance the Good-Luck dance, but she did not want to get up, knowing it was actually a Bad-Luck dance. They urged her, pushed her, pinched her. Little imps stuck pins into her thighs. In the middle of the dance, two she-demons grabbed her by the arms and carried her away into a bedroom which was actually a dark cave full of thistles, scavengers, and rubbish. While these females whispered to her the duties of a bride, they spat in her ear. Then she was thrown upon a heap of mud which was supposed to be linen. For a long while, Hindele lay in that cave, surrounded by darkness, poison weeds and lice. So great was her anxiety that she couldn't even pray. Then the devil to whom she was espoused entered. He assailed her with cruelty, tore off her clothes, martyred her, abused her, shamed her. She wanted to scream for help but she restrained herself knowing that if she uttered a sound she would be lost forever.

All night long Hindele felt herself lying in blood and pus. The one who had raped her snored, coughed, hissed like an adder. Before dawn a group of hags ran into the room, pulled the sheet from under her, inspected it, sniffed it, began to dance. That night never ended. True, the run rose. It was not really the sun, though, but a bloody sphere which somebody hung in the sky. Women came to coax the bride with smooth talk and cunning but Hindele did not pay any attention to their babble. They spat at her, flattered her, said incantations, but she did not answer them. Later a doctor was brought to her, but Hindele saw that he was a horned buck. No, the black powers could not rule her, and Hindele kept on spiting them. Whatever they bade her do, she did the opposite. She threw the soup and marchpane into the slop can. She dumped the chickens and squab which they baked for her into the outhouse. She found a page of a psalter in the mossy forest and she recited psalms furtively. She also remembered a few passages of the Torah and of the prophets. She acquired more and more courage to pray to God-Almighty to save her. She mentioned the names of holy angels as well as those of her illustrious ancestors like the Baal Shem, Rabbi Leib Sarah's, Rabbi Pinchos Korzer and the like.

Strange, that although she was only one and the others were multitudes, they could not overcome her. The one who was disguised as her husband tried to bribe her with sweet-talk and gifts, but she did not satisfy him. He came to her but she turned away from him. He kissed her with his wet lips and petted her with clammy fingers, but she did not let him have her. He forced himself on her, but she tore at his beard, pulled at his sidelocks, scratched his forehead. He ran away from her bloody. It became clear to Hindele that her power was not of this world. Her father was interceding for her. He came to her in his shroud and comforted her. Her mother revealed herself to her and gave her advice. True, the earth was full of evil spirits, but up above angels were hovering. Sometimes Hindele heard the angel Gabriel fighting and fencing with Satan. Bevies of black dogs and crows came to help him, but the saints drove them away with their palm leaves and hosannahs. The barking and the crowing were drowned out by the song which Hindele's grandfather used to sing Saturday evenings and which was called "The Sons of the Mansion."

But horror of horrors, Hindele became pregnant. A devil grew inside her. She could see him through her own belly as through a cobweb: half-frog, half-ape, with eyes of a calf and scales of a fish. He ate her flesh, sucked her blood, scratched her with his claws, bit her with his pointed teeth. He was already chattering, calling her mother, cursing with vile language. She had to get rid of him, stop his gnawing at her liver. Nor was she able to bear this blasphemy and mockery. Besides, he urinated in her and defiled her with his excrement. Miscarriage was the only way out, but how bring it on? Hindele struck her stomach with her fist. She jumped, threw herself down, crawled, all to get rid of that devil's bastard, but to no avail. He grew quickly and showed inhuman strength, pushed and tore at her insides. His skull was of copper, his mouth of iron. He had capricious urges. He told her to eat lime from the wall, the shell of an egg, all kinds of garbage. And if she refused, he squeezed her gall bladder. He stank like a skunk and Hindele fainted from the stench. In her swoon, a giant appeared to her with one eye in his forehead. He talked to her from a hollowed tree saying, "Give yourself up, Hindele, you are one of us."

"No, never."

"We will take revenge."

He flogged her with a fiery rod and yelled abuses. Her head became as heavy as a millstone from fear. The fingers of her hands became big and hard like rolling pins. Her mouth puckered as from eating unripe fruit. Her ears felt as if they were full of water. Hindele was not free any more. The hosts rolled her in muck, mire, slime. They immersed her in baths of pitch. They flayed her skin. They pulled the nipples of her breasts with pliers. They tortured her ceaselessly but she remained mute. Since the males could not persuade her, the female devils attacked her. They laughed with abandon, they braided their hair around her, choked her, tickled her, and pinched her. One giggled, another cried, another wiggled like a whore. Hindele's belly was big and hard as a drum and Belial sat in her womb. He pushed with elbows and pressed with his skull. Hindele lay in labor. One she-devil was a mid-wife and the other an aide. They had hung all kinds of charms over her canopied bed and they put a knife and a Book of

Creation under her pillow, the way the evil ones imitate the humans in all manners. Hindele was in her birth throes, but she remembered that she was not allowed to groan. One sigh and she would be lost. She must restrain herself in the name of her holy forbears.

Suddenly the black one inside her pushed with all his might. A piercing scream tore itself from Hindele's throat and she was swallowed in darkness. Bells were ringing as on a gentile holiday. A hellish fire flared up. It was as red as blood, as scarlet as leprosy. The earth opened like in the time of Korah, and Hindele's canopied bed began to sink into the abyss. Hindele had lost everything, this world and the world to come. In the distance she heard the crying of women, the clapping of hands, blessings and good wishes, while she flew straight into the castle of Asmodeus where Lilith, Namah, Machlath, Hurmizah rule.

In Tzivkev and in the neighborhood the tiding spread that Hindele had given birth to a male child by Reb Simon of Yampol. The mother had died in childbirth.

## *Study questions*

1. *What role in the story is played by Hindele's father? her mother?* 2. *Why is it necessary that Hindele marry?* 3. *Does the fact that Hindele gives birth to a male child support the idea that she is insane?* 4. *At what time in history is this story set? Why?* 5. *Most of the story is focused through Hindele's consciousness. Why is this point of view necessary?*

*Jean-Paul Sartre* (b. 1905), born in Paris, took his degree in philosophy at the École Normale Supérieure in 1929. During 1933–1934 he studied in Germany under Edmund Husserl and Martin Heidegger, after which he became a professor of philosophy. He served in World War II and was taken prisoner by the Germans. When he was released, he returned to Paris and joined the Resistance movement. He founded the radical political journal *Les Temps modernes* in 1945. During the 1940s and 1950s he was one of the leaders of the existential movement in philosophy and in literature. His plays, short stories, and novels are often devised to dramatize and make concrete their philosophical content. Probably his best play is *No Exit* (1944). The novel *Nausea* (1938) remains central to existential thought. A collection of short fiction, *The Wall and Other Stories*, was published in 1937 and in the United States in 1948 under the title *Intimacy.* Sartre was awarded the Nobel Prize in 1964 but declined it on principle, as he had also declined the Legion of Honor. A story of physical and spiritual decay, "The Room" explores schizophrenic behavior not only in Pierre but also in the people around him insofar as his aberrant behavior is a mirror for theirs.

## THE ROOM

### 1

Mme. Darbedat held a *rahat-loukoum* between her fingers. She brought it carefully to her lips and held her breath, afraid that the fine dust of sugar that powdered it would blow away. "Just right," she told herself. She bit quickly into its glassy flesh and a scent of stagnation filled her mouth. "Odd how illness sharpens the sensations." She began to think of mosques, of obsequious Orientals (she had been to Algeria for her honeymoon) and her pale lips started in a smile: the *rahat-loukoum* was obsequious too.

Several times she had to pass the palm of her hand over the pages of her book, for in spite of the precaution she had taken they were covered with a thin coat of white powder. Her hand made the little grains of sugar slide and roll, grating on the smooth paper: "That makes me think of Arcachon, when I used to read on the beach." She had spent the summer of 1907 at the seashore. Then she wore a big straw hat with a green ribbon; she sat close to the jetty, with a novel by Gyp or Colette Yver. The wind made swirls of sand rain down upon her knees, and from time to time she had to shake the book, holding it by the corners. It was the same sensation: only the grains of sand were dry while the small bits of sugar stuck a little to the ends of her fingers. Again she saw a band of pearl grey sky above a black sea. "Eve wasn't born yet." She felt herself all weighted down with memories and precious as a coffer of sandalwood. The name of the book she used to read suddenly came back to mind: it was called *Petite Madame,* not at all boring. But ever since an unknown illness had confined her to her room she preferred memories and historical works.

She hoped that suffering, heavy readings, a vigilant attention to her memories and the most exquisite sensations would ripen her as a lovely hothouse fruit.

She thought, with some annoyance, that her husband would soon be knocking at her door. On other days of the week he came only in the evening, kissed her brow in silence and read *Le Temps,* sitting in the armchair across from her. But Thursday was M. Darbedat's *day:* He spent an hour with his daughter, generally from three to four. Before going he stopped in to see his wife and both discussed their son-in-law with bitterness. These Thursday conversations, predictable to their slightest detail, exhausted Mme. Darbedat. M. Darbedat filled the quiet room with his presence. He never sat, but walked in circles about the room. Each of his outbursts wounded Mme. Darbedat like a glass splintering. This particular Thursday was worse than usual: at the thought that it would soon be necessary to repeat Eve's confessions to her husband, and to see his great terrifying body convulse with fury, Mme. Darbedat broke out in a sweat. She picked up a *loukoum* from the saucer, studied it for a while with hesitation, then sadly set it down: she did not like her husband to see her eating *loukoums.*

She heard a knock and started up. "Come in," she said weakly.

M. Darbedat entered on tiptoe. "I'm going to see Eve," he said, as he did every Thursday. Mme. Darbedat smiled at him. "Give her a kiss for me."

M. Darbedat did not answer and his forehead wrinkled worriedly: every Thursday at the same time, a muffled irritation mingled with the load of his digestion. "I'll stop in and see Franchot after leaving her, I wish he'd talk to her seriously and try to convince her."

He made frequent visits to Dr. Franchot. But in vain. Mme. Darbedat raised her eyebrows. Before, when she was well, she shrugged her shoulders. But since sickness had weighted down her body, she replaced the gestures which would have tired her by plays of emotion in the face: she said *yes* with her eyes, *no* with the corners of her mouth: she raised her eyebrows instead of her shoulders.

"There should be some way to take him away from her by force."

"I told you already it was impossible. And besides, the law is very poorly drawn up. Only the other day Franchot was telling me that they have a tremendous amount of trouble with the families: people who can't make up their mind, who want to keep the patient at home; the doctors' hands are tied. They can give their advice, period. That's all. He would," he went on, "have to make a public scandal or else she would have to ask to have him put away herself."

"And that," said Mme. Darbedat, "isn't going to happen tomorrow."

"No." He turned to the mirror and began to comb his fingers through his beard. Mme. Darbedat looked at the powerful red neck of her husband without affection.

"If she keeps on," said M. Darbedat, "she'll be crazier than he is. It's terribly unhealthy. She doesn't leave his side, she only goes out to see you. She has no visitors. The air in their room is simply unbreathable. She never opens the window because Pierre doesn't want it open. As if you should ask a sick man. I believe they burn incense, some rubbish in a little pan, you'd think it was a church. Really, sometimes I wonder . . . she's got a funny look in her eyes, you know."

"I haven't noticed," Mme. Darbedat said. "I find her quite normal. She looks sad, obviously."

"She has a face like an unburied corpse. Does she sleep? Does she eat? But we aren't supposed to ask her about those things. But I should think that with a fellow like Pierre next to her, she wouldn't sleep a wink all night." He shrugged his shoulders. "What I find amazing is that we, her parents, don't have the right to protect her against herself. Understand that Pierre would be much better cared for by Franchot. There's a big park. And besides, I think," he added, smiling a little, "he'd get along much better with people of his own type. People like that are children, you have to leave them alone with each other; they form a sort of freemasonry. That's where he should have been put the first day and for his own good, I'd say. Of course it's in his own best interest."

After a moment, he added, "I tell you I don't like to know she's alone with Pierre, especially at night. Suppose something happened. Pierre has a very sly way about him."

"I don't know," Mme. Darbedat said, "if there's any reason to worry. He always looked like that. He always seemed to be making fun of the world. Poor boy," she sighed, "to have had his pride and then come to that. He thought he was cleverer than all of us. He had a way of saying 'You're right' simply to end the argument . . . It's a blessing for him that he can't see the state he's in."

She recalled with displeasure the long, ironic face, always turned a little to the side. During the first days of Eve's marriage, Mme. Darbedat asked nothing more than a little intimacy with her son-in-law. But he had discouraged her: he almost never spoke, he always agreed quickly and absent-mindedly.

M. Darbedat pursued his idea. "Franchot let me visit his place," he said. "It was magnificent. The patients have private rooms with leather armchairs, if you please, and day-beds. You know, they have a tennis court and they're going to build a swimming pool."

He was planted before the window, looking out, rocking a little on his bent legs. Suddenly he turned lithely on his heel, shoulders lowered, hands in his pockets. Mme. Darbedat felt she was going to start perspiring: it was the same thing every time: now he was pacing back and forth like a bear in a cage and his shoes squeaked at every step.

"Please, please won't you sit down. You're tiring me." Hesitating, she added, "I have something important to tell you."

M. Darbedat sat in the armchair and put his hands on his knees; a slight chill ran up Mme. Darbedat's spine: the time had come, she had to speak.

"You know," she said with an embarrassed cough, "I saw Eve on Tuesday."

"Yes."

"We talked about a lot of things, she was very nice, she hasn't been so confiding for a long time. Then I questioned her a little, I got her to talk about

Pierre. Well, I found out," she added, again embarrassed, "that she is *very* attached to him."

"I know that too damned well," said M. Darbedat.

He irritated Mme. Darbedat a little: she always had to explain things in such detail. Mme. Darbedat dreamed of living in the company of fine and sensitive people who would understand her slightest word.

"But I mean," she went on, "that she is attached to him *differently* than we imagined."

M. Darbedat rolled furious, anxious eyes, as he always did when he never completely grasped the sense of an allusion or something new.

"What does that all mean?"

"Charles," said Mme. Darbedat, "don't tire me. You should understand a mother has difficulty in telling certain things."

"I don't understand a damned word of anything you say," M. Darbedat said with irritation. "You can't mean . . ."

"Yes," she said.

"They're still . . . now, still . . .?"

"Yes! Yes! Yes!" she said, in three annoyed and dry little jolts.

M. Darbedat spread his arms, lowered his head and was silent.

"Charles," his wife said, worriedly, "I shouldn't have told you. But I couldn't keep it to myself."

"Our child," he said slowly. "With this madman! He doesn't even recognize her any more. He calls her Agatha. She must have lost all sense of her own dignity."

He raised his head and looked at his wife severely. "You're sure you aren't mistaken?"

"No possible doubt. Like you," she added quickly, "I couldn't believe her and I still can't. The mere idea of being touched by that wretch . . . So . . ." she sighed, "I suppose that's how he holds on to her."

"Do you remember what I told you," M. Darbedat said, "when he came to ask for her hand? I told you I thought he pleased Eve *too much.* You wouldn't believe me." He struck the table suddenly, blushing violently. "It's perversity! He takes her in his arms, kisses her and calls her Agatha, selling her on a lot of nonsense about flying statues and God knows what else! Without a word from her! But what in heaven's name's between those two? Let her be sorry for him, let her put him in a sanatorium and see him every day,—fine. But I never thought . . . I considered her a widow. Listen, Jeannette," he said gravely, "I'm going to speak frankly to you; if she had any sense, I'd rather see her take a lover!"

"Be quiet, Charles!" Mme. Darbedat cried.

M. Darbedat wearily took his hat and the cane he had left on the stool. "After what you've just told me," he concluded, "I don't have much hope left. In any case, I'll have a talk with her because it's my duty."

Mme. Darbedat wished he would go quickly.

"You know," she said to encourage him, "I think Eve is more headstrong than . . . than anything. She knows he's incurable but she's obstinate, she doesn't want to be in the wrong."

M. Darbedat stroked his beard absently.

"Headstrong? Maybe so. If you're right, she'll finally get tired of it. He's not always pleasant and he doesn't have much to say. When I say hello to him he gives me a flabby handshake and doesn't say a word. As soon as they're alone, I think they go back to his obsessions: she tells me sometimes he screams as though his throat were being cut because of his hallucinations. He sees statues. They frighten him because they buzz. He says they fly around and make fishy eyes at him."

He put on his gloves and continued, "She'll get tired of it, I'm not saying she won't. But suppose she goes crazy before that? I wish she'd go out a little, see the world: she'd meet some nice young man—well, someone like Schroeder, an engineer with Simplon, somebody with a future, she could see him a little here and there and she'd get used to the idea of making a new life for herself."

Mme. Darbedat did not answer, afraid of starting the conversation up again. Her husband bent over her.

"So," he said, "I've got to be on my way."

"Goodbye, Papa," Mme. Darbedat said, lifting her forehead up to him. "Kiss her for me and tell her for me she's a poor dear."

Once her husband had gone, Mme. Darbedat let herself drift to the bottom of her armchair and closed her eyes, exhausted. "What vitality," she thought reproachfully. As soon as she got a little strength back, she quietly stretched out her pale hand and took a *loukoum* from the saucer, groping for it without opening her eyes.

Eve lived with her husband on the sixth floor of an old building on the Rue du Bac. M. Darbedat slowly climbed the 112 steps of the stairway. He was not even out of breath when he pushed the bell. He remembered with satisfaction the words of Mlle. Dormoy: "Charles, for your age, you're simply marvelous." Never did he feel himself stronger and healthier than on Thursday, especially after these invigorating climbs.

Eve opened the door: that's right, she doesn't have a maid. No girls *can* stay with her. I can put myself in their place. He kissed her. "Hello, poor darling."

Eve greeted him with a certain coldness.

"You look a little pale," M. Darbedat said, touching her cheek. "You don't get enough exercise."

There was a moment of silence.

"Is Mamma well?" Eve asked.

"Not good, not too bad. You saw her Tuesday? Well, she's just the same. Your Aunt Louise came to see her yesterday, that pleased her. She likes to have visitors, but they can't stay too long. Aunt Louise came to Paris for that mortgage business. I think I told you about it, a very odd sort of affair. She stopped in at the office to ask my advice. I told her there was only one thing to do: sell. She found a taker, by the way: Bretonnel. You remember Bretonnel. He's retired from business now."

He stopped suddenly: Eve was hardly listening. He thought sadly that nothing interested her any more. It's like the books. Before you had to tear them away from her. Now she doesn't even read any more.

"How is Pierre?"

"Well," Eve said. "Do you want to see him?"

"Of course," M. Darbedat said gaily, "I'd like to pay him a little call."

He was full of compassion for this poor young man, but he could not see him without repugnance. *I detest unhealthy people.* Obviously, it was not Pierre's fault: his heredity was terribly loaded down. M. Darbedat sighed: *All the precautions are taken in vain, you find out those things too late.* No, Pierre was not responsible. But still he had always carried that fault in him; it formed the base of his character; it wasn't like cancer or tuberculosis, something you could always put aside when you wanted to judge a man as he is. His nervous grace, the subtlety which pleased Eve so much when he was courting her were the flowers of madness. He was already mad when he married her only you couldn't tell.

*It makes you wonder,* thought M. Darbedat, *where responsibility begins, or rather, where it ends.* In any case, he was always analysing himself too much, always turned in on himself. But was it the cause or effect of his sickness? He followed his daughter through a long, dim corridor.

"This apartment is too big for you," he said. "You ought to move out."

"You say that every time, Papa," Eve answered, "but I've already told you Pierre doesn't want to leave his room."

Eve was amazing. Enough to make you wonder if she realized her husband's state. He was insane enough to be in a strait-jacket and she respected his decisions and advice as if he still had good sense.

"What I'm saying is for your own good." M. Darbedat went on, somewhat annoyed, "It seems to me that if I were a woman I'd be afraid of these badly lighted old rooms. I'd like to see you in a bright apartment, the kind they're putting up near Auteuil, three airy little rooms. They lowered the rents because they couldn't find any tenants; this would be just the time."

Eve quietly turned the doorknob and they entered the room. M. Darbedat's throat tightened at the heavy odor of incense. The curtains were drawn. In the shadows he made out a thin neck above the back of an armchair: Pierre's back was turned. He was eating.

"Hello, Pierre," M. Darbedat said, raising his voice. "How are we today?" He drew near him: the sick man was seated in front of a small table; he looked sly.

"I see we had soft boiled eggs," M. Darbedat said, raising his voice higher. "That's good!"

"I'm not deaf," Pierre said quietly.

Irritated, M. Darbedat turned his eyes toward Eve as his witness. But Eve gave him a hard glance and was silent. M. Darbedat realized he had hurt her. Too bad for her. It was impossible to find just the right tone for this boy. He had less sense than a child of four and Eve wanted him treated like a man. M. Darbedat could not keep himself from waiting with impatience for the moment when all this ridiculous business would be finished. Sick people always annoyed him a little—especially madmen because they were wrong. Poor Pierre, for example, was wrong all along the line, he couldn't speak a reasonable word and yet it would be useless to expect the least humility from him, or even temporary recognition of his errors.

Eve cleared away the eggshells and the cup. She put a knife and fork in front of Pierre.

"What's he going to eat now," M. Darbedat said jovially.

"A steak."

Pierre had taken the fork and held it in the ends of his long, pale fingers. He inspected it minutely and then gave a slight laugh.

"I can't use it this time," he murmured, setting it down, "I was warned."

Eve came in and looked at the fork with passionate interest.

"Agatha," Pierre said, "give me another one."

Eve obeyed and Pierre began to eat. She had taken the suspect fork and held it tightly in her hands, her eyes never leaving it; she seemed to make a violent effort. How suspicious all their gestures and relationships are! thought M. Darbedat.

He was uneasy.

"Be careful, Pierre, take it by the middle because of the prongs."

Eve sighed and laid the fork on the serving table. M. Darbedat felt his gall rising. He did not think it well to give in to all this poor man's whims—even from Pierre's viewpoint it was pernicious. Franchot had said: "One must never enter the delirium of a madman." Instead of giving him another fork, it would have been better to have reasoned quietly and made him understand that the first was like all the others.

He went to the serving table, took the fork ostentatiously and tested the prongs with a light finger. Then he turned to Pierre. But the latter was cutting his meat peacefully: he gave his father-in-law a gentle, inexpressive glance.

"I'd like to have a little talk with you," M. Darbedat said to Eve.

She followed him docilely into the salon. Sitting on the couch, M. Darbedat realized he had kept the fork in his hand. He threw it on the table.

"It's much better here," he said.

"I never come here."

"All right to smoke?"

"Of course, Papa," Eve said hurriedly. "Do you want a cigar?"

M. Darbedat preferred to roll a cigarette. He thought eagerly of the discussion he was about to begin. Speaking to Pierre he felt as embarrassed about his reason as a giant about his strength when playing with a child. All his qualities of clarity, sharpness, precision, turned against him; *I must confess it's somewhat the same with my poor Jeannette.* Certainly Mme. Darbedat was not insane, but this illness had . . . stultified her. Eve, on the other hand, took after her father . . . a straight, logical nature; discussion with her was a pleasure; *that's why I don't want them to ruin her.* M. Darbedat raised his eyes. Once again he wanted to see the fine intelligent features of his daughter. He was disappointed with this face; once so reasonable and transparent, there was now something clouded and opaque in it. Eve had always been beautiful. M. Darbedat noticed she was made up with great care, almost with pomp. She had blued her eyelids and put mascara on her long lashes. This violent and perfect make-up made a painful impression on her father.

"You're green beneath your rouge," he told her. "I'm afraid you're getting sick. And the way you make yourself up now! You used to be so discreet."

Eve did not answer and for an embarrassed moment M. Darbedat considered this brilliant, worn-out face beneath the heavy mass of black hair. He thought she looked like a tragedian. *I even know who she looks like. That woman . . . that Roumanian who played* Phèdre *in French at the Mur d'Orange.* He regretted having made so disagreeable a remark: *It escapes me! Better not worry her with little things.*

"Excuse me," he said smiling, "you know I'm an old purist. I don't like all these creams and paints women stick on their face today. But I'm in the wrong. You must live in your time."

Eve smiled amiably at him. M. Darbedat lit a cigarette and drew several puffs.

"My child," he began, "I wanted to talk with you: the two of us are going to talk the way we used to. Come, sit down and listen to me nicely; you must have confidence in your old Papa."

"I'd rather stand," Eve said. "What did you want to tell me?"

"I am going to ask you a single question," M. Darbedat said a little more dryly. "Where will all this lead you?"

"All this?" Eve asked astonished.

"Yes . . . all this whole life you've made for yourself. Listen," he went on, "don't think I don't understand you (he had a sudden illumination) but what you want to do is beyond human strength. You want to live solely by imagination, isn't that it? You don't want to admit he's sick. You don't want to see the Pierre of today, do you? You have eyes only for the Pierre of before. My dear, my darling little girl, it's an impossible bet to win," M. Darbedat continued. "Now I'm going to tell you a story which perhaps you don't know. When we were at Sables-d'Olonne—you were three years old—your mother made the acquaintance of a charming young woman with a superb little boy. You played on the beach with this litle boy, you were thick as thieves, you were engaged to marry him. A while later, in Paris, your mother wanted to see this young woman again; she was told she had had a terrible accident. That fine little boy's head was cut off by a car. They told your mother, 'Go and see her, but above all don't talk to her about the death of her child, she *will not* believe he is dead.' Your mother went, she found a half-mad creature: she lived as though her boy was still alive; she spoke to him, she set his place at the table. She lived in such a state of nervous tension that after six months they had to take her away by force to a sanatorium where she was obliged to stay three years. No, my child," M. Darbedat said, shaking his head, "these things are impossible. It would have been better if she had recognized the truth courageously. She would have suffered once, then time would have erased with its sponge. There is nothing like looking things in the face, believe me."

"You're wrong," Eve said with effort. "I know very well that Pierre is . . ."

The word did not escape. She held herself very straight and put her hands on the back of the armchair: there was something dry and ugly in the lower part of her face.

"So . . .?" asked M. Darbedat, astonished.

"So . . .?"

"You . . .?"

"I love him as he is," said Eve rapidly and with an irritated look.

"Not true," M. Darbedat said forcefully. "It isn't true: you don't love him, you can't love him. You can only feel that way about a healthy, normal person. You pity Pierre, I don't doubt it, and surely you have the memory of three years of happiness he gave you. But don't tell me you love him. I won't believe you."

Eve remained wordless, staring at the carpet absently.

"You could at least answer me," M. Darbedat said coldly. "Don't think this conversation has been any less painful for me than it has for you."

"More than you think."

"Well then, if you love him," he cried, exasperated, "it is a great misfortune for you, for me and for your poor mother because I'm going to tell you something I would rather have hidden from you: before three years Pierre will be sunk in complete dementia, he'll be like a beast."

He watched his daughter with hard eyes: he was angry at her for having compelled him, by stubbornness, to make this painful revelation.

Eve was motionless; she did not so much as raise her eyes.

"I knew."

"Who told you?" he asked stupefied.

"Franchot, I knew six months ago."

"And I told him to be careful with you," said M. Darbedat with bitterness. "Maybe it's better. But under those circumstances you must understand that it would be unpardonable to keep Pierre with you. The struggle you have undertaken is doomed to failure, his illness won't spare him. If there were something to be done, if we could save him by care, I'd say yes. But look: you're pretty, intelligent, gay, you're destroying yourself willingly and without profit. I know you've been admirable, but now it's over . . . done, you've done your duty and more; now it would be immoral to continue. We also have duties to ourselves, child. And then you aren't thinking about us. You must," he repeated, hammering the words, "send Pierre to Franchot's clinic. Leave this apartment where you've had nothing but sorrow and come home to us. If you want to be useful and ease the sufferings of someone else, you have your mother. The poor woman is cared for by nurses, she needs someone closer to her, and *she*," he added, "can appreciate what you do for her and be grateful."

There was a long silence. M. Darbedat heard Pierre singing in the next room. It was hardly a song, rather a sort of sharp, hasty recitative. M. Darbedat raised his eyes to his daughter.

"It's no then?"

"Pierre will stay with me," she said quietly. "I get along well with him."

"By living like an animal all day long?"

Eve smiled and shot a glance at her father, strange, mocking and almost gay. *It's true,* M. Darbedat thought furiously, *that's not all they do; they sleep together.*

"You are completely mad," he said, rising.

Eve smiled sadly and murmured, as if to herself, "Not enough so."

"Not enough? I can only tell you one thing, my child. You frighten me."

He kissed her hastily and left. Going down the stairs he thought: *we should send out two strong-arm men who'd take the poor imbecile away and stick him under a shower without asking his advice on the matter.*

It was a fine autumn day, calm and without mystery; the sunlight gilded the faces of the passers-by. M. Darbedat was struck with the simplicity of the faces; some weather-beaten, others smooth, but they reflected all the happiness and care with which he was so familiar.

*I know exactly what I resent in Eve,* he told himself, entering the Boulevard St. Germain. *I resent her living outside the limits of human nature. Pierre is no longer a human being: in all the care and all the love she gives him she deprives human beings of a little. We don't have the right to refuse ourselves to the world; no matter what, we live in society.*

He watched the faces of the passers-by with sympathy; he loved their clear, serious looks. In these sunlit streets, in the midst of mankind, one felt secure, as in the midst of a large family.

A woman stopped in front of an open-air display counter. She was holding a little girl by the hand.

"What's that?" the little girl asked, pointing to a radio set.

"Mustn't touch," her mother said. "It's a radio; it plays music."

They stood for a moment without speaking, in ecstacy. Touched, M. Darbedat bent down to the little girl and smiled.

## 2

"He's gone." The door closed with a dry snap. Eve was alone in the salon. *I wish he'd die.*

She twisted her hands around the back of the armchair: she had just remembered her father's eyes. M. Darbedat was bent over Pierre with a competent air; he had said "That's good!" the way someone says when they speak to invalids. He had looked and Pierre's face had been painted in the depths of his sharp, bulging eyes. *I hate him when he looks at him because I think he sees him.*

Eve's hands slid along the armchair and she turned to the window. She was dazzled. The room was filled with sunlight, it was everywhere, in pale splotches on the rug, in the air like a blinding dust. Eve was not accustomed to this diligent, indiscreet light which darted from everywhere, scouring all the corners, rubbing the furniture like a busy housewife and making it glisten. However, she went to the window and raised the muslin curtain which hung against the pane. Just at that moment M. Darbedat left the building; Eve suddenly caught sight of his broad shoulders. He raised his head and looked at the sky, blinking, then with the stride of a young man he walked away. *He's straining himself,* thought Eve, *soon he'll have a stitch in the side.* She hardly hated him any longer: there was so little in that head; only the tiny worry of appearing young. Yet rage took her again when she saw him turn the corner of the Boulevard St. Germain and disappear. *He's thinking about Pierre.* A little of their life had escaped from the closed room and was being dragged through the streets, in the sun, among the people. *Can they never forget about us?*

The Rue du Bac was almost deserted. An old lady crossed the street with mincing steps; three girls passed, laughing. Then men, strong, serious men carrying briefcases and talking among themselves. *Normal people,* thought Eve, astonished at finding such a powerful hatred in herself. A handsome, fleshy woman ran heavily toward an elegant gentleman. He took her in his arms and kissed her on the mouth. Eve gave a hard laugh and let the curtain fall.

Pierre sang no more but the woman on the fourth floor was playing the piano; she played a Chopin Etude. Eve felt calmer; she took a step toward Pierre's room but stopped almost immediately and leaned against the wall in anguish; each time she left the room, she was panic-stricken at the thought of going back. Yet she knew she could live nowhere else: she loved the room. She looked around it with cold curiosity as if to gain a little time: this shadowless, odorless room where she waited for her courage to return. *You'd think it was a dentist's waiting room.* Armchairs of pink silk, the divan, the tabourets were somber and discreet, a little fatherly; man's best friends. Eve imagined those grave gentlemen dressed in light suits, all like the ones she saw at the window, entering the room, continuing a conversation already begun. They did not even take time to reconnoiter, but advanced with firm step to the middle of the room; one of them, letting his hand drag behind him like a wake in passing knocked over cushions, objects on the table, and was never disturbed by their contact. And when a piece of furniture was in their way, these poised men, far from making a detour to avoid it, quietly changed its place. Finally they sat down, still plunged in their conversation, without even glancing behind them. *A living-room for normal people,* thought Eve. She stared at the knob of the closed door and anguish clutched her throat: *I must go back. I never leave him alone so long.* She would have to open the door, then stand for a moment on the threshold, trying to accustom her eyes to the shadow and the room would push her back with all its strength. Eve would have to triumph over this resistance and enter all the way into the heart of the room. Suddenly she wanted violently to see Pierre; she would have liked to make fun of M. Darbedat with him. But Pierre had no need of her; Eve could not foresee the welcome he had in store for her. Suddenly she thought with a sort of pride that she had no place anywhere. *Normal people think I belong with them. But I couldn't stay an hour among them. I need to live out there, on the other side of the wall. But they don't want me out there.*

A profound change was taking place around her. The light had grown old and greying: it was heavy, like the water in a vase of flowers that hasn't been changed since the day before. In this aged light Eve found a melancholy she had long forgotten: the melancholy of an autumn afternoon that was ending. She looked around her, hesitant, almost timid: all that was so far away: there was neither day nor night nor season nor melancholy in the room. She vaguely recalled autumns long past, autumns of her childhood, then suddenly she stiffened: she was afraid of memories.

She heard Pierre's voice. "Agatha! Where are you?"

"Coming!" she cried.

She opened the door and entered the room.

The heavy odor of incense filled her mouth and nostrils as she opened her eyes and stretched out her hands—for a long time the perfume and the gloom had meant nothing more to her than a single element, acrid and heavy, as simple, as familiar as water, air or fire—and she prudently advanced toward a pale stain which seemed to float in the fog. It was Pierre's face: Pierre's clothing (he dressed in black ever since he had been sick) melted in obscurity. Pierre had thrown back his head and closed his eyes. He was handsome. Eve looked at his long, curved lashes, then sat close to him on the low chair. *He seems to be suffering,* she thought. Little by little her eyes grew used to the darkness. The bureau emerged first, then the bed, then Pierre's personal things: scissors, the pot of glue, books, the herbarium which shed its leaves onto the rug near the armchair.

"Agatha?"

Pierre had opened his eyes. He was watching her, smiling. "You know, that fork?" he said. "I did it to frighten that fellow. There was *almost* nothing the matter with it."

Eve's apprehensions faded and she gave a light laugh. "You succeeded," she said, "You drove him completely out of his mind."

Pierre smiled. "Did you see? He played with it a long time, he held it right in his hands. The trouble is," he said, "they don't know how to take hold of things; they grab them."

"That's right," Eve said.

Pierre tapped the palm of his left hand lightly with the index of his right.

"They take with that. They reach out their fingers and when they catch hold of something they crack down on it to knock it out."

He spoke rapidly and hardly moving his lips; he looked puzzled.

"I wonder what they want," he said at last, "that fellow has already been here. Why did they send him to me? If they want to know what I'm doing all they have to do is read it on the screen, they don't even need to leave the house. They make mistakes. They have the power but they make mistakes. I never make any, that's my trump card. *Hoffka!*" he said. He shook his long hands before his forehead. "The bitch Hoffka! Paffka! Suffka! Do you want any more?"

"Is it the bell?" asked Eve.

"Yes. It's gone." He went on severely. "This fellow, he's just a subordinate. You know him, you went into the living-room with him."

Eve did not answer.

"What did he want?" asked Pierre. "He must have told you."

She hesitated an instant, then answered brutally. "He wanted you locked up."

When the truth was told quietly to Pierre he distrusted it. He had to be dealt with violently in order to daze and paralyze his suspicions. Eve preferred to brutalize him rather than lie: when she lied and he acted as if he believed it she could not avoid a very slight feeling of superiority which made her horrified at herself.

"Lock me up!" Pierre repeated ironically. "They're crazy. What can walls do to me. Maybe they think that's going to stop me. I sometimes wonder if there aren't two groups. The real one, the negro—and then a bunch of fools trying to stick their noses in and making mistake after mistake."

He made his hand jump up from the arm of the chair and looked at it happily.

"I can get through walls. What did you tell them?" he asked, turning to Eve with curiosity.

"Not to lock you up."

He shrugged. "You shouldn't have said that. You made a mistake too . . . unless you did it on purpose. You've got to call their bluff."

He was silent. Eve lowered her head sadly: *"They grab things!" How scornfully he said that—and he was right. Do I grab things too? It doesn't do any good to watch myself, I think most of my movements annoy him. But he doesn't say anything.* Suddenly she felt as miserable as when she was fourteen and Mme. Darbedat told her "You don't know what to do with your hands." She didn't dare make a move and just at that time she had an irresistible desire to change her position. Quietly she put her feet under the chair, barely touching the rug. She watched the lamp on the table—the lamp whose base Pierre had painted black—and the chess set. Pierre had left only the black pawns on the board. Sometimes he would get up, go to the table and take the pawns in his hands one by one. He spoke to them, called them Robots and they seemed to stir with a mute life under his fingers. When he set them down, Eve went and touched them in her turn (she always felt somewhat ridiculous about it). They had become little bits of dead wood again but something vague and incomprehensible stayed in them, something like understanding. *These are* his *things,* she thought. *There is nothing of mine in the room.* She had had a few pieces of furniture before; the mirror and the little inlaid dresser handed down from her grandmother and which Pierre jokingly called "*your* dresser." Pierre had carried them away with him; things showed their true face to Pierre alone. Eve could watch them for hours: they were unflaggingly stubborn and determined to deceive her, offering her nothing but their appearance—as they did to Dr. Franchot and M. Darbedat. *Yet,* she told herself with anguish, *I don't see them quite like my father. It isn't possible for me to see them exactly like him.*

She moved her knees a little: her legs felt as though they were crawling with ants. Her body was stiff and taut and hurt her; she felt it too alive, too demanding. *I would like to be invisible and stay here seeing him without his seeing me. He doesn't need me; I am useless in this room.* She turned her head slightly and looked at the wall above Pierre. Threats were written on the wall. Eve knew it but she could not read them. She often watched the big red roses on the wallpaper until they began to dance before her eyes. The roses flamed in shadow. Most of the time the threat was written near the ceiling, a little to the left of the bed; but sometimes it moved. *I must get up. I can't . . . I can't sit down any longer.* There were also white discs on the wall that looked like slices of onion. The discs spun and Eve's hands began to tremble: *Sometimes I think I'm going mad. But no,* she thought, *I* can't *go mad. I get nervous, that's all.*

Suddenly she felt Pierre's hand on hers.

"Agatha," Pierre said tenderly.

He smiled at her but he held her hand by the ends of his fingers with a sort of revulsion, as though he had picked up a crab by the back and wanted to avoid its claws.

"Agatha," he said, "I would so much like to have confidence in you."

She closed her eyes and her breast heaved. *I mustn't answer anything, if I do he'll get angry, he won't say anything more.*

Pierre had dropped her hand. "I like you, Agatha," he said, "but I can't understand you. Why do you stay in the room all the time?"

Eve did not answer.

"Tell me why."

"You know I love you," she said dryly.

"I don't believe you," Pierre said. "Why should you love me? I must frighten you: I'm haunted." He smiled but suddenly became serious. "There is a wall between you and me, I see you, I speak to you, but you're on the other side. What keeps us from loving? I think it was easier before. In Hamburg."

"Yes," Eve said sadly. Always Hamburg. He never spoke of their real past. Neither Eve nor he had ever been to Hamburg.

"We used to walk along the canal. There was a barge, remember? The barge was black; there was a dog on the deck."

He made it up as he went along; it sounded false.

"I held your hand. You had another skin. I believed all you told me. Be quiet!" he shouted.

He listened for a moment. "They're coming," he said mournfully.

Eve jumped up. "They're coming? I thought they wouldn't ever come again."

Pierre had been calmer for the past three days; the statues did not come. Pierre was terribly afraid of the statues even though he would never admit it. Eve was not afraid: but when they began to fly, buzzing, around the room, she was afraid of Pierre.

"Give me the ziuthre," Pierre said.

Eve got up and took the ziuthre: it was a collection of pieces of cardboard Pierre had glued together; he used it to conjure the statues. The ziuthre looked like a spider. On one of the cardboards Pierre had written "Power over ambush" and on the other, "Black." On a third he had drawn a laughing face with wrinkled eyes: it was Voltaire.

Pierre seized the ziuthre by one end and looked at it darkly.

"I can't use it any more," he said.

"Why?"

"They turned it upside down."

"Will you make another?"

He looked at her for a long while. "You'd like me to, wouldn't you," he said between his teeth.

Eve was angry at Pierre. *He's warned every time they come: how does he do it? He's never wrong.*

The ziuthre dangled pitifully from the ends of Pierre's fingers. *He always finds a good reason not to use it. Sunday when they came he pretended he'd lost it but I saw it behind the paste pot and he couldn't fail to see it. I wonder if he isn't the one who brings them.* One could never tell if he were completely sincere. Sometimes Eve had the impression that despite himself Pierre was surrounded by a swarm of unhealthy thoughts and visions. But at other times Pierre seemed to invent them. *He suffers. But how much does he* believe *in the statues and the negro. Anyhow, I know he doesn't see the statues, he only hears them: when they pass he turns his head away; but he still says he sees them; he describes them.* She remembered the red face of Dr. Franchot: "But my dear madame, all mentally unbalanced persons are liars; you're wasting your time if you're trying to distinguish between what they really feel and what they pretend to feel." She gave a start. *What is Franchot doing here? I don't mean to start thinking like him.*

Pierre had gotten up. He went to throw the ziuthre into the wastebasket: *I want to think like you,* she murmured. He walked with tiny steps, on tiptoe, pressing his elbows against his hips so as to take up the least possible space. He came back and sat down and looked at Eve with a closed expression.

"We'll have to put up black wallpaper," he said. "There isn't enough black in this room."

He was crouched in the armchair. Sadly Eve watched his meagre body, always ready to withdraw, to shrink: the arms, legs and head looked like retractable organs. The clock struck six. The piano downstairs was silent. Eve sighed: the statues would not come right away; they had to wait for them.

"Do you want me to turn on the light?"

She would rather not wait for them in darkness.

"Do as you please," Pierre said.

Eve lit the small lamp on the bureau and a red mist filled the room. Pierre was waiting too.

He did not speak but his lips were moving, making two dark stains in the red mist. Eve loved Pierre's lips. Before, they had been moving and sensual; but they had lost their sensuality. They were wide apart, trembling a little, coming together incessantly, crushing against each other only to separate again. They were the only living things in this blank face; they looked like two frightened animals. Pierre could mutter like that for hours without a sound leaving his mouth and Eve often let herself be fascinated by this tiny, obstinate movement. *I love his mouth.* He never kissed her any more; he was horrified at contacts: at night they touched him—the hands of men, hard and dry, pinched him all over; the longnailed hands of women caressed him. Often he went to bed with his clothes on but the hands slipped under the clothes and tugged at his shirt. Once he heard laughter and puffy lips were placed on his mouth. He never kissed Eve after that night.

"Agatha," Pierre said, "don't look at my mouth."

Eve lowered her eyes.

"I am not unaware that people can learn to read lips," he went on insolently.

His hand trembled on the arm of the chair. The index finger stretched out, tapped three times on the thumb and the other fingers curled: this was a spell. *It's going to start,* she thought. She wanted to take Pierre in her arms.

Pierre began to speak at the top of his voice in a very sophisticated tone.

"Do you remember São Paulo?"

No answer. Perhaps it was a trap.

"I met you there," he said, satisfied. "I took you away from a Danish sailor. We almost fought but I paid for a round of drinks and he let me take you away. All that was only a joke."

*He's lying, he doesn't believe a word of what he says. He knows my name isn't Agatha. I hate him when he lies.* But she saw his staring eyes and her rage melted. *He isn't lying,* she thought, *he can't stand it any more. He feels them coming; he's talking to keep from hearing them.* Pierre dug both hands into the arm of the chair. His face was pale; he was smiling.

"These meetings are often strange," he said, "but I don't believe it's by chance. I'm not asking who sent you. I know you wouldn't answer. Anyhow, you've been smart enough to bluff me."

He spoke with great difficulty, in a sharp, hurried voice. There were words he could not pronounce and which left his mouth like some soft and shapeless substance.

"You dragged me away right in the middle of the party, between the rows of black automobiles, but behind the cars there was an army with red eyes which glowed as soon as I turned my back. I think you made signs to them, all the time hanging on my arm, but I didn't see a thing. I was too absorbed by the great ceremonies of the Coronation."

He looked straight ahead, his eyes wide open. He passed his hand over his forehead very rapidly, in one spare gesture, without stopping his talking. He did not want to stop talking.

"It was the Coronation of the Republic," he said stridently, "an impressive spectacle of its kind because of all the species of animals that the colonies sent for the ceremony. You were afraid to get lost among the monkeys. I said among the monkeys," he repeated arrogantly, looking around him, "I could say *among the negroes!* The abortions sliding under the tables, trying to pass unseen, are discovered and nailed to the spot by my Look. The password is silence. To be silent. Everything in place and attention for the entrance of the statues, that's the countersign. Tralala . . ." he shrieked and cupped his hands to his mouth. "Tralalala, tralalalala!"

He was silent and Eve knew that the statues had come into the room. He was stiff, pale and distrustful. Eve stiffened too and both waited in silence. Someone was walking in the corridor: it was Marie the housecleaner, she had undoubtedly just arrived. Eve thought, *I have to give her money for the gas.* And then the statues began to fly; they passed between Eve and Pierre.

Pierre went "Ah!" and sank down in the armchair, folding his legs beneath him. He turned his face away; sometimes he grinned, but drops of sweat pearled his forehead. Eve could stand the sight no longer, this pale cheek, this mouth deformed by a trembling grimace; she closed her eyes. Gold threads began to dance on the red background of her eyelids; she felt old and heavy. Not far from her Pierre was breathing violently. *They're flying, they're buzzing, they're bending over him.* She felt a slight tickling, a pain in the shoulder and right side.

Instinctively her body bent to the left as if to avoid some disagreeable contact, as if to let a heavy, awkward object pass. Suddenly the floor creaked and she had an insane desire to open her eyes, to look to her right, sweeping the air with her hand.

She did nothing; she kept her eyes closed and a bitter joy made her tremble: *I am afraid too,* she thought. Her entire life had taken refuge in her right side. She leaned towards Pierre without opening her eyes. The slightest effort would be enough and she would enter this tragic world for the first time. *I'm afraid of the statues,* she thought. It was a violent, blind affirmation, an incantation. She wanted to believe in their presence with all her strength. She tried to make a new sense, a sense of touch out of the anguish which paralysed her right side. She *felt* their passage in her arm, in her side and shoulder.

The statues flew low and gently; they buzzed. Eve knew that they had an evil look and that eyelashes stuck out from the stone around their eyes; but she pictured them badly. She knew, too, that they were not quite alive but that slabs of flesh, warm scales appeared on their great bodies; the stone peeled from the ends of their fingers and their palms were eaten away. Eve could not *see* all that: she simply thought of enormous women sliding against her, solemn and grotesque, with a human look and compact heads of stone. *They are bending over Pierre*—Eve made such a violent effort that her hands began trembling—*they are bending over me.* A horrible cry suddenly chilled her. They had touched him. She opened her eyes: Pierre's head was in his hands, he was breathing heavily. Eve felt exhausted: *a game,* she thought with remorse; *it was only a game. I didn't sincerely believe it for an instant. And all that time he suffered as if it were real.*

Pierre relaxed and breathed freely. But his pupils were strangely dilated and he was perspiring.

"Did you see them?" he asked.

"I can't see them."

"Better for you. They'd frighten you," he said. "I am used to them."

Eve's hands were still shaking and the blood had rushed to her head. Pierre took a cigarette from his pocket and brought it up to his mouth. But he did not light it:

"I don't care whether I see them or not," he said, "but I don't want them to touch me: I'm afraid they'll give me pimples."

He thought for an instant, then asked, "Did you hear them?"

"Yes," Eve said, "it's like an airplane engine." (Pierre had told her this the previous Sunday.)

Pierre smiled with condescension. "You exaggerate," he said. But he was still pale. He looked at Eve's hands. "Your hands are trembling. That made quite an impression on you, my poor Agatha. But don't worry. They won't come back again before tomorrow." Eve could not speak. Her teeth were chattering and she was afraid Pierre would notice it. Pierre watched her for a long time.

"You're tremendously beautiful," he said, nodding his head. "It's too bad, too bad."

He put out his hand quickly and toyed with her ear. "My lovely devil-woman. You disturb me a little, you are too beautiful: that distracts me. If it weren't a question of recapitulation . . ."

He stopped and looked at Eve with surprise.

"That's not the word . . . it came . . . it came," he said, smiling vaguely. "I had another on the tip of my tongue . . . but this one . . . came in its place. I forget what I was telling you."

He thought for a moment, then shook his head.

"Come," he said, "I want to sleep." He added in a childish voice, "You know, Agatha, I'm tired. I can't collect my thoughts any more."

He threw away his cigarette and looked at the rug anxiously. Eve slipped a pillow under his head.

"You can sleep too," he told her, "they won't be back."

. . . *Recapitulation* . . .

Pierre was asleep, a candid, half-smile on his face; his head was turned to one side: one might have thought he wanted to caress his cheek with his shoulder. Eve was not sleepy, she was thoughtful: *Recapitulation.* Pierre had suddenly looked stupid and the word had slipped out of his mouth, long and whitish. Pierre had stared ahead of him in astonishment, as if he had seen the word and didn't recognize it; his mouth was open, soft: something seemed broken in it. He stammered. *That's the first time it ever happened to him: he noticed it, too. He said he couldn't collect his thoughts any more.* Pierre gave a voluptuous little whimper and his hand made a vague movement. Eve watched him harshly: *how is he going to wake up.* It gnawed at her. As soon as Pierre was asleep she had to think about it. She was afraid he would wake up wild-eyed and stammering. *I'm stupid,* she thought, *it can't start before a year; Franchot said so.* But the anguish did not leave her; a year: a winter, a springtime, a summer, the beginning of another autumn. One day his features would grow confused, his jaw would hang loose, he would half open his weeping eyes. Eve bent over Pierre's hand and pressed her lips against it: *I'll kill you before that.*

## *Study questions*

*1. What is the relationship between Mme. Darbedat's room and Pierre's room? Compare and contrast M. Darbedat's relationship with his wife and Eve's relationship with Pierre. 2. The story is told in two parts. Do the parts mirror each other in any way? 3. In part 1, Sartre enters the consciousness of Mme. Darbedat and then of M. Darbedat. In part 2, Sartre enters the consciousness of Eve. How does point of view function to help Sartre tell his story? Why doesn't he enter Pierre's mind? 4. Why does Eve stay with Pierre? What does she fear? How does Eve feel about "normal" people? Are M. and Mme. Darbedat "normal"? 5. What contrasting images recur in the story? What do they add?*

*Richard Wright* (1908–1960), the first twentieth-century writer to treat in depth the economic, social, and moral problems of the black people of America, was born of an impoverished family on a cotton plantation near Natchez, Mississippi. His father abandoned the family when Wright was five, and his mother worked as a domestic until her paralysis forced Wright into an orphanage and then into a series of foster homes. When he was old enough he went to Memphis, where he supported himself by doing odd jobs. In 1927, thoroughly disillusioned with American democracy, he went to Chicago, where he joined the Communist party and began to write. His first important work was *Uncle Tom's Children* (1938), a collection of four long stories about black sharecroppers in the rural South. His first novel, *Native Son,* appeared in 1940 and made him a spokesman for a generation of black people. His autobiography, *Black Boy,* appeared in 1945. In 1947 he went to France where he lived as an expatriate until his death. Another short-story collection, *Eight Men,* was published posthumously in 1961. *American Hunger,* a sequel to *Black Boy,* was published posthumously in 1977. "The Man Who Killed a Shadow" develops some of Wright's characteristic themes: subjugation, frustration, alienation, violence, sex.

## THE MAN WHO KILLED A SHADOW

It all began long ago when he was a tiny boy who was already used, in a fearful sort of way, to living with shadows. But what were the shadows that made him afraid? Surely they were not those beautiful silhouettes of objects cast upon the earth by the sun. Shadows of that kind are innocent and he loved trying to catch them as he ran along sunlit paths in summer. But there were subtler shadows which he saw and which others could not see: the shadows of his fears. And this boy had such shadows and he lived to kill one of them.

Saul Saunders was born black in a little Southern town, not many miles from Washington, the nation's capital, which means that he came into a world that was split in two, a white world and a black one, the white one being separated from the black by a million psychological miles. So, from the very beginning, Saul looking timidly out from his black world, saw the shadowy outlines of a white world that was unreal to him and not his own.

It so happened that even Saul's mother was but a vague, shadowy thing to him, for she died long before his memory could form an image of her. And the same thing happened to Saul's father, who died before the boy could retain a clear picture of him in his mind.

People really never became personalities to Saul, for hardly had he ever got to know them before they vanished. So people became for Saul symbols of uneasiness, of a deprivation that evoked in him a sense of the transitory quality of life, which always made him feel that some invisible, unexplainable event was about to descend upon him.

He had five brothers and two sisters who remained strangers to him. There was, of course, no adult in his family with enough money to support them all, and the children were rationed out to various cousins, uncles, aunts, and grandparents.

It fell to Saul to live with his grandmother who moved constantly from one small Southern town to another, and even physical landscapes grew to have but little emotional meaning for the boy. Towns were places you lived in for a while, and then you moved on. When he had reached the age of twelve, all reality seemed to him to be akin to his mother and father, like the white world that surrounded the black island of his life, like the parade of dirty little towns that passed forever before his eyes, things that had names but not substance, things that happened and then retreated into an incomprehensible nothingness.

Saul was not dumb or lazy, but it took him seven years to reach the third grade in school. None of the people who came and went in Saul's life had ever prized learning and Saul did likewise. It was quite normal in his environment to reach the age of fourteen and still be in the third grade, and Saul liked being normal, liked being like other people.

Then the one person—his grandmother—who Saul had thought would endure forever, passed suddenly from his life, and from that moment on Saul did not ever quite know what to do. He went to work for the white people of the South and the shadowlike quality of his world became terribly manifest, continuously present. He understood nothing of this white world into which he had been thrown; it was just there, a faint and fearful shadow cast by some object that stood between him and a hidden and powerful sun.

He quickly learned that the strange white people for whom he worked considered him inferior; he did not feel inferior and he did not think that he was. But when he looked about him he saw other black people accepting this definition of themselves, and who was he to challenge it? Outwardly he grew to accept it as part of that vast shadow-world that came and went, pulled by forces which he nor nobody he knew understood.

Soon all of Saul's anxieties, fears, and irritations became focused upon this white shadow-world which gave him his daily bread in exchange for his labor. Feeling unhappy and not knowing why, he projected his misery out from himself and upon the one thing that made him most constantly anxious. If this had not happened, if Saul had not found a way of putting his burden upon others, he would have early thought of suicide. He finally did, in the end, think of killing himself, but then it was too late . . .

At the age of fifteen Saul knew that the life he was then living was to be his lot, that there was no way to rid himself of his plaguing sense of unreality, no way to relax and forget. He was most self-forgetful when he was with black people, and that made things a little easier for him. But as he grew older, he became more afraid, yet none of his friends noticed it. Indeed, many of Saul's friends liked him very much. Saul was always kind, attentive; but no one suspected that his kindness, his quiet, waiting loyalty came from his being afraid.

Then Saul changed. Maybe it was luck or misfortune; it is hard to tell. When he took a drink of whisky, he found that it helped to banish the shadows, lessened his tensions, made the world more reasonably three-dimensional, and he grew to like drinking. When he was paid off on a Saturday night, he would drink with his friends and he would feel better. He felt that whisky made life complete, that it stimulated him. But, of course, it did not. Whisky really depressed him, numbed him somewhat, reduced the force and number of the shadows that made him tight inside.

When Saul was sober, he almost never laughed in the presence of the white shadow-world, but when he had a drink or two he found that he could. Even when he was told about the hard lives that all Negroes lived, it did not worry him, for he would take a drink and not feel too badly. It did not even bother him when he heard that if you were alone with a white woman and she screamed, it was as good as hearing your death sentence, for, though you had done nothing, you would be killed. Saul got used to hearing the siren of the police car screaming in the Black Belt, got used to seeing white cops dragging Negroes off to jail. Once he grew wildly angry about it, felt that the shadows would some day claim him as he had seen them claim others, but his friends warned him that it was dangerous to feel that way, that always the black man lost, and the best thing to do was to take a drink. He did, and in a little while they were all laughing.

One night when he was mildly drunk—he was thirty years old and living in Washington at the time—he got married. The girl was good for Saul, for she too liked to drink and she was pretty and they got along together. Saul now felt that things were not so bad; as long as he could stifle the feeling of being hemmed in, as long as he could conquer the anxiety about the unexpected happening, life was bearable.

Saul's jobs had been many and simple. First he had worked on a farm. When he was fourteen he had gone to Washington, after his grandmother had died, where he did all kinds of odd jobs. Finally he was hired by an old white army colonel as chauffeur and butler and he averaged about twenty dollars every two weeks. He lived in and got his meals and uniform and remained with the colonel for five years. The colonel too liked to drink, and sometimes they would both get drunk. But Saul never forgot that the colonel, though drunk and feeling fine, was still a shadow, unreal, and might suddenly change toward him.

One day, when whisky was making him feel good, Saul asked the colonel for a raise in salary, told him that he did not have enough to live on, and that prices were rising. But the colonel was sober and hard that day and said no. Saul was so stunned that he quit the job that instant. While under the spell of whisky he had for a quick moment felt that the world of shadows was over, but when he had asked for more money and had been refused, he knew that he had been wrong. He should not have asked for money; he should have known that the colonel was a no-good guy, a shadow.

Saul was next hired as an exterminator by a big chemical company and he found that there was something in his nature that made him like going from house to house and putting down poison for rats and mice and roaches. He liked seeing concrete evidence of his work and the dead bodies of rats were no shadows. They were real. He never felt better in his life than when he was killing with the sanction of society. And his boss even increased his salary when he asked for it. And he drank as much as he liked and no one cared.

But one morning, after a hard night of drinking which had made him irritable and high-strung, his boss said something that he did not like and he spoke up, defending himself against what he thought was a slighting remark. There was an argument and Saul left.

Two weeks of job hunting got him the position of janitor in the National Cathedral, a church and religious institution. It was the solitary kind of work he liked; he reported for duty each morning at seven o'clock and at eleven he was through. He first cleaned the Christmas card shop, next he cleaned the library; and his final chore was to clean the choir room.

But cleaning the library, with its rows and rows of books, was what caught Saul's attention, for there was a strange little shadow woman there who stared at him all the time in a most peculiar way. The library was housed in a separate building and, whenever he came to clean it, he and the white woman would be there alone. She was tiny, blonde, blue-eyed, weighing about 110 pounds, and standing about five feet three inches. Saul's boss had warned him never to quarrel with the lady in charge of the library. "She's a crackpot," he had told Saul. And naturally Saul never wanted any trouble, in fact, he did not even know the woman's name. Many times, however, he would pause in his work, feeling that his eyes were being drawn to her and he would turn around and find her staring at him. Then she would look away quickly, as though ashamed. "What in hell does she want from me?" he wondered uneasily. The woman never spoke to him except to say good morning and she even said that as though she did not want to say it. Saul thought that maybe she was afraid of him; but how could that be? He could not recall when anybody had ever been afraid of him, and he had never been in any trouble in his life.

One morning while sweeping the floor he felt his eyes being drawn toward her and he paused and turned and saw her staring at him. He did not move, neither did she. They stared at each other for about ten seconds, then she went out of the room, walking with quick steps, as though angry or afraid. He was frightened, but forgot it quickly. "What the hell's wrong with that woman?" he asked himself.

Next morning Saul's boss called him and told him, in a nice quiet tone—but it made him scared and mad just the same—that the woman in the library had complained about him, had said that he never cleaned under her desk.

"Under her desk?" Saul asked, amazed.

"Yes," his boss said, amused at Saul's astonishment.

"But I clean under her desk every morning," Saul said.

"Well, Saul, remember, I told you she was a crackpot," his boss said soothingly. "Don't argue with her. Just do your work."

"Yes, sir," Saul said.

He wanted to tell his boss how the woman always stared at him, but he could not find courage enough to do so. If he had been talking with his black friends, he would have done so quite naturally. But why talk to one shadow about another queer shadow?

That day being payday, he got his weekly wages and that night he had a hell of a good time. He drank until he was drunk, until he blotted out almost everything from his consciousness. He was getting regularly drunk now whenever he had the money. He liked it and he bothered nobody and he was happy while doing it. But dawn found him broke, exhausted, and terribly depressed, full of shadows and uneasiness, a way he never liked it. The thought of going to his job made him angry. He longed for deep, heavy sleep. But, no, he had a good job and he had to keep it. Yes, he would go.

After cleaning the Christmas card shop—he was weak and he sweated a lot—he went to the library. No one was there. He swept the floor and was about to dust the books when he heard the footsteps of the woman coming into the room. He was tired, nervous, half asleep; his hands trembled and his reflexes were overquick. "So you're the bitch who snitched on me, hunh?" he said irritably to himself. He continued dusting and all at once he had the queer feeling that she was staring at him. He fought against the impulse to look at her, but he could not resist it. He turned slowly and saw that she was sitting in her chair at her desk, staring at him with unblinking eyes. He had the impression that she was about to speak. He could not help staring back at her, waiting.

"Why don't you clean under my desk?" she asked him in a tense but controlled voice.

"Why, ma'am," he said slowly, "I just did."

"Come here and look," she said, pointing downward.

He replaced the book on the shelf. She had never spoken so many words to him before. He went and stood before her and his mind protested against what his eyes saw, and then his senses leaped in wonder. She was sitting with her knees sprawled apart and her dress was drawn halfway up her legs. He looked from her round blue eyes to her white legs whose thighs thickened as they went to a V clothed in tight, sheer, pink panties; then he looked quickly again into her eyes. Her face was a beet red, but she sat very still, rigid, as though she was being impelled into an act which she did not want to perform but was being driven to perform. Saul was so startled that he could not move.

"I just cleaned under your desk this morning," he mumbled, sensing that he was not talking about what she meant.

"There's dust there now," she said sternly, her legs still so wide apart that he felt that she was naked.

He did not know what to do; he was so baffled, humiliated, and frightened that he grew angry. But he was afraid to express his anger openly.

"Look, ma'am," he said in a tone of suppressed rage and hate, "you're making trouble for me!"

"Why don't you do your work?" she blazed at him. "That's what you're being paid to do, you black nigger!" Her legs were still spread wide and she was sitting as though about to spring upon him and throw her naked thighs about his body.

For a moment he was still and silent. Never before in his life had he been called a "black nigger." He had heard that white people used that phrase as their supreme humiliation of black people, but he had never been treated so. As the insult sank in, as he stared at her gaping thighs, he felt overwhelmed by a sense of wild danger.

"I don't like that," he said and before he knew it he had slapped her flat across her face.

She sucked in her breath, sprang up, and stepped away from him. Then she screamed sharply, and her voice was like a lash cutting into his chest. She screamed again and he backed away from her. He felt helpless, strange; he knew what he had done, knew its meaning for him; but he knew that he could not have helped it. It seemed that some part of him was there in that room watching him do things that he should not do. He drew in his breath and for a moment he felt that he could not stand upon his legs. His world was now full of all the shadows he had ever feared. He was in the worst trouble that a black man could imagine.

The woman was screaming continuously now and he was running toward the stairs. Just as he put his foot on the bottom step, he paused and looked over his shoulder. She was backing away from him, toward an open window at the far end of the room, still screaming. Oh God! In her scream he heard the sirens of the police cars that hunted down black men in the Black Belts and he heard the shrill whistles of white cops running after black men and he felt again in one rush of emotion all the wild and bitter tales he had heard of how whites always got the black who did a crime and this woman was screaming as though he had raped her.

He ran on up the steps, but her screams were coming so loud that when he neared the top of the steps he slowed. Those screams would not let him run any more, they weakened him, tugged and pulled him. His chest felt as though it would burst. He reached the top landing and looked round aimlessly. He saw a fireplace and before it was a neat pile of wood and while he was looking at that pile of wood the screams tore at him, unnerved him. With a shaking hand he reached down and seized in his left hand—for he was lefthanded—a heavy piece of oaken firewood that had jagged, sharp edges where it had been cut with an ax. He turned and ran back down the steps to where the woman stood screaming. He lifted the stick of wood as he confronted her, then paused. He wanted her to stop screaming. If she had stopped, he would have fled, but while she screamed all he could feel was a hotness bubbling in him and urging him to do something. She would fill her lungs quickly and deeply and her breath would come out at full blast. He swung down his left arm and hit her a swinging blow on the side of her head, not to hurt her, not to kill her, but to stop that awful noise, to stop that shadow from screaming a scream that meant death . . . He felt her skull crack and give as she sank to the floor, but she still screamed. He trembled from head to feet. Goddamn that woman . . . Why didn't she stop that yelling?

He lifted his arm and gave her another blow, feeling the oaken stick driving its way into her skull. But still she screamed. He was about to hit her again when he became aware that the stick he held was light. He looked at it and found that half of it had broken off, was lying on the floor. But she screamed on, with blood running down her dress, her legs sprawled nakedly out from under her. He dropped the remainder of the stick and grabbed her throat and choked her to stop her screams. That seemed to quiet her; she looked as though she had fainted. He choked her for a long time, not trying to kill her, but just to make sure that she would not scream again and make him wild and hot inside. He was not reacting to the woman, but to the feelings that her screams evoked in him.

The woman was limp and silent now and slowly he took his hands from her throat. She was quiet. He waited. He was not certain. Yes, take her downstairs into the bathroom and if she screamed again no one would hear her . . . He took her hands in his and started dragging her away from the window. His hands were wet with sweat and her hands were so tiny and soft that time and again her little fingers slipped out of his palms. He tried holding her hands tighter and only succeeded in scratching her. Her ring slid off into his hand while he was dragging her and he stood still for a moment, staring in a daze at the thin band of shimmering gold, then mechanically he put it into his pocket. Finally he dragged her down the steps to the bathroom door.

He was about to take her in when he saw that the floor was spotted with drippings of blood. That was bad . . . He had been trained to keep floors clean, just as he had been trained to fear shadows. He propped her clumsily against a wall and went into the bathroom and took wads of toilet paper and mopped up the red splashes. He even went back upstairs where he had first struck her and found blood spots and wiped them up carefully. He stiffened; she was hollering again. He ran downstairs and this time he recalled that he had a knife in his pocket. He took it out, opened it, and plunged it deep into her throat; he was frantic to stop her from hollering . . . He pulled the knife from her throat and she was quiet.

He stood, his eyes roving. He noticed a door leading down to a recess in a wall through which steam pipes ran. Yes, it would be better to put her there; then if she started yelling no one would hear her. He was not trying to hide her; he merely wanted to make sure that she would not be heard. He dragged her again and her dress came up over her knees to her chest and again he saw her pink panties. It was too hard dragging her and he lifted her in his arms and while carrying her down the short flight of steps he thought that the pink panties, if he would wet them, would make a good mop to clean up the blood. Once more he sat her against the wall, stripped her of her pink panties—and not once did he so much as glance at her groin—wetted them and swabbed up the spots, then pushed her into the recess under the pipes. She was in full view, easily seen. He tossed the wet ball of panties in after her.

He sighed and looked around. The floor seemed clean. He went back upstairs. That stick of broken wood . . . He picked up the two shattered ends of wood and several splinters; he carefully joined the ends together and then fitted the splinters into place. He laid the mended stick back upon the pile before the fireplace. He stood listening, wondering if she would yell again, but there was no sound. It never occurred to him that he could help her, that she might be in pain; he never wondered even if she were dead. He got his coat and hat and went home.

He was nervously tired. It seemed that he had just finished doing an old and familiar job of dodging the shadows that were forever around him, shadows that he could not understand. He undressed, but paid no attention to the blood on his trousers and shirt; he was alone in the room; his wife was at work. When he pulled out his billfold, he saw the ring. He put it in the drawer of his night table, more to keep his wife from seeing it than to hide it. He climbed wearily into bed and at once fell into a deep, sound sleep from which he did not awaken until late afternoon. He lay blinking bloodshot eyes and he could not remember what he had done. Then the vague, shadowlike picture of it came before his eyes. He was puzzled, and for a moment he wondered if it had happened or had someone told him a story of it. He could not be sure. There was no fear or regret in him.

When at last the conviction of what he had done was real in him, it came only in terms of flat memory, devoid of all emotion, as though he were looking when very tired and sleepy at a scene being flashed upon the screen of a movie house. Not knowing what to do, he remained in bed. He had drifted off to sleep again when his wife came home late that night from her cooking job.

Next morning he ate the breakfast his wife prepared, rose from the table and kissed her, and started off toward the Cathedral as though nothing had happened. It was not until he actually got to the Cathedral steps that he became shaky and nervous. He stood before the door for two or three minutes, and then he realized that he could not go back in there this morning. Yet it was not danger that made him feel this way, but a queer kind of repugnance. Whether the woman was alive or not did not enter his mind. He still did not know what to do. Then he remembered that his wife, before she had left for her job, had asked him to buy some groceries. Yes, he would do that. He wanted to do that because he did not know what else on earth to do.

He bought the groceries and took them home, then spent the rest of the day wandering from bar to bar. Not once did he think of fleeing. He would go home, sit, turn on the radio, then go out into the streets and walk. Finally he would end up at a bar, drinking. On one of his many trips into the house, he changed his clothes, rolled up his bloody shirt and trousers, put the blood-stained knife inside the bundle, and pushed it into a far corner of a closet. He got his gun and put it into his pocket, for he was nervously depressed.

But he still did not know what to do. Suddenly he recalled that some months ago he had bought a cheap car which was now in a garage for repairs. He went to the garage and persuaded the owner to take it back for twenty-five dollars; the thought that he could use the car for escape never came to his mind. During that afternoon and early evening he sat in bars and drank. What he felt now was no different from what he had felt all his life.

Toward eight o'clock that night he met two friends of his and invited them for a drink. He was quite drunk now. Before him on the table was a sandwich and a small glass of whisky. He leaned forward, listening sleepily to one of his friends tell a story about a girl, and then he heard:

"Aren't you Saul Saunders?"

He looked up into the faces of two white shadows.

"Yes," he admitted readily. "What do you want?"

"You'd better come along with us. We want to ask you some questions," one of the shadows said.

"What's this all about?" Saul asked.

They grabbed his shoulders and he stood up. Then he reached down and picked up the glass of whisky and drank it. He walked steadily out of the bar to a waiting auto, a policeman to each side of him, his mind a benign blank. It was not until they were about to put him into the car that something happened and whipped his numbed senses to an apprehension of danger. The policeman patted his waist for arms; they found nothing because his gun was strapped to his chest. Yes, he ought to kill himself . . . The thought leaped into his mind with such gladness that he shivered. It was the answer to everything. Why had he not thought of it before?

Slowly he took off his hat and held it over his chest to hide the movement of his left hand, then he reached inside of his shirt and pulled out the gun. One of the policemen pounced on him and snatched the gun.

"So, you're trying to kill us too, hunh?" one asked.

"Naw, I was trying to kill myself," he answered simply.

"Like hell you were!"

A fist came onto his jaw and he sank back limp.

Two hours later, at the police station, he told them everything, speaking in a low, listless voice without a trace of emotion, vividly describing every detail, yet feeling that it was utterly hopeless for him to try to make them understand how horrible it was for him to hear that woman screaming. His narrative sounded so brutal that the policemen's faces were chalky.

Weeks later a voice droned in a court room and he sat staring dully.

". . . The Grand Jurors of the United States of America, in and for the District of Columbia aforesaid, upon their oath, do present:

"That one Saul Saunders, on, to wit, the first day of March, 19——, and at and within the District of Columbia aforesaid, contriving and intending to kill one Maybelle Eva Houseman . . ."

"So *that's* her name," he said to himself in amazement.

". . . Feloniously, wilfully, purposefully, and of his deliberate and premeditated malice did strike, beat, and wound the said Maybelle Eva Houseman, in and upon the front of the head and in and upon the right side of the head of her, the said Maybelle Eva Houseman, two certain mortal wounds and fractures; and did fix and fasten about the neck and throat of her, the said Maybelle Eva Houseman, his hand or hands—but whether it was one of his hands or both of his hands is to the Grand Jury aforesaid unknown—and that he, the said Saul Saunders, with his hand or hands as aforesaid fixed and fastened about the throat of her, did choke and strangle the said Maybelle Eva Houseman, of which said choking and strangling the said Maybelle Eva Houseman, on, to wit, the said first day of March, 19——, and at and within the said District of Columbia, did die."

He longed for a drink, but that was impossible now. Then he took a deep breath and surrendered to the world of shadows about him, the world he had feared so long; and at once the tension went from him and he felt better than he had felt in a long time. He was amazed at how relaxed and peaceful it was when he stopped fighting the world of shadows.

". . . By force and violence and against resistance and by putting in fear, did steal, take, and carry away, from and off the person and from the immediate, actual possession of one Maybelle Eva Houseman, then and there being, a certain finger ring, of the value of, to wit, ten dollars."

He listened now with more attention but no anxiety:

"And in and while perpetrating robbery aforesaid did kill and murder the said Maybelle Eva Houseman; against the form of the statute in such case made and provided, and against the peace and government of the said United States of America."

P.S. Thereupon Dr. Herman Stein was called as a witness and being first duly sworn testified as follows:

". . . On examination of the genital organs there was no evidence of contusion, abrasion, or trauma, and the decedent's hymen ring was intact. This decedent had not been criminally assaulted or attempted to be entered. It has been ascertained that the decedent's age was 40."

## *Study questions*

1. *What tone is attached to the narrative voice of this story? How is it appropriate?* 2. *What constitutes the shadows that Saul lives among? Account for his seeming total isolation. What is he afraid of?* 3. *What events lead inexorably to the murder? Was it premeditated?* 4. *Is Saul's behavior immediately before, during, and after the murder credible?* 5. *Is the librarian's behavior credible?* 6. *How does the report of the Grand Jurors function? the last paragraph of the story?*

*Eudora Welty* (b. 1909) was born in Jackson, Mississippi, and has remained there most of her life. She attended Mississippi State College for Women and, for short periods, the University of Wisconsin and Columbia University. Thereafter she worked as a copywriter and a free-lance writer for newspapers. Her early stories appeared in the *Southern Review*, then edited by Cleanth Brooks and Robert Penn Warren. Since that time she has published several volumes of stories, including *A Curtain of Green* (1941), *The Wide Net* (1943), *The Bride of the Innisfallen* (1955), *The Golden Apples* (1949), and *Thirteen Stories* (1965). She has also published five novels: *Robber Bridegroom* (1942), *Delta Wedding* (1946), *The Ponder Heart* (1954), *Losing Battles* (1970), and *The Optimist's Daughter* (1972), which won the Pulitzer Prize. Most of Welty's fiction is characterized by subtle ambiguity, irony, a multiplicity of vision, mythical patterns, fantasy, sometimes grotesqueries. Probably her best-known stories are "Death of a Traveling Salesman," "Powerhouse," "Livvie," "Petrified Man," "A Worn Path," and "Why I Live at the P.O." "Keela, the Outcast Indian Maiden" documents the horrible atrocities men are capable of visiting upon other men and the kind of expiation some are called upon to attempt.

# KEELA, THE OUTCAST INDIAN MAIDEN

One morning in summertime, when all his sons and daughters were off picking plums and Little Lee Roy was all alone, sitting on the porch and only listening to the screech owls away down in the woods, he had a surprise.

First he heard white men talking. He heard two white men coming up the path from the highway. Little Lee Roy ducked his head and held his breath; then he patted all around back of him for his crutches. The chickens all came out from under the house and waited attentively on the steps.

The men came closer. It was the young man who was doing all of the talking. But when they got through the fence, Max, the older man, interrupted him. He tapped him on the arm and pointed his thumb toward Little Lee Roy.

He said, "Bud? Yonder he is."

But the younger man kept straight on talking, in an explanatory voice.

"Bud?" said Max again. "Look, Bud, yonder's the only little clubfooted nigger man was ever around Cane Springs. Is he the party?"

They came nearer and nearer to Little Lee Roy and then stopped and stood there in the middle of the yard. But the young man was so excited he did not seem to realize that they had arrived anywhere. He was only about twenty years old, very sunburned. He talked constantly, making only one gesture—raising his hand stiffly and then moving it a little to one side.

"They dressed it in a red dress, and it ate chickens alive," he said. "I sold tickets and I thought it was worth a dime, honest. They gimme a piece of paper with the thing wrote off I had to say. That was easy. 'Keela, the Outcast Indian Maiden!' I call it out through a pasteboard megaphone. Then ever' time it was fixin' to eat a live chicken, I blowed the sireen out front."

"Just tell me, Bud," said Max, resting back on the heels of his perforated tan-and-white sport shoes. "Is this nigger the one? Is that him sittin' there?"

Little Lee Roy sat huddled and blinking, a smile on his face. . . . But the young man did not look his way.

"Just took the job that time. I didn't mean to—I mean, I meant to go to Port Arthur because my brother was on a boat," he said. "My name is Steve, mister. But I worked with this show selling tickets for three months, and I never would of knowed it was like that if it hadn't been for that man." He arrested his gesture.

"Yeah, what man?" said Max in a hopeless voice.

Little Lee Roy was looking from one white man to the other, excited almost beyond respectful silence. He trembled all over, and a look of amazement and sudden life came into his eyes.

"Two years ago," Steve was saying impatiently. "And we was travelin' through Texas in those ole trucks.—See, the reason nobody ever come clost to it before was they give it a iron bar this long. And tole it if anybody come near, to shake the bar good at 'em, like this. But it couldn't say nothin'. Turned out they'd tole it it couldn't say nothin' to anybody ever, so it just kind of mumbled and growled, like a animal."

"Hee! hee!" This from Little Lee Roy, softly.

"Tell me again," said Max, and just from his look you could tell that everybody knew old Max. "Somehow I can't get it straight in my mind. Is this the boy? Is this little nigger boy the same as this Keela, the Outcast Indian Maiden?"

Up on the porch, above them, Little Lee Roy gave Max a glance full of hilarity, and then bent the other way to catch Steve's next words.

"Why, if anybody was to even come near it or even bresh their shoulder against the rope it'd growl and take on and shake its iron rod. When it would eat the live chickens it'd growl somethin' awful—you ought to heard it."

"Hee! hee!" It was a soft, almost incredulous laugh that began to escape from Little Lee Roy's tight lips, a little mew of delight.

"They'd throw it this chicken, and it would reach out an' grab it. Would sort of rub over the chicken's neck with its thumb an' press on it good, an' then it would bite its head off."

"O.K.," said Max.

"It skint back the feathers and stuff from the neck and sucked the blood. But ever'body said it was still alive." Steve drew closer to Max and fastened his light-colored, troubled eyes on his face.

"O.K."

"Then it would pull the feathers out easy and neat-like, awful fast, an' growl the whole time, kind of moan, an' then it would commence to eat all the white meat. I'd go in an' look at it. I reckon I seen it a thousand times."

"That was you, boy?" Max demanded of Little Lee Roy unexpectedly.

But Little Lee Roy could only say, "Hee! hee!" The little man at the head of the steps where the chickens sat, one on each step, and the two men facing each other below made a pyramid.

Steve stuck his hand out for silence. "They said—I mean, I said it, out front through the megaphone, I said it myself, that it wouldn't eat nothin' but only live meat. It was supposed to be a Indian woman, see, in this red dress an' stockin's. It didn't have on no shoes, so when it drug its foot ever'body could see. . . . When it come to the chicken's heart, it would eat that too, real fast, and the heart would still be jumpin'."

"Wait a second, Bud," said Max briefly. "Say, boy, is this white man here crazy?"

Little Lee Roy burst into hysterical, deprecatory giggles. He said, "Naw suh, don't think so." He tried to catch Steve's eye, seeking appreciation, crying, "Naw suh, don't think he crazy, mista."

Steve gripped Max's arm. "Wait! Wait!" he cried anxiously. "You ain't listenin'. I want to tell you about it. You didn't catch my name—Steve. You never did hear about that little nigger—all that happened to him? Lived in Cane Springs, Miss'ippi?"

"Bud," said Max, disengaging himself, "I don't hear anything. I got a juke box, see, so I don't have to listen."

"Look—I was really the one," said Steve more patiently, but nervously, as if he had been slowly breaking bad news. He walked up and down the bare-swept ground in front of Little Lee Roy's porch, along the row of princess feathers and snow-on-the-mountain. Little Lee Roy's turning head followed him. "I was the one—that's what I'm tellin' you."

"Suppose I was to listen to what every dope comes in Max's Place got to say, *I'd* be nuts," said Max.

"It's all me, see," said Steve. "I know that. I was the one was the cause for it goin' on an' on an' not bein' found out—such an awful thing. It was me, what I said out front through the megaphone."

He stopped still and stared at Max in despair.

"Look," said Max. He sat on the steps, and the chickens hopped off. "I know I ain't nobody but Max. I got Max's Place. I only run a place, understand, fifty yards down the highway. Liquor buried twenty feet from the premises, and no trouble yet. I ain't ever been up here before. I don't claim to been anywhere. People come to my place. Now. You're the hitchhiker. You're tellin' me, see. You claim a lot of information. If I don't get it I don't get it and I ain't complainin' about it, see. But I think you're nuts, and did from the first. I only come up here with you because I figured you's crazy."

"Maybe you don't believe I remember every word of it even now," Steve was saying gently. "I think about it at night—that an' drums on the midway. You ever hear drums on the midway?" He paused and stared politely at Max and Little Lee Roy.

"Yeh," said Max.

"Don't it make you feel sad. I remember how the drums was goin' and I was yellin', 'Ladies and gents! Do not try to touch Keela, the Outcast Indian Maiden—she will only beat your brains out with her iron rod, and eat them alive!' " Steve waved his arm gently in the air, and Little Lee Roy drew back and squealed. " 'Do not go near her, ladies and gents! I'm warnin' you!' So nobody ever did. Nobody ever come near her. Until that man."

"Sure," said Max. "That fella." He shut his eyes.

"Afterwards when he come up so bold, I remembered seein' him walk up an' buy the ticket an' go in the tent. I'll never forget that man as long as I live. To me he's a sort of—well—"

"Hero," said Max.

"I wish I could remember what he looked like. Seem like he was a tallish man with a sort of white face. Seem like he had bad teeth, but I may be wrong. I remember he frowned a lot. Kept frownin'. Whenever he'd buy a ticket, why, he'd frown."

"Ever seen him since?" asked Max cautiously, still with his eyes closed. "Ever hunt him up?"

"No, never did," said Steve. Then he went on. "He'd frown an' buy a ticket ever' day we was in these two little smelly towns in Texas, sometimes three-four times a day, whether it was fixin' to eat a chicken or not."

"O.K., so he gets in the tent," said Max.

"Well, what the man finally done was, he walked right up to the little stand where it was tied up and laid his hand out open on the planks in the platform. He just laid his hand out open there and said, 'Come here,' real low and quick, that-a-way."

Steve laid his open hand on Little Lee Roy's porch and held it there, frowning in concentration.

"I get it," said Max. "He'd caught on it was a fake."

Steve straightened up. "So ever'body yelled to git away, git away," he continued, his voice rising, "because it was growlin' an' carryin' on an' shakin' its iron bar like they tole it. When I heard all that commotion—boy! I was scared."

"You didn't know it was a fake."

Steve was silent for a moment, and Little Lee Roy held his breath, for fear everything was all over.

"Look," said Steve finally, his voice trembling. "I guess I was supposed to feel bad like this, and you wasn't. I wasn't supposed to ship out on that boat from Port Arthur and all like that. This other had to happen to me—not you all. Feelin' responsible. You'll be O.K., mister, but I won't. I feel awful about it. That poor little old thing."

"Look, you got him right here," said Max quickly. "See him? Use your eyes. He's O.K., ain't he? Looks O.K. to me. It's just you. You're nuts, is all."

"You know—when that man laid out his open hand on the boards, why, it just let go the iron bar," continued Steve, "let it fall down like that—bang—and act like it didn't know what to do. Then it drug itself over to where the fella was standin' an' leaned down an' grabbed holt onto that white man's hand as tight as it could an' cried like a baby. It didn't want to hit him!"

"Hee! hee! hee!"

"No sir, it didn't want to hit him. You know what it wanted?"

Max shook his head.

"It wanted him to help it. So the man said, 'Do you wanta get out of this place, whoever you are?' An' it never answered—none of us knowed it could talk—but it just wouldn't let that man's hand a-loose. It hung on, cryin' like a baby. So the man says, 'Well, wait here till I come back.' "

"Uh-huh?" said Max.

"Went off an' come back with the sheriff. Took us all to jail. But just the man owned the show and his son got took to the pen. They said I could go free. I kep' tellin' 'em I didn't know it wouldn't hit me with the iron bar an' kep' tellin' 'em I didn't know it could tell what you was sayin' to it."

"Yeh, guess you told 'em," said Max.

"By that time I felt bad. Been feelin' bad ever since. Can't hold onto a job or stay in one place for nothin' in the world. They made it stay in jail to see if it could talk or not, and the first night it wouldn't say nothin'. Some time it cried. And they undressed it an' found out it wasn't no outcast Indian woman a-tall. It was a little clubfooted nigger man."

"Hee! hee!"

"You mean it was this boy here—yeh. It was him."

"Washed its face, and it was paint all over it made it look red. It all come off. And it could talk—as good as me or you. But they'd tole it not to, so it never did. They'd tole it if anybody was to come near it they was comin' to git it—and for it to hit 'em quick with that iron bar an' growl. So nobody ever come near it—until that man. I was yellin' outside, tellin' 'em to keep away, keep away. You could see where they'd whup it. They had to whup it some to make it eat all the chickens. It was awful dirty. They let it go back home free, to where they got it in the first place. They made them pay its ticket from Little Oil, Texas, to Cane Springs, Miss'ippi."

"You got a good memory," said Max.

"The way it *started* was," said Steve, in a wondering voice, "the show was just travelin' along in ole trucks through the country, and just seen this little deformed nigger man, sittin' on a fence, and just took it. It couldn't help it."

Little Lee Roy tossed his head back in a frenzy of amusement.

"I found it all out later. I was up on the Ferris wheel with one of the boys—got to talkin' up yonder in the peace an' quiet—an' said they just kind of happened up on it. Like a cyclone happens: it wasn't nothin' it could do. It was just took up." Steve suddenly paled through his sunburn. "An' they found out that back in Miss'ippi it had it a little bitty pair of crutches an' could just go runnin' on 'em!"

"And there they are," said Max.

Little Lee Roy held up a crutch and turned it about, and then snatched it back like a monkey.

"But if it hadn't been for that man, I wouldn't of knowed it till yet. If it wasn't for him bein' so bold. If he hadn't knowed what he was doin'."

"You remember that man this fella's talkin' about, boy?" asked Max, eying Little Lee Roy.

Little Lee Roy, in reluctance and shyness, shook his head gently.

"Naw suh, I can't say as I remembas that ve'y man, suh," he said softly, looking down where just then a sparrow alighted on his child's shoe. He added happily, as if on inspiration, "Now I remembas *this* man."

Steve did not look up, but when Max shook with silent laughter, alarm seemed to seize him like a spasm in his side. He walked painfully over and stood in the shade for a few minutes, leaning his head on a sycamore tree.

"Seemed like that man just studied it out an' knowed it was somethin' wrong," he said presently, his voice coming more remotely than ever. "But I didn't know. I can't look at nothin' an' be sure what it is. Then afterwards I know. Then I see how it was."

"Yeh, but you're nuts," said Max affably.

"You wouldn't of knowed it either!" cried Steve in sudden boyish, defensive anger. Then he came out from under the tree and stood again almost pleadingly in the sun, facing Max where he was sitting below Little Lee Roy on the steps. "You'd of let it go on an' on when they made it do those things—just like I did."

"Bet I could tell a man from a woman and an Indian from a nigger though," said Max.

Steve scuffed the dust into little puffs with his worn shoe. The chickens scattered, alarmed at last.

Little Lee Roy looked from one man to the other radiantly, his hands pressed over his grinning gums.

Then Steve sighed, and as if he did not know what else he could do, he reached out and without any warning hit Max in the jaw with his fist. Max fell off the steps.

Little Lee Roy suddenly sat as still and dark as a statue, looking on.

"Say! Say!" cried Steve. He pulled shyly at Max where he lay on the ground, with his lips pursed up like a whistler, and then stepped back. He looked horrified. "How you feel?"

"Lousy," said Max thoughtfully. "Let me alone." He raised up on one elbow and lay there looking all around, at the cabin, at Little Lee Roy sitting cross-legged on the porch, and at Steve with his hand out. Finally he got up.

"I can't figure out how I could of ever knocked down an athaletic guy like you. I had to do it," said Steve. "But I guess you don't understand. I had to hit you. First you didn't believe me, and then it didn't bother you."

"That's all O.K., only hush," said Max, and added, "Some dope is always giving me the low-down on something, but this is the first time one of 'em ever got away with a thing like this. I got to watch out."

"I hope it don't stay black long," said Steve.

"I got to be going," said Max. But he waited. "What you want to transact with Keela? You come a long way to see him." He stared at Steve with his eyes wide open now, and interested.

"Well, I was goin' to give him some money or somethin', I guess, if I ever found him, only now I ain't got any," said Steve defiantly.

"O.K.," said Max. "Here's some change for you, boy. Just take it. Go on back in the house. Go on."

Little Lee Roy took the money speechlessly, and then fell upon his yellow crutches and hopped with miraculous rapidity away through the door. Max stared after him for a moment.

"As for you"—he brushed himself off, turned to Steve and then said, "When did you eat last?"

"Well, I'll tell you," said Steve.

"Not here," said Max. "I didn't go to ask you a question. Just follow me. We serve eats at Max's Place, and I want to play the juke box. You eat, and I'll listen to the juke box."

"Well . . ." said Steve. "But when it cools off I got to catch a ride some place."

"Today while all you all was gone, and not a soul in de house," said Little Lee Roy at the supper table that night, "two white mens come heah to de house. Wouldn't come in. But talks to me about de ole times when I use to be wid de circus—"

"Hush up, Pappy," said the children.

## *Study questions*

1. *Like the Ancient Mariner in Coleridge's poem, Steve seems compelled to tell a story. How is this compulsion evidenced in the story? Why does Steve seem to take a personal responsibility and, since he has done so, what means of expiation are possible for him?* 2. *What role does Max play? Why does Max allow Steve to hit him? Why does Max give money to Lee Roy?* 3. *What is Lee Roy like? What means of characterization does Welty employ? What is the significance of the first and last paragraphs? of Lee Roy's name? of his association with the chickens?* 4. *Why do they dress Lee Roy up as Keela, the Outcast Indian Maiden? What effect does the masquerade have on Lee Roy? What effect does Lee Roy's attitude have on the story?* 5. *How does Welty maintain suspense in this story?*

*Ralph Ellison* (b. 1914), born in Oklahoma City, Oklahoma, attended Tuskegee Institute from 1933 to 1936, where he was a music major. Later, in 1963, Tuskegee awarded him the degree of doctor of philosophy in humane letters for his accomplishments in literature. He has written short stories, articles, reviews, and criticism, publishing in such journals as *Partisan Review* and the *Quarterly Review of Literature* and in such collections as *Cross Section* (ed. E. Seaver, 1944), *A New Southern Harvest* (eds. Robert Penn Warren and Albert Erskine, 1957), *Best Stories of World War II* (ed. Charles E. Fenton, 1957), and *I Have Seen War* (ed. Dorothy Sterling, 1960). A collection of essays, *Shadow and Act*, was published in 1964. But it is his novel, *Invisible Man* (1952), which has brought him the most attention, including a National Book Award. Hailed as a profoundly American epic of modern life, it recounts the bizarre adventures of a young black man in his search for identity, authenticating nightmarish experiences with rare intensity. Since the publication of *Invisible Man*, Ellison has made frequent lecture tours and has taught at the University of Chicago, Rutgers University, and Yale University. "Flying Home," an early story, written in 1943, in the middle of World War II, documents an encounter between two black men that begins in estrangement and ends in a "new current of communication."

## FLYING HOME

When Todd came to, he saw two faces suspended above him in a sun so hot and blinding that he could not tell if they were black or white. He stirred, feeling a pain that burned as though his whole body had been laid open to the sun which glared into his eyes. For a moment an old fear of being touched by white hands seized him. Then the very sharpness of the pain began slowly to clear his head. Sounds came to him dimly. He done come to. Who are they? he thought. Naw he ain't, I coulda sworn he was white. Then he heard clearly:

"You hurt bad?"

Something within him uncoiled. It was a Negro sound.

"He's still out," he heard.

"Give 'im time. . . . Say, son, you hurt bad?"

Was he? There was that awful pain. He lay rigid, hearing their breathing and trying to weave a meaning between them and his being stretched painfully upon the ground. He watched them warily, his mind traveling back over a painful distance. Jagged scenes, swiftly unfolding as in a movie trailer, reeled through his mind, and he saw himself piloting a tailspinning plane and landing and falling from the cockpit and trying to stand. Then, as in a great silence, he remembered the sound of crunching bone, and now, looking up into the anxious faces of an old Negro man and a boy from where he lay in the same field, the memory sickened him and he wanted to remember no more.

"How you feel, son?"

Todd hesitated, as though to answer would be to admit an inacceptable weakness. Then, "It's my ankle," he said.

"Which one?"

"The left."

With a sense of remoteness he watched the old man bend and remove his boot, feeling the pressure ease.

"That any better?"

"A lot. Thank you."

He had the sensation of discussing someone else, that his concern was with some far more important thing, which for some reason escaped him.

"You done broke it bad," the old man said. "We have to get you to a doctor."

He felt that he had been thrown into a tailspin. He looked at his watch; how long had he been here? He knew there was but one important thing in the world, to get the plane back to the field before his officers were displeased.

"Help me up," he said. "Into the ship."

"But it's broke too bad. . . ."

"Give me your arm!"

"But, son . . ."

Clutching the old man's arm he pulled himself up, keeping his left leg clear, thinking, "I'd never make him understand," as the leather-smooth face came parallel with his own.

"Now, let's see."

He pushed the old man back, hearing a bird's insistent shrill. He swayed giddily. Blackness washed over him, like infinity.

"You best sit down."

"No, I'm O.K."

"But, son. You jus' gonna make it worse. . . ."

It was a fact that everything in him cried out to deny, even against the flaming pain in his ankle. He would have to try again.

"You mess with that ankle they have to cut your foot off," he heard.

Holding his breath, he started up again. It pained so badly that he had to bite his lips to keep from crying out and he allowed them to help him down with a pang of despair.

"It's best you take it easy. We gon' git you a doctor."

Of all the luck, he thought. Of all the rotten luck, now I have done it. The fumes of high-octane gasoline clung in the heat, taunting him.

"We kin ride him into town on old Ned," the boy said.

Ned? He turned, seeing the boy point toward an ox team browsing where the buried blade of a plow marked the end of a furrow. Thoughts of himself riding an ox through the town, past streets full of white faces, down the concrete runways of the airfield made swift images of humiliation in his mind. With a pang he remembered his girl's last letter. "Todd," she had written, "I don't need the papers to tell me you had the intelligence to fly. And I have always known you to be as brave as anyone else. The papers annoy me. Don't you be contented to prove over and over again that you're brave or skillful just because you're black, Todd. I think they keep beating that dead horse because they don't want to say why you boys are not yet fighting. I'm really disappointed, Todd. Anyone with brains can learn to fly, but then what? What about using it, and who will you use it for? I wish, dear, you'd write about this. I sometimes think they're playing a trick on us. It's very humiliating. . . ." He wiped cold sweat from his face, thinking, What does she know of humiliation? She's never been down South. Now the humiliation would come. When you must have them judge you, knowing that they never accept your mistakes as your own, but hold it against your whole race—that was humiliation. Yes, and humiliation was when you could never be simply yourself, when you were always a part of this old black ignorant man. Sure, he's all right. Nice and kind and helpful. But he's not you. Well, there's one humiliation I can spare myself.

"No," he said, "I have orders not to leave the ship. . . ."

"Aw," the old man said. Then turning to the boy, "Teddy, then you better hustle down to Mister Graves and get him to come. . . ."

"No, wait!" he protested before he was fully aware. Graves might be white. "Just have him get word to the field, please. They'll take care of the rest."

He saw the boy leave, running.

"How far does he have to go?"

"Might' nigh a mile."

He rested back, looking at the dusty face of his watch. But now they know something has happened, he thought. In the ship there was a perfectly good radio, but it was useless. The old fellow would never operate it. That buzzard knocked me back a hundred years, he thought. Irony danced within him like the gnats circling the old man's head. With all I've learned I'm dependent upon this "peasant's" sense of time and space. His leg throbbed. In the plane, instead of time being measured by the rhythms of pain and a kid's legs, the instruments would have told him at a glance. Twisting upon his elbows he saw where dust had powdered the plane's fuselage, feeling the lump form in his throat that was always there when he thought of flight. It's crouched there, he thought, like the abandoned shell of a locust. I'm naked without it. Not a machine, a suit of clothes you wear. And with a sudden embarrassment and wonder he whispered, "It's the only dignity I have. . . ."

He saw the old man watching, his torn overalls clinging limply to him in the heat. He felt a sharp need to tell the old man what he felt. But that would be meaningless. If I tried to explain why I need to fly back, he'd think I was simply afraid of white officers. But it's more than fear . . . a sense of anguish clung to him like the veil of sweat that hugged his face. He watched the old man, hearing him humming snatches of a tune as he admired the plane. He felt a furtive sense of resentment. Such old men often came to the field to watch the pilots with childish eyes. At first it had made him proud; they had been a meaningful part of a new experience. But soon he realized they did not understand his accomplishments and they came to shame and embarrass him, like the distasteful praise of an idiot. A part of the meaning of flying had gone then, and he had not been able to regain it. If I were a prizefighter I would be more human, he thought. Not a monkey doing tricks, but a man. They were pleased simply that he was a Negro who could fly, and that was not enough. He felt cut off from them by age, by understanding, by sensibility, by technology and by his need to measure himself against the mirror of other men's appreciation. Somehow he felt betrayed, as he had when as a child he grew to discover that his father was dead. Now for him any real appreciation lay with his white officers; and with them he could never be sure. Between ignorant black men and condescending whites, his course of flight seemed mapped by the nature of things away from all needed and natural landmarks. Under some sealed orders, couched in ever more technical and mysterious terms, his path curved swiftly away from both the shame the old man symbolized and the cloudy terrain of white men's regard. Flying blind, he knew but one point of landing and there he would receive his wings. After that the enemy would appreciate his skill and he would assume his deepest meaning, he thought sadly, neither from those who condescended nor from those who praised without understanding, but from the enemy who would recognize his manhood and skill in terms of hate. . . .

He sighed, seeing the oxen making queer, prehistoric shadows against the dry brown earth.

"You just take it easy, son," the old man soothed. "That boy won't take long. Crazy as he is about airplanes."

"I can wait," he said.

"What kinda airplane you call this here'n?"

"An Advanced Trainer," he said, seeing the old man smile. His fingers were like gnarled dark wood against the metal as he touched the low-slung wing.

" 'Bout how fast can she fly?"

"Over two hundred an hour."

"Lawd! That's so fast I bet it don't seem like you moving!"

Holding himself rigid, Todd opened his flying suit. The shade had gone and he lay in a ball of fire.

"You mind if I take a look inside? I was always curious to see. . . ."

"Help yourself. Just don't touch anything."

He heard him climb upon the metal wing, grunting. Now the questions would start. Well, so you don't have to think to answer. . . .

He saw the old man looking over into the cockpit, his eyes bright as a child's.

"You must have to know a lot to work all these here things."

He was silent, seeing him step down and kneel beside him.

"Son, how come you want to fly way up there in the air?"

Because it's the most meaningful act in the world . . . because it makes me less like you, he thought.

But he said: "Because I like it, I guess. It's as good a way to fight and die as I know."

"Yeah? I guess you right," the old man said. "But how long you think before they gonna let you all fight?"

He tensed. This was the question all Negroes asked, put with the same timid hopefulness and longing that always opened a greater void within him than that he had felt beneath the plane the first time he had flown. He felt light-headed. It came to him suddenly that there was something sinister about the conversation, that he was flying unwillingly into unsafe and uncharted regions. If he could only be insulting and tell this old man who was trying to help him to shut up!

"I bet you one thing . . ."

"Yes?"

"That you was plenty scared coming down."

He did not answer. Like a dog on a trail the old man seemed to smell out his fears and he felt anger bubble within him.

"You sho' scared me. When I seen you coming down in that thing with it a-rollin' and a-jumpin' like a pitchin' hoss, I thought sho' you was a goner. I almost had me a stroke!"

He saw the old man grinning, "Ever'thin's been happening round here this morning, come to think of it."

"Like what?" he asked.

"Well, first thing I know, here come two white fellers looking for Mister Rudolph, that's Mister Graves's cousin. That got me worked up right away. . . ."

"Why?"

"Why? 'Cause he done broke outta the crazy house, that's why. He liable to kill somebody," he said. "They oughta have him by now though. Then here you come. First I think it's one of them white boys. Then doggone if you don't fall outta there. Lawd, I'd done heard about you boys but I haven't never seen one o' you-all. Cain't tell you how it felt to see somebody what look like me in a airplane!"

The old man talked on, the sound streaming around Todd's thoughts like air flowing over the fuselage of a flying plane. You were a fool, he thought, remembering how before the spin the sun had blazed bright against the billboard signs beyond the town, and how a boy's blue kite had bloomed beneath him, tugging gently in the wind like a strange, odd-shaped flower. He had once flown such kites himself and tried to find the boy at the end of the invisible cord. But he had been flying too high and too fast. He had climbed steeply away in exultation. Too steeply, he thought. And one of the first rules you learn is that if the angle of thrust is too steep the plane goes into a spin. And then, instead of pulling out of it and going into a dive you let a buzzard panic you. A lousy buzzard!

"Son, what made all that blood on the glass?"

"A buzzard," he said, remembering how the blood and feathers had sprayed back against the hatch. It had been as though he had flown into a storm of blood and blackness.

"Well, I declare! They's lots of 'em around here. They after dead things. Don't eat nothing what's alive."

"A little bit more and he would have made a meal out of me," Todd said grimly.

"They bad luck all right. Teddy's got a name for 'em, calls 'em jimcrows," the old man laughed.

"It's a damned good name."

"They the damnedest birds. Once I seen a hoss all stretched out like he was sick, you know. So I hollers, 'Gid up from there, suh!' Just to make sho! An' doggone, son, if I don't see two ole jimcrows come flying right up outa that hoss's insides! Yessuh! The sun was shinin' on 'em and they couldn't a been no greasier if they'd been eating barbecue."

Todd thought he would vomit, his stomach quivered.

"You made that up," he said.

"Nawsuh! Saw him just like I see you."

"Well, I'm glad it was you."

"You see lots a funny things down here, son."

"No, I'll let you see them," he said.

"By the way, the white folks round here don't like to see you boys up there in the sky. They ever bother you?"

"No."

"Well, they'd like to."

"Someone always wants to bother someone else," Todd said. "How do you know?"

"I just know."

"Well," he said defensively, "no one has bothered us."

Blood pounded in his ears as he looked away into space. He tensed, seeing a black spot in the sky, and strained to confirm what he could not clearly see.

"What does that look like to you?" he asked excitedly.

"Just another bad luck, son."

Then he saw the movement of wings with disappointment. It was gliding smoothly down, wings outspread, tail feathers gripping the air, down swiftly—gone behind the green screen of trees. It was like a bird he had imagined there, only the sloping branches of the pines remained, sharp against the pale stretch of sky. He lay barely breathing and stared at the point where it had disappeared, caught in a spell of loathing and admiration. Why did they make them so disgusting and yet teach them to fly so well? It's like when I was up in heaven, he heard, starting.

The old man was chuckling, rubbing his stubbled chin.

"What did you say?"

"Sho', I died and went to heaven . . . maybe by time I tell you about it they be done come after you."

"I hope so," he said wearily.

"You boys ever sit around and swap lies?"

"Not often. Is this going to be one?"

"Well, I ain't so sho', on account of it took place when I was dead."

The old man paused, "That wasn't no lie 'bout the buzzards, though."

"All right," he said.

"Sho' you want to hear 'bout heaven?"

"Please," he answered, resting his head upon his arm.

"Well, I went to heaven and right away started to sproutin' me some wings. Six good ones, they was. Just like them the white angels had. I couldn't hardly believe it. I was so glad that I went off on some clouds by myself and tried 'em out. You know, 'cause I didn't want to make a fool outta myself the first thing. . . ."

It's an old tale, Todd thought. Told me years ago. Had forgotten. But at least it will keep him from talking about buzzards.

He closed his eyes, listening.

". . . First thing I done was to git up on a low cloud and jump off. And doggone, boy, if them wings didn't work! First I tried the right; then I tried the left; then I tried 'em both together. Then Lawd, I started to move on out among the folks. I let 'em see me. . . ."

He saw the old man gesturing flight with his arms, his face full of mock pride as he indicated an imaginary crowd, thinking, It'll be in the newspapers, as he heard, ". . . so I went out and found me some colored angels—somehow I didn't believe I was an angel till I seen a real black one, ha, yes! Then I was sho'—but they tole me I better come down 'cause us colored folks had to wear a special kin' a harness when we flew. That was how come they wasn't flyin'. Oh yes, an' you had to be extra strong for a black man even, to fly with one of them harnesses. . . ."

This is a new turn, Todd thought, what's he driving at?

"So I said to myself, I ain't gonna be bothered with no harness! Oh naw! 'Cause if God let you sprout wings you oughta have sense enough not to let nobody make you wear something what gits in the way of flyin'. So I starts to flyin'. Heck, son," he chuckled, his eyes twinkling, "you know I had to let eve'ybody know that old Jefferson could fly good as anybody else. And I could too, fly smooth as a bird! I could even loop-the-loop—only I had to make sho' to keep my long white robe down roun' my ankles. . . ."

Todd felt uneasy. He wanted to laugh at the joke, but his body refused, as of an independent will. He felt as he had as a child when after he had chewed a sugar-coated pill which his mother had given him, she had laughed at his efforts to remove the terrible taste.

". . . Well," he heard, "I was doing all right 'til I got to speeding. Found out I could fan up a right strong breeze, I could fly so fast. I could do all kin'sa stunts too. I started flying up to the stars and divin' down and zooming roun' the moon. Man, I like to scare the devil outa some ole white angels. I was raisin' hell. Not that I meant any harm, son. But I was just feeling good. It was so good to know I was free at last. I accidentally knocked the tips offa some stars and they tell me I caused a storm and a coupla lynchings down here in Macon County—though I swear I believe them boys what said that was making up lies on me. . . ."

He's mocking me, Todd thought angrily. He thinks it's a joke. Grinning down at me . . . His throat was dry. He looked at his watch; why the hell didn't they come? Since they had to, why? One day I was flying down one of them heavenly streets. You got yourself into it, Todd thought. Like Jonah in the whale.

"Justa throwin' feathers in everybody's face. An' ole Saint Peter called me in. Said, 'Jefferson, tell me two things, what you doin' flyin' without a harness; an' how come you flyin' so fast?' So I tole him I was flyin' without a harness 'cause it got in my way, but I couldn'ta been flyin' so fast, 'cause I wasn't usin' but one wing. Saint Peter said, 'You wasn't flyin' with but one wing?' 'Yessuh,' I says, scared-like. So he says, 'Well, since you got sucha extra fine pair of wings you can leave off yo' harness awhile. But from now on none of that there one-wing flyin', 'cause you gittin' up too damn much speed!' "

And with one mouth full of bad teeth you're making too damned much talk, thought Todd. Why don't I send him after the boy? His body ached from the hard ground and seeking to shift his position he twisted his ankle and hated himself for crying out.

"It gittin' worse?"

"I . . . I twisted it," he groaned.

"Try not to think about it, son. That's what I do."

He bit his lip, fighting pain with counter-pain as the voice resumed its rhythmical droning. Jefferson seemed caught in his own creation.

". . . After all that trouble I just floated roun' heaven in slow motion. But I forgot, like colored folks will do, and got to flyin' with one wing again. This time I was restin' my old broken arm and got to flyin' fast enough to shame the devil. I was comin' so fast, Lawd, I got myself called befo' ole Saint Peter again. He said, 'Jeff, didn't I warn you 'bout that speedin'?' 'Yessuh,' I says, 'but it was an accident.' He looked at me sad-like and shook his head and I knowed I was gone. He said, 'Jeff, you and that speedin' is a danger to the heavenly community. If I was to let you keep on flyin', heaven wouldn't be nothin' but uproar. Jeff, you got to go!' Son, I argued and pleaded with that old white man, but it didn't do a bit of good. They rushed me straight to them pearly gates and gimme a parachute and a map of the state of Alabama . . ."

Todd heard him laughing so that he could hardly speak, making a screen between them upon which his humiliation glowed like fire.

"Maybe you'd better stop awhile," he said, his voice unreal.

"Ain't much more," Jefferson laughed. "When they gimme the parachute ole Saint Peter ask me if I wanted to say a few words before I went. I felt so bad I couldn't hardly look at him, specially with all them white angels standin' around. Then somebody laughed and made me mad. So I tole him, 'Well, you done took my wings. And you puttin' me out. You got charge of things so's I can't do nothin' about it. But you got to admit just this: While I was up here I was the flyinest sonofabitch what ever hit heaven!"

At the burst of laughter Todd felt such an intense humiliation that only great violence would wash it away. The laughter which shook the old man like a boiling purge set up vibrations of guilt within him which not even the intricate machinery of the plane would have been adequate to transform and he heard himself screaming, "Why do you laugh at me this way?"

He hated himself at that moment, but he had lost control. He saw Jefferson's mouth fall open, "What—?"

"Answer me!"

His blood pounded as though it would surely burst his temples and he tried to reach the old man and fell, screaming, "Can I help it because they won't let us actually fly? Maybe we are a bunch of buzzards feeding on a dead horse, but we can hope to be eagles, can't we? Can't we?"

He fell back, exhausted, his ankle pounding. The saliva was like straw in his mouth. If he had the strength he would strangle this old man. This grinning, gray-headed clown who made him feel as he felt when watched by the white officers at the field. And yet this old man had neither power, prestige, rank nor technique. Nothing that could rid him of this terrible feeling. He watched him, seeing his face struggle to express a turmoil of feeling.

"What you mean, son? What you talking 'bout . . . ?"

"Go away. Go tell your tales to the white folks."

"But I didn't mean nothing like that. . . . I . . . I wasn't tryin' to hurt your feelings. . . ."

"Please. Get the hell away from me!"

"But I didn't, son. I didn't mean all them things a-tall."

Todd shook as with a chill, searching Jefferson's face for a trace of the mockery he had seen there. But now the face was somber and tired and old. He was confused. He could not be sure that there had ever been laughter there, that Jefferson had ever really laughed in his whole life. He saw Jefferson reach out to touch him and shrank away, wondering if anything except the pain, now causing his vision to waver, was real. Perhaps he had imagined it all.

"Don't let it get you down, son," the voice said pensively.

He heard Jefferson sigh wearily, as though he felt more than he could say. His anger ebbed, leaving only the pain.

"I'm sorry," he mumbled.

"You just wore out with pain, was all. . . ."

He saw him through a blur, smiling. And for a second he felt the embarrassed silence of understanding flutter between them.

"What you was doin' flyin' over this section, son? Wasn't you scared they might shoot you for a cow?"

Todd tensed. Was he being laughed at again? But before he could decide, the pain shook him and a part of him was lying calmly behind the screen of pain that had fallen between them, recalling the first time he had ever seen a plane. It was as though an endless series of hangars had been shaken ajar in the air base of his memory and from each, like a young wasp emerging from its cell, arose the memory of a plane.

The first time I ever saw a plane I was very small and planes were new in the world. I was four-and-a-half and the only plane that I had ever seen was a model suspended from the ceiling of the automobile exhibit at the State Fair. But I did not know that it was only a model. I did not know how large a real plane was, nor how expensive. To me it was a fascinating toy, complete in itself, which my mother said could only be owned by rich little white boys. I stood rigid with admiration, my head straining backwards as I watched the gray little plane describing arcs above the gleaming tops of the automobiles. And I vowed that, rich or poor, someday I would own such a toy. My mother had to drag me out of the exhibit and not even the merry-go-round, the Ferris wheel, or the racing horses could hold my attention for the rest of the Fair. I was too busy imitating the tiny drone of the plane with my lips, and imitating with my hands the motion, swift and circling, that it made in flight.

After that I no longer used the pieces of lumber that lay about our back yard to construct wagons and autos . . . now it was used for airplanes. I built biplanes, using pieces of board for wings, a small box for the fuselage, another piece of wood for the rudder. The trip to the Fair had brought something new into my small world. I asked my mother repeatedly when the Fair would come back again. I'd lie in the grass and watch the sky, and each fighting bird became a soaring plane. I would have been good a year just to have seen a plane again. I became a nuisance to everyone with my questions about airplanes. But planes were new to the old folks, too, and there was little that they could tell me. Only my uncle knew some of the answers. And better still, he could carve propellers from pieces of wood that would whirl rapidly in the wind, wobbling noisily upon oiled nails.

I wanted a plane more than I'd wanted anything; more than I wanted the red wagon with rubber tires, more than the train that ran on a track with its train of cars. I asked my mother over and over again:

"Mamma?"

"What do you want, boy?" she'd say.

"Mamma, will you get mad if I ask you?" I'd say.

"What do you want now? I ain't got time to be answering a lot of fool questions. What you want?"

"Mamma, when you gonna get me one . . . ?" I'd ask.

"Get you one what?" she'd say.

"You know, Mamma; what I been asking you. . . ."

"Boy," she'd say, "if you don't want a spanking you better come on an' tell me what you talking about so I can get on with my work."

"Aw, Mamma, you know. . . ."

"What I just tell you?" she'd say.

"I mean when you gonna buy me a airplane."

"AIRPLANE! Boy, is you crazy? How many times I have to tell you to stop that foolishness. I done told you them things cost too much. I bet I'm gon' wham the living daylight out of you if you don't quit worrying me 'bout them things!"

But this did not stop me, and a few days later I'd try all over again.

Then one day a strange thing happened. It was spring and for some reason I had been hot and irritable all morning. It was a beautiful spring. I could feel it as I played barefoot in the backyard. Blossoms hung from the thorny black locust trees like clusters of fragrant white grapes. Butterflies flickered in the sunlight above the short new dew-wet grass. I had gone in the house for bread and butter and coming out I heard a steady unfamiliar drone. It was unlike anything I had ever heard before. I tried to place the sound. It was no use. It was a sensation like that I had when searching for my father's watch, heard ticking unseen in a room. It made me feel as though I had forgotten to perform some task that my mother had ordered . . . then I located it, overhead. In the sky, flying quite low and about a hundred yards off was a plane! It came so slowly that it seemed barely to move. My mouth hung wide; my bread and butter fell into the dirt. I wanted to jump up and down and cheer. And when the idea struck I trembled with excitement: "Some little white boy's plane's done flew away and all I got to do is stretch out my hands and it'll be mine!" It was a little plane like that at the Fair, flying no higher than the eaves of our roof. Seeing it come steadily forward I felt the world grow warm with promise. I opened the screen and climbed over it and clung there, waiting. I would catch the plane as it came over and swing down fast and run into the house before anyone could see me. Then no one could come to claim the plane. It droned nearer. Then when it hung like a silver cross in the blue directly above me I stretched out my hand and grabbed. It was like sticking my finger through a soap bubble. The plane flew on, as though I had simply blown my breath after it. I grabbed again, frantically, trying to catch the tail. My fingers clutched the air and disappointment surged tight and hard in my throat. Giving one last desperate grasp, I strained forward. My fingers ripped from the screen. I was falling. The ground burst hard against me. I drummed the earth with my heels and when my breath returned, I lay there bawling.

My mother rushed through the door.

"What's the matter, chile! What on earth is wrong with you?"

"It's gone! It's gone!"

"What gone?"

"The airplane . . ."

"Airplane?"

"Yessum, jus' like the one at the Fair. . . . I . . . I tried to stop it an' it kep' right on going. . . ."

"When, boy?"

"Just now," I cried, through my tears.

"Where it go, boy, what way?"

"Yonder, there . . ."

She scanned the sky, her arms akimbo and her checkered apron flapping in the wind as I pointed to the fading plane. Finally she looked down at me, slowly shaking her head.

"It's gone! It's gone!" I cried.

"Boy, is you a fool?" she said. "Don't you see that there's a real airplane 'stead of one of them toy ones?"

"Real . . . ?" I forgot to cry. "Real?"

"Yass, real. Don't you know that thing you reaching for is bigger'n a auto? You here trying to reach for it and I bet it's flying 'bout two hundred miles higher'n this roof." She was disgusted with me. "You come on in this house before somebody else sees what a fool you done turned out to be. You must think these here lil ole arms of you'n is mighty long. . . ."

I was carried into the house and undressed for bed and the doctor was called. I cried bitterly, as much from the disappointment of finding the plane so far beyond my reach as from the pain.

When the doctor came I heard my mother telling him about the plane and asking if anything was wrong with my mind. He explained that I had had a fever for several hours. But I was kept in bed for a week and I constantly saw the plane in my sleep, flying just beyond my fingertips, sailing so slowly that it seemed barely to move. And each time I'd reach out to grab it I'd miss and through each dream I'd hear my grandma warning:

*Young man, young man,*
*Yo' arms too short*
*To box with God. . . .*

"Hey, son!"

At first he did not know where he was and looked at the old man pointing, with blurred eyes.

"Ain't that one of you-all's airplanes coming after you?"

As his vision cleared he saw a small black shape above a distant field, soaring through waves of heat. But he could not be sure and with the pain he feared that somehow a horrible recurring fantasy of being split in twain by the whirling blades of a propeller had come true.

"You think he sees us?" he heard.

"See? I hope so."

"He's coming like a bat outa hell!"

Straining, he heard the faint sound of a motor and hoped it would soon be over.

"How you feeling?"

"Like a nightmare," he said.

"Hey, he's done curved back the other way!"

"Maybe he saw us," he said. "Maybe he's gone to send out the ambulance and ground crew." And, he thought with despair, maybe he didn't even see us.

"Where did you send the boy?"

"Down to Mister Graves," Jefferson said. "Man what owns this land."

"Do you think he phoned?"

Jefferson looked at him quickly.

"Aw sho'. Dabney Graves is got a bad name on accounta them killings but he'll call though. . . ."

"What killings?"

"Them five fellers . . . ain't you heard?" he asked with surprise.

"No."

"Everybody knows 'bout Dabney Graves, especially the colored. He done killed enough of us."

Todd had the sensation of being caught in a white neighborhood after dark.

"What did they do?" he asked.

"Thought they was men," Jefferson said. "An' some he owed money, like he do me. . . ."

"But why do you stay here?"

"You black, son."

"I know, but. . . ."

"You have to come by the white folks, too."

He turned away from Jefferson's eyes, at once consoled and accused. And I'll have to come by them soon, he thought with despair. Closing his eyes, he heard Jefferson's voice as the sun burned blood-red upon his lips.

"I got nowhere to go," Jefferson said, "an' they'd come after me if I did. But Dabney Graves is a funny fellow. He's all the time making jokes. He can be mean as hell, then he's liable to turn right around and back the colored against the white folks. I seen him do it. But me, I hates him for that more'n anything else. 'Cause just as soon as he gits tired helping a man he don't care what happens to him. He just leaves him stone cold. And then the other white folks is double hard on anybody he done helped. For him it's just a joke. He don't give a hilla beans for nobody—but hisself. . . ."

Todd listened to the thread of detachment in the old man's voice. It was as though he held his words arm's length before him to avoid their destructive meaning.

"He'd just as soon do you a favor and then turn right around and have you strung up. Me, I stays outa his way 'cause down here that's what you gotta do."

If my ankle would only ease for a while, he thought. The closer I spin toward the earth the blacker I become, flashed through his mind. Sweat ran into his eyes and he was sure that he would never see the plane if his head continued whirling. He tried to see Jefferson, what was it that Jefferson held in his hand? It was a little black man, another Jefferson! A little black Jefferson that shook with fits of belly-laughter while the other Jefferson looked on with detachment. Then Jefferson looked up from the thing in his hand and turned to speak, but Todd was far away, searching the sky for a plane in a hot dry land on a day and age he had long forgotten. He was going mysteriously with his mother through empty streets where black faces peered from behind drawn shades and someone was rapping at a window and he was looking back to see a hand and a frightened face frantically beckoning from a cracked door and his mother was looking down the empty perspective of the street and shaking her head and hurrying him along and at first it was only a flash he saw and a motor was droning as through the sun-glare he saw it gleaming silver as it circled and he was seeing a burst like a puff of white smoke and hearing his mother yell. Come along, boy, I got no time for them fool airplanes, I got no time, and he saw it a second time, the plane flying high, and the burst appeared suddenly and fell slowly, billowing out and sparkling like fireworks and he was watching and being hurried along as the air filled with a flurry of white pinwheeling cards that caught in the wind and scattered over the rooftops and into the gutters and a woman was running and snatching a card and reading it and screaming and he darted into the shower, grabbing as in winter he grabbed for snowflakes and bounding away at his mother's, Come on here, boy! Come on, I say! and he was watching as she took the card away, seeing her face grow puzzled and turning taut as her voice quavered, "Niggers Stay From The Polls," and died to a moan of terror as he saw the eyeless sockets of a white hood staring at him from the card and above he saw the plane spiraling gracefully, agleam in the sun like a fiery sword. And seeing it soar he was caught, transfixed between a terrible horror and a horrible fascination.

The sun was not so high now, and Jefferson was calling and gradually he saw three figures moving across the curving roll of the field.

"Look like some doctors, all dressed in white," said Jefferson.

They're coming at last, Todd thought. And he felt such a release of tension within him that he thought he would faint. But no sooner did he close his eyes than he was seized and he was struggling with three white men who were forcing his arms into some kind of coat. It was too much for him, his arms were pinned to his sides and as the pain blazed in his eyes, he realized that it was a straitjacket. What filthy joke was this?

"That oughta hold him, Mister Graves," he heard.

His total energies seemed focused in his eyes as he searched their faces. That was Graves; the other two wore hospital uniforms. He was poised between two poles of fear and hate as he heard the one called Graves saying, "He looks kinda purty in that there suit, boys. I'm glad you dropped by."

"This boy ain't crazy, Mister Graves," one of the others said. "He needs a doctor, not us. Don't see how you led us way out here anyway. It might be a joke to you, but your cousin Rudolph liable to kill somebody. White folks or niggers, don't make no difference. . . ."

Todd saw the man turn red with anger. Graves looked down upon him, chuckling.

"This niggah belongs in a straitjacket, too, boys. I knowed that the minit Jeff's kid said something 'bout a nigguh flyer. You all know you cain't let the nigguh git up that high without his going crazy. The nigguh brain ain't built right for high altitudes. . . ."

Todd watched the drawling red face, feeling that all the unnamed horror and obscenities that he had ever imagined stood materialized before him.

"Let's git outta here," one of the attendants said.

Todd saw the other reach toward him, realizing for the first time that he lay upon a stretcher as he yelled.

"Don't put your hands on me!"

They drew back, surprised.

"What's that you say, nigguh?" asked Graves.

He did not answer and thought that Graves's foot was aimed at his head. It landed on his chest and he could hardly breathe. He coughed helplessly, seeing Graves's lips stretch taut over his yellow teeth, and tried to shift his head. It was as though a half-dead fly was dragging slowly across his face and a bomb seemed to burst within him. Blasts of hot, hysterical laughter tore from his chest, causing his eyes to pop and he felt that the veins in his neck would surely burst. And then a part of him stood behind it all, watching the surprise in Graves's red face and his own hysteria. He thought he would never stop, he would laugh himself to death. It rang in his ears like Jefferson's laughter and he looked for him, centering his eyes desperately upon his face, as though somehow he had become his sole salvation in an insane world of outrage and humiliation. It brought a certain relief. He was suddenly aware that although his body was still contorted it was an echo that no longer rang in his ears. He heard Jefferson's voice with gratitude.

"Mister Graves, the Army done tole him not to leave his airplane."

"Nigguh, Army or no, you gittin' off my land! That airplane can stay 'cause it was paid for by taxpayers' money. But you gittin' off. An' dead or alive, it don't make no difference to me."

Todd was beyond it now, lost in a world of anguish.

"Jeff," Graves said, "you and Teddy come and grab holt. I want you to take this here black eagle over to that nigguh airfield and leave him."

Jefferson and the boy approached him silently. He looked away, realizing and doubting at once that only they could release him from his overpowering sense of isolation.

They bent for the stretcher. One of the attendants moved toward Teddy.

"Think you can manage it, boy?"

"I think I can, suh," Teddy said.

"Well, you better go behind then, and let yo' pa go ahead so's to keep that leg elevated."

He saw the white men walking ahead as Jefferson and the boy carried him along in silence. Then they were pausing and he felt a hand wiping his face; then he was moving again. And it was as though he had been lifted out of his isolation, back into the world of men. A new current of communication flowed between the man and boy and himself. They moved him gently. Far away he heard a mockingbird liquidly calling. He raised his eyes, seeing a buzzard poised unmoving in space. For a moment the whole afternoon seemed suspended and he waited for the horror to seize him again. Then like a song within his head he heard the boy's soft humming and saw the dark bird glide into the sun and glow like a bird of flaming gold.

## *Study questions*

1. *Account for Todd's hostile response to the old black man at the beginning of the story.* 2. *In how many ways is Todd isolated?* 3. *How is it significant that Todd is a pilot? a fighter pilot not allowed to fight?* 4. *How many kinds of flying are represented in the story? What does the act of flying symbolize?* 5. *How many images of constraint do you find? How do they function?* 6. *How does the old black man's story relate to the central symbolism?* 7. *What do the buzzards symbolize?* 8. *What does Ellison achieve by having Todd and Jefferson speak a different dialect? What kind of dialect does Graves speak? What role does he play?* 9. *How is Todd's conflict resolved? Explain the last sentence of the story.*

*Arthur C. Clarke* (b. 1917) was born in Minehead, Somersetshire, England, and attended King's College, the University of London, where he graduated with first-class honors and a B.S. in 1948. During his varied career, he has been a member of the British Civil Service, an editor and writer for *Science Abstracts*, an underwater explorer and photographer, and a noted lecturer. He served in the Royal Air Force in World War II and was one of the founders of the British Rocket Society. He has published a number of nonfiction works on various aspects of space and time and more than twenty-five volumes of science fiction. This genre has, in recent years, enjoyed tremendous popularity, and Clarke has been one of its most successful practitioners. Over five million of his books have been sold in twenty languages and more than three hundred articles and stories have been published in magazines, including *Horizon, Holiday, Harper's, Playboy, Life,* and *Vogue.* A vision of the future, "The Deep Range," like many science-fiction stories, calls on a set of allusions to the past to give added significance to its statement.

## THE DEEP RANGE

There was a killer loose on the range. A 'copter patrol, five hundred miles off Greenland, had seen the great corpse staining the sea crimson as it wallowed in the waves. Within seconds, the intricate warning system had been alerted: men were plotting circles and moving counters on the North Atlantic chart—and Don Burley was still rubbing the sleep from his eyes as he dropped silently down to the twenty-fathom line.

The pattern of green lights on the tell-tale was a glowing symbol of security. As long as that pattern was unchanged, as long as none of those emerald stars winked to red, all was well with Don and his tiny craft. Air—fuel—power—this was the triumvirate which ruled his life. If any of them failed, he would be sinking in a steel coffin down toward the pelagic ooze, as Johnnie Tyndall had done the season before last. But there was no reason why they should fail; the accidents one foresaw, Don told himself reassuringly, were never the ones that happened.

He leaned across the tiny control board and spoke into the mike. Sub 5 was still close enough to the mother ship for radio to work, but before long he'd have to switch to the sonics.

"Setting course 255, speed 50 knots, depth 20 fathoms, full sonar coverage. . . . Estimated time to target area, 70 minutes. . . . Will report at 10-minute intervals. That is all. . . . Out."

The acknowledgment, already weakening with range, came back at once from the *Herman Melville.*

"Message received and understood. Good hunting. What about the hounds?"

Don chewed his lower lip thoughtfully. This might be a job he'd have to handle alone. He had no idea, to within fifty miles either way, where Benj and Susan were at the moment. They'd certainly follow if he signaled for them, but they couldn't maintain his speed and would soon have to drop behind. Besides, he might be heading for a pack of killers, and the last thing he wanted do was to lead his carefully trained porpoises into trouble. That was common sense and good business. He was also very fond of Susan and Benj.

"It's too far, and I don't know what I'm running into," he replied. "If they're in the interception area when I get there, I may whistle them up."

The acknowledgment from the mother ship was barely audible, and Don switched off the set. It was time to look around.

He dimmed the cabin lights so that he could see the scanner screen more clearly, pulled the polaroid glasses down over his eyes, and peered into the depths. This was the moment when Don felt like a god, able to hold within his hands a circle of the Atlantic twenty miles across, and to see clear down to the still-unexplored deeps, three thousand fathoms below. The slowly rotating beam of inaudible sound was searching the world in which he floated, seeking out friend and foe in the eternal darkness where light could never penetrate. The pattern of soundless shrieks, too shrill even for the hearing of the bats who had invented sonar a million years before man, pulsed out into the watery night: the faint echoes came tingling back as floating, blue-green flecks on the screen.

Through long practice, Don could read their message with effortless ease. A thousand feet below, stretching out to his submerged horizon, was the scattering layer—the blanket of life that covered half the world. The sunken meadow of the sea, it rose and fell with the passage of the sun, hovering always at the edge of darkness. But the ultimate depths were no concern of his. The flocks he guarded, and the enemies who ravaged them, belonged to the upper levels of the sea.

Don flicked the switch of the depth-selector, and his sonar beam concentrated itself into the horizontal plane. The glimmering echoes from the abyss vanished, but he could see more clearly what lay around him here in the ocean's stratospheric heights. That glowing cloud two miles ahead was a school of fish; he wondered if Base knew about it, and made an entry in his log. There were some larger, isolated blips at the edge of the school—the carnivores pursuing the cattle, insuring that the endlessly turning wheel of life and death would never lose momentum. But this conflict was no affair of Don's; he was after bigger game.

Sub 5 drove on toward the west, a steel needle swifter and more deadly than any other creature that roamed the seas. The tiny cabin, lit only by the flicker of lights from the instrument board, pulsed with power as the spinning turbines thrust the water aside. Don glanced at the chart and wondered how the enemy had broken through this time. There were still many weak points, for fencing the oceans of the world had been a gigantic task. The tenuous electric fields, fanning out between generators many miles apart, could not always hold at bay the starving monsters of the deep. They were learning, too. When the fences were opened, they would sometimes slip through with the whales and wreak havoc before they were discovered.

The long-range receiver bleeped plaintively, and Don switched over to TRANSCRIBE. It wasn't practical to send speech any distance over an ultrasonic beam, and code had come back into its own. Don had never learned to read it by ear, but the ribbon of paper emerging from the slot saved him the trouble.

COPTER REPORTS SCHOOL 50–100 WHALES HEADING 95 DEGREES GRID REF X186475 Y438034 STOP. MOVING AT SPEED. STOP. MELVILLE. OUT.

Don started to set the coordinates on the plotting grid, then saw that it was no longer necessary. At the extreme edge of his screen, a flotilla of faint stars had appeared. He altered course slightly, and drove head-on toward the approaching herd.

The copter was right: they were moving fast. Don felt a mounting excitement, for this could mean that they were on the run and luring the killers toward him. At the rate at which they were traveling he would be among them in five minutes. He cut the motors and felt the backward tug of water bringing him swiftly to rest.

Don Burley, a knight in armor, sat in his tiny dim-lit room fifty feet below the bright Atlantic waves, testing his weapons for the conflict that lay ahead. In these moments of poised suspense, before action began, his racing brain often explored such fantasies. He felt a kinship with all shepherds who had guarded their flocks back to the dawn of time. He was David, among ancient Palestinian hills, alert for the mountain lions that would prey upon his father's sheep. But far nearer in time, and far closer in spirit, were the men who had marshaled the great herds of cattle on the American plains, only a few lifetimes ago. They would have understood his work, though his implements would have been magic to them. The pattern was the same; only the scale had altered. It made no fundamental difference that the beasts Don herded weighed almost a hundred tons, and browsed on the endless savannahs of the sea.

The school was now less than two miles away, and Don checked his scanner's continuous circling to concentrate on the sector ahead. The picture on the screen altered to a fan-shaped wedge as the sonar beam started to flick from side to side; now he could count every whale in the school, and even make a good estimate of its size. With a practiced eye, he began to look for stragglers.

Don could never have explained what drew him at once toward those four echoes at the southern fringe of the school. It was true that they were a little apart from the rest, but others had fallen as far behind. There is some sixth sense that a man acquires when he has stared long enough into a sonar screen—some hunch which enables him to extract more from the moving flecks than he has any right to do. Without conscious thought, Don reached for the control which would start the turbines whirling into life. Sub 5 was just getting under way when three leaden thuds reverberated through the hull, as if someone was knocking on the front door and wanted to come in.

"Well I'm damned," said Don. "How did *you* get here?" He did not bother to switch on the TV; he'd know Benj's signal anywhere. The porpoises must have been in the neighborhood and had spotted him before he'd even switched on the hunting call. For the thousandth time, he marveled at their intelligence and loyalty. It was strange that Nature had played the same trick twice—on land with the dog, in the ocean with the porpoise. Why were these graceful sea-beasts so fond of man, to whom they owed so little? It made one feel that the human race was worth something after all, if it could inspire such unselfish devotion.

It had been known for centuries that the porpoise was at least as intelligent as the dog, and could obey quite complex verbal commands. The experiment was still in progress, but if it succeeded then the ancient partnership between shepherd and sheep-dog would have a new lease on life.

Don switched on the speakers recessed into the sub's hull and began to talk to his escorts. Most of the sounds he uttered would have been meaningless to other human ears; they were the product of long research by the animal psychologists of the World Food Administration. He gave his orders twice to make sure that they were understood, then checked with the sonar screen to see that Benj and Susan were following astern as he had told them to.

The four echoes that had attracted his attention were clearer and closer now, and the main body of the whale pack had swept past him to the east. He had no fear of a collision; the great animals, even in their panic, could sense his presence as easily as he could detect theirs, and by similar means. Don wondered if he should switch on his beacon. They might recognize its sound pattern, and it would reassure them. But the still unknown enemy might recognize it too.

He closed for an interception, and hunched low over the screen as if to drag from it by sheer will power every scrap of information the scanner could give. There were two large echoes, some distance apart, and one was accompanied by a pair of smaller satellites. Don wondered if he was already too late. In his mind's eye, he could picture the death struggle taking place in the water less than a mile ahead. Those two fainter blips would be the enemy—either shark or grampus—worrying a whale while one of its companions stood by in helpless terror, with no weapons of defense except its mighty flukes.

Now he was almost close enough for vision. The TV camera in Sub 5's prow strained through the gloom, but at first could show nothing but the fog of plankton. Then a vast shadowy shape began to form in the center of the screen, with two smaller companions below it. Don was seeing, with the greater precision but hopelessly limited range of ordinary light, what the sonar scanners had already told him.

Almost at once he saw his mistake. The two satellites were calves, not sharks. It was the first time he had ever met a whale with twins; although multiple births were not unknown, a cow could suckle only two young at once and usually only the stronger would survive. He choked down his disappointment; this error had cost him many minutes and he must begin the search again.

Then came the frantic tattoo on the hull that meant danger. It wasn't easy to scare Benj, and Don shouted his reassurance as he swung Sub 5 round so that the camera could search the turgid waters. Automatically, he had turned toward the fourth blip on the sonar screen—the echo he had assumed, from its size, to be another adult whale. And he saw that, after all, he had come to the right place.

"Jesus!" he said softly. "I didn't know they came that big." He'd seen larger sharks before, but they had all been harmless vegetarians. This, he could tell at a glance, was a Greenland shark, the killer of the northern seas. It was supposed to grow up to thirty feet long, but this specimen was bigger than Sub 5. It was every inch of forty feet from snout to tail, and when he spotted it, it was already turning in toward the kill. Like the coward it was, it had launched its attack at one of the calves.

Don yelled to Benj and Susan, and saw them racing ahead into his field of vision. He wondered fleetingly why porpoises had such an overwhelming hatred of sharks; then he loosed his hands from the controls as the autopilot locked on to the target. Twisting and turning as agilely as any other sea-creature of its size, Sub 5 began to close in upon the shark, leaving Don free to concentrate on his armament.

The killer had been so intent upon his prey that Benj caught him completely unawares, ramming him just behind the left eye. It must have been a painful blow: an iron-hard snout, backed by a quarter-ton of muscle moving at fifty miles an hour is something not to be laughed at even by the largest fish. The shark jerked round in an impossibly tight curve, and Don was almost jolted out of his seat as the sub snapped on to a new course. If this kept up, he'd find it hard to use his Sting. But at least the killer was too busy now to bother about his intended victims.

Benj and Susan were worrying the giant like dogs snapping at the heels of an angry bear. They were too agile to be caught in those ferocious jaws, and Don marveled at the coordination with which they worked. When either had to surface for air, the other would hold off for a minute until the attack could be resumed in strength.

There was no evidence that the shark realized that a far more dangerous adversary was closing in upon it, and that the porpoises were merely a distraction. That suited Don very nicely; the next operation was going to be difficult unless he could hold a steady course for at least fifteen seconds. At a pinch he could use the tiny rocket torps to make a kill. If he'd been alone, and faced with a pack of sharks he would certainly have done so. But it was messy, and there was a better way. He preferred the technique of the rapier to that of the hand-grenade.

Now he was only fifty feet away, and closing rapidly. There might never be a better chance. He punched the launching stud.

From beneath the belly of the sub, something that looked like a sting-ray hurtled forward. Don had checked the speed of his own craft; there was no need to come any closer now. The tiny, arrow-shaped hydrofoil, only a couple of feet across, could move far faster than his vessel and would close the gap in seconds. As it raced forward, it spun out the thin line of the control wire, like some underwater spider laying its thread. Along that wire passed the energy that powered the Sting, and the signals that steered it to its goal. Don had completely ignored his own larger craft in the effort of guiding this underwater missile. It responded to his touch so swiftly that he felt he was controlling some sensitive high-spirited steed.

The shark saw the danger less than a second before impact. The resemblance of the Sting to an ordinary ray confused it, as the designers had intended. Before the tiny brain could realize that no ray behaved like this, the missile had struck. The steel hypodermic, rammed forward by an exploding cartridge, drove through the shark's horny skin, and the great fish erupted in a frenzy of terror. Don backed rapidly away, for a blow from that tail would rattle him around like a pea in a can and might even cause damage to the sub. There was nothing more for him to do, except to speak into the microphone and call off his hounds.

The doomed killer was trying to arch its body so that it could snap at the poisoned dart. Don had now reeled the Sting back into its hiding place, pleased that he had been able to retrieve the missile undamaged. He watched without pity as the great fish succumbed to its paralysis.

Its struggles were weakening. It was swimming aimlessly back and forth, and once Don had to sidestep smartly to avoid a collision. As it lost control of buoyancy, the dying shark drifted up to the surface. Don did not bother to follow; that could wait until he had attended to more important business.

He found the cow and her two calves less than a mile away, and inspected them carefully. They were uninjured, so there was no need to call the vet in his highly specialized two-man sub which could handle any cetological crisis from a stomach-ache to a Caesarian. Don made a note of the mother's number, stencilled just behind the flippers. The calves, as was obvious from their size, were this season's and had not yet been branded.

Don watched for a little while. They were no longer in the least alarmed, and a check on the sonar had shown that the whole school had ceased its panicky flight. He wondered how they knew what had happened; much had been learned about communication among whales, but much was still a mystery.

"I hope you appreciate what I've done for you, old lady," he muttered. Then, reflecting that fifty tons of mother love was a slightly awe-inspiring sight, he blew his tanks and surfaced.

It was calm, so he cracked the airlock and popped his head out of the tiny conning tower. The water was only inches below his chin, and from time to time a wave made a determined effort to swamp him. There was little danger of this happening, for he fitted the hatch so closely that he was quite an effective plug.

Fifty feet away, a long slate-colored mound, like an over-turned boat, was rolling on the surface. Don looked at it thoughtfully and did some mental calculations. A brute this size should be valuable; with any luck there was a chance of a double bonus. In a few minutes he'd radio his report, but for the moment it was pleasant to drink the fresh Atlantic air and to feel the open sky above his head.

A gray thunderbolt shot up out of the depths and smashed back onto the surface of the water, smothering Don with spray. It was just Benj's modest way of drawing attention to himself; a moment later the porpoise had swum up to the conning tower, so that Don could reach down and tickle its head. The great, intelligent eyes stared back into his; was it pure imagination, or did an almost human sense of fun also lurk in their depths?

Susan, as usual, circled shyly at a distance until jealousy overpowered her and she butted Benj out of the way. Don distributed caresses impartially and apologized because he had nothing to give them. He undertook to make up for the omission as soon as he returned to the *Herman Melville.*

"I'll go for another swim with you, too," he promised, "as long as you behave yourselves next time." He rubbed thoughtfully at a large bruise caused by Benj's playfulness, and wondered if he was not getting a little too old for rough games like this.

"Time to go home," Don said firmly, sliding down into the cabin and slamming the hatch. He suddenly realized that he was very hungry, and had better do something about the breakfast he had missed. There were not many men on earth who had earned a better right to eat their morning meal. He had saved for humanity more tons of meat, oil and milk than could easily be estimated.

Don Burley was the happy warrior, coming home from one battle that man would always have to fight. He was holding at bay the specter of famine which had confronted all earlier ages, but which would never threaten the world again while the great plankton farms harvested their millions of tons of protein, and the whale herds obeyed their new masters. Man had come back to the sea after aeons of exile; until the oceans froze, he would never be hungry again. . . .

Don glanced at the scanner as he set his course. He smiled as he saw the two echoes keeping pace with the central splash of light that marked his vessel. "Hang around," he said. "We mammals must stick together." Then, as the autopilot took over, he lay back in his chair.

And presently Benj and Susan heard a most peculiar noise, rising and falling against the drone of the turbine. It had filtered faintly through the thick walls of Sub 5, and only the sensitive ears of the porpoises could have detected it. But intelligent beasts though they were, they could hardly be expected to understand why Don Burley was announcing, in a highly unmusical voice, that he was Heading for the Last Round-up. . . .

## *Study questions*

1. *At what point in time is the story set? What kinds of technological advances have been projected? Are human problems any different?* 2. *Why is the mother ship called the* Herman Melville? 3. *What kind of past warriors is Don associated with? Why does Clarke make these associations?* 4. *What is the significance of the title of the story?* 5. *Does Clarke make use of an underlying symbolic structure? From what is the meaning of the story derived?*

*Carson McCullers* (1917–1967), born in Columbus, Georgia, went to New York with the intention of studying music. However, on the second day there she lost her tuition money and began to write, while working at a variety of jobs during the day and going to school at night. Shortly thereafter *Story* magazine bought two of her stories, and she began to write in earnest. *The Heart Is a Lonely Hunter* was published in 1940 and *Reflections in a Golden Eye* in 1941. At the time critics were amazed not only at the technical dexterity but also at the humanity exhibited by one so young. *The Member of the Wedding* (1946) was put into dramatic form for the New York stage in 1950. A collection of stories, *The Ballad of the Sad Café,* was published in 1951. The novel *Clock Without Hands* (1961) continued to exhibit her talent. A variation on Coleridge's "The Rime of the Ancient Mariner," "A Tree, A Rock, A Cloud" tells the story of a transient who is compelled to relate a story to a boy. But, though the boy listens, he is unable to understand.

# A TREE, A ROCK, A CLOUD

It was raining that morning, and still very dark. When the boy reached the streetcar café he had almost finished his route and he went in for a cup of coffee. The place was an all-night café owned by a bitter and stingy man called Leo. After the raw, empty street the café seemed friendly and bright: along the counter there were a couple of soldiers, three spinners from the cotton mill, and in a corner a man who sat hunched over with his nose and half his face down in a beer mug. The boy wore a helmet such as aviators wear. When he went into the café he unbuckled the chin strap and raised the right flap up over his pink little ear; often as he drank his coffee someone would speak to him in a friendly way. But this morning Leo did not look into his face and none of the men were talking. He paid and was leaving the café when a voice called out to him:

"Son! Hey Son!"

He turned back and the man in the corner was crooking his finger and nodding to him. He had brought his face out of the beer mug and he seemed suddenly very happy. The man was long and pale, with a big nose and faded orange hair.

"Hey Son!"

The boy went toward him. He was an undersized boy of about twelve, with one shoulder drawn higher than the other because of the weight of the paper sack. His face was shallow, freckled, and his eyes were round child eyes.

"Yeah Mister?"

The man laid one hand on the paper boy's shoulders, then grasped the boy's chin and turned his face slowly from one side to the other. The boy shrank back uneasily.

"Say! What's the big idea?"

The boy's voice was shrill; inside the café it was suddenly very quiet.

The man said slowly: "I love you."

All along the counter the men laughed. The boy, who had scowled and sidled away, did not know what to do. He looked over the counter at Leo, and Leo watched him with a weary, brittle jeer. The boy tried to laugh also. But the man was serious and sad.

"I did not mean to tease you, Son," he said. "Sit down and have a beer with me. There is something I have to explain.

Cautiously, out of the corner of his eye, the paper boy questioned the men along the counter to see what he should do. But they had gone back to their beer or their breakfast and did not notice him. Leo put a cup of coffee on the counter and a little jug of cream.

"He is a minor," Leo said.

The paper boy slid himself up onto the stool. His ear beneath the upturned flap of the helmet was very small and red. The man was nodding at him soberly. "It is important," he said. Then he reached in his hip pocket and brought out something which he held up in the palm of his hand for the boy to see.

"Look very carefully," he said.

The boy stared, but there was nothing to look at very carefully. The man held in his big, grimy palm a photograph. It was the face of a woman, but blurred, so that only the hat and the dress she was wearing stood out clearly.

"See?" the man asked.

The boy nodded and the man placed another picture in his palm. The woman was standing on a beach in a bathing suit. The suit made her stomach very big, and that was the main thing you noticed.

"Got a good look?" He leaned over closer and finally asked: "You ever seen her before?"

The boy sat motionless, staring slantwise at the man. "Not so I know of."

"Very well." The man blew on the photographs and put them back into his pocket. "That was my wife."

"Dead?" the boy asked.

Slowly the man shook his head. He pursed his lips as though about to whistle and answered in a long-drawn way: "Nuuu—" he said. "I will explain."

The beer on the counter before the man was in a large brown mug. He did not pick it up to drink. Instead he bent down and, putting his face over the rim, he rested there for a moment. Then with both hands he tilted the mug and sipped.

"Some night you'll go to sleep with your big nose in a mug and drown," said Leo. "Prominent transient drowns in beer. That would be a cute death."

The paper boy tried to signal to Leo. While the man was not looking he screwed up his face and worked his mouth to question soundlessly: "Drunk?" But Leo only raised his eyebrows and turned away to put some pink strips of bacon on the grill. The man pushed the mug away from him, straightened himself, and folded his loose crooked hands on the counter. His face was sad as he looked at the paper boy. He did not blink, but from time to time the lids closed down with delicate gravity over his pale green eyes. It was nearing dawn and the boy shifted the weight of the paper sack.

"I am talking about love," the man said. "With me it is a science."

The boy half slid down from the stool. But the man raised his forefinger, and there was something about him that held the boy and would not let him go away.

"Twelve years ago I married the woman in the photograph. She was my wife for one year, nine months, three days, and two nights. I loved her. Yes . . ." He tightened his blurred, rambling voice and said again: "I loved her. I thought also that she loved me. I was a railroad engineer. She had all home comforts and luxuries. It never crept into my brain that she was not satisfied. But do you know what happened?"

"Mgneeow!" said Leo.

The man did not take his eyes from the boy's face. "She left me. I came in one night and the house was empty and she was gone. She left me."

"With a fellow?" the boy asked.

Gently the man placed his palm down on the counter. "Why naturally, Son. A woman does not run off like that alone."

The café was quiet, the soft rain black and endless in the street outside. Leo pressed down the frying bacon with the prongs of his long fork. "So you have been chasing the floozie for eleven years. You frazzled old rascal!"

For the first time the man glanced at Leo. "Please don't be vulgar. Besides, I was not speaking to you." He turned back to the boy and said in a trusting and secretive undertone: "Let's not pay any attention to him. O.K.?"

The paper boy nodded doubtfully.

"It was like this," the man continued. "I am a person who feels many things. All my life one thing after another has impressed me. Moonlight. The leg of a pretty girl. One thing after another. But the point is that when I had enjoyed anything there was a peculiar sensation as though it was laying around loose in me. Nothing seemed to finish itself up or fit in with the other things. Women? I had my portion of them. The same. Afterwards laying around loose in me. I was a man who had never loved."

Very slowly he closed his eyelids, and the gesture was like a curtain drawn at the end of a scene in a play. When he spoke again his voice was excited and the words came fast—the lobes of his large, loose ears seemed to tremble.

"Then I met this woman. I was fifty-one years old and she always said she was thirty. I met her at a filling station and we were married within three days. And do you know what it was like? I just can't tell you. All I had ever felt was gathered together around this woman. Nothing lay around loose in me any more but was finished up by her."

The man stopped suddenly and stroked his long nose. His voice sank down to a steady and reproachful undertone: "I'm not explaining this right. What happened was this. There were these beautiful feelings and loose little pleasures inside me. And this woman was something like an assembly line for my soul. I run these little pieces of myself through her and I come out complete. Now do you follow me?"

"What was her name?" the boy asked.

"Oh," he said. "I called her Dodo. But that is immaterial."

"Did you try to make her come back?"

The man did not seem to hear. "Under the circumstances you can imagine how I felt when she left me."

Leo took the bacon from the grill and folded two strips of it between a bun. He had a gray face, with slitted eyes, and a pinched nose saddled by faint blue shadows. One of the mill workers signaled for more coffee and Leo poured it. He did not give refills on coffee free. The spinner ate breakfast there every morning, but the better Leo knew his customers the stingier he treated them. He nibbled his own bun as though he grudged it to himself.

"And you never got hold of her again?"

The boy did not know what to think of the man, and his child's face was uncertain with mingled curiosity and doubt. He was new on the paper route; it was still strange to him to be out in the town in the black, queer early morning.

"Yes," the man said. "I took a number of steps to get her back. I went around trying to locate her. I went to Tulsa where she had folks. And to Mobile. I went to every town she had ever mentioned to me, and I hunted down every man she had formerly been connected with. Tulsa, Atlanta, Chicago, Cheehaw, Memphis. . . . For the better part of two years I chased around the country trying to lay hold of her."

"But the pair of them had vanished from the face of the earth!" said Leo.

"Don't listen to him," the man said confidentially. "And also just forget those two years. They are not important. What matters is that around the third year a curious thing begun to happen to me."

"What?" the boy asked.

The man leaned down and tilted his mug to take a sip of beer. But as he hovered over the mug his nostrils fluttered slightly; he sniffed the staleness of the beer and did not drink. "Love is a curious thing to begin with. At first I thought only of getting her back. It was a kind of mania. But then as time went on I tried to remember her. But do you know what happened?"

"No," the boy said.

"When I laid myself down on a bed and tried to think about her my mind became a blank. I couldn't see her. I would take out her pictures and look. No good. Nothing doing. A blank. Can you imagine it?"

"Say Mac!" Leo called down the counter. "Can you imagine this bozo's mind a blank!"

Slowly, as though fanning away flies, the man waved his hand. His green eyes were concentrated and fixed on the shallow little face of the paper boy.

"But a sudden piece of glass on a sidewalk. Or a nickel tune in a music box. A shadow on a wall at night. And I would remember. It might happen in a street and I would cry or bang my head against a lamppost. You follow me?"

"A piece of glass . . ." the boy said.

"Anything. I would walk around and I had no power of how and when to remember her. You think you can put up a kind of shield. But remembering don't come to a man face forward—it corners around sideways. I was at the mercy of everything I saw and heard. Suddenly instead of me combing the countryside to find her she began to chase me around in my very soul. *She* chasing *me,* mind you! And in my soul."

The boy asked finally: "What part of the country were you in then?"

"Ooh," the man groaned. "I was a sick mortal. It was like smallpox. I confess, Son, that I boozed. I fornicated. I committed any sin that suddenly appealed to me. I am loath to confess it but I will do so. When I recall that period it is all curdled in my mind, it was so terrible."

The man leaned his head down and tapped his forehead on the counter. For a few seconds he stayed bowed over in this position, the back of his stringy neck covered with orange furze, his hands with their long warped fingers held palm to palm in an attitude of prayer. Then the man straightened himself; he was smiling and suddenly his face was bright and tremulous and old.

"It was in the fifth year that it happened," he said. "And with it I started my science."

Leo's mouth jerked with a pale, quick grin. "Well none of we boys are getting any younger," he said. Then with sudden anger he balled up a dishcloth he was holding and threw it down hard on the floor. "You draggle-tailed old Romeo!"

"What happened?" the boy asked.

The old man's voice was high and clear: "Peace," he answered.

"Huh?"

"It is hard to explain scientifically, Son," he said. "I guess the logical explanation is that she and I had fleed around from each other for so long that finally we just got tangled up together and lay down and quit. Peace. A queer and beautiful blankness. It was spring in Portland and the rain came every afternoon. All evening I just stayed there on my bed in the dark. And that is how the science come to me."

The windows in the streetcar were pale blue with light. The two soldiers paid for their beers and opened the door—one of the soldiers combed his hair and wiped off his muddy puttees before they went outside. The three mill workers bent silently over their breakfasts. Leo's clock was ticking on the wall.

"It is this. And listen carefully. I meditated on love and reasoned it out. I realized what is wrong with us. Men fall in love for the first time. And what do they fall in love with?"

The boy's soft mouth was partly open and he did not answer.

"A woman," the old man said. "Without science, with nothing to go by, they undertake the most dangerous and sacred experience in God's earth. They fall in love with a woman. Is that correct, Son?"

"Yeah," the boy said faintly.

"They start at the wrong end of love. They begin at the climax. Can you wonder it is so miserable? Do you know how men should love?"

The old man reached over and grasped the boy by the collar of his leather jacket. He gave him a gentle little shake and his green eyes gazed down and unblinking and grave.

"Son, do you know how love should be begun?"

The boy sat small and listening and still. Slowly he shook his head. The old man leaned closer and whispered:

"A tree. A rock. A cloud!"

It was still raining outside in the street: a mild, gray, endless rain. The mill whistle blew for the six o'clock shift and the three spinners paid and went away. There was no one in the café but Leo, the old man, and the little paper boy.

"The weather was like this in Portland," he said. "At the time my science was begun. I meditated and I started very cautious. I would pick up something from the street and take it home with me. I bought a goldfish and I concentrated on the goldfish and I loved it. I graduated from one thing to another. Day by day I was getting this technique. On the road from Portland to San Diego—"

"Aw shut up!" screamed Leo suddenly. "Shut up! Shut up!"

The old man still held the collar of the boy's jacket; he was trembling and his face was earnest and bright and wild. "For six years now I have gone around by myself and built up my science. And now I am a master. Son, I can love anything. No longer do I have to think about it even. I see a street full of people and a beautiful light comes in me. I watch a bird in the sky. Or I meet a traveler on the road. Everything, Son. And anybody. All stranger and all loved! Do you realize what a science like mine can mean?"

The boy held himself stiffly, his hands curled tight around the counter edge. Finally he asked: "Did you ever really find that lady?"

"What? What say, Son?"

"I mean," the boy asked timidly. "Have you fallen in love with a woman again?"

The old man loosened his grasp on the boy's collar. He turned away and for the first time his green eyes had a vague and scattered look. He lifted the mug from the counter, drank down the yellow beer. His head was shaking slowly from side to side. Then finally he answered: "No, Son. You see that is the last step in my science. I go cautious. And I am not quite ready yet."

"Well!" said Leo. "Well well well!"

The old man stood in the open doorway. "Remember," he said. Framed there in the gray damp light of the early morning he looked shrunken and seedy and frail. But his smile was bright. "Remember I love you," he said with a last nod. And the door closed quietly behind him.

The boy did not speak for a long time. He pulled down the bangs on his forehead and slid his grimy little forefinger around the rim of his empty cup. Then without looking at Leo he finally asked:

"Was he drunk?"

"No," said Leo shortly.

The boy raised his clear voice higher. "Then was he a dope fiend?"

"No."

The boy looked up at Leo, and his flat little face was desperate, his voice urgent and shrill. "Was he crazy? Do you think he was a lunatic?" The paper boy's voice dropped suddenly with doubt. "Leo? Or not?"

But Leo would not answer him. Leo had run a night café for fourteen years, and he held himself to be a critic of craziness. There were the town characters and also the transients who roamed in from the night. He knew the manias of all of them. But he did not want to satisfy the questions of the waiting child. He tightened his pale face and was silent.

So the boy pulled down the right flap of his helmet and as he turned to leave he made the only comment that seemed safe to him, the only remark that could not be laughed down and despised:

"He sure has done a lot of traveling."

## *Study questions*

1. *Why does the transient choose the boy to tell his story to?* 2. *What role does Leo play? Notice that Leo and the transient are set in juxtaposition with each other.* 3. *What is the point of the story the transient tells? How much of it does the boy understand? What is the point of the story McCullers tells?* 4. *How does setting function in this story? Are there recurrent image patterns?* 5. *Except for the entry into the mind of Leo and the boy at the very end of the story, "A Tree, A Rock, A Cloud" is told from an objective point of view. Is the point of view effective?*

*Flannery O'Connor* (1925–1964) was born in Savannah, Georgia, and lived most of her brief life in Milledgeville, Georgia. She attended Peabody High School and graduated from the Georgia State College for Women in 1945. Thereafter she went to the Writers' Workshop at the University of Iowa, where she received her M.F.A. in 1947. Her fiction first began to appear in such literary journals as *Accent*, *Partisan Review*, and *Kenyon Review* and in other magazines like *Harper's Bazaar* and *Mademoiselle*. She published two collections of stories, *A Good Man Is Hard to Find* (1955) and *Everything That Rises Must Converge* (1965). Her complete stories were collected and published in 1971. She also wrote two novels, *Wise Blood* (1952) and *The Violent Bear It Away* (1960). She died at the age of thirty-nine after a lengthy illness. Her stories are characterized by finely detailed surfaces that move rapidly to the symbolic, often through the grotesque. Well-known stories include "Good Country People," "The Life You Save May Be Your Own," "The Displaced Person," "The Artificial Nigger," "A Good Man Is Hard to Find," and "Everything That Rises Must Converge." The latter is a story about the convergence of attitudes, both public and private, and the tragedy that results.

## EVERYTHING THAT RISES MUST CONVERGE

Her doctor had told Julian's mother that she must lose twenty pounds on account of her blood pressure, so on Wednesday nights Julian had to take her downtown on the bus for a reducing class at the Y. The reducing class was designed for working girls over fifty, who weighed from 165 to 200 pounds. His mother was one of the slimmer ones, but she said ladies did not tell their age or weight. She would not ride the buses by herself at night since they had been integrated, and because the reducing class was one of her few pleasures, necessary for her health, and *free*, she said Julian could at least put himself out to take her, considering all she did for him. Julian did not like to consider all she did for him, but every Wednesday night he braced himself and took her.

She was almost ready to go, standing before the hall mirror, putting on her hat, while he, his hands behind him, appeared pinned to the door frame, waiting like Saint Sebastian for the arrows to begin piercing him. The hat was new and had cost her seven dollars and a half. She kept saying, "Maybe I shouldn't have paid that for it. No, I shouldn't have. I'll take it off and return it tomorrow. I shouldn't have bought it."

Julian raised his eyes to heaven. "Yes, you should have bought it," he said. "Put it on and let's go." It was a hideous hat. A purple velvet flap came down on one side of it and stood up on the other; the rest of it was green and looked like a cushion with the stuffing out. He decided it was less comical than jaunty and pathetic. Everything that gave her pleasure was small and depressed him.

She lifted the hat one more time and set it down slowly on top of her head. Two wings of gray hair protruded on either side of her florid face, but her eyes, sky-blue, were as innocent and untouched by experience as they must have been when she was ten. Were it not that she was a widow who had struggled fiercely to feed and clothe and put him through school and who was supporting him still, "until he got on his feet," she might have been a little girl that he had to take to town.

"It's all right, it's all right," he said. "Let's go." He opened the door himself and started down the walk to get her going. The sky was a dying violet and the houses stood out darkly against it, bulbous liver-colored monstrosities of a uniform ugliness though no two were alike. Since this had been a fashionable neighborhood forty years ago, his mother persisted in thinking they did well to have an apartment in it. Each house had a narrow collar of dirt around it in which sat, usually, a grubby child. Julian walked with his hands in his pockets, his head down and thrust forward and his eyes glazed with the determination to make himself completely numb during the time he would be sacrificed to her pleasure.

The door closed and he turned to find the dumpy figure, surmounted by the atrocious hat, coming toward him. "Well," she said, "you only live once and paying a little more for it, I at least won't meet myself coming and going."

"Some day I'll start making money," Julian said gloomily—he knew he never would—"and you can have one of those jokes whenever you take the fit." But first they would move. He visualized a place where the nearest neighbors would be three miles away on either side.

"I think you're doing fine," she said, drawing on her gloves. "You've only been out of school a year. Rome wasn't built in a day."

She was one of the few members of the Y reducing class who arrived in hat and gloves and who had a son who had been to college. "It takes time," she said, "and the world is in such a mess. This hat looked better on me than any of the others, though when she brought it out I said, 'Take that thing back. I wouldn't have it on my head,' and she said, 'Now wait till you see it on,' and when she put it on me, I said, 'We-ull,' and she said, 'If you ask me, that hat does something for you and you do something for the hat and besides,' she said, 'with that hat, you won't meet yourself coming and going.' "

Julian thought he could have stood his lot better if she had been selfish, if she had been an old hag who drank and screamed at him. He walked along, saturated in depression, as if in the midst of his martyrdom he had lost his faith. Catching sight of his long, hopeless, irritated face, she stopped suddenly with a grief-stricken look, and pulled back on his arm. "Wait on me," she said. "I'm going back to the house and take this thing off and tomorrow I'm going to return it. I was out of my head. I can pay the gas bill with that seven-fifty."

He caught her arm in a vicious grip. "You are not going to take it back," he said. "I like it."

"Well," she said, "I don't think I ought . . ."

"Shut up and enjoy it," he muttered, more depressed than ever.

"With the world in the mess it's in," she said, "it's a wonder we can enjoy anything. I tell you, the bottom rail is on the top."

Julian sighed.

"Of course," she said, "if you know who you are, you can go anywhere." She said this every time he took her to the reducing class. "Most of them in it are not our kind of people," she said, "but I can be gracious to anybody. I know who I am."

"They don't give a damn for your graciousness," Julian said savagely. "Knowing who you are is good for one generation only. You haven't the foggiest idea where you stand now or who you are."

She stopped and allowed her eyes to flash at him. "I most certainly do know who I am," she said, "and if you don't know who you are, I'm ashamed of you."

"Oh hell," Julian said.

"Your great-grandfather was a former governor of this state," she said. "Your grandfather was a prosperous landowner. Your grandmother was a Godhigh."

"Will you look around you," he said tensely, "and see where you are now?" and he swept his arm jerkily out to indicate the neighborhood, which the growing darkness at least made less dingy.

"You remain what you are," she said. "Your great-grandfather had a plantation and two hundred slaves."

"There are no more slaves," he said irritably.

"They were better off when they were," she said. He groaned to see that she was off on that topic. She rolled onto it every few days like a train on an open track. He knew every stop, every junction, every swamp along the way, and knew the exact point at which her conclusion would roll majestically into the station: "It's ridiculous. It's simply not realistic. They should rise, yes, but on their own side of the fence."

"Let's skip it," Julian said.

"The ones I feel sorry for," she said, "are the ones that are half white. They're tragic."

"Will you skip it?"

"Suppose we were half white. We would certainly have mixed feelings."

"I have mixed feelings now," he groaned.

"Well let's talk about something pleasant," she said. "I remember going to Grandpa's when I was a little girl. Then the house had double stairways that went up to what was really the second floor—all the cooking was done on the first. I used to like to stay down in the kitchen on account of the way the walls smelled. I would sit with my nose pressed against the plaster and take deep breaths. Actually the place belonged to the Godhighs but your grandfather Chestny paid the mortgage and saved it for them. They were in reduced circumstances," she said, "but reduced or not, they never forgot who they were."

"Doubtless that decayed mansion reminded them," Julian muttered. He never spoke of it without contempt or thought of it without longing. He had seen it once when he was a child before it had been sold. The double stairways had rotted and been torn down. Negroes were living in it. But it remained in his mind as his mother had known it. It appeared in his dreams regularly. He would stand on the wide porch, listening to the rustle of oak leaves, then wander through the high-ceilinged hall into the parlor that opened onto it and gaze at the worn rugs and faded draperies. It occurred to him that it was he, not she, who could have appreciated it. He preferred its threadbare elegance to anything he could name and it was because of it that all the neighborhoods they had lived in had been a torment to him—whereas she had hardly known the difference. She called her insensitivity "being adjustable."

"And I remember the old darky who was my nurse, Caroline. There was no better person in the world. I've always had a great respect for my colored friends," she said. "I'd do anything in the world for them and they'd . . ."

"Will you for God's sake get off that subject?" Julian said. When he got on a bus by himself, he made it a point to sit down beside a Negro, in reparation as it were for his mother's sins.

"You're mighty touchy tonight," she said. "Do you feel all right?"

"Yes I feel all right," he said. "Now lay off."

She pursed her lips. "Well, you certainly are in a vile humor," she observed. "I just won't speak to you at all."

They had reached the bus stop. There was no bus in sight and Julian, his hands still jammed in his pockets and his head thrust forward, scowled down the empty street. The frustration of having to wait on the bus as well as ride on it began to creep up his neck like a hot hand. The presence of his mother was borne in upon him as she gave a pained sigh. He looked at her bleakly. She was holding herself very erect under the preposterous hat, wearing it like a banner of her imaginary dignity. There was in him an evil urge to break her spirit. He suddenly unloosened his tie and pulled it off and put it in his pocket.

She stiffened. "Why must you look like *that* when you take me to town?" she said. "Why must you deliberately embarrass me?"

"If you'll never learn where you are," he said, "you can at least learn where I am."

"You look like a—thug," she said.

"Then I must be one," he murmured.

"I'll just go home," she said. "I will not bother you. If you can't do a little thing like that for me . . ."

Rolling his eyes upward, he put his tie back on. "Restored to my class," he muttered. He thrust his face toward her and hissed, "True culture is in the mind, the *mind*," he said, and tapped his head, "the mind."

"It's in the heart," she said, "and in how you do things and how you do things is because of who you *are*."

"Nobody in the damn bus cares who you are."

"I care who I am," she said icily.

The lighted bus appeared on top of the next hill and as it approached, they moved out into the street to meet it. He put his hand under her elbow and hoisted her up on the creaking step. She entered with a little smile, as if she were going into a drawing room where everyone had been waiting for her. While he put in the tokens, she sat down on one of the broad front seats for three which faced the aisle. A thin woman with protruding teeth and long yellow hair was sitting on the end of it. His mother moved up beside her and left room for Julian beside herself. He sat down and looked at the floor across the aisle where a pair of thin feet in red and white canvas sandals were planted.

His mother immediately began a general conversation meant to attract anyone who felt like talking. "Can it get any hotter?" she said and removed from her purse a folding fan, black with a Japanese scene on it, which she began to flutter before her.

"I reckon it might could," the woman with the protruding teeth said, "but I know for a fact my apartment couldn't get no hotter."

"It must get the afternoon sun," his mother said. She sat forward and looked up and down the bus. It was half filled. Everybody was white. "I see we have the bus to ourselves," she said. Julian cringed.

"For a change," said the woman across the aisle, the owner of the red and white canvas sandals. "I come on one the other day and they were thick as fleas—up front and all through."

"The world is in a mess everywhere," his mother said. "I don't know how we've let it get in this fix."

"What gets my goat is all those boys from good families stealing automobile tires," the woman with the protruding teeth said. "I told my boy, I said you may not be rich but you been raised right and if I ever catch you in any such mess, they can send you on to the reformatory. Be exactly where you belong."

"Training tells," his mother said. "Is your boy in high school?"

"Ninth grade," the woman said.

"My son just finished college last year. He wants to write but he's selling typewriters until he gets started," his mother said.

The woman leaned forward and peered at Julian. He threw her such a malevolent look that she subsided against the seat. On the floor across the aisle there was an abandoned newspaper. He got up and got it and opened it out in front of him. His mother discreetly continued the conversation in a lower tone but the woman across the aisle said in a loud voice, "Well that's nice. Selling typewriters is close to writing. He can go right from one to the other."

"I tell him," his mother said, "that Rome wasn't built in a day."

Behind the newspaper Julian was withdrawing into the inner compartment of his mind where he spent most of his time. This was a kind of mental bubble in which he established himself when he could not bear to be a part of what was going on around him. From it he could see out and judge but in it he was safe from any kind of penetration from without. It was the only place where he felt free of the general idiocy of his fellows. His mother had never entered it but from it he could see her with absolute clarity.

The old lady was clever enough and he thought that if she had started from any of the right premises, more might have been expected of her. She lived according to the laws of her own fantasy world, outside of which he had never seen her set foot. The law of it was to sacrifice herself for him after she had first created the necessity to do so by making a mess of things. If he had permitted her sacrifices, it was only because her lack of foresight had made them necessary. All of her life had been a struggle to act like a Chestny without the Chestny goods, and to give him everything she thought a Chestny ought to have; but since, said she, it was fun to struggle, why complain? And when you had won, as she had won, what fun to look back on the hard times! He could not forgive her that she had enjoyed the struggle and that she thought *she* had won.

What she meant when she said she had won was that she had brought him up successfully and had sent him to college and that he had turned out so well—good looking (her teeth had gone unfilled so that his could be straightened), intelligent (he realized he was too intelligent to be a success), and with a future ahead of him (there was of course no future ahead of him). She excused his gloominess on the grounds that he was still growing up and his radical ideas on his lack of practical experience. She said he didn't yet know a thing about "life," that he hadn't even entered the real world—when already he was as disenchanted with it as a man of fifty.

The further irony of all this was that in spite of her, he had turned out so well. In spite of going to only a third-rate college, he had, on his own initiative, come out with a first-rate education; in spite of growing up dominated by a small mind, he had ended up with a large one; in spite of all her foolish views, he was free of prejudice and unafraid to face facts. Most miraculous of all, instead of being blinded by love for her as she was for him, he had cut himself emotionally free of her and could see her with complete objectivity. He was not dominated by his mother.

The bus stopped with a sudden jerk and shook him from his meditation. A woman from the back lurched forward with little steps and barely escaped falling in his newspaper as she righted herself. She got off and a large Negro got on. Julian kept his paper lowered to watch. It gave him a certain satisfaction to see injustice in daily operation. It confirmed his view that with a few exceptions there was no one worth knowing within a radius of three hundred miles. The Negro was well dressed and carried a briefcase. He looked around and then sat down on the other end of the seat where the woman with the red and white canvas sandals was sitting. He immediately unfolded a newspaper and obscured himself behind it. Julian's mother's elbow at once prodded insistently into his ribs. "Now you see why I won't ride on these buses by myself," she whispered.

The woman with the red and white canvas sandals had risen at the same time the Negro sat down and had gone further back in the bus and taken the seat of the woman who had got off. His mother leaned forward and cast her an approving look.

Julian rose, crossed the aisle, and sat down in the place of the woman with the canvas sandals. From this position, he looked serenely across at his mother. Her face had turned an angry red. He stared at her, making his eyes the eyes of a stranger. He felt his tension suddenly lift as if he had openly declared war on her.

He would have liked to get in conversation with the Negro and to talk with him about art or politics or any subject that would be above the comprehension of those around them, but the man remained entrenched behind his paper. He was either ignoring the change of seating or had never noticed it. There was no way for Julian to convey his sympathy.

His mother kept her eyes fixed reproachfully on his face. The woman with the protruding teeth was looking at him avidly as if he were a type of monster new to her.

"Do you have a light?" he asked the Negro.

Without looking away from his paper, the man reached in his pocket and handed him a packet of matches.

"Thanks," Julian said. For a moment he held the matches foolishly. A NO SMOKING sign looked down upon him from over the door. This alone would not have deterred him; he had no cigarettes. He had quit smoking some months before because he could not afford it. "Sorry," he muttered and handed back the matches. The Negro lowered the paper and gave him an annoyed look. He took the matches and raised the paper again.

His mother continued to gaze at him but she did not take advantage of his momentary discomfort. Her eyes retained their battered look. Her face seemed to be unnaturally red, as if her blood pressure had risen. Julian allowed no glimmer of sympathy to show on his face. Having got the advantage, he wanted desperately to keep it and carry it through. He would have liked to teach her a lesson that would last her a while, but there seemed no way to continue the point. The Negro refused to come out from behind his paper.

Julian folded his arms and looked stolidly before him, facing her but as if he did not see her, as if he had ceased to recognize her existence. He visualized a scene in which, the bus having reached their stop, he would remain in his seat and when she said, "Aren't you going to get off?" he would look at her as at a stranger who had rashly addressed him. The corner they got off on was usually deserted, but it was well lighted and it would not hurt her to walk by herself the four blocks to the Y. He decided to wait until the time came and then decide whether or not he would let her get off by herself. He would have to be at the Y at ten to bring her back, but he could leave her wondering if he was going to show up. There was no reason for her to think she could always depend on him.

He retired again into the high-ceilinged room sparsely settled with large pieces of antique furniture. His soul expanded momentarily but then he became aware of his mother across from him and the vision shriveled. He studied her coldly. Her feet in little pumps dangled like a child's and did not quite reach the floor. She was training on him an exaggerated look of reproach. He felt completely detached from her. At that moment he could with pleasure have slapped her as he would have slapped a particularly obnoxious child in his charge.

He began to imagine various unlikely ways by which he could teach her a lesson. He might make friends with some distinguished Negro professor or lawyer and bring him home to spend the evening. He would be entirely justified but her blood pressure would rise to 300. He could not push her to the extent of making her have a stroke, and moreover, he had never been successful at making any Negro friends. He had tried to strike up an acquaintance on the bus with some of the better types, with ones that looked like professors or ministers or lawyers. One morning he had sat down next to a distinguished-looking dark brown man who had answered his questions with a sonorous solemnity but who had turned out to be an undertaker. Another day he had sat down beside a cigar-smoking Negro with a diamond ring on his finger, but after a few stilted pleasantries, the Negro had rung the buzzer and risen, slipping two lottery tickets into Julian's hand as he climbed over him to leave.

He imagined his mother lying desperately ill and his being able to secure only a Negro doctor for her. He toyed with that idea for a few minutes and then dropped it for a momentary vision of himself participating as a sympathizer in a sit-in demonstration. This was possible but he did not linger with it. Instead, he approached the ultimate horror. He brought home a beautiful suspiciously Negroid woman. Prepare yourself, he said. There is nothing you can do about it. This is the woman I've chosen. She's intelligent, dignified, even good, and she's suffered and she hasn't thought it *fun*. Now persecute us, go ahead and persecute us. Drive her out of here, but remember, you're driving me too. His eyes were narrowed and through the indignation he had generated, he saw his mother across the aisle, purple-faced, shrunken to the dwarf-like proportions of her moral nature, sitting like a mummy beneath the ridiculous banner of her hat.

He was tilted out of his fantasy again as the bus stopped. The door opened with a sucking hiss and out of the dark, a large, gaily dressed, sullen-looking colored woman got on with a little boy. The child, who might have been four, had on a short plaid suit and a Tyrolean hat with a blue feather in it. Julian hoped that he would sit down beside him and that the woman would push in beside his mother. He could think of no better arrangement.

As she waited for her tokens, the woman was surveying the seating possibilities—he hoped with the idea of sitting where she was least wanted. There was something familiar-looking about her but Julian could not place what it was. She was a giant of a woman. Her face was set not only to meet opposition but to seek it out. The downward tilt of her large lower lip was like a warning sign: DON'T TAMPER WITH ME. Her bulging figure was encased in a green crepe dress and her feet overflowed in red shoes. She had on a hideous hat. A purple velvet flap came down on one side of it and stood up on the other; the rest of it was green and looked like a cushion with the stuffing out. She carried a mammoth red pocketbook that bulged throughout as if it were stuffed with rocks.

To Julian's disappointment, the little boy climbed up on the empty seat beside his mother. His mother lumped all children, black and white, into the common category, "cute," and she thought little Negroes were on the whole cuter than little white children. She smiled at the little boy as he climbed on the seat.

Meanwhile the woman was bearing down upon the empty seat beside Julian. To his annoyance, she squeezed herself into it. He saw his mother's face change as the woman settled herself next to him and he realized with satisfaction that this was more objectionable to her than it was to him. Her face seemed almost gray and there was a look of dull recognition in her eyes, as if suddenly she had sickened at some awful confrontation. Julian saw that it was because she and the woman had, in a sense, swapped sons. Though his mother would not realize the symbolic significance of this, she would feel it. His amusement showed plainly on his face.

The woman next to him muttered something unintelligible to herself. He was conscious of a kind of bristling next to him, a muted growling like that of an angry cat. He could not see anything but the red pocketbook upright on the bulging green thighs. He visualized the woman as she had stood waiting for her tokens—the ponderous figure, rising from the red shoes upward over the solid hips, the mammoth bosom, the haughty face, to the green and purple hat.

His eyes widened.

The vision of the two hats, identical, broke upon him with the radiance of a brilliant sunrise. His face was suddenly lit with joy. He could not believe that Fate had thrust upon his mother such a lesson. He gave a loud chuckle so that she would look at him and see that he saw. She turned her eyes on him slowly. The blue in them seemed to have turned a bruised purple. For a moment he had an uncomfortable sense of her innocence, but it lasted only a second before principle rescued him. Justice entitled him to laugh. His grin hardened until it said to her as plainly as if he were saying aloud: Your punishment exactly fits your pettiness. This should teach you a permanent lesson.

Her eyes shifted to the woman. She seemed unable to bear looking at him and to find the woman preferable. He became conscious again of the bristling presence at his side. The woman was rumbling like a volcano about to become active. His mother's mouth began to twitch slightly at one corner. With a sinking heart, he saw incipient signs of recovery on her face and realized that this was going to strike her suddenly as funny and was going to be no lesson at all. She kept her eyes on the woman and an amused smile came over her face as if the woman were a monkey that had stolen her hat. The little Negro was looking up at her with large fascinated eyes. He had been trying to attract her attention for some time.

"Carver!" the woman said suddenly. "Come heah!"

When he saw that the spotlight was on him at last, Carver drew his feet up and turned himself toward Julian's mother and giggled.

"Carver!" the woman said. "You heah me? Come heah!"

Carver slid down from the seat but remained squatting with his back against the base of it, his head turned slyly around toward Julian's mother, who was smiling at him. The woman reached a hand across the aisle and snatched him to her. He righted himself and hung backwards on her knees, grinning at Julian's mother. "Isn't he cute?" Julian's mother said to the woman with the protruding teeth.

"I reckon he is," the woman said without conviction.

The Negress yanked him upright but he eased out of her grip and shot across the aisle and scrambled, giggling wildly, onto the seat beside his love.

"I think he likes me," Julian's mother said, and smiled at the woman. It was the smile she used when she was being particularly gracious to an inferior. Julian saw everything lost. The lesson had rolled off her like rain on a roof.

The woman stood up and yanked the little boy off the seat as if she were snatching him from contagion. Julian could feel the rage in her at having no weapon like his mother's smile. She gave the child a sharp slap across his leg. He howled once and then thrust his head into her stomach and kicked his feet against her shins. "Be-have," she said vehemently.

The bus stopped and the Negro who had been reading the newspaper got off. The woman moved over and set the little boy down with a thump between herself and Julian. She held him firmly by the knee. In a moment he put his hands in front of his face and peeped at Julian's mother through his fingers.

"I see yoooooooo!" she said and put her hand in front of her face and peeped at him.

The woman slapped his hand down. "Quit yo' foolishness," she said, "before I knock the living Jesus out of you!"

Julian was thankful that the next stop was theirs. He reached up and pulled the cord. The woman reached up and pulled it at the same time. Oh my God, he thought. He had the terrible intuition that when they got off the bus together, his mother would open her purse and give the little boy a nickel. The gesture would be as natural to her as breathing. The bus stopped and the woman got up and lunged to the front, dragging the child, who wished to stay on, after her. Julian and his mother got up and followed. As they neared the door, Julian tried to relieve her of her pocketbook.

"No," she murmured, "I want to give the little boy a nickel."

"No!" Julian hissed. "No!"

She smiled down at the child and opened her bag. The bus door opened and the woman picked him up by the arm and descended with him, hanging at her hip. Once in the street she set him down and shook him.

Julian's mother had to close her purse while she got down the bus step but as soon as her feet were on the ground, she opened it again and began to rummage inside. "I can't find but a penny," she whispered, "but it looks like a new one."

"Don't do it!" Julian said fiercely between his teeth. There was a streetlight on the corner and she hurried to get under it so that she could better see into her pocketbook. The woman was heading off rapidly down the street with the child still hanging backward on her hand.

"Oh little boy!" Julian's mother called and took a few quick steps and caught up with them just beyond the lamp-post. "Here's a bright new penny for you," and she held out the coin, which shone bronze in the dim light.

The huge woman turned and for a moment stood, her shoulders lifted and her face frozen with frustrated rage, and stared at Julian's mother. Then all at once she seemed to explode like a piece of machinery that had been given one ounce of pressure too much. Julian saw the black fist swing out with the red pocketbook. He shut his eyes and cringed as he heard the woman shout, "He don't take nobody's pennies!" When he opened his eyes, the woman was disappearing down the street with the little boy staring wide-eyed over her shoulder. Julian's mother was sitting on the sidewalk.

"I told you not to do that," Julian said angrily. "I told you not to do that!"

He stood over her for a minute, gritting his teeth. Her legs were stretched out in front of her and her hat was on her lap. He squatted down and looked her in the face. It was totally expressionless. "You got exactly what you deserved," he said. "Now get up."

He picked up her pocketbook and put what had fallen out back in it. He picked the hat up off her lap. The penny caught his eye on the sidewalk and he picked that up and let it drop before her eyes into the purse. Then he stood up and leaned over and held his hands out to pull her up. She remained immobile. He sighed. Rising above them on either side were black apartment buildings, marked with irregular rectangles of light. At the end of the block a man came out of a door and walked off in the opposite direction. "All right," he said, "suppose somebody happens by and wants to know why you're sitting on the sidewalk?"

She took the hand and, breathing hard, pulled heavily up on it and then stood for a moment, swaying slightly as if the spots of light in the darkness were circling around her. Her eyes, shadowed and confused, finally settled on his face. He did not try to conceal his irritation. "I hope this teaches you a lesson," he said. She leaned forward and her eyes raked his face. She seemed trying to determine his identity. Then, as if she found nothing familiar about him, she started off with a headlong movement in the wrong direction.

"Aren't you going on to the Y?" he asked.

"Home," she muttered.

"Well, are we walking?"

For answer she kept going. Julian followed along, his hands behind him. He saw no reason to let the lesson she had had go without backing it up with an explanation of its meaning. She might as well be made to understand what had happened to her. "Don't think that was just an uppity Negro woman," he said. "That was the whole colored race which will no longer take your condescending pennies. That was your black double. She can wear the same hat as you, and to be sure," he added gratuitously (because he thought it was funny), "it looked better on her than it did on you. What all this means," he said, "is that the old world is gone. The old manners are obsolete and your graciousness is not worth a damn." He thought bitterly of the house that had been lost for him. "You aren't who you think you are," he said.

She continued to plow ahead, paying no attention to him. Her hair had come undone on one side. She dropped her pocketbook and took no notice. He stooped and picked it up and handed it to her but she did not take it.

"You needn't act as if the world had come to an end," he said, "because it hasn't. From now on you've got to live in a new world and face a few realities for a change. Buck up," he said, "it won't kill you."

She was breathing fast.

"Let's wait on the bus," he said.

"Home," she said thickly.

"I hate to see you behave like this," he said. "Just like a child. I should be able to expect more of you." He decided to stop where he was and make her stop and wait for a bus. "I'm not going any farther," he said, stopping. "We're going on the bus."

She continued to go on as if she had not heard him. He took a few steps and caught her arm and stopped her. He looked into her face and caught his breath. He was looking into a face he had never seen before. "Tell Grandpa to come get me," she said.

He stared, stricken.

"Tell Caroline to come get me," she said.

Stunned, he let her go and she lurched forward again, walking as if one leg were shorter than the other. A tide of darkness seemed to be sweeping her from him. "Mother!" he cried. "Darling, sweetheart, wait!" Crumpling, she fell to the pavement. He dashed forward and fell at her side, crying, "Mamma, Mamma!" He turned her over. Her face was fiercely distorted. One eye, large and staring, moved slightly to the left as if it had become unmoored. The other remained fixed on him, raked his face again, found nothing and closed.

"Wait here, wait here!" he cried and jumped up and began to run for help toward a cluster of lights he saw in the distance ahead of him. "Help, help!" he shouted, but his voice was thin, scarcely a thread of sound. The lights drifted farther away the faster he ran and his feet moved numbly as if they carried him nowhere. The tide of darkness seemed to sweep him back to her, postponing from moment to moment his entry into the world of guilt and sorrow.

## *Study questions*

1. *What kind of myth informs Mrs. Chestny's personal and public world? How do her attitudes determine her behavior?* 2. *What kind of myth informs Julian's personal and public world? How do his attitudes determine his behavior?* 3. *Julian tells his mother that she does not know who she is. Does he know who he is?* 4. *Why does Julian believe that he is a martyr, sacrificed to his mother's pleasure? What does his mother provide for him?* 5. *How many kinds of self-delusion are operative in the story? How does the self-delusion extend to a larger social and moral plane?* 6. *What role does the black woman play? How is it significant that she has a hat the duplicate of Mrs. Chestny's?* 7. *What is the significance of the last paragraph of the story?*

*Edward D. Hoch* (b. 1930) was born in Rochester, New York, and attended the University of Rochester. Thereafter he was employed as a researcher and a copywriter until in 1968 he became a full-time writer. A member of the Mystery Writers of America, he has authored more than three hundred stories, which have appeared under one of five pseudonyms in such periodicals as *Argosy, Ellery Queen's Mystery Magazine*, and *Alfred Hitchcock's Mystery Magazine*. In 1967, he won the Edgar Allan Poe Award for the best mystery story of the year. Poe's C. Auguste Dupin is, of course, considered the first fictional detective and "The Murders in the Rue Morgue" the first locked-room detective story. Hoch's "The Leopold Locked Room" is one of many such stories in the ratiocinative mode, which for more than one hundred and thirty years have baffled hosts of mystery-story fans.

# THE LEOPOLD LOCKED ROOM

Captain Leopold had never spoken to anyone about his divorce, and it was a distinct surprise to Lieutenant Fletcher when he suddenly said, "Did I ever tell you about my wife, Fletcher?"

They were just coming up from the police pistol range in the basement of headquarters after their monthly target practice, and it hardly seemed a likely time to be discussing past marital troubles. Fletcher glanced at him sideways and answered, "No, I guess you never did, Captain."

They had reached the top of the stairs and Leopold turned in to the little room where the coffee, sandwich, and soft-drink machines were kept. They called it the lunchroom, but only by the boldest stretch of the imagination could the little collection of tables and chairs qualify as such. Rather it was a place where off-duty cops could sit and chat, which was what Leopold and Fletcher were doing now.

Fletcher bought the coffee and put the steaming paper cups on the table between them. He had never seen Leopold quite this open and personal before, anxious to talk about a life that had existed far beyond the limits of Fletcher's friendship. "She's coming back," Leopold said simply, and it took Fletcher an instant to grasp the meaning of his words.

"Your wife is coming back?"

"My ex-wife."

"Here? What for?"

Leopold sighed and played with the little bag of sugar that Fletcher had given him with his coffee. "Her niece is getting married. Our niece."

"I never knew you had one."

"She's been away at college. Her name is Vicki Nelson, and she's marrying a young lawyer named Moore. And Monica is coming back east for the wedding."

"I never even knew her name," Fletcher observed, taking a sip of his coffee. "Haven't you seen her since the divorce?"

Leopold shook his head. "Not for fifteen years. It was a funny thing. She wanted to be a movie star, and I guess fifteen years ago lots of girls still thought about being movie stars. Monica was intelligent and very pretty—but probably no prettier than hundreds of other girls who used to turn up in Hollywood every year back in those days. I was just starting on the police force then, and the future looked pretty bright for me here. It would have been foolish of me to toss up everything just to chase her wild dream out to California. Well, pretty soon it got to be an obsession with her, really bad. She'd spend her afternoons in movie theaters and her evenings watching old films on television. Finally, when I still refused to go west with her, she just left me."

"Just walked out?"

Leopold nodded. "It was a blessing, really, that we didn't have children. I heard she got a few minor jobs out there—as an extra, and some technical stuff behind the scenes. Then apparently she had a nervous breakdown. About a year later I received the official word that she'd divorced me. I heard that she recovered and was back working, and I think she had another marriage that didn't work out."

"Why would she come back for the wedding?"

"Vicki is her niece and also her godchild. We were just married when Vicki was born, and I suppose Monica might consider her the child we never had. In any event, I know she still hates me and blames me for everything that's gone wrong with her life. She told a friend once a few years ago she wished I were dead."

"Do you have to go to this wedding, too, Captain?"

"Of course. If I stayed away it would be only because of her. At least I have to drop by the reception for a few minutes." Leopold smiled ruefully. "I guess that's why I'm telling you all this, Fletcher. I want a favor from you."

"Anything, Captain. You know that."

"I know it seems like a childish thing to do, but I'd like you to come out there with me. I'll tell them I'm working and that I can only stay for a few minutes. You can wait outside in the car if you want. At least they'll see you there and believe my excuse."

Fletcher could see the importance of it to Leopold, and the effort that had gone into the asking. "Sure," he said. "Be glad to. When is it?"

"This Saturday. The reception's in the afternoon, at Sunset Farms."

Leopold had been to Sunset Farms only once before, at the wedding of a patrolman whom he'd especially liked. It was a low rambling place at the end of a paved driveway, overlooking a wooded valley and a gently flowing creek. If it had ever been a farm, that day was long past; but for wedding receptions and retirement parties it was the ideal place. The interior of the main building was, in reality, one huge square room, divided by accordion doors to make up to four smaller square rooms.

For the wedding of Vicki Nelson and Ted Moore three quarters of the large room was in use, with only the last set of accordion doors pulled shut its entire width and locked. The wedding party occupied a head table along one wall, with smaller tables scattered around the room for the families and friends. When Leopold entered the place at five minutes of two on Saturday afternoon, the hired combo was just beginning to play music for dancing.

He watched for a moment while Vicki stood, radiant, and allowed her new husband to escort her to the center of the floor. Ted Moore was a bit older than Leopold had expected, but as the pair glided slowly across the floor, he could find no visible fault with the match. He helped himself to a glass of champagne punch and stood ready to intercept them as they left the dance floor.

"It's Captain Leopold, isn't it?" someone asked. A face from his past loomed up, a tired man with a gold tooth in the front of his smile. "I'm Immy Fontaine, Monica's stepbrother."

"Sure," Leopold said, as if he'd remembered the man all along. Monica had rarely mentioned Immy, and Leopold recalled meeting him once or twice at family gatherings. But the sight of him now, gold tooth and all, reminded Leopold that Monica was somewhere nearby, that he might confront her at any moment.

"We're so glad you could come," someone else said, and he turned to greet the bride and groom as they came off the dance floor. Up close, Vicki was a truly beautiful girl, clinging to her new husband's arm like a proper bride.

"I wouldn't have missed it for anything," he said.

"This is Ted," she said, making the introductions. Leopold shook his hand, silently approving the firm grip and friendly eyes.

"I understand you're a lawyer," Leopold said, making conversation.

"That's right, sir. Mostly civil cases, though. I don't tangle much with criminals."

They chatted for a few more seconds before the pressure of guests broke them apart. The luncheon was about to be served, and the more hungry ones were already lining up at the buffet tables. Vicki and Ted went over to start the line, and Leopold took another glass of champagne punch.

"I see the car waiting outside," Immy Fontaine said, moving in again. "You got to go on duty?"

Leopold nodded. "Just this glass and I have to leave."

"Monica's in from the West Coast."

"So I heard."

A slim man with a mustache jostled against him in the crush of the crowd and hastily apologized. Fontaine seized the man by the arm and introduced him to Leopold. "This here's Dr. Felix Thursby. He came east with Monica. Doc, I want you to meet Captain Leopold, her ex-husband."

Leopold shook hands awkwardly, embarrassed for the man and for himself. "A fine wedding," he mumbled. "Your first trip east?"

Thursby shook his head. "I'm from New York. Long ago."

"I was on the police force there once," Leopold remarked.

They chatted for a few more minutes before Leopold managed to edge away through the crowd.

"Leaving so soon?" a harsh unforgettable voice asked.

"Hello, Monica. It's been a long time."

He stared down at the handsome, middle-aged woman who now blocked his path to the door. She had gained a little weight, especially in the bosom, and her hair was graying. Only the eyes startled him, and frightened him just a bit. They had the intense wild look he'd seen before on the faces of deranged criminals.

"I didn't think you'd come. I thought you'd be afraid of me," she said.

"That's foolish. Why should I be afraid of you?"

The music had started again, and the line from the buffet tables was beginning to snake lazily about the room. But for Leopold and Monica they might have been alone in the middle of a desert.

"Come in here," she said, "where we can talk." She motioned toward the end of the room that had been cut off by the accordion doors. Leopold followed her, helpless to do anything else. She unlocked the doors and pulled them apart, just wide enough for them to enter the unused quarter of the large room. Then she closed and locked the doors behind them, and stood facing him. They were two people, alone in a bare unfurnished room.

They were in an area about thirty feet square, with the windows at the far end and the locked accordion doors at Leopold's back. He could see the afternoon sun cutting through the trees outside, and the gentle hum of the air-conditioner came through above the subdued murmur of the wedding guests.

"Remember the day we got married?" she asked.

"Yes. Of course."

She walked to the middle window, running her fingers along the frame, perhaps looking for the latch to open it. But it stayed closed as she faced him again. "Our marriage was as drab and barren as this room. Lifeless, unused!"

"Heaven knows I always wanted children, Monica."

"You wanted nothing but your damned police work!" she shot back, eyes flashing as her anger built.

"Look, I have to go. I have a man waiting in the car."

"Go! That's what you did before, wasn't it? *Go, go!* Go out to your damned job and leave me to struggle for myself. Leave me to—"

"You walked out on me, Monica. Remember?" he reminded her softly. She was so defenseless, without even a purse to swing at him.

"Sure I did! Because I had a career waiting for me! I had all the world waiting for me! And you know what happened because you wouldn't come along? You know what happened to me out there? They took my money and my self-respect and what virtue I had left. They made me into a tramp, and when they were done they locked me up in a mental hospital for three years. Three years!"

"I'm sorry."

"Every day while I was there I thought about you. I thought about how it would be when I got out. Oh, I thought. And planned. And schemed. You're a big detective now. Sometimes your cases even get reported in the California papers." She was pacing back and forth, caged, dangerous. "Big detective. But I can still destroy you just as you destroyed me!"

He glanced over his shoulder at the locked accordion doors, seeking a way out. It was a thousand times worse than he'd imagined it would be. She was mad—mad and vengeful and terribly dangerous. "You should see a doctor, Monica."

Her eyes closed to mere slits. "I've seen doctors." Now she paused before the middle window, facing him. "I came all the way east for this day, because I thought you'd be here. It's so much better than your apartment, or your office, or a city street. There are one hundred and fifty witnesses on the other side of those doors."

"What in hell are you talking about?"

Her mouth twisted in a horrible grin. "You're going to know what I knew. Bars and cells and disgrace. You're going to know the despair I felt all those years."

"Monica—"

At that instant perhaps twenty feet separated them. She lifted one arm, as if to shield herself, then screamed in terror. "No! Oh, God, no!"

Leopold stood frozen, unable to move, as a sudden gunshot echoed through the room. He saw the bullet strike her in the chest, toppling her backward like the blow from a giant fist. Then somehow he had his own gun out of its belt holster and he swung around toward the doors.

They were still closed and locked. He was alone in the room with Monica.

He looked back to see her crumple on the floor, blood spreading in a widening circle around the torn black hole in her dress. His eyes went to the windows, but all three were still closed and unbroken. He shook his head, trying to focus his mind on what had happened.

There was noise from outside, and a pounding on the accordion doors. Someone opened the lock from the other side, and the gap between the doors widened as they were pulled open. "What happened?" someone asked. A woman guest screamed as she saw the body. Another toppled in a faint.

Leopold stepped back, aware of the gun still in his hand, and saw Lieutenant Fletcher fighting his way through the mob of guests. "Captain, what is it?"

"She—Someone shot her."

Fletcher reached out and took the gun from Leopold's hand—carefully, as one might take a broken toy from a child. He put it to his nose and sniffed, then opened the cylinder to inspect the bullets. "It's been fired recently, Captain. One shot." Then his eyes seemed to cloud over, almost to the point of tears. "Why the hell did you do it?" he asked. "Why?"

Leopold saw nothing of what happened then. He only had vague and splintered memories of someone examining her and saying she was still alive, of an ambulance and much confusion. Fletcher drove him down to headquarters, to the commissioner's office, and he sat there and waited, running his moist palms up and down his trousers. He was not surprised when they told him she had died on the way to Southside Hospital. Monica had never been one to do things by halves.

The men—the detectives who worked under him—came to and left the commissioner's office, speaking in low tones with their heads together, occasionally offering him some embarrassed gesture of condolence. There was an aura of sadness over the place, and Leopold knew it was for him.

"You have nothing more to tell us, Captain?" the commissioner asked. "I'm making it as easy for you as I can."

"I didn't kill her," Leopold insisted again. "It was someone else."

"Who? How?"

He could only shake his head. "I wish I knew. I think in some mad way she killed herself, to get revenge on me."

"She shot herself with *your* gun, while it was in *your* holster, and while *you* were standing twenty feet away?"

Leopold ran a hand over his forehead. "It couldn't have been my gun. Ballistics will prove that."

"But your gun had been fired recently, and there was an empty cartridge in the chamber."

"I can't explain that. I haven't fired it since the other day at target practice, and I reloaded it afterwards."

"Could she have hated you that much, Captain?" Fletcher asked. "To frame you for her murder?"

"She could have. I think she was a very sick woman. If I did that to her—if I was the one who made her sick—I suppose I deserve what's happening to me now."

"The hell you do," Fletcher growled. "If you say you're innocent, Captain, I'm sticking by you." He began pacing again and finally turned to the commissioner. "How about giving him a paraffin test, to see if he's fired a gun recently?"

The commissioner shook his head. "We haven't used that in years. You know how unreliable it is, Fletcher. Many people have nitrates or nitrites on their hands. They can pick them up from dirt, or fertilizers, or fireworks, or urine, or even from simply handling peas or beans. Anyone who smokes tobacco can have deposits on his hands. There are some newer tests for the presence of barium or lead, but we don't have the necessary chemicals for those."

Leopold nodded. The commissioner had risen through the ranks. He wasn't simply a political appointee, and the men had always respected him. Leopold respected him. "Wait for the ballistics report," he said. "That'll clear me."

So they waited. It was another forty-five minutes before the phone rang and the commissioner spoke to the ballistics man. He listened, and grunted, and asked one or two questions. Then he hung up and faced Leopold across the desk.

"The bullet was fired from your gun," he said simply. "There's no possibility of error. I'm afraid we'll have to charge you with homicide."

The routines he knew so well went on into Saturday evening, and when they were finished Leopold was escorted from the courtroom to find young Ted Moore waiting for him. "You should be on your honeymoon," Leopold told him.

"Vicki couldn't leave till I'd seen you and tried to help. I don't know much about criminal law, but perhaps I could arrange bail."

"That's already been taken care of," Leopold said. "The grand jury will get the case next week."

"I—I don't know what to say. Vicki and I are both terribly sorry."

"So am I." He started to walk away, then turned back. "Enjoy your honeymoon."

"We'll be in town overnight, at the Towers, if there's anything I can do."

Leopold nodded and kept on walking. He could see the reflection of his guilt in young Moore's eyes. As he got to his car, one of the patrolmen he knew glanced his way and then quickly in the other direction. On a Saturday night no one talked to wife murderers. Even Fletcher had disappeared.

Leopold decided he couldn't face the drab walls of his office, not with people avoiding him. Besides, the commissioner had been forced to suspend him from active duty pending grand-jury action and the possible trial. The office didn't even belong to him anymore. He cursed silently and drove home to his little apartment, weaving through the dark streets with one eye out for a patrol car. He wondered if they'd be watching him, to prevent his jumping bail. He wondered what he'd have done in the commissioner's shoes.

The eleven-o'clock news on television had it as the lead item, illustrated with a black-and-white photo of him taken during a case last year. He shut off the television without listening to their comments and went back outside, walking down to the corner for an early edition of the Sunday paper. The front-page headline was as bad as he'd expected: DETECTIVE CAPTAIN HELD IN SLAYING OF EX-WIFE.

On the way back to his apartment, walking slowly, he tried to remember what she'd been like—not that afternoon, but before the divorce. He tried to remember her face on their wedding day, her soft laughter on their honeymoon. But all he could remember were those mad vengeful eyes. And the bullet ripping into her chest.

Perhaps he had killed her after all. Perhaps the gun had come into his hand so easily he never realized it was there.

"Hello, Captain."

"I—Fletcher! What are you doing here?"

"Waiting for you. Can I come in?"

"Well . . ."

"I've got a six-pack of beer. I thought you might want to talk about it."

Leopold unlocked his apartment door. "What's there to talk about?"

"If you say you didn't kill her, Captain, I'm willing to listen to you."

Fletcher followed him into the tiny kitchen and popped open two of the beer cans. Leopold accepted one of them and dropped into the nearest chair. He felt utterly exhausted, drained of even the strength to fight back.

"She framed me, Fletcher," he said quietly. "She framed me as neatly as anything I've ever seen. The thing's impossible, but she did it."

"Let's go over it step by step, Captain. Look, the way I see it there are only three possibilities: Either you shot her, she shot herself, or someone else shot her. I think we can rule out the last one. The three windows were locked on the outside and unbroken, the room was bare of any hiding place, and the only entrance was through the accordion doors. These were closed and locked, and although they could have been opened from the other side, you certainly would have seen or heard it happen. Besides, there were one hundred and fifty wedding guests on the other side of those doors. No one could have unlocked and opened them and then fired the shot, all without being seen."

Leopold shook his head. "But it's just as impossible that she could have shot herself. I was watching her every minute. I never looked away once. There was nothing in her hands, not even a purse. And the gun that shot her was in my holster, on my belt. I never drew it till *after* the shot was fired."

Fletcher finished his beer and reached for another can. "I didn't look at her close, Captain, but the size of the hole in her dress and the powder burns point to a contact wound. The medical examiner agrees, too. She was shot from no more than an inch or two away. There were grains of powder in the wound itself, though the bleeding had washed most of them away."

"But she had nothing in her hand," Leopold repeated. "And there was nobody standing in front of her with a gun. Even I was twenty feet away."

"The thing's impossible, Captain."

Leopold grunted. "Impossible—unless I killed her."

Fletcher stared at his beer. "How much time do we have?"

"If the grand jury indicts me for first-degree murder, I'll be in a cell by next week."

Fletcher frowned at him. "What's with you, Captain? You almost act resigned to it! Hell, I've seen more fight in you on a routine holdup!"

"I guess that's it, Fletcher. The fight is gone out of me. She's drained every drop out of me. She's had her revenge."

Fletcher sighed and stood up. "Then I guess there's really nothing I can do for you, Captain. Good night."

Leopold didn't see him to the door. He simply sat there, hunched over the table. For the first time in his life he felt like an old man.

Leopold slept late Sunday morning and awakened with the odd sensation that it had all been a dream. He remembered feeling the same way when he'd broken his wrist chasing a burglar. In the morning, on just awakening, the memory of the heavy cast had always been a dream, until he moved his arm. Now, rolling over in his narrow bed, he saw the Sunday paper where he'd tossed it the night before. The headline was still the same. The dream was a reality.

He got up and showered and dressed, reaching for his holster out of habit before he remembered he no longer had a gun. Then he sat at the kitchen table staring at the empty beer cans, wondering what he would do with his day. With his life.

The doorbell rang and it was Fletcher. "I didn't think I'd be seeing you again," Leopold mumbled, letting him in.

Fletcher was excited, and the words tumbled out of him almost before he was through the door. "I think I've got something, Captain! It's not much, but it's a start. I was down at headquarters first thing this morning, and I got hold of the dress Monica was wearing when she was shot."

Leopold looked blank. "The dress?"

Fletcher was busy unwrapping the package he'd brought. "The commissioner would have my neck if he knew I brought this to you, but look at this hole!"

Leopold studied the jagged, blood-caked rent in the fabric. "It's large," he observed, "but with a near-contact wound the powder burns would cause that."

"Captain, I've seen plenty of entrance wounds made by a thirty-eight slug. I've even caused a few of them. But I never saw one that looked like this. Hell, it's not even round!"

"What are you trying to tell me, Fletcher?" Suddenly something stirred inside him. The juices were beginning to flow again.

"The hole in her dress is much larger and more jagged than the corresponding wound in her chest, Captain. That's what I'm telling you. The bullet that killed her couldn't have made this hole. No way! And that means maybe she wasn't killed when we thought she was."

Leopold grabbed the phone and dialed the familiar number of the Towers Hotel. "I hope they slept late this morning."

"Who?"

"The honeymooners." He spoke sharply into the phone, giving the switchboard operator the name he wanted, and then waited. It was a full minute before he heard Ted Moore's sleepy voice answering on the other end. "Ted, this is Leopold. Sorry to bother you."

The voice came alert at once. "That's all right, Captain. I told you to call if there was anything—"

"I think there is. You and Vicki between you must have a pretty good idea of who was invited to the wedding. Check with her and tell me how many doctors were on the invitation list."

Ted Moore was gone for a few moments and then he returned. "Vicki says you're the second person who asked her that?"

"Oh? Who was the first?"

"Monica. The night before the wedding, when she arrived in town with Dr. Thursby. She casually asked if he'd get to meet any other doctors at the reception. But Vicki told her he was the only one. Of course we hadn't invited him, but as a courtesy to Monica we urged him to come."

"Then after the shooting, it was Thursby who examined her? No one else?"

"He was the only doctor. He told us to call an ambulance and rode to the hospital with her."

"Thank you, Ted. You've been a big help."

"I hope so, Captain."

Leopold hung up and faced Fletcher. "That's it. She worked it with this guy Thursby. Can you put out an alarm for him?"

"Sure can," Fletcher said. He took the telephone and dialed the unlisted squad-room number. "Dr. Felix Thursby? Is that his name?"

"That's it. The only doctor there, the only one who could help Monica with her crazy plan of revenge."

Fletcher completed issuing orders and hung up the phone. "They'll check his hotel and call me back."

"Get the commissioner on the phone, too. Tell him what we've got."

Fletcher started to dial and then stopped, his finger in mid-air. "What *have* we got, Captain?"

The commissioner sat behind his desk, openly unhappy at being called to headquarters on a Sunday afternoon, and listened bleakly to what Leopold and Fletcher had to tell him. Finally he spread his fingers on the desktop and said, "The mere fact that this Dr. Thursby seems to have left town is hardly proof of his guilt, Captain. What you're saying is that the woman wasn't killed until later—that Thursby killed her in the ambulance. But how could he have done that with a pistol that was already in Lieutenant Fletcher's possession, tagged as evidence? And how could he have fired the fatal shot without the ambulance attendants hearing it?"

"I don't know," Leopold admitted.

"Heaven knows, Captain, I'm willing to give you every reasonable chance to prove your innocence. But you have to bring me more than a dress with a hole in it."

"All right," Leopold said. "I'll bring you more."

"The grand jury gets the case this week, Captain."

"I know," Leopold said. He turned and left the office, with Fletcher tailing behind.

"What now?" Fletcher asked.

"We go talk to Immy Fontaine, my ex-wife's stepbrother."

Though he'd never been friendly with Fontaine, Leopold knew where to find him. The tired man with the gold tooth lived in a big old house overlooking the Sound, where on this summer Sunday they found him in the back yard, cooking hot dogs over a charcoal fire.

He squinted into the sun and said, "I thought you'd be in jail, after what happened."

"I didn't kill her," Leopold said quietly.

"Sure you didn't."

"For a stepbrother you seem to be taking her death right in stride," Leopold observed, motioning toward the fire.

"I stopped worrying about Monica fifteen years ago."

"What about this man she was with? Dr. Thursby?"

Immy Fontaine chuckled. "If he's a doctor I'm a plumber! He has the fingers of a surgeon, I'll admit, but when I asked him about my son's radius that he broke skiing, Thursby thought it was a leg bone. What the hell, though, I was never one to judge Monica's love life. Remember, I didn't even object when she married you."

"Nice of you. Where's Thursby staying while he's in town?"

"He was at the Towers with Monica."

"He's not there anymore."

"Then I don't know where he's at. Maybe he's not even staying for her funeral."

"What if I told you Thursby killed Monica?"

He shrugged. "I wouldn't believe you, but then I wouldn't particularly care. If you were smart you'd have killed her fifteen years ago when she walked out on you. That's what I'd have done."

Leopold drove slowly back downtown, with Fletcher grumbling beside him. "Where are we, Captain? It seems we're just going in circles."

"Perhaps we are, Fletcher, but right now there are still too many questions to be answered. If we can't find Thursby I'll have to tackle it from another direction. The bullet, for instance."

"We're agreed it could not have been fired by my gun, either while it was in my holster or later, while Thursby was in the ambulance with Monica. Therefore, it must have been fired earlier. The last time I fired it was at target practice. Is there any possibility—any chance at all—that Thursby or Monica could have gotten one of the slugs I fired into that target?"

Fletcher put a damper on it. "Captain, we were both firing at the same target. No one could sort out those bullets and say which came from your pistol and which from mine. Besides, how would either of them gain access to the basement target range at police headquarters?"

"I could have an enemy in the department," Leopold said.

"Nuts! We've all got enemies, but the thing is still impossible. If you believe people in the department are plotting against you, you might as well believe that the entire ballistics evidence was faked."

"It was, somehow. Do you have the comparison photos?"

"They're back at the office. But with the narrow depth of field you can probably tell more from looking through the microscope yourself."

Fletcher drove him to the lab, where they persuaded the Sunday-duty officer to let them have a look at the bullets. While Fletcher and the officer stood by in the interests of propriety, Leopold squinted through the microscope at the twin chunks of lead.

"The death bullet is pretty battered," he observed, but he had to admit that the rifling marks were the same. He glanced at the identification tag attached to the test bullet: *Test slug fired from Smith & Wesson .38 Revolver, serial number 2420547.*

Leopold turned away with a sigh, then turned back.

*2420547.*

He fished into his wallet and found his pistol permit. *Smith & Wesson 2421622.*

"I remembered those two's on the end," he told Fletcher. "That's not my gun."

"It's the one I took from you, Captain. I'll swear to it!"

"And I believe you, Fletcher. But it's the one fact I needed. It tells me how Dr. Thursby managed to kill Monica in a locked room before my very eyes, with a gun that was in my holster at the time. And it just might tell us where to find the elusive Dr. Thursby."

By Monday morning Leopold had made six long-distance calls to California, working from his desk telephone while Fletcher used the squad-room phone. Then, a little before noon, Leopold, Fletcher, the commissioner, and a man from the district attorney's office took a car and drove up to Boston.

"You're sure you've got it figured?" the commissioner asked Leopold for the third time. "You know we shouldn't allow you to cross the state line while awaiting grand-jury action."

"Look, either you trust me or you don't," Leopold snapped. Behind the wheel Fletcher allowed himself a slight smile, but the man from the D.A.'s office was deadly serious.

"The whole thing is so damned complicated," the commissioner grumbled.

"My ex-wife was a complicated woman. And remember, she had fifteen years to plan it."

"Run over it for us again," the D.A.'s man said.

Leopold sighed and started talking. "The murder gun wasn't mine. The gun I pulled after the shot was fired, the one Fletcher took from me, had been planted on me sometime before."

"How?"

"I'll get to that. Monica was the key to it all, of course. She hated me so much that her twisted brain planned her own murder in order to get revenge on me. She planned it in such a way that it would have been impossible for anyone but me to have killed her."

"Only a crazy woman would do such a thing."

"I'm afraid she was crazy—crazy for vengeance. She set up the entire plan for the afternoon of the wedding reception, but I'm sure they had an alternate in case I hadn't gone to it. She wanted some place where there'd be lots of witnesses."

"Tell them how she worked the bullet hitting her," Fletcher urged.

"Well, that was the toughest part for me. I actually saw her shot before my eyes. I saw the bullet hit her and I saw the blood. Yet I was alone in a locked room with her. There was no hiding place, no opening from which a person or even a mechanical device could have fired the bullet at her. To you people it seemed I must be guilty, especially when the bullet came from the gun I was carrying.

"But I looked at it from a different angle—once Fletcher forced me to look at it at all! I *knew* I hadn't shot her, and since no one else physically could have, I knew no one did! If Monica was killed by a thirty-eight slug, it must have been fired *after* she was taken from that locked room. Since she was dead on arrival at the hospital, the most likely time for her murder—to me, at least—became the time of the ambulance ride, when Dr. Thursby must have hunched over her with careful solicitousness."

"But you *saw* her shot!"

"That's one of the two reasons Fletcher and I were on the phones to Hollywood this morning. My ex-wife worked in pictures, at times in the technical end of movie-making. On the screen there are a number of ways to simulate a person being shot. An early method was a sort of compressed-air gun fired at the actor from just off-camera. These days, especially in the bloodiest of the Western and war films, they use a tiny explosive charge fitted under the actor's clothes. Of course the body is protected from burns, and the force of it is directed outward. A pouch of fake blood is released by the explosion, adding to the realism of it."

"And this is what Monica did?"

Leopold nodded. "A call to her Hollywood studio confirmed the fact that she worked on a film using this device. I noticed when I met her that she'd gained weight around the bosom, but I never thought to attribute it to the padding and the explosive device. She triggered it when she raised her arm as she screamed at me."

"Any proof?"

"The hole in her dress was just too big to be an entrance hole from a thirty-eight, even fired at close range—too big and too ragged. I can thank Fletcher for spotting that. This morning the lab technicians ran a test on the bloodstains. Some of it was her blood, the rest was chicken blood."

"She was a good actress to fool all those people."

"She knew Dr. Thursby would be the first to examine her. All she had to do was fall over when the explosive charge ripped out the front of her dress."

"What if there had been another doctor at the wedding?"

Leopold shrugged. "Then they would have postponed it. They couldn't take that chance."

"And the gun?"

"I remembered Thursby bumping against me when I first met him. He took my gun and substituted an identical weapon—identical, that is, except for the serial number. He'd fired it just a short time earlier, to complete the illusion. When I drew it I simply played into their hands. There I was, the only person in the room with an apparently dying woman, and a gun that had just been fired."

"But what about the bullet that killed her?"

"Rifling marks on slugs are made by the lands in the rifled barrel of a gun causing grooves in the lead of a bullet. A bullet fired through a smooth tube has no rifling marks."

"What in hell kind of gun has a smooth tube for a barrel?" the commissioner asked.

"A homemade one, like a zip gun. Highly inaccurate, but quite effective when the gun is almost touching the skin of the victim. Thursby fired a shot from the pistol he was to plant on me, probably into a pillow or some other place where he could retrieve the undamaged slug. Then he reused the rifled slug on another cartridge and fired it with his homemade zip gun, right into Monica's heart. The original rifling marks were still visible and no new ones were added."

"The ambulance driver and attendant didn't hear the shot?"

"They would have stayed up front, since he was a doctor riding with a patient. It gave him a chance to get the padded explosive mechanism off her chest, too. Once that was away, I imagine he leaned over her, muffling the zip gun as best he could, and fired the single shot that killed her. Remember, an ambulance on its way to a hospital is a pretty noisy place—it has a siren going all the time."

They were entering downtown Boston now, and Leopold directed Fletcher to a hotel near the Common. "I still don't believe the part about switching the guns," the D.A.'s man objected. "You mean to tell me he undid the strap over your gun, got out the gun, and substituted another one—all without your knowing it?"

Leopold smiled. "I mean to tell you only one type of person could have managed it—an expert, professional pickpocket. The type you see occasionally doing an act in nightclubs and on television. That's how I knew where to find him. We called all over southern California till we came up with someone who knew Monica and knew she'd dated a man named Thompson who had a pickpocket act. We called Thompson's agent and discovered he's playing a split week at a Boston lounge, and is staying at this hotel."

"What if he couldn't have managed it without your catching on? Or what if you hadn't been wearing your gun?"

"Most detectives wear their guns off-duty. If I hadn't been, or if he couldn't get it, they'd simply have changed their plan. He must have signaled her when he'd safely made the switch."

"Here we are," Fletcher said. "Let's go up."

The Boston police had two men waiting to meet them, and they went up in the elevator to the room registered in the name of Max Thompson. Fletcher knocked on the door, and when it opened, the familiar face of Felix Thursby appeared. He no longer wore the mustache, but he had the same slim surgeonlike fingers that Immy Fontaine had noticed. Not a doctor's fingers, but a pickpocket's.

"We're taking you in for questioning," Fletcher said, and the Boston detectives issued the standard warnings of his legal rights.

Thursby blinked his tired eyes at them and grinned a bit when he recognized Leopold. "She said you were smart. She said you were a smart cop."

"Did you have to kill her?" Leopold asked.

"I didn't. I just held the gun there and she pulled the trigger herself. She did it all herself, except for switching the guns. She hated you that much."

"I know," Leopold said quietly, staring at something far away. "But I guess she must have hated herself just as much."

## *Study questions*

1. *How much characterization does Hoch employ in this story? Are the characters also symbols?* 2. *How significant is the setting?* 3. *How is suspense initiated and maintained? What kinds of foreshadowing are present?* 4. *Who is the protagonist in this story?* 5. *What role does Fletcher play?*

*Shirley Ann Grau* (b. 1929), born in New Orleans, Louisiana, now maintains a permanent residence in a suburb near that city. Grau attended Newcomb College, graduating in 1950, then completed two years of postgraduate work at Tulane University. She has taught fiction in schools of the area and lectures around the country. Her short stories were first published in such magazines and periodicals as the *New Yorker*, *New World Writing*, and the *New Mexico Quarterly*. The publication of *The Black Prince and Other Stories* (1955) brought her immediate literary recognition. Another collection of stories, *The Wind Shifting West*, was published in 1973. Her novels include *The Hard Blue Sky* (1958), *The House on Coliseum Street* (1961), the Pulitzer Prize–winning *The Keepers of the House* (1964), *The Condor Passes* (1971), and *Evidence of Love* (1977). Her writing is characterized by a multiplicity of viewpoints, a dense texture, and a style that shifts according to the subject matter. Her work can be crisp, sparse, brittle, or poetic and evocative. "The Black Prince" was written while she was a student at Tulane. A brilliant story, it is all lyricism.

## THE BLACK PRINCE

*"How art thou fallen from heaven,*
*O Lucifer, son of the morning!"*

Winters are short and very cold; sometimes there is even a snow like heavy frost on the ground. Summers are powdery hot; the white ball sun goes rolling around and around in a sky behind the smoke from the summer fires. There is always a burning somewhere in summer; the pines are dry and waiting; the sun itself starts the smoldering. A pine fire is quiet; there is only a kind of rustle from the flames inside the trunks until the branches and needles go up with a whistling. A whole hill often burns that way, its smoke rising straight up to the white sun, and quiet.

In the plowed patches, green things grow quickly: the ground is rich and there are underground rivers. But there are no big farms: only patches of corn, green beans, and a field or two of cotton (grown for a little cash to spend on Saturdays at Luther's General Store or Willie's Café; these are the only two places for forty miles in any direction). There is good pasture: the green places along the hillsides with pines for shade and sure water in the streams that come down from the Smokies to the north; even in the burnt-out land of five seasons back, shrubs are high. But in the whole county there are only fifty cows, gone wild most of them and dry because they were never milked. They are afraid of men and feed in the farthest ridges and the swamps that are the bottoms of some littlest of the valleys. Their numbers are slowly increasing because no one bothers them. Only once in a while some man with a hankering for cow meat takes his rifle and goes after them. But that is not often; the people prefer pork. Each family keeps enough razorbacks in a run of bark palings.

It is all colored people here, and it is the poorest part of the smallest and worst county in the state. The place at the end of the dirt road leading from the state highway, the place where Luther's Store and Willie's Café stand, does not even have a name in the county records.

The only cool time of the summer day is very early, before the mists have shriveled away. There is a breeze then, a good stiff one out of the Smokies. During the day there is no sound: it is dead hot. But in the early mornings, when the breeze from the north is blowing, it is not so lonesomely quiet: crickets and locusts and the birds that flutter about hunting them, calling frantically as if they had something of importance to settle quick before the heat sets in. (By seven they are quiet again, in the invisible places they have chosen to wait out the day.)

A pine cone rattled down on Alberta's head and bounced from her shoulder. She scooped it from the ground and threw it upward through the branches. "You just keep your cone, mister birds. I got no cause to want it." With a pumping of wings the birds were gone, their cries sliding after them, back down the air. "You just yell your head off. I can hit you any time I want. Any time I want." There was a small round piece of granite at her feet and she tossed it, without particular aim, into the biggest of the bay trees: a gray squirrel with a thin rattail tumbled from the branches and peeped at her from behind the trunk with a pointed little rat face. She jammed her hands in the pockets of her dress and went on, swaggering slightly, cool and feeling good.

She was a handsome girl, taller than most people in her part of the county, and light brown—there had been a lot of white blood in her family, back somewhere, they'd forgot where exactly. She was not graceful—not as a woman is—but light on her feet and supple as a man. Her dress, which the sun had bleached to a whitish color, leaving only a trace of pink along the seams, had shrunk out of size for her: it pulled tight across her broad, slightly hunched, muscled back, even though she had left all the front buttons open down to the waist.

As she walked along, the birds were making even more of a row, knocking loose cones and dry pine needles and old broad bay leaves, and twice she stopped, threw back her head, and called up to them: "Crazy fool birds. Can't do nothing to me. Fool jackass birds." Up ahead, a couple of minutes' walk, was the field and the cotton, bursting white out of the brown cups and waiting to be picked. And she did not feel like working. She leaned against a tree, stretching so that the bark crumbled in her fingers, listening to the birds.

Something different was in their calling. She listened, her head bent forward, her eyes closed, as she sorted the sounds. One jay was wrong: its long sustained note ended with the cluck of a quail. No bird did that. Alberta opened her eyes and looked slowly around. But the pines were thick and close and full of blue night shadow and wrapped with fog that moved like bits of cloth in the wind. Leaving the other bird calls, the whistle became distinct, high, soaring, mocking, like some rare bird proudly, insolently.

Alberta moved a few steps out from the tree and turned slowly on her heels. The whistle was going around her now, in slow circles, and she turned with it, keeping her eye on the sound, seeing nothing. The birds were still calling and fluttering in the branches, sending bits of twig and bark tumbling down.

Alberta said: "A fool thing you doing. A crazy fool jackass thing." She sat down on a tumbled pile of bricks that had been the chimney of a sugarhouse burned during the Civil War. She spoke in her best tone, while the whistling went round and round her faster. "I reckon you got nothing better to do than go around messing up folks. You got me so riled up I don't reckon I know what way I'm heading in." The sound went around her and around her, but she held her head steady, talking to the pine directly in front of her. "I don't reckon there's nothing for me but set here till you tires out and goes away." The whistle circled her twice and then abruptly stopped, the last high clear note running off down the breeze. Alberta stood up, pulling down her faded dress. "I am mighty glad you come to stopping. I reckon now I can tell what direction I got to go in."

He was right there, leaning on the same pine she had been staring at, cleaning his front teeth with a little green twig and studying her, and she told him to his face: "That was a crazy mean thing, and you ain't got nothing better to do."

"Reckon not," he said, moving the little green twig in and out of the hole between his lower front teeth.

She pushed her hands in the pockets of her dress and looked him over. "Where you come from?"

"Me?" The little green twig went in and out of his teeth with each breath. "I just come straight out the morning."

She turned and walked away. "I be glad to see you go."

He stood in front of her: he had a way of moving without a sound, of popping up in places. "I be sorry to see you go, Alberta Lacy."

She studied him before she answered: tall, not too big or heavy, and black (no other blood but his own in him, she thought). He was dressed nice—a leather jacket with fringe on the sleeves, a red plaid shirt, and new blue denim pants. "How you know what I'm called?" she asked him politely.

He grinned, and his teeth were white and perfect. "I done seen it in the fire," he said. "I done seen it in the fire and I read it clear: Alberta Lacy."

She frowned. "I don't see as how I understand."

He blew the little green twig out of his mouth. "I might could be seeing you again real soon, Alberta Lacy." Then he slipped around the tree like the last trail of night shadow and disappeared.

Alberta stood listening: only the birds and the insects and the wind. Then everything got quiet, and the sun was shining white all around, and she climbed down the slope to the field.

A little field—just a strip of cotton tucked in between two ridges. Her father and her two biggest brothers had planted it with half a morning's work, and they hadn't gone back to tend it once. They didn't even seem to remember it: whatever work they did was in the older fields closer to home. So Alberta had taken it over. Sometimes she brought along the twins: Sidney and Silvia; they were seven: young enough for her to order around and big enough to be a help. But usually she couldn't find them; they were strange ones, gone out of the house for a couple of days at a time in summer, sleeping out somewhere, always sticking together. They were strange little ones and not worth trouble looking for. So most times Alberta worked with Maggie Mary Evans, who was Josh Evans's daughter and just about the only girl her age she was friendly with. From the field there'd be maybe three bales of real early stuff; and they'd split the profit. They worked all morning, pulling off the bolls and dropping them in the sacks they slung crosswise across their shoulders. They worked very slowly, so slowly that at times their hands seemed hardly to move, dozing in the heat. When it got to be noon, when they had no shadow any more, they slipped off the sacks, leaving them between the furrows, and turned to the shade to eat their lunch.

He was waiting for them there, stretched out along the ground with his head propped up on the slender trunk of a little bay tree. He winked lazily at Alberta; his eyes were big and shiny black as oil. "How you, Miss Alberta Lacy?"

Alberta looked down at him, crooking her lips. "You got nothing to do but pester me?"

"Sure I got something to do, but ain't nothing nice like this."

Alberta looked at him through half-closed lids, then sat down to the lunch.

"You hungry, mister?" Maggie Mary asked. She had stood watching, both hands jammed into the belt of her dress, and her eyes moving from one to the other with the quickness and the color of a sparrow.

The man rolled over and looked up at her. "Reckon I am."

"You can have some of our lunch," Maggie Mary said.

Crazy fool, Alberta thought, standing so close with him on the ground like that. He must can see all the way up her. And from the way he lay there, grinning, he must be enjoying it.

"That real nice," he said to Maggie Mary, and crawled over on his stomach to where the lunch bucket was.

Alberta watched his smooth, black hand reaching into the bucket and suddenly she remembered. "How you called?"

He put a piece of corn bread in his mouth, chewed it briefly, and swallowed it with a gulp. "I got three names."

"No fooling," Maggie Mary said, and giggled in her hand. "I got three names, too."

"Stanley Albert Thompson."

"That a good-sounding name," Alberta said. She began to eat her lunch quickly, her mouth too full to talk. Stanley Albert was staring at her, but she didn't raise her eyes. Then he began to sing, low, pounding time with the flat of his hand against the ground.

*"Alberta, let you hair hang low,*
*Alberta, let you hair hang low,*
*I'll give you more gold than you apron can hold*
*If you just let you hair hang low."*

Alberta got up slowly, not looking at him. "We got work to finish."

Stanley Albert turned over so that his face was pressed in the grass and pine needles. "All you get's the muscles in you arm."

"That right." Maggie Mary nodded quickly. "That right."

"Maggie Mary," Alberta said, "iffen you don't come with me I gonna bop you so hard you land in the middle of tomorrow."

"Good-by, Mr. Stanley Albert Thompson," Maggie Mary said, but he had fallen asleep.

By the time they finished work he was gone; there wasn't even a spot in the pine needles and short grass to show where he had been.

"Ain't that the strangest thing?" Maggie Mary said.

Alberta picked up the small bucket they carried their lunch in. "I reckon not."

"Seemed like he was fixing to wait for us."

"He ain't fixing to wait for nobody, that kind." Alberta rubbed one hand across her shoulders, sighing slightly. "I got a pain fit to kill."

Maggie Mary leaned one arm against a tree and looked off across the little field where they had spent the day. "You reckon he was in here most all morning watching us?"

"Maybe." Alberta began to walk home. Maggie Mary followed slowly, her head still turned, watching the field.

"He musta spent all morning just watching."

"Nothing hard about doing that, watching us break our back out in the sun."

Maggie Mary took one long, loping step and came up with Alberta. "You reckon he coming back?"

Alberta stared full at her, head bent, chewing on her lower lip. "Maggie Mary Evans," she said, "you might could get a thought that he might be wanting you and you might could get a thought that you be wanting him—"

Maggie Mary bent down and brushed the dust off her bare feet carefully, not answering.

"You a plain crazy fool." Alberta planted both hands on her hips and bent her body forward slightly. "A plain crazy fool. You wouldn't be forgetting Jay Mastern?" Jay Mastern had gone off to Ramsey to work at the mill and never come back, but left Maggie Mary to have his baby. So one day Maggie Mary took her pa's best mule and put a blanket on it for a saddle and rode over to Blue Goose Lake, where the old woman lived who could tell her what to do. The old woman gave her medicine in a beer can: whisky and calomel and other things that were a secret. Maggie Mary took the medicine in one gulp, because it tasted so bad, waded way out into Blue Goose Lake so that the water came up to her neck, then dripping wet got up on the mule and whipped him up to a good fast pace all the way home. The baby had come off all right: there wasn't one. And Maggie Mary nearly died. It was something on to three months before she was able to do more than walk around, her arms hanging straight down and stiff and her black skin overtinged with gray.

"You wouldn't be forgetting Jay Mastern?"

"Sure," Maggie Mary said, brushing the dust off her bare feet lightly. "I clean forgot about him."

"Don't you be having nothing to do with this here Stanley Albert Thompson."

Maggie Mary began to walk again, slowly, smiling, just a little bit with one corner of her mouth. "Sounds like you been thinking about him for yourself."

Alberta jammed both hands down in the pockets of her dress. "I been thinking nothing of the sort."

"Willie'll kill him."

Alberta chewed on one finger. "I reckon he could care for himself."

Maggie Mary smiled to herself softly, remembering. "I reckon he could; he's real fine-appearing man."

"He was dressed good."

"Where you reckon he come from?" Maggie Mary asked.

Alberta shrugged. "He just come walking out of the morning fog."

That was how he came into this country: he appeared one day whistling a bird call in the woods in high summer. And he stayed on. The very first Saturday night he went down to Willie's and had four fights and won them all.

Willie's was an ordinary house made of pine slabs, older than most of the other houses, but more solid. There were two rooms: a little one where Willie lived (a heavy scrolled ironwork bed, a square oak dresser, a chest, a three-footed table, and on its cracked marble top a blue-painted mandolin without strings). And a big room: the café. Since anybody could remember, the café had been there with Willie's father or his grandfather, as long as there had been people in these parts. And that had been a long while: long before the Civil War even, runaways were settling here, knowing they'd be safe and hidden in the rough, uneven hills and the pines.

Willie had made some changes in the five or six years since his father died. He painted the counter that was the bar with varnish; that had not been a good idea: the whisky took the varnish off in a few weeks. And he painted the walls: bright blue. Then he went over them again, shaking his brush so that the walls were flecked like a mockingbird's eggs. But Willie used red to fleck—red against blue. And the mirror, gilt-edged, and hanging from a thick gold cord: that had been Willie's idea, too. He'd found it one day, lying on the shoulder alongside the state highway; it must have fallen from a truck somehow. So he took it home. It was cracked in maybe two dozen pieces. Anyone who looked into it would see his face split up into a dozen different parts, all separate. But Willie hung it right over the shelves where he kept his whisky and set one of the kerosene lamps in front of it so that the light would reflect yellow-bright from all the pieces. One of them fell out (so that Willie had to glue it back with flour and water) the night Stanley Albert had his fourth fight, which he won like the other three. Not a man in the country would stand up like that, because fighting at Willie's on Saturday night is a rough affair with razors, or knives, or bottles.

Not a man in the country could have matched the way Stanley Albert fought that night, his shirt off, and his black body shining with sweat, the muscles along his neck and shoulders twisting like grass snakes. There wasn't a finer-looking man and there wasn't a better: he proved that.

The first three fights were real orderly affairs. Everybody could see what was coming minutes ahead, and Willie got the two of them out in the yard before they got at each other. And everybody who was sober enough to walk went out on the porch and watched Stanley Albert pound first Ran Carey's and then Henry Johnson's head up and down in the dust. Alberta sat on the porch (Willie had brought her a chair from inside) and watched Stanley Albert roll around the dust of the yard and didn't even blink an eye, not even during the third fight when Tim Evans, who was Maggie Mary's brother, pulled a razor. The razor got Stanley Albert all down one cheek, but Tim didn't have any teeth left and one side of his face got punched in so that it looked peculiar always afterward. Maggie Mary went running down into the yard, not bothering with her brother, to press her finger up against the little cut across Stanley Albert's cheek.

The fourth fight came up so suddenly nobody had time hardly to get out of the way: Joe Turner got one arm hooked around Stanley Albert's neck from behind. There wasn't any reason for it, except maybe that Joe was so drunk he didn't see who he had and that once there's been a couple of fights there's always more. Stanley Albert swung a bottle over his shoulder to break the hold and then nobody could see exactly what was happening: they were trying so hard to get clear. Willie pulled Alberta over the bar and pushed her down behind it and crouched alongside her, grinning. "That some fighter." And when it was all over they stood up again; first thing they saw was Joe Turner down on the floor and Stanley Albert leaning on a chair with Maggie dabbing at a cut on his hand with the edge of her petticoat.

He got a reputation from that Saturday night, and everybody was polite to him, and he could have had just about any of the girls he wanted. But he didn't seem to want them; at least he never took to coming to the houses to see them or to taking them home from Willie's. Maggie Mary Evans swore up and down that he had got her one day when she was fishing in Scanos River, but nobody paid her much attention. She liked to make up stories that way.

He had a little house in a valley to the east. Some boys who had gone out to shoot a cow for Christmas meat said they saw it. But they didn't go close even if there was three of them with a shotgun while Stanley Albert only carried a razor. Usually people only saw him on Saturday nights, and after a while they got used to him, though none of the men ever got to be friendly with him. There wasn't any mistaking the way the girls watched him. But after four or five Saturdays, by the time the summer was over, everybody expected him and waited for him, the way you'd wait for a storm to come or a freeze: not liking it, but not being able to do anything either. That's the way it went along; he'd buy his food for the coming week at Luther's Store, and then he'd come next door to Willie's.

He never stood up at the counter that was the bar. He'd take his glass and walk over to a table and sit down, and pull out a little bottle from his pocket, and add white lightning to the whisky. There wasn't anything could insult Willie more. He made the whisky and it was the best stuff in the county. He even had some customers drive clear out from Montgomery to buy some of his corn, and, being good stuff, there wasn't any call to add anything: it had enough kick of its own; raw and stinging to the throat. It was good stuff; nobody added anything to it—except Stanley Albert Thompson, while Willie looked at him and said things under his breath. But nothing ever came of it, because everybody remembered how good a job Stanley Albert had done the first night he came.

Stanley Albert always had money, enough of it to pay for the groceries and all the whisky he wanted. There was always the sound of silver jingling in his trouser pocket. Everybody could hear that. Once when Willie was standing behind the bar, shuffling a pack of cards with a wide fancy twirl—just for amusement—Stanley Albert, who had had a couple of drinks and was feeling especially good, got up and pulled a handful of coins out of his pocket. He began to shuffle them through the air, the way Willie had done with the cards. Stanley Albert's black hands flipped the coins back and forth, faster and faster, until there was a solid silver ring hanging and shining in the air. Then Stanley Albert let one of his hands drop to his side and the silver ring poured back into the other hand and disappeared with a little clinking sound. And he dropped the money into his pocket with a short quick laugh.

That was the way Stanley Albert used his money: he had fun with it. Only thing, one night when Stanley Albert had had maybe a bit too much and sat dozing at his table, Morris Henry slipped a hand into the pocket. He wouldn't have ever dared to do that if Stanley Albert hadn't been dozing, leaning back in his chair, the bottle of white lightning empty in one hand. And Morris Henry slipped his little hand in the pocket and felt all around carefully. Then he turned his head slowly in a circle, looked at everybody in the room. He was a little black monkey Negro and his eyes were shiny and flat as mirrors. He slipped his hand back and scurried out into the yard and hid in the blackberry bushes. He wouldn't move until morning came; he just sat there, chewing on his little black fingers with his wide flaring yellow teeth. Anybody who wanted to know what was happening had to go out there and ask him. And ever afterwards Morris Henry swore that there hadn't been anything at all in Stanley Albert Thompson's pocket. But then everybody knew Morris Henry was crazy because just a few minutes later when Stanley Albert woke up and walked across to the bar, the change jingled in the pocket and he laid five quarters on the counter. And the money was good enough because Willie bounced it on the counter and it gave the clear ring of new silver.

Stanley Albert had money all right and he spent it; there wasn't anything short about him. He'd buy drinks for anybody who'd come over to his table; the only ones who came were the girls. And he didn't seem to care how much they drank. He'd just sit there, leaning way back in his chair, grinning, his teeth white and big behind his black lips, and matching them drink for drink, and every now and then running his eye up and down their length just to let them know he was appreciating their figures. Most often it was Maggie Mary who would be sitting there, warning all the other girls away with a little slanting of her eyes when they got near. And sometimes he'd sing a song: a song about whisky that would make everyone forget they didn't like him and laugh; or a song about poor boys who were going to be hanged in the morning. He had a good voice, strong and clear, and he pounded time with the flat of his hand on the table. And he'd always be looking at Alberta when he was singing until she'd get up, holding her head high and stiff, and march over to where Willie was and take hold of his arm real sweet and smile at him. And Willie would give Stanley Albert a quick mean look and then pour her a drink of his best whisky.

Stanley Albert had a watch, a big heavy gold one, round almost as a tomato, that would strike the hours. (That was how you could tell he was around sometimes—hearing his watch strike.) It was attached to a broad black ribbon and sometimes he held it up, let it swing before the eyes of whatever girl it happened to be at the time, let it swing slowly back and forth, up and down, so that her head moved with it. He had a ring too, on his right little finger: a white-colored band with a stone big as a chip of second coal and dark green. And when he fought, the first time he came into Willie's, the ring cut the same as a razor in his hand; it was maybe a little more messy, because its edges were jagged.

Those were two things—the watch and the ring—that must have cost more than all the money around here in a year. That was why all the women liked him so; they kept thinking of the nice things he could give them if he got interested. And that was why the men hated him. Things can go as smooth as glass if everybody's got about the same things and the same amount of money knocking around in a jean pocket on Saturday night. But when they don't, things begin happening. It would have been simpler maybe if they could have fought Stanley Albert Thompson, but there wasn't any man keen to fight him. That was how they started fighting each other. A feud that nobody'd paid any mind to for eight or ten years started up again.

It began on Sunday morning along toward dawn when everyone was feeling tired and leaving Willie's. Stanley Albert had gone out first and was sitting aside the porch railing. Jim Mastern was standing on the lowest step not moving, just staring across the fields, not being able to see anything in the dark, except maybe the bright-colored patterns the whisky set shooting starwise before his eyes. And Randall Stevens was standing in the doorway, looking down at his own foot, which he kept moving in a little circle around and around on the floor boards. And Stanley Albert was looking hard at him. Randall Stevens didn't lift his head; he just had his razor out and was across the porch in one minute, bringing down his arm in a sweeping motion to get at Jim Mastern's neck. But he was too drunk to aim very straight and he missed; but he did cut the ear away so that it fell on the steps. Jim Mastern was off like a bat in the daylight, running fast, crashing into things, holding one hand to the side of his head. And Randall Stevens folded up the razor and slipped it back in his pocket and walked off slowly, his head bent over, as if he was sleepy. There wasn't any more sense to it than that; but it started the feud again.

Stanley Albert swung his legs over the railing and stretched himself and yawned. Nobody noticed except Alberta, they were so busy listening to the way Jim Mastern was screaming and running across the fields, and watching Randall Stevens march off, solemnly, like a priest.

And the next night Randall Stevens tumbled down the steps of his cabin with his head full of scatter shot. It was a Monday night in November. His mother came out to see and stepped square on him, and his blood spattered on the hoar-frost. Randall Stevens had six brothers, and the next night they rode their lanky burred horses five miles south and tried to set fire to the Mastern house. That was the beginning; the fighting kept up, off and on, all through the winter. The sheriff from Gloverston came down to investigate. He came driving down the road in the new shiny white state police patrol car—the only one in the county—stopped in Willie's Café for a drink and went back taking two gallons of home brew with him. That wasn't exactly right, maybe, seeing that he had taken an oath to uphold the law; but he couldn't have done much, except get killed. And that was certain.

The Stevenses and their friends took to coming to Willie's on Friday nights; the Masterns kept on coming on Saturday. That just made two nights Willie had to keep the place open and the lamps filled with kerosene; the crowd was smaller; shotguns were leaning against the wall.

That's the way it went all winter. Everybody got on one side or the other—everybody except Stanley Albert Thompson. They both wanted him: they had seen what he could do in a fight. But Stanley Albert took to coming a night all by himself: Sunday night, and Willie had to light all the lamps for just him and stand behind the counter and watch him sit at the table adding lightning to the whisky.

Once along toward the end of February when Cy Mastern was killed and the roof of his house started burning with pine knots tossed from the ground, Stanley Albert was standing just on the rim of the light, watching. He helped the Masterns carry water, but Ed Stevens, who was hiding up on top of a pine to watch, swore that the water was like kerosene in his hands. Wherever he'd toss a bucketful, the fire would shoot up, brighter and hotter than before.

By March the frosts stopped, and there weren't any more cold winds. The farmers came out every noon, solemnly, and laid their hands on the bare ground to see if it was time to put in their earliest corn and potatoes. But the ground stayed cold a long time that year so that there wasn't any plowing until near May. All during that time from March till May there wasn't anything doing; that was the worst time for the fighting. In the winter your hand shakes so with the cold that you aren't much good with a gun or knife. But by March the air is warmer and you don't have any work to get you tired, so you spend all the time thinking.

That spring things got bad. There wasn't a crowd any more at Willie's though he kept the place open and the lights on for the three nights of the week-end. Neither the Stevenses nor the Masterns would come; they were too easy targets in a house with wall lamps burning. And on Sunday night the only person who ever came was Stanley Albert Thompson. He'd sit and drink his whisky and lightning and maybe sing a song or two for the girls who came over to see him. By the end of April that was changed too. He finally got himself the girl he wanted; the one he'd been waiting around nearly all winter for. And his courting was like this:

Thomas Henry Lacy and his sons, Luke and Tom, had gone for a walk, spoiling for a fight. They hadn't seen anything all evening, just some of the cows that had gone wild and went crashing away through the blueberry bushes. Alberta had taken herself along with them, since she was nearly as good as a man in a fight. They had been on the move all night but keeping in the range of a couple of miles and on the one side of the Scanos River. They were for Stevens and there was no telling what sort of affair the Masterns had rigged up on their ground. They rested for a while on the bluff of the river. Tom had some bread in his pocket and they ate it there, wondering if there was anybody in the laurels across the river just waiting for them to show themselves. Then they walked on again, not saying very much, seeing nothing but the moon flat against the sky and its light shiny on the heavy dew.

Alberta didn't particularly care when they left her behind. She turned her head to listen to the plaintive gargling call of a night quail, and when she looked again her father and the boys were gone. She knew where she was: on the second ridge away from home. There was just the big high ridge there to the left. The house was maybe twenty minutes away, but a hard walk, and Alberta was tired. She'd been washing all day, trying to make the clear brook water carry off the dirt and grease from the clothes, her mother standing behind her, yelling at each spot that remained, her light face black almost as her husband's with temper, and her gray fuzzy hair tied into knots like a pickaninny's. The boys had spent the whole day dozing in the shed while they put a new shoe on the mule.

Alberta listened carefully; there was nothing but night noises; her father and the boys would be halfway home by now, scrambling down the rain-washed sides of the ridge. For a moment she considered following them. "Ain't no raving rush, girl," she told herself aloud. The night was cool, but there wasn't any wind. With her bare feet she felt the dry pine needles, then sat down on them, propping her back against a tree. She slipped the razor from the cord around her neck and held it open loosely in the palm of her hand; then she fell asleep.

She woke when the singing started, opening her eyes but not moving. The moon was right overhead, shining down so that the trunks of the pines stuck straight up out of the white shiny ground. There wasn't a man could hide behind a pine, yet she didn't see him. Only the singing going round and round her.

*"Alberta, what's on you mind,*
*Alberta, why you treat me so unkind?*
*You keep me worried; you keep me blue*
*All the time,*
*Alberta, why you treat me so unkind?"*

She pushed herself up to a sitting position, still looking straight ahead, not following the song around and around. She let the hand that held the razor fall in her lap, so that the moon struck on the blade.

*"Alberta, why you treat me so unkind?"*

Nothing grows under pines, not much grass even, not any bushes big enough to hide a man. Only pine trees, like black matches stuck in the moonlight. Black like matches, and thin like matches. There wasn't a man could hide behind a pine under a bright moon. There wasn't a man could pass a bright open space and not be seen.

*"Alberta, let you hair hang low,*
*Alberta, let you hair hang low.*
*I'll give you more gold*
*Than you apron can hold."*

"That ain't a very nice song," she said.

*"I'll give you more gold*
*Than you apron can hold."*

She lifted her right hand and turned the razor's edge slowly in the light. "I got silver of my own right here," she said. "That enough for me."

The song went round in a circle, round and round, weaving in and out of the pines, passing invisible across the open moon filled spaces.

*"Alberta, let you hair hang low,*
*I'll give you more gold*
*Than you apron can hold*
*If you just let you hair hang low."*

There wasn't a man alive could do that. Go round and round.

*"Alberta, why you treat me so unkind?"*

Round and round, in and out the thin black trees. Alberta stood up, following the sound, turning on her heel.

*"You keep me worried, you keep me blue*
*All the time."*

"I plain confused," she said. "I don't reckon I understand."

*"I'll give you more gold*
*Than you apron can hold."*

"I ain't got no apron," she said.

*"Alberta, let you hair hang low,*
*Just let you hair hang low."*

The song stopped and Stanley Albert Thompson came right out of a patch of bright moon ground, where there were only brown pine needles.

Alberta forgot she was tired; the moon-spotted ground rolled past her feet like the moon in the sky—effortless. She recognized the country they passed through: Blue Goose Lake, Scanos River, and the steeper rough ground of the north part of the country, toward the Tennessee border. It was a far piece to walk and she wondered at the lightness of her feet. By moonset they had got there—the cabin that the boys had seen one day while they were hunting cows. She hesitated a little then, not afraid, not reluctant, but just not sure how to go on. Stanley Albert Thompson had been holding her hand all evening; he still held it. Right at the beginning when he had first taken her along with him, she'd shook her head, no, she could walk; no man needed to lead her. But he'd grinned at her, and shook his head, imitating her gesture, so that the moon sparkled on his black curly hair, and his black broad forehead, and he took her hand and led her so that the miles seemed nothing and the hours like smooth water.

He showed her the cabin, from the outside first: mustard color, trimmed with white, like the cabins the railroad company builds. One room with high peaked roof.

"A real fine house," she said. "A real fine house. You work for the railroad?"

"No."

He took her inside. "You light with candles," she said.

"I ain't ever been able to stand the smell of lamps," he said.

"But it's a real nice house. I might could learn to like it."

"No might could about it." He smoothed the cloth on the table with his fingers. "You going to like it."

She bent her head and looked at him through her eyelashes. "Now I don't rightly know. Seems as how I don't know you."

"Sure you do," he said. "I'm standing right here."

"Seems as how I don't know nothing. You might could have a dozen girls all over this here state."

"I reckon there's a dozen," he said.

She glared at him, hands on hips. "You old fool jackass," she said. "I reckon you can just keep everything."

He jammed his hands into the back pockets of his denim pants and bent backward staring at the ceiling.

"Ain't you gonna try to stop me?"

"Nuh-uh."

She leaned against the doorjamb and twisted her neck to look at him. "Ain't you sorry I going?"

"Sure." He was still staring upward at the ceiling with its four crossed beams. "Sure, I real sorry."

"I don't see as how I could stay though."

"Sure you could." He did not look at her.

"I don't see as how. You ain't give me none of the things you said."

"You a driving woman," he said, and grinned, his mouth wide and white in the dark of his face.

Then he sat down at the table. There were five candles there, stuck in bottles, but only one was lighted, the one in the center. Wax had run all down the side of the candle and down the bottle in little round blobs, nubby like gravel. He picked one off, dirty white between his black fingers. He rolled it slowly between his flat palms, back and forth. Then he flipped it toward Alberta. It flashed silvery through the circle of lamplight and thudded against her skirt. She bent forward to pick it up: a coin, new silver. As she bent there, another one struck her shoulder, and another. Stanley Albert Thompson sat at the table, grinning and tossing the coins to her, until she had filled both pockets of her dress.

He pushed the candle away from him. "You all right, I reckon, now."

She held one coin in her hands, turning it over and over.

"That ain't what you promised. I remember how you came and sang:

*'I give you more gold*
*Than you apron can hold.' "*

"Sure," he said and lifted a single eyebrow, very high. "I can do that all right, iffen you want it. I reckon I can do that."

She stood for a moment studying him. And Stanley Albert Thompson, from where he still sat at the table, curled up one corner of his mouth.

And very slowly Alberta began to smile. "I might could like it here," she said. "If you was real nice."

He got up then and rubbed her cheek very gently with his first finger. "I might could do that," he said. "I don't reckon it would be too heavy a thing to do."

The candle was on the table to one side. It caught the brightness of Alberta's eyes as she stood smiling at Stanley Albert Thompson. The steady yellow light threw her shadow over his body, a dark shadow that reached to his chin. His own shadow was on the wall behind. She glanced at it over his shoulder and giggled. "You better do something about your shadow there, Mr. Thompson. That there is a ugly shadow, sure."

He turned his head and glanced at it briefly. "Reckon so," he said.

It was an ugly shadow, sure. Alberta looked at Stanley Albert Thompson and shook her head. "I can't hardly believe it," she said. "You a right pretty man."

He grinned at her and shook himself so that the shadow on the wall spun around in a wild turn.

"I don't reckon you can do anything about it?"

"No," he said briefly. "I can't go changing my shadow." He hunched his back so that the figure on the wall seemed to jump up and down in anger.

She stepped over to him, putting her hands behind her, leaning backward to see his face. "If he don't do any more than dance on a wall, I ain't complaining."

Stanley Albert stood looking down at her, looking down the length of his face at her, and rocking slowly back and forth on his heels. "No," he said. "He ain't gonna do more than wiggle around the wall sometimes. But you can bet I am."

The coins weighed down the pockets of her dress, and his hands were warm against her skin. "I reckon I'm satisfied," she said.

That was the way it began. That was the courting. The woman was young and attractive and strong. The man could give her whatever she wanted. There were other courtings like that in this country. Every season there were courtings like that.

People would see them around sometimes; or sometimes they'd only hear them when they were still far off. Sometimes it would be Stanley Albert Thompson singing:

> *"Alberta, let you hair hang low,*
> *Alberta, let you hair hang low.*
> *I"ll give you more gold*
> *Than you apron can hold*
> *If you just let you hair hang low."*

He had a strong voice. It could carry far in a quiet day or night. And if any of the people heard it, they'd turn and look at each other and nod their heads toward it, not saying anything, but just being sure that everyone was listening. And whenever Willie heard it, he'd close his eyes for a minute, seeing Alberta; and then he'd rub his hands all over his little black kinky head and whistle: "Euuuu," which meant that he was very, very sorry she had left him.

And sometimes all you could hear of them would be the chiming of Stanley Albert's watch every quarter-hour. One night that August, when the moon was heavy and hot and low, Maggie Mary was out walking with Jack Belden. She heard the clear high chime and remembered the nights at Willie's and the dangling gold watch. And she turned to Jack Belden, who had just got her comfortable in one arm, and jammed her fingers in his eyes and ran off after the sound. She didn't find them; and it wouldn't have much mattered if she had. Stanley Albert was much too gone on Alberta to notice any other woman in more than a passing appraising way.

And sometimes people would come on them walking alone, arms around each other's waist; or sitting in a shady spot during the day's heat, his head on her lap and both of them dozing and smiling a little. And everybody who saw them would turn around and get out of there fast; but neither of them turned a head or looked up: there might not have been anyone there.

And then every night they'd go down to Willie's. The first night they came —it was on a Thursday—the place was closed up tight. There wasn't ever anybody came on Thursday. Stanley Albert went around back to where Willie lived and pounded on the door, and when Willie didn't answer he went around to the front again where Alberta was waiting on the steps and kicked in the front panel of the wood door. Willie came scuttling out, his eyes round and bewildered like a suckling's and saw them sitting at one of the tables drinking his home brew, only first putting lightning into it. After that they came every night, just them. It was all most people could do to afford a drink on Saturday or the week-end, but some of them would walk over to Willie's just to look at Stanley Albert and Alberta sitting there. They'd stand at the windows and look in, sweating in the hot summer nights and looking. Maybe a few of them would still be there waiting when Stanley and Alberta got ready to go, along toward morning.

That's what they did every single night of the year or so they were together.

If they fell asleep, Willie would just have to stand waiting. They'd go out with their arms around each other's waist, staggering some, but not falling. And an hour or so later, people who were going out before dawn to get a little work done in the cool would see them clear over on the other side of the county, at Goose Lake, maybe, a good three hours' walk for a man cold sober. Willie had his own version of how they got around. They just picked up their feet, he said, and went sliding off down the winds. Once, he said, when they were sitting over on the bench against the wall, Stanley Albert flat on it with his head on her lap, when the whisky made the man in him come up sudden, so he couldn't wait, they went straight out the window, up the air, like a whistle sound. Willie had the broken glass to show the next morning, if you wanted to believe him.

Willie hated them, the two of them, maybe because they broke his glass, maybe because they made him stay up late every single night of the week, so that he had to hold his eyes open with his fingers, and watch them pour lightning into his very best whisky, maybe because he had wanted Alberta mighty bad himself. He'd been giving her presents—bottles of his best stuff—but he just couldn't match Stanley Albert. Those are three reasons; maybe he had others. And Maggie Mary hated them; and she had only one reason.

Once Pete Stokes shot at Stanley Albert Thompson. He hadn't wanted to: he was scared like everybody else. But Maggie Mary Evans talked him into it. She was a fine-looking girl; she could do things like that. He hid behind the privy and got a perfect bead on Stanley Albert as he came out the door. The bullet just knocked off a piece of Willie's doorframe. When Pete saw what happened he dropped the gun and began to run, jumping the rail fence and crashing face-first through the thick heavy berry bushes. Stanley Albert pursed his lips together and rubbed his hands on his chin, slow, like he was deciding what to do. Then he jumped down from the porch and went after Pete. He ran through the hackberries too; only with him it did not seem difficult: none of the crackling and crashing and waving arms. Stanley Albert just put his head down and moved his legs, and the sprays of the bushes, some of them thick as a rooster's spur, seemed to pull back and make way. Nobody saw the fight: the brave ones were too drunk to travel fast; and the sober ones didn't want to mix with a man like Stanley Albert, drunk and mad. Alberta, she just ran her hand across her mouth and then wiped it along the side of her green satin dress, yawning like she was tired. She stood listening for a while, her head cocked a little, though there wasn't anything to hear, then walked off, pulling down the dress across her hips. And the next night she and Stanley Albert were back at Willie's, and Pete never did turn up again. Willie used to swear that he ended up in the Scanos River and that if the water wasn't so yellow muddy, that if you could see to the bottom, you would see Pete lying there, along with all the others Stanley Albert had killed.

At the last it was Willie who got the idea. For a week, carefully, he put aside the coins Stanley Albert gave him. There were a lot of them, all new silver, because Stanley Albert always paid in silver. Then one morning very early, just after Stanley Albert and Alberta left, Willie melted the coins down, and using the molds he kept for his old outsized pistol, he cast four bullets.

He made a special little shelf for the pistol under the counter so that it would be near at hand. And he waited all evening, sometimes touching the heavy black handle with the tips of his fingers; and he waited, hoping that Stanley Albert would drink enough to pass out. But of course nothing like that happened. So Willie poured himself three or four fingers of his best stuff and swallowed it fast as his throat would stand, then he blinked his little eyes fast for a second or so to clear his vision, and he reached for the gun. He got two shots over the bar, two good ones: the whole front of Stanley Albert's plaid shirt folded together and sank in, after the silver bullets went through. He got up, holding the table edge, unsteady, bending over, looking much smaller, his black skin gray-filmed and dull. His eyes were larger: they reached almost across his face—and they weren't dark any more; they were silver, two polished pieces of silver. Willie was afraid to fire again; the pistol shook where he held it in his two hands.

Then Stanley Albert walked out, not unsteady any more, but bent over the hole in his chest, walked out slowly with his eyes shining like a flat metal, Alberta a few steps behind. They passed right in front of Willie, who still hadn't moved; his face was stiff with fear. Quietly, smoothly, in a single motion, almost without interrupting her step, Alberta picked up a bottle (the same one from which he had poured his drink moments before) and swung it against Willie's head. He slipped down in a quiet little heap, his legs folded under him, his black kinky head on top. But his idea had worked: over by Stanley Albert's chair there was a black pool of blood.

All that was maybe eight or ten years ago. People don't see them any more—Stanley and Alberta. They don't think much about them, except when something goes wrong—like weevils getting in the cotton, or Willie's burning down and Willie inside it—then they begin to think that those two had a hand in it. Brad Tedrow swore that he had seen Stanley Albert that night, just for a second, standing on the edge of the circle of light, with a burning faggot in his hand. And the next morning Brad went back to look, knowing that your eyes play tricks at night in firelight; he went back to look for footprints or some sign. All he found was a burnt-out stick of pine wood that anybody could have dropped.

And kids sometimes think they hear the jingle of silver in Stanley Albert's pocket, or the sound of his watch. And when women talk—when there's been a miscarriage or a stillbirth—they remember and whisper together.

And they all wonder if that's not the sort of work they do, the two of them. Maybe so; maybe not. The people themselves are not too sure. They don't see them around any more.

## *Study questions*

1. *What is the mood of this story? How does the style contribute to the mood?*
2. *Who is Stanley Albert Thompson? Is Alberta an appropriate mate for him?*
3. *What role is played by Maggie Mary? Willie?* 4. *Does Stanley Albert create the problems that emerge in the community or does he act as a kind of catalyst for them?* 5. *What elements of the supernatural are present in the story? How many are associated with devil lore?* 6. *How does Grau make credible the seduction scene? What is the purpose of the song Stanley Albert sings?* 7. *How is the story like a legend?*

*Ann Beattie* (b. 1947), who presently lives in Somerville, Massachusetts, was born in Washington, D.C. She received her B.A. from American University and her M.A. from the University of Connecticut, where she also taught for four years. In addition, she has taught classes in both creative writing and short fiction at the University of Virginia. At Harvard University, she has been the Briggs-Copeland Lecturer in English. She has also received a Guggenheim Fellowship.

A frequent contributor to the *New Yorker*, her stories have also appeared in *TriQuarterly, Fiction, Texas Quarterly,* the *Virginia Quarterly Review,* the *New York Times Magazine,* and *Canto.* In 1976, she published two highly acclaimed books, *Distortions,* a collection of stories, and *Chilly Scenes of Winter,* a novel. "Shifting" is a closely wrought story about a contemporary woman whose life is characterized by means of a series of images and relationships which, combined, create the story's central metaphor.

# SHIFTING

The woman's name was Natalie, and the man's name was Larry. They had been childhood sweethearts; he had first kissed her at an ice-skating party, when they were ten. She had been unlacing her skates and had not expected the kiss. He had not expected to do it, either—he had some notion of getting his face out of the wind that was blowing across the iced-over lake, and he found himself ducking his head toward her. Kissing her seemed the natural thing to do. When they graduated from high school he was named "class clown" in the yearbook, but Natalie didn't think of him as being particularly funny. He spent more time than she thought he needed to studying chemistry, and he never laughed when she joked. She really did not think of him as funny. They went to the same college, in their home town, but he left after a year to go to a larger, more impressive university. She took the train to be with him on weekends, or he took the train to see her. When he graduated, his parents gave him a car. If they had given it to him when he was still in college it would have made things much easier. They waited to give it to him until graduation day, forcing him into attending the graduation exercises. He thought his parents were wonderful people, and Natalie liked them in a way, too, but she resented their perfect timing, their careful smiles. They were afraid that he would marry her. Eventually, he did. He had gone on to graduate school after college, and he set a date six months ahead for their marriage, so that it would take place after his first-semester final exams. That way, he could devote his time to studying for the chemistry exams.

When she married him, he had had the car for eight months. It still smelled like a brand-new car. There was never any clutter in the car. Even the ice scraper was kept in the glove compartment. There was not even a sweater or a lost glove in the back seat. He vacuumed the car every weekend, after washing it at the car wash. On Friday nights, on their way to some cheap restaurant and a dollar movie, he would stop at the car wash, and she would get out, so he could vacuum all over the inside of the car. She would lean against the metal wall of the car wash and watch him clean it.

It was expected that she would not become pregnant. She did not. It had also been expected that she would keep their apartment clean, and keep out of the way as much as possible in such close quarters while he was studying. The apartment was messy, though, and when he was studying late at night she would interrupt him and try to talk him into going to sleep. He gave a chemistry-class lecture once a week, and she would often tell him that over-preparing was as bad as under-preparing. She did not know if she believed this, but it was a favorite line of hers. Sometimes he listened to her.

On Tuesdays, when he gave the lecture, she would drop him off at school and then drive to a supermarket to do the week's shopping. Usually she did not make a list before she went shopping, but when she got to the parking lot she would take a tablet out of her purse and write a few items on it, sitting in the car in the cold. Even having a few things written down would stop her from wandering aimlessly in the store and buying things that she would never use. Before this, she had bought several pans and cans of food that she had not used, or that she could have done without. She felt better when she had a list.

She would drop him at school again on Wednesdays, when he had two seminars that together took up all the afternoon. Sometimes she would drive out of town then, to the suburbs, and shop there if any shopping needed to be done. Otherwise, she would go to the art museum, which was not far away but was hard to get to by bus. There was one piece of sculpture in there that she wanted very much to touch, but the guard was always nearby. She came so often that in time the guard began to nod hello. She wondered if she could ever persuade the man to turn his head for a few seconds—only that long—so she could stroke the sculpture. Of course she would never dare ask. After wandering through the museum and looking at least twice at the sculpture, she would go to the gift shop and buy a few postcards and then sit on one of the museum benches, padded with black vinyl, with a Calder mobile hanging overhead, and write notes to friends. (She never wrote letters.) She would tuck the postcards in her purse and mail them when she left the museum. But before she left, she often had coffee in the restaurant: she saw mothers and children struggling there, and women dressed in fancy clothes talking with their faces close together, as quietly as lovers.

On Thursdays he took the car. After his class, he would drive to visit his parents and his friend Andy, who had been wounded in Vietnam. About once a month she would go with him, but she had to feel up to it. Being with Andy embarrassed her. She had told him not to go to Vietnam—told him that he could prove his patriotism in some other way—and finally, after she and Larry had made a visit together and she had seen Andy in the motorized bed in his parents' house, Larry had agreed that she need not go again. Andy had apologized to her. It embarrassed her that this man, who had been blown sky-high by a land mine and had lost a leg and lost the full use of his arms, would smile up at her ironically and say, "You were right." She also felt as though he wanted to hear what she would say now, and that now he would listen. Now she had nothing to say. Andy would pull himself up, relying on his right arm, which was the stronger, gripping the rails at the side of the bed, and sometimes he would take her hand. His arms were still weak, but the doctors said he would regain complete use of his right arm with time. She had to make an effort not to squeeze his hand when he held hers, because she found herself wanting to squeeze energy back into him. She had a morbid curiosity about what it felt like to be blown from the ground—to go up, and to come crashing down. During their visit, Larry put on the class-clown act for Andy, telling funny stories and laughing uproariously.

Once or twice, Larry had talked Andy into getting in his wheelchair and had loaded him into the car and taken him to a bar. Larry called her once, late, pretty drunk, to say that he would not be home that night—that he would sleep at his parents' house. "My God," she said. "Are you going to drive Andy home when you're drunk?" "What the hell else can happen to him?" he said.

Larry's parents blamed her for Larry's not being happy. His mother could only be pleasant with her for a short while, and then she would veil her criticisms by putting them as questions. "I know that one thing that helps enormously is good nutrition," his mother said. "He works so hard that he probably needs quite a few vitamins as well, don't you think?" Larry's father was the sort of man who found hobbies in order to avoid his wife. His hobbies were building model boats, repairing clocks, and photography. He took pictures of himself building the boats and fixing the clocks, and gave the pictures, in cardboard frames, to Natalie and Larry for Christmas and birthday presents. Larry's mother was very anxious to stay on close terms with her son, and she knew that Natalie did not like her very much. Once she had visited them during the week, and Natalie, not knowing what to do with her, had taken her to the museum. She had pointed out the sculpture, and his mother had glanced at it and then ignored it. Natalie hated her for her bad taste. She had bad taste in the sweaters she gave Larry, too, but he wore them. They made him look collegiate. That whole world made her sick.

When Natalie's uncle died and left her his 1965 Volvo, they immediately decided to sell it and use the money for a vacation. They put an ad in the paper, and there were several callers. There were some calls on Tuesday, when Larry was in class, and Natalie found herself putting the people off. She told one woman that the car had too much mileage on it, and mentioned body rust, which it did not have; she told another caller, who was very persistent, that the car was already sold. When Larry returned from school, she explained that the phone was off the hook because so many people were calling about the car and she had decided not to sell it after all. They could take a little money from their savings account and go on the trip, if he wanted. But she did not want to sell the car. "It's not an automatic shift," he said. "You don't know how to drive it." She told him that she could learn. "It will cost money to insure it," he said, "and it's old and probably not even dependable." She wanted to keep the car. "I know," he said, "but it doesn't make sense. When we have more money, you can have a car. You can have a newer, better car."

The next day, she went out to the car, which was parked in the driveway of an old lady next door. Her name was Mrs. Larsen and she no longer drove a car, and she told Natalie she could park their second car there. Natalie opened the car door and got behind the wheel and put her hands on it. The wheel was covered with a flaky yellow-and-black plastic cover. She eased it off. A few pieces of foam rubber stuck to the wheel. She picked them off. Underneath the cover, the wheel was a dull red. She ran her fingers around and around the circle of the wheel. Her cousin Burt had delivered the car—a young opportunist, sixteen years old, who said he would drive it the hundred miles from his house to theirs for twenty dollars and a bus ticket home. She had not even invited him to stay for dinner, and Larry had driven him to the bus station. She wondered if it was Burt's cigarette in the ashtray or her dead uncle's. She could not even remember if her uncle smoked. She was surprised that he had left her his car. The car was much more comfortable than Larry's, and it had a nice smell inside. It smelled a little the way a field smells after a spring rain. She rubbed the side of her head back and forth against the window and then got out of the car and went in to see Mrs. Larsen. The night before, she had suddenly thought of the boy who brought the old lady the evening newspaper every night; he looked old enough to drive, and he would probably know how to shift. Mrs. Larsen agreed with her —she was sure that he could teach her. "Of course, everything has its price," the old lady said.

"I know that. I meant to offer him money," Natalie said, and was surprised, listening to her voice, that she sounded old too.

She took an inventory and made a list of things in their apartment. Larry had met an insurance man one evening while playing basketball at the gym, who told him that they should have a list of their possessions, in case of theft. "What's worth anything?" she said when he told her. It was their first argument in almost a year—the first time in a year, anyway, that their voices were raised. He told her that several of the pieces of furniture his grandparents gave them when they got married were antiques, and the man at the gym said that if they weren't going to get them appraised every year, at least they should take snapshots of them and keep the pictures in a safe-deposit box. Larry told her to photograph the pie safe (which she used to store linen), the piano with an inlaid mother-of-pearl decoration on the music rack (neither of them knew how to play), and the table with hand-carved wooden handles and a marble top. He bought her an Instamatic camera at the drugstore, with film and flashbulbs. "Why can't you do it?" she said, and an argument began. He said that she had no respect for his profession and no understanding of the amount of study that went into getting a master's degree in chemistry.

That night, he went out to meet two friends at the gym, to shoot baskets. She put the little flashcube into the top of the camera, dropped in the film, and closed the back. She went first to the piano. She leaned forward so that she was close enough to see the inlay clearly, but she found that when she was that close the whole piano wouldn't fit into the picture. She decided to take two pictures. Then she photographed the pie safe, with one door open, showing the towels and sheets stacked inside. She did not have a reason for opening the door, except that she remembered a Perry Mason show in which detectives photographed everything with the doors hanging open. She photographed the table, lifting the lamp off it first. There were still eight pictures left. She went to the mirror in their bedroom and held the camera above her head, pointing down at an angle, and photographed her image in the mirror. She took off her slacks and sat on the floor and leaned back, aiming the camera down at her legs. Then she stood up and took a picture of her feet, leaning over and aiming down. She put on her favorite record: Stevie Wonder singing "For Once in My Life." She found herself wondering what it would be like to be blind, to have to feel things to see them. She thought about the piece of sculpture in the museum—the two elongated mounds intertwined, the smooth gray stone as shiny as sea pebbles. She photographed the kitchen, bathroom, bedroom, and living room. There was one picture left. She put her left hand on her thigh, palm up, and with some difficulty—with the camera nestled into her neck like a violin—snapped a picture of it with her right hand. The next day would be her first driving lesson.

He came to her door at noon, as he said he would. He had on a long maroon scarf, which made his deep blue eyes very striking. She had only seen him from her window when he carried the paper in to the old lady. He was a little nervous. She hoped that it was just the anxiety of any teen-ager confronting an adult. She needed to have him like her. She did not learn about mechanical things easily (Larry had told her that he would have invested in a "real" camera, except that he did not have the time to teach her about it), so she wanted him to be patient. He sat on the footstool in her living room, still in coat and scarf, and told her how a stick shift operated. He moved his hand through the air. The motion he made reminded her of the salute spacemen gave to earthlings in a science-fiction picture she had recently watched on late-night television. She nodded. "How much —" she began, but he interrupted and said, "You can decide what it was worth when you've learned." She was surprised and wondered if he meant to charge a great deal. Would it be her fault and would she have to pay him if he named his price when the lessons were over? But he had an honest face. Perhaps he was just embarrassed to talk about money.

He drove for a few blocks, making her watch his hand on the stick shift. "Feel how the car is going?" he said. "Now you shift." He shifted. The car jumped a little, hummed, moved into gear. It was an old car and didn't shift too easily, he said. She had been sitting forward, so that when he shifted she rocked back hard against the seat—harder than she needed to. Almost unconsciously, she wanted to show him what a good teacher he was. When her turn came to drive, the car stalled. "Take it easy," he said. "Ease up on the clutch. Don't just raise your foot off of it like that." She tried it again. "That's it," he said. She looked at him when the car was in third. He sat in the seat, looking out the window. Snow was expected. It was Thursday. Although Larry was going to visit his parents and would not be back until late Friday afternoon, she decided she would wait until Tuesday for her next lesson. If he came home early, he would find out that she was taking lessons, and she didn't want him to know. She asked the boy, whose name was Michael, whether he thought she would forget all he had taught her in the time between lessons. "You'll remember," he said.

When they returned to the old lady's driveway, the car stalled going up the incline. She had trouble shifting. The boy put his hand over hers, and kicked the heel of his hand forward. "You'll have to treat this car a little roughly, I'm afraid," he said. That afternoon, after he left, she made spaghetti sauce, chopping little pieces of pepper and onion and mushroom. When the sauce had cooked down, she called Mrs. Larsen and said that she would bring over dinner. She usually ate with the old lady once a week. The old lady often added a pinch of cinnamon to her food, saying that it brought out the flavor better than salt, and that since she was losing her sense of smell, food had to be strongly flavored for her to taste it. Once, she had sprinkled cinnamon on a knockwurst. This time, as they ate, Natalie asked the old lady how much she paid the boy to bring the paper.

"I give him a dollar a week," the old lady said.

"Did he set the price, or did you?"

"He set the price. He told me he wouldn't take much, because he has to walk this street to get to his apartment anyway."

"He taught me a lot about the car today," Natalie said.

"He's very handsome, isn't he?" the old lady said.

She asked Larry, "How were your parents?"

"Fine," he said. "But I spent almost all the time with Andy. It's almost his birthday, and he's depressed. We went to see Mose Allison."

"I think it stinks that hardly anyone else ever visits Andy," she said.

"He doesn't make it easy. He tells you everything that's on his mind, and there's no way you can pretend that his troubles don't amount to much. You just have to sit there and nod."

She remembered that Andy's room looked like a gymnasium. There were handgrips and weights scattered on the floor. There was even a psychedelic pink hula hoop that he was to put inside his elbow and then move his arm in circles wide enough to make the hoop spin. He couldn't do it. He would lie in bed with the hoop in back of his neck and, holding the sides, lift his neck off the pillow. His arms were barely strong enough to do that, really, but he could raise his neck with no trouble, so he just pretended that his arms pulling the loop were raising it. His parents thought that it was a special exercise that he had mastered.

"What did you do today?" Larry said now.

"I made spaghetti," she said. She had made it the day before, but she thought that since he was mysterious about the time he spent away from her ("in the lab" and "at the gym" became interchangeable), she did not owe him a straight answer. That day she had dropped off the film and then she had sat at the drugstore counter to have a cup of coffee. She bought some cigarettes, though she had not smoked since high school. She smoked one mentholated cigarette and then threw the pack away in a garbage container outside the drugstore. Her mouth still felt cool inside.

He asked if she had planned anything for the weekend.

"No," she said.

"Let's do something you'd like to do. I'm a little ahead of myself in the lab right now."

That night they ate spaghetti and made plans, and the next day they went for a ride in the country, to a factory where wooden toys were made. In the showroom, he made a bear marionette shake and twist. She examined a small rocking horse, rhythmically pushing her finger up and down on the back rung of the rocker to make it rock. When they left they took with them a catalogue of toys they could order. She knew that they would never look at the catalogue again. On their way to the museum, he stopped to wash the car. Because it was the weekend there were quite a few cars lined up waiting to go in. They were behind a blue Cadillac that seemed to inch forward of its own accord, without a driver. When the Cadillac moved into the washing area, a tiny man hopped out. He stood on tiptoe to reach the coin box to start the washing machine. She doubted if he was five feet tall.

"Look at that poor son of a bitch," he said.

The little man was washing his car.

"If Andy could get out more," Larry said. "If he could get rid of that feeling he has that he's the only freak . . . I wonder if it wouldn't do him good to come spend a week with us."

"Are you going to take him in the wheelchair to the lab with you?" she said. "I'm not taking care of Andy all day."

His face changed. "Just for a week was all I meant," he said.

"I'm not doing it," she said. She was thinking of the boy, and of the car. She had almost learned how to drive the car.

"Maybe in the warm weather," she said. "When we could go to the park or something."

He said nothing. The little man was rinsing his car. She sat inside when their turn came. She thought that Larry had no right to ask her to take care of Andy. Water flew out of the hose and battered the car. She thought of Andy, in the woods at night, stepping on the land mine, being blown into the air. She wondered if it threw him in an arc, so he ended up somewhere away from where he had been walking, or if it just blasted him straight up, if he went up the way an umbrella opens. Andy had been a wonderful ice skater. They all envied him his long sweeping turns, with his legs somehow neatly together and his body at the perfect angle. She never saw him have an accident on the ice. Never once. She had known Andy, and they had skated at Parker's pond, for eight years before he was drafted.

The night before, as she and Larry were finishing dinner, he had asked her if she intended to vote for Nixon or McGovern in the election. "McGovern," she said. How could he not have known that? She knew then that they were farther apart than she had thought. She hoped that on Election Day she could drive herself to the polls—not go with him and not walk. She planned not to ask the old lady if she wanted to come along, because that would be one vote she could keep Nixon from getting.

At the museum, she hesitated by the sculpture but did not point it out to him. He didn't look at it. He gazed to the side, above it, at a Francis Bacon painting. He could have shifted his eyes just a little and seen the sculpture, and her, standing and staring.

After three more lessons, she could drive the car. The last two times, which were later in the afternoon than their first lesson, they stopped at the drugstore to get the old lady's paper, to save him from having to make the same trip back on foot. After the final lesson, when he came out of the drugstore with the paper she asked him if he'd like to have a beer to celebrate.

"Sure," he said.

They walked down the street to a bar that was filled with college students. She wondered if Larry ever came to this bar. He had never said that he did.

She and Michael talked. She asked why he wasn't in high school. He told her that he had quit. He was living with his brother, and his brother was teaching him carpentry, which he had been interested in all along. On his napkin he drew a picture of the cabinets and bookshelves he and his brother had spent the last week constructing and installing in the house of two wealthy old sisters. He drummed the side of his thumb against the edge of the table in time with the music. They each drank beer, from heavy glass mugs.

"Mrs. Larsen said your husband was in school," the boy said. "What's he studying?"

She looked up, surprised. Michael had never mentioned her husband to her before. "Chemistry," she said.

"I liked chemistry pretty well," he said. "Some of it."

"My husband doesn't know you've been giving me lessons. I'm just going to tell him that I can drive the stick shift, and surprise him."

"Yeah?" the boy said. "What will he think about that?"

"I don't know," she said. "I don't think he'll like it."

"Why?" the boy said.

His question made her remember that he was sixteen. What she had said would never have provoked another question from an adult. The adult would have nodded, or said, "I know."

She shrugged. The boy took a long drink of beer. "I thought it was funny that he didn't teach you himself, when Mrs. Larsen told me you were married," he said.

They had discussed her. She wondered why Mrs. Larsen wouldn't have told her that, because the night she ate dinner with her she had talked to Mrs. Larsen about what an extraordinarily patient teacher Michael was. Had Mrs. Larsen told him that Natalie talked about him?

On the way back to the car, she remembered the photographs and went back to the drugstore and picked up the prints. As she took money out of her wallet, she remembered that today was the day she would have to pay him. She looked around at him, at the front of the store, where he was flipping through magazines. He was tall and he was wearing a very old black jacket. One end of his long, thick maroon scarf was hanging down his back.

"What did you take pictures of?" he said when they were back in the car.

"Furniture. My husband wanted pictures of our furniture, in case it was stolen."

"Why?" he said.

"They say if you have proof that you had valuable things the insurance company won't hassle you about reimbursing you."

"You have a lot of valuable stuff?" he said.

"My husband thinks so," she said.

A block from the driveway, she said, "What do I owe you?"

"Four dollars," he said.

"That's nowhere near enough," she said, and looked over at him. He had opened the envelope with the pictures in it while she was driving. He was staring at the picture of her legs. "What's this?" he said.

She turned into the driveway and shut off the engine. She looked at the picture. She could not think what to tell him it was. Her hands and heart felt heavy.

"Wow," the boy said. He laughed. "Never mind. Sorry. I'm not looking at any more of them."

He put the pack of pictures back in the envelope and dropped it on the seat between them.

She tried to think what to say, of some way she could turn the pictures into a joke. She wanted to get out of the car and run. She wanted to stay, not to give him the money, so he would sit there with her. She reached into her purse and took out her wallet and removed four one-dollar bills.

"How many years have you been married?" he asked.

"One," she said. She held the money out to him. He said, "Thank you," and leaned across the seat and put his right arm over her shoulder and kissed her. She felt his scarf bunched up against their cheeks. She was amazed at how warm his lips were in the cold car.

He moved his head away and said, "I didn't think you'd mind if I did that." She shook her head no. He unlocked the door and got out.

"I could drive you to your brother's apartment," she said. Her voice sounded hollow. She was extremely embarrassed, but she couldn't let him go.

He got back in the car. "You could drive me and come in for a drink," he said. "My brother's working."

When she got back to the car two hours later she saw a white parking ticket clamped under the windshield wiper, flapping in the wind. When she opened the car door and sank into the seat, she saw that he had left the money, neatly folded, on the floor mat on his side of the car. She did not pick up the money. In a while, she started the car. She stalled it twice on the way home. When she had pulled into the driveway she looked at the money for a long time, then left it lying there. She left the car unlocked, hoping the money would be stolen. If it disappeared she could tell herself that she had paid him. Otherwise, she would not know how to deal with the situation.

When she got into the apartment, the phone rang.

"I'm at the gym to play basketball," Larry said. "Be home in an hour."

"I was at the drugstore," she said. "See you then."

She examined the pictures. She sat on the sofa and laid them out, the twelve of them, in three rows on the cushion next to her. The picture of the piano was between the picture of her feet and the picture of herself that she had shot by aiming into the mirror. She picked up the four pictures of their furniture and put them on the table. She picked up the others and examined them closely. She began to understand why she had taken them. She had photographed parts of her body, fragments of it, to study the pieces. She had probably done it because she thought so much about Andy's body and the piece that was gone—the leg, below the knee, on his left side. She had had two bourbon-and-waters at the boy's apartment, and drinking always depressed her. She felt very depressed looking at the pictures, so she put them down and went into the bedroom. She undressed. She looked at her body—whole, not a bad figure—in the mirror. It was an automatic reaction with her to close the curtains when she was naked, so she turned quickly and went to the window and did that. She went back to the mirror; the room was darker now and her body looked better. She ran her hands down her sides, wondering if the feel of her skin was anything like the way the sculpture would feel. She was sure that the sculpture would be smoother—her hands would move more quickly down the slopes of it than she wanted—that it would be cool, and that somehow she could feel the grayness of it. Those things seemed preferable to her hands lingering on her body, the imperfection of her skin, the overheated apartment. If she were the piece of sculpture and if she could feel, she would like her sense of isolation.

This was in 1972, in Philadelphia.

## *Study questions*

1. *What details characterize Larry? his parents? What kinds of strictures do they place on Natalie?* 2. *What does the piece of sculpture mean to Natalie? Why does she sit under the Calder mobile?* 3. *What role does Andy play? his motorized bed? his missing limbs?* 4. *How do the cars function? the camera and the various photographs Natalie takes?* 5. *What does Natalie find attractive in Michael?* 6. *What is the significance of the title of the story? On how many levels does it function?*

SECTION THREE

# Contemporary

*Franz Kafka* (1883–1924) was born in Prague, the son of a successful Jewish merchant, and attended the German University of Prague, where he received a doctorate in jurisprudence in 1906. In 1908 he went to work as a civil servant. He took part in World War I and in 1917 learned that he had tuberculosis. He died at the age of forty-one. He published two volumes of short stories during his lifetime, *Metamorphosis* (1915) and *In the Penal Colony* (1919). Before he died he directed his friend and executor of his estate, Max Brod, to destroy all his manuscripts. This Brod did not do; rather, he published in the three years following Kafka's death *The Trial* (1925), *The Castle* (1926), and *Amerika* (1927), all unfinished novels. During the 1930s, Brod published additional stories and parables, and during the 1950s the remaining stories and Kafka's *Diaries* were published. All of Kafka's books have been widely translated. Most of them were translated into English in the 1930s. Kafka's themes have had particular significance to modern readers. His protagonists are trapped, lonely, alienated, directed by forces beyond their control. They are filled with anxieties and consumed by nameless guilt. In *The Trial,* for example, Joseph K., the protagonist, wakes up one morning to find that he has been arrested. During the course of the novel, one year in the life of Joseph K., he tries to find out what he is charged with, where the courts are, indeed, what is the law. He fails, and on the morning of his thirty-first birthday he is killed by nameless executioners. But perhaps more important than themes is the form most of Kafka's fiction takes—dreamscapes, which replicate the nightmares of Everyman. "The Hunter Gracchus" and "A Country Doctor" must be read as surreal structures, dream narratives, exploring areas of public and private guilt.

# THE HUNTER GRACCHUS

Two boys were sitting on the harbor wall playing with dice. A man was reading a newspaper on the steps of the monument, resting in the shadow of a hero who was flourishing his sword on high. A girl was filling her bucket at the fountain. A fruit-seller was lying beside his wares, gazing at the lake. Through the vacant window and door openings of a café one could see two men quite at the back drinking their wine. The proprietor was sitting at a table in front and dozing. A bark was silently making for the little harbor, as if borne by invisible means over the water. A man in a blue blouse climbed ashore and drew the rope through a ring. Behind the boatman two other men in dark coats with silver buttons carried a bier, on which, beneath a great flower-patterned fringed silk cloth, a man was apparently lying.

Nobody on the quay troubled about the newcomers; even when they lowered the bier to wait for the boatman, who was still occupied with his rope, nobody went nearer, nobody asked them a question, nobody accorded them an inquisitive glance.

The pilot was still further detained by a woman who, a child at her breast, now appeared with loosened hair on the deck of the boat. Then he advanced and indicated a yellowish two-storeyed house that rose abruptly on the left near the water; the bearers took up their burden and bore it to the low but gracefully pillared door. A little boy opened a window just in time to see the party vanishing into the house, then hastily shut the window again. The door too was now shut; it was of black oak, and very strongly made. A flock of doves which had been flying around the belfry alighted in the street before the house. As if their food were stored within, they assembled in front of the door. One of them flew up to the first storey and pecked at the windowpane. They were bright-hued, well-tended, lively birds. The woman on the boat flung grain to them in a wide sweep; they ate it up and flew across to the woman.

A man in a top hat tied with a band of black crêpe now descended one of the narrow and very steep lanes that led to the harbor. He glanced around vigilantly, everything seemed to distress him, his mouth twisted at the sight of some offal in a corner. Fruit skins were lying on the steps of the monument; he swept them off in passing with his stick. He rapped at the house door, at the same time taking his top hat from his head with his black-gloved hand. The door was opened at once, and some fifty little boys appeared in two rows in the long entry hall, and bowed to him.

The boatman descended the stairs, greeted the gentleman in black, conducted him up to the first storey, led him around the bright and elegant loggia which encircled the courtyard, and both of them entered, while the boys pressed after them at a respectful distance, a cool spacious room looking toward the back, from whose window no habitation, but only a bare, blackish-gray rocky wall was to be seen. The bearers were busied in setting up and lighting several long candles at the head of the bier, yet these did not give light, but only disturbed the shadows which had been immobile till then, and made them flicker over the walls. The cloth covering the bier had been thrown back. Lying on it was a man with wildly matted hair, who looked somewhat like a hunter. He lay without motion and, it seemed, without breathing, his eyes closed; yet only his trappings indicated that this man was probably dead.

The gentleman stepped up to the bier, laid his hand on the brow of the man lying upon it, then kneeled down and prayed. The boatman made a sign to the bearers to leave the room; they went out, drove away the boys who had gathered outside, and shut the door. But even that did not seem to satisfy the gentleman, he glanced at the boatman; the boatman understood, and vanished through a side door into the next room. At once the man on the bier opened his eyes, turned his face painfully toward the gentleman, and said: "Who are you?" Without any mark of surprise the gentleman rose from his kneeling posture and answered: "The Burgomaster of Riva."

The man on the bier nodded, indicated a chair with a feeble movement of his arm, and said, after the Burgomaster had accepted his invitation: "I knew that, of course, Burgomaster, but in the first moments of returning consciousness I always forget, everything goes around before my eyes, and it is best to ask about anything even if I know. You too probably know that I am the Hunter Gracchus."

"Certainly," said the Burgomaster. "Your arrival was announced to me during the night. We had been asleep for a good while. Then toward midnight my wife cried 'Salvatore'—that's my name—'look at that dove at the window.' It was really a dove, but as big as a cock. It flew over me and said in my ear: 'Tomorrow the dead Hunter Gracchus is coming; receive him in the name of the city.' "

The Hunter nodded and licked his lips with the tip of his tongue: "Yes, the doves flew here before me. But do you believe, Burgomaster, that I shall remain in Riva?"

"I cannot say that yet," replied the Burgomaster. "Are you dead?"

"Yes," said the Hunter, "as you see. Many years ago, yes, it must be a great many years ago, I fell from a precipice in the Black Forest—that is in Germany—when I was hunting a chamois. Since then I have been dead."

"But you are alive too," said the Burgomaster.

"In a certain sense," said the Hunter, "in a certain sense I am alive too. My death ship lost its way; a wrong turn of the wheel, a moment's absence of mind on the pilot's part, the distraction of my lovely native country, I cannot tell what it was; I only know this, that I remained on earth and that ever since my ship has sailed earthly waters. So I, who asked for nothing better than to live among my mountains, travel after my death through all the lands of the earth."

"And you have no part in the other world?" asked the Burgomaster, knitting his brow.

"I am forever," replied the Hunter, "on the great stair that leads up to it. On that infinitely wide and spacious stair I clamber about, sometimes up, sometimes down, sometimes on the right, sometimes on the left, always in motion. The Hunter has been turned into a butterfly. Do not laugh."

"I am not laughing," said the Burgomaster in self-defense.

"That is very good of you," said the Hunter. "I am always in motion. But when I make a supreme flight and see the gate actually shining before me I awaken presently on my old ship, still stranded forlornly in some earthly sea or other. The fundamental error of my onetime death grins at me as I lie in my cabin. Julia, the wife of the pilot, knocks at the door and brings me on my bier the morning drink of the land whose coasts we chance to be passing. I lie on a wooden pallet, I wear—it cannot be a pleasure to look at me—a filthy winding sheet, my hair and beard, black tinged with gray, have grown together inextricably, my limbs are covered with a great flowered-patterned woman's shawl with long fringes. A sacramental candle stands at my head and lights me. On the wall opposite me is a little picture, evidently of a bushman who is aiming his spear at me and taking cover as best he can behind a beautifully painted shield. On shipboard one often comes across silly pictures, but that is the silliest of them all. Otherwise my wooden cage is quite empty. Through a hole in the side the warm airs of the southern night come in, and I hear the water slapping against the old boat.

"I have lain here ever since the time when, as the Hunter Gracchus living in the Black Forest, I followed a chamois and fell from a precipice. Everything happened in good order. I pursued, I fell, bled to death in a ravine, died, and this ship should have conveyed me to the next world. I can still remember how gladly I stretched myself out on this pallet for the first time. Never did the mountains listen to such songs from me as these shadowy walls did then.

"I had been glad to live and I was glad to die. Before I stepped aboard, I joyfully flung away my wretched load of ammunition, my knapsack, my hunting rifle that I had always been proud to carry, and I slipped into my winding sheet like a girl into her marriage dress. I lay and waited. Then came the mishap."

"A terrible fate," said the Burgomaster, raising his hand defensively. "And you bear no blame for it?"

"None," said the Hunter. "I was a hunter; was there any sin in that? I followed my calling as a hunter in the Black Forest, where there were still wolves in those days. I lay in ambush, shot, hit my mark, flayed the skins from my victims: was there any sin in that? My labors were blessed. 'The Great Hunter of the Black Forest' was the name I was given. Was there any sin in that?"

"I am not called upon to decide that," said the Burgomaster, "but to me also there seems to be no sin in such things. But then, whose is the guilt?"

"The boatman's," said the Hunter. "Nobody will read what I say here, no one will come to help me; even if all the people were commanded to help me, every door and window would remain shut, everybody would take to bed and draw the bed-clothes over his head, the whole earth would become an inn for the night. And there is sense in that, for nobody knows of me, and if anyone knew he would not know where I could be found, and if he knew where I could be found, he would not know how to deal with me, he would not know how to help me. The thought of helping me is an illness that has to be cured by taking to one's bed.

"I know that, and so I do not shout to summon help, even though at moments—when I lose control over myself, as I have done just now, for instance—I think seriously of it. But to drive out such thoughts I need only look around me and verify where I am, and—I can safely assert—have been for hundreds of years."

"Extraordinary," said the Burgomaster, "extraordinary. And now do you think of staying here in Riva with us?"

"I think not," said the Hunter with a smile, and, to excuse himself, he laid his hand on the Burgomaster's knee. "I am here, more than that I do not know, further than that I cannot go. My ship has no rudder, and it is driven by the wind that blows in the undermost regions of death."

## *Study questions*

1. *What are the characteristic elements of dreams that Kafka replicates in "The Hunter Gracchus"?* 2. *What do the details of the first paragraph suggest? Are these details "realistic"? What is to be made of the matter-of-fact tone of the story?* 3. *At what point in the story does it become clear that the story as a whole is not "realistic" in the ordinary sense? Is it, therefore, not "true"?* 4. *How do the religious allusions function?* 5. *Why is Gracchus a hunter? Is he also hunted? Did he do anything wrong? What was his life like before he "died"? What is his "life" like now?* 6. *Is there any suggestion that in his previous life he was living in a state of innocence? Could his "death" be a "birth" into a fallen world?* 7. *Why do quotation marks have to be put around so many words in*

*this set of questions?* 8. *Could Gracchus be an Everyman and the world that Kafka pictures a microcosm? What, then, would it be like to be living in a world like this?*

## A COUNTRY DOCTOR

I was in great perplexity; I had to start on an urgent journey; a seriously ill patient was waiting for me in a village ten miles off; a thick blizzard of snow filled all the wide spaces between him and me; I had a gig, a light gig with big wheels, exactly right for our country roads; muffled in furs, my bag of instruments in my hand, I was in the courtyard all ready for the journey; but there was no horse to be had, no horse. My own horse had died in the night, worn out by the fatigues of this icy winter; my servant girl was now running around the village trying to borrow a horse; but it was hopeless, I knew it, and I stood there forlornly, with the snow gathering more and more thickly upon me, more and more unable to move. In the gateway the girl appeared, alone, and waved the lantern; of course, who would lend a horse at this time for such a journey? I strode through the courtyard once more; I could see no way out; in my confused distress I kicked at the dilapidated door of the yearlong uninhabited pigsty. It flew open and flapped to and fro on its hinges. A steam and smell as of horses came out from it. A dim stable lantern was swinging inside from a rope. A man, crouching on his hams in that low space, showed an open blue-eyed face. "Shall I yoke up?" he asked, crawling out on all fours. I did not know what to say and merely stooped down to see what else was in the sty. The servant girl was standing beside me. "You never know what you're going to find in your own house," she said, and we both laughed. "Hey there, Brother, hey there, Sister!" called the groom, and two horses, enormous creatures with powerful flanks, one after the other, their legs tucked close to their bodies, each well-shaped head lowered like a camel's, by sheer strength of buttocking squeezed out through the door hole which they filled entirely. But at once they were standing up, their legs long and their bodies steaming thickly. "Give him a hand," I said, and the willing girl hurried to help the groom with the harnessing. Yet hardly was she beside him when the groom clipped hold of her and pushed his face against hers. She screamed and fled back to me; on her cheek stood out in red the marks of two rows of teeth. "You brute," I yelled in fury, "do you want a whipping?" but in the same moment reflected that the man was a stranger; that I did not know where he came from, and that of his own free will he was helping me out when everyone else had failed me. As if he knew my thoughts he took no offense at my threat but, still busied with the horses, only turned around once toward me. "Get in," he said then, and indeed: everything was ready. A magnificent pair of horses, I observed, such as I had never sat behind, and I climbed in happily. "But I'll drive, you don't know the way," I said. "Of course," said he, "I'm not coming with you anyway, I'm staying with Rose." "No," shrieked Rose, fleeing into the house with a justified presentiment that her fate was inescapable; I heard the door chain rattle as she put it up; I heard the key turn in the lock; I could see, moreover, how she put out the lights in the entrance hall and in further flight all through the rooms to keep herself from being discovered. "You're coming with me," I said to the groom, "or I won't go, urgent as my journey is. I'm not thinking of paying for it by handing the girl over to you." "Gee up!" he said; clapped his hands; the gig whirled off like a log in a freshet; I could just hear the door of my house splitting and bursting as the groom charged at it and then I was deafened and blinded by a storming rush that steadily buffeted all my senses. But this only for a moment, since, as if my patient's farmyard had opened out just before my courtyard gate, I was already there; the horses had come quietly to a standstill; the blizzard had stopped; moonlight all around; my patient's parents hurried out of the house, his sister behind them; I was almost lifted out of the gig; from their confused ejaculations I gathered not a word; in the sickroom the air was almost unbreathable; the neglected stove was smoking; I wanted to push open a window; but first I had to look at my patient. Gaunt, without any fever, not cold, not warm, with vacant eyes, without a shirt, the youngster heaved himself up from under the feather bedding, threw his arms around my neck, and whispered in my ear: "Doctor, let me die." I glanced around the room; no one had heard it; the parents were leaning forward in silence waiting for my verdict; the sister had set a chair for my handbag; I opened the bag and hunted among my instruments; the boy kept clutching at me from his bed to remind me of his entreaty; I picked up a pair of tweezers, examined them in the candlelight, and laid them down again. "Yes," I thought blasphemously, "in cases like this the gods are helpful, send the missing horse, add to it a second because of the urgency, and to crown everything bestow even a groom——" And only now did I remember Rose again; what was I to do, how could I rescue her, how could I pull her away from under that groom at ten miles' distance, with a team of horses I couldn't control. These horses, now, they had somehow slipped the reins loose, pushed the windows open from outside, I did not know how; each of them had stuck a head in at a window and, quite unmoved by the startled cries of the family, stood eyeing the patient. "Better go back at once," I thought, as if the horses were summoning me to the return journey, yet I permitted the patient's sister, who fancied that I was dazed by the heat, to take my fur coat from me. A glass of rum was poured out for me, the old man clapped me on the shoulder, a familiarity justified by this offer of his treasure. I shook my head; in the narrow confines of the old man's thoughts I felt ill; that was my only reason for refusing the drink. The mother stood by the bedside and cajoled me toward it; I yielded, and, while one of the horses whinnied loudly to the ceiling, laid my head to the boy's breast, which shivered under my wet beard. I confirmed what I already knew; the boy was quite sound, something a little wrong with his circulation, saturated with coffee by his solicitous mother, but sound and best turned out of bed with one shove.

I am no world reformer and so I let him lie. I was the district doctor and did my duty to the uttermost, to the point where it became almost too much. I was badly paid and yet generous and helpful to the poor. I had still to see that Rose was all right, and then the boy might have his way and I wanted to die too. What was I doing there in that endless winter! My horse was dead, and not a single person in the village would lend me another. I had to get my team out of the pigsty; if they hadn't chanced to be horses I should have had to travel with swine. That was how it was. And I nodded to the family. They knew nothing about it, and, had they known, would not have believed it. To write prescriptions is easy, but to come to an understanding with people is hard. Well, this should be the end of my visit, I had once more been called out needlessly, I was used to that, the whole district made my life a torment with my night bell, but that I should have to sacrifice Rose this time as well, the pretty girl who had lived in my house for years almost without my noticing her—that sacrifice was too much to ask, and I had somehow to get it reasoned out in my head with the help of what craft I could muster, in order not to let fly at this family, which with the best will in the world could not restore Rose to me. But as I shut my bag and put an arm out for my fur coat, the family meanwhile standing together, the father sniffing at the glass of rum in his hand, the mother, apparently disappointed in me—why, what do people expect?—biting her lips with tears in her eyes, the sister fluttering a blood-soaked towel, I was somehow ready to admit conditionally that the boy might be ill after all. I went toward him, he welcomed me smiling as if I were bringing him the most nourishing invalid broth—ah, now both horses were whinnying together; the noise, I suppose, was ordained by heaven to assist my examination of the patient—and this time I discovered that the boy was indeed ill. In his right side, near the hip, was an open wound as big as the palm of my hand. Rose-red, in many variations of shade, dark in the hollows, lighter at the edges, softly granulated, with irregular clots of blood, open as a surface mine to the daylight. That was how it looked from a distance. But on a closer inspection there was another complication. I could not help a low whistle of surprise. Worms, as thick and as long as my little finger, themselves rose-red and blood-spotted as well, were wriggling from their fastness in the interior of the wound toward the light, with small white heads and many little legs. Poor boy, you were past helping. I had discovered your great wound; this blossom in your side was destroying you. The family was pleased; they saw me busying myself; the sister told the mother, the mother the father, the father told several guests who were coming in, through the moonlight at the open door, walking on tiptoe, keeping their balance with outstretched arms. "Will you save me?" whispered the boy with a sob, quite blinded by the life within his wound. That is what people are like in my district. Always expecting the impossible from the doctor. They have lost their ancient beliefs; the parson sits at home and unravels his vestments, one after another; but the doctor is supposed to be omnipotent with his merciful surgeon's hand. Well, as it pleases them; I have not thrust my services on them; if they misuse me for sacred ends, I let that happen to me too; what better do I want, old country doctor that I am, bereft of my servant girl! And so they came, the family and the village elders, and stripped my clothes off me; a school choir with the teacher at the head of it stood before the house and sang these words to an utterly simple tune:

*Strip his clothes off, then he'll heal us,*
*If he doesn't, kill him dead!*
*Only a doctor, only a doctor.*

Then my clothes were off and I looked at the people quietly, my fingers in my beard and my head cocked to one side. I was altogether composed and equal to the situation and remained so, although it was no help to me, since they now took me by the head and feet and carried me to the bed. They laid me down in it next to the wall, on the side of the wound. Then they all left the room; the door was shut; the singing stopped; clouds covered the moon; the bedding was warm around me; the horses' heads in the open windows wavered like shadows. "Do you know," said a voice in my ear, "I have very little confidence in you. Why, you were only blown in here, you didn't come on your own feet. Instead of helping me, you're cramping me on my deathbed. What I'd like best is to scratch your eyes out." "Right," I said, "it is a shame. And yet I am a doctor. What am I to do? Believe me, it is not too easy for me either." "Am I supposed to be content with this apology? Oh, I must be, I can't help it. I always have to put up with things. A fine wound is all I brought into the world; that was my sole endowment." "My young friend," said I, "your mistake is: you have not a wide enough view. I have been in all the sickrooms, far and wide, and I tell you: your wound is not so bad. Done in a tight corner with two strokes of the ax. Many a one proffers his side and can hardly hear the ax in the forest, far less that it is coming nearer to him." "Is that really so, or are you deluding me in my fever?" "It is really so, take the word of honor of an official doctor." And he took it and lay still. But now it was time for me to think of escaping. The horses were still standing faithfully in their places. My clothes, my fur coat, my bag were quickly collected; I didn't want to waste time dressing; if the horses raced home as they had come, I should only be springing, as it were, out of this bed into my own. Obediently a horse backed away from the window; I threw my bundle into the gig; the fur coat missed its mark and was caught on a hook only by the sleeve. Good enough. I swung myself onto the horse. With the reins loosely trailing, one horse barely fastened to the other, the gig swaying behind, my fur coat last of all in the snow. "Gee up!" I said, but there was no galloping; slowly, like old men, we crawled through the snowy wastes; a long time echoed behind us the new but faulty song of the children:

*O be joyful, all you patients,*
*The doctor's laid in bed beside you!*

Never shall I reach home at this rate; my flourishing practice is done for; my successor is robbing me, but in vain, for he cannot take my place; in my house the disgusting groom is raging; Rose is his victim; I do not want to think about it anymore. Naked, exposed to the frost of this most unhappy of ages, with an earthly vehicle, unearthly horses, old man that I am, I wander astray. My fur coat is hanging from the back of the gig, but I cannot reach it, and none of my limber pack of patients lifts a finger. Betrayed! Betrayed! A false alarm on the night bell once answered—it cannot be made good, not ever.

## *Study questions*

1. *If this story is a dream, who is the dreamer? What do the details of the dream tell us about the anxieties and frustrations of the dreamer? What is his conflict?* 2. *Is the groom someone the doctor fears? emulates?* 3. *Does the doctor desire Rose or want to protect her or both?* 4. *Who is the sick boy? What is the point of the doctor's getting into bed with the boy? What is the significance of the wound on the boy's side? Is the boy in any way similar to Rose?* 5. *Is the doctor supposed to be a savior figure? Is he sick too? Is the boy's wound also his?* 6. *Does the doctor accept or reject the notion of the underlying absurdity of human existence? Is the story a moral allegory? On how many levels does the allegory function?* 7. *Chart the plot line. What kind of plot does Kafka use?*

*Jorge Luis Borges* (b. 1899), one of the world's most prestigious authors, was born in Buenos Aires, Argentina. He traveled widely in Europe, attending secondary school in Geneva and, later, Cambridge University in England. Thereafter, he spent three years in Spain, returning to Buenos Aires in 1921. Because of his opposition to Nazism and Juan Perón during World War II, he was fired from his post as a librarian. After Perón was ousted in 1955, however, Borges became director of the Argentine National Library. At the same time he was appointed professor of English and American literature at the University of Buenos Aires. A poet, short-story writer, essayist, and film critic, he has also translated works by Gide, Melville, Faulkner, Joyce, and Woolf, among others. He was the first to translate Kafka into Spanish. Among his works that have been translated into English are *Ficciones* (tr. 1962), *Labyrinths* (tr. 1962), *Other Inquisitions* (tr. 1965), *Dr. Brodie's Report* (tr. 1972), and *The Book of Sand* (1978). His stories are a combination of myth, parable, and poetry. Always elusive, they are an attempt to find order in a four-dimensional universe. Operating in a time-space continuum where "reality" and "illusion" cease to be separate realms, they are often fabulous conundrums. "The Babylon Lottery" is a piece of four-dimensional science fiction. In it all possibilities exist in a space-time that is at the same time both real and unreal. "The Garden of Forking Paths" is itself a labyrinth of labyrinths mirroring a world where all possible outcomes of every single act occur at some place and in some time.

## THE BABYLON LOTTERY

Like all men in Babylon I have been a proconsul; like all, a slave; I have also known omnipotence, opprobrium, jail. Look: the index finger of my right hand is missing. Look again: through this rent in my cape you can see a ruddy tatoo on my belly. It is the second symbol, Beth. This letter, on nights of full moon, gives me power over men whose mark is Ghimel; but it also subordinates me to those marked Aleph, who on moonless nights owe obedience to those marked Ghimel. In a cellar at dawn, I have severed the jugular vein of sacred bulls against a black rock. During one lunar year, I have been declared invisible: I shrieked and was not heard, I stole my bread and was not decapitated. I have known what the Greeks did not: uncertainty. In a bronze chamber, faced with the silent handkerchief of a strangler, hope has been faithful to me; in the river of delights, panic has not failed me. Heraclitus of Pontica admiringly relates that Pythagoras recalled having been Pyrrho, and before that Euphorbus, and before that some other mortal. In order to recall analogous vicissitudes I do not need to have recourse to death, nor even to imposture.

I owe this almost atrocious variety to an institution which other republics know nothing about, or which operates among them imperfectly and in secret:

the lottery. I have not delved into its history; I do know that the wizards have been unable to come to any agreement; of its powerful designs I know what a man not versed in astrology might know of the moon. I come from a vertiginous country where the lottery forms a principal part of reality: until this very day I have thought about all this as little as I have about the behavior of the indecipherable gods or about the beating of my own heart. Now, far from Babylon and its beloved customs, I think of the lottery with some astonishment and ponder the blasphemous conjectures murmured by men in the shadows at twilight.

My father related that anciently—a matter of centuries; of years?—the lottery in Babylon was a game of plebeian character. He said (I do not know with what degree of truth) that barbers gave rectangular bits of bone or decorated parchment in exchange for copper coins. A drawing of the lottery was held in the middle of the day: the winners received, without further corroboration from chance, silver-minted coins. The procedure, as you see, was elemental.

Naturally, these "lotteries" failed. Their moral virtue was nil. They did not appeal to all the faculties of men: only to their hope. In the face of public indifference, the merchants who established these venal lotteries began to lose money. Someone attempted to introduce a slight reform: the interpolation of a certain small number of adverse outcomes among the favored numbers. By means of this reform, the purchasers of numbered rectangles stood the double chance of winning a sum or of paying a fine often considerable in size. This slight danger—for each thirty favored numbers there would be one adverse number—awoke, as was only natural, the public's interest. The Babylonians gave themselves up to the game. Anyone who did not acquire lots was looked upon as pusillanimous, mean-spirited. In time, this disdain multiplied. The person who did not play was despised, but the losers who paid the fine were also scorned. The Company (thus it began to be known at that time) was forced to take measures to protect the winners, who could not collect their prizes unless nearly the entire amount of the fines was already collected. The Company brought suit against the losers: the judge condemned them to pay the original fine plus costs or to spend a number of days in jail. Every loser chose jail, so as to defraud the Company. It was from this initial bravado of a few men that the all-powerful position of the Company—its ecclesiastical, metaphysical strength—was derived.

A short while later, the reports on the drawings omitted any enumeration of fines and limited themselves to publishing the jail sentences corresponding to each adverse number. This laconism, almost unnoticed at the time, became of capital importance. *It constituted the first appearance in the lottery of non-pecuniary elements.* Its success was great. Pushed to such a measure by the players, the Company found itself forced to increase its adverse numbers.

No one can deny that the people of Babylonia are highly devoted to logic, even to symmetry. It struck them as incoherent that the fortunate numbers should be computed in round figures of money while the unfortunate should be figured in terms of days and nights in jail. Some moralists argued that the possession of money does not determine happiness and that other forms of fortune are perhaps more immediate.

There was another source of restlessness in the lower depths. The members of the sacerdotal college multiplied the stakes and plumbed the vicissitudes of terror and hope; the poor, with reasonable or inevitable envy, saw themselves excluded from this notoriously delicious exhiliration. The just anxiety of all, poor and rich alike, to participate equally in the lottery, inspired an indignant agitation, the memory of which the years have not erased. Certain obstinate souls did not comprehend, or pretended not to comprehend, that a new order had come, a necessary historical stage. . . . A slave stole a crimson ticket, a ticket which earned him the right to have his tongue burned in the next drawing. The criminal code fixed the same penalty for the theft of a ticket. A number of Babylonians argued that he deserved a red-hot poker by virtue of the theft; others, more magnanimous, held that the public executioner should apply the penalty of the lottery, since chance had so determined. . . .

Disturbances broke out, there was a lamentable shedding of blood; but the people of Babylon imposed their will at last, over the opposition of the rich. That is: the people fully achieved their magnanimous ends. In the first place, it made the Company accept complete public power. (This unification was necessary, given the vastness and complexity of the new operations.) In the second place, it forced the lottery to be secret, free, and general. The sale of tickets for money was abolished. Once initiated into the mysteries of Bel, every free man automatically participated in the sacred drawings of lots, which were carried out in the labyrinths of the gods every seventy nights and which determined every man's fate until the next exercise. The consequences were incalculable. A happy drawing might motivate his elevation to the council of wizards or his condemnation to the custody of an enemy (notorious or intimate), or to find, in the peaceful shadows of a room, the woman who had begun to disquiet him or whom he had never expected to see again. An adverse drawing might mean mutilation, a varied infamy, death. Sometimes a single event—the tavern killing of C, the mysterious glorification of B—might be the brilliant result of thirty or forty drawings. But it must be recalled that the individuals of the Company were (and are) all-powerful and astute as well. In many cases, the knowledge that certain joys were the simple doing of chance might have detracted from their excellence; to avoid this inconvenience the Company's agents made use of suggestion and magic. Their moves, their management, were secret. In the investigation of people's intimate hopes and intimate terrors, they made use of astrologers and spies. There were certain stone lions, there was a sacred privy called Qaphqa, there were fissures in a dusty aqueduct which, according to general opinion, *lead to the Company;* malign or benevolent people deposited accusations in these cracks. These denunciations were incorporated into an alphabetical archive of variable veracity.

Incredibly enough, there were still complaints. The Company, with its habitual discretion, did not reply directly. It preferred to scribble a brief argument—which now figures among sacred scriptures—in the debris of a mask factory. That doctrinal piece of literature observed that the lottery is an interpolation of chance into the order of the world and that to accept errors is not to contradict fate but merely to corroborate it. It also observed that those lions and that sacred recipient, though not unauthorized by the Company (which did not renounce the right to consult them), functioned without official guaranty.

This declaration pacified the public unease. It also produced other effects, not foreseen by the author. It deeply modified the spirit and operations of the Company. (I have little time left to tell what I know; we have been warned that the ship is ready to sail; but I will attempt to explain it.)

Improbable as it may be, no one had until then attempted to set up a general theory of games. A Babylonian is not highly speculative. He reveres the judgments of fate, he hands his life over to them, he places his hopes, his panic terror in them, but it never occurs to him to investigate their labyrinthian laws nor the giratory spheres which disclose them. Nevertheless, the unofficial declaration which I have mentioned inspired many discussions of a juridico-mathematical nature. From one of these discussions was born the following conjecture: if the lottery is an intensification of chance, a periodic infusion of chaos into the cosmos, would it not be desirable for chance to intervene at all stages of the lottery and not merely in the drawing? Is it not ridiculous for chance to dictate the death of someone, while the circumstances of his death—its silent reserve or publicity, the time limit of one hour or one century—should remain immune to hazard? These eminently just scruples finally provoked a considerable reform, whose complexities (intensified by the practice of centuries) are not understood except by a handful of specialists, but which I will attempt to summarize, even if only in a symbolic manner.

Let us imagine a first drawing, which eventuates in a sentence of death against some individual. To carry out the sentence, another drawing is set up, and this drawing proposes (let us say) nine possible executioners. Of these executioners, four can initiate a third drawing which will reveal the name of the actual executioner, two others can replace the adverse order with a fortunate order (the finding of a treasure, let us say), another may exacerbate the death sentence (that is: make it infamous or enrich it with torture), still others may refuse to carry it out. . . .

Such is the symbolic scheme. In reality, *the number of drawings is infinite.* No decision is final, all diverge into others. The ignorant suppose that an infinite number of drawings require an infinite amount of time; in reality, it is quite enough that time be infinitely subdivisible, as is the case in the famous parable of the Tortoise and the Hare. This infinitude harmonizes in an admirable manner with the sinuous numbers of Chance and of the Celestial Archetype of the Lottery adored by the Platonists. . . .

A certain distorted echo of our ritual seems to have resounded along the Tiber: Aelius Lampridius, in his *Life of Antoninus Heliogabalus,* tells of how this emperor wrote down the lot of his guests on seashells, so that one would receive ten pounds of gold and another ten flies, ten dormice, ten bears. It is only right to remark that Heliogabalus was educated in Asia Minor, among the priests of the eponymous god.

There are also impersonal drawings, of undefined purpose: one drawing will decree that a sapphire from Taprobane be thrown into the waters of the Euphrates; another, that a bird be released from a tower roof; another, that a grain of sand be withdrawn (or added) to the innumerable grains on a beach. The consequences, sometimes, are terrifying.

Under the beneficent influence of the Company, our customs have become thoroughly impregnated with chance. The buyer of a dozen amphoras of Damascus wine will not be surprised if one of them contains a talisman or a viper. The scribe who draws up a contract scarcely ever fails to introduce some erroneous datum; I myself, in making this hasty declaration, have falsified or invented some grandeur, some atrocity; perhaps, too, a certain mysterious monotony. . . .

Our historians, the most discerning in the world, have invented a method for correcting chance. It is well known that the operations of this method are (in general) trustworthy; although, naturally, they are not divulged without a measure of deceit. In any case, there is nothing so contaminated with fiction as the history of the Company. . . .

A paleographic document, unearthed in a temple, may well be the work of yesterday's drawing or that of one lasting a century. No book is ever published without some variant in each copy. Scribes take a secret oath to omit, interpolate, vary.

The Company, with divine modesty, eludes all publicity. Its agents, as is only natural, are secret. The orders which it is continually sending out do not differ from those lavishly issued by imposters. Besides, who can ever boast of being a mere imposter? The inebriate who improvises an absurd mandate, the dreamer who suddenly awakes to choke the woman who lies at his side to death, do they not both, perhaps, carry out a secret decision by the Company? This silent functioning, comparable to that of God, gives rise to all manner of conjectures. One of them, for instance, abominably insinuates that the Company is eternal and that it will last until the last night of the world, when the last god annihilates the cosmos. Still another conjecture declares that the Company is omnipotent, but that it exerts its influence only in the most minute matters: in a bird's cry, in the shades of rust and the hues of dust, in the cat naps of dawn. There is one conjecture, spoken from the mouths of masked heresiarchs, to the effect that *the Company has never existed and never will.* A conjecture no less vile argues that it is indifferently inconsequential to affirm or deny the reality of the shadowy corporation, because Babylon is nothing but an infinite game of chance.

## *Study questions*

1. *Who is the narrator? Where is he?* 2. *How did the lottery of Babylon start? What changes were made in it? Why? What did it finally come to be?* 3. *What does the narrator mean when he says, "In reality,* the number of drawings is infinite. *No decision is final, all diverge into others."* 4. *Is the narrator reliable?* 5. *Does the lottery exist? Does Babylon exist?* 6. *Is Babylon a microcosm? Is the story an allegory?*

# THE GARDEN OF FORKING PATHS

TO VICTORIA OCAMPO

In his *A History of the World War* (page 212), Captain Liddell Hart reports that a planned offensive by thirteen British divisions, supported by fourteen hundred artillery pieces, against the German line at Serre-Montauban, scheduled for July 24, 1916, had to be postponed until the morning of the 29th. He comments that torrential rain caused this delay—which lacked any special significance. The following deposition, dictated by, read over, and then signed by Dr. Yu Tsun, former teacher of English at the Tsingtao *Hochschule,* casts unsuspected light upon this event. The first two pages are missing.

. . . and I hung up the phone. Immediately I recollected the voice that had spoken in German. It was that of Captain Richard Madden. Madden, in Viktor Runeberg's office, meant the end of all our work and—though this seemed a secondary matter, *or should have seemed so to me*—of our lives also. His being there meant that Runeberg had been arrested or murdered.* Before the sun set on this same day, I ran the same risk. Madden was implacable. Rather, to be more accurate, he was obliged to be implacable. An Irishman in the service of England, a man suspected of equivocal feelings if not of actual treachery, how could he fail to welcome and seize upon this extraordinary piece of luck: the discovery, capture and perhaps the deaths of two agents of Imperial Germany?

I went up to my bedroom. Absurd though the gesture was, I closed and locked the door. I threw myself down on my narrow iron bed, and waited on my back. The never changing rooftops filled the window, and the hazy six o'clock sun hung in the sky. It seemed incredible that this day, a day without warnings or omens, might be that of my implacable death. In despite of my dead father, in despite of having been a child in one of the symmetrical gardens of Hai Feng, was I to die now?

Then I reflected that all things happen, happen to one, precisely *now*. Century follows century, and things happen only in the present. There are countless men in the air, on land and at sea, and all that really happens happens to me. . . . The almost unbearable memory of Madden's long horseface put an end to these wandering thoughts.

In the midst of my hatred and terror (now that it no longer matters to me to speak of terror, now that I have outwitted Richard Madden, now that my

* A malicious and outlandish statement. In point of fact, Captain Richard Madden had been attacked by the Prussian spy Hans Rabener, alias Viktor Runeberg, who drew an automatic pistol when Madden appeared with orders for the spy's arrest. Madden, in self defense, had inflicted wounds of which the spy later died.—*Note by the manuscript editor.*

neck hankers for the hangman's noose), I knew that the fast-moving and doubtless happy soldier did not suspect that I possessed the Secret—the name of the exact site of the new British artillery park on the Ancre. A bird streaked across the misty sky and, absently, I turned it into an airplane and then that airplane into many in the skies of France, shattering the artillery park under a rain of bombs. If only my mouth, before it should be silenced by a bullet, could shout this name in such a way that it could be heard in Germany. . . . My voice, my human voice, was weak. How could it reach the ear of the Chief? The ear of that sick and hateful man who knew nothing of Runeberg or of me except that we were in Staffordshire. A man who, sitting in his arid Berlin office, leafed infinitely through newspapers, looking in vain for news from us. I said aloud, "I must flee."

I sat up on the bed, in senseless and perfect silence, as if Madden was already peering at me. Something—perhaps merely a desire to prove my total penury to myself—made me empty out my pockets. I found just what I knew I was going to find. The American watch, the nickel-plated chain and the square coin, the key ring with the useless but compromising keys to Runeberg's office, the notebook, a letter which I decided to destroy at once (and which I did not destroy), a five shilling piece, two single shillings and some pennies, a red and blue pencil, a handkerchief—and a revolver with a single bullet. Absurdly I held it and weighed it in my hand, to give myself courage. Vaguely I thought that a pistol shot can be heard for a great distance.

In ten minutes I had developed my plan. The telephone directory gave me the name of the one person capable of passing on the information. He lived in a suburb of Fenton, less than half an hour away by train.

I am a timorous man. I can say it now, now that I have brought my incredibly risky plan to an end. It was not easy to bring about, and I know that its execution was terrible. I did not do it for Germany—no! Such a barbarous country is of no importance to me, particularly since it had degraded me by making me become a spy. Furthermore, I knew an Englishman—a modest man—who, for me, is as great as Goethe. I did not speak with him for more than an hour, but during that time, he *was* Goethe.

I carried out my plan because I felt the Chief had some fear of those of my race, of those uncountable forebears whose culmination lies in me. I wished to prove to him that a yellow man could save his armies. Besides, I had to escape the Captain. His hands and voice could, at any moment, knock and beckon at my door.

Silently, I dressed, took leave of myself in the mirror, went down the stairs, sneaked a look at the quiet street, and went out. The station was not far from my house, but I thought it more prudent to take a cab. I told myself that I thus ran less chance of being recognized. The truth is that, in the deserted street, I felt infinitely visible and vulnerable. I recall that I told the driver to stop short of the main entrance. I got out with a painful and deliberate slowness.

I was going to the village of Ashgrove, but took a ticket for a station further on. The train would leave in a few minutes, at eight-fifty. I hurried, for the next would not go until half past nine. There was almost no one on the platform. I walked through the carriages. I remember some farmers, a woman dressed in mourning, a youth deep in Tacitus' *Annals* and a wounded, happy soldier.

At last the train pulled out. A man I recognized ran furiously, but vainly, the length of the platform. It was Captain Richard Madden. Shattered, trembling, I huddled in the distant corner of the seat, as far as possible from the fearful window.

From utter terror I passed into a state of almost abject happiness. I told myself that the duel had already started and that I had won the first encounter by besting my adversary in his first attack—even if it was only for forty minutes—by an accident of fate. I argued that so small a victory prefigured a total victory. I argued that it was not so trivial, that were it not for the precious accident of the train schedule, I would be in prison or dead. I argued, with no less sophism, that my timorous happiness was proof that I was man enough to bring this adventure to a successful conclusion. From my weakness I drew strength that never left me.

I foresee that man will resign himself each day to new abominations, that soon only soldiers and bandits will be left. To them I offer this advice: *Whosoever would undertake some atrocious enterprise should act as if it were already accomplished, should impose upon himself a future as irrevocable as the past.*

Thus I proceeded, while with the eyes of a man already dead, I contemplated the fluctuations of the day which would probably be my last, and watched the diffuse coming of night.

The train crept along gently, amid ash trees. It slowed down and stopped, almost in the middle of a field. No one called the name of a station. "Ashgrove?" I asked some children on the platform. "Ashgrove," they replied. I got out.

A lamp lit the platform, but the children's faces remained in a shadow. One of them asked me: "Are you going to Dr. Stephen Albert's house?" Without waiting for my answer, another said: "The house is a good distance away but you won't get lost if you take the road to the left and bear to the left at every crossroad." I threw them a coin (my last), went down some stone steps and started along a deserted road. At a slight incline, the road ran downhill. It was a plain dirt way, and overhead the branches of trees intermingled, while a round moon hung low in the sky as if to keep me company.

For a moment I thought that Richard Madden might in some way have divined my desperate intent. At once I realized that this would be impossible. The advice about turning always to the left reminded me that such was the common formula for finding the central courtyard of certain labyrinths. I know something about labyrinths. Not for nothing am I the great-grandson of Ts'ui Pên. He was Governor of Yunnan and gave up temporal power to write a novel with more characters than there are in the *Hung Lou Mêng,* and to create a maze in which all men would lose themselves. He spent thirteen years on these oddly assorted tasks before he was assassinated by a stranger. His novel had no sense to it and nobody ever found his labyrinth.

Under the trees of England I meditated on this lost and perhaps mythical labyrinth. I imagined it untouched and perfect on the secret summit of some mountain; I imagined it drowned under rice paddies or beneath the sea; I imagined it infinite, made not only of eight-sided pavilions and of twisting paths but also of rivers, provinces and kingdoms. . . . I thought of a maze of mazes, of a sinuous, ever growing maze which would take in both past and future and would somehow involve the stars.

Lost in these imaginary illusions I forgot my destiny—that of the hunted. For an undetermined period of time I felt myself cut off from the world, an abstract spectator. The hazy and murmuring countryside, the moon, the decline of the evening, stirred within me. Going down the gently sloping road I could not feel fatigue. The evening was at once intimate and infinite.

The road kept descending and branching off, through meadows misty in the twilight. A high-pitched and almost syllabic music kept coming and going, moving with the breeze, blurred by the leaves and by distance.

I thought that a man might be an enemy of other men, of the differing moments of other men, but never an enemy of a country: not of fireflies, words, gardens, streams, or the West wind.

Meditating thus I arrived at a high, rusty iron gate. Through the railings I could see an avenue bordered with poplar trees and also a kind of summer house or pavilion. Two things dawned on me at once, the first trivial and the second almost incredible: the music came from the pavilion and that music was Chinese. That was why I had accepted it fully, without paying it any attention. I do not remember whether there was a bell, a push-button, or whether I attracted attention by clapping my hands. The stuttering sparks of the music kept on.

But from the end of the avenue, from the main house, a lantern approached; a lantern which alternately, from moment to moment, was crisscrossed or put out by the trunks of the trees; a paper lantern shaped like a drum and colored like the moon. A tall man carried it. I could not see his face for the light blinded me.

He opened the gate and spoke slowly in my language.

"I see that the worthy Hsi P'eng has troubled himself to see to relieving my solitude. No doubt you want to see the garden?"

Recognizing the name of one of our consuls, I replied, somewhat taken aback.

"The garden?"

"The garden of forking paths."

Something stirred in my memory and I said, with incomprehensible assurance:

"The garden of my ancestor, Ts'ui Pên."

"Your ancestor? Your illustrious ancestor? Come in."

The damp path zigzagged like those of my childhood. When we reached the house, we went into a library filled with books from both East and West. I recognized some large volumes bound in yellow silk—manuscripts of the Lost Encyclopedia which was edited by the Third Emperor of the Luminous Dynasty. They had never been printed. A phonograph record was spinning near a bronze phoenix. I remember also a rose-glazed jar and yet another, older by many centuries, of that blue color which our potters copied from the Persians. . . .

Stephen Albert was watching me with a smile on his face. He was, as I have said, remarkably tall. His face was deeply lined and he had gray eyes and a gray beard. There was about him something of the priest, and something of the sailor. Later, he told me he had been a missionary in Tientsin before he "had aspired to become a Sinologist."

We sat down, I upon a large, low divan, he with his back to the window and to a large circular clock. I calculated that my pursuer, Richard Madden, could not arrive in less than an hour. My irrevocable decision could wait.

"A strange destiny," said Stephen Albert, "that of Ts'ui Pên—Governor of his native province, learned in astronomy, in astrology and tireless in the interpretation of the canonical books, a chess player, a famous poet and a calligrapher. Yet he abandoned all to make a book and a labyrinth. He gave up all the pleasures of oppression, justice, of a well-stocked bed, of banquets, and even of erudition, and shut himself up in the Pavilion of the Limpid Sun for thirteen years. At his death, his heirs found only a mess of manuscripts. The family, as you doubtless know, wished to consign them to the fire, but the executor of the estate—a Taoist or a Buddhist monk—insisted on their publication."

"Those of the blood of Ts'ui Pên," I replied, "still curse the memory of that monk. Such a publication was madness. The book is a shapeless mass of contradictory rough drafts. I examined it once upon a time: the hero dies in the third chapter, while in the fourth he is alive. As for that other enterprise of Ts'ui Pên . . . his Labyrinth. . . ."

"Here is the Labyrinth," Albert said, pointing to a tall, laquered writing cabinet.

"An ivory labyrinth?" I exclaimed. "A tiny labyrinth indeed . . . !"

"A symbolic labyrinth," he corrected me. "An invisible labyrinth of time. I, a barbarous Englishman, have been given the key to this transparent mystery. After more than a hundred years most of the details are irrecoverable, lost beyond all recall, but it isn't hard to image what must have happened. At one time, Ts'ui Pên must have said; 'I am going into seclusion to write a book,' and at another, 'I am retiring to construct a maze.' Everyone assumed these were separate activities. No one realized that the book and the labyrinth were one and the same. The Pavilion of the Limpid Sun was set in the middle of an intricate garden. This may have suggested the idea of a physical maze.

"Ts'ui Pên died. In all the vast lands which once belonged to your family, no one could find the labyrinth. The novel's confusion suggested that *it* was the labyrinth. Two circumstances showed me the direct solution to the problem. First, the curious legend that Ts'ui Pên had proposed to create an infinite maze, second, a fragment of a letter which I discovered."

Albert rose. For a few moments he turned his back to me. He opened the top drawer in the high black and gilded writing cabinet. He returned holding in his hand a piece of paper which had once been crimson but which had faded with the passage of time: it was rose colored, tenuous, quadrangular. Ts'ui Pên's calligraphy was justly famous. Eagerly, but without understanding, I read the words which a man of my own blood had written with a small brush: "I leave to various future times, but not to all, my garden of forking paths."

I handed back the sheet of paper in silence. Albert went on:

"Before I discovered this letter, I kept asking myself how a book could be infinite. I could not imagine any other than a cyclic volume, circular. A volume whose last page would be the same as the first and so have the possibility of continuing indefinitely. I recalled, too, the night in the middle of *The Thousand and One Nights* when Queen Scheherezade, through a magical mistake on the part of her copyist, started to tell the story of *The Thousand and One Nights,* with the risk of again arriving at the night upon which she will relate it, and thus on to infinity. I also imagined a Platonic hereditary work, passed on from father to son, to which each individual would add a new chapter or correct, with pious care, the work of his elders.

"These conjectures gave me amusement, but none seemed to have the remotest application to the contradictory chapters of Ts'ui Pên. At this point, I was sent from Oxford the manuscript you have just seen.

"Naturally, my attention was caught by the sentence, 'I leave to various future times, but not to all, my garden of forking paths.' I had no sooner read this, than I understood. *The Garden of Forking Paths* was the chaotic novel itself. The phrase 'to various future times, but not to all' suggested the image of bifurcating in time, not in space. Re-reading the whole work confirmed this theory. In all fiction, when a man is faced with alternatives he chooses one at the expense of the others. In the almost unfathomable Ts'ui Pên, he chooses—simultaneously—all of them. He thus *creates* various futures, various times which start others that will in their turn branch out and bifurcate in other times. This is the cause of the contradictions in the novel.

"Fang, let us say, has a secret. A stranger knocks at his door. Fang makes up his mind to kill him. Naturally there are various possible outcomes. Fang can kill the intruder, the intruder can kill Fang, both can be saved, both can die and so on and so on. In Ts'ui Pên's work, all the possible solutions occur, each one being the point of departure for other bifurcations. Sometimes the pathways of this labyrinth converge. For example, you come to this house; but in other possible pasts you are my enemy; in others my friend.

"If you will put up with my atrocious pronunciation, I would like to read you a few pages of your ancestor's work."

His countenance, in the bright circle of lamplight, was certainly that of an ancient, but it shone with something unyielding, even immortal.

With slow precision, he read two versions of the same epic chapter. In the first, an army marches into battle over a desolate mountain pass. The bleak and somber aspect of the rocky landscape made the soldiers feel that life itself was of little value, and so they won the battle easily. In the second, the same army passes through a palace where a banquet is in progress. The splendor of the feast remained a memory throughout the glorious battle, and so victory followed.

With proper veneration I listened to these old tales, although perhaps with less admiration for them in themselves than for the fact that they had been thought out by one of my own blood, and that a man of a distant empire had given them back to me, in the last stage of a desperate adventure, on a Western island. I remember the final words, repeated at the end of each version like a secret command: "Thus the heroes fought, with tranquil heart and bloody sword. They were resigned to killing and to dying."

At that moment I felt within me and around me something invisible and intangible pullulating. It was not the pullulation of two divergent, parallel, and finally converging armies, but an agitation more inaccessible, more intimate, prefigured by them in some way. Stephen Albert continued:

"I do not think that your illustrious ancestor toyed idly with variations. I do not find it believable that he would waste thirteen years laboring over a never ending experiment in rhetoric. In your country the novel is an inferior genre; in Ts'ui Pên's period, it was a despised one. Ts'ui Pên was a fine novelist but he was also a man of letters who, doubtless, considered himself more than a mere novelist. The testimony of his contemporaries attests to this, and certainly the known facts of his life confirm his leanings toward the metaphysical and the mystical. Philosophical conjectures take up the greater part of his novel. I know that of all problems, none disquieted him more, and none concerned him more than the profound one of time. Now then, this is the *only* problem that does not figure in the pages of *The Garden*. He does not even use the word which means *time*. How can these voluntary omissions be explained?"

I proposed various solutions, all of them inadequate. We discussed them. Finally Stephen Albert said: "In a guessing game to which the answer is chess, which word is the only one prohibited?" I thought for a moment and then replied:

"The word is *chess*."

"Precisely," said Albert. "*The Garden of Forking Paths* is an enormous guessing game, or parable, in which the subject is time. The rules of the game forbid the use of the word itself. To eliminate a word completely, to refer to it by means of inept phrases and obvious paraphrases, is perhaps the best way of drawing attention to it. This, then, is the tortuous method of approach preferred by the oblique Ts'ui Pên in every meandering of his interminable novel. I have gone over hundreds of manuscripts, I have corrected errors introduced by careless copyists, I have worked out the plan from this chaos, I have restored, or believe I have restored, the original. I have translated the whole work. I can state categorically that not once has the word *time* been used in the whole book.

"The explanation is obvious. *The Garden of Forking Paths* is a picture, incomplete yet not false, of the universe such as Ts'ui Pên conceived it to be. Differing from Newton and Schopenhauer, your ancestor did not think of time as absolute and uniform. He believed in an infinite series of times, in a dizzily growing, ever spreading network of diverging, converging and parallel times. This web of time—the strands of which approach one another, bifurcate, intersect or ignore each other through the centuries—embraces *every* possibility. We do not exist in most of them. In some you exist and not I, while in others I do, and you do not, and in yet others both of us exist. In this one, in which chance has favored me, you have come to my gate. In another, you, crossing the garden, have found me dead. In yet another, I say these very same words, but am an error, a phantom."

"In all of them," I enunciated, with a tremor in my voice. "I deeply appreciate and am grateful to you for the restoration of Ts'ui Pên's garden."

"Not in *all*," he murmured with a smile. "Time is forever dividing itself toward innumerable futures and in one of them I am your enemy."

Once again I sensed the pullulation of which I have already spoken. It seemed to me that the dew-damp garden surrounding the house was infinitely saturated with invisible people. All were Albert and myself, secretive, busy and multiform in other dimensions of time. I lifted my eyes and the short nightmare disappeared. In the black and yellow garden there was only a single man, but this man was as strong as a statue and this man was walking up the path and he was Captain Richard Madden.

"The future exists now," I replied. "But I am your friend. Can I take another look at the letter?"

Albert rose from his seat. He stood up tall as he opened the top drawer of the high writing cabinet. For a moment his back was again turned to me. I had the revolver ready. I fired with the utmost care: Albert fell without a murmur, at once. I swear that his death was instantaneous, as if he had been struck by lightning.

What remains is unreal and unimportant. Madden broke in and arrested me. I have been condemned to hang. Abominably, I have yet triumphed! The secret name of the city to be attacked got through to Berlin. Yesterday it was bombed. I read the news in the same English newspapers which were trying to solve the riddle of the murder of the learned Sinologist Stephen Albert by the unknown Yu Tsun. The Chief, however, had already solved this mystery. He knew that my problem was to shout, with my feeble voice, above the tumult of war, the name of the city called Albert, and that I had no other course open to me than to kill someone of that name. He does not know, for no one can, of my infinite penitence and sickness of the heart.

## *Study questions*

1. *Who is the narrator of this story? How is the narrator related to Dr. Yu Tsun?* 2. *How many scramblings of nations and nationalities occur in the story? How many scramblings in time? in space?* 3. *The labyrinth is an important symbol in the story. How many mazes can you find?* 4. *How does Ts'ui Pên's* The Garden of Forking Paths *function in the story?* 5. *What role does Stephen Albert play? Why does Dr. Yu Tsun kill him?* 6. *Is the "spy" story related to the story's larger meaning?* 7. *Is the world that you experience anything like the world that Borges presents? Is Borges's world consonant with recent scientific discoveries?*

*Vladimir Nabokov* (1899–1977), perhaps the most brilliant writer of the second half of the century and certainly the most original English prose stylist since Joyce, was born in St. Petersburg, Russia, to a rich and aristocratic family. Trilingual as a child, he was educated in Russia and Trinity College at Cambridge University, where he took an honors degree in Slavic and Romance languages. For the next eighteen years he lived in France and Germany where his family, exiled by the Bolshevik Revolution, took up residence. He came to the United States in 1940 and became an American citizen in 1945. From 1941 to 1948 he taught at Wellesley, and from 1948 to 1959 he taught at Cornell. His first novel published in English was *The Real Life of Sebastian Knight* (1941). With the publication of *Lolita* in Paris in 1955 and in the United States in 1958, he received worldwide acclaim and monetary reward that enabled him to resign from teaching and devote himself full-time to writing. Some of his important later novels are *Pnin* (1957), *Pale Fire* (1962), and *Ada* (1969). His stories have been collected in several volumes, including *Nabokov's Dozen* (1958) and *A Russian Beauty and Other Stories* (1973). Some time before his death in Switzerland, he embarked on a project with his son to translate his Russian writings into English, so that now more than twenty-five volumes of his collected works are available in English. Like his novels, his short stories are characterized by a dazzling technical dexterity and a verbal magic. His narratives are involuted, self-referential, games of words where "reality," "fantasy," "dream," and "memory" merge in surreal perspective. "The Leonardo" operates by means of a double reversal. The artist turns out to be a counterfeiter, but the counterfeiter is, after all, an artist. "The Visit to the Museum" merges time and space, illusion and reality, questioning ordinary perspective. " 'That in Aleppo Once . . .' " is a brilliant exercise in the surreal.

## THE LEONARDO

The objects that are being summoned assemble, draw near from different spots; in doing so, some of them have to overcome not only the distance of space but that of time: which nomad, you may wonder, is more bothersome to cope with, this one or that, the young poplar, say, that once grew in the vicinity but was cut down long ago, or the singled-out courtyard which still exists today but is situated far away from here? Hurry up, please.

Here comes the ovate little poplar, all punctated with April greenery, and takes its stand where told, namely by the tall brick wall, imported in one piece from another city. Facing it, there grows up a dreary and dirty tenement house, with mean little balconies pulled out one by one like drawers. Other bits of scenery are distributed about the yard: a barrel, a second barrel, the delicate shade of leaves, an urn of sorts, and a stone cross propped at the foot of the wall. All this is only sketched and much has to be added and finished, and yet two live people—Gustav and his brother Anton—already come out on their tiny balcony, while rolling before him a little pushcart with a suitcase and a heap of books, Romantovski, the new lodger, enters the yard.

As seen from the yard, and especially on a bright day, the rooms of the house seem filled up with dense blackness (night is always with us, in this or that place, inside, during one part of twenty-four hours, outside, during the other). Romantovski looked up at the black open windows, at the two frog-eyed men watching him from their balcony, and shouldering his bag—with a forward lurch as if someone had banged him on the back of the head—plunged into the doorway. There remained, sunlit: the pushcart with the books, one barrel, another barrel, the nictating young poplar and an inscription in tar on the brick wall: VOTE FOR (illegible). Presumably it had been scrawled by the brothers before the elections.

Now this is the way we'll arrange the world: every man shall sweat, every man shall eat. There will be work, there will be belly-cheer, there will be a clean, warm, sunny—

(Romantovski became the occupant of the adjacent one. It was even drabber than theirs. But under the bed he discovered a small rubber doll. He concluded that his predecessor had been a family man.)

Despite the world's not having yet conclusively and totally turned into solid matter and still retaining sundry regions of an intangible and hallowed nature, the brothers felt snug and confident. The elder one, Gustav, had a furniture-moving job; the younger happened to be temporarily unemployed, but did not lose heart. Gustav had an evenly ruddy complexion, bristling fair eyebrows, and an ample, cupboard-like torso always clothed in a pullover of coarse gray wool. He wore elastic bands to hold his shirt-sleeves at the joints of his fat arms, so as to keep his wrists free and prevent sloppiness. Anton's face was pockmarked, he trimmed his mustache in the shape of a dark trapezoid, and wore a dark red sweater over his spare wiry frame. But when they both leaned their elbows on the balcony railings, their backsides were exactly the same, big and triumphant, with identically checkered cloth enclosing tightly their prominent buttocks.

Repeat: the world shall be sweaty and well-fed. Idlers, parasites, and musicians are not admitted. While one's heart pumps blood one should *live,* damn it! For two years now Gustav had been saving money to marry Anna, acquire a sideboard, a carpet.

She would come every other evening, that plump-armed buxom woman, with freckles on the broad bridge of her nose, a leaden shadow under her eyes, and spaced teeth one of which, moreover, had been knocked out. The brothers and she would swill beer. She had a way of clasping her bare arms behind her nape, displaying the gleaming-wet red tufts of her armpits. With head thrown back, she opened her mouth so generously that one could survey her entire palate and uvula, which resembled the tail end of a boiled chicken. The anatomy of her mirth was greatly to the liking of the two brothers. They tickled her with zest.

In the daytime, while his brother worked, Anton sat in a friendly pub or sprawled among the dandelions on the cool, still vividly green grass along the canal bank and observed with envy exuberant roughs loading coal on a barge, or else stared stupidly at the empty blue of the sleep-inducing sky. But presently in the well-oiled life of the brothers some obstruction occurred.

From the very moment he had appeared, rolling his pushcart into the yard, Romantovski had provoked a mixture of irritation and curiosity in the two brothers. Their infallible flair let them sense that here was someone different from other people. Normally, one would not discern anything special in him at a casual glance, but the brothers did. For example, he walked differently: at every step he rose on a buoyant toe in a peculiar manner, stepping and flying up as if the mere act of treading allowed him a chance to perceive something uncommon over the common heads. He was what is termed a "slank," very lean, with a pale sharp-nosed face and appallingly restless eyes. Out of the much too short sleeves of his double-breasted jacket his long wrists protruded with a kind of annoying and nonsensical obviousness ("here we are: what should we do?"). He went out and came home at unpredictable hours. On one of the first mornings Anton caught sight of him near a bookstand: he was pricing, or had actually bought something, because the vendor nimbly beat one dusty volume against another and carried them to his nook behind the stand. Additional eccentricities were noted: his light remained on practically until dawn; he was oddly unsociable.

We hear Anton's voice:

"That fine gentleman shows off. We should give him a closer look."

"I'll sell him the pipe," said Gustav.

The misty origins of the pipe. Anna had brought it over one day, but the brothers recognized only cigarillos. An expensive pipe, not yet blackened. It had a little steel tube inserted in its stem. With it came a suede case.

"Who's there? What do you want?" asked Romantovski through the door.

"Neighbors, neighbors," answered Gustav in a deep voice.

And the neighbors entered, avidly looking around. A stump of sausage lay on the table next to an uneven pile of books; one of them was opened on a picture of ships with numerous sails and, flying above, in one corner, an infant with puffed-out cheeks.

"Let's get acquainted," rumbled the brothers. "Folks live side by side, one can say, but never meet somehow or other."

The top of the commode was shared by an alcohol burner and an orange.

"Delighted," said Romantovski softly. He sat down on the edge of the bed, and with bent forehead, its V-vein inflamed, started to lace his shoes.

"You were resting," said Gustav with ominous courtesy. "We come at the wrong time?"

Not a word, not a word, did the lodger say in reply; instead he straightened up suddenly, turned to the window, raised his finger, and froze.

The brothers looked but found nothing unusual about that window; it framed a cloud, the tip of the poplar, and part of the brick wall.

"Why, don't you see anything?" asked Romantovski.

Red sweater and gray went up to the window and actually leaned out, becoming identical twins. Nothing. And both had the sudden feeling that something was wrong, very wrong! They wheeled around. He stood near the chest of drawers in an odd attitude.

"I must have been mistaken," said Romantovski, not looking at them. "Something seemed to have flown by. I saw once an airplane fall."

"That happens," assented Gustav. "Listen, we dropped in with a purpose. Would you care to buy this? Brand new. And there's a nice sheath."

"Sheath? Is that so? Only, you know, I smoke very seldom."

"Well, you'll smoke oftener. We sell it cheap. Three-fifty."

"Three-fifty. I see."

He fingered the pipe, biting his nether lip and pondering something. His eyes did not really look at the pipe, they moved to and fro.

Meanwhile the brothers began to swell, to grow, they filled up the whole room, the whole house, and then grew out of it. In comparison to them the young poplar was, by then, no bigger than one of those toy treelets, made of dyed cotton wool, that are so unstable on their round green supports. The doll-house, a thing of dusty pasteboard with mica windowpanes, barely reached up to the brothers' knees. Gigantic, imperiously reeking of sweat and beer, with beefy voices and senseless speeches, with fecal matter replacing the human brain, they provoke a tremor of ignoble fear. I don't know why they push against me; I implore you, do leave me alone. I'm not touching you, so don't you touch me either; I'll give in, only do leave me alone.

"All right, but I don't have enough change," said Romantovski in a low voice. "Now if you can give me six-fifty—"

They could, and went away, grinning. Gustav examined the ten-mark bill against the light and put it away in an iron money box.

Nevertheless, they did not leave their room neighbor in peace. It just maddened them that despite their having got acquainted with him, a man should remain as inaccessible as before. He avoided running into them: one had to waylay and trap him in order to glance fleetingly into his evasive eyes. Having discovered the nocturnal life of Romantovski's lamp, Anton could not bear it any longer. He crept up barefoot to the door (from under which showed a taut thread of golden light) and knocked.

Romantovski did not respond.

"Sleep, sleep," said Anton slapping the door with his palm.

The light peered silently through the chink. Anton shook the door handle. The golden thread snapped.

Thenceforth both brothers (but especially Anton, thanks to his lacking a job) established a watch over their neighbor's insomnia. The enemy, however, was astute and endowed with a fine hearing. No matter how quietly one advanced toward his door, his light went out instantly, as if it never had been there; and only if one stood in the cold corridor for a goodish length of time, holding one's breath, could one hope to see the return of the sensitive lamp beam. Thus beetles faint and recover.

The task of detection turned out to be most exhausting. Finally, the brothers chanced to catch him on the stairs and jostled him.

"Suppose it's my habit to read at night. What business of yours is it? Let me pass, please."

When he turned away, Gustav knocked off his hat in jest. Romantovski picked it up without a word.

A few days later, choosing a moment at nightfall—he was on his way back from the W.C. and failed to dart back into his room quickly enough—the brothers crowded around him. There were only two of them, yet they managed to form a crowd. They invited him to their room.

"There will be some beer," said Gustav with a wink.

He tried to refuse.

"Oh, come along!" cried the brothers; they grabbed him under the arms and swept him off (while at it, they could feel how thin he was—that weakness, that slenderness below the shoulder offered an irresistible temptation—ah, to give a good squeeze so as to make him crunch, ah, hard to control oneself, let us, at least, dig into him on the move, just once, lightly . . .).

"You are hurting me," said Romantovski. "Leave me alone, I can walk by myself."

The promised beer, the large mouth of Gustav's fiancée, a heavy smell in the room. They tried to make him drunk. Collarless, with a copper stud under his conspicuous and defenseless Adam's apple, long-faced and pale, with quivering eyelashes, he sat in a complicated pose, partly doubled up, partly bent out, and when he got up from his chair he seemed to unwind like a spiral. However, they forced him to fold up again and, upon their suggestion, Anna sat in his lap. He kept glancing askance at the swell of her instep in the harness of a tight shoe, but mastered his dull anguish as best he could, not daring to get rid of the inert red-haired creature.

There was a minute when it seemed to them that he was broken, that he had become one of them. In fact, Gustav said, "You see, you were silly to look down on our company. We find offensive the way you have of keeping mum. What do you read all night?"

"Old, old tales," replied Romantovski in such a tone of voice that the brothers suddenly felt very bored. The boredom was suffocating and grim, but drink prevented the storm from bursting out, and, on the contrary, weighed the eyelids down. Anna slipped off Romantovski's knee, brushing the table with a drowsy hip; empty bottles swayed like ninepins, one collapsed. The brothers stooped, toppled, yawned, still looking through sleepy tears at their guest. He, vibrating and diffusing rays, stretched out, thinned, and gradually vanished.

This cannot go on. He poisons the life of honest folks. Why, it can well happen that he will move at the end of the month—intact, whole, never taken to pieces, proudly strutting about. It is not enough that he moves and breathes differently from other people; the trouble is that we just cannot put our finger upon the difference, cannot catch the tip of the ear by which to pull out the rabbit. Hateful is everything that cannot be palpated, measured, counted.

A series of trivial torments began. On Monday they managed to sprinkle his bedclothes with potato flour, which is said to provoke a maddening itch. On Tuesday they ambushed him at the corner of their street (he was carrying books hugged to his breast) and hustled him so neatly that his load landed in the puddle they had picked out for it. On Wednesday they painted the toilet seat with carpenter's glue. By Thursday the brothers' imagination was exhausted.

He said nothing, nothing whatever. On Friday, he overtook Anton, with his flying step, at the gate of the yard, and offered him an illustrated weekly—

maybe you'd like to look at it? This unexpected courtesy perplexed the brothers and made them glow still hotter.

Gustav ordered his fiancée to stir up Romantovski, which would give one the opportunity to pick a quarrel with him. You involuntarily tend to set a football rolling before kicking it. Frolicsome animals also prefer a mobile object. And though Anna, no doubt, greatly repelled Romantovski with those bug-brown freckles on her milky skin, the vacant look in her light eyes, and the little promontories of wet gums between her teeth, he found fit to conceal his distaste, fearing to infuriate Anna's lover by spurning her.

Since he went all the same to the cinema once a week, he took her with him on Saturday in the hope that this attention would be enough. Unnoticed, at a discreet distance, both wearing new caps and orange-red shoes, the brothers stole after the pair, and on those dubious streets, in that dusty dusk, there were hundreds of their likes but only one Romantovski.

In the small elongated movie house night had started to flicker, a self-manufactured lunar night, when the brothers, furtively hunching, seated themselves in the back row. They sensed the darkly delicious presence of Romantovski somewhere in front. On the way to the cinema, Anna failed to worm anything out of her disagreeable companion, nor did she quite understand what exactly Gustav wanted of him. As they walked, the mere sight of his lean figure and melancholy profile made her want to yawn. But once the picture started, she forgot about him, pressing an insensate shoulder against him. Specters conversed in trumpet tones on the newfangled speaking screen. The baron tasted his wine and carefully put his glass down—with the sound of a dropped cannon-ball.

And after a while the sleuths were pursuing the baron. Who would have recognized in him the master crook? He was hunted passionately, frenziedly. Automobiles sped with bursts of thunder. In a nightclub they fought with bottles, chairs, tables. A mother was putting an enchanting child to bed.

When it was all over, and Romantovski, with a little stumble, followed her out into the cool darkness, Anna exclaimed, "Oh, that was wonderful!"

He cleared his throat and said after a pause, "Let's not exaggerate. In real life, it is all considerably duller."

"It's you who's dull," she retorted crossly, and presently chuckled softly as she recalled the pretty child.

Behind them, gliding along at the same distance as before, came the brothers. Both were gloomy. Both were pumping themselves up with gloomy violence. Gloomily, Anton said, "That's not done, after all—going out walking with another's bride."

"And especially on Saturday night," said Gustav.

A passer-by, coming abreast of them, happened to glance at their faces—and could not help walking faster.

The night wind chased rustling rubbish along the fences. It was a dark and desolate part of Berlin. Far to the left of the road, above the canal, blinked scattered lights. On the right were vacant lots from which a few hastily silhouetted houses had turned their black backs away. After a little while the brothers accelerated their step.

"My mother and sister live in the country," Anna was telling him in a rather cosy undertone amid the velvety night. "As soon as I get married, I hope to visit them with him. Last summer my sister—"

Romantovski suddenly looked back.

"—won a lottery prize," continued Anna, mechanically looking back too.

Gustav emitted a sonorous whistle.

"Why, it's them!" exclaimed Anna, and joyfully burst out laughing. "Ah, the rascals!"

"Good evening, good evening," said Gustav hastily, in a panting voice. "What are you doing here, you ass, with my girl?"

"I'm not doing anything. We have just been—"

"Now, now," said Anton and, drawing back his elbow, hit Romantovski crisply in the lower ribs.

"Please, don't use your fists. You know perfectly well that—"

"Leave him alone, fellows," said Anna with a soft snigger.

"Must teach him a lesson," said Gustav, warming up and forefeeling with a poignant glow how he, too, would follow his brother's example and feel those cartilages, that crumpy backbone.

"Apropos, a funny thing happened to me one day," Romantovski started to say, talking fast, but here Gustav began to jam and twist the huge lumps of his knuckles into his victim's side, causing utterly indescribable pain. In lurching back Romantovski slipped and nearly fell: to fall would have meant perishing then and there.

"Let him go," said Anna.

He turned and, holding his side, walked off along the dark rustling fences. The brothers followed, all but treading upon his heels. Gustav rumbled in the anguish of blood lust, and that rumble might turn any moment into a pounce.

Far away before him a bright twinkle promised safety; it meant a lighted street, and although what could be seen was probably one lone lamp, that slit in the blackness seemed a marvelous festive blaze, a blissful region of radiance, full of rescued men. He knew that if he started to run it would be the end, since he could not get there sufficiently fast; he should go at a quiet and smooth walk, then he might cover that distance, keeping silent the while and trying not to press his hand against his burning ribs. So he strode on, with his usual springy step, and the impression was that he did so on purpose, to mock non-flyers, and that next moment he might take off.

Anna's voice: "Gustav, don't tangle with him. You know quite well you won't be able to stop. Remember what you did once to that bricklayer."

"Hold your tongue, old bitch, don't teach him what must be done." (That's Anton's voice.)

Now at last, the region of light—where one could distinguish a chestnut's foliage, and what looked like a Morris pillar, and farther still, to the left, a bridge—that breathlessly waiting imploring light, at last, at last, was not so very remote. . . . And still one should not run. And though he knew he was making a fatal mistake, all at once, beyond the control of his will, he flew up and, with a sob, dashed forward.

He ran and seemed, as he ran, to be laughing exultingly. Gustav overtook him in a couple of leaps. Both fell, and amid the fierce rasping and crunching there occurred a special sound—smooth and moist, once, and a second time, up to the hilt—and then Anna instantly fled into the darkness, holding her hat in her hand.

Gustav stood up. Romantovski was lying on the ground and speaking in Polish. Abruptly his voice broke off.

"And now let's be gone," said Gustav. "I stuck him."

"Take it out," said Anton, "take it out of him."

"I did," said Gustav. "God, how I stuck him."

They scurried off, though not toward the light, but across dark vacant lots. After skirting the cemetery they reached a back alley, exchanged glances, and slowed down to a normal walk.

Upon coming home, they immediately fell asleep. Anton dreamed he was sitting on the grass and watching a barge drift by. Gustav did not dream of anything.

Early next morning police agents arrived; they searched the murdered man's room and briefly questioned Anton, who had come out into the passage. Gustav stayed in bed, replete and somnolent, his face the color of Westphalian ham, in contrast to the whitish tufts of his eyebrows.

Presently, the police left and Anton returned. He was in an unusual state of elation, choking with laughter, flexing his knees, noiselessly hitting his palm with his fist.

"What fun!" he said. "Do you know who the fellow was? A leonardo!"

In their lingo a leonardo (from the name of the painter) meant a maker of counterfeit bills. And Anton related what he had managed to find out: the fellow, it appeared, belonged to a gang and had just got out of jail. Before that he had been designing fake paper money; an accomplice had knifed him, no doubt.

Gustav shook with mirth, too, but then his expression changed suddenly.

"He slipped us his slither, the rogue!" cried Gustav and ran, naked, to the wardrobe where he kept his money box.

"Doesn't matter, we'll pass it," said his brother. "A non-expert won't see the difference."

"Yes, but what a rogue!" Gustav kept repeating.

My poor Romantovski! And I who believed with them that you were indeed someone exceptional. I believed, let me confess, that you were a remarkable poet whom poverty obliged to dwell in that sinister district. I believed, on the strength of certain indices, that every night, by working on a line of verse or nursing a growing idea, you celebrated an invulnerable victory over the brothers. My poor Romantovski! It is all over now. Alas, the objects I had assembled wander away. The young poplar dims and takes off—to return where it had been fetched from. The brick wall dissolves. The house draws in its little balconies one by one, then turns, and floats away. Everything floats away. Harmony and meaning vanish. The world irks me again with its variegated void.

## *Study questions*

1. *What is the function of the opening paragraphs? Notice that the narrator makes the reader constantly aware of the artifice. What happens is similar to certain cartoons where one can see the hand of the artist drawing lines that take shapes, and then the shapes assume a life of their own.* 2. *What are Gustav and Anton like? How are they similar? different? What is their world like?* 3. *Why does Romantovski irritate the brothers? Is his name significant? In the Russian, this story was titled "Korolyok," which means little king, but the word is also slang for counterfeiter. Nabokov chose the title "The Leonardo" for the English translation so he could call upon the same kind of double association.* 4. *What does the narrator mean when he says, "Hateful is everything that cannot be palpated, measured, counted." To whom does this statement refer?* 5. *What is the relationship between the movie that Romantovski sees and the larger story in which he is an actor?* 6. *Why do the brothers kill Romantovski? Why do they enjoy it?* 7. *What is the point of the last paragraph of the story?* 8. *What is the relationship between Romantovski and the narrator?*

# THE VISIT TO THE MUSEUM

Several years ago a friend of mine in Paris—a person with oddities, to put it mildly—learning that I was going to spend two or three days at Montisert, asked me to drop in at the local museum where there hung, he was told, a portrait of his grandfather by Leroy. Smiling and spreading out his hands, he related a rather vague story to which I confess I paid little attention, partly because I do not like other people's obtrusive affairs, but chiefly because I had always had doubts about my friend's capacity to remain this side of fantasy. It went more or less as follows: after the grandfather died in their St. Petersburg house back at the time of the Russo-Japanese War, the contents of his apartment in Paris were sold at auction. The portrait, after some obscure peregrinations, was acquired by the museum of Leroy's native town. My friend wished to know if the portrait was really there; if there, if it could be ransomed; and if it could, for what price. When I asked why he did not get in touch with the museum, he replied that he had written several times, but had never received an answer.

I made an inward resolution not to carry out the request—I could always tell him I had fallen ill or changed my itinerary. The very notion of seeing sights, whether they be museums or ancient buildings, is loathsome to me; besides, the good freak's commission seemed absolute nonsense. It so happened, however, that while wandering about Montisert's empty streets in search of a stationery store, and cursing the spire of a long-necked cathedral, always the same one, that kept popping up at the end of every street, I was caught in a violent downpour which immediately went about accelerating the fall of the maple leaves, for the fair weather of a southern October was holding on by a mere thread. I dashed for cover and found myself on the steps of the museum.

It was a building of modest proportions, constructed of many-colored stones, with columns, a gilt inscription over the frescoes of the pediment, and a lion-legged stone bench on either side of the bronze door. One of its leaves stood open, and the interior seemed dark against the shimmer of the shower. I stood for a while on the steps, but, despite the overhanging roof, they were gradually growing speckled. I saw that the rain had set in for good, and so, having nothing better to do, I decided to go inside. No sooner had I trod on the smooth, resonant flagstones of the vestibule than the clatter of a moved stool came from a distant corner, and the custodian—a banal pensioner with an empty sleeve—rose to meet me, laying aside his newspaper and peering at me over his spectacles. I paid my franc and, trying not to look at some statues at the entrance (which were as traditional and as insignificant as the first number in a circus program), I entered the main hall.

Everything was as it should be: gray tints, the sleep of substance, matter dematerialized. There was the usual case of old, worn coins resting in the inclined velvet of their compartments. There was, on top of the case, a pair of owls, Eagle Owl and Long-eared, with their French names reading "Grand Duke" and "Middle Duke" if translated. Venerable minerals lay in their open graves of dusty papier-mâché; a photograph of an astonished gentleman with a pointed beard dominated an assortment of strange black lumps of various sizes. They bore a great resemblance to frozen frass, and I paused involuntarily over them, for I was quite at a loss to guess their nature, composition and function. The custodian had been following me with felted steps, always keeping a respectful distance; now, however, he came up, with one hand behind his back and the ghost of the other in his pocket, and gulping, if one judged by his Adam's apple.

"What are they?" I asked.

"Science has not yet determined," he replied, undoubtedly having learned the phrase by rote. "They were found," he continued in the same phony tone, "in 1895, by Louis Pradier, Municipal Councillor and Knight of the Legion of Honor," and his trembling finger indicated the photograph.

"Well and good," I said, "but who decided, and why, that they merited a place in the museum?"

"And now I call your attention to this skull!" the old man cried energetically, obviously changing the subject.

"Still, I would be interested to know what they are made of," I interrupted.

"Science. . . ." he began anew, but stopped short and looked crossly at his fingers, which were soiled with dust from the glass.

I proceeded to examine a Chinese vase, probably brought back by a naval officer; a group of porous fossils; a pale worm in clouded alcohol; a red-and-green map of Montisert in the seventeenth century; and a trio of rusted tools bound by a funereal ribbon—a spade, a mattock and a pick. "To dig in the past,"

I thought absentmindedly, but this time did not seek clarification from the custodian, who was following me noiselessly and meekly, weaving in and out among the display cases. Beyond the first hall there was another, apparently the last, and in its center a large sarcophagus stood like a dirty bathtub, while the walls were hung with paintings.

At once my eye was caught by the portrait of a man between two abominable landscapes (with cattle and "atmosphere"). I moved closer and, to my considerable amazement, found the very object whose existence had hitherto seemed to me but the figment of an unstable mind. The man, depicted in wretched oils, wore a frock coat, whiskers and a large pince-nez on a cord; he bore a likeness to Offenbach, but, in spite of the work's vile conventionality, I had the feeling one could make out in his features the horizon of a resemblance, as it were, to my friend. In one corner, meticulously traced in carmine against a black background, was the signature *Leroy* in a hand as commonplace as the work itself.

I felt a vinegarish breath near my shoulder, and turned to meet the custodian's kindly gaze. "Tell me," I asked, "supposing someone wished to buy one of these paintings, whom should he see?"

"The treasures of the museum are the pride of the city," replied the old man, "and pride is not for sale."

Fearing his eloquence, I hastily concurred, but nevertheless asked for the name of the museum's director. He tried to distract me with the story of the sarcophagus, but I insisted. Finally he gave me the name of one M. Godard and explained where I could find him.

Frankly, I enjoyed the thought that the portrait existed. It is fun to be present at the coming true of a dream, even if it is not one's own. I decided to settle the matter without delay. When I get in the spirit, no one can hold me back. I left the museum with a brisk, resonant step, and found that the rain had stopped, blueness had spread across the sky, a woman in besplattered stockings was spinning along on a silver-shining bicycle, and only over the surrounding hills did clouds still hang. Once again the cathedral began playing hide-and-seek with me, but I outwitted it. Barely escaping the onrushing tires of a furious red bus packed with singing youths, I crossed the asphalt thoroughfare and a minute later was ringing at the garden gate of M. Godard. He turned out to be a thin, middle-aged gentleman in high collar and dickey, with a pearl in the knot of his tie, and a face very much resembling a Russian wolfhound; as if that were not enough, he was licking his chops in a most doglike manner, while sticking a stamp on an envelope, when I entered his small but lavishly furnished room with its malachite inkstand on the desk and a strangely familiar Chinese vase on the mantel. A pair of fencing foils hung crossed over the mirror, which reflected the narrow gray back of his head. Here and there photographs of a warship pleasantly broke up the blue flora of the wallpaper.

"What can I do for you?" he asked, throwing the letter he had just sealed into the wastebasket. This act seemed unusual to me; however, I did not see fit to interfere. I explained in brief my reason for coming, even naming the substantial sum with which my friend was willing to part, though he had asked me not to mention it, but wait instead for the museum's terms.

"All this is delightful," said M. Godard. "The only thing is, you are mistaken—there is no such picture in our museum."

"What do you mean there is no such picture? I have just seen it! Portrait of a Russian nobleman, by Gustave Leroy."

"We do have one Leroy," said M. Godard when he had leafed through an oilcloth notebook and his black fingernail had stopped at the entry in question. "However, it is not a portrait but a rural landscape: The Return of the Herd."

I repeated that I had seen the picture with my own eyes five minutes before and that no power on earth could make me doubt its existence.

"Agreed," said M. Godard, "but I am not crazy either. I have been curator of our museum for almost twenty years now and know this catalogue as well as I know the Lord's Prayer. It says here Return of the Herd and that means the herd is returning, and, unless perhaps your friend's grandfather is depicted as a shepherd, I cannot conceive of his portrait's existence in our museum."

"He is wearing a frock coat," I cried. "I swear he is wearing a frock coat!"

"And how did you like our museum in general?" M. Godard asked suspiciously. "Did you appreciate the sarcophagus?"

"Listen," I said (and I think there was already a tremor in my voice), "do me a favor—let's go there this minute, and let's make an agreement that if the portrait is there, you will sell it."

"And if not?" inquired M. Godard.

"I shall pay you the sum anyway."

"All right," he said. "Here, take this red-and-blue pencil and using the red—the red, please—put it in writing for me."

In my excitement I carried out his demand. Upon glancing at my signature, he deplored the difficult pronunciation of Russian names. Then he appended his own signature and, quickly folding the sheet, thrust it into his waistcoat pocket.

"Let's go," he said, freeing a cuff.

On the way he stepped into a shop and bought a bag of sticky-looking caramels which he began offering me insistently; when I flatly refused, he tried to shake out a couple of them into my hand. I pulled my hand away. Several caramels fell on the sidewalk; he stopped to pick them up and then overtook me at a trot. When we drew near the museum we saw the red tourist bus (now empty) parked outside.

"Aha," said M. Godard, pleased. "I see we have many visitors today."

He doffed his hat and, holding it in front of him, walked decorously up the steps.

All was not well at the museum. From within issued rowdy cries, lewd laughter, and even what seemed like the sound of a scuffle. We entered the first hall; there the elderly custodian was restraining two sacrilegists who wore some kind of festive emblems in their lapels and were altogether very purple-faced and full of pep as they tried to extract the municipal councillor's merds from beneath the glass. The rest of the youths, members of some rural athletic organization, were making noisy fun, some of the worm in alcohol, others of the skull. One joker was in rapture over the pipes of the steam radiator, which he pretended was an exhibit; another was taking aim at an owl with his fist and forefinger.

There were about thirty of them in all, and their motion and voices created a condition of crush and thick noise.

M. Godard clapped his hands and pointed at a sign reading "Visitors to the Museum must be decently attired." Then he pushed his way, with me following, into the second hall. The whole company immediately swarmed after us. I steered Godard to the portrait; he froze before it, chest inflated, and then stepped back a bit, as if admiring it, and his feminine heel trod on somebody's foot.

"Splendid picture," he exclaimed with genuine sincerity. "Well, let's not be petty about this. You were right, and there must be an error in the catalogue."

As he spoke, his fingers, moving as it were on their own, tore up our agreement into little bits which fell like snow-flakes into a massive spittoon.

"Who's the old ape?" asked an individual in a striped jersey, and, as my friend's grandfather was depicted holding a glowing cigar, another funster took out a cigarette and prepared to borrow a light from the portrait.

"All right, let us settle on the price," I said, "and, in any case, let's get out of here."

"Make way, please!" shouted M. Godard, pushing aside the curious.

There was an exit, which I had not noticed previously, at the end of the hall and we thrust our way through to it.

"I can make no decision," M. Godard was shouting above the din. "Decisiveness is a good thing only when supported by law. I must first discuss the matter with the mayor, who has just died and has not yet been elected. I doubt that you will be able to purchase the portrait but nonetheless I would like to show you still other treasures of ours."

We found ourselves in a hall of considerable dimensions. Brown books, with a half-baked look and coarse, foxed pages, lay open under glass on a long table. Along the walls stood dummy soldiers in jack boots with flared tops.

"Come, let's talk it over," I cried out in desperation, trying to direct M. Godard's evolutions to a plush-covered sofa in a corner. But in this I was prevented by the custodian. Flailing his one arm, he came running after us, pursued by a merry crowd of youths, one of whom had put on his head a copper helmet with a Rembrandtesque gleam.

"Take it off, take it off!" shouted M. Godard, and someone's shove made the helmet fly off the hooligan's head with a clatter.

"Let us move on," said M. Godard, tugging at my sleeve, and we passed into the section of Ancient Sculpture.

I lost my way for a moment among some enormous marble legs, and twice ran around a giant knee before I again caught sight of M. Godard, who was looking for me behind the white ankle of a neighboring giantess. Here a person in a bowler, who must have clambered up her, suddenly fell from a great height to the stone floor. One of his companions began helping him up, but they were both drunk, and, dismissing them with a wave of the hand, M. Godard rushed on to the next room, radiant with Oriental fabrics; there hounds raced across azure carpets, and a bow and quiver lay on a tiger skin.

Strangely, though, the expanse and motley only gave me a feeling of oppressiveness and imprecision, and, perhaps because new visitors kept dashing by or perhaps because I was impatient to leave the unnecessarily spreading museum and amid calm and freedom conclude my business negotiations with M. Godard, I began to experience a vague sense of alarm. Meanwhile we had transported ourselves into yet another hall, which must have been really enormous, judging by the fact that it housed the entire skeleton of a whale, resembling a frigate's frame; beyond were visible still other halls, with the oblique sheen of large paintings, full of storm clouds, among which floated the delicate idols of religious art in blue and pink vestments; and all this resolved itself in an abrupt turbulence of misty draperies, and chandeliers came aglitter and fish with translucent frills meandered through illuminated aquariums. Racing up a staircase, we saw, from the gallery above, a crowd of gray-haired people with umbrellas examining a gigantic mock-up of the universe.

At last, in a somber but magnificent room dedicated to the history of steam machines, I managed to halt my carefree guide for an instant.

"Enough!" I shouted. "I'm leaving. We'll talk tomorrow."

He had already vanished. I turned and saw, scarcely an inch from me, the lofty wheels of a sweaty locomotive. For a long time I tried to find the way back among models of railroad stations. How strangely glowed the violet signals in the gloom beyond the fan of wet tracks, and what spasms shook my poor heart! Suddenly everything changed again: in front of me stretched an infinitely long passage, containing numerous office cabinets and elusive, scurrying people. Taking a sharp turn, I found myself amid a thousand musical instruments; the walls, all mirror, reflected an enfilade of grand pianos, while in the center there was a pool with a bronze Orpheus atop a green rock. The aquatic theme did not end here as, racing back, I ended up in the Section of Fountains and Brooks, and it was difficult to walk along the winding, slimy edges of those waters.

Now and then, on one side or the other, stone stairs, with puddles on the steps, which gave me a strange sensation of fear, would descend into misty abysses, whence issued whistles, the rattle of dishes, the clatter of typewriters, the ring of hammers and many other sounds, as if, down there, were exposition halls of some kind or other, already closing or not yet completed. Then I found myself in darkness and kept bumping into unknown furniture until I finally saw a red light and walked out onto a platform that clanged under me—and suddenly, beyond it, there was a bright parlor, tastefully furnished in Empire style, but not a living soul, not a living soul . . . . By now I was indescribably terrified, but every time I turned and tried to retrace my steps along the passages, I found myself in hitherto unseen places—a greenhouse with hydrangeas and broken windowpanes with the darkness of artificial night showing through beyond; or a deserted laboratory with dusty alembics on its tables. Finally I ran into a room of some sort with coatracks monstrously loaded down with black coats and astrakhan furs; from beyond a door came a burst of applause, but when I flung the door open, there was no theater, but only a soft opacity and splendidly counterfeited fog with the perfectly convincing blotches of indistinct streetlights. More than convincing! I advanced, and immediately a joyous and unmistakable sensation of reality at last replaced all the unreal trash amid which I had just been dashing to and fro. The stone beneath my feet was real sidewalk, powdered with wonderfully fragrant, newly fallen snow, in which the infrequent pedestrians had already left fresh black tracks. At first the quiet and the snowy coolness of the night, somehow strikingly familiar, gave me a pleasant feeling after my feverish wanderings. Trustfully, I started to conjecture just where I had come out, and why the snow, and what were those lights exaggeratedly but indistinctly beaming here and there in the brown darkness. I examined and, stooping, even touched a round spur stone on the curb, then glanced at the palm of my hand, full of wet granular cold, as if hoping to read an explanation there. I felt how lightly, how naively I was clothed, but the distinct realization that I had escaped from the museum's maze was still so strong that, for the first two or three minutes, I experienced neither surprise nor fear. Continuing my leisurely examination, I looked up at the house beside which I was standing and was immediately struck by the sight of iron steps and railings that descended into the snow on their way to the cellar. There was a twinge in my heart, and it was with a new, alarmed curiosity that I glanced at the pavement, at its white cover along which stretched black lines, at the brown sky across which there kept sweeping a mysterious light, and at the massive parapet some distance away. I sensed that there was a drop beyond it; something was creaking and gurgling down there. Further on, beyond the murky cavity, stretched a chain of fuzzy lights. Scuffling along the snow in my soaked shoes, I walked a few paces, all the time glancing at the dark house on my right; only in a single window did a lamp glow softly under its green-glass shade. Here, a locked wooden gate . . . . There, what must be the shutters of a sleeping shop . . . . And by the light of a streetlamp whose shape had long been shouting to me its impossible message, I made out the ending of a sign—"*. . . inka Sapog*" ("*. . . oe Repair*")—but no, it was not the show that had obliterated the "hard sign" at the end. "No, no, in a minute I shall wake up," I said aloud, and, trembling, my heart pounding, I turned, walked on, stopped again. From somewhere came the receding sound of hooves, the snow sat like a skullcap on a slightly leaning spur stone and indistinctly showed white on the woodpile on the other side of the fence, and already I knew, irrevocably, where I was. Alas, it was not the Russia I remembered, but the factual Russia of today, forbidden to me, hopelessly slavish, and hopelessly my own native land. A semiphantom in a light foreign suit, I stood on the impassive snow of an October night, somewhere on the Moyka or the Fontanka Canal, or perhaps on the Obvodny, and I had to do something, go somewhere, run; desperately protect my fragile, illegal life. Oh, how many times in my sleep I had experienced a similar sensation! Now, though, it was reality. Everything was real—the air that seemed to mingle with scattered snowflakes, the still unfrozen canal, the floating fish house, and that peculiar squareness of the darkened and the yellow windows. A man in a fur cap, with a briefcase under his arm, came toward me out of the fog, gave me a startled glance, and turned to look again when he had passed me. I waited for him to disappear and then, with a tremendous haste, began pulling out everything I had in my pockets, ripping up papers, throwing them into the snow and stamping them down. There were some documents, a letter from my sister in Paris, five hundred francs, a handkerchief, cigarettes; however, in order to shed all the integument of exile, I would have to tear off and destroy my clothes, my linen, my shoes, everything, and remain ideally naked; and, even though I was already shivering from my anguish and from the cold, I did what I could.

But enough. I shall not recount how I was arrested, nor tell of my subsequent ordeals. Suffice it to say that it cost me incredible patience and effort to get back abroad, and that, ever since, I have foresworn carrying out commissions entrusted one by the insanity of others.

## *Study questions*

1. *What elements of dream structure are present in this story?* 2. *At what point does the story seem to abandon "ordinary" perspective?* 3. *How is the museum changed between the first and second visits?* 4. *Does the movement of the protagonist through the museum and the artifacts displayed there have a symbolic significance?* 5. *Who is the narrator? Whose nightmare is he living? How is the nightmare related to the dream the narrator mentions when he says: "It is fun to be present at the coming true of a dream, even if it is not one's own."* 6. *The narrator knows he is in Russia when he sees a "hard sign" missing. In a note to the translation Nabokov notes that the orthography adopted by the Soviets is different from that used in Old Russia. What is the narrator's response to his awareness of where he is?* 7. *Can this story be dismissed as simply a dream?*

# "THAT IN ALEPPO ONCE. . ."

Dear V.—Among other things, this is to tell you that at last I am here, in the country whither so many sunsets have led. One of the first persons I saw was our good old Gleb Alexandrovich Gekko gloomily crossing Columbus Avenue in quest of the *petite café du coin* which none of us three will ever visit again. He seemed to think that somehow or other you were betraying our national literature, and he gave me your address with a deprecatory shake of his gray head, as if you did not deserve the treat of hearing from me.

I have a story for you. Which reminds me—I mean putting it like this reminds me—of the days when we wrote our first udder-warm bubbling verse, and all things, a rose, a puddle, a lighted window, cried out to us: "I'm a rhyme!" Yes, this is a most useful universe. We play, we die: *ig-rhyme, umi-rhyme.* And the sonorous souls of Russian verbs lend a meaning to the wild gesticulation of trees or to some discarded newspaper sliding and pausing, and shuffling again, with abortive flaps and apterous jerks along an endless wind-swept embankment.

But just now I am not a poet. I come to you like that gushing lady in Chekhov who was dying to be described.

I married, let me see, about a month after you left France and a few weeks before the gentle Germans roared into Paris. Although I can produce documentary proofs of matrimony, I am positive now that my wife never existed. You may know her name from some other source, but that does not matter: it is the name of an illusion. Therefore, I am able to speak of her with as much detachment as I would of a character in a story (one of your stories, to be precise).

It was love at first touch rather than at first sight, for I had met her several times before without experiencing any special emotions; but one night, as I was seeing her home, something quaint she had said made me stoop with a laugh and lightly kiss her on the hair—and of course we all know of that blinding blast which is caused by merely picking up a small doll from the floor of a carefully abandoned house; the soldier involved hears nothing; for him it is but an ecstatic soundless and boundless expansion of what had been during his life a pin point of light in the dark center of his being. And really, the reason we think of death in celestial terms is that the visible firmament, especially at night (above our blacked-out Paris with the gaunt arches of its Boulevard Exelmans and the ceaseless Alpine gurgle of desolate latrines), is the most adequate and ever-present symbol of that vast silent explosion.

But I cannot discern her. She remains as nebulous as my best poem—the one you made such gruesome fun of in the *Literaturnïe Zapiski*. When I want to imagine her, I have to cling mentally to a tiny brown birthmark on her downy forearm, as one concentrates upon a punctuation mark in an illegible sentence. Perhaps, had she used a greater amount of make-up or used it more constantly, I might have visualized her face today, or at least the delicate transverse furrows of dry, hot rouged lips; but I fail, I fail—although I still feel their elusive touch now and then in the blindman's buff of my senses, in that sobbing sort of dream when she and I clumsily clutch at each other through a heartbreaking mist and I cannot see the color of her eyes for the blank luster of brimming tears drowning their irises.

She was much younger than I—not as much younger as was Nathalie of the lovely bare shoulders and long earrings in relation to swarthy Pushkin; but still there was a sufficient margin for that kind of retrospective romanticism which finds pleasure in imitating the destiny of a unique genius (down to the jealousy, down to the filth, down to the stab of seeing her almond-shaped eyes turn to her blond Cassio behind her peacock-feathered fan) even if one cannot imitate his verse. She liked mine though, and would scarcely have yawned as the other was wont to do every time her husband's poem happened to exceed the length of a sonnet. If she has remained a phantom to me, I may have been one to her: I suppose she had been solely attracted by the obscurity of my poetry; then tore a hole through its veil and saw a stranger's unlovable face.

As you know, I had been for some time planning to follow the example of your fortunate flight. She described to me an uncle of hers who lived, she said, in New York: he had taught riding at a Southern college and had wound up by marrying a wealthy American woman; they had a little daughter born deaf.

She said she had lost their address long ago, but a few days later it miraculously turned up, and we wrote a dramatic letter to which we never received any reply. This did not much matter, as I had already obtained a sound affidavit from Professor Lomchenko of Chicago; but little else had been done in the way of getting the necessary papers, when the invasion began, whereas I foresaw that if we stayed on in Paris some helpful compatriot of mine would sooner or later point out to the interested party sundry passages in one of my books where I argued that, with all her many black sins, Germany was still bound to remain forever and ever the laughing stock of the world.

So we started upon our disastrous honeymoon. Crushed and jolted amid the apocalyptic exodus, waiting for unscheduled trains that were bound for unknown destinations, walking through the stale stage setting of abstract towns, living in a permanent twilight of physical exhaustion, we fled; and the farther we fled, the clearer it became that what was driving us on was something more than a booted and buckled fool with his assortment of variously propelled junk—something of which he was a mere symbol, something monstrous and impalpable, a timeless and faceless mass of immemorial horror that still keeps coming at me from behind even here, in the green vacuum of Central Park.

Oh, she bore it gamely enough—with a kind of dazed cheerfulness. Once, however, quite suddenly she started to sob in a sympathetic railway carriage. "The dog," she said, "the dog we left. I cannot forget the poor dog." The honesty of her grief shocked me, as we had never had any dog. "I know," she said, "but I tried to imagine we had actually bought that setter. And just think, he would be now whining behind a locked door." There had never been any talk of buying a setter.

I should also not like to forget a certain stretch of highroad and the sight of a family of refugees (two women, a child) whose old father, or grandfather, had died on the way. The sky was a chaos of black and flesh-colored clouds with an ugly sunburst beyond a hooded hill, and the dead man was lying on his back under a dusty plane tree. With a stick and their hands the women had tried to dig a roadside grave, but the soil was too hard; they had given it up and were sitting side by side, among the anemic poppies, a little apart from the corpse and its upturned beard. But the little boy was still scratching and scraping and tugging until he tumbled a flat stone and forgot the object of his solemn exertions as he crouched on his haunches, his thin, eloquent neck showing all its vertebrae to the headsman, and watched with surprise and delight thousands of minute brown ants seething, zigzagging, dispersing, heading for places of safety in the Gard, and the Aude, and the Drome, and the Var, and the Basses-Pyrénées—we two paused only in Pau.

Spain proved too difficult and we decided to move on to Nice. At a place called Faugères (a ten-minute stop) I squeezed out of the train to buy some food. When a couple of minutes later I came back, the train was gone, and the muddled old man responsible for the atrocious void that faced me (coal dust glittering in the heat between naked indifferent rails, and a lone piece of orange peel) brutally told me that, anyway, I had had no right to get out.

In a better world I could have had my wife located and told what to do (I had both tickets and most of the money); as it was, my nightmare struggle with the telephone proved futile, so I dismissed the whole series of diminutive voices barking at me from afar, sent two or three telegrams which are probably on their way only now, and late in the evening took the next local to Montpellier, farther than which her train would not stumble. Not finding her there, I had to choose between two alternatives: going on because she might have boarded the Marseilles train which I had just missed, or going back because she might have returned to Faugères. I forgot now what tangle of reasoning led me to Marseilles and Nice.

Beyond such routine action as forwarding false data to a few unlikely places, the police did nothing to help: one man bellowed at me for being a nuisance; another sidetracked the question by doubting the authenticity of my marriage certificate because it was stamped on what he contended to be the wrong side; a third, a fat *commissaire* with liquid brown eyes confessed that he wrote poetry in his spare time. I looked up various acquaintances among the numerous Russians domiciled or stranded in Nice. I heard those among them who chanced to have Jewish blood talk of their doomed kinsmen crammed into hell-bound trains; and my own plight, by contrast, acquired a commonplace air of irreality while I sat in some crowded café with the milky blue sea in front of me and a shell-hollow murmur behind telling and re-telling the tale of massacre and misery, and the gray paradise beyond the ocean, and the ways and whims of harsh consuls.

A week after my arrival an indolent plain-clothes man called upon me and took me down a crooked and smelly street to a black-stained house with the word "hotel" almost erased by dirt and time; there, he said, my wife had been found. The girl he produced was an absolute stranger, of course; but my friend Holmes kept on trying for some time to make her and me confess we were married, while her taciturn and muscular bedfellow stood by and listened, his bare arms crossed on his striped chest.

When at length I got rid of those people and had wandered back to my neighborhood, I happened to pass by a compact queue waiting at the entrance of a food store; and there, at the very end, was my wife, straining on tiptoe to catch a glimpse of what exactly was being sold. I think the first thing she said to me was that she hoped it was oranges.

Her tale seemed a trifle hazy, but perfectly banal. She had returned to Faugères and gone straight to the Commissariat instead of making inquiries at the station, where I had left a message for her. A party of refugees suggested that she join them; she spent the night in a bicycle shop with no bicycles, on the floor, together with three elderly women who lay, she said, like three logs in a row. Next day she realized that she had not enough money to reach Nice. Eventually she borrowed some from one of the log-women. She got into the wrong train, however, and traveled to a town the name of which she could not remember. She had arrived at Nice two days ago and had found some friends at the Russian church. They had told her I was somewhere around, looking for her, and would surely turn up soon.

Some time later, as I sat on the edge of the only chair in my garret and held her by her slender young hips (she was combing her soft hair and tossing her head back with every stroke), her dim smile changed all at once into an odd quiver and she placed one hand on my shoulder, staring down at me as if I were a reflection in a pool, which she had noticed for the first time.

"I've been lying to you, dear," she said. "*Ya lgunia.* I stayed for several nights in Montpellier with a brute of a man I met on the train. I did not want it at all. He sold hair lotions."

*The time, the place, the torture. Her fan, her gloves, her mask.* I spent that night and many others getting it out of her bit by bit, but not getting it all. I was under the strange delusion that first I must find out every detail, reconstruct every minute, and only then decide whether I could bear it. But the limit of desired knowledge was unattainable, nor could I ever foretell the approximate point after which I might imagine myself satiated, because of course the denominator of every fraction of knowledge was potentially as infinite as the number of intervals between the fractions themselves.

Oh, the first time she had been too tired to mind, and the next had not minded because she was sure I had deserted her; and she apparently considered that such explanations ought to be a kind of consolation prize for me instead of the nonsense and agony they really were. It went on like that for eons, she breaking down every now and then, but soon rallying again, answering my unprintable questions in a breathless whisper or trying with a pitiful smile to wriggle into the semisecurity of irrelevant commentaries, and I crushing and crushing the mad molar till my jaw almost burst with pain, a flaming pain which seemed somehow preferable to the dull, humming ache of humble endurance.

And mark, in between the periods of this inquest, we were trying to get from reluctant authorities certain papers which in their turn would make it lawful to apply for a third kind which would serve as a steppingstone towards a permit enabling the holder to apply for yet other papers which might or might not give him the means of discovering how and why it had happened. For even if I could imagine the accursed recurrent scene, I failed to link up its sharp-angled grotesque shadows with the dim limbs of my wife as she shook and rattled and dissolved in my violent grasp.

So nothing remained but to torture each other, to wait for hours on end in the Prefecture, filling forms, conferring with friends who had already probed the innermost viscera of all visas, pleading with secretaries, and filling forms again, with the result that her lusty and versatile traveling salesman became blended in a ghastly mix-up with rat-whiskered snarling officials, rotting bundles of obsolete records, the reek of violet ink, bribes slipped under gangrenous blotting paper, fat flies tickling moist necks with their rapid cold padded feet, new-laid clumsy concave photographs of your six subhuman doubles, the tragic eyes and patient politeness of petitioners born in Slutzk, Starodub, or Bobruisk, the funnels and pulleys of the Holy Inquisition, the awful smile of the bald man with the glasses, who had been told that his passport could not be found.

I confess that one evening, after a particularly abominable day, I sank down on a stone bench weeping and cursing a mock world where millions of lives were being juggled by the clammy hands of consuls and *commissaires.* I noticed she was crying too, and then I told her that nothing would really have mattered the way it mattered now, had she not gone and done what she did.

"You will think me crazy," she said with a vehemence that, for a second, almost made a real person of her, "but I didn't—I swear that I didn't. Perhaps I live several lives at once. Perhaps I wanted to test you. Perhaps this bench is a dream and we are in Saratov or on some star."

It would be tedious to niggle the different stages through which I passed before accepting finally the first version of her delay. I did not talk to her and was a good deal alone. She would glimmer and fade, and reappear with some trifle she thought I would appreciate—a handful of cherries, three precious cigarettes or the like—treating me with the unruffled mute sweetness of a nurse that trips from and to a gruff convalescent. I ceased visiting most of our mutual friends because they had lost all interest in my passport affairs and seemed to have turned vaguely inimical. I composed several poems. I drank all the wine I could get. I clasped her one day to my groaning breast, and we went for a week to Caboule and lay on the round pink pebbles of the narrow beach. Strange to say, the happier our new relations seemed, the stronger I felt an undercurrent of poignant sadness, but I kept telling myself that this was an intrinsic feature of all true bliss.

In the meantime, something had shifted in the moving pattern of our fates and at last I emerged from a dark and hot office with a couple of plump *visas de sortie* cupped in my trembling hands. Into these the U.S.A. serum was duly injected, and I dashed to Marseilles and managed to get tickets for the very next boat. I returned and tramped up the stairs. I saw a rose in a glass on the table—the sugar pink of its obvious beauty, the parasitic air bubbles clinging to its stem. Her two spare dresses were gone, her comb was gone, her checkered coat was gone, and so was the mauve hairband with mauve bow that had been her hat. There was no note pinned to the pillow, nothing at all in the room to enlighten me, for of course the rose was merely what French rhymsters call *une cheville.*

I went to the Veretennikovs, who could tell me nothing; to the Hellmans, who refused to say anything; and to the Elagins, who were not sure whether to tell me or not. Finally the old lady—and you know what Anna Vladimirovna is like at crucial moments—asked for her rubber-tipped cane, heavily but energetically dislodged her bulk from her favorite armchair, and took me into the garden. There she informed me that, being twice my age, she had the right to say I was a bully and a cad.

You must imagine the scene: the tiny graveled garden with its blue Arabian Nights jar and solitary cypress; the cracked terrace where the old lady's father had dozed with a rug on his knees when he retired from his Novgorod governorship to spend a few last evenings in Nice; the pale-green sky; a whiff of vanilla in the deepening dusk; the crickets emitting their metallic trill pitched at two octaves above middle C; and Anna Vladimirovna, the folds of her cheeks jerkily dangling as she flung at me a motherly but quite undeserved insult.

During several preceding weeks, my dear V., every time she had visited by herself the three or four families we both knew, my ghostly wife had filled the eager ears of all those kind people with an extraordinary story. To wit: that she had madly fallen in love with a young Frenchman who could give her a turreted home and a crested name; that she had implored me for a divorce and I had refused; that in fact I had said I would rather shoot her and myself than sail to New York alone; that she had said her father in a similar case had acted like a gentleman; that I had answered I did not give a hoot for her *cocu de père*.

There were loads of other preposterous details of the kind—but they all hung together in such a remarkable fashion that no wonder the old lady made me swear I would not seek to pursue the lovers with a cocked pistol. They had gone, she said, to a château in Lozère. I inquired whether she had ever set eyes upon the man. No, but she had been shown his picture. As I was about to leave, Anna Vladimirovna, who had slightly relaxed and had even given me her five fingers to kiss, suddenly flared up again, struck the gravel with her cane, and said in her deep strong voice: "But one thing I shall never forgive you—her dog, that poor beast which you hanged with your own hands before leaving Paris."

Whether the gentleman of leisure had changed into a traveling salesman, or whether the metamorphosis had been reversed, or whether again he was neither the one nor the other, but the nondescript Russian who had courted her before our marriage—all this was absolutely inessential. She had gone. That was the end. I should have been a fool had I begun the nightmare business of searching and waiting for her all over again.

On the fourth morning of a long and dismal sea voyage, I met on the deck a solemn but pleasant old doctor with whom I had played chess in Paris. He asked me whether my wife was very much incommoded by the rough seas. I answered that I had sailed alone; whereupon he looked taken aback and then said he had seen her a couple of days before going on board, namely in Marseilles, walking rather aimlessly he thought, along the embankment. She said that I would presently join her with bag and tickets.

This is, I gather, the point of the whole story—although if you write it, you had better not make him a doctor, as that kind of thing has been overdone. It was at that moment that I suddenly knew for certain that she had never existed at all. I shall tell you another thing. When I arrived I hastened to satisfy a certain morbid curiosity: I went to the address she had given me once; it proved to be an anonymous gap between two office buildings; I looked for her uncle's name in the directory; it was not there; I made some inquiries, and Gekko, who knows everything, informed me that the man and his horsey wife existed all right, but had moved to San Francisco after their deaf little girl had died.

Viewing the past graphically, I see our mangled romance engulfed in a deep valley of mist between the crags of two matter-of-fact mountains: life had been real before, life will be real from now on, I hope. Not tomorrow, though. Perhaps after tomorrow. You, happy mortal, with your lovely family (how is Ines? how are the twins?) and your diversified work (how are the lichens?), can hardly be expected to puzzle out my misfortune in terms of human communion, but you may clarify things for me through the prism of your art.

*Yet the pity of it.* Curse your art, I am hideously unhappy. She keeps on walking to and fro where the brown nets are spread to dry on the hot stone slabs and the dappled light of the water plays on the side of a moored fishing boat. Somewhere, somehow, I have made some fatal mistake. There are tiny pale bits of broken fish scales glistening here and there in the brown meshes. It may all end in *Aleppo* if I am not careful. Spare me, V.: you would load your dice with an unbearable implication if you took that for a title.

BOSTON, 1943

## *Study questions*

1. *What form does this story take? Who is V.? Note the number of storytellers: author, V., letter writer. How is this form functional?* 2. *What was the letter writer's relationship with his wife? Was she ever "real" to him? Was he "real" to her? Was the dog "real"?* 3. *The protagonist's "nightmare struggle" to find his wife is similar to other nightmare struggles in the story. How many are "real"?* 4. *The title of the story refers to Othello's last speech before he kills himself. What does the letter writer mean when he says: "It may all end in* Aleppo *if I am not careful." Are there other allusions to* Othello*? Are they relevant?* 5. *What clarification has taken place through the "prism" of art?*

*Nathalie Sarraute* (b. 1902), born in Ivanovo, Russia, was educated at Oxford and at the Sorbonne. She was a member of the French bar between 1926 and 1941, after which she became a full-time writer. Living now in Paris, she has been a frequent contributor to such journals as the *Times Literary Supplement, Books and Bookmen,* and *Les Temps modernes.* An advocate of the "new novel" in France and a critic of note, some of her essays were published in English translation as *The Age of Suspicion* (1963). Other works available in English include the novels *Portrait of a Man Unknown* (1958), *The Planetarium* (1960), *The Golden Fruits* (1964), and *"Fools Say"* (1977). Her short stories, first published in France in the 1930s, were published in English as *Tropisms* (1964). Her short pieces can be called psychological "soundings" that "show" rather than "comment upon." Called "tropisms" because she considered their spontaneous nature and movement similar to that of certain organisms as they respond to various stimuli, they are, as she says, pieces of precise dramatic action, captured in slow motion and developed by means of cadences, image patterns, and recurring motifs. "Tropism XVIII" is an example of the form.

## TROPISM XVIII

On the outskirts of London, in a little cottage with percale curtains, its little back lawn sunny and all wet with rain.

The big, wisteria-framed window in the studio, opens on to this lawn.

A cat with its eyes closed, is seated quite erect on the warm stone.

A spinster lady with white hair, and pink cheeks that tend towards purple, is reading an English magazine in front of the door.

She sits there, very stiff, very dignified, quite sure of herself and of others, firmly settled in her little universe. She knows that in a few moments the bell will ring for tea.

Down below, the cook, Ada, is cleaning vegetables at a table covered with white oilcloth. Her face is motionless, she appears to be thinking of nothing. She knows that it will soon be time to toast the buns, and ring the bell for tea.

### *Study questions*

1. *Is this a short story? Consider the question in terms of the short story's characteristic elements and devices.* 2. *Whether you do or do not conclude that this is a short story, would you say that it has meaning?*

*Tommaso Landolfi* (b. 1908) was born in Pico, Italy, and lives there still. He studied Russian literature at the University of Lorience and has since put much effort into translating Russian works into Italian. A fiction writer of renown, some of his stories have been translated into English and published as *Gogol's Wife and Other Stories* (1963) and *Cancerqueen* (1971). He is often compared with Dostoevsky and Kafka for his penetrating questioning of the nature of the real and for his use of dream visions and fantasies to concretize psychological conditions and project existential despair. "Hands" records what some may believe is abnormal behavior. Upon consideration, however, one may be led to conclude that Federico's behavior, based as it is on a deep psychological need for atonement, is saner than most.

# HANDS

Federico was retiring for the night. In the courtyard his old hunting bitch, left behind to guard the house, bounced to meet him with a festive welcome. The courtyard was enclosed on three sides, while the fourth opened onto the orchard below and, beyond a row of low houses, a narrow valley which, rising gently, stopped at the high and faraway horizon, running into a line of rounded hills; over it a hazy moon cast its bland and shadowy light. Federico lived in the large deserted house completely alone and for the sake of convenience he came and went by a service entrance which, if one followed a set path across two damp storage rooms and a pantry, brought one out at last to the kitchen, the first room furnished with an electric bulb. Moaning and groaning over the remorseless boredom of country life, faced by the prospect of an empty, lonely evening and the annoying necessity of the small, inevitable chores still required for his late supper, he fitted the massive ancient key into the lock. The small bitch wanted to get inside too and without giving him the time to open, threw herself against the door like a ram, scratching at it with her front paws. Since in the semi-darkness she had sat down between his feet, he chased her away and she suddenly remembered a dry and polished bone she had been saving there close by, went to pick it up and began turning it over loudly in her jaws.

As he was groping through the first storage room, a faint scampering sound attracted Federico's attention. "A mouse," he thought, knowing that some lived there; and indeed, having quickly lit a match, he caught sight of a big corpulent fellow who, leaning clumsily to right and left, was precipitously descending along the edge of one of the room's corners to hide behind the rim of a no longer used cistern. Federico knew of the bitch's hatred for mice (actually, because when he was a child he had often taken her to hunt for mice in the attic, she expressed this dislike more ostentatiously than was called for, in order to please him) and he decided to amuse himself with a nocturnal chase. He called her but, outside, her sonorous gnawing rang unperturbed through the silence of the night. At last he managed to infuse his voice with so urgent and promising a tone that she was induced to interrupt her activity and rush inside greatly excited. Federico pointed to the spot where he assumed the mouse had hidden and, still urging the bitch on, began to pound on the wooden cover of the cistern. The mouse, frightened, frantically abandoned his shelter and a spasmodic scrabble of his big claws across the floor marked his passage between the paws of the dog who failed to snatch him and lost sight of him. Although a man's nose is not worth that of a dog, a human eye is definitely sharper than a canine one: Federico had reason to believe that the mouse—it is difficult to understand why he had not escaped upward—had flattened out beneath a large iron bin that rested not directly on the floor but on the wooden slats of an old bath mat; he led the bitch to the spot and, instead of starting to paw and scratch around the container's base, she halted, her body tensed, at a certain distance, on the route the mouse would have to take in order to escape. But no matter how hard Federico kicked the bin and rattled the slats, the animal did not come out; convinced, therefore, that he had been mistaken and already bored with the game, he gave up the idea and went on inside. From the adjacent room, however, he heard the bitch scratch and whine, a clear indication that the mouse was indeed there; up to that point she had attributed her own certainty to her master, albeit leaving him the initiative, but seeing him desert the battlefield without a blow being struck filled her with despair. This revived Federico's interest in the adventure and induced him to retrace his steps, equipped this time with an ancient candlestick.

He set the candlestick on the floor and decisively lifted one side of the bin; the clever animal had indeed squeezed under it and had given no sign of his presence despite the terrific noise they had made all around him. Discovered, he was incapable of deciding immediately which direction he should take, and flitted frenziedly this way and that under the wooden slats; at least that much could be inferred from the movements of the bitch who lacked a free field and so was unable to pounce once and for all on her enemy.

A frantic struggle ensued between the two beasts, dominated by the shrill squeaks of the mouse. He was evidently confronting his enormous opponent in a very nasty way, because the latter, fearing for the moist safety of her muzzle, could not bring herself to make an open-mouthed grab for him, but snapped viciously and then quickly pulled back her head. Probably the mouse, partially protected by the slats, his most vulnerable parts sheltered, fought only with his powerful snout. At last, his situation having become unbearable, he tricked the bitch with an adroit feint and crashed through in the direction of the courtyard.

The bitch, instantly recovering from her bewilderment, took off in furious pursuit and, jumping over the candle, doused it. Two of her bounds were worth several of the mouse's tiny steps, and so the chase in the courtyard was soon over.

Federico, who had simply participated as a witness, followed them outside. The bitch, having seized the mouse by its tail, was swinging him violently from side to side in order to stun him and also, by the very violence of that movement, to prevent him from sinking his fangs into her delicate flesh; then she would drop him to judge the effects. He, broken and battered, after a moment's immobility would try to drag himself away, and then the bitch would snatch him up again. These were the most painful moments for her quivering sensitivity, because the mouse was selling his life dearly and, throwing himself on his back (that being his fighting position), fought back as best he could with his hands (a mouse has real honest-to-goodness flabby hands) and teeth. Besides, it is quite possible that a kind of squeamishness was restraining the bitch from more direct and sweeping action, or that the tiny snout bristling with stiff whiskers, with its suggestive power, unnerved her.

At this point Federico noticed that the mouse, in his attempts at flight, was dragging behind him a longish, dully glistening string which now wrapped itself around his body, now slithered, fully extended, through the dust on the ground, so that it must have quickly lost whatever sheen it originally had. Bending down to see in the weak light of the moon, he discovered it to be a gut and was astonished by its thinness and length. Seized by something akin to horror he rushed into the house to turn on a light that shone out on the courtyard: it was in fact a strip of gut, by now grimy and unrecognizable, which refused to detach itself from the animal and issued from it like an umbilical cord. But now, during one of the many attempts at escape, the gut caught on a jutting stone and snapped in half; a long section, nevertheless, continued to trail after the small body in its writhings.

At best the mouse had been subdued and lay in a queer position, limp on his belly at the hind part, while the front part rested on one side, so that the front hands were parallel to the ground and the hind ones desperately flung apart and practically flat. His body was wracked by the convulsive shivers of the death agony and the tiny snout gasped for air. Federico found himself unable to endure the sight and prodded the bitch to finish him off; but she was satisfied by now and refused to understand; since the enemy was felled, why endanger her throat's vulnerable softness again? Federico went to fetch a small coal shovel and with it did his utmost to kill the mouse. He was loath to hit its head for fear of splattering himself with blood, yet, on the other hand, at all the other parts of his body he could feel the soft fat flesh under his blows. The mouse seemed to have no bones and continued to writhe in a spasm that looked conscious, now and then scratching the ground with one hand. His eyes, slightly protruding from their sockets, were completely blank. What struck Federico most was the aura of innocence surrounding that body.

The mouse continued to toss and Federico decided to choke him, so he held the shovel perpendicularly and pressed it for a long time against his throat. To no avail: the neck yielded and there was no way to feel the resistance of the vertebrae under the thick padding of flabby flesh. However, the skin, drawn taut, exposed the minuscule fangs among the now drooping whiskers and, pulling back the head, slightly opened the tiny V-shaped mouth in an expression of indescribable charm. Now the mouse looked like a child about to cry, and yet without sadness. You would have also said that he had assumed that pose deliberately. Federico, at his wit's end, once more called the bitch, who at last gave in to his wishes; a sinister crack marked the end of our mouse's earthly sojourn: the dog had crushed his skull.

The struggle had been completely bloodless, not a single drop of blood stained the ground or the mouse's brown fur, nor was any dripping from his mouth. Federico picked him up by the tail whose tip had been stripped of its skin during the battle, exposing its muscle free of its hairy rings, and examined him under the light: a kind of arid and granulated mushroom, and what was left of the long string of gut issued from a gash in the belly, obviously inflicted by one of the dog's fangs; and here, too, there was not a drop of blood.

Federico laid the animal in the middle of the courtyard so that the maid who came every morning might admire it and, possibly, be frightened by it. Then he whistled to the dog and went inside.

Having prepared his salad, gotten a pitcher of water, turned off the lights in all the other rooms, and continued to irritate himself in a thousand different ways, he finally sat down at the dinner table. There is one more thing we have forgotten, the book—there, now we're ready. Ordinarily the chord introducing these solitary evening meals was a chat in French, quite informal, with an imaginary interlocutor; transfixing the first slice of potato, Federico began, "*Ah, oui monsieur, je vous l'assure, c'est un spectacle dont vous devriez vous régaler . . .*" and he went on with his mouth full, staring across the table. But the sudden thought of the mouse flashed through his mind: more than a thought, an intimate and subterranean sensation, something that clanged unexpectedly inside him, gave signs of wanting to burrow deeper, and rapidly faded. Federico resumed his conversation, the inner apparition returned several times, and always with greater intensity: it seemed that a great deal of time had elapsed since the first one, yet only a few seconds had gone by and he had already acquired the physical awareness of the dead mouse that lay outside his door. Although he continued to eat quite heartily, a great sadness, a sense of compassion and above all a restless anguish that had no apparent cause began to trouble him. The bitch stationed herself close to his chair, begging for food; she expected a special treat in view of the happy outcome of her recent exploit. There was no way out, he had to reward her; Federico prepared her a few morsels and fussed over her to tell her what a good dog she was.

After finishing his supper, he began as usual to read. He was reading about the adventures of a namesake of his, a novel called *Sentimental Education,* which had interested him very much up until the preceding session. But now the whole thing seemed insipid, and, anyway, he was quite unable to follow what he was reading because his feeling of nausea and anxiety was increasing immeasurably. He kept trying to find something in the book which would be comparable to his scathing experience, and could only find, it seemed to him, things which were much less poignant. He expected the writer to help him through his ordeal, but the man was barely sufficient unto himself and continued quietly to be distressed wholly on his own account.

There is nothing that gives one the perception of flesh and blood as intestines do, with their warm stench. Federico felt suffocated, throttled by mouse flesh; the taste and putrid smell of that fat and tallowy flesh had become a condition of his being, and he savored it directly through his blood, irremediably. He considered going to bed; but how to sleep, he said to himself, with the murdered victim's body at his doorstep? It even seemed to him that the spirit of the dead mouse hovered over him like an almost tangible presence, both menacing and indulgent, and that it was linked to his own spirit by deep, everlasting ties.

That murder could not be atoned for; it would remain forever unavenged, beyond ransom.

He slept very badly and dreamt gloomily about a long procession of mice wearing plumed helmets who held on to a dark rope with one hand and filed past him one by one, bowing gracefully. A medium-sized mouse arrived, and stopped the column, gazed at him for a long time with great sadness and said to him in a grave human voice: "I have decided, I forgive you"; then everything ended in a storm of squeals and chitters and a kind of saraband that dispersed in the dark air of the night. "I will find him again, I will definitely find him again!" Federico promised himself and thankful for having a lead, he flew off along a slender gut (for that is what the dark rope which the mice had been holding turned out to be), and strained toward the leaden horizon; but there seemed to be no end to the gut and Federico, who had been flying over dark valleys for many hours, felt his breath and strength fail him, and so he woke up.

Dawn was rising over the mouse's small corpse; his protruding eyes, by now curdled, vaguely reflected its light; a great many industrious ants bustled all around him like diligent clerks, still sleepy and puffy-eyed, whom one might meet along the city's streets on winter mornings. The acacia trees in the courtyard were trying to clear their throats for the start of the day. The piece of gut that had broken off lay a little to one side and already half withered. The dog huddled in a ditch, shivering in the first gust of wind.

Federico went outside in his night-shirt, lifted the mouse from the ground, shook the ants off him and examined him again: the torn intestines were covered with dust, poor living flesh. Federico smoothed his whiskers, and clutched him to his breast, rocking him to and fro, belly up like a child. Holding him against his cheek, he stroked his fur smoothly with the grain; he noticed a tooth mark, a bald spot on the tiny shoulder, and delicately caressed it with his index fingers, as though to assuage the pain. "My little mouse, my poor little mouse!" he moaned, and still moaning, he descended the steps to the orchard with the mouse in his arms. There he intoned a strange dirge and walked like a little girl who, singing a lullaby, gives a funeral to her doll; he knelt, dug a small grave, placed the mouse in it with the utmost delicacy and covered him up. "Rest in peace, my poor little mouse!" he repeated and lingered for a long time, contemplating the tiny patch of freshly turned earth; from behind the panes of a window a peasant woman watched him with curiosity. He rose and, full of dignity in his long night-shirt, went back up the garden, loudly singing a church psalm, which had suddenly surfaced from his days as a choirboy.

This is not at all to mean that Federico had gone crazy. On the contrary, I believe that he became one of the best lawyers in his region, and there is no doubt that he got along very well with his little bitch until the end, but he retained one weakness: sometimes, even after his hair had turned gray, he roamed at night through the uninhabited rooms of his house, the storage rooms and odd corners, calling: "Come to me, little mice! Oh, come little mice, and rest in my arms!" The little mice, whenever he chanced to run into them, were amused and frightened, and gazing at him with their tiny round glistening eyes, trotted daintily ahead of him with a faint roll of thunder.

## *Study questions*

1. *How does Landolfi give human characteristics to the dog and to the mouse? Why does he do this?* 2. *Why does Federico keep a hunting bitch?* 3. *What is the significance of the piece of gut that issues from the mouse like an umbilical cord? How is it important that the struggle between dog and mouse is completely bloodless?* 4. *Why does Federico habitually talk to himself?* 5. *At what point and why does Federico consider the killing of the mouse as murder that cannot be atoned for?* 6. *Account for Federico's behavior in the penultimate paragraph.*

*Bernard Malamud* (b. 1914), with a largely affirmative view, celebrates traditional human values. In story after story, filled with the cadences of Jewish life and speech, he demonstrates the resiliency of the human spirit. Born in Brooklyn, New York, he received his B.A. from the City College of New York in 1936 and an M.A. from Columbia University in 1942. His first novel, *The Natural* (1952), was followed by others, including *The Assistant* (1957), *A New Life* (1961), the Pulitzer Prize– and National Book Award–winning *The Fixer* (1966), and *The Tenants* (1971). His short stories have appeared in such publications as *Partisan Review*, the *New Yorker*, *Commentary*, *Harper's Bazaar*, and *Best American Short Stories*. His short-story collections include *The Magic Barrel* (1958), for which he won a National Book Award, *Idiots First* (1963), *Pictures of Fidelman* (1969), and *Rembrandt's Hat* (1973). Malamud has taught at Oregon State University and at Bennington College in Vermont. In "Idiots First," he walks a fine line between humor, pathos, and terror, finally balancing the incongruities in the startling climax.

## IDIOTS FIRST

The thick ticking of the tin clock stopped. Mendel, dozing in the dark, awoke in fright. The pain returned as he listened. He drew on his cold embittered clothing, and wasted minutes sitting at the edge of the bed.

"Isaac," he ultimately sighed.

In the kitchen, Isaac, his astonished mouth open, held six peanuts in his palm. He placed each on the table. "One . . . two . . . nine."

He gathered each peanut and appeared in the doorway. Mendel, in loose hat and long overcoat, still sat on the bed. Isaac watched with small eyes and ears, thick hair graying the sides of his head.

"Schlaf," he nasally said.

"No," muttered Mendel. As if stifling he rose. "Come, Isaac."

He wound his old watch though the sight of the stopped clock nauseated him.

Isaac wanted to hold it to his ear.

"No, it's late." Mendel put the watch carefully away. In the drawer he found the little paper bag of crumpled ones and fives and slipped it into his overcoat pocket. He helped Isaac on with his coat.

Isaac looked at one dark window, then at the other. Mendel stared at both blank windows.

They went slowly down the darkly lit stairs, Mendel first, Isaac watching the moving shadows on the wall. To one long shadow he offered a peanut.

"Hungrig."

In the vestibule the old man gazed through the thin glass. The November night was cold and bleak. Opening the door he cautiously thrust his head out. Though he saw nothing he quickly shut the door.

"Ginzburg, that he came to see me yesterday," he whispered in Isaac's ear.

Isaac sucked air.

"You know who I mean?"

Isaac combed his chin with his fingers.

"That's the one, with the black whiskers. Don't talk to him or go with him if he asks you."

Isaac moaned.

"Young people he don't bother so much," Mendel said in afterthought.

It was suppertime and the street was empty but the store windows dimly lit their way to the corner. They crossed the deserted street and went on. Isaac, with a happy cry, pointed to the three golden balls. Mendel smiled but was exhausted when they got to the pawnshop.

The pawnbroker, a red-bearded man with black horn-rimmed glasses, was eating a whitefish at the rear of the store. He craned his head, saw them, and settled back to sip his tea.

In five minutes he came forward, patting his shapeless lips with a large white handkerchief.

Mendel, breathing heavily, handed him the worn gold watch. The pawnbroker, raising his glasses, screwed in his eyepiece. He turned the watch over once. "Eight dollars."

The dying man wet his cracked lips. "I must have thirty-five."

"So go to Rothschild."

"Cost me myself sixty."

"In 1905." The pawnbroker handed back the watch. It had stopped ticking. Mendel wound it slowly. It ticked hollowly.

"Isaac must go to my uncle that he lives in California."

"It's a free country," said the pawnbroker.

Isaac, watching a banjo, snickered.

"What's the matter with him?" the pawnbroker asked.

"So let be eight dollars," muttered Mendel, "but where will I get the rest till tonight?"

"How much for my hat and coat?" he asked.

"No sale." The pawnbroker went behind the cage and wrote out a ticket. He locked the watch in a small drawer but Mendel still heard it ticking.

In the street he slipped the eight dollars into the paper bag, then searched in his pockets for a scrap of writing. Finding it, he strained to read the address by the light of the street lamp.

As they trudged to the subway, Mendel pointed to the sprinkled sky.

"Isaac, look how many stars are tonight."

"Eggs," said Isaac.

"First we will go to Mr. Fishbein, after we will eat."

They got off the train in upper Manhattan and had to walk several blocks before they located Fishbein's house.

"A regular palace," Mendel murmured, looking forward to a moment's warmth.

Isaac stared uneasily at the heavy door of the house.

Mendel rang. The servant, a man with long sideburns, came to the door and said Mr. and Mrs. Fishbein were dining and could see no one.

"He should eat in peace but we will wait till he finishes."

"Come back tomorrow morning. Tomorrow morning. Mr. Fishbein will talk to you. He don't do business or charity at this time of the night."

"Charity I am not interested—"

"Come back tomorrow."

"Tell him it's life or death—"

"Whose life or death?"

"So if not his, then mine."

"Don't be such a big smart aleck."

"Look me in my face," said Mendel, "and tell me if I got time till tomorrow morning?"

The servant stared at him, then at Isaac, and reluctantly let them in.

The foyer was a vast high-ceilinged room with many oil paintings on the walls, voluminous silken draperies, a thick flowered rug at foot, and a marble staircase.

Mr. Fishbein, a paunchy bald-headed man with hairy nostrils and small patent leather feet, ran lightly down the stairs, a large napkin tucked under a tuxedo coat button. He stopped on the fifth step from the bottom and examined his visitors.

"Who comes on Friday night to a man that he has guests, to spoil him his supper?"

"Excuse me that I bother you, Mr. Fishbein," Mendel said. "If I didn't come now I couldn't come tomorrow."

"Without more preliminaries, please state your business. I'm a hungry man."

"Hungrig," wailed Isaac.

Fishbein adjusted his pince-nez. "What's the matter with him?"

"This is my son Isaac. He is like this all his life."

Isaac mewled.

"I am sending him to California."

"Mr. Fishbein don't contribute to personal pleasure trips."

"I am a sick man and he must go tonight on the train to my Uncle Leo."

"I never give to unorganized charity," Fishbein said, "but if you are hungry I will invite you downstairs in my kitchen. We having tonight chicken with stuffed derma."

"All I ask is thirty-five dollars for the train ticket to my uncle in California. I have already the rest."

"Who is your uncle? How old a man?"

"Eighty-one years, a long life to him."

Fishbein burst into laughter. "Eighty-one years and you are sending him this halfwit."

Mendel, flailing both arms, cried, "Please, without names."

Fishbein politely conceded.

"Where is open the door there we go in the house," the sick man said. "If you will kindly give me thirty-five dollars, God will bless you. What is thirty-five dollars to Mr. Fishbein? Nothing. To me, for my boy, is everything."

Fishbein drew himself up to his tallest height.

"Private contributions I don't make—only to institutions. This is my fixed policy."

Mendel sank to his creaking knees on the rug.

"Please, Mr. Fishbein, if not thirty-five, give maybe twenty."

"Levinson!" Fishbein angrily called.

The servant with the long sideburns appeared at the top of the stairs.

"Show this party where is the door—unless he wishes to partake food before leaving the premises."

"For what I got chicken won't cure it," Mendel said.

"This way if you please," said Levinson, descending.

Isaac assisted his father up.

"Take him to an institution," Fishbein advised over the marble balustrade. He ran quickly up the stairs and they were at once outside, buffeted by winds.

The walk to the subway was tedious. The wind blew mournfully. Mendel, breathless, glanced furtively at shadows. Isaac, clutching his peanuts in his frozen fist, clung to his father's side. They entered a small park to rest for a minute on a stone bench under a leafless two-branched tree. The thick right branch was raised, the thin left one hung down. A very pale moon rose slowly. So did a stranger as they approached the bench.

"Gut yuntif" [Happy holiday], he said hoarsely.

Mendel, drained of blood, waved his wasted arms. Isaac yowled sickly. Then a bell chimed and it was only ten. Mendel let out a piercing anguished cry as the bearded stranger disappeared into the bushes. A policeman came running, and though he beat the bushes with his nightstick, could turn up nothing. Mendel and Isaac hurried out of the little park. When Mendel glanced back the dead tree had its thin arm raised, the thick one down. He moaned.

They boarded a trolley, stopping at the home of a former friend, but he had died years ago. On the same block they went into a cafeteria and ordered two fried eggs for Isaac. The tables were crowded except where a heavy-set man sat eating soup with kasha. After one look at him they left in haste, although Isaac wept.

Mendel had another address on a slip of paper but the house was too far away, in Queens, so they stood in a doorway shivering.

What can I do, he frantically thought, in one short hour?

He remembered the furniture in the house: It was junk but might bring a few dollars. "Come, Isaac." They went once more to the pawnbroker's to talk to him, but the shop was dark and an iron gate—rings and gold watches glinting through it—was drawn tight across his place of business.

They huddled behind a telephone pole, both freezing. Isaac whimpered.

"See the big moon, Isaac. The whole sky is white."

He pointed but Isaac wouldn't look.

Mendel dreamed for a minute of the sky lit up, long sheets of light in all directions. Under the sky, in California, sat Uncle Leo drinking tea with lemon. Mendel felt warm but woke up cold.

Across the street stood an ancient brick synagogue.

He pounded on the huge door but no one appeared. He waited till he had breath and desperately knocked again. At last there were footsteps within, and the synagogue door cracked open on its massive brass hinges.

A darkly dressed sexton, holding a dripping candle, glared at them.

"Who knocks this time of night with so much noise on the synagogue door?"

Mendel told the sexton his troubles. "Please, I would like to speak to the rabbi."

"The rabbi is an old man. He sleeps now. His wife won't let you see him. Go home and come back tomorrow."

"To tomorrow I said goodbye already. I am a dying man."

Though the sexton seemed doubtful he pointed to an old wooden house next door. "In there he lives." He disappeared into the synagogue with his lit candle casting shadows around him.

Mendel, with Isaac clutching his sleeve, went up the wooden steps and rang the bell. After five minutes a big-faced, gray-haired bulky woman came out on the porch with a torn robe thrown over her nightdress. She emphatically said the rabbi was sleeping and could not be waked.

But as she was insisting, the rabbi himself tottered to the door. He listened a minute and said, "Who wants to see me let them come in."

They entered a cluttered room. The rabbi was an old skinny man with bent shoulders and a wisp of white beard. He wore a flannel nightgown and black skullcap; his feet were bare.

"Vey is mir" [Woe is me], his wife muttered. "Put on shoes or tomorrow comes sure pneumonia." She was a woman with a big belly, years younger than her husband. Staring at Isaac, she turned away.

Mendel apologetically related his errand. "All I need more is thirty-five dollars."

"Thirty-five?" said the rabbi's wife. "Why not thirty-five thousand? Who has so much money? My husband is a poor rabbi. The doctors take away every penny."

"Dear friend," said the rabbi, "if I had I would give you."

"I got already seventy," Mendel said, heavy-hearted. "All I need more is thirty-five."

"God will give you," said the rabbi.

"In the grave," said Mendel. "I need tonight. Come, Isaac."

"Wait," called the rabbi.

He hurried inside, came out with a fur-lined caftan, and handed it to Mendel.

"Yascha," shrieked his wife, "not your new coat!"

"I got my old one. Who needs two coats for one body?"

"Yascha, I am screaming—"

"Who can go among poor people, tell me, in a new coat?"

"Yascha," she cried, "what can this man do with your coat? He needs tonight the money. The pawnbrokers are asleep."

"So let him wake them up."

"No." She grabbed the coat from Mendel.

He held on to a sleeve, wrestling her for the coat. Her I know, Mendel thought. "Shylock," he muttered. Her eyes glittered.

The rabbi groaned and tottered dizzily. His wife cried out as Mendel yanked the coat from her hands.

"Run," cried the rabbi.

"Run, Isaac."

They ran out of the house and down the steps.

"Stop, you thief," called the rabbi's wife.

The rabbi pressed both hands to his temples and fell to the floor.

"Help!" his wife wept. "Heart attack! Help!"

But Mendel and Isaac ran through the streets with the rabbi's new fur-lined caftan. After them noiselessly ran Ginzburg.

It was very late when Mendel bought the train ticket in the only booth open.

There was no time to stop for a sandwich so Isaac ate his peanuts and they hurried to the train in the vast deserted station.

"So in the morning," Mendel gasped as they ran, "there comes a man that he sells sandwiches and coffee. Eat but get change. When reaches California the train, will be waiting for you on the station Uncle Leo. If you don't recognize him he will recognize you. Tell him I send best regards."

But when they arrived at the gate to the platform it was shut, the light out.

Mendel, groaning, beat on the gate with his fists.

"Too late," said the uniformed ticket collector, a bulky, bearded man with hairy nostrils and a fishy smell.

He pointed to the station clock. "Already past twelve."

"But I see standing there still the train." Mendel said, hopping in his grief.

"It just left—in one more minute."

"A minute is enough. Just open the gate."

"Too late I told you."

Mendel socked his bony chest with both hands. "With my whole heart I beg you this little favor."

"Favors you had enough already. For you the train is gone. You shoulda been dead already at midnight. I told you that yesterday. This is the best I can do."

"Ginzburg!" Mendel shrank from him.

"Who else?" The voice was metallic, eyes glittered, the expression amused.

"For myself," the old man begged, "I don't ask a thing. But what will happen to my boy?"

Ginzburg shrugged slightly. "What will happen happens. This isn't my responsibility. I got enough to think about without worrying about somebody on one cylinder."

"What then is your responsibility?"

"To create conditions. To make happen what happens. I ain't in the anthropomorphic business."

"Whatever business you in, where is your pity?"

"This ain't my commodity. The law is the law."

"Which law is this?"

"The cosmic universal law, goddamit, the one I got to follow myself."

"What kind of a law is it?" cried Mendel. "For God's sake, don't you understand what I went through in my life with this poor boy? Look at him. For thirty-nine years, since the day he was born, I wait for him to grow up, but he don't. Do you understand what this means in a father's heart? Why don't you let him go to his uncle?" His voice had risen and he was shouting.

Isaac mewled loudly.

"Better calm down or you'll hurt somebody's feelings," Ginzburg said with a wink toward Isaac.

"All my life," Mendel cried, his body trembling, "what did I have? I was poor. I suffered from my health. When I worked I worked too hard. When I didn't work was worse. My wife died a young woman. But I didn't ask from anybody nothing. Now I ask a small favor. Be so kind, Mr. Ginzburg."

The ticket collector was picking his teeth with a match stick.

"You ain't the only one, my friend, some got it worse than you. That's how it goes in this country."

"You dog you." Mendel lunged at Ginzburg's throat and began to choke. "You bastard, don't you understand what it means human?"

They struggled nose to nose, Ginzburg, though his astonished eyes bulged, began to laugh. "You pipsqueak nothing. I'll freeze you to pieces."

His eyes lit in rage and Mendel felt an unbearable cold like an icy dagger invading his body, all of his parts shriveling.

Now I die without helping Isaac.

A crowd gathered. Isaac yelped in fright.

Clinging to Ginzburg in his last agony, Mendel saw reflected in the ticket collector's eyes the depth of his terror. But he saw that Ginzburg, staring at himself in Mendel's eyes, saw mirrored in them the extent of his own awful wrath. He beheld a shimmering, starry, blinding light that produced darkness.

Ginzburg looked astounded. "Who me?"

His grip on the squirming old man slowly loosened, and Mendel, his heart barely beating, slumped to the ground.

"Go," Ginzburg muttered, "take him to the train."

"Let pass," he commanded a guard.

The crowd parted. Isaac helped his father up and they tottered down the steps to the platform where the train waited, lit and ready to go.

Mendel found Isaac a coach seat and hastily embraced him. "Help Uncle Leo, Isaakil. Also remember your father and mother."

"Be nice to him," he said to the conductor. "Show him where everything is."

He waited on the platform until the train began slowly to move. Isaac sat at the edge of his seat, his face strained in the direction of his journey. When the train was gone, Mendel ascended the stairs to see what had become of Ginzburg.

## Study questions

*1. How early in the story can we tell that something is wrong with Isaac? 2. Why does Mendel wait so long to seek help? On what kind of quest does he embark with Isaac? 3. What role is played by the pawnbroker? Mr. Fishbein? the rabbi and his wife? 4. What kinds of image patterns recur in the story? How do they function? 5. Who is Ginzburg? What symbolic role does he play? What happens at the climax of the story? 6. What will happen to Mendel and Isaac? to Ginzburg? 7. How does setting function? tone? mood?*

*Alain Robbe-Grillet* (b. 1922), born in Brest, graduated from the Institute National Agronomique and later worked as an agronomist specializing in tropical fruit. His first novel, published in 1953, was translated as *The Erasers.* There followed *The Voyeur* (1955), *Jealousy* (1957), *In the Labyrinth* (1959), *The House of Assignation* (1966), *Project for a Revolution in New York City* (1972), and *Topology of a Phantom City* (1978). A volume of experimental short fiction was translated as *Snapshots* in 1968. Robbe-Grillet is also a literary critic and scriptwriter—*Last Year at Marienbad* (1961)—of note. A member of the French "new novel" movement, Robbe-Grillet rebels against such traditional fictional techniques as plot and characterization. Plot, for example, supposes a rational, coherent universe, but for Robbe-Grillet the world is a meaningless puzzle and not a subject for mimetic art. "The Secret Room" is like a motion picture with stop action, forward and reverse movements, and cuts out of sequence, but a sequential plot can be deduced: action does take place, characters are involved, and, one must assume, some kind of personal conflict leads to the appalling crime.

# THE SECRET ROOM

TO GUSTAVE MOREAU

The first thing to be seen is a red stain, of a deep, dark, shiny red, with almost black shadows. It is in the form of an irregular rosette, sharply outlined, extending in several directions in wide outflows of unequal length, dividing and dwindling afterward into single sinuous streaks. The whole stands out against a smooth, pale surface, round in shape, at once dull and pearly, a hemisphere joined by gentle curves to an expanse of the same pale color—white darkened by the shadowy quality of the place: a dungeon, a sunken room, or a cathedral—glowing with a diffused brilliance in the semidarkness.

Farther back, the space is filled with the cylindrical trunks of columns, repeated with progressive vagueness in their retreat toward the beginning of a vast stone stairway, turning slightly as it rises, growing narrower and narrower as it approaches the high vaults where it disappears.

The whole setting is empty, stairway and colonnades. Alone, in the foreground, the stretched-out body gleams feebly, marked with the red stain—a white body whose full, supple flesh can be sensed, fragile, no doubt, and vulnerable.

Alongside the bloody hemisphere another identical round form, this one intact, is seen at almost the same angle of view; but the haloed point at its summit, of darker tint, is in this case quite recognizable, whereas the other one is entirely destroyed, or at least covered by the wound.

In the background, near the top of the stairway, a black silhouette is seen fleeing, a man wrapped in a long, floating cape, ascending the last steps without turning around, his deed accomplished. A thin smoke rises in twisting scrolls from a sort of incense burner placed on a high stand of ironwork with a silvery glint. Nearby lies the milkwhite body, with wide streaks of blood running from the left breast, along the flank and on the hip.

It is a fully rounded woman's body, but not heavy, completely nude, lying on its back, the bust raised up somewhat by thick cushions thrown down on the floor, which is covered with Oriental rugs. The waist is very narrow, the neck long and thin, curved to one side, the head thrown back into a darker area where, even so, the facial features may be discerned, the partly opened mouth, the wide-staring eyes, shining with a fixed brilliance, and the mass of long, black hair spread out in a complicated wavy disorder over a heavily folded cloth, of velvet perhaps, on which also rest the arm and shoulder.

It is a uniformly colored velvet of dark purple, or which seems so in this lighting. But purple, brown, blue also seem to dominate in the colors of the cushions—only a small portion of which is hidden beneath the velvet cloth, and which protrude noticeably, lower down, beneath the bust and waist—as well as in the Oriental patterns of the rugs on the floor. Farther on, these same colors are picked up again in the stone of the paving and the columns, the vaulted archways, the stairs, and the less discernible surfaces that disappear into the farthest reaches of the room.

The dimensions of this room are difficult to determine exactly; the body of the young sacrificial victim seems at first glance to occupy a substantial portion of it, but the vast size of the stairway leading down to it would imply rather that this is not the whole room, whose considerable space must in reality extend all around, right and left, as it does toward the faraway browns and blues among the columns standing in line, in every direction, perhaps toward other sofas, thick carpets, piles of cushions and fabrics, other tortured bodies, other incense burners.

It is also difficult to say where the light comes from. No clue, on the columns or on the floor, suggests the direction of the rays. Nor is any window or torch visible. The milkwhite body itself seems to light the scene, with its full breasts, the curve of its thighs, the rounded belly, the full buttocks, the stretched-out legs, widely spread, and the black tuft of the exposed sex, provocative, proffered, useless now.

The man has already moved several steps back. He is now on the first steps of the stairs, ready to go up. The bottom steps are wide and deep, like the steps leading up to some great building, a temple or theater; they grow smaller as they ascend, and at the same time describe a wide, helical curve, so gradually that the stairway has not yet made a half-turn by the time it disappears near the top of the vaults, reduced then to a steep, narrow flight of steps without handrail, vaguely outlined, moreover, in the thickening darkness beyond.

But the man does not look in this direction, where his movement nonetheless carries him; his left foot on the second step and his right foot already touching the third, with his knee bent, he has turned around to look at the spectacle for one last time. The long, floating cape thrown hastily over his shoulders, clasped in one hand at his waist, has been whirled around by the rapid circular motion that has just caused his head and chest to turn in the opposite direction, and a corner of the cloth remains suspended in the air as if blown by a gust of wind; this corner, twisting around upon itself in the form of a loose S, reveals the red silk lining with its gold embroidery.

The man's features are impassive, but tense, as if in expectation—or perhaps fear—of some sudden event, or surveying with one last glance the total immobility of the scene. Though he is looking backward, his whole body is turned slightly forward, as if he were continuing up the stairs. His right arm—not the one holding the edge of the cape—is bent sharply toward the left, toward a point in space where the balustrade should be, if this stairway had one, an interrupted gesture, almost incomprehensible, unless it arose from an instinctive movement to grasp the absent support.

As to the direction of his glance, it is certainly aimed at the body of the victim lying on the cushions, its extended members stretched out in the form of a cross, its bust raised up, its head thrown back. But the face is perhaps hidden from the man's eyes by one of the columns, standing at the foot of the stairs. The young woman's right hand touches the floor just at the foot of this column. The fragile wrist is encircled by an iron bracelet. The arm is almost in darkness, only the hand receiving enough light to make the thin, outspread fingers clearly visible against the circular protrusion at the base of the stone column. A black metal chain running around the column passes through a ring affixed to the bracelet, binding the wrist tightly to the column.

At the top of the arm a rounded shoulder, raised up by the cushions, also stands out well lighted, as well as the neck, the throat, and the other shoulder, the armpit with its soft hair, the left arm likewise pulled back with its wrist bound in the same manner to the base of another column, in the extreme foreground; here the iron bracelet and the chain are fully displayed, represented with perfect clarity down to the slightest details.

The same is true, still in the foreground but at the other side, for a similar chain, but not quite as thick, wound directly around the ankle, running twice around the column and terminating in a heavy iron ring embedded in the floor. About a yard farther back, or perhaps slightly farther, the right foot is identically chained. But it is the left foot, and its chain, that are the most minutely depicted.

The foot is small, delicate, finely modeled. In several places the chain has broken the skin, causing noticeable if not extensive depressions in the flesh. The chain links are oval, thick, the size of an eye. The ring in the floor resembles those used to attach horses; it lies almost touching the stone pavement to which it is riveted by a massive iron peg. A few inches away is the edge of a rug; it is grossly wrinkled at this point, doubtless as a result of the convulsive, but necessarily very restricted, movements of the victim attempting to struggle.

The man is still standing about a yard away, half leaning over her. He looks at her face, seen upside down, her dark eyes made larger by their surrounding eyeshadow, her mouth wide open as if screaming. The man's posture allows his face to be seen only in a vague profile, but one senses in it a violent exaltation, despite the rigid attitude, the silence, the immobility. His back is slightly arched. His left hand, the only one visible, holds up at some distance from the body a piece of cloth, some dark-colored piece of clothing, which drags on the carpet, and which must be the long cape with its gold-embroidered lining.

This immense silhouette hides most of the bare flesh over which the red stain, spreading from the globe of the breast, runs in long rivulets that branch out, growing narrower, upon the pale background of the bust and the flank. One thread has reached the armpit and runs in an almost straight, thin line along the arm; others have run down toward the waist and traced out, along one side of the belly, the hip, the top of the thigh, a more random network already starting to congeal. Three or four tiny veins have reached the hollow between the legs, meeting in a sinuous line, touching the point of the V formed by the outspread legs, and disappearing into the black tuft.

Look, now the flesh is still intact: the black tuft and the white belly, the soft curve of the hips, the narrow waist, and, higher up, the pearly breasts rising and falling in time with the rapid breathing, whose rhythm grows more accelerated. The man, close to her, one knee on the floor, leans farther over. The head, with its long, curly hair, which alone is free to move somewhat, turns from side to side, struggling; finally the woman's mouth twists open, while the flesh is torn open, the blood spurts out over the tender skin, stretched tight, the carefully shadowed eyes grow abnormally larger, the mouth opens wider, the head twists violently, one last time, from right to left, then more gently, to fall back finally and become still, amid the mass of black hair spread out on the velvet.

At the very top of the stone stairway, the little door has opened, allowing a yellowish but sustained shaft of light to enter, against which stands out the dark silhouette of the man wrapped in his long cloak. He has but to climb a few more steps to reach the threshold.

Afterward, the whole setting is empty, the enormous room with its purple shadows and its stone columns proliferating in all directions, the monumental staircase with no handrail that twists upward, growing narrower and vaguer as it rises into the darkness, toward the top of the vaults where it disappears.

Near the body, whose wound has stiffened, whose brilliance is already growing dim, the thin smoke from the incense burner traces complicated scrolls in the still air: first a coil turned horizontally to the left, which then straightens out and rises slightly, then returns to the axis of its point of origin, which it crosses as it moves to the right, then turns back in the first direction, only to wind back again, thus forming an irregular sinusoidal curve, more and more flattened out, and rising, vertically, toward the top of the canvas.

## *Study questions*

1. *What were the circumstances of the murder? What does the position and the condition of the woman imply? Why is she called a "sacrificial victim"? Why does the man examine her with "violent exaltation"?* 2. *Why does Robbe-Grillet move his focus back and forth from the woman and forward and backward in time?* 3. *Why is the actual death of the woman placed near the end of the story? Is this the climax?* 4. *How does the focus on the man shift? From the way the focus shifts, can we speculate concerning his feelings?* 5. *Why is the word "canvas" used in the last sentence? Is this story also like a painting or a series of possible paintings? photographs?* 6. *What is the point of it all?*

*William Gass* (b. 1924), now a professor of philosophy at Washington University in St. Louis, has taught at the College of Wooster in Wooster, Ohio, and at Purdue University. He was born in Fargo, North Dakota, and attended Kenyon College, Ohio Wesleyan University, and Cornell University, where he received his Ph.D. in 1954. His stories, which first began to appear in such journals as *Accent, Perspective,* and the *New American Review,* were collected in *In the Heart of the Heart of the Country* (1968). A novel, *Omensetter's Luck,* was published in 1966. Gass is also a literary critic and essayist, publishing articles and reviews in the *South Atlantic Quarterly,* the *New Republic,* the *Philosophic Review,* and the *New York Review of Books,* among others. Many of these essays were collected in *Fiction and the Figures of Life* (1971). Recent publications include the speculative *On Being Blue* (1977) and *The World Within the Word* (1978). "In the Heart of the Heart of the Country" is a contemporary classic, combining, as it does, many characteristics of the antistory mode.

# IN THE HEART OF THE HEART OF THE COUNTRY

### *A place*

So I have sailed the seas and come . . .
to B . . .
a small . . .
town fastened to a field in Indiana. Twice there have been twelve hundred people here to answer to the census. The town is outstandingly neat and shady, and always puts its best side to the highway. On one lawn there's even a wood or plastic iron deer.

You can reach us by crossing a creek. In the spring the lawns are green, the forsythia is singing, and even the railroad that guts the town has straight bright rails which hum when the train is coming, and the train itself has a welcome horning sound.

Down the back streets the asphalt crumbles into gravel. There's Westbrook's, with the geraniums, Horsefall's, Mott's. The sidewalk shatters. Gravel dust rises like breath behind the wagons. And I am in retirement from love.

### *Weather*

In the Midwest, around the lower Lakes, the sky in the winter is heavy and close, and it is a rare day, a day to remark on, when the sky lifts and allows the heart up. I am keeping count, and as I write this page, it is eleven days since I have seen the sun.

### *My house*

There's a row of headless maples behind my house, cut to free the passage of electric wires. High stumps, ten feet tall, remain, and I climb these like a boy to watch the country sail away from me. They are ordinary fields, a little more uneven than they should be, since in the spring they puddle. The topsoil's thin, but only moderately stony. Corn is grown one year, soybeans another. At dusk starlings darken the single tree—a larch—which stands in the middle. When the sky moves, fields move under it. I feel, on my perch, that I've lost my years. It's as though I were living at last in my eyes, as I have always dreamed of doing, and I think then I know why I've come here: to see, and so to go out against new things—oh god how easily—like air in a breeze. It's true there are moments —foolish moments, ecstasy on a tree stump—when I'm all but gone, scattered I like to think like seed, for I'm the sort now in the fool's position of having love left over which I'd like to lose; what good is it now to me, candy ungiven after Halloween?

### *A person*

There are vacant lots on either side of Billy Holsclaw's house. As the weather improves, they fill with hollyhocks. From spring through fall, Billy collects coal and wood and puts the lumps and pieces in piles near his door, for keeping warm is his one work. I see him most often on mild days sitting on his doorsill in the sun. I noticed he's squinting a little, which is perhaps the reason he doesn't cackle as I pass. His house is the size of a single garage, and very old. It shed its paint with its youth, and its boards are a warped and weathered gray. So is Billy. He wears a short lumpy faded black coat when it's cold, otherwise he always goes about in the same loose, grease-spotted shirt and trousers. I suspect his galluses were yellow once, when they were new.

### *Wires*

These wires offend me. Three trees were maimed on their account, and now these wires deface the sky. They cross like a fence in front of me, enclosing the crows with the clouds. I can't reach in, but like a stick, I throw my feelings over. What is it that offends me? I am on my stump, I've built a platform there and the wires prevent my going out. The cut trees, the black wires, all the beyond birds therefore anger me. When I've wormed through a fence to reach a meadow, do I ever feel the same about the field?

### People

Their hair in curlers and their heads wrapped in loud scarves, young mothers, fattish in trousers, lounge about in the speedwash, smoking cigarettes, eating candy, drinking pop, thumbing magazines, and screaming at their children above the whirr and rumble of the machines.

At the bank a young man freshly pressed is letting himself in with a key. Along the street, delicately teetering, many grandfathers move in a dream. During the murderous heat of summer they perch on window ledges, their feet dangling just inside the narrow shelf of shade the store has made, staring steadily into the street. Where their consciousness has gone I can't say. It's not in the eyes. Perhaps it's diffuse, all temperature and skin, like an infant's, though more mild. Near the corner there are several large overalled men employed in standing. A truck turns to be weighed at the Feed and Grain. Images drift on the drugstore window. The wind has blown the smell of cattle into town. Our eyes have been driven in like the eyes of the old men. And there's no one to have mercy on us.

### Vital data

There are two restaurants here and a tearoom. two bars. one bank. three barbers. one with a green shade with which he blinds his window. two groceries. a dealer in Fords. one drug, one hardware, and one appliance store. several that sell feed, grain, and farm equipment. an antique shop. poolroom. a laundromat. three doctors. a dentist. a plumber. a vet. a funeral home in elegant repair the color of a buttercup. numerous beauty parlors which open and shut like night-blooming plants. a tiny dime and department store of no width but several floors. a hutch, homemade, where you can order, after lying down or squirming in, furniture that's been fashioned from bent lengths of stainless tubing, glowing plastic, metallic thread, and clear shellac. an American Legion Post and a root beer stand. little agencies for this and that: cosmetics, brushes, insurance, greeting cards and garden produce—anything—sample shoes—which do their business out of hats and satchels, over coffee cups and dissolving sugar. a factory for making paper sacks and pasteboard boxes that's lodged in an old brick building bearing the legend, OPERA HOUSE, still faintly golden, on its roof. a library given by Carnegie. a post office. a school. a railroad station. fire station. lumber yard. telephone company. welding shop. garage . . . and spotted through the town from one end to the other in a line along the highway—gas stations to the number five.

### Business

One side section of street is blocked off with sawhorses. Hard, thin, bitter men in blue jeans, cowboy boots and hats, untruck a dinky carnival. The merchants are promoting themselves. There will be free rides, raucous music, parades and coneys, pop, popcorn, candy, cones, awards and drawings, with all you can endure of pinch, push, bawl, shove, shout, scream, shriek, and bellow. Children pedal past on decorated bicycles, their wheels a blur of color, streaming crinkled paper and excited dogs. A little later there's a pet show for a prize—

dogs, cats, birds, sheep, ponies, goats—none of which wins. The whirlabouts whirl about. The ferris wheel climbs dizzily into the sky as far as a tall man on tiptoe might be persuaded to reach, and the irritated operators measure with sour eyes the height and weight of every child to see if they are safe for the machines. An electrical megaphone repeatedly trumpets the names of the generous sponsors. The following day they do not allow the refuse to remain long in the street.

### *My house, this place and body*

I have met with some mischance, wings withering, as Plato says obscurely, and across the breadth of Ohio, like heaven on a table, I've fallen as far as the poet, to the sixth sort of body, this house in B, in Indiana, with its blue and gray bewitching windows, holy magical insides. Great thick evergreens protect its entry. And I live *in*.

Lost in the corn rows, I remember feeling just another stalk, and thus this country takes me over in the way I occupy myself when I am well . . . completely —to the edge of both my house and body. No one notices, when they walk by, that I am brimming in the doorways. My house, this place and body, I've come in mourning to be born in. To anybody else it's pretty silly: love. Why should I feel a loss? How am I bereft? She was never mine; she was a fiction, always a golden tomgirl, barefoot, with an adolescent's slouch and a boy's taste for sports and fishing, a figure out of Twain, or worse, in Riley. Age cannot be kind.

There's little hand in hand here . . . not in B. No one touches except in rage. Occasionally girls will twine their arms about each other and lurch along, school out, toward home and play. I dreamed my lips would drift down your back like a skiff on a river. I'd follow a vein with the point of my finger, hold your bare feet in my naked hands.

### *The same person*

Billy Holsclaw lives alone—how alone it is impossible to fathom. In the post office he talks greedily to me about the weather. His head bobs on a wild flood of words, and I take this violence to be a measure of his eagerness for speech. He badly needs a shave, coal dust has layered his face, he spits when he speaks, and his fingers pick at his tatters. He wobbles out in the wind when I leave him, a paper sack mashed in the fold of his arm, the leaves blowing past him, and our encounter drives me sadly home to poetry—where there's no answer. Billy closes his door and carries coal or wood to his fire and closes his eyes, and there's simply no way of knowing how lonely and empty he is or whether he's as vacant and barren and loveless as the rest of us are—here in the heart of the country.

### *Weather*

For we're always out of luck here. That's just how it is—for instance in the winter. The sides of the buildings, the roofs, the limbs of the trees are gray. Streets, sidewalks, faces, feelings—they are gray. Speech is gray, and the grass where it shows. Every flank and front, each top is gray. Everything is gray: hair, eyes, window glass, the hawkers' bills and touters' posters, lips, teeth, poles and metal signs—they're gray, quite gray. Cars are gray. Boots, shoes, suits, hats, gloves are gray. Horses, sheep, and cows, cats killed in the road, squirrels in the same way, sparrows, doves, and pigeons, all are gray, everything is gray, and everyone is out of luck who lives here.

A similar haze turns the summer sky milky, and the air muffles your head and shoulders like a sweater you've got caught in. In the summer light, too, the sky darkens a moment when you open your eyes. The heat is pure distraction. Steeped in our fluids, miserable in the folds of our bodies, we can scarcely think of anything but our sticky parts. Hot cyclonic winds and storms of dust crisscross the country. In many places, given an indifferent push, the wind will still coast for miles, gathering resource and edge as it goes, cunning and force. According to the season, paper, leaves, field litter, seeds, snow fill up the fences. Sometimes I think the land is flat because the winds have leveled it, they blow so constantly. In any case, a gale can grow in a field of corn that's as hot as a draft from hell, and to receive it is one of the most dismaying experiences of this life, though the smart of the same wind in winter is more humiliating, and in that sense even worse. But in the spring it rains as well, and the trees fill with ice.

### *Place*

Many small Midwestern towns are nothing more than rural slums, and this community could easily become one. Principally during the first decade of the century, though there were many earlier instances, well-to-do farmers moved to town and built fine homes to contain them in their retirement. Others desired a more social life, and so lived in, driving to their fields like storekeepers to their businesses. These houses are now dying like the bereaved who inhabit them; they are slowly losing their senses . . . deafness, blindness, forgetfulness, mumbling, an insecure gait, an uncontrollable trembling has overcome them. Some kind of Northern Snopes will occupy them next: large-familied, Catholic, Democratic, scrambling, vigorous, poor; and since the parents will work in larger, nearby towns, the children will be loosed upon themselves and upon the hapless neighbors much as the fabulous Khan loosed his legendary horde. These Snopes will undertake makeshift repairs with materials that other people have thrown away; paint halfway round their house, then quit; almost certainly maintain an ugly loud cantankerous dog and underfeed a pair of cats to keep the rodents down. They will collect piles of possibly useful junk in the backyard, park their cars in the front, live largely leaning over engines, give not a hoot for the land, the old community, the hallowed ways, the established clans. Weakening widow-ladies have already begun to hire large rude youths from families such as these to rake and mow and tidy the grounds they will inherit.

### *People*

In the cinders at the station boys sit smoking steadily in darkened cars, their arms bent out the windows, white shirts glowing behind the glass. Nine o'clock is the best time. They sit in a line facing the highway—two or three or four of them—idling their engines. As you walk by a machine may growl at you or a pair of headlights flare up briefly. In a moment one will pull out, spinning cinders behind it, to stalk impatiently up and down the dark streets or roar half a mile into the country before returning to its place in line and pulling up.

### *My house, my cat, my company*

I must organize myself. I must, as they say, pull myself together, dump this cat from my lap, stir—yes, resolve, move, do. But do what? My will is like the rosy dustlike light in this room: soft, diffuse, and gently comforting. It lets me do . . . anything . . . nothing. My ears hear what they happen to; I eat what's put before me; my eyes see what blunders into them; my thoughts are not thoughts, they are dreams. I'm empty or I'm full . . . depending; and I cannot choose. I sink my claws in Tick's fur and scratch the bones of his back until his rear rises amorously. Mr. Tick, I murmur, I must organize myself. I must pull myself together. Mr. Tick rolls over on his belly, all ooze.

I spill Mr. Tick when I've rubbed his stomach. Shoo. He steps away slowly, his long tail rhyming with his paws. How beautifully he moves, I think; how beautifully, like you, he commands his loving, how beautifully he accepts. So I rise and wander from room to room, up and down, gazing through most of my forty-one windows. How well this house receives its loving too. Let out like Mr. Tick, my eyes sink in the shrubbery. I am not here; I've passed the glass, passed second-story spaces, flown by branches, brilliant berries, to the ground, grass high in seed and leafage every season; and it is the same as when I passed above you in my aged, ardent body; it's, in short, a kind of love; and I am learning to restore myself, my house, my body, by paying court to gardens, cats, and running water, and with neighbors keeping company.

Mrs. Desmond is my right-hand friend; she's eighty-five. A thin white mist of hair, fine and tangled, manifests the climate of her mind. She is habitually suspicious, fretful, nervous. Burglars break in at noon. Children trespass. Even now they are shaking the pear tree, stealing rhubarb, denting lawn. Flies caught in the screens and numbed by frost awake in the heat to buzz and scrape the metal cloth and frighten her, though she is deaf to me, and consequently cannot hear them. Boards creak, the wind whistles across the chimney-mouth, drafts cruise like fish through the hollow rooms. It is herself she hears, her own flesh failing, for only death will preserve her from those daily chores she climbs like stairs, and all that anxious waiting. Is it now, she wonders. No? Then: is it now?

We do not converse. She visits me to talk. My task to murmur. She talks about her grandsons, her daughter who lives in Delphi, her sister or her husband—both gone—obscure friends—dead—obscurer aunts and uncles—lost—ancient neighbors, members of her church or of her clubs—passed or passing on; and in this way she brings the ends of her life together with a terrifying rush: she is a girl, a wife, a mother, widow, all at once. All at once—appalling—but I believe it; I wince in expectation of the clap. Her talk's a fence—a shade drawn, window fastened, door that's locked—for no one dies taking tea in a kitchen; and as her years compress and begin to jumble, I really believe in the brevity of life; I sweat in my wonder; death is the dog down the street, the angry gander, bedroom spider, goblin who's come to get her; and it occurs to me that in my listening posture I'm the boy who suffered the winds of my grandfather with an exactly similar politeness, that I am, right now, all my ages, out in elbows, as angular as badly stacked cards. Thus was I, when I loved you, every man I could be, youth and child—far from enough—and you, so strangely ambiguous a being, met me, heart for spade, play after play, the whole run of our suits.

Mr. Tick, you do me honor. You not only lie in my lap, but you remain alive there, coiled like a fetus. Through your deep nap, I feel you hum. You are, and are not, a machine. You are alive, alive exactly, and it means nothing to you—much to me. You are a cat—you cannot understand—you are a cat so easily. Your nature is not something you must rise to. You, not I, live in: in house, in skin, in shrubbery. Yes. I think I shall hat my head with a steeple; turn church; devour people. Mr. Tick, though, has a tail he can twitch, he need not fly his Fancy. Claws, not metrical schema, poetry his paws; while smoothing . . . smoothing . . . smoothing roughly, his tongue laps its neatness. O Mr. Tick, I know you; you are an electrical penis. Go on now, shoo. Mrs. Desmond doesn't like you. She thinks you will tangle yourself in her legs and she will fall. You murder her birds, she knows, and walk upon her roof with death in your jaws. I must gather myself together for a bound. What age is it I'm at right now, I wonder. The heart, don't they always say, keeps the true time. Mrs. Desmond is knocking. Faintly, you'd think, but she pounds. She's brought me a cucumber. I believe she believes I'm a woman. Come in, Mrs. Desmond, thank you, be my company, it looks lovely, and have tea. I'll slice it, crisp, with cream, for luncheon, each slice as thin as me.

### *More vital data*

The town is exactly fifty houses, trailers, stores, and miscellaneous buildings long, but in places no streets deep. It takes on width as you drive south, always adding to the east. Most of the dwellings are fairly spacious farmhouses in the customary white, with wide wrap-around porches and tall narrow windows, though there are many of the grander kind—fretted, scalloped, turreted, and decorated with clapboards set at angles or on end, with stained glass windows at the stair landings and lots of wrought iron full of fancy curls—and a few of these look like castles in their rarer brick. Old stables serve as garages now, and the lots are large to contain them and the vegetable and flower gardens which, ultimately, widows plant and weed and then entirely disappear in. The shade is ample, the grass is good, the sky a glorious fall violet; the apple trees are heavy and red, the roads are calm and empty; corn has sifted from the chains of tractored wagons to speckle the streets with gold and with the russet fragments of the cob, and a man would be a fool who wanted, blessed with this, to live anywhere else in the world.

### *Education*

Buses like great orange animals move through the early light to school. There the children will be taught to read and warned against Communism. By Miss

Janet Jakes. That's not her name. Her name is Helen something—Scott or James. A teacher twenty years. She's now worn fine and smooth, and has a face, Wilfred says, like a mail-order ax. Her voice is hoarse, and she has a cough. For she screams abuse. The children stare, their faces blank. This is the thirteenth week. They are used to it. You will all, she shouts, you will all draw pictures of me. No. She is a Mrs.—someone's missus. And in silence they set to work while Miss Jakes jabs hairpins in her hair. Wilfred says an ax, but she has those rimless tinted glasses, graying hair, an almost dimpled chin. I must concentrate. I must stop making up things. I must give myself to life; let it mold me: that's what they say in Wisdom's Monthly Digest every day. Enough, enough—you've been at it long enough; and the children rise formally a row at a time to present their work to her desk. No, she wears rims; it's her chin that's dimpleless. So she grimly shuffles their sheets, examines her reflection crayoned on them. I would not dare . . . allow a child . . . to put a line around me. Though now and then she smiles like a nick in the blade, in the end these drawings depress her. I could not bear it—how can she ask?—that anyone . . . draw me. Her anger's lit. That's why she does it: flame. There go her eyes; the pink in her glasses brightens, dims. She is a pumpkin, and her rage is breathing like the candle in. No, she shouts, no—the cartoon trembling—no, John Mauck, John Stewart Mauck, this will not do. The picture flutters from her fingers. You've made me too muscular.

I work on my poetry. I remember my friends, associates, my students, by their names. Their names are Maypop, Dormouse, Upsydaisy. Their names are Gladiolus, Callow Bladder, Prince and Princess Oleo, Hieronymus, Cardinal Mummum, Mr. Fitchew, The Silken Howdah, Spot. Sometimes you're Tom Sawyer, Huckleberry Finn; it is perpetually summer; your buttocks are my pillow; we are adrift on a raft; your back is our river. Sometimes you are Major Barbara, sometimes a goddess who kills men in battle, sometimes you are soft like a shower of water; you are bread in my mouth.

I do not work on my poetry. I forget my friends, associates, my students, and their names: Gramophone, Blowgun, Pickle, Serenade . . . Marge the Barge, Arena, Uberhaupt . . . Doctor Dildoe, The Fog Machine. For I am now in B, in Indiana: out of job and out of patience, out of love and time and money, out of bread and out of body, in a temper, Mrs. Desmond, out of tea. So shut your fist up, bitch, you bag of death; go bang another door; go die, my dearie. Die, life-deaf old lady. Spill your breath. Fall over like a frozen board. Gray hair grows from the nose of your mind. You are a skull already—*memento mori*—the foreskin retracts from your teeth. Will your plastic gums last longer than your bones, and color their grinning? And is your twot still hazel-hairy, or are you bald as a ditch? . . . bitch . . . . . . bitch . . . . . . . . . bitch. I wanted to be famous, but you bring me age—my emptiness. Was it *that* which I thought would balloon me above the rest? Love? where are you? . . . love me. I want to rise so high, I said, that when I shit I won't miss anybody.

### *Business*

For most people, business is poor. Nearby cities have siphoned off all but a neighborhood trade. Except for feed and grain and farm supplies, you stand a chance to sell only what one runs out to buy. Chevrolet has quit, and Frigidaire. A locker plant has left its afterimage. The lumber yard has been, so far, six months about its going. Gas stations change hands clumsily, a restaurant becomes available, a grocery closes. One day they came and knocked the cornices from the watch repair and pasted campaign posters on the windows. Torn across, by now, by boys, they urge you still to vote for half an orange beblazoned man who as a whole one failed two years ago to win at his election. Everywhere, in this manner, the past speaks, and it mostly speaks of failure. The empty stores, the old signs and dusty fixtures, the debris in alleys, the flaking paint and rusty gutters, the heavy locks and sagging boards: they say the same disagreeable things. What do the sightless windows see, I wonder, when the sun throws a passerby against them? Here a stair unfolds toward the street—dark, rickety, and treacherous—and I always feel, as I pass it, that if I just went carefully up and turned the corner at the landing, I would find myself out of the world. But I've never had the courage.

### *That same person*

The weeds catch up with Billy. In pursuit of the hollyhocks, they rise in coarse clumps all around the front of his house. Billy has to stamp down a circle by his door like a dog or cat does turning round to nest up, they're so thick. What particularly troubles me is that winter will find the weeds still standing stiff and tindery to take the sparks which Billy's little mortarless chimney spouts. It's true that fires are fun here. The town whistle, which otherwise only blows for noon (and there's no noon on Sunday), signals the direction of the fire by the length and number of its blasts, the volunteer firemen rush past in their cars and trucks, houses empty their owners along the street every time like an illustration in a children's book. There are many bikes, too, and barking dogs, and sometimes—hallelujah—the fire's right here in town—a vacant lot of weeds and stubble flaming up. But I'd rather it weren't Billy or Billy's lot or house. Quite selfishly I want him to remain the way he is—counting his sticks and logs, sitting on his sill in the soft early sun—though I'm not sure what his presence means to me . . . or to anyone. Nevertheless, I keep wondering whether, given time, I might not someday find a figure in our language which would serve him faithfully, and furnish his poverty and loneliness richly out.

### *Weather*

I would rather it were the weather that was to blame for what I am and what my friends and neighbors are—we who live here in the heart of the country. Better the weather, the wind, the pale dying snow . . . the snow—why not the snow? There's never much really, not around the lower Lakes anyway, not enough to boast about, not enough to be useful. My father tells how the snow in the Dakotas would sweep to the roofs of the barns in the old days, and he and his friends could sled on the crust that would form because the snow was so fiercely driven. In Bemidji trees have been known to explode. That would be something—if the trees in Davenport or Francisville or Terre Haute were to go blam some winter—blam! blam! blam! all the way down the gray, cindery, snow-sick streets.

A cold fall rain is blackening the trees or the air is like lilac and full of parachuting seeds. Who cares to live in any season but his own? Still I suspect the secret's in this snow, the secret of our sickness, if we could only diagnose it, for we are all dying like the elms in Urbana. This snow—like our skin it covers the country. Later dust will do it. Right now—snow. Mud presently. But it is snow without any laughter in it, a pale gray pudding thinly spread on stiff toast, and if that seems a strange description, it's accurate all the same. Of course soot blackens everything, but apart from that, we are never sufficiently cold here. The flakes as they come, alive and burning, we cannot retain, for if our temperatures fall, they rise promptly again, just as, in the summer, they bob about in the same feckless way. Suppose though . . . suppose they were to rise some August, climb and rise, and then hang in the hundreds like a hawk through December, what a desert we could make of ourselves—from Chicago to Cairo, from Gary to Columbus—what beautiful Death Valleys.

### *Place*

I would rather it were the weather. It drives us in upon ourselves—an unlucky fate. Of course there is enough to stir our wonder anywhere; there's enough to love, anywhere, if one is strong enough, if one is diligent enough, if one is perceptive, patient, kind enough—whatever it takes; and surely it's better to live in the country, to live on a prairie by a drawing of rivers, in Iowa or Illinois or Indiana, say, than in any city, in any stinking fog of human beings, in any blooming orchard of machines. It ought to be. The cities are swollen and poisonous with people. It ought to be better. Man has never been a fit environment for man—for rats, maybe, rats do nicely, or for dogs or cats and the household beetle.

A man in the city has no natural thing by which to measure himself. His parks are potted plants. Nothing can live and remain free where he resides but the pigeon, starling, sparrow, spider, cockroach, mouse, moth, fly, and weed, and he laments the existence of even these and makes his plans to poison them. The zoo? There *is* the zoo. Through its bars the city man stares at the great cats and dully sucks his ice. Living, alas, among men and their marvels, the city man supposes that his happiness depends on establishing, somehow, a special kind of harmonious accord with others. The novelists of the city, of slums and crowds, they call it love—and break their pens.

Wordsworth feared the accumulation of men in cities. He foresaw their "degrading thirst after outrageous stimulation," and some of their hunger for love. Living in a city, among so many, dwelling in the heat and tumult of incessant movement, a man's affairs are touch and go—that's all. It's not surprising that the novelists of the slums, the cities, and the crowds, should find that sex is but a scratch to ease a tickle, that we're most human when we're sitting on the john, and that the justest image of our life is in full passage through the plumbing.

Come into the country, then. The air nimbly and sweetly recommends itself unto our gentle senses. Here, growling tractors tear the earth. Dust roils up behind them. Drivers sit jouncing under bright umbrellas. They wear refrigerated hats and steer by looking at the tracks they've cut behind them, their transistors blaring. Close to the land, are they? good companions to the soil? Tell me: do they live in harmony with the alternating seasons?

It's a lie of old poetry. The modern husbandman uses chemicals from cylinders and sacks, spike-ball-and-claw machines, metal sheds, and cost accounting. Nature in the old sense does not matter. It does not exist. Our farmer's only mystical attachment is to parity. And if he does not realize that cows and corn are simply different kinds of chemical engine, he cannot expect to make a go of it.

It isn't necessary to suppose our cows have feelings; our neighbor hasn't as many as he used to have either; but think of it this way a moment, you can correct for the human imputations later: how would it feel to nurse those strange tentacled calves with their rubber, glass, and metal lips, their stainless eyes?

### *People*

Aunt Pet's still able to drive her car—a high square Ford—even though she walks with difficulty and a stout stick. She has a watery gaze, a smooth plump face despite her age, and jet black hair in a bun. She has the slowest smile of anyone I ever saw, but she hates dogs, and not very long ago cracked the back of one she cornered in her garden. To prove her vigor she will tell you this, her smile breaking gently while she raises the knob of her stick to the level of your eyes.

### *House, my breath and window*

My window is a grave, and all that lies within it's dead. No snow is falling. There's no haze. It is not still, not silent. Its images are not an animal that waits, for movement is no demonstration. I have seen the sea slack, life bubble through a body without a trace, its spheres impervious as soda's. Downwound, the whore at wagtag clicks and clacks. Leaves wiggle. Grass sways. A bird chirps, pecks the ground. An auto wheel in penning circles keeps its rigid spokes. These images are stones; they are memorials. Beneath this sea lies sea: god rest it . . . rest the world beyond my window, me in front of my reflection, above this page, my shade. Death is not so still, so silent, since silence implies a falling quiet, stillness a stopping, containing, holding in; for death is time in a clock, like Mr. Tick, electric . . . like wind through a windup poet. And my blear floats out to visible against the glass, befog its country and bespill myself. The mist lifts slowly from the fields in the morning. No one now would say: the Earth throws back its covers; it is rising from sleep. Why is the feeling foolish? The image is too Greek. I used to gaze at you so wantonly your body blushed. Imagine: wonder: that my eyes could cause such flowering. Ah, my friend, your face is pale, the weather cloudy; a street has been felled through your chin, bare trees do nothing, houses take root in their rectangles, a steeple stands up in your head. You speak of loving; then give me a kiss. The pane is cold. On icy mornings the fog rises to greet me (as you always did); the barns and other buildings, rather than ghostly, seem all the more substantial for looming, as if they grew in themselves while I watched (as you always did). Oh, my approach, I suppose, was like breath in a rubber monkey. Nevertheless, on the road along the Wabash in the morning, though the trees are sometimes obscured by fog, their reflection floats serenely on the river, reasoning the banks, the sycamores in French rows. Magically, the world tips. I'm led to think that only those who grow down live (which will scarcely win me twenty-five from Wisdom's Monthly Digest), but I find I write that only those who live down grow; and what I write, I hold, whatever I really know. My every word's inverted, or reversed—or I am. I held you, too, that way. You were so utterly provisional, subject to my change. I could inflate your bosom with a kiss, disperse your skin with gentleness, enter your vagina from within, and make my love emerge like a fresh sex. The pane is cold. Honesty is cold, my inside lover. The sun looks, through the mist, like a plum on the tree of heaven, or a bruise on the slope of your belly. Which? The grass crawls with frost. We meet on this window, the world and I, inelegantly, swimmers of the glass; and swung wrong way round to one another, the world seems in. The world—how grand, how monumental, grave and deadly, that word is: the world, my house and poetry. All poets have their inside lovers. Wee penis does not belong to me, or any of this foggery. It is *his* property which he's thrust through what's womanly of me to set down this. These wooden houses in their squares, gray streets and fallen sidewalks, standing trees, your name I've written sentimentally across my breath into the whitening air, pale birds: they exist in me now because of him. I gazed with what intensity. . . . A bush in the excitement of its roses would not have bloomed so beautifully as you did then. It was a look I'd like to give this page. For that is poetry: to bring within about, to change.

### *Politics*

Sports, politics, and religion are the three passions of the badly educated. They are the Midwest's open sores. Ugly to see, a source of constant discontent, they sap the body's strength. Appalling quantities of money, time, and energy are wasted on them. The rural mind is narrow, passionate, and reckless on these matters. Greed, however shortsighted and direct, will not alone account for it. I have known men, for instance, who for years have voted squarely against their interests. Nor have I ever noticed that their surly Christian views prevented them from urging forward the smithereening, say, of Russia, China, Cuba, or Korea—Vietnam. And they tend to back their country like they back their local team: they have a fanatical desire to win; yelling is their forte; and if things go badly, they are inclined to sack the coach. All in all, then, Birch is a good name. It stands for the bigot's stick, the wild-child-tamer's cane.

### *Final vital data*

The Modern Homemakers' Demonstration Club. The Prairie Home Demonstration Club. The Night-outers' Home Demonstration Club. The IOOF, FFF, VFW, WCTU, WSCS, 4-H, 40 and 8, Psi Iota Chi, and PTA. The Boy and Girl

Scouts. Rainbows, Masons, Indians and Rebekah Lodge. Also the Past Noble Grand Club of the Rebekah Lodge. As well as the Moose and the Ladies of the Moose. The Elks, the Eagles, the Jaynettes, and the Eastern Star. The Women's Literary Club, the Hobby Club, the Art Club, the Sunshine Society, the Dorcas Society, the Pythian Sisters, the Pilgrim Youth Fellowship, the American Legion, the American Legion Auxiliary, the American Legion Junior Auxiliary, the Garden Club, the What-can-you-do? Club, the Get Together Club, the Coterie Club, the Worthwhile Club, the No Name Club, the Forget-me-not Club, the Merry-go-round Club......

### *Education*

Has a quarter disappeared from Paula Frosty's pocketbook? Imagine the landscape of that face: no crayon could engender it; soft wax is wrong; thin wire in trifling snips might do the trick. Paula Frosty and Christopher Roger accuse the pale and splotchy Cheryl Pipes. But Miss Jakes, I *saw* her. Miss Jakes is so extremely vexed she snaps her pencil. What else is missing? I appoint you a detective, John: search her desk. Gum, candy, paper, pencils, marble, round eraser—whose? A thief. I can't watch her all the time, I'm here to teach. Poor pale fossetted Cheryl, it's determined, can't return the money because she took it home and spent it. Cindy, Janice, John, and Pete—you four who sit around her—you will be detectives this whole term to watch her. A thief. In all my time. Miss Jakes turns, unfists, and turns again. I'll handle you, she cries. To think. A thief. In all my years. Then she writes on the blackboard the name of Cheryl Pipes and beneath that the figure twenty-five with a large sign for cents. Now Cheryl, she says, this won't be taken off until you bring that money out of home, out of home straight up to here, Miss Jakes says, tapping her desk.

Which is three days.

### *Another person*

I was raking leaves when Uncle Halley introduced himself to me. He said his name came from the comet, and that his mother had borne him prematurely in her fright of it. I thought of Hobbes, whom fear of the Spanish Armada had hurried into birth, and so I believed Uncle Halley to honor the philosopher, though Uncle Halley is a liar, and neither the one hundred twenty-eight nor the fifty-three he ought to be. That fall the leaves had burned themselves out on the trees, the leaf-lobes had curled, and now they flocked noisily down the street and were broken in the wires of my rake. Uncle Halley was himself (like Mrs. Desmond and history generally) both deaf and implacable, and he shooed me down his basement stairs to a room set aside there for stacks of newspapers reaching to the ceiling, boxes of leaflets and letters and programs, racks of photo albums, scrapbooks, bundles of rolled up posters and maps, flags and pennants and slanting piles of dusty magazines devoted mostly to motoring and the Christian ethic. I saw a birdcage, a tray of butterflies, a bugle, a stiff straw boater, and all kinds of tassels tied to a coat tree. He still possessed and had on display the steering lever from his first car, a linen duster, driving gloves and goggles, photographs along the wall of himself, his friends, and his various machines, a shell from the first war, a record of Ramona nailed through its hole to a post, walking sticks and fanciful umbrellas, shoes of all sorts (his baby shoes, their counters broken, were held in sorrow beneath my nose—they had not been bronzed, but he might have them done someday before he died, he said), countless boxes of medals, pins, beads, trinkets, toys, and keys (I scarcely saw—they flowed like jewels from his palms), pictures of downtown when it was only a path by the railroad station, a brightly colored globe of the world with a dent in Poland, antique guns, belt buckles, buttons, souvenir plates and cups and saucers (I can't remember all of it—I won't), but I recall how shamefully, how rudely, how abruptly, I fled, a good story in my mouth but death in my nostrils; and how afterward I busily, righteously, burned my leaves as if I were purging the world of its years. I still wonder if this town—its life, and mine now—isn't really a record like the one of Ramona that I used to crank around on my grandmother's mahogany Victrola through lonely rainy days as a kid.

### *The first person*

Billy's like the coal he's found: spilled, mislaid, discarded. The sky's no comfort. His house and his body are dying together. His windows are boarded. And now he's reduced to his hands. I suspect he has glaucoma. At any rate he can scarcely see, and weeds his yard of rubble on his hands and knees. Perhaps he's a surgeon cleansing a wound or an ardent and tactile lover. I watch, I must say, apprehensively. Like mine-war detectors, his hands graze in circles ahead of him. Your nipples were the color of your eyes. Pebble. Snarl of paper. Length of twine. He leans down closely, picks up something silvery, holds it near his nose. Foil? cap? coin? He has within him—what? I wonder. Does he know more now because he fingers everything and has to sniff to see? It would be romantic cruelty to think so. He bends the down on your arms like a breeze. You wrote me: something is strange when we don't understand. I write in return: I think when I loved you I fell to my death.

Billy, I could read to you from Beddoes; he's your man perhaps; he held with dying, freed his blood of its arteries; and he said that there were many wretched love-ill fools like me lying alongside the last bone of their former selves, as full of spirit and speech, nonetheless, as Mrs. Desmond, Uncle Halley and the ferris wheel, Aunt Pet, Miss Jakes, Ramona or the megaphone; yet I reverse him finally, Billy, on no evidence but braggadocio, and I declare that though my inner organs were devoured long ago, the worm which swallowed down my parts still throbs and glows like a crystal palace.

Yes, you were younger. I was Uncle Halley, the museum man and infrequent meteor. Here is my first piece of ass. They weren't so flat in those days, had more round, more juice. And over here's the sperm I've spilled, nicely jarred and clearly labeled. Look at this tape like lengths of intestine where I've stored my spew, the endless worm of words I've written, a hundred million emissions or more: oh I was quite a man right from the start; even when unconscious in my cradle, from crotch to cranium, I was erectile tissue; though mostly, after the manner approved by Plato, I had intercourse by eye. Never mind, old Holsclaw, you are blind. We pull down darkness when we go to bed; put out like Oedipus the actually offending organ, and train our touch to lies. All cats are gray, says Mr. Tick; so under cover of glaucoma you are sack gray too, and cannot be distinguished from a stallion.

I must pull myself together, get a grip, just as they say, but I feel spilled, bewildered, quite mislaid. I did not restore my house to its youth, but to its age. Hunting, you hitch through the hollyhocks. I'm inclined to say you aren't half the cripple I am, for there is nothing left of me but mouth. However, I resist the impulse. It is another lie of poetry. My organs are all there, though it's there where I fail—at the roots of my experience. Poet of the spiritual, Rilke, weren't you? yet that's what you said. Poetry, like love, is—in and out—a physical caress. I can't tolerate any more of my sophistries about spirit, mind, and breath. Body equals being, and if your weight goes down, you are the less.

## *Household apples*

I knew nothing about apples. Why should I? My country came in my childhood, and I dreamed of sitting among the blooms like the bees. I failed to spray the pear tree too. I doubled up under them at first, admiring the sturdy low branches I should have pruned, and later I acclaimed the blossoms. Shortly after the fruit formed there were falls—not many—apples the size of goodish stones which made me wobble on my ankles when I walked down the yard. Sometimes a piece crushed by a heel would cling on the shoe to track the house. I gathered a few and heaved them over the wires. A slingshot would have been splendid. Hard, an unattractive green, the worms had them. Before long I realized the worms had them all. Even as the apples reddened, lit their tree, they were being swallowed. The birds preferred the pears, which were small—sugar pears I think they're called—with thick skins of graying green that ripen on toward violet. So the fruit fell, and once I made some applesauce by quartering and pairing hundreds; but mostly I did nothing, left them, until suddenly, overnight it seemed, in that ugly late September heat we often have in Indiana, my problem was upon me.

My childhood came in the country. I remember, now, the flies on our snowy luncheon table. As we cleared away they would settle, fastidiously scrub themselves and stroll to the crumbs to feed where I would kill them in crowds with a swatter. It was quite a game to catch them taking off. I struck heavily since I didn't mind a few stains; they'd wash. The swatter was a square of screen bound down in red cloth. It drove no air ahead of it to give them warning. They might have thought they'd flown headlong into a summered window. The faint pink dot where they had died did not rub out as I'd supposed, and after years of use our luncheon linen would faintly, pinkly, speckle.

The country became my childhood. Flies braided themselves on the flypaper in my grandmother's house. I can smell the bakery and the grocery and the stables and the dairy in that small Dakota town I knew as a kid; knew as I dreamed I'd know your body, as I've known nothing, before or since; knew as the flies knew, in the honest, unchaste sense: the burned house, hose-wet, which drew a mist of insects like the blue smoke of its smolder, and gangs of boys, moist-lipped, destructive as its burning. Flies have always impressed me; they are so persistently alive. Now they were coating the ground beneath my trees. Some were ordinary flies; there were the large blue-green ones; there were swarms of fruit flies too, and the red-spotted scavenger beetle; there were a few wasps, several sorts of bees and butterflies—checkers, sulphers, monarchs, commas, question marks—and delicate dragonflies . . . but principally houseflies and horse-flies and bottleflies, flies and more flies in clusters around the rotting fruit. They loved the pears. Inside, they fed. If you picked up a pear, they flew, and the pear became skin and stem. They were everywhere the fruit was: in the tree still—apples like a hive for them—or where the fruit littered the ground, squashing itself as you stepped . . . there was no help for it. The flies droned, feasting on the sweet juice. No one could go near the trees; I could not climb; so I determined at last to labor like Hercules. There were fruit baskets in the barn. Collecting them and kneeling under the branches, I began to gather remains. Deep in the strong rich smell of the fruit, I began to hum myself. The fruit caved in at the touch. Glistening red apples, my lifting disclosed, had families of beetles, flies, and bugs, devouring their rotten undersides. There were streams of flies; there were lakes and cataracts and rivers of flies, seas and oceans. The hum was heavier, higher, than the hum of the bees when they came to the blooms in the spring, though the bees were there, among the flies, ignoring me—ignoring everyone. As my work went on and juice covered my hands and arms, they would form a sleeve, black and moving, like knotty wool. No caress could have been more indifferently complete. Still I rose fearfully, ramming my head in the branches, apples bumping against me before falling, bursting with bugs. I'd snap my hand sharply but the flies would cling to the sweet. I could toss a whole cluster into a basket from several feet. As the pear or apple lit, they would explosively rise, like monads for a moment, windowless, certainly, with respect to one another, sugar their harmony. I had to admit, though, despite my distaste, that my arm had never been more alive, oftener or more gently kissed. Those hundreds of feet were light. In washing them off, I pretended the hose was a pump. What have I missed? Childhood is a lie of poetry.

## *The church*

Friday night. Girls in dark skirts and white blouses sit in ranks and scream in concert. They carry funnels loosely stuffed with orange and black paper which they shake wildly, and small megaphones through which, as drilled, they direct and magnify their shouting. Their leaders, barely pubescent girls, prance and shake and whirl their skirts above their bloomers. The young men, leaping, extend their arms and race through puddles of amber light, their bodies glistening. In a lull, though it rarely occurs, you can hear the squeak of tennis shoes against the floor. Then the yelling begins again, and then continues; fathers, mothers, neighbors joining in to form a single pulsing ululation—a cry of the whole community—for in this gymnasium each body becomes the bodies beside it, pressed as they are together, thigh to thigh, and the same shudder runs through all of them, and runs toward the same release. Only the ball moves serenely through this dazzling din. Obedient to law it scarcely speaks but caroms quietly and lives at peace.

## *Business*

It is the week of Christmas and the stores, to accommodate the rush they hope for, are remaining open in the evening. You can see snow falling in the cones of the street lamps. The roads are filling—undisturbed. Strings of red and green lights droop over the principal highway, and the water tower wears a star. The windows of the stores have been bedizened. Shamelessly they beckon. But I am alone, leaning against a pole—no . . . there is no one in sight. They're all at home, perhaps by their instruments, tuning in on their evenings, and like Ramona, tirelessly playing and replaying themselves. There's a speaker perched in the tower, and through the boughs of falling snow and over the vacant streets, it drapes the twisted and metallic strains of a tune that can barely be distinguished—yes, I believe it's one of the jolly ones, it's Joy to the World. There's no one to hear the music but myself, and though I'm listening, I'm no longer certain. Perhaps the record's playing something else.

## *Study questions*

1. *What do we know about the narrator? Can we tell how old he is, what his profession is, what his love affair was like, why he has come to the heart of the country?* 2. *What is the significance of the title of the story? What is it like in the heart of the country? in the heart of the heart of the country?* 3. *What is the function of Billy Holsclaw? Mrs. Desmond? Miss Janet Jakes? Aunt Pet? Uncle Halley? Mr. Tick?* 4. *What is the narrator's conflict? How is it resolved?* 5. *What motifs and image patterns are important to the structure of the story? How is the plot developed?* 6. *What is the mood of the story? How does the mood correspond to the narrator's feelings?* 7. *What kind of ironies are present in the story? Note especially the last two sections.* 8. *Why is it important that the narrator is a poet?* 9. *How is this story like a poem?*

*Robert Creeley* (b. 1926), mainly a poet, has published one novel, *The Island* (1963), and a collection of stories, *The Gold Diggers* (1965). He was born in Arlington, Massachusetts. His matriculation at Harvard was interrupted by World War II, when he served in Burma and India. During the early 1950s he lived in Spain and France. Upon his return to the United States, he entered Black Mountain College, receiving his B.A. there. His M.A. (1960) is from the University of New Mexico. He has taught at New Mexico and the State University of New York at Buffalo. In "Mr Blue," the protagonist comes to doubt his own knowing, and, as he says: "If you lose that, or take it as somehow wrong, the whole thing goes to pieces."

## MR BLUE

I don't want to give you only the grotesqueness, not only what it then seemed. It is useless enough to remember but to remember only what is unpleasant seems particularly foolish. I suspect that you have troubles of your own, and, since you have, why bother you with more. Mine against yours. That seems a waste of time. But perhaps mine are also yours. And if that's so, you'll find me a sympathetic listener.

A few nights ago I wrote down some of this, thinking, trying to think, of what had happened. What had really happened like they say. It seemed, then, that some such effort might get me closer to an understanding of the thing than I was. So much that was not directly related had got in and I thought a little noting of what was basic to the problem might be in order. That is, I wanted to analyze it, to try to see where things stood. I'm not at all sure that it got to anything, this attempt, because I'm not very good at it. But you can look for yourselves.

1) That dwarfs, gnomes, midgets are, by the fact of their SIZE, intense;

2) That dwarfs, gnomes, midgets cause people LARGER than themselves to appear wispy, insubstantial, cardboard;

3) that all SIZE tends toward BIG but in the case of dwarfs, gnomes, midgets.

But perhaps best to begin at the beginning. And, to begin, there are two things that you must know. The first of these is that I am, myself, a tall man, somewhat muscular though not unpleasantly so. I have brown hair and brown eyes though that is not altogether to the point here. What you should remember is that I am a big man, as it happens, one of the biggest in the town.

My wife is also large. This is the second. But she is not so much large as large-boned. A big frame. I sound as though I were selling her, but I'm not. I mean, I don't want to sound like that, as though I were trying to impress you that way. It is just that that I don't want to do. That is, make you think that I am defending her or whatever it is that I may sound like to you. In short, she is an attractive woman and I don't think I am the only one who would find her so. She has, like myself, brown hair but it is softer, very soft, and she wears it long, almost to her waist, in heavy braids. But it is like her eyes, I mean, there is that lightness in it, the way it brushes against her back when she is walking. It makes me feel rather blundering, heavy, to look at her. It seems to me my step jars the house when I walk through a room where she is. We have been married five years.

Five years doesn't seem, in itself, a very long time. So much goes so quickly, so many things that I can think of now that then, when they were happening, I could hardly take hold of. And where she comes into it, those things that had to do with her. I find I missed, perhaps, a lot that I should have held to. At least I should have tried. But like it or not, it's done with. Little good to think of it now.

I did try, though, to do what I could. She never seemed unhappy, and doesn't even now. Perhaps upset when the baby was sick, but, generally speaking, she's a level woman, calm, good-sense.

But perhaps that's where I'm wrong, that I have that assumption, that I think I know what she is like. Strange that a man shouldn't know his wife but I suppose it could be so, that even having her around him for five years, short as they are, he could still be strange to her and she to him. I think I know, I think I know about what she'd do if this or that happened, if I were to say this to her, or something about something, or what people usually talk about. It's not pleasant doubting your own knowing, since that seems all you have. If you lose that, or take it as somehow wrong, the whole thing goes to pieces. Not much use trying to hold it together after that.

Still I can't take seriously what's happened. I can't but still I do. I wish it were different, that in some way I were out of it, shaken but at least out. But here I am. The same place.

It was raining, a bad night for anything. Not hard, but enough to soak you if you were out in it for very long. We thought it would probably be closed but when we got there, all the lights were going and I could see some people up in the ferris-wheel, probably wet to the skin. Still they looked as if they were having fun and some of their shouts reached us as we went through the gate and into the main grounds. It was fairly late, about ten or so, another reason why I had thought it would be closed. Another day and the whole works would be gone and that's why she had insisted.

I feel, usually, uncomfortable in such places. I don't like the crowds, at least not the noise of them. They never seem to stop, always jumping, moving, and the noise. Any one of them, alone, or two or three, that's fine. As it happened, we went by a number of our friends, who yelled at us, fine night, or some such thing. I can't remember exactly what the words were. But I didn't like them, or didn't like them then, with that around them, the noise, and their excitement.

No reason, perhaps, to think she knew where she was going. I didn't. I think we followed only the general movement of the people, where they were going. It was packed and very difficult to go anywhere but where you were pushed. So we were landed in front of the tent without much choice and stood, listening to the barker, to see what might be happening.

I can say, and this is part of it, that I didn't want to go in. For several reasons. The main one is that I don't like freaks, I don't like to look at them or to be near them. They seem to have a particular feeling around them, which is against me, altogether. A good many times I've seen others staring, without the slightest embarrassment, at some hunchback, or some man with a deformity that puts him apart from the rest. I don't see how they can do it, how they can look without any reaction but curiosity. For myself, I want only to get away.

But this time she decided. It seemed that not very much could be inside the tent. They had advertised a midget, a knife-thrower, a man with some snakes, and one or two other things. Nothing like the large circuses and none of the more horrible things such might offer. So I got the tickets and we followed a few of the others in.

They were just finishing a performance. It was so packed at the front, that we stood at the back, waiting until the first crowd was ready to leave. I felt tired myself. It must have been close to eleven at that point. It seemed an effort there was no reason for. But she enjoyed it, looked all around, at everyone, smiled at those she knew, waved to some, kept talking to me, and I would say something or other to hide my own feeling. Perhaps I should have been straight with her, told her I was tired, and ducked out. It would have saved it, or at least got me free. But I kept standing there, with her, waiting for the show to finish and another to start.

It did soon, the first crowd moving out, and our own coming up to take its place. The man on the platform had got down at the end and now we waited for him to come back and the new show to begin. There was talking around us, sounding a little nervous the way most will at those times when something is being waited for, though what one can't say with exactness. At this point, I was almost as expectant as the others. Nothing else to be, perhaps. In any event, I had got over my other feeling.

The first act was a cowboy with a lariat, rope tricks. Not much but he was good with it, could make it spin all kinds of loops, shrinking them, making them grow right while we watched him. It was good fun, I thought, not much but enough. At the end he started stamping with one foot and at the same time, he slipped his loop off and on it, brought it up around both feet at the end, jumping and grinning. I think there may have been some music with it, something for the beat, but it doesn't matter. The man told us he was deaf, couldn't hear a thing. There didn't seem to be much point in telling us that but I guess we're apt to like that adding of what we don't expect.

We enjoyed it, the both of us. It's not often that we can get out, like that, to see anything. And after the first I forgot about being tired and liked it as much as she did. The next act was the knife-thrower. He could put them all in a circle no bigger than my hand, eight of them, so that they shivered there with a force which surprised me, each time one hit, she gripped my arm, and I laughed at her nervousness, but it was a funny thing, even so.

Then came the snake act, which wasn't up to the others, or simply that dullness in it, the snakes much the same, doped, I expect, though perhaps I was wrong to think so. Then sort of a juggling act, a man with a number of colored balls and odd-shaped sticks, which he set into a strange kind of movement, tossing them, one after the other, until he must have had ten somehow, going and all this with an intentness that made us almost clap then, as they did move, through his hands. Altogether a wonder it seemed, his precision, and how it kept him away from us, even though some stood no more than a few feet away. Until at last he stopped them one by one, and then, the last, smiled at us, and we all gave him a good hand.

It's here that I leave, or as I go back to it, this time, or this way, that is, now that I make my way out, through the rest of them, my hand on her arm with just that much pressure to guide her, or that is my intention. Perhaps the lights that make my eyes ache, begin to, or simply, that it's now, this point, that I am happy, that it's ourselves, the two of us, have come to some sort of feel of it, that makes us so. Just that I am, now, running, that it is just that I do.

What she had been doing, or going to that, it was a cigarette she asked me for, and I reached into my pocket for them, had got out the pack, and given her one, and then lit a match for her. She bent a little, got it lit, then looked back to the platform where the juggler had been.

But the trick, that it's him who's there, the midget, as such he is named, but the size, it's that which hits me, at first, that he isn't small, or looking, he must be five feet, or perhaps, a little smaller. Four feet. But not small.

The eyes, catch, get me so into it, that they are so, void, in the head, shaded, the shades like changing shadows, colors, coming in to want, to want to be filled. Seem huge. He looks at all of us, moves over us so, to bite, to have something to be there to bite.

But nothing, certainly, to make of it more or more than what I could see, would be, that is, the barker introduced him, and we stood, as we had, in that group in front of him, the boards which made the platform, that roughness, and the poles on which the lights were strung, the wires sagging between them. That is, what is it had come in, as this was, to be not or to make it not as it had been, if it were, as it was, the same place, which I couldn't say or put my finger on, then, but waited like any of the rest.

I could see the muscle of his arm, where the sleeve had been pulled up, rolled, above it, and with his movement, that slightness of tension made him lift it, slightly, from time to time, the muscle tightened and it looked hard, big, below the roll of the sleeve. As my own would. He was smiling, the face somewhat broad, well-shaped, the smile somewhat dreamy, or like sleep, that vagueness, which couldn't be understood.

The barker had laughed, the pitch of it rolled out, on us, and I wondered if he was as drunk as he looked. He was calling the midget, cute, saying, a cute little fellow. He made a joke of it, looking at the woman and laughing. Saying, who would like to take him home. There was laughing, they liked the joke, and he carried it further, sensing their tolerance, and played it up. It was the joke he seemed intent on making us remember, the cuteness, the idea of the women.

Taking the cigarettes out of my pocket, the pack crumpled, I held it out to her, but she was intent on what was before us, and I expect that I was myself, and only did what I did, took them out, to somehow break it, to make it break down. It seemed that, that is, that gesture or an act, an action, so meant to serve double, to be a break, but what was it, that is, more than the taking, just that, of the cigarettes, which I didn't want to smoke, had even just put one out. I looked, then, around me at the rest of them and they were looking at him, the midget, and I couldn't see one that noticed I looked, or gave the least sign.

The midget stood still, beside the barker, who staggered a little, under the lights, moved from one side to the other, his face to us, that drunkenness. He was still on the joke, fumbling, and it wore down on us, that weight of it, kept at us, and I wanted to get out. There seemed breaks, lengths of silence, hung there, made the other, the midget, the whole of it, in his own silence, which he kept as a distance around him, that the eyes made actual.

I would have gone, or as I think, I should have in spite of it, simply slipped out, when the others weren't looking, just left and waited for her outside. I can't see that she would have been hurt. That is, I would think, or think I would have that right to, that it would make no difference to her, that is, that she would understand my going, seeing that it had begun to tire me, even became painful to stay. I think of it so, being such, that no difference could be in it, since she was enjoying it, or so it seemed.

I tried to, but the people around pressed too tight, pushed me from the back, all forward, to the one on the platform in front of us. Not the barker, I knew that much, but the other, who pulled them, kept them all, because the barker had somehow fallen altogether to pieces, had just the joke he hung on to, and that was played out. But then he switched it, perhaps feeling it had, and turned to the midget, and said, but you should have some say in this. Which one would you like.

The midget turned, then seemed to pull himself out of it, the distance, out of nothing, the eyes pulled in, to focus, to grow, somehow, smaller, larger. The eyes went over us, the voice, when it came, was breath, a breathing but way back in, wire, tight, taut, the scream and I couldn't hear it, saw only his finger move to point at her, beside me, and wanted to say, he's looking at you, but she was turned away from me, as though laughing, but struck, hit. I looked, a flash, sideways, as it then happened. Looked, he looked at me, cut, the hate jagged, and I had gone, then, into it and that was almost that. But she said, then, she had seen him, earlier, that same day, as he was standing by a store, near the door, I think, as it had opened, and she, there, across the street, saw him motion, the gesture, then, a dance, shuffle, the feet crooked, and the arms, as now, loose, and it was before, as before, but not because of this, that made it, or I thought, so made it, was it, or it was that thing I hung to, when, the show over, they motioned us out, and I pushed a way for her out through the crowd.

## *Study questions*

1. *What is the matter with the protagonist? Why is he so upset?* 2. *How does he feel about his wife? How is she related to his conflict?* 3. *Why didn't the narrator want to go to the fair? Why does he go? Why does he attend the side show?* 4. *At what point in the side show does he become apprehensive? Why?* 5. *Why do midgets bother the narrator? What is his wife's response? Why is he bothered by it?* 6. *Describe the style of the story, particularly the sentence structure. Is the style appropriate to the theme? Is the style a mirror of the narrator's mind?* 7. *What is the point of the list the narrator sets down at the beginning of the story?* 8. *Why does the narrator address the reader as "you"?*

*Frank London Brown* (1927–1962), a poet, novelist, and short-story writer, was born in Kansas City, Missouri. He received his B.A. from Roosevelt University and his M.A. from the University of Chicago. He had a varied career, having been employed at different times as a machinist, a union organizer, a bartender, and a jazz musician. He was also an associate editor of *Ebony*, director of the Union Research Center at the University of Chicago, and a candidate for the doctorate as a Fellow of the University of Chicago's Committee on Social Thought. Recipient of the John Hay Whitney Foundation Award for Creative Writing, he published two novels, *Trumbull Park* (1959) and *The Myth Makers* (1969). His poems and stories have appeared in various anthologies, including *Negro Digest*, Hughes and Bontemps's *The Poetry of the Negro*, and Margolies's *A Native Son's Reader*. "The Whole Truth" is a fine story, its surface detail rendered with precision and its rhythms consonant with tone and mood.

## THE WHOLE TRUTH

The bass was walking! Nothing but the bass. And the rhythm section waited, counting time with the tap of a foot or the tip of a finger against the piano top. 'Pro' had just finished his solo and the blood in his neck was pumping so hard it made his head hurt. Sweat shone upon the brown backs of his fingers. And the moisture stained the bright brass of his tenor where he held it.

Jake, a young eyeglass-wearing boy from Dallas, had stopped playing the drums, and he too was sweating. Stains were beginning to appear upon his thin cotton coat. His dark skin caught the purple haze from the overhead spot light and the sweat that gathered on his flat cheekbones seemed purple. Percy R. Brookins leaned over the piano tapping a black key, but not hard enough to make a sound.

Everybody seemed to be waiting.

And the bass was walking!

Doom-de-doom-doom-doom-doom-doom-doom-doom-doom!

A tall, thin, white man holding a tenor loosely at his side stood next to lanky, ginger-brown 'Pro', also known as 'The Man'.

'Pro' had wailed; had blown choruses that dripped with the smell of cornbread and cabbage; had roared like a late 'L'; and had cried like a blues singer on the last night of a good gig. 'Pro' had been 'Pro' and nobody was better than 'Pro' when 'Pro' was 'Pro'.

Now it was the white tenorman's turn, right after the bass solo was over. And he waited, and 'Pro' waited, and so did Jake the drummer and Percy R. Brookins. Little Jug the bassman was going into his eighth chorus and he showed no sign of letting up.

DOOM-DE-DOOM-DOOM-DOOM-DOOM-DOOM-DOOM-DOOM!

Jake looked out into the shadowy faces of the audience. They were hard to see behind the bright-coloured lights that ringed the bandstand. Yet he felt that they, too, waited.

'Pro' had laid down some righteous sounds. He had told so much truth, told it so plainly, so passionately, that he had scared everybody in the place, even himself. And now he waited for the affirming bass to finish so that he could hear what the white man had to say.

And the bass walked!

Jake leaned over his drums and whispered to Percy R. Brookins.

'McDougal sure looks beat, don't he?'

Percy R. Brookins nodded and then put his hand to the side of his mouth and whispered back,

'His old lady's pregnant again.'

'Again? What's that, number three?'

'Number four,' Percy R. Brookins answered.

'Hell, I'd look sad too then. Is he still living down on Forty-Seventh Street?'

The drums slid in underneath the bass and the bass dropped back amid strong applause and a few 'Yeahs!' And Jack, not having realised it, cut in where McDougal was to have begun his solo. He smiled sheepishly at Percy R. Brookins and the piano-player hunched his shoulders and smiled back.

McDougal didn't look around. He didn't change his slouched one-sided stance. He didn't stop staring beyond the lights, beyond the audience, beyond the room itself. Yet his left foot kept time with the light bombs the drummer dropped and the soft scrape of the brushes. And he held his tenor lightly against his leg.

Little Jug pulled a handkerchief from his back pocket and wiped his cheeks and around the back of his neck. He stared at the black, glistening back of McDougal's head and then leaned down and whispered to Percy R. Brookins.

'McDougal sure could stand a haircut. He looks as bad as ol' Theo.' And they both knew how bad ol' Theo looked and they both frowned and laughed.

Percy R. Brookins touched a chord lightly to give some colour to Jake's drum solo and then he said: 'Man, that stud has suffered for that coloured woman.'

Little Jug added: 'And those three little brownskin crumb-crushers.'

Percy R. Brookins hit another chord and then: 'They *almost* wouldn't rent to him down on Forty-Seventh Street.'

Little Jug laughed. 'Crime does not pay.'

Jake the skinman made a couple of breaks on the snare drums which meant that he was about to give it to McDougal.

Percy R. Brookins turned to face his piano and then he got an idea. He looked at Little Jug and spoke with a serious look behind the curious smile on his face: 'You know that cat's out for blood? I mean he's out to blow the real thing. You know what I mean? Like, he's no Guy Lombago. Do you know that?'

Little Jug ran into some triplets and skipped a couple of beats and rolled McDougal in, right on time.

McDougal rode in on a long, hollow, gutbucket note that made Percy R. Brookins laugh, and caused 'Pro, the Man' to cock his head and rub his cheek. The tall, worried-looking white man pulled his tenor close to his stomach, hunched his shoulders, closed his eyes—and blew!

Little Jug stared at McDougal, then he looked at Percy R. Brookins, shaking his head slowly.

'The Cat has found out the real happenings. I mean like where *we* getit from, you dig? I mean like with Leola and those kids, and Forty-Seven and those jive landlords, you dig? The man's been burnt, Percy. Listen to that somitch, listen to him!'

McDougal's eyes were closed and he did not see the dark woman in the cotton suit that ballooned away from the great bulge of her stomach. He did not see her ease into a chair at the back of the dark, smoky room. He didn't see the smile on her face or the sweat upon her flat nose.

He was too busy telling the truth, the whole truth.

## *Study questions*

1. *Summarize the plot of this story. How important is the plot?* 2. *Who is the protagonist? What is the conflict?* 3. *What do we learn about McDougal from what is said about him? from the last two paragraphs?* 4. *Is it significant that the drummer cuts into McDougal's turn?* 5. *How does the point of view function? setting?* 6. *How does the style contribute to tone and mood?*

*Gabriel García Márquez* (b. 1928), with the publication of his masterwork, *One Hundred Years of Solitude* (1967, English translation 1970), became recognized as a writer of international importance. The novel, a story of a family whom García Márquez endows with gigantic mythological proportions, was translated into eighteen languages and won prizes in Italy and France. Another novel, *The Autumn of the Patriarch,* was published in 1976. His short stories are available in English translation as *The Funeral of Mama Grande* (1962), *No One Writes to the Colonel and Other Stories* (1968), *Leaf Storm and Other Stories* (1972), and *Innocent Eréndira and Other Stories* (1978). He was born in Aracataca, a small village in Colombia, and attended the University of Bogotá. He has been a journalist and film critic for the Colombian newspaper *El Espectador* and has traveled widely in Colombia, Venezuela, Mexico, Europe, and the United States. He makes his home in Barcelona. His post-realistic fiction is a fabulous combination of mystery, wonder, miracle, fantasy, extravagance, comedy, sentiment. "The Incredible and Sad Tale of Innocent Eréndira and Her Heartless Grandmother" makes use of a linear plot line, but major interest is centered on the fascinating array of fantastic detail that provides the texture of the story.

# THE INCREDIBLE AND SAD TALE OF INNOCENT ERÉNDIRA AND HER HEARTLESS GRANDMOTHER

Eréndira was bathing her grandmother when the wind of her misfortune began to blow. The enormous mansion of moon-like concrete lost in the solitude of the desert trembled down to its foundations with the first attack. But Eréndira and her grandmother were used to the risks of the wild nature there, and in the bathroom decorated with peacocks and childish mosaics of Roman baths they scarcely paid any attention to the wind.

The grandmother, naked and huge in the marble tub, looked like a handsome white whale. Eréndira had just turned fourteen and was languid, soft-boned, and too meek for her age. With a parsimony that had a sacred rigor about it, she was bathing her grandmother with water in which purifying herbs and aromatic leaves had been boiled, the latter clinging to the succulent back, the flowing metal-colored hair, and the powerful shoulders so mercilessly tattooed as to put sailors to shame.

"Last night I dreamt I was expecting a letter," the grandmother said.

Eréndira, who never spoke when avoidable, asked: "What day was it in the dream?"

"Thursday."

"Then it was a letter with bad news," Eréndira said, "but it will never arrive."

When she had finished bathing her grandmother, Eréndira took her to her bedroom. The grandmother was so fat she could only walk by leaning on Eréndira's shoulder or on a staff that looked like a bishop's crosier, but even during her most difficult efforts the power of an antiquated grandeur was evident. In the bedroom, furnished, like the whole house, with excessive, somewhat demented taste, Eréndira needed two more hours to get her grandmother ready. She untangled her hair strand by strand, perfumed and combed it, put an equatorially flowered dress on her, put talcum powder on her face, bright lipstick on her mouth, rouge on her cheeks, musk on her eyelids, and mother-of-pearl polish on her nails, and when she had the old woman done up like a doll, Eréndira led her to an artificial garden with suffocating flowers, seated her in a large chair that had the foundation and pedigree of a throne, and left her listening to records on a phonograph with a speaker like a megaphone.

While the grandmother floated through the swamps of the past, Eréndira busied herself sweeping the house, which was dark and motley, with bizarre furniture and statues of invented Caesars, chandeliers of teardrops and alabaster angels, a gilded piano, and numerous clocks of unthinkable sizes and shapes. There was a cistern in the courtyard for the storage of water carried over many years from distant springs on the backs of Indians, and hitched to a ring on the cistern wall was a broken-down ostrich, the only feathered creature who could survive the torment of that accursed climate. The house was far from everything, in the heart of the desert, next to a settlement with miserable, burning streets where the goats committed suicide from desolation when the wind of misfortune blew.

That incomprehensible refuge had been built by the grandmother's husband, a legendary smuggler whose name was Amadís, by whom she had a son whose name was also Amadís and who was Eréndira's father. No one knew either the origins or the motivations of that family. The best-known version in the language of the Indians was that Amadís the father had rescued his beautiful wife from a house of prostitution in Antilles, where he had killed a man in a knife fight, and that he had transplanted her forever in the impunity of the desert. When the Amadíses died, one of melancholy fevers and the other of bullets in a fight over a woman, the grandmother buried their bodies in the courtyard, sent away the fourteen barefoot servant girls, and continued ruminating on her dreams of grandeur in the shadows of the furtive house, thanks to the sacrifices of the bastard granddaughter whom she had reared since birth.

Eréndira needed six hours just to set and wind the clocks. But the day when her misfortune began she didn't have to do that because the clocks had enough winding left to last until the next morning. On the other hand, she had to bathe and overdress her grandmother, scrub the floors, cook lunch, and polish the crystal ware. Around eleven o'clock, when she was changing the water in the ostrich's bowl and watering the desert weeds around the twin graves of the

Amadíses, Eréndira had to fight off the anger of the wind, which had become unbearable, but she didn't have the slightest feeling that it was the wind of her misfortune. At twelve o'clock she was wiping the last champagne glasses when she caught the smell of broth and had to perform the miracle of running to the kitchen without leaving a disaster of Venetian glass in her wake. She just managed to take the pot off the stove as it was beginning to boil over. Then she put on a stew she had already prepared and took advantage of a chance to sit down on a stool in the kitchen. She closed her eyes, opened them again, and began pouring the soup into the tureen. She was working as she slept.

The grandmother had sat down alone at the head of a banquet table with silver candlesticks and set for twelve people. She shook her little bell and Eréndira arrived almost immediately with the steaming tureen. As Eréndira was serving the soup, her grandmother noticed the somnambulist look and passed her hand in front of Eréndira's eyes as if wiping a pane of glass. The girl didn't see the hand. The grandmother followed her with her look and when Eréndira turned to go back to the kitchen, the grandmother shouted at her:

"Eréndira."

Having been awakened all of a sudden, the girl dropped the tureen onto the rug.

"That's all right, child," the grandmother said with assuring tenderness. "You fell asleep while you were walking about again."

"My body has that habit," Eréndira said by way of an excuse. She picked up the tureen, still hazy with sleep, and tried to clean the stain on the rug.

"Leave it," her grandmother dissuaded her. "You can wash it this afternoon."

So in addition to her regular afternoon chores, Eréndira had to wash the dining-room rug, and she took advantage of her presence at the washtub to do Monday's laundry as well, while the wind went around the house looking for a way in. She had so much to do, night came upon Eréndira without her realizing it, and when she put the dining-room rug back in its place, it was time to go to bed.

The grandmother had been fooling around on the piano all afternoon, singing the songs of her times to herself. But when she lay down on her bed in her muslin nightgown, the bitterness of fond memories returned.

"Take advantage of tomorrow to wash the living-room rug too," she told Eréndira. "It hasn't seen the sun since the days of all the noise."

"Yes, grandmother," the girl answered.

She picked up a feather fan and began to cool the implacable matron, who recited the list of nighttime orders as she sank into sleep.

"Iron all the clothes before you go to bed so you can sleep with a clear conscience."

"Yes, grandmother."

"Check the clothes closets carefully because moths get hungrier on windy nights."

"Yes, grandmother."

"With the time you have left, take the flowers into the courtyard so they can get a breath of air."

"Yes, grandmother."

"And feed the ostrich."

The grandmother had fallen asleep but she was still giving orders, for it was from her that the granddaugher had inherited the ability to be alive while sleeping. Eréndira left the room without making any noise and did the final chores of the night, still replying to the sleeping grandmother's orders.

"Give the graves some water."

"Yes, grandmother."

"And if the Amadíses arrive, tell them not to come in," the grandmother said, "because Porfirio Galán's gang is waiting to kill them."

Eréndira didn't answer anymore because she knew that the grandmother was getting lost in her delirium, but she didn't miss a single order. When she finished checking the window bolts and put out the last lights, she took a candlestick from the dining room and lighted her way to her bedroom while the pauses in the wind were filled with the peaceful and enormous breathing of her grandmother.

Eréndira's room was also luxurious, piled high with the rag dolls and windup animals of her recent childhood. Overcome by the barbarous chores of the day, she didn't have the strength to get undressed. She put the candlestick on the night table and fell onto the bed.

A short while later the wind of Eréndira's misfortune came into her bedroom like a pack of hounds and knocked the candle over against the curtain.

At dawn, when the wind finally stopped, a few thick and scattered drops of rain began to fall, putting out the last embers and hardening the smoking ashes of the mansion. The people in the village, Indians for the most part, tried to rescue the remains of the disaster: the charred corpse of the ostrich, the frame of the gilded piano, the torso of a statue. The grandmother was contemplating the residue of her fortune. When she was convinced very few things remained intact among the ruins, she looked at her granddaughter with sincere pity.

"My poor child," she sighed. "Life won't be long enough for you to pay me back for this mishap."

Eréndira began to pay it back that very day—beneath the noise of the rain, when she was taken to the village storekeeper, a skinny widower well known in the desert for the good price he paid for virginity. As the grandmother waited undaunted, the widower examined Eréndira with scientific austerity: he considered the strength of her thighs, the size of her breasts, the diameter of her hips. He didn't say a word until he had some calculation of her worth.

"She's still quite immature," he said then. "She has the teats of a bitch."

Then he had her get on a scale to prove his decision with figures. Eréndira weighed ninety pounds.

"She isn't worth more than a hundred pesos," the widower said.

The grandmother was scandalized.

"A hundred pesos for a girl who's completely new!" she shouted. "No, sir, that shows on your part a great lack of respect for virtue."

"I'll make it a hundred and fifty," the widower said.

"This girl caused me damages amounting to more than a million pesos," the grandmother said. "At this rate she'll need two hundred years to pay me back."

"You're lucky, the only good feature she has is her age," the widower said.

The grandmother felt all alone in a world of disaster.

"Just raise it to three hundred," she said.

"Two hundred and fifty."

Finally they agreed on two hundred and twenty pesos in cash and some provisions. The grandmother then signaled Eréndira to go with the widower and he led her by the hand to the back room as if he were taking her to school.

"I'll wait for you here," the grandmother said.

"Yes, grandmother," said Eréndira.

At the widower's first attempt, Eréndira shouted something inaudible and tried to get away. The widower answered her without any voice, twisted her arm by the wrist, and dragged her to the hammock. She fought him off with a scratch on the face and shouted in silence again, but he replied with a solemn slap which lifted her off the ground and suspended her in the air for an instant. He grabbed her about the waist before she touched ground again, flung her into the hammock with a brutal heave, and held her down with his knees. Eréndira then succumbed to terror, and remained as if fascinated by moonbeams from a fish floating through air, while the widower undressed her, tearing off her clothes, scattering them with great tugs of color that waved like streamers and went off with the wind.

When there was no other man left in the village who could pay anything for Eréndira's love, her grandmother put her on a truck to go where the smugglers were. They made the trip on the back of the truck, among sacks of rice and buckets of lard and what had been left by the fire: the headboard of the viceregal bed, a warrior angel, the scorched throne, and other junk. In a trunk with two crosses painted in broad strokes, they carried the bones of the Amadíses.

The grandmother protected herself from the sun with a tattered umbrella and it was hard for her to breathe because of the torment of sweat and dust, but even in that unhappy state she kept control of her dignity. Behind the pile of cans and sacks of rice Eréndira paid for the trip and the cartage by making love for twenty pesos a turn with the truck's loader. At first her system of defense was the same as she had used against the widower's attack, but the loader's approach was different, slow and wise, and he ended up taming her with tenderness. So when they reached the first town after a deadly journey, Eréndira and the loader were relaxing from good love behind the parapet of cargo.

The driver shouted to the grandmother: "Here's where the world begins."

The grandmother observed with disbelief the miserable and solitary streets of a town somewhat larger but just as sad as the one they had abandoned.

"It doesn't look like it to me," she said.

"It's mission country," the driver said.

"I'm not interested in charity; I'm interested in smugglers," said the grandmother.

The grandmother, who had decided to stay in spite of the poverty of the town, called to her granddaughter to help her out of the truck, and Eréndira said good-bye to the loader with a kiss.

The grandmother waited, sitting on her throne in the middle of the street, until they finished unloading the goods. The last item was the trunk with the remains of the Amadíses.

"This thing weighs as much as a dead man," the driver laughed.

"There are two of them," the grandmother said, "so treat them with the proper respect."

"I bet they're marble statues," the driver laughed again.

He put down the trunk with bones among the singed furniture and held out his hand to the grandmother.

"Fifty pesos," he said.

"Your slave has already paid in her own way."

The driver looked at his helper with surprise, and the latter made an affirmative sign, and called to the grandmother:

"Eréndira is coming with me, if it's all right with you. My intentions are honorable."

The grandmother looked him up and down, not to make him feel small but trying to measure the true size of his guts.

"It's all right by me," she told him, "provided you pay me what I lost because of her carelessness. It's eight hundred seventy-two thousand three hundred fifteen pesos, less the four hundred and twenty which she's already paid me, making it eight hundred seventy-one thousand eight hundred ninety-five."

The truck started up.

"Believe me, I'd give you that pile of money if I had it," the loader called. "The girl is worth it."

"Well, then, come back when you have it," the grandmother answered.

The loader jumped onto the back of the truck and off it went.

In the vacant lot where the truck had left them, Eréndira and her grandmother improvised a shelter from sheets of zinc and the remains of oriental rugs. They laid two mats on the ground and slept as well as they had in the mansion until the sun opened holes in the ceiling and burned their faces.

Just the opposite of what normally happened, it was the grandmother who busied herself that morning fixing up Eréndira. She made up her face in the style of sepulchral beauty that had been the vogue in her youth and touched her up with artificial fingernails and an organdy bow on her head.

"You look awful," the grandmother admitted, "but it's better that way: men are stupid when it comes to female matters."

Long before they saw them they both recognized the sound of two mules walking on the flint of the desert. At a command from her grandmother, Eréndira lay down on the mat. Leaning on her bishop's crosier, the grandmother went out of the shelter and sat down on the throne to wait for the mules to pass.

The mailman was coming. He was only twenty years old, but his work had aged him, and he was wearing a khaki uniform, leggings, a pith helmet, and had a military pistol on his cartridge belt. He was riding a good mule and leading a timeworn one on whom the canvas mailbags were piled. As he passed the grandmother he saluted her and kept on going, but she signaled him to look inside the shelter. The man stopped and saw Eréndira lying on the mat in her posthumous makeup.

"Do you like it?" the grandmother asked.

The mailman hadn't understood until then what the proposition was.

"It doesn't look bad to someone who's been on a diet," he smiled.

"Fifty pesos," the grandmother said.

"I can eat for a whole month on that," he said. "Don't be a tightwad," the grandmother said. "The airmail pays even better than being a priest."

"I'm the domestic mail," the man said. "The airmail man travels in a pickup truck."

"In any case, love is just as important as eating," the grandmother said.

"But it doesn't feed you."

The grandmother realized that a man who lived from what other people were waiting for had more than enough time for bargaining.

"How much have you got?" she asked him.

The mailman dismounted, took some chewed-up bills from his pocket and showed them to the grandmother, who snatched them up.

"I'll lower the price for you," she said, "but on one condition: that you spread the word all around."

"That's what I'm for," the mailman said.

Eréndira, who had been unable to blink, took off the artificial eyelashes and moved to one side of the mat, to make room. As soon as the mailman was in the shelter, the grandmother closed the entrance with a tug on the curtain.

It was an effective deal. Taken by the words of the mailman, men came from afar to become acquainted with the newness of Eréndira. Behind the men came gambling tables and food stands, and behind them all came a photographer on a bicycle, who, across from the encampment, set up a camera with a mourning sleeve on a tripod and a backdrop of a lake with listless swans.

The grandmother, fanning herself on her throne, seemed alien to her own bazaar. The only thing that interested her was keeping order in the line of customers waiting their turn and checking the exact amount of money they paid in advance to go in to Eréndira. At first she had been so strict that she refused a good customer because he was five pesos short. But with the passage of months she was assimilating the lessons of reality and she ended up letting people in who completed their payment with religious medals, family relics, wedding rings, anything her bite could prove was bona fide gold.

After a long stay in that first town, the grandmother had money enough to buy a donkey, and off she went into the desert in search of places more propitious for the payment of the debt. She traveled on a litter improvised for the donkey and she was protected from the motionless sun by the half-spoked umbrella

Eréndira held over her head. Behind them walked four Indian bearers with the remnants of the encampment: the sleeping mats, the restored throne, the alabaster angel, and the trunk with the remains of the Amadíses. The photographer followed the caravan on his bicycle, but never caught up, as if he were going to a different festival.

Six months had passed since the fire and now the grandmother could get a complete picture of the business.

"If things go on like this," she told Eréndira, "you will have paid me the debt inside of eight years, seven months, and eleven days." She went back over her calculations with her eyes closed, fumbling with the cords of the pouch where she kept the money, and corrected herself: "All that, of course, not counting the pay and board of the Indians and other minor expenses."

Eréndira, who was keeping in step with the donkey, did not reproach her grandmother for her figures, but had to hold back her tears.

"I've got ground glass in my bones," she said.

"Try to sleep."

"Yes, grandmother."

Eréndira closed her eyes, took in a deep breath of scorching air, and went on walking in her sleep.

A small truck loaded with cages appeared, frightening goats in the dust of the horizon, and the clamor of the birds was like a splash of water on the Sunday torpor of San Miguel del Desierto. At the wheel was a corpulent Dutch farmer, his skin splintered by the outdoors. His son, Ulises, who was riding in the other seat, was a gilded adolescent with lonely, maritime eyes and the look of a furtive angel. The Dutchman noticed the tent where all the soldiers of the local garrison were awaiting their turn, and asked in his language:

"What the devil can they be selling there?"

"A woman," his son answered. "Her name is Eréndira."

"How do you know?"

"Everybody in the desert knows," Ulises answered. The Dutchman stopped at the small hotel in town and got out. Ulises stayed in the truck, and with agile fingers opened the briefcase his father had left on the seat, took out a roll of bills, put several in his pocket, and left everything just the way it had been. That night, while his father was asleep, Ulises climbed out the hotel window and went to stand in line in front of Eréndira's tent.

The festivities were at their height. The drunken recruits were dancing by themselves so as not to waste the free music, and the photographer was taking nighttime pictures with magnesium papers. As she watched over her business, the grandmother counted the bank notes in her lap, dividing them into equal piles and arranging them in a basket. There were only twelve soldiers left, but the line had grown with civilian customers. Ulises was the last one.

It was the turn of a soldier with a woeful appearance. The grandmother not only blocked his way but avoided contact with his money.

"No, son," she told him. "You couldn't go in for all the gold in the world.

You bring bad luck."

The soldier, who wasn't from those parts, was puzzled.

"What do you mean?"

"You bring down the evil shadows," the grandmother said. "A person only has to look at your face."

She waved him off, but without touching him, and made way for the next soldier.

"Go right in, handsome," she told him good-naturedly, "but don't take too long. Your country needs you."

The soldier went in but came right out again because Eréndira wanted to talk to her grandmother, who hung the basket of money on her arm and went into the tent. In the back, on an army cot, Eréndira was unable to repress the trembling in her body. She was in sorry shape, all dirty with soldier sweat.

"Grandmother," she sobbed, "I'm dying."

The grandmother felt her forehead and when she saw Eréndira had no fever, she tried to console her.

"There are only ten soldiers left," she said.

Eréndira began to weep with the shrieks of a frightened animal. Stroking her head, the grandmother murmured: "The trouble is you're weak. Come on, don't cry anymore. Take a bath in sage water to get your blood back in shape."

She left the tent when Eréndira was calmer and she gave the soldier waiting his money back. "That's all for today," she told him. "Come back tomorrow and I'll give you the first place in line." Then she shouted to those lined up: "That's all, boys. Tomorrow morning at nine."

Soldiers and civilians broke ranks with shouts of protest. The grandmother confronted them, brandishing the devastating crosier in earnest. "You're an inconsiderate bunch of slobs!" she shouted. "What do you think the girl is made of, iron? I'd like to see you in her place. You perverts! You shitty bums!"

The men answered her with even cruder insults, but she ended up controlling the revolt and stood guard with her staff until they took away the snack tables and dismantled the gambling stands. She was about to go back into the tent when she saw Ulises, big as life, standing alone where the line of men had been.

"You," the grandmother asked him, "what happened to your wings?"

"The one who had wings was my grandfather," Ulises answered in his natural way, "but nobody believed it."

The grandmother examined him with fascination. "Well, I do," she said. "Put them on and come back tomorrow." She went into the tent and left Ulises burning where he stood.

Eréndira felt better after her bath. She had put on a slip and was drying her hair before going to bed, still making an effort to hold back her tears. Her grandmother was asleep.

"Who are you?" Eréndira called when Ulises suddenly appeared.

"My name is Ulises," he said. He showed her the bills he had stolen. "I've got money."

"You were supposed to get in line," she told him.

"I waited all night long," Ulises said.

"Well, now you have to wait until tomorrow," Eréndira said.

The grandmother began to talk in her sleep.

*"It's going on twenty years since it rained last,"* the grandmother said. *"It was such a terrible storm that the rain was all mixed in with seawater, and the next morning the house was full of fish and snails, and your grandfather Amadís, may he rest in peace, saw a glowing manta ray floating through the air."*

Ulises hid behind the bed. Eréndira showed an amused smile. "Take it easy," she told him. "Grandmother always acts kind of crazy when she's asleep, but not even an earthquake can wake her."

Eréndira looked at him with affection and took the soiled sheet off the mattress. "Come," she said. "Help me change the sheet."

He came from behind the bed and took one end of the sheet. "I was going crazy wanting to see you," he said. "Everybody says you're very pretty and they're right."

"But I'm not going to die," Eréndira said.

"My mother says that people who die in the desert don't go to heaven but to the sea," Ulises said.

Eréndira put the dirty sheet aside and covered the mattress with another that was clean and ironed.

"I never saw the sea," she said.

"It's like the desert but with water," said Ulises.

"Then you can't walk on it."

"My father knew a man who could," Ulises said, "but that was a long time ago."

Eréndira was fascinated but she wanted to sleep.

"If you come very early tomorrow you can be first in line," she said.

"I'm leaving with my father at dawn," said Ulises.

"Won't you be coming back this way?"

"Who can tell?" Ulises said. "We just happened along now because we got lost on the road to the border."

Eréndira looked thoughtfully at her sleeping grandmother.

"All right," she decided. "Give me the money."

Ulises gave it to her, and she lay down on the bed, but he remained trembling where he was. Eréndira took him by the hand.

"Is it the first time?" she said.

Ulises didn't answer but smiled in desolation.

"Breathe slowly," she told him.

She laid him down beside her and while she was taking his clothes off she calmed him.

"What's your name?"

"Ulises."

"That's a gringo name," Eréndira said.

"No, a sailor name."

Eréndira uncovered his chest and sniffed him.

"It's like you were made of gold all over," she said, "but you smell of flowers."

"It must be the oranges," Ulises said.

Calmer now, he gave a smile of complicity.

"We carry a lot of birds along to throw people off the track," he added, "but what we're doing is smuggling a load of oranges across the border."

"Oranges aren't contraband," Eréndira said.

"These are," said Ulises. "Each one is worth fifty thousand pesos."

Eréndira laughed for the first time in a long while.

"What I like about you," she said, "is the serious way you make up nonsense."

She had become talkative, as if Ulises' innocence had changed not only her mood but her character. The grandmother, such a short distance away from misfortune, was still talking in her sleep.

"*Around those times, at the beginning of March, they brought you home,*" the grandmother said. "*You looked like a lizard wrapped in cotton. Amadís, your father, who was young and handsome, was so happy that he sent for twenty carts loaded with flowers and arrived strewing them along the street until the whole village was gold with flowers like the sea.*"

She ranted on with great shouts and with a stubborn passion for several hours. But Ulises couldn't hear her because Eréndira had loved him so much and so truthfully that she loved him again for half price while her grandmother was raving and kept on loving him for nothing until dawn.

A group of missionaries holding up their crucifixes stood shoulder to shoulder in the middle of the desert. A wind as fierce as the wind of misfortune shook their burlap habits and their rough beards and they were barely able to stay on their feet. Behind them was the mission, a colonial pile of stone with a tiny belfry atop the harsh whitewashed walls.

The youngest missionary, who was in charge, pointed to a crack in the ground of glassy clay.

"You shall not pass beyond this line!" he shouted.

The four Indian bearers carrying the grandmother in her litter stopped when they heard the shout. Eréndira was on foot. Behind the litter came a file of eight Indians carrying the baggage, and to the rear was the photographer on his bicycle.

"The desert doesn't belong to anyone," the grandmother said.

"It belongs to God," the missionary said, "and you are violating his sacred laws with your filthy business."

"I don't understand your mysteries, son," the grandmother said.

The missionary pointed at Eréndira.

"That child is underage."

"But she's my granddaughter."

"So much the worse," the missionary replied. "Put her under our care willingly or we'll have to seek recourse in other ways."

The grandmother had not expected them to go so far.

"All right, if that's how it is," she surrendered in fear. "But sooner or later I'll pass, you'll see."

Three days after this encounter, the grandmother and Eréndira were sleeping in a village near the mission when a group of sly novices, creeping along like an infantry patrol, slipped into the tent. Without making a sound they cloaked Eréndira in mosquito netting, picked her up without waking her, and carried her off like a fish.

There were no means left untried by the grandmother in her effort to rescue Eréndira from the protection of the missionaries. Only when all had failed did she turn to the civil authority, which was vested in a military man. She found him in the courtyard of his home, his chest bare, shooting with an army rifle at a solitary cloud in the burning sky. He was trying to perforate it to bring rain, and his shots were furious and useless.

"I can't do anything," he explained to her when he had heard her out. "The priesties, according to the Concordat, have the right to keep the girl until she comes of age. Or until she gets married."

"Then why do they have you here as mayor?" the grandmother asked.

"To make it rain," was the mayor's answer.

Then, seeing that the cloud had moved out of range, he interrupted his official duties and gave his full attention to the grandmother.

"What you need is someone with a lot of weight who will vouch for you," he told her. "Someone who can swear to your moral standing and your good behavior in a signed letter. Do you know Senator Onésimo Sánchez?"

Sitting under the naked sun on a stool that was too narrow for her astral buttocks, the grandmother answered with solemn rage: "I'm just a poor woman all alone in the vastness of the desert."

The mayor, his right eye twisted from the heat, looked at her with pity. "Then don't waste your time, ma'am," he said. "You'll rot in hell."

She didn't rot, of course. She set up her tent across from the mission and sat down to think, like a solitary warrior besieging a fortified city. The wandering photographer loaded his gear in readiness to leave when he saw her with her eyes fixed on the mission.

"Let's see who gets tired first," the grandmother said, "they or I."

"They've been here for three hundred years and they can still take it," the photographer said. "I'm leaving."

"Where are you going?"

"Wherever the wind takes me. It's a big world," the photographer said, and he left.

The grandmother sighed. "Not as big as you think, you ingrate."

But in spite of her anger she didn't move her head so as not to lose sight of the mission. She didn't move her head for many, many days of mineral heat and many, many nights of wild winds. All the time she was meditating, but no one came out of the mission. The Indians built a lean-to of palm leaves beside the tent and hung their hammocks there, but the grandmother stood watch, nodding on her throne and chewing the grain in her pouch with the invincible laziness of an ox.

One night a convoy of covered trucks passed very close to her and the only lights they carried were wreaths of colored bulbs which gave them the ghostly aspect of sleepwalking altars. The grandmother recognized them at once because they were just like the trucks of the Amadíses. The last truck in the convoy slowed, stopped, and a man got out to adjust something in back. He looked like a replica of the Amadíses, wearing a hat with a turned-up brim, high boots, two crossed cartridge belts across his chest, an army rifle, and two pistols. Overcome, the grandmother called to the man.

"Don't you know who I am?" she asked him.

The man directed his flashlight at her and studied the face worn out by vigil.

"The only thing I know for sure is that you're not the Virgin of Perpetual Help," he said.

"Quite the contrary," the grandmother said with a very sweet voice. "I'm the Lady."

The man put his hand to his pistol.

"What lady?"

"Big Amadís's."

"Then you're not of this world," he said, tense. "What is it you want?"

"For you to help me rescue my granddaughter, Big Amadís's granddaughter, the daughter of our son Amadís, held captive in that mission."

"You knocked on the wrong door," he said. "If you think we're about to get mixed up in God's affairs, you're not the one you say you are, you never knew the Amadíses and you haven't got the whoriest notion of what smuggling's all about."

At dawn the grandmother lay awake pondering things, and she had to tighten her heart with her hand so as not to be suffocated by the memory of the house with the great red flowers where she had been happy. She remained thus until the mission bell rang and the first lights went on in the windows and the desert became saturated with the smell of the hot bread of matins. Only then did she abandon her fatigue, tricked by the illusion that Eréndira had got up and was looking for a way to escape and come back to her.

Eréndira, however, had not lost a single night's sleep since they had taken her to the mission. They had cut her hair until her head was like a brush, and put a rough cassock on her and given her a bucket of whitewash and broom so that she could freshen the stairs every time someone went up or down. It was mule work, but Eréndira felt as if every day were Sunday after the fearsome galley that had been her bed. One morning, while she was preparing the whitewash in her bucket, she heard string music like a light. Captivated, she peeped into an immense salon and in the center of the room she saw a beautiful nun playing an Easter oratorio on the clavichord. Eréndira listened, and then she spoke for the first time since she had entered the mission.

"I'm happy," she said, which put an end to the grandmother's hopes.

Meanwhile, the missionaries were combing the desert in search of pregnant concubines in order to get them married. For several days the grandmother saw the little truck loaded with women heading for the mission, but she failed to recognize her opportunity. She recognized it on Pentecost Sunday itself, when she heard the rockets and the ringing of the bells and saw the miserable and merry crowd that was going to the festival, and she saw that among the crowd there were pregnant women with the veil and crown of a bride holding the arms of the mates they would legitimize in the collective wedding.

Among the last in the procession there was a boy, innocent of heart with gourd-cut Indian hair and dressed in rags. He carried an Easter candle with a silk bow in his hand. The grandmother called him over.

"Tell me something, son," she asked with her smoothest voice, "what part do you have in this affair?"

"The priests are going to give me my first communion," the boy said.

"How much did they pay you?"

"Five pesos," the boy said.

The grandmother took a roll of bills from her pouch. "I'm going to give you twenty," she said. "Not to make your first communion, but to get married."

"Who to?" the boy inquired.

"My granddaughter," the grandmother replied.

So Eréndira was married in the courtyard of the mission, for the missionaries could find no way to oppose the wile of that unforeseen marriage. After the ceremony, in the presence of the Apostolic Prefect, the mayor who shot at clouds, her new husband, and her old grandmother, they asked Eréndira what her free and true will was, and she didn't even give a sigh of hesitation.

"I want to leave," she said, and then pointing to her husband, she added: "But not with him, with my grandmother."

Ulises had wasted a whole afternoon trying to steal an orange from the grove because his father kept careful watch while they pruned the trees, and his mother kept watch from the house. So he gave up his plan, for that day at least, and helped his father until they had pruned the last orange tree.

The grove was quiet and hidden; the Dutchman's house had copper grating over the windows and a porch set on pilings. Ulises' mother was on the porch with smoked leaves on her temples to relieve her headache, and her Indian stare followed her son to the corners of the orange grove. She was quite beautiful, much younger than her husband, and not only did she still wear the garb of her tribe, but she knew the ancient secrets of her blood.

When Ulises returned to the house with the pruning tools, his mother asked him for her four o'clock medicine, which was on a nearby table, and as soon as he touched them, the glass and the bottle changed color. Then, out of play, he touched a pitcher and the pitcher turned blue. His mother observed him while taking her medicine and when she was sure that it was not a delirium of her pain, she asked him in Guajiro:

"How long has that been happening to you?"

"Ever since we came back from the desert," Ulises said, also in Guajiro. "It only happens with glass things."

In order to demonstrate, he touched the tumblers that were on the table and each turned a different color.

"Those things only happen because of love," his mother said. "Who is it?"

Ulises didn't answer. His father, who couldn't understand the Guajiro, was at that moment passing by the porch with a cluster of oranges.

"What are you two talking about?" he asked Ulises in Dutch.

"Nothing special," Ulises answered.

Ulises' mother didn't know Dutch. When her husband went into the house, she asked her son in Guajiro:

"What did he say?"

"Nothing special," Ulises answered, watching his father through the window of his office.

"Tell me who it is," Ulises' mother repeated.

"It's nobody," Ulises said.

He studied his father's movements in the office, and saw him put the oranges on top of the safe while he worked the combination.

"You haven't eaten any bread for a long time," his mother observed.

"I don't like it."

"It's because you're love-sick," she said. "People who are love-sick can't eat bread." Her voice passed from entreaty to threat. "It would be better if you told me who it was," she said, "or I'll make you take purifying baths."

In the office the Dutchman opened the safe, put the oranges inside, and closed the armored door.

"I already told you, there wasn't anyone," Ulises said.

Ulises couldn't sleep. He rolled about in his hammock until he made his decision. Then he put on his cowboy pants, his plaid shirt, and his riding boots, jumped through the window, and fled from the house in the truck loaded with birds. As he went through the groves he picked the three ripe oranges he had been unable to steal that afternoon.

He traveled across the desert for the rest of the night and at dawn he asked in towns and villages after the whereabouts of Eréndira. They informed him she was traveling in the electoral campaign retinue of Senator Onésimo Sánchez, who was probably in Nueva Castilla. Ulises found him there but Eréndira was no longer among his retinue, for the grandmother had managed to get the senator to vouch for Eréndira's morality in a letter written in his own hand, and with it the old woman was going about opening the most tightly barred doors in the desert.

"They're heading toward the sea," the townspeople told Ulises, and he followed in that direction until he spotted the broad tent the grandmother had bought from a circus. The wandering photographer had come back to her, convinced that the world was really not as large as he had thought, and he had set up his backdrops nearby. A band of brass-blowers was entertaining Eréndira's clientele with a taciturn waltz.

Ulises waited for his turn to go in, and was much impressed by the interior of the tent. The grandmother's bed had recovered its viceregal splendor, the statue of the angel was in its place beside the trunk of the Amadíses, and there was a pewter bathtub with lion's feet. Lying on her new canopied bed, Eréndira was naked and placid, sleeping with her eyes open. Ulises moved to her, oranges in hand, and noticed that she was looking without seeing. He passed his hand over her eyes and called her by name.

Eréndira woke up, let out a squeak, and covered herself with the sheet.

"Don't look at me," she said. "I'm horrible."

"I only came to show you this," Ulises said. "Look here."

He broke open an orange, split it in two, and showed Eréndira what was inside: stuck in the heart of the fruit was a diamond.

"With three like these we can take a trip around the world," Ulises said. "I've got a pickup truck. And besides that . . . look!"

From beneath his shirt he took out a pistol.

"I can't leave for ten years," Eréndira said.

"You'll leave," Ulises said. "Tonight, when the whale falls asleep, I'll be outside calling like an owl."

"It's my grandmother," she said. "No one can leave for anywhere without her grandmother's permission."

"There's no reason to say anything," said Ulises.

"She'll find out in any case," Eréndira said. "She can dream things."

"When she starts to dream that you're leaving we'll already be across the border," Ulises said.

Pointing the pistol, he imitated the sound of shots to excite Eréndira with his audacity. She didn't say yes, but her eyes gave a sigh. Ulises, touched, whispered: "Tomorrow we'll be watching the ships go by."

That night, while Eréndira was combing her grandmother's hair, the wind of her misfortune blew again. In the shelter of the tent were the Indian bearers and the leader of the brass band waiting to be paid. The grandmother finished counting out the bills, and after consulting a ledger she paid the oldest of the Indians.

"Here you are," she told him. "Twenty pesos for the week, less eight for meals, less three for water, less fifty cents on account for the new shirts. That's eight-fifty. Count it."

The oldest Indian counted the money and they all withdrew with a bow. "Thank you, white lady."

Next came the leader of the band. The grandmother consulted her ledger and turned to the photographer. "What's it going to be?" she asked him. "Will you or won't you pay a quarter of the cost of the music?"

The photographer didn't even raise his head to answer.

"Music doesn't come out in pictures."

"But it makes people want to have their pictures taken," the grandmother said.

"On the contrary," said the photographer. "It reminds them of the dead, and then they come out in the picture with their eyes closed."

The bandleader intervened.

"What makes them close their eyes isn't the music," he said, "it's the lightning you make taking pictures at night."

"It's the music," the photographer insisted.

The grandmother put an end to the dispute. "Don't be a cheapskate," she said to the photographer. "Look how well things have been going for Senator Onésimo Sánchez and it's thanks to the musicians he has along." Then, in a harsh tone, she concluded, "So pay what you ought to or go follow your fortune by yourself. It's not right for that poor child to carry the whole burden of expenses."

"I'll follow my fortune by myself," the photographer said. "After all, an artist is what I am."

The grandmother shrugged her shoulders and took care of the bandleader. She handed him a bundle of bills that matched the figure written in her ledger.

"Two hundred and fifty-four numbers," she told him. "At fifty cents apiece, plus thirty-two on Sundays and holidays at sixty cents apiece, that's one hundred fifty-six twenty."

The musician would not accept the money. "It's one hundred eighty-two forty," he said. "Waltzes cost more because they're sadder."

The grandmother made him take the money. "Well, this week you'll play us two happy numbers for each waltz I owe you for and we'll be even."

The musician didn't understand the grandmother's logic, but he accepted the figures while he unraveled the tangle. At that moment the fearsome wind threatened to uproot the tent, and in the silence that it left behind the call of an owl was heard.

Eréndira didn't know what to do to disguise her distress. "Don't be frightened," the grandmother told her, "there are always owls on windy nights."

The grandmother finally went to bed with her usual ritual, and while her granddaughter fanned she gave orders.

"You have to get up early," she said, "so you can boil the infusion for my bath before the customers get here."

"Yes, grandmother."

"With the time you have left, wash the Indians' dirty laundry and that way we'll have something else to take off their pay next week."

"Yes, grandmother," Eréndira said.

"And sleep slowly so that you won't get tired, because tomorrow is Thursday, the longest day of the week."

"Yes, grandmother."

"And feed the ostrich."

"Yes, grandmother," Eréndira said.

She left the fan at the head of the bed and lighted two altar candles in front of the trunk with their dead. The grandmother, asleep now, was lagging behind with her orders.

"Don't forget to light the candles for the Amadíses."

"Yes, grandmother."

Eréndira heard the wind barking about the tent, but she didn't recognize it as the wind of her misfortune this time either. She looked out into the night until the owl called again and her instinct for freedom prevailed over her grandmother's spell.

She hadn't taken five steps outside when she came across the photographer lashing his equipment to the bicycle. His smile of complicity calmed her.

"I don't know anything," the photographer said. "I haven't seen anything, and I won't pay for the music."

He took his leave with a blessing for all. Then Eréndira ran toward the desert, and was swallowed up in the shadows of the wind where the owl was calling.

The grandmother went to the civil authorities at once. The commandant of the local detachment leaped out of his hammock when she put the senator's letter before his eyes. Ulises' father was waiting at the door.

"How in hell do you expect me to know what it says?" the commandant shouted. "I can't read."

"It's a letter of recommendation from Senator Onésimo Sánchez," the grandmother said.

Without further questions, the commandant took down a rifle and began to shout orders to his men. Minutes later they were all in a military truck flying toward the border against a contrary wind that had erased all trace of the fugitives. The commandant rode in the front seat beside the driver. In back were the Dutchman and the grandmother, with an armed policeman on each running board.

The wind became drier as they headed north and the sun was fiercer than the wind. It was hard to breathe for the heat and dust.

The grandmother was the first to spot the photographer. He was pedaling along in the same direction as the one in which they were flying.

"There he is," she pointed. "He was their accomplice, the lowlife."

The commandant ordered one of the policemen on the running board to take charge of the photographer. The policeman jumped off and shouted twice for the photographer to halt. But the photographer didn't hear because of the wind, nor did he hear the shot. He flipped into the air and fell dead.

Before noon they began to see feathers in the wind. The Dutchman recognized them because they were from his birds. The driver changed direction, pushed the pedal to the floor, and in half an hour they could make out the pickup truck on the horizon.

It was around that time that I came to know them, their moment of greatest splendor, but I didn't look into the details of their lives until many years later when Rafael Escalona, in a song, revealed the terrible ending of the drama and I thought it would be good to tell the tale. I was traveling about selling encyclopedias and medical books in the province of Riohacha. Alvaro Cepeda Samudio, who was also traveling in the region selling beer-cooling equipment, took me through the desert towns in his truck with the intention of talking to me about something, and we talked so much about nothing and drank so much beer that we crossed the entire desert and reached the border. There was the tent of wandering love under hanging canvas signs: ERÉNDIRA IS BEST/ERÉNDIRA WAITS FOR YOU/ THERE'S NO LIFE WITHOUT ERÉNDIRA. The endless line of men of all races and ranks snaked through vacant lots and squares, through bazaars and marketplaces, until it left the city behind.

Among the throng was Blacamán the Good, up on a table asking for a real serpent in order to test an antidote of his invention on his flesh. There was the woman transformed into a spider for having disobeyed her parents, who would let herself be touched for fifty cents so that people would see it was no trick. There was an envoy from the eternal life who announced the imminent coming of the fearsome astral bat whose brimstone breath would overturn the order of nature and bring the mysteries of the sea to the surface.

The only restful backwater was the red-light district. Women from the four quadrants of the nautical rose yawned with boredom in the abandoned cabarets. They had slept their siestas sitting up, unawakened by people who wanted them, and they were still waiting for the astral bat under the fans that spun on the ceilings. Suddenly one of them got up and went to a balcony that overlooked the street where the row of Eréndira's suitors was passing.

"Come on," the woman shouted at them. "What's that one got that we don't have?"

"A letter from a senator," someone shouted.

Attracted by the shouts and the laughter, other women came out onto the balcony.

"The line's been like that for days," one of them said. "Just imagine, fifty pesos apiece."

The one who had come out first spoke again:

"I'm going to go find out what that baby has got."

"Me too," another said. "It'll be better than sitting here warming our chairs."

On the way others joined them and when they got to Eréndira's tent they made up a rowdy procession. They went in without announcement, used pillows to chase away the man they found spending as best he could the money he had paid, and they picked up Eréndira's bed and carried it out into the street.

"This is an outrage!" the grandmother shouted. "You pack of traitors, you bandits!" And then, turning to the men in line: "And you, you sissies, where do you keep your balls, letting this attack against a poor defenseless child go on? Damned fags!"

She kept on shouting as far as her voice would carry, distributing whacks with her crosier against all who came within reach, but her rage was inaudible against the shouts and whistles of the crowd.

Eréndira couldn't escape the ridicule, prevented as she was by the dog chain that the grandmother used to hitch her to her bed ever since she had tried to run away. But the whores didn't harm her. They exhibited her along the noisiest streets and finally they set her down in the center of the main square. Eréndira stayed that way under the terrible sun in the square, biting with shame and rage at the chain of her evil destiny until someone was charitable enough to cover her with a shirt.

That was the only time I saw them, but I found out they stayed in that border town under the protection of the public forces until the grandmother's chests were bursting, and then they left the desert and headed for the sea. Never had such opulence been seen gathered together in that realm of poor people. It was a procession of ox-drawn carts with replicas of what was lost in the disaster piled on, not just the imperial busts and rare clocks, but also a secondhand piano and a victrola and the records of nostalgia. A team of Indians took care of the cargo and a band of musicians announced the triumphal arrival in the villages.

The grandmother traveled on a litter with paper wreaths, chomping on the grains in her pouch. Under her blouse she wore a vest of sailcloth where she kept her gold bars stored. Eréndira was beside her, dressed in gaudy fabrics and with trinkets hanging, the dog chain on her ankle.

"You've got no reason to complain," the grandmother had said. "You've got the clothes of a queen, a luxurious bed, a musical band of your own, and fourteen Indians at your service. Don't you think that's splendid?"

"Yes, grandmother," Eréndira replied.

"When I leave you," the grandmother went on, "you won't be left to the mercy of men because you'll have your own home in a city."

It was a new and unforeseen vision of the future. On the other hand, the grandmother no longer spoke about the original debt, the details of which had become twisted and the payments due confused as the costs of the business became more complicated. Still, Eréndira submitted in silence to the torture of the bed in the saltpeter pits, in the torpor of the lakeside towns, in the lunar craters of the talcum mines, while her grandmother sang the vision of the future. One afternoon, as they came out of an oppressive canyon, they noticed a wind of ancient laurels and felt a knot in their hearts. They had reached the sea.

"There it is," the grandmother said, breathing in the glassy light of the Caribbean after half a lifetime of exile. "Don't you like it?"

"Yes, grandmother."

They pitched the tent. The grandmother spent the night talking and sometimes she mixed up her nostalgia with the future. She slept later than usual, awoke relaxed by the sound of the sea, and Eréndira bathed her while she made her predictions.

"You'll be a noble lady," the grandmother said. "A lady of quality, venerated by those under your protection and favored and honored by the highest authorities. Ships' captains will send you postcards from every port in the world."

The warm water perfumed with oregano was pouring into the bathtub through a tube fed from outside. Eréndira picked it up in a gourd and poured it over her grandmother with one hand while she soaped her with the other.

"The prestige of your house will fly from mouth to mouth from the string of the Antilles to the realm of Holland," the grandmother was saying. "And it will be more important than the presidential palace, because the affairs of government will be discussed there and the fate of the nation will be decided."

That night Eréndira lay thinking until quite late while her grandmother sang in her sleep. Then, her arms on her breast and her eyes open, she called with all the strength of her inner voice:

"Ulises!"

Ulises woke up in the house on the orange plantation. He had heard Eréndira's voice. In an instant he made a bundle of his clothing and shoes and left the bedroom. He was crossing the porch when his father's voice surprised him:

"Where are you going?"

"Into the world," Ulises answered.

"This time I won't stop you," the Dutchman said. "But I warn you, wherever you go your father's curse will follow."

"So be it," said Ulises.

This time Ulises didn't have to ask anyone where Eréndira was. He crossed the desert hiding in passing trucks, stealing to eat and sleep and stealing for the pure pleasure of it until he found the tent in a seaside town where ships weighed anchor for the island of Aruba. Eréndira was asleep, chained to her bed. Ulises stood looking at her with such intensity that Eréndira awoke. They kissed in the darkness, caressed each other slowly, got undressed wearily, with a tenderness and a happiness that was more than ever like love.

At the other end of the tent the sleeping grandmother gave a monumental turn and began to rant.

*"That was during the time the Greek ship arrived,"* she said, *"and a crew of madmen who made the women happy and didn't pay them with money but with sponges, living sponges that later on walked about the houses moaning like patients in a hospital and making the children cry so that they could drink the tears."*

The grandmother made a subterranean movement and sat up in bed.

*"That was when he arrived, my God,"* she shouted, *"stronger, taller, and much more of a man than Amadís."*

Ulises tried to hide when he saw the grandmother sitting up in bed.

"Take it easy," Eréndira told him. "Every time she gets to that part she sits up in bed, but she doesn't wake up."

*"I was singing with the sailors that night and I thought it was an earthquake,"* the grandmother went on. *"They all must have thought the same thing because they ran away shouting, dying with laughter, and only he remained under the star-song canopy. I remember as if it had been yesterday that I was singing the song everyone was singing those days. Even the parrots in the courtyard sang it. There he was,"* she was saying, *"with a macaw on his shoulder and a cannibal-killing blunderbuss, the way Guatarral arrived in the Guianas, and I felt his breath of death when he stood opposite me and said: 'I've been around the world a thousand times and seen women of every nation, so I can tell you on good authority that you are the haughtiest and the most pleasing, the most beautiful woman on earth.'"*

She lay down again and sobbed on her pillow. Ulises and Eréndira remained silent for a long time, rocked in the shadows by the old woman's great breathing. Suddenly, without the slightest quiver in her voice, Eréndira asked:

"Would you dare to kill her?"

"Would you dare?" Ulises said.

"I can't," Eréndira said. "She's my grandmother."

Ulises looked at the enormous body as if measuring its quantity of life.

"For you I could do anything," he said.

Ulises bought a pound of rat poison, mixed it with whipped cream and raspberry jam, and poured that fatal cream into a piece of pastry from which he had removed the filling. Then he put some thicker cream on top, smoothing it with a spoon until there was no trace of his sinister maneuver, and he completed the trick with seventy-two little pink candles.

The grandmother sat up on her throne waving her threatening crosier when she saw him come into the tent with the birthday cake.

"You brazen devil!" she shouted. "How dare you set foot in this place?"

Ulises hid behind his angel face.

"I've come to ask your forgiveness," he said, "on this day, your birthday."

Disarmed by his lie, the grandmother had the table set as if for a feast. She sat Ulises down on her right while Eréndira served them, and, after blowing out the candles with one devastating gust, she cut the cake into two equal parts and gave one to Ulises.

"A man who knows how to get himself forgiven has earned half of heaven," the grandmother said. "I give you the first piece, which is the piece of happiness."

"I don't like sweet things," Ulises said. "You take it."

The grandmother ate the cake all by herself. She put the pieces into her mouth and swallowed them without chewing, moaning with delight and looking at Ulises from the limbo of her pleasure. When there was no more on her plate, she picked up the crumbs from the tablecloth and put them into her mouth.

She had eaten enough arsenic to exterminate a whole generation of rats, yet she played the piano, sang until midnight, and went to bed happy.

From the other bed Eréndira and Ulises kept watch over her, waiting for the grandmother's death rattle. But the voice was as alive as ever when she began to rave.

*"I went crazy, my God, I went crazy!"* she shouted. *"I put two bars on the bedroom door so he couldn't get in; I put the dresser and table against the door and the chairs on the table, and all he had to do was give a little knock with his ring for the defenses to fall apart, the chairs to fall off the table, the table and dresser to separate, the bars to move out of their slots."*

Eréndira and Ulises listened with growing surprise as the delirium became more profound and dramatic.

*"I felt I was going to die, soaked in the sweat of fear, begging inside for the door to open without opening, for him to enter without entering, for him never to go away but never to come back so I wouldn't have to kill him!"*

She went on with her drama for hours, the most intimate details, and a little before dawn she rolled with a movement of seismic magnitude and the voice broke with sobs.

*"I warned him and he laughed,"* she screamed. *"I warned him again and he laughed again, until he opened his eyes in terror, saying, 'Agh, queen! Agh, queen!' and his voice wasn't coming out of his mouth but through the cut the knife had made in his throat."*

Ulises, terrified, grabbed Eréndira's hand.

"Murdering old woman!" he cried.

Eréndira didn't pay any attention. The clocks struck five.

"Go!" Eréndira said. "She's going to wake up now."

"She's got more life in her than an elephant," Ulises whispered. "It can't be!"

"The whole trouble," Eréndira said, "is that you're no good for killing anybody."

So shocked was he by the crudeness of the reproach, Ulises left the tent, whereas Eréndira kept on studying the sleeping grandmother with her secret hate until the sun rose and the air of the birds awakened. Then the grandmother opened her eyes and looked at Eréndira with a placid smile.

"God be with you, child."

The only noticeable change was a slight disorder in the daily routine. It was Wednesday, but the grandmother wanted her Sunday dress and then she decided Eréndira would receive no customers until eleven o'clock.

"I never had so much of an urge to have my picture taken," the grandmother exclaimed.

Eréndira had no more news of Ulises until two weeks later when she caught the call of the owl outside the tent. The grandmother was playing the piano and was too absorbed in her nostalgia to notice the signal.

Eréndira answered the call and only then did she see the wick that led from the piano and stretched out through the underbrush and was lost in the darkness. She ran to where Ulises was, hid next to him among the bushes, and with tight hearts they both watched the little blue flame that crept along the fuse, crossed the dark space and entered the tent.

"Cover your ears," Ulises said.

They did, but needlessly, for there was no explosion. The tent lighted up with a radiance, burst in silence, and disappeared in a wind of powder. When Eréndira dared enter to examine the corpse, she found the grandmother singed and in tatters, but more alive than ever.

"It's like the work of the evil one," the grandmother said. "Pianos don't explode just like that."

She made all kinds of conjectures to establish the cause of the latest disaster, threading suppositions together and calculating the loss until dawn. In the morning, when Eréndira took the vest with the gold bars off her grandmother, she found fire blisters on her shoulders and raw flesh on her breast. "I had good reason to be turning over in my sleep," she said as Eréndira put egg whites on the burns. "And, besides, I had a strange dream." She made an effort at concentration to evoke the image.

"It was a peacock in a white hammock," she said.

"A good sign," Eréndira lied. "Peacocks in dreams are animals with long lives."

"May God hear you," the grandmother said, "because we're back where we started. We have to begin all over."

Her face expressionless, Eréndira left her grandmother with her torso soaked in egg white and her skull daubed with mustard. She was putting more egg whites into a plate under the palm shelter that served as a kitchen when she saw Ulises appear from behind the stove.

"The only thing you've managed to do is increase my debt," she said to him.

Ulises' eyes clouded with anxiety. He looked at Eréndira in silence, watching her crack the eggs. Then he searched over the things in the kitchen, the hanging pots, the strings of annatto, the carving knife, and took down the knife.

"Be careful," Eréndira warned, "she's already had an omen of death. She dreamed about a peacock in a white hammock."

The grandmother saw Ulises come to her with the knife and raised her arms.

"Boy!" she shouted. "Have you gone mad?"

Ulises jumped on her and plunged the knife into her breast. The grandmother moaned, fell on him, and tried to strangle him with her powerful arms.

"Son of a bitch," she growled. "I discover too late you have the face of a traitor angel."

She was unable to say anything more because Ulises stabbed her a second time. Then he gave her a third stab, without pity, and a spurt of blood, released under high pressure, squirted in his face: it was oily blood, shiny and green. Huge, roaring with pain, the grandmother grasped Ulises' body. Her arms, her legs, were green with blood. Her enormous breathing filled the air. Ulises freed his arms with the weapon once more, opened a cut in her belly, and a violence of blood soaked him in green from head to toe. The grandmother toppled, and Ulises delivered the vast fallen body a final thrust.

Eréndira leaned over the grandmother, inspecting her. When she was convinced of death, her face took on the look her twenty years of misfortune had not given her. With quick and precise movements, she grabbed the gold vest and fled.

Ulises remained sitting by the corpse, exhausted by the fight. In time he noticed Eréndira's absence.

He shouted, but got no answer. He looked and saw her running along the shore away from the city. He made a last effort to chase her, calling with painful cries, but he was overcome by the terrible drain of having killed a woman without anybody's help. The grandmother's Indians caught up to him lying face-down on the beach, weeping from solitude and fear.

Eréndira had not heard him. She was running into the wind, swifter than a deer, and no voice of this world could stop her. Without turning her head she ran past the saltpeter pits, the talcum craters, the torpor of the shacks, until the natural science of the sea ended and the desert began. But she still kept on running with the gold vest beyond the arid winds and the never-ending sunsets, and she was never heard of again nor was the slightest trace of her misfortune ever found.

## *Study questions*

1. *Who is the storyteller? What characteristics of the oral tale does this story have? Why is a storyteller necessary?* 2. *With what mythological proportions does García Márquez invest his characters and situations?* 3. *How "realistic" is*

*this story? On what epistemological grounds is it possible to accept the story?* 4. *Are the characters endowed with human qualities?* 5. *Where does the story take place? when? How is the setting functional?* 6. *What role does the wind play?* 7. *What is the tone of the story? How are we supposed to respond to the torture Eréndira is put through? Why does she run away in the end, leaving Ulises behind?* 8. *Does García Márquez make a serious statement in this story?*

*John Barth* (b. 1930), born in Cambridge, Maryland, studied music at the Juilliard School of Music, then attended Johns Hopkins, where he received a B.A. in 1951 and an M.A. in 1952. Frequently on the lecture circuit, where he "performs" his works with great skill, he has taught at Pennsylvania State University and at Buffalo. His novels include *The Floating Opera* (1956), *The End of the Road* (1958), *The Sot-Weed Factor* (1960), and *Giles Goat-Boy* (1966). He was co-winner of the National Book Award for *Chimera* (1972), a collection of three long stories. His short stories, appearing first in such publications as *Esquire, Atlantic,* and the *New American Review,* were collected in *Lost in the Funhouse* (1968). In his stories Barth insists on art as artifice in which the real and fictional worlds are inseparable. "Lost in the Funhouse" is an example of metafiction (fiction about fiction) raised to the level of an epistemological act.

## LOST IN THE FUNHOUSE

For whom is the funhouse fun? Perhaps for lovers. For Ambrose it is *a place of fear and confusion.* He has come to the seashore with his family for the holiday, *the occasion of their visit is Independence Day, the most important secular holiday of the United States of America.* A single straight underline is the manuscript mark for italic type, *which in turn* is the printed equivalent to oral emphasis of words and phrases as well as the customary type for titles of complete works, not to mention. Italics are also employed, in fiction stories especially, for "outside," intrusive, or artificial voices, such as radio announcements, the texts of telegrams and newspaper articles, et cetera. They should be used *sparingly.* If passages originally in roman type are italicized by someone repeating them, it's customary to acknowledge the fact. *Italics mine.*

Ambrose was "at that awkward age." His voice came out high-pitched as a child's if he let himself get carried away; to be on the safe side, therefore, he moved and spoke with *deliberate calm* and *adult gravity.* Talking soberly of unimportant or irrelevant matters and listening consciously to the sound of your own voice are useful habits for maintaining control in this difficult interval. *En route* to Ocean City he sat in the back seat of the family car with his brother

Peter, age fifteen, and Magda G_____, age fourteen, a pretty girl an exquisite young lady, who lived not far from them on B_____ Street in the town of D_____, Maryland. Initials, blanks, or both were often substituted for proper names in nineteenth-century fiction to enhance the illusion of reality. It is as if the author felt it necessary to delete the names for reasons of tact or legal liability. Interestingly, as with other aspects of realism, it is an *illusion* that is being enhanced, by purely artificial means. Is it likely, does it violate the principle of verisimilitude that a thirteen-year-old boy could make such a sophisticated observation? A girl of fourteen is *the psychological coeval* of a boy of fifteen or sixteen; a thirteen-year-old boy, therefore, even one precocious in some other respects, might be three years *her emotional junior.*

Thrice a year—on Memorial, Independence, and Labor Days—the family visits Ocean City for the afternoon and evening. When Ambrose and Peter's father was their age, the excursion was made by train, as mentioned in the novel *The 42nd Parallel* by John Dos Passos. Many families from the same neighborhood used to travel together, with dependent relatives and often with Negro servants; schoolfuls of children swarmed through the railway cars; everyone shared everyone else's Maryland fried chicken, Virginia ham, deviled eggs, potato salad, beaten biscuits, iced tea. Nowadays (that is, in 19___, the year of our story) the journey is made by automobile—more comfortably and quickly though without the extra fun though without the *camaraderie* of a general excursion. It's all part of the deterioration of American life, their father declares; Uncle Karl supposes that when the boys take *their* families to Ocean City for the holidays they'll fly in Autogiros. Their mother, sitting in the middle of the front seat like Magda in the second, only with her arms on the seat-back behind the men's shoulders, wouldn't want the good old days back again, the steaming trains and stuffy long dresses; on the other hand she can do without Autogiros, too, if she has to become a grandmother to fly in them.

Description of physical appearance and mannerisms is one of several standard methods of characterization used by writers of fiction. It is also important to "keep the senses operating"; when a detail from one of the five senses, say visual, is "crossed" with a detail from another, say auditory, the reader's imagination is oriented to the scene, perhaps unconsciously. This procedure may be compared to the way surveyors and navigators determine their positions by two or more compass bearings, a process known as triangulation. The brown hair on Ambrose's mother's forearms gleamed in the sun like. Though right-handed, she took her left arm from the seat-back to press the dashboard cigar lighter for Uncle Karl. When the glass bead in its handle glowed red, the lighter was ready for use. The smell of Uncle Karl's cigar smoke reminded one of. The fragrance of the ocean came strong to the picnic ground where they always stopped for lunch, two miles inland from Ocean City. Having to pause for a full hour almost within sound of the breakers was difficult for Peter and Ambrose when they were younger; even at their present age it was not easy to keep their anticipation, *stimulated by the briny spume,* from turning into short temper. The Irish author James Joyce, in his unusual novel entitled *Ulysses,* now available in this country, uses the adjectives *snot-green* and *scrotum-tightening* to describe the sea. Visual, auditory, tactile, olfactory, gustatory. Peter and Ambrose's father, while steering their black 1936 LaSalle sedan with one hand, could with the other remove the first cigarette from a white pack of Lucky Strikes, and, more remarkably, light it with a match forefingered from its book and thumbed against the flint paper without being detached. The matchbook cover merely advertised U. S. War Bonds and Stamps. A fine metaphor, simile, or other figure of speech, in addition to its obvious "first-order" relevance to the thing it describes, will be seen upon reflection to have a second order of significance: it may be drawn from the *milieu* of the action, for example, or be particularly appropriate to the sensibility of the narrator, even hinting to the reader things of which the narrator is unaware; or it may cast further and subtler lights upon the thing it describes, sometimes ironically qualifying the more evident sense of the comparison.

To say that Ambrose's and Peter's mother was *pretty* is to accomplish nothing; the reader may acknowledge the proposition, but his imagination is not engaged. Besides, Magda was also pretty, yet in an altogether different way. Although she lived on B_____ Street she had very good manners and did better than average in school. Her figure was very well developed for her age. Her right hand lay casually on the plush upholstery of the seat, very near Ambrose's left leg, on which his own hand rested. The space between their legs, between her right and his left leg, was out of the line of sight of anyone sitting on the other side of Magda, as well as anyone glancing into the rearview mirror. Uncle Karl's face resembled Peter's—rather, vice versa. Both had dark hair and eyes, short husky statures, deep voices. Magda's left hand was probably in a similar position on her left side. The boy's father is difficult to describe; no particular feature of his appearance or manner stood out. He wore glasses and was principal of a T_____ County grade school, Uncle Karl was a masonry contractor.

Although Peter must have known as well as Ambrose that the latter, because of his position in the car, would be the first to see the electrical towers of the power plant at V_____, the halfway point of their trip, he leaned forward and slightly toward the center of the car and pretended to be looking for them through the flat pinewoods and tuckahoe creeks along the highway. For as long as the boys could remember, "looking for the Towers" had been a feature of the first half of their excursions to Ocean City, "looking for the standpipe" of the second. Though the game was childish, their mother preserved the tradition of rewarding the first to see the Towers with a candy-bar or piece of fruit. She insisted now that Magda play the game; the prize, she said, was "something hard to get nowadays." Ambrose decided not to join in; he sat far back in his seat. Magda, like Peter, leaned forward. Two sets of straps were discernible through the shoulders of her sun dress; the inside right one, a brassiere-strap, was fastened or shortened with a small safety pin. The right armpit of her dress, presumably the left as well, was damp with perspiration. The simple strategy for being first to espy the Towers, which Ambrose had understood by the age of four, was to sit on the right-hand side of the car. Whoever sat there, however, had also to put up with the worst of the sun, and so Ambrose, without mentioning the matter, chose sometimes the one and sometimes the other. Not impossibly

Peter had never caught on to the trick, or thought that his brother hadn't simply because Ambrose on occasion preferred shade to a Baby Ruth or tangerine.

The shade-sun situation didn't apply to the front seat, owing to the windshield; if anything the driver got more sun, since the person on the passenger side not only was shaded below by the door and dashboard but might swing down his sunvisor all the way too.

"Is that them?" Magda asked. Ambrose's mother teased the boys for letting Magda win, insinuating that "somebody [had] a girlfriend." Peter and Ambrose's father reached a long thin arm across their mother to butt his cigarette in the dashboard ashtray, under the lighter. The prize this time for seeing the Towers first was a banana. Their mother bestowed it after chiding their father for wasting a half-smoked cigarette when everything was so scarce. Magda, to take the prize, moved her hand from so near Ambrose's that he could have touched it as though accidentally. She offered to share the prize, things like that were so hard to find; but everyone insisted it was hers alone. Ambrose's mother sang an iambic trimeter couplet from a popular song, femininely rhymed:

*"What's good is in the Army;*
*What's left will never harm me."*

Uncle Karl tapped his cigar ash out the ventilator window; some particles were sucked by the slipstream back into the car through the rear window on the passenger side. Magda demonstrated her ability to hold a banana in one hand and peel it with her teeth. She still sat forward; Ambrose pushed his glasses back onto the bridge of his nose with his left hand, which he then negligently let fall to the seat cushion immediately behind her. He even permitted the single hair, gold, on the second joint of his thumb to brush the fabric of her skirt. Should she have sat back at that instant, his hand would have been caught under her.

Plush upholstery prickles uncomfortably through gabardine slacks in the July sun. The function of the *beginning* of a story is to introduce the principal characters, establish their initial relationships, set the scene for the main action, expose the background of the situation if necessary, plant motifs and foreshadowings where appropriate, and initiate the first complication or whatever of the "rising action." Actually, if one imagines a story called "The Funhouse," or "Lost in the Funhouse," the details of the drive to Ocean City don't seem especially relevant. The *beginning* should recount the events between Ambrose's first sight of the funhouse early in the afternoon and his entering it with Magda and Peter in the evening. The *middle* would narrate all relevant events from the time he goes in to the time he loses his way; middles have the double and contradictory function of delaying the climax while at the same time preparing the reader for it and fetching him to it. Then the *ending* would tell what Ambrose does while he's lost, how he finally finds his way out, and what everybody makes of the experience. So far there's been no real dialogue, very little sensory detail, and nothing in the way of a *theme*. And a long time has gone by already without anything happening; it makes a person wonder. We haven't even reached Ocean City yet: we will never get out of the funhouse.

The more closely an author identifies with the narrator, literally or metaphorically, the less advisable it is, as a rule, to use the first-person narrative viewpoint. Once three years previously the young people *aforementioned* played Niggers and Masters in the backyard; when it was Ambrose's turn to be Master and theirs to be Niggers Peter had to go serve his evening papers; Ambrose was afraid to punish Magda alone, but she led him to the whitewashed Torture Chamber between the woodshed and the privy in the Slaves Quarters; there she knelt sweating among bamboo rakes and dusty Mason jars, pleadingly embraced his knees, and while bees droned in the lattice as if on an ordinary summer afternoon, purchased clemency at a surprising price set by herself. Doubtless she remembered nothing of this event; Ambrose on the other hand seemed unable to forget the least detail of his life. He even recalled how, standing beside himself with awed impersonality in the reeky heat, he'd stared the while at an empty cigar box in which Uncle Karl kept stone-cutting chisels: beneath the words *El Producto,* a laureled, loose-toga'd lady regarded the sea from a marble bench; beside her, forgotten or not yet turned to, was a five-stringed lyre. Her chin reposed on the back of her right hand; her left depended negligently from the bench-arm. The lower half of scene and lady was peeled away; the words EXAMINED BY ______ were inked there into the wood. Nowadays cigar boxes are made of pasteboard. Ambrose wondered what Magda would have done, Ambrose wondered what Magda would do when she sat back on his hand as he resolved she should. Be angry. Make a teasing joke of it. Give no sign at all. For a long time she leaned forward, playing cow-poker with Peter against Uncle Karl and Mother and watching for the first sign of Ocean City. At nearly the same instant, picnic ground and Ocean City standpipe hove into view; an Amoco filling station on their side of the road cost Mother and Uncle Karl fifty cows and the game; Magda bounced back, clapping her right hand on Mother's right arm; Ambrose moved clear "in the nick of time."

At this rate our hero, at this rate our protagonist will remain in the funhouse forever. Narrative ordinarily consists of alternating dramatization and summarization. One symptom of nervous tension, paradoxically, is repeated and violent yawning; neither Peter nor Magda nor Uncle Karl nor Mother reacted in this manner. Although they were no longer small children, Peter and Ambrose were each given a dollar to spend on boardwalk amusements in addition to what money of their own they'd brought along. Magda too, though she protested she had ample spending money. The boys' mother made a little scene out of distributing the bills; she pretended that her sons and Magda were small children and cautioned them not to spend the sum too quickly or in one place. Magda promised with a merry laugh and, having both hands free, took the bill with her left. Peter laughed also and pledged in a falsetto to be a good boy. His imitation of a child was not clever. The boys' father was tall and thin, balding, fair-complexioned. Assertions of that sort are not effective; the reader may acknowledge the proposition, but. We should be much farther along than we are; something has gone wrong; not much of this preliminary rambling seems relevant. Yet everyone begins in the same place; how is it that most go along without difficulty but a few lose their way?

"Stay out from under the boardwalk," Uncle Karl growled from the side of his mouth. The boys' mother pushed his shoulder *in mock annoyance.* They were all standing before Fat May the Laughing Lady who advertised the funhouse. Larger than life, Fat May mechanically shook, rocked on her heels, slapped her thighs while recorded laughter—uproarious, female—came amplified from a hidden loudspeaker. It chuckled, wheezed, wept; tried in vain to catch its breath; tittered, groaned, exploded raucous and anew. You couldn't hear it without laughing yourself, no matter how you felt. Father came back from talking to a Coast-Guardsman on duty and reported that the surf was spoiled with crude oil from tankers recently torpedoed offshore. Lumps of it, difficult to remove, made tarry tidelines on the beach and stuck on swimmers. Many bathed in the surf nevertheless and came out speckled; others paid to use a municipal pool and only sunbathed on the beach. We would do the latter. We would do the latter. We would do the latter.

Under the boardwalk, matchbook covers, grainy other things. What is the story's theme? Ambrose is ill. He perspires in the dark passages; candied apples-on-a-stick, delicious-looking, disappointing to eat. Funhouses need men's and ladies' room at intervals. Others perhaps have also vomited in corners and corridors; may even have had bowel movements liable to be stepped in in the dark. The word *fuck* suggests suction and/or and/or flatulence. Mother and Father; grandmothers and grandfathers on both sides; great-grandmothers and great-grandfathers on four sides, et cetera. Count a generation as thirty years: in approximately the year when Lord Baltimore was granted charter to the province of Maryland by Charles I, five hundred twelve women—English, Welsh, Bavarian, Swiss—of every class and character, received into themselves the penises the intromittent organs of five hundred twelve men, ditto, in every circumstance and posture, to conceive the five hundred twelve ancestors of the two hundred fifty-six ancestors of the et cetera et cetera et cetera et cetera et cetera et cetera et cetera et cetera of the author, of the narrator, of this story, *Lost in the Funhouse.* In alleyways, ditches, canopy beds, pine-woods, bridal suites, ship's cabins, coach-and-fours, coaches-and-four, sultry toolsheds; on the cold sand under boardwalks, littered with *El Producto* cigar butts, treasured with Lucky Strike cigarette stubs, Coca-Cola caps, gritty turds, cardboard lollipop sticks, matchbook covers warning that A Slip of the Lip Can Sink a Ship. The shluppish whisper, continuous as seawash round the globe, tidelike falls and rises with the circuit of dawn and dusk.

Magda's teeth. She *was* left-handed. Perspiration. They've gone all the way, through, Magda and Peter, they've been waiting for hours with Mother and Uncle Karl while Father searches for his lost son; they draw french-fried potatoes from a paper cup and shake their heads. They've named the children they'll one day have and bring to Ocean City on holidays. Can spermatozoa properly be thought of as male animalcules when there are no female spermatozoa? They grope through hot, dark windings, past Love's Tunnel's fearsome obstacles. Some perhaps lose their way.

Peter suggested then and there that they do the funhouse; he had been through it before, so had Magda, Ambrose hadn't and suggested, his voice cracking on account of Fat May's laughter, that they swim first. All were chuckling, couldn't help it; Ambrose's father, Ambrose's and Peter's father came up grinning like a lunatic with two boxes of syrup-coated popcorn, one for Mother, one for Magda; the men were to help themselves. Ambrose walked on Magda's right; being by nature left-handed, she carried the box in her left hand. Up front the situation was reversed.

"What are you limping for?" Magda inquired of Ambrose. He supposed in a husky tone that his foot had gone to sleep in the car. Her teeth flashed. "Pins and needles?" It was the honeysuckle on the lattice of the former privy that drew the bees. Imagine being stung there. How long is this going to take?

The adults decided to forego the pool; but Uncle Karl insisted they change into swimsuits and do the beach. "He wants to watch the pretty girls," Peter teased, and ducked behind Magda from Uncle Karl's pretended wrath. "You've got all the pretty girls you need right here," Magda declared, and Mother said: "Now that's the gospel truth." Magda scolded Peter, who reached over her shoulder to sneak some popcorn. "Your brother and father aren't getting any." Uncle Karl wondered if they were going to have fireworks that night, what with the shortages. It wasn't the shortages, Mr. M_____ replied; Ocean City had fireworks from pre-war. But it was too risky on account of the enemy submarines, some people thought.

"Don't seem like Fourth of July without fireworks," said Uncle Karl. The inverted tag in dialogue writing is still considered permissible with proper names or epithets, but sounds old-fashioned with personal pronouns. "We'll have 'em again soon enough," predicted the boys' father. Their mother declared she could do without fireworks: they reminded her too much of the real thing. Their father said all the more reason to shoot off a few now and again. Uncle Karl asked *rhetorically* who needed reminding, just look at people's hair and skin.

"The oil, yes," said Mrs. M_____.

Ambrose had a pain in his stomach and so didn't swim but enjoyed watching the others. He and his father burned red easily. Magda's figure was exceedingly well developed for her age. She too declined to swim, and got mad, and became angry when Peter attempted to drag her into the pool. She always swam, he insisted; what did she mean not swim? Why did a person come to Ocean City?

"Maybe I want to lay here with Ambrose," Magda teased.

Nobody likes a pedant.

"Aha," said Mother. Peter grabbed Magda by one ankle and ordered Ambrose to grab the other. She squealed and rolled over on the beach blanket. Ambrose pretended to help hold her back. Her tan was darker than even Mother's and Peter's. "Help out, Uncle Karl!" Peter cried. Uncle Karl went to seize the other ankle. Inside the top of her swimsuit, however, you could see the line where the sunburn ended and, when she hunched her shoulders and squealed again, one nipple's auburn edge. Mother made them behave themselves. "*You* should certainly know," she said to Uncle Karl. Archly. "That when a lady says she doesn't feel like swimming, a gentleman doesn't ask questions." Uncle Karl said excuse *him;* Mother winked at Magda; Ambrose blushed; stupid Peter kept saying "Phooey on *feel like!*" and tugging at Magda's ankle; then even he got the point, and cannonballed with a holler into the pool.

"I swear," Magda said, in mock *in feigned* exasperation.

The diving would make a suitable literary symbol. To go off the high board you had to wait in a line along the poolside and up the ladder. Fellows tickled girls and goosed one another and shouted to the ones at the top to hurry up, or razzed them for bellyfloppers. Once on the springboard some took a great while posing or clowning or deciding on a dive or getting up their nerve; others ran right off. Especially among the younger fellows the idea was to strike the funniest pose or do the craziest stunt as you fell, a thing that got harder to do as you kept on and kept on. But whether you hollered *Geronimo!* or *Sieg heil!*, held your nose or "rode a bicycle," pretended to be shot or did a perfect jack-knife or changed your mind halfway down and ended up with nothing, it was over in two seconds, after all that wait. Spring, pose, splash. Spring, neat-o, splash. Spring, aw fooey, splash.

The grown-ups had gone on; Ambrose wanted to converse with Magda; she was remarkably well developed for her age; it was said that that came from rubbing with a turkish towel, and there were other theories. Ambrose could think of nothing to say except how good a diver Peter was, who was showing off for her benefit. You could pretty well tell by looking at their bathing suits and arm muscles how far along the different fellows were. Ambrose was glad he hadn't gone in swimming, the cold water shrank you up so. Magda pretended to be uninterested in the diving; she probably weighed as much as he did. If you knew your way around in the funhouse like your own bedroom, you could wait until a girl came along and then slip away without ever getting caught, even if her boyfriend was right with her. She'd think *he* did it! It would be better to be the boyfriend, and act outraged, and tear the funhouse apart.

Not act; *be.*

"He's a master diver," Ambrose said. In feigned admiration. "You really have to slave away at it to get that good." What would it matter anyhow if he asked her right out whether she remembered, even teased her with it as Peter would have?

There's no point in going farther; this isn't getting anybody anywhere; they haven't even come to the funhouse yet. Ambrose is off the track, in some new or old part of the place that's not supposed to be used; he strayed into it by some one-in-a-million chance, like the time the roller-coaster car left the tracks in the nineteen-teens against all the laws of physics and sailed over the boardwalk in the dark. And they can't locate him because they don't know where to look. Even the designer and operator have forgotten this other part, that winds around on itself like a whelk shell. That winds around the right part like the snakes on Mercury's caduceus. Some people, perhaps, don't "hit their stride" until their twenties, when the growing-up business is over and women appreciate other things besides wisecracks and teasing and strutting. Peter didn't have one-tenth the imagination *he* had, not one-tenth. Peter did this naming-their-children thing as a joke, making up names like Aloysius and Murgatroyd, but Ambrose knew *exactly* how it would feel to be married and have children of your own, and be a loving husband and father, and go comfortably to work in the mornings and to bed with your wife at night, and wake up with her there. With a breeze coming through the sash and birds and mockingbirds singing in the Chinese-cigar trees. His eyes watered, there aren't enough ways to say that. He would be quite famous in his line of work. Whether Magda was his wife or not, one evening when he was wise-lined and gray at the temples he'd smile gravely, at a fashionable dinner party, and remind her of his youthful passion. The time they went with his family to Ocean City; the *erotic fantasies* he used to have about her. How long ago it seemed, and childish! Yet tender, too, *n'est-ce pas?* Would she have imagined that the world-famous whatever remembered how many strings were on the lyre on the bench beside the girl on the label of the cigar box he'd stared at in the toolshed at age ten while she, age eleven. Even then he had felt *wise beyond his years;* he'd stroked her hair and said in his deepest voice and correctest English, as to a dear child: "I shall never forget this moment."

But though he had breathed heavily, groaned as if ecstatic, what he'd really felt throughout was an odd detachment, as though someone else were Master. Strive as he might to be transported, he heard his mind take notes upon the scene: *This is what they call* passion. *I am experiencing it.* Many of the digger machines were out of order in the penny arcades and could not be repaired or replaced for the duration. Moreover the prizes, made now in USA, were less interesting than formerly, pasteboard items for the most part, and some of the machines wouldn't work on white pennies. The gypsy fortune-teller machine might have provided a foreshadowing of the climax of this story if Ambrose had operated it. It was even dilapidateder than most: the silver coating was worn off the brown metal handles, the glass windows around the dummy were cracked and taped, her kerchiefs and silks long-faded. If a man lived by himself, he could take a department-store mannequin with flexible joints and modify her in certain ways. *However:* by the time he was that old he'd have a real woman. There was a machine that stamped your name around a white-metal coin with a star in the middle: *A*_____. His son would be the second, and when the lad reached thirteen or so he would put a strong arm around his shoulder and tell him calmly: "It is perfectly normal. We have all been through it. It will not last forever." Nobody knew how to be what they were right. He'd smoke a pipe, teach his son how to fish and softcrab, assure him he needn't worry about himself. Magda would certainly give, Magda would certainly yield a great deal of milk, although guilty of occasional solecisms. It don't taste so bad. Suppose the lights came on now!

*The day wore on.* You think you're yourself, but there are other persons in you. Ambrose gets hard when Ambrose doesn't want to, *and obversely.* Ambrose watches them disagree; Ambrose watches him watch. In the funhouse mirror-room you can't see yourself go on forever, because no matter how you stand, your head gets in the way. Even if you had a glass periscope, the image of your eye would cover up the thing you really wanted to see. The police will come; there'll be a story in the papers. That must be where it happened. Unless he can find a surprise exit, an unofficial backdoor or escape hatch opening on an alley, say, and then stroll up to the family in front of the funhouse and ask where everybody's been; *he's* been out of the place for ages. That's just where it happened, in that last lighted room: Peter and Magda found the right exit; he found one that you weren't supposed to find and strayed off into the works somewhere. In a perfect funhouse you'd be able to go only one way, like the divers off the highboard; getting lost would be impossible; the doors and halls would work like minnow traps or the valves in veins.

On account of German U-boats, Ocean City was "browned out": streetlights were shaded on the seaward side; shop-windows and boardwalk amusement places were kept dim, not to silhouette tankers and Liberty-ships for torpedoing. In a short story about Ocean City, Maryland, during World War II, the author could make use of the image of sailors on leave in the penny arcades and shooting galleries, sighting through the crosshairs of toy machine guns at swastika'd subs, while out in the black Atlantic a U-boat skipper squints through his periscope at real ships outlined by the glow of penny arcades. After dinner the family strolled back to the amusement end of the boardwalk. The boys' father had burnt red as always and was masked with Noxzema, a minstrel in reverse. The grownups stood at the end of the boardwalk where the Hurricane of '33 had cut an inlet from the ocean to Assawoman Bay.

"Pronounced with a long *o*," Uncle Karl reminded Magda with a wink. His shirt sleeves were rolled up; Mother punched his brown biceps with the arrowed heart on it and said his mind was naughty. Fat May's laugh came suddenly from the funhouse, as if she'd just got the joke; the family laughed too at the coincidence. Ambrose went under the boardwalk to search for out-of-town matchbook covers with the aid of his pocket flashlight; he looked out from the edge of the North American continent and wondered how far their laughter carried over the water. Spies in rubber rafts; survivors in lifeboats. If the joke had been beyond his understanding, he could have said: *"The laughter was over his head."* And let the reader see the serious wordplay on second reading.

He turned the flashlight on and then off at once even before the woman whooped. He sprang away, heart athud, dropping the light. What had the man grunted? Perspiration drenched and chilled him by the time he scrambled up to the family. "See anything?" his father asked. His voice wouldn't come; he shrugged and violently brushed sand from his pants legs.

"Let's ride the old flying horses!" Magda cried. I'll never be an author. It's been forever already, everybody's gone home, Ocean City's deserted, the ghost-crabs are tickling across the beach and down the littered cold streets. And the empty halls of clapboard hotels and abandoned funhouses. A tidal wave; an enemy air raid; a monster-crab swelling like an island from the sea. *The inhabitants fled in terror.* Magda clung to his trouser leg; he alone knew the maze's secret. "He gave his life that we might live," said Uncle Karl with a scowl of pain, as he. The fellow's hands had been tattooed; the woman's legs, the woman's fat white legs had. *An astonishing coincidence.* He yearned to tell Peter. He wanted to throw up for excitement. They hadn't even chased him. He wished he were dead.

One possible ending would be to have Ambrose come across another lost person in the dark. They'd match their wits together against the funhouse, struggle like Ulysses past obstacle after obstacle, help and encourage each other. Or a girl. By the time they found the exit they'd be closest friends, sweethearts if it were a girl; they'd know each other's inmost souls, be bound together *by the cement of shared adventure;* then they'd emerge into the light and it would turn out that his friend was a Negro. A blind girl. President Roosevelt's son. Ambrose's former archenemy.

Shortly after the mirror room he'd groped along a musty corridor, his heart already misgiving him at the absence of phosphorescent arrows and other signs. He'd found a crack of light—not a door, it turned out, but a seam between the plyboard wall panels—and squinting up to it, espied a small old man, *in appearance not unlike* the photographs at home of Ambrose's late grandfather, nodding upon a stool beneath a bare, speckled bulb. A crude panel of toggle- and knife-switches hung beside the open fuse box near his head; elsewhere in the little room were wooden levers and ropes belayed to boat cleats. At the time, Ambrose wasn't lost enough to rap or call; later he couldn't find that crack. Now it seemed to him that he'd possibly dozed off for a few minutes somewhere along the way; certainly he was exhausted from the afternoon's sunshine and the evening's problems; he couldn't be sure he hadn't dreamed part or all of the sight. Had an old black wall fan droned like bees and shimmied two flypaper streamers? Had the funhouse operator—gentle, somewhat sad and tired-appearing, in expression not unlike the photographs at home of Ambrose's late Uncle Konrad—murmured in his sleep? Is there really such a person as Ambrose, or is he a figment of the author's imagination? Was it Assawoman Bay or Sinepuxent? Are there other errors of fact in this fiction? Was there another sound besides the little slap slap of thigh on ham, like water sucking at the chine-boards of a skiff?

When you're lost, the smartest thing to do is stay put till you're found, hollering if necessary. But to holler guarantees humiliation as well as rescue; keeping silent permits some saving of face—you can act surprised at the fuss when your rescuers find you and swear you weren't lost, if they do. What's more you might find your own way yet, *however belatedly*.

"Don't tell me your foot's still asleep!" Magda exclaimed as the three young people walked from the inlet to the area set aside for ferris wheels, carrousels, and other carnival rides, they having decided in favor of the vast and ancient merry-go-round instead of the funhouse. What a sentence, everything was wrong from the outset. People don't know what to make of him, he doesn't know what to make of himself, he's only thirteen, *athletically and socially inept*, not astonishingly bright, but there are antennae; he has . . . some sort of receivers in his head; things speak to him, he understands more than he should, the world winks at him through its objects, grabs grinning at his coat. Everybody else is in on some secret he doesn't know; they've forgotten to tell him. Through simple *procrastination* his mother put off his baptism until this year. Everyone else had it done as a baby; he'd assumed the same of himself, as had his mother, so she claimed, until it was time for him to join Grace Methodist-Protestant and the oversight came out. He was mortified, but pitched sleepless through his private catechizing, intimidated by the ancient mysteries, a thirteen year old would never say that, resolved to experience conversion like St. Augustine. When the water touched his brow and Adam's sin left him, he contrived by a strain like defecation to bring tears into his eyes—but felt nothing. There was some simple, radical difference about him; he hoped it was genius, feared it was madness, devoted himself to amiability and inconspicuousness. Alone on the seawall near his house he was seized by the terrifying transports he'd thought to find in toolshed, in Communion-cup. The grass was alive! The town, the river, himself, were not imaginary; time roared in his ears like wind; the world was *going on!* This part ought to be dramatized. The Irish author James Joyce once wrote. Ambrose M_____ is going to scream.

There is no *texture of rendered sensory detail,* for one thing. The faded distorting mirrors beside Fat May; the impossibility of choosing a mount when one had but a single ride on the great carrousel; the *vertigo attendant on his recognition* that Ocean City was worn out, the place of fathers and grandfathers, straw-boatered men and parasoled ladies survived by their amusements. Money spent, the three paused at Peter's insistence beside Fat May to watch the girls get their skirts blown up. The object was to tease Magda, who said: "I swear, Peter M_____, you've got a one-track mind! Amby and me aren't *interested* in such things." In the tumbling-barrel, too, just inside the Devil's-mouth entrance to the funhouse, the girls were upended and their boyfriends and others could see up their dresses if they cared to. Which was the whole point, Ambrose realized. Of the entire funhouse! If you looked around, you noticed that almost all the people on the boardwalk were paired off into couples except the small children; in a way, that was the whole point of Ocean City! If you had X-ray eyes and could see everything going on at that instant under the boardwalk and in all the hotel rooms and cars and alleyways, you'd realize that all that normally *showed,* like restaurants and dance halls and clothing and test-your-strength machines, was merely preparation and intermission. Fat May screamed.

Because he watched the goings-on from the corner of his eye, it was Ambrose who spied the half-dollar on the boardwalk near the tumbling-barrel. Losers weepers. The first time he'd heard some people moving through a corridor not far away, just after he'd lost sight of the crack of light, he'd decided not to call to them, for fear they'd guess he was scared and poke fun; it sounded like roughnecks; he'd hoped they'd come by and he could follow in the dark without their knowing. Another time he'd heard just one person, unless he imagined it, bumping along as if on the other side of the plywood; perhaps Peter coming back for him, or Father, or Magda lost too. Or the owner and operator of the funhouse. He'd called out once, as though merrily: "Anybody know where the heck we are?" But the query was too stiff, his voice cracked, when the sounds stopped he was terrified: maybe it was a queer who waited for fellows to get lost, or a longhaired filthy monster that lived in some cranny of the funhouse. He stood rigid for hours it seemed like, scarcely respiring. His future was shockingly clear, in outline. He tried holding his breath to the point of unconsciousness. There ought to be a button you could push to end your life absolutely without pain; disappear in a flick, like turning out a light. He would push it instantly! He despised Uncle Karl. But he despised his father too, for not being what he was supposed to be. Perhaps his father hated *his* father, and so on, and his son would hate him, and so on. Instantly!

Naturally he didn't have nerve enough to ask Magda to go through the funhouse with him. With incredible nerve and to everyone's surprise he invited

Magda, quietly and politely, to go through the funhouse with him. "I warn you, I've never been through it before," he added, *laughing easily;* "but I reckon we can manage somehow. The important thing to remember, after all, is that it's meant to be a *fun*house; that is, a place of amusement. If people really got lost or injured or too badly frightened in it, the owner'd go out of business. There'd even be lawsuits. No character in a work of fiction can make a speech this long without interruption or acknowledgment from the other characters."

Mother teased Uncle Karl: "Three's a crowd, I always heard." But actually Ambrose was relieved that Peter now had a quarter too. Nothing was what it looked like. Every instant, under the surface of the Atlantic Ocean, millions of living animals devoured one another. Pilots were falling in flames over Europe; women were being forcibly raped in the South Pacific. His father should have taken him aside and said: "There is a simple secret to getting through the funhouse, as simple as being first to see the Towers. Here it is. Peter does not know it; neither does your Uncle Karl. You and I are different. Not surprisingly, you've often wished you weren't. Don't think I haven't noticed how unhappy your childhood has been! But you'll understand, when I tell you, why it had to be kept secret until now. And you won't regret not being like your brother and your uncle. *On the contrary!*" If you knew all the stories behind all the people on the boardwalk, you'd see that *nothing* was what it looked like. Husbands and wives often hated each other; parents didn't necessarily love their children; et cetera. A child took things for granted because he had nothing to compare his life to and everybody acted as if things were as they should be. Therefore each saw himself as the hero of the story, when the truth might turn out to be that he's the villain, or the coward. And there wasn't one thing you could do about it!

Hunchbacks, fat ladies, fools—that no one chose what he was was unbearable. In the movies he'd meet a beautiful young girl in the funhouse; they'd have hairs-breadth escapes from real dangers; he'd do and say the right things; she also; in the end they'd be lovers; their dialogue lines would match up; he'd be perfectly at ease; she'd not only like him well enough, she'd think he was *marvelous;* she'd lie awake thinking about *him,* instead of vice versa—the way *his* face looked in different lights and how he stood and exactly what he'd said—and yet that would be only one small episode in his wonderful life, among many many others. Not a *turning point* at all. What had happened in the toolshed was nothing. He hated, he loathed his parents! One reason for not writing a lost-in-the-funhouse story is that either everybody's felt what Ambrose feels, in which case it goes without saying, or else no normal person feels such things, in which case Ambrose is a freak. "Is anything more tiresome, in fiction, than the problems of sensitive adolescents?" And it's all too long and rambling, as if the author. For all a person knows the first time through, the end could be just around any corner; perhaps, *not impossibly* it's been within reach any number of times. On the other hand he may be scarcely past the start, with everything yet to get through, an intolerable idea.

*Fill in:* His father's raised eyebrows when he announced his decision to do the funhouse with Magda. Ambrose understands now, but didn't then, that his father was wondering whether he knew what the funhouse was *for*—especially since he didn't object, as he should have, when Peter decided to come along too. The ticket-woman, witchlike, mortifying him when inadvertently he gave her his name-coin instead of the half-dollar, then unkindly calling Magda's attention to the birthmark on his temple: "Watch out for him, girlie, he's a marked man!" She wasn't even cruel, he understood, only vulgar and insensitive. Somewhere in the world there was a young woman with such splendid understanding that she'd see him entire, like a poem or story, and find his words so valuable after all that when he confessed his apprehensions she would explain why they were in fact the very things that made him precious to her . . . and to Western Civilization! There was no such girl, the simple truth being. Violent yawns as they approached the mouth. Whispered advice from an old-timer on a bench near the barrel: "Go crabwise and ye'll get an eyeful without upsetting!" Composure vanished at the first pitch: Peter hollered joyously, Magda tumbled, shrieked, clutched her skirt; Ambrose scrambled crabwise, tight-lipped with terror, was soon out, watched his dropped name-coin slide among the couples. Shame-faced he saw that to get through expeditiously was not the point; Peter feigned assistance in order to trip Magda up, shouted "I see Christmas!" when her legs went flying. The old man, his latest betrayer, cackled approval. A dim hall then of black-thread cobwebs and recorded gibber: he took Magda's elbow to steady her against revolving discs set in the slanted floor to throw your feet out from under, and explained to her in a calm, deep voice his theory that each phase of the funhouse was triggered either automatically, by a series of photoelectric devices, or else manually by operators stationed at peepholes. But he lost his voice thrice as the discs unbalanced him; Magda was anyhow squealing; but at one point she clutched him about the waist to keep from falling, and her right cheek pressed for a moment against his belt-buckle. Heroically he drew her up, it was his chance to clutch her close as if for support and say: "I love you." He even put an arm lightly about the small of her back before a sailor-and-girl pitched into them from behind, sorely treading his left big toe and knocking Magda asprawl with them. The sailor's girl was a string-haired hussy with a loud laugh and light blue drawers; Ambrose realized that he wouldn't have said "I love you" anyhow, and was smitten with self-contempt. How much better it would be to be that common sailor! A wiry little Seaman 3rd, the fellow squeezed a girl to each side and stumbled hilarious into the mirror room, closer to Magda in thirty seconds than Ambrose had got in thirteen years. She giggled at something the fellow said to Peter; she drew her hair from her eyes with a movement so womanly it struck Ambrose's heart; Peter's smacking her backside then seemed particularly coarse. But Magda made a pleased indignant face and cried, "All right for *you*, mister!" and pursued Peter into the maze without a backward glance. The sailor followed after, leisurely, drawing his girl against his hip; Ambrose understood not only that they were all so relieved to be rid of his burdensome company that they didn't even notice his absence, but that he himself shared their relief. Stepping from the treacherous passage at last into the mirror-maze, he saw once again, more clearly than ever, how readily he deceived himself into supposing he was a person. He even foresaw, wincing at his dreadful self-knowledge, that he would repeat the deception, at ever-rarer intervals, all his wretched life, so fearful were the alternatives. Fame, madness, suicide; perhaps all three. It's not believable that so young a boy could articulate that reflection, and in fiction the merely true must always yield to the plausible. Moreover, the symbolism is in places heavy-footed. Yet Ambrose M______ understood, as few adults do, that the famous loneliness of the great was no popular myth but a general truth—furthermore, that it was as much cause as effect.

All the preceding except the last few sentences is exposition that should've been done earlier or interspersed with the present action instead of lumped together. No reader would put up with so much with such *prolixity.* It's interesting that Ambrose's father, though presumably an intelligent man (as indicated by his role as grade-school principal), neither encouraged nor discouraged his sons at all in any way—as if he either didn't care about them or cared all right but didn't know how to act. If this fact should contribute to one of them's becoming a celebrated but wretchedly unhappy scientist, was it a good thing or not? He too might someday face the question; it would be useful to know whether it had tortured his father for years, for example, or never once crossed his mind.

In the maze two important things happened. First, our hero found a name-coin someone else had lost or discarded: *AMBROSE,* suggestive of the famous lightship and of his late grandfather's favorite dessert, which his mother used to prepare on special occasions out of coconut, oranges, grapes, and what else. Second, as he wondered at the endless replication of his image in the mirrors, second, as he *lost himself in the reflection* that the necessity for an observer makes perfect observation impossible, better make him eighteen at least, yet that would render other things unlikely, he heard Peter and Magda chuckling somewhere together in the maze. "Here!" "No, here!" they shouted to each other; Peter said, "Where's Amby?" Magda murmured. "Amb?" Peter called. In a pleased, friendly voice. He didn't reply. The truth was, his brother was a *happy-go-lucky youngster* who'd've been better off with a regular brother of his own, but who seldom complained of his lot and was generally cordial. Ambrose's throat ached; there aren't enough different ways to say that. He stood quietly while the two young people giggled and thumped through the glittering maze, hurrah'd their discovery of its exit, cried out in joyful alarm at what next beset them. Then he set his mouth and followed after, as he supposed, took a wrong turn, strayed into the pass *wherein he lingers yet.*

The action of conventional dramatic narrative may be represented by a diagram called Freitag's Triangle:

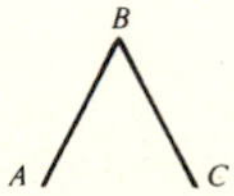


or more accurately by a variant of that diagram:

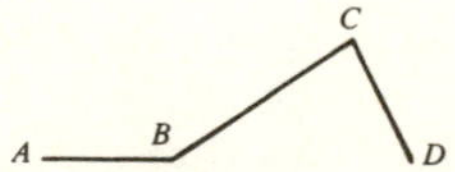

in which *AB* represents the exposition, *B* the introduction of conflict, *BC* the "rising action," complication, or development of the conflict, *C* the climax, or turn of the action, *CD* the dénouement, or resolution of the conflict. While there is no reason to regard this pattern as an absolute necessity, like many other conventions it became conventional because great numbers of people over many years learned by trial and error that it was effective; one ought not to forsake it, therefore, unless one wishes to forsake as well the effect of drama or has clear cause to feel that deliberate violation of the "normal" pattern can better can better effect that effect. This can't go on much longer; it can go on forever. He died telling stories to himself in the dark; years later, when that vast unsuspected area of the funhouse came to light, the first expedition found his skeleton in one of its labyrinthine corridors and mistook it for part of the entertainment. He died of starvation telling himself stories in the dark; but unbeknownst unbeknownst to him, an assistant operator of the funhouse, happening to overhear him, crouched just behind the plyboard partition and wrote down his every word. The operator's daughter, an exquisite young woman with a figure unusually well developed for her age, crouched just behind the partition and transcribed his every word. Though she had never laid eyes on him, she recognized that here was one of Western Culture's truly great imaginations, the eloquence of whose suffering would be an inspiration to unnumbered. And her heart was torn between her love for the misfortunate young man (yes, she loved him, though she had never laid though she knew him only—but how well!—through his words, and the deep, calm voice in which he spoke them) between her love et cetera and her womanly intuition that only in suffering and isolation could he give voice et cetera. Lone dark dying. Quietly she kissed the rough plyboard, and a tear fell upon the page. Where she had written in shorthand *Where she had written in shorthand* Where she had written in shorthand *Where she* et cetera. A long time ago we should have passed the apex of Freitag's Triangle and made brief work of the *dénouement;* the plot doesn't rise by meaningful steps but winds upon itself, digresses, retreats, hesitates, sighs, collapses, expires. The climax of the story must be its protagonist's discovery of a way to get through the funhouse. But he has found none, may have ceased to search.

What relevance does the war have to the story? Should there be fireworks outside or not?

Ambrose wandered, languished, dozed. Now and then he fell into his habit of rehearsing to himself the unadventurous story of his life, narrated from the third-person point of view, from his earliest memory parenthesis of maple leaves stirring in the summer breath of tidewater Maryland end of parenthesis to the present moment. Its principal events, on this telling, would appear to have been *A*, *B*, *C*, and *D*.

He imagined himself years hence, successful, married, at ease in the world, the trials of his adolescence far behind him. He has come to the seashore with his family for the holiday: how Ocean City has changed! But at one seldom at one ill-frequented end of the boardwalk a few derelict amusements survive from times gone by: the great carrousel from the turn of the century, with its monstrous griffins and mechanical concert band; the roller coaster rumored since 1916 to have been condemned; the mechanical shooting gallery in which only the image of our enemies changed. His own son laughs with Fat May and wants to know what a funhouse is; Ambrose hugs the sturdy lad close and smiles around his pipestem at his wife.

The family's going home. Mother sits between Father and Uncle Karl, who teases him good-naturedly who chuckles over the fact that the comrade with whom he'd fought his way shoulder to shoulder through the funhouse had turned out to be a blind Negro girl—to their mutual discomfort, as they'd opened their souls. But such are the walls of custom, which even. Whose arm is where? How must it feel. He dreams of a funhouse vaster by far than any yet constructed; but by then they may be out of fashion, like steamboats and excursion trains. Already quaint and seedy: the draperied ladies on the frieze of the carrousel are his father's father's mooncheeked dreams; if he thinks of it more he will vomit his apple-on-a-stick.

He wonders: will he become a regular person? Something has gone wrong; his vaccination didn't take; at the Boy-Scout initiation campfire he only pretended to be deeply moved, as he pretends to this hour that it is not so bad after all in the funhouse, and that he has a little limp. How long will it last? He envisions a truly astonishing funhouse, incredibly complex yet utterly controlled from a great central switchboard like the console of a pipe organ. Nobody had enough imagination. He could design such a place himself, wiring and all, and he's only thirteen years old. He would be its operator: panel lights would show what was up in every cranny of its cunning of its multifarious vastness; a switch-flick would ease this fellow's way, complicate that's, to balance things out; if anyone seemed lost or frightened, all the operator had to do was.

He wishes he had never entered the funhouse. But he has. Then he wishes he were dead. But he's not. Therefore he will construct funhouses for others and be their secret operator—though he would rather be among the lovers for whom funhouses are designed.

## *Study questions*

1. *In the ninth paragraph of the story the narrator points out how this story would be shaped if it were told in a conventional way. Does any part of this story follow a traditional plot line?* 2. *How many narrative lines does Barth set in motion? How do they interact with each other?* 3. *Who is the narrator? How is the narrator connected to Ambrose?* 4. *What kind of boy is Ambrose? What is his conflict? What is the narrator's conflict?* 5. *How does the toolshed episode function? Fat May?* 6. *Is it significant that the story takes place on July 4, during wartime?* 7. *What is the funhouse? When does Ambrose get in? Does he ever get out? How about the narrator? Is he involved in the funhouse also?* 8. *What is the tone of this story?*

*Donald Barthelme* (b. 1931) was born in Philadelphia and grew up in Texas, where he attended the University of Houston. He has been a reporter, editor of an art and literature review, museum director, and teacher of creative writing. He now lives and works in New York. He has published two novels, *Snow White* (1967) and *The Dead Father* (1975), and several collections of short stories, including, *Come Back, Dr. Caligari* (1964), *Unspeakable Practices, Unnatural Acts* (1968), *City Life* (1970), *Sadness* (1973), and *Amateurs* (1976). Many of his stories were first published in the *New Yorker*. Characterized by surreal surfaces, which combine in varying degrees elements of the fantastic, incongruous, absurd, and clichéd, his stories are satiric thrusts at the insanities of our world. "Views of My Father Weeping" owes much to writers like Gogol, Dostoevsky, Kafka, and Borges, whose dreamscapes provide a suprarational way of knowing, though Barthelme mixes times and places to heighten the surreal effect. "A City of Churches" has a much simpler surface and a linear plot, but the highly charged resolution moves the story from fantasy to nightmare.

## VIEWS OF MY FATHER WEEPING

An aristocrat was riding down the street in his carriage. He ran over my father.

After the ceremony I walked back to the city. I was trying to think of the reason my father had died. Then I remembered: he was run over by a carriage.

I telephoned my mother and told her of my father's death. She said she supposed it was the best thing. I too supposed it was the best thing. His enjoyment was diminishing. I wondered if I should attempt to trace the aristocrat whose carriage had run him down. There were said to have been one or two witnesses.

Yes it is possible that it is not my father who sits there in the center of the bed weeping. It may be someone else, the mailman, the man who delivers the groceries, an insurance salesman or tax collector, who knows. However, I must say, it resembles my father. The resemblance is very strong. He is not smiling through his tears but frowning through them. I remember once we were out on the ranch shooting peccadillos (result of a meeting, on the plains of the West, of the collared peccary and the nine-banded armadillo). My father shot and missed. He wept. This weeping resembles that weeping.

❂ ❂ ❂

"Did you see it?" "Yes but only part of it. Part of the time I had my back turned." The witness was a little girl, eleven or twelve. She lived in a very poor quarter and I could not imagine that, were she to testify, anyone would credit her. "Can you recall what the man in the carriage looked like?" "Like an aristocrat," she said.

❂ ❂ ❂

The first witness declares that the man in the carriage looked "like an aristocrat." But that might be simply the carriage itself. Any man sitting in a handsome carriage with a driver on the box and perhaps one or two footmen up behind tends to look like an aristocrat. I wrote down her name and asked her to call me if she remembered anything else. I gave her some candy.

❂ ❂ ❂

I stood in the square where my father was killed and asked people passing by if they had seen, or knew of anyone who had seen, the incident. At the same time I felt the effort was wasted. Even if I found the man whose carriage had done the job, what would I say to him? "You killed my father." "Yes," the aristocrat would say, "but he ran right in under the legs of the horses. My man tried to stop but it happened too quickly. There was nothing anyone could do." Then perhaps he would offer me a purse full of money.

❂ ❂ ❂

The man sitting in the center of the bed looks very much like my father. He is weeping, tears coursing down his cheeks. One can see that he is upset about something. Looking at him I see that something is wrong. He is spewing like a fire hydrant with its lock knocked off. His yammer darts in and out of all the rooms. In a melting mood I lay my paw on my breast and say, "Father." This does not distract him from his plaint, which rises to a shriek, sinks to a pule. His range is great, his ambition commensurate. I say again, "Father," but he ignores me. I don't know whether it is time to flee or will not be time to flee until later. He may suddenly stop, assume a sternness. I have kept the door open and nothing between me and the door, and moreover the screen unlatched, and on top of that the motor running, in the Mustang. But perhaps it is not my father weeping there, but another father: Tom's father, Phil's father, Pat's father, Pete's father, Paul's father. Apply some sort of test, voiceprint reading or

❂ ❂ ❂

My father throws his ball of knitting up in the air. The orange wool hangs there.

❂ ❂ ❂

My father regards the tray of pink cupcakes. Then he jams his thumb into each cupcake, into the top. Cupcake by cupcake. A thick smile spreads over the face of each cupcake.

❂ ❂ ❂

Then a man volunteered that he had heard two other men talking about the accident in a shop. "What shop?" The man pointed it out to me, a draper's shop on the south side of the square. I entered the shop and made inquiries. "It was your father, eh? He was bloody clumsy if you ask me." This was the clerk behind the counter. But another man standing nearby, well-dressed, even elegant, a gold watchchain stretched across his vest, disagreed. "It was the fault of the driver," the second man said. "He could have stopped them if he had cared to." "Nonsense," the clerk said, "not a chance in the world. If your father hadn't been drunk—" "He wasn't drunk," I said. "I arrived on the scene soon after it happened and I smelled no liquor."

❂ ❂ ❂

This was true. I had been notified by the police, who came to my room and fetched me to the scene of the accident. I bent over my father, whose chest was crushed, and laid my cheek against his. His cheek was cold. I smelled no liquor but blood from his mouth stained the collar of my coat. I asked the people standing there how it had happened. "Run down by a carriage," they said. "Did the driver stop?" "No, he whipped up the horses and went off down the street and then around the corner at the end of the street, toward King's New Square." "You have no idea as to whose carriage . . ." "None." Then I made the arrangements for the burial. It was not until several days later that the idea of seeking the aristocrat in the carriage came to me.

❂ ❂ ❂

I had had in my life nothing to do with aristocrats, did not even know in what part of the city they lived, in their great houses. So that even if I located someone who had seen the incident and could identify the particular aristocrat involved, I would be faced with the further task of finding his house and gaining admittance (and even then, might he not be abroad?). "No, the driver was at fault," the man with the gold watchchain said. "Even if your father was drunk—and I can't say about that, one way or another, I have no opinion—even if your father was drunk, the driver could have done more to avoid the accident. He was dragged, you know. The carriage dragged him about forty feet." I had noticed that my father's clothes were torn in a peculiar way. "There was one thing," the clerk said, "don't tell anyone I told you, but I can give you one hint. The driver's livery was blue and green."

❁ ❁ ❁

It is someone's father. That much is clear. He is fatherly. The gray in the head. The puff in the face. The droop in the shoulders. The flab on the gut. Tears falling. Tears falling. Tears falling. Tears falling. More tears. It seems that he intends to go further along this salty path. The facts suggest that this is his program, weeping. He has something in mind, more weeping. O lud lud! But why remain? Why watch it? Why tarry? Why not fly? Why subject myself? I could be somewhere else, reading a book, watching the telly, stuffing a big ship into a little bottle, dancing the Pig. I could be out in the streets feeling up eleven-year-old girls in their soldier drag, there are thousands, as alike as pennies, and I could be—Why doesn't he stand up, arrange his clothes, dry his face? He's trying to embarrass us. He wants attention. He's trying to make himself interesting. He wants his brow wrapped in cold cloths perhaps, his hands held perhaps, his back rubbed, his neck kneaded, his wrists patted, his elbows anointed with rare oils, his toenails painted with tiny scenes representing God blessing America. I won't do it.

❁ ❁ ❁

My father has a red bandana tied around his face covering the nose and mouth. He extends his right hand in which there is a water pistol. "Stick 'em up!" he says.

❁ ❁ ❁

But blue and green livery is not unusual. A blue coat with green trousers, or the reverse, if I saw a coachman wearing such livery I would take no particular notice. It is true that most livery tends to be blue and buff, or blue and white, or blue and a sort of darker blue (for the trousers). But in these days one often finds a servant aping the more exquisite color combinations affected by his masters. I have even seen them in red trousers although red trousers used to be reserved, by unspoken agreement, for the aristocracy. So that the colors of the driver's livery were not of much consequence. Still it was something. I could now go about in the city, especially in stables and gin shops and such places, keeping a weather eye for the livery of the lackeys who gathered there. It was possible that more than one of the gentry dressed his servants in this blue and green livery, but on the other hand, unlikely that there were as many as half a dozen. So that in fact the draper's clerk had offered a very good clue indeed, had one the energy to pursue it vigorously.

❁ ❁ ❁

There is my father, standing alongside an extremely large dog, a dog ten hands high at the very least. My father leaps on the dog's back, straddles him. My father kicks the large dog in the ribs with his heels. "Giddyap!"

❁ ❁ ❁

My father has written on the white wall with his crayons.

❁ ❁ ❁

I was stretched out on my bed when someone knocked at the door. It was the small girl to whom I had given candy when I had first begun searching for the aristocrat. She looked frightened, yet resolute: I could see that she had some information for me. "I know who it was," she said. "I know his name." "What is it?" "First you must give me five crowns." Luckily I had five crowns in my pocket; had she come later in the day, after I had eaten, I would have had nothing to give her. I handed over the money and she said, "Lars Bang." I looked at her in some surprise. "What sort of name is that for an aristocrat?" "His coachman," she said. "The coachman's name is Lars Bang." Then she fled.

❁ ❁ ❁

When I heard this name, which in its sound and appearance is rude, vulgar, not unlike my own name, I was seized with repugnance, thought of dropping the whole business, although the piece of information she had brought had just cost me five crowns. When I was seeking him and he was yet nameless, the aristocrat and, by extension, his servants, seemed vulnerable: they had, after all, been responsible for a crime, or a sort of crime. My father was dead and they were responsible, or at least involved; and even though they were of the aristocracy or servants of the aristocracy, still common justice might be sought for; they might be required to make reparation, in some measure, for what they had done. Now, having the name of the coachman, and being thus much closer to his master than when I merely had the clue of the blue and green livery, I became afraid. For, after all, the unknown aristocrat must be a very powerful man, not at all accustomed to being called to account by people like me; indeed, his contempt for people like me was so great that, when one of us was so foolish as to stray into the path of his carriage, the aristocrat dashed him down, or permitted his coachman to do so, dragged him along the cobblestones for as much as forty feet, and then went gaily on his way, toward King's New Square. Such a man, I reasoned, was not very likely to take kindly to what I had to say to him. Very possibly there would be no purse of money at all, not a crown, not an öre; but rather he would, with an abrupt, impatient nod of his head, set his servants upon me. I would be beaten, perhaps killed. Like my father.

✿ ✿ ✿

But if it is not my father sitting there in the bed weeping, why am I standing before the bed, in an attitude of supplication? Why do I desire with all my heart that this man, my father, cease what he is doing, which is so painful to me? Is it only that my position is a familiar one? That I remember, before, desiring with all my heart that this man, my father, cease what he is doing?

✿ ✿ ✿

Why! . . . there's my father! . . . sitting in the bed there! . . . and he's *weeping!* . . . as though his heart would burst! . . . Father! . . . how is this? . . . who has wounded you? . . . name the man! . . . why I'll . . . I'll . . . here, Father, take this handkerchief! . . . and this handkerchief! . . . and this handkerchief! . . . I'll run for a towel . . . for a doctor . . . for a priest . . . for a good fairy . . . is there . . . can you . . . can I . . . a cup of hot tea? . . . bowl of steaming soup? . . . shot of Calvados? . . . a joint? . . . a red jacket? . . . a blue jacket? . . . Father, please! . . . look at me, Father . . . who has insulted you? . . . are you, then, compromised? . . . ruined? . . . a slander is going around? . . . an obloquy? . . . a traducement? . . . 'sdeath! . . . I won't permit it! . . . I won't abide it! . . . I'll . . . move every mountain . . . climb . . . every river . . . etc.

✿ ✿ ✿

My father is playing with the salt and pepper shakers, and with the sugar bowl. He lifts the cover off the sugar bowl, and shakes pepper into it.

✿ ✿ ✿

Or: My father thrusts his hand through a window of the doll's house. His hand knocks over the doll's chair, knocks over the doll's chest of drawers, knocks over the doll's bed.

✿ ✿ ✿

The next day, just before noon, Lars Bang himself came to my room. "I understand that you are looking for me." He was very much of a surprise. I had expected a rather burly, heavy man, of a piece with all of the other coachmen one saw sitting up on the box; Lars Bang was, instead, slight, almost feminine-looking, more the type of the secretary or valet than the coachman. He was not threatening at all, contrary to my fears; he was almost helpful, albeit with the slightest hint of malice in his helpfulness. I stammeringly explained that my father, a good man although subject to certain weaknesses, including a love of the bottle, had been run down by an aristocrat's coach, in the vicinity of King's New Square, not very many days previously; that I had information that the coach had dragged him some forty feet; and that I was eager to establish certain facts about the case. "Well then," Lars Bang said, with a helpful nod, "I'm your man, for it was my coach that was involved. A sorry business! Unfortunately I haven't the time right now to give you the full particulars, but if you will call round at the address written on this card, at six o'clock in the evening, I believe I will be able to satisfy you." So saying, he took himself off, leaving me with the card in my hand.

❁ ❁ ❁

I spoke to Miranda, quickly sketching what had happened. She asked to see the white card; I gave it to her, for the address meant nothing to me. "Oh my," she said. "17 rue du Bac, that's over by the Vixen Gate—a very special quarter. Only aristocrats of the highest rank live there, and common people are not even allowed into the great park that lies between the houses and the river. If you are found wandering about there at night, you are apt to earn yourself a very severe beating." "But I have an appointment," I said. "An appointment with a coachman!" Miranda cried, "how foolish you are! Do you think the men of the watch will believe that, or even if they believe it (you have an honest enough face) will allow you to prowl that rich quarter, where so many thieves would dearly love to be set free for an hour or so, after dark? Go to!" Then she advised me that I must carry something with me, a pannier of beef or some dozen bottles of wine, so that if apprehended by the watch, I could say that I was delivering to such and such a house, and thus be judged an honest man on an honest errand, and escape a beating. I saw that she was right; and going out, I purchased at the wine merchant's a dozen bottles of a rather good claret (for it would never do to be delivering wine no aristocrat would drink); this cost me thirty crowns, which I had borrowed from Miranda. The bottles we wrapped round with straw, to prevent them banging into one another, and the whole we arranged in a sack, which I could carry on my back. I remember thinking, how they rhymed, fitted together, *sack* and *back*. In this fashion I set off across the city.

❁ ❁ ❁

There is my father's bed. In it, my father. Attitude of dejection. Graceful as a mule deer once, the same large ears. For a nanosecond, there is a nanosmile. Is he having me on? I remember once we went out on the ups and downs of the West (out past Vulture's Roost) to shoot. First we shot up a lot of old beer cans, then we shot up a lot of old whiskey bottles, better because they shattered. Then we shot up some mesquite bushes and some parts of a Ford pickup somebody'd left lying around. But no animals came to our party (it was noisy, I admit it). A long list of animals failed to arrive, no deer, quail, rabbit, seals, sea lions, condylarths. It was pretty boring shooting up mesquite bushes, so we hunkered down behind some rocks, Father and I, he hunkered down behind his rocks and I hunkered down behind my rocks, and we commenced to shooting at each other. That was interesting.

❂ ❂ ❂

My father is looking at himself in a mirror. He is wearing a large hat (straw) on which there are a number of blue and yellow plastic jonquils. He says: "How do I look?"

❂ ❂ ❂

Lars Bang took the sack from me and without asking permission reached inside, withdrawing one of the straw-wrapped bottles of claret. "Here's something!" he exclaimed, reading the label. "A gift for the master, I don't doubt!" Then, regarding me steadily all the while, he took up an awl and lifted the cork. There were two other men seated at the pantry table, dressed in the blue-and-green livery, and with them a dark-haired, beautiful girl, quite young, who said nothing and looked at no one. Lars Bang obtained glasses, kicked a chair in my direction, and poured drinks all round. "To your health!" he said (with what I thought an ironical overtone) and we drank. "This young man," Lars Bang said, nodding at me, "is here seeking our advice on a very complicated business. A murder, I believe you said?" "I said nothing of the kind. I seek information about an accident." The claret was soon exhausted. Without looking at me, Lars Bang opened a second bottle and set it in the center of the table. The beautiful dark-haired girl ignored me along with all the others. For my part, I felt I had conducted myself rather well thus far. I had not protested when the wine was made free of (after all, they would be accustomed to levying a sort of tax on anything entering through the back door). But also I had not permitted his word "murder" to be used, but instead specified the use of the word "accident." Therefore I was, in general, comfortable sitting at the table drinking the wine, for which I have no better head than had my father. "Well," said Lars Bang, at length, "I will relate the circumstances of the accident, and you may judge for yourself as to whether myself and my master, the Lensgreve Aklefeldt, were at fault." I absorbed this news with a slight shock. A count! I had selected a man of very high rank indeed to put my question to. In a moment my accumulated self-confidence drained away. A count! Mother of God, have mercy on me.

❂ ❂ ❂

There is my father, peering through an open door into an empty house. He is accompanied by a dog (small dog; not the same dog as before). He looks into the empty room. He says: "Anybody home?"

❁ ❁ ❁

There is my father, sitting in his bed, weeping.

❁ ❁ ❁

"It was a Friday," Lars Bang began, as if he were telling a tavern story. "The hour was close upon noon and my master directed me to drive him to King's New Square, where he had some business. We were proceeding there at a modest easy pace, for he was in no great hurry. Judge of my astonishment when, passing through the drapers' quarter, we found ourselves set upon by an elderly man, thoroughly drunk, who flung himself at my lead pair and began cutting at their legs with a switch, in the most vicious manner imaginable. The poor dumb brutes reared, of course, in fright and fear, for," Lars Bang said piously, "they are accustomed to the best of care, and never a blow do they receive from me, or from the other coachman, Rik, for the count is especially severe upon this point, that his animals be well-treated. The horses, then, were rearing and plunging; it was all I could do to hold them; I shouted at the man, who fell back for an instant. The count stuck his head out of the window, to inquire as to the nature of the trouble; and I told him that a drunken man had attacked our horses. Your father, in his blindness, being not content with the mischief he had already worked, ran back in again, close to the animals, and began madly cutting at their legs with his stick. At this renewed attack the horses, frightened out of their wits, jerked the reins from my hands, and ran headlong over your father, who fell beneath their hooves. The heavy wheels of the carriage passed over him (I felt two quite distinct thumps), his body caught upon a projection under the boot, and he was dragged some forty feet, over the cobblestones. I was attempting, with all my might, merely to hang on to the box, for, having taken the bit between their teeth, the horses were in no mood to tarry; nor could any human agency have stopped them. We flew down the street . . ."

❁ ❁ ❁

My father is attending a class in good behavior.

"Do the men rise when friends greet us while we are sitting in a booth?"

"The men do not rise when they are seated in a booth," he answers, "although they may half-rise and make apologies for not fully rising."

❁ ❁ ❁

". . . the horses turning into the way that leads to King's New Square; and it was not until we reached that place that they stopped and allowed me to quiet them. I wanted to go back and see what had become of the madman, your father, who had attacked us; but my master, vastly angry and shaken up, forbade it. I have never seen him in so fearful a temper as that day; if your father had survived, and my master got his hands on him, it would have gone ill with your father, that's a certainty. And so, you are now in possession of all the facts. I trust you are satisfied, and will drink another bottle of this quite fair claret you have brought us, and be on your way." Before I had time to frame a reply, the dark-haired girl spoke. "Bang is an absolute bloody liar," she said.

Etc.

## *Study questions*

1. *List all the details that Barthelme uses to situate this story in time and place. How many inconsistencies do you find?* 2. *What kinds and levels of absurd details does Barthelme employ? to what effect?* 3. *How many narrative lines are there? How are they juxtaposed? Why?* 4. *What is the narrator's father like? Can we know? Can we know what the narrator thinks his father is like? How does the narrator feel about his father?* 5. *What kind of son is the narrator?* 6. *What is the significance of the fact that Lars Bang's name sounds like that of the narrator? Is it significant that Bang may be a liar?* 7. *How does the story end? Why?* 8. *What is the tone of the story? serious? comic? hysterical?* 9. *Did anything in this story actually take place? Does it matter?*

# A CITY OF CHURCHES

"Yes," Mr. Phillips said, "ours is a city of churches all right."

Cecelia nodded, following his pointing hand. Both sides of the street were solidly lined with churches, standing shoulder to shoulder in a variety of architectural styles. The Bethel Baptist stood next to the Holy Messiah Free Baptist, St. Paul's Episcopal next to Grace Evangelical Covenant. Then came the First Christian Science, the Church of God, All Souls, Our Lady of Victory, the Society of Friends, the Assembly of God, and the Church of the Holy Apostles. The spires and steeples of the traditional buildings were jammed in next to the broad imaginative flights of the "contemporary" designs.

"Everyone here takes a great interest in church matters," Mr. Phillips said.

Will I fit in? Cecelia wondered. She had come to Prester to open a branch office of a car-rental concern.

"I'm not especially religious," she said to Mr. Phillips, who was in the real-estate business.

"Not *now*," he answered. "Not *yet*. But we have many fine young people here. You'll get integrated into the community soon enough. The immediate problem is, where are you to live? Most people," he said, "live in the church of their choice. All of our churches have many extra rooms. I have a few belfry apartments that I can show you. What price range were you thinking of?"

They turned a corner and were confronted with more churches. They passed St. Luke's, the Church of the Epiphany, All Saints Ukrainian Orthodox, St. Clement's, Fountain Baptist, Union Congregational, St. Anargyri's, Temple Emanuel, the First Church of Christ Reformed. The mouths of all the churches were gaping open. Inside, lights could be seen dimly.

"I can go up to a hundred and ten," Cecelia said. "Do you have any buildings here that are *not* churches?"

"None," said Mr. Phillips. "Of course many of our fine church structures also do double duty as something else." He indicated a handsome Georgian façade. "That one," he said, "houses the United Methodist and the Board of Education. The one next to it, which is Antioch Pentecostal, has the barbershop."

It was true. A red-and-white striped barber pole was attached inconspicuously to the front of the Antioch Pentecostal.

"Do many people rent cars here?" Cecelia asked. "Or would they, if there was a handy place to rent them?"

"Oh, I don't know," said Mr. Phillips. "Renting a car implies that you want to go somewhere. Most people are pretty content right here. We have a lot of activities. I don't think I'd pick the car-rental business if I was just starting out in Prester. But you'll do fine." He showed her a small, extremely modern building with a severe brick, steel, and glass front. "That's St. Barnabas. Nice bunch of people over there. Wonderful spaghetti suppers."

Cecelia could see a number of heads looking out of the windows. But when they saw that she was staring at them, the heads disappeared.

"Do you think it's healthy for so many churches to be gathered together in one place?" she asked her guide. "It doesn't seem . . . *balanced,* if you know what I mean."

"We are famous for our churches," Mr. Phillips replied. "They are harmless. Here we are now."

He opened a door and they began climbing many flights of dusty stairs. At the end of the climb they entered a good-sized room, square, with windows on all four sides. There was a bed, a table, and two chairs, lamps, a rug. Four very large bronze bells hung in the exact center of the room.

"What a view!" Mr. Phillips exclaimed. "Come here and look."

"Do they actually ring these bells?" Cecelia asked.

"Three times a day," Mr. Phillips said, smiling. "Morning, noon, and night. Of course when they're rung you have to be pretty quick at getting out of the way. You get hit in the head by one of these babies and that's all she wrote."

"God Almighty," said Cecelia involuntarily. Then she said, "Nobody lives in the belfry apartments. That's why they're empty."

"You think so?" Mr. Phillips said.

"You can only rent them to new people in town," she said accusingly.

"I wouldn't do that," Mr. Phillips said. "It would go against the spirit of Christian fellowship."

"This town is a little creepy, you know that?"

"That may be, but it's not for you to say, is it? I mean, you're new here. You should walk cautiously, for a while. If you don't want an upper apartment I have a basement over at Central Presbyterian. You'd have to share it. There are two women in there now."

"I don't want to share," Cecelia said. "I want a place of my own."

"Why?" the real-estate man asked curiously. "For what purpose?"

"Purpose?" asked Cecelia. "There is no particular purpose. I just want—"

"That's not usual here. Most people live with other people. Husbands and wives. Sons with their mothers. People have roommates. That's the usual pattern."

"Still, I prefer a place of my own."

"It's very unusual."

"Do you have any such places? Besides bell towers, I mean?"

"I guess there are a few," Mr. Phillips said, with clear reluctance. "I can show you one or two, I suppose."

He paused for a moment.

"It's just that we have different values, maybe, from some of the surrounding communities," he explained. "We've been written up a lot. We had four minutes on the C.B.S. Evening News one time. Three or four years ago. 'A City of Churches,' it was called."

"Yes, a place of my own is essential," Cecelia said, "if I am to survive here."

"That's kind of a funny attitude to take," Mr. Phillips said. "What denomination are you?"

Cecelia was silent. The truth was, she wasn't anything.

"I said, what denomination are you?" Mr. Phillips repeated.

"I can will my dreams," Cecelia said. "I can dream whatever I want. If I want to dream that I'm having a good time, in Paris or some other city, all I have to do is go to sleep and I will dream that dream. I can dream whatever I want."

"What do you dream, then, mostly?" Mr. Phillips said, looking at her closely.

"Mostly sexual things," she said. She was not afraid of him.

"Prester is not that kind of a town," Mr. Phillips said, looking away.

They went back down the stairs.

The doors of the churches were opening, on both sides of the street. Small groups of people came out and stood there, in front of the churches, gazing at Cecelia and Mr. Phillips.

A young man stepped forward and shouted, *"Everyone in this town already has a car! There is no one in this town who doesn't have a car!"*

"Is that true?" Cecelia asked Mr. Phillips.

"Yes," he said. "It's true. No one would rent a car here. Not in a hundred years."

"Then I won't stay," she said. "I'll go somewhere else."

"You must stay," he said. "There is already a car-rental office for you. In

Mount Moriah Baptist, on the lobby floor. There is a counter and a telephone and a rack of car keys. And a calendar."

"I won't stay," she said. "Not if there's not any sound business reason for staying."

"We want you," said Mr. Phillips. "We want you standing behind the counter of the car-rental agency, during regular business hours. It will make the town complete."

"I won't," she said. "Not me."

"You must. It's essential."

"I'll dream," she said. "Things you won't like."

"We are discontented," said Mr. Phillips. "Terribly, terribly discontented. Something is wrong."

"I'll dream the Secret," she said. "You'll be sorry."

"We are like other towns, except that we are perfect," he said. "Our discontent can only be held in check by perfection. We need a car-rental girl. Someone must stand behind the counter."

"I'll dream the life you are most afraid of," Cecelia threatened.

"You are ours," he said, gripping her arm. "Our car-rental girl. Be nice. There is nothing you can do."

"Wait and see," Cecelia said.

## *Study questions*

1. *What is the city like? Why are there so many churches? Are they harmless, as Mr. Phillips suggests? Can the city be seen as a microcosm?* 2. *What kind of man is Mr. Phillips? What kinds of ironies are involved in the contrast between what he is and what he should be?* 3. *What role does Cecelia play? Does she seem as strong-willed as Mr. Phillips?* 4. *What is wrong in Prester? What does Cecelia threaten Mr. Phillips with? How does he threaten her?* 5. *Toward what is Barthelme's satire directed?*

*Irene Musillo Mitchell* (b. 1931), born in Italy, graduated from Hunter College in New York in 1953 with a music major and an English minor. Her M.A. from Columbia University in 1956 was in musicology. Thereafter she spent four years at Columbia working on a Ph.D. in English literature. She has taught in New Jersey, New York, and in Vermont, where she now lives. A volume of poetry, *Portraits*, was published in 1972. Other poems from a collection, *Chrysalis*, have been published singly or in groups. "Scenes from the Thistledown Theatre," published in 1976, are her first efforts in the area of short prose fiction. Reluctant to call the "Scenes" short stories and unwilling to call them vignettes, she suggests that they are situations, depictions, focusing on a character at a single moment and revealing the substance of the character's thoughts, emotions, and sensations as they relate to the depicted scenes. The technique, she believes, is particularly suited to the modern age's keen sense of the transience of things, a sense heightened by what she calls the universal triumph of the camera.

## SCENES FROM THE THISTLEDOWN THEATRE

### *Weltschmerz and the Boy*

It was spring's human hand caressing her face, fondling her hair that disturbed. Winter's piled snows had locked memories and old wounds; she had been austere and preserved like an arctic zone. But this south wind infected like a pathology. Yes, spring was a vulnerability, a breaking into feeling. It was a new port of call, a country of gnawing sensibilities.

She felt lonely, an existential loneliness, a weltschmerz. Middle aged, within, the folding of wings, the gathering of silences, the principle of spring could not be addressed to her. There was a black-winged irreversibility between her and the cherry blossom air, between her and the innocence of these first blue hyacinths.

Nothing, no one could console. In eyes everywhere she saw extinguished dawns; in hands gesturing or still, formulations of deep, primal desertion.

Then she saw Charles her eight-year-old playing "Trucks" in the small dirt pile on the meadow, his straight blond hair over his eyes. She knew his hand accompanied by proper acoustics from his voice was guiding a Matchbox truck around roads meticulously built; she knew he was following the classic dictates of the game: in snowtime the truck must slip on ice and go off the road; in non-snow it must get stuck in mud; there must always be occasion for the tow truck; and there must always be occasion for trucks or cars to "peel off," leaving convulsive marks on dirt or part of tires on asphalt.

Charles! the mode of the child, his ease in nature, his trustful gaze at the giant maple, bare, leafing, turning in autumn; his unity of self like a bright integer amidst irreconcilable dualities. He must walk with her; they must walk together through the pines down to the stream.

But would he? Of course, he would have to park his truck: in whatever urgency—including bedtime—he could no more break the integrity of the game than a rushed artist could leave colors or lines out of a painting. And usually parking was complicated, entailing not only repeated movements in drive and reverse (with acoustics) but prior to this a professional determination of the proper spot. . . . And there was Tommy who might come to play with him.

She walked across the meadow, heard the casualness of her voice as she addressed him, and saw the far blue eyes gazing at her from the distances of childhood. She heard her voice again . . . the snowy owl. No, that was a blunder—who would see a snowy owl now?

She barely heard his slow, awkward reply, barely heard trucks, Tommy. A negative had entered his eyes; he did not want to go! She heard his "if you want me to go. . . ." But it was his wholeness, his inner truth she needed. Suddenly, she did not want to go. And then she saw Tommy—"But you will go, won't you," Charles was saying. Oh, certainly, she would go.

He stood waiting. She started across the meadow, turned; he was still standing there, watching; he waved. She waved and walked towards the pines.

## *Return to the Childhood Locus*

She stood at the corner of the city block. There, both sides the wide street were the two-family houses, each diverse in brick or stucco, one shingled. Of course, every vacant lot had since been built upon, and visible from the next block were apartment houses. But only six houses on one side and seven on the other were significant; only they stood within the glowing dimensions of memory and dream; only they were pervaded with a metaphysical mortar that rendered their substance as intangible as it was solid, as far, rainbow-hued as it was approximate and commonplace. In particular, the sixth house down from the corner where she stood (she could not see it): brick, porches on first and second floors, the former leading through two thick pillars into another, outer porch; there, up the concrete staircase onto the first floor where she lived ten childhood-through-adolescent years was the locus that had fastened onto her psyche with the sphinx-strange truths of myth.

Three hundred miles, a costly train fare, excuses to return to the city to replenish supplies; then two subways and a bus to stand here. It did not matter that she had lived in other parts of the country; that she had married, had children, had arrived at middle age; that the whole context of her life was different: How could that noble yet baroque immigrant household live in her now?

How could that furniture, that wallpaper; the Latinate Christmases and the strange Mediterranean admixture of severity and lyricism claim her who had graduated to a different order of tastes. Nonetheless, in dreams night after night she was here. And now, more than twenty years later, here she returned.

She must walk casually down the block, not too fast, not too slow—walk this very sidewalk she would run up on summer evenings to kiss her father coming home from work, hold his hand, and walk home together to dinner. Now she must slow her pace; she was coming to the stucco house where her Polish friend used to live. (A man walking a dog was coming towards her. He passed.) Here at the side of the house was the passage leading to the back gate, which she would open, and then standing in the yard, call, Natalie! Natalie! She laughed at this childhood figure, even loved her maternally; she remembered Junior, the bully, and herself incensed calling beneath his windows, Junior's mother! Junior's mother!

But now she was approaching—suddenly, children ran out of a yard and started a game on the sidewalk close by. One more house and—here! here it was. She must look at it—no, not look but with a North Star fixity, an arch-intelligence penetrate this solidity to the weightless, translucent structure of her dreams, where she still lived. Was it not recently she was sleeping again in her childhood bedroom—that very room there that gives with two windows onto the porch (on sleepless nights, she would imagine she saw a shadow on the window shades)—but instead of her sister, her youngest child was sleeping in the other bed.

She must touch this brick, which in her dream was curiously liquid and suffused with light, an acute material vibrant with the bright-condensed, symptomatic logic of the psyche. She pretended to drop something, moved closer to the house, and put one foot on the first step of that concrete staircase where her father had stood, hands over eyes, when he learned of the death of his mother 3,000 miles away; that staircase that had supported the still-less, sun-flickering aspen feet of childhood and a first pair of silk stockings as exotic and aromatic as perfumes and spices from the East; the staircase that like wise, metamorphosed fairy tales had been an intermediary between the patriarchal indoors and the measureless principles of the outer world, instilling incredible wisdom in childhood eyes.

But she was lingering too long. The children had stopped playing and were watching her. She smiled at them and continued down the block. And although she knew within days she would be here again in dream, she wept, weepless. She wept for the child that had been; she wept for the father that was dead. She wept for the far, nameless loneliness that had brought her here, that now returned with her on bus, on subway, on a train speeding 300 miles away.

## *The Woman in the Laundromat*

Fels, Non-Polluting Laundry Detergent, Clorox; three boxes of clothes—four o'clock; she would be here till six. One must dispose dry and efficiently with such chores, with long-accustomed economy of thought and movement. In fact, one must almost not be there; one must fight continually the gargantuan appetite of *domesticus,* which feeds on women's brains and energies; one must preserve oneself for—for this volume of poetry, for example, under fifty dirty socks.

Quickly, sort whites and colors; quickly, throw them into the impassive machine, which hopefully upon ingesting two quarters will set its metallic digestion in motion; soap, extra Clorox certain to clean—if calamitously—the clothes; and now, poetry.

"Good-by, Lorry," someone said. She looked up from her book at "Lorry." Lorry waved and continued an apparent arbitration before three stepladder children: Now it was Jane's turn; then it would be Diana's. She seemed good-hearted, fair; the children appeared healthy and reasonably, tumbingly smudged. She rose to insert a dime in the dryer. She was fleshy and vague like cells that had lost some long-ago motivation lapsing into shapelessness. A symptomatic incoherence rested unopposed upon her face, and the dandruff-specked jersey and lax gesture exuded an imminence of slovenliness. . . . Yes, she was a victim; something critical in her had been eaten up.

Of course, women succumbed in various ways. Many, strong-minded and organized, sated *domesticus* by assimilating it, making it not a means but an end. They, too, had been eaten, but they possessed purpose, method, a commendable intelligence.

But Lorry . . . one could imagine the sad, irredeemable succession of hours reduced only to straggly, deep-stained chores: dishes into the next meal; disorderly rooms still disorderly, recalling a first elan of housekeeping; the continual children—and spilt milk; if nothing else, the indomitable elemental dirt of existence: what shoes bring in; what clings to the pile of coats; hair! maddeningly omnipresent and unriddable; the vitality of pores! oils, sweat, even celestial acids from children's bodies—whole days, whole years of turbid domestic inundation, of nonmind; a gestalt sans concept, sans category, like a thick, sprawling, unsavory gravy.

It was a relief to look away from Lorry at the book of poetry, the precise fixing of thought, the neat divisions into stanzas. Almost half-past four: the clothes must still be put into dryers and then folded. Of course, folding must be quick, economical of concentration—if the four corners of sheets did not meet in all their multiples, what of it? If the king-size sheet were slightly bunched somewhere in its folds, it would be pressed in the linen closet, and besides, it would be on the bed in six days. After all, cleanliness was the first honesty. And given today's crease-resistance—more or less—even casual shirts and blouses folded hastily and pressed in bureaus sat reasonably well on the body—or in any case, the modern unstarched eye preferred a natural look. . . . If she folded this way, how would Lorry fold—or would she?

In fact, at this moment Lorry was folding clothes: a pillow case—she flapped it, then lengthwise corner to corner, laid it down, smoothed it, folded, another fold, smoothed—a perfect rectangle any mathematician could apply a compass to; other pillow cases; now sheets criminal to unfold for future use; children's blouses (destined for immediate crumpling and spilt milk), collars and sleeves professionally manipulated; and on the table a slow mounting of categories of clothes like axioms.

Lorry's face was absorbed, intent upon this act of structuring reality into clean, bright arrangements. The blank spaces and succumbed features of her face transmuted into a definition of person. Some potential in her inferred itself through the positive movements and unproblematic completion of each folding. Perhaps it responded to the soap-smelling cleanliness of the materials of this experience; perhaps it was grateful for a chore that implied the satisfactions of form; a definite beginning, a logic of procedure, finis and concomitant perception of achievement.

Accidentally, one of the children upset a stack, and although Lorry had almost finished and must remove the clothes into her laundry basket, she straightened the stack and patted down the collar.

## *Study questions*

1. *What image patterns and motifs tie together these separate scenes into an integrated whole?* 2. *What is the woman in the section called "Weltschmerz and the Boy" concerned about? the woman in "Return to the Childhood Locus"? the woman in "The Woman in the Laundromat"? Are these the same woman?* 3. *Who is the protagonist? What is the conflict?* 4. *Who is Lorry? What does she represent?* 5. *How does the style of this story function?*

*Robert Coover* (b. 1932), a novelist, playwright, and short-story writer, was born in Charles City, Iowa. He received his B.A. from Indiana University in 1953 and his M.A. from the University of Chicago in 1965. He has taught at Bard College, the University of Iowa, Wisconsin State University, Washington University at St. Louis, and Princeton University. His novel *The Origin of the Brunists* won the William Faulkner Award in 1966 as the best first novel of the year. Another novel, *The Universal Baseball Association, J. Henry Waugh, Prop.*, was published in 1968. A collection of stories, *Pricksongs & Descants*, followed in 1969. *A Theological Position*, a collection of four plays, was published in 1972; his novel *The Public Burning* followed in 1977. Acclaimed as one of the strongest and most original writers on the contemporary scene, Coover combines fantasy, romance, nightmare, and daydream in his stories and uses the fabulous to probe beyond sometimes humdrum surfaces. "The Babysitter" is a collage of events and fantasies that get all mixed up, if someone were rapidly switching channels on a television set.

## THE BABYSITTER

She arrives at 7:40, ten minutes late, but the children, Jimmy and Bitsy, are still eating supper, and their parents are not ready to go yet. From other rooms come the sounds of a baby screaming, water running, a television musical (no words: probably a dance number—patterns of gliding figures come to mind). Mrs. Tucker sweeps into the kitchen, fussing with her hair, and snatches a baby bottle full of milk out of a pan of warm water, rushes out again. "Harry!" she calls. "The babysitter's here already!"

That's My Desire? I'll Be Around? He smiles toothily, beckons faintly with his head, rubs his fast balding pate. Bewitched, maybe? Or, What's the Reason? He pulls on his shorts, gives his hips a slap. The baby goes silent in mid-scream. Isn't this the one who used their tub last time? Who's Sorry Now, that's it.

Jack is wandering around town, not knowing what to do. His girlfriend is babysitting at the Tuckers', and later, when she's got the kids in bed, maybe he'll drop over there. Sometimes he watches TV with her when she's babysitting, it's about the only chance he gets to make out a little since he doesn't own wheels, but they have to be careful because most people don't like their sitters to have boyfriends over. Just kissing her makes her nervous. She won't close her eyes because she has to be watching the door all the time. Married people really have it good, he thinks.

❂ ❂ ❂

"Hi," the babysitter says to the children, and puts her books on top of the refrigerator. "What's for supper?" The little girl, Bitsy, only stares at her obliquely. She joins them at the end of the kitchen table. "I don't have to go to bed until nine," the boy announces flatly, and stuffs his mouth full of potato chips. The babysitter catches a glimpse of Mr. Tucker hurrying out of the bathroom in his underwear.

❂ ❂ ❂

Her tummy. Under her arms. And her feet. Those are the best places. She'll spank him, she says sometimes. Let her.

❂ ❂ ❂

That sweet odor that girls have. The softness of her blouse. He catches a glimpse of the gentle shadows amid her thighs, as she curls her legs up under her. He stares hard at her. He has a lot of meaning packed into that stare, but she's not even looking. She's popping her gum and watching television. She's sitting right there, inches away, soft, fragrant, and ready: but what's his next move? He notices his buddy Mark in the drugstore, playing the pinball machine, and joins him. "Hey, this mama's cold, Jack baby! She needs your touch!"

❂ ❂ ❂

Mrs. Tucker appears at the kitchen doorway, holding a rolled-up diaper. "Now, don't just eat potato chips, Jimmy! See that he eats his hamburger, dear." She hurries away to the bathroom. The boy glares sullenly at the babysitter, silently daring her to carry out the order. "How about a little of that good hamburger now, Jimmy?" she say perfunctorily. He lets half of it drop to the floor. The baby is silent and a man is singing a love song on the TV. The children crunch chips.

❂ ❂ ❂

He loves her. She loves him. They whirl airily, stirring a light breeze, through a magical landscape of rose and emerald and deep blue. Her light brown hair coils and wisps softly in the breeze, and the soft folds of her white gown tug at her body and then float away. He smiles in a pulsing crescendo of sincerity and song.

"You mean she's alone?" Mark asks. "Well, there's two or three kids," Jack says. He slides the coin in. There's a rumble of steel balls tumbling, lining up. He pushes a plunger with his thumb, and one ball pops up in place, hard and glittering with promise. His stare? to say he loves her. That he cares for her and would protect her, would shield her, if need be, with his own body. Grinning, he bends over the ball to take careful aim: he and Mark have studied this machine and have it figured out, but still it's not that easy to beat.

❂ ❂ ❂

On the drive to the party, his mind is partly on the girl, partly on his own high-school days, long past. Sitting at the end of the kitchen table there with his children, she had seemed to be self-consciously arching her back, jutting her pert breasts, twitching her thighs: and for whom if not for him? So she'd seen him coming out of there, after all. He smiles. Yet what could he ever do about it? Those good times are gone, old man. He glances over at his wife, who, readjusting a garter, asks: "What do you think of our babysitter?"

❂ ❂ ❂

He loves her. She loves him. And then the babies come. And dirty diapers and one goddamn meal after another. Dishes. Noise. Clutter. And fat. Not just tight, her girdle actually hurts. Somewhere recently she's read about women getting heart attacks or cancer or something from too-tight girdles. Dolly pulls the car door shut with a grunt, strangely irritated, not knowing why. Party mood. Why is her husband humming, "Who's Sorry Now?" Pulling out of the drive, she glances back at the lighted kitchen window. "What do you think of our babysitter?" she asks. While her husband stumbles all over himself trying to answer, she pulls a stocking tight, biting deeper with the garters.

❂ ❂ ❂

"Stop it!" she laughs. Bitsy is pulling on her skirt and he is tickling her in the ribs. "Jimmy! Don't!" But she is laughing too much to stop him. He leaps on her, wrapping his legs around her waist, and they all fall to the carpet in front of the TV, where just now a man in a tuxedo and a little girl in a flouncy white dress are doing a tapdance together. The babysitter's blouse is pulling out of her skirt, showing a patch of bare tummy: the target. "I'll spank!"

❂ ❂ ❂

Jack pushes the plunger, thrusting up a steel ball, and bends studiously over the machine. "You getting any off her?" Mark asks, and clears his throat, flicks ash from his cigarette. "Well, not exactly, not yet," Jack says, grinning awkwardly, but trying to suggest more than he admits to, and fires. He heaves his weight gently against the machine as the ball bounds off a rubber bumper. He can feel her warming up under his hands, the flippers suddenly coming alive, delicate rapid-fire patterns emerging in the flashing of the lights. 1000 WHEN LIT: *now!* "Got my hand on it, that's about all." Mark glances up from the machine, cigarette dangling from his lip. "Maybe you need some help," he suggests with a wry one-sided grin. "Like maybe together, man, we could do it."

❀ ❀ ❀

She likes the big tub. She uses the Tuckers' bath salts, and loves to sink into the hot fragrant suds. She can stretch out, submerged, up to her chin. It gives her a good sleepy tingly feeling.

❀ ❀ ❀

"What do you think of our babysitter?" Dolly asks, adjusting a garter. "Oh, I hardly noticed," he says. "Cute girl. She seems to get along fine with the kids. Why?" "I don't know." His wife tugs her skirt down, glances at a lighted window they are passing, adding: "I'm not sure I trust her completely, that's all. With the baby, I mean. She seems a little careless. And the other time, I'm almost sure she had a boyfriend over." He grins, claps one hand on his wife's broad gartered thigh. "What's wrong with that?" he asks. Still in anklets, too. Bare thighs, no girdles, nothing up there but a flimsy pair of panties and soft adolescent flesh. He's flooded with vague remembrances of football rallies and movie balconies.

❀ ❀ ❀

How tiny and rubbery it is! she thinks, soaping between the boy's legs, giving him his bath. Just a funny jiggly little thing that looks like it shouldn't even be there at all. Is that what all the songs are about?

❀ ❀ ❀

Jack watches Mark lunge and twist against the machine. Got her running now, racking them up. He's not too excited about the idea of Mark fooling around with his girlfriend, but Mark's a cooler operator than he is, and maybe, doing it together this once, he'd get over his own timidity. And if she didn't like it, there were other girls around. If Mark went too far, he could cut him off, too. He feels his shoulders tense: enough's enough, man . . . but sees the flesh, too. "Maybe I'll call her later," he says.

❀ ❀ ❀

"Hey, Harry! Dolly! Glad you could make it!" "I hope we're not late." "No, no, you're one of the first, come on in! By golly, Dolly, you're looking younger every day! How do you do it? Give my wife your secret, will you?" He pats her on her girdled bottom behind Mr. Tucker's back, leads them in for drinks.

❀ ❀ ❀

8:00. The babysitter runs water in the tub, combs her hair in front of the bathroom mirror. There's a western on television, so she lets Jimmy watch it while she gives Bitsy her bath. But Bitsy doesn't want a bath. She's angry and crying because she has to be first. The babysitter tells her if she'll take her bath quickly, she'll let her watch television while Jimmy takes his bath, but it does no good. The little girl fights to get out of the bathroom, and the babysitter has to squat with her back against the door and forcibly undress the child. There are better places to babysit. Both children mind badly, and then, sooner or later, the baby is sure to wake up for a diaper change and more bottle. The Tuckers do have a good color TV, though, and she hopes things will be settled down enough to catch the 8:30 program. She thrusts the child into the tub, but she's still screaming and thrashing around. "Stop it now, Bitsy, or you'll wake the baby!" "I have to go potty!" the child wails, switching tactics. The babysitter sighs, lifts the girl out of the tub and onto the toilet, getting her skirt and blouse all wet in the process. She glances at herself in the mirror. Before she knows it, the girl is off the seat and out of the bathroom. "Bitsy! Come back here!"

❀ ❀ ❀

"Okay, that's enough!" Her skirt is ripped and she's flushed and crying. "Who says?" "I do, man!" The bastard goes for her, but he tackles him. They roll and tumble. Tables tip, lights topple, the TV crashes to the floor. He slams a hard right to the guy's gut, clips his chin with a rolling left.

❀ ❀ ❀

"We hope it's a girl." That's hardly surprising, since they already have four boys. Dolly congratulates the woman like everybody else, but she doesn't envy her, not a bit. That's all she needs about now. She stares across the room at Harry, who is slapping backs and getting loud, as usual. He's spreading out through the middle, so why the hell does he have to complain about her all the time? "Dolly, you're looking younger every day!" was the nice greeting she got tonight. "What's your secret?" And Harry: "It's all those calories. She's getting back her baby fat!" "Haw haw! Harry, have a heart!"

❀ ❀ ❀

"Get her feet!" he hollers at Bitsy, his fingers in her ribs, running over her naked tummy, tangling in the underbrush of straps and strange clothing. "Get her shoes off!" He holds her pinned by pressing his head against her soft chest.

"No! No, Jimmy! Bitsy, stop!" but though she kicks and twists and rolls around, she doesn't get up, she can't get up, she's laughing too hard, and the shoes come off, and he grabs a stockinged foot and scratches the sole ruthlessly, and she raises up her legs, trying to pitch him off, she's wild, boy, but he hangs on, and she's laughing, and on the screen there's a rattle of hooves, and he and Bitsy are rolling around and around on the floor in a crazy rodeo of long bucking legs.

❂ ❂ ❂

He slips the coin in. There's a metallic fall and a sharp click as the dial tone begins. "I hope the Tuckers have gone," he says. "Don't worry, they're at our place," Mark says. "They're always the first ones to come and the last ones to go home. My old man's always bitching about them." Jack laughs nervously and dials the number. "Tell her we're coming over to protect her from getting raped," Mark suggests, and lights a cigarette. Jack grins, leaning casually against the door jamb of the phonebooth, chewing gum, one hand in his pocket. He's really pretty uneasy, though. He has the feeling he's somehow messing up a good thing.

❂ ❂ ❂

Bitsy runs naked into the livingroom, keeping a hassock between herself and the babysitter. "Bitsy . . . !" the babysitter threatens. Artificial reds and greens and purples flicker over the child's wet body, as hooves clatter, guns crackle, and stagecoach wheels thunder over rutted terrain. "Get outa the way, Bitsy!" the boy complains. "I can't see!" Bitsy streaks past and the babysitter chases, cornering the girl in the back bedroom. Bitsy throws something that hits her softly in the face: a pair of men's undershorts. She grabs the girl scampering by, carries her struggling to the bathroom, and with a smart crack on her glistening bottom, pops her back into the tub. In spite, Bitsy peepees in the bathwater.

❂ ❂ ❂

Mr. Tucker stirs a little water into his bourbon and kids with his host and another man, just arrived, about their golf games. They set up a match for the weekend, a threesome looking for a fourth. Holding his drink in his right hand, Mr. Tucker swings his left through the motion of a tee-shot. "You'll have to give me a stroke a hole," he says. "I'll give you a stroke!" says his host: "Bend over!" Laughing, the other man asks: "Where's your boy Mark tonight?" "I don't know," replies the host, gathering up a trayful of drinks. Then he adds in a low growl: "Out chasing tail probably." They chuckle loosely at that, then shrug in commiseration and return to the livingroom to join their women.

❂ ❂ ❂

Shades pulled. Door locked. Watching the TV. Under a blanket maybe. Yes, that's right, under a blanket. Her eyes close when he kisses her. Her breasts, under both their hands, are soft and yielding.

A hard blow to the belly. The face. The dark beardy one staggers. The lean-jawed sheriff moves in, but gets a spurred boot in his face. The dark one hurls himself forward, drives his shoulder into the sheriff's hard midriff, her own tummy tightens, withstands, as the sheriff smashes the dark man's nose, slams him up against a wall, slugs him again! and again! The dark man grunts rhythmically, backs off, then plunges suicidally forward—her own knees draw up protectively—the sheriff staggers! caught low! but instead of following through, the other man steps back—a pistol! the dark one has a pistol! the sheriff draws! shoots from the hip! explosions! she clutches her hands between her thighs—no! the sheriff spins! wounded! the dark man hesitates, aims, her legs stiffen toward the set, the sheriff rolls desperately in the straw, fires: dead! the dark man is dead! groans, crumples, his pistol drooping in his collapsing hand, dropping, he drops. The sheriff, spent, nicked, watches weakly from the floor where he lies. Oh, to be whole! to be good and strong and right! to embrace and be embraced by harmony and wholeness! The sheriff, drawing himself painfully up on one elbow, rubs his bruised mouth with the back of his other hand.

"Well, we just sorta thought we'd drop over," he says, and winks broadly at Mark. "Who's we?" "Oh, me and Mark here." "Tell her, good thing like her, gotta pass it around," whispers Mark, dragging on his smoke, then flicking the butt over under the pinball machine. "What's that?" she asks. "Oh, Mark and I were just saying, like two's company, three's an orgy," Jack says, and winks again. She giggles. "Oh, Jack!" Behind her, he can hear shouts and gunfire. "Well, okay, for just a little while, if you'll both be good." Way to go, man.

Probably some damn kid over there right now. Wrestling around on the couch in front of his TV. Maybe he should drop back to the house. Just to check. None of that stuff, she was there to do a job! Park the car a couple doors down, slip in the front door before she knows it. He sees the disarray of clothing, the young thighs exposed to the flickering television light, hears his baby crying. "Hey, what's going on here! Get outa here, son, before I call the police!" Of course, they haven't really been doing anything. They probably don't even know how. He stares benignly down upon the girl, her skirt rumpled loosely around her thighs. Flushed, frightened, yet excited, she stares back at him. He smiles. His finger touches a knee, approaches the hem. Another couple arrives. Filling up here with people. He wouldn't be missed. Just slip out, stop back casually to pick up something or other he forgot, never mind what. He remembers that the other time they had this babysitter, she took a bath in their house. She had a date afterwards, and she'd just come from cheerleading practice or something. Aspirin maybe. Just drop quietly and casually into the bathroom to pick up some aspirin. "Oh, excuse me, dear! I only . . . !" She gazes back at him, astonished, yet strangely moved. Her soft wet breasts rise and fall in the water, and her tummy looks pale and ripply. He recalls that her pubic hairs, left in the tub, were brown. Light brown.

❁ ❁ ❁

She's no more than stepped into the tub for a quick bath, when Jimmy announces from outside the door that he has to go to the bathroom. She sighs: just an excuse, she knows. "You'll have to wait." The little nuisance. "I can't wait." "Okay, then come ahead, but I'm taking a bath." She supposes that will stop him, but it doesn't. In he comes. She slides down into the suds until she's eye-level with the edge of the tub. He hesitates. "Go ahead, if you have to," she says, a little awkwardly, "but I'm not getting out." "Don't look," he says. She: "I will if I want to."

❁ ❁ ❁

She's crying. Mark is rubbing his jaw where he's just slugged him. A lamp lies shattered. "Enough's enough, Mark! Now get outa here!" Her skirt is ripped to the waist, her bare hip bruised. Her panties lie on the floor like a broken balloon. Later, he'll wash her wounds, help her dress, he'll take care of her. Pity washes through him, giving him a sudden hard-on. Mark laughs at it, pointing. Jack crouches, waiting, ready for anything.

❁ ❁ ❁

Laughing, they roll and tumble. Their little hands are all over her, digging and pinching. She struggles to her hands and knees, but Bitsy leaps astride her neck, bowing her head to the carpet. "Spank her, Jimmy!" His swats sting: is her skirt up? The phone rings. "The cavalry to the rescue!" she laughs, and throws them off to go answer.

❁ ❁ ❁

Kissing Mark, her eyes closed, her hips nudge toward Jack. He stares at the TV screen, unsure of himself, one hand slipping cautiously under her skirt. Her hand touches his arm as though to resist, then brushes on by to rub his leg. This blanket they're under was a good idea. "Hi! This is Jack!"

❁ ❁ ❁

Bitsy's out and the water's running. "Come on, Jimmy, your turn!" Last time, he told her her took his own baths, but she came in anyway. "I'm not gonna take a bath," he announces, eyes glued on the set. He readies for the struggle. "But I've already run your water. Come on, Jimmy, please!" He shakes his head. She can't make him, he's sure he's as strong as she is. She sighs. "Well, it's up to you. I'll use the water myself then," she says. He waits until he's pretty sure she's not going to change her mind, then sneaks in and peeks through the keyhole in the bathroom door: just in time to see her big bottom as she bends over to stir in the bubblebath. Then she disappears. Trying to see as far down as the keyhole will allow, he bumps his head on the knob. "Jimmy, is that you?" "I—I have to go to the bathroom!" he stammers.

❂ ❂ ❂

Not actually in the tub, just getting in. One foot on the mat, the other in the water. Bent over slightly, buttocks flexed, teats swaying, holding on to the edge of the tub. "Oh, excuse me! I only wanted . . . !" He passes over her astonishment, the awkward excuses, moves quickly to the part where he reaches out to—"What on earth are you doing, Harry?" his wife asks, staring at his hand. His host, passing, laughs. "He's practicing his swing for Sunday, Dolly, but it's not going to do him a damn bit of good!" Mr. Tucker laughs, sweeps his right hand on through the air as though lifting a seven-iron shot onto the green. He makes a *dok!* sound with his tongue. "In there!"

❂ ❂ ❂

"No, Jack, I don't think you'd better." "Well, we just called, we just, uh, thought we'd, you know, stop by for a minute, watch television for thirty minutes, or, or something." "Who's we?" "Well, Mark's here, I'm with him, and he said he'd like to, you know, like if it's all right, just—" "Well, it's *not* all right. The Tuckers said no." "Yeah, but if we only—" "And they seemed awfully suspicious about last time." "Why? We didn't—I mean, I just thought—" "No, Jack, and that's period." She hangs up. She returns to the TV, but the commercial is on. Anyway, she's missed most of the show. She decides maybe she'll take a quick bath. Jack might come by anyway, it'd make her mad, that'd be the end as far as he was concerned, but if he should, she doesn't want to be all sweaty. And besides, she likes the big tub the Tuckers have.

❂ ❂ ❂

He is self-conscious and stands with his back to her, his little neck flushed. It takes him forever to get started, and when it finally does come, it's just a tiny trickle. "See, it was just an excuse," she scolds, but she's giggling inwardly at the boy's embarrassment. "You're just a nuisance, Jimmy." At the door, his hand on the knob, he hesitates, staring timidly down on his shoes. "Jimmy?" She peeks at him over the edge of the tub, trying to keep a straight face, as he sneaks a nervous glance back over his shoulder. "As long as you bothered me," she says, "you might as well soap my back."

❀ ❀ ❀

"The aspirin . . ." They embrace. She huddles in his arms like a child. Lovingly, paternally, knowledgeably, he wraps her nakedness. How compact, how tight and small her body is! Kissing her ear, he stares down past her rump at the still clear water. "I'll join you," he whispers hoarsely.

❀ ❀ ❀

She picks up the shorts Bitsy threw at her. Men's underwear. She holds them in front of her, looks at herself in the bedroom mirror. About twenty sizes too big for her, of course. She runs her hand inside the opening in front, pulls out her thumb. How funny it must feel!

❀ ❀ ❀

"Well, man, I say we just go rape her," Mark says flatly, and swings his weight against the pinball machine. "Uff! Ahh! Get in there, you mother! Look at that! Hah! Man, I'm gonna turn this baby over!" Jack is embarrassed about the phone conversation. Mark just snorted in digust when he hung up. He cracks down hard on his gum, angry that he's such a chicken. "Well, I'm game if you are," he says coldly.

❀ ❀ ❀

8:30. "Okay, come on, Jimmy, it's time." He ignores her. The western gives way to a spy show. Bitsy, in pajamas, pads into the livingroom. "No, Bitsy, it's time to go to bed." "You said I could watch!" the girl whines, and starts to throw another tantrum. "But you were too slow and it's late. Jimmy, you get in that bathroom, and right now!" Jimmy stares sullenly at the set, unmoving. The babysitter tries to catch the opening scene of the television program so she can follow it later, since Jimmy gives himself his own baths. When the commercial interrupts, she turns off the sound, stands in front of the screen. "Okay, into the tub, Jimmy Tucker, or I'll take you in there and give you your bath myself!" "Just try it," he says, "and see what happens."

❀ ❀ ❀

They stand outside, in the dark, crouched in the bushes, peeking in. She's on the floor, playing with the kids. Too early. They seem to be tickling her. She gets to her hands and knees, but the little girl leaps on her head, pressing her face to the floor. There's an obvious target, and the little boy proceeds to beat on it. "Hey, look at that kid go!" whispers Mark, laughing and snapping his fingers softly. Jack feels uneasy out here. Too many neighbors, too many cars going by, too many people in the world. That little boy in there is one up on him, though: he's never thought about tickling her as a starter.

❁ ❁ ❁

His little hand, clutching the bar of soap, lathers shyly a narrow space between her shoulderblades. She is doubled forward against her knees, buried in rich suds, peeking at him over the edge of her shoulder. The soap slithers out of his grip and plunks into the water. "I . . . I dropped the soap," he whispers. She: "Find it."

❁ ❁ ❁

"I dream of Jeannie with the light brown pubic hair!" "Harry! Stop that! You're drunk!" But they're laughing, they're all laughing, damn! he's feeling pretty goddamn good at that, and now he just knows he needs that aspirin. Watching her there, her thighs spread for him, on the couch, in the tub, hell, on the kitchen table for that matter, he tees off on Number Nine, and—*whap!*—swats his host's wife on the bottom. "Hole in one!" he shouts. "Harry!" Why can't his goddamn wife Dolly ever get happy-drunk instead of sour-drunk all the time? "Gonna be tough Sunday, old buddy!" "You're pretty tough right now, Harry," says his host.

❁ ❁ ❁

The babysitter lunges forward, grabs the boy by the arms and hauls him off the couch, pulling two cushions with him, and drags him toward the bathroom. He lashes out, knocking over an endtable full of magazines and ashtrays. "You leave my brother alone!" Bitsy cries and grabs the sitter around the waist. Jimmy jumps on her and down they all go. On the silent screen, there's a fade-in to a dark passageway in an old apartment building in some foreign country. She kicks out and somebody falls between her legs. Somebody else is sitting on her face. "Jimmy! Stop that!" the babysitter laughs, her voice muffled.

❁ ❁ ❁

She's watching television. All alone. It seems like a good time to go in. Just remember: really, no matter what she says, she wants it. They're standing in the bushes, trying to get up the nerve. "We'll tell her to be good," Mark whispers, "and if she's not good, we'll spank her." Jack giggles softly, but his knees are weak. She stands. They freeze. She looks right at them. "She can't see us," Mark whispers tensely. "Is she coming out?" "No," says Mark, "she's going into—that must be the bathroom!" Jack takes a deep breath, his heart pounding. "Hey, is there a window back there?" Mark asks.

❁ ❁ ❁

The phone rings. She leaves the tub, wrapped in a towel. Bitsy gives a tug on the towel. "Hey, Jimmy, get the towel!" she squeals. "Now stop that, Bitsy!" the babysitter hisses, but too late: with one hand on the phone, the other isn't enough to hang on to the towel. Her sudden nakedness awes them and it takes them a moment to remember about tickling her. By then, she's in the towel again. "I hope you got a good look," she says angrily. She feels chilled and oddly a little frightened. "Hello?" No answer. She glances at the window—is somebody out there? Something, she saw something, and a rustling—footsteps?

❂ ❂ ❂

"Okay, I don't care, Jimmy, don't take a bath," she says irritably. Her blouse is pulled out and wrinkled, her hair is all mussed, and she feels sweaty. There's about a million things she'd rather be doing than babysitting with these two. Three: at least the baby's sleeping. She knocks on the overturned endtable for luck, rights it, replaces the magazines and ashtrays. The one thing that really makes her sick is a dirty diaper. "Just go on to bed." "I don't have to go to bed until nine," he reminds her. Really, she couldn't care less. She turns up the volume on the TV, settles down on the couch, poking her blouse back into her skirt, pushing her hair out of her eyes. Jimmy and Bitsy watch from the floor. Maybe, once they're in bed, she'll take a quick bath. She wishes Jack would come by. The man, no doubt the spy, is following a woman, but she doesn't know why. The woman passes another man. Something seems to happen, but it's not clear what. She's probably already missed too much. The phone rings.

❂ ❂ ❂

Mark is kissing her. Jack is under the blanket, easing her panties down over her squirming hips. Her hand is in his pants, pulling it out, pulling it toward her, pulling it hard. She knew just where it was! Mark is stripping, too. God, it's really happening! he thinks with a kind of pious joy, and notices the open door. "Hey! What's going on here?"

❂ ❂ ❂

He soaps her back, smooth and slippery under his hand. She is doubled over, against her knees, between his legs. Her light brown hair, reaching to her gleaming shoulders, is wet at the edges. The soap slips, falls between his legs. He fishes for it, finds it, slips it behind him. "Help me find it," he whispers in her ear. "Sure Harry," says his host, going around behind him. "What'd you lose?"

❂ ❂ ❂

Soon be nine, time to pack the kids off to bed. She clears the table, dumps paper plates and leftover hamburgers into the garbage, puts glasses and silverware into the sink, and the mayonnaise, mustard, and ketchup in the refrigerator. Neither child has eaten much supper finally, mostly potato chips and ice cream, but it's really not her problem. She glances at the books on the refrigerator. Not much chance she'll get to them, she's already pretty worn out. Maybe she'd feel better if she had a quick bath. She runs water into the tub, tosses in bubblebath salts, undresses. Before pushing down her panties, she stares for a moment at the smooth silken panel across her tummy, fingers the place where the opening would be if there were one. Then she steps quickly out of them, feeling somehow ashamed, unhooks her brassiere. She weighs her breasts in the palms of her hands, watching herself in the bathroom mirror, where, in the open window behind her, she sees a face. She screams.

❀ ❀ ❀

She screams: "Jimmy! Give me that!" "What's the matter?" asks Jack on the other end. "Jimmy! Give me my towel! Right now!" "Hello? Hey, are you still there?" "I'm sorry, Jack," she says, panting. "You caught me in the tub. I'm just wrapped in a towel and these silly kids grabbed it away!" "Gee, I wish I'd been there!" "Jack!—!" "To protect you, I mean." "Oh, sure," she says, giggling. "Well, what do you think, can I come over and watch TV with you?" "Well, not right this minute," she says. He laughs lightly. He feels very cool. "Jack?" "Yeah?" "Jack, I . . . I think there's somebody outside the window!"

❀ ❀ ❀

She carries him, fighting all the way, to the tub, Bitsy pummeling her in the back and kicking her ankles. She can't hang on to him and undress him at the same time. "I'll throw you in, clothes and all, Jimmy Tucker!" she gasps. "You better not!" he cries. She sits on the toilet seat, locks her legs around him, whips his shirt up over his head before he knows what's happening. The pants are easier. Like all little boys his age, he has almost no hips at all. He hangs on desperately to his underpants, but when she succeeds in snapping these down out of his grip, too, he gives up, starts to bawl, and beats her wildly in the face with his fists. She ducks her head, laughing hysterically, oddly entranced by the spectacle of that pale little thing down there, bobbing and bouncing rubberily about with the boy's helpless fury and anguish.

❀ ❀ ❀

"Aspirin? Whaddaya want aspirin for, Harry? I'm sure they got aspirin here, if you—" "Did I say aspirin? I meant, uh, my glasses. And, you know, I thought, well, I'd sorta check to see if everything was okay at home." Why the hell is it his mouth feels like it's got about six sets of teeth packed in there, and a tongue the size of that liverwurst his host's wife is passing around? "Whaddaya want your glasses for, Harry? I don't understand you at all!" "Aw, well, honey, I was feeling kind of dizzy or something, and I thought—" "Dizzy is right. If you want to check on the kids, why don't you just call on the phone?"

❀ ❀ ❀

They can tell she's naked and about to get into the tub, but the bathroom window is frosted glass, and they can't see anything clearly. "I got an idea," Mark whispers. "One of us goes and calls her on the phone, and the other watches when she comes out." "Okay, but who calls?" "Both of us, we'll do it twice. Or more."

❂ ❂ ❂

Down forbidden alleys. Into secret passageways. Unlocking the world's terrible secrets. Sudden shocks: a trapdoor! a fall! or the stunning report of a rifle shot, the *whaaii-ii-iing!* of the bullet biting concrete by your ear! Careful! Then edge forward once more, avoiding the light, inch at a time, now a quick dash for an open doorway—*look out!* there's a knife! a struggle! no! the long blade glistens! jerks! thrusts! *stabbed!* No, no, it missed! The assailant's down, yes! the spy's on top, pinning him, a terrific thrashing about, the spy rips off the assailant's mask: *a woman!*

❂ ❂ ❂

Fumbling behind her, she finds it, wraps her hand around it, tugs. "Oh!" she gasps, pulling her hand back quickly, her ears turning crimson. "I . . . I thought it was the soap!" He squeezes her close between his thighs, pulls her back toward him, one hand sliding down her tummy between her legs. I Dream of Jeannie—"I have to go to the bathroom!" says someone outside the door.

❂ ❂ ❂

She's combing her hair in the bathroom when the phone rings. She hurries to answer it before it wakes the baby. "Hello, Tuckers." There's no answer. "Hello?" A soft click. Strange. She feels suddenly alone in the big house, and goes in to watch TV with the children.

❂ ❂ ❂

"Stop it!" she screams. "Please, stop!" She's on her hands and knees, trying to get up, but they're too strong for her. Mark holds her head down. "Now, baby, we're gonna teach you how to be a nice girl," he says coldly, and nods at Jack. When she's doubled over like that, her skirt rides up her thighs to the leg bands of her panties. "C'mon, man, go! This baby's cold! She needs your touch!"

❂ ❂ ❂

Parks the car a couple blocks away. Slips up to the house, glances in his window. Just like he's expected. Her blouse is off and the kid's shirt is unbuttoned. He watches, while slowly, clumsily, childishly, they fumble with each other's clothes. My God, it takes them forever. "Some party!" "You said it!" When they're more or less naked, he walks in. "Hey! What's going on here?"

They go white as bleu cheese. Haw haw! "What's the little thing you got sticking out there, boy?" "Harry, behave yourself!" No, he doesn't let the kid get dressed, he sends him home bareassed. "Bareassed!" He drinks to that. "Promises, promises," says his host's wife. "I'll mail you your clothes, son!" He gazes down on the naked little girl on his couch. "Looks like you and me, we got a little secret to keep, honey," he says coolly. "Less you wanna go home the same way your boyfriend did!" He chuckles at his easy wit, leans down over her, and unbuckles his belt. "Might as well make it two secrets, right?" "What in God's name are you talking about, Harry?" He staggers out of there, drink in hand, and goes to look for his car.

❀ ❀ ❀

"Hey! What's going on here?" They huddle half-naked under the blanket, caught utterly unawares. On television: the clickety-click of frightened running feet on foreign pavements. Jack is fumbling for his shorts, tangled somehow around his ankles. The blanket is snatched away. "On your feet there!" Mr. Tucker, Mrs. Tucker, Mark's mom and dad, the police, the neighbors, everybody comes crowding in. Hopelessly, he has a terrific erection. So hard it hurts. Everybody stares down at it.

❀ ❀ ❀

Bitsy's sleeping on the floor. The babysitter is taking a bath. For more than an hour now, he's had to use the bathroom. He doesn't know how much longer he can wait. Finally, he goes to knock on the bathroom door. "I have to use the bathroom." "Well, come ahead, if you have to." "Not while you're in there." She sighs loudly. "Okay, okay, just a minute," she says, "but you're a real nuisance, Jimmy!" He's holding on, pinching it as tight as he can. "*Hurry!*" He holds his breath, squeezing shut his eyes. No. Too late. At last, she opens the door. "Jimmy!" "I *told* you to hurry!" he sobs. She drags him into the bathroom and pulls his pants down.

❀ ❀ ❀

He arrives just in time to see her emerge from the bathroom, wrapped in a towel, to answer the phone. His two kids sneak up behind her and pull the towel away. She's trying to hang onto the phone and get the towel back at the same time. It's quite a picture. She's got a sweet ass. Standing there in the bushes, pawing himself with one hand, he lifts his glass with the other and toasts her sweet ass, which his son now swats. Haw haw, maybe that boy's gonna shape up, after all.

❀ ❀ ❀

They're in the bushes, arguing about their next move, when she comes out of the bathroom, wrapped in a towel. They can hear the baby crying. Then it stops. They see her running, naked, back to the bathroom like she's scared or something. "I'm going in after her, man, whether you're with me or not!" Mark whispers, and he starts out of the bushes. But just then, a light comes sweeping up through the yard, as a car swings in the drive. They hit the dirt, hearts pounding. "Is it the cops?" "I don't know!" "Do you think they saw us?" "Sshh!" A man comes staggering up the walk from the drive, a drink in his hand, stumbles on in the kitchen door and then straight into the bathroom. "It's Mr. Tucker!" Mark whispers. A scream. "Let's get outa here, man!"

❁ ❁ ❁

9:00. Having missed most of the spy show anyway and having little else to do, the babysitter has washed the dishes and cleaned the kitchen up a little. The books on the refrigerator remind her of her better intentions, but she decides that first she'll see what's next on TV. In the livingroom, she finds little Bitsy sound asleep on the floor. She lifts her gently, carries her into her bed, and tucks her in. "Okay, Jimmy, it's nine o'clock, I've let you stay up, now be a good boy." Sullenly, his sleepy eyes glued still to the set, the boy backs out of the room toward his bedroom. A drama comes on. She switches channels. A ballgame and a murder mystery. She switches back to the drama. It's a love story of some kind. A man married to an aging invalid wife, but in love with a younger girl. "Use the bathroom and brush your teeth before going to bed, Jimmy!" she calls, but as quickly regrets it, for she hears the baby stir in its crib.

❁ ❁ ❁

Two of them are talking about mothers they've salted away in rest homes. Oh boy, that's just wonderful, this is one helluva party. She leaves them to use the john, takes advantage of the retreat to ease her girdle down awhile, get a few good deep breaths. She has this picture of her three kids carting her off to a rest home. In a wheelbarrow. That sure is something to look forward to, all right. When she pulls her girdle back up, she can't seem to squeeze into it. The host looks in. "Hey, Dolly, are you all right?" "Yeah, I just can't get into my damn girdle, that's all." "Here, let me help."

❁ ❁ ❁

She pulls them on, over her own, standing in front of the bedroom mirror, holding her skirt bundled up around the waist. About twenty sizes too big for her, of course. She pulls them tight from behind, runs her hand inside the opening in front, pulls out her thumb. "And what a good boy am I!" She giggles: how funny it must feel! Then, in the mirror, she sees him: in the doorway behind her, sullenly watching. "Jimmy! You're supposed to be in bed!" "Those are my daddy's!" the boy says. "I'm gonna tell!"

❁ ❁ ❁

"Jimmy!" She drags him into the bathroom and pulls his pants down. "Even your shoes are wet! Get them off!" She soaps up a warm washcloth she's had with her in the bathtub, scrubs him from the waist down with it. Bitsy stands in the doorway, staring. "Get out! Get out!" the boy screams at his sister. "Go back to bed, Bitsy. It's just an accident." "Get out!" The baby wakes and starts to howl.

❂ ❂ ❂

The young lover feels sorry for her rival, the invalid wife; she believes the man has a duty toward the poor woman and insists she is willing to wait. But the man argues that he also has a duty toward himself: his life, too, is short, and he could not love his wife now even were she well. He embraces the young girl feverishly; she twists away in anguish. The door opens. They stand there grinning, looking devilish, but pretty silly at the same time. "Jack! I thought I told you not to come!" She's angry, but she's also glad in a way: she was beginning to feel a little too alone in the big house, with the children all sleeping. She should have taken that bath, after all. "We just came by to see if you were being a good girl," Jack says and blushes. The boys glance at each other nervously.

❂ ❂ ❂

She's just sunk down into the tubful of warm fragrant suds, ready for a nice long soaking, when the phone rings. Wrapping a towel around her, she goes to answer: no one there. But now the baby's awake and bawling. She wonders if that's Jack bothering her all the time. If it is, brother, that's the end. Maybe it's the end anyway. She tries to calm the baby with the half-empty bottle, not wanting to change it until she's finished her bath. The bathroom's where the diapers go dirty, and they make it stink to high heaven. "Shush, shush!" she whispers, rocking the crib. The towel slips away, leaving an airy empty tingle up and down her backside. Even before she stoops for the towel, even before she turns around, she knows there's somebody behind her.

❂ ❂ ❂

"We just came by to see if you were being a good girl," Jack says, grinning down at her. She's flushed and silent, her mouth half open. "Lean over," says Mark amiably. "We'll soap your back, as long as we're here." But she just huddles there, down in the suds, staring up at them with big eyes.

❂ ❂ ❂

"Hey! What's going on here?" It's Mr. Tucker, stumbling through the door with a drink in his hand. She looks up from the TV. "What's the matter, Mr. Tucker?" "Oh, uh, I'm sorry, I got lost—no, I mean, I had to get some aspirin.

Excuse me!" And he rushes past her into the bathroom, caroming off the living-room door jamb on the way. The baby wakes.

❂ ❂ ❂

"Okay, get off her, Mr. Tucker!" "Jack!" she cries, "what are *you* doing here?" He stares hard at them a moment: so that's where it goes. Then, as Mr. Tucker swings heavily off, he leans into the bastard with a hard right to the belly. Next thing he knows, though, he's got a face full of an old man's fist. He's not sure, as the lights go out, if that's his girlfriend screaming or the baby . . .

❂ ❂ ❂

Her host pushes down on her fat fanny and tugs with all his might on her girdle, while she bawls on his shoulder: "I don't *wanna* go to a rest home!" "Now, now, take it easy, Dolly, nobody's gonna make you—" "Ouch! Hey, you're hurting!" "You should buy a bigger girdle, Dolly." "You're telling me?" Some other guy pokes his head in. "Whatsamatter? Dolly fall in?" "No, she fell out. Give me a hand."

❂ ❂ ❂

By the time she's chased Jack and Mark out of there, she's lost track of the program she's been watching on television. There's another woman in the story now for some reason. That guy lives a very complicated life. Impatiently, she switches channels. She hates ball-games, so she settles for the murder mystery. She switches just in time, too: there's a dead man sprawled out on the floor of what looks like an office or a study or something. A heavyset detective gazes up from his crouch over the body: "He's been strangled." Maybe she'll take that bath, after all.

❂ ❂ ❂

She drags him into the bathroom and pulls his pants down. She soaps up a warm washcloth she's had in the tub with her, but just as she reaches between his legs, it starts to spurt, spraying her arms and hands. "Oh, Jimmy! I thought you were done!" she cries, pulling him toward the toilet and aiming it into the bowl. How moist and rubbery it is! And you can turn it every which way. How funny it must feel!

❂ ❂ ❂

"Stop it!" she screams. "Please stop!" She's on her hands and knees and Jack is holding her head down. "Now we're gonna teach you how to be a nice girl," Mark says and lifts her skirt. "Well, I'll be damned!" "What's the matter?"

asks Jack, his heart pounding. "Look at this big pair of men's underpants she's got on!" "Those are my daddy's!" says Jimmy, watching them from the doorway. "I'm gonna tell!"

❂ ❂ ❂

People are shooting at each other in the murder mystery, but she's so mixed up, she doesn't know which ones are the good guys. She switches back to the love story. Something seems to have happened, because now the man is kissing his invalid wife tenderly. Maybe she's finally dying. The baby wakes, begins to scream. Let it. She turns up the volume on the TV.

❂ ❂ ❂

Leaning down over her, unbuckling his belt. It's all happening just like he's known it would. Beautiful! The kid is gone, though his pants, poor lad, remain. "Looks like you and me, we got a secret to keep, child!" But he's cramped on the couch and everything is too slippery and small. "Lift your legs up, honey. Put them around my back." But instead, she screams. He rolls off, crashing to the floor. There they all come, through the front door. On television, somebody is saying: "Am I a burden to you, darling?" "Dolly! My God! Dolly, I can explain . . . !"

❂ ❂ ❂

The game of the night is Get Dolly Tucker Back in Her Girdle Again. They've got her down on her belly in the livingroom and the whole damn crowd is working on her. Several of them are stretching the girdle, while others try to jam the fat inside. "I think we made a couple inches on this side! Roll her over!" Harry?

❂ ❂ ❂

She's just stepped into the tub, when the phone rings, waking the baby. She sinks down in the suds, trying not to hear. But that baby doesn't cry, it screams. Angrily, she wraps a towel around herself, stamps peevishly into the baby's room, just letting the phone jangle. She tosses the baby down on its back, unpins its diaper hastily, and gets yellowish baby stool all over her hands. Her towel drops away. She turns to find Jimmy staring at her like a little idiot. She slaps him in the face with her dirty hand, while the baby screams, the phone rings, and nagging voices argue on the TV. There are better things she might be doing.

❂ ❂ ❂

What's happening? Now there's a young guy in it. Is he after the young girl or the old invalid? To tell the truth, it looks like he's after the same man the women are. In disgust, she switches channels. "The strangler again," growls the fat detective, hands on hips, staring down at the body of a half-naked girl. She's considering either switching back to the love story or taking a quick bath, when a hand suddenly clutches her mouth.

❂ ❂ ❂

"You're both chicken," she says, staring up at them. "But what if Mr. Tucker comes home?" Mark asks nervously.

❂ ❂ ❂

How did he get here? He's standing pissing in his own goddamn bathroom, his wife is still back at the party, the three of them are, like good kids, sitting in there in the livingroom watching TV. One of them is his host's boy Mark. "It's a good murder mystery, Mr. Tucker," Mark said, when he came staggering in on them a minute ago. "Sit still!" he shouted, "I'm just home for a moment!" Then whump thump on into the bathroom. Long hike for a weewee, Mister. But something keeps bothering him. Then it hits him: the girl's panties, hanging like a broken balloon from the rabbit-ear antennae on the TV! He barges back in there, giving his shoulder a helluva crack on the livingroom door jamb on the way—but they're not hanging there any more. Maybe he's only imagined it. "Hey, Mr. Tucker," Mark says flatly. "Your fly's open."

❂ ❂ ❂

The baby's dirty. Stinks to high heaven. She hurries back to the livingroom, hearing sirens and gunshots. The detective is crouched outside a house, peering in. Already, she's completely lost. The baby screams at the top of its lungs. She turns up the volume. But it's all confused. She hurries back in there, claps an angry hand to the baby's mouth. "Shut up!" she cries. She throws the baby down on its back, starts to unpin the diaper, as the baby tunes up again. The phone rings. She answers it, one eye on the TV. *"What?"* The baby cries so hard it starts to choke. Let it. "I said, hi, this is Jack!" Then it hits her: oh no! the diaper pin!

❂ ❂ ❂

"The aspirin . . ." But she's already in the tub. Way down in the tub. Staring at him through the water. Her tummy looks pale and ripply. He hears sirens, people on the porch.

❂ ❂ ❂

Jimmy gets up to go to the bathroom and gets his face slapped and smeared with baby poop. Then she hauls him off to the bathroom, yanks off his pajamas, and throws him into the tub. That's okay, but next she gets naked and acts like she's gonna get in the tub, too. The baby's screaming and the phone's ringing like crazy and in walks his dad. Saved! he thinks, but, no, his dad grabs him right back out of the tub and whales the dickens out of him, no questions asked, while she watches, then sends him—*whack!*—back to bed. So he's lying there, wet and dirty and naked and sore, and he still has to go to the bathroom, and outside his window he hears two older guys talking. "Listen, you know where to do it if we get her pinned?" "No! Don't you?"

❁ ❁ ❁

"Yo ho heave ho! *Ugh!*" Dolly's on her back and they're working on the belly side. Somebody got the great idea of buttering her down first. Not to lose the ground they've gained, they've shot it inside with a basting syringe. But now suddenly there's this big tug-of-war under way between those who want to stuff her in and those who want to let her out. Something rips, but she feels better. The odor of hot butter makes her think of movie theaters and popcorn. "Hey, has anybody seen Harry?" she asks. "Where's Harry?"

❁ ❁ ❁

Somebody's getting chased. She switches back to the love story, and now the man's back kissing the young lover again. What's going on? She gives it up, decides to take a quick bath. She's just stepping into the tub, one foot in, one foot out, when Mr. Tucker walks in. "Oh, excuse me! I only wanted some aspirin . . ." She grabs for a towel, but he yanks it away. "Now, that's not how it's supposed to happen, child," he scolds. "Please! Mr. Tucker . . . !" He embraces her savagely, his calloused old hands clutching roughly at her backside. "Mr. Tucker!" she cries, squirming. "Your wife called—!" He's pushing something between her legs, hurting her. She slips, they both slip—something cold and hard slams her in the back, cracks her skull, she seems to be sinking into a sea . . .

❁ ❁ ❁

They've got her over the hassock, skirt up and pants down. "Give her a little lesson there, Jack baby!" The television lights flicker and flash over her glossy flesh. 1000 WHEN LIT. Whack! Slap! Bumper to bumper! He leans into her, feeling her come alive.

❁ ❁ ❁

The phone rings, waking the baby. "Jack, is that you? Now, you listen to me—!" "No, dear, this is Mrs. Tucker. Isn't the TV awfully loud?" "Oh, I'm sorry, Mrs. Tucker! I've been getting—" "I tried to call you before, but I couldn't hang on. To the phone, I mean. I'm sorry, dear." "Just a minute, Mrs. Tucker, the baby's—" "Honey, listen! Is Harry there? Is Mr. Tucker there, dear?"

❁ ❁ ❁

"Stop it!" she screams and claps a hand over the baby's mouth. "Stop it! Stop it! *Stop it!*" Her other hand is full of baby stool and she's afraid she's going to be sick. The phone rings. "No!" she cries. She's hanging on to the baby, leaning woozily away, listening to the phone ring. "Okay, okay," she sighs, getting ahold of herself. But when she lets go of the baby, it isn't screaming any more. She shakes it. Oh no . . .

❂ ❂ ❂

"Hello?" No answer. Strange. She hangs up and, wrapped only in a towel, stares out the window at the cold face staring in—she screams!

❂ ❂ ❂

She screams, scaring the hell out of him. He leaps out of the tub, glances up at the window she's gaping at just in time to see two faces duck away, then slips on the bathroom tiles, and crashes to his ass, whacking his head on the sink on the way down. She stares down at him, trembling, a towel over her narrow shoulders. "Mr. Tucker! Mr. Tucker, are you all right . . . ?" Who's Sorry Now? Yessir, who's back is breaking with each . . . He stares up at the little tufted locus of all his woes, and passes out, dreaming of Jeannie . . .

❂ ❂ ❂

The phone rings. "Dolly! It's for you!" "Hello?" "Hello, Mrs. Tucker?" "Yes, speaking." "Mrs. Tucker, this is the police calling . . ."

❂ ❂ ❂

It's cramped and awkward and slippery, but he's pretty sure he got it in her, once anyway. When he gets the suds out of his eyes, he sees her staring up at them. Through the water. "Hey, Mark! Let her up!"

❂ ❂ ❂

Down in the suds. Feeling sleepy. The phone rings, startling her. Wrapped in a towel, she goes to answer. "No, he's not here, Mrs. Tucker." Strange. Married people act pretty funny sometimes. The baby is awake and screaming. Dirty, a real mess. Oh boy, there's a lot of things she'd rather be doing than babysitting in this madhouse. She decides to wash the baby off in her own bathwater. She removes her towel, unplugs the tub, lowers the water level so the baby can sit. Glancing back over her shoulder, she sees Jimmy staring at her. "Go back to bed, Jimmy." "I have to go to the bathroom." "Good grief, Jimmy! It looks like you already have!" The phone rings. She doesn't bother with the towel—what can Jimmy see he hasn't already seen?—and goes to answer. "No, Jack, and that's final." Sirens, on the TV, as the police move in. But wasn't that the channel with the love story? Ambulance maybe. Get this over with so she can at least catch the news. "Get those wet pajamas off, Jimmy, and I'll find clean ones. Maybe you better get in the tub, too." "I think something's wrong with the baby," he says. "It's down in the water and it's not swimming or anything."

❁ ❁ ❁

She's staring up at them from the rug. They slap her. Nothing happens. "You just tilted her, man!" Mark says softly. "We gotta get outa here!" Two little kids are standing wide-eyed in the doorway. Mark looks hard at Jack. "No, Mark, they're just little kids . . . !" "We gotta, man, or we're dead."

❁ ❁ ❁

"Dolly! My God! Dolly, I can explain!" She glowers down at them, her ripped girdle around her ankles. "What the four of you are doing in the bathtub with *my* babysitter?" she says sourly. "I can hardly wait!"

❁ ❁ ❁

Police sirens wail, lights flash. "I heard the scream!" somebody shouts. "There were two boys!" "I saw a man!" "She was running with the baby!" "My God!" somebody screams, "they're *all* dead!" Crowds come running. Spotlights probe the bushes.

❁ ❁ ❁

"Harry, where the hell you been?" his wife whines, glaring blearily up at him from the carpet. "I can explain," he says. "Hey, whatsamatter, Harry?" his host asks, smeared with butter for some goddamn reason. "You look like you just seen a ghost!" Where did he leave his drink? Everybody's laughing, everybody except Dolly, whose cheeks are streaked with tears. "Hey, Harry, you won't let them take me to a rest home, will you, Harry?"

❁ ❁ ❁

10:00. The dishes done, children to bed, her books read, she watches the news on television. Sleepy. The man's voice is gentle, soothing. She dozes—awakes with a start: a babysitter? Did the announcer say something about a babysitter?

❁ ❁ ❁

"Just want to catch the weather," the host says, switching on the TV. Most of the guests are leaving, but the Tuckers stay to watch the news. As it comes on, the announcer is saying something about a babysitter. The host switches channels. "They got a better weatherman on four," he explains. "Wait!" says Mrs. Tucker. "There was something about a babysitter . . . !" The host switches back. "Details have not yet been released by the police," the announcer says. "Harry, maybe we'd better go . . ."

They stroll casually out of the drugstore, run into a buddy of theirs. "Hey! Did you hear about the babysitter?" the guy asks. Mark grunts, glances at Jack. "Got a smoke?" he asks the guy.

"I think I hear the baby screaming!" Mrs. Tucker cries, running across the lawn from the drive.

She wakes, startled, to find Mr. Tucker hovering over her. "I must have dozed off!" she exclaims. "Did you hear the news about the babysitter?" Mrs. Tucker asks. "Part of it," she says, rising. "Too bad, wasn't it?" Mr. Tucker is watching the report of the ball scores and golf tournaments. "I'll drive you home in just a minute, dear," he says. "Why, how nice!" Mrs. Tucker exclaims from the kitchen. "The dishes are all done!"

"What can I say, Dolly?" the host says with a sigh, twisting the buttered strands of her ripped girdle between his fingers. "Your children are murdered, your husband gone, a corpse in your bathtub, and your house is wrecked. I'm sorry. But what can I say?" On the TV, the news is over, and they're selling aspirin. "Hell, *I* don't know," she says. "Let's see what's on the late late movie."

## *Study questions*

1. *Line up the various characters by means of what they are doing and where they are. Who are the major characters whose actions we follow and fantasies we enter into?* 2. *At what point in the story does it become difficult to separate action from fantasy and to assign characters to various actions and fantasies?* 3. *How is television related to the actions and fantasies?* 4. *What can we learn about ourselves from television programming?* 5. *Who is the protagonist in this story? Before you answer this question you may need to determine what the major conflict is as it is similar to or different from the separate conflicts of individual characters.*

*Ronald Sukenick* (b. 1932), born in Brooklyn, New York, received his B.A. from Cornell University in 1955, his M.A. from Brandeis University in 1957, and his Ph.D. from Brandeis in 1962. He has taught at Sarah Lawrence College, at Cornell, and at the University of California at Irvine. His publications include a scholarly work, *Wallace Stevens: Musing the Obscure* (1967), a novel, *Up* (1968), and a collection of stories, *The Death of the Novel and Other Stories* (1969). From this collection, "The Birds" is a poetic collage of images, recurrent motifs, realistic episodes based on factual accounts, and fantastic events based in fictional modes, arranged to suggest chance encounters. At the same time, it is a piece of metafiction, attempting to be itself what the narrator conceives is the function of art as a way of knowing. About the sounds of the birds, the narrator comments: "But then again, what does it matter what they say? What matters is that they carve shapes from nothingness, decorate the silence, make melodious distinctions to distinguish one moment finely from the next."

## THE BIRDS

The the the

Nuthatch walks up the tree a Prussian soldier pivots walks back down

birds

the

Nuthatch slick arctic acrobat seal bullets through blank air silence of page the stream carries mainly on its glassy surface rippled clouds inventing themselves from minutes to minute toss in a stone

The the I want to tell you the story about "ear-tree." It was on Icelandic that eighteen-hour flight from Luxemburg where your feet swell up. We cruised among fantastic shapes, formations piling shifting flowing, distortions of distortions of distortions at all altitudes. The plane skimmed across a kind of ocean of streaming transformations, the wings clipped white tumuli, and on the actual ocean waves were ripples were wrinkles, viscid metal crawling across the earth, the land itself a slower lava, somewhat thicker, especially that of Iceland, where that was what it was. I was looking out over the wing as I watched a wisp of white blew back from the engine, then another, another, and after a pause, a band of grey I looked up the aisle for the stewardess when I looked back the smoke was roiling from the engine a greasy black plume with suddenly red at its root . . .

Wings pulled in it allowed itself to fall, a stroke of scarlet from green to green.

It began in '62 a Chinese restaurant naturally midtown I remember very well because that was the phase when I had a thing with fortune cookies I am always interested in any overt confrontation

with chance though if you stop to think about it every moment is such a confrontation for each of us as likely to provide the cue for something tasty an

adventure something other than sex a coincidence in any case one was tired of sex I mean of thinking about it preferably a

coincidence such things renew my faith in the unknown however the fortune merely said, "You will soon plan another oriental meal" but that wasn't the interesting thing.

Corrosive chatter. Starlings are a bore, despite iridescences. They're too precocious, and have no intelligence. "We put the snake live into the freezer it was at least two feet long and when we took it out it was frozen into this really interesting shape stiff as a board but then we hung it up and it began to smell. What ever happened to Phillip Morris? And mockies? There always used to be a lot of mockies. I had an aunt who always used to smoke Phillip Morris. She got lung cancer though. She was a mockie. She's dead now. I guess that's what happens to them."

The Yellow-shafted Flicker appears around April. The male has a black "mustache." Its strange laugh haunts the woods but seems to be a courtship cry. Lovemaking involves reciprocal undulations of the long necks like oriental dancers. The underwing is an astonishing pink-gold. Note the pure white rump in flight.

The dress was made of clinging white nylon jersey of a thinness that in certain angles of light would outline the thighs or reveal the curve of a breast and which, when taut against the skin, assumed something of the warm flesh tone. The loose ankle-length curtain of skirt was slit at the side to the top of the thigh. The backless halter scooped down to the point at which the swell and division of the buttocks become apparent, and was slashed to the waist in front, baring both the inner and outer curves of the breasts, leaving the nipples free to poke and bob through the material.

"A pattern was seen in the use of females to bite and kick the policemen" *New York Times* 5/7/68.

Its drumming, distinct from other peckers, resembles the sound of a muffled machine gun, a soft, hollow automatic weapon.

He came stumbling up in Tompkins Square with his red scabby face and clapped a hand on my shoulder: "Say buddy I'm a junkie no I mean not a junkie a wino." That was how I met Sparrow. Oh nobody knew what his name really was we called him Sparrow. After the saying, "Hot as a Sparrow." He used to say things to me like, "The salient fact about American culture is that we all have to get back to nipples and start over again. Whole cockamanie country." He's also the one who said, "I wuz-a fuck 'is-a wife." When he talked like that we used to call him "the Cardinal" because he seemed so intellectual. Like a Cardinal I mean, if you really look at one.

With one stroke rose half an arc then wings pulled in allowed itself to fall like diving over a wave.

I want to write a story that does a lot of infolding and outfolding. Majestic infolding and outfolding. No petty invective and venom. No comic bits, no noodgy satire like Shawanga Lodge casino. Calm, slow exfoliations. The life cycle of Whistling Swans. Inexorable curves of passion. Rise and fall of continents. Concrete. Innocent. Beautiful. No meaning.

30 million Americans living in poverty
it says in I. F. Stone
in the richest country in the world
people eat clay to still the pains of an empty belly
children come to school too hungry to learn
and the infants of the poor suffer
irreversible brain damage from protein deprivation
the 42.7% of our farmers
with incomes of less than $2,500 a year
received only 4.5% of total farm subsidies
while the top 10%
many of them farm corporations or vertical trusts
received 64.5%
with a budget allocated 80% to the Pentagon
and 10% to health education and welfare

This is what I call pure poetry. This is the New American Poetry, the poetry of pure fact. This is the purity that has been missing from our poems.

Red-winged Blackbirds floating in like Piper Cubs, suns on shoulders. Phoebe brooding on her egg. Towhee, Picasso camouflage, comic butler in tails. Catbird chat. Brown Thrasher variations. Oriole riff. Pheasants waltz across the road. In the field a Crow barks. A Hawk hangs in the air, absolutely still. Grouse explode in the underbrush. Doves at their vespers. Invisible, huge in the night sky, a train of Canada Geese goes honking and gabbling full five minutes from engine to caboose.

There was an item on the menu and the Chinese was translated as "Ear-tree." It was right between Shar Ding Op (chickens, Chinese frankfurter, water chestnut) and Hong Hong Duk (lobster nails, pig flesh, Chinese vegetable). Myself I was all for getting the "Ten Ingredient." I felt expansive and experimental. But Phoebe, who was a big girl, tended toward "Mile High Rice," with maybe an order of "Stopped Duck," or "Blistered Beef," whatever that was. So then we asked ourselves, well, what would "the Sparrow" do? Our eyes met for an instant. There was no doubt about it: "Ear-tree." We didn't even have to speak.

"Seen as how I'm a nice guy, I'll give you a tip. We like to stop guys with long hair, especially in old cars. They look like students. You're a teacher. Teach and be taught."

I put the ticket in my pocket. "Yeah. Well I didn't know driving with studded snow tires was illegal in this state after May first as of ten days ago." I opened my car door.

"Hey. Come 'ere."

I walked back to the patrol car.

"It's not illegal."

"No?"

"No. It's unlawful."

"Oh."

I walked back to my car and opened the door.

"Hey. Come 'ere."

I walked back to the patrol car.

"Ya know what illegal is?"

"No, what?"

"It's a sick bird. Hah hah hah."

Q. When does a bird break the law?

A. When it's a Robin.

Q. What characteristic distinguishes the Bald Eagle?

A. Its balls.

Q. When is a bird not a bird?

A. When it's a horse.

poor Americans are four times as likely to die
before the age of 35 as the average citizen
Negro women in Mississippi die
six times as often in childbirth as white women
in some urban ghettos of the North
one child in ten dies in infancy
the health gap between rich and poor is growing
in 1940 the infant mortality rate for non-whites
was 70% higher than that for whites
in 1962 the rate was 90% greater
the life expectancy of an American Negro is 61 years
that of a white American
is 68
it says
in the *Sunday*
*Times*

The Downy Woodpecker, in his prison outfit, is easily confused with the Hairy, which in fact is almost identical. However the Downy is smaller than the Hairy, and its call, *pik*, is softer than Hairy's. The Black-capped Chickadee is the friendliest of acrobats. The Bobwhite is a gallinaceous bird, very henny in other words, and acts it. But let us ascend from the ridiculous to the majestic. The Whistling Swan is common. It has a wingspan of over seven feet. Like other swans, it has a "deep, ponderous flight," neck extended. When swimming neck is stiff and straight; secondaries are not raised.

Q. What bird would you be glad to see if you were out of gas?
A. The Petrel.
Q. What birds can't fly straight?
A. Terns.
Q. What birds are often run over by trains?
A. Rails.
Q. What bird's ass would you not want to sit on?
A. The Pintail's.
Q. Which-a bird is not-a yours-a?
A. Myna.
Q. When does a bird make a sacrifice?
A. When it's a Bunting.
Q. What bird blows his whistle?
A. Old Dickcissel, old Dickcissel.

birds

the

what do they say

through the empty air

keep-back keep-back

peter-peter-peter

tea-cher tea-cher

o-say mari-a

hurry worry flurry blurry

drink-your-tea drink-your-tea

old sam peabodypeabodypeabody

ticket-ticket-ticket-ticket

wide-a-wake

rounde-lay rounde-lay

trees trees if you please

witchery-witchery-witchery

whip-three-beers

chicky-tucky-tuck

chicky-tucky-tuck

We are all, of course, familiar with that kind of anthropomorphic slop. What do the birds really say when you listen hard and understand what they are saying? They say k-a-a-a. They say kwrrk. They say

kow-kow-kow

keeur

kleep

kzrrt

prrrp

bzee

plick

rronk

tlu-tlu

krr-oww

zrurrr

wheet

peent

tsweep

cuh-cuh

churree

che-bunk

kraaa

che-bek

jeet

hooah

tschizzik

kirrik

ssllick

karr-reek

kwuririp

kek-kek-kek

kee-oo

auw

churweeoo

pchip ee pcheewee

ooah-ooo-oo-oo

breep

But then again, what does it matter what they say? What matters is that they carve shapes from nothingness, decorate the silence, make melodious distinctions to distinguish one moment finely from the next.

I call waiter. What thisee here, I say. He say, That is "ear-tree," a delicious Oriental specialty. But Phoebe no likee. What is? she ask. She little girl, no muchee eatee. "Ear-tree" is a popular and delicious Cantonese dish, say waiter. He Chinee fella. It is highly recommended, he say. But what is? I say. Waiter shrug and stare to other sidee room with inscrutable Chinee face. No likee, Phoebe say. You got Chicken Chow Mein. Waiter nod. I order Chop Suey. Then other customer come. They order "ear-tree." Waiter go in kitchen, we hear yellee to cook: Two spaghettis! I callee waiter. What this "ear-tree," I say. I pointee at menu. You say is Canton dish. Then waiter answer: It doesn't matter what you say. What matters is to hurl the words at the silence of the page like hand grenades. With feeling. Look out! someone screamed. He's got a gun!

"But why 'ear-tree'?" asked Phoebe, wide-eyed. She was a slim, light-haired pale face on summer vacation from Bryn Mawr College, but with very big boobs.

"Ah, these ees the ow-you-say question my young chérie," answered Sparrow. She was at the same time flattered and offended by his insistence that she use his first name, for it implied both a compliment and an impropriety. Why, she wondered, as she stared out the porthole and watched the clouds transform themselves from moment to moment, feeling the touch of his sharkskin on her bare microskirted thigh, did her parents allow a trip to Europe in the company of this strange, dark, manly business acquaintance of her father's, with his profile, his greying sideburns, and his carriage and skin texture that reminded her so much of an erect cock? She quivered a bit in her seat, and fastened her safety belt. He was mainly Latin in descent, from a Franco-Italian Spanish family with an intermixture of Greco-Moorish blood, that settled on the island of Malta some centuries ago in the wake of the conquest of Jerusalem. Sparrow. Spiro? Ero? She wondered if it was his real name. He was the kind of person that might be incognito. The jetliner shuddered through a cumulonimbus. She pulled a lever easing her seat into a reclining position that thrust her long full firm young thighs up and forward from the pelvis where the thin stuff of her microgarb caught and bunched under her seatbelt.

"But why 'ear-tree'?" asked Phoebe.

"My charming eediot," rejoined his vibrant basso, "if we knew these . . ." His middle and index fingers grazed her thigh confidentially, and came to rest near the hem of her skirt. She pretended not to notice, since she didn't know what else to do, and turned to look through the porthole where she saw a sheep running across the wing, no not a sheep a puff of smoke, another, another then after a pause a band of grey a plume of roiling black with suddenly red at its root . . .

"Built entirely without design precedent or orderly planning, created bit by bit on sheer impulse, a natural artist's instinct, and the fantasy of the moment": Simone Rodia's Watts Towers. Connections proliferate, meanings drop away.

Sparrow left England traveling as a young Greek sailor named George and Nick. I found him easily before the ship had cleared harbor leaning against the starboard rail in tight white pants and striped blue shirt. The day was blue with white clouds, whitecaps, gulls dove and hung above the churning stern. The gulls of Dover scream like Harpies and fly on wings of rusty iron. Sparrow was traveling as a young Greek sailor named George and Nick, but he spoke with a thick Italian accent. "'owza da boy?" he greeted me. His theory was that from his Italian accent he would be taken for a notorious Neapolitan intellectual known as "the Cardinal" who was inclined to proletarian dress and argot as a disguise. If however he were recognized as the Greek sailor boy George and Nick masquerading as the Cardinal in proletdrag, he would still be ahead of the game. This was the evasive measure known as bifurcation. While the authorities are interrogating George and Nick, Sparrow slips out between the two of them. Or if they settle on George, Nick sidles off and meantime George subdivides into

Sparrow-Spiro-Ero. The principle here is progressive fission as in certain microorganisms. They never catch up with you, whoever you are. But this, ironically, is the hang-up of the method, since some agents have been left stranded in a maze of sloughed identities nursing a king-size identity problem. Often you will see an old hand slap a green agent on the back, wink, and growl avuncularly, "Say kid, what you say we go fission?" This is the process referred to, so beware.

Sparrow pointed toward a couple standing on the bridge next to the skipper, and slipped a homing pigeon out of his attaché case. The man was tall and slender, suntanned, and of a distinguished allure in the French sense. The woman was tall and slender, suntanned, and also of a distinguished allure, etc. At this distance it was a little difficult to tell them apart, though they were both quite distinct from the skipper, who was pale and squat and emanated banality. The bird ruffled and fluttered, happy to escape its confinement. Sparrow set it on his wrist, raised it high in the air, and whispered "Dai! Dai!" The pigeon flapped off while Sparrow began reciting the Paolo and Francesca episode from the fifth canto of the *Commedia.* We watched as the bird hovered over the woman's head for a moment, then perched on her shoulder. We watched as she reached up and removed the message from the bird's leg, still looking straight ahead. We watched as she swallowed the note, took the pigeon, twisted its neck, and let it flop to the deck. Then the suntanned man was standing alone on the bridge, near the squat skipper, still looking straight ahead. Sparrow pointed to the man and shrugged: "I wuz-a fuck 'iz-a wife," he said in explanation. Just then said lady appeared at the rail near us and stood there looking straight ahead. "Beh!" said Sparrow. Was he as surprised as I was to recognize Phoebe? There was probably no telling. She looked straight ahead, her eyes on the horizon. The gulls dipped and hung in our wake. Sparrow cleared his throat. "Ear-tree," he said. Phoebe turned to him, her charcoal eyes smouldering in her olive face: "Millions of people are starving. A sixth of the population lives in poverty. In the richest nation in the world, in the history of the world. Abroad we practice mass murder, at home slow genocide. How long can we continue to regard as democratic a nation run like a company town for corporate profit, built-in poverty, endemic racism? Starving children suffer irreversible brain damage while Senators get rich. Soldiers die while profits soar. Democracy by tear gas, Mace, and political assassination. What are we going to do?"

"We like to stop guys with long hair and old cars," he said. "First of all old cars are a drug on the market like. I mean seen as how you got an old car it means you ain't got a new car right. And if all you was to pay is a few bucks on an old car you ain't puttin much back into the system are yiz? And that breaks the law of the market which is free enterprise.

"Now we ain't got nothin against long hair see. But what about all these guys that set up shop as barbers, they gotta make their profit, right? That breaks the law of supply and demand.

"Now another thing is long hair ain't neat like. And if it ain't neat it's unruly. And if it's unruly it's unlawful in this state according to a law on the books as of ten days ago by which appearance can be considered an extension of overt behavior during periods of national emergency such as for example now.

"Now seen as how guys with long hair and old cars don't fit in a system for guys with old hair and long cars, what that means is you're a troublemaker which is an offense by the new law that considers mental attitude an extension of overt behavior during times of national emergency 063589 state penal code and authorizes the arresting officer to put certain questions to the accused according to the mental stop-and-search provision on grounds of reasonable suspicion like long hair and old cars. Wrong answers are considered grounds for perjury.

Part I *Short Answer* (10 points)

1. How would you define "illegal"?
2. What characteristic distinguishes the Bald Eagle?
3. When does a bird break the law?
4. What birds can't fly straight?
5. What bird's ass would you not want to sit on?

Part II *Essay* (90 points)

Choose *one* of the following:

a) This story is "entirely without design precedent or orderly planning, created bit by bit on sheer impulse, a natural artist's instinct, and the fantasy of the moment." Why do you think the police don't like that? Discuss.

b) What is "ear-tree"? Give examples.

In Part II, I answered b). This was my answer: "Connections proliferate, meanings disperse. The painter studies his nude, his landscape."

IN A SPIRIT OF JOY AND REVOLUTIONARY EXULTATION, THOUSANDS OF STUDENTS OCCUPIED THE SORBONNE TODAY.

THE STUDENTS STARTED MOVING INTO THE UNIVERSITY LATE LAST NIGHT, AFTER COMPLETING THEIR JOINT PROTEST MARCH WITH THE WORKERS OF PARIS AND SPENDING THE EVENING DANCING ON THE COBBLED STREETS OF THE LATIN QUARTER.

IN THE GRANDIOSE COBBLED COURTYARD OF THE MAIN BUILDING A SMALL JAZZ BAND PLAYED ALL THROUGH THE NIGHT.

AFTER 10 DAYS OF BLOODY CLASHES WITH THE POLICE, NOT A SINGLE POLICEMAN WAS IN SIGHT. STUDENTS IN WHITE HELMETS DIRECTED TRAFFIC. THE GOVERNMENT HAD SURRENDERED THIS PART OF THE CITY TO THE STUDENTS.

HUNDREDS OF THOUSANDS OF STUDENTS TOOK TO THE STREETS NOT ONLY IN PARIS BUT IN MOST PROVINCIAL CITIES.

MANY HAD A FEAR THAT GOVERNMENTAL POWER HAD BROKEN DOWN.

THE STUDENTS THEMSELVES DELIBERATELY HARKED BACK TO THE BATTLE CRIES THAT HAD SERVED EARLIER FRENCH REVOLUTIONARIES.

TWO THOUSAND WORKERS, IMITATING THE REBELLIOUS STUDENTS OF THE SORBONNE, HAVE OCCUPIED THE AIRCRAFT CONSTRUCTION PLANT OF SUD-AVIATION AT NANTES, ON THE ATLANTIC

COAST, AND ARE HOLDING THE PLANT MANAGER AND HIS PRINCIPAL AIDES PRISONERS.

THE WORKERS, WHO WERE ALREADY ON STRIKE, MOVED INTO THE PLANT EARLY LAST NIGHT AND WELDED THE MAIN GATE CLOSED. THEY THREW UP BARRICADES ON THE ROADS LEADING TO THE PLANT. THEY CLOSED DOWN THE NANTES AIRPORT, WHICH IS ADJACENT TO THE FACTORY.

FRANCE'S SOCIAL REVOLT SPREAD AND CHANGED IN NATURE TODAY AS AN ESTIMATED 100,000 STRIKERS OCCUPIED DOZENS OF FACTORIES IN ALL PARTS OF THE COUNTRY.

THE STRIKE MOVEMENT SPREAD SO SWIFTLY THAT, WITHIN HALF AN HOUR EARLY THIS EVENING, REPORTS REACHED PARIS THAT SEVEN MAJOR INDUSTRIAL PLANTS AND SHIPYARDS HAD BEEN TAKEN OVER IN LE HAVRE ALONE.

PRODUCERS AND DIRECTORS OF THE GOVERNMENT'S TELEVISION AND RADIO SYSTEM WENT ON STRIKE AND THE SYSTEM'S NEWSMEN VOTED TO REFUSE TO ACCEPT ANY FURTHER DIRECTIVES FROM THE INFORMATION MINISTRY OR OTHER GOVERNMENT AGENCIES ON THEIR NEWS REPORTS.

WORKERS SEIZED THE GOLD-DOMED OPERA AND THE OPERA COMIQUE.

THE SPEECHES AT THE NATIONAL ASSEMBLY SEEMED STRANGELY IRRELEVANT. FRANCOIS MITTERAND, THE OPPOSITION LEADER, AND WALDECK ROCHET, THE HEAD OF THE COMMUNIST PARTY, WERE AS HOPELESSLY OUT OF TOUCH AS PREMIER GEORGES POMPIDOU. THEY WERE ALL PART OF THE "ESTABLISHMENT."

ONE OF THE STUDENT LEADERS, DANIEL COHN-BENDIT, CALLED THE COMMUNISTS "STALINIST CREEPS." MR. COHN-BENDIT, CALLED DANNY THE RED, APPEARS TO HOLD VIEWS CLOSE TO ANARCHISM.

THE BLACK FLAG OF THE ANARCHISTS MADE ITS APPEARANCE DURING THE MASSIVE PARADE OF STUDENTS AND WORKERS YESTERDAY.

THE RED FLAG WAS HOISTED OVER SEVERAL PLANTS.

THE RED AND THE BLACK FLAGS APPEARED TOGETHER, AN ABNORMAL SITUATION BECAUSE THE COMMUNISTS AND ANARCHISTS HAVE LONG BEEN ENEMIES. THE JOINT APPEARANCE WAS ONE OF THE MANY SIGNS THAT SOMETHING NEW HAD HAPPENED.

IF THE MOVEMENT IS AN UNCONTROLLED REVOLUTIONARY UPSURGE, THE COUNTRY MAY BE PLUNGED INTO ANARCHY.

THE DECISION OF THE WORKERS APPEARS TO HAVE BEEN A SPONTANEOUS MOVE BY THE RANK-AND-FILE STRIKERS, WHO ACTED WITHOUT ORDERS FROM POLITICAL PARTIES OR LABOR UNIONS.

THE STUDENT REVOLT WAS SIMILARLY UNOFFICIAL IN ITS ORIGIN.

IT IS THIS POPULAR AND REVOLUTIONARY CHARACTER OF THE MOVEMENT THAT LEADS MANY OBSERVERS TO FEEL THAT THE STU-

DENTS MAY HAVE UNLEASHED FORCES THAT CANNOT BE HARNESSED OR TAMED BY CONVENTIONAL MEANS, EITHER BY THE GOVERNMENT OR THE TRADITIONAL OPPOSITION PARTIES, INCLUDING THE COMMUNISTS.

JUST WHAT CAUSED THE STUDENTS' AND WORKERS' REVOLT TO ASSUME SUCH EXPLOSIVE DIMENSIONS IS STILL A MYSTERY TO MOST OBSERVERS HERE.

MANY HAVE LINKED THE DISILLUSION OF THE FRENCH STUDENT TO A GLOBAL STUDENT MALAISE.

THE GAULLIST ADMINISTRATION, LIKE MANY PRIVATE CITIZENS, IS CONVINCED THAT A TRULY REVOLUTIONARY SITUATION EXISTS AND THAT THE DEMOCRATIC INSTITUTIONS OF FRANCE ARE THREATENED.

THE PRINCIPAL THREAT LIES IN THE SPONTANEOUS, POPULAR AND UTTERLY UNCONTROLLED NATURE OF THE MOVEMENT.

THE REVOLT, BY ITS SPONTANEOUS, TOTALLY UNCONTROLLED AND UNCONTROLLABLE NATURE HAD BECOME A TRULY REVOLUTIONARY EVENT.

IF THE COMMUNIST PARTY HAS MANAGED TO TAKE OVER THE MOVEMENT, THEN, IRONICALLY, THE INSTITUTIONS ARE SAFE AND THE POLITICAL CONTEST IS LIKELY TO MOVE BACK INTO THE NATIONAL ASSEMBLY, WITH VOTES OF CONFIDENCE AND VOTES OF CENSURE AND TRADITIONAL SPEECHES—AND SOONER OR LATER A NEW ELECTION.

SOMETHING HAS BEEN CREATED THAT IS IRREVERSIBLE. THERE WILL BE NO GOING BACK TO THE STATUS QUO.

The police want an end to this disorder and that depends on one question and one question only: What is "ear-tree"? This in turn leads us to the matter of the identity of the man called "Ero." Destroy this as you read. It is printed in a soluble ink which you can lick off the page sentence by sentence. The ink has various flavors depending on the parts of speech to make this easier to understand and swallow.

To get to the point, the police suspect a plot, yet all they see is disorder. They suspect that disorder is part of the plot, if not the point of it. They imagine that they merely have to figure out the plot to put an end to the disorder. But they don't understand the plot and believe the explanation lies with the meaning of the word "ear-tree." In turn they believe that this meaning will lead them to a man called Ero. In real life Ero is an eminent ornithologist, but the police believe that he is the leader of an international liberation conspiracy, and that only in his mind are all the connections coherently held together, the whole matter fully understood. To make matters worse, they aren't even sure whether Ero is dead or alive, or for that matter whether that is his right name.

I first met Ero in Tompkins Square Park. He was disguised as a bum. Although he was given to a kind of banal chattering—he sometimes compared himself to a Starling—I soon realized that this was a mere verbal subterfuge, so to speak, which could not prevent the escape of sudden flashes of the profoundest insight. For example he once remarked, almost as a non sequitur, that the whole country had to get back to nipples. It was not long before I was captivated by his brilliance and charisma. At about that point I met another of his admirers, an English "bird" named Phoebe. Though she attended an American college, she was married; however, she had an ambiguous relation with her husband, and while she traveled with him a good deal, she spent much of the time in the protection of her parents. Ero once indicated to me quite clearly that there had been something between them, but then, she was beautiful and he—he was Ero.

To continue, at that time Phoebe and I used to frequent Chinese restaurants. That was because it used to be Ero's way to plant his messages in fortune cookies and leave strictly to chance whether you received them or not—Ero favored chance because he said we must remain open to the unknown. They say that he still does this, and that you might for all you know receive a message from him yourself in your very next fortune cookie—a message that might change your life. Anyway we were sitting in this Cantonese place in midtown, speaking Pigeon English to put the natives at ease and to confuse the police. The waiter recommended "ear-tree"—could he have been Ero?—but when he ordered it for someone else called it "spaghetti."

At first I thought that "ear-tree" had something to do with birds—a kind of tree that birds liked to sing in, or to. Ero was of course filled with bird lore. Birds were something special for him. He said that bird songs constituted a kind of code which, when correctly deciphered, turned out to have absolutely no meaning. On the other hand he had a whole system of private symbolism worked out on the basis of what the various species meant to him, and would often express himself in its terms. This was a code the police never cracked, though God knows they tried. For example, he once sent me a message composed completely of bird images. These involved the Red-winged Blackbird, the Phoebe, the Rufous-sided Towhee, the Catbird, the Brown Thrasher, the Oriole (Orchard), the Pheasant, the Crow, the Hawk, the Grouse, the Dove, the Canada Goose, in that order. Knowing his system based on his emotional response to different birds, I worked the symbols out as follows:

Red-winged Blackbird = calm dash
Phoebe = domestic
Rufous-sided Towhee = human comedy
Catbird = eccentric relativism
Brown Thrasher = rich
Oriole (Orchard) = hot butter
Pheasant = beautiful fortune, pathetic sacrifice
Crow = wisdom floats intensely
Hawk = kill with grace
Grouse = explosion
Dove = dumb animals
Canada Goose = away, away

Decoded and allowing for variation in the given images in which the birds appeared, this means, roughly: "The *calm dash* of our once *domestic* culture has faded along with our old *human comedy.* In its place we have an *eccentric relativism* that is as *rich* as experience itself, yet as slippery as *hot butter.* Today's tragic hero is a man of *beautiful fortune, pathetic sacrifice*—his role as rich as the flux itself, and his denouement as meaningless. But in this streaming chaos *wisdom floats intensely* could one but be deadly enough with the fine net of intelligence. For wisdom and art mean precisely to kill the quick of our experience as it races past, but to *kill with grace* so that the victim may be preserved, as if alive, from oblivion. The universe is a long, an infinite *explosion* in which we are driven for an instant like *dumb animals* as it rushes *away, away.*"

Unfortunately, when I showed this interpretation to Ero, he got very angry and tore it up. When I asked what his system of bird symbolism meant to him he replied: "Nothing. A feather here and there, a color, a squawk, disconnected, opaque, totally self-contained, ending in a triumph of birdness, song and soar, itself opaque and without equivalent, but the feeling ordered and defined—like that of a bird's song, or of its flight."

That was my last encounter with Ero, as such. Immediately after that he assumed the guise of Spiro the spy, then of the Cardinal, then of George and Nick, and then literally disappeared in a welter of dividing and subdividing identities—Orson, Chet Nexus, the Beach Boy, Madame Lafayette, the Light-fingered Trio—to name just a few. Originally intended as an evasive measure against an assassination plot, this frenzy of transformations, some believe, may have made him a victim of terminal identity fission, a malignant psychological disorder which progressively rarefies the ego so that it ultimately loses consciousness of itself and in effect ceases to exist. Some say that he was seized and murdered in one of his ephemeral metamorphoses—thrown overboard by the squat skipper and the pimply homosexual second mate as George and Nick, on board a plane that crashed in mysterious circumstances off Iceland, shot dead in a Chinese restaurant by a Cuban exile who ordered "ear-tree" and got spaghetti. No one really knows.

What we do now know definitely, or at least what I know and you will in thirty seconds, is the meaning of "ear-tree." Shhh. It was on Icelandic that eighteen-hour flight from Luxemburg where your feet swell up when the insight came to me. Three A.M. and I couldn't sleep. We had been traveling maybe nine, ten hours. Nothing could have been further from my mind than that old riddle. I leaned back against my pillow and thought *oreiller,* French for pillow. I had been in France. Then I thought *pommier,* apple tree, *cerisier,* cherry tree, *pêcher,* peach tree, *oranger,* orange tree. Then I thought *oreille,* ear. Then I thought *voilà! oreiller,* "ear-tree." But why "ear-tree" on a Chinese menu? Of course! Spaghetti. In Chinese restaurants in France, *lo-mein,* which as we know was brought from China to Italy as *spaghetti,* is often called *pilaf* or *pilaw,* from the Arabic, because it is used as a pillow for some kind of ragout or sauce. So some Chinese who knew neither French nor English nor Arabic very well, translated *lo-mein* to *pilaw, pilaw* to *oreiller,* and *oreiller* from French to English as "ear-tree." I immediately dropped off into a profound slumber from which I awoke next morning completely refreshed.

When I arrived in New York, I went back to that same Chinese restaurant and ordered a large "ear-tree." It was of excellent quality, at least three stars, and I polished it off with tremendous satisfaction. The message in my fortune cookie read: "Connections proliferate, meanings are dispelled. The traveler studies out his map."

"Je suis réellement désolé I'm really sorry to have waited so long before answering you but I am totally caught up in the events that have taken place in May and in June in France. You've undoubtedly had some echoes but it's difficult to imagine the extraordinary enthusiasm that sustained the young people during the month of May."

"To form a perfect conception of the beauty and elegance of these Swans, you must observe them when they are not aware of your proximity . . . the neck, which at other times is held stiffly upright, moves in graceful curves . . . with a sudden effort a flood of water is thrown over the back and wings, when it is seen rolling off in sparkling globules, like so many large pearls. The bird then shakes its wings, beats the water, and as if giddy with delight shoots away, gliding . . . with surprising agility and grace. Imagine, reader, that a flock of fifty Swans are thus sporting before you, as they have more than once in my sight, and you will feel, as I have felt, more happy and void of care than I can describe."

The dress was made of clinging white nylon jersey of a thinness that in certain angles of light would outline the thighs or reveal the curve of a breast and which, when taut against the skin, assumed something of the warm flesh tone. Slashed to the waist, it left the nipples free to poke and bob through the material.

in the richest country in the world/ people eat clay to still the pains of an empty belly/ children come to school too hungry to learn/ and the infants of the poor suffer/ irreversible brain damage from protein deprivation

JUST WHAT CAUSED THE STUDENTS' AND WORKERS' REVOLT TO ASSUME SUCH EXPLOSIVE DIMENSIONS IS STILL A MYSTERY TO MOST OBSERVERS HERE. MANY HAVE LINKED THE DISILLUSION OF THE FRENCH STUDENT TO A GLOBAL STUDENT MALAISE

Ero is an eminent ornithologist, but the police believe that he is the leader of an international liberation conspiracy, and that only in his mind are all the connections coherently held together

"A pattern was seen in the use of females to bite and kick the policemen" *New York Times* 5/7/68. Its drumming, distinct from other peckers, resembles the sound of a muffled machine gun, a soft, hollow automatic weapon.

"Les manifestations sur les barricades the demonstrations on the barricades were only one aspect, perhaps secondary, of this surprising movement, much more astonishing was the climate in the streets. We organized every day and during the month of May all-day meetings each of which gathered up to a hundred people sometimes until two in the morning."

THE REVOLT BY ITS SPONTANEOUS TOTALLY UNCONTROLLED AND UNCONTROLLABLE NATURE HAD BECOME A TRULY REVOLUTIONARY EVENT

"Spontanément spontaneously, the people raised the real problems, confusedly felt and it was this, exactly that was extraordinary—it was not a question of the usual political theories struggling but of notions as vague as human dignity, the responsibility of each man, the infinite resources of the emotion of enthusiasm facing efficiency, the power of technology—"

IF THE MOVEMENT IS AN UNCONTROLLED REVOLUTIONARY UPSURGE THE COUNTRY MAY BE PLUNGED INTO ANARCHY "entirely without design precedent or orderly planning, created bit by bit on sheer impulse"

coincidence such things renew my faith in the unknown I am always interested in any overt confrontation with chance though if you stop to think about it every moment is such a confrontation for each of us Ero favored chance because he said we must remain open to the unknown

the stream carries mainly on its glassy surface rippled clouds inventing themselves from minute to minute, fantastic shapes, formations piling shifting flowing, distortions of distortions of distortions

"Nous attendons we await November, December but also the movements that cannot fail to appear in Italy, Germany perhaps the United States . . ."

in the richest country in the world

an international liberation conspiracy

the children of the poor

caused the revolt to assume such explosive

spontaneous totally uncontrolled and uncontrollable

a soft hollow automatic weapon

left the nipples free to poke and bob

much more astonishing was the climate in the streets

a small jazz band played all through the night

the infinite resources of the motion of enthusiasm

created bit by bit on sheer impulse

we await November December

formations piling shifting flowing

we must remain open to the unknown

the bird then shakes its wings beats the water
and shoots away gliding like other Swans it has a deep ponderous flight the
underwing is an astonishing pink-gold stroke of scarlet from green to green
Nuthatch bullets through blank air Red-winged Blackbirds floating in in the field
a Crow barks

Pheasants waltz across the road
Grouse explode in the underbrush
a Hawk

hangs
in the air

birds

the

## *Study questions*

1. *What are the various bits and pieces that form the collage which structures this story? It will help if you discern where an image cluster or motif begins and how it recurs in rhythmic patterning. Note how all the parts fall together toward the end of the story and how the end of the story circles back to its beginning.*
2. *Who is the protagonist? What is his conflict? One could argue that it is as pointless to try to find a protagonist and a conflict in this story as it is to lament the absence of a linear plot. Still, the narrator answers the question: What is "ear-tree"? "This was my answer: 'Connections proliferate, meanings disperse. The painter studies his nude, his landscape.'" Is this statement close to what may be called the governing principle of the story?* 3. *The story suggests a coming revolution, spontaneous, totally uncontrolled, and irreversible. On how many fronts will such a revolution occur? How is such a revolution related to the concept of coincidence?* 4. *At what point in time is this story told? Where is the narrator?* 5. *What happened to the airplane with the smoke coming from the engine?* 6. *What are the birds doing in the story?*

*Imamu Amiri Baraka* (LeRoi Jones, b. 1934), novelist, poet, playwright, essayist, and short-story writer, was born in Newark, New Jersey, where he now lives. He attended the State University at Rutgers, Howard University, Columbia University, and the New School for Social Research. He has taught at the New School, the University of Buffalo, Columbia University, and San Francisco State University. He was founder and director of the Black Arts Repertory Theatre in Harlem and has been director of Spirit House, a black community theater in Newark. He served in the United States Air Force from 1954 to 1957. His novel, *The System of Dante's Hell,* was published in 1965. His best-known collection of poems, *The Dead Lecturer and Other Poems,* was published in 1964. His most important plays include *The Slave* (1964), *Dutchman* (1964), and *The Toilet* (1967). His essays have been collected in such volumes as *Blues People* (1963), *In Our Terribleness* (1970), and *Raise, Race, Rays, Raze: Essays Since 1965* (1971). His short stories were collected in *Tales* (1967). A black militant, Baraka espouses violence as a necessary corollary to the kind of social change he thinks necessary in the United States. From *Tales,* "Answers in Progress" is a projection of a revolutionary holocaust, but the vision is not from the outside in. It is, rather, from the inside out.

## ANSWERS IN PROGRESS

*Can you die in airraid jiggle*
*torn arms flung through candystores*
*Touch the edge of answer. The waves of nausea*
*as change sweeps the frame of breath and meat.*

"Stick a knife through his throat,"
he slid
in the blood
got up running toward
the blind newsdealer. He screamed
about "Cassius Clay," and slain there in the
street, the whipped figure of jesus, head opened
eyes flailing against his nose. They beat him to
pulpy answers. We wrote Muhammad Ali across his
face and chest, like a newspaper of bleeding meat.

The next day the spaceships landed. Art Blakey records was what they were looking for. We gave them Buttercorn Lady and they threw it back at us. They wanted to know what happened to The Jazz Messengers. And right in the middle, playing the Sun-Ra tape, the blanks staggered out of the department store. Omar had missed finishing the job, and they staggered out, falling in the snow, red all over the face chest, the stab wounds in one in the top of a Adam hat.

The space men thought that's what was really happening. One beeped (Ali mentioned this in the newspapers) that this was evolution. Could we dig it? Shit, yeh. We were laughing. Some blanks rounded one corner, Yaa and Dodua were behind them, to take them to the Center. Nationalized on the spot.

The space men could dig everything. They wanted to take one of us to a spot and lay for a minute, to dig what they were in to. Their culture and shit. Whistles Newark was broke up in one section. The dead mayor and other wops carried by in black trucks. Wingo, Rodney and them waving at us. They stopped the first truck and Cyril wanted to know about them thin cats hopping around us. He's always very fast finger.

Space men wanted to know what happened after Blakey. They'd watched but couldn't get close enough to dig exactly what was happening. Albert Ayler they dug immediately from Russell's mouth imitation. That's later. Red spam cans in their throats with the voices, and one of them started to scat. It wigged me. Bamberger's burning down, dead blancos all over and a cat from Sigma Veda, and his brothers, hopping up and down asking us what was happening.

We left Rachel and Lefty there to keep explaining. Me and Pinball had to go back to headquarters, and report Market Street Broad Street rundown. But we told them we'd talk to them. I swear one of those cats had a hip walk. Even thought they was hoppin and bopadoppin up and down, like they had to pee. Still this one cat had a stiff tentacle, when he walked. Yeh; long blue winggly cats, with soft liquid sounds out of their throats for voices. Like, "You know where Art Blakey, Buhainia, is working?" We fell out.

❀ ❀ ❀

*Walk through life*
*beautiful more than anything*
*stand in the sunlight*
*walk through life*
*love all the things*
*that make you strong, be lovers, be anything*
*for all the people of*
*earth.*

*You have brothers*
*you love each other, change up*
*and look at the world*
*now, it's*
*ours, take it slow*
*we've long time, a long way*
*to go,*

*we have*
*each other, and the*
*world,*
*don't be sorry*
*walk on out through sunlight life, and know*
*we're on the go*
*for love*
*to open*
*our lives*
*to walk*
*tasting the sunshine*
*of life.*

Boulevards played songs like that and we rounded up blanks where we had to. Space men were on the south side laying in some of the open houses. Some brothers came in from the west, Chicago, they had a bad thing going out there. Fires were still high as the buildings, but Ram sent a couple of them out to us, to dig what was happening. One of them we sent to the blue cats, to take that message, back. Could W dig what was happening with them? We sent our own evaluation back, and when I finished the report me and Pinball started weaving through the dead cars and furniture. Waving at the brothers, listening to the sounds, we had piped through the streets.

Smokey Robinson was on now. But straight up fast and winging. No more unrequited love. Damn Smokey got his thing together too. No more tracks or mirages. Just the beauty of the whole. I hope they play Sun-Ra for them blue cats, so they can dig where we at.

Magic City played later. By time we got to the courthouse. The whole top of that was out. Like you could look inside from fourth or fifth floor of the Hall of Records. Cats were all over that joint. Ogun wanted the records intact.

Past the playgrounds and all them blanks in the cold standing out there or laying on the ground crying. The rich ones really were funny. This ol cat me an Pinball recognized still had a fag thing going for him. In a fur coat, he was some kind of magistrate. Bobby and Moosie were questioning him about some silver he was supposed to have stashed. He was a silver freak. The dude was actually weeping. Crying big sobs; the women crowded away from him. I guess they really couldn't feel sorry for him because he was crying about money.

By the time we got to Weequahic Avenue where the space men and out-of-town brothers were laying I was tired as a dog. We went in there and wanted to smoke some bush, but these blue dudes had something better. Taste like carrots. It was a cool that took you. You thought something was mildly amusing and everything seemed interesting.

I talked with Pinball and the blue leader about Ben Caldwell's paintings . . . the one where the guy is smoking the reefer. We thought about the changing reference, of our new world. As it stood already in the old ruins. And we all felt like Bird. The old altosaxophonist . . . but the limits opened out into the pure lyric tone of powerful beings. But when the Sun-Ra tape came on this blue dude really opened up. He dug the hell out of it. Perfect harmony these cats had too. Boooooo—Iiiiiiiiiooooooooooooo . . . daaaaa ahhhhhhhh aaaaahhhhhh . . . booooo OOOOOOOOOOOOO ooooooooooaaaaaaaaaoooaaaaa

Claude McKay I started quoting. Four o'clock in the morning to a blue dude gettin cooled out on carrots. We didn't have no duty until ten o'clock the next day, and me and Lorenzo and Ish had to question a bunch of prisoners and stuff for the TV news. Chazee had a play to put on that next afternoon about the Chicago stuff. Ray talked to him. And the name of the play was Big Fat Fire.

Man I was tired. We had taped the Sigma. They were already infested with Buddhas there, and we spoke very quietly about how we knew it was our turn. I had burned my hand somewhere and this blue cat looked at it hard and cooled it out. White came in with the design for a flag he'd been working on. Black heads, black hearts, and blue fiery space in the background. Love was heavy in the atmosphere. Ball wanted to know what the blue chicks looked like. But I didn't. Cause I knew after tomorrow's duty, I had a day off, and I knew somebody waitin for me at my house, and some kids, and some fried fish, and those carrots, and wow.

That's the way the fifth day ended.

MARCH 1967

## *Study questions*

1. *Who are the spacemen? Why are they blue? Is it significant that the spacemen are interested in the music and have a "perfect harmony" with it?* 2. *How can we tell that some kind of battle is going on?* 3. *Who is the narrator? Whose side is he on? Who is fighting whom? Who wins?* 4. *What is the tone of this story? How is the violence handled? Why?* 5. *What is the significance of the design of the new flag?* 6. *What is the significance of the title? of the last sentence of the story?*

*Joyce Carol Oates* (b. 1938) was born in Lockport, New York, and received her B.A. from Syracuse University and her M.A. in English from the University of Wisconsin. She has taught at the University of Windsor, Ontario, Canada, and now teaches at Princeton University. A novelist, short-story writer, poet, playwright, and essayist, she began writing while she was in high school and began to publish when she was twenty-one years old. Her novel *Them* (1969) won the National Book Award. Other important novels include *A Garden of Earthly Delights* (1967), *Do with Me What You Will* (1973), and *Childwold* (1976). Her stories have been collected in several volumes, including *By the North Gate* (1963), *Upon the Sweeping Flood and Other Stories* (1966), *The Wheel of Love* (1970), *Marriage and Infidelities* (1972), *The Goddess and Other Women* (1974), and *The Poisoned Kiss and Other Stories from the Portuguese* (1975). "How I Contemplated The World from the Detroit House of Correction and Began My Life Over Again" tells a story by means of a series of notes, but, as is common in stories of this mode, one must come to question what, if anything, took place. Still further consideration leads to one to conclude that events must be considered at deeper than a circumstantial level. The protagonist in this story is profoundly troubled, whether she experienced all of the events set down or whether they are imaginative projections of her fears.

# HOW I CONTEMPLATED THE WORLD FROM THE DETROIT HOUSE OF CORRECTION AND BEGAN MY LIFE OVER AGAIN

NOTES FOR AN ESSAY FOR AN ENGLISH CLASS AT BALDWIN COUNTRY DAY SCHOOL; POKING AROUND IN DEBRIS; DISGUST AND CURIOSITY; A REVELATION OF THE MEANING OF LIFE; A HAPPY ENDING . . .

## *I Events*

1. The girl (myself) is walking through Branden's, that excellent store. Suburb of a large famous city that is a symbol for large famous American cities. The event sneaks up on the girl, who believes she is herding it along with a small fixed smile, a girl of fifteen, innocently experienced. She dawdles in a certain style by a counter of costume jewelry. Rings, earrings, necklaces. Prices from $5 to $50, all within reach. All ugly. She eases over to the glove counter, where everything is ugly too. In her close-fitted coat with its black fur collar she con-

templates the luxury of Branden's, which she has known for many years: its many mild pale lights, easy on the eye and the soul, its elaborate tinkly decorations, its women shoppers with their excellent shoes and coats and hairdos, all dawdling gracefully, in no hurry.

Who was ever in a hurry here?

2. The girl seated at home. A small library, paneled walls of oak. Someone is talking to me. An earnest, husky, female voice drives itself against my ears, nervous, frightened, groping around my heart, saying, "If you wanted gloves, why didn't you say so? Why didn't you ask for them?" That store, Branden's, is owned by Raymond Forrest who lives on Du Maurier Drive. We live on Sioux Drive. Raymond Forrest. A handsome man? An ugly man? A man of fifty or sixty, with gray hair, or a man of forty with earnest, courteous eyes, a good golf game; who is Raymond Forrest, this man who is my salvation? Father has been talking to him. Father is not his physician; Dr. Berg is his physician. Father and Dr. Berg refer patients to each other. There is a connection. Mother plays bridge with . . . On Mondays and Wednesdays our maid Billie works at . . . The strings draw together in a cat's cradle, making a net to save you when you fall. . . .

3. *Harriet Arnold's.* A small shop, better than Branden's. Mother in her black coat, I in my close-fitted blue coat. Shopping. Now look at this, isn't this cute, do you want this, why don't you want this, try this on, take this with you to the fitting room, take this also, what's wrong with you, what can I do for you, why are you so strange . . . ? "I wanted to steal but not to buy," I don't tell her. The girl droops along in her coat and gloves and leather boots, her eyes scan the horizon, which is pastel pink and decorated like Branden's, tasteful walls and modern ceilings with graceful glimmering lights.

4. Weeks later, the girl at a bus stop. Two o'clock in the afternoon, a Tuesday; obviously she has walked out of school.

5. The girl stepping down from a bus. Afternoon, weather changing to colder. Detroit. Pavement and closed-up stores; grill-work over the windows of a pawnshop. What is a pawnshop, exactly?

## *II Characters*

1. The girl stands five feet five inches tall. An ordinary height. Baldwin Country Day School draws them up to that height. She dreams along the corridors and presses her face against the Thermoplex glass. No frost or steam can ever form on that glass. A smudge of grease from her forehead . . . could she be boiled down to grease? She wears her hair loose and long and straight in suburban teen-age style, 1968. Eyes smudged with pencil, dark brown. Brown hair. Vague green eyes. A pretty girl? An ugly girl? She sings to herself under her breath, idling in the corridor, thinking of her many secrets (the thirty dollars she once took from the purse of a friend's mother, just for fun, the basement

window she smashed in her own house just for fun) and thinking of her brother who is at Susquehanna Boys' Academy, an excellent preparatory school in Maine, remembering him unclearly... he has long manic hair and a squeaking voice and he looks like one of the popular teen-age singers of 1968, one of those in a group, *The Certain Forces, The Way Out, The Maniacs Responsible.* The girl in her turn looks like one of those fieldsful of girls who listen to the boys' singing, dreaming and mooning restlessly, breaking into high sullen laughter, innocently experienced.

2. The mother. A Midwestern woman of Detroit and suburbs. Belongs to the Detroit Athletic Club. Also the Detroit Golf Club. Also the Bloomfield Hills Country Club. The Village Women's Club at which lectures are given each winter on Genet and Sartre and James Baldwin, by the Director of the Adult Education Program at Wayne State University. . . . The Bloomfield Art Association. Also the Founders Society of the Detroit Institute of Arts. Also . . . Oh, she is in perpetual motion, this lady, hair like blown-up gold and finer than gold, hair and fingers and body of inestimable grace. Heavy weighs the gold on the back of her hairbrush and hand mirror. Heavy heavy the candlesticks in the dining room. Very heavy is the big car, a Lincoln, long and black, that on one cool autumn day split a squirrel's body in two unequal parts.

3. The father. Dr. . He belongs to the same clubs as #2. A player of squash and golf; he has a golfer's umbrella of stripes. Candy stripes. In his mouth nothing turns to sugar, however; saliva works no miracles here. His doctoring is of the slightly sick. The sick are sent elsewhere (to Dr. Berg?), the deathly sick are sent back for more tests and their bills are sent to their homes, the unsick are sent to Dr. Coronet (Isabel, a lady), an excellent psychiatrist for unsick people who angrily believe they are sick and want to do something about it. If they demand a male psychiatrist, the unsick are sent by Dr. (my father) to Dr. Lowenstein, a male psychiatrist, excellent and expensive, with a limited practice.

4. Clarita. She is twenty, twenty-five, she is thirty or more? Pretty, ugly, what? She is a woman lounging by the side of a road, in jeans and a sweater, hitchhiking, or she is slouched on a stool at a counter in some roadside diner. A hard line of jaw. Curious eyes. Amused eyes. Behind her eyes processions move, funeral pageants, cartoons. She says, "I never can figure out why girls like you bum around down here. What are you looking for anyway?" An odor of tobacco about her. Unwashed underclothes, or no underclothes, unwashed skin, gritty toes, hair long and falling into strands, not recently washed.

5. Simon. In this city the weather changes abruptly, so Simon's weather changes abruptly. He sleeps through the afternoon. He sleeps through the morning. Rising, he gropes around for something to get him going, for a cigarette or a pill to drive him out to the street, where the temperature is hovering around 35°. Why doesn't it drop? Why, why doesn't the cold clean air come down from Canada; will he have to go up into Canada to get it? Will he have to leave the Country of his Birth and sink into Canada's frosty fields . . . ? Will the F.B.I.

(which he dreams about constantly) chase him over the Canadian border on foot, hounded out in a blizzard of broken glass and horns . . . ?

"Once I was Huckleberry Finn," Simon says, "but now I am Roderick Usher." Beset by frenzies and fears, this man who makes my spine go cold, he takes green pills, yellow pills, pills of white and capsules of dark blue and green . . . he takes other things I may not mention, for what if Simon seeks me out and climbs into my girl's bedroom here in Bloomfield Hills and strangles me, what then . . . ? (As I write this I begin to shiver. Why do I shiver? I am now sixteen and sixteen is not an age for shivering.) It comes from Simon, who is always cold.

## *III World Events*

Nothing.

## *IV People & Circumstances Contributing to This Delinquency*

Nothing.

## *V Sioux Drive*

George, Clyde G. 240 Sioux. A manufacturer's representative; children, a dog, a wife. Georgian with the usual columns. You think of the White House, then of Thomas Jefferson, then your mind goes blank on the white pillars and you think of nothing. Norris, Ralph W. 246 Sioux. Public relations. Colonial. Bay window, brick, stone, concrete, wood, green shutters, sidewalk, lantern, grass, trees, blacktop drive, two children, one of them my classmate Esther (Esther Norris) at Baldwin. Wife, cars. Ramsey, Michael D. 250 Sioux. Colonial. Big living room, thirty by twenty-five, fireplaces in living room, library, recreation room, paneled walls wet bar five bathrooms five bedrooms two lavatories central air conditioning automatic sprinkler automatic garage door three children one wife two cars a breakfast room a patio a large fenced lot fourteen trees a front door with a brass knocker never knocked. Next is our house. Classic contemporary. Traditional modern. Attached garage, attached Florida room, attached patio, attached pool and cabana, attached roof. A front door mail slot through which pour *Time Magazine, Fortune, Life, Business Week,* the *Wall Street Journal,* the *New York Times,* the *New Yorker,* the *Saturday Review, M.D., Modern Medicine, Disease of the Month* . . . and also. . . . And in addition to all this, a quiet sealed letter from Baldwin saying: *Your daughter is not doing work compatible with her performance on the Stanford-Binet.* . . . And your son is not doing well, not well at all, very sad. Where is your son anyway? Once he stole trick-and-treat candy from some six-year-old kids, he himself being a robust ten. The beginning. Now your daughter steals. In the Village Pharmacy she made off with, yes she did, don't deny it, she made off with a copy of *Pageant Magazine* for no reason, she swiped a roll of Life Savers in a green wrapper and was in no need of saving her life or even in need of sucking candy; when she was no more than eight years old she stole, don't blush, she stole a package of Tums only because it was out on the counter and available, and the nice lady behind the counter (now dead) said nothing. . . . Sioux Drive. Maples, oaks, elms. Diseased elms cut down. Sioux Drive runs into Roosevelt Drive. Slow, turning lanes, not streets, all drives and lanes and ways and passes. A private police force. Quiet private police, in unmarked cars. Cruising on Saturday evenings with paternal smiles for the residents who are streaming in and out of houses, going to and from parties, a thousand parties, slightly staggering, the women in their furs alighting from automobiles bought of Ford and General Motors and Chrysler, very heavy automobiles. No foreign cars. Detroit. In 275 Sioux, down the block in that magnificent French-Normandy mansion, lives                himself, who has the C                account itself, imagine that! Look at where he lives and look at the enormous trees and chimneys, imagine his many fireplaces, imagine his wife and children, imagine his wife's hair, imagine her fingernails, imagine her bathtub of smooth clean glowing pink, imagine their embraces, his trouser pockets filled with odd coins and keys and dust and peanuts, imagine their ecstasy on Sioux Drive, imagine their income tax returns, imagine their little boy's pride in his experimental car, a scaled-down C          , as he roars around the neighborhood on the sidewalks frightening dogs and Negro maids, oh imagine all these things, imagine everything, let your mind roar out all over Sioux Drive and Du Maurier Drive and Roosevelt Drive and Ticonderoga Pass and Burning Bush Way and Lincolnshire Pass and Lois Lane.

When spring comes, its winds blow nothing to Sioux Drive, no odors of hollyhocks or forsythia, nothing Sioux Drive doesn't already possess, everything is planted and performing. The weather vanes, had they weather vanes, don't have to turn with the wind, don't have to contend with the weather. There is no weather.

## *VI Detroit*

There is always weather in Detroit. Detroit's temperature is always 32°. Fast-falling temperatures. Slow-rising temperatures. Wind from the north-northeast four to forty miles an hour, small-craft warnings, partly cloudy today and Wednesday changing to partly sunny through Thursday . . . small warnings of frost, soot warnings, traffic warnings, hazardous lake conditions for small craft and swimmers, restless Negro gangs, restless cloud formations, restless temperatures aching to fall out the very bottom of the thermometer or shoot up over the top and boil everything over in red mercury.

Detroit's temperature is 32°. Fast-falling temperatures. Slow-rising temperatures. Wind from the north-northeast four to forty miles an hour. . . .

## *VII Events*

1. The girl's heart is pounding. In her pocket is a pair of gloves! In a plastic bag! Airproof breathproof plastic bag, gloves selling for twenty-five dollars on Branden's counter; In her pocket! Shoplifted! . . . In her purse is a blue comb, not very clean. In her purse is a leather billfold (a birthday present from

her grandmother in Philadelphia) with snapshots of the family in clean plastic windows, in the billfold are bills, she doesn't know how many bills. . . . In her purse is an ominous note from her friend Tykie *What's this about Joe H. and the kids hanging around at Louise's Sat. night? You heard anything?* . . . passed in French class. In her purse is a lot of dirty yellow Kleenex, her mother's heart would break to see such very dirty Kleenex, and at the bottom of her purse are brown hairpins and safety pins and a broken pencil and a ballpoint pen (blue) stolen from somewhere forgotten and a purse-size compact of Cover Girl Make-Up, Ivory Rose. . . . Her lipstick is Broken Heart, a corrupt pink; her fingers are trembling like crazy; her teeth are beginning to chatter; her insides are alive; her eyes glow in her head; she is saying to her mother's astonished face *I want to steal but not to buy.*

2. At Clarita's. Day or night? What room is this? A bed, a regular bed, and a mattress on the floor nearby. Wallpaper hanging in strips. Clarita says she tore it like that with her teeth. She was fighting a barbaric tribe that night, high from some pills; she was battling for her life with men wearing helmets of heavy iron and their faces no more than Christian crosses to breathe through, every one of those bastards looking like her lover Simon, who seems to breathe with great difficulty through the slits of mouth and nostrils in his face. Clarita has never heard of Sioux Drive. Raymond Forrest cuts no ice with her, nor does the C            account and its millions; Harvard Business School could be at the corner of Vernor and 12th Street for all she cares, and Vietnam might have sunk by now into the Dead Sea under its tons of debris, for all the amazement she could show . . . her face is overworked, overwrought, at the age of twenty (thirty?) it is already exhausted but fanciful and ready for a laugh. Clarita says mournfully to me *Honey somebody is going to turn you out let me give you warning.* In a movie shown on late television Clarita is not a mess like this but a nurse, with short neat hair and a dedicated look, in love with her doctor and her doctor's patients and their diseases, enamored of needles and sponges and rubbing alcohol. . . . Or no: she is a private secretary. Robert Cummings is her boss. She helps him with fantastic plots, the canned audience laughs, no, the audience doesn't laugh because nothing is funny, instead her boss is Robert Taylor and they are not boss and secretary but husband and wife, she is threatened by a young starlet, she is grim, handsome, wifely, a good companion for a good man. . . . She is Claudette Colbert. Her sister too is Claudette Colbert. They are twins, identical. Her husband Charles Boyer is a very rich handsome man and her sister, Claudette Colbert, is plotting her death in order to take her place as the rich man's wife, no one will know because they are *twins*. . . . All these marvelous lives Clarita might have lived, but she fell out the bottom at the age of thirteen. At the age when I was packing my overnight case for a slumber party at Toni Deshield's she was tearing filthy sheets off a bed and scratching up a rash on her arms. . . . Thirteen is uncommonly young for a white girl in Detroit, Miss Brock of the Detroit House of Correction said in a sad newspaper interview for the *Detroit News;* fifteen and sixteen are more likely. Eleven, twelve, thirteen are not surprising in colored . . . they are more precocious. What can we do?

Taxes are rising and the tax base is falling. The temperature rises slowly but falls rapidly. Everything is falling out the bottom, Woodward Avenue is filthy, Livernois Avenue is filthy! Scraps of paper flutter in the air like pigeons, dirt flies up and hits you right in the eye, oh Detroit is breaking up into dangerous bits of newspaper and dirt, watch out. . . .

Clarita's apartment is over a restaurant. Simon her lover emerges from the cracks at dark. Mrs. Olesko, a neighbor of Clarita's, an aged white wisp of a woman, doesn't complain but sniffs with contentment at Clarita's noisy life and doesn't tell the cops, hating cops, when the cops arrive. I should give more fake names, more blanks, instead of telling all these secrets. I myself am a secret; I am a minor.

3. My father reads a paper at a medical convention in Los Angeles. There he is, on the edge of the North American continent, when the unmarked detective put his hand so gently on my arm in the aisle of Branden's and said, "Miss, would you like to step over here for a minute?"

And where was he when Clarita put her hand on my arm, that wintry dark sulphurous aching day in Detroit, in the company of closed-down barber shops, closed-down diners, closed-down movie houses, homes, windows, basements, faces . . . she put her hand on my arm and said, "Honey, are you looking for somebody down here?"

And was he home worrying about me, gone for two weeks solid, when they carried me off . . . ? It took three of them to get me in the police cruiser, so they said, and they put more than their hands on my arm.

4. I work on this lesson. My English teacher is Mr. Forest, who is from Michigan State. Not handsome, Mr. Forest, and his name is plain, unlike Raymond Forrest's, but he is sweet and rodentlike, he has conferred with the principal and my parents, and everything is fixed . . . treat her as if nothing has happened, a new start, begin again, only sixteen years old, what a shame, how did it happen? —nothing happened, nothing could have happened, a slight physiological modification known only to a gynecologist or to Dr. Coronet. I work on my lesson. I sit in my pink room. I look around the room with my sad pink eyes. I sigh, I dawdle, I pause, I eat up time, I am limp and happy to be home, I am sixteen years old suddenly, my head hangs heavy as a pumpkin on my shoulders, and my hair has just been cut by Mr. Faye at the Crystal Salon and is said to be very becoming.

(Simon too put his hand on my arm and said, "Honey, you have got to come with me," and in his six-by-six room we got to know each other. Would I go back to Simon again? Would I lie down with him in all that filth and craziness? Over and over again.

a Clarita is being betrayed as in front of a Cunningham Drug Store she is nervously eying a colored man who may or may not have money, or a nervous white boy of twenty with sideburns and an Appalachian look, who may or may not have a knife hidden in his jacket pocket, or a husky red-faced man of friendly countenance who may or may not be a member of the Vice Squad out for an early twilight walk.)

I work on my lesson for Mr. Forest. I have filled up eleven pages. Words pour out of me and won't stop. I want to tell everything . . . what was the song Simon was always humming, and who was Simon's friend in a very new trench coat with an old high school graduation ring on his finger . . . ? Simon's bearded friend? When I was down too low for him, Simon kicked me out and gave me to him for three days, I think, on Fourteenth Street in Detroit, an airy room of cold cruel drafts with newspapers on the floor. . . . Do I really remember that or am I piecing it together from what they told me? Did they tell the truth? Did they know much of the truth?

## *VIII Characters*

1. Wednesdays after school, at four; Saturday mornings at ten. Mother drives me to Dr. Coronet. Ferns in the office, plastic or real, they look the same. Dr. Coronet is queenly, an elegant nicotine-stained lady who would have studied with Freud had circumstances not prevented it, a bit of a Catholic, ready to offer you some mystery if your teeth will ache too much without it. Highly recommended by Father! Forty dollars an hour, Father's forty dollars! Progress! Looking up! Looking better! That new haircut is so becoming, says Dr. Coronet herself, showing how normal she is for a woman with an I.Q. of 180 and many advanced degrees.

2. Mother. A lady in a brown suede coat. Boots of shiny black material, black gloves, a black fur hat. She would be humiliated could she know that of all the people in the world it is my ex-lover Simon who walks most like her . . . self-conscious and unreal, listening to distant music, a little bowlegged with craftiness. . . .

3. Father. Tying a necktie. In a hurry. On my first evening home he put his hand on my arm and said, "Honey, we're going to forget all about this."

4. Simon. Outside, a plane is crossing the sky, in here we're in a hurry. Morning. It must be morning. The girl is half out of her mind, whimpering and vague; Simon her dear friend is wretched this morning . . . he is wretched with morning itself . . . he forces her to give him an injection with that needle she knows is filthy, she has a dread of needles and surgical instruments and the odor of things that are to be sent into the blood, thinking somehow of her father. . . . This is a bad morning, Simon says that his mind is being twisted out of shape, and so he submits to the needle that he usually scorns and bites his lip with his yellowish teeth, his face going very pale. *Ah baby!* he says in his soft mocking voice, which with all women is a mockery of love, *do it like this—Slowly*—And the girl, terrified, almost drops the precious needle but manages to turn it up to the light from the window . . . is it an extension of herself then? She can give him this gift then? *I wish you wouldn't do this to me,* she says, wise in her terror, because

it seems to her that Simon's danger—in a few minutes he may be dead—is a way of pressing her against him that is more powerful than any other embrace. She has to work over his arm, the knotted corded veins of his arm, her forehead wet with perspiration as she pushes and releases the needle, staring at that mixture of liquid now stained with Simon's bright blood. . . . When the drug hits him she can feel it herself, she feels that magic that is more than any woman can give him, striking the back of his head and making his face stretch as if with the impact of a terrible sun. . . . She tries to embrace him but he pushes her aside and stumbles to his feet. *Jesus Christ,* he says. . . .

5. Princess, a Negro girl of eighteen. What is her charge? She is closed-mouthed about it, shrewd and silent, you know that no one had to wrestle her to the sidewalk to get her in here; she came with dignity. In the recreation room she sits reading *Nancy Drew and the Jewel Box Mystery,* which inspires in her face tiny wrinkles of alarm and interest: what a face! Light brown skin, heavy shaded eyes, heavy eyelashes, a serious sinister dark brow, graceful fingers, graceful wristbones, graceful legs, lips, tongue, a sugar-sweet voice, a leggy stride more masculine than Simon's and my mother's, decked out in a dirty white blouse and dirty white slacks; vaguely nautical is Princess' style. . . . At breakfast she is in charge of clearing the table and leans over me, saying, *Honey you sure you ate enough?*

6. The girl lies sleepless, wondering. Why here, why not there? Why Bloomfield Hills and not jail? Why jail and not her pink room? Why downtown Detroit and not Sioux Drive? What is the difference? Is Simon all the difference? The girl's head is a parade of wonders. She is nearly sixteen, her breath is marvelous with wonders, not long ago she was coloring with crayons and now she is smearing the landscape with paints that won't come off and won't come off her fingers either. She says to the matron *I am not talking about anything,* not because everyone has warned her not to talk but because, because she will not talk; because she won't say anything about Simon, who is her secret. And she says to the matron, *I won't go home,* up until that night in the lavatory when everything was changed. . . . "No, I won't go home I want to stay here," she says, listening to her own words with amazement, thinking that weeds might climb everywhere over that marvelous $180,000 house and dinosaurs might return to muddy the beige carpeting, but never never will she reconcile four o'clock in the morning in Detroit with eight o'clock breakfasts in Bloomfield Hills. . . . oh, she aches still for Simon's hands and his caressing breath, though he gave her little pleasure, he took everything from her (five-dollar bills, ten-dollar bills, passed into her numb hands by men and taken out of her hands by Simon) until she herself was passed into the hands of other men, police, when Simon evidently got tired of her and her hysteria. . . . *No, I won't go home, I don't want to be bailed out.* The girl thinks as a *Stubborn and Wayward Child* (one of several charges lodged against her), and the matron understands her crazy white-rimmed eyes that are seeking out some new violence that will keep her in jail, should someone threaten to let her out. Such children try to strangle the matrons, the attendants, or one another . . . they want the locks locked forever, the doors

nailed shut . . . and this girl is no different up until that night her mind is changed for her. . . .

### *IX That Night*

Princess and Dolly, a little white girl of maybe fifteen, hardy however as a sergeant and in the House of Correction for armed robbery, corner her in the lavatory at the farthest sink and the other girls look away and file out to bed, leaving her. God, how she is beaten up! Why is she beaten up? Why do they pound her, why such hatred? Princess vents all the hatred of a thousand silent Detroit winters on her body, this girl whose body belongs to me, fiercely she rides across the Midwestern plains on this girl's tender bruised body . . . revenge on the oppressed minorities of America! revenge on the slaughtered Indians! revenge on the female sex, on the male sex, revenge on Bloomfield Hills, revenge revenge. . . .

### *X Detroit*

In Detroit, weather weighs heavily upon everyone. The sky looms large. The horizon shimmers in smoke. Downtown the buildings are imprecise in the haze. Perpetual haze. Perpetual motion inside the haze. Across the choppy river is the city of Windsor, in Canada. Part of the continent has bunched up here and is bulging outward, at the tip of Detroit; a cold hard rain is forever falling on the expressways. . . . Shoppers shop grimly, their cars are not parked in safe places, their windshields may be smashed and graceful ebony hands may drag them out through their shatterproof smashed windshields, crying, *Revenge for the Indians!* Ah, they all fear leaving Hudson's and being dragged to the very tip of the city and thrown off the parking roof of Cobo Hall, that expensive tomb, into the river. . . .

### *XI Characters We Are Forever Entwined With*

1. Simon drew me into his tender rotting arms and breathed gravity into me. Then I came to earth, weighed down. He said, *You are such a little girl,* and he weighed me down with his delight. In the palms of his hands were teeth marks from his previous life experiences. He was thirty-five, they said. Imagine Simon in this room, in my pink room: he is about six feet tall and stoops slightly, in a feline cautious way, always thinking, always on guard, with his scuffed light suede shoes and his clothes that are anyone's clothes, slightly rumpled ordinary clothes that ordinary men might wear to not-bad jobs. Simon has fair long hair, curly hair, spent languid curls that are like . . . exactly like the curls of wood shavings to the touch, I am trying to be exact . . . and he smells of unheated mornings and coffee and too many pills coating his tongue with a faint green-white scum. . . . Dear Simon, who would be panicked in this room and in this house (right now Billie is vacuuming next door in my parents' room; a vacuum cleaner's roar is a sign of all good things), Simon who is said to have come from

a home not much different from this, years ago, fleeing all the carpeting and the polished banisters. . . . Simon has a deathly face, only desperate people fall in love with it. His face is bony and cautious, the bones of his cheeks prominent as if with the rigidity of his ceaseless thinking, plotting, for he has to make money out of girls to whom money means nothing, they're so far gone they can hardly count it, and in a sense money means nothing to him either except as a way of keeping on with his life. *Each Day's Proud Struggle,* the title of a novel we could read at jail. . . . Each day he needs a certain amount of money. He devours it. It wasn't love he uncoiled in me with his hollowed-out eyes and his courteous smile, that remnant of a prosperous past, but a dark terror that needed to press itself flat against him, or against another man . . . but he was the first, he came over to me and took my arm, a claim. We struggled on the stairs and I said, *Let me loose, you're hurting my neck, my face,* it was such a surprise that my skin hurt where he rubbed it, and afterward we lay face to face and he breathed everything into me. In the end I think he turned me in.

2. Raymond Forrest. I just read this morning that Raymond Forrest's father, the chairman of the board at          , died of a heart attack on a plane bound for London. I would like to write Raymond Forrest a note of sympathy. I would like to thank him for not pressing charges against me one hundred years ago, saving me, being so generous . . . well, men like Raymond Forrest are generous men, not like Simon. I would like to write him a letter telling of my love, or of some other emotion that is positive and healthy. Not like Simon and his poetry, which he scrawled down when he was high and never changed a word . . . but when I try to think of something to say, it is Simon's language that comes back to me, caught in my head like a bad song, it is always Simon's language:

*There is no reality only dreams*
*Your neck may get snapped when you wake*
*My love is drawn to some violent end*
*She keeps wanting to get away*
*My love is heading downward*
*And I am heading upward*
*She is going to crash on the sidewalk*
*And I am going to dissolve into the clouds*

## *XII Events*

1. Out of the hospital, bruised and saddened and converted, with Princess' grunts still tangled in my hair . . . and Father in his overcoat looking like a prince himself, come to carry me off. Up the expressway and out north to home. Jesus Christ, but the air is thinner and cleaner here. Monumental houses. Heartbreaking sidewalks, so clean.

2. Weeping in the living room. The ceiling is two stories high and two chandeliers hang from it. Weeping, weeping, though Billie the maid is *probably*

# INDEX

ABCDEFGHIJ—BP—798